OVEN TEMPERATURES

Very slow oven	250°—275° F.
Slow oven	300°—325° F.
Moderate oven	350°—375° F.
Hot oven	400°—425° F.
Very hot oven	450°—475° F.
Extremely hot oven	500°—525° F.

Internal Temperatures for
DONENESS IN MEAT AND POULTRY

Beef, rare	140° F.
medium	160° F.
well done	170° F.
Lamb	175°—180° F.
Pork (loin)	170° F.
Pork (other cuts)	185° F.
Veal	170° F.
Ham (uncooked)	160°—170° F.
Ham (fully cooked)	130° F.
Turkey (whole)	180°—185° F.
Chicken	185° F.
Capon and Duckling	190° F.

Temperatures for
DEEP-FAT FRYING

Chicken	350° F.
Doughnuts and fritters	350°—375° F.
Fish and seafood	350°—375° F.
Croquettes	375°—385° F.
Vegetables	375°—385° F.
Potatoes	385°—395° F.

Temperatures for
CANDY, FROSTING AND JELLY-MAKING

Jellying point	220° F.
Thread	230°—234° F.
Soft ball	234°—240° F.
Firm ball	244°—248° F.
Hard ball	250°—266° F.
Soft crack	270°—290° F.
Hard crack	300°—310° F.

WORLD SAVINGS
AND LOAN ASSOCIATION

Woman's Day
COLLECTOR'S
COOK BOOK REVISED AND ENLARGED

A treasury of over 2,700 recipes selected from the highly esteemed collector's cook books published monthly in Woman's Day since 1957

PREPARED AND EDITED BY THE EDITORS OF **WOMAN'S DAY**

Editor **Geraldine Rhoads**

Food Editor **Glenna McGinnis**

Art Consultant **Harold Sitterle**

Associates **Charlotte Scripture, Sally W. Smith, Jennifer C. Schmid**

Special Project Editor **Isabel S. Cornell**

SIMON AND SCHUSTER   **NEW YORK**

SBN 671-21986-3
Manufactured in the United States of America
Printed by Deven Lithographers Inc., Long Island City, N.Y.
Bound by The Book Press, Brattleboro, Vermont

1   2   3   4   5   6   7   8   9   10

This is a cook book for connoisseur cooks—a new and unique collection of wonderful food adventures. The recipes it contains have been carefully culled from over 6,500 in the special clip-out sections called Collector's Cook Books that appear each month in Woman's Day. The great classics are well represented, and in addition the book offers hundreds of recipes for dishes so unusual that they have seldom or never been published elsewhere. All are organized simply enough for an inexperienced cook to undertake.

Because ingredients, cooking methods and tastes change through the years, every recipe has been brought completely up to date. Final selection was based on testing and tasting by the Woman's Day Kitchen staff and panels of tasters, as well as on the comments sent to us by millions of our readers.

Believing it will make your menu planning easier, your cooking more imaginative and your family's eating more pleasurable than ever, we dedicate the book to all who use and enjoy it.

The Editors

CONTENTS

WHAT EVERY GOOD COOK SHOULD KNOW

TO YOUR SUCCESS WITH THESE RECIPES

You will enjoy uniform success with these recipes if you bear in mind the methods, ingredients and measurements with which we developed and tested them.

• All recipes in this book have been tested in the Woman's Day Kitchens with standard American measuring cups (8 fluid ounces = 16 tablespoons), measuring spoons (1 tablespoon = 3 teaspoons) and other standard kitchen equipment.
• Before starting to cook or bake, read the recipe carefully. Assemble all ingredients and equipment, taking care to use the exact pan size specified. Follow recipe exactly. Ingredients are listed in the order of their use. Where directions refer to ingredients by numbers, such as "first 3" or "next 5," a listing with 2 items—"½ teaspoon each cinnamon and nutmeg," for instance—is counted as 1 ingredient.
• Do not increase or decrease recipes unless you are a skilled enough cook to recognize what adjustments must be made as to ingredients, pan sizes and/or cooking times. Increasing or dividing recipes can be hazardous.
• Preheat oven before baking unless otherwise specified.
• Number of servings given at end of recipe denotes average portions, not number of people the recipe will serve.
• Recipes are not for high altitudes.
• All sugar is granulated white sugar unless otherwise specified.
• Cake flour is sifted before measuring into cup unless otherwise specified. (All-purpose flour need not be sifted before measuring.) To measure either flour, spoon into cup and level off with a straight knife or spatula. No self-rising or unbleached flour is used.
• All baking powder is double-acting.
• All soda is baking soda.
• The exact type of chocolate is specified in each recipe, such as unsweetened squares, semisweet squares, semisweet pieces and sweet cooking chocolate.
• All cornmeal is regular (not waterground) yellow cornmeal unless otherwise specified. No self-rising cornmeal is used.

• All vinegar is cider vinegar unless otherwise specified.
• All brown sugar is firmly packed when measured.
• All confectioners' sugar is sifted before using, unless otherwise specified.
• All commercial syrups are clearly designated as to the type needed for each recipe unless it is not important; i.e., if we do not say dark or light when referring to molasses or corn syrup, either may be used.
• All pepper is ground black pepper unless otherwise specified.
• Fats and shortening are measured at room temperature, packed firmly into measuring cup and leveled off with a straight knife. They should be scraped out of the cup with a rubber spatula.
• Salted butter or margarine, packed in ¼-pound sticks, is used unless otherwise specified. 1 stick = ½ cup = 8 tablespoons = ¼ pound. No whipped butter or whipped cream cheese is used unless specified.
• 1 tall can undiluted evaporated milk (13 fluid ounces) contains 1⅔ cups. Sweetened condensed milk (about 14 ounces) is an entirely different product and *cannot* be used *interchangeably* with evaporated milk. A substitute for buttermilk can be made by putting 1 to 2 tablespoons vinegar in a cup and filling cup with sweet milk. Let stand 5 minutes before using.
• ⅓ to ½ teaspoon dried herbs can be substituted for each tablespoon fresh herbs. Crumble herbs before using, to release flavor.

COOKING CUES

CANDY, JELLY AND FROSTINGS

Use a good candy-jelly-frosting thermometer. One first-rate vertical (non-dial-type) thermometer does all three jobs.

When not in use, hang the thermometer up if possible rather than laying it in a drawer.

Before using each time, test thermometer by boiling in water. If it reads 212° F., cook all recipes to the temperatures given. If it shows a higher or lower temperature reading than 212°F., adjust the temperatures accordingly.

Use a small enough utensil so that the bulb end of the thermometer can be completely submerged in the candy, jelly or frosting, without touching the bottom or side of pot.

Allow plenty of time when making most candies. Many, such as caramels, take long cooking and stirring.

In humid or rainy weather, cook candies 2° higher than the recipe directions

Use a heavy saucepan, and an asbestos mat, if available, for candies made with milk or cream, since they burn easily.

Watch candy carefully, especially during last few minutes of cooking. Temperature rises quickly at end.

For best results, don't double any of the recipes or make substitutions in ingredients in candies, jellies or frostings.

Store different kinds of candies separately. Brittles soften if stored with creamy candies. Airtight storage in a cool place is best for all candies unless otherwise indicated in recipe.

DEEP-FAT FRYING

This means cooking food in enough fat to cover the food completely. When food is properly deep-fried, a thin coating forms on its outer surface, keeping its juices inside and preventing the fat from penetrating into the food.

Properly prepared deep-fried foods are crisp outside, moist and delicate inside. What is more, they have absorbed less fat than foods cooked in a smaller amount of fat. Fat absorption increases with the length of frying time and the size of the surface exposed to the fat. Thus, foods to be deep-fried should either take little time to cook, or should be precooked. Foods should also be cut into small pieces, not more than 2" to 3" in diameter, and the pieces should be uniform so that they will cook evenly.

Success with deep-fried foods depends largely on the heat of the fat. It must be hot enough to cause rapid browning of the food's surfaces but the fat should not be so hot that it smokes. The right temperature for most foods is 375°F., although some foods require a higher temperature. Recipes will generally specify the correct temperature when this is so.

Equipment Equipment need not be elaborate. A deep heavy 3- to 4-quart kettle that will hold about 3 pounds of fat is a necessity. There must be enough fat in the kettle to cover the food completely and enough space for the food pieces to move around freely. The kettle should have a flat bottom so that it will sit firmly on the burner, and a short handle to avoid any danger of being overturned. Since the proper temperature is crucial to successful deep-frying, an electric fryer is desirable because the heat is thermostatically controlled.

A wire basket is almost a necessity when deep-frying any quantities of food such as French-fried potatoes. The food is placed in it and then lowered into the fat. The basket makes it easier to get the food in and out and it insures even browning.

A frying thermometer is needed to measure the temperature of the fat. The importance of such a thermometer cannot be sufficiently stressed. While the fat is heating, keep the thermometer in a bowl of hot water to prevent its cracking when it is lowered into the hot fat. Be sure to wipe it very dry before using, because water makes hot fat spatter.

A slotted metal spoon and long-handled metal tongs are also useful for raising and lowering food into the hot fat. And you will need absorbent paper for draining the food.

Fats used in deep-frying should have a high smoking point, i.e., heat to a high temperature before burning. Hydrogenated (solid) fats, lard, and oils such as corn, cottonseed, peanut, olive, sesame and soy are suited for the purpose. Butter and margarine are not; they have low smoking points and burn easily.

After fat has cooled, strain it through several layers of cheesecloth. Use fat again for frying similar foods, such as fat used to fry fish for fish, etc.

When deep-frying frozen foods, remove them from their package, defrost, and thoroughly drain and dry before frying.

Caution Keep a metal lid near the kettle. In case fat should catch fire, drop the lid on the kettle. Fire can also be smothered with salt or baking soda; keep either close at hand. *Never* use water, since this will only spread the flame.

FREEZING

Nearly every type of fresh food can be frozen. Exceptions are: lettuce, celery, cabbage, cucumbers, radishes, cake batters, bananas, custards, cream pie fillings, custard pie, mayonnaise or salad dressing, and cooked egg white. Always freeze fresh foods of high quality and at the peak of perfection. Freeze as quickly as possible and don't try to freeze too much food at one time.

Foods must be kept airtight, so select packing materials or containers that are vapor- and moisture-proof. Materials may be made of foil, laminates or polyethylene films. The latter need tape or string. Adjust sizes of packages to fit your family's needs and label and date all foods.

Keep food frozen at 0°F. or lower and do not refreeze if completely thawed. Follow manufacturer's directions for freezing in your particular freezer.

FRUITS AND COCONUT

Buying Fresh Coconuts Fresh coconuts are available year-round but are at their peak during the early winter months. Select coconuts heavy for their size that sound full of liquid when shaken. Avoid those with wet or moldy eyes.

Storing Fresh Coconuts Store unopened coconuts at room temperature. Grated coconut and unused pieces should be kept tightly covered in refrigerator or freezer.

Preparing Fresh Coconuts Pierce eyes in end of coconut and drain off liquid; reserve if needed in individual recipe. Put coconut in shallow pan in moderate oven (350°F.) 20 minutes, or until shell cracks in several places. Remove from oven and pound with hammer or mallet to crack shell open. Remove coconut meat and cut off black outer shell. Coconut pieces can then be eaten like any nut. Or for use in recipes, grate meat on grater or whirl a few small pieces at a time in blender until finely grated or shredded.

Packaged Coconut Sweetened coconut, in cans or bags, comes flaked, grated (cookie coconut) and shredded. Length of shreds and moisture content vary. Frozen unsweetened coconut and coconut syrup, honey and chips are also available. Coconut syrup is made by adding sugar to the emulsion obtained by pressing coconut and cooking it to form a syrup. It is used for milk shakes and as a sauce. Coconut honey is similar but the cooking time is longer and the brown skin on the coconut meat is not removed. The honey is used as a spread. Coconut chips are thin chips of toasted coconut, salted and used as a snack.

Dried-fruit Tips Most dried fruits available nowadays don't need soaking or long cooking. Occasional exceptions are fruits sold in bulk. To cook these, cover with water and slowly bring to boil. Cover and simmer until tender. Cook apples and apricots 20 to 30 minutes; nectarines and peaches, 45 minutes; pears, 35 minutes; prunes, 45 minutes; raisins, 10 minutes. Pitted prunes are available now and are a great convenience. Follow directions on label for cooking packaged fruits. Sweeten after cooking. (Honey makes a delicious sweetener.)

To snip dates and raisins Oil scissors or rinse in hot water before using.

To plump prunes Put fruit in jar or bowl and cover with cold water, allowing 1 quart water to 1 pound prunes. Cover and soak 24 hours. Refrigerate and use as needed.

To store dried fruits Store fruits tightly covered in cool, dry, well-ventilated place; in hot weather, in refrigerator.

FRUITCAKE TIPS

Preparation Different combinations of fruits and nuts can be used in any fruitcake, but the total amount should be the same as given in the recipe. Chop or slice the fruits and nuts a day or so before making the cake, if more convenient, and refrigerate.

Glazing and Decorating Before serving or gift-wrapping cakes, you can glaze and decorate them. Melted tart jelly or equal parts of honey or corn syrup and water, boiled 2 minutes, can be brushed warm on cold cakes. Press into glaze designs made of candied cherries and nuts; leaves cut from citron angelica or green candied cherries; and slices of red or green candied pineapple. Brush again with glaze and put in slow oven (300°F.) about 10 minutes to set. Glazed dried fruits such as prunes and apricots make attractive decorations. To prepare, cover fruits with water and simmer, covered, 10 minutes; drain. Bring to boil equal parts of honey, sugar and water. Add fruits and simmer about 15 minutes. Drain on cake rack. Remaining mixture can be used to glaze cake. Fruitcakes aren't usually frosted but the top can be spread with almond paste and a thin layer of confectioners'-sugar frosting. For the frosting, mix 1 cup sifted confectioners' sugar, 1 egg white and a few drops of almond extract. Melted semisweet chocolate is a good substitute for the frosting on white fruitcakes.

Serving Fruitcakes, especially dark ones, are better if allowed to age a week or two before eating. Chilled cakes usually cut best. Slice thin with a serrated knife, if available. If not, use a thin sharp knife.

Storage Dark fruitcakes keep better than light ones since the larger proportion of fruit to batter adds moisture. Both types keep better if refrigerated. They can also be frozen. When refrigerated, they should be wrapped in foil, waxed paper or plastic and, if possible, put in airtight container. Dark cakes can be wrapped first with a cloth soaked in brandy, wine or bourbon. Liquor should not be put on white fruitcakes since it may make them soggy. Wrapped and refrigerated, dark cakes will keep several months, light ones about 2 weeks. Dark cakes will, of course, ship better.

GARNISHES

Garnishes are the small decorative touches you add to a plate or platter to make a dish more attractive and to give food color and taste contrast. They may be sweet, spicy or simply crisp and cool. Often they are merely raw fruits or vegetables cut into fanciful shapes. However you use them, just keep these three rules in mind.

• Don't overlook the beauty of the food itself. When carefully selected and well prepared, food is attractive by virtue of its natural goodness and freshness and its varying textures, colors and aromas. Just a row of thinly cut, beautifully roasted meat slices, delicately crusted, covered with a silky shimmer of sauce and garnished with mushroom slices and fresh perky bunches of watercress, is beautiful to look at. Good food, good design involving color, form and pleasing combinations all add up to successful garnishing.

• Be sure the garnishes are in keeping with the food itself, and that the food is arranged on platters or in dishes suitable for it.

GELATIN

Large Molds Attractive molds are available in a variety of shapes and sizes. There are shells, pineapples, fish and many other shapes. However, square cake pans, loaf pans or mixing bowls can also be used. Mixtures can be unmolded and cut in squares or slices, or scooped out with an ice cream scoop.

Individual Molds A selection of scalloped, fluted and other shapes is available. Mixtures can also be molded in custard cups, coffee cups or even paper cups. Some mixtures need not be molded but can be spooned directly into sherbet or parfait glasses before chilling.

Molding Allow at least 3 hours chilling time for gelatin-based mixtures to become firm. Some may need to chill overnight before being turned out of mold. Refrigerators also vary in degree of coldness and this must be considered.

Unmolding Dip mold in warm water to the depth of the gelatin. Loosen around edge with the point of a paring knife. Put serving dish on top of mold and turn upside down. Shake, holding the dish tightly to mold.

Using Fruit Juice or Syrup Fresh or frozen pineapple juice and fruit must be boiled 2 minutes before being added to gelatin mixtures. Fresh pineapple contains an enzyme that destroys the gelling power of the gelatin. Use not more than $1/2$ to $3/4$ cup canned-fruit syrup in a recipe calling for a total of 2 cups liquid. These syrups may be too heavy and sweet and prevent the mixture from gelling properly.

GIFTS OF FOOD

Containers A glass or plastic container or a covering of transparent plastic is perfect for many food gifts since they are so attractive and look so appetizing they really need no further decoration. Foil containers, such as loaf pans, trays and fluted cupcake pans, and reusable containers, such as apothecary jars, baskets, brandy snifters, trays, painted wood or metal boxes and miniature bread trays, can also be used. Frozen-pudding containers and coffee cans with snap-on lids are also fine; the pudding containers have attractive colored lids. Plastic drinking glasses can be used for some foods. Cotton rug yarn comes in many colors and is convenient and is inexpensive for tying gifts.

Decorating Jar Lids Jelly or pickle jars make attractive containers. To decorate the lids, cover with foil, felt or crepe paper; or attach bows, artificial fruits or flowers, or a small ornament with double-faced masking tape.

Decorating Glass Containers Use notary seals (they come in several sizes and colors), make stripes with colored plastic tape, cut designs out of self-adhesive plastic, or make appropriate holiday drawings with china markers.

To Trim Jar Lids with Yarn or Cord With toothpick, thinly spread screw-type jar lids with white glue. Starting at edge of rim, carefully wind red or green yarn or cord around lid, keeping rows very close together. (Guiding yarn or cord with toothpick prevents it from sticking to fingers.) Reapply small amounts of glue, if necessary. At center, cut yarn or cord, leaving about $1/2$" length. Apply small amount of glue to end and tuck under, using a clean toothpick. Let stand until glue is dry.

When to Make Sealed gifts: anytime. Refrigerated gifts: no more than a day or two before giving. Cakes: unless frozen, no more than a week ahead. Candies: no more than a week ahead. Breads: unless frozen, no more than two days ahead. Label food gifts that require refrigeration. Serving suggestions are helpful, too.

Cookies for Mailing Select ones that keep their fresh flavor at least a week under average conditions. Those low in eggs are best. Choose thick, firm cookies that won't break easily and end up in crumbs.

Wrapping for Mailing Wrap separately in transparent plastic wrap or foil. Pack in crumpled tissue paper in a firm box so cookies cannot slide around. Gift-wrap, then cover with corrugated cardboard. Put in a slightly larger box and mark it "Fragile." *Important* Food gifts that require refrigeration should be so labeled, and those that require reheating should carry a decorative tag or label with the reheating directions. Serving suggestions might prove helpful, too.

Something Extra Include the recipe for your gift either typed or neatly handwritten on a small card that the recipient can transfer to her recipe file for future use. Sign your name and add the date.

GRATING AND SHREDDING

These are not the same and should not be confused.

To grate is to reduce a hard food into smaller pieces by rubbing against a rough or indented surface. Spices, hard cheeses, lemon or orange peel, onions, cabbage and potatoes are grated to bring out their flavor and to make them easier to mix with other food. There are hand graters, wire graters and mechanical graters in different shapes so they may be placed over a bowl or loaf pan, or stand on the table for grating.

To shred is to tear or cut into fragments or strips. It may be done with a sharp knife by cutting on a board or on a mechanical or hand shredder. Some hand and mechanical shredders also have disks or sides with different-size cuts for making small, medium or large cuts.

HONEY

Measuring Honey When baking with honey, measure the shortening first and then measure the honey in the same cup. The honey will slide out more easily.

Storing Honey Store honey in a dry place, because it absorbs and retains moisture. Do not refrigerate. Refrigeration or freezing won't harm the color or flavor, but it may hasten granulation. If granulation, or solidification, does occur, put the container in a bowl of warm water (no warmer than the hand can bear), until the crystals melt and the honey liquefies.

Kinds of Honey Five types of honey are on the market today: liquid (used in our recipes); granulated, or solid, sometimes called candied, creamed or honey spread; comb; cut comb, which comes in bars about 4" long and 1½" wide; and chunk, which is small pieces of comb honey in liquid honey.

Buying Honey Buy the flavor of honey you prefer, either very mild or strong. The flavor depends on the flower from which the bees gather nectar. As a rule, the lighter the color of the honey, the milder the flavor. Mild-flavored clover honey should be used in baking. The moisture content varies in the less common types of honey, such as tupelo, sage, orange-blossom, buckwheat and many others, and this may unbalance the recipe. Serve these stronger types as spreads in order to appreciate more fully their unusual flavors.

KNIVES

Cut working time by having good-quality and sharp knives. Do not let these precious tools of your trade be misused by anyone. Use the type of sharpener recommended by the manufacturer. Buy knives to fit your hand and purpose. If you have not mastered the art of using French knives and a good solid wooden chopping board or block, learn how. Properly used, a French knife requires a minimum of time, energy and clean-up to chop or mince almost any food.

LUNCH BOXES
Soups

● Freeze individual cans of flavored bouillon (or fruit or vegetable juice) and pack them frozen. At lunchtime they'll be the right temperature for drinking. Use miniature can openers for these.

● Tie a string around a frankfurter and dangle frankfurter in thermos of hot tomato juice, tomato soup, pea or bean soup. At lunchtime, remove heated frankfurter and put in split roll. Drink liquid.

● Put soups in wide-mouthed vacuum containers and include a sturdy plastic ladle spoon.

Sandwiches and Such

● For non-soggy sandwiches, spread softened butter or margarine evenly to the edge of each bread slice. Peanut butter and moistened cream cheese also keep moist fillings from soaking into the bread.

● For easier eating, use several thin slices of meat rather than a single thick one.

● Wrap lettuce, tomato slices, pickle slices and other juicy items separately in moisture-proof wrapping to be added to sandwich later.

● Tuck in small salt and pepper shakers and little packets of catsup, jelly, mustard and mustard relish, whichever are appropriate. Tiny plastic containers with covers can also be used for mustard, etc.

Tips on Freezing Prepare a week's supply of sandwiches, wrap individually and freeze. Pack in lunch boxes while still frozen and they'll be just thawed by lunchtime. Don't keep frozen longer than 2 to 3 weeks. All fresh breads freeze well. For fillings, use cooked egg yolk, peanut butter, cooked chicken, turkey, meat, fish, dried beef or drained crushed pineapple. Do not use very moist fillings, cooked egg white or raw vegetables. For binders use lemon, orange, pineapple or other fruit juice; milk; dairy sour cream or applesauce. Avoid mayonnaise or salad dressing, which separate when they are frozen. Good combinations are: minced hard-cooked egg yolk with sour cream and chopped dill pickle, grated cheese with sour cream and chili sauce, thinly sliced ham with cream cheese and chopped chives, chopped chicken with sour cream and red-pepper relish, and liver pâté with crumbled crisp bacon.

Quickies

● Alternate cheese and ham cubes on small skewers or picks. Wrap with bread-butter sandwiches.

● Hollow out frankfurter or sandwich rolls and fill with tuna or chicken salad.

MERINGUES

A meringue is a mixture of beaten egg whites and granulated sugar. It may be soft or hard depending on the amount of sugar added during the beating. Soft meringue may be used as a topping for pies, cakes and puddings; hard meringue as a pastry shell for fruit or ice cream. Here, rules for perfect meringues:

- Separate eggs while they are cold.
- Allow egg whites to warm to room temperature, since at this temperature they can be beaten to incorporate more air.
- Use a small deep bowl and a beater free from grease, as fat interferes with the proper beating of egg whites. The whites will increase to 2½ to 4 times their original volume. A rotary hand beater can be used in making a soft meringue; an electric mixer is necessary for a hard meringue.
- When egg whites have been beaten to the foamy stage, add salt and cream of tartar (1 teaspoon to one cup unbeaten egg whites).
- The addition of sugar determines the type of meringue produced. Two tablespoons granulated sugar per egg white results in soft meringue. Four to 5 tablespoons of sugar for each egg white are added for hard meringues. Beat in sugar gradually, 1 tablespoon at a time, until no grains of sugar can be felt when a little is rubbed between the fingers. Meringue should form pointed peaks that are so stiff they stand upright and don't curl over.
- When spreading a meringue on a pie or cake, be sure to spread it over the entire surface, so the filling is completely covered and the meringue is attached to the edge of the dish. This prevents shrinkage of the meringue during baking.
- When preparing a hard meringue, spoon or pipe it onto unglazed brown paper for easier removal when done.
- To prevent "weeping" in a soft meringue, bake it in a preheated moderate oven (350°F.) for 12 to 15 minutes, or until golden brown. Cool at room temperature and it will not bead. Bake an individual hard meringue (tart size) in a preheated very slow oven (275°F.) for 45 minutes, then reduce heat to 250°F. and bake another 15 minutes until very lightly golden and hard to the touch. Bake larger hard meringues (pie size) in a preheated very slow oven (275°F.) for 1 hour. The oven temperature should always be low to dry the meringues and make them crisp instead of gummy.
- A meringue mixture can also be poached in milk and used to top a soft custard.
- Allow hard meringues to cool in the oven.

OVEN-TEMPERATURE CONTROL

In baking, exact temperature control is extremely important for some foods—namely cakes, pies, breads, soufflés, popovers, cream puffs, meringues and custards. In others, a little variation can be tolerated; for example, some casserole dishes, baked potatoes, beans, meat loaves, etc. However, it is always desirable to have oven temperatures as accurate as possible. And since temperatures may vary for any one of a number of reasons, we suggest the following checks.

- When a range has no thermostatic oven control, a portable oven thermometer can be a great help. Check the temperature frequently and adjust the amount of heat manually.

- Use a portable oven thermometer to determine the accuracy of an automatic thermostatic control. If, for example, your oven is set at 375°F. but the thermometer shows 350°F., turn the control up an extra 25° to compensate.

- Some thermostatic controls are accurate in the middle temperature range but inaccurate at very high or very low temperatures. So whenever you're baking one of the dishes listed above it's a good idea to check your oven out.

SHEARS

Good sharp kitchen shears are most useful in the kitchen. It pays to buy a good quality of stainless steel; the type that separates into 2 parts for cleaning is most convenient. These may be sharpened easily, and washed in the dishwasher (nonstainless shears rust in the dishwasher). Here are a few tips for putting shears to work for you.

1. Snip small amounts of parsley, green onion, celery, watercress, capers, pimiento, etc.

2. Use in boning fish or poultry.

3. Cut off bread crust if doing only one or two slices.

4. Snip raw or cooked bacon into small pieces for recipe use.

5. Disjoint poultry.

6. Open frozen food package wrappings.

7. Snip cord for trussing poultry, tying meat rolls, etc.

8. Cut up dried fruits.

9. Cut marshmallows and dates (wet first).

10. Cut out membranes from liver, kidneys, etc.

11. Trim fat off chops, cutlets, steaks, etc.

12. Cut cross in baked potato skin before serving.

13. Cut around sections and remove center from grapefruit halves.

GLOSSARY

BAKE To cook in an oven or oven-type appliance. Covered or uncovered containers may be used. When meats are baked in uncovered containers, the method is called roasting.

BAKING SHEET A flat, rectangular utensil closed on all four sides. Used where protection of the sides is necessary to prevent juicy fillings or other mixtures from running off sheet into the oven.

BARBECUE To roast slowly on a grill or spit, over coals or under free flame or oven electric unit, usually basting with a highly seasoned sauce. Popularly applied to foods cooked in or served with barbecue sauce.

BASTE To moisten meat or other foods while cooking to add flavor and to prevent drying of the surface. The liquid is often melted fat, meat drippings, fruit juice or sauce.

BATTER A mixture of flour and liquid, usually combined with other ingredients, as in baked products. The mixture is of such consistency that it may be stirred with a spoon and is thin enough to pour or drop from a spoon.

BEAT To mix rapidly 1 or more ingredients, to make mixture lighter, frothier or smoother, with a brisk, regular motion that lifts the mixture over and over, using a fork, spoon or whisk, or with a rotary motion as with an egg beater or electric mixer.

BLANCH (precook) To preheat in boiling water or steam. (1) Process used to inactivate enzymes and shrink some foods for canning, freezing or drying. Vegetables are blanched in boiling water or steam, and fruits in boiling fruit juice, syrup, water or steam. (2) Process used to aid in removal of skins from nuts, fruits and some vegetables.

BLAND Mild-flavored, not stimulating to the taste.

BLEND To mix thoroughly two or more ingredients.

BOIL To cook in water or a liquid consisting mostly of water in which bubbles rise continually and break on the surface. The boiling temperature of water at sea level is 212°.

BRAISE To cook meat or poultry slowly in a covered utensil in a small amount of liquid or in steam. (Meat may or may not be browned in a small amount of fat before braising.)

BREAD CRUMBS *Soft bread crumbs* are made by crumbling day-old or slightly stale bread. Firm bread is best for these. *Dry bread crumbs* are made from dry, hard bread. Crumbs can be made by whirling broken bread in blender or rolling with rolling pin. *Fine dry bread crumbs* are commercially packaged crumbs. They are sold plain or seasoned and are used for breading, etc.

BREADED Coated with crumbs of bread or other food; or coated with crumbs, then with diluted slightly beaten egg or evaporated milk, and again with crumbs.

BROIL To cook by direct heat.

CAKE PAN Utensil for baking cake. It may be round, square or oblong, with straight or slightly flared sides. Some have removable bottoms and some, a tube in the center. Size is designated by dimensions (to nearest 1/4") of top inside rim.

CANDIED (1) When applied to fruit, fruit peel or ginger, cooked in a heavy syrup until plump and translucent, then drained and dried. The product is also known as crystallized fruit, fruit peel or ginger. (2) When applied to sweet potatoes and carrots, cooked in sugar or syrup.

CARAMELIZE To heat sugar or foods containing sugar until a brown color and characteristic flavor develop.

CASSEROLE A covered utensil in which food may be baked and served. It may have one or two handles. Size is stated in liquid measurements.

CHAFING DISH A utensil used to cook food at the table, consisting of a deep, lidded skillet that sits on a stand over a burner. Some are like a double boiler, with a pan for hot water into which the skillet may be placed.

CHICKEN FRYER A deep, covered frypan or skillet.

CHOPPED Cut in pieces with a knife or other sharp tool.

CLARIFIED BUTTER The upper portion of butter, clear, liquefied and oil-like, formed when butter is melted slowly, then cooled without stirring.

CLARIFY To make a liquid clear and free from solids, such as broth made clear by the use of egg white.

COOKIE SHEET A flat, rectangular utensil that may be open on one, two or three sides. Especially designed for baking cookies and biscuits.

CREAMED (1) One or more foods worked until soft and creamy, using a spoon, wooden paddle or other implement. Applied frequently to mixing or blending fat and sugar together. (2) Applied to foods cooked in or served with a white sauce.

CUSTARD CUPS Small, deep, bowl-shaped utensils for oven use. They contain individual servings.

CUT IN To distribute solid fat in dry ingredients by chopping with knives or pastry blender until finely divided.

DASH Less than 1/8 teaspoon of an ingredient, usually a spice.

DECORATE To embellish a dessert with ingredients that add color or flavor, such as whipped cream or topping, bits of candied fruit, maraschino cherries, etc.

DICE To cut into small cubes.

DOUBLE BOILER Consists of two saucepans (each with a handle or side handles) that fit one on top of the other. Food that must be cooked at a low temperature is placed in top pan over hot or boiling water in the lower pan.

DREDGE To coat or sprinkle food with specified ingredient, such as flour.

DRIPPINGS Fat and juices drawn from meat during cooking.

DRIZZLE To sprinkle in small amounts or particles.

DUTCH OVEN A large heavy pot with a tight-fitting cover, especially good for long, slow cooking.

FOLD To gently combine ingredients for maximum volume and lightness by using two motions, one that cuts vertically through the mixture and another that turns the mixture over as the implement slides across bottom of mixing bowl.

FREEZE-DRYING A process to preserve foods by freezing and drying them in a vacuum. Freeze-dried food is porous, brittle and lightweight. It also retains its original shape when rehydrated, and can be stored without refrigeration.

FREEZING A method of preserving food by chilling it very rapidly at a low temperature (usually −10°F. or below) and maintaining it at a temperature below 0°F. Freezing is accomplished by direct immersion in a refrigerating medium, such as brine; by indirect contact with a refrigerant, such as conduction through metal plates; or by a blast of cold air. In flash freezing, food is frozen at very low temperatures in a medium such as liquid nitrogen.

FRENCH FRYER An uncovered cooking utensil with a perforated, meshed or sieve-like insert basket with one handle, used for deep-fat frying of foods.

FRICASSEE To cook by braising. Usually applied to meat, poultry and game cut into pieces.

FRY To cook in fat. Applied especially to (1) cooking in a small amount of fat, also called sautéing or panfrying; (2) cooking in a deep layer of fat, also called deep-fat frying.

FRYPAN OR SKILLET A shallow covered or uncovered pan with one handle. Size is stated by the top diameter in inches.

GARNISH To embellish a main dish or salad with ingredients that add color or flavor, such as parsley, paprika, radish roses, carrot curls, etc.

GLACE To coat with a thin sugar syrup cooked to the hard-crack stage (300°F.). When used for pies and certain types of bread, the mixture may contain thickening, but is not cooked to such a concentrated form, or it may be uncooked.

GRIDDLE A very shallow, uncovered, smooth, heavy utensil (occasionally with pouring lip) equipped with one or two handles. Size is stated by top outside dimension.

GRILL To cook by direct heat. Also a utensil or appliance used for such cooking.

GRIND To reduce to particles by cutting or crushing.

KETTLE A covered or uncovered cooking utensil with a bail handle. Capacity is stated in liquid measurement.

KNEAD To manipulate with a pressing motion accompanied by folding and stretching.

LARD To cover with strips of fat, or to insert fat strips into meat with a larding needle.

LOAF PAN A deep, narrow, rectangular utensil with slightly flared sides; designed for oven use.

LUKEWARM Approximately 95°F.; tepid. Lukewarm liquids or foods sprinkled on the wrist will not feel warm.

MARINATE To put food in a marinade, a seasoned or flavored liquid, to give flavor.

MASK To cover completely. Usually applied to the use of mayonnaise or other thick sauce.

MINCE To cut or chop into very small pieces.

MIX To combine ingredients in any way that effects a distribution.

MUFFIN OR CUPCAKE PAN A tray-like utensil consisting of a number of suspended individual cups that are almost straight-sided and that are an integral part of the pan.

OPEN ROASTING AND BAKING PAN A large rectangular pan especially designed for roasting meats and poultry and for baking.

PANBROIL To cook uncovered on a hot surface, usually in a frypan. Fat is poured off as it accumulates.

PANFRY To cook in a small amount of fat. (See FRY and SAUTÉ.)

PARBOIL To boil until partially cooked. Usually cooking is completed by another method.

PARE To cut off the outside covering.

PEEL To strip off the outside covering.

PIEPANS OR PIE PLATES Round, open utensils with flared sides, especially designed for baking pies.

POACH To cook in a hot liquid using precautions to retain shape. The temperature used varies with the food.

POT ROAST A term applied to cooking large cuts of meat by braising or to the meat so cooked. (See BRAISE.)

PRESSURE COOKER An airtight container for cooking food at a high temperature under steam pressure. It is equipped with a gauge for measuring and indicating the pressure on a graduated dial or with some other device. Pressure cookers are used in canning low-acid foods, for cooking less tender cuts of meat and poultry in reduced time and for cooking some vegetables.

RECONSTITUTE To restore concentrated foods to their normal state, usually by adding water. Applied to such foods as dry milk (for fluid milk) or frozen orange juice (for liquid juice).

REHYDRATION To soak, cook or use other procedures with dehydrated foods to restore water lost during drying.

RENDER To free fat from connective tissue at low heat.

ROAST To cook uncovered in hot air. Usually done in an oven, but occasionally in ashes, under coals or on heated stones or metals. The term is usually applied to meats, but may refer to other foods such as potatoes, corn or chestnuts.

ROASTER A covered pan, with or without a rack. Especially designed for cooking meats and poultry. Length and width are measured overall outside the pan, including handles.

ROTISSERIE An appliance designed to roast meat or poultry by dry heat on a turning spit.

SAUCEPAN A covered or uncovered cooking utensil with one handle. Capacity is stated in liquid measurement.

SAUTÉ To brown or cook in a small amount of fat. (See FRY.)

SCALD (1) To heat milk to just below the boiling point, when tiny bubbles form at edge. (2) To dip certain foods in boiling water. (See BLANCH.)

SCALLOP To bake food (usually cut in pieces) with a sauce or other liquid. The food and sauce may be mixed together or arranged in alternate layers in a baking dish, with or without a topping of crumbs.

SEAR To brown the surface of meat by a short exposure to intense heat.

SIMMER To cook in a liquid just below the boiling point, at temperatures of 185° F. to 210°F. Bubbles form slowly and collapse below the surface.

STEAM To cook in steam with or without pressure. The steam may be applied directly to the food, as in a steamer or pressure cooker.

STEAMER A covered saucepan or sauce pot having one or more perforated insert pans equipped with a handle or handles.

STEEP To allow a substance to stand in liquid below the boiling point for the purpose of extracting flavor, color or other qualities.

STERILIZE To destroy microorganisms. For culinary purposes this is most often done at a high temperature with steam, hot air or boiling liquid.

STEW To simmer in a small quantity of liquid.

STIR To mix food materials with a circular motion for the purpose of blending or securing uniform consistency.

TEXTURE Properties of food including roughness, smoothness, graininess, etc., that are visible or sensed with the skin and the muscles in the mouth.

TOAST To brown by means of dry heat.

UTENSILS FOR BAKING AND TOP-OF-RANGE COOKING Inside dimensions (to nearest 1/4") of baking utensils are used to designate size. Most utensils are measured from the top inside for length, width or diameter. In general, capacities are stated in liquid measurements when level-full.

WARM A temperature of 105°F. to 115°F. for liquid or food.

WHIP To beat rapidly to incorporate air and produce expansion. Generally applied to cream, eggs and gelatin dishes.

COOKING FOR TWO

There are two times in a woman's life when she experiences the joys of cooking for two. The first is obviously when she is a bride—learning the ropes, finding out what her husband likes and loathes, what he *will* eat, *won't* eat and *might* be tempted to try. The second generally occurs when, after years of big-family cooking, she waves the last child off to college and settles down to relearn the techniques of planning, buying and preparing meals for a duo again.

Especially on this second go-around, cooking for two can be the most rewarding cooking of a lifetime. It can and should be more exciting and experimental than big-family cooking dares to be. The investment is smaller, the occasional failure more easily written off, and if the results are sheer disaster, the substitute meal more quickly and easily prepared. With cupboard space liberated from giant-economy-size packages of staples you have room for an exciting variety of herbs, spices and all the things that make a dish different. There's also more time to plan, shop, sample and create.

So there's really no reason at all to fall into the delicatessen-dinner habit or the tuna-salad-three-nights-a-week syndrome. In fact there is every reason, now as never before, to cook up a storm. Keep firmly in mind that no kind of food is off limits for two. True, you can now serve the double lamb chops, the individual steaks, the broiled lobsters that were prohibitive on a big-family budget. But if you hanker for the aroma of a roast in the oven, or the taste of a succulent turkey, don't despair. These too can be tailored to two, without waste or monotony, if you program them ahead. Take a pork loin roast, for example. Depending on the size, you can first ask the butcher to cut off two, four or six loin chops to freeze for future reference. (They're considerably cheaper than if you bought them individually.) From the other end have him cut off another hunk to give you 1/2 to 3/4 pound of boneless meat for an exotic Chinese dish. Freeze for future use. Now, roast the rest for an evocative big-family kind of dinner.

Look for the ever-increasing number of foreign foods, browse through cookbooks of national or regional dishes, and regularly try something you've never cooked, perhaps never even tasted. You may come an occasional cropper but you'll guarantee a note of real interest in his voice when your husband asks "What's for dinner tonight?"

TIPS FOR TWOSOMES

- Buy a pound of ground beef and shape in patties. Wrap in foil and freeze any not used.
- Use a small double boiler for creamed vegetables or other foods. Small amounts of food dry out quickly in a saucepan, but stay moist over hot water.
- In general, it's better not to halve large recipes. Cooking time and amounts of liquid have different proportions.
- Store leftovers in covered containers so they will retain their freshness. Meat or prepared dishes need not cool more than 15 minutes before being refrigerated.
- Invest in small-size saucepans and skillets for everyday use, with perhaps large ones of each for company.

- Avoid fresh milk spoilage by keeping evaporated and instant nonfat milk on hand for cooking. They are convenient and less expensive.
- Learn can sizes and buy the ones best suited for your use.

CHICKEN SOUP DELUXE

2 teaspoons instant chicken bouillon
2 tablespoons slivered almonds
1/2 cup shredded carrots
1 cup minced cooked chicken
Salt and pepper
1 tablespoon instant parsley

Bring 2 cups water to boil. Add first 4 ingredients and bring again to boil. Season to taste and sprinkle with parsley. Makes 2 servings.

FISH CHOWDER

2 tablespoons butter or margarine
1 medium onion, minced
1 large potato, chopped
1 can (1 pint 2 ounces) tomato juice
1 package (12 ounces) unthawed frozen cod, haddock or flounder
1/2 teaspoon each thyme and basil
Salt and pepper

Melt butter in 2-quart saucepan. Add onion and potato and cook slowly, 10 minutes, stirring occasionally. Add tomato juice and bring to boil. Add fish cut in 4 pieces; bring to boil, cover and simmer 10 minutes, or until fish is white, firm and flakes easily. (Do not overcook.) Add herbs, and salt and pepper to taste. Makes about 1 quart, or 2 hearty servings.

SAVORY MEAT LOAF

Fine dry bread crumbs
1 cup milk
1 small onion, minced
1-1/2 teaspoons butter or margarine
1 pound ground beef
1/2 cup grated carrot
1 egg
1 tablespoon chili sauce
1 teaspoon salt
Freshly ground pepper
1/2 teaspoon ginger
1/2 teaspoon curry powder
1 teaspoon anchovy paste
Prepared mustard

Soak 1/3 cup crumbs in milk. Sauté onion in butter. Combine all ingredients, except mustard, and blend well. Shape in a smooth loaf in greased shallow baking dish. Spread thin coat of mustard on the surface and sprinkle lightly with some dry bread crumbs. Bake in moderate oven (350°F.) 50 to 60 minutes. Good with creamed potatoes and broiled tomatoes. Serve hot at one meal, cold at another. Makes 4 servings.

BARBECUED FRANKFURTERS WITH NOODLES

1/2 large onion, chopped
1 clove garlic, minced
2/3 cup catsup
1 teaspoon chili powder
1-1/2 teaspoons each salt and dry
   mustard
2 tablespoons red-wine vinegar
1/2 pound frankfurters
Hot cooked wide noodles or thin
   spaghetti

Put all ingredients, except last 2, in large heavy saucepan with 1 cup water. Bring to boil, cover and simmer 15 minutes. Add frankfurters and simmer 10 minutes longer. Meanwhile, arrange noodles on heated platter. Cover with frankfurters; top with some of the sauce. Serve with remaining sauce. Makes 2 servings.

BEEF CHEESEBURGERS DE LUXE

3/4 pound ground beef chuck
1 cup shredded sharp Cheddar cheese
1-1/2 tablespoons grated onion
2 to 3 teaspoons steak sauce
Pepper to taste
4 slices bacon, partially cooked
Hot buttered sliced French bread
2 tablespoons soft butter or margarine
1 tablespoon minced stuffed olives

Mix first 5 ingredients and shape in 4 patties. Wrap a slice of bacon around each and secure with a wooden pick. Sauté about 5 minutes on each side and serve on French bread. Top each patty with a dab of butter and olives mixed together. Makes 2 to 4 servings.

FISH MORNAY

1/2 pound frozen flounder or cod fillets
Salt
1 tablespoon butter or margarine
2 teaspoons flour
Dash of pepper
2/3 cup milk
Grated Parmesan cheese

Poach fish in small amount of boiling salted water in skillet until it flakes easily with fork; drain. Break apart in large pieces and put in broiler-proof dish. Melt butter in saucepan and stir in flour, 1/4 teaspoon salt and the pepper. Add milk and cook, stirring, until thickened and bubbly. Remove from heat and stir in 2 tablespoons grated cheese. Pour over fish; sprinkle generously with additional cheese. Broil until lightly browned. Makes 2 servings.

BROILED FRANKFURTERS WITH HOT POTATO SALAD

3 potatoes, cooked
3 or 4 slices bacon
1 egg, hard-cooked and diced
1 small onion, minced
2 teaspoons white vinegar
Salt and pepper
Chopped parsley
1/2 teaspoon chopped capers
1/2 pound frankfurters
Prepared mustard
Hot potato salad

Cut potatoes in slices 1/4" thick. Sauté bacon until crisp, drain and crumble. Leave 1-1/2 tablespoons bacon drippings in skillet; add potatoes, bacon, egg, onion, vinegar and salt and pepper to taste. Mix gently and heat. Garnish with parsley and capers. Split frankfurters lengthwise almost through and open out. Score 3 or 4 times diagonally on skin side and brush with mustard. Arrange on rack in baking pan skin side up. Broil 5" from unit 5 minutes, or until heated and browned. Serve with the salad. Makes 2 servings.

CHICKEN WITH MUSHROOMS

2 small whole chicken breasts
1 teaspoon dry sherry
2 teaspoons cornstarch
1-1/2 teaspoons salt
1/4 teaspoon monosodium glutamate
1 can (4 ounces) sliced mushrooms,
   drained and liquid reserved
1 cup pea pods or 1/2 cup partially
   cooked fresh or frozen peas
1/4 cup vegetable oil
2 slices gingerroot
Hot cooked rice

Remove skin and bone chicken breasts. Trim off membrane and any fat and cut meat in thin slices. Mix with the sherry, 1 teaspoon cornstarch, 1 teaspoon salt and the monosodium glutamate in bowl. Blend remaining cornstarch with mushroom liquid and set aside. Remove strings from pea pods, rinse pods and pat dry. Put oil in hot skillet over medium-high heat; add ginger and chicken. Cook, stirring, for less than 2 minutes, just until chicken meat turns white. Drain chicken in strainer over bowl, reserving oil; discard ginger. Put oil back in skillet, add mushroom and remaining salt. Stir a few times, then add pea pods and cook, stirring, until pods turn darker green. Stir in cornstarch mixture and chicken. Cook, stirring, until thickened. Serve on the rice. Makes 2 to 3 servings.

BROILED GINGERED SPARERIBS

1 pound fresh spareribs in serving pieces
1-3/4 cups ginger ale
1/4 cup soy sauce
2 tablespoons sherry
1 tablespoon brown sugar
1/8 teaspoon white pepper
1/2 teaspoon ground ginger

Put spareribs in large saucepan, add ginger ale and bring to boil. Cover and simmer 1 hour. Drain and put in large bowl. Combine remaining ingredients and pour mixture over ribs. Marinate, tossing occasionally, 1 hour or longer. Arrange ribs on foil-lined broiler pan and broil under low heat 10 minutes on each side. Serves 2.

PORK CHOPS, SHANGHAI STYLE

3 tablespoons soy sauce
1 tablespoon sugar, preferably brown
1/4 teaspoon monosodium glutamate
1 tablespoon vegetable oil
4 thin pork chops or 4 thin slices pork tenderloin
1/2 cup thinly sliced onion

Mix first 3 ingredients and ½ cup water in small bowl. Put oil in hot skillet over medium-high heat. Add chops and brown on both sides. Remove chops, leaving as much oil as possible in skillet. Add onion and cook, stirring, until edges are light brown. Put chops back in skillet and pour soy sauce mixture over top. Cover and cook slowly, turning once, 5 minutes. Uncover and cook, basting, ½ minute. Makes 2 or 3 servings.

BEAN SANDWICH

For each sandwich, mix 3 tablespoons baked beans, 3 tablespoons minced watercress, 2 slices broken cooked crisp bacon, 1 teaspoon sweet-pickle relish and salad dressing or mayonnaise to bind. Spread between slices of buttered whole-wheat or white toast and add a lettuce leaf.

GOLDEN FLEECE

1 package (3 ounces) cream cheese
6 tablespoons milk
2 eggs
1/4 teaspoon salt
1/4 teaspoon dry mustard

Heat cheese in top part of double boiler over hot water until softened. Remove from heat, add remaining ingredients and beat until blended. Pour into individual baking dishes or custard cups. Bake in pan of hot water in moderate oven (375°F.) 20 to 25 minutes. Makes 2 servings.

HEARTY OMELET

4 eggs, separated
1/4 cup milk
1/2 cup leftover mashed potato
Salt and pepper
1 tablespoon butter or margarine
1/2 cup grated Cheddar cheese

Beat egg whites until stiff; set aside. Beat yolks and add milk and potato. Fold in whites and season to taste. Melt butter in skillet with cover. Pour in egg mixture and sprinkle with cheese. Cover and cook slowly until browned on the bottom. Fold and serve. Serves 2.

CURRIED SCALLOPED POTATOES

3 medium potatoes, peeled and very thinly sliced
1/2 small onion, minced
1/2 teaspoon curry powder
1 tablespoon butter or margarine
2 teaspoons flour
1/2 teaspoon salt
1/8 teaspoon pepper
2/3 cup milk
Chopped parsley

Put potatoes in shallow 1-quart baking dish. Sauté onion with curry powder in butter 2 to 3 minutes. Blend in flour, salt and pepper. Gradually add milk and cook, stirring, until slightly thickened. Pour over potatoes, cover with lid or foil and bake in moderate oven (350°F.) about 1¼ hours; sprinkle with parsley. Serves 2.

FAMILY FAVORITE

3/4 pound ground beef
1/2 small onion, chopped
1/2 carrot, shredded
1 tablespoon flour
Seasoned salt and pepper

Cook beef and onion until lightly browned, breaking up meat with fork. Add carrot. Blend flour and ¼ cup water and stir into mixture. Cook, stirring, until thickened. Season to taste. Good on mashed potatoes. Serves 2.

CHEESE RABBIT

1 cup diced sharp Cheddar cheese
1 tablespoon flour
1/2 teaspoon dry mustard
1/4 teaspoon salt
1-1/2 teaspoons butter
1/3 cup hot milk

Combine all ingredients in blender and whirl at high speed until smooth. Heat over simmering water. Good on hot toast or crackers. Makes 2 servings.

BUTTERFLY CUTLETS

With a very sharp knife, slice 2 boneless pork chops or veal cutlets, ³/₄" thick, almost in half and open out to form "butterfly" shapes. Season with salt and paprika. Brown 1 tablespoon margarine lightly in skillet, add cutlets and brown slowly on both sides until crisp. Cover each cutlet with a slice of ham and a slice of Swiss cheese, folded. Sprinkle cheese lightly with paprika, cover pan and sauté 5 minutes, or until cheese melts. Serves 2.

SKILLET FISH DINNER

1 package (12 ounces) frozen flounder, cod or haddock fillets, thawed and separated
Salt and paprika
1 tablespoon each margarine and vegetable oil
1/2 cup orange juice
1 teaspoon grated orange rind
2 green onions, sliced
1/4 cup water chestnuts, sliced
1 can (8 ounces) cut green beans, drained

Cut each fillet in 2 pieces if large. Pat dry on absorbent paper. Sprinkle lightly on each side with salt and paprika. Slowly brown fish in margarine and oil on one side. Turn and add remaining ingredients. Bring to boil, cover and simmer until fish is firm, white and flakes easily. (Cooking time depends on kind of fish.) Serve at once. Good with mashed potatoes or rice. Serves 2.

STOVE-TOP CHICKEN DINNER

1 frying chicken (about 3-1/2 pounds) with giblets
Juice of 1/2 lemon
1-1/2 teaspoons salt
1/8 teaspoon pepper
1 teaspoon rosemary leaves, crushed
1/2 cup orange juice
4 medium potatoes, peeled
6 small carrots, scraped
Chopped parsley
Green salad (optional)

Rinse chicken under running cold water and pat dry. Rub well inside and out with a mixture of next 4 ingredients. Put chicken, with giblets, in heavy pot. Add next 3 ingredients and ¹/₂ cup water. Bring to boil, cover, reduce heat and simmer 45 minutes, or until everything is tender. Sprinkle breasts and thighs with parsley; serve with a green salad, if desired. Reserve wings and legs for Hearty Chicken Salad, page 18. Use remaining parts for Chicken Soup Deluxe, page 14. Serves 2.

SKILLET LONDON BROIL

Lightly score both sides of half of a 1¹/₂-pound flank steak. Brush with soy sauce and sprinkle with pepper and garlic powder. Let stand 30 minutes. Sprinkle salt lightly in bottom of heavy skillet and heat until very hot. Panbroil steak in skillet 5 minutes on one side, or until well browned. Then turn and panbroil other side 5 minutes. Put steak on carving board; let stand a few minutes before cutting diagonally in thin slices against the grain. Steak will be rare. Cook longer for medium Makes 2 servings.

CREAMED CRAB MEAT

Melt 2 tablespoons butter in saucepan; blend in 2 tablespoons flour, stirring until mixture bubbles. Gradually add ¹/₂ cup milk. Cook, stirring, until thickened. Add 1 package (6 ounces) frozen king crab meat and let thaw over low heat. Do not boil. Season to taste. Add 1 tablespoon sherry; heat through. Serves 2.

HAM-VEGETABLE GRILL

Slash edges of ³/₄-pound slice fully cooked ham 1" thick, to prevent curling. Place on foil-covered shallow pan and broil 5 minutes in preheated broiler. Turn, spread with 2 teaspoons mustard and sprinkle with 1 tablespoon brown sugar. Surround with 2 to 4 cooked or canned sweet potatoes and 2 to 4 small cooked or canned onions. Broil 8 to 10 minutes. Makes 2 servings.

CURRIED BEEF

1 tablespoon curry powder
2 tablespoons flour
Half of 1-1/2 pound flank steak, sliced diagonally very thin (see Note)
2 tablespoons margarine
Salt and pepper to taste

Mix curry powder and flour in paper or plastic bag. Add meat slices and shake until well coated. Heat margarine in skillet. Add meat and brown only until pink color disappears. Add ³/₄ cup boiling water. Bring to boil, stirring, and simmer until gravy thickens. Season. Good with seasoned hot cooked rice, chutney and cucumbers. Makes 2 servings. *Note* Meat will be easier to cut in very thin slices if partially frozen.

EASY CREAMED SPINACH

In top part of double boiler over direct heat prepare 1 package white sauce mix, omitting ¼ cup of the liquid called for. Place over boiling water; add 1 package (10 ounces) frozen chopped spinach. Cover and cook 15 to 20 minutes, stirring occasionally. Season to taste with salt, pepper, onion salt and nutmeg; add more liquid if needed. Makes 2 to 3 servings.

PAN-BROWNED POTATOES

Drain 1 can (8 ounces) whole potatoes; dry on paper toweling. Mix 1 to 2 tablespoons fine dry bread crumbs, ½ teaspoon salt, ⅛ teaspoon pepper and dash of paprika. Roll potatoes in crumbs and sauté in 1 tablespoon hot oil in skillet, sprinkling with any remaining crumbs. Brown evenly. Makes 2 servings.

SAUTÉED CHERRY TOMATOES

Allow 6 to 8 tomatoes per serving. Sauté in a little butter or margarine in small saucepan until skins burst and tomatoes are heated. Season with salt, pepper, and oregano, thyme or basil.

HEARTY CHICKEN SALAD

Salad greens
Cooked chicken legs and wings
3 strips crisp cooked bacon
2 hard-cooked eggs, halved
1 can (2-1/2 ounces) whole mushroom caps, drained
1 tomato, cut in wedges
French dressing

Arrange salad greens on individual plates and put chicken pieces in center. Sprinkle with crumbled bacon and surround with egg halves, mushroom caps and tomato wedges. Chill. At serving time, sprinkle with French dressing. Serves 2.

GARLIC BREAD

Peel 1 clove garlic and cut in 4 slivers. Press slivers into ¼ cup softened butter or margarine and let stand at room temperature at least 30 minutes. Remove garlic. Cut one 8" hero loaf in 8 diagonal slices almost to bottom. Spread butter generously between slices and on top of bread. Sprinkle with grated Parmesan cheese and paprika; bake in very hot oven (450°F.) about 10 minutes. Serves 2.

ORANGE PANCAKES

3 tablespoons butter or margarine, softened
1/3 cup confectioners' sugar
Grated rind of 1 orange
1 recipe Thin Pancakes, page 355
1/2 cup orange juice

Mix first 3 ingredients and spread on cooled pancakes. Roll up and put in skillet. Add orange juice and heat until juice bubbles. Serve at once. Makes 8.

QUICK VANILLA SAUCE

Mix 2 tablespoons instant vanilla-pudding powder, 1 cup half-and-half or light cream, 1 teaspoon vanilla extract and few drops of yellow food coloring; beat until smooth. Chill. If sauce gets too thick, add more liquid. Makes about 1 cup.

PEARS HÉLÈNE

Place a drained chilled canned pear half in each dish. Top with vanilla ice cream and Quick Chocolate Sauce, below.

QUICK CHOCOLATE SAUCE

1 package (6 ounces) semisweet chocolate pieces or 6 squares semisweet chocolate
1 small can (5-1/2 ounces) undiluted evaporated milk
1/8 teaspoon salt
1 teaspoon vanilla extract

Melt chocolate over hot water. Beat in remaining ingredients. Serve hot or cold. Store in refrigerator and dilute with water if sauce becomes too thick. Makes about 1½ cups.

BAKED BANANAS WITH COCONUT

Put 2 bananas, cut in half lengthwise, in shallow baking dish. Pour ¼ cup orange juice and 2 teaspoons lemon juice over fruit and dot with butter. Sprinkle with grated coconut and bake in hot oven (400°F.) 10 to 15 minutes. Makes 2 servings.

BERRIES DELUXE

Add small amount of rum, orange liqueur or kirsch to fresh or frozen raspberries or strawberries. Serve with a scoop of raspberry or strawberry sherbet.

Cranberry-Orange Punch

Lime Punch with
Lemon-Lime Molds

Citrus Punch

IRWIN HOROWITZ

HOW TO MAKE GOOD COFFEE

1. Coffee brands do differ. Try them until you find the one you like best, then stick with it.

2. Choose the correct grind for your coffee maker. Use drip or all-purpose grind for a drip pot, fine grind for a vacuum maker and regular grind for a percolator.

3. Have coffee maker thoroughly clean. Scrub with a light-duty detergent and a soft cloth or sponge after each use, and rinse well.

4. Fresh coffee makes the best. Once opened, store coffee in refrigerator. Store unopened cans in freezer.

5. If possible, use the full capacity of the coffee maker, but never less than half the capacity, for most successful operation.

6. Start with cold fresh water, not water from hot water tap.

7. Use the correct measurement: For each serving, use 2 level measuring-tablespoons (or 1 coffee measure) and $3/4$ measuring-cup water. For demitasse coffee, use $1/2$ measuring-cup water.

8. To make the clearest coffee, use a filter or filter paper that fits the coffee basket.

9. Time the brewing accurately. When coffee is overbrewed, undesirable flavors develop.

Drip Method

1. Measure cold water into tea kettle and heat to boiling. Meanwhile, preheat coffeepot by rinsing with very hot water.

2. Measure drip-grind coffee into cone with filter paper or into filter section of coffeepot, depending on the drip pot used.

3. Pour measured freshly boiling water into cone or upper container of drip pot. Cover, depending on pot used.

4. When dripping is completed, in 4 to 6 minutes, remove upper section. Stir and serve.

Vacuum Method

1. Measure fresh cold water into lower bowl. Put on heat and bring to boil. Place filter in upper bowl. When water boils, measure fine-grind coffee into upper bowl.

2. Remove boiling water from heat. Insert upper bowl with slight twist to insure tight seal. Put back over reduced heat. (When using electric range, turn off electricity.)

3. Most of water will rise into upper bowl. Allow to mix with ground coffee.

1 minute, stirring thoroughly in zigzag fashion first 20 seconds.

4. Remove from heat. Brew will return to lower bowl within 2 minutes. Remove upper bowl and serve coffee.

Percolator Method

1. Remove basket and stem and measure cold fresh water into percolator. Put over heat until water boils. Remove from heat.

2. Measure regular-grind coffee into basket.

3. Insert basket and stem in percolator, cover, return to gentle heat and percolate slowly 6 to 8 minutes. (Water level should always be below the bottom of coffee basket.)

4. Remove basket and stem and serve coffee.

For automatic coffee makers, follow manufacturer's directions.

Instant Coffee

Follow directions on label for amount. Pour freshly boiled water over coffee in cups. For a flavor more like freshly brewed coffee, prepare several cups at a time in a pot.

THREE METHODS FOR MAKING GOOD ICED COFFEE

1. Brew extra breakfast coffee and freeze into coffee ice cubes. Then make iced coffee by pouring regular-strength coffee over the cubes.

2. Make demitasse coffee by using only $1/2$ cup water to each 2 tablespoons coffee. Pour hot over regular ice cubes.

3. Put into a tall glass twice the amount of instant coffee you would use for a cup. Dissolve in a little warm water. Fill glass with ice cubes and cold water.

HOT TEA

Heat teapot by filling it with hot water. Fill teakettle with cold fresh water from tap and bring to full rolling boil. Do not use reheated water. Allow 1 tea bag or 1 teaspoon loose tea for $3/4$ measuring-cup water and pour water directly over tea in preheated pot. Brew 3 to 5 minutes before serving. If tea is not to be served at once, remove tea bags or loose-tea holder, or strain.

ICED TEA

Make tea as for Hot Tea, above, using 50 percent more tea. Pour tea into ice-filled glasses and serve with lemon and sugar. (Instant tea is handy for making iced tea.)

CRISPY CRAB APPETIZERS

1 tablespoon grated onion
1/4 cup butter or margarine, melted
1/4 cup flour
1 cup milk
1 egg yolk, beaten
1/2 teaspoon Worcestershire
1/4 teaspoon salt
Dash pepper
Pinch of garlic powder
1 pound crab meat
3/4 cup fine cracker or dry bread
   crumbs
Fat for frying

Cook onion in the butter until golden; blend in flour. Gradually add milk and cook until thickened, stirring constantly. Combine egg yolk and seasonings and add to sauce, stirring. Carefully add crab meat. Blend into a paste and cool. Shape crab mixture into balls with a teaspoon, roll in crumbs and fry in hot deep fat (375°F. on a frying thermometer) 2 minutes. Drain on paper toweling. Serve hot or cold on toothpicks. Makes about 50. These can be impaled on toothpicks and arranged on a cauliflower head with stuffed green and black olives.

MARINATED APPETIZER FRANKFURTERS

3/4 pound cocktail frankfurters
1/2 cup soy sauce
1 tablespoon sugar
1 teaspoon instant minced onion
1/2 teaspoon ground ginger

Marinate frankfurters for 2 hours in mixture of remaining ingredients, turning and basting occasionally. Drain and reserve marinade. Place frankfurters in shallow baking dish. Pour marinade over them. Bake in moderate oven (350°F.) 15 to 20 minutes, or until thoroughly heated. Drain and serve on cocktail picks.

HOT CHILI-BEEF APPETIZERS

1 pound ground beef
1 tablespoon chili powder
1 teaspoon salt
Dash of hot pepper sauce
1/4 cup catsup
12 slices toast, buttered

Heat all ingredients, except toast, in skillet, stirring with fork, until meat loses its red color but is still spreadable. Spread on toast. When ready to serve, cut each slice in 4 triangles. Bake in very hot oven (450°F.) about 10 minutes. Makes 4 dozen.

MUSHROOM APPETIZERS

Drain 1 can (4 ounces) mushroom caps. Marinate overnight in 1/2 cup tarragon French dressing. Add dash of hot pepper sauce. Roll Flaky French Pastry (page 24) to 1/8" thickness and cut in 36 squares, 2" square. Put a well-drained mushroom in center of each, rounded side up. Fold corners to center. Bake in very hot oven (450°F.) 12 to 15 minutes.

EGGPLANT MARINARA APPETIZER

1 unpeeled large eggplant cut in 1"
   cubes
1/2 cup white vinegar (preferably wine
   vinegar)
1 teaspoon salt
1/2 teaspoon white pepper
1 clove garlic, minced
1 teaspoon dried oregano
1/2 teaspoon dried basil
3/4 cup olive oil

Boil eggplant in boiling water to cover 8 to 10 minutes. Drain. Cubes should be soft but retain their shape. Mix other ingredients, except oil. Place drained eggplant in large bowl and pour marinade over. Toss thoroughly. Marinate overnight, or at least 8 hours. Before serving, toss with oil. Makes 6 to 8 servings. This will keep about a week in the refrigerator.

TWO-CHEESE APPETIZERS

1/2 pound (2 cups) Swiss cheese, grated
1/2 cup grated Parmesan cheese
1/2 cup butter at room temperature
3/4 cup all-purpose flour
3/4 teaspoon salt
1/8 teaspoon cayenne
1/8 teaspoon nutmeg
1 egg
Paprika

Knead together in bowl 1 1/2 cups Swiss cheese and next 6 ingredients. Form into ball and chill 15 minutes. Divide dough in 6 equal pieces. Shape each piece into a rope 6" long. Put ropes parallel to each other and cut ropes in 1/2" pieces. Shape each piece into a ball and flatten into a circle about 1/4" thick. Arrange on baking sheet, leaving 2" space between. Brush with egg beaten with 1 teaspoon water. Sprinkle each with a little of the remaining Swiss cheese. Bake in hot oven (425°F.) 10 minutes, or until puffed and lightly browned. Cool on rack. Sprinkle with paprika and store in air-tight container. Makes about 6 dozen.

HAM-CHEESE APPETIZERS

1-1/2 cups grated process American
   cheese
1/4 cup evaporated milk
1 cup ground cooked ham
1/4 cup catsup
1 teaspoon dry mustard
6 slices toast, crusts removed

Melt cheese in milk in top of double
boiler over boiling water. Add remaining ingredients, except toast;
mix well. Spread one side of toast
with mixture. Cut in fingers and reheat in moderate oven (350°F.).
Makes 1½ dozen.

DANISH BEEF CANAPÉ

Butter thin slices of tiny rye bread.
Top with thin slices of cold, rare
roast beef and paper-thin onions,
fried crisp and dark brown.

CRAB CANAPÉ

2 cups crab meat
1/4 cup mayonnaise (about)
1/4 teaspoon Worcestershire
1 large cucumber
Salt and pepper
24 sautéed small bread rounds
Parsley sprigs

Shred crab meat fine. Mix with
enough mayonnaise to hold it together and season with Worcestershire. Peel cucumber and chop very
fine. Season lightly with salt and pepper. Spread a thin layer of cucumber
on each bread round. Cover with a
mound of crab meat. Brown lightly
under broiler. Decorate with parsley
sprigs before serving. Makes 24
canapés.

TOMATO CAVIAR

1 can (28 ounces) tomatoes
1 package (3 ounces) cream cheese
1 tablespoon onion juice
1 tablespoon cream (about)
12 rounds of sautéed bread
1/4 cup mayonnaise (about)
1 small jar red caviar

Drain tomatoes for at least 2 hours,
reserving juice for other purposes.
Beat cheese with onion juice and
enough cream to make it spreadable.
Spread each sautéed bread round
with cheese. Mash tomatoes and
spread a little over cheese on each
round. Cover with mayonnaise and
put a few dots of red caviar in the
center of each round. Makes 2 dozen.

APPLE APPETIZERS

1 cup creamed cottage cheese
1 small can deviled ham
1 teaspoon grated onion
2 tablespoons chopped black olives
1 tablespoon minced pimiento
2 teaspoons dry sherry
3 unpeeled red eating apples cut in
   wedges

Combine all ingredients, except apples, and mix well. Pile in small bowl
and surround with apple wedges. Using cocktail picks, dip wedges in mixture. Makes about 1½ cups.

HOT TUNA CANAPÉS

1/2 cup tuna, drained and broken in
   small pieces
1 hard-cooked egg, chopped
1 tablespoon minced green pepper
6 anchovies, chopped
3 tablespoons well-drained diced fresh
   tomato
Dash of steak sauce
Dash of hot pepper sauce
1 tablespoon chili sauce
1 tablespoon mayonnaise
Small toast rounds

Mix all ingredients, except toast
rounds. Spread on toast and put under broiler until hot. Makes about 1
cup mixture.

REMOULADE DIP FOR SCALLOPS

2 cups mayonnaise
1 clove garlic, crushed
1 tablespoon prepared mustard
1 tablespoon chopped capers
1 tablespoon minced parsley
2 teaspoons chives minced
Cooked scallops

Mix all together well; chill. Serve in
a bowl on a large plate, surrounded
by boiled scallops, each stuck with a
toothpick. Makes about 2 cups.

TUNA DIP, FINES HERBES

1 can (6-7 ounce) tuna
1 package (3 ounces) cream cheese
1/4 cup sherry
2 tablespoons minced parsley
2 tablespoons minced chives (or 1
   teaspoon dried)
1 teaspoon minced tarragon (or 1/4
   teaspoon dried)
Dairy sour cream
Salt to taste

Combine all ingredients, adding
enough sour cream for dunking
consistency. Add 1 or 2 tablespoons
of chopped capers or nuts, if desired.
Makes about 1 cup.

BACON DIP

1 package (8 ounces) cream cheese
3 tablespoons finely cut chives
1 cup dairy sour cream
1 teaspoon fresh horseradish
Dash of garlic salt
Cayenne
6 strips bacon, cooked crisp

Soften cheese at room temperature. Blend with next 5 ingredients. Mix with 4 strips crumbled bacon. Top with a sprinkling of remaining bacon, crumbled. Makes about 3 cups.

SOUR-CREAM HAM DIP

1 cup dairy sour cream
1/2 cup ground cooked ham, packed
   well
1-1/4 teaspoons dry sherry
1-1/4 teaspoons prepared mustard
3/4 teaspoon instant minced onion

Mix all ingredients and chill until ready to serve. Makes about 1½ cups.

DIPSIDOODLE CRAB DIP

1 cup dairy sour cream
1/4 cup mayonnaise
1/2 pound crab meat, flaked
1 tablespoon capers
1 tablespoon grated onion
1 tablespoon lemon juice
Salt and pepper to taste

Combine all ingredients and chill thoroughly. Makes about 2 cups.

COTTAGE-CLAM DIP

Drain 1 can (10 ounces) white clam sauce, reserving liquid. Sieve 1 pound cottage cheese. Add clams, 2 tablespoons liquid, ¾ teaspoon salt and 1 teaspoon curry powder. Serve as a dip for crackers or chips. Makes 2 cups.

FRANKFURTER-AVOCADO DIP

1 medium avocado
1 tablespoon lemon juice
1 package (3 ounces) cream cheese
1/2 teaspoon instant minced onion
1/4 teaspoon salt
1/8 teaspoon hot pepper sauce
3 skinless frankfurters, ground or very
   finely minced
1/4 cup milk or dairy sour cream

Peel avocado and whirl in blender with ¼ lemon juice. Add all other ingredients. Add more milk or sour cream if needed for dipping consistency. Makes about 2 cups.

CREAMY CHEESE DIP

2 cups shredded sharp Cheddar cheese
8 ounces cream cheese
1 small clove garlic, crushed
2/3 cup beer
1 tablespoon poppy seed
2 tablespoons sweet-pickle relish

Let cheeses stand at room temperature about ½ hour. Blend smooth Cheddar, cream cheese and garlic; continue creaming. Add beer slowly and beat until creamy. Stir in poppy seed and relish. Keep refrigerated. Makes about 2½ cups.

NUT DIP

1 cup peanut butter
1 pint sour cream
1 cup apple with red peel, grated and
   drained
1 tablespoon fresh horseradish
1 teaspoon hot prepared mustard
Parsley
Apple slices

Let peanut butter soften at room temperature. Blend all ingredients except parsley and apple slices. Chill several hours. Serve with parsley topping and apple slices for dipping. Makes about 3 cups.

GUACAMOLE DIP

3 avocados, peeled and mashed
3 tomatoes, peeled, seeded and diced
1/2 cup minced mild onion
Juice and grated rind of 1 lime
2 tablespoons lemon juice
1/2 teaspoon salt (coarse if possible)
1/2 cup mayonnaise
1 cup dairy sour cream
3 dashes hot pepper sauce
Parsley
Cayenne

Blend together all ingredients, except parsley and cayenne. Top with parsley sprigs and dash of cayenne. Serve as a dip for corn chips or potato chips. Makes about 4 cups.

CURRY-CHEESE DIP

1 package (8 ounces) cream cheese,
   softened
1/2 cup dairy sour cream
1-1/2 tablespoons curry powder
1 tablespoon lemon juice
3/4 cup chutney, finely chopped

Combine all ingredients and beat until smooth. Makes about 2 cups.

BLACK-BEAN DIP

Combine 1 can (10½ ounces) condensed black-bean soup, 1 clove garlic, crushed, and 1 teaspoon chili powder and mix well. Chill a few hours to develop flavors. Serve with corn chips. Makes about 1⅓ cups.

TWO-CHEESE AND ONION DIP

1 cup creamed cottage cheese
4 ounces blue cheese
1/3 cup light cream
1 can (3-1/2 ounces) French-fried onions, crushed
Paprika
Minced parsley

Put cheeses and cream in blender and whirl until smooth. Stir in onions, put in serving bowl and sprinkle with paprika and parsley. Serve with potato chips and/or crisp crackers. Makes about 2 cups.

SARDINE DIP

1 package (8 ounces) cream cheese, softened
1/2 cup dairy sour cream
1 can (4-3/8 ounces) skinless and boneless sardines in oil, drained
1 tablespoon minced red or green onion
1 tablespoon lemon juice
1/4 teaspoon salt
Paprika

Beat cheese with sour cream and sardines until smooth. Add next 3 ingredients and blend well. Pour into serving dish, sprinkle with paprika and serve with potato chips, crackers or pretzels. Makes about 2 cups.

ABERDEEN SAUSAGE

1 pound ground beef
1/2 pound smoked ham, ground
1 cup soft bread crumbs
2 tablespoons Worcestershire
2 teaspoons grated lemon rind
1 teaspoon each sugar and salt
2 eggs
Flour

Mix thoroughly all ingredients, except flour. Shape in a roll about 2½″ in diameter. Roll in flour and tie in double thickness of cheesecloth. Tie each end of cloth with string. Put on rack in kettle and cover with boiling water. Bring to boil and simmer 1½ hours. Cool in the broth. Chill and slice thin. Serve with thin slices of rye bread as appetizer or hors d'oeuvre. Good with mustard, mayonnaise and horseradish. Makes 12 to 16 appetizer servings.

CREAMY LIVERWURST DIP

8 ounces liverwurst, coasely chopped
1 cup dairy sour cream
2 tablespoons minced red or green onion
1 tablespoon drained capers, chopped
1/4 cup finely chopped water chestnuts
1/2 teaspoon seasoned salt
Finely chopped parsley

Beat liverwurst, then add sour cream and beat until well blended. Add next 4 ingredients and blend well. Pour into serving dish and garnish edge with parsley. Chill until serving time. Serve with corn chips, potato chips or crackers. Makes 2 cups.

WISCONSIN CHEESE ROLL

Force through food chopper ¼ pound Cheddar cheese and ½ cup unblanched almonds. Add 2 packages (3 ounces each) cream cheese and 1 tablespoon minced canned pimiento. Season to taste with garlic salt and shape in a 1½″ roll. Sprinkle a thick layer of paprika on waxed paper. Coat cheese with paprika and roll up in paper. Store in refrigerator.

AVOCADO EGGS

2 large or 3 small avocados, peeled
6 eggs, hard-cooked, cooled
1 large onion, chopped
1/2 teaspoon ground dried chili peppers
1/4 cup minced parsley
2 tablespoons vinegar
2 teaspoons salt
Lettuce cups

Combine first 3 ingredients and whirl briefly in blender or chop very fine; mixture should be relatively smooth but not mushy. Add remaining ingredients except lettuce and mix well. Serve in lettuce cups as a first course. Makes 6 servings.

FROSTED HAM BALL

1/2 pound cooked ham, ground or finely chopped
1/3 cup raisins
1 tablespoon grated onion
1/4 teaspoon curry powder
1/4 cup mayonnaise
1 package (3 ounces) cream cheese
1 tablespoon milk
Chopped parsley

Mix first 5 ingredients, shape in ball and put on serving plate; chill. Mix cream cheese with milk until smooth and spread on ball. Sprinkle with parsley and chill until serving time. Makes about 2 cups.

BROILED HAM AND CHUTNEY

2 cups minced cooked ham
1/3 cup mayonnaise
1/3 cup chutney chopped fine
2 dozen 1" toast rounds

Mix ham with mayonnaise and chutney, using a little chutney liquid. Spread on toast; broil 5 minutes.

TURKEY PÂTÉ

2 cups ground turkey meat and skin, lightly packed
1 onion, minced
2 hard-cooked eggs, minced
1/2 cup ground almonds
Salt and pepper
A generous dash of hot pepper sauce
2 tablespoons Cognac
Enough mayonnaise to bind

Combine all ingredients, except mayonnaise. Then bind with mayonnaise just until a stiff paste is formed. Place in a bowl or container. You can decorate with aspic, and truffles or sliced olives. Chill. Serve as an hors d'oeuvre or as a snack.

PÂTÉ DE CAMPAGNE PROVENÇALE

2 pounds lean pork
2 pounds veal
1 pound pork liver
6 cloves garlic
1 pound fresh pork siding
3 eggs
1/3 cup Cognac
1 tablespoon chopped fresh basil or 1 teaspoon dried
1 tablespoon salt
1 teaspoon black pepper
Slices of bacon

Force pork, veal, liver and garlic through medium blade of food chopper. Repeat, forcing mixture through fine blade. Cut pork siding into small dice and add to first mixture. Beat together eggs, Cognac and seasonings. Add to first mixture and blend thoroughly. Press into a straight-sided casserole or baking dish (a 2½-quart soufflé dish, a heavy pottery dish or large round glass dish is ideal). Place a few strips of bacon on top. Bake at 325°F. for 2 to 2½ hours. The loaf will break away from the sides a bit when done. (Place a sheet of foil on top for the first hour of cooking.) Remove from the oven and cool. After half an hour, weight down the top. Chill thoroughly. Turn out on platter and decorate with mayonnaise piped through a pastry tube. Garnish with diamonds of red and green pepper and surround with diced aspic. To serve cut in slices.

RUBY-GLAZED CHICKEN-LIVER PÂTÉ

1/2 pound chicken livers
2 tablespoons butter
2 hard-cooked eggs
6 ounces cream cheese
2 tablespoons chopped parsley
3/4 teaspoon salt
Dash of cayenne
1 tablespoon Cognac
1 can consommé madrilene

Sauté chicken livers in butter until lightly browned. Put chicken livers and eggs through fine blade of food chopper or blend in electric blender. Cream cheese with next 4 ingredients. Blend mixtures thoroughly. Pack into container. Pour consommé over pâté to cover. Refrigerate. Makes 1½ cups.

MUSHROOM LIVER PÂTÉ

1/2 pound mushrooms, sliced
1 tablespoon butter
1 pound liverwurst
1 tablespoon chopped scallions
1 teaspoon soy sauce
1 cup dairy sour cream
4 tablespoons Cognac or brandy
Dash of cayenne
1 teaspoon sharp prepared mustard
Parsley
Melba rounds

Sauté mushrooms in butter. Have liverwurst at room temperature; mash and blend with mushrooms and rest of ingredients, except last two. Pile in dish, garnish with parsley and chill. Serve with melba rounds. Makes about 4 cups.

WINE-PICNIC PÂTÉ

3/4 cup butter
1 pound chicken livers
1/2 pound fresh mushrooms
1 teaspoon salt
1/3 cup finely chopped green onions
1/2 cup dry white wine
1 clove garlic, minced
1/16 teaspoon dillweed
4 drops hot pepper sauce
Pimientos

Melt ¼ cup butter in skillet. Add chicken livers, mushrooms, salt and green onions; simmer 5 minutes. Add wine, garlic, dillweed and hot pepper sauce. Cover and cook slowly 10 minutes, or until chicken livers and mushrooms are very tender. Cool slightly and whirl in a blender until smooth; or press through a sieve. Blend in ½ cup butter. Pack in a crock; chill well. Garnish with pimientos. Makes 3 cups.

REDHEADED PÂTÉ

1 envelope unflavored gelatin
1 can (13 ounces) condensed red
  consommé madrilène, heated
1 package (3 ounces) cream cheese
1 can (4-1/2 ounces) liver pâté
Parsley

Soften gelatin in ¼ cup cold water; add heated consommé to gelatin and stir until gelatin is dissolved. Pour about ½ cup in 3-cup mold. Chill until firm. Add cheese and pâté to remaining mixture; beat lightly with rotary beater. Pour over first mixture and chill until firm. Unmold and garnish with parsley. Serve with crisp crackers.

LIVER PÂTÉ

1 pound pork liver
Milk
2 eggs
1/2 cup all-purpose flour
1 cup light cream
2 teaspoons salt
1-1/2 teaspoons sugar
1/2 teaspoon white pepper
1/4 teaspoon ginger
1/4 teaspoon allspice
1/4 pound fresh-pork fat
1 small onion
Parsley
Pickled Cucumber appetizer (below right)

Cover liver with milk and let stand while preparing other ingredients. Combine next 8 ingredients with ½ cup milk and beat until smooth. Drain liver and pat dry with paper towels. Cut liver, fat and onion in small cubes. Put half the amount at a time in electric blender and whirl until smooth. Put in mixing bowl and add first mixture a little at a time, beating well after each addition, until smooth and well blended. Pour into buttered 9" x 5" x 3" loaf pan, cover with foil and bake in a water bath in slow oven (325°F.) 1 hour. Remove foil and bake 30 minutes longer. Cool, then run a small spatula around edges to loosen; turn out on platter. Garnish with parsley and serve with cucumbers. Serves 20.

MARINATED MUSHROOMS

1/2 pound fresh mushrooms, sliced
1/4 teaspoon salt
Freshly ground black pepper
1/2 teaspoon oregano leaves
2 tablespoons lemon juice
1/3 cup olive oil

Combine all ingredients and let stand at room temperature an hour or so. Drain and serve.

SMALL MEATBALLS

2 tablespoons minced onion
Butter or margarine
1/2 pound ground beef
1/4 pound each ground veal and pork
1/2 cup fine dry bread crumbs
1/2 cup light cream
1 egg
3/4 teaspoon salt
1/4 teaspoon ground allspice

Brown onion in 1 tablespoon butter until golden. Mix with remaining ingredients until blended. Using a heaping measuring-teaspoonful for each meatball, dip hands in cold water and shape mixture in smooth balls. Brown 2 dozen at a time in browned butter, shaking skillet occasionally to brown evenly. When all are browned, add a small amount of hot water to skillet and loosen drippings. Return meatballs to skillet and simmer 15 minutes, or until done. Serve as appetizer or main dish. Makes about 5 dozen.

SWEDISH HORS D'OEUVRES

3 to 4 medium baking potatoes, peeled
  and cut in matchsticks
3/4 cup minced onion
Butter
Pepper
1 can (3-1/4 ounces) Swedish anchovy
  fillets (about 18), drained and cut in
  pieces (see Note)
1 cup each heavy cream and milk, scalded

In shallow 1½-quart baking dish, put half the potato and onion, dots of butter, a few grindings of pepper and half the anchovy fillets. Repeat layers. Carefully pour in hot cream and milk. Dot with butter. Bake in hot oven (400°F.) 45 to 60 minutes, or until most of liquid has cooked into potato and top is flecked with brown. Makes 4 supper servings or 8 for smorgasbord. **Note** Anchovies canned in Sweden are smelts pickled in salt, spices and sugar and not the true anchovy.

PICKLED CUCUMBERS

1/2 cup white vinegar
1/4 cup sugar
1/2 teaspoon salt
1/8 teaspoon white pepper
2 medium cucumbers, peeled and sliced
2 tablespoons chopped parsley or dill

In small saucepan, mix first 4 ingredients and 2 tablespoons water; bring to boil. Cool. Put cucumbers in serving dish and add vinegar mixture. Sprinkle with parsley. Refrigerate 2 to 3 hours before serving. Serve with Liver Pâté (left) or other meats. Makes 4 servings.

CREAM-CHEESE PASTRY

1 cup butter
1 package (8 ounces) regular cream
cheese
1/2 teaspoon salt
2 cups all-purpose flour
1 egg yolk
2 teaspoons cream or milk

Using electric mixer, beat first 3 ingredients together until smooth and blended. With fingertips or fork work in flour to form smooth dough. Flatten dough in foil in 8″ x 6″ rectangle and chill overnight. Remove from refrigerator and warm 8 to 10 minutes. Keep unrolled portions in refrigerator until ready to use. Roll one portion on floured pastry cloth with floured rolling pin (first rub cloth and pin with flour, then shake out excess). Shape as directed and chill before baking. Brush tops only of all pastries with egg yolk beaten with cream. Bake as indicated. **Note** Pastry can be reworked and rerolled to the last scrap. It still remains tender and flaky.

MUSHROOM TURNOVERS

Prepare 1 recipe Cream-cheese Pastry, above. Prepare Mushroom Filling. Divide pastry in half and roll each half in 9″ x 6″ rectangle, using floured pastry cloth and stockinette-covered rolling pin. Fold over in thirds, roll, fold over again and roll dough to 1/8″ thickness. Cut in 2 1/2″ rounds. Reroll trimmings. Put 1 teaspoonful filling in center of each round. Moisten edges with water and fold double. Seal edges with fork. Put on ungreased baking sheet. Brush with 1 egg yolk beaten with 2 teaspoons milk or cream; chill 1 hour. Bake in moderate oven (350°F.) 25 to 30 minutes, or until golden. Serve warm, cold or reheated. Makes 5 to 6 dozen.

Mushroom Filling

2 cans (4 ounces each) mushrooms stems
and pieces, drained and minced
1/2 cup minced onion
2 tablespoons butter or margarine
1/2 teaspoon salt
1/8 teaspoon white pepper
1 teaspoon lemon juice
2 teaspoons flour
1/2 cup light cream
1 tablespoon sherry or dry vermouth

In small saucepan, sauté mushrooms and onion in the butter 5 minutes. Sprinkle with next 4 ingredients; stir and simmer 2 minutes longer. Gradually stir in light cream and simmer, stirring, until thickened and smooth. Stir in sherry and chill.

PARMESAN TWISTS

Prepare 1/2 recipe Cream-cheese Pastry (left) and chill; divide in half and roll each half in rectangle a generous 1/4″ thick. Sprinkle heavily with finely grated Parmesan cheese, pressing it lightly into dough with rolling pin. Fold dough over itself in thirds and roll again. Sprinkle with more cheese, press with pin and fold again. Roll in 18″ x 4″ rectangle 1/4″ thick. Brush with 1 egg yolk beaten with 2 teaspoons milk; sprinkle with cheese. Cut in strips about 4″ x 3/4″. Twist strips in spirals, put on ungreased cookie sheet and brush ends with remaining egg-yolk mixture. Chill 1 hour. Bake in moderate oven (350°F.) 15 to 20 minutes, or until crisp and golden. Remove from sheet at once. Makes about 2 dozen.

COSSACK'S DELIGHT

1 pound button-size mushrooms
2 tablespoons each butter and olive oil
1 large clove garlic, crushed
1 small onion, grated
Soy sauce
1/8 teaspoon each (or more to taste) dry
mustard, paprika, seasoned salt and
monosodium glutamate
Dash of Worcestershire
Salt and pepper to taste
1 tablespoon flour
1 cup dairy sour cream

Wash mushrooms. Heat butter and oil in Dutch oven. Add mushrooms, garlic, onion, 1/2 teaspoon soy sauce and other seasonings. Cook, stirring, about 1 minute. Cover, reduce heat and simmer, stirring occasionally, about 5 minutes. Blend flour and sour cream, beating with rotary or electric beater until smooth. Add to mushroom mixture and turn off heat. Add more soy sauce if necessary.

TOASTED AROMATIC PECANS

4 cups pecan halves (1-1/4 pounds)
1/4 cup butter or margarine
1 teaspoon (or more) Angostura bitters
Seasoned salt

Put pecans in 13″ x 9″ x 2″ pan and toast in slow oven (300°F.) 20 minutes. Meanwhile melt butter in small saucepan. Add bitters and 1 teaspoon seasoned salt and stir to blend. Pour over pecans and toast, stirring occasionally to get an even coating, 15 minutes longer. Sprinkle with additional seasoned salt, if desired. Makes 4 cups.

SHAPED CHEESE SPREADS

Dried-beef and Cream-cheese Spread

1 jar (2-1/2 ounces) dried beef, minced
1 pound cream cheese, softened
2 teaspoons (or to taste) curry powder
Garnish: paprika and curry powder

Two-cheese Brandy-Nut Spread

3 ounces blue cheese, softened
8 ounces cream cheese, softened
2 tablespoons brandy
1/2 cup minced pecans
Garnish: minced pecans and dried parsley

Cheddar-Burgundy Spread

8 ounces sharp Cheddar cheese, finely
shredded and softened
1/2 cup butter, softened
1/3 cup Burgundy
Garnish: 10 drops yellow food coloring,
4 drops green food coloring and 1/2
cup toasted minced almonds

To prepare each spread combine all ingredients, except garnish, in bowl and mix well. Turn out on waxed paper and mold into desired shape. As a guide, put cracker of desired shape at each end and mold with fingers so that cheese when sliced will fit cracker. Sprinkle beef shape generously with paprika and curry powder, 2-cheese shape with pecans and parsley and Cheddar shape with green-tinted nuts. To tint nuts, mix 1 teaspoon water and food colorings and toss with almonds. Refrigerate.

LIPTAUER CHEESE POT

1 package (8 ounces) cream cheese,
softened
1/2 green pepper, minced
1 small onion, minced
1 large clove garlic, minced
2 tablespoons caraway seed
2 tablespoons bright-red paprika
1 can (3/4 ounces) anchovies, undrained
1 tablespoon olive oil
1/4 teaspoon dry mustard

Mix all ingredients until thoroughly blended. Store in crock in refrigerator. Make 1½ cups.

ONION-COATED PECANS

4 cups shelled pecans
1 envelope (1-3/8 ounces) dried onion-
soup mix
1/4 cup buttery-flavor oil

Toast pecans in shallow roasting pan in slow oven (300°F.) 30 minutes. Crush soup mix in blender or with rolling pin. Mix with oil and nuts. Roast, stirring often, 15 minutes. Cool on absorbent paper. Store airtight.

OLIVE-ALMOND ROLL-UPS

1 package (8 ounces) cream cheese,
softened
1/4 cup mayonnaise
Dash of hot pepper sauce
1/3 cup finely chopped pimiento-stuffed
olives
1/4 cup finely chopped blanched almonds
24 thin slices firm-type white bread,
crusts trimmed
Finely chopped parsley

Beat cheese until fluffy. Add next 4 ingredients and mix well. (Makes about 1½ cups.) Put bread slices between 2 clean towels that have been put in cold water, then wrung out; roll until bread becomes very thin and moist. Spread each slice generously with mixture and roll up tight. Store, seam side down, covered, in refrigerator. At serving time, cut each roll crosswise in 2 or 3 pieces and roll in parsley. Makes 48 to 72.

CHEESE-SANDWICH APPETIZERS

Cut out rounds of white or dark bread (or use a favorite cracker) and spread thinly with butter or margarine. Cover with slices of Swedish cheese such as *Herrgardsost* (a mild cheese with nutty flavor and large holes) or *Vasterbottensost* (a sharp cheese resembling Cheddar with small holes). Garnish with radish slices and tiny sprigs of parsley.

BLUE-CHEESE AND CELERY APPETIZER

Cut tops from bunch of celery. Separate stalks, wash and dry. Blend 3 ounces blue cheese, 1 package (3 ounces) cream cheese and 1 tablespoon Worcestershire. Stuff stalks with mixture, then press together to resemble a bunch of celery. Tie with string and chill. To serve, cut in slices with sharp knife. Serve to be eaten with forks.

TUNA-HORSERADISH CANAPES

1 can (7 ounces) tuna, drained and flaked
1 tablespoon minced celery
3 tablespoons mayonnaise
1/2 cup butter or margarine, softened
3 tablespoons well-drained prepared
horseradish
8 slices toast, each cut in 4 triangles
Minced parsley

Mix first 3 ingredients to a paste. Mix in butter and horseradish. Spread on toast and sprinkle with parsley.

CARAWAY CHEDDAR CHEESE

Beat together 1/2 cup soft butter or margarine, 3 cups grated sharp Cheddar cheese, 1 tablespoon caraway seed and 2 tablespoons brandy. Pack in cheese crock. Makes 2 cups.

BRANDIED CHEESE

Combine 1/2 pound (2 cups) crumbled blue or Roquefort cheese with 1 cup butter and 1/3 to 1/2 cup brandy. Blend until well mixed and smooth. Put in crocks and cover with paraffin. Refrigerate. Makes about 3 cups.

ROMANO-CHEDDAR CHEESE SPREAD

1/2 cup grated Romano cheese
1 cup grated Cheddar cheese
1/3 cup undiluted evaporated milk
1/8 teaspoon cayenne
1/2 teaspoon salt
1 teaspoon Worcestershire

Combine cheeses, add milk and seasonings and beat well. Refrigerate. Makes about 1 cup.

THREE-CHEESE NUT SPREAD

8 ounces blue cheese
2 jars (5 ounces each) pasteurized process pineapple-cheese spread
1 package (8 ounces) cream cheese, softened
1/4 teaspoon onion powder
1 cup chopped pecans or other nuts
1 teaspoon Worcestershire or steak sauce
1/2 teaspoon salt
1/2 teaspoon paprika

Mix all ingredients, using electric blender or mixer. Pack into small crocks or glasses and refrigerate. Makes 4 cups.

ALMOND-ROQUEFORT BALLS

1 package (3 ounces) soft cream cheese
4 ounces Roquefort cheese
1 teaspoon instant minced onion
1 tablespoon chopped parsley
1 tablespoon drained finely chopped chutney
Pitted ripe olives, drained
1/2 cup toasted almonds, finely chopped

Blend cheeses, onion, parsley and chutney together. Refrigerate mixture until firm enough to handle. Then shape around olives. Roll in chopped almonds. Cover tightly and refrigerate. Makes about 16.

COCKTAIL MOUSSE

1 envelope unflavored gelatin
3 ounces Camembert cheese
1/4 pound Roquefort cheese, crumbled
1 egg, separated
1 teaspoon Worcestershire
1/2 cup heavy cream, whipped
Parsley

Soften gelatin in 1/4 cup cold water; dissolve over hot water. Cream cheeses together. Beat in gelatin, egg yolk and Worcestershire. Fold in stiffly beaten egg white and whipped cream. Pour into 3-cup mold and chill 3 hours, or until firm. Unmold and garnish with parsley. Serve with crisp crackers. Makes 8 to 10 servings.

ANTIPASTO PLATES

The antipasto (meaning "before the meal") plate can be a little salad or a meal in itself. The idea is to combine vegetables, meats, fish and eggs, in as colorful an assortment as possible.

1. In an attractive and orderly way arrange the following on a platter: slices of Italian salami; rolled-up prosciutto or other ham; tuna in olive oil; black and green olives; eggs sliced or stuffed and topped, in both cases, with a sprig of parsley or 3 capers; pickled mushrooms; radish roses; tomato slices, strips of red pimientos and green peppers marinated in olive oil; celery stuffed with mashed Gorgonzola or other blue cheese; eggplant salad, artichoke hearts marinated in a mixture of olive oil, white wine, basil or any other herb and salt and pepper; rolled anchovies, sardines and any Italian-style relishes such as pickled peppers, cauliflower, artichokes, sold in jars in supermarkets.
2. Pare a chilled cantaloupe or honeydew melon and cut in wedges. Wrap with wafer-thin slices of prosciutto. Allow 2 melon wedges for each person.
3. Mushroom salad, anchovy-stuffed eggs, tomatoes, sliced fennel.
4. Slices of Italian salami, potato salad, pimiento marinated in olive oil, green olives, anchovies, sardines.
5. Meatless antipasto: overlapping slices of tomatoes and hard-cooked eggs, surrounded by chunks of tuna in olive oil and rolled anchovies, garnished with mayonnaise and decorated with parsley sprigs.
6. Alternate layers of cooked cleaned shrimps and cold cooked cauliflowerets. Top with mayonnaise and chopped parsley.

MUSHROOM-STUFFED DEVILED EGGS

6 tablespoons ground raw mushrooms
2 tablespoons lemon juice
6 eggs, hard-cooked
1/2 teaspoon salt
Cracked pepper to taste
6 pimiento-stuffed olives, chopped
2 tablespoons (about) mayonnaise
Parsley sprigs

Sprinkle mushrooms with lemon juice. Mash egg yolks with fork and add seasonings. Mix mushrooms, egg yolks, olives and mayonnaise. Fill egg whites and garnish with sprig of parsley.

CLAM BITES

1 can (10-1/2 ounces) minced clams
1 egg, separated
1 teaspoon melted butter
1/2 cup all-purpose flour
Salt and pepper
Fat for frying

Drain clams, reserving liquid. Beat egg yolk until light. Add butter, flour, ¼ teaspoon salt and clam liquid. (Add milk, if necessary, to make ¼ cup.) Fold in stiffly beaten egg white. Add clams and let stand at least an hour at room temperature. Drop by teaspoonfuls into hot deep fat (375°F. on a frying thermometer) and fry until golden brown (5 to 6 minutes). Drain on absorbent paper. Sprinkle with salt and pepper and serve hot on toothpicks. Makes about 2 dozen.

TERIYAKI MEATBALLS

Bite-size appetizers baked in Hawaiian sauce.

2 eggs
2 pounds ground round steak
1/2 cup cornflake crumbs
1/2 cup milk
2 tablespoons grated onion
1 teaspoon salt
1/4 teaspoon pepper
Teriyaki sauce

Beat eggs and mix thoroughly with remaining ingredients, except sauce. Shape in balls about 1½" in diameter and arrange in a layer in shallow baking pan. Pour sauce over balls and bake in slow oven (300°F.) about 45 minutes, turning and basting every 15 minutes. Makes about 3 dozen balls. **Teriyaki Sauce** Mix 1 cup soy sauce, ½ cup water, 2 teaspoons ginger juice (or 1 teaspoon powdered ginger), 2 cloves garlic, minced, and 1 teaspoon sugar.

AMERICAN COCKTAIL SAUCE

Serve on shrimp or other seafood.

Mix 1 cup catsup, ¼ cup chili sauce, juice 1 lemon, ⅛ teaspoon hot pepper sauce, 1 tablespoon chopped parsley, 1 tablespoon horseradish and 1 teaspoon each Worcestershire and prepared mustard. Season. Makes 1⅓ cups.

TOASTED BRAZIL-NUT CHIPS

Cover 1½ cups shelled Brazil nuts with cold water in saucepan. Bring slowly to boil and simmer 5 minutes. Drain and cut in thin lengthwise slices. Spread out in shallow baking pan. Dot with 2 tablespoons butter; sprinkle with 1 teaspoon salt. Bake in 350°F. oven 12 to 15 minutes; stir occasionally. Makes 2 cups.

SOYED ALMONDS

4 cups blanched almonds (1-1/4 pounds)
1/4 cup butter or margarine
1/4 cup soy sauce

Put almonds in large roasting pan. Roast in 400°F. oven about 15 minutes, stirring several times. Add butter and soy sauce; stir. Roast 12 to 15 minutes longer, stirring often, until nuts are coated and fairly dry. Makes 4 cups.

EAST INDIA MIX

2 tablespoons butter
1 teaspoon mustard seed
1 teaspoon curry powder
Dash of pepper
2 cans (2-1/4 ounces each) potato sticks
1 cup salted peanuts

Melt butter, add mustard seed, cover and cook until seed pops. Add remaining ingredients and stir until heated. Makes about 4 cups.

SAVORY SNACK MIX

1/3 cup butter or margarine
1/4 cup steak sauce
2 teaspoons seasoned salt
2 cups bite-size shredded-rice cereal
2 cups bite-size shredded-wheat cereal
2 cups bite-size shredded-corn cereal
1 cup shelled nuts

Melt butter in shallow pan over low heat. Stir in steak sauce and salt. Add cereals and nuts. Mix over low heat until all pieces are coated. Heat in very slow oven (250°F.) 1 hour. Stir every 15 minutes. Spread out on absorbent paper to cool. Store airtight. Makes 7 cups.

COLD SHRIMPS WITH SPICY SAUCE

3 tablespoons horseradish
1 cup catsup
1/4 cup chili sauce
3 tablespoons lemon juice
2 dashes hot pepper sauce
1-1/2 pounds cooked cleaned shrimps

Mix all ingredients, except shrimps, and use as a dip or sauce for the shrimps. Makes 6 servings.

MELON COCKTAIL WITH GUAVA JELLY

Cut equal portions of watermelon, cantaloupe and honeydew or other melon in cubes, diamonds and balls. Drizzle over fruit a half-and-half mixture of melted guava jelly and lemon juice.

SPICED TOMATO COCKTAIL

1 cucumber
1 can (1 quart 14 ounces) tomato juice
3 green onions, chopped
3 tablespoons lemon juice
Dash of hot pepper sauce
1 tablespoon Worcestershire
1 tablespoon horseradish, drained
Salt and pepper to taste

Peel and grate cucumber. Add remaining ingredients and mix thoroughly. Cover and let stand in refrigerator about 2 hours. Strain through a coarse sieve. Serves 8.

RUMAKI

Broil your own appetizers, Japanese style.

1/3 cup soy sauce
2 tablespoons dry sherry
1 clove garlic, minced
1/8 teaspoon each pepper and monosodium glutamate
1/2 pound chicken livers, cleaned and cut in half
1 can (5 ounces) water chestnuts, drained
About 1/2 pound bacon, each slice halved

Combine first 4 ingredients, pour over chicken livers and marinate 30 minutes. Cut each water chestnut in 3 crosswise slices. Wrap a chicken-liver half and piece of water chestnut together in a half slice of bacon, securing with 1 or 2 toothpicks. Grill over charcoal, turning occasionally, until bacon is crisp. Or put on wire rack set over a shallow pan and bake in hot oven (400°F.) 20 minutes, or until bacon is crisp; do not turn. Makes about 20.

PROSCIUTTO WITH MELON

Cut 1 honeydew melon in half, remove seeds and peel. Cut into individual portions. Serve with rolls of paper-thin prosciutto. (You will need about 1/4 pound for 1 melon.) Serve with a pepper mill handy. Makes about 2 dozen.

CHEESE STRAWS

Add 1 cup grated sharp Cheddar cheese to 1 package pastry mix and prepare as directed on package. Roll 1/8" thick and cut in 4" x 1/2" strips with pastry wheel. Put on baking sheet. Bake in hot oven (400°F.) until lightly browned (about 8 minutes). Sprinkle with paprika. Makes about 8 dozen.

CHICKEN-LIVER TURNOVERS

Cook until crisp 2 slices bacon; crumble. In bacon fat, cook 1/2 pound chicken livers. Chop livers fine; mix with bacon and a little mayonnaise. Season. Roll Flaky French Pastry (page 24) about 1/8" thick. Cut in 2" rounds. Put a dab of filling on one side of each round and fold over, pinching together. Prick with fork and crimp around edge. Brush with an egg yolk beaten with 1 tablespoon milk. Bake in very hot oven (450°F.) 10 minutes. Makes about 3 dozen.

CLAM PASTRIES

1/2 cup vegetable shortening
1 cup all-purpose flour
1/2 teaspoon salt
1/2 cup cold riced potato
1 can (10-1/2 ounces) minced clams, drained
1 tablespoon instant minced onion
1/4 cup minced green pepper
1 egg
1/2 cup heavy cream
2 tablespoons minced celery and leaves
1/2 cup fine dry bread crumbs
1 tablespoon melted margarine
Dash of cayenne
Seasoning to taste

To make potato pastry, cut shortening into flour and salt. Stir in potato with fork and put about 1 rounded teaspoonful into each of 2 dozen 1¾" muffin-pan sections. Press firmly with finger onto bottom and sides of pans, leaving centers hollow. Bake in very hot oven (450°F.) about 12 minutes. Mix remaining ingredients and fill baked shells. Broil until golden brown. Serve hot. Makes 2 dozen.

CHEESE SQUARES

8 slices firm-type white bread
Butter or margarine
1/4 pound (1 cup packed) finely
  shredded sharp Cheddar cheese
1/4 teaspoon Worcestershire
Dash of cayenne
1 egg white, stiffly beaten

Cut crusts from bread. Spread 4 slices bread very lightly with butter, then top with remaining 4 slices. Cut each in 9 squares (about 1"). Put on baking sheet about 1" apart. Cover while preparing topping. Cream 1/4 cup butter, add next 3 ingredients and beat until fluffy. Mix in egg white. Top each square generously with some of mixture. Bake in hot oven (400°F.) 8 minutes, or until puffy and very lightly browned. Serve on cocktail picks. Makes 3 dozen.

HOT CRAB TRIANGLES

1 package (8 ounces) cream cheese,
  softened
1/2 teaspoon dry mustard
1 tablespoon milk
1/4 teaspoon salt
Dash of cayenne
1 can (6 ounces) white crab meat,
  drained
2 tablespoons minced chives or green
  onion
2 tablespoons finely chopped blanched
  almonds
12 slices firm-type white bread, crusts
  trimmed
Paprika

Beat cheese, mustard and milk until fluffy. Add next 5 ingredients. Mix well and spread generously on bread slices. Sprinkle lightly with paprika. Cut each slice in 4 triangles, put on baking sheet and bake in hot oven (400°F.) 10 to 12 minutes, or until well browned. Serve on cocktail picks. Makes 4 dozen.

MARINATED APPETIZER FRANKS

1/2 cup soy sauce
1 tablespoon sugar
1 teaspoon instant minced onion
1/2 teaspoon ground ginger
3/4 pound cocktail frankfurters

Mix all ingredients, except frankfurters, in shallow baking dish. Marinate frankfurters in mixture, turning occasionally, 2 hours. Bake in moderate oven (350°F.) 15 to 20 minutes, basting once or twice with marinade. Drain and serve on cocktail picks.

DEVILED-HAM QUICHE

Pastry for 9" one-crust pie
1 can (4-1/2 ounces) deviled ham
3 tablespoons fine dry bread crumbs
1 cup (about 4 ounces) shredded
  Switzerland Swiss cheese
1 small onion, minced
4 eggs
2 cups heavy or light cream
3/4 teaspoon salt
1/4 teaspoon sugar
1/8 teaspoon cayenne

Butter generously a 9" piepan. Adjust rolled pastry in pan and flute to make a high rim. Mix ham and crumbs and spread on bottom of shell. Sprinkle with cheese and onion. Beat eggs slightly, then beat in remaining ingredients. Pour into shell and bake in hot oven (425°F.) 15 minutes. Reduce heat to 300°F. and bake 35 minutes longer, or until firm. Remove from oven and let stand 20 minutes before cutting in wedges. Makes 6 main-dish servings, or 8 to 10 appetizer servings. To be served with forks.

SAVORY SAUSAGE APPETIZERS

1 pound pork-sausage meat
1/2 teaspoon sweet-basil leaves
1/3 cup minced water chestnuts
Paprika

Combine first 3 ingredients with hands until well blended. Dip hands in cold water and shape mixture in smooth small balls. Put in small baking dish and sprinkle with paprika. Bake in moderate oven (375°F.) 15 minutes. Remove from oven, drain off all fat, shake meatballs and sprinkle with additional paprika. Return to oven and bake 15 minutes longer. Drain, keep warm and serve with cocktail picks. Good with Curry-Cheese Dip (page 23). Makes 4 dozen.

CHEESY APPETIZERS

2/3 cup grated Parmesan cheese
1/3 cup mayonnaise
1 small onion, grated
Dash of Worcestershire
9 slices firm-type bread, crusts trimmed

Mix well first 4 ingredients. Cut bread slices in fourths and brown on one side under broiler. Spead untoasted side of each piece with 1 measuring-teaspoonful mixture. Put under broiler until golden brown and serve hot. Makes 3 dozen. Serve on cocktail picks.

CURRIED SHRIMP DIAMONDS

2/3 cup soft butter or margarine
1-1/2 cups all-purpose flour
1/2 teaspoon salt
1 teaspoon instant minced onion
1 teaspoon Worcestershire
1 cup finely chopped cooked shrimps
1 teaspoon curry powder
1 egg yolk
1 tablespoon milk

Cut butter into flour and salt. Soak onion a few minutes in 1 teaspoon water and the Worcestershire. Add with shrimps and curry powder to first mixture, stirring with fork until blended. Roll out on floured board 1/2″ thick and cut in 1 1/2″ diamonds. Put on greased cookie sheet. Brush with egg yolk beaten with milk. Bake in moderate oven (375°F.) about 30 minutes. Serve hot or cold. Makes about 2 dozen.

CHEESE BITES

1 cup coarsely shredded sharp Cheddar
   cheese, at room temperature
1/2 cup butter, at room temperature
1 cup crisp rice cereal
1 cup all-purpose flour
1/8 teaspoon salt
1/2 teaspoon hot pepper sauce

Put all ingredients on board or in bowl and mix well. Pinch off marble-size pieces and put on lightly greased baking sheet. Bake in moderate oven (350°F.) 10 to 15 minutes, or until lightly browned. Store airtight. Makes about 4 dozen.

SKEWERED PORK APPETIZERS

1 pound lean pork, cut in 3/4″ cubes
2 tablespoons soy sauce
Juice of 1 lemon
2 tablespoons vegetable oil
1 teaspoon coriander seed, crushed
1 clove garlic, minced
1 teaspoon brown sugar
1/2 teaspoon freshly ground pepper

Put pork in small mixing bowl. Add remaining ingredients; toss well. Cover and refrigerate overnight. Arrange on individual skewers; grill or broil slowly, turning occasionally, 25 minutes, or until done. Makes 6 servings.

SMITHFIELD HAM IN HOT BISCUITS

Make little baking powder biscuits, or heat packaged beaten biscuits and place bits of Smithfield ham, sliced paper-thin, between halves. Serve with a little bowl of Dijon mustard for additional seasoning.

CURRY STICKS

Put 1 box (11 ounces) pastry mix and 1 tablespoon curry powder in bowl and mix. Add amount of liquid called for on pastry-mix label (usually 4 tablespoons water) and mix with fork to form ball. Divide in half and roll each half between sheets of waxed paper to form a 9″ x 6″ rectangle. (Moisten counter top to prevent bottom sheet of paper from sliding.) Remove top sheet and sprinkle pastry lightly with salt. Cut in sticks 6″ long and 1/4″ wide. Arrange carefully on ungreased baking sheet and bake in moderate oven (375°F.) about 10 minutes. Carefully remove to cake rack to cool. Store airtight. Makes about 6 dozen.

WATER-CHESTNUT AND PINEAPPLE ROLL-UPS

Cut bacon slices in thirds, slice water chestnuts and drain canned pineapple chunks. Wrap a bacon slice around a chunk of pineapple and a slice of water chestnut. Secure with a toothpick. Broil until bacon is crisp, turning once or twice. Drain on paper towel. Put on rack in shallow baking pan. Just before serving, reheat in moderate oven (350°F.) about 5 minutes.

PIROSHKI

2 cups all-purpose flour
1/2 teaspoon salt
Butter or margarine
Dairy sour cream
1 cup cooked chicken, veal or chicken
   livers
1 can (3 ounces) chopped mushrooms,
   drained
1 hard-cooked egg, minced
Dash each garlic salt and cayenne
Paprika and chopped fresh dill or
   dillweed

Sift flour and salt. Blend in 1/2 cup soft butter. Work in 1/2 cup sour cream. Wrap in waxed paper and chill overnight. To make filling, cook meat and mushrooms in 1 tablespoon butter 2 or 3 minutes. Add egg, garlic salt, cayenne, and paprika and dill to taste. Moisten with enough sour cream to hold mixture together. Roll pastry to 1/4″ thickness. Cut out with floured 3 1/2″ cutter. Put 1 tablespoon filling on one side of each round, wet edges and fold over. Pinch edges to seal. Put on greased cookie sheet and bake in moderate oven (375°F.) about 15 minutes. Serve hot. Makes about 16.

SHRIMP PUFFS

Substitute canned shrimp for the anchovies in Anchovy Puffs, below. Put ½ teaspoon sandwich spread or tartar sauce on shrimp. Proceed as directed.

ANCHOVY PUFFS

Roll Flaky French Pastry (at right) to ⅛" thickness. Cut in 1½" rounds. Put half on cookie sheet. Put an anchovy in center of each. Top with remaining rounds. Prick tops and crimp edges with fork. Brush with egg yolk beaten with 1 tablespoon milk. Bake in very hot oven (450°F.) 10 minutes.

EMPANADAS

Filling

1/4 pound ground lean beef
1 medium onion, chopped
3 chili peppers, crushed
1 green pepper, chopped
2 tablespoons butter
1 large tomato, peeled and chopped
6 ripe olives, chopped
2 tablespoons seedless raisins
1 hard-cooked egg, chopped
1 teaspoon sugar
Salt and pepper

Fry beef, onion, chili peppers and green pepper in butter until meat loses its red color, stirring constantly. Add tomato, stir well and simmer 5 minutes. Add olives, raisins, egg and sugar, and salt and pepper to taste. Mix all ingredients well.

Dough

1/2 cup butter
1/4 cup lard
2-1/4 cups all-purpose flour
Salt
1 egg, beaten

Cut butter and lard into sifted flour and ⅓ teaspoon salt until small, even particles are formed. Add ⅓ cup ice water slowly, using only enough to make the particles hold together. Form lightly into a ball, wrap in waxed paper and chill in refrigerator. Roll dough out ⅛" thick and cut in rounds with 3" cutter. Place a little of meat mixture on each round and fold over, pressing tightly on edges to hold together. Place on lightly greased cookie sheet and refrigerate until 15 minutes before serving. Brush with beaten egg, sprinkle with salt and bake in hot oven (425°F.) 15 minutes, or until pastries are browned. Makes about 2 dozen empanadas.

FLAKY FRENCH PASTRY

2 cups plus 2 tablespoons all-purpose flour
3/4 teaspoon salt
1 cup soft butter
2 egg yolks
1/4 cup light cream
2 tablespoons dry white wine

Sift flour and salt into bowl. Cut in butter. Add combined egg yolks, cream and wine; mix with fork until blended and smooth. Knead lightly in bowl until bubbles begin to appear on the surface of dough. Cover and chill 1 hour. Roll to ⅛" thickness on floured board. Fold twice lengthwise and then twice crosswise. Chill 15 minutes. Roll and fold twice more. Store, wrapped in moistureproof paper, in refrigerator until needed.

FRIED CHEESE

2-1/4 cups all-purpose flour
1/2 teaspoon salt
1 cup beer
4 egg whites, beaten stiff
2 packages (3 ounces each) process Swiss Gruyère-cheese wedges
Fat for deep frying

Mix flour and salt with beer. Fold in egg whites. Let stand 4 to 6 hours in a warm, not hot, place. Cut cheese wedges in half lengthwise. Dip into batter and fry in hot deep fat (375°F. on frying thermometer) until golden brown. Drain on absorbent paper. Makes 24.

MUSHROOM BEIGNETS
(French Cream Puffs)

Put ½ cup water, ¼ cup butter and a dash of salt into a small saucepan and bring to a boil. Add ½ cup all-purpose flour all at once. Stir hard, cooking until mixture leaves sides of pan and forms a ball. Remove from heat. Beat in 2 eggs, one at a time, beating (easiest with electric beater) until mixture is thick and shining. Using 2 teaspoons, shape little rounds of the mixture (about 1 teaspoonful each) on a baking sheet, 2" apart. Bake in very hot oven (450°F.) 15 minutes; lower heat to 350°F. and bake 20 minutes longer. Cool. Slit puff shells on one side and fill with Mushroom Filling. Stem ½ pound mushrooms. Chop mushrooms fine. Sauté in 1 tablespoon butter about 5 minutes. Add 1 tablespoon flour and stir until smooth. Add ½ cup heavy cream gradually, stirring constantly until thickened. Add ¼ teaspoon curry powder, salt and pepper to taste. Makes about 48.

CRANBERRY-ORANGE PUNCH

2-1/2 quarts apple juice, chilled
1 quart cranberry-juice cocktail, chilled
1/2 cup lemon juice
1 apple
Whole cloves
Few orange and lemon slices

Mix first 3 ingredients and pour over ice cubes in punch bowl. Core apple and slice in thin rounds. Carefully cut out each round with scalloped cutter and stud with 3 cloves. With sharp knife, scallop edges of citrus slices. Decorate punch with apple and citrus slices. Makes about 4 quarts.

APPLE PICK-ME-UP

Peel 1 medium-large eating apple, cut in small pieces and put in electric blender with 1 cup milk and 1 to 2 tablespoons honey. Cover and blend until thick and frothy. Sprinkle with cinnamon or nutmeg; serve at once. Makes about 2 cups.

ORANGE-BANANA SHAKE

1/2 can (6-ounce size) frozen orange-juice concentrate, partially thawed
2 bananas, cut up
1 pint vanilla ice cream, softened
2 cups cold milk

Whirl all ingredients in blender, or beat with rotary beater. (Mash banana first if beater is used.) Makes 1 quart.

CEYLON SPICED TEA

Open 12 cardamom pods, remove seed and crush slightly. Add 1½ teaspoons cracked cinnamon, 1 tablespoon dried, grated orange peel (from store), the crushed heads of 8 whole cloves and ½ cup loose tea. Use 1 rounded teaspoon for each cup of tea and brew 5 or 6 minutes.

HOT SPICED CRANBERRY TEA

1 envelope (2 ounces) sweetened lemon-flavored iced-tea mix
3 cups cranberry-juice cocktail
Lemon slices
Whole cloves and cinnamon sticks

Combine mix, 3 cups boiling water and cranberry cocktail. Top each serving with a lemon slice decorated with cloves, and a cinnamon-stick muddler. Makes 6 cups.

HOT BUTTERED RUM

1 quart apple juice
1/4 cup packed light-brown sugar
2 tablespoons butter or margarine
Rum

Heat apple juice and brown sugar until mixture comes to a boil. Add butter. Pour into mugs. Add 1 jigger rum to each. Makes 4 servings.

THREE-FRUIT DRINK

1 can (6 ounces) frozen grapefruit-juice concentrate, reconstituted
1 can (6 ounces) frozen orange-juice concentrate, reconstituted
1 can (8-1/2 ounces) crushed pineapple, undrained
1/4 cup grenadine
Maraschino cherries

Combine all ingredients, except cherries, in large pitcher or punch bowl. Chill thoroughly. Serve with ice cubes and top with cherries. Makes about 1³/₄ quarts.

APPLE-APRICOT COOLER

2 quarts apple juice, chilled
1 quart apricot nectar, chilled
1 bottle (28 ounces) carbonated water, chilled
1/4 cup lime juice

Combine all ingredients and pour over ice in punch bowl. Makes 4 quarts.

CHOCOLATE-PEPPERMINT FLIP

1/2 cup quick chocolate-flavored beverage mix
1/3 cup marshmallow cream
3-1/2 cups milk
1/4 teaspoon peppermint extract

Whirl all ingredients in blender until well mixed. Makes about 4 cups.

APPLE-BERRY CHILLER

1 can (6 ounces) frozen apple juice, reconstituted
1 package (10 ounces) frozen raspberries, thawed
1 bottle (28 ounces) carbonated water, chilled

Combine all ingredients just before serving. Serve with ice cubes, if desired. Makes about 2 quarts.

APRICOT-WINE MEDLEY

Mix equal parts of chilled apricot nectar and white wine. Delicious for a special brunch or an afternoon party.

ALMOND TEA

2/3 cup cooked rice
2 tablespoons almond paste
1 teaspoon almond extract
1/3 cup granulated sugar
Light-brown sugar

Blend rice, almond paste and 1/2 cup water in blender at low speed 5 minutes. While still blending, add 1/2 cup water, a small amount at a time, until mixture forms a smooth thin paste. Pour into large saucepan. Use 3 cups water, 1 cup at a time, to rinse blender and put in saucepan. Beat well with rotary beater or force through sieve. Bring to boil, stirring. Add flavoring and granulated sugar and serve hot in tea cups, small bowls or rice bowls with a sprinkling of brown sugar on each serving. Makes 4 to 6 servings.

SPICED ICED TEA

1/2 cup sugar
Grated rind and juice of 1 lemon
Grated rind and juice of 1 orange
1" cinnamon stick
1/2 teaspoon whole cloves
4 cups hot double-strength tea

Put all ingredients, except last 2, and 1/2 cup water in small saucepan; bring to boil and simmer, stirring occasionally, 5 minutes. Strain, add to tea and chill. When ready to serve, pour into ice-filled tall glasses. Makes 1 1/2 quarts.

SPICED INSTANT TEA

1 cup grapefruit-flavored instant
    breakfast drink
1 teaspoon grated lemon rind
1 cup sugar
1/2 cup instant tea
1 teaspoon cinnamon
1/2 teaspoon each ground cloves and
    allspice

Combine all ingredients and mix well. Store in tightly covered jar. Use 2 to 3 teaspoons to each cup boiling water.

CUCUMBER-TOMATO COCKTAIL

1 medium cucumber, peeled
2-1/4 cups tomato juice
2 tablespoons chopped green onions
1 teaspoon Worcestershire
Juice of 1 lemon
2 teaspoons prepared horseradish
1/8 teaspoon hot pepper sauce
1/2 teaspoon salt
1/8 teaspoon pepper
Parsley or watercress

Grate cucumber into tomato juice. Add remaining ingredients, except parsley; chill 2 hours. Strain; serve with parsley. Serves 4.

BLENDER VEGETABLE COCKTAIL

Combine in blender 1 1/2 cups tomato juice, 1 stalk celery (cut up), 1 carrot (cut up), 1 teaspoon instant minced onion, 1 tablespoon lemon juice, 1/2 teaspoon Worcestershire and a dash of pepper. Blend and chill. Serve over ice cubes in glasses. Makes 2 cups.

CHRISTMAS BEVERAGE

1/4 teaspoon cardamom seed
1/2 cup sugar
1/2 cup Madeira or port wine
2 bottles (about 12 ounces each) stout or
    porter, chilled
2 bottles (12 ounces each) beer, chilled

Crush cardamom seed and mix with sugar and wine. Shortly before serving, add stout and beer. Serves 8.

SPICED WINE

1/2 cup sugar
1/2 cup raisins
1/4 teaspoon cardamom seed
5 whole cloves
2" piece whole cinnamon
1 small piece whole ginger
1 cup Swedish aquavit, gin or vodka
1 bottle Burgundy
1/4 cup Madeira or port wine
1/2 cup blanched whole almonds

Combine first 7 ingredients in heavy saucepan. Heat slowly until hot (do not boil). Add wines and continue to heat (do not boil) about 30 minutes. Add almonds. Serve hot with spoons. Makes about 10 servings.

SPICED "WINE" FOR CHILDREN

2 cups apple juice
2 cups cranberry-juice cocktail
1/2 cup raisins
1 small piece whole ginger
5 whole cloves
2" piece whole cinnamon
1/2 cup blanched whole almonds

Combine first 6 ingredients in heavy saucepan. Bring to boil and simmer 20 minutes. Add almonds; serve hot with spoons. Serves 8.

HONEYCREEPER PUNCH

1 can (46 ounces) red fruit punch, chilled
1 can (6 ounces) frozen orange-juice
    concentrate, thawed
1 can (6 ounces) frozen limeade or
    lemonade concentrate, thawed
1 quart Bacardi rum, light or dark
Orange, lemon or lime slices

Stir first 3 ingredients together in large punch bowl. Stir in rum. Add ice and citrus slices. Makes about 2 1/2 quarts.

CHOCOLATE EGGNOG

For 1 serving, put 3 tablespoons chocolate syrup, 1 cup cold milk, 1 egg yolk and a dash of salt into bowl, blender or beverage maker. Blend until thoroughly mixed. Beat egg white until foamy. Gradually beat in 1 tablespoon sugar. Pile lightly on eggnog and sprinkle with chocolate shot.

ORANGE-BUTTERMILK NOG

1 cup orange juice
1 cup buttermilk
2 tablespoons honey
2 eggs
Nutmeg

Combine all ingredients, except nutmeg, in blender. Whirl 1 minute until frothy. Serve in tall glasses with a sprinkling of nutmeg. Makes 2½ cups. *Note* Eggs can be omitted. Makes about 2 cups.

ORANGE EGGNOG PUNCH

6 eggs
1/4 cup sugar
1/4 teaspoon cinnamon
1/4 teaspoon ginger
1/8 teaspoon ground cloves
2 cans (6 ounces each) frozen orange-juice concentrate, reconstituted
1 quart vanilla ice cream
1 bottle (28 ounces) ginger ale, chilled
Nutmeg

Beat eggs until light-colored. Add sugar, cinnamon, ginger and cloves. Then stir in orange juice. Cut ice cream in small cubes into punch bowl. Pour in orange mixture and ginger ale and sprinkle with nutmeg. Makes about 3½ quarts.

CITRUS PUNCH

1 can each (6 ounces each) frozen orange-juice concentrate, lemonade and limeade
1 bottle (28 ounces) ginger ale or 1 bottle white wine or 1/2 bottle of each
Fruited Ice Mold

In punch bowl, reconstitute frozen beverages as directed on cans. Add 4 cups more cold water. Just before serving, add ginger ale and ice mold. Makes about 4 quarts. **Fruited Ice Mold** Cover bottom of ring or other mold with ice cubes. Arrange lemon, orange, lime or apple slices, strawberries or grape clusters around or between ice cubes. Fill with water and freeze. (Ice cubes help hold fruit in place.)

BLOSSOM PUNCH

1 can (6 ounces) frozen pineapple-grapefruit juice, thawed
1 pint lemon sherbet, softened
1 bottle (28 ounces) citrus-flavor carbonated water, or Collins mix
1/3 cup (or to taste) gin (optional)

Combine all ingredients in punch bowl. Serve at once. Makes about 1½ quarts.

TANGY PUNCH

1 quart cranberry-juice cocktail, chilled
1 can (1 quart 14 ounces) pink pineapple-grapefruit drink, chilled
Juice of 1 lemon
1 bottle (28 ounces) citrus-flavor carbonated beverage, chilled

Combine first 3 ingredients. Just before serving, add carbonated beverage and pour into large pitcher. Makes about 3 quarts.

MINT SPARKLE PUNCH

1 quart orange sherbet
4 cups apple juice, chilled
4 cups orange juice, chilled
1 bottle (28 ounces) lemon-lime-flavor carbonated beverage, chilled
Fresh mint

Ahead of time, make small scoops of sherbet and freeze. When ready to serve, combine fruit juices and carbonated beverage in a chilled large punch bowl. Add frozen sherbet balls and decorate with sprigs of mint. Makes about twenty 5-ounce servings.

LIME PUNCH WITH LEMON-LIME MOLDS

5 cups lemon-lime-flavor carbonated beverage
1 teaspoon lemon extract
Green food coloring
2 cans (6 ounces each) frozen limeade
1 lime, cut in wedges
Mint sprigs
Fresh strawberries

Mix carbonated beverage and flavoring. Tint with food coloring and pour into individual gelatin molds, filling only about three fourths full since liquid expands when frozen. Freeze until firm. Shortly before serving, mix limeade and 8 cans cold water and put in punch bowl. Add molds and decorate with lime wedges, mint sprigs and berries. Makes about 3 quarts. *Note* Gin, vodka or green crème de menthe can be added.

CRANBERRY-APPLE PUNCH

2 pints cranberry-apple juice
1/2 cup lemon juice
1/3 cup sugar
1/4 teaspoon nutmeg
1 cinnamon stick
1/4 teaspoon salt
6 whole cloves
Additional cinnamon sticks (optional)

Combine all ingredients, except last, with 2 cups water. Bring to boil and simmer 10 minutes. Strain and serve hot in mugs. Use cinnamon sticks as muddlers, if desired. Makes about 1¹/₂ quarts.

FESTIVE MILK PUNCH

1 cup each sherry and port
1/2 cup brandy
1 quart milk
Sugar to taste
1 cup heavy cream
Nutmeg

Mix liquors in punch bowl. Add milk, sugar and cream. Sprinkle with nutmeg. Serve at room temperature. Makes 2 quarts.

SANGRÍA
(Spanish Red-wine Punch)

1 tablespoon sugar
1 bottle Spanish red wine, Burgundy, rosé or dry red wine, chilled
1 bottle (12 ounces) carbonated water, chilled
Spirals of lemon peel
Orange slices

Put sugar in large glass pitcher. Add wine, ice cubes and carbonated water. Drop in lemon peel and decorate with orange slices. Makes about 1¹/₂ quarts.

YOGURT-CHOCOLATE SHAKE

1 cup plain yogurt
1/3 cup chocolate syrup
1/2 teaspoon vanilla extract
2 cups skim milk

Whirl all ingredients in electric blender, or beat with rotary beater. Makes 2¹/₃ cups.

APRICOT-MILK COOLER

1 cup apricot nectar, chilled
1 to 2 tablespoons sugar
1 tablespoon lemon juice
2 cups cold milk
Dash of salt

Combine all ingredients and stir until sugar is dissolved. Makes 3 cups.

FROSTY PINK PUNCH

1/2 cup fine granulated sugar
1/2 cup lemon juice
1 cup orange juice
2 cups cranberry-juice cocktail
1 pint raspberry sherbet
1 bottle (28 ounces) ginger ale, chilled

Combine first 4 ingredients in punch bowl or large pitcher and stir until sugar is dissolved. Spoon in sherbet. Pour ginger ale over all. Serve with ice, if desired. Makes about 2 quarts.

MULLED APPLE-JUICE PUNCH

4 cups apple juice
6 whole cloves
1 cinnamon stick
1 bottle (28 ounces) ginger ale, chilled
Festive Ice Cubes

Bring first 3 ingredients to boil and cool. Just before serving, mix with ginger ale in punch bowl or pitcher. Add ice cubes. Makes about 2 quarts. *Note* Grape juice or cranberry-juice cocktail can be substituted for the apple juice. For a less sweet punch, substitute carbonated water for the ginger ale. **Festive Ice Cubes** Cut leaves from angelica or green candied cherries. Arrange a stemmed red maraschino cherry and 2 leaves in each section of ice-cube tray. Fill with water and freeze.

MULLED CIDER

1/2 teaspoon whole cloves
Two 2" cinnamon sticks
2/3 cup loose tea or 30 tea bags
1/4 cup sugar
2 quarts apple cider or apple juice
1/2 cup lemon juice

Put cloves and cinnamon sticks in saucepan with 2 quarts water. Bring to boil. Add tea, cover and brew about 4 minutes. Stir and strain. Stir in sugar, cider and lemon juice and heat gently but do not boil. Makes 4 quarts.

MULLED APRICOT NECTAR

1 can (46 ounces) apricot nectar
1/2 cup orange juice
1/2 lemon, sliced
2 tablespoons honey
8 whole cloves
4 whole allspice
1 cinnamon stick

Combine all ingredients in large saucepan, bring to boil and simmer 10 minutes. Remove from heat and let stand, covered, 30 minutes. Reheat; strain and serve. Makes about 1¹/₂ quarts.

HOT MULLED APPLE JUICE

Combine 1 quart apple juice; 2" stick cinnamon, broken; 4 whole cloves and 1/4 cup sugar. Bring to boil, cover and simmer 10 minutes. Strain. Serve hot. Serves 4 to 6.

CHERRY SHAKE-O

1/2 can (1 cup) cherry pie filling
1 pint vanilla ice cream, softened
2 cups milk
2 tablespoons lemon juice
Additional ice cream

Put all ingredients, except last, in blender; whirl until mixed. Or blend with rotary beater. Serve in tall glasses with a scoop of ice cream, a soda spoon and a straw. Thin with a little milk, if desired. Makes about 1¼ quarts.

HONEY COFFEE

4 tablespoons honey
2 cups hot very strong coffee
2 cups hot milk

Put 1 tablespoon honey in each coffee cup. Half-fill cup with coffee. Then fill cup with milk and stir well. Makes 4 cups.

FRENCH CHOCOLATE

2-1/2 squares unsweetened chocolate
1/2 cup sugar
Dash of salt
1/2 cup heavy cream, whipped
6 cups milk, heated

Put chocolate in heavy saucepan with 1/2 cup water. Heat, stirring, until chocolate is melted and blended. Add sugar and salt and boil, stirring, 4 minutes. Cool and fold into cream. To serve, put 1 rounded teaspoonful of mixture into each chocolate cup. Add hot milk to fill cup and stir until chocolate and milk are well blended. Makes 8 (6-ounce) cups.

SPICY PARTY COFFEE

1 cup heavy cream
2 tablespoons coffee liqueur
1 teaspoon sugar
Cinnamon
Hot double-strength coffee

Whip cream with coffee liqueur, sugar and 1/8 teaspoon cinnamon until stiff peaks form. Pour coffee into cups and top with cream mixture. Add more cinnamon, if desired. Makes 6 servings.

CLARET LEMONADE

Fill chilled glass three fourths full with cold lemonade. Tip glass slightly and slowly pour small amount of chilled claret down side of glass so that it settles on the bottom.

MINTED-TEA LEMONADE

2 tablespoons mint jelly
1 quart hot tea
1 can (6 ounces) frozen lemonade, reconstituted

Dissolve jelly in the tea. Mix with lemonade. Chill thoroughly before serving. Makes about 1½ quarts.

GUESTS' DESSERT DELIGHT

4 cups hot chocolate
1-1/2 cups strong hot coffee
1 cup brandy or rum
1 cup heavy cream, whipped with 2 tablespoons sugar

Beat together chocolate, coffee and brandy. Fold in heavy cream. Serve at once. Makes about 8 cups.

CAFÉ BRÛLOT

4 ounces (½ cup) Cognac
2 small cinnamon sticks
8 whole cloves
10 small lumps sugar
2 tablespoons canned chocolate syrup
2 long strips orange peel
2 strips lemon peel
2 cups hot strong coffee

Heat Cognac gently in top pan of chafing dish. Add remaining ingredients, except coffee, and ignite with match. Stir until mixture is blended and sugar is melted. Slowly stir in coffee. Strain into demitasse cups. Makes 4 servings.

BRAZILIAN CHOCOLATE

2 squares unsweetened chocolate
1/4 cup sugar
3 cups milk
1 tablespoon grated orange rind
1/4 teaspoon almond extract
Cinnamon sticks

Melt chocolate in 1 cup water in top of double boiler over hot water. Stir in sugar; bring to a boil over direct heat. Boil 5 minutes, stirring constantly. Stir in milk, orange rind and almond extract. Heat thoroughly. Before serving, beat with rotary beater until frothy. Serve with cinnamon sticks as muddlers. Makes 5 cups.

PINK FLUFF

1 bottle (28 ounces) lime-flavored
   carbonated beverage, chilled
Juice of 1 lemon
1 pint raspberry sherbet

Combine all ingredients in pitcher.
Makes about 1½ quarts.

BANANA-ORANGE BREAKFAST

1 can (6 ounces) frozen orange-juice
   concentrate, reconstituted
1 large ripe banana
1/3 cup lemon juice
2 tablespoons honey

Whirl all ingredients in blender,
or mash banana with fork, add
remaining ingredients and beat with
rotary beater. Makes about 1 quart.

ORANGE BLUSH

Combine in pitcher 1 can (6 ounces)
partially thawed frozen orange-juice
concentrate, 1½ cups cranberry-juice
cocktail, ¼ cup sugar and 2 cups carbonated water. Serve over ice cubs.
Makes 1 quart, or four 8-ounce servings.

BANANA MILK SHAKE

Peel 1 fully ripe banana; slice into
bowl and beat with rotary beater
or electric mixer until smooth. Add 1
cup cold milk and mix well. Serve at
once. Makes 1 large or 2 medium servings. **Note** Use blender if available.

Banana-Chocolate Shake Add 1 tablespoon chocolate syrup before beating.

Banana-frosted Shake Add a small
scoop of vanilla ice cream before
beating.

BANANA FROSTED

1 banana, sliced
1 cup milk
1 cup ice cream or ice milk
1/8 teaspoon cinnamon

Reserve 2 banana slices. Combine remaining banana and other
ingredients in blender container and
blend until frothy. Serve in tall
glasses with a banana slice perched
on rim of glass. Makes 2½ cups, or
2 servings.

BEVERAGES BASED ON COFFEE

Café au Lait (French breakfast coffee)
Using two pots, pour simultaneously
into each cup equal amounts of
strong hot freshly brewed coffee and
hot rich milk.

Viennese Coffee Brew strong coffee,
sweeten to taste and top with whipped
cream.

Spiced Dessert Coffee For 6 servings,
brew 6 cups coffee with seed from 1
cardamom pod. Pour slowly into tall
glasses, having coffee run down spoon
in glass to prevent breakage. Top with
generous spoonful of whipped cream
and wedge of thinly sliced orange.

Frosted Coffee Hawaii Combine
2 cups strong cold coffee, 1 cup
chilled pineapple juice and 1 pint
coffee ice cream. Whirl in blender or
beat with rotary beater until smooth
and foamy. Pour into tall glasses.
Serves 4 or 5.

Mocha Frosted Combine 2 cups
strong cold coffee, ¼ cup chocolate syrup and 1 pint coffee ice
cream. Whirl in blender or beat with
rotary beater until smooth. Pour into
tall glasses. Serves 4.

Spiced Iced Coffee Pour 3 cups hot
very strong coffee over 2 cinnamon
sticks, 4 whole cloves and 4 whole
allspice. Let stand 1 hour, then strain
and pour over ice in 4 tall glasses.
Add cream and sugar.

Café Olé In each glass, put 2 tablespoons light cream, 1 tablespoon
chocolate syrup and cold coffee to
half fill glass; mix well. Then fill glass
with carbonated cola drink and stir
gently.

Coffee Ice Cubes Pour about 3 cups
cooled coffee into ice-cube tray.
Freeze until firm. Use in any iced-
coffee beverage.

COFFEE ICE CREAM SODAS

Pour ¼ cup coffee syrup into each
tall glass. Add 2 tablespoons heavy
cream and a little chilled carbonated
water and stir. Put 1 to 2 scoops coffee ice cream in each glass; fill with
carbonated water and stir gently.

Coffee Syrup In saucepan, dissolve
¼ cup instant-coffee granules (not
freeze-dried) in ½ cup hot water.
Blend in 2 cups dark corn syrup and
¼ teaspoon salt. Bring to boil and
simmer 5 minutes; skim and add 2
teaspoons vanilla. Store, tightly covered, in refrigerator. Makes 2 cups.

Philadelphia Pepper Pot

Bombay Refresher

French Tarragon Soup

BEN CALVO

SELECTING A SOUP

Although there are hundreds, possibly thousands of soups, each of them falls into one of three groups:

1. **Thin, clear soups** based on bouillon, consommé or broth. This type is suitable as a first course at dinner.

2. **Thin, light, delicate soups** such as bisques, thin cream soups and vegetable broths. This kind can be served as a first course, or for lunch with a hearty sandwich or salad.

3. **Heavy, thick soups,** including beef or other meat soups, vegetable soups such as minestrone, poultry soups such as mulligatawny, fish soups, chowders and thick cream soups. These are hearty enough to be served as the main course for dinner.

Chilled or jellied soups may fall into any of these three main types. These are, of course, most suitable for hot weather.

PREPARED AND SEMIPREPARED SOUPS

Canned soups are packed in ready-to-serve, condensed and frozen condensed forms.

The condensed and frozen condensed soups require the addition of water or milk before heating. These soups, undiluted, also make excellent sauces.

Dried soups are of various types. Most contain dehydrated vegetables and some grain produce such as noodles.

Bouillon cubes, meat extract, seasoned stock bases and instant bouillon can be used to reinforce the flavor of meat stock for soups and sauces.

GARNISHES FOR SOUPS

Vary the flavor and appearance of a simple soup with one of the following garnishes:

Avocado slices or strips
Whipped cream colored with a little
   mashed pimiento
Paprika
Chopped fresh herbs
Popcorn
Toasted chopped nuts
Grated cheese
Thin rounds of cooked frankfurter or
   sausage
Diced fresh tomato
Dairy sour cream
Croutons
Thin lemon slices
Sliced stuffed olives
Crisp bacon bits
Browned onion rings
Paper-thin carrot or radish slices
Thin celery rings
Crisp ready-to-eat cereal
Snipped chives or watercress
Crumbled blue cheese.

SOUP ACCOMPANIMENTS

Try some of the new crackers such as those flavored with bacon, onion or potato; sesame crackers; Swiss- and ham-flavored crackers; vegetable crackers; shredded-wheat wafers; oblong buttery crackers; whole-wheat wafers; round cheese crackers; as well as the old favorites: oyster crackers, saltines, soda crackers, rye wafers, pretzels and pilot crackers. Or try one of the recipes at the end of this chapter.

BOMBAY REFRESHER

1 can (10-1/2 ounces) condensed
   cream of chicken soup
1 soup-can milk
1 tablespoon curry powder
3 tablespoons lemon juice
Chutney, sliced green apples, pistachio
   nuts and coconut

Mix first 4 ingredients. Chill until icy cold. When serving, add chutney, tart sliced apples and pistachio nuts to taste. Crush nuts if preferred, but whole nuts seem to add to the texture. Top with coconut. Makes 2½ cups.

CHILLED HERBED CHICKEN SOUP

Put 1 can condensed cream of chicken soup, 1 cup chicken broth, ½ cup heavy cream and 1 teaspoon fresh tarragon in container of electric blender. Run blender until mixture is smooth. Chill thoroughly. Makes 4 servings.

CHILLED FRUIT SOUP

The fruit: prunes, apricots, raisins, cherries, pears.

1/2 cup each dried prunes and apricots
1/2 cup seedless raisins
1 stick cinnamon
2 cooking apples, peeled
2 fresh pears
1 can (1 pound) unsweetened sour red
   cherries
1 box cherry-flavored gelatin
Lemon slices

In large kettle, soak prunes, apricots and raisins in 3 cups cold water 1 hour. Add cinnamon stick, sliced apples and pears. Cover and simmer 15 minutes, or until fruit is tender. Add undrained cherries and bring to boil. Dissolve gelatin in 1 cup boiling water; stir gently into fruit. Chill overnight. Serve with lemon. Serves 8.

CHILLED ROQUEFORT BOUILLON

1 envelope unflavored gelatin
2 cans condensed beef bouillon
Juice of 1/2 lemon
1/4 cup crumbled Roquefort cheese
Dairy sour cream
Chopped chives

Soften gelatin in ½ cup cold water; dissolve over low heat. Stir into bouillon; add lemon juice. Chill until slightly thickened. Lightly fold in cheese. Serve in bouillon cups with sour cream and a sprinkling of chives. Makes 4 to 6 servings.

FRENCH TARRAGON SOUP

5 cups clear chicken bouillon
4 teaspoons chopped fresh tarragon or
   2 teaspoons crumbled dried tarragon
1 envelope unflavored gelatin
Lime or lemon slices and chopped
   parsley or chives

Simmer chicken bouillon about 5 minutes, then add tarragon. Dissolve gelatin in ¼ cup cold water and add to chicken bouillon. Chill 4 hours. Serve in individual cups topped with a lime slice and chopped parsley. Makes 5 cups.

VICHYSSOISE

3 leeks (white only), diced
1 white onion, sliced
2 tablespoons sweet butter
2 cups chicken or veal stock or
   consommé
3 cups peeled diced potato
Salt and white pepper
2 cups rich milk
1/2 cup heavy cream
Chopped chives

Sauté leeks and onion gently in butter until soft; do not brown. Add to soup stock with potato and seasonings. Simmer until potato is soft. Put through fine strainer, cool and add 1 cup of the milk and the cream. Bring just to boil. If any lumps form, strain again. Add rest of milk and stir again until blended. Chill thoroughly and serve with ¼ teaspoon chopped chives in each bowl. It should be like iced velvet. Makes about 1½ quarts.

GAZPACHO

1 medium loaf French bread (about 1
   pound)
2 cloves garlic
1 pound tomatoes, peeled
1 large onion
1 cucumber, peeled
1/2 cup olive oil
1/2 cup wine vinegar
Salt and pepper
Croutons
Finely diced cucumber, tomato, onion,
   parsley and hard-cooked egg

Cut up bread; soak in water and squeeze almost dry. Put in blender with garlic and coarsely cut tomatoes, onion and cucumber. Blend until thoroughly mixed. Remove cover, put blender on low and add oil gradually. Pour into bowl; stir in vinegar, and salt and pepper to taste. Chill. Serve in large flat bowls. Put croutons and remaining ingredients in individual bowls to be passed at the table. Makes 4 to 6 servings.

CHILLED SEAFOOD BISQUE

Beat 1 can condensed tomato soup and 1 soup-can milk until smooth. Add 1 can (4½ ounces) small shrimp, drained, and 1 can (6½ ounces) crab meat, flaked. Season to taste with salt, pepper and lemon juice. Chill. Sprinkle with chopped chives. Makes 4 servings.

LOBSTER BISQUE

Remove any bone from 1 can (6½ ounces) lobster. Separate meat in small pieces, put in bowl and cover with ⅓ cup dry sherry. Let stand 20 minutes. In top part of double boiler over simmering water, melt ¼ cup butter or margarine. Blend in 3 tablespoons flour. Gradually add 3 cups milk and cook, stirring, until thickened. Season with 1 teaspoon steak sauce and salt, seasoned salt and pepper to taste. Add soaked lobster with the sherry; cook, covered, 10 minutes. Makes about 4 cups.

TOMATO SHRIMP BISQUE

2 cans (19 ounces each) tomatoes
2 cups beef stock or bouillon
1 cup chopped celery and leaves
2 onions, sliced
2 carrots, sliced
2 sprigs parsley
4 whole cloves
6 whole black peppercorns
Small piece of bay leaf
Pinch of thyme
2 teaspoons salt
3 tablespoons rice
1-1/2 pounds shrimp, cooked and cut up
1 pint light cream
Sherry
Croutons
Thin slices of lemon
Chopped parsley

Put tomatoes, stock, vegetables, seasonings and rice in kettle; bring to boil. Cover and simmer 1 hour. Force through fine sieve or blend smooth in electric blender. Just before serving, add shrimp; heat. Heat cream and add to tomato mixture. Season to taste. Serve at once with sherry and croutons. Garnish with lemon and parsley. Makes about 2½ quarts.

TURKEY-CORN CHOWDER

In saucepan mix 1 can condensed turkey-noodle soup, 1 soup-can milk, 1 can (8 ounces) cream-style corn, ¼ teaspoon salt and a dash of pepper. Heat, stirring occasionally. Serve in hot soup bowls topped with paprika. Makes 4 servings.

CURRIED CHICKEN SOUP

2 cans condensed cream of chicken soup
2 cups cold milk
2 tablespoons finely chopped green onions or chives
1 teaspoon curry powder
Paprika
Slivered lemon rind
1 hard-cooked egg, chopped

Mix all ingredients, except last 3. Chill several hours, or overnight. Garnish each serving with paprika, lemon rind and chopped egg. Serves 4.

MANHATTAN CLAM CHOWDER

1/4 pound salt pork, diced
1 large onion, sliced
1/2 medium green pepper, chopped
1/2 cup each diced celery, carrot and turnip
3 cups diced potato
Salt
1 pint clams and liquid
Pinch of thyme
2 cups tomato juice
1/2 cup tomato purée
Chopped parsley

Brown pork in heavy kettle. Pour off all but 1 tablespoon fat. Add onion, pepper and celery; brown lightly. Add carrot, turnip, potato, 3 cups water and 1 teaspoon salt. Chop hard part of clams and add to soup with clam liquid; reserve soft part of clams. Simmer about 30 minutes. Add coarsely cut soft part of clams, thyme, tomato juice and tomato purée; bring to boil and simmer 5 minutes. Season to taste. Serve garnished with parsley. Makes 4 to 6 servings.

NEW ENGLAND CLAM CHOWDER

18 chowder clams
1 stalk celery
1/4 pound salt pork, diced
2 onions, sliced
2 potatoes, diced
3 cups milk
Salt and pepper
6 pilot crackers, crumbled

Scrub clams and put in large kettle with 1 cup water and celery; cover and simmer 15 minutes, or until shells open. Strain off clam broth and reserve. Cook salt pork slowly in heavy kettle until browned. Pour off all but 2 tablespoons fat. Cook onions with pork until tender but not browned. Mince hard part of clams; add to onions and pork with potatoes and clam broth; bring to boil and simmer 20 minutes, or until potatoes are tender. Scald milk; add to soup with soft part of clams; season. Add crackers. Makes 1½ quarts.

OVEN FISH CHOWDER

2 pounds cod or haddock fillets
4 potatoes, sliced
Few chopped celery leaves
1 bay leaf
2-1/2 teaspoons salt
4 whole cloves
1 clove garlic
3 onions, sliced
1/2 cup butter or margarine
1/4 teaspoon dried dillseed
1/4 teaspoon white pepper
1/2 cup dry white wine
2 cups light cream
Chopped fresh dill or parsley

Put all ingredients, except cream and dill, with 2 cups boiling water in 3-quart casserole. Cover and bake in moderate oven (375°F.) I hour. Heat cream to scalding and add to chowder. Serve with garnish of chopped dill. Makes 6 servings.

CHAMPION CRAB CHOWDER

3 slices salt pork, diced
1 tablespoon instant minced onion
3 tablespoons flour
2 cups chicken stock or bouillon
2 cups undiluted evaporated milk
2 cups tomato juice
1 tablespoon sugar
1 cup cooked diced potato
2 pounds crab meat
1/2 teaspoon salt
1/8 teaspoon pepper
1/8 teaspoon paprika

Parboil salt pork in small amount of water 5 minutes. Drain, put in skillet and fry until crisp. Remove and reserve. Add onion and flour to remaining fat and stir until smooth. Gradually stir in stock and evaporated milk. Cook until slightly thickened. Add remaining ingredients and cook until the consistency of thick purée. Add pork bits. Serve at once, with croutons, if desired. Makes about 2 quarts.

BLENDER CREAM OF CORN SOUP

1-1/2 cups cooked whole-kernel corn
2 cups milk
1 cup light cream
1 small onion, sliced
1-1/2 slices bread, crust-trimmed and torn
3/4 teaspoon salt
Dash of white pepper
1 teaspoon steak sauce
1/4 teaspoon powdered marjoram

Put corn, milk, cream, onion and bread in container of electric blender. Whirl on high speed 20 seconds. Add remaining ingredients and heat. Makes about 4½ cups.

CORN-CLAM CHOWDER

2 slices bacon
2 tablespoons finely chopped onion
1-1/2 cups frozen hashed brown potatoes, southern style
1 package (10 ounces) frozen cut corn
1 can (6-1/2 ounces) minced clams
2 cups milk
1/4 teaspoon thyme leaves
Salt and pepper

Cut bacon in small pieces, then cook until crisp. Remove and reserve. Add onion to fat in pan and sauté a few minutes. Add potatoes, corn and liquid drained from clams. Cover and simmer 8 minutes, or until potatoes are tender. Add milk, thyme, clams and salt and pepper to taste. Bring to boil and simmer gently about 2 minutes. Sprinkle with reserved crisp bacon. Makes 4 to 6 servings.

SALMON-CORN CHOWDER

1/4 cup butter or margarine
3/4 cup chopped onion
1/2 cup chopped green pepper
1 small clove garlic, minced
1 can (1 pound) salmon
1 can (1 pound) tomatoes
1 can (8 ounces) whole-kernel corn
1 chicken bouillon cube
1 bay leaf
1/2 teaspoon salt
Dash of pepper

Melt butter in 3-quart saucepan. Add next 3 ingredients and sauté, stirring frequently, 5 minutes. Drain and flake salmon, reserving liquid. Add both salmon and liquid with remaining ingredients and 1 cup water to first mixture. Bring to boil, cover and simmer 10 to 15 minutes. Remove bay leaf. Makes about 1½ quarts, or 6 servings.

CREOLE CHEESE SOUP

1 medium onion, chopped
1/2 cup each chopped green pepper and celery
1 large clove garlic, minced
1/4 teaspoon crushed dried red pepper
1/4 cup bacon fat or margarine
1/4 cup flour
1/4 to 1/2 cup dry white wine
1 pound Cheddar cheese, shredded
4 cups milk
Salt and white pepper
Minced chives or chopped parsley

Sauté first 4 ingredients in fat in kettle until golden. Blend in flour and cook, stirring, about 3 minutes. Over very low heat, stir in wine, cheese and milk. Cook, stirring, until cheese is melted and mixture is smooth and slightly thickened. Add salt and pepper to taste. Serve with chives. Makes 2 quarts.

FISH SOUP, SCANDINAVIAN STYLE

2 packages (1 pound each) frozen fish fillets (any kind)
3 tablespoons olive or vegetable oil
1 cup frozen chopped onion
1/2 cup frozen chopped green pepper
1 can (1 pound) tomatoes
2 packages (10 ounces) frozen lima beans (either kind)
1 bottle (8 ounces) clam broth
2 teaspoons salt
1/4 teaspoon pepper
1/4 cup parsley flakes

Put fillets in kettle or Dutch oven with 2 cups water. Bring to boil, reduce heat, cover and simmer 15 minutes, or until fish flakes easily with fork. Remove fish and flake, removing any bones; reserve broth. Heat oil in same kettle, add onion and green pepper and sauté 2 to 3 minutes. Add tomatoes and simmer 10 minutes. Add reserved broth and remaining ingredients, except parsley. Bring to boil, cover and simmer 10 minutes, or until beans are tender. Add fish and heat. Sprinkle with parsley. Makes 2¹/₂ quarts.

MUSHROOM-CLAM BISQUE

1 can (4 ounces) mushroom stems and pieces
2 tablespoons butter or margarine
1 bottle (8 ounces) clam juice
1 can (7 ounces) minced clams, undrained
1 stalk celery, chopped
1 small onion, chopped
3 or 4 whole cloves
1 cup light cream or milk
1 teaspoon salt
Dash each of cracked pepper, cayenne

Drain mushrooms, reserving liquid. Chop mushrooms and sauté in the butter 1 to 2 minutes. Set aside about ¹/₄ cup. In saucepan, put minced clams and juice, sautéed mushrooms and mushroom liquid, celery, onion and cloves. Simmer about 5 minutes (do not boil). Add cream and seasonings. Add mushrooms and heat gently. Makes 1 quart.

CORN BISQUE

Grate or scrape 6 ears corn. Cover cobs with cold water, bring to boil and simmer 30 minutes. Strain, reserving liquid. To 2 cups liquid, add corn pulp and simmer 15 minutes. Blend 1 tablespoon melted butter and 2 teaspoons flour; add to corn. Add ¹/₈ teaspoon white pepper, 1 teaspoon instant chicken bouillon, 2 cups milk, 1 teaspoon sugar and salt to taste. Bring to boil, stirring. Makes 1 quart.

CLAM SOUP, ITALIAN STYLE

1/4 cup olive oil
4 slices Italian bread
1 clove garlic
2 sprigs parsley, chopped
3/4 cup red wine
1 tablespoon catsup
2 cans (7-1/2 ounces each) minced clams with liquid
1 cup clam juice
1/4 teaspoon pepper
1/2 teaspoon oregano

Heat 2 tablespoons oil in saucepan. Add bread and brown on both sides. Remove bread and add garlic to oil; cook 2 or 3 minutes. Remove garlic. Add remaining ingredients to oil and simmer a few minutes. Put a slice of bread in each bowl. Pour in soup. Makes 1 quart.

SOUTH AMERICAN ONION SOUP

6 onions, thinly sliced
3 tablespoons butter
2 quarts rich stock, or 3 cans of condensed consommé with 3 soup-cans water
1-1/2 cups almonds, blanched and chopped fine
Salt and pepper
Rounds of crusty bread, toasted
1 cup grated Gruyère cheese

Sauté onions in butter slowly until soft. Add stock and nuts and simmer for ¹/₂ hour. Season to taste with salt and pepper and serve with toast rounds sprinkled with cheese. Makes about 2¹/₂ quarts.

HAMBURGER-VEGETABLE SOUP

1/2 pound ground beef
1 large onion, chopped
1 clove garlic, minced
1/2 cup chopped celery and leaves
3 carrots, chopped
1/2 cup diced green beans
2 potatoes, diced
1 tablespoon flour
1-1/2 teaspoons salt
1/4 teaspoon pepper
Dash of cayenne

Brown meat in kettle, stirring to break up. Add onion and garlic and cook until yellowed. Add remaining vegetables and cook, stirring often, 3 minutes. If there is much fat in kettle, remove all but about 1 tablespoon and save the excess fat for other purposes. Stir in flour; add 6 cups boiling water, the salt, pepper and cayenne. Cover and simmer 20 minutes, or until vegetables are tender. Makes 4 servings.

QUICK BORSCH

Empty 1 jar (1 pound) Harvard beets into saucepan. If beets are sliced, chop them. If slivered or diced, leave as is. Add 2 cans condensed onion soup. Heat and add lemon juice to taste. Serve hot with a garnish of sour cream. Makes about 7 cups.

PEANUT-BUTTER CELERY SOUP

1 cup diced celery
1 medium onion, chopped
2 tablespoons butter
4-1/2 cups milk
4 chicken bouillon cubes
2 pimientos, minced
1/8 teaspoon pepper
1/4 cup peanut butter
Sautéed or toasted croutons

In top part of double boiler over direct heat, cook celery and onion in butter 2 or 3 minutes. Put over boiling water and add 4¼ cups milk. Heat to scalding and add next 3 ingredients. Cover and cook 15 minutes. Beat remaining ¼ cup milk and peanut butter until blended. Add to first mixture and blend well. Serve with croutons. Makes 1½ quarts.

MINESTRONE MILANESE

In this northern version of Italy's national soup, rice replaces pasta.

1/4 cup olive oil
1 clove garlic, minced
1 onion, minced
1 leek, washed and diced
1 tablespoon chopped parsley
1 teaspoon dried thyme leaves
1 tablespoon tomato paste
3 canned or fresh tomatoes, peeled, seeded and chopped
3 stalks celery, chopped
2 carrots, diced
2 potatoes, diced
1/4 small cabbage, shredded
2 zucchinis, diced
Salt to taste
1/2 teaspoon black pepper
1/3 cup uncooked rice
1 to 1-1/2 cups drained cooked dried beans
Grated Parmesan cheese

Put olive oil in large kettle. Add next 5 ingredients and cook until soft. Add tomato paste thinned with ¼ cup water and cook 5 minutes. Add all remaining ingredients, except rice, beans and cheese, with 1½ quarts hot water or bouillon. Simmer, covered, 1 hour. Bring to boil, add rice and cook until soft. Add beans; heat. Serve with cheese. Makes 3 quarts.

CURRY CONSOMMÉ-PEA

Mix 1 can each condensed consommé and condensed pea soup. Add 1 soup-can milk and 1 teaspoon curry powder. Heat, stirring occasionally. Makes 4 servings.

PHILADELPHIA PEPPER POT

2 veal shins
Salt
2 pounds boneless veal
1 pound fresh tripe, finely cut
4 cups all-purpose flour
4 cans (10-1/2 ounces each) condensed consommé
4 cans (10-1/2 ounces each) condensed tomato soup
Red pepper
Ground allspice
4 hard-cooked eggs, cut into chunks

Simmer veal shins with 4 quarts water and 2 tablespoons salt for 2 hours. Strain and add veal and tripe to broth. Simmer for 2 hours, or until meats are tender. Cut veal into pieces and return to mixture. Cook flour until golden brown in skillet. Blend in 1 quart water and stir into veal broth. Add consommé and tomato soup. Simmer for 1 hour. Season with salt, red pepper and allspice. Add eggs and simmer for ½ hour. Makes 10 to 12 servings.

BOUILLABAISSE

1 carrot, diced
2 onions, chopped
2 leeks (white part only) or 4 green onions, sliced
1 clove garlic, crushed
1/2 cup olive oil
3 pounds boned white fish, cut in 3" pieces
2 large tomatoes, diced, or 1 cup canned tomatoes
Salt and pepper
1 bay leaf
2 cups fish stock, clam juice or water
1 cup cooked shrimp, crab or lobster
2 dozen scrubbed oysters, clams or mussels in the shell
1 can (4 ounces) pimientos, diced
Few shreds of saffron
Juice of 1 lemon
1 cup dry white wine
French bread, sliced and toasted
Chopped parsley

Cook first 4 ingredients in oil in large kettle until golden brown. Add fish, tomatoes, salt and pepper, bay leaf and stock. Bring to boil, cover and simmer 20 minutes. Add shellfish and simmer 5 minutes, or until shells open. Add remaining ingredients, except last 2. Heat well. Put toast in tureen and add soup. Sprinkle with parsley. Serves 6 to 8.

UKRAINIAN BORSCH

1 pound beef chuck, in one piece
8 cups beef broth
Salt and pepper
1 bay leaf
2 tablespoons margarine
1 medium onion, chopped
2 carrots, sliced
1 stalk celery, sliced
4 medium raw beets, cut in strips
1/2 medium cabbage (about 1 pound), shredded
4 medium potatoes (about 1 pound), cubed
1 can (6 ounces) tomato paste
1 tablespoon vinegar
Lemon slices
Dairy sour cream
Chopped dill or parsley (optional)

Put beef and broth in heavy 4-quart kettle. Add salt and pepper to taste and the bay leaf. Bring to boil and skim. Simmer, covered, about 30 minutes. Melt margarine in deep heavy 6-quart kettle or Dutch oven. Add next 6 ingredients and sauté, stirring, 5 minutes. Add tomato paste and vinegar and simmer 10 minutes. Remove meat from broth and pour broth over vegetables. Put meat in kettle with vegetables and simmer, covered, 1½ hours, or until meat is tender. Remove meat and cut in bite-size pieces. Put back in soup. Add seasoning to taste. Serve in large soup plates or bowls with a lemon slice and a tablespoon sour cream in each plate. Sprinkle lightly with chopped dill, if desired. Makes about 4 quarts. Leftovers can be frozen. **Note** Beef broth can be canned or made out of bouillon cubes and water. Or cook a leftover ham bone in water with seasonings, then strain.

FRENCH POTATO SOUP

4 medium potatoes
3 or 4 leeks, white part only
Butter or margarine
Salt
1-1/2 cups milk, scalded
White pepper
2 egg yolks
Croutons

Peel and dice potatoes and put in large saucepan. Chop leeks fine and brown lightly in 2 tablespoons butter. Add to potatoes. Add boiling water to cover and ½ teaspoon salt. Cover, bring to boil and cook until potatoes are tender. Purée entire mixture in blender. Add milk and heat. Season to taste and beat in egg yolks. Serve with a spoonful of butter and a few croutons in each bowl. Makes 4 servings.

CREAM OF BLACK BEAN SOUP

1/4 cup butter or margarine
1/4 cup flour
4 cups milk
1 cup Black Bean Spread (below)
1 teaspoon steak sauce
Seasoned salt and pepper to taste

Melt butter in saucepan and blend in flour. Gradually add milk and cook, stirring, until smooth and thickened. Add remaining ingredients; heat. Makes 4½ cups.

BLACK BEAN SPREAD

1 pound dried black beans
1 onion, minced
1 clove garlic, minced
1 small fresh chili pepper, minced, or 4 teaspoons chili powder
3 teaspoons salt

Bring 6 cups water to boil in kettle or Dutch oven. Add washed beans and boil 2 minutes. Cover, remove from heat and let stand 1 hour. Then add remaining ingredients, bring again to boil and simmer, covered, until mushy-tender. Without draining, whirl in blender until smooth. (Or force through food mill or sieve.) If desired, chill and serve as a sandwich spread. Makes about 3 cups.

FRANKFURTER-CHEESE SOUP

1 large onion, chopped
1 cup chopped celery
3 tablespoons butter or margarine
1/4 cup flour
1 teaspoon dry mustard
2 bouillon cubes
1 package (10 ounces) frozen mixed vegetables
6 cups milk
2 cups (1/2 pound) shredded process American cheese
1 teaspoon Worcestershire
3/4 pound frankfurters, sliced
1 tablespoon vegetable oil
Salt and pepper
Chopped parsley and pimiento

In heavy 4-quart kettle, sauté onion and celery in the butter 5 minutes. Stir in flour and mustard. Gradually stir in 2 cups water, bring to boil and cook, stirring, until thickened. Add bouillon cubes and vegetables and cook 3 minutes. Add milk and heat just to boiling. Add cheese and Worcestershire and stir until cheese is melted. Sauté frankfurters lightly in the oil and add to soup. Season to taste and garnish with parsley and pimiento. Makes about 3 quarts.

BLACK-BEAN AND SALAMI SOUP

In saucepan, mix 2 cans condensed black-bean soup, 1 can condensed consommé, 6 ounces hard salami, cut in strips, and 3 cups water. Bring to boil and simmer 5 minutes. Garnish each bowl with slices of hard-cooked egg. Serves 4.

FRANKFURTER AND RICE SOUP

3 tablespoons butter
1 onion, chopped
1/4 cup chopped green pepper
1/4 cup diced celery
3 cups chicken broth
1 cup canned or stewed tomatoes
1/4 cup uncooked rice
2 tablespoons chopped parsley
1/2 bay leaf
1/2 teaspoon salt
1/8 teaspoon pepper
1/2 pound frankfurters, sliced

Melt butter and sauté onion, green pepper and celery in it until soft. Add all other ingredients, bring to a boil and reduce heat. Simmer, covered, stirring frequently, 20 to 30 minutes. Makes about 1½ quarts.

GARBURE BASQUE
(Ham and Bean Soup with Vegetables)

1 pound dried navy or pea beans
1 ham butt, 3 to 4 pounds, or a
    smoked pork tenderloin
6 onions, sliced
8 cloves garlic, chopped
1 green pepper, cut in strips
1 hot pepper
1 pound fava beans or lima beans,
    or 1 box (10 ounces) frozen limas
4 carrots, sliced
6 turnips, sliced
1 cabbage, shredded
1 pound peas or 1 box (10 ounces)
    frozen peas
Salt and pepper
12 to 16 pork sausages

Cover dried beans with 6 cups water, bring to boil and boil 2 minutes. Cover and let stand 1 hour. Then cook until just tender. Add next 8 ingredients and more water, if necessary. Cover kettle and simmer gently 3 to 4 hours. Add cabbage, peas and any other vegetable you may have. Cook until vegetable mixture is a thick purée. Season to taste. Remove ham from soup when tender; cut in slices and keep warm. Grill the sausages. Serve big bowls of this thick soup with slices of ham, sausages and plenty of crusty bread. This is a good rib-sticking winter dish that's a full meal in itself. Makes about 4 quarts.

FRESH-TOMATO WINE SOUP

This is an appetizer soup. In the summertime, Californians use big, ripe, flavorful beefsteak tomatoes for this.

2 cups peeled and diced ripe fresh
    tomatoes
1/4 cup butter
2 tablespoons flour
1 teaspoon salt
1/8 teaspoon each ground nutmeg and
    basil
Pinch of pepper
1/4 teaspoon baking soda
1 cup half-and-half (half milk and half
    cream), or light cream
1/2 cup dry white table wine

In saucepan, simmer tomatoes in butter for 5 minutes. Whirl in blender or press through strainer to purée. Return purée to saucepan. Blend in flour, salt, nutmeg, basil and pepper. Stirring constantly, bring mixture to a boil; reduce heat and simmer 2 minutes, stirring. Stir in soda and half-and-half. Cook over low heat, stirring, until very slightly thickened. Stir in wine; heat to simmering. Makes 4 servings.

HAMBURGER-TOMATO SOUP
WITH RICE DUMPLINGS

1 pound ground beef chuck
1-1/2 tablespoons butter
1 can (30 ounces) tomatoes
1 envelope onion-soup mix
1/4 teaspoon paprika
1 can (1 pound) red kidney beans
1 teaspoon seasoned salt
1/4 teaspoon pepper
1 bay leaf
Rice Dumplings

In Dutch oven or 12″ skillet with cover, brown beef in butter, stirring with fork. Add 1½ cups water and remaining ingredients, except Dumplings. Bring to boil, cover and simmer 10 minutes. Drop dumpling batter by tablespoonfuls into soup. Cover and simmer 20 minutes without removing cover. Serves 6.
Rice Dumplings Sift 1¾ cups all-purpose flour, 2 teaspoons baking powder and ½ teaspoon salt. Cut in 3 tablespoons shortening. Add ¾ cup cold cooked rice and 2 tablespoons minced parsley. Mix ½ cup milk, add 1 egg and beat with fork. Add to first mixture, stirring with fork until dry ingredients are dampened. (Mixture will be stiff, but do not add more milk.) *Note* If preferred, 2 cups biscuit mix can be substituted for the flour, baking powder, salt and shortening in the above recipe.

QUICK TOMATO SOUP

2 cans condensed tomato soup
3/4 cup chicken broth
1/2 cup mashed potato
1 teaspoon curry powder
Dash of pepper

Beat all ingredients together with 1 soup-can water in blender or with rotary beater; heat. Serves 4.

OYSTER STEW

3 dozen oysters with liquid
1/2 cup butter or margarine
1/8 teaspoon Worcestershire
Dash of cayenne
1/2 cup clam juice
4 cups hot milk
4 cups hot light cream
Salt and pepper
Paprika

Cook first 4 ingredients in large skillet just until edges of oysters begin to curl. Add clam juice, milk and cream; heat but do not boil. Add salt and pepper to taste. Sprinkle with paprika. Makes about 2½ quarts. For a simpler stew, allow 2 dozen oysters for every pint of half-and-half (milk and cream). Heat the half-and-half; add the oysters and 1 tablespoon butter for each 2 dozen oysters. Heat and season with salt and pepper.

BACON-POTATO SOUP

2/3 cup diced lean bacon
3 mild white onions, chopped
4 green onions, chopped
2 tablespoons flour
6 cups bouillon
4 boiling potatoes, thinly sliced
   crosswise
1/2 cup dairy sour cream
1/2 cup light cream
2 egg yolks
1 tablespoon each minced parsley and
   chervil

In deep heavy pot, sauté bacon a few minutes. Add onions and cook 5 to 10 minutes, or until soft but not brown. Blend in flour. Gradually stir in bouillon. Add potato, cover and simmer 1 hour. Have sour cream at room temperature. Mix with light cream and beat in egg yolks. Spoon a little hot soup into cream mixture, mix well, then slowly stir back into hot soup. Simmer (*do not boil*), stirring frequently, 5 to 8 minutes. Add herbs and ladle into warm soup bowls. Makes 6 to 8 servings. *Note* No salt or pepper is needed. The bouillon adds enough seasoning.

CREAM OF CORN AND TOMATO SOUP

A good way to use leftover corn.

Prepare 1 can condensed cream of tomato soup as directed on the label. Add 1 cup cooked cream-style corn (or use canned). Add 1 teaspoon instant minced onion and season to taste with basil or rosemary. Add a little more milk or water, if necessary. Heat through. Serve with a little dairy sour cream and top with chopped chives, if desired. Makes about 3 cups, or 4 servings.

SPICY TOMATO BOUILLON

1 can (1 pound 3 ounces) tomatoes or
   2 cups chopped ripe tomatoes
1 can (10-1/2 ounces) condensed beef
   broth
1 onion, sliced
1/4 teaspoon each celery seed and
   whole black peppercorns
3 whole cloves
Salt
Chopped parsley

Heat all ingredients, except salt and parsley. Simmer about 10 minutes. Season to taste with salt and serve topped with parsley. Serves 4.

PETITE MARMITE

3 medium onions, sliced
1 tablespoon butter
2 pounds beef chuck in one piece
2 pounds beef soupbones
1 stewing chicken
Salt
2 bay leaves
3 whole black peppercorns
Few sprigs of parsley
1/2 teaspoon thyme
2 whole cloves
1 cup diced celery
4 carrots, diced
3 sliced leeks, white part only
1/4 small green cabbage, slivered
1 box frozen peas
Pepper
Grated cheese

Brown onions in butter in large kettle. Add beef, bones, chicken, 3 quarts water, 1 tablespoon salt, bay leaves, whole peppers, parsley, thyme and cloves. Bring to boil and simmer, covered, 4 hours, or until meats are tender. Remove meats, cool and slice thin. Cook remaining vegetables for garnish until barely tender in a little boiling salted water. Drain. Strain soup mixture and reheat. Season to taste with salt and pepper. Put some vegetables and meat slices in individual marmites or soup bowls. Cover with broth. Serve with grated cheese. Makes 6 to 8 servings.

CREAM OF CLAM

Drain 1 can (10½ ounces) minced clams. Put clams in container of electric blender with 1 cup light cream. Run blender until mixture is smooth. Heat with 2 cups chicken broth, 2 tablespoons lemon juice and ½ cup white wine or sherry. Serve hot with a sprinkling of paprika. Makes 4 servings.

CHICKEN SOUP WITH SWEDISH DUMPLINGS

1-1/2 quarts chicken broth
2 cups diced cooked chicken
1/4 cup flour
1 cup milk
3/4 teaspoon salt
2 cardamom seeds, crushed, or 1/8
    teaspoon nutmeg
1 tablespoon sugar
2 tablespoons butter
1 egg, beaten
8 blanched almonds, minced
2 sprigs parsley, minced

Bring broth and chicken to boil in kettle. For dumplings, blend flour and a little milk to a smooth paste in saucepan. Add remaining milk, salt, cardamom and sugar. Cook until thickened, stirring constantly. Add butter and stir until melted. Pour over egg, mix and cool. Add almonds and parsley. Drop into gently boiling soup. Cook 2 minutes, or until dumplings rise to top. Makes 4 servings.

HAM-CHEESE SOUP

1 medium onion, chopped
1/2 cup chopped celery
3 tablespoons butter or margarine
1/4 cup flour
3/4 teaspoon dry mustard
2 bouillon cubes
6 cups milk
2 cups (1/2 pound) shredded process
    American cheese
1 box frozen mixed vegetables, cooked
1 teaspoon Worcestershire
1 to 1-1/2 cups finely diced ham
Chopped parsley
Chopped pimiento

Cook onion and celery in the butter about 8 minutes; do not brown. Blend in flour and mustard. Dissolve bouillon cubes in 2 cups hot water. Gradually add to first mixture and cook, stirring, until thickened. Then cook 3 minutes longer. Add milk and heat just to boiling. Add cheese and stir until melted. Stir in remaining ingredients, except last 2, and heat. Sprinkle with parsley and pimiento. Makes 2½ quarts.

POLISH BORSCH

1-1/2 pounds beef chuck, cut up
4 medium beets, cooked and sliced
2 stalks celery, diced
1 onion, minced
Salt and pepper
1/4 cup dairy sour cream
2 tablespoons flour
1 egg
Hot boiled potatoes

Put meat in kettle and add 1½ quarts water. Bring to boil and simmer, covered, 2 hours, or until meat is almost tender. Add beets, celery and onion; cook about 30 minutes longer. Season to taste. Blend sour cream, flour and egg. Stir into soup and bring again to boil. Serve in hot soup bowls. Pass potatoes. Makes 4 to 6 servings.

SENATE BEAN SOUP

1 pound dried marrow, navy, Great
    Northern, or pea beans
1 large smoked ham hock
3 potatoes, cooked and mashed
2 onions, chopped
1 cup diced celery
2 cloves garlic, minced
Salt and pepper

Wash beans and cover with 5 quarts water. Bring to boil and boil 2 minutes. Remove from heat and let stand 1 hour. Bring again to boil and simmer, covered, 2 hours, or until beans begin to mush. Add all ingredients, except salt and pepper, and simmer 1 hour longer. Remove bone, cut up meat and return to soup. Season. Makes about 4 quarts.

SCOTCH BARLEY BROTH

2 pounds lamb neck or breast
1/2 cup pearl barley
Salt
6 whole black peppercorns
3/4 cup each chopped onion and celery
3/4 cup each diced yellow turnip and
    carrot
1 carrot, grated
1 leek, sliced
1 cup cooked peas
2 tablespoons minced parsley
Pepper

Put lamb, barley, 1 teaspoon salt and the peppercorns in a large heavy pan; add 2 quarts water. Simmer about 1½ hours. Cool; skim. Remove meat, trim off fat and bones and dice meat; put meat back in soup. Add onion, celery, turnip and diced carrot. Bring to a boil and simmer 30 minutes, or until vegetables are tender. Add remaining ingredients and season to taste. Heat through. Makes 1½ quarts.

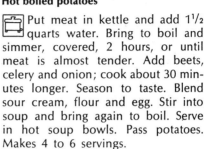

ACCOMPANIMENTS

CROUTONS

Trim crusts from bread slices and dice bread. Sauté in butter until an even brown. Or butter slices of trimmed bread, cut in dice and brown in moderate oven.

CHEESE CROUTONS

3 cups hot croutons
1 teaspoon salt
1 teaspoon paprika
Grated Parmesan cheese
Very finely minced chives, parsley or
  other herb

Drop hot croutons in bag containing remaining ingredients and shake until croutons are evenly coated. Good with hot soup or in Caesar salad.

HERBED WHEAT CROUTONS

1/3 cup margarine
1/2 teaspoon rosemary, crushed
1/4 teaspoon seasoned garlic salt
1/4 teaspoon salt
1/4 teaspoon thyme
1/4 teaspoon mace
2 cups spoon-size shredded-wheat
  biscuits

Melt margarine in roasting pan in hot oven (400°F.). Add seasonings. Stir in shredded wheat and toss with spoon until evenly coated. Toast in oven, stirring at least twice, about 15 minutes. Delicious sprinkled on hot broth or your favorite green salad, or serve as a snack.

MELBA TOAST

Cut white bread or other bread into the very thinnest slices possible and remove crusts. Put bread in a barely warm oven until crisp and slightly browned. Cool and store in a tightly closed container in cool place or refrigerator.

CORN CRISPS

1 cup cornmeal
1 tablespoon pork drippings
1/2 teaspoon salt

Combine all ingredients with ⅞ cup boiling water; make balls, using 1 tablespoon mixture for each. Place on baking sheet greased with extra pork drippings. Pat into 3" rounds. Bake in oven (400°F.) 30 minutes. Makes 2 dozen.

SALTY RYE-BREAD CHIPS

Spread small thin slices of salty rye bread with soft butter. Put on baking sheet. Broil until lightly browned.

CARAWAY CHEESE STICKS

1/2 cup butter
2-1/2 cups sifted flour
3/4 cup grated Swiss cheese
1/2 teaspoon salt
1/2 cup milk
2 teaspoons baking powder
1/2 teaspoon curry powder
2 eggs
Caraway seed
Coarse salt

Cut butter into flour and cheese. Add next 4 ingredients and 1 egg; mix until blended. Let rest for 1 hour. On lightly floured board, roll to ¼" thickness. Cut in strips 4" x 1". Beat remaining egg. Brush each bar with egg and sprinkle with caraway seed and salt. Bake in hot oven (425°F.) 10 to 12 minutes. Store airtight. Makes about 4½ dozen.
Poppy-seed Cheese Sticks Follow above recipe, substituting poppy seed for the caraway seed.

PARMESAN CORN CRISPS

1/2 cup white cornmeal
1 cup all-purpose flour
1/2 teaspoon salt
1/2 teaspoon paprika
1/4 teaspoon dry mustard
1/3 cup butter or vegetable shortening
  (not margarine)
1/2 cup grated Parmesan cheese
1/4 cup milk

Put cornmeal in mixing bowl. Sift next 4 ingredients over meal and mix with fork or slotted spoon. Add butter and cut in with pastry blender or mix with fingers. Mixture should resemble coarse crumbs. Add cheese, freshly grated if possible. Mix again with fork or spoon. Add milk, stir, then knead just enough to hold mixture together. Make dough into a ball and roll in flour. Shake off excess and divide dough in half. Place each half on a cookie sheet without sides. Using a rolling pin covered with stockinet and floured, roll very thin, about ⅛", to a 10" x 7" rectangle, pushing in sides of dough while rolling. With a fluted pastry wheel or dull knife, cut in sticks about 1" wide and 3½" long. Do not try to reroll scraps; bake as is. Bake in hot oven (400°F.) 6 to 10 minutes, or until done. Remove from oven and loosen sticks with a pancake turner. Leave on sheets until cold. Makes about 3 dozen.

BEEF

Hungarian Goulash

Beef a la Mode

Swiss Steak

HOW TO BUY BEEF

America's favorite meat, beef is guaranteed as to wholesomeness and graded as to tenderness by government inspectors: the purple "U. S. Inspected and Passed" stamp on the individual cut indicates that it measures up to health standards. And many beef cuts also carry the shield-shaped purple U. S. D. A. grade stamp to indicate quality. The grades of beef are:

U. S. D. A. Prime Highest grade, but most of this beef goes to restaurants and hotels so is not widely available to the housewife.

U. S. D. A. Choice Highest grade commonly found in retail stores. This grade is well-marbled meat, tender and juicy. The lean is usually bright red, firm and velvety to the touch. It is well streaked with little veins of fat and has a thick, white or creamy white, firm fat covering. The meat is especially flavorsome and tender. Top Choice is the best meat of this grade.

U. S. D. A. Good has slightly less marbling, meat is slightly darker red and fat covering is somewhat thinner than that found in U. S. A. Choice.

Amount to Buy

● Buy ¼ to ⅓ pound per serving for boneless cuts such as ground beef, boneless stew, boned roasts and steaks, flank and variety meats.
● Buy ½ to ¾ pound per serving for cuts with some bone such as rib roast, unboned steak.
● Buy ¾ to 1 pound per serving for bony and fatty cuts such as short ribs, plate, brisket.

Keeping Times for Raw Beef

Remove or loosen wrapper and store unwrapped in meat container or loosely wrapped in coldest part of refrigerator.

Refrigerator shelf
Ground beef: 1 day
Stew meat, cut up: 2 days
Steak: 2 to 4 days
Roasts: 3 to 6 days

Refrigerator frozen-food compartment, prepared for freezing
Ground beef: 2 to 4 days
Other cuts: 1 week

Freezer, prepared for freezing
Wrap closely and seal tightly in moisture-vaporproof material and freeze quickly. Store at 0°F., or lower, a maximum of 3 to 4 months for ground beef and 6 to 8 months for other beef.

Keeping Times for Cooked Beef

To keep cooked beef and gravy, cool quickly, cover tightly and put in coldest part of refrigerator. Prepared for freezing, it may be kept 4 to 5 days in refrigerator frozen-food compartment. When stored in freezer, use within 2 to 3 months.

COOKING BEEF

● Use dry heat for the more tender cuts of beef. This method includes roasting, broiling, grilling, deep-fat frying, pan-frying.
● Use moist heat for the less tender cuts of beef. This method includes braising, pot-roasting, stewing and fricasseeing.
● Marinades with tomatoes and vinegar are often helpful as tenderizers. Commercial meat tenderizers may also be used, following manufacturer's directions.

HOW TO STRETCH CERTAIN CUTS OF BEEF

CUTTING TIPS

Raw meat cuts most easily when cold. At room temperature it tends to get mushy and unmanageable.

Before you attempt to cut it, chill meat in the freezing compartment of refrigerator about 10 minutes, or until it is about as firm as a ripe tomato. If you are aiming for thin, even slices, this rule holds especially true.

For easy handling, cut chilled meat on a butcher's block, cutting board or plain wood surface. The board will hold the meat firm and help you to have a steady hand.

Grip knife in most comfortable position. Hold meat firmly with other hand. Always cut away from your body and pull the meat toward you. If inexperienced, work slowly.

After cutting meat, wipe with damp paper towels and dry. Use at once or wrap loosely and store in refrigerator or wrap securely for freezer.

THE PORTERHOUSE EXTENSION

Purchase two 2¹/₂- to 3-pound porterhouse steaks, 1" to 1¹/₂" thick.
Cut two 5- to 8-ounce filets mignons, four 5- to 6-ounce shell steaks, 1 to 1¹/₂ pounds cubed beef.

Follow the same cutting procedure for both steaks:

1 Place each steak flat on cutting surface. Insert tip of knife in narrowest part of steak and slice straight across to remove tail. One smart stroke of the knife will do it.

2 To remove filet mignon (otherwise known as the tenderloin or eye), cut in as closely to top part of T bone as possible, working slowly with tip of knife.

3 Continue scooping along and around bone to about its center. At this point you will be able to remove tenderloin.

4 Trim tenderloin of excess fat. Each tenderloin will weigh 5 to 8 ounces. The section remaining with the bone is known as a T-bone or club steak.

5 Using same cutting method on the T-bone steak as used to remove tenderloin, cut in as close to bone as possible and remove entirely. The result will be a 10- to 12-ounce boneless shell or strip steak. Trim off excess fat.

6 Slice meat vertically from thick end. Cut each shell in half for two 5- to 6-ounce supper-size servings.

7 Trim fat from tails that were removed first and cut in 1" cubes for

stew or kabobs. There will be enough cubed beef to make 4 servings.

STRETCHING SIRLOIN STEAK

Purchase two 3-pound center-cut sirloin steaks with filet, each 1" to 1¹/₂" thick.
Cut 4 small filets mignons, about 12 sandwich steaks, 1¹/₄ pounds cubed beef for kabobs.

Follow same cutting procedure for both steaks:

1 Place steak flat on cutting surface and insert tip of knife in meat at end of flat bone.

2 Turn meat and cut in to remove the filet (or eye). Trim any excess fat from filet and rechill in freezer about 10 minutes.

3 After meat has chilled, split each filet through center horizontally with knife (this will make 4 small filet-mignon portions). Flatten filets with palm of hand to make uniformly thick throughout. To store, wrap each filet individually.

4 To remove balance of meat from bone, push knife straight along edge of bone; peel bone away from meat.

5 Remove tail by slicing along natural seam, separating it from sirloin's center. Reserve tail for cubing.

6 Use meat from center of sirloin for sandwich steaks. Trim center portion of excess fat, then cut vertically or

diagonally in thin slices, beginning at oval end of meat. There will be 6 or more sandwich-size portions.

7 Trim any excess fat from tail and cut in 1" cubes. Tails from both sirloins will provide enough beef cubes for kabobs or stew to serve 4 to 6.

Includes material from The Meat Book: A Consumer's Guide to Selecting, Buying, Cutting, Storing, Freezing and Carving the Various Cuts *by Travers Moncure Evans and David Greene with*

illustrations by Dana J. Greene, to be published by Charles Scribner's Sons. Text Copyright © 1973 Travers Moncure Evans. Illustrations Copyright © 1973 Dana J. Greene.

STRACOTTO

Stracotto means overcooked—over-cooking the sauce is the secret of its delicious flavor

Tails from 2 sirloin steaks
1/4 cup butter or margarine
1 onion, minced
1 carrot, minced
1 rib celery, minced
1/2 cup minced parsley
1/2 cup dry Marsala or Madeira wine
1/2 cup bouillon
1 ounce dried mushrooms, soaked to soften, then chopped
Salt and pepper
1 teaspoon grated lemon rind
1 pound spaghetti or linguine, cooked

Remove any fat from tails and cut meat in tiny cubes or force through coarse blade of food chopper. In heavy saucepan, sauté meat in butter with next 4 ingredients, stirring frequently, 5 minutes. Add wine, bouillon and mushrooms. Add salt and pepper to taste and lemon rind. Cover and simmer, stirring occasionally, 3 to 4 hours. Serve on hot spaghetti. Makes 4 servings.

SKILLET KABOBS

Tails from 2 sirloin steaks
2 tomatoes, each cut in 8 wedges
2 green peppers, cut in 1" pieces
1 can (8 ounces) onions, drained
Salt and pepper
Vegetable oil

Cut meat in 1" pieces. Thread alternately with vegetables on 8 short skewers and sprinkle with salt and pepper. Heat small amount of oil in large skillet and brown kabobs quickly on all sides. Reduce heat, cover and cook 5 to 10 minutes, or until foods are of desired doneness. Serve on or off skewers. Serves 4.

STEAK-RICE CASSEROLE

3 cups hot unsalted cooked rice
1 envelope onion-soup mix
2 tablespoons butter or margarine
4 minute steaks, or tails from 2 sirloin steaks
Salt and pepper
1 can (4 ounces) button mushrooms

Mix first 3 ingredients and put in greased 1½-quart casserole. Brown steaks on both sides in skillet, sprinkle with salt and pepper and cut in strips 2" to 3" long and ½" wide. Arrange in spoke fashion on rice. Pour mushrooms with the liquid over top. Bake uncovered in slow oven (325°F.) about 30 minutes. Makes 4 to 6 servings.

BEEF STEW, GERMAN STYLE

1-1/4 pounds beef stew meat, or tails from 2 sirloin steaks
2 tablespoons margarine
1 onion, chopped
2 teaspoons salt
1/4 teaspoon pepper
2 carrots, peeled and cut in chunks
4 medium potatoes, peeled and sliced
1/2 cup undiluted evaporated milk
2 tablespoons catsup
1 tablespoon flour

Brown meat on all sides in margarine in kettle. Add onion and brown lightly. Add 1½ cups water and the seasonings. Bring to boil, cover and simmer 1 hour, or until meat is almost tender. Add vegetables and cook 20 minutes, or until vegetables are tender. Blend remaining ingredients and stir into mixture. Cook, stirring, until slightly thickened. Makes 4 servings.

RANCH-HOUSE CHILI CASSEROLE

4 slices bacon
2 pounds boneless beef chuck, or tails from 2 sirloin steaks, cut in 1" cubes
2 medium onions, chopped
1 clove garlic, minced
2 cans (8 ounces each) tomato sauce
1 tablespoon chili powder
2 teaspoons sugar
2 dashes hot pepper sauce
2 cans (20 ounces each) red kidney beans, drained
1-1/4 teaspoons salt

Cook bacon in large skillet until crisp. Remove bacon, drain and crumble. Pour off all but 3 tablespoons fat. Brown meat in the fat and put in 3-quart casserole. Cover and bake in moderate oven (375°F.) 30 minutes. Add onions, garlic and 1 cup water. Then add tomato sauce and stir in chili powder mixed with the sugar. Cover and bake in 300° F. oven 45 minutes. Add remaining ingredients, mix well and bake in 350° F. oven 20 minutes. Just before serving, sprinkle with bacon. Makes 4 to 6 servings.

CHINESE BEEF AND MUSHROOMS

2 tablespoons minced onion
3 tablespoons vegetable oil
Tails from 2 sirloin steaks in 1/4" slivers
2 cans (4 ounces each) sliced mushrooms, drained

Sauté onion in hot oil until soft. Add beef and sauté 3 minutes, stirring constantly. Push meat to side of skillet and stir in soy sauce. Add mushrooms and sauté in pan juices until tender. Mix with meat. Cook, covered, 3 minutes longer. Makes 4 servings.

STEAKS

The best steaks for grilling or broiling are porterhouse, T-bone, sirloin, strip and tenderloin. If cut from prime-grade beef, lesser cuts such as rump steak and sirloin tip can be used. Ideally, steaks should be cut at least 1½" thick and should be cooked rare, but tastes vary. Brush surface with oil or melted butter and grill over medium-hot fire until of desired doneness, from 4 minutes on each side for very rare, to 12 to 15 minutes for well-done. Or broil under high heat 2" below heat. For best results, remove steak from refrigerator far enough in advance to bring it to room temperature—3 to 4 hours for a 1½" steak, longer for thicker ones —before it is put on the fire.

BARBECUED BEEF

Sesame seed suggests Korean origin.

1 cup soy sauce
1/4 cup sugar
2 tablespoons vegetable oil
1 green onion, thinly sliced
1 clove garlic, minced
1 teaspoon monosodium glutamate
1/2 teaspoon coarsely ground pepper
2 tablespoons sesame seed, toasted and crushed (see note)
3 pounds steak round or sirloin, sliced 1/2" thick

Combine all ingredients, except steak. Pour over meat and marinate 1 to 2 hours, turning occasionally. Broil quickly, preferably over charcoal. Makes 6 to 8 servings. *Note* Toast sesame seed in a dry pan over moderate heat or in moderate oven until golden, then crush.

FLANK STEAK TERIYAKI BARBECUE

3/4 cup vegetable oil
1/4 cup each soy sauce and honey
2 tablespoons each vinegar and finely chopped green onions
1 large clove garlic, minced
1-1/2 teaspoons ground ginger
1 flank steak (about 1-1/2 pounds) (not scored)

Combine all ingredients except meat. Pour over flank steak and marinate 4 hours or more; turn occasionally. Broil under high heat, 2" from heat, or grill steak over hot coals, turning once, until done as desired, about 5 minutes each side for medium rare. Baste occasionally with marinade. Carve in thin slices, cutting diagonally across the grain from top to bottom of steak. Makes 4 servings.

TERIYAKI

Use round steak, 1" thick. Cut in very thin ¼" to ½" slices. Marinate meat strips for 1 hour in mixture of ½ cup soy sauce, ½ cup oil, 2 teaspoons sugar, ½ cup orange juice, a pressed clove of garlic and 1 teaspoon grated fresh ginger (or ½ teaspoon ground ginger). Remove meat from marinade and weave strips back and forth on bamboo or metal skewers. Grill them very quickly over a fairly hot fire, about 30 seconds on a side.

PINEAPPLE TERIYAKI

1 slice boneless beef sirloin 1" thick (about 1-1/4 pounds)
1 can (13-1/2 ounces) pineapple chunks
1/4 cup soy sauce
1 clove garlic, crushed
3/4 teaspoon ground ginger
Stuffed olives
Hot cooked rice (optional)

Cut meat in 1" to 1¼" cubes. Drain ½ cup syrup from pineapple. Mix syrup, soy sauce, garlic and ginger and pour over meat cubes. Stir and let stand at room temperature at least 1 hour, then thread olives, meat and pineapple chunks on skewers. Broil, turning once, to desired doneness, 8 to 10 minutes for rare. Baste once with drippings in pan. Serve with rice, if desired. Makes 4 or 5 servings.

BEEF-BIRD AND VEGETABLE CASSEROLE

A rich, stewlike dish.

8 thin slices round steak (about 2-1/2 pounds)
1 envelope onion-soup mix
3 tablespoons margarine
1 can beef gravy
8 small white onions, peeled
4 potatoes, peeled and halved
4 to 6 carrots, cut in 2" pieces
4 stalks celery, cut in 2" pieces
4 zucchini, cut in 2" pieces
Salt and pepper
1 cup cooked baby lima beans

Sprinkle meat slices with onion-soup mix, roll up and tie with string. Brown on all sides in margarine in Dutch oven or top-stove casserole. Add 2 cups water, cover and bake in moderate oven (350°F.) 1 hour. Add beef gravy and a little more water if necessary to almost cover meat. Add vegetables, except lima beans, and sprinkle lightly with salt and pepper. Bake, covered, in moderate oven (375°F.) about 1 hour, or until meat and vegetables are tender. Garnish with lima beans. Makes 6 to 8 servings.

FILET OF BEEF À LA SUISSE

1 filet of beef (3 to 4 pounds)
Oil
1 cup dry red wine
Salt and pepper

Heat the oven to 475°F. Rub the filet well with oil and arrange on a rack in a roasting pan. Roast 15 minutes and then baste with the wine. Season to taste and roast for another 15 minutes. Baste with the pan juices and additional red wine. Roast 10 minutes more. Baste and let stand 10 minutes. Serves 8 to 12.

BEEF STROGANOFF I

2 pounds lean sirloin steak
3 tablespoons sweet butter
2 onions, thinly sliced
1 pound mushrooms, sliced
1 tablespoon flour
1/4 teaspoon white pepper
1/2 teaspoon paprika
Dash of cayenne
1 cup dairy sour cream
Hot buttered noodles, seasoned with
    poppy seed
Chopped chives or dill

With sharp knife, cut beef across grain into narrow strips. Heat 2 tablespoons butter in large heavy skillet and add meat and onions. Cook over high heat a few minutes, turning meat to brown all sides. Reduce heat, add mushrooms and cook, covered, 10 minutes longer. Remove mixture to top of double boiler or chafing dish and put over hot water to keep warm. To juices in skillet, add remaining butter and blend in flour and seasonings. Gradually add sour cream, blending to keep smooth. Add to meat. Serve with noodles and a sprinkling of chives. Serves 6.

BEEF STROGANOFF II

2 pounds sirloin of beef
Flour
1/3 cup butter
3 medium onions, chopped
1/2 pound mushrooms, sliced
Salt and pepper
2/3 cup tomato juice
1/2 cup sherry
2/3 cup dairy sour cream

Cut meat in thin strips; dredge with flour. Brown quickly in skillet in half the butter. Remove meat; add remaining butter. Add onions and mushrooms and cook 5 minutes. Add meat and sprinkle with salt and pepper. Add tomato juice, sherry and 1½ cups water. Bring to boil; cover and simmer 2 hours, or until meat is tender. Season to taste. Stir in sour cream and serve at once. Serves 6.

LONDON BROIL

Mushrooms and onions are an excellent accompaniment and blend deliciously with the steak juices, which can be thickened if desired.

Salt both sides of flank steak well and smear generously with French dressing. Let steak marinate in the refrigerator several hours. Broil below high heat, allowing 5 to 7 minutes for each side. Carve diagonally across the grain in thin wide slices. Use a board containing a gravy well, or a tray or deep platter. Makes 4 to 6 servings.

TOURNEDOS BÉARNAISE

A tournedos is a slice 1½" to 2" thick cut from the filet after it has been surrounded with a layer of pounded beef fat and tied in a roll. Grill over a medium charcoal fire about 5 minutes on a side for rare, 7 to 8 minutes on a side for medium, longer if you want it well done. Or broil 2" below high heat. When done, sprinkle with salt and pepper and serve with Béarnaise Sauce, page 61. **Tournedos Rossini** Grill or broil the tournedos, as desired, place each one on a round of fried toast, top with a slice of foie gras and one of truffle and pour Bordelaise Sauce (page 68) or Sauce Madeira (page 61) over.

MUSSELBURGH PIE

Oysters lend an elusive, nutty flavor to this elegant steak pie.

1 pound lean round steak
1 dozen oysters
1/4 cup butter or margarine
Flour
1 cup beef stock, or 1 bouillon cube
    and 1 cup hot water
1/2 recipe Standard Pastry (page 419)
Milk

Cut off any fat from steak and cut meat in 24 thin diagonal strips. Cut the oysters in half. Roll each half-oyster, plus ½ teaspoon butter, in a strip of beef. Dredge each roll generously with flour; then pack tightly in a 10" piepan. Invert a small funnel (can be made with foil) in the center of the dish. Pour stock over the steak rolls. Cover with pastry, leaving a hole for the funnel spout in the middle (this makes a chimney for the steam). Brush pastry with milk. Bake in hot oven (425°F.) 15 minutes, then at 350°F. about 1 hour. Makes 6 servings.

CHATEAUBRIAND STEAK

Broil or grill a slice of tenderloin at least 2" thick and larded with beef fat or bacon, until done as desired. Slice diagonally across the grain. Pour prepared sauce over slices. **Chateaubriand Sauce** Cook together 1 cup brown gravy (or sauce espagnol) and 1 cup white wine until very thick. Add ¼ pound butter, 3 tablespoons lemon juice, 1 tablespoon minced parsley, and salt and pepper to taste. Beat well and serve when the butter is melted. Makes about 1 cup.

BEEF CHOP SUEY

1 tablespoon sugar
1-1/2 pounds round steak
2 onions, sliced
1 teaspoon each salt and ginger
3 tablespoons soy sauce
1 bouillon cube
1 can (3 ounces) chopped mushrooms, drained
1 cup sliced celery
1 can (1 pound) bean sprouts, drained
2 tablespoons cornstarch

Brown sugar in large skillet. Trim any fat from steak and cut meat in ½" cubes. Brown in skillet, stirring. Add 1½ cups water, onions, seasonings and bouillon cube. Cover and simmer about 45 minutes. Add vegetables and heat. Stir in cornstarch blended with a little cold water; cook, stirring, until thickened. Makes 6 servings.

SWISS STEAK

3 pounds boneless chuck steak, about 1-1/2" thick
Salt and pepper
Flour
2 onions, sliced
2 cans (1 pound each) tomatoes

Remove excess fat from steak and cut meat in 6 pieces. Season and put on a well-floured cutting board. Cover steak with 1 cup flour; pound with a meat hammer or edge of a heavy saucer. Flour and pound both sides of the meat until 1 cup flour is taken up. Melt a little fat from steak in skillet. Brown onion in the hot fat, remove and brown the steak on both sides. Put the onion on top of the steak. Add tomatoes, cover and simmer 2½ to 3 hours, or until fork-tender. Or bake in a moderate oven (350°F.). Remove steak to hot serving dish, top with onion rings and serve with gravy made by thickening drippings in skillet with a little flour blended with cold water. Serves 6.

STEAK AU POIVRE

Crush coarsely 1½ tablespoons peppercorns (crushed, coarse ground or seasoned pepper may be substituted in lesser amounts). Press pepper firmly into both sides of a 2"-thick top sirloin steak, using heel of hand. Let the steak stand for half to three quarters of an hour. Now grill it over a medium fire for 6 to 8 minutes on each side or broil 2" below high heat. Remove the steak to a hot platter, sprinkle with salt and place a large chunk of sweet butter on top. Let this melt and run over the surface before carving. Or flame it with Cognac before serving. Serve with boiled new potatoes rolled in butter and minced tarragon.

RUNDERLAPPEN
(Dutch Pickled Beef)

1-1/2 teaspoons salt
1/2 teaspoon freshly ground black pepper
2 to 3 tablespoons flour
2 pounds round steak, about 1-1/2" thick
1/2 cup vegetable oil
2 medium onions, thinly sliced
2 tablespoons wine vinegar
1-1/2 teaspoons prepared mustard
1 bay leaf

Combine salt and pepper with flour and pound into the steak. Heat the oil and brown the steak well on both sides. Reduce heat and add the onions. When just wilted, add ¾ cup boiling water, vinegar and seasonings. Cover and simmer 2 hours, or until steak is tender, turning once or twice during the cooking. Serve with the pan sauce. Makes 6 to 8 servings.

BEEFSTEAK BIRDS

4 cube steaks (about 1 pound)
Salt and pepper
Italian herbs
Meat tenderizer
1 small carrot, cut in strips
1 green pepper, cut in strips
1 teaspoon flour
1/2 teaspoon paprika
2 teaspoons fat
1 small onion, chopped
1 cup bouillon
Dash of hot pepper sauce

Sprinkle steaks with salt, pepper, herbs and tenderizer. Put a few strips of carrot and pepper on each, roll up and tie with string. Dredge with flour mixed with paprika. Brown on all sides in fat. Add remaining ingredients; cover. Simmer 1½ hours, or until meat is tender. Serves 4.

BROILED BEEF-VEGETABLE KABOBS

Tails from 2 sirloin steaks, cut in
  1" to 1-1/2" cubes
1 cup bottled Italian dressing
2 medium zucchini, cut in 1" pieces
12 cherry tomatoes
Hot cooked rice (optional)

Put beef cubes in bowl, add dressing and stir to coat thoroughly. Cover and refrigerate, stirring once or twice, 4 hours or overnight. When ready to use, pour off marinade and reserve. Thread four 12" skewers alternately with beef, zucchini and tomatoes. Brush with marinade. Put kabobs on rack in broiler pan 3" to 4" from heat and broil, turning and brushing occasionally with marinade, 12 to 18 minutes, depending on desired doneness. Serve on rice. Makes 4 servings.

BEEF PIE WITH SESAME-SEED PUFFS

1 pound round steak, cut in bite-size
  pieces
1/4 cup solid vegetable shortening
1-1/2 cups chopped onion
2 tablespoons flour
1 cup canned tomatoes
1 can (6 ounces) tomato paste
1 tablespoon sugar
1-1/2 teaspoons salt
1/8 teaspoon pepper
1/4 teaspoon Worcestershire
1 can (6 ounces) sliced mushrooms,
  drained
1 cup dairy sour cream
1 can (15 ounces) artichoke hearts,
  drained on paper towel
Sesame-seed Puffs

Brown meat in shortening in skillet. Add onion and flour and cook until onion is tender. Then add 1 cup water and next 6 ingredients, bring to boil, cover and simmer, stirring occasionally, 1½ hours, or until meat is tender. Add remaining ingredients, except puffs, and put in greased shallow 2½-quart baking dish. Top with puffs and bake in hot oven (400°F.) 20 to 25 minutes. Serves 6 to 8.

Sesame-seed Puffs

1-1/4 cups all-purpose flour
2 teaspoons baking powder
1/2 teaspoon salt
1/4 cup solid vegetable shortening
3/4 cup dairy sour cream
Milk
Sesame seed

Mix dry ingredients, then cut in shortening. Mixing with fork, stir in sour cream. Pat out on floured board to ½" thickness and cut in rounds with biscuit cutter. Brush with milk, then sprinkle with sesame seed.

BEEF WITH MUSHROOMS

1 pound flank or other steak, cut in
  1/4" slices about 2" long
1//4 cup soy sauce
1 tablespoon cornstarch
1 tablespoon dry sherry
1 teaspoon sugar
1/4 teaspoon monosodium glutamate
4 tablespoons vegetable oil
1/2 teaspoon salt
6 to 8 ounces fresh mushrooms, sliced,
  or 2 cans (4 ounces each) sliced
  mushrooms, drained
1 slice gingerroot or 1/4 cup sliced onion

Mix first 6 ingredients and set aside. Put 2 tablespoons oil in hot skillet over high heat. Add salt and mushrooms. Cook, stirring, about 2 minutes. Remove from skillet. Add remaining oil to skillet and add ginger. Add beef mixture and sauté quickly, stirring, less than 2 minutes. Add mushrooms and mix well. Serve at once. Makes 2 or 3 servings.

Beef with Green Peppers Follow above recipe, substituting 2 medium green peppers for the mushrooms. Wash peppers and dry before cutting. Discard white membrane and cut peppers in chunks. Cook in the oil less than 1 minute. Proceed as directed.

Beef with Pea Pods Follow basic recipe, substituting ¼ pound pea pods for the mushrooms. Cook in the oil less than 1 minute. Proceed as directed.

BEEF WITH BROCCOLI

1 pound flank or other steak, cut in 1/4"
  slices about 2" long
1/4 cup soy sauce
1 tablespoon cornstarch
1 tablespoon dry sherry
1 teaspoon sugar
1/4 teaspoon monosodium glutamate
1/2 bunch broccoli
5 tablespoons vegetable oil
1/2 teaspoon salt
1 slice gingerroot or 1/4 cup sliced onion

Mix first 6 ingredients and set aside. Cut broccoli in florets about 2" long, peel stalk and slice in 2" lengths less than ½" thick. Put 2 tablespoons oil in hot skillet over high heat. Add salt and broccoli and stir-fry, turning constantly, until broccoli is dark green—not over 2 minutes. Remove from skillet. Put remaining oil in skillet and add ginger and beef mixture. Stir-fry, turning constantly, not more than 2 minutes. Add broccoli and mix well. Serve at once. Makes 2 or 3 servings. **Note** Broccoli tends to make oil spatter, so drain thoroughly after washing. Precooked broccoli can also be used.

MADEIRA SAUCE

Heat a can of beef gravy with 2 beef bouillon cubes. Add ¼ cup of Madeira wine, heat and serve. Makes about 1¼ cups.

FONDUE BOURGUIGNONNE

1/2 pound butter
1 cup peanut oil (or 2 cups oil and no butter)
2-1/2 pounds filet of beef, well trimmed and cut into 1/2" cubes

Melt butter in a fondue pan over an alcohol burner or in an electric skillet. Add oil; heat until bubbling hot. Give each guest one fondue fork for cooking and one regular fork for eating. Warn guests not to eat with the fork they use in cooking or they may burn themselves severely. Each guest spears a piece of meat and cooks it in hot fat, rare, medium or well done to suit. He then dips the meat into any of several sauces. Sauces may include Béarnaise, Barbecue, Anchovy Butter or any favorites that you choose. With this meat dish go crisp French-fried potatoes and a good salad. Allow a generous quarter-pound of beef per person. Serves 6 to 8.
Suggested Sauces Prepare at least a cup of each kind of sauce. **Béarnaise Sauce I** Chop 1 small onion or 6 green onions very fine and mix them with 1½ teaspoons fresh or ½ teaspoon dried tarragon and ¼ cup wine vinegar. Cook down until it is merely a glaze. Add this to ⅔ cup freshly made hollandaise sauce and stir in a little chopped parsley and a few chopped leaves of fresh tarragon. Makes 1 cup. **Barbecue Sauce** Sauté 1 small finely chopped onion and 1 finely chopped garlic clove in ¼ cup oil. Add 6 peeled, seeded and chopped tomatoes, 1 teaspoon fresh or ¼ teaspoon dried basil, 2 tablespoons chopped parsley and salt to taste. Cover and cook gently over medium heat 10 minutes. Add 2 tablespoons tomato paste and ½ teaspoon freshly ground black pepper and cook down for another 20 minutes. If the sauce begins to get dry, add a little vermouth. Finally, add 1 or 2 finely chopped hot Italian peppers or a little hot pepper sauce. Makes about 2 cups. **Anchovy Butter** Cream 1 cup butter or margarine. Gradually work in 2 finely chopped garlic cloves and 12 finely chopped anchovy fillets. Season with a dash of hot pepper sauce and 1 teaspoon lemon juice. Serve soft but not melted. Makes 1 cup.

WINE-SHALLOT SAUCE

Sauté 1 cup chopped shallots or green onions in ¼ cup butter until soft. Add 1 cup white wine, 2 tablespoons wine vinegar, 1 teaspoon salt and some freshly ground black pepper, and cook 5 minutes. Cut in ¼ pound butter and cook until melted. Makes about 1⅔ cups.

FLANK STEAK WITH VEGETABLES

1 flank steak (about 2 pounds)
1/2 cup chopped celery tops
1 onion, chopped
Few sprigs of parsley, chopped
1/2 teaspoon dried thyme
2 teaspoons salt
1/2 teaspoon pepper
1 tablespoon fat
8 small whole carrots
8 small potatoes

Put steak on board and pound with rolling pin or mallet until both sides are slightly flattened. Sprinkle with next 4 ingredients, 1 teaspoon salt and ¼ teaspoon pepper. Roll up jelly-roll fashion, beginning at the pointed end. Tie with string. Brown on all sides in hot fat in heavy kettle. Add 1 cup water, cover and simmer 1½ hours, turning meat occasionally and adding more water if necessary. Add vegetables and remaining salt and pepper. Simmer 30 minutes longer. To serve, slice meat diagonally. Makes 6 servings.

GOOBER BEEF CASSEROLE

1-1/2 pounds round steak, cut 1/4" thick
1 large onion, chopped
3 cups green-pepper strips
3 tablespoons vegetable oil
1/2 cup peanut butter
1 teaspoon basil
1-1/2 teaspoons salt
1/4 teaspoon pepper
1 teaspoon steak sauce
1 can condensed mushroom soup
2 cups buttered soft bread crumbs

Cut excess fat from beef and cut meat in strips 1½" long and ½" wide. Sauté onion and green pepper in hot oil 2 or 3 minutes. Remove from skillet and brown meat lightly in fat remaining in pan. Add onion and pepper, 1½ cups water and remaining ingredients, except last 2. Bring to boil, cover and simmer 30 minutes, or until meat is tender. Stir in soup. Pour in shallow 2-quart baking dish and sprinkle with crumbs. Bake in moderate oven (350°F.) about 30 minutes. Makes 6 servings.

SWISS CUBED STEAKS

1-1/2 pounds cubed steaks
2 tablespoons flour
1/2 teaspoon salt
1/8 teaspoon pepper
2 tablespoons fat
1 can (8 ounces) tomato sauce
1 teaspoon Worcestershire
1 stalk celery, diced
1 onion, chopped
1 clove garlic, minced

Shake steaks in a plastic bag with flour, salt and pepper until steaks are well coated. Brown on both sides in hot fat. Add 1 cup water and remaining ingredients. Cover and simmer 1 hour, or until meat is tender. Makes 4 servings.

CHINESE BEEF CASSEROLE

1 flank steak (about 1-1/2 pounds)
2 tablespoons flour
1/2 teaspoon salt
Dash of pepper
1 clove garlic, minced
2 tablespoons vegetable oil
1 can beef gravy
2 tablespoons soy sauce
1 teaspoon sugar
1 green pepper, sliced
1 can (10 ounces) tomatoes, drained

Pound steak with edge of saucer or meat hammer; cut diagonally across the grain in thin slices. Mix flour, salt and pepper. Dredge meat with the mixture. Brown meat and garlic in oil. Add next 3 ingredients; heat and pour into 2-quart casserole. Cover and bake in moderate oven (350°F.) 1 hour. Add green pepper and tomatoes; bake, covered, 1 hour longer. Makes 4 servings.

BAVARIAN BEEF STEW

1-1/2 pounds round steak, cubed
2 medium onions, sliced
3 tablespoons butter or margarine
1 bay leaf
1-1/2 teaspoons salt
1/4 teaspoon pepper
1 teaspoon caraway seed
1/4 cup vinegar
1 small head cabbage, cut in wedges
1/4 cup finely crushed gingersnaps

Brown beef and onion in butter. Add 3 cups boiling water, seasonings and seed. Bring to boil, cover and simmer 1½ to 2 hours. Add vinegar and cabbage. Cover and simmer about 45 minutes. Remove cabbage and arrange around edge of platter. Pile meat in center. Soften gingersnap crumbs in ¼ cup warm water and stir into gravy. Add additional vinegar and seasonings if necessary. Pour over meat. Makes 6 servings.

GREEN-PEPPER STEAK

Cut 1 pound round steak, ½" thick, in 4 pieces. Brown on both sides in greased skillet. Cover with 1 small onion, sliced, and 3 green peppers, quartered. Add ½ cup consommé, ¼ teaspoon ginger, 1 tablespoon soy sauce and ½ teaspoon monosodium glutamate. Cover; cook slowly 1 hour, or until meat is tender. Makes 4 servings.

INDIVIDUAL DEVILED MINUTE STEAKS

For 4 steaks, have ready 1½ to 2 cups of toasted buttered crumbs and about ¼ pound of butter. Grill or broil the steaks quickly, undercooking them a little, less than 2 minutes a side, then spread them with butter and roll in crumbs, pressing the crumbs in firmly. Replace them on the grill for just long enough for the crumbs to brown and crisp, about a minute. Serve with prepared sauce.
Sauce Diable Cook 3 tablespoons of minced shallots in 3 tablespoons butter until wilted. Add ¼ cup lemon juice or vinegar, 2 teaspoons each Worcestershire and prepared mustard, a dash of hot pepper sauce and a can of beef gravy. Heat well and serve. Makes about ³/₄ cup.

STEAK AND KIDNEY PIE

1-1/2 pounds round steak
3 lamb kidneys
Flour
Salt and pepper
2 tablespoons butter or margarine
1 large onion, minced
1 tablespoon Worcestershire
1/2 recipe Standard Pastry (page 419)
Milk

Trim fat from round steak. Cut meat into ³/₄" cubes. Remove skin, fat and tubes from kidneys. Cut kidneys in 1½" cubes. Dredge steak and kidney cubes with 3 tablespoons flour mixed with 1 teaspoon salt and ¼ teaspoon pepper. Melt butter in heavy pan. Add onion, 1 cup boiling water and Worcestershire. Cover tightly. Simmer gently 30 minutes, or until meats are tender. Mix 2 tablespoons flour in a little cold water and add to gravy to thicken. Pour mixture into a 10" piepan. Invert a custard cup in center to support crust. Roll out pastry and cover pie. Cut small slits in pastry to allow steam to escape. Crimp edge of pastry to rim of piepan. Brush pastry with milk. Bake in hot oven (425°F.) about 30 minutes. Makes 6 servings.

BRAISED STEAK WITH PEANUT-BUTTER SAUCE

2 pounds round steak, 3/4" thick
1/4 cup flour
1 teaspoon salt
1/8 teaspoon pepper
1/4 cup vegetable oil
1 clove garlic, minced
1 onion, chopped
1 can (1 pound) tomatoes
1 cup chicken or beef broth
3/4 cup peanut butter

Cut steak in 6 servings. Coat meat with mixture of flour, salt and pepper. Brown meat on both sides in hot oil in skillet. Remove meat and pour off most of fat. Add garlic and onion to remaining fat and cook 2 to 3 minutes. Add meat, tomatoes and broth. Bring to boil, cover and simmer about 15 minutes. Add peanut butter and simmer, covered, about 15 minutes longer. Makes 6 servings.

HUNGARIAN BEEF GOULASH

1 pound round steak
1-1/4 teaspoons salt
2 teaspoons sweet Hungarian paprika
2 tablespoons margarine
2 cups thinly sliced onion
1/3 cup dairy sour cream
Hot cooked wide noodles

Cut meat in 1½" pieces. Season with salt and paprika. Melt margarine in heavy kettle or Dutch oven. Add onion and cook slightly. Add meat and cook, uncovered, stirring occasionally, 20 minutes, or until liquid cooks down. Add 1 cup water, cover and cook slowly 1½ hours, or until meat is tender, adding more water if necessary to make additional gravy. Stir in sour cream and serve with noodles. Makes 4 servings.

CURRIED BEEF AMANDINE

1-1/2 pounds round steak, cut in strips
    1-1/2" x 1/2" x 1/2"
3 tablespoons fat
1/2 pound fresh mushrooms, sliced
1 can (10-1/2 ounces) condensed cream
    of mushroom soup, undiluted
1 can (10-1/2 ounces) condensed beef
    consommé, undiluted
1 tablespoon Worcestershire
1-1/2 teaspoons curry powder
1/4 teaspoon coarsely ground pepper
1/2 cup sliced blanched almonds
3 tablespoons chopped parsley

Brown meat in the fat in large skillet. Add mushrooms and cook over low heat until soft. Mix next 5 ingredients in small bowl. Add to meat and mushrooms, cover and simmer 40 minutes. Add almonds and parsley. Makes 4 to 6 servings.

PRESSED BEEF

1 flank steak (about 2 pounds)
2 teaspoons salt
1/4 cup vinegar
1/2 teaspoon peppercorns
1 small bay leaf
Grated fresh or prepared horseradish

Put meat in kettle or Dutch oven with 6 cups boiling water and remaining ingredients, except horseradish. Bring to boil and simmer, covered, 3 hours, or until meat is very tender. Drain, reserving liquid. Chop beef fine and pack into 9" x 5" x 3" loaf pan. Strain liquid and reduce to ½ cup by boiling uncovered. Pour over meat; cover with waxed paper and a heavy weight. Chill overnight. Turn out and slice thin. Serve with horseradish. Makes 6 servings.

BEEF-PASTA SKILLET

1 pound round steak, 1/2" thick
Flour
2 tablespoons butter or margarine
1 can (1 pound) tomatoes
1-1/4 teaspoons salt
1/4 teaspoon each pepper and thyme
1 large onion, quartered
3 sprigs parsley
2 cups shell macaroni, cooked

Cover steak with flour and pound well with back of heavy knife; turn and repeat, then cut in 8 pieces. Brown in hot butter in skillet. Combine in blender tomatoes, salt, pepper, thyme, onion and parsley. Whirl until blended and pour over meat. Cover and simmer 1 hour. Add macaroni and heat through. Makes 4 servings.

FORFAR BRIDIES

(Cornish Pasties)

1 pound lean round steak
1 box (10 ounces) pie-crust mix
1/3 cup minced onion
Butter or margarine
Salt and pepper
Milk

Cut steak in very thin diagonal slices, 1" to 2" long. Prepare pastry as directed on package and roll out about ¼" thick; cut in six 6" circles. Divide meat among circles. Sprinkle each with minced onion and dot with butter. Season with salt and pepper. Wet rims of pastry circles with an ice cube. Fold over to make crescent-shaped tarts. Pinch edges tightly together. Cut holes in top of each tart. Brush pastry with milk. Bake in hot oven (400°F.) 45 minutes, or until done. Good hot or cold. Makes 6 servings.

THE THREE-RIB ROAST TRANSFORMED

Purchase first three ribs of semi-boned rib roast (self-service supermarkets generally sell rib roasts semi-boned, which means that the chine, backbone and short ribs have been removed).

Cut 6 to 12 rib steaks.

1 With tip of knife, cut across the three exposed ribs and down to the thick end.

2 If successfully accomplished, all three bones can easily be removed in one piece.

3 Place the now-boneless roast fat side up and shave some of the fat off top with knife. Leave just enough fat to provide flavor and moisture. A thin layer should do the trick.

4 After removing excess fat, leave roast upright and divide in eight steaks this way: With tip of knife, score seven long, vertical, equidistant lines on fat.

5 Following lines as guide, slice straight down through roast vertically. Use long, slender knife and start from thick end. If you prefer thinner steaks, divide roast in twelfths. For thicker steaks, divide in sixths.

6 Remove any excess exterior fat.

Note Save rib bones for a great addition to the stock pot.

THE THREE-MEAL RIB ROAST

Purchase 10- to 12-pound end-cut rib roast, including last 2 or 3 ribs with chine and backbone removed (have short ribs sawed off by meat cutter and reserve).

Cut 6- to 8-pound rib roast, 2½- to 4-pound top-rib pot roast, 2 or 3 short ribs.

1 Separate short ribs by cutting between rib bones. With knife, trim away any excess fat.

2 To separate pot-roast meat from whole rib roast, stand roast up and insert tip of knife in extreme end of roast, where short ribs were removed, just above large section of fat that divides the two layers of meat. Cut around fatty section, lifting upper layer from lower until entire upper layer can be removed completely.

3 Trim excess fat from meat you have removed and, starting at one end, roll meat in cylindrical shape. To help hold shape, encircle with kitchen twine and tie several times.

4 The remaining piece of meat, including rib bones, needs no tailoring. Any excess scraps of fat remaining can

be added to exterior surface of meat to keep it juicy as it roasts.

MARINATED CHUCK STEAK

Sprinkle a large chuck steak, about ¾" thick, with tenderizer, following manufacturer's directions. Marinate steak overnight in well-seasoned French dressing. Refrigerate. Drain; broil or pan-fry.

MAKING THE MOST OF CHUCK ROAST

Purchase a boneless 4-pound chuck roast (first cut, with an inside chuck roll).

Cut one 1½-pound well-marbled chuck eye roast and one lean pot roast or four 6-ounce steaks and up to ten sandwich-size steaks.

1 Place roast on flat surface. If tied, remove string. Turn roast over and look for the little gap in the solid meat. This is where the rib bone was removed.

2 Start at gap with tip of knife and cut straight across, following natural dividing line of fat. This will divide roast in 2 pieces, one lean, the other highly marbled. Lean piece can be left whole, marinated, then pot-roasted, providing enough meat for 6 or more servings. Marbled piece can be broiled or roasted and will make 4 servings.

3 As an alternative, marbled piece can be divided in 4 individual steaks, lean part can be halved. Slicing vertically, cut each half in 5 sandwich-size steaks (tenderize before cooking).

Includes material from The Meat Book: A Consumer's Guide to Selecting, Buying, Cutting, Storing, Freezing and Carving the Various Cuts by Travers Moncure Evans and David Greene with

illustrations by Dana J. Greene, to be published by Charles Scribner's Sons. Text Copyright © 1973 Travers Moncure Evans. Illustrations Copyright © 1973 Dana J. Greene.

BEEF A LA MODE

4 pounds beef for pot roast
Salt and pepper
2 cups dry white wine (Sauterne or
   Chablis)
2 tablespoons each fat and flour
2 cups meat stock
1 cup canned tomatoes
1 clove garlic
Few sprigs of parsley
2 stalks celery
1 bay leaf
1/8 teaspoon thyme
6 carrots, cut in pieces
3 onions, quartered

Season meat with salt and pepper. Put in bowl and pour wine over top. Let stand in refrigerator 5 to 6 hours, turning occasionally. Then remove from wine and wipe dry. Brown on all sides in hot fat. Remove meat and pour off fat. Brown flour in kettle. Add meat, marinade and remaining ingredients, except last 2. Bring to boil, cover and simmer about 2 hours. Remove meat and skim off fat. Return meat to kettle with vegetables. Cover and simmer 1½ to 2 hours longer, or until meat and vegetables are tender. Then remove the meat and vegetables to a heated platter and season gravy with salt and pepper to taste. Makes about 6 servings.

POT ROAST FONTAINE

5 pounds beef for pot roast
2 cloves garlic, split
Salt and pepper
Flour
2 tablespoons olive oil
1/4 cup brandy
1 bay leaf
Pinch each of thyme and marjoram
2 onions, sliced
1/2 cup chopped celery
4 carrots, split
2 tomatoes, cut up
1 cup dry red wine
1/2 cup cooked mushrooms
1 tablespoon cornstarch

Make small cuts in meat and stick with garlic. Sprinkle with salt and pepper and rub with flour. Brown on all sides in oil. Slip rack under the meat. Turn off heat (be sure the kettle is in safe place as flame will come up over meat), add brandy and ignite. Let the brandy burn itself out. Add ½ cup water and next 7 ingredients. Cover and simmer 3½ hours, or until meat is tender. Remove meat and carrots; strain liquid for gravy. Add a little water, if necessary. Add mushrooms, and cornstarch mixed with cold water. Cook until thickened. Season to taste. Slice meat and serve with gravy and mashed potatoes, or rice, if desired. Makes 6 to 8 servings, with meat left over.

PARTY POT ROAST

6 pounds boneless fresh brisket
1 onion, sliced
Salt and pepper
12 medium potatoes, peeled
Flour

In a large heavy kettle, brown beef in its own fat. Pour off fat. Add onion, cover and cook over low heat 1 hour. Put meat in shallow pan to cool. Cut into attractive serving-size slices. Return to kettle and sprinkle with salt and pepper. Cover and simmer 2 hours, or until tender. Turn slices once. Add potatoes during last 45 minutes of cooking. Remove meat and potatoes to hot platter. To make gravy, skim off fat; stir in a little flour blended with cold water. Cook until slightly thickened. Serves 8.

SKILLET POT ROAST WITH VEGETABLES

3 to 4 pounds beef for pot roast (bottom
   or top round, eye or chuck)
2 tablespoons fat
Salt and pepper
Onion salt
8 small new potatoes
8 carrots, peeled
3/4 pound whole green beans
1 to 2 small summer squash or zucchini
8 green onions

In 12" skillet, brown meat in hot fat on all sides. Sprinkle with seasonings. Add ½ cup water, cover tightly and simmer about 2½ hours, adding more water if necessary. Add potatoes and carrots. Cook 30 minutes. Add beans, squash and onions. Cover; simmer about 30 minutes. Makes 4 servings, with meat left over.

PEPPERY BEEF

4 pounds boneless beef brisket
1 tablespoon whole black peppercorns
1-1/2 teaspoons salt
1/4 teaspoon ground allspice
2 tablespoons fine dry bread crumbs
1 teaspoon garlic salt
1 onion, sliced

Have butcher pound brisket flat. Put on board and with a heavy knife, score the meat lengthwise and crosswise on both sides. Put the peppers in a small cloth bag and crush with hammer. Sprinkle meat with crushed peppers and next 4 ingredients. Roll very tightly lengthwise. Cut in 2 crosswise pieces. Tie firmly with string. Put on a rack in heavy kettle. Add 1 cup hot water and the onion; cover and simmer 4 hours, or until tender, adding more water, if necessary. Serve hot. Or cool in the broth, then chill. Makes 8 servings.

LEMON POT ROAST

1 clove garlic, minced
1/4 cup lemon juice
3 slices lemon, cut in quarters
1 small onion, chopped
1/2 teaspoon each seasoned salt,
  celery salt and pepper
1/4 teaspoon marjoram
3 pounds lean boneless chuck

Mix ¼ cup water with all ingredients, except meat, and refrigerate 24 hours. Brown meat in greased kettle and add sauce. Cover and simmer about 3 hours. Makes 6 to 8 servings.

BARBECUED POT ROAST

4 pounds beef for pot roast
2 tablespoons fat
Salt and pepper
1 can (8 ounces) tomato sauce
3 medium onions, sliced
2 cloves garlic, minced
2 tablespoons brown sugar
1/2 teaspoon dry mustard‑
1/4 cup lemon juice
1/4 cup vinegar
1/4 cup catsup
1 tablespoon Worcestershire
Dash of hot pepper sauce

Brown meat in fat. Sprinkle with salt and pepper. Add 1 cup water, tomato sauce, onion and garlic. Cover and simmer 2 hours. Add remaining ingredients, cover and continue cooking 1½ hours longer, or until tender, adding more water if necessary. Remove meat and skim off excess fat from gravy. Makes 6 to 8 servings.

BRISKET OF BEEF IN HORSERADISH SAUCE

4 pounds boneless fresh brisket
2 medium onions, sliced
2 carrots
1 stalk celery
2 bay leaves
Salt and pepper to taste
Horseradish Sauce
Chopped parsley

Put meat in heavy kettle. Add next 5 ingredients. Cover with water. Cover and simmer 3 to 4 hours or until meat is tender. Remove, slice and serve in Horseradish Sauce with a sprinkling of parsley. Serves 6.
Horseradish Sauce Brown 1 chopped onion in ¼ cup butter. Stir in 2 tablespoons flour. Add 2 cups strained meat stock, ½ cup prepared horseradish, 1 cup vinegar, 2 cloves and ¼ cup sugar. Season to taste. Simmer about 10 minutes.

MIRACLE ROAST OF BEEF

To. roast beef rare all the way through, use this method for standing rib roast, bone in. Place roast in shallow pan, fat side up. Season with salt and pepper and insert meat thermometer in center of meat. Roast in very slow oven (200°F.), allowing about 1 hour per pound. Roast can cook an extra hour more without overcooking. Thermometer reading should be 120°F. for really rare; 130°F. for medium rare, 140°F. for medium. To reheat roast, warm to room temperature and roast uncovered 1 hour at 200°F. These times and temperatures apply to standing rib roast only.

RIB ROAST OF BEEF

Standing Rib Roast Buy a roast. at least 2 ribs wide, allowing ½ to 1 pound per serving. A 10" rib roast means one with ribs 10" long with backbone and small bones on. When part of the long rib is cut off, it is called the short ribs. These are good barbecued or braised (see page 71). The standing rib roast remaining is often known as a Newport-style roast.

Place standing rib roast fat side up in shallow pan. Season with salt and pepper and insert meat thermometer in center, not touching a bone. Roast in slow oven (300°F.) 20 minutes per pound for rare; add 20 minutes to total cooking time for medium and 45 minutes for well-done.

Boned and Rolled Roast Rib roast may be boned, rolled and tied. Use the bones and meat scraps for making stock and soup. Allow ⅓ pound of rolled roast per serving. Place meat on a rack in shallow pan. Season with salt and pepper and insert meat thermometer in center. Roast in slow oven (300°F.) 33 to 35 minutes per pound for rare; add 15 minutes to total cooking time for medium and 30 minutes for well-done.

Consider 120° on meat thermometer for really rare beef, 130°F. for medium rare and 140° for medium well-done. Remove roast from heat, let "rest" at room temperature 15 to 20 minutes. It will be easier to carve.

If meat is taken directly from the refrigerator, you will need to add a little more time. Watch meat thermometer for accurate gauge of inside temperature, because size and shape of roast also influence cooking time.

OVEN POT ROAST

Put 3 pounds lean boneless beef for pot roast on a large sheet of heavy foil. Sprinkle with 1/2 envelope onion-soup mix and lightly with salt and pepper. Add 1 can (3 ounces) chopped mushrooms, drained. Wrap tightly in foil and put in a shallow baking dish. Bake in moderate oven (350°F.) about 3 1/2 hours. Makes 8 servings.

FRENCH POT ROAST AND VEGETABLES

1 large marrow bone
3 pounds boneless beef chuck
1 tablespoon salt
1/4 teaspoon pepper
1 bay leaf
1 onion, stuck with 2 cloves
2 whole allspice
3 sprigs parsley
5 carrots, sliced
3 whole turnips, quartered
3 celery stalks, sliced
5 leeks, sliced
Buttered toast

Put marrow bone and chuck in large kettle or Dutch oven and cover with 2 1/2 quarts water. Bring to boil, add next 6 ingredients, partially cover and simmer 3 hours. Add vegetables and simmer 1 hour longer, or until meat is tender. Remove marrow bone, meat and vegetables. Strain, discarding bay leaf, onion and allspice. Cut beef and marrow in cubes and put back in soup with vegetables. Put a piece of toast in each soup bowl and pour soup over. Makes 8 servings.

FLEMISH POT ROAST WITH NOODLES

3 pounds beef rump roast
Flour, seasoned with salt and pepper
1 tablespoon margarine
2 medium onions, sliced
1/4 cup packed brown sugar
1/4 cup honey
1/4 teaspoon cinnamon
1/8 teaspoon ground allspice
1/8 teaspoon ginger
1 can (12 ounces) beer
1 cup each dried apricots and pitted prunes
8 ounces curly noodles, cooked

Dredge beef with flour. Brown on all sides in margarine in Dutch oven. Add next 6 ingredients and 1/2 cup beer. Cover and cook 2 1/2 hours. Pour remaining beer over fruit and let stand. Add to meat and simmer 30 minutes longer. Remove meat and slice. Thicken liquid with flour-water paste. Serve with meat and hot noodles. Makes 6 servings, with some meat left over.

BEEF POT ROAST

Brown chuck, top rib or other cut for pot roast on all sides in 2 tablespoons fat in kettle or Dutch oven. Remove meat and put rack in kettle. Set meat on rack and season with salt and pepper. Add 1 small onion, sliced, and 1/2 cup water. Cover and simmer chuck roast 2 hours, or until tender (time depends on thickness; a rolled pot roast from rib roast will take 3 hours or longer). Add a little more water during cooking if necessary. Remove meat and skim fat from liquid. Serve liquid as is or thicken with a little flour and water, simmering a few minutes. Good with boiled or mashed potatoes, noodles or rice.

GLAZED BEEF BRISKET

First-cut fresh boneless beef brisket, about 4 pounds
1 tablespoon peppercorns
2-1/2 teaspoons salt
1/8 teaspoon ground allspice
2 tablespoons fine dry bread crumbs
1 teaspoon garlic salt
1 onion, sliced
Glaze
Carrot slices
Green-pepper strips

Wipe meat with damp cloth and put on board. With dull side of heavy knife, pound meat well on both sides. Then score inside of meat lengthwise and crosswise, making scorings about 1/2" apart. Put peppercorns in small cloth bag and crush with hammer or mallet. Sprinkle scored side of meat with the pepper, 1 1/2 teaspoons salt and next 3 ingredients. Roll up tightly lengthwise (the right way for slicing across the grain). Tie firmly in several places with string and put in large heavy kettle. Add onion and remaining salt. Cover with hot water. Bring to boil, cover and simmer 3 hours, or until tender. Chill thoroughly in the broth. Put on serving platter and remove string. Spoon some Glaze over meat to cover. Refrigerate about 10 minutes. Pour remaining Glaze over meat to cover well, letting mixture run onto platter. (If gelatin congeals, set in pan of warm water a few seconds.) Decorate meat with carrot slices and green-pepper strips. Chill until serving time, then dice gelatin on platter and slice meat. Makes 8 servings. **Glaze** Soften 1 envelope unflavored gelatin in 1/4 cup cold water. Heat 1 can (10 1/2 ounces) beef consommé with 1/2 cup water. Add gelatin and stir until dissolved. Chill until cold but not set.

BORDELAISE SAUCE

Cook 2 tablespoons minced shallots or green onions in 2 tablespoons butter. Add ¾ cup red wine and simmer until the liquid is reduced to one half. Add 1 can beef gravy, 2 tablespoons each lemon juice and minced parsley, and salt and cayenne to taste. Heat; add sliced poached beef marrow, if desired. Makes 2 cups.

SAUCE BEARNAISE II

2 shallots or 3 small green onions, chopped
1/2 cup wine vinegar
1 teaspoon dried or 1 tablespoon chopped fresh tarragon
3 egg yolks
1/2 cup butter, softened
Salt

Put shallots, vinegar and tarragon in a pan and bring to boil. Cook down until it is merely a glaze. Put egg yolks and 1 tablespoon warm water in a bowl over hot, not boiling, water. Water beneath bowl must be kept just below the boil. Whisk egg yolks and then slowly add soft butter, 1 tablespoon at a time. Keep whisking as you add butter. When sauce thickens, add glaze and salt to taste. If sauce is too thick, thin with a little heavy cream. Taste for seasoning. For zest, add a touch of lemon juice and a dash of hot pepper sauce. Makes about ½ cup. *Note* You can make sauce in an electric blender. Put egg yolks, glaze and a little salt in blender and flick it on and off quickly. Melt butter and heat until bubbly but not boiling. Turn blender on at high speed and dribble hot butter into beaten yolks until sauce thickens.

HUNGARIAN POT ROAST WITH NOODLES

4 pounds beef for pot roast
Salt and pepper
Flour
2 tablespoons fat
2 onions, quartered
1 teaspoon caraway seed
1 tablespoon paprika
1-1/2 cups tomato juice
Hot cooked noodles

Season meat with salt and pepper. Dredge with flour. Brown well on all sides in fat. Add remaining ingredients, except noodles. Cover and simmer 3½ hours, or until tender. If liquid evaporates, add a little water during cooking. Remove meat and thicken liquid with flour mixed with a little water, if desired. Serve with hot cooked noodles. Serves 6.

CHILI-SAUCE BEEF

3 pounds beef for pot roast
1 tablespoon fat
Salt and pepper
3 onions, sliced
1 bottle (12 ounces) chili sauce
2 dill pickles, chopped

Brown meat in fat in kettle. Add salt and pepper. Put a rack in kettle under meat; add ¼ cup water and onions. Cover and simmer 2 to 2½ hours. Add chili sauce and pickles and simmer 1 hour longer, or until meat is tender. Makes 4 servings.

DAUBE DE BOEUF PROVENÇALE
(Beef Daube, Provence Style)

The Provence daube is made in a daubière, a deep covered pot that's made from the native pottery. Usually cooked on top of the stove, it can be made in the oven. It's best when made a day ahead; cool, skim fat off and reheat, or serve cold.

1 cup red wine
2/3 cup olive oil
1 tablespoon salt
1 teaspoon black pepper
1 teaspoon oregano
1 teaspoon rosemary
1 bay leaf
2 cloves
1 carrot, cut up
5 to 6 pounds bottom round or chuck, firmly tied
1 calf's or pig's foot, if available
1/2 pound salt pork
6 to 8 carrots, peeled
6 garlic cloves, peeled
1 bay leaf
1 teaspoon rosemary
1/2 teaspoon thyme
8 ripe tomatoes, peeled, seeded and chopped
24 black olives, pitted

Place first 9 ingredients for marinade in a pot and bring to boil. Lower heat and simmer 5 minutes. Remove from heat and cool. Put meats in cooled marinade and let stand 12 to 24 hours, turning occasionally. Remove meat from marinade and put in large casserole. Add next 6 ingredients. Strain the marinade and pour it over the meat. Cover tightly and bake in slow oven (300°F.) about 2½ hours. Add tomatoes and olives and bake 35 to 40 minutes. Remove meat and let stand a few minutes before slicing. Slice salt pork. Arrange meats on a platter; surround with vegetables. Mix a little of liquid with boiled noodles or macaroni. Pass rest of liquid in sauceboat. Makes 6 to 8 servings, with meat left over.

BEEF IN SPAGHETTI SAUCE

4 pounds beef for pot roast
2 tablespoons olive oil
1 onion, chopped
1 clove garlic, minced
1 teaspoon Italian herb seasoning
1 teaspoon salt
1/4 teaspoon pepper
2 cans (8 ounces each) tomato sauce
1 pound spaghetti
Grated Parmesan cheese

Brown meat on all sides in oil in heavy kettle. Put meat on rack in kettle. Add next 5 ingredients. Mix tomato sauce with 1 cup water and pour over meat. Cover and simmer 3½ hours, or until meat is tender, adding 2 more cups of water at intervals during the cooking. Cook and drain spaghetti. Remove meat to a hot platter, slice and top with some of the sauce. Toss remaining sauce with the spaghetti and serve with grated cheese. Makes 8 servings.

POT AU FEU
(Boiled Beef with Vegetables)

5 pounds cross rib, short rib or brisket
    of beef
1-1/2 pounds salt pork
1 marrow bone
10 medium onions, peeled
4 whole cloves
9 leeks, well washed
10 carrots, peeled and sliced
1 bay leaf
1 teaspoon thyme
2 or 3 sprigs parsley
1 teaspoon salt
1/4 teaspoon pepper
8 small turnips, peeled
1 medium cabbage, cut in quarters or
    sixths

Put meat, salt pork, marrow bone, 2 onions stuck with cloves, 3 leeks, 2 carrots and the herbs in heavy kettle. Add water to cover 1½" above meat. Bring to boil and boil rapidly 5 minutes. Skim off any scum that forms on top, add salt and pepper and cover kettle. Lower heat and simmer 2 to 2½ hours, or until meat is tender. Remove meat and keep warm. Add remaining vegetables, except cabbage, and cook until done. Add cabbage the last 12 minutes. Cut salt pork and beef in slices and arrange on a hot platter. Surround meat with vegetables and garnish with marrow from marrow bone. Coarse salt, mustard and horseradish are traditional with this dish. Potatoes cooked in jackets and good pickles are also a nice addition. Taste broth for seasoning, pour into bowls and serve separately. Makes 8 servings.

SAUERBRATEN I

4 to 5 pounds round of beef
2 onions, sliced
1 carrot, sliced
1 stalk celery, sliced
2 cups red-wine vinegar
1 tablespoon salt
1 tablespoon mixed pickling spice
1/2 teaspoon dried thyme
1 sprig parsley
4 tablespoons margarine
3 tablespoons all-purpose flour
2 tablespoons red-currant jelly
Gingersnaps

Put meat in deep bowl or crock. Mix next 8 ingredients and pour over meat. Store, covered, in refrigerator 2 to 3 days, turning meat once or twice. Remove meat from marinade and wipe dry. Brown on all sides in 1 tablespoon margarine in heavy kettle or Dutch oven. Remove meat and melt remaining margarine in kettle. Blend in flour. Add strained marinade and meat. Cover and simmer 2½ hours, or until meat is tender. Remove meat and blend jelly and 4 or 5 gingersnaps into liquid in pan. If necessary, add more gingersnaps, or jelly. Serve meat, sliced, with the gravy. Serves 6, with meat left over.

SAUERBRATEN II

4 pounds beef for pot roast
2 teaspoons salt
1 teaspoon ginger
2 cups cider vinegar
2 medium onions, sliced
2 tablespoons mixed pickling spice
2 bay leaves
1 teaspoon whole black peppercorns
8 whole cloves
1/3 cup sugar
2 tablespoons fat
6 gingersnaps, crumbled

Rub meat with salt and ginger; put in large bowl. Combine 2½ cups water and remaining ingredients, except fat and flour, bring to boil and pour over meat. Cool, cover and put in refrigerator for 3 days; turn meat once each day. Remove meat, reserving liquid. Dry meat with paper towel and brown on all sides in fat in heavy kettle. Put on rack, add 1 cup reserved liquid and half the onions and spices from liquid. Cover tightly and simmer very slowly 3½ hours, or until tender, adding more liquid as needed. Remove meat to hot platter. Strain liquid in pan and return to heat; strain in additional liquid to make about 2 cups. Skim off excess fat. Thicken gravy with gingersnaps. Serve with sliced meat; good with mashed potatoes, rice or potato dumplings. Makes about 6 servings.

COFFEE POT ROAST WITH VEGETABLES

2 pounds beef for pot roast
1 cup each canned tomatoes and black coffee
Salt and pepper to taste
1 onion, chopped
6 carrots, peeled and diced
2 cups diced potato
1 box (10 ounces) frozen peas

Brown meat on all sides in heavy kettle or Dutch oven, adding a small amount of fat if necessary. Add tomatoes, coffee, 1 cup water, salt and pepper. Bring to boil, cover and simmer 1 hour. Add onion and carrot and simmer 15 minutes. Add potato and cook until vegetables are tender. Add peas and cook a few minutes. If desired, thicken gravy. Makes 6 servings.

WEST INDIAN POT ROAST

1 can (3-1/2 ounces) flaked coconut
3 pounds beef for pot roast
Flour
2 tablespoons fat
Salt and pepper
1 onion, sliced
1 clove garlic, minced

Put coconut in bowl and cover with 1¼ cups boiling water; let stand until cold. Strain, reserving liquid. Dredge meat with flour and brown on all sides in the fat in heavy kettle or Dutch oven. Pour off fat and put meat on rack in kettle. Season with salt and pepper and add coconut liquid, onion and garlic. Simmer, covered, 3 to 3½ hours, adding water if necessary. Remove meat and thicken liquid, if desired. Serves 4.

SPANISH BEEF STEW

1-1/2 pounds boneless beef chuck, cut in 1" cubes
1/4 cup olive oil
4 medium onions, chopped
1 teaspoon instant minced garlic
3 sprigs parsley, chopped
3 green peppers, cut in strips
2 teaspoons seasoned salt
1/2 teaspoon pepper
1 can (1 pint 2 ounces) tomato juice
3 medium potatoes, peeled and diced
2 pimientos, cut in strips
2 tablespoons flour

Brown meat on all sides in olive oil in kettle. Add next six ingredients and brown lightly. Add tomato juice. Bring to boil, cover and simmer 1½ hours. Add potato and pimiento; simmer 30 minutes longer. Stir in flour blended with ¼ cup cold water; cook, stirring constantly, 5 minutes, or until thickened. Makes 4 servings.

BEEF IN CASSEROLE

3 pounds boneless beef chuck, cut in 1" cubes
1 can (10-1/2 ounces) condensed golden mushroom soup
1 scant soup-can dry red wine
Salt and pepper to taste

Put all ingredients in greased 3-quart casserole. Cover and bake in moderate oven (350°F.), stirring occasionally, about 3 hours. Good with noodles or rice. Makes 6 to 8 servings.

BEEF-VEGETABLE CASSEROLE

Margarine
3 pounds boneless chuck roast, cut in 3/8" slices
Salt and white pepper
Crumbled marjoram leaves
1 can (10-1/2 ounces) condensed golden mushroom soup
6 medium potatoes, peeled and cut in 1/2" slices
4 large carrots, peeled and sliced diagonally
1 can (1 pound) whole onions, drained
Chopped parsley

Brown 2 tablespoons margarine in large heavy skillet. Add meat slices a few at a time and brown on both sides, adding additional margarine as needed. Season with salt, pepper and marjoram and transfer to greased 3- to 4-quart casserole. Add 1 cup boiling water to skillet to loosen pan drippings. Pour over meat together with soup. Cover tightly and bake in slow oven (325° F.) 1½ to 2 hours, or until meat is almost done. Add potatoes, carrots and onions. Bake 1 hour, or until all is done. Sprinkle with parsley. Makes 6 to 8 servings, with some meat left over.

SPICED APPLES AND BEEF

2 pounds boneless beef chuck or round, cut in 1" cubes
2 tablespoons vegetable oil
1/4 cup lemon or lime juice
2 cups sliced onion
1-1/2 teaspoons curry powder
1/4 teaspoon each ground cloves and cinnamon
1 teaspoon salt
3 cups peeled apples in 1" wedges
3/4 cup chopped watermelon pickle
Buttered hot cooked rice

Brown beef cubes in oil in heavy kettle or Dutch oven. Add 1 cup water, the lemon juice, onion and seasonings. Bring to boil, cover and simmer 40 minutes. Add apple wedges and ½ cup water, mixing gently. Cover and simmer 40 minutes, or until meat is tender. Gently mix in pickle. Serve on rice. Makes 4 to 6 servings.

BARBECUED SHORT RIBS

3 pounds short ribs of beef
1 onion, chopped
1/2 cup sliced celery
2 tablespoons Worcestershire
1 teaspoon prepared mustard
1-1/2 teaspoons salt
1/8 teaspoon pepper

Brown short ribs on all sides in heavy kettle; pour off fat. Add ½ cup water, vegetables and seasonings. Cover and simmer 2 hours, or until tender, turning meat several times and adding more water if necessary. Makes 4 servings.

SHORT RIBS, BAYOU STYLE

3 pounds short ribs, cut in 6 pieces
Flour
2 bay leaves
8 whole cloves
1 clove garlic, minced
1/2 green pepper, chopped
1/4 cup chopped celery leaves
1 tablespoon salt
1/4 teaspoon pepper
1 can (8 ounces) tomato sauce
1/2 lemon, sliced

Sprinkle meat lightly with flour. Brown slowly in heavy kettle or Dutch oven without added fat. Pour off any fat that collects. Add 1 cup water and remaining ingredients. Cover and cook very slowly 2 to 3 hours, or until meat is very tender, adding more water, if necessary. Makes 4 to 6 servings.

SPICY SHORT RIBS

They're flavored with cinnamon, clove and allspice.

3 pounds short ribs of beef
1-1/2 teaspoons salt
1/4 teaspoon pepper
1/4 cup flour
1/4 teaspoon each cinnamon, cloves and allspice
1 tablespoon fat
1 cup uncooked dried apricots (optional)
2 tablespoons brown sugar
2 tablespoons vinegar
3 cups beef bouillon

Dredge ribs with next 3 ingredients and spices mixed together. Brown on all sides in the fat in heavy kettle. Pour off fat and sprinkle ribs with 1 tablespoon remaining flour mixture. Mix remaining ingredients and pour over meat. Bring to boil, cover and simmer 2½ hours, or until meat is tender, adding more liquid if necessary and turning often to prevent sticking. Thicken gravy with a flour-and-water paste if desired. Makes 4 to 6 servings.

BEEF STEW WITH HERB DUMPLINGS

3 pounds boneless chuck, cut in cubes
Flour
1 medium onion, chopped
3 tablespoons vegetable oil
1 bay leaf
1 teaspoon celery seed
1 tablespoon salt
1/2 teaspoon pepper
1 pound green beans, cut
Herb Dumplings

Dredge beef with flour and brown with onion in oil in kettle. Add 3 cups water and seasonings. Bring to boil; cover and simmer 1½ hours. Add beans and cook 15 minutes. If necessary, thicken with a paste of flour and water. Drop Herb Dumpling batter by tablespoonfuls into gently boiling stew. Cover and cook 15 minutes. Makes 6 to 8 servings. **Herb Dumplings** Sift 3 cups sifted cake flour, 1¼ teaspoons baking powder and 1 teaspoon salt. With fork blend in 2 tablespoons shortening. Add 2 tablespoons chopped fresh herbs, 1 tablespoon dried herbs or 1 teaspoon poultry seasoning. Stir in 1 cup minus 1 tablespoon milk.

STEFADO
(Greek Beef Stew)

3 pounds lean stew meat, cut in 1-1/2" cubes
Salt and freshly ground black pepper
1/2 cup butter
2-1/2 pounds small onions, peeled
1 can (6 ounces) tomato paste
1/3 cup red table wine
2 tablespoons red-wine vinegar
1 tablespoon brown sugar
1 clove garlic, minced or mashed
1 bay leaf
1 small cinnamon stick
1/2 teaspoon whole cloves
1/4 teaspoon ground cumin

Season meat with salt and pepper. Melt butter in Dutch oven or heavy kettle with cover. Add meat and coat with butter, but do not brown. Arrange onions over meat. Mix remaining ingredients; pour over meat and onions. Cover onions with plate (to hold them intact), cover kettle and simmer 3 hours, or until meat is very tender. (Do not stir.) As you serve, stir sauce gently to blend. Makes 6 servings. *Note* 2 tablespoons currants or raisins can be added with seasonings. Accompany with a red wine and Greek bread with sesame-coated crust, or spread a good white bread with soft butter and sesame seeds and bake or broil to toast seeds.

BEEF AND RED MACARONI

1-1/2 pounds boneless stewing beef
2 tablespoons fat
2 cloves garlic, minced
1 can (6 ounces) tomato paste
1-1/2 teaspoons salt
1/8 teaspoon pepper
1 bay leaf
8 ounces macaroni, broken
1/4 cup grated Parmesan or Italian-style cheese

Cut meat in 1" pieces. Brown in fat in large skillet. Add 3 cups water and next 5 ingredients. Cover and simmer 1 hour, or until meat is tender. Add uncooked macaroni, and more water if needed to cover. Cover and simmer 15 minutes, or until macaroni is tender. Serve with cheese. Makes 4 servings.

BEEF-LIMA CASSEROLE

1 pound dried lima beans
2 pounds boneless beef chuck
1 tablespoon salt
1/2 teaspoon pepper
1/4 cup all-purpose flour
1/3 cup butter or margarine
3 onions, sliced

Cover washed beans with 6 cups water, bring to boil and boil 2 minutes. Cover and let stand 1 hour; then cook until tender. Drain, reserving liquid. Cut meat in 1" cubes, roll in seasoned flour and brown in butter. Add onions and continue browning. Add 2 cups bean liquid and bring to boil. Arrange alternate layers of beans and meat in 3-quart casserole, large bean pot or electric Dutch oven. Add remaining liquid and enough water to cover. Cover and bake in slow oven (300°F.) 2 hours. Makes 6 servings.

BEEF BIRMINGHAM

1 clove garlic, sliced
1 pound stew beef, cut in thin strips
1 cup sliced onion (3 medium)
1 cup sliced celery
2 tablespoons vegetable oil
2 tablespoons peanut butter
2 tablespoons soy sauce
1/2 teaspoon sugar
1 cup beef stock or bouillon
Dash of pepper
Hot cooked rice or noodles

Sauté garlic, beef, onion and celery in hot oil until lightly browned. Add remaining ingredients, except rice, bring to boil, cover and simmer 1 hour, or until meat is tender. Add additional liquid during cooking if needed. Serve on rice. Makes 4 servings.

CARAWAY-CRUST BEEF PIE

1-1/2 pounds round steak, cut in 1" cubes
1 teaspoon salt
1/4 teaspoon pepper
1/2 cup all-purpose flour
1/4 cup butter or margarine
2 onions, sliced
1 can condensed bouillon
1 bay leaf
1/2 pound green beans, cut up
4 carrots, peeled and sliced
12 small white onions, peeled
1/2 recipe Standard Pastry (page 419)
2 teaspoons caraway seed

Dredge meat with seasoned ¼ cup flour and brown on all sides in hot butter in kettle. Add onions and brown lightly. Add 2 cups hot water, bouillon and bay leaf. Cover and simmer 1½ hours, or until meat is almost tender. Add vegetables and simmer 30 minutes, or until onions and meat are tender. Thicken with ¼ cup flour blended with a little cold water. Pour into 3-quart casserole. Make pastry, adding seed to dry ingredients. Roll to fit top of casserole. Make slits for steam to escape. Bake in very hot oven (450°F.) until crust is golden brown. Serves 6 to 8.

BEEF AND VEGETABLE PIE

2-1/2 pounds boneless beef chuck
6 tablespoons all-purpose flour
2 teaspoons salt
1/4 teaspoon pepper
3 tablespoons margarine or other fat
2 onions, sliced
1 teaspoon steak sauce
1 teaspoon seasoned salt
1 can (1 pound) tomatoes
2 carrots, sliced
3 cups sliced potato
1 box or 1 stick pastry mix

Cut beef in 1" cubes and dredge with 3 tablespoons flour seasoned with the salt and pepper. Brown on all sides in the margarine in heavy kettle. Add onions and brown lightly. Add 2 cups water, the steak sauce and seasoned salt. Bring to boil, cover and simmer 1 hour, or until meat is almost tender. Add tomatoes, carrots and potato. Simmer, covered, ½ hour longer. Blend remaining flour with a little cold water and stir into mixture. Cook, stirring gently, until thickened. Pour into 3-quart casserole. Prepare pastry mix as directed on the label. Roll out to fit top of casserole, trim edges and flute. Prick top to allow steam to escape. Bake in hot oven (425°F.) 25 minutes, or until top is browned. Makes 8 servings.

BEEF ROLLS IN WINE

Mix 1/2 cup cooked, chopped mushrooms or cooked sausage meat, and 1 onion, chopped. Put a spoonful on each of 4 large, thin slices of cooked roast beef. Roll up and fasten with a toothpick. Brown in fat and remove from pan. In the same pan put 2 tablespoons flour, more fat if necessary, and cook a few minutes. Add 1/3 cup each red wine, water and meat stock and heat well. Add salt, pepper, 1/2 bay leaf, a pinch of thyme. Put back meat rolls; simmer, covered, 1 hour, adding liquid if necessary. Add 1 can (1 pound) carrots, drained, during last part of cooking. Garnish with chopped parsley. Serves 4.

INDIENNE BEEF STEW

1 pound boneless chuck, cut in 1-1/2"
   cubes
Flour
1 teaspoon salt
1/8 teaspoon pepper
3 tablespoons butter
2 onions, peeled and sliced
1 green pepper, sliced
1 cup dairy sour cream
1 to 2 teaspoons curry powder
Hot cooked rice

Dredge meat with 2 tablespoons flour, salt and pepper. Brown in hot butter. Add 2 cups water, bring to boil, cover and simmer 1 hour. Add onion and green pepper; simmer 30 minutes. Thicken with paste of 2 tablespoons flour mixed with a little cold water. Add sour cream and curry powder and heat gently. Serve on rice. Makes 4 servings.

HUNGARIAN GOULASH

3 pounds boneless beef chuck or
   3-1/2 pounds bone-in chuck
3 pounds large onions, cut in wedge-
   shaped pieces (about 7 cups)
1 tablespoon salt
1/2 teaspoon black pepper
Paprika
Parsley
Cooked noodles
Dairy sour cream

Cut meat in 1" cubes, discarding any excess fat and bone. Put meat, onion, salt, pepper and 2 tablespoons paprika in large heavy kettle or Dutch oven. Cook over medium heat about 20 minutes, stirring often. Cover and simmer 2 hours, stirring occasionally. Uncover and simmer until liquid cooks down to gravy consistency. Garnish with parsley and serve with noodles and a generous dollop of sour cream sprinkled with paprika. Makes 6 servings.

SHEPHERD'S BEEF PIE

Heat together in saucepan cubed cooked beef, gravy, cooked peas, and carrots or green beans. Pour into a casserole. Make a ring of seasoned mashed potatoes on top of meat mixture. Bake in hot oven (400°F.) 20 minutes, or until thoroughly heated and potatoes are golden brown.

BEEF IN SOUR CREAM

Beef, bacon and onions simmer in white wine; then sour cream is added.

4 slices bacon, diced
2 pounds beef stew meat, cut in 1"
   cubes
4 onions, chopped
1 clove garlic, minced
2 teaspoons salt
1/4 teaspoon pepper
1/2 teaspoon marjoram
2/3 cup dry white wine
1 pint dairy sour cream
Chopped parsley
Paprika

Cook bacon in kettle until browned. Remove bacon and set aside. Add beef to fat remaining in kettle and brown on all sides. Add onion and garlic and cook a few minutes. Stir in bacon and next 4 ingredients. Bring to boil, cover and simmer 1 1/2 hours, or until meat is tender. Add a little broth or water if mixture becomes dry. Stir in sour cream and heat gently. Sprinkle with parsley and paprika. Makes 4 to 6 servings.

CHILI CON CARNE

1 cup dried pinto beans
3 pounds lean stew beef
1/4 cup olive oil
1 bay leaf
2 tablespoons chili powder
1 tablespoon salt
4 cloves garlic, minced
1 teaspoon crushed cumin seed
1 teaspoon oregano
3 tablespoons paprika
3 tablespoons cornmeal
1 tablespoon flour

Cover washed beans with 4 cups water, bring to boil and boil 2 minutes. Cover and let stand 1 hour, then cook until tender. Drain. Cut meat in 1/2" cubes and sear in hot oil. Add 6 cups water, cover, bring to boil and simmer 1 hour. Add bay leaf and next 6 ingredients. Simmer 1/2 hour. Blend cornmeal, flour and cold water to make a paste. Stir into mixture; simmer 5 minutes. Add beans and heat. Makes 6 servings.

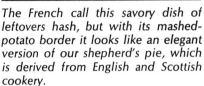

HACHIS DE BOEUF EN BORDURE
(Beef Hash in Potato Border)

The French call this savory dish of leftovers hash, but with its mashed-potato border it looks like an elegant version of our shepherd's pie, which is derived from English and Scottish cookery.

1 onion, chopped
4 tablespoons butter or margarine
3/4 cup leftover or canned beef gravy
1 teaspoon wine vinegar
2 tablespoons Madeira wine
3 cups diced cooked roast beef
1 egg
2 cups hot mashed potato, seasoned
2 tablespoons fine dry bread crumbs

Cook onion in 3 tablespoons butter until soft. Add next 3 ingredients and beef. Heat gently just to boiling. Pile in center of greased shallow baking dish. Beat egg into mashed potato. Spread in puffs or force through pastry bag to make border around hash. Sprinkle potato with bread crumbs and drizzle with remaining tablespoon butter, melted. Bake in hot oven (425°F.) 20 minutes, or until hot and glazed with brown. Makes 4 servings.

AUSTRIAN BEEF GOULASH

Tart dill pickles are added to the sour-cream gravy.

4 large onions, cut in rings
1/3 cup butter
2 pounds lean top round or chuck beef, cut in 1" cubes
1 tablespoon sweet paprika
Dash of cayenne
Dash of garlic salt
Salt and pepper
2 bay leaves
1 tablespoon wine vinegar
Beef stock
Flour
1 cup dairy sour cream
2 tart dill pickles, diced
Cooked noodles

Sauté onions in butter. Place in Dutch oven or heavy pot with cover. In skillet, brown meat and add to onions. To skillet add seasonings, vinegar and 1 cup stock. Simmer a few minutes and pour over meat. Add additional stock if necessary to cover meat. Simmer, covered, at least 2 hours over low heat, checking for dryness; add more stock if necessary. Add a little flour moistened with cold stock to thicken gravy. At last minute, stir in sour cream and heat. Add pickles, drained, and serve with noodles. Makes 6 servings.

SKILLET BEEF AND CABBAGE

1-1/2-pound head of cabbage
Salt and pepper
1 onion, sliced
4 tablespoons butter or margarine
4 servings thinly sliced cooked roast beef

Cut cabbage in quarters; wash, dry and chop fine. Put in saucepan in salted water to cover and cook until barely tender. Drain. Sauté with the onion in 3 tablespoons butter until tender. Season with salt and pepper. In another skillet, sauté beef gently in remaining butter until very hot. Put on platter and top with cabbage and meat drippings. Makes 4 servings.

SOUR-CREAM MENU SAVER

A delicious way to use any leftover meat or poultry.

8 ounces medium noodles, cooked
1 onion, minced
2 tablespoons butter
1-1/2 cups cooked meat, cut in julienne strips
Salt and pepper
2 eggs, beaten
1/2 cup chopped green or ripe olives
1 tablespoon chopped parsley
1 cup dairy sour cream
Buttered bread crumbs

Put drained cooked noodles into greased casserole. Sauté onion lightly in butter. Stir in remaining ingredients, except bread crumbs, and pour over noodles, using fork to let sauce through. Top with crumbs. Bake in moderate oven (375°F.) about 40 minutes. Makes 6 servings.

MEAT AND VEGETABLE STEW WITH CALICO DUMPLINGS

6 peeled white onions
3 medium carrots, diced
2 cups diced yellow turnip
1 or 2 bouillon cubes
3 cups diced cooked beef, lamb or other meat
2 cups leftover gravy or meat stock
Salt and pepper
Flour
Calico Dumplings

Cook first 4 ingredients with 2 cups water until vegetables are tender. Add meat, gravy, and salt and pepper to taste. Thicken, if necessary, with a flour-and-water paste. Drop Calico Dumpling batter by tablespoonfuls onto pieces of vegetable or meat. Cover and simmer 10 minutes, or until dumplings are done. Makes 4 servings. **Calico Dumplings** Add ¾ cup milk to 2 cups biscuit mix. With fork, mix until soft dough is formed. Add 1 chopped pimiento and ¼ cup chopped parsley.

DEVILED ROAST-BEEF SLICES

4 slices cooked roast beef, 1/4" to 1/2"
  thick
Prepared mustard
Fine dry bread crumbs
Beef drippings
1 cup beef gravy
1/2 teaspoon dry mustard
Dash of hot pepper sauce
1 tablespoon Worcestershire
Garlic salt
Freshly ground pepper

Spread slices of roast beef with mustard. Dip in crumbs. Fry in beef drippings until browned. Serve with gravy made by heating remaining ingredients. Makes 4 servings.

BEEF IN SAVORY SAUCE

1 medium onion, chopped
2 tablespoons beef fat
2 tablespoons flour
Pinch of thyme
1/3 cup dry red wine
1 cup beef bouillon
1 can (2 or 3 ounces) mushrooms,
  undrained
1/4 cup tomato sauce
6 slices cooked roast beef
Salt and pepper
Chopped parsley

Fry onion in fat until lightly browned. Stir in flour and thyme. Add next 4 ingredients. Bring to boil and simmer about 5 minutes. Add beef; heat well. Season with salt and pepper. Sprinkle with parsley. Makes 4 servings.

BEEF CURRY

1-1/2 pounds boneless beef chuck
Salt and pepper
2 tablespoons flour
2 large onions, sliced
2 tablespoons margarine
3/4 teaspoon ground coriander
1/2 teaspoon turmeric
1/2 teaspoon ground cumin
Dash of cayenne
1/2 cup tomato juice
Hot cooked rice
Condiments (optional)

Cut meat in 1" cubes and roll in seasoned flour. Cook meat and onion in margarine until meat is well browned. Add 1 cup boiling water and spices. Bring to boil, cover and simmer 1½ hours, or until meat is tender. Stir in tomato juice. Serve on hot cooked rice, accompanied by condiments such as chutney, raisins, coconut, peanuts, cashews, etc., if desired. Makes 4 to 6 servings. *Note* If preferred, 2 teaspoons curry powder can be substituted for the 4 spices in ingredients.

HIGHLAND HOT POT

1 pound lean bottom round
3 tablespoons flour
1/2 pound link sausages
4 medium potatoes, peeled and sliced
  1/4" thick
2 apples, peeled and sliced 1/4" thick
1 onion, peeled and sliced 1/4" thick
Salt and pepper
1 can (1 pint 2 ounces) tomato juice,
  or about 2 cups
3 beef bouillon cubes
Pinch of sage

Cut bottom round in cubes and dredge with flour. Cut sausages in half. In a 2-quart casserole, put half of mixed potato, apple and onion. Add meats, then remaining vegetable mixture. Sprinkle each layer lightly with salt and pepper. Heat tomato juice and dissolve bouillon cubes in it. Add sage. Pour over ingredients in casserole. Cover and bake in moderate oven (350°F.) about 1½ hours. Makes 4 servings.

OVEN BEEF GOULASH

2 pounds boneless beef chuck
1 teaspoon salt
1/4 teaspoon pepper
1 teaspoon seasoned salt
1 teaspoon paprika
1/4 cup all-purpose flour
2 tablespoons fat
1 tablespoon Worcestershire
1 clove garlic, minced
1 teaspoon dry mustard
1 bay leaf
1 teaspoon caraway seed
1 tablespoon vinegar

Cut the beef chuck in 1" cubes. Mix the next 5 ingredients Dredge all sides in hot fat. Put in 2-quart casserole. Sprinkle with any remaining flour. Add 2 cups water and remaining ingredients. Cover and bake in moderate oven (350°F.) 2 hours. Makes 6 servings.

BEEF ALL'ITALIANA

1 clove garlic, minced
2 tablespoons olive oil
1 can (1 pound) tomatoes
1 can (3 ounces) tomato sauce
1/2 teaspoon oregano
3/4 teaspoon salt
1/4 teaspoon pepper
2 cups diced cooked beef
Chopped parsley
Hot cooked spaghetti or noodles

Cook garlic in oil until lightly browned. Add next 5 ingredients. Cook 25 minutes. Add beef. Cook over low heat about 15 minutes. Sprinkle with chopped parsley. Serve with spaghetti or noodles. Serves 4.

MUSHROOM CREAMED BEEF

1/4 pound dried beef
2 tablespoons butter
2 cans condensed cream of mushroom
  soup
1/2 cup light cream or milk
Pepper and Worcestershire to taste

Cover beef with boiling water and let stand 5 minutes; drain. Cut in pieces and put in top of double boiler, add butter and cook over direct heat until beef is frizzled. Add remaining ingredients and put over boiling water. Heat, stirring occasionally. Good on baked potatoes, rice, noodles or toast. Serves 4.

DRIED BEEF IN SOUR-CREAM SAUCE

1/4 cup butter
2 tablespoons minced onion
1/4 pound dried beef
3 tablespoons flour
1 cup each milk and dairy sour cream
1 can (3 ounces) chopped mushrooms,
  drained
1 cup shredded sharp Cheddar cheese
2 tablespoons chopped parsley
Salt and pepper to taste

Put butter and onion in saucepan; add beef cut in julienne strips. Cook 2 or 3 minutes. Blend in flour. Gradually add milk and cook, stirring, until thickened. Add remaining ingredients and heat. Makes 4 servings.

SIMMERED CORNED BEEF

(Basic Recipe)

4- to 5-pound corned-beef brisket or
  rump
1 onion
1 bay leaf
2 cloves garlic
1 leek (optional)
2 carrots
Few whole black peppercorns

Wash beef and put in kettle. Cover with water and add remaining ingredients. Bring to boil, cover and simmer 4 to 4½ hours, or until tender. Serve hot or let stand in the broth until lukewarm to keep beef moist. Then remove and chill.
To cook in pressure cooker Put beef in pressure pan and cover with cold water. Bring to boil and simmer 5 minutes; drain. (If beef seems very salty, simmer 10 minutes before draining.) Put rack under beef and add 3 cups boiling water and remaining ingredients. Bring to 10 pounds pressure and process 25 minutes to the pound for a thick piece, 15 minutes to the pound for a thin piece.

DRIED-BEEF CASSEROLE

1/4 pound dried beef
1/2 cup diced celery
1 can (8-1/2 ounces) peas, undrained
1 can condensed cream of chicken soup
1 can condensed cream of mushroom
  soup
1/4 teaspoon each pepper and garlic salt
1 can (3-1/2 ounces) chow-mein
  noodles

Tear beef in pieces. Cover with boiling water; drain. Mix with remaining ingredients, except noodles. Arrange half of noodles in shallow casserole. Add beef mixture; top with noodles. Bake in moderate oven (375°F.) about 30 minutes. Serves 4 to 6.

GREEN-BEAN AND DRIED-BEEF LUNCHEON DISH

1 box frozen cut green or wax beans
1 package (2-1/4 ounces) cheese sauce
  mix
1-1/2 cups milk
1/4 teaspoon chili powder
Dash of Worcestershire
1 tablespoon instant minced onion
2 pimientos, chopped
1 jar (2-1/2 ounces) dried beef, shredded
Toast or waffles

Cook beans in small amount of boiling water as directed on the label; drain. Put mix in saucepan and gradually stir in milk. Bring to boil, stirring. Add beans and remaining ingredients, except toast. Heat and serve on toast or waffles. Makes 4 servings.

NEW ENGLAND BOILED DINNER

4- to 5-pound corned beef brisket
6 small beets, unpeeled
6 small white turnips, unpeeled
6 medium carrots, peeled
8 medium potatoes, peeled
1 small cabbage, quartered
Vinegar
Prepared mustard

Wash beef and put in large kettle. Cover with cold water. Bring to boil, cover and simmer 4 to 4½ hours, or until tender. Remove meat from kettle. Put beets in saucepan and add some of the broth from the corned beef. Cover and simmer until tender. Add turnips, carrots and potatoes to broth in kettle. Cover and simmer 20 minutes, or until tender. Add cabbage and simmer 15 minutes longer. Remove vegetables and keep hot. Put meat back in broth a few minutes to reheat. Slip skins off beets. Slice beef and arrange in center of hot platter. Surround with the vegetables and serve with vinegar and mustard. Makes 6 servings with meat left over.

CORNED-BEEF CASSEROLE

1 cup milk
2 eggs
1 cup soft bread crumbs
1/2 cup minced onion
1 tablespoon prepared horseradish
1 teaspoon dry mustard
2 cans (12 ounces each) corned beef
Creamy Mustard Sauce (page 132)

Mix first 6 ingredients. Chop corned beef and add; mix well. Put in 8″ square casserole. Bake in moderate oven (375°F.) 30 to 35 minutes. Cut in squares and serve with sauce, and cabbage. Serves 6 to 8.

CHEESY CORNED-BEEF AND CABBAGE CASSEROLE

6 cups chopped cabbage, about 2 pounds
1 can (12 ounces) corned beef, diced
3 tablespoons grated onion
1 tablespoon prepared mustard
1/2 teaspoon salt
1 can condensed cheese soup
1 tall can undiluted evaporated milk
2 tablespoons butter or margarine
4 slices bread, cut in small cubes
4 slices process American cheese

Cook cabbage in 2″ boiling water 10 minutes, or until just tender; drain. Arrange alternate layers of cabbage and corned beef in greased 2½-quart casserole. Mix next 5 ingredients and pour over mixture. Melt butter and toss with bread cubes. Arrange in ring around edge of casserole. Bake in moderate oven (350°F.) 45 minutes, or until mixture is bubbly and croutons are browned. Arrange cheese slices in center. Bake 5 minutes longer, or until cheese is melted. Makes 6 servings.

SAVORY CORNED-BEEF BREAD

2/3 cup chopped green onion with tops
3 tablespoons vegetable oil
2 cups buttermilk biscuit mix
1 cup chopped corned beef
2 eggs, slightly beaten
2/3 cup milk
1/2 teaspoon prepared mustard
1-1/2 cups grated sharp Cheddar cheese
2 tablespoons sesame seed
3 tablespoons butter or margarine

Sauté onion in 1 tablespoon oil about 2 minutes. Combine biscuit mix and corned beef. Mix remaining oil, eggs, milk, mustard, onion and half the cheese. Add to corned beef mixture and stir until mixed. Spread in greased round 10″ casserole. Sprinkle with remaining cheese and the seed, then pour butter over top. Bake in moderate oven (375°F.) 35 to 40 minutes. Cut in wedges and serve hot with butter. Makes 4 to 6 servings.

DILLED CORNED-BEEF AND MACARONI CASSEROLE

4 ounces elbow macaroni
1 can (10-1/2 ounces) condensed cream of celery soup
1/2 cup milk
1/2 cup mayonnaise
Dash of pepper
1/4 teaspoon hot pepper sauce
1-1/2 teaspoons dillseed
1 teaspoon prepared horseradish
1/4 cup chopped pimiento
1 can (12 ounces) corned beef, chopped
1/4 cup fine dry bread crumbs
2 tablespoons butter or margarine, melted

Cook and drain macaroni. Combine with remaining ingredients, except last 2. Pour into greased 1½-quart casserole. Mix crumbs with the butter and sprinkle on top. Bake in moderate oven (350°F.) 20 to 25 minutes, or until bubbly. Makes about 4 servings.

DRIED-BEEF-POTATO QUICKIE

1/4 cup butter or margarine
2 pounds frozen cottage-fried potatoes (or equal amount other frozen potatoes, such as French fries, crinkle-cut French fries or potato rounds)
1 jar (5 ounces) dried beef, torn in 1″ pieces
1 can (3-1/3 ounces) French-fried onions

Put butter in large shallow pan and set in very hot oven (450°F.) to melt. Add potatoes to melted butter and stir gently. Heat, stirring occasionally, 12 minutes. Push potatoes to one side and scatter dried beef over butter. Sprinkle potatoes with onion rings. Bake 3 minutes longer. Toss to mix. Makes 6 servings.

LAYERED CORNED-BEEF CASSEROLE

2 tablespoons margarine
2 tablespoons flour
1-1/4 cups milk
1 teaspoon prepared mustard
1 can (12 ounces) corned beef, cut in 1″ cubes
Salt and pepper
2 large carrots, shredded
4 servings instant mashed potato, prepared with 1 tablespoon instant minced onion
Chopped fresh parsley or flaked parsley

Melt margarine and blend in flour. Gradually add milk and cook, stirring, until thickened. Carefully stir in corned beef and mustard. Add salt and pepper to taste. Pour into greased 2-quart casserole. Cover with carrots, then top with mashed potato. Bake in moderate oven (350°F.) 35 minutes, or until well browned. Sprinkle with parsley. Makes 4 servings.

BAKED SPICY CORNED BEEF

4- to 6-pound corned brisket of beef
2 tablespoons pickling spice
1 orange, sliced
1 onion, sliced
1 stalk celery with leaves, sliced
1 carrot, sliced
1/3 cup packed brown sugar
1 tablespoon prepared mustard

Soak corned beef in water to cover 1/2 hour, or longer if deeply corned. Place a large sheet of heavy foil on a shallow pan. Remove corned beef from water and pat dry to remove any salt on surface. Put in center of foil and pour 1/4 cup fresh water over top. Sprinkle with the spice and arrange orange slices and vegetables over and around the meat. Bring long ends of foil up over meat and seal with a tight double fold. Seal other ends, turning them up so liquid cannot run out. Bake in slow oven (300°F.) 4 hours. Cool slightly, unwrap and put in shallow pan. Spread with brown sugar mixed with mustard. Bake in moderate oven (375°F.) 20 minutes, or until glazed. Makes 8 to 10 servings.

RED-FLANNEL HASH

2 cups chopped cooked corned beef
2 cups chopped cooked beets
4 cups chopped cooked potato
1 large onion, chopped
Salt and pepper to taste
2 tablespoons Worcestershire
Light cream
1/4 cup bacon or pork drippings

Combine beef with beets, potato, onion, seasonings and enough cream to bind mixture. Heat drippings in large skillet. Spoon meat mixture into skillet and spread evenly in pan. Cook over low heat, without stirring, until the bottom is well crusted. Fold as for omelet. Makes 4 to 6 servings.

CORNED-BEEF AND CORN FRITTERS

1 can (8-3/4 ounces) cream-style corn
2 eggs
3/4 cup milk
2 tablespoons baking powder
2 cups all-purpose flour
1 teaspoon salt
1 can (7 ounces) corned beef, chopped
Fat for deep frying

Mix all ingredients, except fat. Drop by tablespoonfuls into hot deep fat (360°F. on a frying thermometer) and fry, turning frequently, 5 to 6 minutes, or until golden brown and done. Drain on absorbent paper and serve hot. Makes 4 to 6 servings.

CORNED BEEF, NEW POTATOES AND PEAS IN CREAM

1 pound small new potatoes
1 teaspoon salt
1 box (10 ounces) frozen peas
1 can (12 ounces) corned beef, diced
2/3 cup heavy cream
1/8 teaspoon pepper

Peel potatoes and cook with salt in 2 cups boiling water until almost tender. Add peas and cook until vegetables are tender. Drain and add beef, cream and pepper. Heat well. Makes 4 servings.

CORNED-BEEF AND RICE CASSEROLE

1 can (12 ounces) corned beef, broken in small pieces
2 tablespoons each minced green pepper, onion and canned pimiento
1 cup cooked rice (about 1/3 cup before cooking)
1 cup dairy sour cream
1/4 pound Cheddar-cheese slices

Mix all ingredients, except cheese. Put in shallow 1 1/2-quart baking dish and top with cheese slices. Bake in hot oven (400°F.) about 20 minutes. Serves 4 to 6.

CORNED-BEEF SUCCOTASH

2 boxes frozen succotash
1 can (12 ounces) corned beef, diced
1/2 teaspoon chili powder
1/2 teaspoon seasoned salt
1/8 teaspoon pepper
1 tablespoon instant minced onion

Cook succotash as directed on the label. Drain off most of water. Add remaining ingredients and heat well. Makes 4 servings.

CORNED BEEF BAKED IN SHERRY

4 pounds corned beef brisket or rump
6 whole allspice
1 stalk celery, diced
1 carrot, diced
Whole cloves
1/4 cup fine dry bread crumbs
2 tablespoons brown sugar
1/2 teaspoon dry mustard
1/2 cup sherry

Cook beef as in Simmered Corned Beef, page 57, adding allspice, celery and carrot. Cool in broth, then remove to shallow baking pan. Score fat in 1" squares and stud with cloves. Mix next 3 ingredients and cover the fat, pressing down firmly. Pour sherry over top. Bake in slow oven (300°F.) 1 hour, basting several times with drippings in pan. Serve hot or cold. Makes 8 servings.

CORNED-BEEF STEW, CAMP STYLE

1 can (12 ounces) corned beef, coarsely chopped
1 can (8 ounces) tomato sauce
1 large onion, chopped
4 cups diced peeled potato
2 cups sliced carrot
2 teaspoons salt
1/2 teaspoon pepper

Put all ingredients in large kettle with 4 cups water. Bring to boil, cover and simmer 30 minutes, or until vegetables are tender. Serve in bowls. Good with seeded breadsticks, toasted French bread or corn muffins. Makes 4 servings. *Note* Carry cooked stew to picnic in thermos jug. Or take ingredients to cook over campfire.

CORNED-BEEF, GREEN-BEAN AND POTATO SKILLET

4 onions, sliced
2 cloves garlic, minced
1/4 cup olive oil
2 cups diced peeled potato
2 cups cooked corned beef in 1" cubes
2 cups cut green beans
1 cup bouillon
Salt and pepper
Chopped parsley

Cook onions and garlic in the oil 2 to 3 minutes. Add potato and beef and cook 5 minutes. Add beans and bouillon. Bring to boil, cover and simmer 15 minutes, or until vegetables are tender, adding a little water if necessary. Season, and sprinkle with parsley. Serves 4 to 6.

CORNED-BEEF AND CABBAGE CASSEROLE

1 small white or green cabbage, cored, quartered and diced
Salt and pepper
2 cups diced cooked corned beef
1/4 cup butter or margarine
1/4 cup flour
2 cups milk
1 cup light cream
1-1/2 tablespoons prepared mustard
1/2 teaspoon Worcestershire
2 tablespoons grated Parmesan cheese

Cook the cabbage in small amount of boiling salted water about 10 minutes, or until almost tender. Drain cabbage and put half in greased 3-quart casserole. Add beef and cover with remaining cabbage. Melt butter and blend in flour. Gradually add milk and cream and cook, stirring, until thickened. Add mustard, Worcestershire, and salt and pepper to taste. Pour over ingredients in casserole. Sprinkle with cheese. Bake in moderate oven (350°F.) about 1 hour. Makes 6 servings.

CORNED-BEEF AND POTATO CAKE

1 pound (3 medium) potatoes, peeled and grated
1 can (12 ounces) corned beef, finely chopped
1/2 cup all-purpose flour
2 eggs, slightly beaten
1 cup milk
Salt and pepper
3 tomatoes, sliced
2 tablespoons grated Cheddar cheese
2 tablespoons chopped parsley

Mix first 5 ingredients. Season with salt and pepper. Pour into well-greased 13" x 9" x 2" baking pan. Bake in hot oven (400°F.) 30 minutes. Remove from oven and top with tomatoes. Sprinkle with cheese. Bake 10 minutes, or until cheese is melted. Sprinkle with parsley. Serves 4 to 6.

CORNED-BEEF AND BEAN BAKE

1 onion, chopped
2 tablespoons butter
2 tablespoons molasses
1 teaspoon dry mustard
1/2 teaspoon salt
Dash of pepper
1 teaspoon steak sauce
1 tablespoon vinegar
1 can (12 ounces) corned beef, coarsely chopped
1 can (1 pound) dried lima beans, undrained
1 can (1 pound) red kidney beans, undrained

Cook onion in the butter 2 to 3 minutes. Add remaining ingredients and pour into shallow 2-quart baking dish. Bake in moderate oven (350°F.) about 30 minutes. Makes 4 to 6 servings. *Note* If preferred, use 2 cans of one kind of beans.

CORNED-BEEF AND VEGETABLE STEW

2 cloves garlic
2 tablespoons olive oil
1 cup chopped onion
2 cups sliced raw potato
2 cups beef bouillon
1 can (12 ounces) corned beef, diced
1 green pepper, diced
1 cup diced celery
1/4 cup minced parsley

In heavy saucepan, sauté garlic in oil 5 minutes. Discard garlic and add onion and potato to skillet. Sauté 10 minutes, stirring frequently. Add bouillon and beef and simmer, covered, until potato is almost tender. Add green pepper and celery and simmer a few minutes longer, or until potato is tender and pepper and celery are still crisp. Sprinkle with parsley. Makes 4 to 6 servings.

SATURDAY-NIGHT SPECIAL

8 ounces elbow macaroni
Salt
1 medium onion, chopped
1 medium green pepper, chopped
2 tablespoons butter or margarine
1 can (1 pound) tomatoes
1 can (6 ounces) tomato paste
1/4 teaspoon pepper
1/2 pound sharp Cheddar cheese, grated
1 can (12 ounces) corned beef, diced

Cook macaroni in boiling salted water 6 to 7 minutes. Drain and rinse with cold water. Cook onion and green pepper in the butter 2 to 3 minutes. Add next 3 ingredients, 1 teaspoon salt and 1 cup water. Bring to boil. In greased 3-quart casserole, make a layer of half the macaroni. Sprinkle with one-third of cheese. Add beef and remaining macaroni. Sprinkle with another third of cheese and top with tomato mixture. Mix lightly and sprinkle with remaining cheese. Bake in slow oven (325°F.) about 1 hour. Makes 8 servings. *Note* Broken straight macaroni or seashells can be substituted for the elbow macaroni.

DEEP-DISH CORNED-BEEF PIE WITH CHEESE CRUST

All-purpose flour
Salt and pepper
1/4 cup grated Parmesan cheese
1/3 cup shortening
1 cup sliced celery
1 can (4 ounces) sliced mushrooms
1/4 cup butter or margarine
1/2 teaspoon dry mustard
2 cups diced cooked corned beef

For crust, mix 1 cup flour, 1/4 teaspoon salt, cheese and shortening with fork. Mix in 2 tablespoons ice water and shape in a ball; chill. Bring 1 1/2 cups water to boil, add celery and cook 5 minutes. Drain, reserving liquid. Drain mushrooms, adding liquid to celery cooking water. Measure 1 1/4 cups. Melt butter; blend in 1/4 cup flour and the mustard. Add liquid; cook, stirring, until thickened. Add celery, mushrooms and beef. Season with salt and pepper to taste. Pour into a casserole 8 1/2" wide and 2" deep. Roll out cheese pastry; cut in 3/4" strips. Arrange lattice-fashion on casserole. Bake in hot oven (425°F.) 20 minutes, or until lightly browned. Makes 4 to 6 servings. *Note* One package pastry mix or 1 stick can be used to make the lattice top. Add cheese to mixture before adding water.

JELLIED CORNED-BEEF RING

3 envelopes unflavored gelatin
2-1/2 cups beef bouillon
3 cups diced cooked corned beef
Prepared horseradish, salt and white pepper to taste
Potato salad (optional)
Parsley

Sprinkle gelatin on 1/2 cup water, add bouillon and heat, stirring, until gelatin is dissolved. Pour 1/2 cup into a 1 1/2-quart ring mold and chill until firm. Mix remainder with corned beef and season with horseradish, salt and pepper. Chill until slightly thickened and pour into mold. Chill until firm. Unmold on serving plate and fill center with potato salad, if desired. Garnish with parsley. Makes 6 to 8 servings. *Note* This is a firm mold resembling head cheese in texture.

QUICK CORNED BEEF AND CABBAGE

6 small white onions, peeled
Salt
6 potatoes, scrubbed and halved
1 medium head cabbage, cored and quartered
Salt and pepper
1 can (12 ounces) corned beef, cut in chunks
Chopped parsley
Prepared mustard

Cook onions in small amount of boiling salted water 15 minutes. Add potatoes and cook 15 minutes. Add cabbage and cook until vegetables are tender. Season with salt and pepper. Add beef, cover and heat. Sprinkle with parsley and serve with mustard. Makes 4 to 6 servings.

CORNED-BEEF AND BEAN CASSEROLE

1 box each frozen cut green beans, wax beans and lima beans
2 tablespoons butter or margarine
2 tablespoons flour
1/2 teaspoon salt
Dash of pepper
1/8 teaspoon Worcestershire
1 cup milk
1 can corned beef, diced
1/3 cup grated Parmesan cheese

Cook beans separately as directed on individual packages. Drain and mix lightly. Melt butter and blend in flour and seasonings. Gradually add milk and cook, stirring, until smooth and thickened. Add corned beef and beans and mix lightly. Put in shallow 2-quart baking dish and sprinkle with cheese. Bake in moderate oven (375°F.) 20 minutes, or until heated and lightly browned. Serves 6.

CORNED-BEEF AND MASHED-POTATO PATTIES

1 cup minced onion
4 tablespoons butter or margarine
3 cups cold mashed potato
1 can (12 ounces) corned beef, finely chopped
1 egg, beaten
1/2 cup all-purpose flour
Salt and pepper
1/4 cup fine dry bread crumbs
Cranberry sauce (optional)

Brown onion slowly in 2 tablespoons butter. Add next 4 ingredients and season lightly with salt and pepper. Shape in ten 3" patties 1/2" thick. Dip both sides in bread crumbs and brown slowly in remaining butter. Serve hot, with cranberry sauce, if desired. Serves 4 to 5.

CORNED-BEEF PICADILLO

3 cups diced cooked corned beef
2 tablespoons olive oil
3 cups diced peeled potato
Salt, pepper and paprika
1 bay leaf, crumbled
1/2 cup each white wine and water, or 1 cup water and pimiento liquid
1 jar (4 ounces) pimientos, chopped
1/4 cup minced parsley

Brown beef lightly in the oil. Add potato and sprinkle with salt, pepper and paprika. Cook over high heat, stirring, until potato browns slightly. Add bay leaf and liquid. Bring to boil, cover and simmer about 20 minutes. Add pimiento and sprinkle with parsley. Makes 4 to 6 servings.

CORNED-BEEF PIZZA

2 cups all-purpose flour
1/2 teaspoon salt
3/4 cup vegetable shortening
1 teaspoon vinegar
1 can (12 ounces) corned beef, chopped
2 tablespoons catsup
4 anchovy fillets, chopped
1/4 cup chopped pimiento-stuffed olives
3 tomatoes, sliced
Freshly ground pepper
1/2 teaspoon oregano
2 tablespoons grated Parmesan cheese

Mix flour and salt in bowl and cut in shortening. Mix 1/4 cup cold water and vinegar and add to flour, mixing lightly with fork to form a ball. Chill, then roll out on slightly greased large baking sheet to form a 12" circle. Flute edges and bake in hot oven (425°F.) 10 minutes. Cool. Mix beef and next 3 ingredients. Spread on pastry, leaving rim uncovered. Top with tomato slices and sprinkle with remaining ingredients. Bake in very hot oven (450°F.) 10 minutes or until crust is well browned. Serves 4 to 6.

CORNED-BEEF AND CHEESE STRATA

7 slices firm bread, crust removed
1/4 pound sharp Cheddar cheese, shredded
1 cup finely diced cooked corned beef
2 eggs, beaten
1-1/4 cups milk
1/2 teaspoon salt
Dash of cayenne
2 teaspoons butter

Put a layer of bread in bottom of greased shallow 1½-quart baking dish, cutting slices to fit. Sprinkle one third of cheese and beef on bread. Repeat twice and top with a layer of bread. Mix eggs, milk, salt and cayenne and pour over bread mixture. Dot with butter. Bake in moderate oven (350°F.) about 30 minutes. Makes 6 servings.

CORNED-BEEF HASH, SWEDISH STYLE

1 cup chopped onion
4 tablespoons butter or margarine
3 cups diced cooked potato
3 cups diced cooked corned beef
Salt, pepper and paprika
Fried or poached eggs, pickles or catsup (optional)

Cook onion in 1 tablespoon butter over low heat until soft and golden. Put in large saucepan. In 2 tablespoons butter in hot skillet, sauté potato until crisp. Add to onion. In remaining butter, quickly brown beef. Mix carefully with potato and onion. Season; heat. Serve with eggs and pickles or catsup, if desired. Serves 6.

CORNED-BEEF TURNOVERS WITH MUSHROOM SAUCE

1 can (7 ounces) corned beef
1 can condensed cream of mushroom soup
1 small onion, grated
2 sprigs parsley, chopped
Pepper
Standard Pastry (page 419)
Undiluted evaporated milk
1/3 cup milk
1/2 teaspoon Worcestershire

Mince beef and add 1/4 cup soup, the onion, parsley and pepper to taste. Roll pastry in a 16" x 8" rectangle and cut in eight 4" squares. Spoon meat mixture on one corner of each square, moisten edges with water and fold over to form triangles. Crimp edges with fork and brush with evaporated milk. Put on baking sheet and bake in hot oven (425°F.) about 20 minutes. Mix remaining soup with fresh milk and Worcestershire. Heat and serve as sauce for turnovers. Makes 4 servings.

CORNED-BEEF CABBAGE ROLLS

8 large white cabbage leaves
Salt
3/4 cup uncooked rice
1 can (12 ounces) corned beef, diced
1 small onion, minced
1 can (12 ounces) vegetable-juice
  cocktail
Pepper
1/2 teaspoon nutmeg
1 can (1 pound) tomatoes, diced
1/2 teaspoon oregano
1 tablespoon brown sugar
1/2 teaspoon garlic salt (optional)

Cook cabbage leaves in small amount of boiling salted water until tender. Drain and remove some of tough membrane. Cook rice in 2 cups boiling water until water is absorbed and rice is tender. Cool and add beef, onion and vegetable juice. Mix well and season with salt, pepper and the nutmeg. Divide evenly into cabbage leaves. Roll up, folding sides toward center. Arrange, seam side down, in shallow baking dish. Mix remaining ingredients and pour over cabbage rolls. Bake in hot oven (400°F.) 45 minutes, or until well browned. Makes 6 to 8 servings.

CORNED-BEEF HASH WITH CHEESE

1 onion, chopped
1 green pepper, chopped
2 tablespoons fat
1 can (1 pound) corned-beef hash
1/2 pound sharp Cheddar cheese, diced

Cook onion and pepper slowly in hot fat in skillet 5 minutes. Add hash and cook until slightly browned, stirring often. Stir in cheese and cook just long enough to melt it partially. Makes 2 servings.

CORNED-BEEF-HASH AND EGG SANDWICHES

4 slices bread
Prepared mustard
1 can (1 pound) corned-beef hash
Onion salt
Melted butter or margarine
1 can condensed celery soup
1/2 cup milk
2 hard-cooked eggs, chopped
4 slices toast
Paprika

Spread bread with mustard, then with hash. Sprinkle with onion salt and brush with butter. Bake in very hot oven (450°F.) about 10 minutes. Heat together soup, milk and eggs. Top corned-beef-hash slices with toast and serve soup mixture for a sauce. Sprinkle with paprika. Serves 4.

DINTY MOORE'S DOLL-UP

1 whole corned beef brisket (9 to 10
  pounds)
1/3 cup sugar
1/4 cup currant jelly
1 medium head cabbage
1/4 pound fat salt pork
8 small potatoes, boiled
Paprika
Parsley (optional)

Cover corned beef with cold water and simmer, covered, 5 to 6 hours, skimming off fat frequently. Add boiling water as often as necessary during cooking. Fifteen minutes before beef is done, add sugar. Cool slightly, put in broiler pan and spread with jelly. Put under broiler for a few minutes, or until well glazed. Wash cabbage, cut in eighths and cook with the salt pork 10 to 15 minutes. Slice corned beef on platter, surround with the cabbage and boiled potatoes. Sprinkle potatoes with a little paprika. Garnish with parsley, if desired. Makes 4 servings, with meat left over.

CORNED-BEEF HASH O'BRIEN

1 medium onion, minced
1 medium green pepper, chopped
2 tablespoons butter or margarine
2 canned pimientos, chopped
2 cans (1 pound each)
  corned-beef hash

Cook onion and green pepper in the butter until onion is lightly browned. Add pimientos and hash and cook, stirring occasionally, until hash is well browned. Makes 4 servings.

CORNED-BEEF AND VEGETABLE BAKE

1 tablespoon instant minced onion
1 can (12 ounces) corned beef, broken
  in pieces
2 cups diced cooked potato
1-1/4 cups undiluted evaporated milk
1 teaspoon salt
1/4 teaspoon pepper
3 tablespoons butter
3 tablespoons flour
1 can (16 ounces) whole-kernel corn,
  undrained
1/3 cup shredded Cheddar cheese

Mix onion, beef, potato, 1/2 cup milk, 1/2 teaspoon salt and 1/8 teaspoon pepper. Press against sides and bottom of shallow 2-quart baking dish. Melt butter and blend in flour and remaining salt and pepper. Add corn liquid and remaining milk and cook, stirring, until thickened. Add corn and pour into lined baking dish. Sprinkle with cheese. Bake in moderate oven (350°F.) about 30 minutes. Makes 4 to 6 servings.

ROBERT E. COATES

LAMB, VEAL, VARIETY MEATS

Puszta Schnitzel

HOW TO BUY LAMB

Wholesome lamb carries the Federal stamp "U. S. Inspected and Passed." It may also have a stamp indicating the quality grade. Grades are Prime, Choice and Good.

A clear clue to the quality of lamb is the color of the uncooked lean meat, which varies with the age of the animal. Young, milk-fed lamb will have light pink lean. Spring lamb (under one year of age) will have deeper pink lean and the average market lamb will have a pinkish-red lean. The texture should always be fine and velvety. The fat should be smooth, firm, white, rather brittle but of a waxy consistency.

The outer fat is covered with a parchment-like tissue called the fell, which helps keep the wholesale cut fresh and protected if the lamb is aged. This is sometimes removed from retail cuts before they are offered for sale.

For lamb for a small family, a practical way to use a leg of lamb is to have it divided into three types of cuts: chops cut from the loin end, a roast from the center, and the meat from the lower leg cut for stewing.

HOW TO BUY VEAL

Veal is beef less than three months old. The inspecting and stamping system is the same as for lamb. The color of lean veal, like lamb, varies with the age of the animal, becoming redder with increasing age. The lean portions of young, milk-fed veal will be grayish-pink. The texture should be fine and velvety.

STORAGE OF LAMB AND VEAL

Keep in the coldest part of the refrigerator, loosely wrapped in waxed paper. Use chops or steaks within 2 to 3 days. Roasts can be kept a little longer, but use ground meat within 24 hours of purchase.

VARIETY MEATS

Variety or organ meats include sweetbreads, liver, kidneys, brains, heart and tongue and are more perishable than the muscle meats. They must be absolutely fresh, firm to the touch and sweet in odor when purchased. They should be kept in coldest part of refrigerator not longer than 2 days. Cooked, these meats can be stored in refrigerator 1 to 2 days.

HOW TO STRETCH CERTAIN CUTS OF LAMB

RACK OF LAMB REVISED

Purchase 1 whole rack of lamb.

Note In supermarkets this cut is almost always cut and sold as chops, so you may have to order it in advance. By purchasing the whole rack you should be able to save 10 to 20 percent of cost. Have meat cutter divide rack in 2 parts and remove backbone.

Cut 1 Frenched rack and 8 Frenched chops or 4 double-thick rib chops.

1 Place half the rack fat-side up. Score fat deeply until tip of knife touches rib bone, working straight across width of rack at a distance of about 2″ from top of rib bone. Continue to cut horizontally with knife. With other hand, lift entire strip of fat from tip of bones (this is purely waste fat; discard it). There will now be 8 or 9 rib bones exposed, depending on how rack was cut originally.

2 With knife, pare away all fat and meat between rib bones. Make sure each protruding rib is virtually bare of meat for about 1½″ to 2″ from tip (this is called Frenching a rib bone).

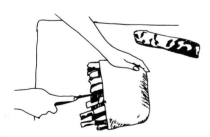

3 Trim excess fat from roast.

4 Cut away tiny blade bone. Roast is now ready to put in oven. Makes 4 servings.

Blade bone

Includes material from The Meat Book: A Consumer's Guide to Selecting, Buying, Cutting, Storing, Freezing and Carving the Various Cuts *by Travers Moncure Evans and David Greene with*

5 Place other half of rack on its flat surface. To make Frenched chops, proceed as above. Turn roast fat-side down and slice between ribs vertically to divide in 8 or 9 chops. (It is not necessary to French chops. Frenching serves no purpose other than making a regular rib chop a bit fancier, but if you like the little touch it adds, you can save money by doing it yourself rather than having it done by a butcher.)

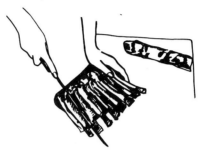

6 For double-thick rib chops, omit first two steps. Remove excess fat and blade bone, then place half rack on its flat surface and slice vertically following every other rib. You will get 4 fat chops.

Note To keep rib bones from charring while lamb cooks, cap each with a piece of foil. If desired, present roast at table with a paper frill atop each rib.

ROAST RACK OF LAMB

To roast lamb rack, put in roasting pan and season with salt, pepper and rosemary. Roast in moderate oven (375°F.) 45 minutes, or until meat thermometer registers 145°F. to 150°F. for rare. Roast 10 to 15 minutes for well done.

ROAST LAMB WITH PEACHES AND CHUTNEY GLAZE

1 can (1 pound) sliced cling peaches
1/3 cup chutney
Frenched lamb rack

Drain peaches, reserving half the syrup. Mix syrup with the chutney. Put lamb in roasting pan and baste with chutney mixture. Roast in moderate oven (375°F.) basting frequently with glaze, 45 minutes, or until meat thermometer registers 145°F. to 150°F. for rare. Roast 10 to 15 minutes longer for well done. When roasted to desired doneness, arrange peaches around meat, baste with glaze and heat in oven a few minutes. Makes 4 servings.

illustrations by Dana J. Greene, to be published by Charles Scribner's Sons. Text Copyright © 1973 Travers Moncure Evans. Illustrations Copyright © 1973 Dana J. Greene.

A LAMB-CHOP TREAT FROM LAMB-STEW MEAT

Purchase two 1½- to 3-pound lamb breasts, with or without the flank, and 1½ pounds ground lamb.

Cut 8 double-thick lamb chops, stuffed.

1 At store if flank portion of lamb breasts is included, have it removed and ground. Add to the 1½ pounds. If store is self-service, bones at thick end of breast will generally have been cracked. If not, have them cracked.

2 Place breasts bone side down. Tuck tip of knife underneath thin layer of meat at widest end of each breast. Probe underneath layer of meat with knife, working full length and width of each breast, until you have inserted pockets about 10″ long and 4″ wide (some people find a long, thin knife makes this easier).

3 If desired, season ground lamb with herbs, garlic and spices. Divide meat in half and insert one half in each breast pocket.

4 Push ground meat all the way down and spread evenly inside breast. As pockets are stuffed, breasts will expand.

5 Turn both breasts of lamb bone side up. According to how they were orig-

inally cut, each will contain 10 to 13 rib bones. To cut double-thick chops, start at exposed end of third rib and slice length of bone all the way through breast. Continue to cut after every second or third rib. Cut each breast in 4 equally thick chops. Chops can be roasted, broiled or braised.

INDONESIAN LAMB CHOPS

1/3 cup finely chopped celery
1/3 cup finely chopped onion
1 clove garlic, crushed
1/3 cup vegetable oil
1/4 cup cider vinegar
2 teaspoons steak sauce
2 tablespoons curry powder
Dash of hot pepper sauce
3 tablespoon honey
1 teaspoon oregano
1 bay leaf
1/3 cup prepared mustard
Juice and grated rind of 1 lemon
4 lamb chops

Sauté first 3 ingredients in the oil until transparent. Add remaining ingredients, except chops, and simmer 3 minutes. Marinate chops in refrigerator, turning occasionally, several hours or overnight. Put in greased 13″ x 9″ x 12″ baking pan, brush with marinade and bake in hot oven (400°F.) about 20 minutes. Heat remaining marinade, remove bay leaf and serve as sauce. Makes 4 servings.

PEANUT-LAMB STEW

2 pounds boneless lamb stew meat
3 large onions, sliced
1-1/2 teaspoons salt
3 large ripe tomatoes, quartered
3 chili peppers, washed and seeded
1 cup peanut butter
2 cups beef bouillon
3 to 4 cups hot cooked rice
6 hard-cooked eggs, shelled

Put first 3 ingredients and 3 cups water in large kettle, bring to boil and simmer, covered, 1 hour, or until meat is almost tender. In saucepan, combine tomatoes, peppers and ½ cup water. Bring to boil and simmer, covered, 8 to 10 minutes. Force through sieve. Mix peanut butter, tomato mixture and bouillon; add to meat and simmer until meat is tender. To serve, put a helping of rice in each soup plate. Put an egg in center and cover with stew. Makes 6 servings. **Note** Dried or pickled chili peppers can be substituted for fresh.

Includes material from The Meat Book: A Consumer's Guide to Selecting, Buying, Cutting, Storing, Freezing and Carving the Various Cuts *by Travers Moncure Evans and David Greene with*

illustrations by Dana J. Greene, to be published by Charles Scribner's Sons. Text Copyright © 1973 Travers Moncure Evans. Illustrations Copyright © 1973 Dana J. Greene.

PECAN STUFFING

1 onion, chopped
1/2 cup chopped celery
1/2 cup butter
1 teaspoon salt
1/2 teaspoon paprika
5 cups diced stale bread
1-1/2 cups chopped pecans
1/2 cup chopped parsley

Cook onion and celery in butter about 5 minutes. Add remaining ingredients. Makes about 1½ quarts stuffing.

SKILLET LAMB CHOPS AND VEGETABLES

4 shoulder lamb chops
Salt and pepper
1/4 teaspoon marjoram
1 chicken bouillon cube
2 medium onions, sliced
4 potatoes, peeled and cut in quarters
1 box frozen peas and carrots

Brown chops on both sides in large skillet. Sprinkle with salt and pepper and remove. To drippings in skillet add marjoram, bouillon cube, 1 teaspoon salt, ⅛ teaspoon pepper and ½ cup water. Bring to boil, stirring. Add onions and potatoes; arrange chops over top. Cover and simmer 30 minutes. Add slightly thawed peas and carrots. Season, cover and cook 7 minutes longer, or until vegetables are tender. Makes 4 servings.

CHEESE-CRUSTED LAMB CHOPS

4 large loin lamb chops, cut 1" thick
Salt and pepper
2 tablespoons butter or margarine
1/3 cup flour
2/3 cup milk
1 egg, beaten
1 small onion, grated
1/2 cup shredded or grated Parmesan
   cheese

Brown chops on one side in oven-proof skillet over medium heat; season with salt and pepper. Turn chops and brown 5 minutes; remove from heat. Melt butter in saucepan and stir in flour to make a smooth paste. Gradually add milk, cooking and stirring to make a smooth thick sauce. Beat in egg. Cook, stirring vigorously until mixture is shiny and pulls away from pan. Mix in onion, cheese, 1 teaspoon salt and ¼ teaspoon pepper. Put one fourth of batter on each chop. Bake in moderate oven (350°F.) 30 minutes or until topping is browned. Makes 4 servings.

ROAST LEG OF LAMB WITH BROWNED POTATOES AND ONIONS

Leg of lamb (8 pounds)
6 medium potatoes, pared
1 can (1 pound) onions, drained
Salt and pepper

Put lamb on rack in roasting pan. Roast in moderate oven (325°F.) 4 to 4½ hours. About 1 hour before meat should be done, parboil potatoes 15 minutes. Drain and put in pan with meat, coating with drippings. Roast 45 minutes longer, basting potatoes occasionally and turning to brown evenly. Add onions during last ½ hour. Season vegetables. Serves 6, with meat left over.

STUFFED LAMB CHOPS

Add a little horseradish or a dash of vinegar to the tomato sauce.

6 thick loin lamb chops
2 tablespoons minced onion
1 tablespoon butter
2 tablespoons minced celery
2 tablespoons fresh white-bread crumbs
1 teaspoon grated lemon rind
1 tablespoon chopped parsley or chives
Salt and pepper
1 egg yolk
Tomato sauce

Cut a pocket in chops. Cook onion in butter until soft and golden. Combine with all other ingredients, except last 2. Moisten with egg yolk. Stuff chops and broil as usual. Serve with hot sauce. Makes 6 servings.

BROILED CHOPS PROVENÇALE

4 servings lean loin or rib lamb chops
4 tomatoes, peeled
1/2 teaspoon sugar
6 tablespoons butter or margarine
1/3 cup minced shallots
1/2 cup dry white table wine
3 cloves garlic, mashed
1/4 cup minced parsley
Salt
Freshly ground black pepper

Grill or panbroil chops to desired doneness; keep warm. Meanwhile, seed tomatoes and cut in sixths; sprinkle with sugar and set aside. Melt 2 tablespoons butter over medium heat in a large skillet. Add shallots and heat through. Add wine and cook, stirring, until slightly reduced. Add tomatoes. Cook gently until heated through but not mushy. Add remaining butter, garlic and parsley. Gently shake and tilt pan over heat to mix ingredients and soften butter. Season, pour over broiled chops and serve at once. Makes 4 servings.

CURRY-BROILED LAMB CHOPS

Trim excess fat from 8 rib lamb chops, about ³/₄″ thick. Marinate in mixture of 1 tablespoon curry powder, ¼ teaspoon ground ginger, 1 crushed clove garlic and ³/₄ cup soy sauce for 1 to 2 hours in refrigerator, turning several times. Broil to desired doneness. Makes 4 servings.

TROPICAL CHOPS

Broil 4 lamb chops, about ³/₄″ thick, to desired degree of doneness. Meanwhile blend ½ teaspoon cornstarch, 1 tablespoon soy sauce, 1 can (13 ounces) pineapple tidbits and syrup, and ⅓ cup flaked coconut. Cook over medium heat, stirring, until slightly thickened. Pour on chops; salt and pepper to taste. Makes 4 servings.

BRAISED LAMB SHANKS WITH VEGETABLES

4 lamb shanks (about 3-1/2 pounds)
2 tablespoons fat
Salt and pepper
8 carrots, peeled
4 medium potatoes, peeled
1/8 teaspoon thyme
2 medium zucchini, sliced

Brown lamb shanks in fat in heavy kettle; pour off fat. Put a low rack under meat. Add ½ cup water and season with salt and pepper. Bring to boil, cover and simmer 1½ hours, or until meat is tender. Remove rack. Add carrots, potatoes and thyme to kettle. Cook 30 minutes longer. Add zucchini and cook 10 to 15 minutes more. Serves 4.

CORN-SAUSAGE STUFFING

2 boxes (10 ounces each) frozen whole-kernel corn
1/2 pound sausage meat
1 cup chopped onion
2-1/2 quarts soft stale-bread crumbs
2 teaspoons salt
1/2 teaspoon pepper
1-1/2 teaspoons poultry seasoning

Cook corn as directed on the label; drain. Cook sausage until browned but not hard, crumbling with a fork. Remove sausage, reserving ¼ cup drippings in skillet. Add onion and cook until golden. Mix onion and drippings with cooked corn, add sausage and remaining ingredients and mix well. Makes about 3½ quarts stuffing, or enough for a 14- to 18-pound turkey.

BAKED ORANGE LAMB STEAKS

2 lamb steaks, trimmed of excess fat
1 teaspoon salt
2 medium oranges, sliced
2 tablespoons brown sugar
1 tablespoon grated orange rind
1/2 teaspoon ginger
1/4 teaspoon cloves
1 teaspoon dried mint flakes
1/4 cup melted butter

Cut lamb steaks in half and arrange in shallow baking dish. Sprinkle with salt; top with oranges. Pour mixture of remaining ingredients over steaks. Bake in moderate oven (325°F.) about 40 minutes, basting often. Makes 4 servings.

LAMB AND BARLEY STEW

1/3 cup medium barley
2 cups diced roast lamb
2 tablespoons butter or margarine
2 medium onions, sliced
2 sprigs parsley, minced
1/2 cup chopped celery tops
2 teaspoons salt
4 medium potatoes, peeled and halved
6 carrots, peeled and quartered

Cover barley with 4 cups water and soak 1 hour. Brown lamb lightly in butter in kettle. Add undrained barley and remaining ingredients, except potato and carrot. Bring to boil, cover and simmer 1½ hours. Add potato and carrot. Simmer 30 minutes, or until vegetables are tender, adding more water if necessary. Makes 6 servings.

LAMB SHANKS BAKED IN FRUITED WINE

4 lamb shanks
Salt and pepper
Flour
1 cup dry red wine
1 cup each dried apricots and pitted prunes, each cooked just until tender
1/2 cup each golden raisins and sugar
2 tablespoons each vinegar, lemon juice and honey
1/2 teaspoon each cinnamon and ground allspice

Season lamb shanks with salt and pepper; dust with flour. Put in baking pan. Cover and bake in moderate oven (350°F.) about 1½ hours, or until meat is tender. Meanwhile, combine remaining ingredients in saucepan. Bring to boil, then simmer 5 minutes. Drain excess fat from lamb; pour wine sauce over. Cover and bake in hot oven (400°F.) 30 minutes longer. Serve lamb with fruit sauce. Makes 4 servings.

BUTTERFLIED LEG OF LAMB

Barbecue outdoors a leg of lamb that's been boned and opened out.

Place butterflied leg of lamb (5 to 6 pounds before boning) on grill, fat side up, over medium coals. Cook 50 to 60 minutes, basting frequently with Wine Sauce and turning occasionally. To carve, start at one end and cut across the grain into thin slices. Makes 8 servings.

Wine Sauce
1 teaspoon salt
1/4 teaspoon ground ginger
1 tablespoon each instant minced onion,
   dried rosemary and marjoram
1 large bay leaf, crumbled
1 cup each dry wine and beef or
   chicken stock
2 tablespoons each orange marmalade
   and wine vinegar

Combine all ingredients in a saucepan; simmer 20 minutes, stirring occasionally. Brush over lamb before and during grilling.

Cheesed Barbecued Lamb Slices Rub surface of butterflied leg of lamb with salt, pepper and 1/4 teaspoon ground cumin. Grill as directed, basting occasionally with simple French dressing. Carve lamb in very thin slices. Top each one with a thin slice of Muenster cheese, using about 1 pound. Arrange overlapping on platter; sprinkle with more cumin.

LAMB ROAST, SOUTHWESTERN

Leg of lamb (6 pounds), boned, rolled
   and tied
1 cup dry red table wine
1/2 cup orange juice
1/4 cup chili sauce
1 onion, minced
2 tablespoons olive oil
1 tablespoon each chili powder and
   brown sugar
1 teaspoon crushed cumin seed
3/4 teaspoon crumbled dried oregano
1/2 teaspoon each salt and pepper

Place lamb in deep pan. Mix remaining ingredients and 1/4 cup water; pour over meat. Let stand in refrigerator 24 hours, turning occasionally. Drain meat; place on rack in an open roasting pan. Roast in a very hot oven (450°F.) 15 minutes. Reduce temperature to moderate (350°F.), pour marinade over meat and continue roasting meat 2 1/2 hours, or until of desired doneness (140°F. on meat thermometer for rare, 185°F. for well done). Baste frequently during roasting. Add a few tablespoons boiling water if necessary to prevent burning. At serving time, skim off fat and serve juices as sauce with meat.

SWEDISH COFFEE-BASTED ROAST LAMB

Leg of lamb (5 to 6 pounds)
Salt and pepper
1 cup strong hot coffee
1/4 cup light cream
2 tablespoons sugar
2 tablespoons flour
Red currant jelly

Rub lamb with salt and pepper. Roast as usual, basting during last hour with coffee mixed with cream and sugar. Make gravy from pan drippings: Skim off excess fat. Lightly brown flour. Mix with cold water to a thin paste; stir into drippings, beating well. Add water as needed for gravy consistency, simmering until thick and smooth. Check seasoning. To each cup of gravy add 1 tablespoon currant jelly; heat and stir until jelly melts. Serve with lamb. Makes 8 servings.

CROWN ROAST OF LAMB

1/2 cup chopped green pepper or
   pimiento
1 cup chopped mushrooms
1/4 cup vegetable oil
1 cup small white onions, cooked
2 cups cooked wild rice or brown rice
Salt and pepper
1/2 teaspoon marjoram
Crown roast of lamb (5 to 6 pounds)

Cook green pepper and mushrooms in oil until barely tender. Add onions, rice and seasonings. Stuff center of lamb. Place on rack in roasting pan. Bake in moderate oven (325°F.) 2 1/2 to 3 hours, to desired degree of doneness. Makes 6 servings.

BASQUE BARBECUED LAMB

During barbecuing, apply the basting sauce with a brush of fresh parsley. Thin portions of the meat will be well done, thick portions slightly pink.

Butterflied leg of lamb (5 to 6 pounds
   before boning)
2 cloves garlic, minced
3/4 cup dry wine
1/4 cup chopped fresh parsley
1 teaspoon mixed dried herbs
1 teaspoon salt
1/2 teaspoon pepper
1/4 cup each olive oil and wine vinegar

Brush meat all over with mixture of remaining ingredients. Put meat on grill, fat side up, over medium coals. Cook 50 to 60 minutes, basting frequently and turning meat occasionally as it cooks. Makes 8 servings.

TRADITIONAL ENGLISH MINT SAUCE FOR ROAST LAMB

Crush 1 cup fresh mint leaves with 2 tablespoons sugar. Add ½ cup hot water. When sugar is dissolved, add ½ cup mild cider vinegar. Let stand about 2 hours before serving. Makes about 1½ cups.

SCANDINAVIAN CUCUMBER HOLLANDAISE FOR ROAST LAMB

Slice 2 peeled cucumbers into quarters lengthwise; slice thin crosswise. Cook in a small amount of boiling salted water just until tender. Drain thoroughly and fold into 1 cup hot Hollandaise sauce with dillweed to season. Makes 8 servings.

SESAME GARLIC BUTTER

Spread on hot broiled salted-and-peppered lamb chops.

Blend together ¼ cup soft butter, 1 small clove garlic, minced, 2 tablespoons toasted sesame seeds and 2 teaspoons lemon juice. Makes topping for 8 chops.

MOUSSAKA

A ground-lamb and eggplant casserole of Greek descent.

1 pound ground lamb
Butter or olive oil
3 onions, sliced
1/4 cup tomato juice
Sprig of parsley, finely chopped
Salt and pepper
4 small eggplants
2 eggs, separated
7 to 8 tablespoons bread crumbs
3 cups Medium White sauce (page 214)
Grated cheese

Brown meat in 2 teaspoons butter. Add next 3 ingredients, seasoning and ¼ cup water. While meat is heating, slice eggplant the long way and fry slices in butter until light brown. Cover bottom of greased casserole with eggplant strips. Add egg whites and about 5 tablespoons bread crumbs to meat mixture and spread half over layer of eggplant strips. Add another layer of eggplant strips and the rest of meat mixture. Add egg yolks to white sauce and spread over top layer of meat. Sprinkle with remaining bread crumbs and grated cheese. Dot with butter; bake in moderate oven (350°F.) about ½ hour. Cut in squares. Makes 4 servings.

CAPER SAUCE

Make 2 cups medium white sauce, using half milk and half lamb stock. To each cup, add 2 tablespoons capers and 1 teaspoon liquid. Makes 8 servings.

ARMENIAN LAMB STEW

2 pounds lamb shoulder, trimmed of excess fat
2 tablespoons vegetable oil
1 cup sliced onion
2 pounds spinach, cut in large pieces
1 cup tomato juice or sauce
Salt and pepper to taste

Cut meat in serving pieces; brown on all sides in oil. Add onion, cover and cook 10 minutes until tender but not brown. Add remaining ingredients and 1 cup water. Cover and simmer until tender, 40 minutes to 1 hour. Serves 4.

LAMB STEAKS IN MARINADE

2 pounds lamb-leg slices, 1" thick
3 tablespoons each olive oil and vinegar
1/2 teaspoon salt
1 small onion, minced
Few sprigs of parsley, chopped
Few leaves of rosemary, chopped
Butter

Pound meat to about ¾" thickness. Marinate several hours or overnight in refrigerator in mixture of remaining ingredients, except butter. Sauté meat quickly on both sides in small amount of hot butter in skillet. Put on hot platter. Heat marinade in skillet and pour over meat. Serves 4.

LAMB IN SOUR CREAM

3 pounds lamb-neck slices
Seasoned flour
2 tablespoons cooking oil
2 medium onions, chopped
1 clove garlic, minced
1/4 cup dry white wine
1/2 teaspoon caraway seed
1/2 teaspoon oregano
1 cup dairy sour cream
Hot cooked noodles
Paprika

Dredge lamb with seasoned flour and brown on all sides in oil in heavy kettle. Pour off fat; add next 5 ingredients and ¼ cup water. Cover and simmer 2 hours, or until meat is tender, basting occasionally. Add more water if necessary. Remove lamb and add sour cream to liquid. Heat gently and season to taste. Pour over lamb and serve with noodles sprinkled with paprika. Makes 4 servings.

DEVILED LAMB RIBLETS

3 pounds lamb riblets, cut in serving
    pieces
2 tablespoons prepared mustard
1 cup all-purpose flour
2 teaspoons salt
1/2 teaspoon pepper
1/3 cup vegetable oil
1/2 cup each chili sauce and lemon
    juice
2 tablespoons Worcestershire
1 teaspoon paprika
1/3 cup chopped onion

Trim lamb of excess fat, brush with mustard and sprinkle with flour, salt and pepper. Cook lamb in hot oil until browned on all sides. Combine remaining ingredients and 2 cups water and pour over lamb. Cover and simmer over low heat about 1½ hours. Makes 4 to 6 servings.

BROWNED FRICASSEE OF LAMB

3 pounds breast of lamb
2/3 cup all-purpose flour
1 tablespoon salt
1/2 teaspoon pepper
1 onion, sliced
Hot cooked rice, mashed potatoes or
    noodles

Cut lamb in pieces about 1½" wide and roll in a mixture of the flour, salt and pepper. Brown slowly in heavy kettle without added fat; pour off any fat that collects. Add onion and 2 cups water. Bring to boil, cover and simmer 1½ hours, or until tender, adding more water if necessary. Serve with rice. Makes 4 to 6 servings.

SHISH KEBAB

2 pounds boneless shoulder or leg of
    lamb
1 cup dry red wine
3 tablespoons red-wine vinegar
1/2 cup olive oil
1 clove garlic, crushed
1 large onion, sliced
Bay leaf, thyme, cumin, oregano, or
    marjoram as desired
Whole boiled small onions
Whole small or quartered tomatoes
Green-pepper chunks
Cubes of eggplant or zucchini

Cut lamb in 1" cubes. Marinate 24 hours in mixture of next 5 ingredients and seasonings as desired; turn cubes occasionally. String meat on skewers, alternating with pieces of vegetable. Broil to desired doneness over charcoal fire or cook in broiler, basting occasionally with the marinade. Makes 4 servings.

BARBECUED LAMB IN FOIL

An ideal meal for picnics, cooked in its own dish.

4 pounds lamb shoulder, trimmed of
    excess fat
1/3 cup flour
1 tablespoon vegetable oil
6 small onions, peeled
6 small potatoes, peeled
6 small tomatoes
1 large eggplant, peeled and cut into
    serving pieces
1/4 cup chopped green pepper
1 teaspoon each salt and seasoned salt
1/2 teaspoon pepper
2 crushed bay leaves
1/2 teaspoon dried thyme or marjoram

Cut six 15" x 15" aluminum-foil squares. Cut lamb into 6 servings; dredge in flour and brown on all sides in oil. On each square of foil place 1 piece of lamb, 1 onion, 1 potato, 1 tomato and one sixth of the eggplant pieces. Sprinkle with remaining ingredients. Fold foil; fasten each portion securely. Place in foil-lined baking pan and cover with more foil. Cook on top of coals about 2½ to 2¾ hours. Or bake in moderate oven (350°F.). Makes 6 servings.

WILD-RICE AND MUSHROOM STUFFING

2 cups wild rice
2 large onions, chopped
1 cup chopped celery with leaves
1/2 cup butter
4 cups chicken broth
1 cup chopped pecans or walnuts
2 cans (3 ounces each) chopped mush-
    rooms, drained
1/2 teaspoon poultry seasoning
Salt and pepper to taste

Cook rice, onion and celery in butter 5 minutes. Add chicken broth and bring to boil. Cover and simmer 30 minutes, or until liquid is absorbed and rice is tender. Mix thoroughly with remaining ingredients. Makes about 6 cups.

MUSTARD SAUCE

Scald ¾ cup light cream and ¼ cup sugar in top part of small double boiler over boiling water. Mix 2 tablespoons dry mustard, 1 tablespoon flour and ¼ teaspoon salt; gradually add ¼ cup cold light cream. Add to hot cream, cooking and stirring until thickened. Stir a little into 1 egg yolk, beaten. Return to double boiler and cook, stirring, 2 minutes. Remove from heat and stir in ½ cup hot water. Makes about 1⅓ cups.

LIMAS AND BREAST OF LAMB

Bring 4 cups water to boil in Dutch oven. Add ³/₄ pound (1¹/₂ cups) dried large lima beans and boil 2 minutes. Cover, remove from heat and let stand 1 hour. Brown 3 pounds breast of lamb, cut in pieces, in shallow roasting pan in hot oven (400°F.) 40 minutes, or until lightly browned. Remove meat to 3- or 4-quart casserole or baking dish, season with seasoned salt, pepper and onion or garlic salt; add 1 cup water. Cover and bake in moderate oven (350°F.) 40 minutes. Add beans and enough bean liquid to almost cover. Season beans. Cover and bake, adding more water if necessary, 1¹/₂ hours longer, or until beans and lamb are very tender. Sprinkle with chopped parsley. Makes 4 servings.

LAMB AND BEANS IN BARBECUE SAUCE

3 pounds boned lamb shoulder, trimmed of fat
1 teaspoon ground allspice
1 large onion, sliced
1/2 cup sliced celery
1 tablespoon prepared horseradish
1 cup bottled barbecue sauce
1 tablespoon chopped parsley
1 can (1 pound) vegetarian baked beans
1 cup canned tomatoes, drained

Sprinkle lamb with allspice and put in greased 3-quart casserole. Bake, uncovered, in hot oven (400°F.) 1 hour. Drain off fat and add remaining ingredients to casserole. Mix well and bake, covered, in moderate oven (375°F.) about 1 hour. Serves 6 to 8.

BARBECUED LAMB WITH VEGETABLES

3 pounds lamb breast, cut in 3" pieces
8 carrots, peeled
4 potatoes, peeled
Barbecue Sauce
1/2 cup hot cooked peas (optional)

Bake meat in shallow pan in very hot oven (500°F.) 30 minutes, or until well browned. Pour off fat and arrange carrots and potatoes in pan with meat. Cover all with Barbecue Sauce. Cover with lid or foil and bake in moderate oven (375°F.), basting several times with the sauce, 2 hours, or until all is tender. Sprinkle with peas, if desired. Makes 4 servings. **Barbecue Sauce** Mix 1 chopped large onion, 2 minced cloves garlic, ¹/₃ cup vinegar, 2 tablespoons Worcestershire, 1¹/₂ teaspoons each salt and chili powder, ¹/₄ teaspoon pepper, 1 can (8 ounces) tomato sauce and ¹/₂ cup water.

ROAST LAMB WITH COFFEE-APRICOT-GRAVY

1 lamb shoulder or leg, boned and rolled
1 tablespoon sugar
2 cups hot coffee
1/4 cup light cream
Flour
3/4 cup diced dried apricots
Salt

Put lamb on rack in shallow roasting pan and insert meat thermometer. Dissolve sugar in hot coffee and add cream. Pour about ½ cup coffee mixture over lamb. Roast in slow oven (325°F.) 30 minutes to the pound, or until meat thermometer registers 175°F. to 180°F., depending on degree of doneness desired. Baste at intervals during roasting with remaining coffee mixture and drippings in pan. Remove lamb from pan and keep warm. Skim off some of fat from liquid and add enough water to liquid to make 1 to 2 cups, or enough to make gravy. Bring to boil, scraping up essence in pan. Stir in flour (about 1 tablespoon to a cup) mixed with a little cold water and cook, stirring, until smooth and thickened. Add apricots and simmer 5 minutes, or just until apricots are plumped. Season with salt to taste. Makes 6 to 8 servings. Good with noodles, rice, mashed or boiled potatoes.

ENGLISH HOT POT

2 pounds sliced lamb neck
3 tablespoons margarine
Salt and pepper
2 medium onions, sliced
1/2 pound mushrooms, sliced
3 lamb kidneys, sliced
2 pounds potatoes, sliced 1/2" thick
3 tablespoons flour
1 teaspoon sugar
1-1/2 cups stock or bouillon

Brown lamb in the margarine. Add salt and pepper and arrange in heavy 3-quart casserole. Brown onions in same skillet used to brown meat and put on top of lamb. Add layer of mushrooms and layer of kidneys. On top, arrange potatoes, overlapping slices in neat spiral pattern. Season potatoes. Add flour and sugar to drippings in pan and blend. Slowly add broth and cook, stirring, until thickened. Pour over potatoes and cover tightly. Bake in moderate oven (350°F.) 2 hours. Remove cover last 15 to 20 minutes to brown potatoes. Makes 6 to 8 servings.

BENGAL CURRY

Serve with condiments like chutney, preserved ginger, coconut and chopped nuts.

2 pounds lamb shoulder, cut in serving pieces
2 tablespoons flour
1-1/2 teaspoons salt
2 tablespoons curry powder
2 large onions, sliced
1/2 cup margarine
2 small apples, pared, cored and chopped
1 lemon, sliced
1 clove garlic, minced
2 tablespoons brown sugar
2 tablespoons seedless raisins, plumped in water
1 tablespoon Worcestershire
2 tablespoons shredded fresh or canned coconut
1/2 cup chopped walnuts or cashews
Hot cooked rice

Dredge meat with next 3 ingredients sifted together. Sauté onions until golden in margarine in heavy skillet. Push onions to one side and brown meat. Add apples and cook over low heat 5 minutes. Stir in remaining ingredients, except rice, and 2 cups water. Bring to a boil, lower heat and cover. Simmer gently about 1 hour, or until meat is tender. Serve with hot rice. Serves 4 to 6.

SAVORY TURKISH LAMB PILAF

1/2 pound boneless lamb, cut in julienne strips
1/4 cup butter
3 medium onions, chopped fine
1/4 cup pine nuts or walnut pieces
2 cups uncooked rice
1 large fresh tomato, peeled, seeded and chopped
1/4 cup currants or chopped seedless raisins
2 teaspoons salt
1 teaspoon pepper
1/2 teaspoon ground sage
1/4 teaspoon allspice
4 cups boiling-hot bouillon
Chopped parsley or mint (optional)

Sauté lamb strips in butter until golden brown. Remove and keep hot. In the same pan cook onion until soft but not brown; add nuts and rice and cook over medium heat 5 minutes, stirring constantly. Add next 7 ingredients; stir thoroughly. Cover tightly. Cook over lowest possible heat until rice is tender and liquid absorbed, about 20 to 30 minutes. Return lamb strips to rice and heat through. Remove from heat. Cover and stand in warm place for about 15 minutes. Sprinkle with 1 to 2 tablespoons parsley or mint, if desired. Makes 6 to 8 servings.

HONEY-LIME GLAZE

Pour into 8-ounce screw-top container ³/₄ cup honey and the grated rind and juice of 1 lime. Shake well. Use for glazing lamb last hour of roasting. Makes almost 1 cup.

LAMB PIE WITH POPPY-SEED CRUST

1/3 cup lamb fat or butter
1/3 cup flour
3 cups lamb broth or bouillon
1 teaspoon gravy-seasoning-and-browning sauce
1 box frozen peas
1 can (1 pound) onions, drained
2 cups cubed roast lamb
Salt and pepper to taste
1 tablespoon poppy seed
1 stick pastry mix

Make gravy with fat, flour, broth and gravy seasoning. Add vegetables and lamb and season. Put in 2-quart casserole. Add poppy seed to pastry mix and prepare as directed on label. Roll out on floured board to fit top of casserole. Prick or cut to allow steam to escape, and fit on lamb mixture. Bake in hot oven (425°F.) 25 minutes, or until well browned. Makes 6 servings.

LANCASHIRE HOT POT

3 pounds lamb-neck slices
Salt
2 sprigs parsley
1 bay leaf
1 carrot
1 stalk celery
3 or 4 whole black peppercorns
8 medium potatoes, peeled and cut in 1/4" slices
4 medium onions, thinly sliced
1/2 pound lamb kidney, cut in 1/2" cubes
1 teaspoon thyme
Pepper

Put lamb in kettle with 3 cups water, 1 teaspoon salt and next 5 ingredients. Bring to boil, cover and simmer 1 hour, or until meat is tender. Remove meat, strain broth and reserve. Remove meat from bones. Put a layer of potato slices in well-greased 2½-quart casserole. Add a layer of onions, then a layer of lamb and kidney. Sprinkle with salt, thyme and pepper. Alternate layers of ingredients, ending with potato. Pour strained broth over top. Cover and bake in moderate oven (350°F.) 2⅓ to 3 hours. Makes 6 servings.

SAUTEED LAMB WITH ONIONS AND PEAS

2 pounds boneless lamb, cut in 1" cubes
1-1/2 tablespoons butter or margarine
1 teaspoon salt
1/2 teaspoon pepper
1 tablespoon flour
1 cup bouillon
3 tablespoons tomato sauce
12 very small white onions, peeled
1 package frozen peas, cooked

Sauté lamb in butter until brown on all sides. Season and sprinkle with flour. Add bouillon, tomato sauce and onions. Cover and simmer gently for 45 minutes to 1 hour, or until tender. Add peas; heat thoroughly. Makes 4 to 6 servings.

LAMB-APPLESAUCE CURRY

3 pounds lean boneless lamb, cut in 1-1/2" cubes
1/2 cup flour
Salt
1/4 cup vegetable oil
1 medium onion, chopped
1-1/2 tablespoons curry powder
1 cup canned applesauce
1 can (10-1/2 ounces) condensed chicken broth
1/2 cup light cream

Toss lamb cubes in flour mixed with 2½ teaspoons salt until well coated. Heat oil in skillet or Dutch oven. Add lamb and sauté until golden brown. Add any remaining flour and mix well. Add onion and next 3 ingredients, bring to boil, cover and simmer 1½ hours, or until lamb is tender. Remove from heat and stir in cream. Season with additional salt to taste. Makes 6 to 8 servings.

FINNISH MAIN-DISH SOUP

2-1/2 pounds lamb shanks
1 cup chopped onion
2 cans (10 ounces each) condensed beef broth
1 tablespoon salt
6 whole allspice
6 whole white peppercorns
1 head cabbage, about 2-1/2 pounds, shredded
1 teaspoon marjoram leaves
Chopped parsley

Brown lamb shanks slowly in heavy 5-quart kettle or Dutch oven. Add next 5 ingredients and 6 cups water. Bring to boil, cover and simmer 1 hour. Remove lamb shanks and cut off meat from bones in small cubes. Put meat back in broth and add cabbage and marjoram. Cover and simmer 45 minutes, or until cabbage and meat are tender. Add parsley to taste. Makes about 3 quarts.

ALGERIAN COUSCOUS

1 large frying chicken, cut up
3 tablespoons margarine
2 pounds boneless lamb, cubed
3 medium onions, chopped
3 tomatoes, diced
2 green peppers, sliced
2 carrots, sliced
Salt and pepper
1/8 teaspoon cayenne
1 can (1 pound) chick-peas, drained
2 cups diced winter squash
1 cup frozen peas
2 cups couscous, semolina or farina

Brown chicken in the margarine in large heavy kettle or Dutch oven. Remove chicken and brown lamb in same kettle. Add onions and cook, stirring, 2 to 3 minutes. Add chicken, water (2½ to 3 cups, or to half-cover), tomatoes, green peppers, carrots, 1 tablespoon salt, ¼ teaspoon pepper and the cayenne. Bring to boil, cover and simmer 1 hour, or until chicken and lamb are tender. Add chickpeas, squash and peas and cook 15 minutes longer, or until squash is tender. Add more salt and pepper if necessary. Cook cereal as directed on package. Serve in bowls with chicken, lamb, vegetables and liquid. Makes 8 servings.

LAMB-BANANA CURRY

2 tablespoons flour
1 teaspoon salt
1/4 teaspoon black pepper
Curry powder
2 pounds shoulder lamb chops, boned
2 large onions, chopped (about 2 cups)
1/2 cup chopped celery
2 cups chicken broth
Rind of 1 lemon, finely shredded
1" piece fresh ginger, minced
1/4 cup seedless raisins
3 large firm bananas
2 tablespoons lemon juice
1 tablespoon butter, melted
1 tablespoon light-brown sugar
Hot cooked rice

Combine first 3 ingredients with 1 tablespoon curry powder and mix well. Add lamb cut in ¾" cubes and toss until coated. Brown in Dutch oven, adding oil if necessary. Add onions and sauté 10 minutes, stirring. Skim off fat. Add next 4 ingredients. Cover and simmer 50 minutes; add raisins and simmer 15 minutes, or until very tender. Meanwhile, cut bananas in ½"-thick diagonal slices. Put in 9" piepan and sprinkle with lemon juice, butter and brown sugar mixed with 1 teaspoon curry powder. Bake in moderate oven (350°F.) 15 to 20 minutes. Serve meat stew over rice topped with bananas. Makes 6 servings.

PRESSED LAMB LOAF

Cover 4 pounds lamb shoulder with warm water in heavy kettle. Season with salt, pepper, marjoram, thyme and a little caraway seed. Bring to boil and simmer over low heat 3 to 4 hours. Remove meat and chop fine. Moisten with broth and 1½ teaspoons lemon juice and pack into 9" x 5" x 3" loaf pan. Cover with waxed paper and weight down. Chill. Unmold and cut in slices. Makes 6 to 8 servings.

LAMB-FRUIT KABOBS

2 oranges
2 pounds boneless leg or shoulder of lamb, cut in 1" cubes
1 can (1 pound) onions, drained
1 clove garlic, crushed
2 tablespoons vegetable oil
1 cup jellied whole-cranberry sauce
1/4 cup soy sauce
1/2 cup orange juice
2 tablespoons lemon juice
Hot cooked rice

Cut oranges in ½" slices; cut slices in half crosswise. Thread lamb cubes, orange slices and onions on skewers. Mix remaining ingredients, except rice, until smooth and blended. Pour over filled skewers and marinate at room temperature 1 hour. Broil 5 minutes on each side, brushing with marinade before and after broiling. Serve on bed of rice. Heat any remaining marinade and serve with kabobs. Makes 4 to 6 servings.

RICE-STUFFED LAMB SHANKS

4 short-cut lamb shanks (about 2-1/2 pounds)
1 tablespoon olive oil
2 slices lemon
3 whole cloves
Salt and pepper
1 cup uncooked rice
Few celery leaves, chopped

Brown meat on all sides in hot oil in heavy kettle. Cover with boiling water and add lemon, cloves, 1 teaspoon salt and ¼ teaspoon pepper. Cover and simmer 1½ hours. Lift out shanks, cool slightly and remove bones. Skim fat from broth and bring broth to boil. Add rice and cook 20 minutes, or until tender, adding more water if necessary. Drain rice, reserving broth. Mix rice with celery leaves; season. Stuff boned shanks with rice, put in shallow baking dish and add 1 cup broth. Bake in moderate oven (350°F.) 15 minutes. Makes 4 servings.

SHERRIED LAMB AND MUSHROOMS

1/2 pound mushrooms, sliced
2 tablespoons butter
1 teaspoon instant minced onion
1 cup leftover lamb gravy
8 slices roast lamb
1 tablespoon each grated Parmesan cheese and sherry

Brown mushrooms in butter. Add next 3 ingredients; heat well. Add cheese and sherry. Serves 4.

BARBECUED LAMB WITH POTATOES

2-1/4 pounds stewing lamb, trimmed of excess fat
1 large onion, chopped
1 can (6 ounces) tomato paste
1 clove garlic, minced
1/3 cup vinegar
2 teaspoons salt
1/2 teaspoon pepper
1 tablespoon dry mustard
1 tablespoon Worcestershire
1 small dried hot pepper, crushed, or dash of hot pepper sauce
8 hot cooked medium potatoes

Put meat in 3-quart casserole. Mix 1¼ cups water and remaining ingredients, except potatoes, in saucepan and bring to a boil; simmer 5 minutes. Pour over meat. Cover and bake in slow oven (325°F.) 2 hours, or until tender, turning twice. Put potatoes in center of hot platter, surround with meat and spoon sauce over. (If necessary, skim some of fat off sauce.) Makes 4 servings.

LAMB, EGGPLANT AND GREEN-BEAN CASSEROLE

1 pound lean lamb, cut in cubes
1 onion, chopped
1 cup diced celery
2 cups bouillon
1 large eggplant, peeled and sliced 1/4" thick
Flour
1/2 teaspoon oregano
Salt and pepper
Olive oil
1 package frozen Italian green beans, cooked
1/2 pound mozzarella cheese, sliced

Simmer first 4 ingredients, covered, until lamb is tender. Meanwhile, dip eggplant in flour seasoned with oregano, salt and pepper. Brown on both sides in 2 tablespoons olive oil, adding oil as necessary. Alternate layers of eggplant, beans, mozzarella and lamb mixture in shallow 2-quart baking dish, ending with lamb. Bake in moderate oven (350°F.) 30 minutes. Serves 4.

POTATO-TOPPED LAMB PIE

2 to 3 cups diced roast lamb
1 medium onion
1 cup lamb gravy
1/4 cup dry white wine
1 teaspoon monosodium glutamate
1/4 teaspoon each crumbled thyme and rosemary
1/2 teaspoon salt (or to taste)
Dash of garlic salt
Freshly ground pepper to taste
2 cups prepared instant mashed potatoes
2 tablespoons butter or margarine
1 egg
1/2 to 1 cup grated Cheddar cheese

Force meat and onion through coarse blade of food chopper. Add gravy, wine and seasonings. Put in shallow 1½-quart baking dish. Beat next 3 ingredients together and spread on meat mixture; sprinkle with cheese. Bake in moderate oven (350°F.) about 40 minutes. Makes 6 servings.

LAMB-POTATO CASSEROLE

1/4 cup minced onion
1/4 cup butter or margarine
4 cups diced roast lamb
6 large potatoes, cooked and diced
1/2 cup each heavy cream and dry red wine
2 tablespoons soy sauce
2 tablespoons chopped parsley
1/4 teaspoon each ground thyme and marjoram
Salt and pepper to taste
1/4 teaspoon paprika

Sauté onion in the butter 2 to 3 minutes. Add remaining ingredients, except paprika, and mix well. Put in 2½- to 3-quart casserole; sprinkle with paprika. Bake in moderate oven (350°F.) about 30 minutes. Serves 6 to 8.

SHEPHERD'S LAMB PIE

1 small onion, minced
4 tablespoons butter or margarine
3 cups ground cooked lamb
1-1/2 cups leftover or canned gravy
1 teaspoon Worcestershire
1/4 teaspoon hot pepper sauce
1-1/2 teaspoons salt
6 medium potatoes, peeled
1/4 teaspoon pepper
1/4 cup hot milk
1 egg, slightly beaten

Sauté onion in 1 tablespoon butter until soft but not brown. Remove from heat; mix in next 4 ingredients and ³/₄ teaspoon salt. Mash potatoes with remaining butter, salt, pepper and hot milk. Beat until fluffy. Put meat mixture in 1½-quart baking dish. Top with mashed potatoes, scoring with fork. Brush with beaten egg. Bake in hot oven (425°F.) 15 to 20 minutes. Makes 4 servings.

LAMB-RICE PIE

3 tablespoons dry onion-soup mix
2 cups chopped cooked lean lamb
1 teaspoon dried mint leaves
1/2 teaspoon curry powder
Dash of pepper
2 cups cooked rice (1/2 cup before cooking)
1 tablespoon dairy sour cream
1 tablespoon lemon juice
1 tablespoon Worcestershire
1 can (10-1/2 ounces) condensed cream of mushroom soup
2 tablespoons margarine, melted
1 cup milk
1 package (11 ounces) pie-crust mix

Mix 2 tablespoons soup mix and remaining ingredients, except pie-crust mix. Prepare pie-crust mix as directed on package, adding remaining soup mix. Roll out about two thirds of pastry to a circle 3" larger than inverted 1½-quart casserole. Fit pastry inside casserole and fill with lamb mixture. Roll remaining pastry to fit top of dish, adjust on mixture and cut slits for steam to escape. If desired, brush with cream. Bake in hot oven (425°F.) 20 to 25 minutes. Makes 4 to 6 servings.

CURRIED LAMB CASSEROLE WITH FLUFFY TOPPING

1 package (6 ounces) rice pilaf
Curry powder
2 cups julienne-cut cooked lamb
2 tablespoons margarine
1/2 cup raisins
1/3 cup each chopped green onion, celery and green pepper
2 tablespoons each chopped chutney, pimiento and pine nuts
1 tablespoon each white vinegar and brown sugar
1 can (10-1/2 ounces) condensed cream of chicken soup
2/3 cup milk
3 egg whites
1/2 teaspoon salt
1/3 cup mayonnaise

Prepare pilaf according to package directions, adding 2 teaspoons curry powder to mixture. Cover bottom of greased shallow 2-quart baking dish with rice mixture. Make a layer of lamb. Melt margarine in skillet, add raisins, onion, celery and pepper and sauté a few minutes. Stir in chutney, pimiento, pine nuts, vinegar and sugar. Spread on lamb. Combine soup with milk and 1 teaspoon curry powder until smooth. Pour on top. Combine egg whites and salt and beat until stiff. Fold in mayonnaise and spread on top of soup. Bake in moderate oven (350°F.) 30 minutes, or until browned, puffed and heated through. Makes 6 servings.

VEAL CHOPS IN FOIL

Brown 1½"-thick chops quickly on both sides over charcoal. Put each chop on square of heavy foil, add 1 large pat butter, salt, pepper and tarragon. Wrap well and finish cooking on grill, about 20 minutes, turning once or twice.

VEAL CHOPS, ITALIAN STYLE

4 loin veal chops, about 1/2" thick
1 teaspoon butter
Salt and pepper
1 can (4 ounces) pimientos, cut in
  pieces
4 large green or stuffed olives, chopped
1 cup tomato purée

Trim any fat from chops and brown on both sides in butter. Put in shallow baking dish and sprinkle lightly with salt and pepper. Top with remaining ingredients. Bake, uncovered, in moderate oven (375°F.) about 45 minutes, or until meat is tender. Makes 4 servings.

VEAL AND PEPPERS, ITALIAN STYLE

Serve it on hot cooked rice, macaroni or spaghetti.

1-1/2 pounds boneless lean veal
3 tablespoons olive oil
2 green peppers, cut in eighths
1 can (3 ounces) sliced mushrooms
Pinch of crushed red pepper
2 cans (8 ounces each) tomato sauce
Salt and pepper to taste

Cut meat in bite-size pieces. Brown on all sides in hot oil in skillet. Add green pepper, cover, reduce heat and cook 10 minutes, stirring occasionally. Add remaining ingredients. Simmer, covered, 30 minutes longer, or until tender. Serves 4.

VEAL PARMIGIANA

1/4 cup fine dry bread crumbs
1/4 cup grated Parmesan
1/2 teaspoon salt
1/2 teaspoon paprika
4 large or 6 small veal loin chops
1 egg, beaten
3 tablespoons butter
4 to 6 thin slices mozzarella cheese
1-1/2 cups well-seasoned tomato sauce

Mix first 4 ingredients. Dip chops in egg and roll in crumb mixture. Heat butter and brown chops on both sides. Cover each with a slice of mozzarella. Pour tomato sauce over chops. Cover and simmer about 45 minutes. If sauce is too thick, add a little hot water. Serves 4.

VEAL CHOPS SUPREME

Bone 4 veal chops about 1½" thick. Dredge in seasoned flour. Brown in hot skillet in 2 tablespoons butter. Place chops in shallow baking dish. Add hot water to skillet, scraping up browned bits. Pour over chops to half cover. Cover and bake in moderate oven (375°F.) 1 hour. Remove chops; stir 1 cup dairy sour cream into pan juices. Serve over chops. Makes 4 servings.

MUSHROOM-VEAL STEW

2-1/2 pounds veal stew meat, cubed
2 tablespoons shortening
2 large onions, quartered
1 teaspoon salt
 Freshly ground pepper
1 teaspoon gravy-seasoning-and-browning
  sauce
1/2 pound mushrooms, sliced
2 tablespoons butter or margarine
1 tablespoon flour
1/2 cup dairy sour cream
Chopped parsley

Brown meat in the shortening. Add onions and cook 8 to 10 minutes. Add ¾ cup water and seasonings. Bring to boil, cover and simmer 1 hour, or until meat is tender. Add mushrooms sautéed lightly in butter, and flour mixed with a little cold water. Cook, stirring, until thickened. Add sour cream and bring almost to boil. Sprinkle with parsley. Makes 6 servings.

VEAL STEW MARENGO

2-1/2 pounds breast of veal
Salt and pepper
6 medium onions, sliced
2 tablespoons butter
2 tablespoons vegetable oil
1/4 cup flour
1 can (29 ounces) tomatoes, drained
  and cut in large pieces
1 cup dry white wine
1 cup consomme or bouillon
1 clove garlic, minced
1/8 teaspoon each thyme and marjoram
1 bay leaf
Few sprigs of parsley, chopped
1 can (4 ounces) sliced mushrooms,
  drained
Boiled potatoes, rice or noodles

Cut meat in 1½" cubes. Season and brown with onion in hot butter and oil in large skillet. Blend in flour; add all ingredients, except last 2. Bring to boil, cover and simmer 45 minutes. Add mushrooms and simmer 15 minutes longer. Serve with potatoes. Makes 4 to 6 servings.

VEAL SCALLOPS MILANESE

An Italian scallopini dish from the town of Milan.

Cover 1½ pounds thin veal scallops with milk; soak 1 hour. Drain milk from veal and add to 2 beaten eggs. Dip scallops in flour, then in egg-milk mixture and then in ⅔ cup fine dry crumbs. Heat 6 tablespoons butter in skillet until bubbly. Sauté veal pieces until tender and browned on both sides. Drain on absorbent paper. Season to taste with salt and freshly ground black pepper. Makes 4 servings.

Veal Scallops Parmesan Add to fine dry bread crumbs used in dipping scallops: ½ cup grated Parmesan, ⅓ cup chopped parsley and 1 tablespoon fresh basil or 1 teaspoon dried basil. After veal is cooked and removed to hot platter, rinse skillet with ½ cup white wine, scraping browned bits from bottom. Pour over scallops.

BLINDE VINKEN
(Stuffed Veal Birds)

A variation of the traditional Dutch recipe.

8 slices leg of veal, about 3" x 4" x 1/2"
4 slices bread, crumbled
1/2 cup milk
1 small onion, finely chopped
2 ounces (or more) sausage meat
Salt and freshly ground pepper
2 eggs
8 thin slices bacon
1 dill pickle, cut in 8 slivers
Fine dry bread crumbs
3 tablespoons each vegetable oil and butter
1/2 cup light cream

Pound veal to ¼" thickness. For stuffing, mix next 4 ingredients with 1 teaspoon salt and a dash of pepper. Separate one egg; brush white over each piece of veal. Place a piece of bacon and a sliver of pickle on each veal slice; spread with 1 tablespoon stuffing. Roll and secure with small skewers or toothpicks. Beat slightly the remaining egg yolk and whole egg. Dip each veal bird in the egg mixture, then roll in crumbs. Chill ½ hour. When ready to cook, heat oil and butter in skillet and brown the birds well on all sides. Add ½ cup boiling water, cover and simmer 20 minutes. Remove birds to a hot platter. Add cream and cook down 1 minute. Correct the seasoning and pour over veal birds. These are especially good with mashed potatoes. Makes 4 servings.

VEAL BREAST GRATELLA

3 pounds breast of veal
2 teaspoons salt
1 stalk celery
1 carrot
1 onion
1/4 teaspoon pepper
1/8 teaspoon nutmeg
1 tablespoon chopped parsley
3 tablespoons olive oil
3 tablespoons lemon juice
2 eggs, beaten
1 tablespoon melted butter
Fine dry bread crumbs

Simmer first 5 ingredients in boiling water to cover 1 hour, or until tender. Remove meat and reserve broth for soup and other uses. Cut meat in 1" or 2" strips. Combine pepper with next 4 ingredients and meat; marinate at least 2 hours, turning occasionally. Remove meat from marinade and dry with paper towels. Mix eggs and melted butter. Dip meat into mixture, roll in crumbs and put in one layer in greased shallow baking dish. Bake in moderate oven (375°F.) 15 minutes. Turn and bake 15 minutes longer. Serves 4 to 6.

ITALIAN VEAL MOZZARELLA

1 egg
1/2 cup milk
1 teaspoon salt
1/8 teaspoon pepper
1-1/2 pounds veal cutlets, sliced 1/4" thick
Fine dry bread crumbs
1/4 cup olive oil
Mushroom-Tomato Sauce
1/4 pound mozzarella or Monterey Jack cheese, sliced

Beat together first 4 ingredients. Dip each cutlet in egg mixture, then in bread crumbs to coat both sides. Brown veal in a skillet in olive oil. Transfer to a shallow baking dish. Pour Mushroom-Tomato Sauce over. Bake in moderate oven (350°F.) 30 minutes. Arrange cheese slices over top and bake about 5 minutes longer. Makes 6 servings.

Mushroom-Tomato Sauce

1 large onion, chopped
3 tablespoons minced green pepper
1/4 pound mushrooms, sliced
2 tablespoons olive oil
2 cloves garlic, minced
2 cans (6 ounces each) tomato paste
2 cans (8 ounces each) tomato sauce
1 bay leaf
1/2 teaspoon salt
1/4 teaspoon each pepper and oregano

Sauté first 3 ingredients in the oil about 5 minutes. Add remaining ingredients, bring to boil and simmer 20 minutes. Makes about 3 cups.

VEAL POT PIE

1-1/2 pounds boneless veal shoulder
1 teaspoon salt
1/8 teaspoon pepper
1 medium onion, minced
1/4 cup flour
1 cup milk
1/2 cup cooked peas
1 cup cooked diced carrots
1/2 cup cooked diced celery
Pastry

Cut veal in 1" cubes. Put in kettle with next 3 ingredients and 4 cups boiling water. Bring to boil, cover and simmer 1¼ hours, or until meat is tender. Blend flour and milk, stir into meat mixture and cook, stirring, until thickened. Add vegetables, heat and pour into 2-quart casserole. Top with baked pastry pieces and serve. Makes 4 to 6 servings. **Pastry** Mix in bowl 2 cups all-purpose flour, ½ teaspoon baking powder and 1 teaspoon salt. Cut in ¾ cup shortening. Mix 1 slightly beaten egg yolk with 5 tablespoons water. Add to dry ingredients and blend with fork. Roll out ½" thick, about the size of top of casserole. Cut in wedges and put on baking sheet. Brush with 1 slightly beaten egg white and bake in hot oven (425°F.) about 20 minutes.

PUSZTA SCHNITZEL

A variation of Paprika Schnitzel, with favorite Hungarian vegetables.

Trim any fat from four ¼"-thick boneless slices from center rump of veal (4 ounces each). Pound each slice to ⅛" thickness. Make small vertical cuts around edge of slices; sprinkle with salt. Dip one side only into flour and fry that side first in smoking-hot lard ½" deep in skillet, 2 to 3 minutes on each side. Remove veal. Add 1 small onion, sliced, and fry until soft. Pour off all but 2 tablespoons fat. Replace veal, sprinkle with ½ teaspoon or more Hungarian sweet paprika and 1 teaspoon flour. Cook over low heat, turning and coating meat and onions with paprika and flour, from 3 to 5 minutes. Add ½ cup or more heavy cream and several tablespoons beef bouillon to give sauce consistency you prefer. Simmer until heated through, stirring. Add chopped green pepper, sautéed sliced mushrooms, tomato cubes, diced cooked carrots and cooked peas; heat through. Serve veal and vegetables smothered in sauce over broad noodles, accompanied by a green salad. Makes 4 servings.

VEAL SCALLOPS WITH WHITE WINE AND TARRAGON

Dust 1½ pounds of thin veal scallops with flour. Heat 3 tablespoons butter and 3 tablespoons oil in skillet. Brown veal pieces quickly on both sides. Season to taste with salt and 1 tablespoon fresh or 1½ teaspoons dried tarragon. Add white wine just to cover the meat. Reduce heat and continue cooking, turning meat occasionally. When the wine has cooked down and the meat is tender, remove scallops to a hot platter. Add ¼ cup more white wine to the pan. Cook rapidly for a minute or two; pour over scallops. Good with small new potatoes browned in butter and puréed spinach. Serves 4.

KIDNEYS BOLO

4 veal kidneys with most of the fat removed
Flour
3 tablespoons butter
2 tablespoons oil
Salt and pepper
1/3 cup Cognac
1 teaspoon Dijon mustard
Juice of 1/2 lemon
Hot cooked rice

Cut kidneys in ½" slices; dust lightly with flour. Brown until done on each side in hot butter and oil in chafing dish or skillet. Season with salt and pepper; flame with heated Cognac. Remove to a hot serving dish. Add mustard and lemon juice to pan juices; blend and spoon over the kidneys. Serve with rice. Makes 4 to 6 servings.

OXTAIL STEW

Cut 2 oxtails in pieces and dredge with ½ cup all-purpose flour. Brown on all sides in 2 tablespoons vegetable oil in large kettle. Add 2 quarts water, 1 teaspoon salt, ¼ teaspoon whole black peppercorns, dash of cayenne and 1 bay leaf. Bring to boil, skim, cover and simmer 3 hours. Remove oxtails, strain broth, cool and remove fat. Separate meat from bones. To broth and meat add ½ cup diced celery, 1 chopped leek or onion and 1 diced carrot. Bring to boil and simmer 30 minutes. Add ½ cup tomato purée, 1 teaspoon steak sauce, few sprigs of chopped parsley, salt and pepper. Simmer 10 minutes longer. Brown 2 tablespoons flour; blend in 1 tablespoon butter. Add to stew and bring to boil. Makes 4 to 6 servings.

VEAL IN ONION GRAVY

1-1/2 pounds thin veal cutlet
Flour
3 tablespoons butter
1 large onion, thinly sliced
1 tablespoon prepared mustard
1 teaspoon horseradish
1 teaspoon salt
1/8 teaspoon pepper
2 tablespoons lemon juice
1 cup chicken bouillon

Cut veal in serving pieces and roll in flour. Brown quickly on both sides in butter in heavy skillet. Remove veal and brown onion. Return veal to skillet with remaining ingredients. Cover and simmer 30 minutes. Makes 4 servings.

SOUR-CREAM VEAL LOAF

1-1/2 pounds ground veal
2 cups grated raw carrot
1 small onion, minced
1 can (3 ounces) chopped mushrooms, drained
1/2 cup fine dry bread crumbs
1 teaspoon salt
1/4 teaspoon pepper
1 teaspoon steak sauce
1 cup dairy sour cream

Put all ingredients in bowl and work lightly with hands until thoroughly mixed. Press into greased 9" x 5" x 3" loaf pan. Bake in moderate oven (375°F.) about 1½ hours. Remove from oven and let stand in pan about 10 minutes. Pour off any liquid and turn loaf out on hot platter. Makes 6 to 8 servings.

SPAGHETTI WITH TREVISANO SAUCE

1/4 pound each salt pork and lean pork meat, cut in 1/2" cubes
1/2 pound each veal and chicken, cut in 1½" cubes
1 clove garlic, minced
2 onions, chopped
2 green peppers, chopped
4 ripe tomatoes, peeled and diced
1 cup dry white wine
1/4 teaspoon pepper
1 bay leaf
1 tablespoon tomato paste
1/2 teaspoon powdered thyme
Salt to taste
Grated Parmesan cheese
8 ounces spaghetti, cooked

Partially cook salt pork and pour off fat. Add other meats and brown lightly. Add next 7 ingredients. Simmer, uncovered, stirring occasionally, 1 hour, or until thick, adding water as needed. Add tomato paste, thyme and salt. Serve with cheese on spaghetti. Makes 4 servings.

VEAL-PORK PIE

1 pound each diced boneless veal and pork
1/4 cup vegetable oil
1 teaspoon salt
1/4 teaspoon pepper
2 cans (10-1/2 ounces) condensed cream of chicken soup
1 cup milk
2 teaspoons dried parsley flakes
14 pimiento-stuffed olives
2 cups buttermilk biscuit mix
2 tablespoons dry onion-soup mix

Lightly brown meats in hot oil in skillet. Sprinkle with the salt and pepper. Mix soup, milk and 1 cup water; mix well with meats. Pour into 2½-quart casserole, cover and bake in moderate oven (350°F.) 1½ hours. Mix in parsley and 8 olives, sliced. Prepare biscuit dough as directed on package, adding remaining olives, sliced, and onion-soup mix. Roll to ½" thickness, cut in rounds and arrange on meat mixture. Bake in very hot oven (450°F.) about 15 minutes. Makes 6 servings. **Note** If preferred, substitute favorite biscuit recipe for the biscuit mix.

JELLIED VEAL

3-1/2 to 4 pounds veal shanks, neck or breast
1 pound pork shank
Salt
5 whole white peppercorns
5 whole allspice
2 bay leaves
1 medium onion, quartered
Ground white pepper
Pickled beets

Put veal and pork shank in heavy kettle. Add water to cover and 1½ tablespoons salt. Bring to rapid boil and skim well. Add whole peppercorns, allspice, bay leaf and onion, and simmer slowly, covered, 1½ hours, or until meat is very tender. Take meat from broth and remove bones and gristle. Put bones back in broth and reduce broth while chopping meat very fine. Strain broth, return to kettle (you should have about equal parts broth and chopped meat) and add meat. Bring to boil and season with salt and white pepper to taste. Pour into mold rinsed in cold water and refrigerate overnight. When ready to serve, run small spatula around edge, dip mold in warm water and shake out on platter. Serve in slices with pickled beets. Makes 12 servings.

GYPSY STEW

1 large onion, minced
3 tablespoons margarine or other fat
1 teaspoon caraway seed
2 tablespoons marjoram
1 teaspoon paprika
1 tablespoon vinegar
2 tablespoons chili sauce
1 pound boneless beef chuck, cut in 1" cubes
1 pound lamb-neck slices
1 pound shoulder pork chops, cut in pieces
Salt and pepper
1 can (10 ounces) condensed beef broth
Hot cooked rice, noodles or mashed potatoes

In Dutch oven sauté onion in 1 tablespoon margarine until lightly browned. Add next 5 ingredients. In heavy skillet brown meats, including bones, in remaining margarine. Season with salt and pepper and add to ingredients in Dutch oven. Add broth and 1 cup water to skillet and bring to boil, scraping up brown bits. Strain over meat. Cover, bring to boil and simmer 2 to 2½ hours, or until meat is tender. Remove bones and serve with rice. Makes 6 servings.

LIVER-BACON-POTATO CASSEROLE

1 pound sliced bacon
2 medium onions, sliced
1 pound liver, sliced (any kind)
1 tablespoon butter or margarine
1 tablespoon flour
1 cup milk
1 teaspoon prepared mustard
1 teaspoon Worcestershire
2 teaspoons prepared horseradish
1/2 teaspoon salt
1/8 teaspoon pepper
1 box (1 pound) frozen potatoes for hashed browns
1/2 cup grated sharp Cheddar cheese

Cook bacon until crisp. Remove from skillet, drain and crumble. Pour off most of fat. Add onion to skillet and sauté until golden. Push aside, add liver and cook until browned and done. Remove liver and cut in cubes. Melt butter in saucepan and blend in flour. Gradually add milk and cook, stirring, until thickened. Add next 5 ingredients. Put liver, onion, potato and 1 cup crumbled bacon in shallow 1½-quart casserole. Add sauce and mix well. Mix remaining bacon and cheese and sprinkle on top. Bake in moderate oven (350° F.) about 30 minutes. Makes 6 servings. **Note** If desired, 4 cups diced cold cooked potatoes can be substituted for hashed browns.

VENETIAN LIVER

Cut 1½ pounds thinly sliced calf liver into strips; dust with flour seasoned with salt, pepper and onion salt. Melt ¼ cup butter with 3 tablespoons oil; add 2 medium onions, sliced. Sauté until soft and golden. Add liver strips and sauté quickly until browned but still pink in the center. Add ⅓ cup dry vermouth. Swirl it around pan to blend with liver and pan juices. Heat through. Serve on hot cooked rice or polenta. Makes 4 servings.

LIVER BAKED IN SPANISH SAUCE

2 pounds beef liver, unsliced
Bacon ends
1/2 cup chopped carrot
1/2 cup chopped celery
1 small onion, sliced
1 can (1 pound) stewed tomatoes
1 teaspoon salt
Dash of pepper
1/2 bay leaf

Put liver in greased 2-quart casserole and arrange bacon ends on top. Mix remaining ingredients and pour around liver. Cover and bake in moderate oven (350° F.) 1 hour. Uncover and bake 30 minutes longer. Makes 6 servings. Good with parsley potatoes, rice, noodles or spaghetti.

SWEDISH LIVER-POTATO PATTIES

3/4 pound beef or pork liver, cut up
3 medium potatoes, peeled and cut up
1 medium tart apple, cored and cut up
1 medium onion, cut up
1-1/2 teaspoons salt
1/4 teaspoon pepper
2 tablespoons margarine
1-1/4 cups milk
1 tablespoon soy sauce
Chopped parsley

 Force liver, potato, apple and onion through fine blade of food chopper. Mix well and add salt and pepper. Brown margarine in skillet and drop in about ¼ cup mixture for each patty. Flatten slightly with spatula and sauté slowly on both sides. Transfer to heat-proof serving dish. Pour milk into skillet and heat gently, scraping pan to loosen pan drippings. Add soy sauce. Pour on top of patties, cover and simmer 5 to 10 minutes. Sprinkle with parsley. Makes 4 to 6 servings.

FARM-STYLE TRIPE

2 pounds fresh tripe
Salt and pepper
1-1/2 cups fine dry bread crumbs
2 eggs, beaten
3/4 cup milk
Fat for deep frying
Parsley

Wash tripe; put in kettle. Cover with water; bring to boil. Simmer, covered, 1 hour, or until tripe is tender. Drain, cool and cut in thin slices. Season with salt and pepper and roll slices in crumbs. Dip in eggs mixed with milk, then again in crumbs. Fry in hot deep fat (375°F. on a frying thermometer) until golden brown. Drain and put on hot platter. Garnish with parsley. Serves 6.

LIVER IN MUSTARD SOUR-CREAM SAUCE

4 slices bacon, diced
1-1/2 pounds pork liver, sliced
1/3 cup flour
Salt, pepper and paprika
3 onions, sliced
2 teaspoons dry mustard
1/2 cup dairy sour cream

Cook bacon in large skillet until crisp; remove. Dredge liver in flour and brown in fat in skillet; season with salt, pepper and paprika. Remove liver and cook onions a few minutes in skillet; return liver to pan. Blend mustard and 1 cup water and pour over liver. Bring to boil, cover and cook 15 to 20 minutes, or until liver is tender. Add sour cream and heat gently. Top with bacon. Makes 4 to 6 servings.

LAMB LIVER WITH RICE

2 lamb livers (about 2 pounds)
Flour
1/4 cup bacon fat or other fat
3 sprigs parsley
1 bay leaf
1/8 teaspoon dried thyme
1/4 teaspoon pepper
2 teaspoons salt
1 onion, sliced
Hot cooked rice

Cover livers with 1½ cups boiling water. Let stand 5 minutes. Drain, reserving water. Dry livers and dredge with 2 tablespoons flour. Brown on all sides in hot fat in skillet. Add next 6 ingredients and reserved water. Cover and simmer 1½ hours, or until done. Remove livers and slice. Thicken liquid with a flour-and-water paste and season to taste. Serve over liver on rice. Serves 6.

BEEF-LIVER STEW

1 pound beef liver
1/3 cup dry red wine
1 onion, chopped
3 tablespoons butter
3 tablespoons flour
1-1/4 teaspoons seasoned salt
1/8 teaspoon pepper
3 carrots, peeled and cut in 1" pieces
12 small white onions, peeled
1/2 teaspoon thyme

Cut liver in 1½" pieces and marinate in wine 1 hour. Meanwhile cook onion in butter 5 minutes. Dredge liver with flour and brown with onions. Add remaining ingredients, including wine. Bring to boil, cover and simmer about 35 minutes. Makes 4 to 6 servings.

PORK LIVER WITH VEGETABLES

1 pork liver (about 2 pounds)
2 tablespoons flour
1/4 cup bacon fat
3 sprigs parsley
1 bay leaf
1/8 teaspoon thyme
2 teaspoons salt
1/4 teaspoon pepper
1 onion, sliced
2 cups sliced carrots
1-1/2 cups sliced parsnips
4 potatoes, cubed

Pour 1½ cups boiling water over liver; drain, reserving water. Remove tough outer membrane from liver; dry meat and dredge with flour. Brown on all sides in fat. Add reserved water and seasonings. Cover and simmer 1 hour. Add vegetables and simmer about ½ hour longer. Serves 6.

BEEF-LIVER SAUTÉ, SWISS STYLE

8 thin slices young beef liver (about
    1-1/2 pounds)
2 cups milk
Flour
8 slices bacon
2 tablespoons butter
Salt and pepper
Juice of 1/2 lemon
8 leaves fresh sage
8 lemon slices

Soak liver in milk for ½ hour. Remove, wipe dry and roll in flour. Sauté bacon and keep warm. Pour off fat. Melt butter in same skillet and heat until bubbly. Sauté the liver gently, turning once to brown on both sides. Season to taste. Remove to a hot platter. Add lemon juice and sage to pan. Pour over liver. Garnish with lemon slices. Makes 4 servings.

FONDUE ORIENTALE

6 lamb kidneys
1 pound each lean beef, veal and pork
8 cups chicken or beef stock
6 tablespoons chopped onion

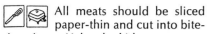 All meats should be sliced paper-thin and cut into bite-size pieces. Halve the kidneys, remove the hard core and then slice the halves very thin. Pour the stock into a chafing dish, electric skillet, or fondue dish that may be brought to the table and kept over a hot plate or alcohol burner. Add chopped onion and bring to a boil. Adjust the heat to keep the stock boiling. Give each guest two fondue forks (long, wooden-handled, two-pronged forks), one for cooking and one for eating. Do not use the cooking fork to eat or you may be seriously burned. Each guest spears a piece of meat, lowers it into the hot stock and cooks until it is done to suit taste. Good with piquant sauces and plain rice. Makes 6 to 8 servings.

STEAK-KIDNEY CASSEROLE

2 beef kidneys
1 pound round steak, cut 1/2" thick
Flour
1 onion, minced
2 tablespoons margarine
Salt and pepper
1 bay leaf
Few sprigs parsley
Few celery leaves
1/2 pound mushrooms, sliced
2 teaspoons steak sauce
Dash of hot pepper sauce
Pastry (recipe made with 1-1/2 cups flour)
    or 1 box (10 ounces) pie-crust mix
1 egg

Remove outer membrane of kidneys. Split kidneys open and remove all fat and white veins. Soak in cold water to cover 30 minutes. Drain and cut kidneys and steak in 1" pieces. Dredge with flour and brown with onion in the margarine in kettle or Dutch oven. Sprinkle with 2 teaspoons salt and 1/4 teaspoon pepper. Add next 4 ingredients and 2 cups water. Bring to boil, cover and simmer 1 hour, or until meats are tender. Then thicken with 2 to 3 tablespoons flour blended with a little cold water. Add remaining seasonings, and salt and pepper to taste. Pour into 1½-quart casserole. Roll pastry to fit top and arrange on casserole; trim and flute edges with fork. Brush with egg beaten with 1 teaspoon cold water. From remaining pastry, cut leaf and stem designs and arrange on pastry. Brush with egg mixture. Bake in very hot oven (450° F.) about 20 minutes. Makes 6 servings.

SKEWERED LAMB KIDNEYS WITH BACON

Clean and halve lamb kidneys, allowing two for each serving. Thread a strip of bacon on a skewer, then half a kidney, then again the bacon. Sprinkle kidneys with salt and pepper and broil about 3" from heat, turning frequently.

KIDNEY PIE AND HAMBURGER

1 beef kidney
1 tablespoon fat
1 pound ground chuck
1 medium onion, chopped
2 tablespoons flour
1-1/2 teaspoons salt
1/4 teaspoon pepper
1 teaspoon steak sauce
1/2 box (10 ounces) pie-crust mix

Cut kidney in crosswise slices; remove fat and gristle; then cut kidney in small pieces. Rinse in cold water and wipe dry. Brown on all sides in fat. Add 2 cups boiling water, cover and simmer 1 hour, or until tender. Meanwhile, cook beef and onion, stirring with fork, until meat loses its red color. Add cooked kidney and liquid. Blend flour with 1/4 cup cold water and stir into mixture. Cook until slightly thickened, stirring. Add seasonings and pour into 1-quart casserole. Prepare pastry as directed on package and roll 1/8" thick; cut in strips. Arrange on mixture, lattice fashion. Brush with undiluted evaporated milk, top milk or slightly beaten egg white, if desired. Bake in hot oven (400°F.) 20 minutes, or until pastry is brown. Makes 4 servings.

DANISH CALF HEARTS

2 calf hearts (about 1-1/2 pounds)
6 sprigs parsley, chopped
2 onions, sliced thin
1 tablespoon fat
1/2 bay leaf
4 whole black peppercorns
1 teaspoon salt
Dash of pepper
2 small carrots, diced
1 stalk celery, diced
1/4 cup heavy cream

Wash hearts and remove large tubes. Stuff hearts with parsley and half the onion; close with skewers or sew with string. Brown on all sides in fat in heavy kettle. Add remaining onion, seasonings, vegetables and 1 cup water. Cover and simmer 2 hours, or until hearts are very tender. Remove to hot serving platter. Strain broth, add cream and pour over hearts. Makes 4 servings.

LAMB KIDNEYS OREGANO

8 lamb kidneys
2 tablespoons margarine or other fat
Few sprigs of fresh oregano or 1 teaspoon
   dried oregano
1/4 cup chopped parsley
1 clove garlic, minced
1 cup sliced fresh mushrooms
1 can condensed mushroom soup
1 cup dairy sour cream
Hot cooked green or white noodles

Cut kidneys in bite-size pieces, discarding any white membranes. Sauté in margarine with next 4 ingredients until done. Add soup and sour cream and heat gently. Serve on noodles. Good with tomato salad, breadsticks and a creamy dessert. Serves 4.

SAVORY STUFFED HEART

1-1/4 cups rice, cooked
Few celery leaves, chopped
3 onions, chopped
1 teaspoon poultry seasoning or 1/2
   teaspoon each thyme and sage
Salt and pepper
1 beef heart, fat removed
2 tablespoons fat
2 cups bouillon

Mix first 4 ingredients and season to taste. Season heart well inside and out with salt and pepper. Fill with part of rice mixture and sew edges together. Brown well in hot fat in heavy kettle. Cover and cook slowly, without added water, 2 hours. Remove meat and pour off all fat. Put remaining rice mixture in pan. Add bouillon and season to taste. Put heart on top, cover and simmer 1 hour longer, or until meat is tender. Makes 8 servings.

BROILED SWEETBREADS

Soak 2 pairs of sweetbreads in ice-cold water for 2 to 3 hours. Drain and blanch in boiling salted water for 3 minutes. Remove sweetbreads, cool and take out the tubes and membranes. Dip sweetbreads in melted butter and place on a broiling rack about 5 inches from the heat. Broil for 4 minutes. Remove, dip again in melted butter and then in seasoned fine bread crumbs. Return to the broiler cooked side down. Continue broiling and brushing with melted butter until the crumbs are brown and crisp. Serve with Hollandaise Sauce, page 222 or Béarnaise Sauce, page 61, and tiny French-style peas with onions. Makes 4 servings.

CORN-AND-TONGUE SUPPER DISH

Heat together 1 can condensed celery soup, 2 cups cooked whole-kernel corn, 1 cup slivered cooked tongue, 1 teaspoon prepared mustard, 1 tablespoon chili sauce and 1/4 teaspoon pepper. Makes 4 servings.

SMOKED TONGUE DINNER

1 smoked beef tongue (3 to 3-1/2 pounds)
1 onion, sliced
1 stalk celery
1 bay leaf
1/2 teaspoon whole black peppercorns
6 whole onions
6 carrots, cut in quarters
1-1/2 pounds whole green beans

Put tongue in kettle and cover with water. Add next 4 ingredients. Bring to boil, cover and simmer 3 to 3½ hours, or until tongue is tender. Remove tongue; pull off skin and remove bones. Add remaining ingredients to kettle. Slice tongue, arrange on top. Cook ½ hour, or until vegetables are tender.

MUSHROOMS AND SWEETBREADS

2 pairs sweetbreads
2 tablespoons lemon juice or vinegar
Salt
1/2 pound mushrooms, sliced
1/4 cup butter or margarine
1/4 cup flour
1 cup chicken broth or bouillon
1/2 cup cream or milk
Dash of cayenne
1/4 teaspoon mace or nutmeg
1/4 teaspoon pepper
Soft bread crumbs
Grated Cheddar cheese
Toast points

Plunge sweetbreads into cold water and let stand about ½ hour. Drain and cover with boiling water. Add lemon juice and a little salt and bring to boil; cover and simmer about 20 minutes. Drain and rinse with cold water. Remove membrane and tubes. Cut sweetbreads in ½" pieces. Sauté mushrooms in butter 2 to 3 minutes. Remove mushrooms and blend flour into drippings in skillet. Gradually add chicken broth and cream. Cook, stirring, until thickened and smooth. Add sweetbreads, mushrooms, 1 teaspoon salt and the other seasonings. Put in shallow 1½-quart baking dish. Sprinkle lightly with bread crumbs and grated cheese. Bake in moderate oven (375°F.) 30 minutes, or until browned on top. Serve on toast. Serves 6.

HOW TO BUY FRESH PORK

Wholesome pork carries the Federal stamp "U. S. Inspected and Passed," but is not graded for quality federally. For flavorful, tender and juicy results, choose pork that is fine and velvety in texture and is well-marbled with fat or has generous amounts of intramuscular fat. Dark meat is less acidic, juicier and shrinks less in cooking.

FRESH-PORK STORAGE

Unless you select your pork from the prepacked counter, remove the butcher's wrapping and cover loosely. Prepackaged pork can be left in its original wrappings. Put pork promptly in the coldest part of the refrigerator and use within 1 to 2 days.

COOKING CAUTION

Whatever method is used, pork should always be cooked until well done. Prolonged heat kills any trichina organisms sometimes present in this meat.

HOW TO BUY SMOKED HAM
Kinds of Ham

Two kinds of ham are generally available—**fully-cooked** or **cook-before-eating hams.** A third kind, the so-called **country-style** ham, is not sold in all localities. Country-style hams are heavily cured and firm-textured. They require soaking and simmering in water before baking. Hams are labeled so that it's easy to tell which kind you are buying.

Styles of Ham

Hams are available in several styles: bone-in; skinless, shankless (shank removed, meat skinned and trimmed of excess fat); semi-boneless; boneless; boneless-skinless (ham rolls); and canned ham, also boneless and skinless. All come in various sizes.

HAM STORAGE

Refrigerate hams at 40°F. or less. Like all meats, ham is at its best when used promptly. Freezing tends to reduce the flavor.

KINDS OF SAUSAGES
Southern European Sausages

In this group dry sausages predominate because in the warm Mediterranean area, when methods of refrigeration were very primitive, preserving meat in summer was a great problem. Some Italian varieties are: salami, pepperoni, Italian sweet, Italian hot, and bologna.

Northern European Sausages

The cooler climate of northern Europe produced mainly fresh and cooked sausages. From Germany come *bockwurst,* bratwurst, fresh Thüringer, mettwurst, frankfurters, *knoblauch,* knackwurst, Berliner sausage, blood sausage, liverwurst, and cervelat. Austria contributed Vienna sausage; Sweden, Göteborg.

American Sausages

America's gifts to the sausage world are fresh and smoked country-style pork sausage, in bulk and link form and brown-and-serve links. But because immigrants from Europe brought their favorite recipes with them, Americans today can enjoy most European varieties.

KINDS OF FRANKFURTERS

Frankfurters range from large dinner franks to tiny cocktail size and may be skinless or in natural casings. Ingredients are listed on packages in descending order of weight. If name is simply "Frankfurters," "Wieners" or "Hot Dogs," approved fillers such as milk powder and soy flour may be present in limited quantities. Frankfurters labeled "All Meat" must contain meat only. "All Beef" means just that. The latter may also be labeled "Kosher." Frankfurter seasonings may include coriander, garlic, mustard, nutmeg, salt, sugar and white pepper.

STORAGE

Frankfurters can be kept refrigerated in their original wrappers about 2 weeks. They can be frozen 1 to 2 months.

HOW TO STRETCH CERTAIN CUTS OF PORK

FOUR-WAY PORK

Purchase 8- to 10-pound pork loin rib roast with backbone removed.

Cut 1 Frenched loin roast or 10 to 13 Frenched chops, or 6 to 8 butterfly chops or 8 cutlets.

1 To French roast, follow first three steps of Rack of Lamb Revised (page 85). You can cook this roast as is, but if you prefer chops or cutlets, proceed to step 2.

2 To make Frenched chops of the roast, leave fat side down. With knife, slice vertically between ribs, allowing one rib per chop. Allow 1 to 2 chops per serving, depending on size.

1 For butterfly chops, place whole roast fat side up. Score fat and remove.

2 Tuck tip of knife in meat at point where excess fat has been removed.

3 Cut close to bone along entire length of roast and remove center core

of meat from all the bones in one large piece (this cut is known as the shell of pork loin).

4 Place shell fat side up and trim away all excess fat. Starting ¹/₂″ from end of shell, slice vertically about three quarters of the way through.

5 Move knife another ¹/₂″ to left— this time about 1″ from end of shell— and slice vertically all the way through. The result is a butterfly chop.

6 Continue to slice shell vertically at ¹/₂″ intervals, alternating three-quarter slice with full slice. Entire shell of pork loin will make about 8 butterfly chops.

1 To make cutlets, spread sides of butterfly chops on flat surface. Pound cutlet with palm of hand to make flat and evenly thick. You may want to flour or bread cutlet before cooking.

BREADED PORK CUTLETS

4 pork cutlets
Seasoned flour
2 eggs, slightly beaten
Fine dry bread crumbs
Butter
Vegetable oil
Lemon slices
Rolled anchovies (optional)
Chopped parsley

Dip each cutlet in flour, then in egg and finally in crumbs. Sauté in ¹/₂″ combined butter and oil in large skillet until well browned on both sides and cooked through. Arrange on hot platter, top each with a slice of lemon. Put an anchovy in center of each lemon slice. Sprinkle with parsley. Makes 4 servings.

ROAST PORK WITH VEGETABLES

Frenched pork loin
Salt and pepper
6 medium yams, cooked and peeled
2 pounds small white onions, peeled and cooked
3/4 cup cider or apple juice

Rub pork loin with salt and pepper and put on rack in shallow baking pan. Roast in moderate oven (325°F.) 35 minutes to the pound, or until meat thermometer registers 170°F. Arrange yams and onions on rack beside pork and bake, basting frequently with the cider, 15 minutes. Put on platter. Makes 6 servings.

Includes material from The Meat Book: A Consumer's Guide to Selecting, Buying, Cutting, Storing, Freezing and Carving the Various Cuts *by Travers Moncure Evans and David Greene with* illustrations by Dana J. Greene, to be published by Charles Scribner's Sons. Text Copyright © 1973 Travers Moncure Evans. Illustrations Copyright © 1973 Dana J. Greene.

LOMO DE PUERCO EN SALSA NEGRA
(Caribbean Pork Loin in Black Sauce)

4 to 5 pounds pork loin, boned if desired
2 teaspoons salt
1 teaspoon pepper
2 large onions, thickly sliced
1/4 cup lard
1/4 cup vinegar
12 black olives, pitted and chopped
1 tablespoon capers
1/3 cup seeded raisins, chopped
1 tablespoon brown sugar or molasses
2 large or 4 small onions, chopped
1-1/2 pounds potatoes, peeled and quartered (4 to 6 medium)

Sprinkle meat with salt and pepper. Brown thoroughly on all sides with sliced onions in hot lard. Discard onions. Pour off excess fat. Sprinkle meat with vinegar. Add next 4 ingredients and 4 cups water. Bring to boil, lower heat and simmer, covered, 1½ to 2 hours. Turn meat occasionally. Add chopped onion and potatoes and cook for 30 to 45 minutes longer over very low heat, until potatoes are done and sauce thickens. Makes 6 to 8 servings.

SIMMERED PORK BUTT WITH VEGETABLES

(Prepare the day before serving)

5- or 6-pound fresh-pork butt (bone in)
1 tablespoon salt
5 whole allspice
1 bay leaf
1 teaspoon dry mustard
1 teaspoon paprika
1/2 teaspoon ground ginger
1 rutabaga, about 2 pounds (1 quart diced)
4 medium baking potatoes, peeled and diced
2 tablespoons each chopped green onion and parsley

Put pork in large heavy kettle. Add water to almost cover. Bring to boil, skim and add next 3 ingredients. Cover and simmer 3½ hours. Cool, then chill overnight in the broth. Next day, remove all fat from broth and reserve for later use. Heat and strain broth. Trim off excess fat and put pork, fat side up, on rack in foil-lined roasting pan. Rub with mixture of mustard, paprika and ginger. Roast in moderate oven (375°F.) 30 minutes, or until well browned and very tender. Meanwhile, peel and dice rutabaga. Put in large saucepan with 2 cups pork broth and cook 5 minutes. Add potatoes and cook 12 minutes longer, or until very soft. Mash and add onion and parsley. Serve with the meat. Serves 6 with some meat left over.

ROAST PORK LOIN WITH CHEESE SAUCE

5 pounds pork-loin roast
1 small clove garlic, minced
1 can (10-3/4 ounces) Cheddar-cheese soup
1/2 cup dairy sour cream
2 tablespoons crumbled Roquefort cheese
2 tablespoons chopped parsley

Roast meat in slow oven (325° F.) 3 hours, or until meat thermometer reaches 170° F. Remove roast to heated platter and keep warm. Spoon off excess fat from pan, reserving 2 tablespoons drippings. In same pan, sauté garlic lightly in the drippings. Blend in ½ cup water and next 3 ingredients. Heat, stirring to loosen browned bits. Sprinkle with parsley. Serve with the meat. Makes 6 servings.

SAGE PORK ROAST

3-1/2 to 4 pounds boneless pork loin, rolled and tied
Salt
1 tablespoon soy sauce
1 to 2 teaspoons crushed dried sage
1/2 teaspoon freshly ground black pepper
4 cups potatoes, cut in 1/4″ slices
Garlic salt (optional)

Put roast in roasting pan. Combine ½ teaspoon salt and next 3 ingredients and rub into roast. Bake in slow oven (325°F.) 1 hour and 45 minutes. Parboil potatoes 5 to 6 minutes in lightly salted boiling water; drain well. Remove roast from oven. Arrange potatoes around meat, sprinkle lightly with garlic salt and baste with pan drippings. Return to oven. Bake 30 minutes longer. Remove string and cut meat in thin slices. Serves 8.

GLAZED ROAST FRESH HAM

1 fresh ham, 10 to 12 pounds
Salt and pepper
1/3 cup dark corn syrup
1 tablespoon soy sauce
1/4 teaspoon ginger
1 tablespoon cornstarch
Halved pineapple rings
Preserved kumquats
Orange wedges
Parsley

Put ham, fat side up, on rack in roasting pan. Sprinkle with salt and pepper and insert meat thermometer into center of thickest muscle. Roast in slow oven (325° F.) 5 to 6 hours, or until thermometer registers 185° F. About ½ hour before meat is done, cover with mixture of corn syrup and next 3 ingredients. Continue roasting until well glazed. Remove to hot platter. Garnish with remaining ingredients. Makes 10 to 12 servings.

ROAST FRESH HAM

It roasts on a bed of sliced onions, carrots and celery.

1 fresh ham
1 clove garlic, cut
Salt and pepper
1 tablespoon caraway seed
4 onions, sliced
2 carrots, sliced
2 medium stalks celery, sliced
1 bay leaf
3 whole cloves
1 cup dry white wine
Raisin Sauce, page 132.

Score skin of ham in two directions, making a diamond pattern. Rub meat on all sides with garlic, salt, pepper and caraway seed. Put next 5 ingredients on bottom of large baking pan. Add 1 cup water. Lay ham, skin side down, on vegetables. Roast, uncovered, in moderate oven (325°F.), 1 hour. Baste frequently with pan juices and wine. Turn meat skin side up and roast until done. Allow 25 minutes per pound total roasting time or roast to 185°F. on a meat thermometer. Baste often with pan juices and wine. Serve with Raisin Sauce or with gravy made with pan juices. Allow ½ pound uncooked meat for each serving.

ROAST PORK, SPANISH STYLE

Make a paste of ¼ teaspoon each powdered sage and ginger, 1 crushed garlic clove, 1 teaspoon each salt and flour, and sherry to moisten. Spread on fat side of 4-pound pork loin. Bake on rack in roasting pan in moderate oven (325°F.) 3 hours, or until meat thermometer registers 185°F., basting frequently with additional sherry during the roasting. Make gravy with drippings in pan. Serves 6 to 8.

BEANS AND ROAST PORK

1 pound dried white beans
1 teaspoon herb-bouquet blend
1 clove garlic
5-pound loin of pork
Salt and pepper

Cover washed beans with 6 cups water, bring to boil and boil 2 minutes. Cover and let stand 1 hour; then cook with herbs and garlic until tender. Drain; remove garlic. Put meat on rack in roasting pan. Surround with beans. Season. Roast in moderate oven (325°F.) 3 hours, or until meat is done. Stir beans occasionally, adding water if necessary. Slice pork; serve with beans. Serves 6 to 8.

ROAST PORK AU VIN BLANC

Rub a 5-pound pork loin with half a lemon, a cut clove of garlic, crumbled marjoram, salt and pepper. Roast on a rack in a moderate oven (375°F.) 2½ to 3 hours, or until meat thermometer registers 185°F. Remove meat and keep warm. Pour off all but ⅓ cup fat from pan. Add ⅓ cup dry white wine to pan; heat, then stir in ¾ cup dairy sour cream and season. Serve with the pork. Makes 6 to 8 servings.

CHINESE ROAST PORK

2 pounds loin of pork, boned and rolled
1/4 cup chicken stock
1 tablespoon soy sauce
4 teaspoons sugar
4 teaspoons honey
1 teaspoon salt
1/4 teaspoon powdered ginger or 1 teaspoon minced gingerroot
1/4 cup prepared mustard
2 tablespoons soy sauce

Marinate meat in mixture of next 6 ingredients 2 hours, turning occasionally. Roast in moderate oven (325°F.) 1 to 1½ hours, basting several times. Serve hot or cold with sauce of mustard mixed with soy sauce. Makes 4 servings.

MEXICAN PORK LOIN IN PEPPER SAUCE

5 tablespoons olive oil
3 cloves garlic, minced
1/4 pound hot sausage, cut in small pieces
4 pounds pork loin
3 onions, chopped
2 tomatoes, peeled and chopped
1 cup chicken bouillon
6 green peppers, sliced thin
Salt and pepper
Flour

Heat 3 tablespoons oil in heavy kettle. Add garlic and sausage. Cook until well browned; remove sausage. Brown pork loin on all sides. Remove pork and pour off fat. Return pork and sausage to kettle with half the onion, the tomatoes and bouillon. Cover and simmer about 2½ hours. In skillet, heat remaining oil. Add remaining onion and peppers. Cook, stirring occasionally, until tender; season. Remove pork and slice. Arrange on hot platter. Thicken liquid in kettle with flour mixed to a thin paste with water; add salt and pepper. Pour some of the gravy over pork; top with peppers and onion. Serve remaining gravy in bowl. Makes 6 servings.

ROAST PORK WITH BROWNED VEGETABLES

Put 5-pound pork loin roast, fat side up, on rack in roasting pan. Rub with cut clove of garlic. Roast in moderate oven (325°F.) about 4¼ hours, or until meat thermometer registers 185°F. About 1¼ hours before meat is done, put 12 each peeled small potatoes, carrots and white onions around the roast. Season with salt and pepper. Turn vegetables occasionally. Makes 6 servings, with some meat left over.

FLORENTINE PORK COOKED IN MILK

4-pound loin of pork, boned
Salt and pepper
1 tablespoon dried rosemary, crumbled
2 tablespoons butter
1 quart milk
1 can (4 ounces) mushrooms, undrained

Trim excess fat from meat. Rub with salt, pepper and rosemary. Brown on all sides in butter; add milk. Cover tightly and simmer over low heat 2 to 2½ hours. (Gravy will be thick and creamy and golden brown.) At serving time, place pork on hot serving platter and slice. Strain liquid, if desired, and add mushrooms. Thicken with flour-and-water paste, if desired. Pour gravy over sliced pork. Makes 6 to 8 servings. *Note* Use ¼ pound fresh mushrooms, sliced and sautéed in butter, if desired.

ROAST PORK SHOULDER WITH PEAR STUFFING

1 onion, minced
1/4 cup butter or margarine
Salt and pepper
1/8 teaspoon thyme
2-1/2 cups soft bread crumbs
1-3/4 cups chopped firm pears (2 medium)
5-pound boned pork shoulder with pocket

Cook onion in the butter 2 to 3 minutes. Add 1 teaspoon salt, dash of pepper, ½ cup boiling water and remaining ingredients, except meat. Fill pocket of pork with stuffing and fasten edges with skewers or roll up and tie with string. Rub outside of meat with salt and pepper. Put on rack in roasting pan and roast in moderate oven (350°F.) 3 hours, or until meat thermometer registers 185°F. (Insert thermometer in thickest part of meat without touching stuffing.) Makes 6 to 8 servings.

PORK LOIN WITH SAGE AND ONIONS

4 pounds pork loin
2 pounds small white onions, peeled
Salt and pepper
1-1/2 teaspoons sage

Put meat on rack in roasting pan and roast in slow oven (325°F.) about 2 hours, or until meat thermometer registers 185°F. In the meantime, cook onions in small amount of boiling water until tender. Drain and chop. Add 1 teaspoon salt, ¼ teaspoon pepper and the sage. Remove roast and rack from pan, pour off drippings and reserve for making gravy. Arrange onions in center of pan and put roast on top. Season with salt and pepper. Roast 1 hour longer. Serve meat with gravy made from drippings. Makes 6 to 8 servings. *Note* Two large cans onions, well drained, can be used; omit salt.

APPLE-STUFFED CROWN ROAST OF PORK

1 onion, chopped
1/4 cup diced celery
2 cups diced tart apple
2 tablespoons butter or margarine
1/4 cup molasses
1 teaspoon grated lemon rind
Juice of 1/2 lemon
1 teaspoon salt
1/2 teaspoon crumbled sage
4 cups bread cubes, toasted
7-pound crown roast of pork

Cook onion, celery and apple in butter 5 minutes. Remove from heat and add ¼ cup water and remaining ingredients, except pork. Fill roast lightly with stuffing, heaping it up in the center. Roast on rack uncovered in moderate oven (325°F.) about 4 hours. Fasten paper frills to rib tips. Makes 8 servings.

SIMPLE CHOUCROUTE GARNIE

(A French and Swiss specialty, featuring sauerkraut.)

6 thick slices bacon
1 quart sauerkraut, rinsed and drained
6 pork chops, about 3/4" thick
1 medium onion, sliced
12 whole black peppercorns
6 juniper berries
2 cups bouillon and 1 cup dry white wine

Arrange bacon in bottom of large saucepan or deep skillet. Top with sauerkraut and pork chops. Combine remaining ingredients and pour over chops. Cover and simmer about 1 hour. Makes 6 servings. *Note* Omit wine and use all bouillon, if desired.

PORK-AND-POTATO SCALLOP

Mix 4 cups thinly sliced potatoes and 1 thinly sliced onion. Measure 2 tablespoons flour. Put a layer of potato and onion in 2-quart casserole. Sprinkle with salt, pepper and some of the flour. Repeat, ending with layer of potatoes. Add 1½ cups hot milk to almost cover potatoes. Brown 4 pork chops (about 1½ pounds) on both sides in hot skillet. Arrange chops on top of potatoes. Bake, covered, in moderate oven (350°F.) 45 minutes. Uncover and bake 15 minutes longer, or until potatoes are tender. Makes 4 servings.

HERB-STUFFED PORK BIRDS

8 very thin end pork chops (about 2-1/2 pounds)
1 onion, chopped
2 tablespoons chopped parsley
2 tablespoons chopped celery and leaves
2 tablespoons butter
1/2 teaspoon salt
1/2 teaspoon poultry seasoning
2 cups soft bread crumbs
2 tablespoons flour
2 tablespoons fat

Cut bones off chops; pound meat slightly. For stuffing, cook onion, parsley and celery in butter; add seasonings. Mix with bread crumbs; add a little water to moisten. Put a portion of stuffing on each chop. Roll and tie with string. Roll in flour; brown in fat in heavy skillet. Add ⅓ cup water, cover and simmer 1¼ hours, or until tender. Cut strings before serving. Make ahead and reheat if desired. Makes 4 servings.

DISNOKARAJ MAGYAROSAN
(Hungarian Pork Chops)

6 pork chops, about 1/2" thick
Salt and pepper
1 medium onion, chopped
1 clove garlic, minced
3 tablespoons lard
1 bay leaf
3/4 cup chicken bouillon
1 cup dairy sour cream
2 teaspoons paprika

Trim excess fat from pork chops; sprinkle with salt and pepper. Sauté onion and garlic in hot lard until soft and golden. Push aside or remove from skillet. Add pork chops and brown on all sides. Pour off fat. Reduce heat, add bay leaf and bouillon and cook, covered, over low heat about 1 hour. Transfer chops to hot serving plate and keep hot. Reduce pan juices to half by cooking over high heat. Blend sour cream and paprika thoroughly with pan juices. Heat through, but do *not* boil. Pour sauce over chops. Serves 4 to 6.

STUFFED PORK CHOPS WITH VEGETABLES

Slit 4 thick loin pork chops from fat side to bone to form a pocket in each. Brown on both sides in Dutch oven. Remove. Cook in drippings for 5 minutes 1 chopped small onion and 2 tablespoons each finely chopped celery and green pepper. Add some margarine if necessary. Add 1½ cups soft bread crumbs and 1 teaspoon salt. Fill pockets in chops; fasten with skewers. Put in Dutch oven with 6 potatoes, sliced thin, and 4 carrots, cut in strips. Season. Cover and bake in moderate oven (350°F.) 1 hour. Remove skewers. Serves 4.

ORIENTAL PORK CHOPS

4 pounds pork chops
1/2 cup soy sauce
2 teaspoons sugar
1 clove garlic, minced
1/2 teaspoon ginger juice (or 1/4 teaspoon ground ginger)
1/2 teaspoon monosodium glutamate

Trim bone and fat from pork chops and render fat in heavy skillet to make 2 tablespoons of drippings. Discard pieces of fat and brown pork on both sides in the drippings. Mix together remaining ingredients and pour over pork. Cover and simmer 30 to 45 minutes, turning occasionally. Makes 6 to 8 servings.

TIN SUAN ROW
(Chinese Sweet-and-Sour Pork)

1-1/2 pounds pork chops
1 egg, beaten
1 tablespoon milk
3 tablespoons flour
1/2 teaspoon salt
4 tablespoons vegetable oil
1 clove garlic, minced
1 cup canned pineapple tidbits
1/2 cup pineapple syrup
1 large carrot, sliced
2 tablespoons vinegar
2 tablespoons soy sauce
1 tablespoon sugar
1 chicken bouillon cube
1 large green pepper, cut in eighths
2 tablespoons cornstarch
4 cups hot cooked rice

Cut meat in ½" strips, discarding bones and fat. Dip meat in the mixture of next 4 ingredients and sauté slowly in 3 tablespoons oil until browned and thoroughly cooked. Sauté garlic in remaining 1 tablespoon oil 1 minute. Add next 6 ingredients and bouillon cube dissolved in 1 cup hot water. Simmer 5 minutes. Add green pepper; cook 1 minute. Add meat. Thicken with cornstarch mixed with a little water. Serve on rice. Makes 4 servings.

GEORGIA PORK CHOPS

Brown 4 large lean pork chops on both sides in small amount of fat. Pour off fat. Top each chop with thick slice of onion. Mix 1/4 cup peanut butter, 1/2 can condensed mushroom soup, 1/4 cup milk, 1 teaspoon each Worcestershire and salt and 1/8 teaspoon pepper. Pour over chops. Cover and cook slowly, 45 minutes. Makes 4 servings.

BARBECUED PORK BIRDS

8 medium-thick center-cut pork chops
  (about 2 pounds)
Italian seasoning
Salt and pepper
Flour
2 tablespoons butter
1 medium onion, chopped
1 clove garlic
1/2 cup catsup
2 tablespoons vinegar
1 tablespoon brown sugar
1 teaspoon Worcestershire
Hot instant mashed potato

Trim off bones and any excess fat from chops. Split almost all the way through, and open out. Pound lightly to flatten. Sprinkle with seasonings. Roll up and tie with string. Dredge with flour and brown in butter. Put in casserole; add onion and garlic. Mix 3/4 cup water with next 4 ingredients. Pour over birds, bring to boil, cover and bake in moderate oven (375°F.) about 1 hour. Serve with mashed potato. Serves 4.

JAMAICAN PORK CHOPS

1 onion, chopped
1 tablespoon fat
8 medium-thick pork chops, boned and
  trimmed of excess fat
2 tablespoons flour
1 teaspoon salt
3/4 teaspoon pepper
1 cup uncooked rice
2/3 cup catsup
1 tablespoon soy sauce

Sauté onion in fat in skillet until lightly brown; remove onion. Dredge chops with flour and brown in same skillet. Remove to shallow baking dish; top with onion. Add salt, pepper and 1½ cups water to skillet; bring to boil, scraping brown bits from bottom. Pour around chops. Cover and bake in moderate oven (350°F.) 1 hour, or until chops are tender. Meanwhile cook rice according to package directions. Add catsup and soy sauce to rice; put a scoop on each chop, spoon some of liquid over rice and bake, uncovered, 30 minutes. Makes 4 servings.

ORANGE BAKED PORK CHOPS

2 pounds lean thick pork chops
Salt and pepper
2 tablespoons flour
1 or 2 oranges, thinly sliced
1/2 cup orange juice

Arrange meat in casserole. Sprinkle with salt, pepper and flour and top with orange slices. Pour juice over meat and oranges, cover and bake in moderate oven (350°F.) 1½ hours, or until tender. Makes 4 to 6 servings.

COTOLETTE DI MAIALE ALLA NAPOLITANA (Pork Chops, Neapolitan Style)

2 green peppers
1 clove garlic
2 tablespoons olive oil
4 large thick pork chops
Salt and pepper
1/4 cup tomato puree
1 pound mushrooms, thinly sliced

Roast peppers in hot oven (400°F.) 30 minutes. Pull skin off and cut each pepper in several strips. Brown garlic lightly in olive oil. Remove garlic; brown chops on both sides in same skillet. Sprinkle with salt and pepper. Remove chops. Put remaining ingredients in skillet, add chops, cover and simmer 30 minutes, or until chops are tender. Makes 4 servings.

FRENCH COUNTRY-STYLE PORK CHOPS

4 medium carrots
2 small white turnips
2 stalks celery
4 leeks, white part only, or 8 green
  onions, white part only
4 small white onions, chopped
1 can (28 ounces) tomatoes
1/8 teaspoon marjoram
1 bay leaf
1/4 cup chopped parsley
3/4 teaspoon salt
1/2 teaspoon pepper
1/3 cup consomme
1-1/2 to 2 pounds rib or shoulder pork
  chops, trimmed of excess fat

Cut first 4 ingredients into 1½"-long julienne strips. Combine with next 8 ingredients in large kettle; bring to a boil. Simmer, covered, 5 minutes. Put pork chops on top of vegetables. Cover and simmer about 1 hour, or until thoroughly done. Arrange vegetables in center of serving dish and surround with pork chops. Makes 4 servings.

PIQUANT PORK-STUFFING CASSEROLE

6 large pork chops, about 1" thick
Salt and pepper
1 package (8 ounces) herb-seasoned
    bread stuffing
3 cups cooked rice
2 large oranges, peeled and separated in
    sections
1 cup fresh or frozen cranberries,
    chopped
1 cup sweet mixed pickles, chopped
1/4 cup pickle liquid
1/2 cup butter or margarine, melted
1 cup orange juice
2 tablespoons light corn syrup

Trim some of fat from edges of chops, leaving about one third of rim. Brown slowly on both sides in own fat. Season with salt and pepper. Mix next 7 ingredients and put in large casserole deep enough to hold stuffing and chops. Arrange chops on top. Mix last 2 ingredients and pour over top. Cover and bake in slow oven (325°F.) about 1 hour. Makes 6 servings.

PORK CHOPS WITH SAUERKRAUT

6 loin pork chops, about 3/4" thick
Salt and pepper
2 pounds sauerkraut
1/4 cup packed brown sugar
2 teaspoons caraway seed
2 large tart apples, cored, peeled and
    cut in wedges
1 cup chopped onion

Brown chops on both sides in large skillet. Season with salt and pepper and add small amount of hot water to skillet. Combine next 5 ingredients and mix well. Spoon half the mixture into large shallow baking dish. Arrange chops on top and spread with remaining sauerkraut mixture. Pour drippings over top and cover tightly with foil. Bake in moderate oven (350°F.) about 1½ hours. Serves 6.

PORK-CHOP SKILLET DINNER

4 end pork chops, about 3/4" thick
Salt and pepper
1 can (10-3/4 ounces) condensed
    Cheddar-cheese soup
1/2 soup-can milk
1 tablespoon instant minced onion
4 medium potatoes, peeled and quartered
Chopped parsley

Brown pork chops on both sides in heavy skillet and pour off excess fat. Season with salt and pepper. Add next 4 ingredients, cover and simmer slowly, stirring once or twice, 35 to 40 minutes, until done. Sprinkle with parsley. Makes 4 servings.

BAKED BREADED PORK CHOPS

2 tablespoons margarine
1 cup coarse cracker crumbs
3 tablespoons grated Parmesan cheese
1/2 teaspoon each salt and oregano
1/4 teaspoon pepper
1 egg, beaten
2 tablespoons milk
6 pork chops, cut 3/4" thick

Use margarine to coat 13" x 9" x 2" baking pan. In shallow pan or piepan, mix next 5 ingredients. In shallow bowl, mix egg and milk. Coat chops wtih crumb mixture, then dip in egg mixture and again in crumbs. Arrange in pan and bake in slow oven (325°F.) 30 minutes. Turn chops carefully; bake 30 minutes longer. Makes 6 servings.

PORK CHOPS HAWAIIAN

4 loin pork chops, cut 3/4" thick
Salt and pepper
1/2 cup white wine
1/4 cup honey
2 tablespoons wine vinegar
1 can (13-1/4 ounces) pineapple chunks,
    drained and syrup reserved
2 green onions, sliced
1 green pepper, cut in 3/4" chunks
1 tablespoon cornstarch
1 tablespoon Hawaiian teriyaki sauce
1 teaspoon finely chopped mint

Brown chops slowly on both sides in fat trimmed from chops in oven-proof skillet. Season with salt and pepper to taste. Combine next 3 ingredients with ¼ cup pineapple syrup and pour over chops. Cover and bake in slow oven (300°F.) 1 hour, or until tender. Remove chops to serving dish and keep warm. Add pineapple, onions and green pepper to skillet and simmer, uncovered, 5 minutes. Combine cornstarch with teriyaki sauce and mint and stir into skillet. Cook, stirring, until mixture boils. Pour over chops. Makes 4 servings.

MEXICAN HOT PORK AND HOMINY

2 medium onions, chopped
2 tablespoons bacon fat or lard
2 tablespoons chili powder
2 pounds lean pork, cut in 1" cubes
1 bay leaf
1 teaspoon salt
1/2 teaspoon oregano
2 cups cooked hominy

Cook onion in hot bacon fat until soft and golden; remove. Stir in chili powder, add pork and brown on all sides. Add onion, 4 cups hot water and remaining ingredients, except hominy. Cover and simmer about 2½ hours. Add hominy; heat. Serves 4 to 6.

PORK-CHOP AND SWEET-POTATO SKILLET

Chops are topped with sweet potatoes, onion, green pepper, tomatoes.

4 pork chops
1 tablespoon fat
Salt and pepper
1/4 teaspoon each thyme and marjoram
1 onion, sliced
4 sweet potatoes, peeled and sliced
1 green pepper, cut in rings
1 can (19 ounces) tomatoes

Brown chops on both sides in fat in skillet. Season with salt, pepper and herbs. Top with onion, potatoes and pepper; add tomatoes. Cover; cook slowly 45 minutes. Makes 4 servings.

PORK CHOPS WITH APPLE-ONION SAUCE

4 center-cut pork chops, 3/4" thick (about 1-1/4 pounds)
Salt and pepper
2 tablespoons butter or margarine
2 cups diced apple
1/2 cup chopped onion
1/2 cup dairy sour cream
1 teaspoon lemon juice
1/2 teaspoon onion salt
Paprika
Chopped parsley

In heavy skillet, brown chops on both sides. Drain off fat, add ¼ cup water and sprinkle with salt and pepper. Cover and cook over low heat 45 minutes. Meanwhile, melt butter in another skillet; add apple and onion. Sauté over low heat 15 minutes, or until quite soft. Add sour cream, lemon juice and onion salt; cook about 5 minutes. Remove chops to hot serving platter. Spoon apple mixture on chops and garnish with paprika and parsley. Makes 4 servings.

MAIALE AFFOGATO (Italian Stewed Pork with Celery)

1 clove garlic
2 tablespoons olive oil
1 carrot, minced
2 pounds lean pork, cubed
1 cup dry red or white wine
1-1/2 teaspoons salt
1/2 teaspoon pepper
2-1/2 cups sliced celery
Bouillon
1 cup chopped tomatoes

Brown garlic in oil and discard garlic. Add next 5 ingredients. Cook, covered, over low heat 1½ hours; meanwhile cook celery in bouillon or water to cover until almost tender; drain. Add cooked celery and tomatoes to pork mixture for the last 15 minutes cooking time. Serves 4 to 6.

PORK CHOW MEIN

Cook 2 sliced onions and 2 cups sliced celery in 1 tablespoon vegetable oil 5 minutes. Add 2 cups diced cooked pork, 3 tablespoons soy sauce, 1 tablespoon molasses and 2 cups water. Simmer 15 minutes. Add 1 can (19 ounces) bean sprouts, drained; heat. Stir in 3 tablespoons cornstarch blended with a little cold water. Cook until thickened. Serve on chow-mein noodles. Serves 4.

CURRIED PORK

1/2 cup all-purpose flour
1/2 teaspoon ground ginger
Salt and pepper
2 pounds lean pork, cut in 1" cubes
1/4 cup butter or margarine
1 tablespoon curry powder
1/8 teaspoon chili powder
1 cup chopped onion
3/4 cup chopped green pepper
2 cups hot bouillon or water

Combine flour, ginger, 1 teaspoon salt and ¼ teaspoon pepper. Coat pork with flour mixture. Brown on all sides in hot butter, stirring occasionally. Add remaining ingredients. Simmer, covered, 1¼ to 1½ hours, or until pork is tender, stirring occasionally. Makes 6 servings.

KOREAN FRIED RICE WITH PORK

1 pound boneless pork
Soy sauce
1 teaspoon sugar
2 teaspoons sesame seed, toasted and crushed
1 clove garlic, minced
4 green onions, finely sliced
1 ounce dried mushrooms
1/2 pound Chinese peas in pods or 1 box (10 ounces) frozen peas
1/4 cup vegetable oil
1/3 cup chicken broth
1 pound fresh bean sprouts or 1 can (1 pound), drained and rinsed
1/2 pound fresh water chestnuts, cooked and sliced, or 1 can (5 ounces), drained
4 cups cooked rice

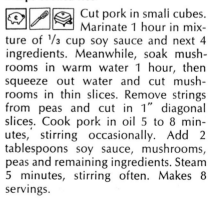 Cut pork in small cubes. Marinate 1 hour in mixture of ⅓ cup soy sauce and next 4 ingredients. Meanwhile, soak mushrooms in warm water 1 hour, then squeeze out water and cut mushrooms in thin slices. Remove strings from peas and cut in 1" diagonal slices. Cook pork in oil 5 to 8 minutes, stirring occasionally. Add 2 tablespoons soy sauce, mushrooms, peas and remaining ingredients. Steam 5 minutes, stirring often. Makes 8 servings.

PORK HASH

2 cups lean pork, cut in 1/4" dice
1 teaspoon dry mustard
1/2 teaspoon paprika
1/4 teaspoon white pepper
2 tablespoons soy sauce
1 cup onion, cut in 1/4" dice
Margarine
2 cups raw potato, cut in 1/4" dice
Fried eggs
Chopped parsley
Pickled beets

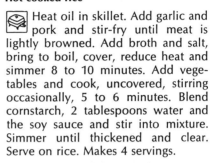 Combine first 5 ingredients in bowl and set aside. Sauté onion in 1 tablespoon margarine in hot skillet over medium heat 6 minutes, or until wilted; remove onion. Reheat skillet and brown potato in 2 tablespoons margarine over high heat, stirring occasionally, 10 minutes, or until well browned and almost done; add to onion. Reheat skillet and brown meat in 1 tablespoon margarine over high heat, stirring occasionally, about 8 minutes. Add onion and potato to skillet and combine carefully to avoid mashing potato. Cover and heat gently 5 to 6 minutes to blend flavors. Prepare the eggs and have ready. Sprinkle the hash with parsley and serve with the eggs and beets. Makes 4 or 5 servings.

PORK-VEGETABLE STEW

3 pounds lean boneless pork, cut in
 1-1/2" cubes
1 tablespoon shortening
1-1/2 cups coarsely chopped onion
1 clove garlic, crushed
3 teaspoons salt
2 tablespoons all-purpose flour
1/4 teaspoon pepper
1/4 teaspoon allspice
Dash of ground nutmeg
1 small bay leaf
2 cups celery, cut in 1" pieces
2 cups carrots, cut in 1" pieces
8 to 10 small white potatoes, peeled
2 tablespoons chopped parsley (optional)

Brown pork cubes well in the shortening in kettle or Dutch oven. Add onion and garlic and sauté until golden. Mix together 2 teaspoons salt, the flour, pepper, allspice and nutmeg and sprinkle on meat. Add 1 cup water and the bay leaf, bring to boil, cover and cook slowly 35 minutes. Add the celery, carrots and potatoes and sprinkle with remaining 1 teaspoon salt. Cover and cook slowly 30 minutes, or until meat is cooked and vegetables are tender. Just before serving, sprinkle with parsley, if desired. Makes 6 to 8 servings.

STIR-FRIED PORK AND PEPPERS

2 tablespoons vegetable oil
1 clove garlic
1 pound lean pork, cut in 1/2" cubes
1-1/4 cups broth or water
3/4 teaspoon salt
2 medium green peppers, diced
2 celery stalks, sliced
2 green onions, cut in 1/2" slices
1 tablespoon cornstarch
1 tablespoon soy sauce
Hot cooked rice

Heat oil in skillet. Add garlic and pork and stir-fry until meat is lightly browned. Add broth and salt, bring to boil, cover, reduce heat and simmer 8 to 10 minutes. Add vegetables and cook, uncovered, stirring occasionally, 5 to 6 minutes. Blend cornstarch, 2 tablespoons water and the soy sauce and stir into mixture. Simmer until thickened and clear. Serve on rice. Makes 4 servings.

PORK-RICE STEW

1 pound lean pork, cut in 1" cubes
2 teaspoons shortening
1 pound smoked ham, diced
1/4 pound Spanish or Italian sausage,
 sliced
1 bay leaf
3 tablespoons instant minced onion
1/2 teaspoon instant minced garlic
1 teaspoon salt
3 cups beef bouillon
1 cup uncooked regular rice
1/8 teaspoon cayenne
1 teaspoon oregano leaves

Brown meat in hot shortening in Dutch oven or 10" skillet. Add ham and sausage and cook, stirring, 5 minutes. Add next 5 ingredients. Cover and cook 10 minutes. Add rice and seasonings. Cover and cook 25 minutes longer. Makes 6 servings.

SWEET-SOUR PORK
WITH PLUM SAUCE

1 pound lean pork, cut in 1" cubes
1 green pepper, cut in strips
1 large onion, chopped
1 cup diced canned pineapple
1/3 cup vinegar
1/4 cup packed brown sugar
1 cup beef bouillon
2 tablespoons each soy sauce and
 cornstarch
1 tablespoon lemon juice
1/2 cup plum jam
Hot cooked rice

Brown pork on all sides. Add next 3 ingredients. Blend remaining ingredients, except rice, and pour over pork. Put in well-greased 1-quart casserole, cover and bake in moderate oven (350° F.) 1 hour, or until tender. Serve with rice. Makes 4 servings.

HEKKA
(Hawaiian Pork and Vegetables)

1 cup konnyaku or bean thread (available in Oriental-food stores)
1-1/2 pounds boneless lean pork
1/4 cup vegetable oil
6 tablespoons soy sauce
1/4 cup sugar
1/2 teaspoon monosodium glutamate
1 can (5 ounces) bamboo shoots in strips
1 cup sliced mushrooms
1 cup sliced green onions
1 cup diced tofu (bean curd), optional
2 tablespoons sake or white wine
Hot steamed rice

Soak konnyaku in warm water ½ hour; drain well. Meanwhile, cut meat into strips about ½" square and 1½" long; brown in oil. Add next 3 ingredients and simmer 10 minutes. Add konnyaku, bamboo shoots and next 3 ingredients. Simmer 5 minutes. Add sake, mix well and serve with rice. Serves 6.

SWEET-AND-SOUR PORK

2 pounds lean pork butt
1/2 cup soy sauce
1/2 teaspoon ground ginger
1/4 teaspoon each salt and monosodium glutamate
1 clove garlic, minced
Cornstarch
Oil for deep frying
Sweet-and-Sour Sauce
2 large green peppers, seeded and cut in 1" squares
2 tablespoons sliced green onions
2 large tomatoes, cut in small wedges
2 cups pineapple chunks
Chinese parsley

Cut pork in thin strips, then in 1" pieces. Marinate ½ hour in mixture of next 4 ingredients. Turn occasionally. Remove pork; dredge in 6 tablespoons cornstarch. Cook meat, a few pieces at a time, in hot deep fat (380°F.) 8 to 10 minutes, or until crisp and brown. Drain on absorbent paper; keep warm. Meanwhile make Sweet-and-Sour Sauce in large skillet, adding green pepper and onions. Cook 1 minute over high heat. Add tomato, pineapple and cooked meat; add 2 tablespoons cornstarch mixed with ¼ cup water. Stir and cook 1 minute, or until sauce is thickened and hot. Turn onto heated serving platter. Garnish with Chinese parsley. Makes 6 to 8 servings. **Sweet-and-Sour Sauce** Combine 1 cup pineapple juice, ½ cup white vinegar, ¼ cup catsup, ³/₄ cup packed brown sugar, 1 tablespoon Worcestershire and a dash of hot pepper sauce. Bring to boil and simmer ½ minute.

SZEGEDI GULYAS
(Hungarian Pork-and-Sauerkraut Goulash)

2 pounds sauerkraut, drained
2 bay leaves
1/4 teaspoon white pepper
1 teaspoon caraway seeds
1 teaspoon sugar
1 large onion, minced
2 tablespoons fat
2 tablespoons paprika
1-1/2 pounds lean pork, cubed
1 cup dairy sour cream
Boiled potatoes

Simmer sauerkraut with 1½ cups water, seasonings and sugar 45 minutes. In large heavy skillet or Dutch oven sauté onion in fat until golden. Add paprika and pork; cook several minutes, stirring. Blend in sauerkraut mixture. Simmer slowly at least 1 hour, covered. Add a little bouillon or water if mixture becomes too dry. Just before serving stir in sour cream and heat. Serve with potatoes. Makes 6 servings.

LOUISVILLE SCRAPPLE

1 pound lean pork shoulder or neck
Salt
Black and red pepper
1 onion
1 bunch celery tops
1/2 cup white cornmeal
1/2 teaspoon crumbled dried sage
Flour

Put pork, 1 teaspoon salt, black and red pepper to taste, the onion, celery tops and 1 quart water in heavy kettle. Bring to boil, cover and simmer 2 hours or until meat is tender, adding more water if necessary. Strain and set broth aside to cool. There should be 2 cups. When meat can be handled, discard any bone, skin, fat or gristle, and grind the lean part. Pour broth back into a saucepan and bring to boil. Slowly add cornmeal, stirring constantly. Cook 5 to 10 minutes to a very thick mush, continuing to stir. Add ground pork, sage and salt and pepper to taste. Remove from heat and pour into greased 8" square pan or 2 lightly greased 2-cup cans. Refrigerate 12 hours until firm. Remove bottoms of cans with can opener, then carefully free outside of scrapple from container and push out. Cut in ½" slices. Dip in flour and brush off excess. Put into hot skillet and fry until golden brown. Turn and brown on other side; be careful not to let burn. Scrapple is served for breakfast, with syrup or a poached egg. It also makes a nice luncheon or supper main dish with applesauce and gingerbread or with sautéed apple wedges and parsley. Serves 6 to 8.

CURRIED PORK

Brown 1 pound diced lean pork in 1 tablespoon fat. Add 1 chopped onion and 2 apples, peeled and diced; brown lightly. Add 2 tablespoons flour, 1 to 2 teaspoons curry powder, 1/4 teaspoon ginger, 1/8 teaspoon garlic salt, 2 cups bouillon and 1 tablespoon lemon juice. Cover; simmer 35 minutes. Serve on hot cooked rice. Makes 4 to 6 servings.

PIKANTES SCHWEINEFLEISCH MIT MEERRETTICH
(Austrian Piquant Pork with Horseradish)

2 pounds lean pork
2 tablespoons butter or margarine
1 cup vinegar
1 medium onion, stuck with 3 cloves
1 medium carrot
1 small celery root (celeriac), peeled, or 1 celery stalk
1 tablespoon salt
1 teaspoon caraway seed
1/2 teaspoon pepper
1/4 cup prepared horseradish
Boiled potatoes (optional)

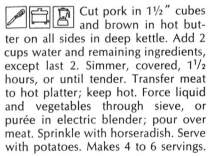 Cut pork in 1½" cubes and brown in hot butter on all sides in deep kettle. Add 2 cups water and remaining ingredients, except last 2. Simmer, covered, 1½ hours, or until tender. Transfer meat to hot platter; keep hot. Force liquid and vegetables through sieve, or purée in electric blender; pour over meat. Sprinkle with horseradish. Serve with potatoes. Makes 4 to 6 servings.

MOCK GOOSE

4 slices fresh ham, 1/2" thick (8 servings)
Salt and pepper
1-1/2 cups dried apple rings, soaked
16 pitted prunes
2 tablespoons margarine
2 jars (1 pound each) sweet-sour red cabbage
2 tablespoons light-brown sugar

Pound meat slices thin and halve lengthwise. Season with salt and pepper. Put 1 apple ring and 1 prune on each, roll up and secure with toothpick. Cook slowly in browned margarine in hot skillet until browned on all sides. In large heavy saucepan, mix cabbage, sugar and remaining apples and prunes. Arrange meat rolls on cabbage. Pour 1 cup boiling water into skillet and scrape up browned bits with spoon. Pour over meat and cabbage. Cover, bring to boil and simmer 1 hour and 15 minutes, or until tender. Add more water if necessary. Makes 8 servings.

SAVORY PORK TENDERLOIN

Roll 8 thin slices pork tenderloin in flour. Brown on both sides in a little fat. Drain off fat and sprinkle meat with salt and pepper. Add 1 chopped medium onion, 1 teaspoon each Worcestershire and sugar, 1/2 teaspoon chili powder and 1 cup canned tomatoes. Cover; simmer 1 hour, turning meat occasionally. Makes 4 servings.

BAKED PORK TENDERLOIN

Season 2 small pork tenderloins and roll in flour. Brown on all sides in 2 tablespoons hot oil. Remove to shallow baking dish. Lightly brown in drippings 1 stalk celery, diced, and 1 small onion, chopped. Put with meat. Mix 1 envelope mushroom-soup mix and 1½ cups water. Pour over meat. Cover; bake in moderate oven (350° F.) 2 hours. Makes 6 to 8 servings.

PORK, STROGANOFF-STYLE

Dredge 1 pound lean pork, cut in thin strips, with 1/4 cup seasoned flour. Brown in 2 tablespoons hot fat. Add 1 cup water, 1 beef bouillon cube, 3 tablespoons catsup or tomato purée, 1 teaspoon Worcestershire and 1 can (3 ounces) sliced mushrooms with liquid. Cover and simmer about 30 minutes. Just before serving, stir in 1 cup dairy sour cream. Serve with hot rice. Makes 4 servings.

PORC À LA FLAMANDE
(Flemish Pork)

2 pounds pork shoulder, diced
2 tablespoons fat
Salt and pepper
2 cups beer
1 teaspoon crushed dried rosemary
4 onions, halved
2 cups bouillon
2 packages (10 ounces each) frozen Brussels sprouts
2 cups cooked sliced potato
1-3/4 cups cooked sliced carrot
1/4 cup flour

Brown pork pieces in fat in large kettle. Sprinkle with salt and pepper. Add beer, rosemary and 1/2 cup boiling water. Simmer, covered, 45 minutes. Add onions and cook 30 minutes. Stir in bouillon and Brussels sprouts. Cover and cook until sprouts are tender, about 10 minutes. Add potato and carrot. Blend flour and water to a smooth paste. Slowly stir into pork mixture. Cook until liquid is thickened, stirring occasionally. Makes 6 to 8 servings.

PORK BUTT WITH CARAWAY SAUERKRAUT

2 pounds lean fresh pork butt
1/4 teaspoon whole black peppercorns
2 pounds sauerkraut
2 tablespoons caraway seed
1/2 cup packed brown sugar
2 cups diced unpeeled green apples

Put pork and peppercorns in 2" boiling water in kettle. Simmer, covered, 1½ to 2 hours, or until tender. Rinse sauerkraut under running cold water and drain thoroughly. Add sauerkraut and remaining ingredients to pork. Cook 20 minutes longer. Makes 4 to 6 servings.

CREAMY PORK HASH

1 medium onion, sliced
3 tablespoons butter or margarine
1 can condensed cream of mushroom soup
1/2 cup milk
1 teaspoon Worcestershire
1/4 teaspoon hot pepper sauce
1 cup diced cooked pork
1 cup diced cooked potato
1/2 cup cooked peas
1 teaspoon paprika

Sauté onion in hot butter until soft and golden. Blend in next 4 ingredients. Add remaining ingredients. Cook over low heat 10 minutes, or until heated through, stirring often. Makes 4 servings.

SATÉ BABI
(Indonesian Skewered Pork)

1 cup salted peanuts
2 tablespoons ground coriander
2 cloves garlic
1 teaspoon crushed red pepper, or 1/4 teaspoon hot pepper sauce
1 cup sliced onions
1/4 cup lemon juice
2 tablespoons brown sugar
1/4 cup soy sauce
1/2 teaspoon pepper
1/2 cup butter or margarine, melted
1/2 cup bouillon
2 pounds lean pork, cut into 1" cubes

Combine all ingredients, except butter, bouillon and pork, in electric blender. Blend mixture to a fine purée. Transfer to a saucepan and bring to boil, add melted butter and bouillon and remove from heat. Cool and pour over pork cubes. Marinate at least 3 hours. Thread pork on skewers and broil slowly over charcoal or under broiler, turning frequently to brown and cook on all sides. Cook 25 to 30 minutes, basting with marinade. If any remains, heat and serve with meat. Serves 4 to 6.

PORK HOCKS WITH VEGETABLES

4 pork hocks
1 bay leaf
1 clove garlic
2 teaspoons salt
1/4 teaspoon pepper
4 sweet potatoes
4 large white turnips, quartered

Put hocks in kettle and cover with water. Add seasonings, cover and simmer 2 hours. Add potatoes and turnips. Cook ½ hour. Skin hocks and arrange on hot platter with vegetables. Makes 4 servings.

SPARERIBS HAWAIIAN

4 pounds spareribs, cut in servings
2 onions, chopped
2 cloves garlic, minced
1-1/2 cups pineapple juice
1/2 cup vinegar
1 teaspoon salt
Dash of pepper
1 teaspoon each paprika, chili powder, sugar and dry mustard
2 tablespoons cornstarch
1 can (9 ounces) crushed pineapple, undrained

Brown spareribs on all sides in heavy kettle. Remove meat and pour off fat. Return ribs to kettle; add onions and garlic. Mix pineapple juice, vinegar and seasonings; pour over meat. Cover and simmer 2 hours or until meat is tender, basting occasionally with liquid. Remove ribs to hot platter. Blend cornstarch and pineapple; stir into liquid in kettle and cook a few minutes, stirring. Serve over ribs. Makes 4 to 6 servings.

SWEET-AND-SOUR SPARERIBS

3 pounds spareribs, cut in 1-1/2"-wide pieces
3 tablespoons flour
1 cup diced celery
1 cup chopped green pepper
1 medium onion, chopped
1/2 cup maple syrup or substitute
1 can (1 pound) pineapple chunks with syrup
1/4 cup vinegar
1/3 cup soy sauce
Salt and pepper to taste

Roast spareribs in hot oven (400°F.) 30 minutes, or until golden brown, stirring occasionally. Remove ribs from roasting pan and drain off all but ¼ cup drippings. Blend in flour, add remaining ingredients and mix well. Put ribs in sauce and bake in moderate oven (375°F.) 1½ hours, or until tender, basting often. Remove ribs to a hot serving dish and top with sauce. Thicken sauce if necessary with 1 tablespoon cornstarch blended with a little water. Serves 4.

SPARERIBS, KOREAN STYLE

4 pounds pork spareribs, cut in
   individual ribs
3/4 cup soy sauce
3/4 cup sherry
1 tablespoon grated fresh gingerroot
1 clove garlic, crushed
1/4 cup sesame seed
Duck Sauce

Cook ribs in Dutch oven, covered, in moderate oven (375°F.)
1 hour. Drain off fat. Combine remaining ingredients, except sauce,
and marinate ribs in the mixture 30 to
60 minutes. Lay ribs in one layer on
rack in large shallow baking pan and
brush with marinade. Bake in hot oven
(400°F.) about 20 minutes, brushing
several times with marinade. Can be
broiled (watch carefully) in oven or
grilled. Marinade can be reused. Serve
with Duck Sauce. Makes 4 to 6 servings. **Note** Ribs can be precooked 1
hour, then refrigerated to be marinated and browned the following day.
Duck Sauce Mix well 2 jars (12 ounces
each) peach jam or preserves; 1/3 cup
cider vinegar; 1 teaspoon onion salt;
1 teaspoon ground ginger; 1/8 teaspoon each ground allspice, cloves
and nutmeg; 1/8 teaspoon dry mustard
and 1/2 teaspoon angostura bitters.

APPLE-STUFFED SPARERIBS

4 pounds fresh spareribs in matching
   sides
2 teaspoons salt
1/2 teaspoon pepper
3 medium cooking apples, cored,
   peeled and cut in wedges
2 tablespoons brown sugar
2 cups apple juice, heated

Rub spareribs on both sides with salt
and pepper. Put one side of ribs, fat
side down, on foil-lined roasting pan.
Cover with apples; sprinkle with sugar.
Put second side of ribs on top, fat side
up. Add apple juice. Bake in moderate
oven (350°F.), basting occasionally, 2½
to 3 hours, until very tender. Serve
hot or cold. Makes 6 to 8 servings.

BROWN PORK HASH

2 cups chopped cold roast pork
2 cups chopped cold boiled potatoes
1/4 cup butter or margarine
1 large onion, sliced
1-1/2 teaspoons salt
1/4 teaspoon pepper
Hot bouillon or water

Brown meat and potatoes in hot
butter in skillet. Add next 3 ingredients and bouillon to cover. Simmer, covered, 45 minutes. Serves 4.

PORK IN OLIVE SAUCE

2 tablespoons flour
2 tablespoons fat
1/2 teaspoon each salt and paprika
2 tablespoons brown sugar
1 tablespoon lemon juice
1 teaspoon instant minced onion
2-1/2 cups cold cooked pork in strips
1/2 cup chopped pimiento-stuffed olives

Brown flour lightly in the hot fat
in skillet. Add 1 cup water and
next 4 ingredients. Cook, stirring, 5
minutes. Add meat and cook, covered,
stirring occasionally, 5 minutes. Add
olives and heat gently. Makes 4 servings.

PORK STEW, HUNGARIAN STYLE

2 tablespoons butter or margarine
4 medium onions, cut in wedges
2 cloves garlic, minced
2 tablespoons paprika
2 teaspoons salt
1/2 teaspoon freshly ground pepper
3 pounds boneless pork in 1-1/2" cubes
1 green pepper, chopped
1 can (8 ounces) tomato sauce
Hot cooked noodles, rice or potatoes

Melt butter in Dutch oven or
heavy stove-top casserole. Add
onions and garlic and sauté over low
heat until onions are golden. Stir in
paprika, salt and pepper; then add remaining ingredients, except noodles.
Cover and simmer over very low heat,
stirring occasionally, 2½ to 3 hours.
Add a little boiling water if stew becomes too thick. Serve on noodles.
Makes 6 to 8 servings.

PORK STEW WITH APPLES AND POTATOES

1 pound boneless pork, cut in 1" cubes
2 tablespoons margarine
1/2 teaspoon paprika
1/4 teaspoon white pepper
2 teaspoons salt
2 tablespoons flour
3 medium onions, sliced
3 cups potato, cut in 1/4" slices
2 tart medium apples, cored, peeled
   and cut in wedges
1-1/2 cups broth or water
Chopped parsley

Brown meat in large heavy saucepan or Dutch oven in browned
margarine. Add seasonings and sauté
while preparing vegetables and apples.
Sprinkle with flour and add remaining
ingredients, except parsley. Cover and
simmer slowly about 40 minutes, or
until all is tender. Sprinkle with parsley. Makes 6 servings.

TON-YUK KUI
(Korean Broiled Pork)

1 pound lean pork
1/3 cup soy sauce
2 tablespoons sugar
1 green onion, chopped
1 clove garlic, minced
1 teaspoon chopped candied ginger
2 tablespoons toasted sesame seed
1/8 teaspoon pepper

Cut pork in very thin pieces. Mix remaining ingredients and mix well with pork. Let stand 15 minutes. Broil under medium heat until browned and done. Makes 4 servings.

BREADED PIGS' KNUCKLES

6 pigs' knuckles
1 medium onion, stuck with 3 cloves
2 teaspoons salt
1 egg, beaten
Fine dry bread crumbs
1/2 cup shortening

Put pigs' knuckles in kettle with boiling water to cover. Cook 15 minutes. Remove with slotted spoon; reserve liquid. Plunge knuckles into cold water. Pull off skins. Return knuckles to liquid. Add onion and salt. Cook, covered, until meat falls off bones, about 2 hours; drain. Pick meat off bones and cut in bite-size pieces. Dip first in egg, then in crumbs. Sauté on all sides in hot shortening until brown. Serves 4.

HAM BISCUIT ROLL WITH CHEESE SAUCE

A beautiful luncheon dish using the small pieces of ham.

1/4 cup butter or margarine
1/4 cup flour
2 cups milk
1-1/2 to 2 cups ground cooked ham
1 tablespoon instant minced onion
Salt and pepper
Dry mustard
Baking-powder biscuit dough, page 307
3/4 cup grated Cheddar cheese

Melt butter and blend in flour. Gradually add milk and cook, stirring, until thickened. Mix ham, onion and 1/4 teaspoon each salt, pepper and dry mustard. Add enough sauce to hold ham mixture together. Roll out biscuit dough to form a rectangle about 12" x 10". Spread with ham mixture. Roll up from 10" end as for jelly roll. Cut in 1" slices and put, cut side down, on greased baking sheet. Bake in very hot oven (450°F.) 15 to 20 minutes. Meanwhile, add cheese to remaining sauce and heat, stirring, until cheese is melted. Season to taste with salt, pepper and dry mustard. Serve on ham biscuits. Serves 6.

BAKED COUNTRY-STYLE HAM

Unwrap cook-before-eating ham and soak 24 to 30 hours in cold water to cover; drain. Put ham in large kettle or old-fashioned wash boiler, cutting off tip of ham if necessary. Cover with water, bring to boil and simmer, covered, until tender (allow about 25 to 30 minutes per pound), or until large bone in heavy end of ham becomes loose and protrudes. Remove ham; cut off skin. If desired, score fat and top with a glaze. (See Glazing Ham and Glazes for Baked Ham, page 121.) Serve hot or cold, sliced paper-thin. *Note* Country-style ham can be bought already cooked. Bake according to label directions.

HAM-AND-EGG PIROSHKI

1 medium onion, minced
2 tablespoons butter
1/2 cup chopped cooked ham
2 hard-cooked eggs, chopped
1 tablespoon chopped parsley
1 teaspoon chopped fresh dill or dillweed
Dairy sour cream
1/2 recipe Standard Pastry, page 419
1 egg, beaten

Cook onion in butter until golden. Add next 4 ingredients and enough sour cream to moisten. Roll pastry to 1/8" thickness. Cut in 2 1/2" to 3" rounds. Put a small spoonful of mixture in center of each, moisten edges and pinch together firmly along the top, making pointed canoe-shaped pastries. Brush with egg and bake in hot oven (400°F.) 10 to 15 minutes, or until brown. Makes 2 dozen.

CURRIED PINEAPPLE HAM

1/2 cup chopped onion
2-1/2 tablespoons butter
3 tablespoons flour
1 cup chicken broth
1 can (1 pound) pineapple chunks
2 tablespoons chutney, chopped
1 tablespoon curry powder
1/2 teaspoon salt
Pepper to taste
2 cups ham chunks
Orange Rice

In skillet, sauté onion in the butter 2 to 3 minutes. Stir in flour, then gradually add broth and pineapple syrup, stirring. Stir in next 4 ingredients and simmer 10 minutes. Add pineapple and ham chunks. Heat thoroughly and serve on Orange Rice. Makes 4 servings. **Orange Rice** Prepare 4 servings rice, adding grated rind of 1 orange before cooking.

HAM À LA KING

1 cup finely chopped green pepper
2 tablespoons butter or margarine
2 tablespoons flour
2 cans (4 ounces each) sliced mushrooms
Milk
1/2 cup heavy cream
2 egg yolks, slightly beaten
2 cups ham in thin strips
1 jar (4 ounces) pimientos, drained and
   cut in small pieces
1 teaspoon lemon juice
2 tablespoons sherry
Salt and pepper to taste
Toast or croustades

Cook green pepper in the butter until soft but not brown. Blend in flour. Drain liquid from mushrooms and add milk to make 1 cup. Gradually add with cream to flour mixture and cook, stirring, until thickened. Mix a little hot cream sauce with egg yolks; then add yolks to sauce in pan. Add remaining ingredients, except toast, and stir over low heat until sauce is thick and hot. Serve on toast or in croustades. Makes 6 servings. **Croustades** Cut unsliced white bread 2" thick; remove crusts. Cut into oblongs and hollow out, leaving a shell 3/8" thick. Brush with melted butter and bake in moderate oven (375°F.) 12 to 15 minutes, or until golden brown.

TO BAKE HAM

To bake ham, put meat, fat side up, on rack in shallow roasting pan. Add no water; do not cover or baste. Insert a meat thermometer in thickest part of meat. Bake in slow oven (325°F.) for time indicated below. Cook-before-eating hams should be baked to an internal temperature of 160°F. Fully-cooked hams, which include all canned hams, can be reheated to an internal temperature of 125°F. to 130°F.

RECOMMENDED BAKING TIME

Type of ham	Minutes per pound
Cook-before-eating	
Whole ham	18 to 20
Half ham	22 to 25
Roll-shaped boned ham	30
Fully-cooked	
Whole ham	10
Half ham	14
Roll-shaped boned ham	12 to 15
Canned, 8 to 13 pounds	10 to 15
6 pounds	15 to 20

Glazing Ham Half an hour before end of baking time, remove ham from oven and carefully remove any skin. With knife, score fat lightly in diamond shapes. Stud ham with whole cloves; cover with desired glaze (see above right). Bake 30 minutes more.

GLAZES FOR BAKED HAM

Molasses Mix 1/2 cup each vinegar and molasses.

Jelly Mash 1 cup cranberry, currant or other tart jelly.

Marmalade Use 1/2 cup orange, peach or apricot marmalade.

Pineapple Mix 1/2 cup crushed pineapple and 3/4 cup packed brown sugar.

Honey Use 3/4 cup strained honey.

Honey and Peanut Butter Mix 1/2 cup each strained honey and smooth peanut butter.

Mustard-Molasses Mix 1/2 cup sugar, 1/3 cup molasses and 1/2 teaspoon dry mustard.

Butterscotch Mix 3/4 cup packed brown sugar, 2 teaspoons dry mustard and small amount of ham fat.

Applesauce Mix 1/2 cup corn syrup, 1 cup strained applesauce and 2 tablespoons prepared mustard.

Sweet-pickle Use liquid drained from gherkins or other sweet pickle.

GLAZED BANANA-HAM ROLLS

Cut 4 firm ripe bananas in half crosswise, then each half in 2 lengthwise pieces. Spread one cut side with peanut butter and cover with matching piece, sandwich fashion. Wrap each of the 8 "sandwiches" in a long, thin slice of cooked ham. Sauté rolls lightly in hot margarine until browned on both sides. Add 1/4 cup honey and 1/2 cup orange juice, mixed together. Cook a few minutes longer, basting to glaze with liquid in the pan. Serves 4.

BAKED HAM SLICE WITH APPLE RINGS

1-1/2-pound center-cut fully-cooked ham
   slice, about 1" thick
3/4 cup packed brown sugar
1/2 teaspoon each ground cloves and
   cinnamon
3 medium tart apples
1/2 cup pineapple juice

Gash fat in ham slice to prevent curling. Mix brown sugar and spices and rub one fourth of mixture into one side of ham. Put sugar side down in shallow baking dish. Peel and core apples and cut in 1/2" slices. Arrange around ham. Sprinkle apples and ham with remaining sugar mixture. Heat juice to boiling and pour over all. Bake, uncovered, in moderate oven (350°F.) about 45 minutes. Remove ham and apples to hot platter and pour liquid over all. Makes 4 servings.

HAM IN RAISIN SAUCE

1/3 cup seedless raisins
1 cup packed brown sugar
2 tablespoons cornstarch
Pinch of salt
1/4 teaspoon ginger
2 tablespoons vinegar
2 cups chunky pieces cooked ham
1 package (8 ounces) wide noodles, cooked

Cook raisins in 2 cups water 5 minutes. Add next 5 ingredients. Cook, stirring, until slightly thickened. Add ham and heat. Put hot cooked noodles in deep platter. Cover with ham and sauce. Serves 4.

BRAISED PORK BUTT WITH ORANGE-CRANBERRY SAUCE

3-pound ready-to-eat smoked pork butt
1/4 teaspoon salt
1/4 teaspoon pepper
1 can (1 pound) whole-cranberry sauce
Grated rind and juice of 1 orange
Additional orange juice (if necessary)

Put meat in kettle just large enough to hold it. Add ¾ cup water and cook slowly, uncovered, until water has evaporated. Brown meat with fat left in pan. Pour off excess fat and sprinkle meat with salt and pepper. Add cranberry sauce, orange rind and juice. Cover and simmer about 1½ hours. Check occasionally for dryness. Add more orange juice, ¼ cup at a time, as necessary. Makes 6 servings.

HAM-CAULIFLOWER CASSEROLE

1 large head cauliflower
Salt
1-1/2 cups diced cooked ham
Butter
3 tablespoons chopped chives or green onions
1 cup dairy sour cream
1/2 teaspoon paprika
Dash of white pepper
Dash of nutmeg
2 egg yolks, lightly beaten
Sharp Cheddar cheese, grated

Cook cauliflower in salted water until almost done. Drain, cool and break into flowerets. Grease casserole and make alternate layers of cauliflower and ham. Dot with butter. Mix ¼ teaspoon salt and remaining ingredients, except cheese. Pour into casserole. Bake, covered, in moderate oven (375°F.) until bubbly, about 30 minutes. Remove cover, top with layer of cheese and bake until browned, about 15 minutes. Or put under broiler to brown. Makes 6 servings.

HAM BAKED IN CLARET

1 center-cut ready-to-eat ham slice, 1" thick (about 2 pounds)
1 teaspoon dry mustard
2 cups chopped peeled tart apples
1/2 cup packed brown sugar
1 cup claret

Put ham in large shallow baking dish. Sprinkle with mustard. Top with apples and sprinkle with brown sugar. Pour claret over ham. Cover and bake in moderate oven (350°F.) 1 hour. Uncover and bake 30 minutes longer, or until ham is tender. Makes 4 servings.

SKILLET HAM AND SWEETS

3 tablespoons minced onion
1/4 cup butter or margarine
2 tablespoons flour
1 can (8 ounces) pineapple tidbits
1/3 cup packed brown sugar
2 cups diced ham
3 cups sliced cooked sweet potato

Cook onion in the butter 2 to 3 minutes. Blend in flour. Drain syrup from pineapple and add water to make ½ cup. Gradually add to first mixture and cook, stirring, until thickened. Stir in pineapple, sugar and ham. Arrange sweet potato on top; bring to boil. Cover and simmer 10 minutes, or until thoroughly heated. Makes 4 servings.

HAM TETRAZZINI

8 ounces thin spaghetti
1/4 cup chopped onion
1/4 cup butter or margarine
3 tablespoons flour
1/2 teaspoon salt
Dash each of pepper and nutmeg
2-3/4 cups milk
1/4 cup chopped green pepper
1 can (3 ounces) sliced mushrooms, undrained
1 can (4 ounces) pimientos, chopped
3/4 cup grated Romano or Parmesan cheese
1-1/2 cups cooked ham strips

Cook spaghetti according to package directions, or until just tender. Meanwhile cook onion in the butter 2 to 3 minutes. Blend in flour and seasonings. Gradually add milk and cook, stirring, until thickened. Stir in next 3 ingredients. Combine half the cheese with the spaghetti and put half of this mixture in 2-quart baking dish about 2" deep. Arrange half the ham over spaghetti. Pour half the sauce over. Repeat layers, ending with sauce. Sprinkle with remaining cheese. Bake in moderate oven (375°F.) 25 minutes, or until lightly browned and bubbly. Makes 4 to 6 servings.

HOW TO STRETCH CERTAIN CUTS OF HAM

HAM THREE WAYS

Purchase 6- to 8-pound shank end of ham (have butcher remove hock).

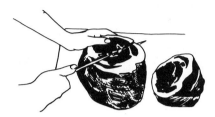

Cut 6 ham steaks and 1 pound diced ham (you'll also have 1 large soup bone and a 1- to 1½-pound ham hock).

1 Place ham on its largest cut surface. One side of ham contains bone; other side is boneless. Insert knife as close to bone as possible, slice down and remove bony side of ham.

2 Cut as much meat as possible away from bone (just hack away until bone is nearly clean). Dice ham you have cut away. Store for use in casseroles, scrambled eggs or omelets.

3 Place boneless side of ham on its freshly cut surface. Slice in 6 equally thick ham steaks.

4 How about brewing up a pot of pea soup with the hock and bone?

DEVILED HAM STEAKS

6 ham steaks
1 teaspoon dry mustard
1/4 cup packed brown sugar
2 tablespoons cider vinegar

Arrange steaks on rack in shallow baking pan. Mix remaining ingredients and sprinkle on steaks. Broil under moderate heat until well browned. Turn and baste with pan drippings. Broil until lightly browned. Makes 6 servings.

HAM A LA CRÉME

2 medium onions, minced
6 tablespoons butter or margarine
6 tablespoons flour
2 cups light cream
1 cup milk
1/4 cup tomato purée
1/2 cup white wine
Salt and pepper to taste
2-pound fully-cooked ham steak, about 1" thick

Sauté onion in butter in top part of double boiler over direct heat until tender but not browned. Stir in flour. Gradually add cream and milk and cook, stirring, until smooth and thickened. Add tomato purée, wine and seasoning. Cook over hot water 15 to 20 minutes, stirring occasionally. Cut ham in ¼" strips and heat in skillet. Put on hot platter and cover with sauce. Makes 6 servings.

FRENCH PARSLEYED HAM

2 to 3 cups broth or bouillon
1-1/2 tablespoons unflavored gelatin
3 cups diced cooked ham, in 1/2" cubes
About 1 cup chopped parsley
Mustard sauce

Use clear meat or chicken broth for aspic. For each 2 cups cold broth use 1 envelope gelatin; heat to dissolve. Cool slightly. Mix diced ham with parsley and press firmly into mold or bowl. Pour cooled gelatin mixture over ham to cover, using knife to help broth reach bottom of mold. Cover with a plate and top with a weight. Chill thoroughly. Unmold on platter, slice and serve with mustard sauce. Makes 6 servings.

Includes material from The Meat Book: A Consumer's Guide to Selecting, Buying, Cutting, Storing, Freezing and Carving the Various Cuts *by Travers Moncure Evans and David Greene with illustrations by Dana J. Greene, to be published by Charles Scribner's Sons. Text Copyright © 1973 Travers Moncure Evans. Illustrations Copyright © 1973 Dana J. Greene.*

SMOKED HOCK CHOPS

Purchase 4 smoked ham hocks of similar size, 1 to 1½ pounds each (make sure they are from the hind shank and not the foreshank, which looks the same but is smaller and is referred to as the knuckles).

Cut 3 hock chops, ½ to ¾ pound diced ham, smoked ham skin (for flavoring).

1 To remove hard-smoked outer skin from ham hocks, grasp shank end of hock firmly in one hand and puncture skin at wider end of hock with tip of knife.

2 Insert knife, blade side up, just inside puncture. Using sharp, upward cutting strokes, split skin in one continuous line until you have freed it completely from bone at opposite shank end.

3 Continue to grasp shank end in one hand and, with the other, hand-peel hard outer skin back in one piece until interior meat is fully exposed and skin is completely removed. Reserve skin (see Note). Repeat above steps until all hocks have been skinned. Skinless hocks, or hock chops, are easier to eat than unskinned ham hocks.

4 Select one hock for de-boning. Insert tip of knife into hock until it touches bone. Cut around bone, freeing meat, until all meat has been removed from bone (neatness does not count).

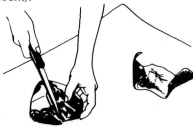

5 Dice hock meat fine and use in omelets, scrambled eggs, soups or stews.

Note Diced smoked ham-hock skin is a flavor booster for hearty soups, greens or beans. Smoked ham hocks are fully cooked and need only reheating by any method; or use them in combination with other foods. The average hock costs less and provides more lean meat than a pound of bacon.

SMOKED HAM HOCK CHOPS

To cook skinned ham hocks, put in large kettle, cover with water and add 1 each sliced onion and carrot. Bring to boil, cover and simmer 2 hours, or until tender. For boiled dinner, add cut carrots and potatoes last ½ hour of cooking and cabbage last 10 to 15 minutes. Use broth to make soup.

SPLIT-PEA SOUP

Ham hock and soup bone
1 pound green split peas
1 onion, chopped
2 carrots, chopped
3 ribs celery, chopped
Salt and pepper

Put bones in large kettle with next 4 ingredients and 2 quarts water. Bring to boil, cover and simmer, stirring several times, 1½ hours, or until peas are mushy. Remove meat from hock and add to soup. Season to taste with salt and pepper. Makes about 2 quarts.

HAM HASH

Force 4 medium potatoes, peeled and cooked; 1 onion, ½ green pepper, and 2 to 3 cups diced ham through coarse blade of food chopper. Stir in ¼ teaspoon salt, ⅛ teaspoon pepper and a dash of dried thyme. Heat 3 tablespoons butter in skillet, add mixture and cook, stirring frequently, until browned. Serves 4.

HAM-CHEESE-POTATO CASSEROLE

Diced ham
2 cups diced process Cheddar cheese
1 can (4 ounces) pimientos, drained
6 medium potatoes, peeled, cooked and diced
3 tablespoons butter or margarine
3 tablespoons flour
1-1/2 cups milk
Salt and pepper

Force first 3 ingredients through medium blade of food chopper. Spread in buttered shallow 1½-quart baking dish. Cover with the potato. Melt butter in saucepan. Blend in flour. Add milk and cook, stirring, until thickened. Season to taste with salt and pepper and pour over potatoes. Bake in moderate oven (350°F.) about 40 minutes. Makes 6 servings.

Includes material from The Meat Book: A Consumer's Guide to Selecting, Buying, Cutting, Storing, Freezing and Carving the Various Cuts by Travers Moncure Evans and David Greene with illustrations by Dana J. Greene, to be published by Charles Scribner's Sons. Text Copyright © 1973 Travers Moncure Evans. Illustrations Copyright © 1973 Dana J. Greene.

HAM AND POTATOES CHANTILLY

3 large potatoes, cooked and riced
1/4 cup hot milk
2 tablespoons butter
Salt and pepper
1/2 cup finely chopped cooked ham
1/2 cup heavy cream
1 cup shredded sharp Cheddar cheese
Paprika

Beat until fluffy the first 3 ingredients; season to taste. Put in shallow 1-quart baking dish. Sprinkle with ham. Whip cream until stiff, fold in cheese and season to taste. Spread on potatoes, sprinkle with paprika. Bake in very hot oven (450°F.) 15 minutes. Makes 4 servings.

HAM HAWAIIAN

1/2 medium green pepper, chopped
2 cups slivered cooked ham
4 tablespoons butter
1 can (8 ounces) pineapple tidbits
2 tablespoons brown sugar
1-1/2 tablespoons cornstarch
1-1/2 tablespoons vinegar
1-1/2 teaspoons prepared mustard
1/8 teaspoon pepper
1-1/3 cups packaged precooked rice
1/8 teaspoon ground cloves

 Sauté green pepper and ham in 2 tablespoons butter in skillet 5 minutes. Drain pineapple, reserving liquid. Mix liquid with next 5 ingredients and ³⁄₄ cup cold water. Stir into ham mixture. Cook, stirring, until thickened. Add pineapple and heat. Prepare rice as directed on the package; add 2 tablespoons butter and the cloves. Serve with ham mixture. Makes 4 servings.

HAM-AND-ASPARAGUS TOAST

1 can (15 ounces) asparagus tips
8 thin slices bread, crusts removed
Butter or margarine
8 thin slices boiled ham
2 tablespoons flour
3/4 cup light cream or half-and-half
Salt and pepper

Drain asparagus, reserving 1/2 cup of the liquid. Brush bread lightly on both sides with melted butter. Place a slice of ham and several asparagus spears on each slice of bread and roll up or fold over; secure with toothpicks. Bake in hot oven (400°F.) 15 minutes, or until browned. Melt 2 tablespoons butter in saucepan and blend in flour. Gradually stir in asparagus liquid and cream; cook, stirring, until thickened. Season with salt and pepper. Put toast rolls on a hot platter and remove toothpicks. Pour sauce over top. Makes 4 servings.

SAUTEED HAM AND POTATOES

1 medium onion, sliced
2 tablespoons butter or margarine
2 cups sliced cooked potato
1 cup cooked ham pieces
Salt, pepper and paprika

 Cook onion in the butter until lightly browned. Add potato and ham and season with salt, pepper and paprika. Cook until lightly browned, turning several times with wide spatula or pancake turner. Makes 4 servings.

HAM IN CIDER

1/2 bone-in, cook-before-eating
    smoked ham (about 6 pounds)
Cider (about 2 to 3 quarts)
2 large carrots, scraped and sliced
3 medium onions, peeled and sliced
3 stalks celery, diced
Few sprigs of parsley
12 whole cloves
6 whole black peppercorns
1 bay leaf

Put ham in kettle; add enough cider to cover. Add remaining ingredients. Bring to boil, cover and simmer 2 hours, or until tender. Serve hot. Or cool in the broth, then chill. Makes 8 servings.

DEVILED-HAM PANCAKES WITH CHEESE SAUCE

3 eggs
1-1/2 cups milk
1-1/2 cups pancake mix
Butter or margarine
2 cans (4-1/2 ounces each) deviled ham
1 cup condensed cheese soup

Beat eggs, add milk and pancake mix and beat until smooth. Let stand 1/2 hour, then beat again. Melt 1 teaspoon butter in 7" skillet and pour in 2 tablespoons batter. Rotate pan so batter completely covers surface. Brown lightly on both sides. Spread with deviled ham, roll and put in warm serving dish. Repeat until all of batter is used, making about 18. Serve with sauce of hot cheese soup. Makes 4 to 6 servings.

FRANKFURTERS, ITALIAN STYLE

Cook 1 small onion, minced, in 2 tablespoons butter until golden. Add 2 large potatoes, peeled and diced, 1 can (6 ounces) tomato paste, 1/2 cup water and salt and pepper to taste. Cover and simmer 20 minutes, until potato is tender. Add 1 pound frankfurters cut lengthwise in quarters; heat through. Makes 4 servings.

PIQUANT FRANKFURTER-POTATO SKILLET

4 large potatoes, peeled and thinly sliced
1/4 cup butter or margarine
1 medium onion, sliced
1/2 cup chopped green pepper
1/4 cup chopped pimiento
1 cup chopped dill pickle
1/4 cup dill-pickle liquid
1/2 teaspoon salt
1/4 teaspoon pepper
1/2 pound frankfurters, cut in 1" pieces

 Cook potatoes in butter until browned on both sides. Add remaining ingredients. Cook, covered, over low heat, stirring occasionally, 15 minutes, or until potatoes are tender. Makes 4 servings.

CREAMED FRANKFURTERS AND CHICKEN

6 large hard rolls
1/2 cup diced celery
1/4 cup butter or margarine
1/4 cup flour
1/2 teaspoon salt
1/8 teaspoon pepper
2-1/2 cups milk
1 cup diced cooked chicken
1/2 pound diced cooked frankfurters
2 tablespoons chopped parsley

Scoop out hard rolls; reserve crumbs for other uses. Sauté celery in butter until tender. Stir in flour, salt and pepper. Gradually add milk. Simmer until mixture thickens, stirring. Add chicken, frankfurters and parsley; heat. Serve in hard-roll shells. Makes 4 to 6 servings.

FRANKFURTER-STUFFED GREEN PEPPERS

6 large green peppers
1 onion, chopped
1/2 teaspoon instant minced garlic
1/4 cup butter or margarine
3/4 pound frankfurters, diced
1/2 cup grated Cheddar cheese
2 cups cooked rice
2 tablespoons chopped parsley
1/4 teaspoon pepper
Salt to taste
1 cup tomato juice

Cut stem ends off peppers and carefully remove the seeds and pith. Parboil 5 minutes. Sauté onion and garlic in butter until onion is soft. Add frankfurters and cook 5 minutes, stirring. Blend in next 5 ingredients. Stuff peppers and arrange in greased baking dish. Pour tomato juice around them. Bake in moderate oven (350°F.) 30 minutes, or until tender, basting occasionally. If peppers dry out, pour more tomato juice over. Makes 6 servings.

FRANKFURTERS AND CREAMED ONIONS

2 packages white-sauce mix
Milk
1/4 teaspoon marjoram
2 cans (1 pound each) white onions, drained
1 pound frankfurters, sliced
2 tablespoons sherry (optional)

Prepare white-sauce mix with milk as directed on package. Add next 3 ingredients. Simmer, covered, about 10 minutes. Add sherry, if desired. Makes 4 to 6 servings.

FRANKFURTER, SWEET-POTATO AND APPLE CASSEROLE

6 medium sweet potatoes, cooked, peeled and sliced
1/8 teaspoon salt
1 can (1 pound) applesauce
1/4 teaspoon nutmeg
2 tablespoons butter or margarine
1 pound frankfurters, scored

Put a layer of sweet potatoes in a shallow 2-quart baking dish. Sprinkle with salt, cover with applesauce and sprinkle with nutmeg. Put remaining potato slices on top and dot with butter. Arrange frankfurters on potatoes. Bake in moderate oven (350°F.) 25 to 30 minutes. Makes 6 servings.

FRANKFURTERS WITH FRUIT SAUCE

1/2 cup brown packed sugar
1-1/2 tablespoons flour
1/2 teaspoon dry mustard
1 can (12 ounces) apricot nectar
1/4 cup cider vinegar
1/2 cup raisins
3/4 pound frankfurters, sliced
Cooked noodles (optional)

Combine first 6 ingredients in saucepan and bring to a boil. Reduce heat and simmer, stirring, until thickened. Add frankfurters; cook 5 minutes. Serve over noodles, if desired. Makes 4 servings.

DEVILED DOGS

1 pound frankfurters
1 cup shredded process American cheese
1/3 cup pickle relish
1 teaspoon prepared mustard
1 tablespoon chili sauce
3 tablespoons salad dressing or mayonnaise

Split frankfurters lengthwise almost all the way through. Mix cheese at room temperature with a fork until smooth and soft. Mix in remaining ingredients. Stuff into frankfurters. Put under broiler until heated and cheese is slightly melted. Makes 4 servings.

DOGS IN BLANKETS

A delectable main dish for a teen-age supper.

8 skinless frankfurters
Flour
1/4 cup white cornmeal
1/4 teaspoon salt
1/4 teaspoon soda
1 egg
1/2 cup buttermilk
Fat for frying (part bacon, part lard)
Cocktail sauce, or catsup with prepared
mustard, or tartar sauce

Halve frankfurters crosswise and put wooden skewer in each. Roll in flour and shake off excess. Sift ½ cup flour and next 3 ingredients into bowl. Add egg and buttermilk and beat with whisk or slotted spoon to form a smooth thick batter. Holding skewer, dip frankfurter pieces in batter, coating well. Drop into hot deep fat (375°F. to 400°F. on a frying thermometer) and fry until golden brown. Drain on absorbent paper and serve at once with cocktail sauce. Good with coleslaw, potato chips, sliced tomatoes and dill pickles, with a piece of pie or cake for dessert. Makes 4 servings.

SOUR-CREAM FRANKFURTERS

1 pound frankfurters
2 tablespoons butter or margarine
1 package sour-cream-sauce mix
Milk
3 tablespoons catsup
Salt and pepper to taste

Cut frankfurters in ½" pieces and brown in butter. Prepare mix as directed on the package, increasing milk to ¾ cup. Stir in catsup. Add to frankfurters and heat a few minutes to blend; season to taste. Makes 4 servings.

THE ORIGINAL CONEY ISLAND HOT DOGS

8 frankfurters
1/3 cup sweet-pickle relish
2 tablespoons sweet-pickle liquid
1 tablespoon melted margarine
1 teaspoon prepared mustard
1/8 teaspoon pepper
1/8 teaspoon onion salt
1/8 teaspoon garlic salt
8 frankfurter rolls

Cut slits into frankfurters lengthwise almost all the way through. Fill with pickle relish; fasten with toothpicks. Combine remaining ingredients, except rolls, and mix well. Brush frankfurters with pickle mixture. Broil or cook on outdoor grill 5 to 7 minutes, brushing frequently with mixture. Serve in rolls. Makes 4 servings.

BARBECUED FRANKFURTERS AND ONIONS

Brown 1 pound small frankfurters lightly in 1 tablespoon margarine. Add ¾ cup bottled barbecue sauce and 1 can (1 pound) onions, drained; simmer about 5 minutes. Good with noodles. Makes 4 servings.

FRANKFURTERS WITH CABBAGE

1 small head red or green cabbage,
shredded
2 unpeeled tart apples, cored and sliced
2 tablespoons bacon fat
1-1/2 teaspoons salt
1/2 teaspoon pepper
1/2 pound frankfurters, halved or cut
into 2" pieces
3 tablespoons vinegar
1 teaspoon sugar
1 tablespoon flour

Put first 6 ingredients in large skillet; add just enough water to cover frankfurters. Bring to a boil, reduce heat and cover. Simmer, stirring frequently, till cabbage is tender but still crisp, about 15 minutes. Drain, reserving liquid. Combine last 3 ingredients in small saucepan and add cabbage liquid. Cook, stirring, until thick and smooth. Blend into cabbage mixture. Serves 4 to 6.

ALSATIAN CHOUCROUTE

4 strips bacon, diced
2 onions, chopped
2 pounds fresh or 1 can (29 ounces)
sauerkraut, drained
1 large carrot, peeled and diced
1 large potato, peeled and grated
3 apples, peeled and diced
1 pound knackwurst or kielbasa
1 slice ham, cut in 1" squares
2 fresh pork hocks
10 dried juniper berries
5 peppercorns
1 cup meat stock
1 cup dry white wine
Boiled potatoes

Sauté bacon and onion until limp but not brown. In large heavy casserole, mix sauerkraut with all vegetables, apple, bacon and bacon fat. Cut 1 knackwurst in ½" slices and add with ham and hocks to casserole. Crush berries; tie with peppercorns in cheesecloth and add to casserole. Pour stock and wine over the mixture; cover tightly and bake in moderate oven (350°F.) for 2 to 2½ hours. Check for dryness the last half hour, adding more stock if needed. Put rest of knackwurst, cut in half, on top. Cover and finish cooking. Remove spices in cloth. Serve with boiled potatoes. Makes 6 to 8 servings.

PIZZA FRANKS

1 clove garlic, minced
2 tablespoons olive or vegetable oil
1 can (10-3/4 ounces) condensed tomato
 soup
2 tablespoons chopped parsley
1/4 teaspoon crushed dried oregano
8 frankfurters, slit lengthwise
8 frankfurter rolls, split
6 ounces sliced mozzarella cheese

Sauté garlic in oil until golden. Add
¹/₄ cup water, soup, parsley and oregano. Bring to boil and simmer, stirring
frequently, 15 minutes. Put a frankfurter on each roll and arrange in large
shallow baking pan. Cover frankfurters with tomato sauce and top with
cheese. Put under broiler 1 minute, or
until cheese is melted and begins to
bubble. Makes 8 servings.

FRANKFURTERS ON ROLLS WITH SAUERKRAUT

8 long thin frankfurters (1 pound),
 partially split
8 tablespoons butter or margarine,
 softened
2 tablespoons prepared mustard
8 frankfurter rolls, partially split
1 small green pepper, slivered
1 small onion, chopped
1 pound sauerkraut, undrained

Sauté frankfurters lightly until
curled. Mix 6 tablespoons butter
and the mustard, spread on rolls and
toast under broiler. Sauté next 2 ingredients lightly in remaining butter.
Add sauerkraut and heat. Put a frankfurter on each roll and top with sauerkraut. Makes 8 servings.

FRANKFURTER-SUCCOTASH SKILLET

1/2 cup uncooked rice
1 medium onion, chopped
2 tablespoons butter or margarine
1 can (1 pound) tomatoes
2 boxes (10 ounces each) frozen
 succotash
2 teaspoons salt
1/4 teaspoon pepper
1 pound frankfurters
1 teaspoon prepared mustard
1 cup light cream or milk
Chopped parsley

Sauté rice and onion in butter in
heavy skillet over medium heat 5
minutes. Add next 4 ingredients and
¹/₂ cup water. Bring to boil, stir well,
cover and simmer 15 minutes. Score
tops of frankfurters at ¹/₂″ intervals.
Arrange on vegetables, scored side up.
Blend mustard with cream and add to
mixture. Simmer, covered, 8 minutes
longer. Sprinkle with parsley. Makes
6 servings.

FRANKFURTER-BUTTERMILK PANCAKES

1 cup buttermilk pancake mix
1 cup buttermilk
1 egg
1/2 pound frankfurters, cut in 1/4″ dice
1/3 cup minced green onion
1 tablespoon butter or margarine

Mix first 3 ingredients with ¹/₂
cup cold water until smooth.
Sauté frankfurters and onion in butter
a few minutes. Add to pancake batter
and mix well. Using about ¹/₄ cup batter for each pancake, drop mixture on
hot greased griddle or heavy skillet.
Bake on both sides until browned and
crisp. Serve at once. Makes about 14.

FRANKFURTERS WITH BROCCOLI AND CREAMED MUSHROOMS

1/4 cup butter or margarine
1 can (4 ounces) sliced mushrooms
1/4 cup flour
1 cup milk
2 teaspoons soy sauce
White pepper
1 package (10 ounces) frozen broccoli
 spears, cooked and drained
8 slices bacon, partially cooked
8 frankfurters
1/2 cup finely shredded Cheddar cheese
Fine dry bread crumbs

Melt butter in small saucepan. Drain
mushrooms, reserving liquid. Add
mushrooms to butter and sauté a few
minutes. Sprinkle with flour and mix
well. Add mushroom liquid and milk
and cook, stirring, until thickened.
Add soy sauce, and pepper to taste.
Pour into greased 10″ shallow baking
dish. Arrange broccoli in pinwheel
fashion on sauce. Wrap a slice of
bacon around each frankfurter and
put between broccoli spears. Sprinkle
with cheese and bread crumbs and
bake in very hot oven (450° F.) 10
minutes, or until heated and golden
brown. Makes 4 servings.

FRANKFURTER-CHEESE CRESCENTS

1 tube of 8 refrigerated crescent dinner
 rolls
Prepared mustard
8 frankfurters
8 strips Cheddar cheese

Unroll crescents and separate into triangles. Spread lightly with mustard.
Cut a shallow slit lengthwise in each
frankfurter and insert a cheese strip in
each. Place a frankfurter on wide end
of triangle and roll up. Put on ungreased cookie sheet, cheese side up.
Bake in moderate oven (375°F.) about
12 minutes. Makes 8 servings.

FRANKFURTERS WITH PUFFY TOPPING

1 pound frankfurters, slit lengthwise
1 jar (8 ounces) process-cheese spread
1/2 cup mayonnaise
1 egg, separated
Paprika

Arrange frankfurters, skin side up, in baking dish. Mix cheese spread with mayonnaise and egg yolk. Fold in stiffly beaten egg white and spread on frankfurters. Sprinkle lightly with paprika and bake in hot oven (400° F.) about 20 minutes. Good with a mixed green salad. Makes 4 servings.

SKILLET FRANKS WITH BEANS

6 frankfurters, sliced
2 teaspoons instant minced onion
1/4 teaspoon instant minced garlic (optional)
1/4 teaspoon crushed dried oregano leaves
1 tablespoon butter or margarine
1 can (28 ounces) New England-style baked beans
1 medium tomato, cut in thin wedges

Sauté first 4 ingredients in butter until frankfurter slices are lightly browned. Add beans and heat well. Add tomato wedges and heat gently. Makes 4 servings.

FRANKFURTER-SPAGHETTI CASSEROLE

4 tablespoons vegetable oil
2 medium onions, chopped
2 cloves garlic, minced
1 can (4 ounces) sliced mushrooms, drained
1-1/2 pounds frankfurters, in 1/2" slices
3 tablespoons catsup
1 tablespoon chopped parsley
1/2 teaspoon each pepper and oregano
1/2 cup small pimiento-stuffed olives
1/2 cup sliced sweet pickles
1 cup dry herb-seasoned bread stuffing
8 ounces spaghetti, broken in half, cooked and drained

Heat 2 tablespoons oil in large skillet. Add onions and garlic and cook until onions are golden. Add mushrooms and frankfurters and cook, stirring, 5 minutes. Add 2 cups boiling water, the parsley, seasonings, olives and pickles. Bring to boil, stirring, and simmer 5 minutes. Brown stuffing crumbs in remaining oil. Put half the spaghetti in shallow 3-quart casserole, pour in frankfurter mixture and top with remaining spaghetti. Sprinkle with browned crumbs and bake in moderate oven (350° F.) 20 to 30 minutes. Makes 6 to 8 servings.

FRANKFURTER-BACON CASSEROLE

1/2 pound bacon, cooked crisp and crumbled
1 pound frankfurters, sliced
1 can (1 pound) pork and beans with tomato sauce
1 can (1 pound) butter beans, drained
1 can (1 pound) pinto or red kidney beans
1/2 cup packed brown sugar
1 small onion, chopped
2 tablespoons wine vinegar
1/4 teaspoon oregano leaves, crushed

Mix half the bacon and remaining ingredients and put in greased 2½-quart casserole. Sprinkle with remaining bacon. Bake, uncovered, in moderate oven (350° F.), stirring occasionally, about 2 hours. Makes 8 servings.

FRANKFURTERS STUFFED WITH MASHED POTATOES

1 small onion, minced
1 tablespoon butter or margarine
2 cups seasoned mashed potatoes (not instant)
1 egg yolk
1/4 cup minced pimiento-stuffed olives
2 tablespoons chopped parsley
6 frankfurters
Grated sharp Cheddar cheese

Sauté onion in butter 2 to 3 minutes. Mix with potatoes, egg yolk, olives and parsley. Split frankfurters lengthwise almost through and open out. Divide potato mixture evenly on frankfurters and put on greased baking sheet. Sprinkle with cheese and bake in very hot oven (450°F.) 10 minutes, or until heated and browned on top. Makes 3 or 4 servings. Good as a hearty snack or luncheon dish.

FRANKFURTER HASH

4 cups fine diced cold boiled potato
1 medium onion, chopped
3 tablespoons flour
Salt and pepper
1/4 cup milk
1/2 pound frankfurters, thinly sliced
3 tablespoons butter or margarine
1/2 cup shredded sharp Cheddar cheese

Combine potato and onion, sprinkle with the flour and season with salt and pepper. Add milk and frankfurters and put in greased shallow baking dish or piepan. Dot with the butter and bake in hot oven (425°F.) 30 minutes. Top with cheese and bake 5 minutes longer, or until cheese is melted. Makes 4 servings. Good with pickled beets or green salad.

ENGLISH SAUSAGES IN ALE

1 pound link pork sausages
1 cup ale
2 bay leaves
5 peppercorns
5 whole cloves
Scrambled eggs, buttered toast, parsley
  (optional)

Put sausage in unheated heavy skillet; cook slowly over low heat until nicely browned but not done. Pour off fat; add ale and spices tied in cloth and simmer, covered, for 1/2 hour. Check for dryness; add more ale if needed. Can be made in chafing dish. Good with scrambled eggs and toast tips garnished with parsley, for brunch or supper treat. Makes 4 servings.

ITALIAN SAUSAGES WITH BEANS

1 pound sweet or hot Italian sausages
2 tablespoons olive oil
2 tablespoons tomato paste
1/4 teaspoon salt
1/8 teaspoon pepper (omit if hot sausages
  are used)
4 cups drained cooked kidney beans
1/4 cup bean liquid

Prick sausages and put in skillet with cold water to cover. Cook over moderate heat until water evaporates. Then cook 20 minutes, browning sausages on all sides. Add oil. Stir in remaining ingredients. Simmer 15 minutes, stirring occasionally. Makes 4 to 6 servings.

SAUSAGE, APPLE AND YAM CASSEROLE

2 packages (8 ounces each) brown-and-
  serve sausage links
1 cup applesauce
Lemon juice (if sauce is canned)
2 cups mashed cooked yams
1 tablespoon melted butter
2 eggs, beaten
1/2 teaspoon salt
1/2 teaspoon each cinnamon and ground
  cloves
Grating of nutmeg
3 tablespoons brown sugar
Coleslaw or sauerkraut slaw

Brown links lightly. Mix applesauce with lemon juice; add next 3 ingredients and seasonings. Put in casserole. Arrange links on top in spoke design. Sprinkle with brown sugar; cover and bake in moderate oven (375°F.) for 30 to 40 minutes, or until set. Serve with coleslaw. Makes 4 servings. Note Try mashed butternut or Hubbard squash in place of yams.

SCALLOPED SAUSAGE AND CORN

1 pound bulk fresh-pork sausage
1 can (1 pound) cream-style corn
6 soda crackers, crumbled
1 cup milk
1 egg, beaten
1/2 teaspoon salt
Dash of pepper, cayenne and nutmeg
1 large tomato, sliced

Use part of sausage to make 6 small balls. Brown balls and remaining sausage in skillet; drain. Crumble bulk sausage and mix with next 4 ingredients and seasonings. Pour in greased casserole, top with tomato slices and sausage balls. Place casserole in pan of hot water in moderate oven (350° F.). Bake until set, about 1 hour. Makes 4 to 6 servings.

CORN AND SAUSAGE, CREOLE

1/2 pound link sausages
1 onion, chopped
1/2 green pepper, chopped
1 tablespoon flour
1 bay leaf
1/2 teaspoon thyme
1 teaspoon salt
1/8 teaspoon pepper
1 can (19 ounces) tomatoes
2 cups cooked whole-kernel corn

Cut sausages in small pieces. Cook slowly in heavy skillet until browned. Add onion and green pepper and continue cooking until sausage is well done. Blend in flour and seasonings. Add tomatoes and corn, stirring constantly. Simmer 20 minutes. Makes 4 to 6 servings.

BAKED SAUSAGE, CABBAGE AND APPLES

1 pound sausage meat
3 tablespoons vinegar
1 teaspoon instant minced onion
2 tablespoons brown sugar
Salt and pepper
1 small cabbage, finely shredded
  (about 4 cups)
4 cups thinly sliced peeled tart apples
Nutmeg

Shape sausage meat in 8 flat patties. Brown on both sides in skillet, cooking until almost done. Remove sausage from skillet and add next 3 ingredients to fat. (If amount of fat seems excessive, pour off some.) Season with salt and pepper. Alternate layers of cabbage and apples in 3-quart casserole, seasoning each layer with salt, pepper and nutmeg. Arrange sausage patties on top and pour vinegar mixture over meat. Cover and bake in moderate oven (375°F.) about 45 minutes. Serves 4.

SAUSAGE HOT POT

1 pound brown-and-serve sausage links
4 onions, sliced thin
4 large raw potatoes, sliced
1 package frozen French-style green
  beans, thawed
1 cup sliced mushrooms
Butter
1 tablespoon flour
1 cup stock
1 teaspoon salt
1/2 teaspoon dry mustard
1/2 teaspoon Worcestershire
1/2 cup undiluted evaporated milk
Cayenne

Brown sausage lightly; put half in greased casserole and cover with all of onions, half of potatoes and all of beans. Sauté mushrooms in a little butter and put over beans; add remaining sausages and top with remaining potatoes. Add 1 tablespoon butter to fat remaining in pan. Add flour, stirring; add stock and seasonings and cook until thickened. Add milk and pour over casserole, parting with fork to let gravy through layers; sprinkle with cayenne and cover. Bake in moderate oven (350° F.) 1½ hours. Remove cover and let brown 20 minutes. Makes 4 to 6 servings.

SAUSAGE-STUFFED EGGPLANT

1 large or 2 medium eggplants
Salt
1 pound pork-sausage meat
1 large onion, chopped
1 clove garlic, minced
1/2 cup diced celery
1/2 cup diced green pepper
1 can (1 pound) tomatoes
1/4 teaspoon dried basil
1 teaspoon salt
Dash each black pepper and cayenne
1/2 teaspoon sugar
1/4 cup each dry bread crumbs and
  grated Parmesan cheese

Cut eggplant in half lengthwise and parboil in salted water 10 minutes. Remove carefully and cool. With sharp-edged spoon, scoop out pulp, leaving a shell ½" thick. Brown sausage quickly; remove, drain on toweling and crumble. Remove all but 2 tablespoons fat from skillet. Sauté the onion, garlic, celery and green pepper in the remaining fat in skillet until limp. Add chopped eggplant pulp, the tomatoes, seasonings and sugar; simmer 5 minutes. Add sausage; cook 5 minutes more. Pile in eggplant shells in greased baking dish. Top with crumbs mixed with cheese. Bake in moderate oven (375°F.) 45 minutes. Makes 4 to 6 servings.

SPICY SAUSAGE-POTATO CASSEROLE

4 to 5 teaspoons vegetable oil
1-1/2 cups thinly sliced peeled potato
1/2 cup chopped green pepper
1/3 cup chopped onion
3/4 pound sweet Italian sausage, cut in
  small pieces
6 eggs
1/2 cup milk
3/4 teaspoon baking powder
1/4 cup grated Parmesan cheese
Salt and pepper
1/2 cup canned tomato sauce
4 ounces mozzarella cheese

Use vegetable oil to grease shallow 2-quart casserole. Arrange vegetables and sausage in casserole. Bake in moderate oven (375°F.) 35 to 40 minutes. Beat together eggs, next 3 ingredients and salt and pepper to taste. Pour over first mixture, reduce heat to 325°F. and bake 30 minutes. Drizzle with sauce. Slice mozzarella, then cut in 1" pieces. Arrange on casserole; bake 10 minutes. Makes 6 servings.

SAVORY SAUSAGE CASSEROLE

1/2 pound pork-sausage meat
1 can (1 pound) red kidney beans,
  drained
1 cup sliced peeled tart apple
1/4 cup packed brown sugar
1 onion, sliced
1/2 cup tomato juice
1/8 teaspoon pepper
1/2 teaspoon chili powder

Cook sausage in skillet; pour off fat. Add remaining ingredients and pour into 1½-quart casserole. Cover and bake in moderate oven (350°F.) about 1 hour and 15 minutes. Makes 4 servings.

BOLOGNA-VEGETABLE DINNER

4 large potatoes, peeled and cut in
  1/2" slices
1 to 2 cups sliced carrots
1 small head cabbage, cut in quarters
  and sliced lengthwise in 1" strips
1 can (8 ounces) tomato sauce
2 teaspoons salt
2 teaspoons whole cumin seed
1/4 teaspoon black pepper
1-1/2 pounds bologna, cut in 1/2" slices
Chopped parsley
Prepared mustard

Layer potatoes in large heavy saucepan. Add next 6 ingredients and 1 cup water. Bring to boil, reduce heat, cover and simmer 20 minutes. Put bologna on top of cabbage, cover and simmer 6 to 8 minutes. Sprinkle generously with parsley and serve with mustard. Makes 6 servings.

BARBECUED BOLOGNA

For charcoal-broiling on a spit.

 Buy 2 pounds bologna in one piece. Score crosswise at 1" intervals to depth of 1/4". Put on spit in·rotisserie over charcoal. Center and lock. Brush with bottled barbecue sauce. Roast about 50 minutes, not too close to coals, brushing every 10 minutes with sauce. Serve, sliced, on toasted sandwich rolls. Serves 4 to 6.

CREAMED LUNCHEON MEAT AND POTATOES

1 can (12 ounces) luncheon meat, cut in 1/2" strips
1 onion, thinly sliced
2 tablespoons margarine
1 can condensed cream of mushroom soup
2/3 cup undiluted evaporated milk
1/2 teaspoon steak sauce
1/8 teaspoon pepper
2-1/2 cups diced cooked potato (4 medium)
Few sprigs of parsley, chopped

Lightly brown luncheon meat and onion in margarine in skillet. Stir in next 4 ingredients. Add potato and cook over low heat about 10 minutes, stirring occasionally. Sprinkle with parsley. Serves 4.

POLENTA CON SALSICCE
(Italian Cornmeal Mush with Sausages)

1 pound Italian sausage, sweet or hot
1 tablespoon olive oil
1 large onion, chopped
2 cloves garlic, minced
1 can (35 ounces) Italian tomatoes
1 can (6 ounces) tomato paste
1 teaspoon sugar
1 tablespoon parsley, chopped
1/4 teaspoon oregano
1/2 teaspoon basil
Cayenne and salt
1 cup cornmeal, yellow or white
1/4 cup butter
Grated Parmesan cheese

Cut sausage in 1/2" slices and brown slowly in oil with onion and garlic until vegetables are limp. Add next 7 ingredients with 1/2 teaspoon salt and simmer 1 to 1 1/2 hours. Combine cornmeal, 3 cups water and 1 teaspoon salt in double boiler. Let simmer 1 hour after thickening. Cool slightly and beat in butter and 1/2 cup grated Parmesan. Spread in 8" x 8" x 2" cake pan. Chill until firm, overnight if possible. Cut in 2" squares; put on large flat shallow baking dish. Top with sauce; put in hot oven (400°F.) 20 minutes. Remove and top with more cheese. Broil until cheese melts. Makes 6 to 8 servings.

CREAMY MUSTARD SAUCE

To serve on cold ham, grilled ham or luncheon meat.

In saucepan mix 1 cup dairy sour cream, 1/4 teaspoon salt and 1 tablespoon each minced onion, prepared mustard and steak sauce. Cook few minutes over low heat. Makes 1 cup.

BEER BARBECUE SAUCE

Mix 1/4 cup corn syrup or packed brown sugar, 1 tablespoon prepared mustard, 1/2 cup catsup, 1 tablespoon Worcestershire, 1 minced small onion, 1/2 teaspoon salt, dash of pepper and 1 cup beer. Simmer, uncovered, about 15 minutes. Good for basting frankfurters. Makes about 1 1/2 cups.

RAISIN SAUCE

1 tablespoon sugar
4 teaspoons flour
1/2 cup seedless raisins
3 tablespoons molasses
1 tablespoon lemon juice
Pinch of salt
1 tablespoon butter

Mix sugar and flour; gradually add 1 cup water. Bring to a boil, add next 4 ingredients. Simmer for about 5 minutes. Add butter, stirring to melt. Serve on hot or cold cooked ham. Makes 1 1/2 cups sauce.

CUMBERLAND SAUCE

Very elegant for thin ham slices.

In saucepan mix 1 teaspoon dry mustard, 1 teaspoon paprika, 1/2 teaspoon ginger, dash of salt, 1 tablespoon water, grated rind of 2 oranges, 2 tablespoons orange juice and 1 tablespoon lemon juice. Let stand 30 minutes. Add 1/4 cup currant or apple jelly and heat, stirring, until jelly is dissolved. Cool and strain. Add 2 tablespoons port wine and quartered slices of 1/2 orange. Makes 4 servings.

FRANKFURTER BARBECUE SAUCE

2 medium onions, chopped
2 green peppers, chopped
2/3 cup sweet-pickle relish
1/2 cup cider vinegar
2 cups chili sauce
1/4 cup packed brown sugar
1 tablespoon prepared mustard
1/4 teaspoon hot pepper sauce

Combine all ingredients in saucepan. Simmer, covered, about 10 minutes, stirring frequently. Makes about 3 cups sauce, or enough for 3 pounds grilled or broiled frankfurters.

Meatballs, Stroganoff Style

ROBERT E. COATES

HOW TO BUY GROUND MEAT

Grinding meats is a method of tenderizing them and is also a good way for butchers to use up the trimmings from larger cuts.

Ground meat may be beef (hamburger), veal, lamb, pork, or meat-loaf mixture, which contains beef, pork and veal.

- Beef, of course, is the most popular kind of ground meat, is available in several types and is usually ground twice. It can be ground to order. **Regular ground beef,** the lowest in price, is the highest in fat content. **Ground chuck,** containing from 10 to 20 percent fat, is medium priced. **Ground round,** with less than 10 percent fat, is usually more expensive.

- Veal flank, breast, shank, neck, shoulder or round is usually ground with added meat fat and often with other meats.

- Lamb neck, shoulder, flank, breast or shank may be ground for use in loaves, patties and casseroles.

- Ground pork is not available pre-packaged but can be ground to order. It is often used in combination with beef to add extra flavor as in meat loaves and meatballs. Always cook it well done.

- Meat-loaf mixture, usually ground beef, veal and pork, is available pre-packaged. Always be sure that it is cooked well done.

STORAGE OF GROUND MEAT

Ground meat should be wrapped loosely in waxed paper and stored in the coldest part of the refrigerator. Use within 24 hours. Beef keeps a little longer than the other meats.

HAMBURGER GUACAMOLE

1 pound ground chuck
4 slices toast
1 avocado
1 tomato, chopped
1 medium onion, chopped
1/4 teaspoon hot pepper sauce
1 tablespoon lemon juice

Shape meat in 4 patties. Cook to desired doneness and set on toast. Mash avocado with rest of ingredients and spoon some on meat. Put under broiler or heat in oven a few minutes. Serve with remaining sauce. Serves 4.

MARTHA'S HAMBURGER PATTIES

1 pound ground beef
1/4 pound hard salami, cut in thin strips
1 cup cooked ham, cut in thin strips
1 egg, beaten
1/4 teaspoon salt
Dash of pepper
1 sprig parsley, minced

Mix all ingredients thoroughly. Shape in patties and brown on both sides in heavy skillet. Serves 4.

GREEN-CHILI AND CHEESE HAMBURGERS

Rinse seed from 1 can (4 ounces) green chilies; dice. Dice ½ pound Cheddar cheese. Add chilies and cheese to 2 pounds ground beef. Shape and broil, grill or fry. Makes 6 to 8 servings.

HAMBURGERS, POLISH STYLE

1 onion, peeled
1 carrot, scraped
1 stalk celery
1 medium potato, peeled
Few sprigs of parsley
3/4 pound chuck, ground
2 slices bread, crumbled
1 egg
1-1/2 teaspoons seasoned salt
1/4 teaspoon seasoned pepper
2 tablespoons butter or margarine
1 cup dairy sour cream
1/2 can French-fried onion rings

Force first 5 ingredients through medium blade of food chopper. Mix lightly but thoroughly with next 5 ingredients. Shape in 8 patties and brown on both sides in butter. Remove from skillet and blend sour cream into drippings. Put patties back in skillet, cover and simmer about 20 minutes. Top with onion rings. Makes 4 servings.

SMOTHERED HAMBURGER STEAKS AND ONIONS

1 pound ground round or chuck
1 teaspoon salt
1/4 teaspoon pepper
1/4 cup fine dry bread crumbs
4 medium onions, sliced
1 can beef gravy

Mix first 4 ingredients with ½ cup water. Shape in 4 patties. Brown on one side, turn, add onion and brown lightly. Add gravy, cover and simmer about 35 minutes. Makes 3 to 4 servings.

CHEESE-NUT BURGERS

Mix lightly 1 pound ground beef chuck, ¼ cup unsweetened wheat germ, ¾ cup finely diced sharp Cheddar cheese, ½ teaspoon instant meat tenderizer, ½ cup chopped cashews or other nuts and ¼ cup water. Shape in 4 to 6 thick patties and broil to desired doneness. Makes 4 to 6 servings.

SHERRIBURGERS

1/2 pound process American cheese, shredded
1/4 cup milk
1/4 cup sherry
1 pound ground beef
1 teaspoon salt
1/4 teaspoon pepper
1/4 cup sweet-pickle relish
4 sandwich rolls

Melt cheese in top of double boiler. Stir in milk and sherry and keep hot. Mix next 4 ingredients. Broil or panfry to desired doneness. Put on toasted roll halves, cover with cheese sauce and top with other roll halves. Makes 4 servings.

BEEF PATTIES WITH SAGE-ONION POTATOES

3 onions, sliced thin
3 tablespoons butter or margarine
5 potatoes, cooked and chopped
1 teaspoon ground sage
1/2 teaspoon ground thyme
Salt and pepper
1 pound ground beef

Cook onions in 2 tablespoons butter until tender. Add next 3 ingredients, ½ teaspoon salt and ¼ teaspoon pepper. Cook until potato is browned, stirring occasionally. Mix 1 teaspoon salt and ¼ teaspoon pepper with meat. Shape in 8 patties and cook in remaining butter to desired doneness. Put potato between 2 patties, sandwich fashion. Serves 4.

SMOKY HAMBURGERS

Brush steak or hamburger patties with bottled smoke before grilling, broiling or frying.

BACON NUTBURGERS

6 slices bacon
1-1/2 pounds ground chuck
1-1/2 teaspoons salt
1/8 teaspoon pepper
6 tablespoons chopped nuts
3 tablespoons chopped parsley
2 tablespoons grated onion

Cook bacon until crisp; drain. Mix beef, salt and pepper; divide in 12 equal portions and roll with rolling pin between 2 sheets of waxed paper to form thin patties about 5" in diameter. Mix last 3 ingredients and spread on 6 patties. Top each with a bacon slice. Cover with remaining 6 patties and crimp edges with fork. Broil to desired doneness, turning once. Makes 6 servings.

ELENA'S CHULETAS

Mix 1 pound hamburger with 1 cup each very finely minced onion and parsley, 1 egg, 1½ teaspoons salt, a little pepper and ¼ teaspoon monosodium glutamate. Form into 16 balls. Mix 1 cup sifted dried bread crumbs with ¼ cup grated Parmesan cheese and spread on a board. One at a time, pat each hamburg ball in the crumbs until thin and flat as a pancake. Turn to coat with crumbs on both sides. Put meat on a flat pan with waxed paper between the layers; chill thoroughly. Brush with melted butter and broil until brown on both sides. Serve with **Salsa Fria (Cold Sauce):** Peel and chop 1 pound very ripe tomatoes and mix with 1 medium onion, chopped, 2 tablespoons olive oil, 1 tablespoon wine vinegar, ¼ teaspoon oregano and 3 canned green chili peppers, chopped (or ½ cup minced green pepper and 1 teaspoon chili powder). Chill well before serving with **Frijoles Refritos (Refried Beans):** Mash 3 cans of undrained kidney beans and put in a heavy pan or skillet with ¼ pound lard or bacon grease. Cook very slowly, stirring the crispy part from the sides and bottom a few times, until the liquid is absorbed and mixture is the consistency of mashed potatoes. Add more lard if necessary. Season with salt. Makes 8 servings.

CRUNCHY BEEF PATTIES

Mix 1 pound ground beef, ¼ cup chopped water chestnuts, and salt and pepper to taste. Make 4 patties and brown on both sides in a little fat. Add 1 can (3 ounces) mushrooms, drained, and 2 tablespoons Burgundy. Simmer, covered, 15 minutes. Makes 4 servings.

BURGERS IN PEPPER RINGS

1 pound ground chuck
3/4 cup soft bread crumbs
1 teaspoon salt
1/8 teaspoon pepper
1/4 cup milk
6 green-pepper rings, about 1/2" thick
1 tablespoon fat
Bottled barbecue sauce
6 split sandwich rolls, heated

Mix first 5 ingredients and shape in 6 patties. Press the mixture into pepper rings, having meat cover cut edge of pepper on both sides. Brown patties on both sides in hot fat in skillet. Baste generously with sauce. Cook to desired doneness and serve in rolls. Makes 6 servings.

DILL BURGERS

Add ½ teaspoon crushed dillseed and ¼ cup chopped olives or sweet pickles to 1 pound ground beef. Season to taste and shape in patties; cook to desired doneness. Serves 3.

SESAME BURGERS

Toast ¼ cup sesame seed in moderate oven (350°F.) 10 to 15 minutes. Add to 1 pound ground beef; season, shape in patties and broil or panfry to desired doneness. Serves 3.

HAMBURGER TOPPINGS

Spread on broiled, grilled or panfried hamburgers just before serving.

Cranberry-Celery Sauce Mix 1 cup cranberry sauce, ¼ cup sliced celery, 1 teaspoon lemon juice and 1 teaspoon minced onion.
Savory Butter Cream ½ cup butter. Stir in 2 tablespoons each chopped parsley and green-onion tops.
Blue-cheese Topping Mix 2 ounces blue cheese and ½ teaspoon steak sauce.
Steak-sauce Butter Mix ¼ cup soft butter and 2 tablespoons steak sauce.

HAMBURGER FLUFFS

1 pound ground beef
2 tablespoons flour
1/2 teaspoon Worcestershire
1/2 teaspoon pepper
1 teaspoon salt
1/2 medium onion, minced
Pinch of thyme
Pinch of marjoram
3/4 cup undiluted evaporated milk

Put beef in large bowl; add all ingredients, except milk. Whip mixture with large spoon or electric mixer. Add milk and 3/4 cup water slowly, beating constantly. When all liquid has been absorbed, cover bowl and let stand in refrigerator a few hours. (Mixture can be cooked at once, but texture improves on standing.) Drop in 16 mounds on hot greased griddle. Brown 1 1/2 minutes on each side. Makes 4 to 6 servings.

HAMBURGERS WITH SAUCE FELIPE

Mince 2 medium onions and brown lightly in 1 tablespoon butter. Add 1/3 cup dry white wine and 1 tablespoon vinegar. Simmer 2 or 3 minutes. Add 2 tablespoons catsup and 1 can beef gravy. Simmer about 10 minutes. Blend in 1 teaspoon dry mustard, 1 teaspoon minced parsley and seasoned salt and pepper to taste. Serve on hamburgers, cooked to desired doneness. Makes 2 cups sauce for 6 to 8 servings.

HAMBURGERS AND MUSHROOMS

2 chicken bouillon cubes
1-1/2 pounds ground beef
3/4 teaspoon salt
1/4 teaspoon pepper
3/4 teaspoon poultry seasoning
2 teaspoons Worcestershire
1 egg
1 can (6 ounces) sliced mushrooms
2 tablespoons flour
Hot toast triangles

Dissolve bouillon cubes in 3/4 cup boiling water; cool. Mix thoroughly with next 6 ingredients. Shape in 4 oval loaves and put in shallow baking pan. Broil to desired doneness, about 5 minutes on each side. Remove to hot platter. Drain mushrooms, reserving liquid. Cook mushrooms in drippings in baking pan a few minutes. Blend in flour. Add mushroom liquid and cook until thickened. Put hamburgers on hot toast and cover with gravy. Makes 4 to 6 servings.

HAMBURGERS WITH NIPPY CHEESE SAUCE

Divide 1 pound ground beef in quarters; form each quarter into a fat patty, tucking a chip of ice and a bit of butter in center. Brush tops with melted butter. Grill, broil or panfry to desired doneness. Serve on split toasted buns with **Nippy Cheese Sauce:** To 1 cup Medium White Sauce (page 214), add 1/2 cup shredded sharp Cheddar cheese and 1/4 to 1/2 teaspoon chili powder. Simmer over very low heat, stirring, just until cheese melts. Makes 4 servings.

BURGUNDY HAMBURGERS

Mix 1 pound of ground beef with 1 teaspoon salt, 1/4 cup Burgundy, some freshly ground pepper and 1 tablespoon each minced parsley and chives. Form in cakes and broil, grill or panfry to desired doneness. Serves 3 to 4.

STUFFED HAMBURGER PATTIES

1 pound ground chuck
1 medium onion, minced
1 teaspoon salt
Cracked pepper
1-1/3 cups soft bread crumbs
1/4 teaspoon poultry seasoning
1/4 teaspoon seasoned salt
1/4 cup margarine, melted
2 tablespoons lemon juice

Mix beef, onion, salt and 1/8 teaspoon pepper. Divide in 8 equal parts. With rolling pin, flatten pieces between pieces of waxed paper to make thin patties 5" in diameter. Mix 1/8 teaspoon pepper and remaining ingredients. Spread on 4 patties and top with remaining 4 patties. Crimp edges with a fork. Broil to desired doneness, turning once. Makes 4 servings.

TENNESSEE HAMBURGER

1 pound ground round or chuck
1 teaspoon salt
1/8 teaspoon pepper
1 clove garlic, minced
1/4 cup prepared mustard
2 cups thinly sliced onion

Mix first 4 ingredients; shape in 2 large thin patties. Put one in a piepan or layer-cake pan. Spread with mustard and cover with onion. Put second patty on top. Put under broiler until top browns lightly. Carefully turn and brown the other side of the double patty. Cover pan and bake in moderate oven (350°F.) about 50 minutes. Makes 4 servings.

HAMBURGER PRINCESS

1 pound ground chuck
Salt
1/2 cup all-purpose flour
1 teaspoon sugar
1 egg
3/4 cup tomato juice
Butter or margarine
6 slices process American cheese

Mix meat and 1 teaspoon salt; shape in six 4" patties. Mix flour, sugar and 1/2 teaspoon salt. Beat egg with tomato juice and add to flour mixture; beat until smooth. Melt 1 teaspoon butter in 6" skillet. Pour in enough tomato-juice batter to cover pan thinly (one-sixth of mixture). When done on bottom, turn and place a meat patty on cooked side. When underside is done, turn again. Sauté about 4 minutes for medium to well done. Lift onto baking sheet and roll up pancake with meat on inside and edges underneath. Repeat until 6 rolls are made. Top each with a slice of cheese and put under broiler until cheese is just melted. Makes 4 servings.

LEMON PIEPAN STEAK

1-1/2 pounds ground beef chuck
1 onion, sliced
6 lemon slices
1 cup catsup
1 tablespoon Worcestershire

Pat beef into deep 9" or 10" piepan. Top with onion and lemon slices. Mix remaining ingredients with 1/4 cup water and pour over top of meat. Bake in hot oven (400°F.) about 30 minutes. Pour off some of the fat and cut pie in wedges. Makes 4 to 6 servings.

ITALIAN MEAT PATTIES

1/2 pound ground beef chuck
1/2 pound sweet Italian sausages, casings removed
1/2 large clove garlic, minced
2 tablespoons chopped parsley
1/2 teaspoon salt
1/8 teaspoon pepper
3 slices white bread, soaked in milk and squeezed dry
1 egg, beaten
Fine dry bread crumbs
Olive oil
Tomato Sauce (page 241)

Mix all ingredients, except crumbs and oil. Shape in 1 1/2" patties. Dredge in dry crumbs and sauté in oil until well browned on both sides. Serve with Tomato Sauce, if desired. Makes 4 servings.

BARBECUE PEARS WITH HAMBURGERS

1 can (1 pound 13 ounces) pear halves
1/2 cup catsup
1/4 cup packed brown sugar
1 tablespoon lemon juice
Butter or margarine
1-1/2 pounds ground beef
1-1/2 teaspoons salt
1/4 teaspoon pepper

Drain pears, reserving syrup. Put halves, cut side up, in shallow baking pan. Pour 1 cup syrup over top. Mix next 3 ingredients and spoon over pears. Dot with butter. Bake in hot oven (400°F.) 10 to 15 minutes. Mix remaining ingredients lightly and shape in 4 large or 8 small patties. Panbroil in small amount of butter in skillet to desired doneness. Put on hot platter and serve with the pears. Makes 4 to 6 servings.

SMOTHERED SAUSAGE-BEEF PATTIES

Mix 1/2 pound each pork-sausage meat and ground chuck, 1 1/2 cups soft bread crumbs and 1/2 teaspoon poultry seasoning. Shape in 8 patties. Brown on both sides in skillet. Drain off fat. Blend 1/2 can condensed cream-of-mushroom soup, 1 cup water and 2 tablespoons flour. Pour around patties and cook until mixture is thickened and meat done. Makes 4 servings.

HAMBURGERS A LA PROVENCALE

Fluffy white rice would be a good accompaniment.

2/3 cup coarsely chopped onion
1 small clove garlic, minced
Butter or margarine
1 can (15 ounces) tomato sauce with tomato tidbits
Small piece of bay leaf
1/8 teaspoon thyme leaves
Pinch of sugar
1/4 cup coarsely cut green olives
1/4 cup dry white wine
Salt and pepper
2 pounds ground round or chuck

Cook onion and garlic in 2 tablespoons butter about 10 minutes, stirring frequently. Add next 6 ingredients, 1/2 teaspoon salt and 1/8 teaspoon pepper. Bring to boil and simmer about 10 minutes. Shape meat in 6 large patties and sauté in small amount of butter until of desired doneness. Season with salt and pepper, put on hot platter and top with the sauce. Make 6 to 8 servings.

OLD DOMINION HAMBURGER-CABBAGE LOAF

2 pounds lean ground beef
2-1/2 cups finely shredded cabbage
1/2 green pepper, chopped
1 medium onion, chopped
1/2 clove garlic, minced
3 eggs
1 teaspoon salt
1/8 teaspoon pepper
6 slices bacon
1 can (6 ounces) tomato paste

Mix the beef and next 7 ingredients together and press into a 9″ x 5″ x 3″ loaf pan. Put bacon slices on top. Bake in moderate oven (350°F.) about 1½ hours. Pour tomato paste over top the last 15 minutes of cooking. Makes 8 servings.

PIZZA MEAT LOAF

1 pound ground beef
1 teaspoon salt
1/4 teaspoon pepper
1 cup well-drained canned tomatoes
1/2 cup shredded sharp Cheddar cheese
Garlic salt
Onion salt
1/4 teaspoon basil
Few sprigs of parsley, chopped
1 can (2 ounces) flat anchovy fillets

Mix first 3 ingredients lightly but thoroughly and press into an 8″ pie-pan, making a shell. Bake in hot oven (400°F.) 10 minutes. Remove from oven and pour off fat and liquid. Spread with tomatoes and cover with cheese. Sprinkle lightly with garlic and onion salts, the basil and parsley. Arrange anchovies spoke-fashion on top. Return to oven and bake 15 minutes longer. Cut in wedges. Serves 4.

GLAZED BEEF-AND-LUNCHEON-MEAT LOAF

1 can (12 ounces) luncheon meat
1 pound ground beef
1/2 cup drained canned crushed pineapple
1/2 cup pineapple juice
1 egg
2 tablespoons quick-cooking tapioca
1 teaspoon salt
Dash of pepper
1/2 cup packed brown sugar
1/2 teaspoon dry mustard
1/4 cup vinegar

Force luncheon meat through food chopper. Add to next 7 ingredients and mix lightly but thoroughly. Shape in loaf in a shallow baking pan. Mix remaining ingredients with ¼ cup water and pour over loaf. Bake in moderate oven (350°F.) about 1 hour, basting occasionally with the drippings in pan. Serves 6.

CATSUP-GLAZED MEAT LOAF

1 egg, slightly beaten
1/3 cup milk
2 cups soft stale-bread crumbs
1 pound ground beef
1 pound pork sausage meat
1/2 teaspoon salt
2 tablespoons minced onion
Catsup
2 tablespoons brown sugar
2 tablespoons prepared mustard

Mix first 3 ingredients. Add next 4 ingredients and 2 tablespoons catsup. Mix lightly but thoroughly. Shape in a loaf in shallow baking pan. Mix ⅓ cup catsup, brown sugar and mustard. Spread on loaf. Bake in moderate oven (350°F.) about 1 hour and 15 minutes. Makes 8 servings.

PORCUPINE MEAT LOAF

1-1/2 pounds ground beef
1/2 cup uncooked rice
1 teaspoon salt
1/4 teaspoon each pepper and powdered marjoram
1/8 teaspoon powdered thyme
1 medium onion, minced
1/2 green pepper, minced
1 can (12 ounces) vegetable-juice cocktail
1 can condensed beef broth
1/2 teaspoon chili powder

Mix first 7 ingredients. Mix cocktail, broth and chili powder; add ½ cup to first mixture. Shape in a loaf and put in baking pan. Pour remaining liquid over meat loaf. Cover with foil; bake in moderate oven (375°F.) 1 hour. Makes 6 servings.

VEGETABLE-BURGER LOAF

1 large carrot
1 large onion
1 stalk celery
1/2 green pepper
3 tablespoons margarine
2 pounds ground beef
1/4 teaspoon poultry seasoning
1/2 teaspoon dried dill, crushed
1 teaspoon prepared mustard
2 teaspoons salt
1/2 cup Italian tomatoes
1/4 teaspoon dried basil
1/2 teaspoon sugar
1 egg
1/2 cup quick-cooking rolled oats
Juice of 1/2 lemon
Catsup (optional)

Finely chop first 4 vegetables. Cook in the margarine about 5 minutes. Add remaining ingredients, except catsup, and mix well. Put in 9″ x 5″ x 3″ loaf pan. Let stand about an hour before baking. Bake in moderate oven (350°F.) 1¼ hours. Serve with catsup, if desired. Serves 8.

BEEF-OATMEAL LOAF

2 pounds ground beef
2-1/2 teaspoons salt
1/4 teaspoon each pepper and nutmeg
1 onion, minced
1 cup quick-cooking rolled oats
1 can (19 ounces) tomatoes

Mix first 5 ingredients. Force tomatoes through coarse sieve; combine with meat mixture. Shape in large flat loaf or 2 small loaves in baking pan; crisscross top surface with a knife. Bake in moderate oven (350°F.) 1½ hours for large loaf, 1 hour for small loaves. Serves 8 to 10.

MUSHROOM MEAT LOAF

1 can condensed cream of mushroom
   soup
1-1/2 pounds ground beef
1-1/2 cups soft bread crumbs
1 medium onion, chopped
1/4 cup chopped parsley
1 egg
1 tablespoon Worcestershire
1-1/4 teaspoons salt
1/4 teaspoon pepper
1/4 cup milk
1 pimiento, chopped

Combine ½ cup soup with next 8 ingredients. Pack into 9" x 5" x 3" loaf pan. Bake in moderate oven (350°F.) 1¼ hours. Pour off liquid; turn loaf out on hot platter. Heat remaining soup with milk. Add pimiento and pour over loaf. Serves 6.

BISCUIT-COVERED
BEEF-SAUSAGE LOAF

1 pound ground beef
1/2 pound sausage meat
1 onion, grated
1 egg
3/4 cup soft bread crumbs
1/3 cup milk
1 teaspoon salt
1/4 teaspoon each pepper, allspice and
   nutmeg
Baking-powder-biscuit dough (page 307)
Undiluted evaporated milk

Mix all ingredients, except last 2. Shape in loaf about 8" long and 4" wide. Put in shallow baking pan and bake in moderate oven (350°F.) 1 hour. Remove from oven and increase heat to 425°F. Roll biscuit dough in a rectangle about 16" x 14". Moisten edges with water. Put loaf upside down on rolled dough; bring dough up around loaf and pinch edges together. Put in baking pan, pinched side down, and score top lightly with knife. Brush with evaporated milk. Bake 20 minutes, or until well browned. Serve hot, with brown gravy if desired, or cold. Makes 6 to 8 servings.

CHILI BEEF LOAF

2 pounds ground beef
1 package chili seasoning mix
1 egg, slightly beaten
1 can (8 ounces) tomato sauce with
   cheese
1 small onion, minced
1/2 teaspoon salt

Mix all ingredients lightly but thoroughly. Pack lightly into 9" x 5" x 3" loaf pan. Bake in moderate oven (375°F.) 1 hour, or until firm. Let stand 5 minutes before turning out of pan. Good with kidney beans. Makes 6 to 8 servings.

MEAT LOAF, MEXICAN STYLE

1-1/2 pounds ground beef
1 cup drained whole-kernel corn
2 medium onions, minced
3/4 cup unsweetened wheat germ
1-1/2 teaspoons salt
1 tablespoon chili powder
Dash of pepper
2 teaspoons Worcestershire
2 eggs
1 can (8 ounces) tomato sauce
Spanish Sauce (page 161)

Mix all ingredients, except Spanish Sauce, lightly but thoroughly. Press into 9" x 5" x 3" loaf pan. Bake in moderate oven (350°F.) about 1 hour. Let stand in pan 10 minutes. Turn out and serve with the sauce. Makes 6 to 8 servings.

HERB MEAT LOAF
WITH CHEESE

2 pounds meat-loaf mixture
2 teaspoons salt
1/4 teaspoon pepper
1 teaspoon mixed fresh or 1/4 teaspoon
   dried herbs (basil, marjoram, rosemary,
   sage, savory)
1/2 cup soft bread crumbs
1/2 cup milk or other liquid
1 small onion, minced
3 or 4 slices bacon (optional)
4 or 5 slices process American cheese,
   cut in thirds
Parsley
Cherry tomatoes

Mix first 7 ingredients lightly but thoroughly. Put in 9" x 5" x 3" loaf pan and top with bacon, if desired. Bake in moderate oven (350°F.) about 1 hour. Let stand about 10 minutes. Transfer right side up to shallow baking pan. Cut 1" slices about one fourth of the way through loaf and insert a cheese strip in each cut. Return loaf to oven 2 or 3 minutes, or until cheese melts slightly. Put on hot platter; garnish with parsley and tomatoes. Makes 6 to 8 servings.

TOMATO MEAT LOAF WITH HERB BUTTER

2-1/2 pounds ground beef
3 medium tomatoes, chopped
1/3 cup chopped pickle
3 tablespoons prepared horseradish
1 large onion, minced
2-1/2 teaspoons salt
1/4 teaspoon pepper
4 slices bread, cubed
1 cup undiluted evaporated milk
Herb Butter Sauce

Mix all ingredients, except sauce. Pack into 9" x 5" x 3" loaf pan. Score top with back of knife. Bake in moderate oven (350°F.) about 2 hours. Remove loaf to hot platter. Top with the sauce. Makes 8 to 10 servings. **Herb Butter Sauce** Mix 2 tablespoons butter, ¼ teaspoon each powdered thyme and sage and 1 tablespoon chopped parsley. Spread on hot loaf just before serving. Makes enough for one 9" x 5" x 3" loaf.

POT-ROASTED BEEF LOAF

1/4 cup fine dry bread crumbs
2 pounds ground beef
2 eggs
2 teaspoons salt
1/4 teaspoon pepper
1 onion, minced
2 tablespoons chopped parsley
2 tablespoons butter
12 small carrots
6 new potatoes
1 pound green beans

Soak bread crumbs in ½ cup water. Mix with next 6 ingredients. Shape into a loaf. Brown in butter. Cover and cook over low heat for 1 hour, adding a little water if necessary. Add vegetables and cook 45 minutes longer. Makes 8 servings.

BEEF-CARROT-OLIVE LOAF

2 pounds ground beef chuck
1-1/2 cups cornflakes
1/2 cup chopped parsley
1/2 cup shredded raw carrot
1 can (4-1/2 ounces) chopped ripe olives
1 medium onion, chopped
2 cloves garlic, minced
2 tablespoons butter or margarine
2 teaspoons salt
1/2 teaspoon pepper
1/2 teaspoon each sage and oregano
1-1/2 cups milk
1 egg

Mix first 5 ingredients. Add onion and garlic, browned in butter, and remaining ingredients. Mix well and shape in a loaf in a baking pan. Bake in moderate oven (350°F.) about 1 hour. Makes 8 servings.

INDIVIDUAL SAUERBRATEN MEAT LOAVES

1-1/2 pounds ground beef
1/3 cup fine dry bread crumbs
1 small onion, minced
Dash of pepper
1 cup undiluted evaporated milk
2 teaspoons salt
1/4 cup margarine
2 tablespoons each vinegar and catsup
1 tablespoon brown sugar
8 whole black peppercorns
1 bay leaf
1/3 cup seedless raisins
6 gingersnaps, crushed

Mix first 5 ingredients and 1½ teaspoons salt. Shape in 6 individual loaves and brown on both sides in margarine in skillet. Remove loaves and pour off fat. Put ½ teaspoon salt and remaining ingredients in skillet; bring to boil. Add loaves, cover and simmer 15 minutes. Stir sauce and add a little more water, if necessary. Cover and simmer 15 minutes longer, or until meat is done. Makes 6 servings.

MEAT LOAF WITH OVERCOAT

2 pounds ground beef
1 egg
1 cup soft bread crumbs
1/2 cup milk
1 teaspoon poultry seasoning
2 teaspoons salt
1/4 teaspoon pepper
1 medium onion, minced
Mashed-potato Coating
Melted butter or margarine

Mix all ingredients, except last 2. Pack into 9" x 5" x 3" loaf pan. Bake in moderate oven (350°F.) about 1½ hours. Let stand 10 minutes. Drain off liquid and turn meat onto an ovenproof platter. Spread thickly with Mashed-potato Coating, covering loaf completely. Crimp with a fork, or use a pastry tube, to finish edges. Brush with melted butter. Brown under medium heat in broiler; or bake in very hot oven (450°F.) 10 minutes, or until browned. Makes 8 servings.

Mashed-potato Coating

6 medium potatoes
Salt
1/4 cup butter
1/2 cup hot milk
1 egg yolk
Pepper

Cook peeled potatoes in boiling salted water until tender. Drain and mash well. Add butter, milk and egg yolk; season to taste. Beat until fluffy.

MEATBALL SHEPHERD'S PIE

1 pound ground beef
1 egg
2 cups soft bread crumbs
Salt and pepper
3 tablespoons butter or margarine
1 large onion, minced
1 tablespoon flour
1 can (3 ounces) mushrooms, undrained
1 can (1 pound) tomatoes
1 box frozen peas and carrots, thawed
1/8 teaspoon oregano
1 box frozen whipped potatoes,
    thawed

Mix beef, egg, crumbs, 1 teaspoon salt and 1/8 teaspoon pepper. Shape in 12 large balls. Brown on all sides in 2 tablespoons butter in Dutch oven or large skillet. Remove meatballs and brown onion in drippings. Blend in flour; add mushrooms and tomatoes. Add meatballs and bring to boil. Cover and simmer 30 minutes. Add peas and carrots and bring to boil. Add oregano and season to taste. Pour into shallow 2-quart baking dish. Melt remaining 1 tablespoon butter in small saucepan, add potatoes and heat. Spread on top of meat mixture. Put under broiler until lightly browned. Makes 4 to 6 servings.

MEATBALL-NOODLE SKILLET

1 pound ground beef
1 egg
1/2 cup fine dry bread crumbs
1/3 cup chopped parsley
1 medium onion, minced
1 tablespoon grated lemon rind
1/8 teaspoon nutmeg
2 teaspoons salt
1/2 teaspoon pepper
1/4 cup olive or vegetable oil
2 tablespoons margarine
1 can (29 ounces) tomatoes
1 teaspoon oregano leaves
2 bay leaves
8 ounces medium egg noodles

Mix lightly but thoroughly first 7 ingredients, 1 teaspoon salt and 1/4 teaspoon pepper. Shape in 1½" balls. Heat oil and margarine, add meatballs and brown on all sides. Cover and cook over low heat 15 minutes. Drain tomatoes. Add enough water to juice to make 4 cups liquid. Add remaining salt and pepper, oregano and bay leaves and pour over meatballs. Bring to boil, gradually add noodles and cook, uncovered, stirring frequently, 12 to 15 minutes, or until noodles are almost tender. Add tomatoes and cook 5 minutes longer. Makes 4 to 6 servings.

PEANUT-HAMBURGER BALLS

3/4 pound ground chuck
3/4 cup crunchy peanut butter
1 onion, minced
3 tablespoons chili sauce
1-1/4 teaspoons salt
1/8 teaspoon pepper
1 egg, beaten
2 tablespoons fat
2 cans (8 ounces each) tomato sauce

Mix first 7 ingredients and shape in 12 balls. Brown on all sides in hot fat. Remove meat and pour off fat. Put meat back in skillet with tomato sauce, cover and simmer about 30 minutes. Makes 4 servings.

MEATBALLS

1/2 pound ground beef
1/2 pound ground pork
2 medium onions, minced
1 clove garlic, minced
1/4 cup chopped parsley
1/2 cup grated Parmesan cheese
1/2 cup fine dry bread crumbs
1 egg
2 teaspoons salt
1/2 teaspoon pepper
2 tablespoons olive oil

Combine all ingredients except oil; mix thoroughly. Add a little water if mixture seems dry. Shape in 24 balls and brown slowly in hot oil until cooked through. Makes 4 servings.

KONIGSBERGER MEATBALLS

Parsley boiled potatoes go well with this German favorite.

1 roll or 1 slice firm-type bread
3/4 pound ground chuck
1/4 pound ground pork
2 medium potatoes, cooked and mashed
2 anchovies, chopped
1 egg
Flour
Salt and pepper
3 tablespoons butter
1 beef bouillon cube
1 tablespoon capers
Juice of 1/2 lemon

Moisten roll or bread with a little water and squeeze dry. Mix very thoroughly with next 5 ingredients, 3 tablespoons flour, 1 teaspoon salt and 1/8 teaspoon pepper. Shape in 16 balls, dredge with flour and drop into simmering salted water. Cover and simmer about 15 minutes. Melt butter and blend in 2 tablespoons flour. Add 1 cup water and bouillon cube; cook, stirring, until thickened. Add capers, lemon juice and pepper to taste. Add cooked meatballs and simmer a few minutes. Makes 4 servings.

SWEET-AND-SOUR MEATBALLS

You cook pineapple chunks with them and serve them on hot rice.

1 can (3 ounces) chopped mushrooms
1 pound ground chuck
1/2 pound ground lean pork
1 tablespoon sherry
1 teaspoon instant minced onion
Soy sauce
1 tablespoon vegetable oil
1 beef bouillon cube
1 small onion, thinly sliced
1 medium green pepper, slivered
1 can (13-1/2 ounces) pineapple chunks
1/4 cup sugar
1/4 cup vinegar
3 tablespoons cornstarch
Hot cooked rice

Drain mushrooms, reserving liquid. Add enough water to liquid to make 1 cup and set aside. Mix next 4 ingredients with 2 tablespoons soy sauce. Shape in 12 to 16 balls and brown on all sides in hot oil. Drain off fat. Add mushroom liquid and bouillon cube. Cover and simmer 30 minutes. Add next 3 ingredients. Blend 2 teaspoons soy sauce with sugar, vinegar and cornstarch. Stir into hot mixture. Cover and cook 10 minutes, stirring. Serve on rice. Serves 4 to 6.

SWEDISH MEATBALLS

1 onion, minced
Butter
1 pound ground lean beef
1/2 pound each ground lean pork and veal
1 cup dry stale-bread crumbs
1 cup milk
2 eggs, beaten
Dash of nutmeg
1 teaspoon salt
1/8 teaspoon pepper
3 tablespoons flour
2 cups meat stock or consommé
Pinch of grated lemon rind
1 cup dairy sour cream
Chopped dill or parsley
Cooked noodles

Sauté onion in 1 tablespoon butter; add to next 8 ingredients, mixing with hands to get even texture. Roll in small balls. Brown in 2 tablespoons butter. Remove meatballs. To pan juices, add flour and stock to make gravy. Stir until hot. Check seasoning and add lemon rind. (Gravy should not be too thick at this point.) Return meatballs to gravy and simmer over very low heat 1 hour. Remove meatballs to serving dish with slotted spoon. Stir sour cream into gravy and heat. Pour over meat; add dill. Serve with noodles. Makes 6 to 8 servings.

MEATBALLS, STROGANOFF STYLE

1-1/2 pounds ground beef
1/4 cup fine dry bread crumbs
1 teaspoon grated lemon rind
Salt and pepper
1/4 cup minced onion
1 tablespoon butter or margarine
1 can (3 ounces) sliced mushrooms, drained (reserve liquid)
2 tablespoons flour
1 bouillon cube
2 tablespoons catsup
1/2 cup dairy sour cream
Chopped parsley
1 package (6 ounces) yellow rice, cooked

Mix lightly first 3 ingredients, 1½ teaspoons salt, ¼ teaspoon pepper, 2 tablespoons onion and ⅓ cup ice water. Shape in 18 balls and brown slowly in butter in skillet. Remove meatballs and sauté remaining onion and the mushrooms in drippings in skillet. Blend in flour. Gradually add mushroom liquid and bouillon cube dissolved in 1 cup boiling water and bring to boil, stirring. Add meatballs, cover and simmer about 15 minutes. Remove meatballs to hot serving dish. Stir catsup and sour cream into liquid in skillet, heat and correct seasoning. Pour sauce over meatballs. Sprinkle with parsley. Serve with rice, prepared as directed on label. Makes 6 servings.

DUTCH-OVEN DINNER

Meatballs, vegetables, noodles and Cheddar-cheese cubes.

1 pound ground beef
1/2 teaspoon onion salt
1 egg
1-1/2 teaspoons salt
1/2 cup dry bread crumbs
3 tablespoons margarine
1 can (12 ounces) whole-kernel corn, undrained
1 can (3 ounces) mushroom stems and pieces, undrained
1 can (29 ounces) tomatoes
1 large onion, sliced
1 green pepper, sliced
8 ounces wide or medium noodles
1 cup diced Cheddar cheese

Mix first 3 ingredients, ½ teaspoon salt and bread crumbs, soaked in ½ cup water. Shape in 1½" balls and brown on all sides in margarine. Combine next 6 ingredients and 1 teaspoon salt in Dutch oven. Bring to boil, cover and simmer over very low heat 15 minutes, stirring occasionally. Add cheese and meatballs, cover and simmer 10 to 15 minutes longer, adding a little water if mixture becomes too dry. Makes 4 to 6 servings.

STUFFED BEEF ROLLS

2 pounds ground chuck
1 teaspoon bottled thick meat sauce
Salt and pepper
1 cup soft bread crumbs
1 egg
1 teaspoon instant minced onion
1/4 teaspoon celery salt
1/2 teaspoon poultry seasoning
2 tablespoons melted butter or margarine
1 tablespoon fat
1/2 cup beef bouillon
4 carrots, cut in strips
1 can (1 pound) potatoes, drained
1 can (1 pound) onions, drained
1 large green pepper, cut in chunks
Canned beef gravy, heated

Mix beef, meat sauce, 2 teaspoons salt and 1/4 teaspoon pepper. Roll between 2 sheets of waxed paper to a rectangle 12" x 8". Mix 1/2 teaspoon salt, 1/8 teaspoon pepper and next 6 ingredients; spread on meat. Roll up and cut in half crosswise. Brown on all sides in fat. Pour off fat and put a rack under meat rolls. Add bouillon, cover and simmer 15 minutes. Add carrots, season and simmer 1/2 hour longer. Then add potatoes, onion and peppers; simmer 15 minutes. Serve with the gravy. Makes 6 to 8 servings.

HAMBURGER PASTIES

Wrap cooked pasties in foil, take on a picnic and reheat over hot coals

1 onion, minced
1 tablespoon fat
1 pound ground beef
1 teaspoon salt
1/4 teaspoon pepper
1 teaspoon Worcestershire
1 tablespoon tomato paste
1/4 cup dairy sour cream
Special Pastry

Brown onion in fat in skillet. Add meat and cook until lightly browned, breaking up with fork. Add next 4 ingredients and mix well. Remove from heat and stir in sour cream. Spoon about 3 tablespoons meat mixture onto a pastry square. Top with another pastry square. Crimp edges together and prick with fork. Repeat with remaining pastry squares and filling. Bake on cookie sheet in hot oven (400°F.) 15 minutes, or until lightly browned. Makes 4 to 6 servings.

Special Pastry
1 cup all-purpose flour
1/2 cup butter or margarine
1 package (3 ounces) cream cheese
1/2 teaspoon poppy seed

Mix all ingredients until well blended. Chill several hours, or overnight if possible. When ready to use, roll thin and cut into twelve 4" squares.

HAMBURGER PIZZA PIE

1 pound ground chuck or round
1 teaspoon instant seasoned meat tenderizer
1 small clove garlic, minced
1 can (8 ounces) tomato sauce
1/4 teaspoon garlic salt
1/2 teaspoon sugar
1/4 teaspoon Italian herb seasoning
1 sweet onion, thinly sliced
1/4 pound Italian salami in thin slices
1/2 pound mozzarella cheese, thinly sliced
1 can (8 ounces) chopped mushrooms, drained
1/4 teaspoon oregano
1/4 cup grated Parmesan cheese

Mix first 3 ingredients and pat into 12" pizza pan. Mix tomato sauce with next 3 ingredients and spread on beef. Arrange next 4 ingredients on beef in order given. Sprinkle with oregano and cheese. Bake in very hot oven (450°F.) about 15 minutes, or until mozzarella is bubbly. Makes 4 to 6 servings.

MEXICAN STACK

1 pound ground beef
1 large onion, chopped
2 small cloves garlic, minced
1 can (8 ounces) tomato sauce
Salt and pepper
Grated Parmesan cheese
1-1/2 cups yellow cornmeal
1-1/2 cups all-purpose flour
2 eggs
Vegetable oil
1 can (4 ounces) green chilies
Tomato-mushroom sauce
Shredded Cheddar cheese
Raw-onion rings
Shredded lettuce

Cook beef, breaking up with fork, in skillet until it loses its red color. Add chopped onion and garlic and cook 5 minutes longer. Add tomato sauce, 1 teaspoon salt and 1/4 teaspoon pepper and simmer a few minutes. Add 1/2 cup Parmesan cheese and set aside. Mix next 3 ingredients with 2 1/2 cups water and season with salt and pepper. Shape in very thin flat cakes like tortillas, about 7" in diameter, and cook on both sides in a little oil until done. Put half in greased individual serving dishes or piepans. Divide filling among tortillas. Drain and chop chilies and sprinkle on filling. Top with remaining tortillas, cover with sauce and sprinkle with Cheddar cheese. Cover with foil and bake in hot oven (400°F.) 15 minutes, or until piping hot. Top with onion rings and lettuce and pass extra Parmesan cheese. Makes 4 to 6 servings.

CHILI BEANS AND BEEF, SUN VALLEY STYLE

4 cups dried pinto beans
Salt
1 large onion, peeled
1 large bay leaf
1 large clove garlic, thinly sliced
1-1/2 to 2 pounds ground beef
1 cup beef stock, tomato juice or water
3 tablespoons chili powder (or to taste)
1-1/2 teaspoons ground cumin

Put beans in large kettle with 3 quarts (12 cups) water and bring to boil. Boil rapidly, uncovered, 2 minutes. Remove from heat, cover and let stand 1 hour. Add 4 teaspoons salt and next 3 ingredients. Bring to boil, cover and simmer 2 hours, or until beans are tender. Remove onion and bay leaf. Brown meat in skillet, breaking up with fork. Add to beans. Add stock to skillet and heat, stirring up brown bits. Add to mixture. Mix chili powder and cumin with a little liquid from beans and stir into mixture. Bring to boil, cover and simmer 1 to 1½ hours. Add more salt to taste. Makes 8 to 10 servings.

DOLMATHES (Stuffed Grape Leaves)

1 pound ground lean beef
3 eggs
1 medium onion, chopped
1/2 cup uncooked rice
1/4 cup chopped parsley
1 teaspoon chopped fresh mint leaves
   (or 1/2 teaspoon dried)
2 tablespoons olive oil
Salt and pepper
Grape or cabbage leaves
2 cans condensed beef bouillon, heated
Juice of 1 lemon

Mix beef, 1 egg, beaten, next 5 ingredients and ¼ cup water. Season. Soak fresh grape or cabbage leaves in hot water 5 minutes to soften. (Remove core of cabbage and soak whole head so that leaves can be peeled off without breaking.) Rinse canned grape leaves in warm water. Place a spoonful of meat mixture on a leaf (shiny side is down) and roll, folding ends to seal in mixture. Place folded side down in skillet, making 2 layers if necessary. Add beef bouillon and 1½ cups water. Cover and simmer 45 minutes. Remove to hot platter. For sauce, add lemon juice to remaining eggs, beaten. Slowly add some hot broth to eggs; continue to beat. Stir egg mixture into remaining broth. Remove from heat, cover and allow to stand 5 minutes to thicken. Pour over Dolmathes. Makes 6 servings.

HAMBURGER-ZUCCHINI SKILLET

1 pound ground beef
1 can (3 ounces) mushrooms, drained
2 tablespoons flour
1 teaspoon salt
1/4 teaspoon pepper
1 teaspoon onion salt
1/4 teaspoon garlic salt
1/2 teaspoon hot pepper sauce
1/2 teaspoon monosodium glutamate
2 medium zucchini, sliced thin
1 can (10 ounces) tomatoes
1 tablespoon vinegar
1/2 teaspoon seasoned salt

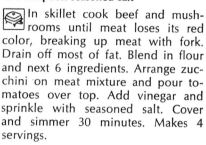

In skillet cook beef and mushrooms until meat loses its red color, breaking up meat with fork. Drain off most of fat. Blend in flour and next 6 ingredients. Arrange zucchini on meat mixture and pour tomatoes over top. Add vinegar and sprinkle with seasoned salt. Cover and simmer 30 minutes. Makes 4 servings.

POTATO MOUSSAKA (Meat and Potatoes, Greek Style)

This savory Mediterranean dish varies with the available vegetables and preferred seasonings of the country.

1 large onion, chopped
2 tablespoons vegetable oil
1 clove garlic, minced
1 pound ground beef (or lamb or veal)
Salt
1/4 teaspoon each pepper and cinnamon
2 tablespoons minced parsley
1 teaspoon chopped mint
1/2 bay leaf, crumbled
4 cups thinly sliced peeled potato
1/4 cup tomato paste
1 cup bouillon
Cream Topping
1/4 cup grated Parmesan cheese

Cook onion in oil until soft. Add garlic and meat and cook, stirring, until meat is lightly browned. Add 1 teaspoon salt and next 4 ingredients and cook a few minutes longer. Layer in 8" square glass baking dish with potato sprinkled with salt, ending with potato. Mix tomato paste with ¼ cup hot water and the bouillon; pour into skillet. Bring to boil; pour carefully over layers in pan. Bake in moderate oven (375°F.) 30 minutes, or until most of the liquid has been absorbed and potato is nearly tender. Remove from oven and pour topping carefully over potato; sprinkle with cheese. Bake in moderate oven (350°F.) 15 minutes, or until custard is set and top is a rich brown. Makes 4 to 6 servings. **Cream Topping** Whisk 2 teaspoons flour with 1 cup light cream. Blend in 2 beaten egg yolks.

HAMBURGER PIE

This recipe comes from Canada.

1 box pastry mix
1/2 cup grated sharp Cheddar cheese
1/2 teaspoon paprika
Dash of cayenne
1-1/2 pounds ground beef chuck
1 small onion, minced
1-1/2 cups dry bread cubes
1 can condensed beef bouillon or consommé
1/2 teaspoon salt
1/2 teaspoon pepper
1/4 teaspoon each thyme and marjoram
2 teaspoons Worcestershire

Prepare pastry mix as directed on the label, adding cheese, paprika and cayenne before adding the liquid. Roll half of pastry on lightly floured board and fit in 9" piepan. Cook beef and onion in skillet until meat loses its red color, breaking up meat with fork. Mix bread cubes and bouillon and let stand a few minutes. Add beef mixture and remaining ingredients. Mix well and pour into pie shell. Roll remaining pastry and put over top, crimping edges. Bake in moderate oven (375°F.) about 45 minutes. Serve warm or cold. Makes 6 servings.

STUFFED CABBAGE, HUNGARIAN STYLE

1 large head cabbage
1 pound ground beef
1 onion, minced
1/2 cup uncooked rice
1 clove garlic, minced
1-1/2 teaspoons salt
1/4 teaspoon pepper
1 large onion, sliced
2 tablespoons fat
1 can (1 pint 2 ounces) tomato juice
1 cup sauerkraut, undrained
1 teaspoon brown sugar

Cut core from cabbage; wash cabbage and put in large pot of boiling water. Cook 10 minutes. Remove from heat and let stand 10 to 15 minutes to soften leaves, then drain. Mix thoroughly next 6 ingredients. Separate cabbage leaves carefully, keeping them whole. Put a leaf on a board and, with sharp knife, shave off rib to thickness of leaf. Put spoonful of meat mixture at base of leaf and roll up loosely to permit swelling of rice. Cook sliced onion in fat in large skillet until golden. Add tomato juice and sauerkraut. Sprinkle with brown sugar. Arrange stuffed cabbage in skillet. Pour 1 cup water over all. Cover and simmer over low heat 1-1/2 hours. Makes 18 rolls, or 6 servings.

BEEF AND SAUSAGE LASAGNA

1 pound ground chuck
1/2 pound sliced sweet Italian sausage, skin removed
2 cloves garlic, minced
1 onion, chopped
1/4 cup olive oil
1 can (2 pounds 3 ounces) Italian tomatoes
1 can (6 ounces) tomato paste
1 teaspoon basil
1 teaspoon oregano
1/2 teaspoon pepper
Salt
1/2 pound lasagna noodles
1 pound ricotta cheese
1 pound mozzarella cheese, sliced
2/3 cup grated Parmesan cheese

Brown first 4 ingredients in olive oil. Add next 5 ingredients, 1½ teaspoons salt and 1 cup water. Bring to boil and simmer, covered, 2 to 3 hours. Cook noodles in boiling salted water until tender; drain. Put a layer of meat mixture in large shallow baking dish. Add a layer of noodles, then a layer each of ricotta, mozzarella and Parmesan. Repeat layers, ending with Parmesan. Bake in moderate oven (350°F.) about 45 minutes. Makes 4 to 6 servings.

HAMBURGER AND EGGPLANT

1 medium eggplant
Vegetable oil
3 medium onions, sliced
2 tablespoons margarine
1 clove garlic, minced
1 pound ground beef
3/4 teaspoon salt
1/2 teaspoon thyme
1/2 teaspoon oregano
1/2 cup canned tomatoes
1/2 cup dry white wine
2 egg whites
1/2 cup fine dry bread crumbs
Sauce

Wash eggplant but do not peel. Cut in lengthwise slices about ½" thick. Brown in oil and set aside. In same pan, sauté onions in margarine until yellowed. Add next 7 ingredients. Bring to boil, stirring with fork. Cover and simmer about ½ hour. Cool; mix in egg whites and ¼ cup crumbs. Butter a baking dish and sprinkle some of remaining crumbs in bottom. Arrange eggplant and meat mixture in layers; top with Sauce and sprinkle with remaining crumbs. Bake in moderate oven (350°F.) about 1 hour. Makes 6 servings. **Sauce** Melt 2 tablespoons butter and stir in 2 tablespoons flour. Add 1½ cups milk and ½ teaspoon salt; cook until thickened. Stir gradually into 2 egg yolks and add ⅛ teaspoon nutmeg.

CREAMED HAMBURGER AND CABBAGE

3/4 pound ground chuck
1 medium onion, minced
3 tablespoons butter or margarine
4 cups coarsely chopped cabbage
3 tablespoons flour
2 teaspoons salt
1/4 teaspoon pepper
3/4 teaspoon paprika
1/2 teaspoon celery seed
1-1/2 cups milk

Brown meat and onion lightly in butter, breaking up meat with fork. Add cabbage and sauté lightly. Blend in flour and seasonings. Add milk, cover and simmer 15 to 20 minutes. Makes 4 servings.

CHINESE BEEF WITH GREEN PEPPERS

1 pound lean ground beef
4 tablespoons soy sauce
2 teaspoons cornstarch
1/8 teaspoon pepper
6 medium green peppers
6 tablespoons vegetable oil
1 teaspoon salt
1/4 teaspoon monosodium glutamate

Mix beef with 2 tablespoons soy sauce, the cornstarch and pepper. Seed peppers and cut in julienne strips. Fry in 3 tablespoons oil. Remove, add remaining 3 tablespoons oil and fry beef until redness disappears. Add peppers, salt, monosodium glutamate and remaining 2 tablespoons soy sauce. Serves 4 to 6.

STUFFED PEPPERS WITH CHEESE SAUCE

4 green peppers
Salt and pepper
1 pound ground beef
1 small onion, sliced
5 tablespoons butter or margarine
1/2 cup raisins
1/4 cup flour
2 cups milk
1 cup diced Cheddar cheese

Split peppers lengthwise, discard seeds and parboil in boiling salted water about 5 minutes; drain well. Cook beef and onion in 1 tablespoon butter, breaking up meat with fork, until meat loses its red color. Add raisins, 1 teaspoon salt and dash of pepper. Fill peppers with mixture and arrange in shallow baking dish. Melt remaining butter and blend in flour. Gradually add milk and cook, stirring, until thickened. Stir in cheese and season to taste. Pour over peppers and bake in moderate oven (350°F.) about 30 minutes. Makes 4 servings.

EASY CHILI CON CARNE WITH BEANS

1 pound ground beef
1 large onion, chopped
2 cloves garlic, crushed
1/2 teaspoon salt
2 to 3 teaspoons chili powder
Dash of pepper
1 tablespoon shortening
1 can condensed tomato soup
2 cans (1 pound each) kidney beans, undrained
1 teaspoon vinegar

Brown first 6 ingredients lightly in the shortening. Add remaining ingredients and 1/2 cup water. Bring to boil, cover and cook over low heat, stirring occasionally, about 30 minutes. Makes 4 servings.

HAMBURGER POTPOURRI

1/2 pound each ground beef and lean pork
1/4 pound ground smoked ham
1 teaspoon salt
1/4 teaspoon pepper
1/4 cup slivered blanched almonds
1/3 cup seedless raisins
1 clove garlic, minced
1 egg
1/2 cup milk
1/2 cup sherry
Few sprigs of parsley, chopped

Cook meats with next 5 ingredients in skillet about 10 minutes, breaking up meat with fork until it loses color. Cool slightly and add remaining ingredients. Pour into 1-quart baking dish. Bake in moderate oven (350°F.) 20 minutes, or until firm. Makes 4 to 6 servings.

HAMBURGER STEW

A savory blend of meat and vegetables.

1 pound ground beef
1 tablespoon butter
1 onion, sliced
1-1/2 teaspoons salt
1/4 teaspoon pepper
1 tablespoon steak sauce
1 can (19 ounces) tomatoes
3 medium potatoes, peeled and sliced
3 medium carrots, sliced
2 stalks celery, diced
Hot biscuits, split (optional)

Brown beef lightly in butter, stirring with fork to break up meat. Add onion and cook a few minutes longer. Add remaining ingredients, except biscuits. Bring to boil and simmer, covered, 30 minutes, or until vegetables are tender. Serve on biscuits. Makes 4 to 6 servings.

HAMBURGER CUPS WITH MUSHROOMS

Serve with mashed potatoes or potatoes Boulangère (page 258).

Shape 1½ pounds ground chuck or round steak in 6 inch patties, making a large depression in center of each. Put in shallow baking dish. Wash 12 large mushrooms and cut off part of stems. Put mushrooms around meat. Bake in hot oven (400°F.) 10 to 20 minutes to desired degree of doneness. Turn mushrooms once during cooking and sprinkle with salt and pepper. Remove meat to platter; put 2 mushrooms in center of each patty and top with a spoonful of **Savory Butter:** Cream together ⅓ cup butter and 2 tablespoons each chopped parsley and green-onion tops. Makes 6 servings.

HAMBURGER HARVEST CASSEROLE

1 onion, chopped
2 green peppers, sliced
1/4 cup margarine
1 pound ground beef
1-1/2 teaspoons salt
1/4 teaspoon pepper
2 cups fresh whole-kernel corn
4 tomatoes, sliced
1/2 cup soft bread crumbs

Brown onion and peppers in the margarine. Add meat, breaking up with fork. Cook a few minutes until it loses its red color. Season with salt and pepper. In 2-quart casserole, arrange layers of half the corn, meat and tomatoes. Repeat. Cover with crumbs. Bake in moderate oven (350°F.) about 35 minutes. Makes 4 servings.

CABBAGE NORWAY

1 medium head cabbage
1-1/2 pounds ground beef
1/2 pound ground pork
1 cup cracker crumbs
1 onion, grated
2 teaspoons salt
1/8 teaspoon pepper
2 eggs, beaten
Tomato sauce or catsup

Cut top from the head of cabbage. Scoop out center of head with sharp knife. Mix next 7 ingredients; stuff into hollow cabbage head. Replace top and tie securely with string. Wrap with cheesecloth and tie ends together. Put in large kettle, cover with boiling water and simmer 1 hour. Remove cloth and string. Cut cabbage in slices and serve with tomato sauce. Makes 4 to 6 servings.

CANADIAN PORK PIE

1 pound ground lean pork
1 teaspoon salt
1/2 teaspoon pepper
1/4 teaspoon nutmeg
1/8 teaspoon mace
2 teaspoons cornstarch
Pastry for 2-crust 8" pie

Combine all ingredients, except pastry, with 1 cup water. Blend thoroughly. Simmer, covered, stirring frequently, 30 minutes. Line 8" piepan with pastry, pour in meat mixture and cover with remaining pastry. Press edges together and prick with fork to allow steam to escape during baking. Bake in hot oven (425°F.) 10 minutes. Reduce heat to 350°F. and bake 35 minutes longer, or until top is brown. Serve hot. Makes 4 to 6 servings.

MUSAKA, YUGOSLAV STYLE

3 medium eggplants
Salt
Flour
7 eggs
2/3 cup vegetable oil
3 large onions, minced
1/2 cup butter or margarine
1/2 pound each ground lean pork and beef
1 pound ground lamb
1/4 cup fine dry bread crumbs
1/2 teaspoon pepper
1 clove garlic, minced
2 cups milk
1/8 teaspoon nutmeg
3 egg yolks, beaten
Dairy sour cream (optional)

Peel eggplants and cut in ¼" lengthwise slices. Sprinkle generously with salt and let stand 15 minutes. Dust with flour. Then dip in 5 eggs, beaten, and brown quickly on both sides in hot oil. Set aside. In skillet cook onion in ¼ cup butter until golden. Mix meats with next three ingredients, ½ teaspoon salt and 2 eggs. Add to onion. Cook and stir until meat is crumbled and lightly browned. In saucepan melt ¼ cup butter and blend in 6 tablespoons flour. Gradually add milk and cook, stirring, until smooth and thickened. Stir in ½ teaspoon salt and the nutmeg. Stir a little of the hot sauce into the egg yolks; stir mixture into sauce. Line a 3½- to 4-quart shallow baking dish or roasting pan with a layer of eggplant. Top with a layer of meat mixture. Repeat layers until all eggplant and meat are used, ending with eggplant. Pour sauce over top. Bake in moderate oven (375°F.) 1 hour. Cut in squares. Serve with sour cream if desired. Makes 10 servings.

SPICY BEEF-MACARONI CASSEROLE

1/4 cup peanut oil
3 medium onions, sliced
1 pound ground round
2 cans (1 pound each) tomatoes
2 teaspoons salt
1/4 teaspoon each garlic salt and pepper
1 teaspoon hot pepper sauce
2 teaspoons Worcestershire
1 teaspoon each rosemary leaves and parsley flakes
1/2 teaspoon celery seed
1/2 pound Cheddar cheese, grated
1 cup milk
1 can condensed cream of mushroom soup
1 pound small seashell macaroni
1/4 cup cracker crumbs

Heat oil in skillet, add onions and brown lightly. Add beef and cook, breaking up with fork, until meat loses its red color. Add tomatoes and seasonings. Bring to boil and simmer while preparing remaining ingredients. Over low heat, melt cheese in the milk and soup. Cook and drain macaroni. Mix all ingredients, except crumbs, and pour into two greased 2-quart casseroles. Sprinkle with crumbs and bake in moderate oven (350°F.) 35 to 40 minutes, or until browned. Makes 9 to 12 servings.

HAMBURGER-SPINACH BLINTZES IN TOMATO SAUCE

1/2 pound ground beef
1/4 pound sausage meat
1 small onion, minced
1 clove garlic, minced
1 cup chopped cooked spinach
3/4 teaspoon salt
1/8 teaspoon pepper
2 eggs, beaten
1 cup milk
2/3 cup all-purpose flour
1 can (16 ounces) tomato sauce
Grated Parmesan cheese

Cook first 4 ingredients in skillet until sausage is well done, breaking up with fork. Add spinach, $^1/_2$ teaspoon salt and the pepper. Remove from heat. Combine eggs, milk and $^1/_4$ teaspoon salt. Add flour and beat until smooth. Pour about $^1/_4$ cup batter into greased 10″ skillet, tilting pan to spread batter very thin over bottom. Cook slowly until lightly browned on one side only. Remove pan from heat and spoon about $^1/_3$ cup meat-spinach mixture into center of pancake; roll pancake around meat and place in shallow baking dish. Repeat with remaining batter and filling to make 6 blintzes. Pour sauce over blintzes and sprinkle with cheese. Bake in moderate oven (350°F.) about 30 minutes. Makes 4 to 6 servings.

HOT TAMALE PIE

1-1/2 pounds lean ground beef
1 onion, chopped
1/2 cup chopped green pepper
1 teaspoon seasoned salt
1 package chili seasoning mix
1 can (1 pound) tomatoes
1-1/2 cups cooked whole-kernel corn, drained
1 can (3-1/4 ounces) pitted black olives, drained (about 1 cup)
1 cup yellow cornmeal
1 teaspoon salt
1/4 can chopped canned pimiento
1 cup shredded Cheddar cheese

Brown beef in skillet, breaking up meat with fork. Add next 5 ingredients and simmer 5 minutes. Stir in corn and olives. Combine cornmeal, salt and $2^1/_2$ cups cold water. Cook, stirring, until thick. Add pimiento. Line greased shallow 2-quart baking dish with some of cornmeal mush. Pour in beef mixture and make a border of remaining mush around edge of baking dish. Bake in moderate oven (350°F.) about 40 minutes. Sprinkle with cheese and bake 5 minutes longer. Makes 6 servings.

HAMBURGER ROLL

Hamburger ready for a company dinner.

1 pound ground beef
1 teaspoon salt
1/4 teaspoon pepper
1 can (2 ounces) mushroom pieces
1 small onion, minced
1/4 cup chopped sweet pickle
2 sprigs parsley, chopped
1/4 teaspoon dry mustard
2 tablespoons flour
Herb-biscuit Dough
Milk
1 can (10-3/4 ounces) beef gravy

Sauté beef, stirring with fork, until it loses its red color. Add next 7 ingredients; simmer 10 minutes. Pour off any fat. Blend in flour; add $^1/_3$ cup water and cook until thickened, stirring constantly. Cool. Roll Herb-biscuit Dough in 12″ x 9″ rectangle. Spread meat mixture on dough to within $^1/_2$″ of edges. Moisten edges with water; roll like jelly roll and pinch edges together. Put roll in greased shallow pan and brush with milk. Bake in hot oven (425°F.) about 30 minutes. Slice and serve with heated gravy. Makes 4 servings. **Herb-biscuit Dough** Sift 2 cups all-purpose flour, 2 teaspoons baking powder, $^1/_2$ teaspoon poultry seasoning and 1 teaspoon salt. Cut in $^1/_4$ cup shortening. Add $^3/_4$ cup milk and mix only until dry ingredients are moistened.

CREAMED HAMBURGER

1 pound ground beef
1 onion, minced
1 tablespoon butter
2 tablespoons flour
1-1/2 cups milk
Salt and pepper
Hot rice, toast or mashed or baked
    potatoes

Brown meat and onion lightly in the butter. Blend in flour. Gradually add milk and cook, stirring, until thickened. Season to taste. Serve on hot rice. Makes 4 servings.

CREOLE STUFFED PEPPERS

4 large green peppers
1 pound ground beef
2 cups cooked rice
1/2 teaspoon monosodium glutamate
Pepper and seasoned salt to taste
Creole Sauce

Split peppers; discard seeds and membrane and wash. Parboil 5 minutes; drain. Cook beef until it loses its red color. Pour off fat. Mix beef, rice, seasonings and 1/4 cup sauce. Pack peppers with the mixture. Put in large shallow baking dish. Pour about three fourths of remaining sauce around peppers. Cover; bake in moderate oven (350°F.) 45 minutes. Serve with remaining sauce, heated. Makes 8 servings. **Creole Sauce** Cook 1 chopped onion and 1/2 cup diced celery in 2 tablespoons butter 5 minutes. Add 1 can (15 1/2 ounces) spaghetti sauce, 1 can (8 ounces) tomato sauce, 1 cup water, 1 bay leaf, 2 whole cloves and salt and pepper. Simmer 15 minutes.

CANDIED SWEET POTATOES AND HAM BALLS

They have a brown-sugar-mustard-vinegar sauce.

1 egg
1/3 cup instant powdered cream
1-1/2 cup soft stale-bread crumbs
2 cups ground cooked ham
1 teaspoon dry mustard
4 sweet potatoes, cooked, peeled and
    halved
3/4 cup packed brown sugar
1/4 cup vinegar

Beat egg lightly; add next 3 ingredients, 1/2 teaspoon mustard and 1/3 cup water. Mix well and shape in 12 balls. Put in large shallow baking dish, making one layer only. Arrange potatoes around edge. Mix sugar, vinegar, 1/2 teaspoon mustard and 1/4 cup water. Pour over ham balls and potatoes. Bake in moderate oven (375°F.) about 45 minutes, basting several times with the syrup. Serves 4.

POTATO-BEEF BAKE

Cook 8 small peeled potatoes 15 minutes. Put in casserole. Sauté over low heat 1/2 pound ground beef until it loses its red color, breaking up with fork. Add 1 can (15 1/2 ounces) spaghetti sauce, 1 minced clove garlic, 1 minced onion and 1 tablespoon chopped parsley; bring to boil. Pour over potatoes. Sprinkle with 1/4 cup grated Parmesan or Romano cheese. Bake in moderate oven (350°F.) about 1 hour. Serves 4.

GLAZED FRUITED HAM LOAF

2 pounds ground cooked ham
1 pound ground fresh pork
3 eggs
1-1/2 cups fine cracker crumbs
1-1/2 cups milk
1/2 teaspoon salt
1/8 teaspoon pepper
12 dried apricot halves
3/4 cup packed brown sugar
2 teaspoons dry mustard
1/4 cup vinegar
Cooked unpitted whole prunes
Parsley

Mix first 7 ingredients lightly but thoroughly. Arrange apricot halves in circle in bottom of round 2-quart casserole. Mix next 3 ingredients and carefully pour over apricots. Top with meat mixture, packing it firmly over apricots. Bake in moderate oven (350°F.) about 1 1/2 hours. Turn out on a hot platter and garnish with prunes and parsley. Serves 8 to 10.

HAM CROQUETTES

1/4 cup each butter and flour
1 small onion, minced
1 cup milk
2 eggs
1 tablespoon lemon juice
1-1/2 cups ground cooked ham
Salt and pepper
Fine dry bread crumbs
Fat for deep frying
Creamy Horseradish Sauce (page 156) or
    Mustard Sauce (page 91)

Melt butter; blend in flour and onion. Add milk; cook, stirring constantly, until very thick. Stir into 1 egg beaten with lemon juice. Add ham, and salt and pepper to taste. Pour into a shallow dish; cool. Shape into 4 croquettes and chill. Dip in crumbs, then in 1 egg beaten with 2 tablespoons water. Dip again in crumbs and let stand 1/2 hour. Fry in hot deep fat (390°F. on a frying thermometer) 2 minutes, or until done. Serve with Creamy Horseradish or Mustard Sauce. Makes 4 servings.

GOLDEN VEAL BALLS WITH LEMON GRAVY

1 pound ground veal
1 cup milk
1 cup soft stale-bread crumbs
Yellow peel of 1/2 lemon, cut in very
  thin strips
1 teaspoon each salt and celery salt
2 cups chicken broth
Lemon Gravy
Chopped parsley

Mix well all ingredients, except last 3. Bring broth to boil in saucepan. With oval tablespoon, shape meatballs and drop, 4 at a time, into broth. Simmer 6 minutes, or until done. Remove to covered serving dish and keep warm. Repeat until all are done. Strain broth and reserve for gravy. Pour gravy over top and garnish with parsley. Makes 4 to 6 servings. **Lemon Gravy** Melt 2 tablespoons butter and blend in 2 tablespoons flour. Gradually add broth and cook, stirring, until thickened. Beat together 2 egg yolks and ³/₄ cup half-and-half. Add to hot sauce, stirring briskly. Cook, stirring, 2 minutes. Add 2 tablespoons lemon juice.

SWEET-SOUR PORK BALLS

1 pound ground lean pork
1/4 cup minced green onion
1 egg
1/2 teaspoon each salt and ground ginger
5 tablespoons soy sauce
4 tablespoons cornstarch
2-1/4 cups vegetable oil
1 cup cooked sliced carrots, drained
  and liquid reserved
1 package (7 ounces) frozen snow-pea
  pods, thawed
1 can (13-1/3 ounces) pineapple chunks,
  drained and syrup reserved
1/4 cup sliced water chestnuts
3 tablespoons sugar
2 to 3 tablespoons white vinegar
Hot cooked rice

Combine first 5 ingredients with 2 tablespoons soy sauce and 2 tablespoons cornstarch and mix well. Shape in even round balls, using a measuring tablespoonful for each. Heat 2 cups oil in deep heavy skillet until bubbling (370°F. on frying thermometer). Fry balls until well browned; drain. Heat remaining oil in large skillet, add next 4 ingredients and sauté about 3 minutes, then add meatballs. In small saucepan, mix sugar, remaining soy sauce and cornstarch with reserved carrot liquid and pineapple syrup (add water to make 1¹/₂ cups). Bring to boil, stirring, until thickened and clear. Correct seasoning and pour over meatballs and vegetables in skillet. Simmer 5 minutes and serve with rice. Makes 4 to 6 servings.

FRIKADELLER
(Danish Meatballs)

1 pound ground veal
1 pound ground pork
3 tablespoons flour
1/4 cup minced onion
1 teaspoon salt
Freshly ground pepper
2 eggs, slightly beaten
2 cups carbonated water
Butter or margarine
Seasoned cooked red cabbage

Combine first 7 ingredients and mix well. Add carbonated water ¹/₄ cup at a time and beat well. Cover with foil and chill 1 hour. With hands dipped in cold water, shape meat in oblong patties about 4″ long and 2¹/₂″ wide. Sauté on both sides in browned butter in skillet until well browned. Remove to heavy saucepan. Add small amount of hot water to skillet to loosen browned bits. Pour over frikadeller, cover and simmer 15 minutes or until done. Serve with cabbage. Makes 6 to 8 servings.

CURRIED LAMB PATTY

1 pound ground lamb
1 tablespoon instant minced onion
1 tablespoon curry powder
1/2 teaspoon salt
1 tablespoon lemon juice
1 tablespoon chopped chutney
1/2 cup wheat germ
1 egg, slightly beaten
1/2 cup milk
1/4 cup slivered almonds

Combine all ingredients, except nuts, and mix well. Pat into 9″ piepan and sprinkle with almonds. Bake in moderate oven (350°F.) about 45 minutes. Serve in wedges. Makes 4 servings.

CHILI MEATBALLS

1 pound meat-loaf mixture
1/4 cup white cornmeal
1 clove garlic, crushed or minced
1 small onion, grated
1 teaspoon ground coriander
1 teaspoon salt
1/4 teaspoon pepper
Sauce

Mix lightly all ingredients, except Sauce. Shape in balls about ³/₄″ in diameter. Drop into boiling Sauce, cover and simmer 10 to 15 minutes. Makes 4 servings. **Sauce** Melt 1 tablespoon butter in saucepan; add 1 small onion, chopped and 1 clove garlic, crushed and minced. Cook slowly until lightly browned. Add 1 tablespoon chili powder and 1 can (1 pint 2 ounces) tomato juice; simmer 10 minutes. Season with salt and pepper.

LAMB BALLS AND CURRIED TOMATO

1-1/2 pounds ground lamb
1 onion, minced
3/4 cup soft stale-bread crumbs
1-1/2 cups milk
2 teaspoons salt
1/4 teaspoon pepper
Cooking oil
Curried Tomatoes

Mix first 6 ingredients. Shape into balls and brown on all sides in hot oil. Reduce heat and cook, covered, until done. Serve with tomatoes. Makes 6 servings.

Curried Tomatoes

1 can (28 ounces) tomatoes
1 teaspoon each salt, sugar, instant minced onion and curry powder
1/4 teaspoon pepper
1/4 cup soft stale-bread crumbs

Simmer all ingredients together 15 minutes.

SOUDZOUKAKIA SMYRNAYKA (Greek Meatballs)

1 pound ground lamb
1/2 cup soft bread crumbs
1/2 cup dry white wine
2 cloves garlic, minced
1 teaspoon salt
1/4 teaspoon pepper
1/2 teaspoon caraway seed
Olive oil or butter
1 can (8 ounces) tomato sauce
1/2 teaspoon sugar
Mashed potatoes or cooked rice

Mix first 7 ingredients. Shape into 6 rolls about 5" long and 1" in diameter. Brown rolls lightly in olive oil. Add tomato sauce, sugar and $1/2$ cup water. Heat slowly to boiling. Simmer 5 minutes, or until done. Serve with mashed potato or rice. Serves 4.

LOULE KEBAB (Armenian Lamb Hamburgers)

Traditional shape for the Armenian lamb "hamburger" is an elongated patty, almost frankfurter shape. Serve the Loule Kebab hot with pilaf or vegetables.

2 pounds ground lamb
1 medium onion, minced
1-1/2 teaspoons salt
1 teaspoon ground coriander
3/4 teaspoon freshly ground black pepper

Mix together all ingredients and shape into 8 to 12 elongated patties. Broil on both sides until browned. Makes 4 to 6 servings.

ARMENIAN LAMB PATTIES

1 pound ground lamb
1 small onion, minced
1-1/2 teaspoons salt
1/4 teaspoon pepper
Few sprigs of parsley, minced
1 cup soft bread crumbs
Cooking oil
Clove of garlic, halved

Mix first 6 ingredients and 2 tablespoons oil. Shape into 4 patties. Heat small amount of oil in skillet; add garlic. Brown patties quickly on both sides in hot oil. Reduce heat and cook slowly 10 minutes. Makes 4 servings.

FILLED LAMBURGERS

1-1/2 pounds lean ground lamb
1 teaspoon salt
1/4 teaspoon each pepper and rosemary
1 large onion, chopped
4 tablespoons butter
1 can (3 ounces) chopped mushrooms, undrained
1 teaspoon bottled gravy sauce
Rolls (optional)

Mix meat and seasonings. Shape in 8 patties, 4" in diameter. Cook onion in 2 tablespoons butter 2 to 3 minutes. Add mushrooms and cook until liquid evaporates. Put mushroom mixture on 4 meat patties and cover with remaining patties. Press edges together. Mix remaining 2 tablespoons butter and the gravy sauce. Brush on patties. Broil about 5 minutes on each side. Serve on rolls, if desired. Serves 4.

LAMB CABBAGE ROLLS

1 white cabbage (about 4 pounds)
1 pound ground lamb
1/2 cup uncooked rice
1 medium onion, minced
2 cloves garlic, minced
1 egg
2 teaspoons salt
1/4 teaspoon pepper
1 pound sauerkraut
1 can (28 ounces) Italian tomatoes
1/4 cup butter

Cut core out of cabbage to depth of 3". Put cabbage into a large kettle of boiling water over high heat. With tongs, remove about 18 leaves as they wilt. Cool; cut out coarsest part of ribs. Chop remaining cabbage coarsely and put half into a large kettle. Mix next 7 ingredients. Put a spoonful of mixture on each cabbage leaf and roll up. Put cabbage rolls on top of cabbage in kettle. Top with remaining cabbage, sauerkraut, tomatoes and butter. Check seasoning. Add $1^{1}/_{2}$ cups boiling water, cover and simmer about 45 minutes. Serves 6.

INDIVIDUAL HAM LOAVES

1 pound ground ham
1-1/2 pounds ground pork
2 eggs, well beaten
1 cup cracker crumbs
1 cup milk
1 teaspoon dry mustard
1/4 cup prepared horseradish
1 small onion, grated
1/4 teaspoon salt
1/4 teaspoon pepper
Sweet-and-Sour Mustard Sauce (page 156)

Mix all ingredients, except sauce. Pack into 12 sections of 3" muffin pan. Put on shallow baking pan and bake in moderate oven (350°F.) about 1 hour. Serve hot with sauce. Serves 6.

HAM-AND-VEAL LOAF

1-1/2 pounds ground cooked ham
1/2 pound ground veal
2 eggs
1-1/2 cups fine dry bread crumbs
1 teaspoon celery salt
1/8 teaspoon pepper
3/4 cup milk
1 envelope sour-cream sauce mix
2 to 3 tablespoons horseradish

Mix all ingredients, except last 2. Shape in 2 rolls and fit in 2 greased 1-pound coffee cans. Shake mixture; then press down lightly. Cover each can with foil and tie securely. Set upright on rack in large kettle. Pour in water to reach halfway up on cans. Cover kettle and bring water to boil. Reduce heat and simmer 3 hours. Cut rolls into slices and serve hot or cold with sauce prepared as directed on envelope, with horseradish added to taste. Makes 8 servings.

PORK LOAF WITH CREAM GRAVY

1 pound ground lean pork
1 cup soft bread crumbs
1 egg, slightly beaten
1 small onion, minced
1/4 teaspoon poultry seasoning
1 teaspoon salt
1/8 teaspoon pepper
Fine dry bread crumbs
4 slices bacon
2 tablespoons flour
1 cup light cream
Seasoned salt and pepper

Mix first 7 ingredients and shape in a loaf. Roll in crumbs and put in shallow baking pan. Arrange bacon strips on loaf. Bake in moderate oven (350°F.) about 1 hour. Remove loaf to a hot platter. Pour off all but 2 tablespoons fat from pan. Blend flour into fat in pan. Gradually add cream and cook, stirring, until thickened. Add seasoned salt and pepper to taste. Serve with the loaf. Makes 4 servings.

FLAMING HAM LOAF

2 cups ground cooked ham
1-1/2 cups soft bread crumbs
2 eggs, slightly beaten
1 tablespoon instant minced onion
1/8 teaspoon pepper
1 cup milk
2 tablespoons minced parsley
1/4 teaspoon dry mustard
3 to 4 tablespoons brown sugar
1/4 cup brandy

Mix first 8 ingredients and pack in greased 9" x 5" x 3" loaf pan. Bake in moderate oven (350°F.) about 50 minutes. Remove from oven and turn out on a platter. Pat brown sugar over loaf. Warm brandy and put in ladle. At the table, set the brandy alight and pour over ham loaf. Makes 4 servings.

ORANGE-GLAZED VEAL-AND-HAM LOAF

1 pound each ground ham and veal
2 eggs, beaten
1 cup orange juice
1/2 teaspoon salt
1/4 teaspoon pepper
1 cup fine dry bread crumbs
Orange Glaze
Orange slices

Mix meats thoroughly with next 5 ingredients. Shape in a loaf and put in shallow baking pan. Bake in moderate oven (350°F.) 1½ hours, basting frequently with half of the glaze. Top with orange slices last 10 minutes of baking. Serve with remaining glaze. Makes 6 servings. **Orange Glaze** Mix 3 tablespoons sugar and 1 tablespoon cornstarch in saucepan. Add 1½ cups orange juice. Cook, stirring, until thickened.

CURRIED PORK AND SMOKED-HAM LOAF

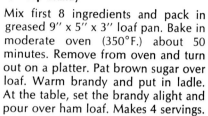 Force 1 pound each lean pork and ham ends through food chopper twice, using medium blade. Add 1 minced clove garlic, 1 chopped small onion, 3 teaspoons salt, 1 teaspoon pepper, 2 teaspoons curry powder, 1 to 2 teaspoons crumbled sage, 1 egg white and ½ cup undiluted evaporated milk. Mix lightly but thoroughly; shape in an oval loaf about 9" long. Lay 4 slices bacon out on a square of cheesecloth; put meat loaf on bacon. Roll up in cloth; tie ends with cord. Put on trivet in large kettle. Add 2 quarts boiling water, ¼ cup vinegar and 1 teaspoon salt. Cover; simmer 2½ hours. Remove from liquid; let stand until cold. Chill; unwrap and slice thin. Serves 6 to 8.

GREEN-PEPPER HAM LOAF

2 pounds ground ham
1/2 cup soft bread crumbs
1/2 green pepper, minced
1 teaspoon prepared mustard
1 teaspoon chopped fresh or 1/4
   teaspoon dried oregano, crushed
2 eggs
1/2 cup milk
Dash of hot pepper sauce
Salt to taste

Combine all ingredients, pack in a loaf pan and bake in moderate oven (350°F.) 1 hour. Serve plain or with desired sauce. Makes 6 servings.

BAKED HAM-PORK BALLS

3/4 pound ground fully-cooked smoked
   ham
1/2 pound lean pork, ground
1/2 cup milk
1/2 cup cracker crumbs
3/4 cup packed brown sugar
1/2 cup vinegar
6 whole cloves
1 tablespoon dry mustard

Mix first 4 ingredients and shape in 12 balls about 2" in diameter. Put in shallow baking dish. Bring remaining ingredients and ½ cup water to boil and pour over ham balls. Bake, uncovered, in slow oven (325°F.) about 2 hours. Makes 4 servings.

MEATBALLS WITH ORANGE SOUR-CREAM SAUCE

1 pound meat-loaf mixture
1 teaspoon salt
1/4 teaspoon pepper
1 tablespoon parsley flakes
1 egg
3/4 cup soft bread crumbs
1 cup orange juice
Orange Sour-cream Sauce
Chopped parsley
Hot cooked noodles (optional)

In bowl combine first 6 ingredients with ½ cup orange juice. Shape in 24 small meatballs and brown in skillet. Add remaining ½ cup orange juice, cover and simmer 15 minutes. Put in serving dish; top with sauce. Sprinkle with parsley; serve with noodles, if desired. Serves 4 to 6.

Orange Sour-cream Sauce

1/4 cup butter or margarine
2 tablespoons flour
1 cup dairy sour cream
Grated rind of 1 orange
1 can (2 ounces) mushroom stems and
   pieces, undrained

In saucepan, melt butter, blend in flour and cook, stirring, until flour is lightly browned. Stir in sour cream, orange rind and mushrooms and heat through.

MEAT-AND-VEGETABLE CASSEROLE

1/4 pound salt pork
1 pound meat-loaf mixture
6 small whole onions
2 carrots, diced
1 cup cut green beans
1 cup diced turnip
1 teaspoon salt
1/4 teaspoon pepper

Cut pork in thin slices and put in 1½-quart casserole with cover. Shape ground meat in 4 patties and put on pork. Mix remaining ingredients and spread over patties. Cover and bake in moderate oven (350°F.) 1¼ hours, or until vegetables are tender. Makes 4 servings.

LAYERED MEAT-RICE LOAVES

2-2/3 cups packaged precooked rice
3 teaspoons salt
1 onion, minced
1 cup soft bread crumbs
1 cup milk
2 pounds meat-loaf mixture
2 eggs, slightly beaten
Dash of pepper
2 tablespoons minced parsley
2 teaspoons steak sauce
1/2 cup catsup
Mustard Sauce (page 91)

Add rice, 1 teaspoon salt and 2 tablespoons onion to 2⅔ cups boiling water in saucepan. Mix just enough to moisten all the rice. Cover; remove from heat and let stand 5 minutes. Soak bread in the milk and add remaining salt and onion and other ingredients, except Mustard Sauce. Mix lightly but thoroughly. Press a layer of meat mixture in bottom of each of 2 greased 9" x 5" x 3" loaf pans. Add a layer of half of rice mixture, then a layer of half of remaining meat; repeat. Bake in moderate oven (350°F.) about 45 minutes. Let stand 5 minutes. Turn out on hot platter and serve with sauce. Serves 8 to 10.

PICKLE-RELISH LAMB LOAF

2 cups soft bread crumbs
2/3 cup milk
2 eggs
1 onion, minced
1-1/2 pounds ground lamb
1 canned pimiento, chopped
1/2 cup drained sweet-pickle relish
2 teaspoons salt

Mix all ingredients lightly but thoroughly. Press into greased 9" x 5" x 3" loaf pan. Bake in moderate oven (375°F.) about 1 hour. Let stand 10 minutes. Turn out of pan and serve plain or with any desired sauce. Makes 6 servings.

APRICOT VEAL LOAF

1 cup dried apricots
3/4 cup diced celery
3 tablespoons minced onion
1 tablespoon minced parsley
1 cup cooked rice
1 teaspoon salt
1/8 teaspoon pepper
1/4 teaspoon savory
1 egg, slightly beaten
1-1/4 pounds ground veal
2 tablespoons honey
4 slices bacon, slightly cooked and
  drained
Sweet-Sour Sauce

Cover apricots with boiling water and let stand 10 minutes. Drain and cut in pieces with scissors; mix with next 9 ingredients. Put in 9" x 5" x 3" loaf pan. Drizzle with honey; arrange bacon slices on top. Bake in moderate oven (350°F.) about 1 hour. Serve with sauce. Makes 6 to 8 servings.

Sweet-Sour Sauce

1 tablespoon cider vinegar
1 teaspoon dry mustard
3 tablespoons honey
1/2 cup chili sauce
1/2 cup golden raisins
2 tablespoons sherry
Any pan drippings available

Combine all ingredients with 2 tablespoons water and simmer about 10 minutes. Makes about 1 cup.

OLD-FASHIONED VEAL LOAF

Mix thoroughly 2 pounds ground veal, 1 pound ground pork, 1 cup fine bread crumbs, 2 finely chopped garlic cloves, 1/4 cup grated onion, 1/2 cup chopped parsley, 2 lightly beaten eggs, 1 teaspoon thyme and 1 teaspoon each salt and freshly ground black pepper. Form into a firm loaf. Place a layer of bacon slices on the bottom of a shallow roasting pan or baking dish and arrange the loaf on top. Put more bacon slices on top of the meat. Roast in moderate oven (350°F.) for 1½ hours, basting occasionally with pan juices. Serve hot with creamy mashed potatoes and green beans. Makes 8 servings.

Veal Loaf with Italian Sausages This is an elegant buffet dish to be served hot or cold. Prepare recipe for Old-fashioned Veal Loaf. Boil 6 to 8 Italian sausages for 10 minutes. Cool and remove the skins. Arrange half of the veal-pork mixture on bacon slices in the bottom of a baking dish. Put the skinned sausages on the meat and add the rest of the mixture. Press down firmly. Top with more bacon and bake as above. Makes 8 to 10 servings.

LIVER LOAF

1-1/2 pounds calf's or beef liver
1/2 cup fine dry bread crumbs
4 anchovy fillets
1 onion, minced
3/4 pound sausage meat
1-1/2 teaspoons salt
1/4 teaspoon freshly ground pepper
1 to 2 teaspoons mixed fresh or 1/4 to
  1/2 teaspoon dried herbs (basil,
  marjoram, rosemary, sage, savory),
  crushed; or 1/2 teaspoon ginger
1/3 cup undiluted evaporated milk
4 slices bacon

Cut raw liver in strips, coat with crumbs, then force through food chopper, using medium blade; grind anchovies. Combine with remaining ingredients, except bacon. Mix lightly but thoroughly and pack into a 9" x 5" x 3" loaf pan. Cut bacon slices in half and cover top. Bake in moderate oven (350°F.) about 1 hour. This needs no sauce, though it can be served with a tomato one. It's as delicious cold as it is hot. Serves 8.

MEAT-LOAF SQUARES

2 cups ground cooked lamb, beef or veal
1 cup soft bread crumbs
3/4 cup leftover gravy or milk
1 small onion, minced
2 eggs
1 teaspoon curry powder
1/2 teaspoon seasoned salt
1 tablespoon lemon juice or vinegar
2 tablespoons chopped parsley
2 tablespoons catsup
Salt and pepper to taste

Mix all ingredients and press into a greased 8" square pan. Bake in moderate oven (350°F.) about 45 minutes. Cut in squares. Good served plain, with creamed eggs, catsup, hot gravy or any sauce desired. Serves 4.

STUFFED GREEN PEPPERS

4 large green peppers
1-1/2 cups ground cooked meat
1/4 cup uncooked rice
1/4 cup minced onion
1-1/2 teaspoons salt
1/4 teaspoon pepper
1 can (8 ounces) tomato sauce
Dash of cayenne
2 basil leaves, or pinch of dried basil

Cut off tops of peppers and remove seeds. Mix next 5 ingredients. Stuff peppers three fourths full. Stand up in deep heavy skillet with tight-fitting lid. Pour remaining ingredients mixed with 1 cup water over peppers. Cover and cook very slowly 40 minutes. If necessary, add a little more water. Makes 4 servings.

CREOLE MEAT LOAF AND MACARONI

1 onion, minced
1/2 green pepper, minced
2 tablespoons butter or margarine
1 can (28 ounces) tomatoes
1-1/4 cups elbow or broken macaroni
1 bay leaf
1 teaspoon Worcestershire
1 to 1-1/2 cups leftover meat loaf, cubed
Seasoned salt and pepper

Cook onion and green pepper in butter 2 or 3 minutes. Add next 4 ingredients and 1 cup water. Bring to boil and simmer, covered, about ½ hour, stirring frequently. Add meat loaf and seasoned salt and pepper to taste; heat through. Makes 4 servings.

SCALLOPED POTATOES WITH MEAT LOAF

1/4 teaspoon pepper
1 can condensed cream of chicken soup
3/4 cup milk
1 teaspoon salt
5 large potatoes, peeled and thinly sliced
8 slices cooked meat loaf

Mix first 4 ingredients. Put in greased 2-quart casserole in alternate layers with potato and meat loaf. Bake in moderate oven (375°F.) 1 hour, or until potatoes are tender. Makes 6 servings.

LAMB BISCUIT ROLL WITH BROWN SAUCE

2 cups ground cooked lamb
3/4 teaspoon salt
1/4 teaspoon pepper
1 tablespoon lamb fat
1 can (2 ounces) chopped mushrooms, drained
1 small onion, minced
1 sprig parsley, chopped
2 tablespoons chopped stuffed olives
2 tablespoons chopped sweet pickles
1/4 teaspoon dry mustard
Baking-powder-biscuit dough (page 307)
1 tablespoon milk
Brown Sauce (above right)

Put first 10 ingredients in heavy skillet. Cook over low heat 10 minutes. Cool. Turn biscuit dough out on lightly floured board and roll into rectangle ¼" thick. Spread meat mixture over dough to within ½" of edge. Roll up like jelly roll; moisten edges with water and seal. Put roll in greased shallow pan and brush with 1 tablespoon milk. Bake in hot oven (425°F.) about 30 minutes, or until crust is nicely browned. Slice while hot and serve on heated platter with Brown Sauce poured over slices. Makes 4 to 6 servings.

BROWN SAUCE

2 tablespoons lamb fat
1 small onion, minced
1 sprig parsley, minced
1/2 carrot, grated
Pinch of thyme
1 bay leaf
1-1/2 tablespoons flour
1 bouillon cube
Salt and pepper

Put first 8 ingredients in skillet. Cook slowly 10 minutes, or until browned. Add 1½ cups boiling water. Season to taste and simmer 2 minutes. Strain.

DILL SOUR-CREAM SAUCE

In saucepan blend 2 tablespoons flour, 1 tablespoon snipped fresh dill, ½ teaspoon sugar and 1 cup dairy sour cream. Vigorously stir in 1 cup pan juices or beef broth. Cook, stirring, until bubbly. Makes 1¾ cups.

SWEET-AND-SOUR MUSTARD SAUCE

Mix 1 cup water, ½ cup brown sugar, ¼ cup vinegar, 2 tablespoons dry mustard, ¼ teaspoon salt and a dash each of pepper and cayenne. Bring to boil and thicken with 3 tablespoons cornstarch mixed with little cold water. Makes about 1⅓ cups.

CREAMY HORSERADISH SAUCE

Whip 1 cup heavy cream until stiff. Add ½ teaspoon salt and 3 or 4 tablespoons prepared horseradish. Makes about 2 cups.

HERB SAUCE

1 tablespoon each butter and flour
1 cup milk
1 tablespoon minced parsley
1 tablespoon minced chives
1 teaspoon chopped fresh tarragon or basil
Salt and pepper to taste

Melt butter and blend in flour. Gradually add milk and cook, stirring, until thickened. Add remaining ingredients. Makes 1 cup.

BROWN MUSHROOM SAUCE

1 tablespoon chopped shallot
1/4 pound mushrooms, thinly sliced
3 tablespoons butter or margarine
1 teaspoon lemon juice
1 can beef gravy

Cook shallot and mushrooms in the butter 5 minutes, stirring occasionally. Add remaining ingredients and heat. Makes about 2 cups.

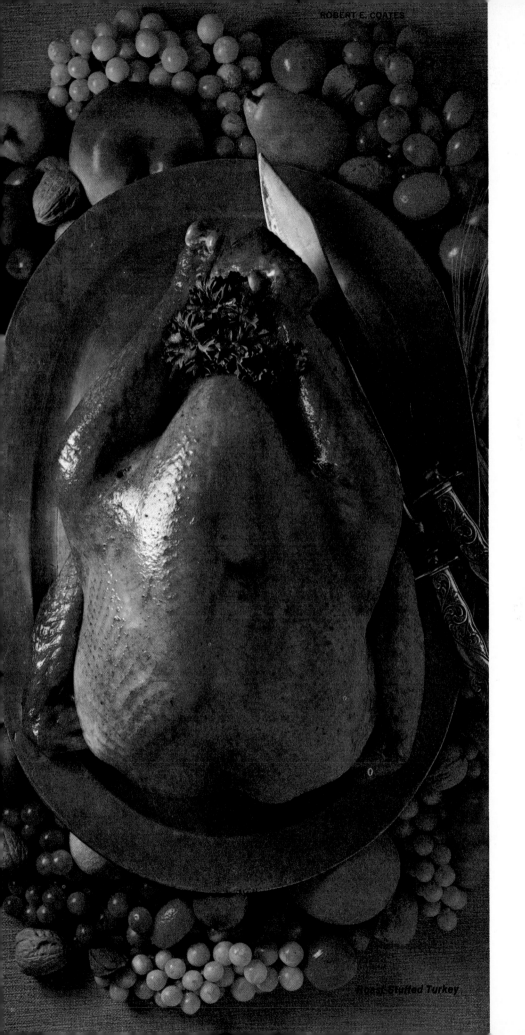

ROBERT E. COATES

Roast Stuffed Turkey

HOW TO BUY POULTRY

Today most poultry comes from the market in ready-to-cook form. Whole birds are sold eviscerated with edible giblets wrapped separately in the body cavity. Most markets sell both chilled freshly-killed and frozen birds. There is also a choice, in the case of chicken and turkey, of whole or cut-up birds and parts (breasts, thighs, wings, necks and backs) and frozen boneless chicken and turkey rolls. Chicken livers and giblets are also sold separately.

Amounts to buy

Allow ½ to ¾ pound per person for ready-to-cook chicken; ¾ to 1 pound for turkey, guinea hen and capon; 1 to 1½ pounds for duck and geese.

POULTRY STORAGE

If **chilled fresh ready-to-cook,** remove wrapper. Remove giblets and neck from cavity. Wrap bird loosely in waxed paper, foil or plastic wrap and store in coldest part of refrigerator. Use within 24 hours. If **quick-frozen ready-to-cook,** put bird in freezer as quickly as possible. Keep frozen stored at 0°F., or less, until ready to thaw for cooking. Completely thaw bird before cooking, following label directions. Once thawed, remove giblets and neck and cook bird at once. **To store leftover roast bird,** remove stuffing while bird is still warm and refrigerate separately. It is not necessary for poultry to cool at room temperature longer than 15 to 20 minutes before refrigerating.

Caution

Do not stuff bird with warm stuffing and store in refrigerator until ready to roast. If stuffing must be made ahead, refrigerate separately and stuff bird just before roasting.

ROAST STUFFED CHICKEN

1 roasting chicken (3 to 4 pounds)
1/2 lemon
Butter or margarine
1 small onion, minced
1/2 teaspoon dried thyme leaves
2 tablespoons chopped parsley
1/2 cup chopped cooked ham
1-1/2 cups soft stale-bread crumbs
1 egg, beaten
1/4 cup cream
Salt and pepper

Rub chicken cavity with lemon. Butter the giblets and place them inside
the bird. Sauté onion in butter 2 or
3 minutes. Add next 6 ingredients
and salt and pepper to taste. Use to
stuff bird. Sew openings or cover
with foil. Truss, tie securely and rub
with butter. Put on one side on rack
in shallow roasting pan. Roast in
moderate oven (375°F.) 20 minutes.
Turn on other side and baste well
with pan drippings and melted butter. Roast 20 minutes. Turn bird on
its back; baste again. Roast until
tender, about 30 more minutes. Serve
with crisp pork sausages, new potatoes and green peas. Serves 4 to 6.

ROAST CHICKEN WITH SAUSAGE-NUT STUFFING

1 roasting chicken (3 to 4 pounds)
1 lemon
1/4 cup sausage meat
1/4 cup butter or margarine
3 tablespoons minced onion
1/2 teaspoon paprika
3/4 teaspoon salt
1/4 cup chopped celery
1/4 cup chopped parsley
3-1/2 cups soft stale-bread crumbs
1/3 cup chopped pecans
Milk
1 tablespoon chicken or sausage fat
Celery leaves and rosemary
1/2 cup cream
2 tablespoons brown sugar

Wash and dry chicken. Rub skin with
cut lemon. Cook sausage until golden
brown, breaking up with fork. Add
butter and 2 tablespoons of the
onion. Cook 2 or 3 minutes. Remove
from heat and add next 6 ingredients.
Mix well with enough milk to moist-
en. Stuff body and neck cavities of
chicken lightly and truss. Rub with
fat; then sprinkle with celery leaves,
rosemary and remaining 1 tablespoon
onion. Wrap loosely in foil and put
on rack in open shallow pan. Roast
in slow oven (325°F.) 1½ hours.
Pull foil away from chicken. Brush
with mixture of cream and brown
sugar. Continue roasting and basting
1 hour, or until chicken is tender and
well browned. Serves 4 to 6.

CHICKEN WITH GINGER-CREAM SAUCE

1 frying chicken (about 2-1/2 pounds),
    cut up
1/4 cup flour
1/2 teaspoon salt
1/8 teaspoon pepper
1 teaspoon ginger
3 tablespoons butter
1 chicken bouillon cube
1/2 cup cream
Hot cooked green lima beans

Roll chicken in mixture of flour,
salt, pepper and ginger. Brown
in butter. Stir in remaining flour mixture. Add bouillon cube dissolved in
³/₄ cup boiling water and bring to
boil. Cover and simmer 45 minutes,
or until tender. Stir in cream and
heat. Serve with lima beans. Makes
4 servings.

BARBECUED CHICKEN

1 broiling chicken (about 1-1/2 pounds),
    quartered
1/2 cup lemon juice
2 tablespoons vegetable oil
1/4 teaspoon each dried rosemary,
    thyme and marjoram
1/2 teaspoon each salt, pepper and
    celery seed

Put chicken, skin side down, on
greased rack of broiler pan.
Brush chicken with sauce made of
remaining ingredients. Broil 30 minutes in preheated broiler, 3" to 4"
below heat, brushing several times
with sauce. Turn and broil 15 minutes longer, basting with sauce, until
tender. Makes 4 servings.

CHICKEN CACCIATORA

1/4 cup olive oil
1 chicken (2-1/2 to 3 pounds), cut up
2 onions, sliced
2 cloves garlic, minced
1 can (1 pound) Italian tomatoes
1 can (8 ounces) tomato sauce
1 teaspoon salt
1/4 teaspoon pepper
1/2 teaspoon celery seed
1 teaspoon crushed dried oregano
2 bay leaves
1/2 cup dry white wine

Heat oil in large deep skillet. Brown
chicken on all sides. Remove chicken
pieces and keep hot. Cook onions
and garlic in oil in skillet until tender.
Blend in next 7 ingredients. Cook 5
minutes. Return chicken to skillet.
Cover and simmer 45 minutes. Add
wine and cook, uncovered, about 15
minutes. Arrange on hot platter. Skim
excess fat from sauce and remove bay
leaves. Pour sauce over chicken.
Makes 4 to 6 servings.

CHICKEN BAKED WITH CHICKEN LIVERS

3 small chickens (about 1-1/2 pounds
    each), halved
Butter or margarine
Paprika
2 tablespoons minced onion
3 tablespoons chopped green pepper
2 tablespoons minced celery
1 clove garlic, crushed
3 tablespoons chopped parsley
1/2 pound chicken livers, diced
1 teaspoon salt
1/4 teaspoon pepper
1 cup soft bread crumbs
1/2 cup chicken stock
2 tablespoons fine dry bread crumbs

Wash and dry chicken halves; put in baking pan or casserole, skin side up. Brush with melted butter, sprinkle with paprika and add ½ cup water. Bake in moderate oven (375°F). 30 minutes. In the meantime, cook onion, green pepper and celery in 3 tablespoons butter for 2 or 3 minutes. Add next 7 ingredients. Turn chickens over and fill cavity with onion mixture. Sprinkle with fine dry crumbs and melted butter. Dust with paprika and bake in moderate oven (350°F.) about 30 minutes. Makes 6 servings.

CHICKEN VELVET

1/2 pound chicken breasts
5 egg whites
1 teaspoon cornstarch
1/2 teaspoon salt
3 tablespoons vegetable oil
Chicken Gravy

Separate chicken meat from skin and bones. Cut into 1″ cubes and put into blender with 1 egg white, cornstarch and salt. Blend until mushy; gradually add ¼ cup water, continuing to blend. (Or, if you have no blender, grind meat twice with finest blade, mix thoroughly with unbeaten egg white, cornstarch and salt, then mix in water a few drops at a time.) Beat remaining 4 egg whites until stiff and gradually fold into the chicken mixture. Heat a heavy skillet and add oil. Quickly stir 2 tablespoons hot oil into the chicken mixture before pouring it into pan. Cook over low heat until set but not browned. (If it begins to brown on bottom, put the pan in a 350°F. oven to finish setting.) Serve hot with Chicken Gravy. Makes 4 to 6 servings. **Chicken Gravy** Blend 4 teaspoons cornstarch and 1 teaspoon sherry with 1 cup chicken stock and cook until thickened, stirring constantly. Season to taste.

CHICKEN, JAMAICA STYLE

1 roasting chicken (about 4 pounds)
2 tablespoons butter or margarine
1-1/2 cups chicken broth
3/4 cup sliced celery
1 medium onion, chopped
1/2 teaspoon garlic salt
2 dried red peppers, crushed
1 tablespoon vinegar
1/4 teaspoon allspice
1/2 cup sliced green olives
1 medium green pepper, sliced
2 tablespoons cornstarch
Salt and pepper

Brown chicken on all sides in butter in heavy kettle. Put chicken on rack in kettle. Add next 7 ingredients, cover and simmer 1½ hours, or until chicken is tender. Add olives and green pepper and cook 10 minutes longer. Remove chicken and thicken liquid with cornstarch blended with a little cold water. Pour over chicken. Season. Serves 4.

ROAST CHICKEN, INDIA STYLE

1 roasting chicken (3 to 3-1/2 pounds)
1/2 cup uncooked rice
1 can condensed mushroom soup
1/2 teaspoon curry powder
6 ripe olives, chopped
2 tablespoons chopped onion
2 tablespoons butter or margarine, melted

Wash and dry chicken. Cook and drain rice. Mix rice, ½ cup soup, ¼ teaspoon curry powder, olives and onion. Stuff chicken and truss. Put in baking pan; brush with butter. Cover lightly with foil; roast in slow oven (325°F.) 2½ to 3 hours, removing foil for last 45 minutes, to brown. Serve with sauce of heated soup and ¼ teaspoon curry powder. Serves 4.

MALAYAN CHICKEN

1 frying chicken (2-1/2 pounds), cut up
1/4 cup vegetable oil
1/2 cup orange juice
1 teaspoon each ginger and salt
1/8 teaspoon garlic salt
1 can (8 ounces) pitted ripe olives,
    halved
1 can (5-1/4 ounces) water chestnuts,
    sliced
1 cup white wine
2 tablespoons cornstarch

Wash and dry chicken pieces. Brown on all sides in hot oil. Reduce heat and stir in next 6 ingredients. Cover and simmer about 30 minutes. Remove chicken; keep warm. Blend cornstarch and 2 tablespoons water; stir into skillet. Cook, stirring, until thickened. Serve with the chicken. Makes 4 servings.

BUTTER-FRIED CHICKEN WITH HOMINY DRESSING

1 broiling chicken (about 2 pounds),
   quartered
Salt and pepper
1/4 cup butter
1 medium onion, chopped
1/4 teaspoon poultry seasoning
1/4 teaspoon marjoram
1 can (1 pound 13 ounces) hominy,
   drained
2 tablespoons fine dry bread crumbs

Season chicken with salt and pepper. Brown in butter. Cover and simmer 20 minutes. Remove from pan. To drippings in pan add onion and cook 5 minutes. Add next 3 ingredients, 1 teaspoon salt and 1/8 teaspoon pepper. Cook about 5 minutes, stirring. Put in shallow baking dish; sprinkle with bread crumbs. Top with chicken. Bake in moderate oven (375°F.) 25 minutes, or until chicken is tender. Makes 4 servings.

SESAME FRIED CHICKEN

1 frying chicken (about 2-1/2 pounds),
   cut up
1/2 cup all-purpose flour
1/4 cup sesame seed
1 teaspoon monosodium glutamate
1 teaspoon salt
1 teaspoon paprika
1 teaspoon poultry seasoning
1/4 teaspoon pepper
Fat

Wash chicken pieces, but do not dry. Roll wet chicken pieces in mixture of next 7 ingredients. Heat 1/2" fat in large skillet. Using large, meaty pieces first, put chicken, skin side down, in hot fat. Fry, uncovered, 15 to 25 minutes on each side, until tender. Makes 4 servings.

CHICKEN KABOBS, IRANIAN STYLE

2 pounds chicken breasts, boned and
   cut in 1-1/2" cubes
1/4 cup smooth peanut butter
1-1/2 teaspoons ground coriander
1-1/2 teaspoons salt
1/4 to 1/2 teaspoon cayenne
1 teaspoon ground cumin
4 medium onions, minced
1/2 teaspoon pepper
1 clove garlic, minced
1-1/2 tablespoons lemon juice
1 tablespoon brown sugar
3 tablespoons soy sauce

Toss chicken pieces in mixture of remaining ingredients, coating on all sides. Cover and refrigerate several hours. Thread chicken on skewers and broil under broiler or over charcoal about 10 minutes, turning to brown all sides. Makes 4 servings.

SOUTHERN FRIED CHICKEN WITH CREAM GRAVY

1 frying chicken (about 2-1/2 pounds),
   cut up
All-purpose flour
1-1/2 teaspoons salt
3/4 teaspoon pepper
Butter
Solid vegetable shortening
2 cups light cream
Hot corn bread

Shake moist pieces of chicken, a few at a time, in a paper bag with 1/2 cup flour, the salt and the pepper until thoroughly coated. Melt equal amounts of butter and shortening to 1/2" depth in large, heavy, covered skillet. Put in chicken; cover and brown quickly in hot fat on all sides. Reduce heat and continue frying slowly 25 minutes, turning once or twice. Remove cover during last 10 minutes cooking. Remove chicken. Drain off all but 2 tablespoons fat from pan; stir in 2 tablespoons flour. Add cream gradually, stirring constantly. Season and cook until thickened. Serve with gravy and corn bread. Makes 4 servings.

CHICKEN ALLA MELANZANA (Italian Chicken with Eggplant)

3 tablespoons butter
1 frying chicken (about 2-1/2 pounds),
   cut up
Salt
Pepper
1 medium eggplant, peeled
Flour
Cooking oil
1 medium onion, chopped
1 clove garlic, minced
1 chicken bouillon cube
1/3 cup dry red wine
1/4 cup sliced stuffed green olives
2 pimientos, cut in strips

Melt butter in large heavy skillet. Fry chicken pieces until golden brown on all sides. Season with salt and pepper. Cover and simmer 45 minutes or until tender. Cut eggplant in slices about 1/2" thick. Season with salt, dip in flour and brown in oil until tender. Remove chicken to shallow baking dish. In drippings in pan, brown onion and garlic about 5 minutes. Stir in 2 tablespoons flour; add 1 cup water, bouillon cube and wine. Bring to boil and cook until thickened, stirring. Pour over chicken. Sprinkle with half of olives and pimiento. Cover with fried eggplant and remaining olives and pimiento. Bake in hot oven (400°F.) 25 minutes, or until thoroughly heated. Makes 4 servings.

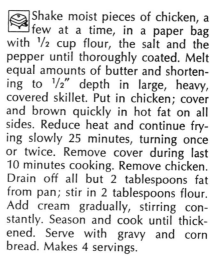

STREAMLINED PAELLA

1 frying chicken (3 pounds), cut up
Salt
Paprika
3 tablespoons vegetable oil
1/4 cup chopped onion
1/4 cup chopped green pepper
1 clove garlic, minced
1 can (10-3/4 ounces) condensed tomato soup
2-1/2 cups canned beef broth
1 tablespoon lemon juice
1/8 teaspoon saffron
1 cup uncooked rice
1 can (4-1/2 ounces) large or jumbo shrimps, drained
1 can (5 ounces) lobster (optional)
1/2 cup cooked peas
1 or 2 canned pimientos, cut up

Sprinkle chicken lightly with salt and paprika. In large skillet or Dutch oven, brown chicken on both sides in the oil. Push chicken to one side of skillet, add next 3 ingredients and cook 2 to 3 minutes, stirring. Stir in tomato soup and next 3 ingredients. Bring to boil, cover and simmer 20 minutes. Stir in rice, cover and simmer 30 minutes, stirring gently occasionally to prevent rice from sticking. Add shrimps, lobsters if used, the peas and pimiento; stir gently and heat. Makes 4 to 6 servings.

CHICKEN NORMANDY

2 broiler-fryers (about 3 pounds each), cut up (omit necks and backs)
1/2 cup butter or margarine
1/4 cup brandy
Seasoned salt and pepper
1 medium onion, thinly sliced
3/4 cup thinly sliced celery
2 tart medium apples, peeled and diced (if not tart, sprinkle with lemon juice)
2 tablespoons chopped parsley
1/4 teaspoon marjoram leaves
1/3 cup sherry
1/3 cup heavy cream

Sauté chicken pieces in the butter in skillet until browned. Transfer to large Dutch oven or casserole. Reserve drippings in skillet. Heat brandy in small saucepan, ignite and pour over chicken. Sprinkle with seasoned salt and pepper. Add next 4 ingredients to drippings in skillet and cook, stirring frequently, 2 to 3 minutes. Sprinkle with seasoned salt and pepper. Add marjoram and sherry and pour over chicken. Cover and bake in moderate oven (350°F.) about 2 hours. Add cream to gravy in Dutch oven, stir to mix and spoon over chicken. Or remove chicken to serving dish, stir cream into gravy and pour over chicken. Makes 6 servings.

ITALIAN CHICKEN, HUNTER STYLE

1 frying chicken (about 3-1/2 pounds), cut up
2 tablespoons olive oil
1 tablespoon minced parsley
1/2 stalk celery, chopped
1/2 clove garlic, crushed
1 teaspoon salt
1/8 teaspoon pepper
2 bay leaves
1/2 cup dry white wine

Brown chicken on all sides in the oil in skillet. Add next 3 ingredients and brown lightly. Sprinkle with the salt and pepper and add bay leaves and wine. Simmer, uncovered, until wine is almost evaporated. Then add 2 tablespoons water, cover and cook slowly 30 minutes, or until chicken is tender. Makes 4 servings.

CHICKEN-POTATO CASSEROLE

4 cups thinly sliced peeled potatoes
4 or 5 medium onions, sliced
Salt, pepper and ground thyme
1 tall can undiluted evaporated milk
2 slices bacon
2 tablespoons margarine
2 broiler-fryers (about 3 pounds each), cut up
Paprika

Put potatoes and onions in large roasting pan and sprinkle with seasonings; add 1/2 cup hot water. Reserve 1/4 cup milk and pour remainder over vegetables. Put in hot oven (400°F.) while preparing chicken. In large skillet, cook bacon until browned, remove bacon and drain. Add margarine to skillet, then add chicken and brown on all sides, removing as it browns. Put chicken in pan with potatoes and sprinkle with more seasonings. Crumble bacon over top. Cover tightly wtih foil and bake in hot oven (400°F.) 1 hour. Uncover and pour reserved milk over top and sprinkle with paprika. Bake 30 minutes longer. Makes 6 to 8 servings.

CURRIED CHICKEN AND RICE

1 package (6 ounces) curry rice
1 can (13 ounces) boned chicken with broth
1 can (1 pound) Chinese mixed vegetables
1 cup frozen peas

Prepare rice as directed on label. When done, stir in remaining ingredients. Cook gently a few minutes, or until peas are done. Makes 4 servings.

BAKED CHICKEN AND SWEET POTATOES

1 fryer (about 2-1/2 pounds), cut up
Salt and pepper
Fine dry bread crumbs
1 egg
4 sweet potatoes, cooked and peeled
1/2 cup butter, melted

Sprinkle chicken with salt and pepper and roll in crumbs. Dip chicken in mixture of egg beaten with 3 tablespoons water; roll again in crumbs. Put in shallow baking dish or pan in single layer with sweets. Baste with butter. Bake in hot oven (400°F.) about 1 hour, basting several times with remaining butter. Makes 4 servings.

DEVILED CHICKEN

1 large frying chicken (about 2-1/2 pounds), cut up
Dry mustard
Seasoned flour
Bacon fat
1 can condensed cream of mushroom soup
1 soup-can milk
1 can condensed tomato soup

Wash and dry chicken pieces. Mix mustard with enough water to make a thick paste. Spread chicken liberally with the paste. Dredge with seasoned flour and fry in fat until crisp and golden brown. Remove chicken from skillet. Add remaining ingredients and mix well. Put chicken back in skillet. Cover and simmer 30 minutes, or until tender. Makes 4 servings.

CHICKEN NORMANDY

2 broiling chickens (1-1/2 to 2 pounds each), cut up
1/2 cup butter or margarine
1/4 cup brandy
1 medium onion, thinly sliced
2 celery hearts, thinly sliced
2 tart apples, peeled, cored and chopped
2 tablespoons chopped parsley
1/8 teaspoon marjoram
1/3 cup sherry
Salt and pepper
1/3 cup heavy cream

Wash and dry chicken pieces and brown lightly in butter. Pour brandy over chicken and ignite. Let flame burn out. Remove chicken. Sauté onion, celery and apple in drippings about 5 minutes. Add parsley, marjoram and sherry. Season to taste with salt and pepper. Add chicken and baste with the sauce. Bring to boil, cover and simmer 35 minutes. Stir in cream. Makes 4 to 6 servings.

BAKED CHICKEN, PAKISTANI STYLE

1 fryer (about 3 pounds), cut in pieces
1/4 cup soft butter
1 teaspoon salt
1/4 teaspoon each ground cloves and pepper
1/2 teaspoon crushed dried red chili peppers
2 cardamom seeds, crushed
1/4 cup chopped almonds
Small piece of fresh ginger, minced, or 1/4 teaspoon ground ginger
4 cloves garlic, minced
2 medium onions, chopped

Arrange chicken pieces in casserole. Cover with remaining ingredients combined. Bake in hot oven (400°F). about 1 hour. Serves 4.

HAM-STUFFED CHICKEN

8 chicken thighs
8 cooked-ham pieces, about 2" x 1" x 1"
2 eggs, beaten
Fine dry bread crumbs
Melted butter

Remove bone from chicken pieces, keeping skin intact. With skin side down, pound chicken to flatten slightly. In center of each, put a piece of cooked ham. Fold chicken over, pull skin to cover and fasten with skewer or strong wooden toothpicks. Dip in egg and roll in crumbs. Put in shallow baking dish and pour over each a little melted butter. Cover and bake in slow oven (325°F.) about 1¼ hours. Remove skewers; serve plain or with gravy made from drippings in baking dish. Serves 4.

CHICKEN DIVAN

1 frying chicken (about 2-1/2 pounds), split
Salt and pepper
1 package frozen broccoli spears
2 tablespoons butter
3 tablespoons flour
Milk
2 tablespoons sherry
Grated Parmesan cheese

Simmer chicken in 2 cups water with 1 teaspoon salt 45 minutes, or until very tender. Reserve broth. Remove meat from bones in large pieces, then cut in long slices. Cook broccoli until just tender; drain and put in shallow casserole. Arrange chicken pieces on top. Melt butter in heavy saucepan and stir in flour. Add chicken broth and enough milk to make 2 cups. Cook, stirring constantly, until thickened. Add sherry and season to taste. Pour over chicken. Sprinkle with cheese. Bake in hot oven (400°F.) about 12 minutes. Serves 4.

CHICKEN IN LEMON-CAPER BUTTER

1/2 cup butter
2 tablespoons lemon juice
1 teaspoon salt
1 clove garlic
1/8 teaspoon pepper
1/2 teaspoon paprika
1 can (6 ounces) sliced mushrooms, drained
1 tablespoon capers
1 frying chicken (about 2-1/2 pounds), cut up

Put first 8 ingredients in skillet and bring to boil. Add chicken, bring again to boil and cover. Simmer 30 minutes, or until chicken is tender, turning several times. Serves 4.

CHICKEN-AND-OYSTER CASSEROLE

1 large fryer (about 2-1/2 pounds), cut up
1/4 cup flour
1-1/4 teaspoons salt
1/4 teaspoon pepper
2 tablespoons shortening
1/2 cup heavy cream
18 oysters
2 tablespoons toasted slivered almonds
Baking-powder biscuits (optional)

Reserve back, wings and neck of chicken for another recipe. Wash and dry remaining pieces. Dredge with flour mixed with ½ teaspoon salt and ⅛ teaspoon pepper. Brown on all sides in hot fat. Remove to 1½-quart casserole. Add ½ cup boiling water, cover and bake in moderate oven (350°F.) 1 hour, or until tender. Add cream, remaining ¾ teaspoon salt, ⅛ teaspoon pepper and the oysters. Cover and bake 10 minutes longer. Sprinkle with almonds and serve at once, with hot baking-powder biscuits, if desired. Makes 4 servings.

PASTEL DE MAIZ CON GALLINA (Chicken Pie with Corn Crust)

Grate the kernels from 12 large ears of raw corn as directed on page 189. Season with 2 tablespoons melted butter, 1 teaspoon salt and a little freshly ground pepper. Put in heavy pot a 4-pound roasting chicken, cut up; 1 sliced onion; herb bouquet; 2 cups water and 1 teaspoon salt. Cover and simmer until tender, adding a little water if needed. Cool slightly and remove bones; cut meat in fairly large pieces. Put half the corn mixture in a buttered 2-quart casserole, add chicken in a layer, cover with remaining corn, drizzle 1 tablespoon melted butter over top and bake in moderate oven (350°F.) about 45 minutes. Serves 6.

OLD HOMESTEAD CHICKEN PIE

1 stewing chicken (about 4 pounds), cut up
1 onion
2 stalks celery
2 sprigs parsley
Salt and pepper
1 can (1 pound) onions
1 package frozen carrots and peas, cooked
Chicken fat and butter
6 tablespoons flour
1/2 recipe Standard Pastry (page 419)
1 egg, slightly beaten

Mix first 4 ingredients and 1 teaspoon salt with 5 cups water. Simmer, covered, 3 hours, or until tender. Remove chicken; cool broth. Remove meat from bones and cut into large pieces. Put in 2-quart baking dish with onions and carrots and peas. Remove fat from broth. Melt 4 tablespoons fat and stir in flour. Add 3 cups broth. Cook until thickened. Season to taste. Pour over chicken and vegetables; keep hot. Roll pastry to fit top of baking dish. Make slits in crust to let steam escape. Brush with egg. Bake in hot oven (425°F.) 30 minutes. Serves 6.

PAELLA

2 fryers (about 2 pounds each)
Cooking oil
Salt
1-1/2 cups uncooked rice
2 cloves garlic, minced
1 bay leaf, crumbled
Large pinch of saffron (from drugstore)
1/4 teaspoon pepper
1 cup canned tomatoes
1 green pepper, slivered
1 pimiento, sliced
Dash of cayenne
1 pound hot Spanish or Italian sausage
1 dozen littleneck clams, shucked
1 pound shrimp, cooked, shelled and cleaned
1 lobster tail, cooked and cut up
1 cup cooked peas

Cut chickens in 20 pieces. Fry in shallow hot oil in skillet until browned. Put in large casserole and sprinkle with 1 teaspoon salt. In same skillet, brown rice and garlic. Add next 7 ingredients, 2½ teaspoons salt and 3 cups water. Bring to boil and pour on chicken. Cover and bake in hot oven (425°F.) 25 minutes. Cut sausage in 1" pieces and fry until browned. Add sausage and remaining ingredients to casserole, stirring lightly with fork. Reduce heat to moderate (375°F.) and bake, covered, 15 minutes, or until thoroughly heated. Makes 8 to 10 servings.

BROILED CHICKEN BREASTS

Bone 2 whole raw chicken breasts and pound meat thin, using a mallet. Be careful not to make holes. Spread the breasts with a mixture of 1 small mashed clove of garlic and 1/4 pound of butter. Roll tightly, then roll in foil and chill. Slice rolls 1/2" thick, like a jelly roll, and thread on skewers (have end of roll pinned in). Broil about 5 minutes, using white wine or diluted lemon juice and melted butter as a baste.

FILIPINO CHICKEN

1 frying chicken (about 3 pounds),
  cut up
1/3 cup soy sauce
Juice of 1 lemon
1 teaspoon poultry seasoning
1/2 teaspoon pepper
1 teaspoon ginger
Flour
1/4 cup fat
2 onions, cut in half

Wash chicken and put in bowl. Combine soy sauce, lemon juice and seasonings. Pour over chicken and let stand 1/2 hour. Lift chicken from sauce, roll in flour and brown in hot fat. Place chicken, marinade, onions and 1 cup boiling water in covered roaster or casserole. Bake in moderate oven (350°F.) 45 minutes, or until chicken is tender. Serves 4.

BRUNSWICK STEW

1 frying chicken (about 2-1/2 pounds),
  cut up
2 ounces lean salt pork, diced
1 dried red pepper or 1/4 teaspoon
  crushed dried red pepper
1 clove garlic
1 tablespoon salt
1/2 teaspoon pepper
1 teaspoon monosodium glutamate
3 medium potatoes, peeled and diced
2 medium onions, chopped
2 cups fresh lima beans or 1 box (10
  ounces) frozen limas
1 can (1 pound) tomatoes
2 cups fresh whole-kernel corn

Put first 7 ingredients and 2 quarts water in large kettle, bring to boil and simmer, covered, 2 hours, or until chicken meat drops off bones. Cool, skim off excess fat and remove bones. Add 1 quart water, bring to boil and add potato, onion and limas. Cover and simmer 15 minutes, or until vegetables are tender. Add tomatoes and simmer about 30 minutes. Add corn and bring to full rolling boil. For a thicker stew, cook to desired consistency, stirring frequently. Makes about 3 quarts.

CHICKEN, JAPANESE STYLE

Soy sauce brightens rice and leftover chicken.

3 tablespoons butter or margarine
1 clove garlic, cut
3 tablespoons flour
1-1/2 cups chicken broth
2 teaspoons soy sauce
2 cups slivered cooked chicken
Salt and pepper
2/3 cup uncooked rice
Chopped parsley

Heat butter and garlic in skillet; remove garlic. Blend in flour. Gradually add chicken broth and cook, stirring, until thickened. Add soy sauce and chicken and season to taste. Cook and drain rice and spread on top of chicken mixture. Cover and heat gently. Sprinkle with parsley. Makes 4 servings.

CHICKEN STEW WITH DUMPLINGS

1 fowl (about 4 pounds), cut up
2 stalks celery with leaves, chopped
1 onion, sliced
2 sprigs parsley, chopped
1 bay leaf
Salt and pepper
12 small white onions, peeled
8 small carrots, peeled and cut in halves
1/4 cup flour
1 box (10 ounces) frozen peas
Dumpling Batter
1 teaspoon monosodium glutamate
1/2 cup light cream

Put first 5 ingredients in heavy kettle with 6 cups boiling water, 1 teaspoon salt and 1/4 teaspoon pepper. Bring to boil, cover and simmer 2 hours, or until fowl is tender. Cool chicken, remove bones and skin; cut meat in bite-size pieces. Skim fat from broth if necessary. Add enough water to broth to make 4 cups. Add onions and carrots and cook, covered, about 35 minutes, or until tender. Blend flour with small amount of cold water and stir into mixture. Cook, stirring, until thickened. Add chicken and peas. Put dumplings on top; cover and simmer about 10 minutes. Remove dumplings and add last 2 ingredients to stew; heat. Serve with dumplings. Makes 6 servings.

Dumpling Batter

1 cup all-purpose flour
1 teaspoon baking powder
3/4 teaspoon salt
Dash of mace or nutmeg
1 teaspoon minced onion
2 egg yolks
1/3 cup milk

Sift together dry ingredients. Add onion. Beat egg yolks with milk and add to dry mixture. Mix until blended.

BRAISED CURRIED CHICKEN

1 medium onion, chopped
2 tablespoons vegetable oil
1 frying chicken (about 2-1/2 pounds),
  cut up
1 tablespoon flour
1 to 2 tablespoons curry powder
1/4 teaspoon ground ginger
2 tablespoons each honey and soy sauce
2 cans condensed chicken consommé
  or broth
2 or 3 medium potatoes, each cut in 6
  wedges
Salt

Sauté onion in oil until light-ly browned. Add chicken and brown on both sides. Sprinkle with flour, curry powder and ginger and stir. Then add honey, soy sauce and broth. Simmer, covered, about 35 minutes. Add potatoes and simmer 20 minutes longer, or until chicken and potato are tender. Season lightly with salt if needed. Makes 4 servings.

CHICKEN PAPRIKA

2 frying chickens (2 to 2-1/2 pounds
  each), cut up
Salt and pepper
4 mild onions, sliced thin
3 tablespoons sweet butter
2 tablespoons sweet paprika
1 cup chicken stock
1 pint dairy sour cream
Cooked noodles

Rub chicken with salt and pep-per. In Dutch oven, sauté onions in butter until limp. Stir in paprika, add chicken and brown quickly over medium heat. Add stock, cover and bake in moderate oven (350°F.) 1 hour. Remove chicken from pan. Re-duce sauce to about ³/₄ cup and stir in sour cream. Return chicken to oven; cover and bake 20 minutes longer. Serve with hot noodles. Makes 6 to 8 servings.

CHICKEN, NIGERIAN STYLE

From Nigeria, a smooth peanut-butter gravy.

1 frying chicken (about 2-1/2 pounds),
  cut up
1 large onion, chopped
1 fresh or canned tomato, chopped
2 cloves garlic, minced
1 teaspoon salt
1 tablespoon catsup
3/4 cup crunchy-style peanut butter
1/8 teaspoon cayenne
3 hard-cooked eggs, sliced
Hot cooked rice

Combine first 5 ingredients and 2 cups water. Bring to boil, cover and sim-mer 30 minutes. Add next 3 ingre-dients and 1 cup water. Cover and simmer 1 hour longer, stirring oc-casionally. Add eggs. Serve on rice. Makes 4 servings.

POULET AU TARRAGON
(Roast Chicken with Tarragon)

Rub with cut lemon and salt the in-side and outside of 5- to 6-pound roasting chicken or capon. Put 5 to 6 tablespoons butter and a good-size sprig or two of fresh tarragon or a little dried tarragon in the cavity. Rub skin with butter and a little tar-ragon. Put chicken on its side on rack in roasting pan. Roast in moder-ate oven (375°F.) 20 minutes. Turn to other side, baste with drippings and melted butter and roast 20 minutes. Turn chicken on its back, baste and roast 20 minutes. Chicken should be done. (Legs should move easily at the thigh joints.) Serve with the pan juices. Makes 4 servings.

CHICKEN NEWBURG

1/2 cup butter or margarine
2 cups diced cooked chicken
1-1/2 cups light cream
4 tablespoons sherry
4 egg yolks
3/4 cup drained canned seedless grapes
1/4 cup flaked coconut
Seasoned salt and white pepper
Hot toast, rice or patty shells
Paprika

Heat first 3 ingredients and 2 table-spoons sherry in top part of double boiler over simmering water. Beat re-maining 2 tablespoons sherry with egg yolks. Add small amount of hot mixture. Put back in double boiler and cook, stirring, until thickened. Add grapes and coconut and season. Serve on toast, rice or in patty shells. Sprinkle with paprika. Serves 4.

SCOTCH COCK-A-LEEKIE

1 fowl (about 5 pounds), cut up
3 onions, quartered
1/4 cup chopped parsley
2 stalks celery, slivered
1/4 cup chopped celery leaves
1/2 teaspoon poultry seasoning
Salt and pepper
1 bay leaf
2 tablespoons barley
12 leeks with tops, sliced
3 potatoes, peeled and diced
Chopped parsley

Place all ingredients, except last 4, in kettle; add 2¹/₂ quarts cold water. Bring to boil, simmer for 2 hours, or until chicken is tender. Re-move chicken and slice thin; put aside. Strain broth, add barley, leeks and potatoes; simmer ¹/₂ hour. Place chicken in tureen, pour soup over and garnish with chopped parsley. Serve with crusty bread and salad. Makes about 3 quarts.

CHICKEN KIEV

From Russia, thin pieces of chicken wrapped around butter.

1-1/2 sticks butter (6 ounces)
6 chicken breasts
Fine dry bread crumbs
3 eggs
Fat for deep frying

Halve butter lengthwise; cut in twelve 2″ pieces. Chill until very firm. Cut chicken breasts in half; remove bones. On wet board, pound chicken into thin cutlets. Put a piece of butter in center of each. Roll chicken around butter; fold securely so butter cannot escape during cooking. Secure with toothpicks. Roll in bread crumbs; dip in eggs beaten with 2 tablespoons cold water; roll again in crumbs. Fry in hot deep fat (375°F. on frying thermometer) 3 to 5 minutes. Drain and put on cookie sheet in hot oven (425°F.) 5 minutes. Makes 6 servings.

CHICKEN, HAWAIIAN STYLE

A luscious party dish, rich with herbs and spices.

1 frying chicken (about 2-1/2 pounds), cut up
1/4 cup soy sauce
1/2 cup dry white wine
Juice of 1 lime
1 clove garlic, crushed
1 teaspoon curry powder
1 teaspoon minced fresh ginger or ground ginger to taste
1/4 teaspoon each thyme, oregano and pepper
2 medium onions, thinly sliced
5 tablespoons butter or margarine
Seasoned flour
1-1/2 cups uncooked rice
4 canned pineapple slices, halved
1/2 cup toasted slivered almonds
8 soft prunes, pitted and cut up
1 pimiento, minced

Wash and dry chicken pieces. Mix soy sauce, ¼ cup wine and next 5 ingredients. Pour over chicken and marinate several hours, turning occasionally. Cook onions in 4 tablespoons butter until golden. Remove onions. Remove chicken from marinade, dry and dredge with flour. Brown in drippings in skillet. Add onions and marinade, cover and cook 45 minutes, uncovering pan last 15 minutes. Meanwhile, cook and drain rice and keep hot. Brown pineapple slices in 1 tablespoon butter. To serve, mix rice, almonds, prunes and pimiento and heap on large serving platter. Arrange chicken and pineapple slices around edge. Add ¼ cup wine to drippings. Heat well and serve as sauce. Makes 4 servings.

SMOKED CHICKEN

Rub 1 whole frying chicken (about 2½ pounds) inside and out with soy sauce and let stand ½ hour. Cover with boiling salted water and simmer 40 minutes. Drain and pat dry. Line a kettle slightly larger than the chicken with a large piece of foil. Put ⅓ cup packed brown sugar on foil. Put chicken in kettle on a trivet above the sugar. Draw foil over top of chicken and seal with double fold. Put kettle over low heat and smoke chicken 20 minutes. Remove from foil; cut in thin slices. Makes 4 servings.

LEMON BROILED CHICKEN

1 broiler-fryer (about 2-1/2 pounds), cut up
1/2 cup lemon juice
3 tablespoons vegetable oil
2 tablespoons corn syrup or honey
1/2 teaspoon each thyme and marjoram leaves
1 teaspoon salt
2 teaspoons grated lemon rind

Arrange chicken pieces on broiler pan. Combine remaining ingredients and brush on chicken. Broil in preheated broiler about 3″ from heat about ½ hour on each side. Baste frequently, using all the sauce. Makes 4 servings.

SOUR-CREAM CHICKEN MOLD

1 envelope unflavored gelatin
1 cup chicken stock
1/2 teaspoon salt
Dash of hot pepper sauce
1 tablespoon lemon juice
2 tablespoons sherry
1/2 cup sliced stuffed olives
2 cups diced cooked chicken
1/2 cup each diced celery and green pepper
1 tablespoon chopped parsley
1 cup dairy sour cream
Watercress and radishes
Sour-cream Dressing

Soften gelatin in stock. Bring to boil. Add next 4 ingredients. Chill until thickened but not firm. Spoon a little gelatin in mold and arrange a few olive slices. Chill until firm. Mix remaining gelatin and olives with next 3 ingredients. Fold in sour cream. Put in mold and chill until firm. Unmold and garnish with watercress and radishes. Serve with Sour-cream Dressing. Makes 6 servings. **Sour-cream Dressing** Mix equal parts dairy sour cream and mayonnaise. Season with garlic salt and cayenne.

CHICKEN THIGHS PARMESAN

12 to 16 chicken thighs, boned
5 tablespoons flour
Salt and white pepper
1 teaspoon paprika
2 tablespoons margarine
1 can (1 pound) small onions, drained
Chicken broth
1/2 cup light cream
2 tablespoons sherry (optional)
Gravy seasoning-browning sauce
2 egg yolks
3 cups seasoned firm mashed potatoes
  (not instant)
2 tablespoons grated Parmesan cheese

Keep thigh meat in one piece; roll each to form a bundle. Mix 2 tablespoons flour, 1½ teaspoons salt, ½ teaspoon pepper and the paprika. Roll chicken thighs lightly in the mixture. Heat margarine in large skillet until browned. Add chicken, seam side down, and when browned, turn and brown other side. Then turn skin side up. Add onions and ½ cup boiling water. Cover and simmer 20 to 25 minutes, or until chicken is tender. Pile chicken and onions in center of oven-proof platter or shallow baking dish. Strain pan juices and add enough chicken broth to make 2 cups. Bring to boil in small saucepan. Blend remaining flour and the cream until smooth and stir into broth. Bring to boil and simmer, stirring, until thickened. Add salt and pepper to taste, sherry, if desired, and enough gravy sauce to give desired color. Pour over chicken and onions. Add egg yolks to potatoes and mix well. Flute or spoon potatoes around edge of platter. Sprinkle with cheese and bake in very hot oven (450°F.) 12 minutes, or until potatoes are well browned. Serves 6.

CHICKEN DELICIOUS

6 medium potatoes, peeled and quartered
1 teaspoon each oregano and paprika
1/2 teaspoon garlic salt
1-1/2 teaspoons salt
1/2 teaspoon pepper
1 frying chicken, about 3 pounds, cut up
1 pound sweet or hot Italian-sausage
  links, cut up
1/3 cup vegetable oil

Arrange potatoes in greased large shallow 3-quart casserole. Mix seasonings and sprinkle some on potatoes. Arrange chicken and sausage on top. Pour oil over mixture and sprinkle with remaining seasonings. Cover and bake in hot oven (425°F.) 1 hour. Reduce heat to 375°F., uncover casserole and bake 30 minutes longer, or until chicken and potatoes are well browned. Makes 4 to 6 servings.

STUFFED CHICKEN BREASTS

1 large onion, sliced
1 can (3 ounces) sliced mushrooms,
  drained and liquid reserved
1 stalk celery, thinly sliced
2 tablespoons vegetable oil
1 egg
1 tablespoon chopped parsley
2 tablespoons fine dry bread crumbs
1 tablespoon grated Parmesan cheese
1 cup shredded mozzarella
Salt
White pepper
6 whole chicken breasts, boned
2 cans (10-3/4 ounces each) condensed
  tomato soup
1/2 teaspoon basil leaves

Sauté first 3 ingredients in the oil until limp. Add next 5 ingredients and ¼ teaspoon each salt and pepper. Mix well. Sprinkle chicken breasts lightly with salt and pepper and fill generously with the mixture. Roll up and secure with toothpicks. Arrange in greased shallow 3-quart baking dish. Empty soup into bowl. Put mushroom liquid in one empty soup can and add enough water to half-fill can. Add liquid and basil to soup and mix well. Pour over chicken. Bake in moderate oven (350°F.) 1 hour, basting occasionally with sauce in dish. Remove toothpicks and serve. Good with rice. Makes 6 large or 12 small servings.

CHICKEN-LIVER PIE

18 chicken livers, cut in bite-size pieces
3/4 cup cream sherry or Madeira
1 clove garlic, minced
1 teaspoon monosodium glutamate
1 teaspoon soy sauce
1/4 cup butter or margarine
1/4 cup flour
1 can (4 ounces) sliced mushrooms
2-1/2 cups chicken broth
1 small box frozen peas, partially thawed
1/2 cup thinly sliced celery
Salt and pepper
1/3 cup slivered blanched almonds
Standard Pastry (page 419)

Marinate livers in next 4 ingredients in refrigerator overnight. Next day, remove livers and sauté lightly in butter in skillet. Stir in flour. Drain mushrooms and add enough water to liquid to make ½ cup. Combine marinade, mushroom liquid and chicken broth with livers. Bring to boil and cook, stirring gently, until thickened. Add mushrooms, peas and celery and simmer about 5 minutes. Add salt and pepper to taste and pour into greased shallow 1½-quart baking dish. Sprinkle with almonds. Roll out pastry to fit top of dish; adjust on mixture. Bake in very hot oven (450°F.) 15 to 20 minutes. Serves 8.

ARROZ CON POLLO
(Spanish Chicken with Rice)

From Spain, chicken, onion, pepper, tomatoes and rice, cooked together.

1 frying chicken (about 2-1/2 pounds), cut up
Salt
3 tablespoons olive oil
1 large onion, chopped
1 clove garlic, minced
1 medium green pepper, chopped
1 can (19 ounces) tomatoes
1/3 cup sherry
1/4 teaspoon pepper
Pinch of saffron
1/2 teaspoon paprika
2 whole cloves
1 bay leaf
1-1/4 cups uncooked long-grain rice
1 cup cooked peas
1 pimiento, cut up

Season chicken with salt. Brown in oil. Add onion, garlic and green pepper; brown about 5 minutes. Add next 7 ingredients and 1 cup water. Cover; simmer 15 minutes. Add rice, bring to boil and stir. Cover; simmer about 30 minutes. Garnish with peas and pimiento. Serves 4 to 6.

BREAST OF CHICKEN, TROPICALE

4 large chicken breasts
Salt and pepper
Butter
8 ounces medium noodles
1 pound mushrooms, chopped
2 tablespoons minced onion
Few sprigs of parsley, chopped
1/2 cup fine dry bread crumbs
4 slices canned pineapple
3 tablespoons flour
2-1/2 cups milk
1/2 cup pineapple juice
2 egg yolks, beaten
1/2 cup heavy cream, whipped
1/4 cup grated Parmesan cheese

Wash and dry chicken breasts. Season with salt and pepper and sauté in 1/4 cup butter until lightly browned. Cover and cook 25 minutes, or until tender, turning occasionally. Cook and drain noodles. Season with salt, pepper and butter and put in flat broiler-proof dish. Arrange chicken on top and keep warm. Cook mushrooms and onion in butter remaining in chicken skillet. Add parsley and crumbs and mix well; season. Put a pineapple slice on each chicken breast and top with a mound of mushroom mixture. Melt 3 tablespoons butter and blend in flour. Add milk and pineapple juice and cook until slightly thickened. Add small amount of mixture to egg yolks. Put back in saucepan; cook, stirring, a few minutes longer. Fold in whipped cream and season. Pour over chicken; sprinkle with cheese. Put under broiler until browned. Serves 4.

CHICKEN IN JELLY

This chicken dish is worthy of your most beautiful mold.

1 frying chicken (about 2-1/2 pounds), cut up
1/3 cup soy sauce
1/4 cup sherry
1 small onion
4 slices fresh gingerroot
1 teaspoon salt
20 whole black peppercorns
2 cloves star anise
1/4 cup cooked peas
Lettuce

Cover chicken with water; add next 5 ingredients and simmer 30 minutes, or until chicken is tender. Cool and skim off fat. Separate meat and cut into 1/2" cubes; arrange in a fancy mold or loaf pan. Return skin and bones to stock in saucepan, add peppers and anise and simmer 1 hour. Strain stock and pour enough over chicken cubes to just cover. When partially set, arrange peas on top and pour more stock over to cover peas. Chill until set. To serve, wrap mold in a cloth wrung out in hot water and carefully invert on platter lined with lettuce. Makes 4 to 6 servings.

WALNUT CHICKEN

2 pounds chicken breasts
2 tablespoons cornstarch
2 egg whites, unbeaten
1 cup walnut meats
Fat for deep frying
1/4 cup vegetable oil
1 cup diced celery
1 can (5 ounces) water chestnuts, quartered
1/3 cup chicken broth
3 tablespoons soy sauce
1 tablespoon sherry
1 teaspoon sugar
3 slices fresh ginger, minced

Remove chicken meat from bones and cut in 1/2" cubes. Mix 1 tablespoon cornstarch with 1 tablespoon water and beat into egg whites with a fork. Add chicken and mix until each piece is coated. Boil walnuts in water to cover 3 minutes. Drain and dry between paper towels. Deep-fry in hot fat (375°F. on a frying thermometer) until golden brown (or brown nuts in 1/4 cup oil in skillet). Remove and keep warm. Heat vegetable oil in skillet, add chicken, celery and water chestnuts. Fry 3 or 4 minutes. Add next 5 ingredients and 1 tablespoon cornstarch. Cook, stirring, until thickened. Serve garnished with walnuts. Makes 4 to 6 servings.

CUSTARDY BAKED CHICKEN

1 broiler-fryer (about 3 pounds), cut up
1 medium onion
2 stalks celery
1 tablespoon salt
1 small onion, minced
7 tablespoons margarine
1/4 teaspoon ground thyme
1/2 teaspoon ground sage
1/4 teaspoon celery salt
2 cups soft bread crumbs or cubes
3 tablespoons flour
3 eggs, well beaten
Pepper
Chopped parsley

Put chicken in kettle or Dutch oven with next 3 ingredients. Add 4 cups water and bring to boil. Cover and simmer 45 minutes, or until chicken is tender. Remove chicken and cool. Strain broth and, if necessary, skim off fat. Sauté onion in 4 tablespoons margarine in skillet 2 to 3 minutes. Add herbs, celery salt and crumbs. Mix well and put evenly in bottom of greased shallow 2-quart baking dish. (Reserve skillet for later use.) Remove chicken meat from bones and cut in bite-size pieces. Put on top of dressing in dish. In reserved skillet, melt remaining 3 tablespoons margarine. Blend in flour. Gradually add 3 cups broth and cook, stirring, until slightly thickened. Remove from heat and very gradually stir about 1 cup into eggs. Very gradually stir back into mixture in skillet and cook, stirring, over very low heat 2 to 3 minutes. Add pepper to taste, pour over chicken and bake in moderate oven (350°F.) 30 minutes, or until firm. Sprinkle with parsley. Makes 6 servings.

CHICKEN BREASTS GRUYÈRE

2 whole chicken breasts
Salt and pepper
3 tablespoons butter or margarine
4 large mushrooms, chopped
2 tablespoons flour
1-1/4 cups milk
1/4 pound natural Gruyère cheese, finely
    shredded (about 1 cup)

Split, skin and bone breasts. Sprinkle with salt and pepper. In skillet, sauté chicken, turning, in 1 tablespoon melted butter 10 minutes, or until **done**. Remove to broiler-proof platter. Sauté mushrooms in same skillet and spoon over chicken. Melt remaining 2 tablespoons butter in skillet and stir in flour. Slowly stir in milk and simmer about 5 minutes. Stir in cheese until melted. Add additional salt to taste. Spoon over chicken (sauce will be very thick). Broil until browned. Makes 4 servings.

MANDARIN CHICKEN

3 large whole chicken breasts, split
1/2 cup butter or margarine, melted
1/2 cup Sauterne or other white wine
2 tablespoons soy sauce
1 can (8 ounces) tomato sauce
1 clove garlic, minced or crushed
1/2 teaspoon ginger
2 cans (11 ounces each) mandarin
    oranges
1 tablespoon flour
Hot cooked rice

Bone chicken and put in shallow baking dish. Mix next 3 ingredients and pour over chicken. Cover and marinate in refrigerator 3 hours. Drain marinade into saucepan and add tomato sauce, garlic, ginger and syrup from oranges. Bring to boil and boil over medium heat 5 to 10 minutes. Pour over chicken and add half the oranges. Bake in moderate oven (350°F). 35 minutes. Add remaining oranges and bake 10 minutes longer. Put chicken on hot platter. Pour liquid into saucepan. Blend flour with small amount of cold water and stir into liquid. Bring to boil and cook, stirring, until slightly thickened. Pour over chicken and serve with rice. Makes 6 servings.

EMPRESS CHICKEN

4 chicken wings
4 whole chicken legs
1 green onion
1 cup dried black mushrooms
1/2 cup soy sauce
2 cups broth or water
1 tablespoon sugar
Few cloves star anise
2 slices gingerroot
1 tablespoon dry sherry
1/2 teaspoon salt
2 cans (6 ounces each) diced bamboo
    shoots, drained

With sharp heavy cleaver, chop chicken in big chunks and scald in boiling water. Rinse and drain well. (Care should be taken to avoid bone splinters. Remove any small loose bones or pieces before cooking. If cleaver is unavailable, cut chicken in as small pieces as possible with knife.) Fold whole green onion in 2" to 3" length and tie with thread. Cover mushrooms with boiling water, soak 15 minutes, or until soft, then drain. Put chicken, green onion, mushrooms and remaining ingredients, except bamboo shoots, in kettle or Dutch oven. Bring to boil, cover and simmer, stirring occasionally, 1/2 hour, or until tender. Add bamboo shoots and heat. Makes 4 servings.

RUMANIAN-STYLE CHICKEN STEW

2 frying chickens (about 2-1/2 pounds each), cut up
Salt and pepper
1 clove garlic, crushed
3 onions, thinly sliced
3 tablespoons sweet butter
1/2 cup white wine
1/4 teaspoon monosodium glutamate
1 pint dairy sour cream
1/2 cup chopped ripe olives
Rumanian-style Cornmeal

Wash and dry chicken pieces and season with salt and pepper. Cook garlic and onion in butter in Dutch oven 2 to 3 minutes. Remove vegetables and reserve. Add chicken to drippings; brown on both sides. Add onion, wine, seasoning and ½ cup water. Cover and simmer 1 hour. Stir in sour cream and olives. Simmer about 20 minutes longer. Serve with cornmeal. Makes 6 to 8 servings. **Rumanian-style Cornmeal** Mix 1 cup cornmeal with 2 cups cold water. Gradually stir in 2 cups boiling water. Cook, stirring, until thickened. Add salt, cover and simmer about 25 minutes, stirring occasionally. Spread in greased 8" x 8" x 2" pan and chill overnight. Cut in 1½" squares and put in shallow baking dish. Dot with butter and sprinkle with ½ cup grated Cheddar cheese and a little cayenne. Bake in moderate oven (375°F.) 30 minutes. If desired, brown under broiler.

MURGHA CURRY

From India, curry, apple and ginger flavor creamed chicken and rice.

1 medium onion, minced
1 peeled apple, chopped
1/4 cup butter
1/3 cup flour
1 to 2 tablespoons curry powder
1-1/2 teaspoons salt
1/8 teaspoon pepper
1/4 teaspoon ginger
1 cup chicken broth
1 cup milk
1/2 cup heavy cream
Juice of 1/2 lemon
3 cups coarsely cut cooked chicken
4 cups hot cooked rice

Cook onion and apple in butter in top part of double boiler over direct heat until onion is yellowed. Blend in flour and seasonings. Slowly add broth, milk and cream; cook over boiling water, stirring constantly, until mixture is thickened. Cover and cook 10 minutes longer. Add lemon juice and chicken and heat well. Serve with the rice. Makes 6 servings.

CHICKEN ENCHILADAS

Cook 12 tortillas in hot lard or oil a few seconds, then dip in mixture of 2 cups cream and 1 cup very rich chicken stock. Spread Filling on tortillas, roll and place seam side down on a baking dish. Pour remaining cream mixture over and sprinkle with 1½ cups grated Jack cheese. Bake in moderate oven (350°F.) until enchiladas are hot and cheese is melted, about 25 minutes.

Filling
1/2 cup chopped onion
2 tablespoons butter
2 cups chopped cooked chicken
1 cup hot chili sauce
1 cup dairy sour cream
Salt to taste

Sauté onions in butter. Add remaining ingredients. Makes 6 servings.

CURRIED CHICKEN

1 can each condensed cream of chicken and cream of mushroom soup
1 tablespoon curry powder
3/4 cup light cream
2 cups diced cooked chicken
1/2 cup broken cashew nuts
Hot cooked rice

Put first 3 ingredients in top of double boiler over boiling water. Cover and heat, stirring occasionally. Add chicken and heat. Sprinkle with nuts and serve with rice. Makes 4 servings.

BANANA-CHICKEN CURRY

Bake this in a dish that can go to the table. To serve, spoon it over hot rice.

1/4 cup butter or margarine
1/4 cup flour
2 teaspoons curry powder
1/2 teaspoon salt
1/4 teaspoon pepper
2 cups chicken broth
3 green-tipped bananas
2 cups diced cooked chicken
Grated coconut (optional)
Hot steamed rice

Melt butter; add next 4 ingredients and stir until smooth. Gradually add chicken broth and cook, stirring constantly, until smooth and thickened. Peel bananas and cut in 1" lengths. Arrange in 1½-quart casserole. Pour half of curry sauce over bananas and bake in moderate oven (350°F.) 15 minutes. Arrange chicken on top and add remaining sauce. Bake 5 to 10 minutes. Sprinkle with grated coconut, if desired, and serve on rice. Makes 4 servings.

FAR EAST BARBECUED CHICKEN

1 onion, chopped
2 cloves garlic, minced
1/2 teaspoon chili powder
1/2 cup peanut butter
1 teaspoon salt
2 teaspoons vegetable oil
2 tablespoons soy sauce
2 tablespoons lime or lemon juice
2 broilers (about 2-1/2 pounds each),
    quartered

In saucepan cook first 6 ingredients 2 or 3 minutes, stirring. Add soy sauce, lime juice and 1 cup water. Bring to boil and simmer 5 minutes. Cool, pour over chicken and let stand 1 hour, turning once. Broil chicken pieces for 30 minutes until done. Turn several times and brush with marinade. Heat any remaining marinade and serve with chicken. Makes 8 servings.

CRUSTY SPICED CHICKEN

1-1/2 cups finely crushed potato chips
1 teaspoon salt
1/4 teaspoon pepper
1/2 teaspoon curry powder
1/8 teaspoon ginger
1 frying chicken (about 3 pounds), cut up
2 eggs, beaten
1/4 cup milk
1/3 cup butter, melted

Mix first 5 ingredients. Wash and dry chicken pieces. Combine eggs and milk. Pour butter into a large shallow baking dish. Dip chicken pieces in chips, then in egg mixture, then in chips again. Put pieces side by side in butter in dish. Bake in moderate oven (375°F.) 45 minutes. Makes 4 servings.

CHICKEN, SUMMER STYLE

1 frying chicken (about 3 pounds), cut up
3 tablespoons butter or margarine
Seasoned salt and pepper
3/4 cup chicken broth
1 can (2 ounces) sliced mushrooms,
    drained
1 can (1 pound) whole potatoes, drained
1 can (8 ounces) onions, drained
Salt and paprika
1 box (10 ounces) frozen peas, thawed,
    or 1 can (1 pound) peas, drained
4 tomatoes, halved

Brown chicken pieces in butter in large skillet. Sprinkle with seasoned salt and pepper. Add chicken broth, bring to boil, cover and simmer 35 minutes, or until tender. Add next 3 ingredients. Season potatoes and onions lightly with salt and paprika. Add a little more broth if dry. Cook 5 minutes. Add peas and tomatoes; cook a few minutes longer, or until tomatoes are heated. Serves 4.

CHICKEN AND CREAM-CHEESE LOAF

2 packages (3 ounces each) cream cheese
1/4 cup milk or chicken broth
3 eggs, separated
1 teaspoon sugar
1-1/2 teaspoons salt
Dash of pepper
3 tablespoons sherry
4-1/2 cups finely ground cooked chicken
Mushroom-Pimiento Sauce

Work cheese with spoon until softened; gradually beat in milk. Beat egg whites until stiff; set aside. Beat egg yolks until light. Stir into cheese mixture with next 4 ingredients. Fold in chicken, then egg whites. Put in well-greased 9" x 5" x 3" loaf pan. Set in a baking pan; pour in hot water to reach one third of height of loaf pan. Bake in moderate oven (350°F.) about 45 minutes. Turn out of pan onto a hot platter and serve with Mushroom-Pimiento Sauce. Makes 6 servings. **Mushroom-Pimiento Sauce** Heat, stirring, 1 can condensed cream of mushroom soup, 1/4 cup light cream and 1 teaspoon steak sauce. Stir in 2 pimientos, chopped. Makes about 1 1/2 cups.

CHICKEN TETRAZZINI

Chicken, mushrooms and spaghetti with a creamy sauce and cheese topping.

Butter or margarine
1/2 cup all-purpose flour
1 cup hot milk
1 cup hot chicken broth
1/2 teaspoon salt
1/2 teaspoon pepper
1/8 teaspoon nutmeg
1/4 cup dry sherry
3/4 cup heavy cream
1 pound thin spaghetti
1/2 pound mushrooms, sliced, or 2 cans
    (4 ounces each) mushrooms, drained
2 to 3 cups diced cooked chicken
1/2 cup grated Parmesan or Romano
    cheese

Heat 1/2 cup butter and stir in flour. Stir in milk and broth. Cook, stirring, until sauce is smooth and thickened. Blend in next 5 ingredients; remove from heat. Cook and drain spaghetti. Sauté mushrooms in 2 tablespoons butter 5 minutes. Mix half of sauce with spaghetti and mushrooms. Place in buttered shallow baking dish. Make a well in center of spaghetti mixture. Mix remaining sauce with chicken and place in well. Sprinkle with Parmesan cheese. Bake in hot oven (400°F.) 20 minutes. Makes 6 to 8 servings.

CURRIED CHICKEN-SALAD CASSEROLE

2 cups diced cooked chicken
2 cups diced celery
1 teaspoon curry powder
1 cup mayonnaise
Salt and pepper
1/4 cup toasted slivered almonds

Mix chicken, celery, curry powder and mayonnaise. Add salt and pepper to taste. Put in 4 individual baking dishes or shallow 1½-quart baking dish. Sprinkle with almonds. Bake in moderate oven (350°F.) 20 to 25 minutes. Makes 4 servings.

CHICKEN-HAM CASSEROLE

2 packages (10 ounces each) frozen Brussels sprouts
2 cups sliced cooked chicken
1 cup slivered cooked ham
1/2 cup mayonnaise
1/2 teaspoon lemon juice
1 can condensed cream of chicken soup
1/4 teaspoon Italian herb seasoning
1/2 cup fine dry bread crumbs
1/4 cup grated sharp Cheddar cheese
2 tablespoons butter or margarine, melted

Cook and drain Brussels sprouts and put in shallow 2-quart baking dish. Top with chicken and ham. Mix next 4 ingredients and pour over chicken. Sprinkle with crumbs and cheese and drizzle butter on top. Bake in moderate oven (350°F.) 25 minutes, or until browned. Makes 6 servings.

CHICKEN PARMESAN

2 frying chickens (about 2-1/2 pounds each), cut up
Prepared garlic spread
Grated Parmesan cheese
3 tablespoons olive oil
2 tablespoons flour
1-1/2 cups chicken broth
1/4 pound fresh mushrooms, sliced, or 1 can (4 ounces) sliced mushrooms
1/3 cup sherry
Salt and pepper
8 ounces spaghetti, cooked
Chopped parsley

Coat chicken with garlic spread. Rub with 3 tablespoons cheese. Cook in oil about 5 minutes. Stir in flour, add broth, mushrooms and sherry. Bring to boil. Cover and simmer 45 minutes, or until tender. Season with salt and pepper. Remove chicken. Mix spaghetti with sauce and sprinkle with parsley. Arrange on hot platter; put chicken on top. Serve with additional Parmesan cheese. Serves 6 to 8.

CHICKEN À L'ORANGE

The oranges give both color and flavor.

1 frying chicken (2-1/2 pounds), cut up
Salt and pepper
1/4 cup flour
1/4 cup vegetable shortening or oil
1 cup orange juice
1/2 cup chili sauce
1/4 cup chopped green pepper
1 teaspoon prepared mustard
1/2 to 1 teaspoon garlic salt
2 tablespoons soy sauce
1 tablespoon molasses
3 medium oranges, peeled and sliced in half-cartwheels

Wash and dry chicken pieces and dredge with seasoned flour. Heat shortening in skillet; brown chicken lightly on all sides. Remove chicken to 3-quart casserole. Drain fat from pan. To skillet, add remaining ingredients except orange slices and simmer 2 or 3 minutes. Pour sauce over chicken in casserole. Cover and bake in moderate oven (350°F.) 50 to 60 minutes, or until chicken is tender. Just before serving, add oranges. Makes 4 servings.

PINEAPPLE CHICKEN AND VEGETABLES

A subtle blend of flavors.

2 tablespoons vegetable oil
1/2 teaspoon salt
1 clove garlic, crushed
1-1/2 cups diced raw white chicken meat
1/2 cup finely diced lean raw pork
1 teaspoon finely shredded fresh gingerroot
1 tablespoon soy sauce
1 cup diced bamboo shoots
1 can (4 ounces) chopped mushrooms, drained
1 cup sliced Chinese cabbage
1 cup sliced celery
1 onion, chopped
1 cup chicken broth
2 tablespoons cornstarch
1 teaspoon monosodium glutamate
1 teaspoon sugar
1 cup thawed frozen peas
1 cup pineapple tidbits
1/2 cup toasted almonds

Heat oil, salt and garlic in large skillet. Add chicken and pork; cook until lightly browned. Add ginger and soy sauce; mix well. Add next 5 ingredients and cook 5 minutes. Add chicken broth, cover and cook 5 minutes. Mix next 3 ingredients and ¼ cup cold water and stir into first mixture. Cook until thickened. Add peas and pineapple and cook 2 or 3 minutes. Add almonds; serve on rice. Makes 6 servings.

BAKED CHICKEN HASH

2 cups chopped cooked chicken
1 medium onion, chopped
1 raw potato, chopped
2 pimientos, diced
2 carrots, shredded
1/2 teaspoon salt
2 tablespoons chopped parsley
1/2 teaspoon poultry seasoning
1 can chicken gravy and 1 cup leftover
   chicken gravy, heated

Combine all ingredients and mix well. Put in 1½-quart casserole. Cover and bake in moderate oven (350°F.) 45 minutes. Uncover and bake about 15 minutes longer. Serve with additional gravy. Makes 4 servings.

CHICKEN PILAF

Serve with a mixed green salad.

2 cups cooked chicken in strips
1/2 cup butter
1/3 cup coarsely chopped walnuts
1 tablespoon instant minced onion
1 teaspoon salt
1/2 teaspoon pepper
1/4 teaspoon ground coriander
2 cups uncooked rice
4 cups boiling chicken bouillon
2 medium tomatoes, peeled, seeded and
   chopped

Cook chicken in butter over low heat 3 minutes. Add walnuts and cook 2 minutes longer. Add next 5 ingredients, mix and cook 5 minutes, stirring. Pour in boiling bouillon and tomatoes; bring to boil, cover and simmer 20 minutes, or until rice is tender and liquid completely absorbed. Remove from heat and let stand 5 minutes before serving. Makes 4 to 6 servings.

CHICKEN AMANDINE

A deliciously simple way to dress up leftover chicken.

3 tablespoons butter or margarine
3 tablespoons flour
1 cup milk
1 cup chicken broth
Salt and pepper
Sliced cooked chicken for 4 servings
2 tablespoons sherry
1/3 cup toasted slivered almonds
Biscuits, noodles or rice

Melt butter and blend in flour. Gradually stir in milk and broth. Cook, stirring, until thickened. Season with salt and pepper. Add chicken and heat. Just before serving, blend in sherry. Sprinkle with nuts and serve over split hot biscuits, cooked noodles or rice. Serves 4.

CHICKEN CHINOIS

1/4 cup butter
1/4 cup flour
2 cups chicken broth or bouillon
1/4 teaspoon garlic salt
1 tablespoon soy sauce
1/4 teaspoon pepper
1/4 teaspoon ginger
1/2 teaspoon paprika
Salt to taste
3 cups diced cooked chicken
Hot cooked rice

Melt butter in top pan of double boiler over direct heat. Blend in flour, broth and seasonings. Cook, stirring occasionally, until thickened. Add chicken, put over boiling water, cover and heat. Serve with rice and additional soy sauce, if desired. Makes 4 to 6 servings.

COMPANY CHICKEN MARENGO

2 frying chickens (2 to 2-1/2 pounds
   each), cut up
Seasoned salt
2 packages (1-1/2 ounces each)
   spaghetti-sauce mix
1 cup fine dry bread crumbs
1/2 to 3/4 cup vegetable oil
1 cup sauterne
6 tomatoes, peeled and quartered
1/2 pound mushrooms, sliced

Sprinkle chicken pieces with seasoned salt. Blend sauce mix and crumbs and roll chicken in the mixture. Heat part of oil in Dutch oven. Brown chicken pieces, a few at a time, in the oil. When all are browned, put back in Dutch oven. Add remaining crumb mixture and other ingredients. Bring to boil, cover and simmer 45 minutes, or until chicken is tender. Makes 8 servings.

HAWAIIAN PINEAPPLE
AND CHICKEN

1/2 cup each sliced water chestnuts,
   bamboo shoots and celery
1/4 cup sliced Chinese cabbage
2 tablespoons vegetable oil
2 cups diced cooked chicken
1 tablespoon brown sugar
1 tablespoon vinegar
1 teaspoon monosodium glutamate
3 tablespoons soy sauce
2 cups chicken broth
1 cup drained pineapple cubes
3 tablespoons cornstarch
1/4 cup chopped green onion
Chow mein noodles

Cook vegetables in oil 5 minutes, stirring. Add next 7 ingredients and bring to boil. Stir in cornstarch blended with 3 tablespoons water; cook, stirring, until thickened. Sprinkle with onion and serve on noodles. Makes 4 servings.

CHICKEN OR TURKEY STOCK

Put bones and skin from chicken or turkey (raw or cooked) in heavy kettle and almost cover with water. Add 1 onion, 1 celery stalk, 1 carrot, few sprigs of parsley, 1 teaspoon salt and 1/4 teaspoon pepper. Cover and simmer 2 hours. Strain, check seasoning and chill. Remove fat from top of stock; fat may be used for frying. Use stock for sauces, soups and molded salads.

SAUTEED CHICKEN LIVERS, PEAS AND CARROTS

1/4 cup all-purpose flour
1 teaspoon salt
1/4 teaspoon pepper
1/2 teaspoon poultry seasoning
1 pound chicken livers, halved
1/4 cup butter
3/4 cup chicken broth or bouillon
1 box frozen peas and carrots, cooked

Mix first 4 ingredients and dredge livers. Heat butter in top of double boiler over direct heat until it begins to brown. Add livers and sauté until lightly browned. Add broth and simmer a few minutes. Put over boiling water, add vegetables, cover and heat. Makes 4 servings.

CHICKEN GIZZARDS IN SAUCE PIETRO

It's served on spaghetti or fine egg noodles.
1/4 pound salt pork, chopped fine
1 tablespoon olive oil
1 small onion, minced
2 cloves garlic, minced
1 pound chicken gizzards, chopped
2 sprigs parsley, minced
1/4 to 1/2 teaspoon crushed dried red pepper
1/4 teaspoon ground cloves
1/2 teaspoon marjoram
1/2 teaspoon salt
1 cup dry red wine
1 can (1 pound) Italian-style tomatoes
2 cans (6 ounces each) tomato paste
1 package (8 ounces) thin spaghetti or fine egg noodles
Grated Romano or Parmesan cheese

Put salt pork in kettle with next 3 ingredients and cook until pork is golden brown. Add gizzards, herbs and salt and cook a few minutes. Add wine and simmer about 25 minutes. Add tomatoes, paste and 4 cups water and simmer until fairly thick. Cook and drain spaghetti. Sprinkle platter with cheese, add some spaghetti, more cheese and some sauce. Repeat until all is used, ending with sauce and cheese. Makes 6 servings.

SELECTING A TURKEY

If you decide on a whole bird, buy a large one since the proportion of meat to bone is higher on larger birds. Any leftover meat can be used for later meals (recipes follow). However, small turkeys take less time to cook, and if you serve two small roasters, you can have four drumsticks, four wings and two kinds of stuffing. For medium or heavy birds of 12 pounds or over, allow 1/2 to 3/4 pound per serving. For turkeys under 12 pounds, allow 3/4 to 1 pound per serving.

THAWING A FROZEN BIRD

In many markets you can order your bird well in advance and ask that it be thawed completely or partially. Thaw turkey according to directions on bag or at room temperature using the paper-bag method.

Or thaw in partially opened or punctured plastic bag on tray in refrigerator 2 to 4 days, or 24 hours for each 5 pounds of turkey. When turkey is pliable, take off bag and remove giblets and neck. Cover turkey and refrigerate until ready to roast.

Or thaw in unopened plastic bag in cool water, changing water frequently, 6 to 8 hours (do not use warm or hot water). When turkey is pliable, remove bag and proceed as above.

Or put turkey in plastic bag inside a heavy paper bag. Close bag securely and let stand at room temperature 5 to 7 hours. (Closed paper bag allows turkey to thaw partially but keeps outside surface temperature low enough for safety.) Remove paper bag and refrigerate in punctured plastic bag 16 to 18 hours. When turkey is pliable, take off bag. Remove giblets from thawed turkey and cook as directed below.

COOKING THE GIBLETS

Wash giblets and neck and put in large saucepan with 2 teaspoons salt, 1 carrot, a few celery tops and 1 bay leaf. Cover with water, bring to boil and simmer, covered, 15 minutes. Remove liver and cook remaining giblets 1 1/2 hours longer, or until tender. Drain, reserving broth for gravy (there will be about 3 cups). Remove meat from neck and grind or chop with the heart, gizzard and liver. (Giblets can be prepared a day ahead and refrigerated.) Add to stuffing or gravy.

ROAST STUFFED TURKEY

Wash turkey and wipe dry. Spoon stuffing lightly into cavities. Sew or close openings with skewers. Draw skin of neck to back and fasten with skewer, then fold wing tips onto back. Tie legs. Place, breast side up, in roasting pan and rub lightly with butter. Cover with foil. Roast as directed on chart, basting several times with drippings in pan. Remove foil last ½ hour for more browning. Remove from oven and let stand ½ hour before carving.

STUFFED WHOLE TURKEY ROASTING CHART

Roast in slow oven (325°F.).

Ready-to-cook Weight	Total Roasting Time
6 to 8 pounds	2 to 2½ hours
8 to 12 pounds	2½ to 3 hours
12 to 16 pounds	3 to 3¾ hours
16 to 20 pounds	3¾ to 4½ hours
20 to 24 pounds	4½ to 5½ hours

Unstuffed turkeys require about 5 minutes less per pound. Meat thermometer should register 185°F. and drumstick should be easy to move up and down. **Stuffing** Stuffing can be made the day before and stored, covered, in refrigerator. If you prefer to make it the day you're going to use it, you can prepare crumbs, onion and celery ahead.

Though turkeys vary a great deal in weight, the capacity of the body cavities does not vary in proportion. A 12- to 16-pound turkey will hold about 5 cups stuffing in the body cavity and 2 cups in the neck. If you're serving a large number of people, you may need more stuffing than you can get in the bird. The remainder can be wrapped in foil and baked with the turkey about 40 minutes. This makes a moist stuffing. For a crisp stuffing, pack lightly into a casserole and bake, allowing about ¾ cup stuffing per serving. Pan drippings, extra butter or margarine, broth or bouillon can be used to season stuffing baked separately.

TURKEY HALVES AND QUARTERS ROASTING CHART

Roast in slow oven (325°F.).

Ready-to-cook Weight	Total Roasting Time
5 to 8 pounds	2-1/2 to 3 hours
8 to 10 pounds	3 to 3-1/2 hours
10 to 12 pounds	3-1/2 to 4 hours

TO ROAST TURKEY HALVES AND QUARTERS

For a small family, buy a turkey half or quarter. Or have a large turkey cut in halves or quarters and freeze the unused portion until ready to use. Thaw as directed on page 175. Rinse, drain and pat dry. Skewer skin to meat along cut edges to prevent shrinking during roasting. Rub cavity of roast lightly with salt and tie leg to tail. Lay wing flat over white meat and tie string around breast end to hold wing down. Put, skin side up, in shallow roasting pan and brush with fat. Roast following chart at left.

TO FREEZE COOKED TURKEY

Remove any stuffing from bird, put in covered container and store in refrigerator or freeze. Remove meat from bones and separate large slices from scraps. Package types and amounts of meat for the particular recipes you plan to use. Tear off generous strips of heavy-duty foil, put meat in center and fold ends over tightly, making several double folds. Fold sides in the same way. Secure with string or freezer tape and mark contents and date with freezer pencil. Frozen cooked turkey will retain its good quality for up to 3 months.

BONELESS-TURKEY ROASTING CHART

Roast in slow oven (325°F.).

Ready-to-cook Weight	Total Roasting Time
3 to 5 pounds	2 to 2-1/2 hours
5 to 7 pounds	2-1/2 to 3-1/2 hours
7 to 9 pounds	3-1/2 to 4 hours

TO COOK BONELESS TURKEY ROLL OR ROAST

Leave uncooked roll or roast in original bag and thaw in refrigerator 1 to 2 days. Remove bag and leave string in place while roasting. If roast is not pre-seasoned, rub lightly with salt and pepper and put on rack in shallow roasting pan. Brush with melted butter or margarine and roast following chart above until thermometer registers 170°F. to 175°F. Baste or brush occasionally with melted butter or pan drippings during roasting. If meat becomes too brown, cover loosely with foil. Let stand 20 to 30 minutes before slicing.

MAKING THE GRAVY

• Remove turkey from pan to heated platter and keep warm. (A heavy foil tent helps keep heat in.) Pour fat drippings from pan into heat-proof measuring cup. (Some brown bits usually adhere to pan; don't wash pan.) Let drippings stand 1 minute, or until fat comes to top of meat juices. From chart below, determine amount of fat required for desired amount of gravy; skim that amount off juices and put into heavy saucepan or skillet. *Do not turn heat on.*

• Using spoon or wire whisk, stir in required amount of flour.

• Remove remaining fat from juices in cup. Note amount of juices in cup and, allowing for the amount, add enough broth, bouillon, consommé, vegetable cooking water or water from simmering giblets to make the number of cups of gravy desired. (Amount of liquid determines amount of gravy.) Return juices to roasting pan. Put pan over one or two burners and bring liquid to boil. Using pancake turner, scrape brown bits from bottom. *Strain.* You now have the liquid called for in chart.
  Turn heat under saucepan to low and, stirring constantly, brown fat-flour mixture *lightly.*

• Remove from heat and stir in strained liquid. Return to low heat and cook, stirring constantly, until slightly thickened. (For giblet gravy, add minced giblets at this point.) Simmer about 5 minutes. Add salt and pepper to taste. **Note** This makes a gravy of average thickness. You can make a thinner gravy by using less flour, a thicker one by using more flour. Dripping amounts need not be changed. For a browner gravy, add enough gravy seasoning-browning sauce to give color desired.

GRAVY MAKING CHART

Liquid (equals gravy desired)	Fat Drippings and All-purpose Flour (equal quantities of each)
1 cup	1-1/2 tablespoons
2 cups	3 tablespoons
3 cups	4-1/2 tablespoons
4 cups	6 tablespoons
5 cups	7-1/2 tablespoons
6 cups	1/2 cup plus 1 tablespoon

MUSHROOM-GIBLET STUFFING

1 pound mushrooms, sliced
2 medium onions, chopped
1 cup chopped parsley
2 teaspoons each dried marjoram and sage
2 teaspoons salt
1 teaspoon pepper
1/2 cup butter or margarine
Chopped or ground cooked giblets and neck meat from turkey
2 cups giblet-cooking broth
6 cups firm-type bread-crumbs or cubes

Cook mushrooms and onions with seasonings in the butter 5 minutes. Add remaining ingredients and mix well. Makes about 8 cups.

SAUSAGE STUFFING

1-1/2 pounds sweet Italian sausage
2 large onions, chopped
2/3 cup chopped parsley
1 clove garlic, minced
2 teaspoons oregano or sage
Salt and pepper
Dash of cayenne
2 cups grated Parmesan cheese
5 cups soft stale-bread cubes

Remove sausage casing and brown meat in skillet. Add onion and cook until golden. Add remaining ingredients and mix well. Use as stuffing for poultry. Makes about 8 cups.

RICE STUFFING

1-1/2 cups uncooked rice
1 cup butter or margarine
1 cup minced onion
1 teaspoon each thyme, sage and marjoram
1-1/2 teaspoons salt
3/4 teaspoon pepper
1/3 cup chopped parsley
3/4 cup chopped celery and leaves

Cook rice according to package directions. Meanwhile, melt butter in skillet, add remaining ingredients and cook 5 minutes. Add rice. Makes about 6 cups.

PRUNE-APPLE-RAISIN STUFFING

1/2 cup chopped cooked prunes
2 cups chopped tart apples
1/2 cup seedless raisins
5 cups toasted bread cubes
1/4 cup melted butter or margarine
1/4 cup brown sugar
Grated rind of 1 lemon
1/2 teaspoon paprika
1/2 teaspoon cinnamon
1 teaspoon salt
3/4 cup apple juice or apple cider

Mix all ingredients. Makes about 8 cups.

CHEESE-TURKEY SHORTCAKES

In top part of double boiler over boiling water, melt ¹/₂ pound process Cheddar cheese. Stir in ²/₃ cup chicken broth, 2 cups diced cooked turkey, 1 teaspoon instant minced onion and pepper to taste. Heat and serve on hot biscuits with a garnish of pimiento strips. Makes 4 servings.

TURKEY TETRAZZINI

3/4 pound mushrooms, sliced
1 small green pepper, slivered
1/4 cup butter or margarine
3 tablespoons flour
2 teaspoons salt
1/4 teaspoon pepper
2-1/2 cups light cream
4 cups diced cooked turkey
2 pimientos, chopped
2 tablespoons sherry
6 ounces fine spaghetti, cooked
2 egg yolks, beaten
Grated Parmesan cheese

Cook mushrooms and green pepper in the butter 5 minutes. Blend in flour and seasonings. Add cream and cook, stirring, until thickened. Add next 3 ingredients and heat. Divide spaghetti into 6 broiler-proof individual baking dishes or put in shallow baking dish. Add small amount of turkey mixture to egg yolks, then return, stirring, to turkey mixture. Pour over spaghetti and sprinkle with cheese. Bake in slow oven (300°F.) about 45 minutes. Put under broiler to brown lightly. Makes 6 servings.

TURKEY PIE WITH SAGE PASTRY

1/2 cup butter
1/2 cup all-purpose flour
1-1/4 teaspoons salt
1/4 teaspoon ground sage
1/8 teaspoon pepper
1/8 teaspoon mace
1 teaspoon lemon juice
1-1/2 cups turkey or chicken broth
1 cup milk
3 cups diced cooked turkey
Sage pastry

Melt butter; blend in flour and seasonings. Add lemon juice, stock and milk. Cook, stirring, until thickened. Add turkey and heat. Pour into shallow 1¹/₂-quart casserole. Roll Sage Pastry to fit top of casserole. Set in place, trim and flute edges. Cut 2 or 3 gashes in top to allow steam to escape. Bake in hot oven (425°F.) about 20 minutes. Makes 6 servings. **Sage Pastry** Mix ¹/₂ cup all-purpose flour, ¹/₂ cup cornmeal, ¹/₂ teaspoon each salt and ground sage. Cut in ¹/₃ cup butter or margarine. Add 3 tablespoons water; mix lightly with fork.

TURKEY PACIFICA

1/2 cup all-purpose flour
2 teaspoons seasoned salt
1/2 teaspoon seasoned pepper
1 whole turkey breast (about 4 pounds), boned and split
1 egg, beaten
1/2 cup fine dry bread crumbs
1/3 cup sesame seed
1/4 cup butter or margarine

Mix first 3 ingredients. Coat turkey pieces with the mixture, brush with egg and roll in combined crumbs and seed. Melt butter in shallow baking dish, add turkey pieces and bake in slow oven (325°F.) 1¹/₂ hours, or until tender, basting occasionally with the drippings in pan. Good with sautéed pineapple rings. Makes 6 to 8 servings.

ROAST TURKEY ROLL WITH VEGETABLES

1 frozen seasoned turkey roll (3 to 4 pounds), thawed
Butter or margarine
12 to 16 small new potatoes
Salt, pepper and sugar
12 to 16 small carrots or 1 can (1 pound) whole carrots, drained
2 tablespoons flour
1/2 cup light cream
12 to 16 green onions

Put roll on rack in shallow roasting pan and brush with melted butter. Roast in moderate oven (350°F.) 1¹/₂ hours, basting occasionally with pan drippings. If roast becomes too brown, cover loosely with foil. Peel potatoes, wash and pat dry. Score crosswise at ¹/₈″ intervals almost to bottom. Sprinkle lightly with salt, pepper and sugar. Add the potatoes and carrots to roasting pan. (If canned carrots are used, add during last 10 minutes of roasting.) If necessary, add more butter. Continue roasting 1 hour longer, or until turkey and vegetables are tender, turning and basting turkey occasionally with pan drippings. Remove turkey to cutting board and cover with foil. Remove vegetables to a hot platter. Add enough boiling water to roasting pan to make 1¹/₂ cups liquid. Scrape up browned bits from bottom of pan and strain liquid into saucepan. Bring to boil. Blend flour with small amount of cold water and stir into liquid. Cook, stirring, until thickened, and simmer 3 minutes. Add cream and heat. Season with salt and pepper. Cover green onions with boiling water and drain. Cut roast in thin slices and arrange on platter with vegetables. Serve with the gravy. Makes 6 to 8 servings.

TURKEY CURRY

2 tablespoons butter or margarine
1/3 cup finely chopped onion
1 to 2 tablespoons curry powder
1 can (10-1/2 ounces) condensed cream
 of chicken soup
2 cups diced cooked turkey
Lemon juice
4 servings prepared packaged precooked
 rice

Melt butter, add onion and cook until tender. Stir in curry powder and heat a few seconds. Add ⅔ cup water and soup, and heat, stirring. Add turkey and heat. Add lemon juice to taste and serve on rice. Makes 4 servings.

TURKEY AND RICE PROVENCE

1 box (5-1/2 ounces) rice with chicken-
 sauce mix
1-1/2 cups diced cooked turkey

Prepare rice according to package directions and add turkey. Cover and bake as directed. Sprinkle with crumbs from rice package. Serves 4 to 6.

TURKEY PUFF

1 can (10-1/2 ounces) condensed cream
 of mushroom soup
1-1/2 cups diced cooked turkey
1-1/2 cups leftover turkey stuffing
1 can (8 ounces) cut green or wax beans,
 drained
4 eggs, separated
1 can French-fried onion rings

Mix soup and ⅓ cup water in greased 2-quart casserole. Arrange turkey, stuffing and beans in layers on soup. Beat egg whites until stiff, then beat yolks until thick; fold in whites. Pile on casserole and bake in slow oven (300°F.) about 40 minutes. Sprinkle with onions and bake 5 minutes longer. Makes 6 servings.

TURKEY WITH TAMALES

2 cans (15 ounces each) tamales
1 can (12 ounces) whole-kernel corn,
 drained
1 can (8 ounces) tomato sauce
1 tablespoon vegetable oil
1 tablespoon Worcestershire
2 cups diced cooked turkey
1/2 cup diced pitted black olives
1/2 cup turkey broth
1 envelope grated Cheddar cheese

Line greased shallow 1½ quart baking dish with tamales. Mix remaining ingredients, except cheese, and put in lined dish. Sprinkle with cheese; bake in slow oven (300°F.) about 1 hour. Makes 6 servings.

ALMOND TURKEY

1 envelope chicken-gravy mix
1 cup light cream
1 cup diced cooked turkey
1/4 cup toasted slivered almonds
4 servings prepared packaged precooked
 rice
Dried parsley

Put gravy mix in skillet and gradually stir in cream. Cook as directed on envelope. Stir in turkey and almonds and pour over rice. Sprinkle with parsley. Makes 2 to 3 servings.

SHORTCUT TURKEY PIE

1-1/2 cups leftover turkey gravy or
 canned giblet gravy
1 tablespoon red currant jelly (optional)
1 cup frozen peas
2 cups diced cooked turkey
1 tube (8 ounces) crescent dinner rolls
Milk or slightly beaten egg
1 tablespoon each sesame seed and
 grated Parmesan cheese
1/8 teaspoon paprika

Combine gravy and jelly in saucepan and heat. Gently mix in peas and turkey. Pour into greased shallow rectangular 1½-quart baking dish. Cover top with 6 unrolled crescents, pinching seams together. Unroll remaining dough and cut in strips, twist and place around edges. Brush with milk or egg and sprinkle with mixture of remaining ingredients. Bake in moderate oven (375°F.) 30 to 35 minutes, or until golden brown and done. Makes 4 to 6 servings.

TURKEY SCRAPPLE

4 cups turkey broth (or part broth and
 part water)
1-1/2 teaspoons salt
1/4 teaspoon pepper
1 teaspoon poultry seasoning
1 cup quick-cooking grits
1 cup finely chopped cooked turkey
Flour
Shortening or margarine

Combine first 4 ingredients. Bring to boil and slowly add grits, stirring. When mixture begins to boil again, reduce heat and cook, stirring occasionally, 6 minutes, or until thickened. Add turkey and stir gently over heat about 1 minute. Pour into greased 9″ x 5″ x 3″ loaf pan. Chill several hours or overnight. Remove from pan and slice ¼″ to ½″ thick. Coat with flour and sauté in 2 to 3 tablespoons hot shortening until browned on both sides. Good with applesauce. Makes 4 servings.

TURKEY DIVAN

12 slices (6 servings) cooked turkey
2 boxes frozen asparagus spears, cooked
1 tablespoon steak sauce
1 can (10-1/2 ounces) condensed cream
   of chicken soup
3/4 cup shredded Cheddar cheese

Arrange turkey slices in shallow broiler-proof baking dish. Cover with asparagus spears. Mix steak sauce and soup and pour over top. Sprinkle with cheese. Bake in moderate oven (375°F.) about 20 minutes, then put under broiler until bubbly. Serves 6.

SAVORY TURKEY SQUARES WITH MUSHROOM SAUCE

3 cups coarsely chopped or ground
   cooked turkey
2 cups soft bread crumbs
1 cup turkey broth
2/3 cup minced celery
2 tablespoons minced parsley
1 teaspoon monosodium glutamate
3 eggs, slightly beaten
1 tablespoon lemon juice
2 tablespoons instant minced onion
1 pimiento, chopped
2/3 cup light cream
Salt
Pepper
Mushroom Sauce

Mix all ingredients, except the last 3. Season to taste with salt and pepper. Pour into 12" x 7" x 2" baking dish and put in pan of hot water. Bake in moderate oven (350°F.) 1 hour. Cut in squares and serve with sauce. Makes 6 to 8 servings. **Mushroom Sauce** In saucepan blend ¼ cup soft turkey fat or butter and ¼ cup flour; heat until bubbly, stirring. Gradually stir in 2 cups turkey broth and cook, stirring, until thickened. Drain 1 can (3 ounces) chopped mushrooms. Add to sauce and season to taste with salt, pepper and poultry seasoning.

TURKEY SUKIYAKI

1 cup minced green pepper
1 cup thinly sliced celery
1 can (4 ounces) sliced mushrooms,
   drained
1 cup green onions in 1" pieces, tops
   included
3 tablespoons vegetable oil
1-1/2 cups diced canned or cooked
   turkey
1/4 cup soy sauce

Cook vegetables in oil in skillet over medium heat 6 to 8 minutes, or until barely tender. Stir in turkey and soy sauce. Heat through and serve at once. Good with rice or noodle dishes. Makes 4 servings.

PRESSED TURKEY

It must be made a day ahead.

Mix 1 cup turkey broth and 3 cups minced cooked turkey in saucepan. Simmer until broth is nearly evaporated. Season to taste with salt and pepper. Cool. Pour into a 3-cup bowl; press down with a plate. Chill overnight. Unmold and cut in slices. Garnish with parsley and serve with mayonnaise. Makes 4 to 6 servings.

BROILED TURKEY SALAD

Turkey salad topped with potato chips and cheese, then broiled.

2 cups diced cooked turkey
1-1/2 cups diced celery
1/4 cup toasted slivered almonds
1/4 cup French dressing
Salt and pepper to taste
1/2 cup salad dressing or mayonnaise
1/3 cup dairy sour cream
2 cups finely crushed potato chips
1 cup grated Cheddar cheese
Salad greens

Marinate first 3 ingredients in French dressing for 1 hour; season. Add salad dressing and sour cream and chill. About 15 minutes before serving, put salad in 4 individual ramekins or a 9" layer-cake pan. Mix potato chips and cheese and completely cover salad. Put under broiler until cheese melts. Tuck greens under salad and serve. Makes 4 servings.

TURKEY DRUMSTICKS PAPRIKASH

2 turkey drumsticks with thighs
Butter or margarine
2 teaspoons paprika
1 cup chopped onion
2 tablespoons flour
2 cups chicken broth
1 cup sliced celery
1 cup sliced carrot
1/2 cup dairy sour cream
Salt and pepper
Chopped parsley

Brown drumsticks in 2 tablespoons butter in skillet. Remove to small shallow roasting pan. Melt 2 tablespoons butter in saucepan, add paprika and onion and sauté 5 minutes, stirring. Sprinkle with flour. Gradually add broth and cook, stirring, until thickened. Add celery and carrot. Cover and simmer 5 minutes. Stir in sour cream and season with salt and pepper. Pour over turkey. Cover lightly with foil. Bake in moderate oven (350°F.) 1½ to 2 hours, or until tender. Remove drumsticks, slice meat from bones and add to sauce. Sprinkle with parsley. Good with mashed potatoes. Serves 4.

TURKEY BREAST WITH HAM SAUCE

1 whole turkey breast (about 4 pounds), split
2 tablespoons butter or margarine
1 teaspoon instant minced onion
1 can (4-1/2 ounces) deviled ham
1 cup dairy sour cream
1/4 teaspoon dry mustard
Chopped parsley

 Brown turkey pieces in butter in skillet. Remove to shallow roasting pan. Add ³/₄ cup water and onion to skillet, bring to boil and pour over turkey. Cover lightly with foil. Bake in moderate oven (350°F.) 1 hour. Meanwhile, mix ham, sour cream and mustard. Spread on turkey. Bake, uncovered, 40 minutes longer, or until done. Sprinkle with chopped parsley and serve with drippings in pan. Good with new potatoes in jackets. Makes 8 servings.

GRILLED TURKEY STEAKS

The trick with these is not to overcook them. Buy a frozen turkey; have butcher slice center portion (between wing joint and thigh joint) crosswise into ³/₄″ pieces. Save ends for roasting. Lay slices in large flat pans and pour over them a marinade of 1 cup wine to ¹/₂ cup oil; turn steaks several times while thawing. Cook on greased grill over moderate fire or under hot broiler 10 to 15 minutes on each side, basting with marinade. Test by tasting. Arrange on hot platter, pour remaining marinade over; sprinkle with salt and pepper.

ROAST GUINEA HENS WITH WILD-RICE STUFFING

1 cup wild rice
1 large onion, chopped
1/2 cup chopped celery with leaves
Butter or margarine
2 cups chicken broth
1/2 cup chopped nuts
1 can (3 ounces) chopped mushrooms, drained
Poultry seasoning, salt and pepper
2 guinea hens (2 to 3 pounds each)

Cook rice, onion and celery in ¹/₄ cup butter 5 minutes. Add broth and bring to boil. Cover and simmer 30 minutes, or until liquid is absorbed and rice is tender. Add nuts and mushrooms and seasoning to taste. Stuff guinea hens and truss. Put breast down on rack in roasting pan and brush with melted butter. Bake in moderate oven (350°F.) 1 hour. Turn over and brush again with butter. Roast 1 hour longer, or until tender. Makes 4 to 6 servings.

ROAST DUCK AND SAUERKRAUT

1 duckling (about 5 pounds)
Salt and pepper
1 clove garlic
3 apples, pared and quartered
1 cup seedless raisins
2 quarts sauerkraut
1 cup orange juice
1 tablespoon brown sugar

Rub inside of duckling with salt, pepper and garlic clove. Stuff with apples and raisins. Put in roasting pan and roast in slow oven (325°F.) 1 hour. Pour off fat. Mix sauerkraut, orange juice and sugar; arrange around but not on top of duck. Cover and roast in slow oven (325°F.) 1³/₄ to 2 hours longer, or until duck is tender and brown. Makes 4 servings.

DUCK SPANISH-STYLE

1 duckling (4 to 5 pounds)
1 onion, chopped
1 cup chicken broth or stock
1 teaspoon salt
1/4 teaspoon pepper
1/2 teaspoon celery salt
1/2 teaspoon garlic salt
1 can (8 ounces) tomato sauce
1 tablespoon paprika
1 can (4 ounces) mushroom stems and pieces, drained
1/4 cup dry sherry

Brown duck slowly on all sides in heavy kettle; pour off fat. Put duck on rack in kettle. Add next 8 ingredients. Simmer, covered, 1¹/₂ hours, or until duck is tender, basting frequently with the liquid in kettle. Remove duck to a hot platter. Add mushrooms and sherry to kettle; heat and pour over duck. Serves 3 to 4.

GINGER-PINEAPPLE DUCKLING WITH ORANGE RICE

1 duckling (4 to 5 pounds)
2 tablespoons lemon juice
1/2 teaspoon salt
1 teaspoon ground ginger
1 can (1 pound 4-1/2 ounces) sliced pineapple
Orange Rice (page 246)
Strawberries

Rub duckling inside and out with lemon juice; then outside with salt and ginger. Truss and put, breast up, on rack in shallow roasting pan. Roast in slow oven (325°F.) 1 hour. Pour off fat from pan. Add 1 cup syrup drained from pineapple to pan. Continue roasting 2 hours, or until tender, basting every 10 minutes with drippings. Duckling should be well glazed. Arrange on a bed of Orange Rice on hot platter and garnish with the fruit. Makes 3 to 4 servings.

LEMON-GLAZED DUCK

1 duckling (4 to 5 pounds)
Salt and pepper
Grated rind and juice of 1 lemon
1/2 cup honey
1 lemon, peeled and thinly sliced
Watercress or parsley

Wash duckling and dry on absorbent paper. Sprinkle inside and out with salt and pepper. Truss bird and place on rack in shallow roasting pan. If desired, prick skin all over to allow fat to drain out. Roast in slow oven (325°F.) about 3 hours. Pour off fat during roasting. Mix lemon rind and juice and honey. During last hour of roasting, brush frequently with the mixture. Remove to serving platter and garnish with sliced lemon and watercress. Makes 3 to 4 servings.

ROAST DUCK WITH SAGE AND ONION STUFFING

2 ducklings (4 to 5 pounds each)
Salt
2 large onions, chopped
6 tablespoons butter
1/2 pound ground veal
1 teaspoon dried sage leaves
3 to 4 cups soft stale-bread crumbs
1/4 cup chopped parsley
2 eggs, beaten
Pepper
Light cream
1 lemon
3 tablespoons flour

Put the duck giblets in a pan with salted water and boil 30 minutes, or until giblets are tender. Drain, reserving broth; chop giblets. Sauté onion in butter until transparent. Add veal and cook 3 to 4 minutes, blending well. Remove from heat, stir in next 4 ingredients, season to taste and add a little cream if stuffing seems too dry. Rub cavities and skin of ducks with lemon and salt and pepper. Stuff and sew up cavities or close with foil. Truss birds and arrange on rack in shallow baking pan. Roast in slow oven (325°F.) about 2 hours. Increase heat to 350°F. and puncture the skin in several places. Roast 15 minutes to crisp skin. Remove ducks to hot platter and pour off liquid. Skim off 3 tablespoons fat and put in pan over medium heat; blend in flour. Then slowly stir in 1½ cups broth from giblets. Cook and stir until sauce is smooth, thickened and bubbling. Add chopped giblets and check seasoning. With the ducks, serve gravy, applesauce and boiled or mashed potatoes, as desired. An orange-watercress salad is good too. Makes 6 to 8 servings.

BAKED ALMOND CAPON

1 capon (4 to 5 pounds), cut up
1 can condensed golden mushroom soup
2 cups (1/2 pound) shredded Cheddar cheese
1/2 cup sliced almonds

Put capon pieces in shallow 3-quart baking dish or roasting pan. Spoon soup over. Cover with lid or foil and bake in moderate oven (350°F.) 1½ hours. Uncover and sprinkle with cheese and almonds. Bake, uncovered, 30 minutes longer, or until tender. Makes 6 to 8 servings.

CAPON SOUP

2 tablespoons butter
1/4 cup slivered almonds
1/4 cup minced green pepper
1/4 cup thinly sliced green onions with tops
1 cup thinly sliced celery
4 cups capon broth
1 cup finely diced leftover cooked capon
Salt and pepper
Chopped parsley

Melt butter in saucepan. Add next 4 ingredients and sauté, stirring, about 5 minutes. Add broth and bring to boil. Add meat and season with salt and pepper to taste. Sprinkle with parsley. Makes about 5 cups.

ROAST MUSHROOM-STUFFED CAPON, SAUCE CAFÉ-CRÈME

1 capon (4 to 5 pounds)
1/2 lemon
Salt and pepper
1 can (3 ounces) chopped mushrooms, undrained
1 cup soft bread crumbs
1 can (2-2/3 ounces) liver pâté
2 tablespoons flour
1 tablespoon instant-coffee powder
1/2 cup light cream

Rub cavity of capon with lemon and sprinkle lightly with salt and pepper. Mix mushrooms with bread crumbs and liver pâté until blended. Stuff capon with mixture and truss. Put on rack in shallow roasting pan. Roast in slow oven (325°F.) 2 to 2½ hours, or until tender. Baste occasionally with pan drippings. When tender, remove to a hot platter. Pour off drippings and add enough boiling water to make 1 cup. Put in saucepan. Blend flour and coffee with ¼ cup cream. Add to liquid and bring to boil, stirring. Simmer 3 to 5 minutes. Add remaining cream and season to taste. Serve as sauce with the capon. Makes 6 servings.

BROILED CORNISH HENS

2 Rock Cornish hens, split
Salt and white pepper
1 teaspoon crushed dried marjoram or
    thyme leaves
Melted butter or margarine

Rub hens with salt, pepper and marjoram; let stand about 1 hour. Put, skin side down, in preheated broiler. Brush with melted butter and broil about 5" from unit 12 to 15 minutes. Turn and brush with butter, broil 12 to 15 minutes, or until tender and well browned. Makes 4 servings.

GLAZED ROAST STUFFED ROCK CORNISH HENS

6 frozen Rock Cornish hens
Pecan Stuffing, page 87
1/2 cup butter or margarine, melted
Salt and pepper
2 tablespoons cornstarch
1 cup bouillon

Thaw Cornish hens lightly; stuff with Pecan Stuffing. Secure with toothpicks and tie legs together. Put in shallow roasting pan; pour butter over and sprinkle with salt and pepper. Roast in hot oven (425°F.) 1 to 1¼ hours, basting twice with drippings in pan. Mix cornstarch with a little cold water in small saucepan. Add bouillon and bring to boil, stirring. Spoon over hens to glaze. Makes 6 servings.

CORNISH HENS BONNE FEMME

2 Rock Cornish hens, split
1 tablespoon lemon juice
Salt and white pepper
1/4 cup butter or margarine
1/2 cup hot chicken broth
1/2 cup white wine
8 small white onions
8 small carrots
1 can (3 ounces) mushroom caps
Chopped parsley

Sprinkle hen pieces with lemon juice, salt and pepper. Brown on all sides in the butter in large heavy skillet. Transfer to a large casserole and cover with chicken broth and wine. Bake, uncovered, in moderate oven (350°F.) 30 minutes, basting frequently with liquid in dish. Partially cook onions and carrots in liquid drained from mushrooms plus a small amount of water. Add with mushrooms to Cornish hens and bake 30 minutes longer, or until hens and vegetables are tender. Season to taste; garnish with parsley. Good with rice. If gravy is desired, thicken liquid with 2 teaspoons cornstarch blended with a little water. Makes 4 servings.

ROAST STUFFED PHEASANT

Many special markets sell pheasants. One bird will usually serve two persons. Pheasant can be very dry; a moist stuffing helps.

1 medium onion, minced
1/4 cup butter or margarine
1 pound pork or sausage meat
1 pound ground veal
2 tablespoons chopped parsley
1 teaspoon dried thyme leaves
1 cup soft stale-bread crumbs
1 egg
Salt and pepper
2 pheasants
2 slices salt pork or bacon
Bread Sauce (page 184)

Sauté onion in butter, add meats and mix well, breaking up with a fork. Add next 4 ingredients and season to taste. Stuff the birds and close cavities with foil. Truss and tie a piece of salt pork or bacon strip over the breast of each bird. Arrange in a roasting pan, breast side down. Roast in moderate oven (350°F.) 25 minutes. Turn breast side up and roast 20 minutes. Remove the pork fat or bacon and roast about 15 minutes longer to brown the breast skin. Serve with Bread Sauce. Makes 4 servings.

ROAST GOOSE WITH SAVORY FRUIT STUFFING

1 junior goose (about 12 pounds)
1 lemon
Salt and pepper
1-1/2 cups chopped pitted prunes
1-1/2 cups cranberries
1-1/2 cups each finely diced celery and
    apple
1/2 teaspoon salt

Remove excess fat and rub goose inside and out with cut lemon. Sprinkle with salt and pepper. Mix remaining ingredients and lightly stuff cavity of goose. Skewer or sew opening, truss bird and put breast down on rack in shallow roasting pan. Roast in slow oven (325°F.) 4½ hours, or until drumstick meat feels very soft. Prick skin occasionally and pour off fat as it accumulates in pan. After about 3 hours of roasting, turn goose over and finish roasting. Makes 8 to 10 servings. *Note* Seasoned with apple and onion, goose fat makes an excellent fat for frying potatoes, or shortening for biscuits or other hot breads. Rinse fat and cut in small pieces. Put in heavy saucepan and cover with cold water. Add 1 apple, cut in wedges, and 1 small onion. Cook, uncovered, over low heat until all water is evaporated. Strain into container, cool and chill.

SQUABS WITH SAVORY STUFFING

16 to 18 green onions, tops removed, cut finely
2/3 cup shredded ham (try Smithfield)
1/3 cup chopped green pepper
1/3 cup chopped parsley
1-1/2 teaspoons chopped fresh basil
Butter
4 cups cooked rice
2 eggs
Soy sauce
Salt and pepper
6 squabs
1/2 cup vegetable oil
1 teaspoon paprika
Watercress and cherry tomatoes (optional)

Sauté first 5 ingredients in ½ cup butter. Add rice and mix well. Stir in eggs and 2 tablespoons soy sauce. Check seasoning. Stuff birds with the mixture and close cavities with a small piece of foil. Truss and tie the birds; arrange them on their sides on a rack in a shallow pan. Brush well with melted butter. Roast in moderate oven (375°F.) 20 minutes; turn and roast another 20 minutes; then turn them on their backs and roast till tender, about 30 minutes. Baste the birds 4 times during roasting with mixture of ½ cup soy sauce, the oil and paprika. Transfer squabs to hot platter. Remove excess fat from pan and baste birds again. Serve whole, garnished with watercress and cherry tomatoes, if desired. Serves 6.

PEACH BARBECUE SAUCE

1 jar (7-3/4 ounces) peach cobbler junior dessert
1/4 cup honey
1/4 cup vinegar
1 tablespoon grated onion
2 tablespoons brown sugar
1/4 teaspoon garlic salt
1/2 teaspoon Worcestershire

Mix all ingredients in saucepan. Bring to boil and remove from heat. Use as a glaze when broiling poultry. Makes 1⅓ cups.

BREAD SAUCE

1 small onion, peeled
1 cup soft stale-bread crumbs
Dash of hot pepper sauce
1/2 teaspoon salt
1 cup milk
1/2 cup heavy cream
1 tablespoon butter

Combine all ingredients, except butter, in a saucepan and bring to boil. Lower heat and simmer for 5 minutes. Remove onion. Add butter and let melt. Makes about 1¾ cups.

BARBECUE SAUCE

To brush over meat about halfway through the cooking period.

3/4 teaspoon salt
1/4 teaspoon pepper
1/2 small onion, minced
2 tablespoons Worcestershire
1 tablespoon dry mustard
1 can (8 ounces) tomato sauce
1 cup juice from sweet pickles
1 clove garlic, minced
2 tablespoons flour

Combine all ingredients in saucepan. Bring to boil, stirring; boil 2 minutes. Cool. Refrigerate. Makes 2 cups.

PLUM SAUCE

Chinese duck sauce to go with roast duck; good, too, with meats.

1 can (1 pound 13 ounces) purple plums
3/4 cup crushed pineapple, drained
1 medium apple, diced
1 can (4 ounces) pimientos, drained
1/2 cup white vinegar
1/2 cup sugar
1/4 teaspoon salt

Drain plums, reserving 1 cup syrup. Remove stones from plums and put fruit with reserved syrup in saucepan. Add remaining ingredients and simmer about 1 hour; stir occasionally. Whirl in blender or force through a coarse sieve. Makes about 2 cups.

GINGER-CRANBERRY RELISH

4 cups (1 pound) cranberries
1 large thin-skinned orange, quartered and seeded
1 cup seedless raisins
1/4 cup honey
3/4 cup sugar
1-1/2 teaspoons ground ginger

Force cranberries and orange through food chopper, using coarse blade. Mix with remaining ingredients and ripen in refrigerator several hours before serving. Store in refrigerator. Makes 4 cups.

GINGER PEAR CHIPS

1 cup sugar
2 tablespoons lemon juice
3 or 4 thin slices lemon
1 tablespoon chopped candied ginger or 1/2 teaspoon ginger
3 or 4 winter pears

Bring to a boil sugar and ½ cup water. Stir in lemon juice, lemon slices and ginger. Quarter and core pears and cook in syrup a few at a time until tender. Serve warm or chilled as accompaniment to meat or poultry. Makes 6 to 8 servings.

Cioppino

HOW TO BUY FISH
AND SHELLFISH

Although canned, frozen and dried fish
and shellfish are available everywhere
all through the year, fresh fish is another
story. The kind you can buy in one
area may not be in another. Seasonal
factors, weather and yearly fluctuations
affect the catch and determine the kind
and amount of fish that comes to our
markets. And since fresh fish is highly
perishable, market storage is often a
problem. So it's a good idea to buy with
special care. Fresh fish should smell
fresh and have firm elastic flesh and
bulging eyes. Shells of oysters and clams
should be tightly closed. Uncooked
lobsters or crabs should be alive when
purchased. Fresh scallops are at their
best from November to April; oysters,
September through April. Fresh Northern
lobsters are most plentiful in summer.

Amounts of fish to buy

Allow about 1½ pounds fresh or frozen
fillets for 4 servings, about 2 pounds
steaks and about 3 pounds whole fish.

1 dozen live clams or oysters = 2 servings
1 pint shucked clams = 3 servings
1 dozen live crabs = 4 servings
1 pound crab or lobster meat = 6 servings
1 pound live lobster = 1 serving
1 pint shucked oysters = 3 servings
1 pound scallops = 3 servings
1 pound shelled shrimps = 3 servings
1 pound lobster tails = 2 servings

FISH AND SHELLFISH STORAGE

All fresh fish and shellfish should be
cooked as soon as possible after buying.
If frozen fish has thawed, do not attempt
to refreeze it, but cook it promptly.

Equivalents

6½-ounce can crab meat = ¾ cup meat
6½-ounce can lobster = 1 cup meat
6-ounce frozen lobster tail = ½ cup
    diced meat
4½-ounce can shrimps = 22 to 28 shrimps

CANNED-SALMON TIPS

Salmon color varies from deep red to
light pink or almost white. The deep-red
varieties are more oily and more
expensive. The less expensive types are
just as nutritious and can be used in
any recipe where color is not important,
such as sandwiches, casseroles and loaves.
Where possible, use the salmon liquid,
skin and the soft bones (which may be
mashed) because they contain nutrients.

SESAME BAKED FISH

2 pounds fish fillets or steaks
Salt
Melted butter
3 cups soft bread cubes
1/4 teaspoon pepper
1/4 cup sesame seed, toasted
1/2 teaspoon thyme

Put fish in a shallow baking dish. Sprinkle with salt and pour on 1/4 cup melted butter. Mix 1 teaspoon salt, 1/3 cup melted butter and remaining ingredients. Spread on fish. Bake in moderate oven (375°F.) about 30 minutes. Makes 6 to 8 servings.

FINNAN HADDIE IN CREAM

1 fillet of finnan haddie
2 cups milk
1 bay leaf
Pinch of thyme
10 whole black peppercorns
1 slice onion
1/4 cup butter or margarine
1/4 cup flour
Dash of cayenne
1/4 cup light cream
1 pimiento, chopped
2 hard-cooked eggs, chopped
Hot buttered toast

Soak fish 1 hour in mixture of next 5 ingredients. Put over low heat and simmer 10 minutes. Remove fish, flake and discard skin. Strain milk and reserve. Melt butter and blend in flour. Gradually add milk and cook, stirring, until thickened. Add fish and remaining ingredients, except toast. Heat and serve on toast. Serves 4.

FLOUNDER FILLETS SUPREME

1 onion, sliced
1/2 lemon, sliced
1 bay leaf
Few celery leaves
Salt and pepper
1 pound flounder
1/4 cup butter
2 tablespoons flour
1/2 cup milk
1/2 cup dry white wine or sherry
1 egg, beaten

Put first 4 ingredients in skillet with 1 1/2 cups water. Add salt and pepper to taste. Bring to boil, add fish and reduce heat. Simmer gently 5 minutes. Remove fish to shallow broiler-proof baking dish; reserve stock. Melt 2 tablespoons butter and blend in flour. Gradually add milk and 1/2 cup fish liquid and cook until thickened, stirring constantly. Add wine and heat to boiling. Add remaining butter and pour slowly over egg, stirring. Pour over fish and brown lightly under broiler. Makes 4 servings.

SPUDS AND STICKS

1 box (6 ounces) oven-ready scalloped potatoes
1 box (8 ounces) frozen fish sticks
2 hard-cooked eggs, chopped
1/4 cup chopped parsley
1-1/4 cups milk
2 tablespoons butter or margarine

Empty potatoes into 1 1/2-quart baking dish. Add frozen fish sticks, cut in half, eggs and parsley. Mix gently. Add milk, butter and 2 cups boiling water. Bake in hot oven (400°F.) about 40 minutes. Makes 4 servings.

BUTTERFISH WITH SOUR-CREAM SAUCE

2 pounds butterfish
Salt and pepper
3/4 cup sifted all-purpose flour
1 egg, beaten
1/2 cup milk
1 tablespoon melted butter
Fat for deep frying
1 cup dairy sour cream
1 tablespoon minced parsley
1 tablespoon minced green onion
Juice of 1/2 lemon
Dash of cayenne

Sprinkle fish with salt and pepper. Combine 1/2 teaspoon salt with next 4 ingredients. Beat until smooth. Dip fish in batter and fry in hot deep fat until golden brown. Combine 1/2 teaspoon salt and remaining ingredients. Heat slightly. Serve with fried fish. Makes 4 servings.

BACALAO VERACRUZANA (Mexican Codfish in a Spicy Tomato Sauce)

1 pound salt codfish
Bouquet garni (bay leaf, parsley, thyme)
1 large clove garlic
1/4 cup olive oil
1 onion, chopped
1 tablespoon butter
1 cup tomato purée
2 chopped pimientos
1 chopped canned green chili
1/4 cup chopped green olives
1 tablespoon capers

Freshen the codfish by soaking in cold water 3 or 4 hours. Drain; cover with water, add bouquet garni and simmer until tender. Drain and reserve stock. Crush garlic and cook in the olive oil until golden. Remove garlic. Cut codfish in pieces, discarding any bone, and lightly brown in the garlic oil. In the meantime, cook onion in butter until wilted, add 1 cup fish stock and next 4 ingredients. Simmer 10 minutes, then add capers and combine with the codfish. Good with crusty bread. Makes 6 servings.

DEVILED HALIBUT STEAKS

Mix 2 tablespoons prepared mustard, 1 tablespoon oil, 2 tablespoons chili sauce, 2 tablespoons horseradish and 1 teaspoon salt. Spread half of mixture on 4 halibut steaks (about 2 pounds). Put on greased broiler rack and broil about 6 minutes under medium heat. Turn fish, spread with remaining sauce and broil 5 or 6 minutes longer. Makes 4 servings.

GRILLED MAHIMAHI

"Mahimahi" is the Hawaiian word for dolphin, but halibut is a good substitute.

1/4 cup butter, melted
1 teaspoon vegetable oil
1/8 teaspoon garlic salt
1 teaspoon soy sauce
1/2 teaspoon lemon juice
1-1/2 pounds mahimahi or halibut steak
Lemon wedges

Mix first 5 ingredients. Add fish and marinate 30 minutes. Grill over charcoal or broil 5 to 6 minutes on each side, or until fish flakes easily with a fork. Serve with lemon wedges. Makes 4 servings.

FISH-RICE PUFF

2 cups flaked cooked cod or haddock
2 cups cooked rice
1 cup milk
2 tablespoons butter or margarine, melted
Juice of 2 lemons
4 eggs, separated
Salt and pepper

Mix first 5 ingredients. Fold in beaten egg yolks, then stiffly beaten egg whites. Add salt and pepper to taste. Put in greased 1½-quart casserole. Bake in moderate oven (375°F.) 30 minutes. Makes 4 servings.

TROUT WITH ANCHOVY SAUCE

4 trout
Seasoned flour
Olive oil
3 tablespoons butter
4 anchovy fillets, cut fine
1/2 cup white wine
1 teaspoon chopped fresh or dried mint
1 tablespoon chopped parsley
Juice of 1 lemon

Roll fish in seasoned flour. Heat enough olive oil to cover bottom of skillet. Panfry fish about 5 minutes on each side. Meanwhile, melt butter, add anchovy fillets and heat 5 minutes. Add next 3 ingredients, simmer 3 minutes; add lemon juice. Put fish on hot platter and pour sauce over all. Makes 4 servings.

SOLE IN VERMOUTH

1 cup dry vermouth
1-1/2 pounds sole fillets
4 egg yolks
2/3 cup butter or margarine
1 tablespoon heavy cream
Salt and pepper

Heat vermouth in skillet. Wrap fish loosely in cheesecloth and poach in the vermouth about 10 minutes. Put fish on broilerproof platter. Boil vermouth to reduce to about ⅔ cup. Put in top of double boiler with next 3 ingredients. Cook over hot, not boiling, water, stirring until mixture just begins to thicken. Season, pour over fish and brown very quickly under broiler. Serves 4 to 6.

STUFFED SOLE FILLETS

6 large or 12 small (2 pounds) sole fillets
Melted butter or margarine
Chopped parsley
2 carrots, peeled and shredded
6 slices bread, cubed
2 pimientos, minced
2 green onions, chopped, or 1 small onion, minced
Salt and pepper to taste
Paprika

Cut fillets in serving pieces if necessary. Mix ¼ cup melted butter, 2 tablespoons parsley and remaining ingredients, except paprika. Divide onto fillets and roll up from small end, securing with toothpicks. Put in baking dish and brush with melted butter. Bake in moderate oven (375°F.) 30 minutes. Sprinkle with parsley and paprika. Makes 6 servings.

Quick Stuffed Fillets Prepare ½ package stuffing mix and use to stuff fillets. Proceed as directed above.

PANFRIED PORGIES WITH SHERRY-ALMOND SAUCE

4 porgies (about 1 pound each)
1/2 cup undiluted evaporated milk
1/3 cup each flour and yellow cornmeal
1 tablespoon salt
1/4 teaspoon pepper
Fat for frying
1/2 cup slivered blanched almonds
1/4 cup melted butter
1/4 cup dry sherry
Parsley or watercress

Wipe fish with a paper towel. Dip in evaporated milk. Combine next 4 ingredients; roll fish in mixture. Heat enough fat to cover bottom of skillet and panfry fish about 5 minutes on each side, adding more fat as needed. Cook almonds in butter until lightly browned, add sherry and heat thoroughly. Remove fish to a hot platter and cover with the sauce. Garnish with sprigs of parsley. Serves 4.

HANGCHOW SWEET-SOUR FISH

1 large- or small-mouthed bass (1-1/2
   to 2 pounds), dressed
1 tablespoon dry sherry
Few slices gingerroot
1/2 cup sugar
1/3 cup cider vinegar
1 tablespoon soy sauce
1/4 teaspoon gingerroot juice
2 tablespoons cornstarch
1 clove garlic, crushed (optional)

Rinse fish in cold water and drain. Slash crosswise on each side along backbone in meaty part, making three equal diagonal cuts for even cooking. Boil enough water in large oval roasting pan or other shallow pan to completely cover fish. Lower fish gently into the boiling water; and sherry and ginger slices. Cover tightly and remove at once from heat. Let stand 15 to 20 minutes (fish will be cooked). Meanwhile, combine remaining ingredients in small saucepan and cook, stirring, until thickened. Discard garlic if used. Remove fish carefully to serving platter and pour hot sauce over top. Makes 2 servings.

LEMON BAKED FISH

1 pound fish fillets
Juice of 1 lemon
1 teaspoon salt
1-1/2 teaspoons dried dill
1/2 teaspoon paprika
1 tablespoon butter or margarine
1 lemon, peeled and thinly sliced
1 tablespoon parsley flakes

Place fish in greased baking dish and sprinkle with lemon juice and seasonings. Dot with butter. Arrange lemon slices on fish. Bake in slow oven (325°F.) 20 minutes, or until fish flakes easily with work. Sprinkle with parsley flakes. Makes 4 servings.

CURRIED COD FILLETS

2 packages (1 pound each) frozen cod,
   thawed and cut in 6 pieces
3/4 teaspoon salt
1/4 cup butter or margarine
1 tablespoon curry powder
1 cup each chopped onion and
   chopped peeled apple
3/4 cup each catsup and light cream

Arrange fish in buttered shallow 2-quart baking dish. Sprinkle with salt. Melt butter in skillet; add curry, onion and apple. Simmer, stirring, about 5 minutes. Divide on fish. Add catsup and cream to skillet, stir to mix and pour around fish. Bake in moderate oven (350°F.) 30 minutes, or until fish is opaque and flakes easily with fork. Makes 4 to 6 servings.

FISH-VEGETABLE PIE

1 pound fish fillets, cut in 1" pieces
6 carrots, diced
4 medium potatoes, diced
4 medium onions, sliced
Salt
3 tablespoons butter or margarine
3 tablespoons flour
1-1/2 cups milk
1/4 teaspoon pepper
1 can (8 ounces) refrigerated biscuits

Cook fish and vegetables in boiling salted water 10 minutes, or until vegetables are just tender. Drain; reserve liquid, adding water if necessary to make 1½ cups. Melt butter and blend in flour. Add liquid from vegetables, the milk, 1 teaspoon salt and the pepper and cook, stirring, until thickened. Put fish and vegetables in greased 9" round or square baking dish, pour on sauce and top with biscuits. Bake in hot oven (400°F.) about 20 minutes. Makes 4 servings.

STUFFED FISH ROLLS

1 pound fish fillets
2 tablespoons soy sauce
1 tablespoon shredded fresh gingerroot
1/2 pound spinach
1/2 cup ground ham
1/2 clove garlic, minced
1 egg
1 cup all-purpose flour
1/4 teaspoon salt
1/2 teaspoon sesame seed
Oil for deep frying

Marinate fillets in soy sauce and ginger. Blanch spinach in boiling water, drain and mince. Add ham and garlic. Spread some of mixture on fish fillets and roll each, like a jelly roll. Fasten with toothpicks. Beat egg; add flour and ½ cup water alternately to make a batter. Add salt. Dip fillets in batter, then into sesame seed. Fry in hot deep oil (375° F. on frying thermometer) until golden. Serves 4.

FISH-NOODLE-CLAM CASSEROLE

1 pound cod fillets, cooked
4 cups medium noodles, cooked
1 can (8 ounces) minced clams
Salt and pepper
1 tablespoon butter or margarine
1 package (9 ounces) prepared frozen
   creamed spinach

Break fish in chunks; mix with noodles in greased 2-quart casserole. Drain clams; add to noodles with ½ cup of drained liquid. Salt and pepper to taste. Dot wth butter. Pour cooked spinach over top. Bake in moderate oven (350°F.) 25 minutes, or until hot and bubbly. Serves 4 to 6.

FISH FILLETS FLORENTINE

Cook and drain 2 boxes frozen chopped spinach. Put in shallow casserole. Poach 1 pound white fish fillets in boiling salted water. Put fish on spinach. Thaw 1 can frozen condensed cream of shrimp soup and dilute with 1/4 cup milk. Pour over fish. Bake in hot oven (400°F.) 15 to 20 minutes. Makes 3 to 4 servings.

LITTLE FISH IN PAPILLOTES

Small fresh fish cooked in envelopes.

Vegetable oil
6 to 8 small whole fish, cleaned
3 tablespoons chopped parsley
1/4 cup chopped mushrooms
Salt and pepper
2 peeled tomatoes, sliced
6 to 8 lemon slices

Cut 6 to 8 heart-shaped pieces of foil or parchment large enough to hold the fish with some room left for expansion. Place a well-oiled fish to one side of each piece of paper. Sprinkle with chopped parsley, mushrooms and salt and pepper. Top with a slice of tomato and a slice of lemon. Fold over the other half of the foil or parchment to envelop the fish and crimp the edges together to make the package airtight. Arrange the *papillotes* in a baking pan and bake in a hot oven (400°F.) 20 to 25 minutes. Place the fish in their envelopes on plates and serve. Serves 6 to 8.

GERMAN FISH PUDDING

3 cups (about 1-1/2 pounds raw)
  flaked, boiled or poached fish
1 onion, chopped
1/4 cup butter or margarine
2 tablespoons flour
2 cups milk
1 teaspoon salt
2 tablespoons capers
3 tablespoons grated Parmesan cheese
1/2 teaspoon lemon juice
1-1/2 quarts potatoes, peeled and thinly
  sliced (about 1-1/2 pounds)
2 tablespoons fine dry bread crumbs
1 tablespoon butter

Bone fish; flake or cut in small pieces. Cook onion in butter until soft but not brown. Stir in flour. Gradually add milk and stir over low heat until sauce bubbles and thickens a little. Add next 4 ingredients. Layer potatoes and fish in 2-quart casserole, ending with potato. Cover with sauce. Sprinkle top with crumbs and dot with butter. Bake in moderate oven (350°F.) 1 hour, or until potato is tender. Makes 6 servings.

MUSTARD FISH AND CHIPS

Put 1 pound fish fillets in baking dish. Mix 1/4 cup salad dressing, 2 teaspoons prepared mustard and 2 tablespoons minced onion. Spread on fish. Sprinkle with paprika. Bake in extremely hot oven (500°F.) 15 minutes, along with 1 box frozen French fries. Makes 2 to 3 servings.

FISH AND CHIPS

Cut white or any mild-flavored fish in narrow strips and roll lightly in salted flour or Fritter Batter. Fry in hot deep fat (370°F. on a frying thermometer) until crisp and golden brown. Drain on paper towels. Serve hot with crisp hot French fries. If fish strips are dipped in batter they will be puffy and light like fried shrimp. Two kettles of fat are usually used in fish-and-chips shops, but at home you may pre-fry the French fries, then brown quickly in hot fat after removing fish. Or you can always heat frozen French fries until crisp in the oven. **Fritter Batter** Sift 2 cups all-purpose flour with 1 tablespoon salt and 2 teaspoons baking powder. Roll fish strips lightly in this. Beat 2 eggs and add enough milk to make 1 1/2 cups. Stir in flour, and 1 tablespoon vegetable oil, if desired. Dip floured fish in batter, then fry.

KEDGEREE

1 pound cod fillets, cooked and flaked
2 cups hot cooked rice
4 hard-cooked eggs, chopped
1/8 teaspoon pepper
3 tablespoons minced parsley
1/2 cup light cream
1 tablespoon butter or margarine
1 teaspoon salt
1/4 teaspoon curry powder

Put fish in top part of double boiler with remaining ingredients. Heat thoroughly over hot water. Serves 4.

BAKED WHOLE FISH

Stuff whole red snapper, bluefish or haddock lightly with well-seasoned bread stuffing. Cut 3 or 4 gashes in skin and insert thin slices of salt pork or bacon. Put a pinch of thyme or marjoram, 1 minced onion, 3 tablespoons minced parsley and 2 tablespoons fat in baking pan. Put fish in pan; bake in moderate oven (350°F.) until fish flakes easily with a fork. Makes 4 to 6 servings.

FIFTEEN-MINUTE FISH DINNER

1 can (1 pound) tomatoes
2 tablespoons butter or margarine
1-1/2 cups thinly sliced celery
2 medium onions, sliced
1 pound frozen fish fillets, cut in 1/2"
 slices
Salt and pepper
1 can (1 pound) sliced potatoes, drained
1/4 cup minced parsley

Drain liquid from tomatoes; put it in skillet with butter. Bring to boil and add celery and onions; simmer 5 minutes. Arrange a layer of fish slices on celery and onions and sprinkle with salt and pepper. Add tomatoes and potatoes, cover and simmer 10 minutes. Add parsley and season. Makes 4 servings.

POACHED FISH, SICILIAN STYLE

4 slices halibut or swordfish or other
 thick fish (1-3/4 to 2 pounds)
1/4 cup olive oil
1 tablespoon chopped parsley
1 clove garlic, minced
1/2 cup white vinegar
2 pounds tomatoes, peeled, seeded and
 chopped
Salt and pepper
1 package (10 ounces) frozen peas,
 thawed

In skillet, brown fish in hot oil. Add next 3 ingredients. Cook until liquid has almost evaporated. Add tomatoes, salt and pepper. Simmer, covered, 20 minutes. Add peas. Simmer, covered, about 15 minutes. Put fish on hot platter and pour sauce over it. Makes 4 to 6 servings.

FRIDAY NIGHT CASSEROLE

1 box each frozen lima beans and cut
 corn
1/4 cup soft butter or margarine
1 can condensed cream of celery soup
1/2 cup undiluted evaporated milk
3/4 teaspoon celery salt
Salt and pepper
1 pound frozen cod or haddock fillets,
 thawed
3 tablespoons mayonnaise

Put beans and corn in saucepan and cover with 2 cups boiling water. Let stand 8 minutes; drain. Add 2 tablespoons butter. Mix next 3 ingredients, 1/2 teaspoon salt and 1/8 teaspoon pepper. Mix with vegetables. Put fish in shallow baking dish and spread with soft butter. Sprinkle with salt and pepper. Pour vegetable mixture over top. Bake in hot oven (425°F.) 25 minutes. Spread mayonnaise over top and bake 10 minutes longer. Makes 4 servings.

SEAFOOD SUPREME

2 cans (6-1/2 ounces each) king crab
 meat or 2 boxes (6 ounces each)
 frozen crab meat, thawed
2 lobster tails, cooked and cut up
1 pound cod fillets, poached
1 can frozen condensed cream of shrimp
 soup, thawed
1 can condensed cream of mushroom
 soup
1/2 cup heavy cream
2 tablespoons sherry
Dash of pepper
2 tablespoons fine dry bread crumbs
1/4 cup grated Parmesan cheese
Paprika
2 tablespoons butter or margarine

Flake crab meat. Add all but last 4 ingredients and mix well. Pour into shallow 1½-quart baking dish. Sprinkle with crumbs, cheese and paprika. Dot with butter. Bake in moderate oven (350°F.) about 30 minutes. Makes 6 to 8 servings.

TONGFILLETS MET GARNALEN
(Dutch Fillets of Sole
with Shrimps)

1 cup white wine
1 small onion
1/2 teaspoon thyme
4 slices lemon
1 bay leaf
Salt and white pepper to taste
Parsley
6 portions fillets of sole (or flounder)
3 tablespoons butter
3 tablespoons flour
1 cup heavy cream
2 egg yolks
1 cup cooked medium shrimps, fresh,
 frozen or canned

In shallow saucepan, combine the first 5 ingredients, salt and pepper, 1 sprig parsley and 4 cups water for court bouillon; simmer 10 minutes. Sprinkle fillets with salt and pepper, roll up and secure with toothpicks. Place in the bouillon; simmer 6 to 8 minutes, or until fish flakes easily when tested with a fork. Be careful not to overcook, for they are to be reheated. Drain well and put on a hot plate; remove toothpicks. Reduce broth to about 2 cups over high heat. Strain. Melt butter in a saucepan and blend in flour. Simmer 3 minutes. Gradually stir in 1¼ cups reduced broth and continue stirring until thickened. Combine cream and egg yolks; add a little of the hot sauce. Stir egg mixture into hot sauce in pan; heat through but keep below boiling point. Add salt and pepper to taste and shrimps, reserving a few for garnishing. Heat and pour over fish. Garnish with reserved shrimps and chopped parsley. Makes 6 servings.

FISH-STICK PASTRIES

Prepare 1 box pastry mix as directed on package; roll to form 12″ x 6″ rectangle. Cut in eight 3″ squares. Spread some prepared mustard in center of each square. Put a narrow strip of sharp Cheddar cheese diagonally across each square. Cover with a fish stick. Fold opposite corners over center of stick and secure with toothpick. Put on a cookie sheet and bake in very hot oven (450°F.) about 15 minutes. Makes 4 servings.

JANSSON'S TEMPTATION

3 to 4 medium baking potatoes, peeled
  and cut in matchsticks (1 quart)
3/4 cup minced onion
Butter
Freshly grated pepper
1 can (2 ounces) anchovy fillets, drained
  and cut in pieces
1 cup each light cream and milk, scalded

In shallow 1½-quart baking dish, put half the potato and onion, dot with butter and sprinkle with pepper and half the anchovy fillets. Repeat layers. Carefully pour in hot cream and milk. Dot with more butter. Bake in slow oven (325°F.) 45 to 60 minutes, or until most of liquid has cooked into potato and top is flecked with brown. Makes 4 supper servings, or 8 for smorgasbord.

PIQUANT WHITEFISH

1 pound whitefish fillets
1 tablespoon oil
1 tablespoon vinegar
2 tablespoons minced onion
1 teaspoon salt
2 teaspoons Worcestershire
1/3 cup catsup
1 tablespoon capers
1 cup cooked green peas

Cut fish in serving-size pieces. Bring next 6 ingredients and ¼ cup water to boil in top part of double boiler. Add capers and fish. Cover and cook over boiling water 25 minutes, stirring several times. Add peas and heat. Makes 4 servings.

MARINATED WHITING

Cut 1½ pounds whiting fillets in serving-size pieces. Pour ½ cup highly seasoned French dressing over fish and chill for several hours. Arrange fish on broiler rack; broil under medium heat 5 minutes on each side, brushing with marinade. To serve, pour drippings over fish and sprinkle with paprika. Makes 4 servings.

HADDOCK-POTATO PATTIES

4 medium potatoes
1 pound haddock fillets, cooked and
  flaked
1 egg, beaten
2 tablespoons minced onion
1 teaspoon poultry seasoning
Salt and pepper
Flour
Fat for frying

Cook potatoes; mash. Add next 4 ingredients and salt and pepper to taste. Shape into 8 flat patties, roll in flour and panfry in hot fat until brown. Makes 4 servings.

SCANDINAVIAN FISH STEW

2 pounds fish with skin and bones
6 medium potatoes, peeled and diced
1 large onion, diced
2 teaspoons salt, or to taste
10 whole allspice
1/4 teaspoon coarse black pepper
Butter or margarine
Chopped parsley

Cut fish crosswise in serving-size chunks. Put in kettle with vegetables, seasonings and ½ cup butter. Add just enough water to cover. Bring slowly to boil and cook gently 15 minutes, or until potato is tender. Remove fish, pour a little melted butter over top and sprinkle with parsley. Serve soup separately in bowls. Makes 6 servings.

RED-SNAPPER STEW

1/2 cup olive or vegetable oil
2 tablespoons flour
2 onions, chopped
1 clove garlic, minced
Few sprigs of parsley, chopped
2 or 3 green onions, chopped
1 can (1 pound) tomatoes
1 green pepper, chopped
2 celery stalks, diced
Dash of thyme
2 bay leaves
1 tablespoon Worcestershire
3 thin slices lemon
Salt and pepper
Dash of hot pepper sauce
Pinch of allspice
1/2 cup claret
1 tablespoon port (optional)
2 pounds red-snapper steaks, cut 1″
  thick

Blend first 2 ingredients in skillet. Add onion and garlic; brown lightly. Add remaining ingredients, except fish; simmer, covered, 15 minutes. Add fish, cook 10 minutes, turn and cook 10 minutes longer. Makes 6 servings.

POACHED SALMON TROUT WITH TOMATO HOLLANDAISE

1 onion
1 carrot
1 stalk celery
1 teaspoon vinegar
1 teaspoon dried tarragon
1/2 teaspoon salt
1/4 teaspoon pepper
Parsley
1 salmon trout (4 to 5 pounds)
Lemon wedges
Hollandaise Sauce (page 222)
1 teaspoon prepared mustard
1 teaspoon tomato paste

Put first 7 ingredients, 1 sprig parsley and 2 to 3 cups water in large heavy skillet. Boil rapidly 10 minutes. Wrap fish in cheesecloth, leaving long ends of cloth for handles. (Or use regular fish boiler with rack.) Lower fish into bouillon, add more boiling water if needed to cover fish and poach gently. Cook 5 or 6 minutes per pound, or until flesh flakes easily when tested with a fork or toothpick. Remove from bouillon; carefully unwrap onto a serving platter. Garnish with parsley and lemon wedges. Serve with Hollandaise Sauce flavored with mustard and tomato paste. Makes 8 servings.

MAMA MIA'S SALMON SPECIAL

1 medium onion, minced
1 clove garlic, minced
1/4 cup olive oil
2 cans (1 pound each) tomatoes, chopped
1 can (6 ounces) tomato paste
1 teaspoon salt
1/2 teaspoon pepper
1 teaspoon basil
1/2 teaspoon oregano
1/4 cup chopped parsley
1 pound broad green noodles or mafalde
8 ounces mozzarella, sliced
1 pound ricotta or creamed cottage cheese
1 can (1 pound) red or pink salmon, drained and flaked
1/2 cup grated Parmesan cheese

Cook onion and garlic in hot olive oil until soft. Add next 7 ingredients and simmer 30 minutes, stirring frequently. Cook and drain noodles. Spread about one fourth of sauce on bottom and sides of greased shallow 2-quart baking dish. Top with a layer of noodles placed lengthwise, a layer of mozzarella, one of ricotta and one of salmon; sprinkle with Parmesan cheese. Repeat layers, ending with noodles. Cover top with remaining sauce and sprinkle with remaining Parmesan. Bake in moderate oven (350°F.) 30 minutes. Makes 6 to 8 servings.

BROILED SALMON WITH HERBS

2 pounds salmon steaks, about 3/4" thick
1 tablespoon grated onion
Juice of 1 lemon
6 tablespoons melted butter or margarine
1 teaspoon salt
1/4 teaspoon pepper
1/2 teaspoon marjoram
1 tablespoon minced watercress or chives
2 tablespoons minced parsley

Arrange fish on greased broiler rack. Mix remaining ingredients and pour half over steaks. Broil about 6 minutes under medium heat; turn and pour remaining sauce over. Broil 5 or 6 minutes longer. Serves 4 to 6.

BAKED SALMON WITH CAPER BUTTER

4 salmon steaks, 1" to 1-1/2" thick
1/3 cup lemon juice
1/2 cup butter
Salt and pepper
1/4 cup chopped parsley
1/2 cup chopped capers

Rub salmon steaks with part of lemon juice, brush well with melted butter and sprinkle with salt and pepper. Arrange in baking dish and bake in hot oven (425°F.) about 20 minutes, basting several times with melted butter and lemon juice. Do not turn. Add parsley and capers and baste again. If additional liquid is needed, add a little dry vermouth or white wine. Makes 4 servings.

SALMON MOUNDS WITH CURRY-MUSHROOM SAUCE

1 small onion, minced
1/4 cup melted butter
1 can (1 pound) salmon
Milk
3 cups soft bread crumbs
2 eggs
1/4 teaspoon poultry seasoning
1/4 cup minced parsley
1/4 teaspoon salt
Dash of nutmeg
1 can condensed cream of mushroom soup
1/2 teaspoon curry powder
1/2 teaspoon paprika
2 stuffed olives, sliced

Cook onion in butter until golden. Drain salmon, reserving liquid. Add enough milk to liquid to make 1/2 cup. Mix onion, salmon, liquid, crumbs and next 5 ingredients. Shape into 6 mounds in large shallow baking dish. Mix 1/2 cup milk, the soup, curry powder and paprika. Pour around salmon. Top each salmon mound with a slice of olive. Bake, uncovered, in moderate oven (350°F.) about 45 minutes. Serves 6.

SALMON-NOODLE BAKE

1 medium onion, minced
1 clove garlic, minced
1/4 cup olive oil
2 cans (1 pound each) tomatoes, chopped
1 can (6 ounces) tomato paste
1 teaspoon salt
1/2 teaspoon pepper
1 teaspoon basil
1/2 teaspoon oregano
1/4 cup chopped parsley
1 pound broad spinach noodles or mafalde
8 ounces mozzarella, sliced
1 pound ricotta or creamed cottage cheese
1 can (1 pound) salmon, drained, flaked
1/2 cup grated Parmesan cheese

In saucepan, cook onion and garlic in hot olive oil until soft. Add next 7 ingredients and simmer, stirring frequently, 30 minutes. Cook and drain noodles. Spread about one-fourth of sauce on bottom and sides of buttered shallow 2-quart baking dish. Top with a layer of noodles, a layer of mozzarella, one of ricotta and one of salmon; sprinkle with Parmesan cheese. Repeat layers, ending with noodles. Cover with remaining sauce and sprinkle with remaining Parmesan. Bake in moderate oven (350°F.) about 30 minutes. Serves 6.

SALMON BISCUIT ROLL WITH LEMON SAUCE

1/2 cup each chopped celery and green pepper
1/4 cup sliced green onion
2 tablespoons butter or margarine
1/2 cup chopped black olives
1 can (1 pound) salmon
1-3/4 cups all-purpose flour
2-1/2 teaspoons double-acting baking powder
3/4 teaspoon salt
1/3 cup shortening
Milk
Sesame seed
Lemon Sauce (above right)

Sauté vegetables lightly in butter; add olives. Drain salmon, reserving liquid for sauce, flake and add to vegetables. Mix next 3 ingredients and cut in shortening. With fork, stir in ³/₄ cup milk, or just enough to hold ingredients together. Turn out on lightly floured board and knead about 12 turns. Roll to a rectangle about 12″ x 9″. Spread with salmon mixture and roll up lengthwise as for jelly roll. Put in greased shallow baking dish, brush with 1 tablespoon milk and sprinkle with sesame seed. Bake in hot oven (400°F.) 25 to 30 minutes. Slice and serve hot with sauce. Makes 6 servings.

Lemon Sauce Melt 2 tablespoons butter and blend in 2 tablespoons flour. Add enough milk to salmon liquid to make 1¹/₂ cups and stir gradually into first mixture. Cook, stirring, until thickened. Season and add 1 tablespoon lemon juice.

POACHED SALMON STEAKS

1 tablespoon white vinegar or lemon juice
1 tablespoon salt
2 onion slices
Fresh dill or parsley sprigs
4 or 5 white peppercorns
4 small salmon steaks
Béarnaise Sauce (page 61)

Put 4 cups boiling water and first 5 ingredients in large skillet. Bring to boil and carefully add salmon steaks in single layer (need not be thawed if frozen). Bring again to boil, cover and simmer 6 to 8 minutes, or until fish flakes easily with fork. Remove with slotted spoon to hot platter and serve with sauce. Makes 4 servings. **Note** To serve cold, cool fish in the broth, cover and chill until ready to serve.

GRAVAD LAX (Cured salmon, Scandinavian style)

For each pound of salmon, use 2 tablespoons salt, 1¹/₂ tablespoons sugar, 5 white peppercorns (crushed) and plenty of fresh dill sprigs. Select a middle cut of fresh salmon, if possible. Scrape and dry with paper towels (do not rinse). Cut salmon in fillets and pull out any small bones (a sharp, thin-bladed knife is best for this). Make a layer of dill sprigs in deep china or stainless-steel casserole. Mix seasonings and rub some on both sides of salmon fillets. Put 1 fillet, skin side down, on dill and cover with more dill. Cover with second fillet and sprinkle with remaining spice mixture. Add more dill and put a weighted dish on top. Refrigerate 24 hours or longer, turning salmon each day. Can be stored 1 to 3 weeks. When ready to serve, scrape off spices, cut salmon diagonally in thin slices away from skin and arrange in single layer (or roll up) on serving plate. Serve as hors d'oeuvre on toast with Green Sauce (page 202), fresh dill sprigs and coarsely grated pepper. Skin can be cut in strips and quickly sautéed to serve as a hot hors d'oeuvre. For a main dish, cut salmon in thin slices and sauté quickly in a little butter or margarine.

HOT SALMON MOUSSE

1 can (1 pound) red salmon
3/4 teaspoon salt
1/4 teaspoon pepper
1 teaspoon Worcestershire
1 teaspoon onion juice
3 egg whites
1 cup heavy cream
Mayonnaise or Many-purpose Sauce
    (page 261)

Drain salmon and remove skin. Whirl salmon in blender or force through food chopper, using fine blade. Add seasonings and mix well. Add egg whites one at a time, blending thoroughly after each addition. Add cream and mix well. Pour into well-oiled 1½-quart mold and set in pan of hot water. Bake in moderate oven (375°F.) 30 to 40 minutes, or until mixture is firm and inserted knife comes out clean. Unmold on hot platter and serve with mayonnaise. Makes 4 to 6 servings.

SALMON-EGG QUICHE

Unbaked deep 9" pie shell
1 can (1 pound) salmon
Juice of 1/2 lemon
1 onion, minced
2 tablespoons butter or margarine
2 tablespoons chopped parsley
6 eggs, beaten
1-1/2 cups light cream or milk
1 teaspoon seasoned salt
1/4 teaspoon pepper

Bake shell in very hot oven (450°F.) 5 minutes. Drain salmon liquid into bowl. Remove bones and skin and flake salmon. Put in pie shell and sprinkle with lemon juice. Cook onion lightly in the butter. Sprinkle onion and parsley on salmon. Mix salmon liquid and remaining ingredients. Pour over salmon. Bake in moderate oven (350°F.) 50 minutes, or until firm. Cut in wedges and serve hot. Makes 6 servings.

FISH FILLETS IN MUSHROOM-CHEESE SAUCE

1-1/2 pounds fish fillets
Salt and pepper
1 can condensed cream of mushroom
    soup
1 cup grated sharp Cheddar cheese
1/4 cup sherry
Paprika

Cut fish in serving pieces and arrange in baking dish. Season. Mix next 3 ingredients and spread on fish. Top with paprika and bake in moderate oven (375°F.) about 25 minutes. Makes 4 to 6 servings.

BAKED SWORDFISH, MAYONNAISE

Season 2 pounds swordfish with salt and pepper. Spread generously with mayonnaise and sprinkle lightly with instant minced onion, then with corn-flake crumbs, fine dry bread crumbs or cracker crumbs. Bake in hot oven (400°F.) about 30 minutes. Serves 4.

SWORDFISH AMANDINE

1/2 cup chopped almonds
8 tablespoons butter
Few sprigs of parsley, chopped
1 lemon
4 swordfish steaks
Sherry
Pepper
2 green onions, chopped
8 slices crumbled crisp bacon
Paprika

Brown almonds lightly in 2 tablespoons butter. Melt remaining 6 tablespoons butter; add some chopped parsley and the grated rind and juice of ½ lemon. Put fish on foil-covered broiler pan. Put 1 tablespoon sherry on each steak and sprinkle with pepper. Spoon some of butter mixture over each. Broil under medium heat 10 minutes, basting with sherry-butter mixture. Turn fish; baste. Broil 10 minutes longer. Sprinkle with almonds, green onion and bacon. Garnish with lemon slices and paprika. Makes 4 servings.

SWORDFISH WITH TOMATO SAUCE

1-1/2 pounds swordfish, 1-1/2" thick
7 tablespoons olive oil
1 cup finely chopped parsley
2 cloves garlic, minced
Juice of 1 lemon
1 can (8 ounces) tomato sauce
Salt and pepper

Cut fish in serving pieces and arrange in baking dish. Simmer next 3 ingredients 10 minutes. Add lemon juice and sauce; heat and season. Pour over fish. Bake in hot oven (425°F.) 25 minutes. Makes 3 or 4 servings.

CHILI BAKED PERCH

Put 1 pound ocean-perch fillets in shallow baking dish. Mix ³/₄ cup chili sauce, ¼ cup red Burgundy and 2 tablespoons instant minced onion. Spread on fish and sprinkle with ³/₄ cup grated process American cheese. Bake in very hot oven (450° F.) 15 to 20 minutes. Makes 4 servings.

GOLDEN FLOUNDER FILLETS

Season flounder fillets and sauté in hot butter 3 to 5 minutes on each side. Serve with **Maître d'Hôtel Butter:** Melt 1/2 cup butter; add 1 tablespoon lemon juice, 1/8 teaspoon each salt and pepper and 1 teaspoon minced parsley.

OVEN FISH CHOWDER

2 pounds cod or haddock fillets
4 potatoes, sliced
Few chopped celery leaves
1 bay leaf
2-1/2 teaspoons salt
4 whole cloves
1 clove garlic
3 onions, sliced
1/4 pound butter
1/4 teaspoon dried dillweed
1/4 teaspoon white pepper
1/2 cup dry white wine
2 cups light cream
Chopped parsley

Put all ingredients, except last 2, in 3-quart casserole. Cover and bake in moderate oven (375°F.) 1 hour. Heat cream to scalding. Add to chowder. Serve with garnish of chopped parsley. Makes 6 servings.

SHERRIED TUNA

2 cans (about 7 ounces each) tuna in oil
2 tablespoons flour
1/8 teaspoon salt
2/3 cup milk
1/3 cup sherry
1 tablespoon lemon juice
1 tablespoon chopped parsley
1/4 cup canned toasted diced almonds

Drain oil from tuna into skillet or chafing dish. Blend in flour and salt. Gradually add milk and cook, stirring, until thickened. Add remaining ingredients, except nuts, and heat. Sprinkle with nuts. Serves 4.

TUNA MARKA

2 cans (7 ounces each) white tuna in oil
1/2 cup chopped green onions
1 tablespoon butter
1/2 cup sliced water chestnuts
2 teaspoons slivered fresh or candied
  ginger
2 cups dairy sour cream
Salt and pepper to taste
Hot cooked rice

Drain tuna oil into pan, add onion and butter and cook until wilted. Add tuna, broken in large flakes, and remaining ingredients, except rice. Heat gently. Serve with rice. Makes 6 servings.

SOUTHERN FISH GRILL

Wrap cleaned and washed small fish in bacon and pin with toothpicks. Cook slowly on grill over coals, turning carefully once or twice. They're done when fish flakes easily with fork. Thawed frozen fish fillets cut in individual servings can also be cooked this way.

SMELTS WITH CAPER SAUCE

2 pounds smelts
1/3 cup undiluted evaporated milk
1/3 cup flour
1/2 cup yellow cornmeal
2 teaspoons salt
1/8 teaspoon pepper
Fat for frying
1/4 cup butter
Juice of 1/2 lemon
1 tablespoon capers
1 tablespoon minced parsley

Dip fish in milk, then roll in combined flour, cornmeal and seasonings. Heat enough fat to cover the bottom of skillet. Fry fish 5 minutes on each side, or until well-browned and done. Meanwhile, melt butter; add lemon juice, capers and parsley. Pour over hot fish. Makes 4 servings.

BARCELONA TUNA AND EGGS

In 2 tablespoons olive oil, cook 1 chopped medium green pepper and 1 chopped onion 5 minutes. Beat 8 eggs; add 1 can (9 1/4 ounces) tuna, flaked, 1/2 teaspoon salt and 1/8 teaspoon pepper. Mix well and pour into skillet with vegetables. Cook, lifting edges with spatula and tilting skillet to allow uncooked egg to run under. Divide in portions and turn each to brown. Serve on toast spread with mayonnaise. Serves 4 to 6.

TUNA EGGS FOO YUNG

Pour boiling water over 1/4 pound of bean sprouts, let stand 1 minute and drain (or use a 1-pound can, drained). Mix with 1/2 cup thinly sliced green onions, 1/2 cup minced water chestnuts, 5 slightly beaten eggs, 1 tablespoon soy sauce, and 1 can (7 ounces) tuna, broken up. Cook by the spoonful on a griddle or in a skillet. Turn and brown other side. Serve with a sauce made by seasoning 1 cup chicken stock with 2 tablespoons soy sauce, thickened with 4 teaspoons cornstarch moistened with 2 tablespoons cold water. Cook until thickened and clear. Makes 4 servings.

SOUR-CREAM TUNA CASSEROLE

2 cans (7 ounces each) tuna, drained
  and flaked
1 tablespoon lemon juice
1 can (1 pound) whole potatoes, drained
1 medium onion, minced
1 clove garlic, crushed
1 small green pepper, chopped
2 tablespoons butter
1 teaspoon curry powder
Salt and pepper
Dash each of monosodium glutamate and
  cayenne
1 cup dairy sour cream

Toss tuna with lemon juice. Put potatoes in greased shallow 1½-quart casserole. Cook onion, garlic and green pepper in butter 2 or 3 minutes. Add tuna, seasonings and sour cream; mix well. Pour over potatoes. Bake in moderate oven (375°F.) 35 to 40 minutes. Makes 6 servings.

SHERRIED TUNA

1 can (10-1/2 ounces) condensed cream
  of chicken soup
Milk
2 cans (7 ounces each) water-packed
  tuna, drained and liquid reserved
1 teaspoon paprika
2 tablespoons sherry

Heat soup in saucepan. Add enough milk to tuna liquid to measure ⅓ cup. Add with paprika to soup and mix well. Break tuna in chunks and fold into mixture. Add sherry and heat gently. Good on cooked rice, mashed or riced potatoes or as a filling for crepes or omelets. Makes 4 servings.

TUNA AND CABBAGE PIROG

1 package hot-roll mix
4 cups finely chopped cabbage
1 onion, chopped
1/4 cup butter
1 can (7 ounces) tuna
2 tablespoons dillweed
Salt and pepper
1 egg

Make hot-roll mix according to directions on the box. Cook cabbage and onion in butter until wilted. Add tuna, flaked, and dillweed. Season to taste with salt and pepper. After dough has risen, divide in half and roll each half into a rectangle about 9″ x 11″. Put one rectangle on a greased shallow baking pan and spread with tuna-cabbage mixture. Moisten edges and top with second rectangle; seal. Brush top with egg beaten with 1 tablespoon water. Bake in hot oven (400°F.) for 15 to 20 minutes, or until nicely browned. Cut in squares to make 12 servings.

TUNA-SWISS CASSEROLE

1-1/2 cups milk or light cream
2 tablespoons butter
1 cup soft bread crumbs
1 canned pimiento, chopped
2 tablespoons chopped parsley
2 tablespoons minced onion
1-1/2 cups grated Swiss cheese
1/2 teaspoon salt
Dash each of pepper and paprika
3 eggs, beaten
3 cans (7 ounces each) white-meat
  tuna, drained and flaked

Heat milk and butter until butter is melted and pour over crumbs. Add all ingredients, except last 2, and mix well. Slowly stir in eggs. Arrange tuna in greased 1½-quart casserole, then pour in mixture. Set casserole in pan of hot water and bake in slow oven (325°F.) about 1 hour and 15 minutes. Makes 6 to 8 servings.

TUNA FRIED RICE

4 green onions, sliced
2 tablespoons peanut, soy or corn oil
6 cups dry cooked rice
1 egg, slightly beaten
3 tablespoons soy sauce
1 can (7 ounces) tuna, flaked

Cook 3 tablespoons onion in oil for 1 minute. Add rice and stir until hot. Add egg mixed with soy sauce. Cook, stirring, until the egg is set, then fold in tuna and heat. Serve sprinkled with the remaining onion. Serves 6.

TUNA PAPRIKA WITH GREEN RICE

1 cup packaged parboiled long-grain rice
Salt
2 cans (7 ounces each) tuna
1 can (10-1/2 ounces) condensed cream
  of mushroom soup
1 to 2 tablespoons paprika
1 can (4 ounces) sliced mushrooms,
  undrained
3/4 cup dairy sour cream
Pepper
1/2 cup each chopped green onion and
  parsley
Cherry tomatoes

Cook rice in boiling salted water as directed on label. Meanwhile, flake tuna, reserving liquid. Heat soup and add paprika, the mushrooms, tuna and liquid; fold in sour cream. Heat gently. Season to taste with salt and pepper. Add green onion and parsley to hot cooked rice and mix carefully. With spoon, press rice mixture into oiled half measuring cup. Unmold around edge of heated platter. Repeat until all of mixture is used, or use greased 3-cup ring mold. Fill center with tuna mixture and garnish with tomatoes. Makes 6 servings.

TUNA GREEN-BEAN CASSEROLE

2 tablespoons minced onion
Butter
2 tablespoons flour
1 cup milk
1/4 cup chicken stock
1 tablespoon (or more) prepared mustard
1/2 pound green beans, cooked
2 hard-cooked eggs, chopped
1 can (7 ounces) tuna, flaked
1 tablespoon minced parsley
1/2 teaspoon dried tarragon (optional)
Salt and pepper
1/4 cup fine dry bread crumbs

Cook onion in 2 tablespoons butter until wilted. Add next 4 ingredients and cook, stirring, until thickened. Add green beans and next 4 ingredients. Season to taste. Put in greased 1-quart casserole and sprinkle with crumbs mixed with 2 tablespoons melted butter. Bake in oven about 20 minutes. Makes 4 servings.

TUNA-PEA CASSEROLE

1 can (7 ounces) tuna, undrained
1 can (8 ounces) green peas, drained
Pinch of dried thyme leaves
1/2 cup chopped black olives
1 can (10-1/2 ounces) condensed cream of mushroom soup

Break tuna in chunks and make a layer, including liquid, in greased shallow 1-quart baking dish. Sprinkle with the peas. Season lightly with thyme. Add olives and spread soup on top to cover. Bake in slow oven (300°F.) 30 minutes, or until heated. Makes 4 servings.

DOUBLE-BOILER TUNA SOUFFLÉ

2 tablespoons butter
1 small onion, minced
3 tablespoons flour
3/4 teaspoon salt
1/2 teaspoon celery salt
1/8 teaspoon pepper
3/4 cup milk
2 eggs, separated
1 can (7 ounces) tuna, drained and flaked
Juice of 1/2 small lemon

Melt butter in top part of double broiler. Add onion and cook over direct heat until golden. Blend in flour and seasonings. Put over boiling water and gradually add milk, stirring. Cook until thickened, stirring. Beat egg whites until stiff; set aside. Beat yolks until thick and lemon-colored. Add with tuna and lemon juice to first mixture. Fold in egg whites. Cover and cook over simmering water 45 minutes, or until firm. Makes 4 servings.

SAVORY TUNA PIE

1/2 cup all-purpose flour
1/4 cup yellow cornmeal
Dash of cayenne
3 tablespoons grated Cheddar cheese
3 tablespoons shortening
2 cans (7 ounces each) tuna, drained and liquid reserved
1 small green pepper, chopped
1 can (10-3/4 ounces) condensed tomato soup
1/4 cup milk
2 bay leaves

To make pastry, combine first 4 ingredients and cut in shortening. Sprinkle with 2 tablespoons cold water and shape in a ball. Chill until ready to use. Heat reserved tuna liquid in saucepan. Add green pepper, soup, milk and bay leaves. Bring to boil, reduce heat and simmer 15 minutes. Discard bay leaves and add tuna. Pat or roll pastry to 1/4″ thickness and cut in 10 rounds with scalloped 2½″ cutter. Arrange on baking sheet and bake in very hot oven (450°F.) about 8 minutes. Pour hot tuna into serving dish and top with pastries. Serves 6.

TUNA PIE WITH CHEESE ROLLS

1/2 cup each chopped green pepper, onion and celery
1/4 cup butter or margarine
6 tablespoons flour
3 cups milk
2 cans (7 ounces each) tuna, drained and flaked
Salt and pepper to taste
3 tablespoons dry white wine (optional)
Few sprigs parsley, finely chopped
Cheese Rolls

Sauté vegetables in the butter until limp. Stir in flour, then gradually add milk and cook, stirring, until thickened. Add tuna, salt and pepper. Add parsley and wine if used, and put in shallow 2-quart baking dish. Top with rolls and bake in very hot oven (450°F.) 20 minutes, or until rolls are well browned. Makes 6 servings.

Cheese Rolls

1-1/2 cups all-purpose flour
2 teaspoons baking powder
Dash of cayenne
1/2 teaspoon salt
1/2 cup solid vegetable shortening
1/2 cup (about) milk
1 jar (2 ounces) sliced pimientos, drained
3/4 cup grated mild Cheddar cheese

Mix dry ingredients, then cut in shortening. Mixing with fork, add enough milk to hold ingredients together. Shape in ball and roll out in rectangle as for pastry. Spread with pimientos and cheese and roll up as for jelly roll. Cut in 1″ slices.

TUNA MORNAY IN RICE RING

Mix well 5 cups hot cooked rice, 1/2 cup slivered almonds and 6 tablespoons melted butter. Pack in 8" or 9" ring mold and keep warm. Heat 2 cans (about 7 ounces each) tuna in top of double boiler. Add 1 cup Mornay Sauce. Keep tuna mixture and remaining sauce hot while you unmold rice. Fill center with tuna; top with remaining sauce. Makes 6 servings.

Mornay Sauce

1/4 cup butter
1/4 cup flour
2 cups milk
2 tablespoons grated Parmesan cheese
1/4 cup grated Swiss cheese
1/2 teaspoon dry mustard
Salt and pepper to taste

Cook butter and flour together for a minute, add milk and stir until thickened. Add remaining ingredients. Cook, stirring, for 10 minutes.

TUNA NOODLES ROMANOFF

1 package (5-3/4 ounces) Noodles Romanoff
1 teaspoon salt
2 tablespoons butter or margarine
1/2 cup milk
1 can (7 ounces) tuna, flaked
1 tablespoon dried chives
2 pimientos, chopped
Pepper to taste

Cook noodles 7 to 8 minutes with salt in boiling water. Drain and add remaining ingredients, including sauce mix from package. Mix lightly and heat gently. Serves 4.

TUNA PATTIES, FINES HERBES

Serve on broiled or fried tomato slices.

Potatoes
2 cans (about 7 ounces each) tuna
3 eggs, beaten
Dash of pepper
2 tablespoons minced parsley
1/2 teaspoon thyme or marjoram
2 tablespoons minced chives
1 small clove garlic
1/2 teaspoon salt
Cracker crumbs
Olive oil, butter or other fat

Cook, drain and mash enough potatoes to make 3 cups. (Do not add milk.) Cool. Combine potatoes with next 6 ingredients. Add garlic peeled and mashed with salt. Form into patties, roll in crumbs and sauté in olive oil until browned on both sides. Makes 6 servings.

LORD BALTIMORE CRAB CAKES

1 pound crab meat
1-1/2 teaspoons salt
1 teaspoon white pepper
1 teaspoon dry mustard
2 teaspoons Worcestershire
1 egg yolk
1 tablespoon mayonnaise
1 teaspoon chopped parsley
2 eggs, beaten
Fine dry bread crumbs
Fat for frying

Mix well first 8 ingredients. Shape in 4 large cakes or 8 smaller cakes, pressing firmly together. Dip in beaten eggs, then in bread crumbs, coating well. Fry quickly in hot shallow fat until browned. Makes 4 servings.

CRAB-MEAT SOUFFLÉ SPECIAL

1/2 pound crab meat
2 tablespoons grated onion
1 tablespoon fine dry bread crumbs
2 tablespoons minced parsley
1 pimiento, minced
3/4 teaspoon salt
1/4 teaspoon pepper
4 eggs, separated

Shred crab meat. Add next 4 ingredients and mix well. Beat salt and pepper with egg yolks until light in color. Combine with crab-meat mixture. Gently fold in stiffly beaten egg whites. Pour into an ungreased 1 1/2-quart soufflé dish. Put in shallow pan of hot water; bake in moderate oven (350°F.) about 30 minutes. Serves 4.

CHESAPEAKE CRAB CAKES

2 slices stale bread, crumbled
1 pound crab meat
2 egg yolks, beaten
1 teaspoon dry mustard
1 tablespoon butter, melted
1 tablespoon Worcestershire
Salt and pepper to taste
Fat for frying
Crackers
Tartar Sauce
Pickles

Mix all ingredients, except last 4, blend well and shape into 4 large or 8 smaller cakes. Chill at least 2 hours. Fry in 1" fat in skillet, turning to brown. Drain on absorbent paper. If preferred, fry in deep fat. Serve with crackers, tartar sauce and pickles. Makes 4 servings. **Tartar Sauce** Mix 1 cup mayonnaise, 1 teaspoon grated onion, 2 tablespoons chopped sweet pickle, and enough lemon juice to thin to desired consistency. For variety, add chopped parsley, chopped celery, capers, chopped olives, chili sauce or hot pepper sauce.

SAUTÉED CRABS À LA MEUNIÈRE

Sprinkle soft-shell crabs with salt, pepper and lemon juice. Sauté in hot butter 5 minutes on each side. Serve crabs with pan juice and sprinkle with minced parsley.

DOWN-DIXIE CRAB CASSEROLE

1/4 cup butter or margarine
1/4 cup minced onion
1/4 cup minced celery
1/4 cup minced green pepper
1 pound mushrooms, sliced
1/4 cup flour
3/4 teaspoon salt
Dash of ground ginger
2 cups chicken stock
1 pound crab meat
2 egg yolks, slightly beaten
1/4 cup grated Cheddar cheese

Melt butter in saucepan and add next 3 ingredients. Cook until golden. Add mushrooms and cook 10 minutes. Blend in next 3 ingredients. Add chicken stock and crab meat and cook until mixture is thickened. Remove from heat and stir mixture slowly into egg yolks. Pour into shallow 1½-quart baking dish, sprinkle with cheese and bake in moderate oven (350°F.) 30 minutes, or until browned. Makes 6 to 8 servings.

IMPERIAL CRAB MARYLAND

2 pounds choice back-fin crab meat
Mayonnaise
2 eggs
1 hard-cooked egg, mashed into a paste
3 slices soft stale white bread, crumbled fine
3 tablespoons minced pimiento
3 tablespoons minced green pepper, parboiled 5 minutes
2 tablespoons minced parsley
1/4 cup Worcestershire
Salt and pepper to taste
2 tablespoons melted butter or margarine
Milk or cream
Paprika

Carefully remove any bits of shell from crab meat and save about one fourth of the largest lumps for garnish. Mix remaining crab meat with ¼ cup mayonnaise and remaining ingredients, except last 2. Blend well. Pile greased crab shells or ramekins high with mixture. Partially flatten top surface and press reserved lumps of crab meat on it. Thin ½ cup mayonnaise with a little milk or cream and pour some over each dish of crab, letting it run down sides of heaped-up filling. Sprinkle with paprika and bake in moderate oven (350°F.) 15 minutes, or until brown. Makes 8 servings.

NOVEL CRAB NEWBURG

2 tablespoons butter or margarine
2 tablespoons flour
1/2 cup milk
1 can frozen condensed cream of shrimp soup
1 pound lump crab meat
2 tablespoons sherry

Melt butter and blend in flour. Stir in milk and soup, cooking slowly and stirring constantly 3 to 5 minutes, or until soup thaws and sauce thickens. Simmer 1 minute. Add crab meat and heat through. Blend in wine. Good on hot waffles. Makes 4 servings.

CRAB STEW MARYLAND

1 can (29 ounces) tomatoes
2 chicken bouillon cubes
1-3/4 cups fresh cut corn or 1 box frozen cut corn
2 stalks celery, diced
1 cup sliced fresh okra or 1/2 package frozen okra
1 teaspoon salt
1/4 teaspoon pepper
2 bay leaves
1 pound lump crab meat
Flour (optional)

Mash tomatoes thoroughly. Put in large saucepan. Add 2 cups water and next 7 ingredients. Simmer 30 minutes. Add crab meat gently and simmer gently, covered, 15 minutes longer. Thicken slightly with a flour-and-water paste, if desired. Makes about 1½ quarts, or 4 servings.

GOVERNOR'S LADY DEVILED CRAB

2 teaspoons lemon juice
2 teaspoons Worcestershire
1 pound crab meat
8 tablespoons butter
2 tablespoons flour
1 teaspoon prepared mustard
1/4 cup milk
1 cup light cream
Salt and pepper
6 soda crackers, crushed
Hot potato sticks
Parsley and lemon wedges

Add lemon juice and Worcestershire to crab meat. Melt 6 tablespoons butter. Blend in flour and mustard. Add milk and cream and cook, stirring, until thick. Season with salt and pepper to taste. Add crab meat and mix well. Pack into 4 or 5 buttered crab shells or ramekins. Melt remaining butter and mix with crackers; sprinkle on crab mixture. Bake in hot oven (400°F.) about 15 minutes. Serve with hot potato sticks. Garnish with parsley and lemon wedges. Makes 4 or 5 servings.

CRAB EGGS FOO YUNG

6 eggs
1 can (1 pound) bean sprouts, drained
2 tablespoons instant minced onion
1 teaspoon salt
1/2 teaspoon pepper
1 cup crab meat, or shrimps
Vegetable oil
Sauce

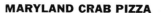 Beat eggs well. Add drained bean sprouts, onion, salt, pepper and crab meat. Cook like pancakes in a little oil in small skillet. Serve with Sauce. Makes 6 servings. **Sauce** Mix 1 tablespoon each cornstarch and sugar. Add 3 tablespoons soy sauce and 1½ cups water. Cook, stirring, until thickened.

CRAB-MEAT CASSEROLE

8 slices white bread, crusts trimmed
1 can (6-1/2 ounces) crab meat, flaked
1/4 cup each chopped onion and green pepper
2 eggs, slightly beaten
1-1/2 cups milk
1/4 teaspoon each salt, pepper and monosodium glutamate
1 can (10-1/2 ounces) condensed cream of mushroom soup
1/4 cup grated Cheddar cheese

Butter a 10″ square baking dish and put 4 slices bread in dish. Sprinkle with crab meat, onion and green pepper. Top with remaining bread. Mix eggs, milk and seasonings and pour over mixture. Let stand at room temperature 1 hour. Bake in moderate oven (350°F.) 15 minutes. Pour soup over top and sprinkle with cheese. Bake about 45 minutes longer. Makes 6 servings.

CRAB-MEAT PIE

1/2 cup each chopped onion and green pepper
1/2 cup butter or margarine
1/2 cup flour
1/2 teaspoon monosodium glutamate
1 cup milk
1/2 cup shredded American cheese
1 can (6-1/2 ounces) crab meat
1-1/2 cups canned tomatoes, drained
1 teaspoon Worcestershire
1/2 teaspoon salt
1 package (8 ounces) refrigerated biscuits

Sauté onion and green pepper in the butter 2 to 3 minutes. Stir in flour and monosodium glutamate. Gradually add milk and cook, stirring, until very thick. Remove from heat and stir in cheese. When melted, add remaining ingredients, except biscuits. Put in greased shallow 1½-quart baking dish and arrange biscuits on top. Bake in moderate oven (350°F.) about 25 minutes. Makes 4 servings.

CRAB POULETTE

Lobster meat or chopped shrimp may be substituted for the crab meat.

12 hard-cooked eggs
2 tablespoons mayonnaise
1-1/2 teaspoons prepared mustard
Salt and pepper
1 can (6 ounces) sliced mushrooms
1 pound lump crab meat
Milk
3 tablespoons butter or margarine
3 tablespoons flour
1 cup grated Cheddar cheese
1 teaspoon instant minced onion
1 tablespoon minced parsley

Cut eggs in halves lengthwise. Remove yolks and mash with mayonnaise, mustard, salt and pepper to taste. Fill halves of egg whites with mixture and arrange in greased shallow baking dish. Drain mushrooms, reserving liquid. Put mushrooms and crab meat around eggs. Add enough milk to mushroom liquid to make 1 cup. Melt butter and blend in flour. Add milk and cook, stirring, until thick. Add last 3 ingredients and salt and pepper to taste. Pour over eggs, crab and mushrooms and bake in moderate oven (350°F.) about 15 minutes. Makes 6 servings.

MARYLAND CRAB PIZZA

1 package hot-roll mix
1/4 cup minced green pepper
1/4 cup minced onion
1 garlic clove, minced
2 tablespoons vegetable oil
1 can (29 ounces) tomatoes
Salt and pepper
1/2 teaspoon sugar
Provolone cheese
1/4 cup butter or margarine, melted
1 pound back-fin crab meat
Oregano
1/2 cup grated Parmesan cheese

Prepare hot-roll mix as directed and let rise until double in bulk. Punch down lightly. Divide in half; roll out ¼″ thick and large enough to cover bottoms of two 8″ piepans. Fry pepper, onion and garlic in oil about 10 minutes, or until onion is golden brown. Add tomatoes and cook until thick. Add salt and pepper to taste and the sugar. Slice enough Provolone cheese to cover each pan of dough. Mix butter with crab lumps. Put on top of cheese. Cover with tomato mixture, sprinkle generously with oregano and Parmesan cheese. Bake in hot oven (425°F.) until crust is golden and filling bubbly. Cut in wedges and serve hot. Makes 6 servings.

GREEN SAUCE

Good on boiled fish, beef, tongue or hard-cooked eggs for antipasto.

3/4 cup chopped parsley
2 tablespoons capers
1 small cucumber pickle, diced
1/4 cup olive oil
1/2 cup vinegar
1 slice white bread, trimmed and crumbled
1/2 teaspoon sugar
1/2 teaspoon salt
1/4 teaspoon pepper

Combine all ingredients in blender. Whirl until smooth. Makes about 1 cup sauce.

CURRIED SHELLFISH

1 onion, minced
1/2 green pepper, minced
1/4 cup butter
1 to 2 tablespoons curry powder
1/4 cup flour
2 cups chicken bouillon or consomme
1 tablespoon lemon juice
1 can (4-1/2 ounces) shrimps, drained and rinsed
1 can (5 ounces) lobster, drained
1 can (6-1/2 ounces) crab meat, drained
Cooked rice (optional)

Cook onion and green pepper in butter 2 or 3 minutes. Add curry powder and cook 1 or 2 minutes. Blend in flour. Gradually stir in bouillon and cook, stirring, until thickened. Add remaining ingredients, except rice, and and heat. Serve over rice, if desired. Makes 6 servings.

CREOLE CRAB CASSEROLE

2/3 cup uncooked rice
1 small onion, minced
1 small green pepper, chopped
2 tablespoons butter or margarine
1 can (1 pound) tomatoes
1 teaspoon seasoned salt
1/4 teaspoon seasoned pepper
1 teaspoon sugar
1/2 teaspoon Worcestershire
1 bay leaf
6 whole black peppercorns
2 whole cloves
1 can (6-1/2 ounces) crab meat
Salt and pepper
1/4 cup grated Parmesan cheese

Cook and drain rice. Cook onion and green pepper in butter 2 to 3 minutes. Add next 5 ingredients. Tie whole spices in small piece of cheesecloth and add. Simmer, uncovered, 10 minutes. Remove spice bag. Add crab meat, rice, and salt and pepper to taste. Put in 1½-quart casserole and sprinkle with cheese. Bake in moderate oven (375°F.) about 20 minutes. Makes 4 to 6 servings.

CORN-CRAB CUSTARD

2 tablespoons butter or margarine
1-1/2 cups milk
1/2 cup light cream
1 can (17 ounces) cream-style corn
1 box (6 ounces) frozen crab meat, thawed and coarsely chopped
1 teaspoon sugar
1-1/2 teaspoons salt
1 tablespoon steak sauce
3 eggs, beaten

Heat first 3 ingredients until butter is melted. Add remaining ingredients and mix well. Pour into shallow 1½-quart baking dish. Set in a pan of hot water and bake in slow oven (325°F.) 1¼ hours, or until firm. Serves 4 to 6.

HOT SEAFOOD SALAD

1 can (6 ounces) crab meat
1 can (4-1/2 ounces) shrimps, drained
1 cup diced celery
1 small onion, minced
1/2 medium green pepper, chopped
4 sprigs parsley, chopped
Juice of 1/2 lemon
1/2 teaspoon salt
Dash of cayenne
2 tablespoons Worcestershire
1 cup mayonnaise
3/4 cup soft bread crumbs
2 tablespoons salad oil

Flake crab meat. Rinse and clean shrimps. Mix all ingredients lightly, except crumbs and oil. Pile in 4 oiled baking shells. Sprinkle with crumbs mixed with oil. Bake in moderate oven (350°F.) about 25 minutes. Makes 4 servings.

SEAFOOD NEWBURG

1 can (6 ounces) crab meat
1 can (5-1/2 ounces) lobster
1 can (4-1/2 ounces) shrimps
3 tablespoons butter
2 tablespoons flour
1/2 teaspoon salt
1/8 teaspoon white pepper
Dash each of cayenne, and nutmeg or mace
2 cups milk
2 egg yolks, slightly beaten
2 tablespoons sherry
Toast points

Pick over seafood; rinse shrimps. In double boiler or chafing dish over direct heat cook seafood lightly in butter 2 or 3 minutes. Blend in flour and seasonings. Gradually add milk and cook over boiling water, stirring, until thickened. Stir small amount of mixture into egg yolks, return to pan and cook, stirring, 2 or 3 minutes. Stir in sherry and serve on toast. Serves 6.

CURRIED ROCK LOBSTER

6 frozen South African rock lobster
   tails
1 teaspoon salt
1 bay leaf
2 tablespoons minced onion
2 stalks celery, minced
1/4 teaspoon thyme
2 tablespoons minced parsley
3 tablespoons butter or margarine
3 tablespoons flour
1 bouillon cube
2 or more teaspoons curry powder
1 teaspoon paprika
1/2 cup cream
Juice of 1/2 lemon
Hot cooked rice

Cook lobster tails for 6 minutes in boiling water seasoned with the salt and bay leaf. Remove tails and rinse with cold water; reserve stock and reduce to 1½ cups by boiling. Discard bay leaf. Remove lobster meat from shells and dice. Cook onion and next 3 ingredients in butter 2 or 3 minutes. Blend in flour. Add next 3 ingredients and reduced stock. Cook, stirring, until thickened. Add cream, lemon juice and lobster; heat. Serve on rice. Makes 6 servings.

QUICHE DE LANGOUSTE
(Lobster Pie)

2 lobsters (1-1/2 pounds each), cooked,
   or 3 or 4 lobster tails, cooked, or 1 can
   (12 ounces) frozen lobster meat,
   thawed
Lobster coral and tomalley (optional)
Pastry for 9" pie shell
2 tablespoons chopped onion
1/4 cup butter
1/4 cup Cognac or whiskey
Salt and pepper
1-1/4 cups medium cream
4 eggs
Dash of nutmeg

Remove lobster meat from shells and cut in convenient pieces. If you are using whole lobsters, remove coral and tomalley and reserve. Line 9" piepan with pastry. Prick with fork. Chill. Bake in hot oven (425°F.) 10 minutes. Sauté onion in butter in skillet until tender. Add lobster and heat through. Add Cognac and season to taste with salt and pepper. Arrange lobster and onion in shell. If desired, put coral and tomalley in skillet with 1 tablespoon cream. Cook a second or two and pour over the lobster. Beat eggs and remaining cream together and season with salt. Pour over lobster in pie shell and dust with a little nutmeg. Bake in moderate oven (375°F.) 35 minutes, or until firm. Serve at once. This will serve 6 for a first course, or 4 for a main luncheon course.

SCALLOPS WITH LEMON BUTTER

1-1/2 pounds scallops
Fine dry bread crumbs (about 1/3 cup)
1/2 cup butter
1/4 teaspoon salt
1/8 teaspoon pepper
Dash of paprika
1 tablespoon chopped parsley
3 tablespoons lemon juice

Roll scallops in crumbs. Melt half of butter in skillet. Add next 3 ingredients. Sauté scallops slowly 8 minutes, turning gently to brown evenly. Remove scallops to hot serving dish. Put remaining butter, parsley and lemon juice in skillet. Heat and pour over scallops. Makes 4 to 6 servings.

COQUILLES ST. JACQUES
(Scallops in Shells)

1-1/2 pounds scallops
Butter
6 shallots or green onions, chopped
Bouquet garni (parsley, celery, thyme,
   bay leaf)
1-1/2 cups dry white wine
Salt
12 mushrooms chopped fine
Juice of 1 lemon
1/4 teaspoon pepper
3 tablespoons flour
4 egg yolks
1 cup heavy cream
Grated Parmesan cheese
Bread crumbs

Dry scallops on paper towels. Place in saucepan with 2 tablespoons butter, shallots and bouquet garni. Barely cover with white wine. Season with a little salt. Bring just to boil, reduce to a gentle simmer (the liquid should be just barely moving) and simmer 4 or 5 minutes, or until scallops are just tender. Drain and save broth for the sauce. Cut scallops in small pieces or slices. Sauté mushrooms a minute in 2 tablespoons butter. Add ⅓ cup water, the lemon juice, ½ teaspoon salt and the pepper. Simmer gently a few minutes. Drain and reserve liquid. Prepare a *beurre manié* with 3 tablespoons butter and the flour kneaded in small balls about the size of peas. Combine liquids from scallops and mushrooms in saucepan and heat. Stir in *beurre manié*. Cook and stir until sauce is thickened and smooth; cook 2 or 3 minutes. Add scallops and heat through. Beat egg yolks and mix with cream; add to sauce and cook gently, stirring, until smooth and thick. Do not let sauce boil. Add mushrooms and season. Spoon into individual ramekins or shells, sprinkle with Parmesan cheese and crumbs and lightly brown a minute under broiler. Makes 6 servings.

SCALLOPS EN BROCHETTE

Skewer alternately whole scallops, fresh mushrooms and squares of uncooked bacon. Grill over charcoal or in broiler about 10 minutes, turning often and brushing frequently with highly seasoned French dressing.

SCALLOPS NEWBURG

1 box (12 ounces) frozen scallops, thawed
3 tablespoons butter or margarine
1 teaspoon lemon juice
1 teaspoon flour
1/2 cup heavy cream
2 egg yolks, slightly beaten
2 tablespoons sherry
Salt and pepper
4 sandwich rolls
Paprika

Cut scallops in half and cook 3 minutes in 2 tablespoons butter. Add lemon juice and cook 1 minute. In another saucepan, melt remaining butter and blend in flour. Add cream and cook until thickened, stirring constantly. Add egg yolks, sherry and scallops; season to taste. Cut tops from sandwich rolls; scoop out centers and heat rolls in oven. Fill with scallops mixture. Garnish with paprika. Makes 4 servings.

BROILED CURRIED SCALLOPS

2 pounds sea scallops
1/4 cup honey
2 teaspoons curry powder
1/4 cup prepared mustard
1 teaspoon lemon juice

Line broiler pan with foil and arrange scallops in pan. Mix remaining ingredients and brush generously on scallops. Broil scallops under low heat 10 minutes, turn, brush with mixture and broil 10 minutes longer, or until just tender. Makes 4 servings.

ROCK LOBSTER IN ALMOND SAUCE

6 frozen South African rock lobster tails
Salt and pepper
1 cup slivered blanched almonds
6 tablespoons butter
3 tablespoons flour
1/2 teaspoon paprika
2 cups milk

Cook lobster tails in boiling salted water 6 minutes. Drain and drench with cold water. Remove meat from shells and slice. Brown almonds in butter. Blend in flour, paprika, and salt and pepper to taste; add milk and cook, stirring, until thickened. Add lobster. Makes 6 servings.

CIOPPINO

The versions of this stew are many. Traditional seasonings vary from area to area and the fish varies with the day's catch. In addition, individual cooks often change the ingredients to suit their own tastes. Some prefer white wine to red; others use sherry. Many like to add exotic tidbits such as octopus, squid or eel. Sometimes only shellfish are used. Soaked dried mushrooms are often included. This is the basic recipe. To prepare the fish and shellfish:

3 pounds sea bass, barracuda, halibut or a variety of any firm fish
1 large live Dungeness (hard-shell) crab or a live lobster
1 pound jumbo shrimps (or more)
1 pint clams, mussels or oysters, or all three

Cut the fish into good-size serving pieces. Crack the crab and remove the top shell but keep it for making stock. If you use lobster, cut the tail in pieces and reserve the body to make stock; if you use Eastern lobster, cut the tail in sections and crack the claws. Split the shrimp shells down the back and remove the black vein. Steam the mollusks (clams, mussels or oysters) in a small amount of water just until they open. Remove the top shells and save the juice. To prepare the sauce:

1-1/2 cups chopped onion
1 cup chopped green pepper
1/4 cup olive oil
3 cloves garlic thoroughly mashed with 1 teaspoon salt
1 can (29 ounces) tomatoes
Juice from the mollusks
2 cups red table wine
2 cups tomato juice
2 cups fish stock made from the crab shell or lobster body and fish trimmings
Herb bouquet (bay leaf, parsley, basil)
1/2 cup minced parsley

Sauté onion and green pepper in olive oil until just soft. Add rest of the ingredients, except parsley, and cook for 10 minutes. Remove herb bouquet and taste for seasoning. Arrange in layers all fish except the mollusks in large casserole or kettle with a cover. Pour sauce over fish. Simmer, covered, over low heat or in the oven for 20 to 30 minutes, or until the fish is just done. Add the mollusks for last 3 minutes. Serve in deep bowls, shells and all, and sprinkle liberally with minced parsley. This is finger food. Have plenty of big paper napkins on hand. Serve hot crusty sourdough bread and a robust red wine. For dessert, fruit and a variety of cheeses. Makes 4 servings.

OYSTERS ROCKEFELLER

2 dozen oysters with shells
1 tablespoon minced green onion
1 tablespoon chopped parsley
2 tablespoons butter or margarine
Salt, pepper and paprika
2 tablespoons minced bacon
2 tablespoons finely chopped cooked
   spinach
1/3 cup fine dry bread crumbs
Lemon wedges

Drain oysters on a paper towel. Wash shells and set on baking sheets with sides. Put an oyster in each shell. Mix onion, parsley and 1 tablespoon butter; dab on each oyster. Season with salt, pepper and paprika. Top with bacon, spinach and crumbs. Dot with 1 tablespoon butter. Bake in very hot oven (450°F.) 8 to 10 minutes. Serve with lemon. Serves 4.

SAVORY OYSTERS WITH MASHED POTATOES

2 dozen shucked oysters
2 tablespoons minced green pepper or
   pimiento
1-1/2 teaspoons minced onion
2 tablespoons butter or margarine
4-1/2 teaspoons cornstarch
1/2 teaspoon each salt and celery salt
1/8 teaspoon pepper
Milk (optional)
1 tablespoon lemon juice
Dash of mace
2 cups mashed potato or 1 envelope
   instant mashed potato, prepared

Heat oysters in their liquor until edges begin to curl. Drain, reserving 1 cup liquor. Cook green pepper and onion in butter 2 or 3 minutes. Blend in cornstarch and seasonings. Add oyster liquor, plus milk if necessary to make 1 cup. Cook, stirring, until thickened. Add lemon juice, mace and oysters. Border a deep 9″ ovenware dish with mashed potato. Pour oyster mixture into center. Put under broiler until potato is browned. Serves 4.

SHRIMP CAKES WITH DILL SAUCE

Cook ¼ cup chopped onion in ¼ cup butter until wilted. Stir in 3 tablespoons flour, 1 teaspoon prepared mustard, 1 cup cream, and salt and pepper to taste. When thick and smooth, add 1 pound cooked chopped shrimps. Chill, form in cakes, roll in cracker crumbs and sauté in plenty of butter. Serve with **Dill Sauce:** Combine 1 cup mayonnaise, ½ cup chopped ripe olives, 1 tablespoon fresh dillweed and 1 tablespoon lemon juice. Serves 4.

SCALLOPED OYSTERS

2/3 cup butter, melted
3 cups coarse unsalted-cracker crumbs
3 dozen shucked oysters
2 teaspoons salt
1/4 teaspoon pepper
1/8 teaspoon hot pepper sauce
1/4 cup oyster liquor
1/2 cup heavy cream

Mix butter and crumbs. Drain oysters, reserving ¼ cup liquor. Arrange alternate layers of crackers and oysters in shallow 1½-quart baking dish, making crumbs the last layer. Sprinkle with mixed salt and pepper. Mix last 3 ingredients and pour over top. Bake in moderate oven (350°F.) about 30 minutes. Makes 6 to 8 servings.

MYDIA PILAFI (Clams with Rice)

1 medium onion, chopped
2 tablespoons butter
2 tablespoons olive oil
2 cans (7 ounces each) tiny whole clams
1-1/2 cups canned tomatoes
1 cup uncooked rice
1/2 teaspoon dried oregano leaves
Salt and pepper

Sauté onion in butter and olive oil until golden brown. Drain the clams and add enough water to liquid to make 1½ cups. Combine all ingredients, cover and simmer about 25 minutes. Makes 6 servings.

CLAM HASH

4 cups diced cold boiled potatoes
1/2 cup diced cooked carrot
1 onion, chopped
1/4 teaspoon crushed thyme
1 can (10-1/2 ounces) minced clams
3 tablespoons bacon fat or margarine
Salt and pepper

Mix first 5 ingredients and let stand about 20 minutes to allow clam liquid to soak into vegetables. Heat bacon fat in skillet and add mixture. Cook slowly, turning occasionally, until lightly browned. Season to taste. Makes 4 servings.

SHRIMP FRIED RICE

Melt ¼ cup butter in large skillet. Add 2 cups cold cooked rice, 1 pound chopped cooked shrimps and ½ cup minced water chestnuts. Simmer until heated through. Stir in 2 eggs beaten with 2 tablespoons soy sauce. Cook, stirring until eggs are set. Serve sprinkled with chopped green onions. Makes 4 servings.

JUMBO SHRIMPS EN BROCHETTE

2 pounds jumbo shrimps (20 to 24)
3 cloves garlic, minced
1 medium onion, minced
1/4 cup minced parsley
1 teaspoon each basil, prepared mustard
  and salt
1/2 cup olive oil
Juice of 1 lemon

Split shrimp shells up the back with scissors and remove sand veins but leave shells on. Marinate 1 hour in mixture of remaining ingredients. Broil over brisk fire about 3 minutes on each side. (For easier turning, put shrimps on skewers or use a folding wire grill.) Serve with plenty of napkins or with fingertip towels wrung out in hot water. Each guest shells his own. Makes 4 to 6 servings.

PRAWNS IN CREAM

2 pounds green (raw) prawns or jumbo
  shrimps
1/4 cup butter
1/2 cup heavy cream
1/4 cup dry sherry
2 tablespoons minced parsley
Salt and pepper
Toast points

Drop prawns into boiling water to cover and cook gently 5 minutes. Drain, shell and devein. Melt butter in large skillet or chafing dish; add prawns and cook, turning gently, until lightly browned. Add next 3 ingredients, and salt and pepper to taste. Heat. Spoon onto toast. Makes 6 servings.

SHRIMPS IN THE PINK

2 boxes (10 ounces each) frozen cleaned
  shelled shrimps
1/2 cup chopped celery tops
1/4 cup mixed pickling spices
2 cups onion slices
7 or 8 bay leaves
1-1/4 cups salad oil
3/4 cup white vinegar
2 tablespoons capers with liquid
2-1/2 teaspoons celery seed
1-1/2 teaspoons salt
Dash of hot pepper sauce

Cover frozen shrimps with boiling water. Tie celery tops and spices loosely in a cheesecloth bag. Add to shrimps and cook 5 minutes, or until shrimps turn pink, separating with fork. Remove spice bag, drain shrimps and cool. Arrange shrimps and onion slices in alternate layers in bowl. Add bay leaves. Mix remaining ingredients and pour over shrimps. Cover and chill at least 24 hours. Drain before serving. Makes 4 servings.

SHRIMPS CREOLE

1 medium onion, chopped
1/2 cup diced green pepper
2 tablespoons vegetable oil
1 clove garlic, minced
1 teaspoon salt
1/8 teaspoon pepper
1 can (1 pound) tomatoes
1 bay leaf
2 whole cloves
1-1/2 pounds shrimps, cooked, shelled
  and cleaned

Cook onion and green pepper in the oil about 5 minutes. Add next 6 ingredients, bring to boil, cover and simmer 30 minutes. Remove cloves and bay leaf. Add shrimps and heat. Serve on rice. Makes 4 to 6 servings.

SHRIMPS AND PINEAPPLE, CHINESE STYLE

1/4 cup packed brown sugar
1-1/2 tablespoons cornstarch
1/2 teaspoon salt
1/4 cup vinegar
1 tablespoon soy sauce
1/2 teaspoon ground ginger
1 can (1 pound 4-1/2 ounces) pineapple
  chunks
1 green pepper, cut in strips
1 medium onion, cut in rings
1 pound cleaned shelled cooked shrimps
Hot cooked rice

Blend first 3 ingredients in large saucepan or skillet. Add next 3 ingredients and syrup from pineapple. Cook, stirring, until thickened. Add pineapple, pepper and onion; cook 2 or 3 minutes. Add shrimps and bring to boil, stirring. Serve on hot rice. Makes 4 to 6 servings.

SWEET-AND-SOUR SHRIMPS

1 pound raw shrimps, shelled
2 eggs
1/2 cup all-purpose flour
1/4 teaspoon salt
Fat for deep frying
1/4 cup pineapple juice
1/3 cup vinegar
1/2 cup sugar
2 teaspoons soy sauce
1 tablespoon cornstarch

Remove veins from shrimps. Beat eggs and add flour and salt to make a batter. (If too thick, add a little milk). Dip shrimps in batter and fry in hot deep oil (375°F. on a frying thermometer) until golden brown. Drain on absorbent paper. Mix remaining ingredients and simmer, stirring, until thickened. Arrange shrimps on a heated platter and pour pineapple sauce over. Makes 4 servings.

SESAME SHRIMPS

Marinate peeled jumbo shrimps in equal parts of sesame oil, bourbon and soy sauce for 2 hours. Grill or broil 3 or 4 minutes on each side. Dip again in the marinade, roll in sesame seed to cover and return to the grill or broiler until the seed on both sides of the shrimps are lightly colored.

SHRIMP POT PIE

1 can (4 ounces) chopped mushrooms, drained
1 small onion, minced
5 tablespoons butter or margarine
1 pound shrimps, cooked and deveined
3 tablespoons flour
1 teaspoon salt
1/8 teaspoon pepper
2 cups milk
1 tablespoon chopped parsley
1 cup cooked diced potato
1/2 cup cooked green peas
1/2 recipe Standard Pastry (page 419)

Cook mushrooms and onion in 2 tablespoons butter 5 minutes; add shrimps. Prepare white sauce with remaining 3 tablespoons butter, the flour, salt, pepper and milk. Pour over shrimp mixture and add remaining ingredients, except pastry. Turn into 1-quart casserole; top with pastry, rolled and cut to fit. Bake in hot oven (425°F.) about 20 minutes. Serves 4.

SHRIMPS TEMPURA

1-1/2 pounds large shrimps
1/2 cup cornstarch
1/2 cup all-purpose flour
1 teaspoon salt
1/4 teaspoon monosodium glutamate
1 egg
Oil for deep frying
Sweet-Sour Sauce or Chinese mustard

Shell and clean shrimps, leaving tails on. Split shrimps through back, cutting almost through. Open to butterfly shape. Mix dry ingredients. Add egg and $^1/_2$ cup water and beat until smooth. Holding shrimps by tail, dip in batter and drop gently, a few at a time, into hot deep oil (375°F. on a frying thermometer). When shrimps rise to surface, turn and continue cooking until golden brown. Serve with sauce or mustard. Makes 4 servings. **Sweet-Sour Sauce** Mix 2 tablespoons each cornstarch and brown sugar, 3 tablespoons soy sauce and $^1/_4$ cup vinegar; gradually add 1 cup hot fish stock or chicken broth. Cook, stirring, until thick and clear. Makes about $1^1/_2$ cups.

SHRIMP NEWBURG

Sauté 1 pound raw cleaned shrimps in $^1/_4$ cup butter in a chafing dish for 5 minutes. Pour in a jigger of Cognac and flame. Heat 1 cup heavy cream in another pan; beat $^1/_4$ cup into 3 beaten egg yolks. Return to pan with remaining cream, season with salt and paprika and cook gently, stirring, until the sauce thickens. Pour over hot shrimps and serve at once. Serves 3.

SHRIMP JAMBALAYA

1 large onion, chopped
1 clove garlic, minced
1/2 green pepper, chopped
1/4 cup butter or margarine
2 tablespoons flour
1 cup uncooked rice
2 teaspoons salt
1/4 teaspoon pepper
1 can (19 ounces) tomatoes
1 can (8 ounces) tomato sauce
1/8 teaspoon hot pepper sauce
1 cup (4 ounces) ground cooked ham
2 cans (4-1/2 ounces each) medium shrimps, drained and rinsed

Cook first 3 ingredients in butter 5 minutes. Blend in flour. Add $1^1/_2$ cups water and remaining ingredients, except shrimps. Bring to boil, cover and simmer about 30 minutes. Add half the shrimps, put jambalaya in serving dish and top with remaining shrimps. Makes 4 to 6 servings.

GRILLED JUMBO SHRIMPS, VENETIAN STYLE

2 pounds raw jumbo shrimps
1 clove garlic, crushed
Freshly ground black pepper
Juice of 1 lime
1/4 cup olive oil
Garlic Butter

With scissors or sharp knife, split each shrimp shell on underside down to tail; try not to cut meat. Put shrimps in bowl with remaining ingredients, except Garlic Butter. Stir well to coat shrimps. Cover and refrigerate at least 2 hours. Push onto skewers and grill 6" from heat over low charcoal fire, turning frequently until done, or about 15 minutes. (If grilling in broiler, remove shells first.) Serve with Garlic Butter. Makes 4 servings. **Garlic Butter** Mix $^1/_2$ cup melted butter, 1 teaspoon Worcestershire, 1 tablespoon lemon juice, $^1/_4$ teaspoon hot pepper sauce, 1 mashed clove garlic and salt to taste. Serve in saucers as a dip for shrimps.

SUNSET SHRIMP CASSEROLE

5 slices white bread
Butter or margarine, softened
1 can (4-1/2 ounces) shrimps
1/2 pound Cheddar cheese, shredded
Dry mustard
3 eggs, slightly beaten
1/2 teaspoon salt
Pepper, paprika and cayenne to taste
2 cups milk

Spread bread with butter and cut in 1/2" cubes. Sprinkle half in greased shallow 1½-quart baking dish. Drain shrimps and rinse. Sprinkle half on bread, then sprinkle with half the cheese and dust lightly with mustard. Add remaining bread, a sprinkling of cheese and remaining shrimps. Mix remaining ingredients and pour over mixture. Sprinkle with remaining cheese and bake in slow oven (325°F.) 40 minutes, or until firm. Makes 4 to 6 servings.

SHRIMP-FILLED AVOCADOS

1/2 cup mayonnaise
1/2 teaspoon curry powder
Lemon juice
1-1/2 cups coarsely chopped cooked
   shrimps (about 3/4 pound)
1 tablespoon capers
2 hard-cooked eggs, chopped
2 avocados, peeled, halved and seeded
1/2 cup soft bread crumbs
1 tablespoon butter, melted

Mix mayonnaise with curry powder and 2 tablespoons each water and lemon juice. Heat gently, add next 3 ingredients and heat through. Brush avocados with lemon juice and fill with shrimp mixture. Combine crumbs and butter and sprinkle over filled avocado halves. Put under broiler until lightly browned. Serves 4.

BUTTERFLY SHRIMP

1 pound raw jumbo shrimps
3 tablespoons flour
1-1/2 tablespoons cornstarch
1 tablespoon white cornmeal
3/4 teaspoon baking powder
3/4 teaspoon salt
1/2 cup milk
Fat for deep frying
1/2 recipe Sweet-Sour Sauce (page 207)

Peel shrimps, leaving tails on. Make a deep slit along the back to "butterfly" shrimp, removing black vein as you do so. Mix next 5 ingredients. Beat in milk to make a thin batter. Dip each shrimp in batter and fry in hot deep oil (375°F. on a frying thermometer) 2 or 3 minutes, or until golden brown. Serve with Sweet-Sour Sauce. Makes 3 or 4 servings.

SHRIMP WITH WILD RICE, ROMAGNA

1 cup uncooked wild rice
Salt and pepper
1 clove garlic, minced
1/4 cup olive oil
2 cans (8 ounces each) tomato sauce
1/2 teaspoon oregano
1/2 teaspoon sweet basil
1 large green pepper, cut in chunks
2 packages (10 ounces each) frozen
   shelled cleaned shrimp, thawed

Cook rice in boiling salted water; drain and put in greased 2-quart casserole. Cook garlic in olive oil 5 minutes. Add all ingredients, except shrimp, with ½ cup water. Bring to boil and simmer 10 minutes. Add shrimp, and salt and pepper to taste. Pour on rice. Cover and make in moderate oven (350°F.) about 30 minutes. Makes 6 servings.

SHRIMP COOKED IN BEER

Prepare court bouillon for boiling shrimp, using 3 parts stale beer to 1 part water. Add 1 tablespoon salt for each quart liquid, a few whole black peppercorns, 1 or 2 bay leaves and a sprinkling of celery seed. Added shelled deveined shrimp and simmer, covered, 2 to 5 minutes, or until pink; drain. Use in recipes requiring cooked shrimp, or serve with favorite sauce.

BITTERBALLEN

2 cups cooked shrimps, finely chopped
   or ground
Thick White Sauce
1/4 teaspoon mace
Salt and pepper to taste
1 teaspoon lemon juice
1 tablespoon each chopped parsley and
   chopped chives
2 egg yolks
2 tablespoons light cream
Flour
Fine dry bread crumbs
Vegetable oil for deep frying
Creamy Mustard Sauce (page 132) or
   Tartar Sauce (page 199)

Combine the shrimps with white sauce and seasonings and pour into bowl to cool thoroughly. Form into 1" balls. Beat together egg yolks and cream. Dip balls in flour, then into egg-cream mixture, and roll in crumbs. Chill. Fry in hot deep oil (375°F. on a frying thermometer) until crisp and brown. Serve with sauce desired. Makes about 30. **Thick White Sauce** Melt 3 tablespoons butter or margarine; blend in 3 tablespoons flour. Slowly add 1 cup milk, stirring until thick and smooth.

una-Cheddar Chowder

Top-hat Cheese Soufflé

Quiche Lorraine

TONI FICALORA

HOW TO BUY CHEESE

Versatile and varied, cheese can be served at any meal in any form—mixed into casseroles, melted into vegetable sauces, sprinkled on pasta or potatoes, or coupled with fruit for dessert. Cheese products are divided in four groups: **Natural cheese** (non-processed), made directly from milk curds or from whey; **process cheese,** composed of one or more natural cheeses; **process cheese food,** made with less cheese and more milk or water than process cheese; and **process cheese spread,** with an edible stabilizer added. Cheeses can also be classified as soft, semisoft, hard and very hard.

CHEESE STORAGE

Soft cheeses such as cottage cheese should be tightly covered and stored in the coldest part of the refrigerator. Hard natural cheeses should be tightly wrapped in a double thickness of waxed paper, foil or plastic wrap and refrigerated. Cut edges can be buttered or coated with melted paraffin. Strong cheeses should be wrapped as above and put in a tightly covered container in the refrigerator. Mold on natural cheeses is not harmful and can be cut off. Process cheeses can be kept in their original wrapper or container in the refrigerator. Cheese spread in jars or crocks should be refrigerated after opening.

HOW TO BUY EGGS

Eggs are sold in cartons according to size, which is determined by weight per dozen as follows:

Jumbo	30 ounces or more
Extra large	27 ounces or more
Large	24 ounces or more
Medium	21 ounces or more
Small	18 ounces or more
Peewee	15 ounces or more

Buy the size that best suits your needs—smaller eggs may be an economy when used in cooking. Eggs are graded according to freshness. Grade AA and Grade A eggs are top quality. They are best for poaching, frying and cooking in the shell. Grade B and Grade C eggs have thinner whites and rather flat yolks that may break easily. They are less expensive and are good to use for scrambling, baking, thickening sauces and to combine with other foods. Shell color is a matter of personal preference and has no effect on the taste or nutritional quality of the egg.

EGG STORAGE

Eggs should be stored, covered, in the refrigerator, away from strong-smelling foods and with small ends down.

To freeze eggs

WHOLE EGGS OR YOLKS To each 8-ounce cupful, add 1 tablespoon sugar or 1 teaspoon salt. Mix well with fork; freeze in freezer container. (Use sugared in cakes, puddings; salted in omelets, etc.) **WHITES** Freeze unbeaten.

Leftover yolks or whites

YOLKS They will keep 2 to 3 days in refrigerator if placed, covered with water, in jar with lid. **WHITES** They will keep up to 10 days in refrigerator if stored in covered jar.

COOKING CAUTION

Whether cooking eggs on top of range or in oven, always use low or moderate and even heat. If cooked at too high a temperature, eggs become tough. If adding hot liquids to beaten eggs, add just a little at a time, continuing to beat.

TO MEASURE EGGS

2 medium eggs = $\frac{1}{3}$ cup
2 large eggs or 3 medium eggs = $\frac{1}{2}$ cup
4 large eggs = 1 cup
6 large egg whites = 1 cup
12 large egg yolks = 1 cup

TARTLETS

A delicious luncheon dish.

Tart Pastry (page 419) or Standard
  Pastry (page 419)
2 cups grated Swiss cheese
1 cup milk
2 eggs
1/4 teaspoon salt
1/4 teaspoon dry mustard
Dash of hot pepper sauce

Line with pastry 16 well-greased tart-
let pans 3" across and 1" deep. Half-
fill with beaten cheese, milk and egg
mixture seasoned to taste. Bake in hot
oven (425°F.) 15 minutes. Makes 16.

STOVE-TOP CHEESE FONDUE

2 slices firm bread
2-3/4 cups (3/4 pound) diced sharp
  Cheddar cheese
3/4 cup milk
1 teaspoon dry mustard
1/4 teaspoon salt
Dash of cayenne
1 egg, slightly beaten
1 tablespoon butter
6 slices toast or crisp crackers
Paprika

Cut crusts from bread and cut bread
in 1/4" cubes. Put in top of double
boiler. Add next 5 ingredients. Put
over hot water until cheese melts and
mixture thickens, stirring constantly.
Beat in egg and butter and cook, stirring, about 5 minutes. Serve on toast
with a sprinkling of paprika. Serves 6.

TRUE SWISS FONDUE

4 cups (1 pound) shredded Swiss cheese
3 tablespoons flour
1 large clove garlic
2 cups dry white wine (such as
  Neufchâtel, Rhine wine, Riesling or
  Chablis)
1/2 teaspoon nutmeg
Salt and pepper
6 tablespoons kirsch

Dredge cheese with flour. Rub chafing
dish or earthenware cooking pot or
heatproof china casserole with garlic.
Pour in wine and put over low heat
to keep mixture just below boiling
point (when the air bubbles rise to
the surface). Add cheese by spoonfuls, stirring with a fork until each
spoonful is completely absorbed.
Keep stirring until mixture starts bubbling lightly. It must not boil or the
cheese will become stringy. Season
with nutmeg, salt and pepper. Stir in
kirsch thoroughly. Remove fondue
from heat and place on preheated
serving equipment. Keep warm but
do not boil. Makes 4 to 6 servings.

SHRIMP FONDUE

1 can condensed frozen shrimp soup
1 cup shredded Swiss cheese
2 tablespoons dry white wine
Cubes of rye or French bread

Heat shrimp soup in top pan of double boiler over boiling water. Add
cheese and stir occasionally until
melted. Stir in wine. Serve as a dunk
with the cubes of bread. Serves 4.

ONIONS, SWISS STYLE

2 sweet onions, sliced thin
2 tablespoons butter
Salt and pepper
2 cups grated Swiss cheese
1 can condensed cream of chicken soup
1 cup milk
1 cup buttered bread crumbs
Crisp toast

Separate onion slices into rings
and sauté in butter until golden,
then cover pan and simmer 10 minutes. Put in buttered baking dish,
season and cover with cheese. Dilute
soup with milk and pour over cheese.
Top with crumbs and bake in moderate oven (375°F.) 1/2 hour. Serve as
a dunk snack with crisp toast. Makes
4 servings.

ITALIAN TOMATO PIES

1 package dry yeast
1-1/2 teaspoons sugar
2-1/2 teaspoons salt
1/2 cup shortening
6 cups all-purpose flour
2 cans (2 ounces each) flat anchovy
  fillets
2 or 3 cloves garlic, minced
2 cans (29 ounces each) Italian-style
  tomatoes, drained
Pepper, cayenne and salt
1 pound mozzarella cheese, thinly sliced
2/3 cup grated Parmesan cheese
Oregano

Soften yeast in 1/4 cup lukewarm
water. Put sugar, salt and shortening
in bowl; add 1 3/4 cups boiling water
and stir until shortening is melted.
Cool to lukewarm. Stir in yeast mixture. Add half the flour; beat until
smooth. Gradually stir in remaining
flour. Divide dough into 4 portions.
Roll each on floured board to about
13" in diameter. Shape on bottom
and sides of lightly greased 12" pizza
pans. Let rise in warm place until
light. Drain anchovies; mix anchovy
oil with garlic and brush on dough.
Cover with tomatoes; season. Arrange
mozzarella and anchovies on top.
Sprinkle with Parmesan cheese and
oregano. Bake in hot oven (425°F.)
15 to 20 minutes. Cut in wedges and
serve at once. Makes four 12" pies.

CHEESE FONDUE

Tradition says that if a lady drops bread into the fondue, the men at the table may kiss her; if a man drops bread into the cheese, he may kiss any girl he chooses.

1 clove garlic
2 cups dry white wine
1 pound Swiss cheese, finely cut
1 teaspoon cornstarch
3 tablespoons kirsch, Cognac, applejack or vodka
Pinch of nutmeg
Dash of hot pepper sauce
2 loaves Italian or French bread with hard crust

Rub an enameled metal casserole with garlic. Pour in wine and set over low heat. Heat until air bubbles rise to the surface and then add cheese by handfuls, stirring constantly with a wooden spoon or fork. Keep stirring until the cheese is melted. Add cornstarch dissolved in kirsch. Stir again for 2 or 3 minutes and season with nutmeg and hot pepper sauce. Place casserole on the table on a hot plate or over an alcohol burner to keep it barely bubbling. Cut bread into bite-size pieces, each with one side of crust. Guests spear pieces of bread on fondue forks and dip them into the cheese. Makes 4 to 6 servings.

WESTERN CHEESE CASSEROLE

Two kinds of cheese flavor this hearty casserole.

1 can (4 ounces) green chilies
1 medium onion, finely chopped
2 tablespoons butter
1 can (8 ounces) tomato sauce
1/2 teaspoon salt
2 eggs, slightly beaten
1 cup half-and-half (half milk, half cream)
1 bag (6 ounces) corn chips
1/2 pound Jack cheese or mild Cheddar, cut in 1/2" cubes
1 cup dairy sour cream
1/2 cup shredded Cheddar cheese
Paprika

Remove seed from chilies and chop chilies coarsely. Sauté onion in the butter 2 to 3 minutes. Add chilies, tomato sauce and salt and simmer 5 minutes. Remove from heat. Mix eggs and half-and-half and stir into sauce. Put half the corn chips in greased shallow 1½-quart baking dish. Add half the Jack cheese, then half the sauce. Repeat layers and top with sour cream. Sprinkle with Cheddar and paprika. Bake in moderate oven (350°F.) about 30 minutes. Makes 6 servings.

CHEESE RISOTTO

1 cup chopped onion
3 tablespoons butter or margarine
1 cup uncooked regular rice
1 can (1 pound) tomatoes
2 chicken bouillon cubes
1 can (3 ounces) sliced mushrooms, drained
1 cup shredded sharp Cheddar cheese

Cook onion in the butter in large heavy saucepan until tender. Add rice and cook, stirring, until very lightly browned. Add remaining ingredients, except cheese. Bring to boil, stirring until bouillon cubes are dissolved. Cover and simmer 20 to 25 minutes, or until rice is tender and all liquid absorbed. Add cheese and stir gently into rice with fork so that cheese melts. Serve at once. Makes 6 servings.

DOUBLE-CHEESE AND MASHED-POTATO PIE

2 cups firm mashed potatoes
1/2 cup finely diced mozzarella cheese
1/2 cup finely diced sharp Cheddar cheese
2 eggs, well beaten
1 teaspoon dried parsley flakes
Freshly ground black pepper to taste
1/4 cup sliced or slivered almonds or other nuts, chopped
Garlic salt
Butter or margarine

Combine and mix well first 6 ingredients. Put in buttered 9" piepan and sprinkle with almonds. Sprinkle lightly with garlic salt, then dot with butter. Bake in hot oven (400°F.) 15 to 20 minutes, or until puffy and golden brown. Makes 6 servings.

HOT CHEESE-MACARONI SALAD

2 cups bowknots or other macaroni
Salt
1/4 pound bacon, diced
1/2 teaspoon paprika
1 teaspoon dry mustard
1 tablespoon blue-cheese salad-dressing mix
1/4 cup wine vinegar with garlic
1/2 cup dairy sour cream
1 cup chopped celery
1/2 cup chopped green onions
1/2 cup shredded carrot
1/2 cup chopped filberts

Cook macaroni in boiling salted water until tender; drain. Cook bacon until crisp and drain on paper towel. Mix next 5 ingredients and stir into macaroni. Fold in remaining ingredients. Put in greased 1½- to 2-quart casserole, sprinkle with bacon and bake in slow oven (300°F.) 20 minutes, or until heated. Makes 6 servings.

QUICHE LORRAINE

France's classic cheese pie, with bacon.

1-1/2 cups grated Swiss cheese
   (6 ounces)
8 slices crisp bacon, crumbled
Unbaked 9" pie shell
3 eggs
1 cup heavy cream
1/2 cup milk
1/2 teaspoon salt
1/4 teaspoon pepper
Dash of cayenne
1/2 teaspoon dry mustard

Sprinkle cheese and bacon in pie shell. Beat remaining ingredients together and pour into pie shell. Bake in moderate oven (375°F.) 45 minutes, or until firm and browned. Cut in wedges and serve warm. Serves 6.

COTTAGE-CHEESE QUICHE

With a tossed green salad, it makes a satisfying luncheon.

1/2 cup grated Swiss cheese
Deep 9" pie shell, partially baked
1-1/2 cups onion-chive cottage cheese
4 eggs
1/2 cup light cream
1-1/2 teaspoons salt
Dash of pepper
3/4 cup canned French-fried onion rings

Sprinkle Swiss cheese in pie shell. Beat together next 5 ingredients. Pour into shell. Bake in moderate oven (350°F.) 40 to 45 minutes. About 15 minutes before quiche is done, sprinkle top with onions. Finish baking. Cool slightly before serving. Makes 6 servings.

CORN QUICHE

1 can (12 ounces) whole-kernel corn,
   drained
1/4 cup grated Swiss or Parmesan cheese
Unbaked 9" pie shell
5 eggs
1-1/2 cups light cream
1 teaspoon instant minced onion
1 teaspoon seasoned salt
1/8 teaspoon pepper
4 slices crisp bacon, crumbled

Mix corn and cheese and put in bottom of pie shell. Beat next 5 ingredients. Pour over corn. Sprinkle with bacon. Bake in hot oven (400°F.) 25 minutes. Reduce heat to 350°F. and bake about 20 minutes longer. Serve at once. Makes 4 to 6 servings.

POTATO, CHEESE AND ONION PIE

3 cups sliced onion
2 tablespoons butter or margarine
1 can condensed cream of mushroom
   soup
Salt and pepper
Pinch of sage
6 cooked medium potatoes, sliced
1/4 pound Cheddar cheese, sliced
Pastry Wedges

Brown onion lightly in butter; cover and cook slowly until tender. Add soup and ½ cup water; season with salt, pepper and sage. Arrange potatoes and half of cheese in 2-quart casserole. Pour onion mixture over and top with remaining cheese. Bake in hot oven (400°F.) 15 minutes, until cheese is lightly browned. Top with baked Pastry Wedges. Makes 4 servings. **Pastry Wedges** Prepare ½ recipe Standard Pastry (page 311). Roll pastry ½" thick to fit top of casserole. Cut in 4 wedges and brush with beaten egg yolk or cream. Bake on cookie sheet in oven while pie bakes.

SCOTCH WOODCOCK

2 egg yolks
2 tablespoons butter or margarine
2 tablespoons light cream
1 tablespoon chopped parsley
Salt and pepper
Anchovy paste
2 slices hot toast, cut in halves or
   quarters

Beat egg yolks in top part of double boiler until thick. Add butter, cream and parsley. Cook over hot water, stirring until thick. Add salt and pepper to taste. Spread anchovy paste on hot toast. Pour egg mixture over toast and serve at once. Serves 4 to 8.

SOUTH-OF-THE-BORDER RABBIT

1 green pepper, chopped
1/2 small onion, minced
1/4 cup butter
1/4 cup undiluted evaporated milk
1/2 pound sharp Cheddar cheese,
   cut in pieces
1/2 teaspoon Worcestershire
2 tablespoons catsup
1 can (1 pound) red kidney beans,
   undrained
Toast points or crisp crackers

Sauté green pepper and onion in butter in top part of double boiler over direct heat. Add milk and cheese and cook until cheese is melted, stirring occasionally. Put over boiling water and add next 3 ingredients; cover and heat about 15 minutes. Serve on toast. Makes 6 servings.

WELSH RABBIT

2 tablespoons butter
1 pound Cheddar cheese, cubed
1/2 teaspoon each salt and dry mustard
Dash of cayenne
1 teaspoon Worcestershire
1/2 cup milk
2 eggs, slightly beaten
8 slices hot toast

Melt butter in top part of double boiler over boiling water. Add cheese; stir until melted. Add next 5 ingredients. Cook, stirring, until thickened. Serve hot on toast. Serves 4 to 6.

GOLDEN FLEECE

2 packages (3 ounces each) cream cheese
3/4 cup milk
4 eggs
1/2 teaspoon salt
1/2 teaspoon dry mustard

Heat cheese in top of double boiler over hot water until softened. Remove from heat. Add remaining ingredients and beat until blended. Pour into individual baking dishes or custard cups and bake in pan of hot water in moderate oven (375°F.) 20 to 25 minutes. Makes 4 servings.

RINGTUM DITTY

1 can condensed tomato soup
2 medium onions, sliced
1 pound American cheese, sliced
1 teaspoon salt
1 teaspoon paprika
1 teaspoon dry mustard
1/2 teaspoon pepper
1 teaspoon Worcestershire
3 eggs, separated
Toast or crackers

Mix 1/2 cup water with soup in saucepan. Add onions and simmer 10 minutes. Add cheese and cook, stirring, until cheese is melted. Add seasonings beaten with egg yolks. Fold in stiffly beaten egg whites. Serve on toast or crackers. Prepare this dish in saucepan ahead of time, and reheat over boiling water in chafing dish. Makes 4 to 6 servings.

CHEESE SAUCE

Melt 2 tablespoons butter in saucepan. Stir in 2 tablespoons flour. Add 1 cup chicken broth slowly, continuing to stir. Add 1/2 cup heavy cream, and salt and pepper to taste. Cook until medium thick. Fold in 1/2 cup grated Parmesan or shredded Swiss or Gruyère cheese. Stir until cheese begins to melt. Makes about 2 cups of sauce.

MEDIUM WHITE SAUCE

Melt 2 tablespoons butter and blend in 2 tablespoons flour. Gradually add 1 cup milk and cook, stirring, 5 minutes, until smooth and thickened. Add salt and pepper to taste. Makes about 1 cup sauce.

CHEESE SPINACH PIE

You can cook it in 20 minutes.

Cook and drain 1 box (10 ounces) frozen chopped spinach. Add 1 cup cottage cheese, 2 beaten eggs, 1 teaspoon caraway seed, 1 teaspoon seasoned salt, 1/4 teaspoon seasoned pepper and a dash of nutmeg. Put in small shallow casserole or 8" piepan. Sprinkle with 2 tablespoons grated Parmesan cheese and dot with 1 tablespoon butter. Sprinkle with paprika. Bake in moderate oven (350°F.) about 20 minutes. Makes 4 servings.

FRIED TOAST WITH ANCHOVIES

1/2 pound mozzarella cheese, sliced thin
8 anchovy fillets
16 slices bread, 1/2" thick, from long French loaf
1/2 teaspoon pepper
1/2 cup all-purpose flour
2 eggs, beaten
Olive oil

Put a slice of mozzarella and 1 anchovy fillet on each of 8 slices of bread. Sprinkle with pepper and cover with another slice of bread. Dip in cold water and roll in flour. Then dip in beaten egg and fry in olive oil until golden brown on each side. Serves 4.

PUFFED TOAST SQUARES

1/2 pound Cheddar cheese, softened
1/2 cup butter or margarine, softened
Mustard
Curry powder
Caraway or celery seed
Salt and pepper, or paprika
White bread, cut in 1-1/2" cubes

Blend cheese, butter and seasonings. Cover bread cubes with the cheese spread. Keep chilled until ready for use. Put on baking sheet and put in moderate oven (375°F.) until browned and puffed. Makes 4 servings. *Note* Any of the following seasonings are also delicious creamed with the butter: chili powder, dillseed, grated lemon rind, parsley or pimiento.

TWO-CHEESE PUDDING

4 eggs, beaten
1/8 teaspoon salt
1/2 teaspoon paprika
1 cup creamed small-curd cottage cheese
1/4 cup shredded sharp Cheddar cheese

Combine all ingredients in mixing bowl and blend well. Pour into buttered shallow 1-quart baking dish and bake in moderate oven (350°F.) 25 minutes, or until set. Serve at once. Good with creamed vegetables, mixed salad or frankfurters. Make 4 servings.

EASY TWO-CHEESE LASAGNA

1/2 pound curly lasagna noodles
1 pound ground beef
1 can (10-3/4 ounces) condensed
   Cheddar-cheese soup
1 soup-can milk
Garlic salt, pepper
2 cups coarsely shredded sharp Cheddar
   cheese
3 cups ricotta cheese
2 eggs, beaten

Cook noodles as directed on package, drain well and keep separated by laying flat between sheets of waxed paper. Cook meat, breaking up with fork, in skillet until lightly browned (drain off excess fat). In bowl, mix meat, soup and milk and season to taste with garlic salt and pepper. Line bottom of greased shallow baking dish about 13″ x 9″ x 2″ with noodles and cover with half the meat sauce. Sprinkle with a third of the Cheddar cheese. Mix ricotta cheese and eggs. Dot casserole with half the mixture. Repeat layers, ending with ricotta mixture, then sprinkle with remaining third of Cheddar cheese. Bake in moderate oven (350°F.) about 40 minutes. Let stand 10 minutes, then cut in squares with shears. Make 8 servings.

CHEESE TOAST SPECIAL

2 tablespoons butter or margarine
1-1/2 tablespoons all-purpose flour
1/2 cup milk
1/2 cup grated Swiss cheese
3 tablespoons dry white wine
1/2 teaspoon dry mustard
1 clove garlic, minced
1 egg, beaten
Salt and white pepper to taste
Slices of diagonally cut French bread

Melt butter, blend in flour, add milk and cook, stirring, until thick and smooth. Cool 15 minutes. Stir in remaining ingredients, except bread. Toast bread on one side. Spread untoasted side with ¹/₂″ layer of cheese mixture. Heat and lightly brown under broiler. Makes 4 servings.

CHEESE CROQUETTES WITH GREEN NOODLES

1/2 pound green noodles
1/3 cup butter
1/2 pound Gruyère, cut in strips 2″ x 1″
1 egg, beaten
Fine dry bread crumbs
Olive or peanut oil
1/2 cup grated Romano cheese
2 tablespoons chopped parsley
Pine nuts
Paprika

Cook noodles in boiling salted water until just tender. Drain and combine with butter. Dip strips of cheese into egg and roll in crumbs. Brown in hot oil. Sprinkle grated Romano cheese and parsley on noodles in a serving dish. Arrange cheese croquettes on the noodles and sprinkle with pine nuts and paprika. Serves 4 to 6.

RICH CHEESE-MACARONI CASSEROLE

8 ounces Swiss cheese, coarsely shredded
1/4 cup grated Romano or Parmesan
   cheese
3 tablespoons butter or margarine
2 tablespoons all-purpose flour
1 cup milk
1 cup heavy cream, slightly whipped
1/2 teaspoon salt
Freshly ground black pepper to taste
2 cups elbow macaroni, cooked and
   drained
Paprika

Put half the Swiss cheese in buttered deep 2-quart casserole and sprinkle with half the Romano cheese. Melt butter in small saucepan, stir in flour and cook over low heat, stirring, 2 minutes. Gradually stir in milk and simmer until smooth and thickened. Fold in whipped cream and add salt and pepper. Pour over macaroni in mixing bowl and toss until well mixed. Pour into cheese-lined casserole. Sprinkle with remaining Swiss and Romano cheeses and, lightly, with paprika. Bake in moderate oven (350°F.) 20 minutes, or until cheese is melted and top is golden brown. Good with fruit salad. Serves 6.

EGGS LORRAINE

For each serving, put a slice of Canadian bacon or smoked pork tenderloin in lightly buttered shirred-egg dish. Cover with a thin slice of Swiss cheese. Top with 1 egg; season with salt and white pepper. Top with 1 tablespoon sour or heavy cream. Bake in hot oven (400°F.) 12 minutes, or until done.

BACON-CHEESE TOAST

🕐 Blend well 8 strips lean bacon, minced, and ½ pound Cheddar cheese, grated. Spread on lightly buttered bread. Broil on baking sheet until cheese is melted. Makes 4 to 6 servings.

FRENCH CHEESE TOAST

1/2 pound grated or minced Cheddar cheese
1/2 teaspoon salt
Dash of cayenne
1/4 cup milk
3 tablespoons butter or margarine
French toast
Chopped chives (optional)

Mix first 5 ingredients and stir over very low heat until smooth. Spread on browned French toast. Arrange on shallow ovenproof platter. Brown lightly in moderate oven (350°F.). Sprinkle with chives, if desired.

DUTCH ONION PIE

3 cups thinly sliced onions
2 tablespoons butter
1 pound cottage cheese
1/4 cup heavy cream
Baked 9" pie shell
Salt and pepper
Cayenne

Fry onions in butter until soft. Moisten cheese with cream and pour into shell. Season lightly with salt and pepper. Cover with onions, add more salt and pepper and dash of cayenne. Bake in hot oven (400°F.) 15 minutes. Makes 6 servings.

COTTAGE CHEESE AND BROCCOLI AU GRATIN

Seasoned salt and pepper add zest to this simple dish.

1 box (10 ounces) frozen chopped broccoli
1 cup cottage cheese
2 eggs, slightly beaten
1/4 teaspoon salt
1 teaspoon seasoned salt
1/4 teaspoon pepper
1/4 teaspoon steak sauce
1 teaspoon instant minced onion
1/4 cup butter, melted
1/4 cup soft bread crumbs

🕐 Cook and drain broccoli. Mix with next 7 ingredients. Stir in 2 tablespoons butter and put mixture in small shallow baking dish or 8" piepan. Mix remaining butter and crumbs; sprinkle on top. Bake in moderate oven (350°F.) 30 minutes. Makes 4 servings.

TUNA-CHEDDAR CHOWDER

Salt
1 large potato, peeled and cut in 1/2" dice
1/2 cup each diced carrot and celery
1 small onion, chopped
1/4 cup butter or margarine
1/4 cup flour
2 cups milk
3/4 pound sharp Cheddar cheese, shredded
1 can (6-1/2 ounces) tuna, drained and flaked
1 can (8 ounces) cream-style corn
Pinch of dried rosemary
Few drops of hot pepper sauce
Chopped chives

🍲 Put 2 cups boiling water in saucepan and season with one teaspoon salt. Add next 3 ingredients, bring to boil, cover and simmer 10 minutes; do not drain. In Dutch oven melt butter and blend in flour. Gradually stir in milk and cook, stirring, until smooth and thickened. Add cheese and stir until melted. Add vegetables, liquid, tuna, corn and rosemary. Salt to taste. Serve with a garnish of chives. Makes about 2 quarts, or 6 servings.

MANICOTTI

1 cup all-purpose flour
Salt
7 eggs
Vegetable oil
2 pounds ricotta cheese
Grated Parmesan or Romano cheese
1/4 teaspoon pepper
1/2 pound mozzarella, cut in 12 strips
3 cans (8 ounces each) tomato sauce

To make pancakes, combine flour, 1 cup water and ¼ teaspoon salt and beat until smooth. Beat in 4 eggs, one at a time. Heat a 5" to 6" skillet and grease with a few drops of oil. Put about 3 tablespoons batter in hot skillet and roll pan around to distribute evenly. Cook over low heat until firm (do not brown). Turn and cook lightly on other side. Continue making pancakes until all batter is used. (Do not grease skillet a second time.) Makes 12 to 14 pancakes. To make filling, mix ½ teaspoon salt, 3 eggs, ricotta, ¼ cup grated cheese and the pepper. Put about 2 tablespoons filling and a strip of mozzarella on each pancake and roll up. Pour 1 can tomato sauce into large shallow baking dish. Put pancakes, seam side down, in sauce. Cover with remaining 2 cans sauce and sprinkle with ½ cup grated cheese. Bake in moderate oven (350° F.) 45 minutes. Makes 6 generous servings.

CHEESE FRITTERS

1 egg, beaten
1/2 cup milk
1 teaspoon Worcestershire
1 tablespoon instant minced onion or 1 small onion, minced
Dash of hot pepper sauce
2 cups biscuit mix
1-1/2 cups diced process American cheese
Fat for deep frying
Tart jelly

Mix first 6 ingredients well; stir in cheese. Drop by tablespoons into hot deep fat (365°F. on a frying thermometer) and fry until golden brown. Drain on absorbent paper. Serve with jelly. Makes about 20.

FRIED MOZZARELLA

A Roman and Neapolitan dish that's good for lunch or meatless days.

8 slices bread
4 slices mozzarella about 1/4" thick
Flour
2 eggs, lightly beaten
Olive oil for frying
White Anchovy Sauce, page 241

Trim crusts from bread. Dip mozzarella in flour and put each slice between 2 slices of bread, sandwich fashion. Dip in beaten egg. Heat oil. Fry sandwiches, turning once, until bread is golden and cheese begins to melt. Serve with sauce. Makes 4.

EGGPLANT PARMIGIANA

Hearty enough for a main course.

2 cups olive oil
1 clove garlic, minced
1 large onion, chopped
5 cups canned Italian-style tomatoes
1/2 teaspoon basil
Salt and pepper
1 cup all-purpose flour
2 eggs, beaten
1 cup milk
2 medium eggplants, cut in 1/2" slices
1 cup grated Parmesan
8 ounces mozzarella cheese, diced
1/4 cup butter

Heat 1/4 cup oil in skillet. Sauté garlic and onion in it until soft. Add next 3 ingredients. Cook, covered, stirring occasionally, 30 minutes. Mix flour, eggs and milk. Dip eggplant slices in mixture; fry in remaining hot oil until just browned. Add more olive oil after each frying. Arrange alternate layers of eggplant, sauce and cheeses in casserole, sprinkling each with salt and pepper. Dot with butter; bake in moderate oven (350°F.) 30 minutes. Serves 6 to 8.

ROMANO-CHEESE ROLLS

Add enough finely grated Romano cheese and garlic salt to mayonnaise to season well. Separate sections of flaked butter rolls or make 4 crosswise slits in dinner rolls, cutting almost to bottom crust. Fill slits with mayonnaise mixture and fasten with toothpicks. Bake in hot oven (400°F.) about 10 minutes, or until heated.

GNOCCHI PARMESAN
(Italian Dumplings with Cheese)

1/2 cup milk
1/2 cup butter
Salt
1-1/3 cups all-purpose flour
5 eggs
Cheese Sauce
Paprika
Grated Parmesan cheese

Heat 1/2 cup water, the milk and butter to boiling. Add 1/4 teaspoon salt and the flour all at once and stir vigorously until mixture leaves the sides of the saucepan and forms a ball. Remove from heat and add eggs, one at a time, beating well after each. Drop a measuring-half-teaspoonful at a time into boiling salted water. When balls come to the surface, remove to a bowl of cold water. Drain well and mix with Cheese Sauce. Put in a shallow baking dish and sprinkle with paprika and 1/2 cup grated Parmesan cheese. Bake in moderate oven (375° F.) about 30 minutes. Makes 4 servings. **Cheese Sauce** Cook 1 small minced onion in 2 tablespoons butter 5 minutes. Blend in 1 1/2 tablespoons flour, 1/2 teaspoon salt, 1/4 teaspoon pepper and a dash of nutmeg. Gradually add 1 cup milk; cook, stirring, until thickened. Remove from heat; stir in 1/2 cup grated Parmesan cheese. **Gnocchi Mornay** Layer drained cooked gnocchi in buttered shallow baking dish with 2 cups Mornay Sauce and 1/2 cup grated Parmesan or Gruyère cheese. Dot with butter. Bake in hot oven (400°F.) 15 to 20 minutes, or until bubbly-hot and glazed on top. **Mornay Sauce** Melt 2 tablespoons butter in saucepan and blend in 3 tablespoons flour. Stir over low heat about 2 minutes, but do not brown. Gradually stir in 2 cups scalded milk. Stir over moderate heat with wooden spoon or wire whisk until mixture comes to full boil. Boil 1 minute, stirring constantly. Season with salt, white pepper or cayenne and a dash of nutmeg. Remove from heat and blend in 1/3 cup grated Swiss or Parmesan cheese, or a mixture of both. Makes 2 cups sauce.

FARMER BROWN'S POTATO BAKE

3 tablespoons butter
1 small onion, minced
3 medium potatoes, cooked and thinly sliced
Ground rosemary
Salt and pepper
1 pound cottage cheese, beaten smooth
1/4 cup dairy sour cream
2 eggs, slightly beaten
2 tablespoons flour

Melt butter in skillet, add onion and potatoes. Cook, turning occasionally, until lightly browned. Put in shallow 1½-quart baking dish. Sprinkle lightly with seasonings. Mix remaining ingredients, a dash of rosemary, 1 teaspoon salt and a dash of pepper. Pour over potato mixture. Bake in moderate oven (375°F.) ½ hour, or until set. Serves 4 to 6.

SCALLOPED COTTAGE CHEESE AND ONIONS

A really hearty vegetable dish.

6 medium onions
3 tablespoons butter or margarine
3 tablespoons flour
1 cup milk
1 teaspoon salt
Dash of pepper
1/4 teaspoon paprika
1 cup dry cottage cheese
1 green pepper, minced
1 cup soft stale-bread crumbs

Slice onions very thin; cook in boiling water until soft. Melt 2 tablespoons butter and stir in flour. Gradually add milk, stirring until thick. Add next 5 ingredients. Drain onions; arrange in buttered baking dish in alternate layers with cheese mixture and cover with bread crumbs. Dot with remaining butter or margarine. Bake in moderate oven (350°F.) about 20 minutes. Makes 4 servings.

EGGS IN SOUR-CREAM SAUCE

3/4 cup chopped green onions and tops
2 tablespoons butter
8 eggs
Salt and pepper
1/4 cup minced sweet pickle
1 cup dairy sour cream
Paprika

Cook onion in butter in skillet 5 minutes. Break eggs onto onion and sprinkle with salt and pepper. Mix pickle and sour cream; pour over eggs. Sprinkle with paprika, cover and simmer 15 minutes to desired doneness. Makes 4 servings.

COTTAGE-CHEESE GREEN-NOODLE CASSEROLE

A wonderful accompaniment for cold meats on a buffet table.

1/4 pound green noodles
Salt and pepper
1 cup cottage cheese
1/2 cup dairy sour cream
1 onion, minced
1 small clove garlic, minced
1 teaspoon steak sauce
1 teaspoon seasoned salt
1/2 cup soft bread crumbs
1/2 cup shredded Cheddar cheese

Cook noodles in salted boiling water until tender. Drain and mix with next 7 ingredients. Put in shallow 1-quart baking dish. Sprinkle with combined crumbs and cheese. Bake in moderate oven (350°F.) 30 minutes. Makes 4 servings.

STEAK DE FROMAGE

A delicious luncheon dish.

1 pound Swiss or Gruyere cheese
Beer Batter
Butter
8 eggs
Dash of hot pepper sauce
Salt and pepper

Cut 3" by 5" slices of cheese ½" thick. Dip in batter and sauté in butter to brown on both sides. Arrange in a 15" x 10" baking pan. Beat eggs well; add 2 teaspoons water and seasonings. Pour over cheese and bake in moderate oven (375°F.) about 12 minutes. Makes 6 servings. **Beer Batter** Combine 2 slightly beaten eggs, ²/₃ cup beer and ¼ teaspoon hot pepper sauce. Slowly beat in 1 cup all-purpose flour, ½ teaspoon salt and 2 tablespoons oil.

EGGS MORNAY

6 tablespoons butter or margarine
6 tablespoons flour
1-3/4 cups milk
1 cup chicken broth
4 ounces sharp Cheddar cheese, diced
1/2 cup grated Parmesan cheese
1/4 cup sherry
1/2 teaspoon Worcestershire
Salt and white pepper
12 hard-boiled eggs, shelled
Croutons
Chopped parsley

Make a sauce with first 8 ingredients. Add salt and pepper to taste. Put eggs in shallow baking dish. Surround with sauce and sprinkle with croutons. Reheat in slow oven (300°F.) and sprinkle with parsley. Makes 6 servings.

EGGS POACHED IN CREAM

Heat ½ cup heavy cream, seasoned with salt and pepper, in large skillet. Break in 8 eggs. Cover and poach to desired doneness. Serve on hot toast. Makes 4 servings.

WAFFLE EGG OMELET

Make a smooth paste with ¼ cup each flour and cold water. Add 4 well-beaten egg yolks, ½ teaspoon salt, ⅛ teaspoon pepper and 2 tablespoons melted butter or margarine. Mix well and fold in 4 stiffly beaten egg whites. Put in moderately hot large waffle iron and bake about 3 minutes. Cut in quarters; serve with jelly. Makes 3 to 4 servings.

MUSHROOM OMELET

1/2 pound mushrooms, thinly sliced
4 tablespoons butter or margarine
Salt, pepper and paprika
6 eggs

Sauté mushrooms in 2 tablespoons butter 3 to 4 minutes. Add seasonings to taste and keep warm. With fork, lightly beat eggs, ⅓ cup water, ½ teaspoon salt and ⅛ teaspoon pepper. Heat remaining butter in 10" skillet. Pour in egg mixture; it should set at edges at once. Draw edges toward center with fork so that uncooked portion flows to side and bottom. Tilt skillet to hasten flow of uncooked egg. When egg is set and surface is still moist, increase heat to quickly brown bottom. Remove from heat. Spoon mushrooms evenly in center; and fold sides over filling. Turn out on hot platter and serve at once. Makes 3 to 4 servings.
Corn Omelet Omit mushrooms. Cook 2 tablespoons each green pepper and onion in 3 tablespoons butter 2 or 3 minutes. Add 1 cup cooked whole-kernel corn, ¼ cup heavy cream and salt and pepper to taste; let simmer while preparing omelet. When omelet is done, top with corn mixture. Fold over and put on a hot platter. Sprinkle with ¼ cup grated Cheddar cheese.

Chicken Omelet Omit mushrooms. Heat ¼ cup milk, ¼ teaspoon pepper, 1 can condensed cream of chicken soup, 1 cup diced cooked chicken, 1 teaspoon Worcestershire and ½ cup chopped ripe olives. When omelet is done, cover center with some of the chicken mixture, fold sides over and turn out on hot platter. Top with remaining sauce; sprinkle with parsley.

SAILOR'S OMELET

Garlic
3 tablespoons anchovy paste
2 tablespoons heavy cream
8 eggs
2 tablespoons chopped parsley
Dash of cayenne
4 slices smoked salmon

Rub a bowl with garlic; add anchovy paste and cream; mix until smooth. Add eggs, parsley and cayenne. Beat well and pour into greased skillet. Cook, lifting edges with spatula to allow uncooked egg to run under. When firm, fold and serve garnished with salmon. Makes 4 servings.

FLUFFY CRAB-FLAKE OMELET

3 tablespoons lemon juice or vinegar
1 pound crab meat, flaked
4 eggs, separated
1/2 cup milk
1 teaspoon salt
1/4 teaspoon black pepper
2 tablespoons chopped parsley
2 tablespoons grated onion
1/4 cup butter, melted

Add lemon juice to crab flakes. Beat egg whites stiff and set aside. Beat egg yolks and stir in next 5 ingredients. Mix well with crab flakes. Fold in stiffly beaten egg whites and pour into hot butter in ovenproof skillet. Cook slowly on top of stove 5 to 10 minutes. When cooked through, put in slow oven (300°F.) a few minutes to dry top. When dry enough to touch, remove and cut edges loose from pan. Fold over onto hot platter. Makes 4 servings.

SPANISH SAUCE

1 small clove garlic, minced
1 small onion, chopped
8 black or pimiento-stuffed olives, chopped
1 can (4 ounces) mushroom stems and pieces, drained
2 tablespoons butter or margarine
1 can (8 ounces) tomato sauce
2 tablespoons chopped parsley
1/4 teaspoon salt
1/4 teaspoon oregano or basil
Cracked pepper to taste
1 tablespoon dry sherry or Madeira wine (optional)

Sauté first 4 ingredients in the butter 2 to 3 minutes. Add remaining ingredients. Simmer, uncovered, 10 minutes, or until most of liquid has evaporated. When omelet is done, spoon half the sauce on omelet and fold omelet over. Pour remaining sauce on top. Makes 4 servings.

BAKED EGGS, SHRIMP AND MUSHROOMS

6 hard-cooked eggs
1/2 teaspoon instant minced onion
8 tablespoons butter or margarine
Salt and pepper
1/4 cup flour
1-1/2 cups half-and-half, or milk
12 cooked shelled cleaned shrimp
1/2 pound mushrooms, sliced
1/3 cup grated Parmesan cheese

Cut eggs lengthwise and scoop out yolks. Mash yolks with onion and 2 tablespoons butter. Season with salt and pepper. Beat until light and fluffy. Fill egg whites with the mixture. Put egg halves in shallow baking dish. Heat 4 tablespoons butter and blend in flour. Gradually add half-and-half and cook, stirring, until smooth and thickened. Add shrimp. Cook mushrooms in remaining butter until slightly browned. Add to shrimp mixture. Pour over eggs and sprinkle with cheese. Bake in hot oven (425°F.) 10 to 15 minutes. Makes 4 to 6 servings.

EGG ROLLS

1 cup all-purpose flour
4 eggs
1 teaspoon salt
Filling
Fat for frying
Dry mustard

Sift flour and salt into bowl. Beat eggs. Reserve 2 tablespoons beaten egg and add rest to flour, beating until smooth. Gradually add 1 cup water and mix well. Lightly grease a 7" skillet. Pour in just enough batter to cover bottom of pan. Cook over medium heat until batter is set. Remove and cool. Repeat until all batter is used. You should have 12 pancakes. Divide Filling into 12 even portions and place a mound in the center of each pancake. Roll tightly, folding sides over as you go, moistening the edges with the reserved beaten egg and sealing. Fry rolls in 1" hot oil (350°F. on a frying thermometer) until golden brown; turn and brown other side. Serve hot with dry mustard mixed to a paste with a little water. Makes 12 rolls. **Filling** Soak 2 large dried mushrooms in warm water 20 minutes. Squeeze dry and dice finely. Fry with 2 tablespoons each grated carrot, minced celery and minced green onion in 1 tablespoon oil 2 minutes. Add 1 cup each ground cooked pork and shrimp, 2 tablespoons minced water chestnuts and 2 teaspoons each salt and sugar.

BACON-EGG STRATA

8 slices bread, crust-trimmed
1/4 pound bacon, diced
4 eggs, slightly beaten
3 cups milk, scalded
1 teaspoon instant minced onion
3/4 teaspoon seasoned salt
1/4 teaspoon pepper

Cut each slice of bread in 3 strips and arrange half in shallow baking dish. Cook bacon crisp and spoon bacon and fat over bread. Cover with remaining bread. Mix remaining ingredients and pour over bread. Put in pan of hot water and bake in moderate oven (350°F.) 45 minutes, or until firm. Makes 4 to 6 servings.

HAM-EGG ALL-IN-ONE

1/2 cup butter or margarine
6 eggs, separated
3/4 cup grated Parmesan cheese
1/2 cup dairy sour cream
1-1/4 teaspoons salt
1/4 teaspoon pepper
1/4 cup flour
1/4 pound cooked ham, minced
1 can (8-1/2 ounces) peas, drained
1 small cauliflower, cooked and sliced
1 can (3 ounces) sliced mushrooms, drained

Cream butter, egg yolks, 2 tablespoons cheese and next 4 ingredients. Fold in stiffly beaten egg whites. Spread half of mixture in shallow baking dish. Sprinkle with ham and 2 tablespoons cheese. Cover with peas and 2 tablespoons more cheese. Repeat with cauliflower, more cheese, then mushrooms and remaining cheese. Spread remaining egg mixture over top. Bake in moderate oven (350°F.) about 45 minutes. Serves 6.

EGGS FOO YUNG

6 eggs
1 can (1 pound) bean sprouts, well drained
4 green onions, thinly sliced
1/2 cup minced water chestnuts
Soy sauce
1 tablespoon vegetable oil
1 cup chicken stock
1 tablespoon cornstarch

Beat eggs slightly and add next 3 ingredients and 1 tablespoon soy sauce. Heat oil in large skillet and pour in egg mixture. Cook, lifting edges to allow egg to run under. When set and browned on bottom, fold and put on a hot platter. Serve with sauce of chicken stock, cornstarch and 1 tablespoon soy sauce mixed in saucepan. Cook, stirring, until thickened. Makes 4 servings.

POACHED EGGS AL ROMANO

**1 can (8 ounces) meatless spaghetti
  sauce**
4 eggs
Salt and pepper
4 slices toast
Grated Romano cheese

Heat spaghetti sauce in skillet. Carefully drop eggs, one at a time, into sauce. Sprinkle with salt and freshly ground pepper. Cover and poach 5 minutes over low heat for medium-done eggs. Put one egg and some of the sauce on each slice of toast. Sprinkle with cheese. Makes 4 servings.

EGGS BENEDICT

Panfry 8 small thin ham slices until browned and done; keep warm. Split, butter and toast 4 English muffins under broiler. In large skillet, poach 8 eggs in boiling salted water. Top each of 8 muffin halves with a ham slice, then a poached egg. Serve at once with Hollandaise Sauce (page 222) and a garnish of parsley. Makes 4 servings.

VELVET EGGS

3 onions, sliced
3 tablespoons butter
2-1/2 tablespoons flour
1 teaspoon seasoned salt
1/4 teaspoon pepper
1-1/2 cups milk
1/2 cup light cream
1/2 cup grated Parmesan cheese
6 hard-cooked eggs, sliced
Chow-mein noodles or rice

Cook onions in butter until tender but not browned. Blend in flour and seasonings. Add liquids and cook, stirring, until thickened. Add cheese and eggs, heat and serve on noodles. Makes 4 servings.

SAVORY STUFFED EGGS

Halve 6 hard-cooked eggs lengthwise. Remove yolks; cream with ¼ cup butter or margarine, ¼ teaspoon salt, 1 tablespoon minced parsley and 1 teaspoon each Worcestershire and prepared mustard. Mix well. Fill egg whites with mixture; put in baking dish. Surround with 1 box frozen peas, partly cooked. Top with 1 can condensed cream of mushroom soup mixed with ½ cup milk and dash of pepper. Sprinkle with 1 cup grated Cheddar cheese and paprika. Bake in moderate oven (350°F.) 30 minutes. Serves 4.

EGGS ASTORIA

Spread buttered toast very lightly with anchovy paste. Top with a slice or more of smoked salmon and a poached egg. Serve with hot white sauce made with part cream.

HOT SKILLET SALAD

1/2 green pepper, chopped
1 small onion, minced
2 cups shredded lettuce
2 ripe tomatoes, chopped
6 eggs
2 tablespoons milk
1 teaspoon salt
1/8 teaspoon pepper
2 tablespoons olive oil

Mix all ingredients, except the oil. Heat oil in large skillet; add mixture and cook, stirring, until eggs are set. Makes 4 servings.

HOT SAVORY EGG SALAD

2 tablespoons butter
2 tablespoons flour
1-1/2 teaspoons salt
Pepper
1 cup milk
4 cups diced cooked potato
1 onion, minced
1 pimiento, chopped
1 cup diced celery
1/3 cup minced ripe olives
6 hard-cooked eggs, chopped
2/3 cup salad dressing

Melt butter, blend in flour and seasonings, gradually add milk and cook, stirring, until thickened. Add potato and heat gently. Just before serving, add remaining ingredients, reserving some of the chopped egg to garnish top. Mix lightly. Add more salt and pepper, if necessary. Serve hot. Makes 4 servings.

HUEVOS CARAQUEÑOS

A Venezuelan dish of eggs and dried beef.

2 ounces dried beef, shredded
2 tablespoons butter or margarine
1 cup chopped peeled tomatoes
**1-1/2 teaspoons chili powder (or more
  to taste)**
1/4 pound Monterey Jack cheese, grated
4 eggs, beaten
1/2 teaspoon salt

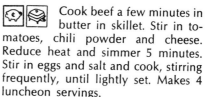 Cook beef a few minutes in butter in skillet. Stir in tomatoes, chili powder and cheese. Reduce heat and simmer 5 minutes. Stir in eggs and salt and cook, stirring frequently, until lightly set. Makes 4 luncheon servings.

CREAMED EGGS SUPREME

Melt ¼ cup butter, blend in ¼ cup flour, 1 teaspoon Worcestershire, 1½ cups milk and ½ cup cream. Cook, stirring, until thickened. Add a dash of hot pepper sauce, 2 tablespoons chopped parsley, 1 chopped pimiento and 8 hard-cooked eggs, cut in chunks. Heat. Season to taste. Makes 4 to 6 servings.

BASQUE EGGS AND POTATOES

4 large potatoes, peeled
1/4 cup sausage fat or vegetable oil
1 medium onion, thinly sliced
Salt and pepper
4 eggs, slightly beaten
1/4 cup minced green onions or chives
2 tablespoons minced parsley
1/4 teaspoon each fresh marjoram and thyme

Slice potatoes. Heat fat in heavy skillet and add potatoes and onion. Cook, without stirring, until golden brown on bottom. Turn and season with salt and pepper. Pour eggs over top and sprinkle with remaining ingredients. Cook over low heat until eggs are just set. Serves 4.

ZIPPY EGGS

1/2 pound sharp Cheddar cheese
1 can condensed cream of celery soup
1 teaspoon prepared mustard
1 teaspoon Worcestershire
Dash of hot pepper sauce
1/4 teaspoon pepper
1/2 cup milk
6 hard-cooked eggs, cut in quarters
Toasted French bread

Cut cheese in chunks and melt in top pan of double boiler over boiling water. Add next 6 ingredients, cover and heat, stirring occasionally. Add eggs and reheat. Serve on toast. Makes 4 servings.

SCOTCH EGGS

This savory makes a sumptuous breakfast or brunch, or a lunchbox meal.

4 hard-cooked eggs
1 egg, beaten
1 pound sausage meat
Cracker meal
Fat for deep frying

Dip eggs in beaten egg. Wrap each in a coat of sausage meat. Dip again in egg. Roll in cracker meal. Fry in hot deep fat (375°F. on a frying thermometer) 5 to 6 minutes. Drain well on paper towels. Makes 4 servings.

HOLLANDAISE SAUCE

In top part of double boiler, beat 3 egg yolks with whisk. Add ¼ teaspoon salt, dash of cayenne and 1 tablespoon lemon juice. Stir in ½ cup melted butter or margarine. Add 3 tablespoons hot water. Put over hot (not boiling) water and cook, stirring, 4 or 5 minutes, or until thickened. Makes about ¾ cup.

EGGS RALEIGH

Melt ½ cup butter in skillet. Just before butter turns brown, break in 4 eggs, one at a time. Sprinkle with salt and paprika. Put a pat of butter on each yolk and pour over it ½ teaspoon Worcestershire a few drops at a time. Cook a few seconds longer. Pour butter from skillet onto 4 slices fresh white bread. Put eggs, sunny side down, on bread. Serve at once. Makes 4 servings.

FRITTATA ITALIANA
(Italian Omelet)

2 large sweet onions, sliced wafer-thin
4 tablespoons olive oil
Salt and pepper
6 eggs

Sauté onions in half of oil 5 minutes. Season eggs and beat lightly. Stir in onions. Add rest of oil to pan, add eggs and cook over low heat until set. Turn carefully to brown slightly on other side. Makes 4 servings.

THOUSAND-ISLAND EGGS

A wonderful luncheon dish served with salad and crusty bread.

1/2 cup dairy sour cream
1/4 cup chopped stuffed olives
1 tablespoon chopped chives
1/4 cup catsup
Salt and freshly ground black pepper
Dash each of garlic salt and hot pepper sauce
4 teaspoons butter
4 eggs

Mix all ingredients, except butter and eggs. Melt 1 teaspoon butter in each of 4 individual casseroles or baking cups. Put dishes few minutes in heated oven. Remove from oven and break 1 raw egg in each (egg will begin to cook immediately). Pour one fourth of sour-cream mixture over each. Bake in moderate oven (350°F.) 15 minutes. Makes 4 servings.

GOLDEN EGG CASSEROLE

3 teaspoons butter or margarine
3 tablespoons cornstarch
1/2 teaspoon salt
1/8 teaspoon pepper
1 cup milk
4 eggs, separated

Melt butter, blend in cornstarch and seasonings; gradually add milk and cook, stirring, until smooth and thickened. Remove from heat and gradually pour over beaten egg yolks, mixing well. Spoon stiffly beaten egg whites into greased shallow 1½-quart baking dish. Make 4 depressions in egg white and spoon in sauce mixture. Set in pan of warm water; bake in moderate oven (350°F.) 45 minutes, or until lightly browned. Good with broccoli and other green vegetables. Makes 4 servings.

SWISS EGGS

Butter
8 eggs
8 tablespoons heavy cream
Salt and fine pepper
1 cup grated Swiss cheese

Use shirred-egg dishes or small individual casseroles and butter them well. Into each dish break 2 very fresh eggs and top whites with 2 tablespoons heavy cream. Season with salt and pepper and sprinkle each with a wreath of grated cheese. Bake in moderate oven (350°F.) 15 to 20 minutes. Makes 4 servings.

POACHED EGGS A LA RHINE

1/2 pound mushrooms, sliced
Butter
4 slices hot buttered toast
2 tablespoons flour
1 cup milk
Grated Parmesan cheese
Salt and pepper
4 eggs, poached
Pimiento strips

Cook mushrooms in 2 tablespoons butter 5 minutes. Put toast on a broiler-proof platter or baking dish; cover with mushrooms. Melt 2 tablespoons butter and blend in flour; add milk gradually and cook, stirring, until thickened. Stir in ½ cup cheese and seasonings to taste. Put an egg on each slice of toast and cover with sauce. Sprinkle with cheese. Broil until tops are golden brown and serve with a garnish of pimiento. Makes 4 servings.

EGGS CHASSEUR

Cook 1 minced green onion with top and 3 chopped mushrooms in 1 tablespoon butter 5 minutes. Add ¼ cup chicken stock or bouillon and simmer 10 minutes. Add 1 tablespoon sherry and salt and pepper to taste. Pour into 9″ piepan. Poach 4 eggs, put into pan and season. Top with 2 tablespoons heavy cream and sprinkle with 2 tablespoons grated Parmesan cheese. Broil until golden. Makes 4 servings.

TOMATO-EGG SUPPER DISH

4 tablespoons butter or margarine
3 tablespoons flour
1-1/2 cups milk
1/2 cup shredded Cheddar cheese
Salt and pepper
6 hard-cooked eggs, sliced
3 large tomatoes, peeled and cut in thick slices
3 cooked carrots, cut in strips
1/4 cup fine cracker crumbs

Melt 3 tablespoons butter and blend in flour. Gradually add milk and cook, stirring, until thickened. Stir in cheese and season to taste with salt and pepper. Arrange a layer of egg slices in greased 1½-quart casserole. Reserve 6 tomato slices for top and put remainder in a layer over egg slices. Cover with some of sauce. Add carrot strips and remaining eggs and sauce. Arrange reserved tomatoes on top and sprinkle with crumbs. Dot with remaining butter. Bake in moderate oven (375°F.) about 30 minutes. Makes 6 servings.

PUERTO RICAN EGGS

2 onions, sliced
2 green peppers, chopped
3 tablespoons butter or margarine
1 cup chopped fresh tomatoes, or 1 can (19 ounces) whole tomatoes, drained and chopped
Salt and pepper
1/2 teaspoon chili powder
1 can (17 ounces) whole-kernel corn, drained
2 tablespoons olive oil
12 eggs

Cook onion and peppers in butter 5 minutes; add tomatoes, 1 teaspoon salt, ¼ teaspoon pepper and the chili powder. Cover and cook 2 to 3 minutes. Put in greased shallow baking dish. Add corn and sprinkle with oil. Drop in eggs; season. Bake in moderate oven (375°F.) 20 minutes, to desired doneness. Makes 6 servings.

BREAD-CHEESE CUSTARD

A fine meatless main dish.

6 slices dry bread
1/2 pound process American cheese,
    sliced
1-3/4 cups hot milk
1 onion, grated
1 teaspoon salt
Dash of cayenne
Dash of paprika
1/2 teaspoon Worcestershire
2 eggs, beaten

Arrange alternate layers of bread and
cheese in 1½-quart casserole, ending
with cheese. Heat milk with onion
and seasonings; pour slowly over
eggs, stirring constantly. Pour milk
mixture over bread and cheese; let
stand 5 minutes or longer. Bake in
moderate oven (375°F.) 20 minutes,
or until custard is set and bread and
cheese puffy. Makes 3 to 4 servings.

BACON-EGG-CORN CAKES

1/2 cup chopped bacon ends
1-1/4 cups cornmeal
1/4 cup all-purpose flour
1/2 teaspoon baking soda
1 hard-cooked egg, chopped
1 egg, beaten
1 cup buttermilk

Cook bacon until crisp; reserve fat.
Mix dry ingredients; add bacon and
chopped egg. Mix bacon fat, raw egg
and buttermilk. Add to dry ingredients and mix well. Spoon into hot
greased skillet and brown cakes on
both sides. Makes 4 servings.

CURRIED EGGS

3 onions, sliced
1/4 teaspoon salt
1/2 cup butter
1/4 cup flour
2 tablespoons curry powder
2 cups stock or broth
12 small eggs, hard-cooked
2 to 3 cups cooked rice
1/4 cup sultana or white raisins
1/4 cup toasted almonds

Sauté onion and salt in ¼ cup
butter until nicely browned. Remove from skillet. Melt ¼ cup butter
in same skillet and stir in flour and
curry powder. When well blended,
add stock; cook, stirring, until thick
and smooth. Add onion and whole
eggs. Cover and simmer 30 minutes.
On a platter or serving plate, make
a ring of rice. Place eggs in the center and pour sauce around them.
Garnish with sultanas and toasted almonds. Makes 4 to 6 servings.

EGG-POTATO PIE, INDIENNE

1/2 teaspoon onion salt
6 medium potatoes, cooked, mashed
    and seasoned
6 hard-cooked eggs, cut in chunks
2 tablespoons butter
1 tablespoon flour
1/2 teaspoon salt
1/2 teaspoon curry powder
1/8 teaspoon pepper
3/4 cup milk
Few sprigs of parsley, chopped

Add onion salt to potatoes and line
a shallow 1½-quart baking dish with
the mixture. Fill center with the eggs.
Melt butter and blend in flour and
seasonings. Gradually add milk and
cook, stirring constantly, until thickened. Add parsley and pour over
eggs. Bake in moderate oven (375°F.)
about 30 minutes. Makes 6 servings.

EGG-VEGETABLE LOAF

1/4 cup butter or margarine
1/4 cup flour
2 cups milk
1/2 cup each cooked diced celery and
    carrots
1/2 cup cooked peas
2 hard-cooked eggs, chopped
Few sprigs of parsley, chopped
1 tablespoon instant minced onion
4 eggs, beaten
Salt and pepper
Grated Cheddar cheese

Prepare a sauce with first 3 ingredients. Measure ½ cup and mix with
remaining ingredients, except cheese.
Pour into greased 8" x 4" x 3" loaf
pan and bake in moderate oven (350°
F.) about 45 minutes. Unmold on
small platter. Heat remaining sauce
and add cheese to taste. Season and
serve on sliced hot loaf. Serves 4 to 6.

EGGS FLORENTINE

1 box frozen chopped spinach, cooked
    and drained
4 eggs, poached
Puffy Cream Sauce
1/4 cup grated Parmesan cheese

Put spinach in hot shallow broiler-
proof baking dish and make 4 depressions in it. Put 1 egg in each hollow.
Cover with sauce and sprinkle with
cheese. Lightly brown under broiler
a few minutes. Makes 4 servings.
Puffy Cream Sauce Melt 3 tablespoons
butter and blend in 3 tablespoons
flour, ½ teaspoon salt and a dash of
cayenne. Gradually add 1¼ cups milk
and cook, stirring, until thickened.
Remove from heat and fold in ¼ cup
heavy cream, whipped.

CREAMY EGGS AND CHEESE

1 tablespoon butter
1/2 cup shredded process American
    cheese
5 eggs, beaten
Salt and pepper
Chopped chives

 Melt butter in skillet. Add cheese and 2 tablespoons water; cook over low heat, stirring, until cheese is melted and smooth. Add eggs and season. Cook over low heat until eggs are just set, stirring several times. Sprinkle with chives. Makes 4 servings.

EGG-TOMATO SCRAMBLE

6 eggs, beaten
2 medium tomatoes, chopped
1/2 teaspoon salt
1/8 teaspoon pepper
Few fresh basil leaves, chopped
2 tablespoons butter

Combine first 5 ingredients. Melt butter in skillet; add egg mixture and cook, stirring occasionally, until scramble thickens. Makes 4 servings.

BACON, CORN AND EGGS

4 slices bacon or frizzled boiled ham
    slices
1 small green pepper, chopped
1 small onion, minced
1 can (16 or 17 ounces) cream-style corn
1/2 teaspoon salt
1/8 teaspoon pepper
4 eggs, beaten

Cook bacon until crisp. Remove from skillet and pour off most of fat. Sauté green pepper and onion in remaining fat 2 or 3 minutes; stir in remaining ingredients. Stir until eggs are set. Add crumbled bacon. Serves 4.

ORIENTAL SCRAMBLE

1 tablespoon butter
1/2 cup peanut butter
1 small onion, chopped
1/2 cup finely diced celery
1/2 cup chopped green pepper
3 eggs
1-1/2 teaspoons salt
Dash of pepper
1/2 cup milk
1 cup cooked rice
2 tablespoons chopped parsley

Heat first 2 ingredients in skillet. Add next 3 ingredients and sauté 2 or 3 minutes, stirring. Beat eggs and add remaining ingredients. Stir quickly into first mixture. Cook over low heat, stirring, until eggs are cooked to desired consistency. Makes 4 servings.

ONIONS AND EGGS, FAUST

6 hard-cooked eggs
2 cups chopped onions
2 tablespoons butter
1/2 cup dry white wine
3/4 teaspoon salt
1/4 teaspoon pepper
Paprika
Dry mustard
1/4 cup chili sauce
1/4 cup buttered fine dry bread crumbs

Slice eggs and place them in buttered baking dish. Brown onions lightly in butter and add remaining ingredients, except crumbs. Pour over eggs. Sprinkle with crumbs and bake in hot oven (425°F.) about 15 minutes. Makes 4 to 6 servings.

ASPARAGI ALL'UOVO
(Italian Asparagus with Eggs)

1 bunch asparagus (2-1/2 pounds)
Salt and pepper
6 tablespoons olive oil
1/3 cup grated Parmesan cheese
1 clove garlic
8 eggs

Cook asparagus in boiling salted water until tender; drain well. Put whole asparagus spears in shallow baking pan. Pour 3 tablespoons oil over asparagus and sprinkle with salt, pepper and cheese. Cut garlic in half and cook slowly in remaining oil about 5 minutes; do not brown. Remove garlic. Drop eggs into oil; cover and cook slowly 3 minutes. Put asparagus under broiler and brown lightly under medium heat. Serve 2 eggs on each portion of asparagus. Serves 4.

EGG-STUFFED FRENCH LOAF

1 oval loaf French bread
1/2 cup milk
1 egg
1 clove garlic, minced
Salt and pepper to taste
1/2 teaspoon ground coriander seed
1-1/2 cups diced celery
1/3 cup diced stuffed olives
6 hard-cooked eggs, chopped
1/2 cup mayonnaise
2 tablespoons melted butter

Cut a slice from top of bread and reserve. Scoop out enough crumbs from loaf to make 2 cups. Mix crumbs with all ingredients, except melted butter. Cut 6 thick slices almost all the way through loaf. Fill loaf tightly with salad mixture. Add top piece, marking loaf slices. Brush with butter, wrap in foil and bake in hot oven (425°F.) about 30 minutes. Serve hot. Makes 6 servings.

BREAKFAST EGGS

4 eggs
3/4 teaspoon salt
Dash of pepper
1-1/3 cups milk

Beat eggs with salt and pepper until very light. Add milk and pour into well-greased top of double boiler. Set over boiling water, cover and cook, without stirring, 20 to 25 minutes, or until set and spongy. Do not remove cover during first 15 minutes. Makes 4 servings.

EGG-CHEESE TOAST

Make well-seasoned scrambled eggs. Toast one slice of bread for each serving and spread with chutney or catsup. Heap scrambled eggs on toast; cover thickly with grated Cheddar cheese. Brown lightly under broiler. Sprinkle with chopped parsley or garnish with narrow strips of green pepper and pimiento.

SHIRRED EGGS CARUSO

4 teaspoons melted butter
8 eggs
8 tablespoons heavy cream
Salt and pepper
Sautéed chicken livers

Put 1 teaspoon butter in each of 4 individual baking dishes or ramekins. Break 2 eggs into each. Add 2 tablespoons cream and sprinkle with salt and pepper. Bake in moderate oven (350°F.) 10 to 15 minutes to desired doneness. Garnish with chicken livers. Makes 4 servings.

MRS. BROWN'S POTATO CASSEROLE

6 medium potatoes
Salt
3 teaspoons steak sauce
1/2 cup undiluted evaporated milk or light cream
3 tablespoons soft butter or margarine
6 eggs
Pepper and paprika
1/2 cup grated sharp Cheddar cheese

Cook potatoes with 1 teaspoon salt in small amount of boiling water until tender. Drain and mash. Beat in next 3 ingredients. Put in shallow 1½-quart baking dish. Make 6 depressions in potato and drop 1 egg in each. Sprinkle with salt, pepper and paprika. Top with cheese. Bake in very hot oven (450°F.) 10 to 15 minutes, or to desired doneness. Makes 6 servings.

SKILLET EGGS AND POTATOES

4 cups diced raw potatoes
1-1/2 teaspoons salt
1/2 teaspoon pepper
1 onion, minced
1/4 cup butter or margarine
6 hard-cooked eggs, cut in chunks
3/4 cup milk
Chopped parsley

Put potatoes, salt and 2 cups boiling water in skillet, cover and cook 10 minutes. Uncover; cook until water is evaporated. Add next 3 ingredients; cook, stirring occasionally, until lightly browned. Add eggs and milk; heat. Top with parsley. Serves 4.

HUEVOS RANCHEROS (Mexican Ranch-style Eggs)

2 tablespoons chopped onion
2 tablespoons olive oil
1 clove garlic, minced
3 chopped canned green chilies
1 teaspoon oregano
1 pound (3 medium) ripe tomatoes, peeled and chopped
1 teaspoon salt
6 eggs
6 crisp-fried tortillas or toast slices

Cook onion in oil until wilted; add other ingredients, except eggs and tortillas, and simmer for 10 minutes. Serve over fried or poached eggs on tortillas. Makes 6 servings.

EGG AND TOMATO SQUARES, MOUSSELINE

1 can condensed tomato soup
2 tablespoons butter or margarine
1 teaspoon instant minced onion
3/4 cup fine dry bread crumbs
3/4 teaspoon seasoned salt
1/4 teaspoon pepper
1/2 teaspoon monosodium glutamate
1/2 teaspoon Worcestershire
1/4 cup grated Parmesan cheese
4 eggs, separated
Mousseline Sauce

Heat first 8 ingredients in saucepan, stirring until butter melts. Remove from heat and add 2 tablespoons cheese and well-beaten egg yolks. Cool and fold in stiffly beaten whites. Put in shallow baking dish and sprinkle with remaining cheese. Bake in moderate oven (350°F.) 30 minutes, or until firm. Cut in squares and serve with **Mousseline Sauce:** Mix 2 tablespoons each butter and flour and 1 cup chicken stock; cook until smooth over low heat. Pour over 2 beaten egg yolks, stirring. Season, add 2 tablespoons lemon juice, ¼ teaspoon grated lemon rind and 1 tablespoon chopped parsley Makes 6 servings.

EGG AND COTTAGE-CHEESE PANCAKES WITH TOMATO-MUSHROOM SAUCE

2 cups (1 pound) small-curd creamed cottage cheese
2/3 cup fine dry bread crumbs
1/2 cup chopped green onion
2 tablespoons chopped fresh or dried parsley
1 teaspoon salt
1/4 teaspoon nutmeg
4 eggs
3 tablespoons butter or margarine
Tomato-Mushroom Sauce

Combine all ingredients, except butter and sauce. Beat with wooden spoon until well blended. Melt butter in large skillet. When butter begins to bubble, drop in batter by ¼ measuring-cupfuls. Cook until browned on both sides. Serve with Tomato-Mushroom Sauce. Makes about 16 pancakes.

Tomato-Mushroom Sauce

2 tablespoons olive oil
1 can (4 ounces) mushroom stems and pieces, drained
1/3 cup chopped green pepper
1 can (15 ounces) tomato sauce with tidbits
1/2 teaspoon basil
1/4 teaspoon oregano
Salt and pepper to taste

Heat oil in skillet. Add mushrooms and green pepper and cook until barely tender. Add tomato sauce and seasonings. Simmer about 10 minutes.

CREAMY CHICKEN WITH EGGS, PARISIAN STYLE

5 tablespoons butter or margarine
1 medium green pepper, chopped
3 tablespoons flour
1-1/2 cups milk
Salt and pepper
2 cups diced cooked chicken
1 canned pimiento, chopped
Six 3" rounds of bread
6 eggs, poached
Paprika

Melt 3 tablespoons butter, add green pepper and cook 2 to 3 minutes. Blend in flour. Gradually add milk and cook, stirring, until smooth and thickened. Season to taste with salt and pepper. Add chicken and pimiento and heat. Sauté bread rounds in remaining butter until golden brown on both sides. Put a round on each individual serving plate; top with hot chicken mixture, then with eggs. Sprinkle with paprika and serve at once. Makes 6 servings.

EGG FRITTERS WITH HOLLANDAISE SAUCE

4 eggs, hard-cooked
2 slices liverwurst, 1/4" thick, peeled
Salt and cayenne to taste
1 egg, beaten
1/2 cup fine soft bread crumbs
3 tablespoons butter or margarine
Hollandaise Sauce (page 164)

Cut eggs in half lengthwise, remove yolks and mash. Mash liverwurst and season with salt and cayenne; add yolks and blend well. Fill whites, using entire mixture. Press halves together to reshape eggs. There will be a layer of filling between halves; smooth edges with spoon. Dip whole eggs in beaten egg and roll in crumbs. Sauté in the butter until golden brown and serve with hollandaise. Makes 4 servings.

EGG-STUFFED TOMATOES

4 tomatoes
8 eggs
1 clove garlic, minced
Chopped parsley
Salt and pepper
1/4 cup grated sharp Cheddar cheese
1/4 cup browned bread crumbs
3 tablespoons butter or margarine

Halve tomatoes; scrape out center, pressing with spoon to extract most of juice. Put tomato shells in shallow baking dish and bake in moderate oven (350°F.) 10 minutes. Then break an egg into each. Add a little garlic and parsley; season. Sprinkle thickly with mixture of cheese, crumbs and chopped parsley. Dot with butter. Bake in hot oven (425°F.) 15 minutes, or until top is golden and eggs set. Makes 4 servings.

EGGS A LA FERMIERE

1/2 pound chicken livers
2 tablespoons butter or bacon fat
2 tablespoons canned deviled chicken
1 slice cooked bacon, crumbled
1 teaspoon minced onion
1 teaspoon minced parsley
Salt and pepper to taste
4 slices toast
8 eggs, scrambled

Brown chicken livers in 1 tablespoon butter, cover and cook slowly 10 minutes, or until done. Force through food chopper or whirl in blender and mix with chicken and bacon. Sauté onion and parsley in remaining 1 tablespoon butter 1 minute. Add with drippings to liver mixture. Add seasonings and mix well. If too dry, moisten with cream or broth. Spread on toast and top with eggs. Makes 4 servings.

EGGS SCRAMBLED IN CHEESE SOUP

Melt 1/4 cup butter or margarine in large skillet. Add 2 diced tomatoes; cook a few minutes. Stir 1 can condensed cheese soup until smooth. Blend with 8 slightly beaten eggs; pour into skillet. Pepper to taste; cook, stirring once or twice, until eggs are set. Serves 4 to 6.

MILE-HIGH CHEESE SOUFFLÉ

Butter or margarine
1/2 cup all-purpose flour
2 teaspoons salt
1/2 teaspoon paprika
Dash of cayenne
2 cups milk
2 cups (1/2 pound) sharp Cheddar
  cheese, cut fine
8 eggs, separated

Melt 1/2 cup butter in top part of double boiler over hot water. Add flour and seasonings and mix well. Stir in milk and cook, stirring constantly, until sauce is thick and smooth. Add cheese and stir until melted. Remove from heat. Beat yolks until light and gradually stir into cheese sauce. Beat whites until stiff but not dry and carefully fold sauce into whites. Brush 3-quart casserole generously with melted butter and pour in mixture. Bake in very hot oven (475°F.) 10 minutes. Reduce heat to 400°F.; bake 25 minutes. Serves 6.

TOP-HAT CHEESE SOUFFLÉ

6 tablespoons butter or margarine
6 tablespoons flour or 3 tablespoons
  cornstarch
1 teaspoon salt
1/8 teaspoon dry mustard
Dash of cayenne
1-1/2 cups milk
2 cups grated sharp Cheddar cheese
6 eggs, separated

Melt butter in top part of double boiler over boiling water. Blend in flour and seasonings. Gradually stir in milk and cook, stirring, until smooth and thickened. Add cheese and stir until melted. Remove from heat and cool slightly. Beat egg whites until stiff but not dry. Beat yolks until thick and lemon-colored. Stir cheese mixture slowly into yolks and blend thoroughly. Pour slowly over egg whites and fold together quickly and lightly. Pour into 3-quart soufflé dish or casserole. For top-hat effect, use a teaspoon tip to flatten a border 1 1/4" wide around outside edge of soufflé. Bake in slow oven (300°F.) 1 hour and 15 minutes Serves 4 to 6.

SUNDAY BREAKFAST SUPREME

1 package (3 ounces) cream cheese
1 cup milk, scalded
6 eggs, slightly beaten
1 cup diced ham
Salt and pepper
2 tablespoons vegetable oil or drippings

Beat cheese until fluffy; gradually stir in milk. Add eggs, ham, and salt and pepper to taste. Heat oil in skillet; add egg mixture. Cook slowly, stirring, until eggs are just set. Serves 4.

SURPRISE SOUFFLÉS

3 tablespoons butter or margarine
1-1/2 tablespoons cornstarch
1 teaspoon salt
1/2 teaspoon dry mustard
3/4 cup milk
1/4 pound Port du Salut or Oka cheese,
  cut in bits
4 eggs, separated
6 whole eggs

Melt butter and blend in cornstarch, salt and mustard. Gradually stir in milk and cheese. Cook, stirring, until smooth and thickened. Cool slightly. Beat 4 egg whites until stiff but not dry. Beat yolks until thick and lemon-colored. Stir yolks into sauce mixture. Pour over whites, folding to blend completely. Half-fill 6 individual dishes or ramekins. Break 1 egg into each and add remaining mixture. Bake in hot oven (400°F.) about 20 minutes. Makes 6 servings.

CHEESE-TAPIOCA SOUFFLÉ

1/4 cup quick-cooking tapioca
1/2 teaspoon salt
Dash of freshly ground black pepper
1 teaspoon dry mustard
1/4 teaspoon ginger
Dash of hot pepper sauce
1-1/3 cups milk
1 cup lightly packed shredded Cheddar
  cheese
4 eggs, separated
Grated Cheddar cheese or fine dry
  bread crumbs

Combine first 6 ingredients. Stir in milk and let stand about 5 minutes. Then cook, stirring, over medium heat until mixture comes to a full boil. Add shredded cheese and stir until melted. Remove from heat and cool slightly. Then stir in egg yolks beaten until thick and lemon-colored. Mix thoroughly. Fold in stiffly beaten egg whites and pour into well-buttered 1 1/2-quart casserole dusted lightly with grated cheese. Bake in moderate oven (350°F.) about 35 minutes. Makes 4 to 6 servings.

DEVILED-HAM BLENDER SOUFFLÉ

5 eggs, separated
1/4 cup butter or margarine, softened
1/4 cup flour
1/4 teaspoon salt
Dash of freshly ground pepper
1/2 teaspoon prepared mustard
1/2 teaspoon powdered horseradish
1 can (4-1/2 ounces) deviled ham
1 cup hot milk

Set egg whites aside to warm to room temperature. Blend remaining ingredients in blender about 1 minute. Pour into saucepan and cook, stirring briskly, until thickened; cool. Gently fold in stiffly beaten egg whites. Pour into well-buttered 1½-quart casserole and bake in moderate oven (375°F.) 25 to 30 minutes. Makes 4 servings.

SOUFFLÉ LORRAINE

4 eggs, separated
1/3 cup light cream
3 tablespoons flour
1-1/2 cups cottage cheese
1/2 cup grated Parmesan
6 slices bacon, cooked crisp and crumbled
1/2 teaspoon salt
Dash of pepper

Beat egg whites until stiff but not dry; set aside. Beat egg yolks until thick. Beat in next 3 ingredients until almost smooth. Add remaining ingredients; fold in egg whites. Put in buttered 1½-quart soufflé dish or casserole. Bake in slow oven (300°F.) about 1 hour. Makes 6 servings.

CORNED-BEEF AND CHEESE SOUFFLÉ

1/4 cup butter or margarine
1/4 cup flour
1 cup milk
4 egg yolks, beaten
1/4 pound Cheddar cheese
1 can (7 ounces) corned beef, finely chopped
6 egg whites, stiffly beaten
Salt and pepper
1/4 cup grated Parmesan cheese

Melt butter and blend in flour. Gradually add milk and cook, stirring, until thickened. Add egg yolks and blend well. Stir in Cheddar cheese and beef. Fold in egg whites carefully. Season with salt and pepper. Put in buttered 2-quart casserole and sprinkle with Parmesan cheese. Bake in moderate oven (350°F.) 50 minutes, or until puffed and firm. Serve immediately. Makes 4 to 6 servings.

OMELET SOUFFLÉ

Melt 3 tablespoons butter or margarine. Blend in 3 tablespoons flour, ¾ teaspoon salt and ⅛ teaspoon pepper. Add 1 cup milk and cook, stirring, until thickened. Separate 6 eggs and beat whites until stiff. Then beat yolks until thick and lemon-colored. Stir first mixture into yolks; fold into whites. Pour into 3-quart casserole and set in pan of hot water. Bake in moderate oven (350°F.) 35 minutes, or until tip of knife inserted in center comes out clean. Serve at once. Makes 6 servings.
Chicken Soufflé Prepare Omelet Soufflé, folding in with egg whites 1 cup ground or minced cooked chicken, a few sprigs of parsley, minced, and 1 tablespoon instant minced onion. Bake as directed.

CHEESE AND MASHED-POTATO SOUFFLÉ

4 eggs, separated
4 servings instant mashed potato, prepared as directed on package
1 cup dairy sour cream or yogurt
2 cups shredded, grated or finely cut Cheddar cheese
1 teaspoon Worcestershire
Dash of hot pepper sauce
1 tablespoon finely minced onion

Add egg yolks to potato one at a time, beating well after each. Add next 5 ingredients. Fold in stiffly beaten egg whites. Turn into well-buttered 2-quart casserole and bake in moderate oven (350°F.) 50 to 60 minutes. Makes 6 servings.

SQUASH SOUFFLÉ

2 packages (12 ounces each) frozen squash, heated
2 tablespoons butter or margarine
1 teaspoon salt
Generous dash of freshly ground black pepper
2 teaspoons sugar
2 tablespoons dairy sour cream
2 eggs, separated
2 tablespoons fine dry bread crumbs

Mix well first 6 ingredients. Beat in egg yolks one at a time. Cool slightly and gently fold in stiffly beaten egg whites. Generously butter 1½-quart casserole, sprinkle with bread crumbs and shake surplus into soufflé mixture. Turn mixture into prepared dish, set in shallow pan of hot water and bake in moderate oven (375°F.) 35 to 40 minutes, or until firm. Makes 4 to 6 servings.

SWEDISH FISH SOUFFLÉ

1 pound frozen haddock or cod fillets
1 small bay leaf
1 small onion, halved, or 1 teaspoon
   instant minced onion
Salt
3 tablespoons butter or margarine
1/4 cup flour
1 teaspoon Worcestershire
Pepper
1-1/2 cups milk
4 eggs, separated
Fine dry bread crumbs
Grated Parmesan cheese

Cook fish with bay leaf, onion and 1 teaspoon salt in water to cover 30 minutes, or until fish flakes easily with fork. Cool enough to handle. Discard bones and skin. Flake fish and force through food chopper. There should be 2 to 3 cups. Strain stock and reserve. Melt butter and blend in flour, Worcestershire and salt and pepper to taste. Gradually add milk and 1 cup reserved fish stock and cook, stirring, until thickened. Add egg yolks one at a time, stirring well after each addition. Cook, stirring, 1 minute longer. Beat egg whites until stiff but not dry. Fold in gently but thoroughly. Turn into well-buttered 2-quart casserole dusted with bread crumbs. Sprinkle with grated cheese and crumbs. Bake in moderate oven (350° F.) about 30 minutes. Serves 6.

CHEESE SOUFFLÉ ON BROILED TOMATOES

1/4 cup butter or margarine
1/4 cup flour
Salt and pepper
1 cup milk
1 cup Cheddar cheese, shredded or in
   fine pieces
4 eggs, separated
4 large tomatoes, peeled
16 rounds buttered toast
1/2 pound bacon, cooked until crisp
Watercress

Melt butter and blend in flour, 1 teaspoon salt and a dash of pepper. Gradually add milk and cook, stirring, until thickened. Add cheese and stir until melted. Remove from heat, cool slightly, and add well-beaten egg yolks. Cut tomatoes in 4 slices and season with salt and pepper. Broil 1 minute on each side. Transfer tomato slices to toast and arrange in long shallow baking pan. Fold beaten egg whites into cheese sauce and heap each tomato slice with some of the mixture. Bake in hot oven (400°F.) 15 minutes. Garnish with bacon and watercress. Makes 4 servings.

DOUBLE-CORN SOUFFLÉ

2 tablespoons butter or margarine
1 tablespoon flour
1 teaspoon salt
1/8 teaspoon pepper
1 tablespoon sugar
1 can (16 or 17 ounces) cream-style corn
1 cup cooked whole-kernel corn
4 eggs, separated
1 carrot, peeled and shredded
1 cup dairy sour cream
2 tablespoons fine dry bread crumbs

Melt butter and blend in flour, seasonings and sugar. Stir in corn, beaten egg yolks, carrot and sour cream. Fold in stiffly beaten egg whites and pour into shallow 1½-quart baking dish. Sprinkle with crumbs. Bake in moderate oven (350°F.) about 35 minutes. Serves 6.

HOMINY-GRITS SOUFFLÉ

2-1/2 cups milk
1 teaspoon salt
1 cup quick-cooking hominy grits
2 tablespoons butter or margarine
3 eggs, separated

In heavy saucepan, heat together 2½ cups water, the milk and salt. Stir in grits and butter and cook, stirring, until thickened. Cool to lukewarm, then stir in well-beaten egg yolks. Fold in stiffly beaten egg whites. Pour into well-buttered 1½-quart casserole or ring mold. Set in pan of hot water 1" deep. Bake in slow oven (325°F.) about 1¼ hours, increasing temperature to 350°F. last 15 minutes. Makes 4 to 6 servings.

YAM SOUFFLÉ

3 cups mashed cooked yams or sweet
   potatoes
2 teaspoons grated orange rind
1-1/2 cups milk
1/3 cup butter or margarine, softened
1/4 cup sherry or orange juice
Dash of pepper
1/2 teaspoon nutmeg
1/2 teaspoon ginger
1 teaspoon salt
2 tablespoons brown sugar
4 eggs, separated

Mix well all ingredients, except eggs. Add egg yolks beaten until light and lemon-colored. When thoroughly combined, gently fold in stiffly beaten egg whites. Turn into well-buttered 2½-quart casserole or 10 individual well-buttered soufflé dishes or glass custard cups. Bake in moderate oven (375°F.) 45 minutes for casserole or 20 to 25 minutes for individual dishes. Makes 8 to 10 servings.

Pasta Rustica

HOW TO BUY DRIED BEANS

Dried beans should be clean, and uniform in size and quality. Since they are usually packaged, a reliable brand will guarantee such beans. Beans come in many sizes and varieties, including limas, black-eye, yellow-eyed, red kidney, pinto, pink, and white beans such as marrow, Great Northern, navy and pea beans.

BEAN STORAGE

After package is opened, beans stored in clean covered container on pantry shelf will keep 1 year. Store cooked beans, covered, in refrigerator 1 to 4 days.

COOKING HINTS

• Fast cooking causes beans to break. Simmering keeps them whole and prevents sticking to bottom of pot.
• A tablespoon of fat added to beans during cooking minimizes foaming.
• Be sure to wait until beans are almost done to add tomatoes, lemon juice, vinegar or wine to beans. The reason: Acid slows down the softening process.
• Cooked beans and bean dishes freeze well.

HOW TO BUY PASTA

The term "pasta" embraces the many kinds of macaroni, spaghetti and noodles that make up the family of flour-paste products. The best quality is made from durum wheat; they don't splinter when broken as do cheaper grades. If noodles contain eggs rather than coloring, it will be so indicated on the label. Always look on the label for pasta products that are enriched with vitamins B_1 and B_2, niacin and iron. Pasta products keep almost indefinitely stored covered on the pantry shelf.

HOW TO BUY RICE

There are a number of different types of rice. Your choice will depend on how you wish to use it. **Regular white milled rice** is washed, cleaned and graded during milling. Use long-grain for salads, stews; short-grain for croquettes, puddings. **Parboiled rice** is prepared by a special process that retains most of the food value, even after milling. **Instant or precooked rice** needs only to steam in boiling water to be ready to serve. **Brown rice** is the whole, unpolished grain of rice with only the inedible hull removed. Its texture is chewy, its flavor nutlike. There are also flavored rices, such as chicken, roast-beef and curry, available in both precooked and cooking styles. Combinations of rice and wild rice (not a cereal), or rice and pasta are also available. Many brands of rice are vitamin-enriched.

RICE STORAGE

Rice, stored covered, keeps almost indefinitely on the pantry shelf. Brown rice is an exception and should be stored, covered, in the refrigerator, as it may become rancid.

MAPLE BAKED BEANS

1 pound dried white beans
1 onion, sliced
1/2 pound salt pork, sliced
1 teaspoon salt
1 teaspoon dry mustard
1/2 cup maple syrup
2 tablespoons maple sugar or brown
  sugar

Cover washed beans with 6 cups water, bring to boil and boil 2 minutes. Cover and let stand 1 hour. Add onion and salt pork; then cook until tender; drain, reserving liquid. Mix ½ cup liquid, salt, mustard and maple syrup. Pour over beans. Put in shallow baking dish. Put pork on top; sprinkle with sugar. Bake, uncovered, in hot oven (400°F.) 45 minutes. Makes 6 to 8 servings.

BAKED BEANS WITH HAM

1 pound dried beans
1 onion, sliced
2 teaspoons salt
1 smoked ham shank (3 pounds)
1/4 cup catsup
1/4 cup light molasses
1 tablespoon vinegar
1/4 teaspoon hot pepper sauce
1 teaspoon dry mustard

Cover washed beans with 6 cups water, bring to boil and boil 2 minutes. Cover and let stand 1 hour; then add onion and salt. Cook until tender. Drain, reserving 1½ cups liquid. Put ham in 3-quart casserole. Put beans around ham and pour liquid mixed with remaining ingredients over top. Cover and bake in slow oven (325°F.) 1½ hours. Remove ham and put beans back in oven. Bake, uncovered, 1 hour. Meanwhile, remove rind from ham and cut meat in bite-size pieces. Add to beans and bake 30 minutes longer. Makes 6 servings.

BLACK BEANS WITH RICE

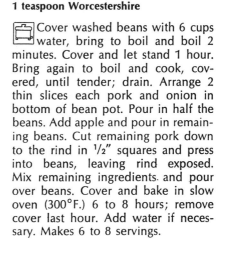 Cover 1 pound washed dried black beans with 6 cups water, bring to boil and boil 2 minutes. Cover and let stand 1 hour. Cook 1 cup chopped onion, 1 chopped green pepper and 1 minced clove garlic in ½ cup olive oil 5 minutes. Add to beans with 2 bay leaves, 2 teaspoons salt, ¼ teaspoon pepper, 1 smoked-ham bone (optional) and 1 minced slice of bacon. Bring to boil and simmer, covered, 2 hours, adding more water if necessary. Add ¼ cup wine vinegar and serve with hot cooked rice. Garnish with hard-cooked egg and parsley. Makes 6 to 8 servings.

BEST BAKED BEANS

1 pound dried pea beans
1/2 to 3/4 pound salt pork
1 medium onion, sliced
1 tart apple, peeled and quartered
1/2 cup tomato pulp
1/2 cup dark molasses
1-1/2 cups meat broth
2 teaspoons salt
1/2 teaspoon pepper
1/2 teaspoon celery salt
1 teaspoon dry mustard
1 teaspoon Worcestershire

Cover washed beans with 6 cups water, bring to boil and boil 2 minutes. Cover and let stand 1 hour. Bring again to boil and cook, covered, until tender; drain. Arrange 2 thin slices each pork and onion in bottom of bean pot. Pour in half the beans. Add apple and pour in remaining beans. Cut remaining pork down to the rind in ½" squares and press into beans, leaving rind exposed. Mix remaining ingredients and pour over beans. Cover and bake in slow oven (300°F.) 6 to 8 hours; remove cover last hour. Add water if necessary. Makes 6 to 8 servings.

FRIJOLES
(Mexican Beans)

Mexican beans are as important as tortillas and, like them, are served morning, noon and night. They freeze well, so keep a batch on hand.

1 pound Mexican pink or pinto beans
1/2 teaspoon ground cumin (optional)
2 cloves garlic (optional)
2 teaspoons salt
2 tablespoons bacon fat or lard

Cover beans with 6 cups water, add cumin and garlic as you wish and simmer over very low heat 1½ hours. Add salt and bacon fat and continue cooking until beans are tender. Top with a little chopped red pepper, if desired. Makes 6 servings.

Frijoles Fritos (Fried Beans) Prepare Frijoles. Heat ¼ cup of bacon fat or lard in a heavy skillet and add cooked beans, a few at a time. Mash them into the fat. Add bean liquid and beans until all are added and mashed. Cook, stirring occasionally, until beans are a thick mush. Makes 6 servings.

Frijoles Refritos (Crisp Fried Beans) Prepare Frijoles Fritos and fry until they are crispy around the edges. Use additional lard or bacon fat as needed. Add small cubes of tart cheese, as desired. Makes 6 servings.

BAKED BEANS WITH CHOPS

Cover 1½ cups washed dried white beans with 6 cups water, bring to boil and boil 2 minutes. Cover and let stand 1 hour; then cook until tender. Drain, reserving ½ cup liquid; add to liquid 1 can (8 ounces) tomato sauce, 1 tablespoon brown sugar, ½ teaspoon salt and dash of pepper. Put with beans in 2-quart casserole; top with 6 browned pork chops. Cover and bake in moderate oven (350°F.) 1 hour. Makes 6 servings.

TOMATO-CHEESE SOY BEANS

1 cup dried soy beans
2 cups cooked corn
1 can (19 ounces) tomatoes
1 teaspoon each sugar and seasoned salt
1/2 teaspoon monosodium glutamate
1/8 teaspoon pepper
1 cup soft bread crumbs
1/4 cup melted butter or margarine
1/2 cup grated Cheddar cheese
Paprika

Cover washed beans with 4 cups water, bring to boil and boil 2 minutes. Cover and let stand 1 hour; then cook until tender. Drain and arrange beans in alternate layers with corn in shallow baking dish. Mix tomatoes, sugar and seasonings; pour over bean mixture. Top with crumbs, drizzle butter over top, and sprinkle with cheese and paprika. Bake, uncovered, in moderate oven (375°F.) about 30 minutes. Makes 6 servings.

LAMB AND BEAN RAGOUT

1 cup dried white beans
2 pounds boneless lamb shoulder, cut in cubes
1/4 cup bacon fat or butter
2 onions, sliced
1 clove garlic, minced
1 can (19 ounces) tomatoes
1 bay leaf
1-1/2 teaspoons salt
1/2 teaspoon each pepper and paprika
1/2 teaspoon Italian herb seasoning
1-1/2 cups lamb or chicken broth
3 tablespoons flour

Wash beans and cover with water. Bring to boil and boil 2 minutes. Let stand 1 hour; then simmer until tender. Brown lamb in hot fat. Add onions and garlic; cook a few minutes. Add drained beans, tomatoes and seasonings. Cover and bake in moderate oven (350°F.) 2 hours. Thicken broth with flour blended with ¼ cup cold water. Stir into lamb mixture and bake about 15 minutes longer. Makes 6 servings.

BAKED BEANS WITH SOUR CREAM

2 cans (1 pound each) baked beans in tomato sauce
Dairy sour cream
Salt, pepper and garlic salt

Mix beans and ½ cup sour cream. Season with salt, pepper and garlic salt. Put in 1½-quart baking dish and bake in hot oven (400°F.) until beans are bubbly. Serve with more sour cream. Makes 4 servings.

CASSOULET

1 pound dried kidney beans
1/2 pound pork sausage links
1 pound lean lamb, cubed
2 onions, chopped
2 cloves garlic, minced
1/2 teaspoon dried rosemary
2 teaspoons salt
Dash of pepper
3/4 cup red wine

Cover beans with 6 cups water, bring to boil and boil 2 minutes. Let stand 1 hour; then cook, covered, until almost tender. Drain, reserving 1½ cups liquid. Cut sausages in half and fry until browned. Remove sausage. Brown lamb, onion and garlic in fat remaining. Put in 3-quart casserole. Add seasonings and wine. Cover and bake in 350°F. oven 1 hour. Add beans, sausage and bean liquid. Cover and bake 1½ hours. Makes 6 servings.

CHILI CON CARNE

1 cup dried pinto beans
3 pounds lean beef
1/4 cup olive oil
1 bay leaf
2 tablespoons chili powder
1 tablespoon salt
4 cloves garlic, minced
1 teaspoon crushed cumin seed
1 teaspoon oregano
3 tablespoons paprika
3 tablespoons cornmeal
1 tablespoon flour

Cover washed beans with 4 cups water, bring to boil and boil 2 minutes. Cover and let stand 1 hour; then cook, covered, until tender; drain. Cut meat in ½" cubes and sear in hot oil. Add 6 cups water, cover, bring to boil and simmer 1 hour. Add next 7 ingredients. Simmer ½ hour. Blend cornmeal, flour and cold water to make a paste. Stir into mixture and simmer 10 minutes. Add beans and heat. Makes 8 to 10 servings.

BRETON BEANS

Cover 1½ cups washed dried pea beans with 6 cups water, bring to boil and boil 2 minutes. Cover and let stand 1 hour; then cook until tender. Drain and put in 2-quart casserole. Mix 1 cup chicken stock, 1 cup strained canned tomatoes, 1 minced onion, 1 minced clove garlic, ¼ cup melted margarine, 4 mashed pimientos, and salt and pepper to taste. Pour over beans. Cover and bake in moderate oven (350°F.) 1 hour. Uncover and bake 30 minutes. Makes 4 to 6 servings.

BEAN-AND-BACON CASSEROLE

6 slices bacon (3 diced, 3 cut in half)
1 small onion, minced
1/2 cup catsup
2 tablespoons prepared mustard
1/4 cup molasses
1/3 cup packed brown sugar
1 can (1 pound) pork and beans
1 can (1 pound 5 ounces) red kidney
  beans
1 can condensed bean-and-bacon soup

Put diced bacon and onion in skillet and cook until bacon is translucent but not crisp. Add next 4 ingredients. Cook until heated and bubbling. Put remaining ingredients in shallow 2-quart baking dish. Pour first mixture over top and mix gently. Top with bacon slices. Bake in moderate oven (350°F.) about 45 minutes. Serves 6.

BAKED BEANS, SOUTHERN STYLE

1 pound dried marrow beans
2 cloves garlic, minced
1 onion, sliced
1 small dried hot red pepper
1 bay leaf
3/4 pound salt pork, sliced
3 tablespoons molasses
1/4 cup catsup
1 teaspoon dry mustard
1/2 teaspoon ginger
1-1/2 teaspoons Worcestershire
1/2 teaspoon salt
1/4 cup packed brown sugar

Cover beans with 6 cups water, bring to boil and boil 2 minutes. Cover and let stand 1 hour. Add next 5 ingredients and cook until beans are tender. Drain, reserving 2 cups liquid. To liquid (or water), add remaining ingredients, except sugar. Put beans in shallow 2-quart baking dish. Arrange pork slices on top. Add liquid. Sprinkle with sugar. Bake, uncovered, in hot oven (400°F.) about 1 hour. Makes 6 to 8 servings.

ERWTENSOEP
(Dutch Pea Soup)

This hearty soup is even better the next day.

2 to 3 cups dried split peas
Salt
2 pigs' feet, split
1/2 pound bacon in one piece
2 or 3 leeks
1 cup diced celery
1 cup diced celery root (celeriac)
1 large onion, coarsely chopped
Pepper
6 frankfurters, quartered
2 tablespoons sherry (optional)
Crisp garlic-buttered toast

Soak the peas overnight unless they are the quick-cooking variety. Put them to boil in 3 quarts water with 1 tablespoon salt. After 1 hour, add pigs' feet and bacon. After another hour, add next 4 ingredients. Simmer 2 more hours, adding water if the soup becomes too thick. Add salt and pepper to taste. Remove the pigs' feet and bacon; cut the bacon in dice. Strain soup and add diced bacon, frankfurters and sherry. Simmer ½ hour. Serve with the toast. Makes about 3 quarts, or 6 servings.

PASTA RUSTICA

2 cups dried brown or pinto beans
1 clove garlic
1 large onion
2 sprigs parsley
2 carrots
1 leek
1 turnip
1/4 cup oil
1 pound tomatoes, peeled
1 cup solid-pack canned tomatoes,
  drained
1/2 pound sliced bacon, diced
1/2 teaspoon basil
Salt and pepper to taste
3 small zucchini, sliced
1/2 small head cabbage, shredded
1/2 pound rigatoni, cooked
Grated Parmesan cheese
French bread
Parsley-and-chive butter

Soak beans overnight in water to cover; cook until almost tender. Chop next 3 ingredients; slice next 3 vegetables in rounds. Brown prepared vegetables lightly in oil; add tomatoes, bacon and basil. Check seasoning. Simmer until beans are tender. Add zucchini and cabbage and check seasoning; add broth or water if necessary. Combine with rigatoni and sprinkle with cheese. Serve with French bread, split, spread with parsley-and-chive butter, wrapped in foil and heated through. Serves 6 to 8.

LENTIL-VEGETABLE SOUP

1 pound quick-cooking dried lentils
2-1/2 quarts chicken broth or water
1-1/2 cups diced potato
1 medium onion, chopped
1/2 cup sliced carrots
1 cup sliced celery
1 pound Polish-style sausage, skin removed and meat sliced
Salt
Chopped parsley to taste

Put lentils and broth in large heavy kettle or Dutch oven. Bring to boil, cover, reduce heat and simmer 35 minutes. Add next 4 ingredients and simmer 20 minutes. Add sausage, cover and heat 10 minutes. Salt to taste and add parsley. Makes about 3 quarts.

BAKED LENTILS WITH BACON

1/2 pound bacon, diced
1 pound quick-cooking dried lentils
2 teaspoons salt
2 cans (8 ounces each) or 1 can (15 ounces) tomato sauce
1/2 cup packed brown sugar
2 tablespoons prepared mustard
1/2 cup molasses
1 teaspoon onion salt
1/2 cup catsup

Partially cook bacon and drain. Put in kettle or Dutch oven with lentils, salt and 4 cups water. Bring to boil, cover and simmer 30 minutes, or until lentils are tender but not mushy. Add remaining ingredients and pour into greased 2-quart casserole. Cover and bake in very slow oven (250°F.) 2 hours, or until most of liquid is absorbed. Makes 6 servings.

CALICO BEANS

1/4 pound bacon, cut in 1/2" pieces
1 medium onion, chopped
1 pound ground beef, lamb or meat-loaf mixture
1/2 cup packed brown sugar
1/2 cup catsup
1 tablespoon prepared mustard
1 teaspoon salt
1 can (1 pound) green baby limas, drained
1 can (1 pound) Boston-style pork and beans
1 can (1 pound) kidney beans, drained

Cook and drain bacon. Brown onion in bacon drippings and set aside. Discard drippings and brown beef in skillet. Drain off excess fat. Combine beef, bacon and onion with remaining ingredients; mix well. Put in greased 2½-quart casserole, cover and bake in slow oven (300°F.) about 1½ hours. Makes 6 to 8 servings.

BEANS CREOLE-STYLE

1 pound dried large limas
1/2 pound bacon, diced
1 onion, chopped
1 green pepper, diced
1 tablespoon flour
2 teaspoons seasoned salt
1/2 teaspoon salt
1/4 teaspoon pepper
2 teaspoons prepared mustard
1 teaspoon Worcestershire
2 tablespoons brown sugar
1 can (19 ounces) tomatoes

Cover washed beans with 6 cups water, bring to boil and boil 2 minutes. Cover and let stand 1 hour; then cook until tender; drain. Cook bacon in large skillet until crisp. Remove bacon and drain. Add onion and green pepper to fat in skillet and cook 5 minutes. Blend in remaining ingredients, except beans and bacon. Simmer, uncovered, 10 minutes. Add beans and heat. Sprinkle with bacon. Makes 6 to 8 servings. **Note** Beans can be soaked overnight if preferred. Other dried beans such as marrow or white beans can be substituted for the limas.

WINTERTIME LIMAS

1 cup dried large lima beans
Salt
1 pound pork-sausage meat, cut in patties and browned (reserve fat)
1 medium onion, chopped
1 can (3 ounces) chopped mushrooms, drained and liquid reserved
2 tablespoons flour
2 teaspoons dry mustard
1 cup milk
1 small bay leaf, crushed
2 tablespoons lemon juice
Pepper

In heavy saucepan, bring 4 cups water to boil. Add washed limas and boil 2 minutes. Cover, remove from heat and let stand 1 hour. Simmer 1 hour, or until tender. Add 1 teaspoon salt last half hour. Drain and reserve liquid. Put beans in greased shallow 2-quart baking dish and top with sausage patties. Sauté onion and mushrooms in 2 tablespoons sausage fat a few minutes. Combine mushroom liquid with bean liquid, then add water to measure 1 cup. Sprinkle flour and mustard over onion-mushroom mixture and simmer, stirring, 1 minute. Add liquids and milk, bring to boil and cook, stirring, until thickened. Add bay leaf, lemon juice and salt and pepper to taste. Pour over beans and pork patties. Bake in moderate oven (350°F.) 30 to 45 minutes. Makes 4 servings.

SPAGHETTI, EGGPLANT SAUCE

2 cloves garlic, minced
1/4 cup olive oil
1 can (29 ounces) Italian tomatoes
2 tablespoons chopped green olives
1 tablespoon capers
Pinch of dried basil
1-1/2 teaspoons salt
1/2 teaspoon pepper
1 medium eggplant, peeled and diced
Grated Parmesan cheese
8 ounces spaghetti, cooked

Brown garlic lightly in oil. Add next 6 ingredients. Simmer, covered, about 45 minutes, stirring occasionally. Add eggplant and simmer ½ hour. Season and serve with grated cheese on spaghetti. Makes 4 servings.

MANICOTTI WITH MEAT SAUCE

2 pounds ricotta or creamed cottage
  cheese
1/2 pound mozzarella, diced
2 eggs, well beaten
2 tablespoons chopped parsley
1/2 teaspoon pepper
1/4 teaspoon nutmeg
1/2 cup slivered blanched almonds
Salt
Grated Parmesan
1 pound ground beef
3 cans (10-1/4 ounces each) mushroom
  or meat sauce
16 manicotti, cooked

Make filling by blending first 7 ingredients, 1 teaspoon salt and 1 cup Parmesan. Cook meat until lightly browned, breaking up with fork; sprinkle with salt. Add mushroom sauce and bring to boil. Spread one third of mixture in large shallow baking dish. Stuff manicotti with cheese filling and arrange in dish. Cover with remaining sauce and sprinkle with ½ cup Parmesan. Bake in moderate oven (350°F.) 20 minutes. Makes 8 servings.

Manicotti à la Béchamel Prepare Baked Manicotti with Meat Sauce, omitting beef and mushroom sauce. For sauce, prepare 4 cups medium white sauce, using ½ cup butter or margarine, ½ cup all-purpose flour, 2 cups light cream and 2 cups milk. Season with instant minced onion. Proceed as directed.

Meat-filled Manicotti Prepare Baked Manicotti with Meat Sauce, omitting beef. Heat 1 tablespoon butter. Add ½ pound each ground beef, veal and pork; cook until browned, stirring. Add 2 teaspoons instant minced onion, 1 teaspoon grated lemon rind, ½ teaspoon oregano, ⅛ teaspoon hot pepper sauce, 1 teaspoon salt, ½ teaspoon pepper, 2 beaten eggs and ½ pound mozzarella, diced. Fill manicotti and proceed as directed.

SPAGHETTI WITH BACON-BOUILLON SAUCE

3 slices bacon, dried
1/4 cup olive oil
1 green pepper, chopped
2 large onions, chopped
1 can (6 ounces) tomato paste
2 cups bouillon
1 bay leaf
1/2 teaspoon dried thyme leaves
1 clove garlic, crushed
1 whole clove
Salt and pepper to taste
1/4 pound fresh mushrooms, sliced
Grated Parmesan cheese
8 ounces spaghetti, cooked

Cook bacon in oil until golden. Add remaining ingredients, except last 3. Simmer 2½ to 3 hours, adding more bouillon if necessary. Add mushrooms last 10 minutes. Serve with grated cheese on spaghetti. Makes 4 servings.

SPAGHETTI WITH MEATBALLS

A superior version of an all-time favorite.

1 can (1 pound 13 ounces) tomatoes
3 cans (6 ounces each) tomato paste
1 onion, minced
1 clove garlic, minced
1/4 pound salt pork, minced
2 tablespoons olive oil
2 tablespoons chopped parsley
2 teaspoons salt
1/2 teaspoon each pepper and oregano
1 teaspoon sugar
1 bay leaf, crushed
Meatballs
1/4 cup grated Parmesan or Romano
  cheese
12 ounces spaghetti

Combine tomatoes, tomato paste and 2½ cups water and bring to boil. Sauté onion, garlic and salt pork in hot olive oil. Add to tomato mixture. Add remaining ingredients, except last 3, and simmer, covered, about 1 hour, stirring frequently. Add Meatballs and simmer, covered, about 40 minutes, stirring occasionally. Before serving, stir in grated cheese. Pour over hot spaghetti. Makes 6 to 8 servings.

Meatballs

1/2 pound each ground beef, veal and
  pork
2 eggs, beaten
1 teaspoon salt
1/4 teaspoon pepper
1/4 teaspoon dried oregano
1/3 cup grated Parmesan
2 tablespoons chopped parsley
2 teaspoons grated lemon rind
1/4 cup fine dry bread crumbs

Combine all ingredients and mix thoroughly with hands; shape in balls.

RED TUNA SPAGHETTI

2 medium onions, chopped
1 clove garlic, minced
1/2 cup diced celery
1/4 cup butter or margarine
2 cans (1 pound each) tomatoes
1 can (6 ounces) tomato paste
1-1/2 teaspoons salt
1/4 teaspoon pepper
1 teaspoon Italian herb seasoning
1 bay leaf, crushed
2 cans (7 ounces each) tuna fish
2 cups shredded sharp Cheddar cheese
1 pound spaghetti, cooked

Cook onion, garlic and celery in butter in large skillet. Add next 6 ingredients and ¼ cup water. Bring to boil and simmer, covered, 1 hour. Add tuna and heat through. Combine tuna mixture, cheese and spaghetti. Makes 8 servings.

CLAM SPAGHETTI

1 small clove garlic, minced
1/4 cup minced onion
1/2 cup olive oil
1/2 cup minced green pepper or
   pimiento
2 cans (7 ounces each) minced clams,
   undrained
1/4 cup minced parsley
1/4 teaspoon thyme
1/2 teaspoon salt
1/4 teaspoon pepper
1/2 cup tomato juice or white wine
1 pound spaghetti, cooked

Cook garlic and onion in olive oil until soft and golden. Add green pepper and cook 5 minutes. Add next 6 ingredients. Simmer 15 minutes, stirring occasionally. Toss sauce with hot spaghetti. Makes 6 to 8 servings.

SICILIAN PASTA

3 tablespoons olive oil
1 clove garlic, minced
2 tablespoons minced parsley
1 tablespoon minced fresh basil or 1
   teaspoon dry basil
1 tablespoon minced celery
1 tablespoon capers
12 pitted black olives, minced
4 anchovy fillets, minced
Dash of hot pepper sauce
3 cups plain tomato sauce
1 pound spaghetti, cooked

Heat olive oil in large skillet. Add next 8 ingredients and cook 5 minutes over low heat, stirring. Add tomato sauce and simmer, covered, over low heat about 30 minutes. Toss spaghetti and sauce. Serves 6 to 8.

SPAGHETTI WITH BEEF-ANCHOVY SAUCE

2 cups ground cooked roast beef or pot
   roast
1 onion, ground
2 cloves garlic, crushed
1/2 green pepper, ground
1 can (2 ounces) chopped mushrooms,
   undrained
1 can (8 ounces) tomato sauce
1/2 teaspoon herb seasoning
1/4 teaspoon pepper
1 teaspoon Worcestershire
Pinch of allspice
1 bay leaf
1/2 cup dry wine
Beef gravy plus bouillon to make 2 cups
1 can (3/4 ounce) flat anchovies,
   drained and crushed
Salt
Grated Parmesan cheese
12 ounces spaghetti, cooked

Put all ingredients, except last 3, in large skillet. Simmer, covered, about 45 minutes. Add salt to taste. Serve with grated cheese on spaghetti. Makes 6 to 8 servings.

TWO-CHEESE SPAGHETTI TWISTS

8 ounces spaghetti twists
3 tablespoons butter or margarine
3 tablespoons flour
1 cup each hot milk and cream
1 teaspoon salt
1/2 teaspoon pepper
2 cups grated Cheddar cheese
1/2 pound Swiss cheese, diced
Paprika

Cook and drain spaghetti twists. Melt butter and stir in flour. Stir in combined hot milk and cream. Cook until sauce is smooth and thickened. Stir in next 3 ingredients. Cook until cheese is melted. In buttered dish, arrange a layer of spaghetti twists, diced Swiss cheese and ⅓ of the cheese sauce. Repeat twice. Sprinkle with paprika. Bake in moderate oven (350°F.) about 20 minutes. Makes 4 to 6 servings.

Olive Two-cheese Twists Add ¾ cup chopped pitted black or sliced pimiento-stuffed olives with cheese to sauce in above recipe. Proceed as directed.

Pimiento Two-cheese Twists Add ¾ cup chopped pimiento with cheese to sauce in above recipe. Proceed as directed.

Poppy-seed Two-cheese Twists Add 1 tablespoon poppy seeds with cheese to sauce in above recipe. Proceed as directed.

SHRIMP AND SPAGHETTI

Cook 1 large clove garlic, crushed, in 1/2 cup each butter and olive oil until soft. Mash smooth; add 1 pound chopped cooked shrimps and 2 fresh tomatoes, peeled, seeded and chopped. Add 3 tablespoons minced parsley, and salt and pepper to taste; heat. Mix with 1 pound of spaghetti, cooked *al dente*. Serves 6 to 8.

SHERRIED SPAGHETTI

1/3 cup olive oil
1 clove garlic, minced
1/3 cup cooking sherry
8 ounces spaghetti, cooked
Grated Parmesan or Romano cheese
Salt and pepper

Heat oil and garlic in top of double boiler over direct heat. Add sherry, spaghetti and 1/2 cup cheese. Season to taste. Toss well and reheat over boiling water. Serve with more cheese. Makes 4 servings.

SPAGHETTI AMATRICIANA

1/4 pound lean bacon, diced
1 pound peeled, seeded and chopped tomatoes
1 teaspoon salt
1/2 teaspoon pepper
3/4 cup dry white wine
1 pound spaghetti or other pasta, cooked

Cook bacon until soft and transparent, not crisp. Add next 4 ingredients. Simmer 15 minutes, stirring often. Serve on spaghetti. Makes 6 to 8 servings.

CARUSO SPAGHETTI

2 medium onions, minced
2 tablespoons butter
6 fresh tomatoes, peeled, seeded and chopped
1 cup fat-free beef or veal gravy
1/4 cup olive oil
1 can (4 ounces) sliced mushrooms, drained
4 canned artichoke bottoms, diced
1 cup chopped chicken livers
1 teaspoon salt
1/2 teaspoon pepper
1 teaspoon grated lemon rind
2 tablespoons chopped parsley
12 ounces spaghetti, cooked

Sauté onions in butter until soft and golden. Add tomatoes and gravy; simmer 10 minutes. Heat olive oil and sauté mushrooms, artichoke bottoms and chicken livers about 5 minutes. Add to tomato sauce with next 4 ingredients. Cover and simmer 10 to 15 minutes, stirring frequently. Serve on hot cooked spaghetti. Serves 6.

SAUCES FOR SPAGHETTI

TOMATO-SOUP MEAT SAUCE

Cook 1/2 pound ground beef, 1 chopped onion and 1 minced clove garlic in 2 tablespoons fat until browned. Add 1 can condensed tomato soup, 1 can (1 pound) tomatoes, 1 teaspoon salt, 1/2 teaspoon oregano and 1/8 teaspoon pepper. Simmer, uncovered, 1 hour. Serve with grated cheese on 8 ounces spaghetti, cooked. Makes 4 servings.

WHITE CLAM SAUCE

1 clove garlic, minced
3 tablespoons butter
1 tablespoon flour
2 cans (10-1/2 ounces each) minced clams
1/4 cup chopped parsley
Salt and pepper to taste
3/4 teaspoon dried thyme leaves or basil
8 ounces spaghetti, cooked

Cook garlic in butter 1 minute. Blend in flour; add remaining ingredients, except spaghetti, and simmer, covered, about 10 minutes, stirring frequently. Serve over hot spaghetti. Makes 4 servings.

KIDNEY-BEAN SAUCE

Cook 1 cup diced celery, 1 minced onion, 1/4 cup chopped parsley, 2 chopped green peppers and 1 minced clove garlic in 1/4 cup fat 5 minutes. Add 1 bay leaf, 1/2 teaspoon paprika, 1 teaspoon each salt and chili powder, a dash of pepper, 1 can (19 ounces) tomatoes and 1 can (21 ounces) red kidney beans. Simmer, covered, 1 hour. Uncover; simmer 1/2 hour. Serve with grated cheese on 8 ounces spaghetti, cooked. Serves 4.

ITALIAN-SAUSAGE SAUCE

Cut 1 pound sweet or hot Italian sausage in pieces. Cook 10 minutes with 1/4 cup water. When sausage begins to brown, add 1 chopped onion and a few sprigs of chopped parsley. Cook until onion is lightly browned. Add 1/4 cup water, 1 can (19 ounces) tomatoes, 2 cans (8 ounces) tomato sauce and 1 bay leaf. Simmer, uncovered, 1 1/4 hours. Season. Serve with grated cheese on 12 ounces spaghetti, cooked. Makes 6 to 8 servings.

ANCHOVY SAUCE

1 tablespoon flour
1/4 cup olive oil
2 tablespoons dry wine
1 can (6 ounces) tomato paste
1 bay leaf
1 can (2 ounces) flat anchovy fillets,
  mashed
Salt and pepper
8 ounces spaghetti, cooked
Grated Parmesan or Romano cheese

Brown flour lightly in oil. Add wine,
³/4 cup water, tomato paste and bay
leaf. Simmer, uncovered, 15 minutes.
Add anchovies, anchovy oil and salt
and pepper to taste. Simmer 5 minutes. Serve with grated cheese on hot
spaghetti. Makes 4 to 6 servings.

BACON-CORN SAUCE

Brown 4 slices diced bacon and set
aside. Pour off all but 2 tablespoons
fat. Lightly brown 1 onion, chopped.
Add ¹/2 cup tomato sauce; ¹/4 cup
chopped parsley; 1 can condensed
tomato soup; 1 can (17 ounces)
whole-kernel corn, drained; ¹/2 teaspoon garlic salt; ¹/2 teaspoon pepper;
¹/4 cup water and seasoned salt to
taste. Simmer 20 minutes. Pour on 8
ounces spaghetti, cooked. Makes 6 to
8 servings.

SAUSAGE SAUCE

1 pound Italian sausage (sweet, hot or
  half and half)
1 tablespoon olive oil
1 medium onion, chopped
2 cloves garlic, minced
1 can (6 ounces) tomato paste
1 can (35 ounces) Italian-style tomatoes
1/2 teaspoon sugar
1/2 cup chopped celery
1/2 teaspoon each salt and basil
1 teaspoon chopped parsley
1 cup sliced fresh mushrooms or 1 can
  (4 ounces) sliced mushrooms, drained
1 tablespoon butter
8 ounces linguine or spaghetti, cooked
Grated Italian cheese

Cut sausage in ¹/2" slices; brown lightly in oil with onion and garlic. Add
next 4 ingredients, seasonings and
herbs; simmer 1¹/2 hours. Sauce will
be cooked down; add water only if
too thick or dry. Sauté mushrooms in
butter and add with pan juices to
sauce for last half hour of cooking.
Serve over cooked linguine or spaghetti, topped with grated cheese.
Makes a meal with tossed green salad
and crusty sesame-seed Italian bread.
Makes 6 servings.

DEVILED-HAM SAUCE

1 onion, minced
1/2 cup chopped celery and leaves
1 carrot, chopped
1/2 clove garlic, minced
Few sprigs of parsley, chopped
2 tablespoons butter or margarine
1 can (6 ounces) tomato paste
1/8 teaspoon pepper
1/4 teaspoon oregano
2 small or 1 large can deviled ham
Salt to taste
8 ounces spaghetti, cooked

Cook first 5 ingredients in butter 10
minutes. Add tomato paste, seasonings and 2 cups water. Simmer, uncovered, stirring occasionally, 30
minutes. Stir in remaining ingredients.
Serve on hot spaghetti. Serves 4 to 6.

TOMATO-JUICE SAUCE

1/4 cup butter or margarine
3 tablespoons flour
3/4 teaspoon salt
1 teaspoon paprika
Dash of hot pepper sauce
1-1/2 cups canned tomato juice
1 bouillon cube
1/4 cup undiluted evaporated milk
Grated Italian cheese
8 ounces spaghetti, cooked

Melt butter in saucepan; blend in flour
and seasonings. Add tomato juice, ¹/2
cup water and bouillon cube; cook,
stirring constantly, until mixture thickens and bouillon cube dissolves. Add
milk. Serve with grated cheese on hot
spaghetti. Makes 6 servings.

SAUCE CALABRESE

Soak 5 slices stale bread in ¹/2 cup
water until softened; squeeze out
water. Mix bread, 1 pound ground
round steak, 2 beaten eggs, 2 or 3
tablespoons grated Romano cheese,
1 teaspoon salt and ¹/4 teaspoon pepper. Shape into balls the size of a
walnut. Heat ¹/4 cup olive oil in large
kettle. Brown 6 center-cut pork chops
on both sides. Sprinkle with salt, pepper and oregano. Remove chops and
brown meatballs in remaining fat, adding more oil if necessary. Sprinkle with
oregano. Add chops, 1 teaspoon salt,
¹/4 teaspoon pepper, ¹/2 teaspoon
oregano, 1 clove garlic, 4 cans (6
ounces each) tomato paste and 2
quarts water. Simmer, covered, stirring occasionally, 4 or 5 hours. Remove chops and meatballs; simmer 2
to 3 hours, or until of desired thickness. Reheat meat in sauce. Serve on
12 ounces spaghetti, cooked. Makes
6 to 8 servings.

SEAFOOD SAUCE

Lightly brown 1 chopped onion and 1 cup diced celery in ¼ cup olive oil. Add 1 can (6 ounces) tomato paste, 1 envelope spaghetti-sauce mix, ½ teaspoon Italian herb seasoning, 2 cups water, 2 teaspoons seasoned salt and ¼ teaspoon pepper. Simmer, uncovered, 25 minutes. Add the juice of ½ lemon; 3 cups mixed cooked shrimp, diced crab meat and lobster; and 1 can (3 ounces) sliced mushrooms, drained. Simmer 5 minutes. Serve on 12 ounces spaghetti, cooked. Makes 6 servings.

HERB TOMATO SAUCE

Sauté 1 clove garlic in ⅓ cup olive oil until golden. Remove garlic and cool oil. Add 2 cans (6 ounces each) tomato paste blended with 2 cups water, 2 leaves fresh sweet basil or ⅛ teaspoon dried basil, and ⅛ teaspoon each dried-herb mixture and oregano. Simmer about 30 minutes. Season. Serve with grated cheese on 12 ounces spaghetti, cooked. Makes 6 to 8 servings.

HAM SAUCE

Melt ¼ cup butter or margarine, blend in ¼ cup flour and add 1 cup each chicken broth and milk. Cook, stirring, until thickened. Stir small amount of mixture into 1 beaten egg yolk. Return to first mixture and cook a few minutes longer. Add ½ pound boiled ham, finely diced, and ¼ cup grated Parmesan cheese. Heat and season to taste. Serve with grated cheese over 8 ounces spaghetti, cooked. Makes 4 servings.

TOMATO SAUCE

1 can (29 ounces) Italian tomatoes
2 small cloves garlic, pressed
2 sprigs thyme
1 teaspoon sugar
Dash of hot pepper sauce or cayenne
3 tablespoons olive oil
Few leaves of rosemary, crushed
Few leaves of basil, crumbled
Salt

Place first 8 ingredients and 1 teaspoon salt in a heavy saucepan. Cover and simmer 20 to 30 minutes, or until mixture is as thick as tomato purée. Stir occasionally to keep from sticking. Strain or put through food mill or whirl in blender. Add salt, if desired. Serves 6.

WHITE ANCHOVY SAUCE

In small skillet, heat 1 clove garlic in ⅓ cup olive oil. Remove. Add 1 can (2 ounces) anchovy fillets, drained and crushed. Pour over 8 ounces spaghetti, cooked. Season to taste. Makes 4 servings.

PEPPER-CHEESE SAUCE

Mix ¼ pound Bel Paese or Pont l'Évêque cheese, flaked; 1 each red and green peppers, chopped fine; 8 to 10 pitted green olives; ¼ cup dry sherry; ¼ cup olive oil; and salt and pepper to taste. Toss with 8 ounces cooled, cooked spaghetti. Serve cold as a salad. Makes 4 servings.

MARINARA SAUCE

Heat ¼ cup olive oil in skillet. Add few sprigs parsley, chopped; 1 minced onion; 1 minced clove garlic; and 6 anchovy fillets. Brown lightly. Add 1 can (29 ounces) Italian tomatoes; and salt, pepper and oregano to taste. Simmer uncovered, about 20 minutes, stirring occasionally. Serve with grated cheese on 12 ounces cooked spaghetti. Serves 6 to 8.

COLD MUSHROOM SAUCE

Sauté ¼ pound mushrooms, sliced, and 2 cloves garlic in 2 tablespoons butter about 5 minutes; cool. Blend 1 tablespoon dry mustard with 1 tablespoon water; gradually blend in 3 tablespoons olive oil, ½ teaspoon sugar, 2 tablespoons heavy cream, 10 diced pitted ripe olives, 2 or 3 teaspoons capers, the mushrooms and the garlic. Pour over 8 ounces spaghetti, cooked and cooled. Toss lightly and season. Makes 4 servings.

GARBANZO SAUCE

Cook 1 chopped onion, 1 minced clove garlic and ½ cup diced celery and tops in 3 tablespoons olive oil until golden. Mash 1 can (19 ounces) garbanzos, reserving liquid; add water to make 2½ cups. Add to onion mixture with 1 can (19 ounces) tomatoes, 1 can (6 ounces) tomato paste, 1 bay leaf, 1 teaspoon salt, a dash of cayenne and ½ teaspoon oregano. Simmer, uncovered, 2 hours, stirring occasionally. Serve with a sprinkling of grated Italian cheese on 1 pound spaghetti, cooked. Serves 8.

FUSILLI WITH GREEN SAUCE

1/3 cup butter
1 clove garlic, minced
3/4 cup minced parsley
Grated Parmesan cheese
8 ounces fusilli macaroni, cooked

Melt butter in top part of double boiler over direct heat. Add garlic and cook about 5 minutes. Add parsley, 1/2 cup cheese and the fusilli. Toss well and heat over boiling water. Serve with additional cheese. Makes 4 servings.

MACARONI, CHEESE AND HAM PUFF

1 cup elbow macaroni
1/2 cup minced cooked ham
1 cup grated Cheddar cheese
2 tablespoons chopped parsley
Salt to taste
3 eggs, separated

Cook macaroni according to package directions; drain. Mix with next 4 ingredients. Add well-beaten egg yolks. Fold in egg whites beaten until stiff but not dry. Turn into buttered 1½-quart baking dish. Bake in moderate oven (325°F.) 35 to 40 minutes. Makes 4 servings.

BAKED CHICKEN SALAD

2 cups (8 ounces) elbow macaroni
4 cups diced cooked chicken
1/3 cup chopped toasted almonds
1 tablespoon lemon juice
1 teaspoon grated lemon rind
1-1/2 cups grated Swiss cheese (about
  1/3 pound)
2 teaspoons celery salt
1/2 teaspoon pepper
1-1/2 cups mayonnaise
Parsley

Cook macaroni according to package directions; drain. Combine with next 8 ingredients. Turn into buttered 2-quart baking dish. Bake in moderate oven (350°F.) 30 minutes. Garnish with parsley. Makes 4 to 6 servings.

ONION RICE

Heat 1 can condensed onion soup and 1/3 cup water to boiling. Stir in 1½ cups packaged precooked rice. Cover, turn off heat and let stand 5 minutes. Fluff with fork, add pepper to taste and serve with grated Parmesan cheese, if desired. Serves 4.

MACARONI PARMESAN

1 cup small soft bread cubes
2 tablespoons butter
1/8 teaspoon garlic salt
8 ounces elbow macaroni
1 cup dairy sour cream
1/2 cup grated Parmesan cheese
2 egg yolks
1/2 teaspoon each paprika and salt
1/4 teaspoon pepper

Brown bread cubes in butter, add garlic salt and set aside. Cook macaroni according to package directions; drain and put in top of double boiler over boiling water. Add remaining ingredients. Sprinkle with browned bread cubes. Serves 4.

SKILLET BACON, MACARONI AND CHEESE

3/4 pound bacon, diced
1 cup chopped onion
1 quart milk
2 teaspoons celery salt
1/2 teaspoon pepper
1/4 teaspoon hot pepper sauce
2 cups (8 ounces) elbow macaroni
1 cup grated Swiss cheese
1/2 cup chopped pimientos

In large skillet cook bacon and onion over low heat 15 minutes. Drain off drippings. Add next 4 ingredients. Heat to boiling point. Gradually add macaroni so that milk continues to boil. Simmer, uncovered, 20 minutes, stirring often. Add cheese and pimiento; stir until cheese melts. Makes 4 to 6 servings.

BAKED RICE AND CHEESE

1 cup uncooked rice
1 small onion, minced
6 tablespoons butter
3 tablespoons flour
1 teaspoon each salt and Worcestershire
1/4 teaspoon pepper
1/2 teaspoon dry mustard
2 cups milk
1/2 pound sharp Cheddar cheese
3 tablespoons fine dry bread crumbs

Cook and drain rice as directed on package. Cook onion 5 minutes in 1/4 cup butter; blend in flour and seasonings. Gradually add milk and cook, stirring constantly, until thickened. Dice half of cheese and add, stirring until blended. Slice remaining cheese. Put half of rice in shallow 1½-quart baking dish. Cover with layer of sliced cheese; pour half of hot mixture over top. Repeat. Sprinkle crumbs on top and dot with remaining 2 tablespoons butter. Bake in hot oven (400°F.) 20 minutes. Makes 4 to 6 servings.

NOODLES POLONAISE

Serve these with goulash or pot roast.

4 cups (8 ounces) broad noodles
1/4 cup butter
1/2 cup fine dry bread crumbs
1 hard-cooked egg, chopped
1 tablespoon chopped chives or parsley
1/2 teaspoon salt

Cook noodles according to package directions; drain. Melt butter in skillet and brown crumbs. Add remaining ingredients and noodles and toss to coat. Heat through, stirring. Makes 4 to 6 servings.

SICILIAN MACARONI-EGGPLANT CASSEROLE

1 eggplant
Olive oil
1/2 pound macaroni twists, cooked
3/4 teaspoon salt
1 teaspoon dried oregano
1/2 teaspoon dried basil
1/2 cup pine nuts
1/2 cup grated Parmesan cheese
1 can (17 ounces) Italian-style tomatoes
2 tablespoons butter

Cut unpeeled eggplant into 1/4" slices. Cook in 2 tablespoons olive oil until well browned on both sides, adding more oil as necessary. Grease a 2-quart casserole. Arrange half of macaroni on bottom. Top with half of eggplant. Mix salt and next 4 ingredients; sprinkle half on eggplant. Repeat layers and top with tomatoes. Dot with butter and bake in moderate oven (350°F.) 30 minutes. Makes 4 servings.

POLENTA WITH MUSHROOMS

This polenta is especially good with chicken or pork.

Polenta (at right)
3 tablespoons chopped onion
1/3 cup butter
1/2 pound mushrooms, sliced
1 tablespoon flour
1/2 teaspoon dried basil
3 tablespoons chopped parsley
1 teaspoon salt
Dash of pepper
2/3 cup tomato purée

Prepare Polenta and steam in a buttered 1-quart mold or loaf pan for 1 hour. Sauté the onion in butter in skillet; add mushrooms and sauté for 3 minutes more. Stir in remaining ingredients. Blend well and cook over medium heat 5 minutes. Unmold the polenta on a serving dish and pour the sauce over. Makes 4 to 6 servings.

SPAETZLE

Mix 3 cups all-purpose flour, 1 teaspoon salt and dash each of nutmeg and paprika. Add 4 eggs and 3/4 cup water. Beat well with spoon until thick and smooth. Put 3/4 cup dough on dampened end of small cutting board. With spatula, smooth a small amount of dough very thin. Cut off small strips into a large kettle of boiling salted water. Dip spatula in water several times during cutting. If dough is too thin to hold together, add a little flour. Cook about 5 minutes, until tender. Lift out, place in dish and pour a little melted butter over strips. Repeat until all of dough is used, adding a little fresh boiling water to kettle each time. Serve hot with goulash and pot roast. Serves 6.

DOUBLE-BOILER MACARONI AND CHEESE

2 cups elbow macaroni
2 teaspoons salt
1 tablespoon instant minced onion
1/2 cup powdered cream
3 tablespoons flour
1/4 teaspoon pepper
1/2 teaspoon dry mustard
1/2 pound sharp Cheddar cheese, cubed
1 teaspoon Worcestershire
1 cup soft bread cubes
2 tablespoons butter or margarine
Seasoned salt

In top part of 2½-quart double boiler, cook first 3 ingredients in 5 cups boiling water until macaroni is tender. (Do not drain.) Stir in next 6 ingredients. Put over boiling water and simmer, covered, 15 minutes, stirring occasionally. Brown bread cubes in butter; sprinkle with seasoned salt and stir into mixture. Serves 4 to 6.

POLENTA

A delicious cornmeal loaf, especially good with Parmesan cheese.

In a very heavy saucepan, mix 1½ cups cornmeal with 2 cups water; add 1 cup more water and 1 teaspoon salt. Bring to boil, stirring constantly to be sure cornmeal does not lump. Continue cooking and stirring until the mixture is smooth and thick. Pour into a mold, or a sieve or strainer lined with cloth. Cover and steam over hot water 2 hours, or until the mixture forms a firm loaf. Cut in slices and serve with plenty of butter, salt, pepper and, if you like, grated Parmesan cheese. Makes 4 servings.

HAM-NOODLE RABBIT

A traditional Cheddar rabbit with ham and noodles added.

3 tablespoons flour
1 teaspoon salt
2 teaspoons dry mustard
1/8 teaspoon hot pepper sauce
1 pound Cheddar cheese, shredded
3 tablespoons butter
12 ounces beer or ale
2 cups diced cooked ham
8 ounces medium noodles, cooked

Mix together first 5 ingredients. Melt butter; stir in cheese mixture and cook over low heat until smooth, stirring. Add beer and continue stirring over low heat until thoroughly blended. Add ham and noodles and mix well. Heat if necessary. Makes 4 to 6 servings.

CANNELLONI WITH TOMATO SAUCE

The word "cannelloni" means "little tubes," and you can stuff them with anything you choose.

1/2 pound mushrooms, minced or ground
1 small clove garlic, pressed
3 tablespoons olive oil
1 cup minced or finely ground cooked chicken
1 hard-cooked egg, sieved
1/8 teaspoon thyme
1/8 teaspoon rosemary, crumbled
2 tablespoons cream or evaporated milk
Salt and pepper
Flour
Foolproof All-purpose Thin Pancakes (page 310)
Tomato Sauce (page 241)
Grated Parmesan cheese

Add mushrooms and garlic to oil in a deep skillet. Brown lightly, covered, 3 or 4 minutes. Add next 6 ingredients and cook stirring. If too stiff, add a little more cream. If too thin, add a dash of flour dissolved in a little water. Cool slightly and spread mixture evenly over **12** cooked thin pancakes. Roll up like little tubes. Allow 2 to each person. Place in lightly buttered shallow individual baking dishes, seam side down, or use one large shallow baking dish. Cover with Tomato Sauce. Sprinkle generously with grated Parmesan cheese. Near serving time place cannelloni in a cold broiler not too near unit. Turn on heat and broil until top is lightly browned and sauce is bubbling. Serve at once, very hot. Makes 6 servings. *Note* Cheese Sauce (page 157) may be used in place of Tomato Sauce.

HUNGARIAN ALMOND POPPY-SEED NOODLES

Cook 1/2 cup slivered blanched almonds in 1/4 cup melted butter until golden. Add 2 tablespoons poppy seed and 1 tablespoon paprika. Cook 3 minutes, stirring. Toss with 8 ounces hot noodles, cooked and drained. Makes 4 to 6 servings.

RUMANIAN NOODLES MUSACA

A noodle-and-pork casserole.

1 pound fine noodles
1 pound ground pork
1 slice bread, soaked in milk and squeezed dry
1 leek, minced
2 teaspoons fennel seed
1/4 cup chopped parsley
1 teaspoon salt
1/2 teaspoon pepper
4 eggs
2/3 cup light cream
1/2 cup grated Cheddar or Parmesan cheese
1/4 cup butter or margarine

Cook noodles only three quarters tender. Combine next 7 ingredients. In large shallow baking dish, place alternate layers of noodles and meat mixture, ending with noodles. Beat eggs with cream and cheese. Pour over noodles. Dot with butter. Bake in moderate oven (350°F.) 40 minutes, or until pork is done. Makes 4 to 6 servings.

LASAGNA

8 ounces lasagna noodles
Salt
1 tablespoon olive oil
1 pound ricotta cheese
8 ounces mozzarella cheese, sliced
Tomato-Meat Sauce
1/2 cup grated Parmesan cheese

Cook noodles in boiling salted water 25 minutes, or until tender, stirring frequently. Drain and add oil. Arrange in shallow 2 1/2-quart baking dish, making 3 layers each of cooked noodles, ricotta, mozzarella, sauce and grated cheese. Bake in slow oven (325°F.) about 45 minutes. Makes 6 servings. **Tomato-Meat Sauce** Brown 1 minced medium onion and 2 minced cloves garlic lightly in 1/4 cup olive oil in large skillet. Add 1 pound ground beef and brown lightly. Add 1 can (29 ounces) tomatoes, 1 can (6 ounces) tomato paste, 2 teaspoons salt, 1/8 teaspoon cayenne, 1 teaspoon sugar, pinch of basil, 1 bay leaf and 2 cups water. Simmer, uncovered, about 1 1/2 hours.

NEAPOLITAN RIGATONI

1 pound rigatoni
1/3 cup olive oil
1 clove garlic, minced
1 can (14-1/2 ounces) stewed tomatoes
1/2 teaspoon salt
1 can (8 ounces) tomato sauce
1/4 teaspoon coarse black pepper
1 teaspoon oregano
2 tablespoons chopped parsley

Cook and drain rigatoni; while pasta is cooking, make sauce. Cook garlic 3 or 4 minutes in oil in heavy saucepan. Add remaining ingredients. Cook, stirring, 10 to 15 minutes. Add to rigatoni and toss well. Makes 6 servings.

MEXICAN HOMINY

1 medium onion, minced
1 medium green pepper, chopped
1/4 cup butter or bacon fat
1 can (29 ounces) whole hominy, drained
1 teaspoon chili powder
1/2 teaspoon salt
1/8 teaspoon pepper

Cook onion and green pepper in butter in skillet over low heat about 10 minutes. Add remaining ingredients and heat. Makes 4 servings.

TACO CASSEROLE

1 tablespoon bacon fat or vegetable oil
1 pound ground beef
3/4 cup chopped green onion
1 clove garlic, minced
1 can (10-1/2 ounces) condensed beef consommé
1/2 cup sauterne
1 can (12 ounces) Mexican-style corn
1 can (6 ounces) tomato paste
1 tablespoon chili powder
1/2 teaspoon ground cumin
4 drops hot pepper sauce
Salt
3 tortillas, each torn in sixths
3/4 cup sharp Cheddar cheese
1 cup shredded lettuce
1 large avocado, cut in thin slices
1 medium tomato, cut in very thin slices

Put bacon fat in skillet, add beef, 1/2 cup onion and the garlic and sauté, breaking up meat with fork, until onions are limp. Add consommé and wine and bring to boil. Simmer 1 minute, then add next 5 ingredients and mix well. Add salt to taste and pour into greased 9" x 9" x 2" baking dish. Poke tortilla pieces into meat mixture and bake, uncovered, in moderate oven (350°F.) about 25 minutes. Remove from oven and sprinkle with cheese. Then top with remaining green onion, the lettuce, avocado and tomato. Serve at once. Makes 4 to 6 servings.

TACOS DE JOCOQUI
(Sour-Cream Tacos)

12 tortillas
Hot lard or oil
1 pound shredded Jack cheese
1 can (4 ounces) peeled green chilies
1-1/2 cups hot tomato sauce
Salt and pepper
1/2 cup white sauce
2-1/2 cups dairy sour cream

Dip tortillas in hot lard. On each one put 1/4 cup of cheese, a third of a chili (in a strip), 2 tablespoons tomato sauce and salt and pepper. Roll and put in baking dish, seam side down. Mix cream sauce and sour cream, pour over all and bake in moderate oven (350°F.) 30 minutes. Makes 6 servings.

LASAGNA WITH SAUSAGE

1 pound bulk sweet Italian sausage
1/2 pound ground beef
1 tablespoon whole basil
Salt
1 can (1 pound) stewed tomatoes
2 cans (6 ounces each) tomato paste
6 large wide lasagna noodles
1 tablespoon olive oil
Cheese Filling
1 pound mozzarella cheese, thinly sliced

Brown meats slowly in skillet or saucepan. Add basil, 1 1/2 teaspoons salt, 1 cup water, tomatoes and paste. Bring to boil and simmer, stirring occasionally, 30 minutes, or until of desired consistency. Meanwhile, cook noodles in boiling salted water with the olive oil until tender. Drain and arrange half in greased 13" x 9" x 2" baking dish. Spread with half the filling, then cover with half the cheese and half the meat sauce. Repeat layers. Bake in moderate oven (375°F.) about 30 minutes. Let stand 10 minutes before cutting in squares. Makes 6 to 8 servings. **Note** Can be frozen.

Cheese Filling

2 cups ricotta or creamed cottage cheese
1/2 cup grated Parmesan or Romano cheese
2 tablespoons chopped parsley
2 eggs, beaten
2 teaspoons salt
1/2 teaspoon pepper

Mix all ingredients together until smooth and well blended.

PASTA TIPS

Look for pasta enriched with thiamin, riboflavin, niacin and iron. Green (spinach) noodles and whole-wheat pastas are also available.

BEEF PILAF WITH HERBS

1/4 cup vermicelli in 1/4" pieces
3/4 cup uncooked rice
1 teaspoon salt
1 teaspoon instant minced onion
1 beef bouillon cube
1/4 teaspoon freshly ground pepper
1/2 teaspoon tarragon
1/4 teaspoon thyme
1/2 teaspoon basil
1 tablespoon butter or margarine

Brown vermicelli in moderate oven (350°F.) about 10 minutes. Mix with next 8 ingredients. Bring to a boil in large saucepan 2 cups water and butter. Add vermicelli mixture, bring to boil, stir and cover. Simmer 15 minutes, or until all moisture is absorbed. Makes 4 servings.

SOUR-CREAM RICE PANCAKES

1 egg
2 tablespoons butter or margarine, melted
1-1/2 cups dairy sour cream
1 cup cooked rice
1 cup all-purpose flour
2 tablespoons sugar
3/4 teaspoon salt
3/4 teaspoon baking soda
1/4 cup milk

Beat egg slightly. Stir in next 3 ingredients. Add sifted dry ingredients and milk and stir until well mixed. Bake on hot lightly greased griddle, turning to brown both sides. Makes eighteen 3" cakes.

SPANISH EGGS AND RICE

3/4 cup uncooked rice
6 eggs
1 can (1 pound) tomatoes
1 teaspoon instant minced onion
1 small bay leaf
3 whole cloves
1 teaspoon sugar
1/4 teaspoon pepper
1/2 teaspoon each salt, celery salt, paprika and Worcestershire
2 tablespoons butter or margarine
2 tablespoons flour
1 cup buttered crumbs
2 tablespoons grated Parmesan cheese

Cook and drain rice; put in shallow baking dish. Make 6 indentations in rice and drop an egg in each. Simmer tomatoes, onion and seasonings 10 minutes. Strain into butter blended with flour; cook until thickened, stirring. Pour over eggs. Sprinkle with crumbs mixed with cheese. Bake in moderate oven (350°F.), about 20 minutes. Makes 6 servings.

YELLOW RICE

Put 1 cup uncooked rice in 1½-quart casserole with 2 cups boiling water, 1 teaspoon each salt and turmeric and 2 tablespoons butter or margarine. Cover and bake in moderate oven (350°F.) about 1¾ hours. Makes 4 servings.

SPANAKORIZO
(Greek Spinach and Rice)

1 cup uncooked rice
1 medium onion, chopped
1/3 cup olive oil
1-1/2 teaspoons salt
1 pound fresh spinach

Sauté rice and onion in olive oil 15 minutes, stirring occasionally. Add 2 cups boiling water and the salt, cover and simmer 10 minutes. Wash spinach; chop in small pieces. Mix thoroughly with rice. Cover and simmer 15 minutes, stirring occasionally. Makes 4 to 6 servings.

ORANGE RICE

3 tablespoons butter or margarine
2/3 cup diced celery with leaves
2 tablespoons finely chopped green onion
1 tablespoon finely chopped parsley
Grated rind of 1 orange
1 cup orange juice
1-1/4 teaspoons salt
1 cup uncooked rice

Melt butter in heavy saucepan. Add next 3 ingredients and sauté about 5 minutes. Add 1½ cups water, orange rind and juice and salt. Bring to boil and slowly stir in rice. Cover, reduce heat and cook 25 minutes, or until rice is tender. Makes 4 to 6 servings.

TUNA WILD RICE, AMANDINE

Cover ¾ cup wild rice with boiling water; cover and let stand 20 minutes; drain. Repeat 3 times until rice is cooked to desired doneness. Drain well and add salt to taste. Brown ½ cup blanched and slivered almonds lightly in 3 tablespoons butter; stir in rice. Pour into 3-cup bowl. Flake 1 can (7 ounces) white tuna and combine with 2 cups medium white sauce and 2 tablespoons sherry. Unmold rice on round platter and surround with tuna mixture. White or brown rice can be used in place of the wild rice and 1 cup sliced sautéed mushrooms may be added to the sauce. Makes 4 to 5 servings.

CHINESE FRIED RICE

1/2 cup diced cooked chicken, ham or
    pork
3 tablespoons butter
1 can (3 ounces) sliced mushrooms,
    drained
1 green onion, chopped
1 pimiento, chopped
1 teaspoon dried green pepper
3 tablespoons soy sauce
3 cups cooked rice
1 egg, beaten

Put all ingredients, except last two,
in top pan of double boiler over
direct heat. When butter is melted,
stir in rice lightly with fork. Heat
over boiling water. Meanwhile, cook
egg in a greased skillet until firm but
not browned. Cut in thin strips and
put on rice. Makes 4 to 6 servings.

RICE NEPTUNE

1 can (10-1/2 ounces) minced clams
1 small onion, minced
1/4 cup butter
2 pimientos, cut in strips
1/4 cup minced parsley
1/2 teaspoon salt
1/4 teaspoon pepper
1-1/3 cups packaged precooked rice
1 box (10 ounces) frozen cleaned shelled
    shrimp, cooked

Drain clams, reserving liquid; add
water to make 1½ cups. Cook onion
in the butter in top pan of double
boiler over direct heat about 10 minutes. Add clam liquid, pimientos,
parsley and seasonings. Heat to boiling; put over boiling water and stir
in rice with fork. Cover and let stand
5 minutes. Add clams and shrimps
and heat through. Serves 4 to 6.

ORIENTAL PINEAPPLE
AND TUNA

1 can (13-1/2 ounces) pineapple chunks
1/4 cup vinegar
1/4 cup sugar
2 teaspoons soy sauce
1/2 teaspoon monosodium glutamate
2 tablespoons cornstarch
1 onion, cut in thin wedges
1 medium green pepper, cut in strips
1 can (7 ounces) tuna, drained
1 canned or peeled fresh tomato
Hot cooked rice

Drain syrup from pineapple into
large saucepan or skillet. Add
next 4 ingredients and ½ cup water
blended with cornstarch. Cook, stirring, until thickened. Add pineapple
and remaining ingredients, except
rice; cover and cook just until ingredients are heated. Serve on rice.
Makes 4 servings.

SAVORY RICE

Prepare 1½ cups packaged precooked rice as directed on the
label. Stir in 1 can (8 ounces) spaghetti sauce and heat. Serve with
grated Parmesan or Romano cheese.
Makes 4 servings.

SAUTEED BROWN RICE
AND MUSHROOMS

1 medium onion, minced
1/4 green pepper, minced
1/4 cup butter or margarine
1 can (3 ounces) mushroom stems and
    pieces, drained
3 cups cooked brown rice
3/4 teaspoon salt
1/2 teaspoon pepper
1/2 teaspoon chili powder

Sauté onion and green pepper in the butter 5 minutes.
Add remaining ingredients and cook
until lightly browned, stirring gently.
Makes 4 servings.

NASI GORENG
(Indonesian Fried Rice)

1-1/2 cups uncooked rice
2 large onions, minced
Margarine
1/2 pound ground beef
1/3 cup minced celery leaves
2 tablespoons soy sauce
1 teaspoon curry powder
1/4 teaspoon dry mustard
Salt and pepper
1 pound shrimps, steamed, shelled and
    cleaned
Egg Topping
6 small bananas

Steam rice, drain, cool and chill.
(This can be done the day before serving.) Sauté onions in ½ cup
margarine until lightly browned. Add
beef and rice and brown lightly, breaking up meat with fork. Add celery
leaves, seasonings and shrimps. Heat,
stirring gently. Put on hot serving
platter and top with strips of Egg Topping. Garnish with bananas lightly
sautéed in a little margarine. Good
with chutney, mustard pickle, a green
salad, and fresh fruit for dessert.
Makes 6 servings. **Egg Topping** Beat
2 eggs with ¼ teaspoon salt and
¼ cup milk until foamy. In a hot,
well-greased large skillet, pour a thin
layer (about half) the egg mixture.
Sauté lightly and quickly on both
sides like a paper-thin omelet. Remove, grease skillet again and repeat
with remaining egg mixture. Cut in
julienne strips.

RICE, VIENNESE STYLE

1 small onion, minced
Butter or margarine
1 cup uncooked rice
Salt and pepper to taste
2 cups hot consommé
1 cup canned peas, heated
1 teaspoon paprika

Brown onion lightly in 1 tablespoon butter; add rice and cook until glazed. Season, add consommé, bring to boil and simmer until rice is done and consommé entirely absorbed. Carefully stir in peas and 2 tablespoons butter. Sprinkle with paprika. Serves 4.

HERB RICE BLEND

1 cup uncooked rice
2 beef bouillon cubes
1/2 teaspoon salt
1/2 teaspoon each rosemary, dried
    marjoram and dried thyme
1 teaspoon dried green onion flakes
1 tablespoon butter

Mix all ingredients and add to 2 cups cold water in heavy saucepan. When mixture boils, stir once with fork; reduce heat to medium-low. Cover tightly and simmer 12 to 14 minutes, or until all liquid is absorbed. Makes 4 servings.

RISOTTO ALLA MILANESE

1/4 cup butter
1/4 cup chopped beef marrow or 2
    tablespoons butter
1 onion, minced
2 cups uncooked rice
1/2 cup dry white wine
About 5 cups boiling hot chicken
    bouillon
1/2 teaspoon saffron
2/3 cup grated Parmesan cheese
Salt to taste
1/2 teaspoon white pepper

In heavy saucepan, melt butter and beef marrow. Cook onion until soft but not brown. Add rice and cook 3 or 4 minutes, stirring. (The rice must be transparent, but not brown.) Stir in wine and cook 3 minutes. Add ½ cup boiling bouillon. Cook, stirring, until bouillon is absorbed. Add remaining bouillon ½ cupful at a time, allowing each addition to become absorbed and stirring constantly. It will take 20 to 25 minutes after the first bouillon has been added, depending on the kind of rice used and the degree of doneness desired. Italians eat it *al dente*. After about 15 minutes, steep saffron in a little bouillon and add. When rice is done, stir in cheese, salt and pepper. Serves 4 to 6.

CHEESE-RICE SOUFFLÉ, INDIENNE

1/3 cup uncooked rice
1-1/2 teaspoons curry powder
3 tablespoons butter or margarine
2 tablespoons flour
1/2 teaspoon salt
3/4 cup milk
1/2 pound mild process cheese, shredded
4 eggs, separated

Cook rice, adding curry powder to the cooking water. Melt butter in top part of double boiler over boiling water. Blend in flour and salt. Gradually add milk and cook, stirring, until smooth and thickened. Stir in cheese. Cool slightly. Beat egg whites until stiff but not dry. Beat egg yolks until thick and lemon-colored. Stir cheese mixture into yolks and blend thoroughly; add rice. Pour mixture slowly over egg whites and fold together quickly and ightly. Pour into 1½-quart soufflé dish or straight-side casserole. Bake in slow oven (325°F.) about 40 minutes. Makes 4 servings.

PILAF
(Greek Rice)

1 cup uncooked rice
1/4 cup butter
2-1/2 cups chicken stock
1 teaspoon salt

Brown rice in butter. Stir in stock and salt. Cover and simmer gently until stock is absorbed, 15 to 20 minutes. Makes 4 servings.

COTTAGE-RICE LOAF WITH SHRIMP SAUCE

1 box (4-5/8 ounces) precooked rice
1 teaspoon salt
2 tablespoons butter
1 teaspoon instant minced onion
3 eggs, beaten
1-1/2 cups milk
2 cups cottage cheese, sieved
1 teaspoon seasoned salt
1/2 teaspoon pepper
Shrimp Sauce

Prepare rice with 1⅓ cups water, salt, butter and onion as directed on label. Add remaining ingredients, except sauce, and mix well. Pour into well-greased 9" x 5" x 3" loaf pan, set in pan of hot water and bake in moderate oven (350°F.) 1 to 1¼ hours, or until set. Remove from water and let stand on cake rack 10 minutes. Turn out, slice and serve with sauce. Makes 6 servings. **Shrimp Sauce** Heat 1 can frozen shrimp soup with ¼ cup milk; add 1 tablespoon sherry.

Savory Tomatoes, Beans and Squash

THYME

BEN CALVO

HOW TO BUY FRESH VEGETABLES

When browsing at the fresh-vegetable bins, look for bright color, crisp or firm texture and unwilted unspotted leaves. All fresh vegetables should be young enough to be tender but mature enough to be ripe and full-flavored. They should also be clean, as sand and soil are time-consuming to remove. Usually, vegetables are at their best and cheapest when they are most plentiful. Buy only enough for 1 to 2 days at a time.

VEGETABLE STORAGE

Store potatoes, sweet potatoes, onions and turnips where cool air can circulate around them. Do not clean until ready to use. Generally, sweet potatoes don't keep well, so use promptly. Refrigerate other fresh vegetables at once in plastic bags or vegetable crisper.

VEGETABLE EQUIVALENTS

Corn

16- and 17-ounce cans = about 2 cups kernels
12-ounce can = about 1½ cups
1 box frozen cut = about 1¾ cups kernels
3 medium ears fresh = about 1 cup kernels
6 medium ears fresh = about 1 cup grated or cream-style

Mushrooms

1 pound fresh = 20 to 24 medium mushrooms
1 pound fresh mushrooms, sliced and cooked = 1 can (8 ounces) sliced mushrooms (there will be slightly less in the can)

2 ounces dried mushrooms, soaked in 1½ cups water = 1⅓ cups chopped mushrooms and liquid
1 pound fresh mushrooms = 20 to 24 frozen (do not go by weight)

FRESH-TOMATO TIPS

TO BUY Select firm, plump, smooth tomatoes with good color and without blemishes. If too green, ripen out of the sun in a moderately warm place. Refrigerate just before using. **TO PEEL** Dip tomato in boiling water 1 minute. Cut out stem end and peel with knife. Or hold tomato on fork over heat until skin wrinkles and splits, then peel off skin. *Note* Beefsteak, oxheart, plum and cherry tomatoes need not be peeled.

HOW TO CHOOSE AND STORE FRESH CORN

To choose Look for bright green, snug husks (this denotes freshness) and dark brown silk at the husk end (a sign of well-filled kernels). Milk should flow from kernels when you press them.
To store Cook fresh corn as soon as possible after buying. Keep in refrigerator until cooking time to preserve tenderness and sweet flavor.

To Freeze Mushrooms

Whole fresh mushrooms frozen by home methods tend to water out and be rubbery when cooked. The best way is to cook them first, then freeze. Partially broil large whole mushrooms or sauté button or sliced mushrooms in a little butter or margarine until almost cooked. Cool quickly, then freeze in plastic containers. Cook and label the right amount needed for your recipes.

GREEN BEANS WITH HERB-BUTTER SAUCE

2 cans (1 pound each) French-style
  green beans
1 small onion, minced
1/4 cup butter
2 tablespoons minced parsley
1/2 teaspoon thyme
3 tablespoons lemon juice
Salt and pepper to taste
1/4 teaspoon paprika

Heat beans, drain and put in serving dish. Sauté onion lightly in the butter, add remaining ingredients and mix well. Heat gently and pour over beans. Makes 6 servings.

BEANS AU GRATIN

1 box each frozen cut green beans,
  wax beans and lima beans
4 tablespoons butter or margarine
2 tablespoons flour
1 teaspoon salt
Dash of pepper
Dash of Worcestershire
1 cup medium cream
1/2 cup grated Parmesan cheese

Cook beans separately according to package directions; drain. Mix lightly and put in shallow baking dish. Melt 2 tablespoons butter and stir in flour, salt, pepper and Worcestershire. Add cream and cook until thickened, stirring. Pour over beans. Dot with remaining butter and sprinkle with cheese. Bake in moderate oven (375°F.) 15 minutes, or until hot and browned. Makes 6 servings.

FAVORITE ITALIAN BROCCOLI

Cook broccoli as usual. Drain; place on serving dish and dress with olive oil, lemon juice and salt and pepper. Good hot or cold. (String beans and cauliflower are also eaten this way. The trick is to dress vegetable while hot so dressing can soak in.)

LIME BEETS

2 cans (1 pound each) small whole beets
1/4 cup sugar
1 tablespoon cornstarch
Juice of 2 limes
1 tablespoon butter or margarine

Drain beets, reserving liquid from 1 can. Put liquid in saucepan. Mix sugar and cornstarch and add to beet liquid. Simmer a few minutes, until clear, stirring. Add beets and lime juice and heat through; stir in the butter. Makes 6 servings.

GREEN BEANS ORIENTALE

1 can (5 ounces) water chestnuts, sliced
2 tablespoons vegetable oil
2 tablespoons soy sauce
1 package (9 ounces) frozen French-cut
  green beans
1 teaspoon sugar
Salt and pepper

Sauté water chestnuts in oil until golden brown. Add soy sauce, beans and sugar and cook over low heat until beans are just tender-crisp and still bright green, separating them with a fork as they defrost. Add salt and pepper to taste. Makes 4 servings.

QUICK SHREDDED BEETS

2 bunches beets
2 tablespoons vinegar
1 teaspoon sugar
2 tablespoons butter or margarine
Salt and pepper

Peel beets and shred on coarse grater. Put beets, 1/4 cup water, vinegar and sugar in heavy saucepan. Cover and cook 10 minutes, or until beets are tender. Stir twice during cooking. Add butter and season. Makes 4 servings.

POLISH BEETS

2 cans (1 pound each) baby beets
1 cup beet liquid
3 tablespoons butter
1 tablespoon brown sugar
1/4 teaspoon monosodium glutamate
Salt and pepper
1 tablespoon lemon juice
2 tablespoons cornstarch
1/2 cup dairy sour cream
Chopped fresh dill or dill salt

Heat beets in beet liquid. (Add consommé to beet juice if necessary to make 1 cup.) Drain, reserving liquid; put beets in bowl. In same pan make sauce with butter, the hot liquid drained from beets, sugar, seasonings, lemon juice and cornstarch blended with a little cold water. Cook until clear. Add sour cream. Heat, stirring, and add hot beets. Top with dill. Makes 6 to 8 servings.

ZANAHORIAS NATAS

A favorite Mexican way with carrots. Peel and julienne 10 young carrots. Braise slowly in 1 tablespoon butter until tender. Add 1/4 teaspoon salt and 1 cup dairy sour cream. Stir gently. Top with chopped chives. (Also good with summer squash, zucchini or asparagus.) Serves 6.

BROCCOLI WITH SOUR CREAM

2 pounds fresh broccoli or 2 boxes
  frozen broccoli spears
Salt
1 cup dairy sour cream
1/4 cup mayonnaise
2 tablespoons tomato paste
1/4 teaspoon dried basil
2 teaspoons minced drained capers

Discard some of the larger leaves and
a little of the stalk from fresh broccoli.
Put broccoli in saucepan and add 1"
boiling salted water. Cover and cook
10 to 15 minutes. (Cook frozen broccoli as directed on the box.) Drain
and cool. Mix 3/4 teaspoon salt and remaining ingredients; chill. Serve on
broccoli. Makes 4 servings.

SWEET-SOUR RED CABBAGE

1 onion, chopped
3 tablespoons butter or margarine
9 cups shredded red cabbage
1 large tart apple, peeled and diced
3 tablespoons cider vinegar
3 tablespoons brown sugar
1 tablespoon caraway seed
1-1/4 teaspoons salt
1/4 teaspoon pepper
1/3 cup seedless raisins

Cook onion in the butter 5 minutes.
Add cabbage; cover and cook 5 minutes longer. Add 1 cup water and
remaining ingredients, cover and simmer about 10 minutes. Serves 6.

CABBAGE SCALLOP

2-pound head of young cabbage
Salt
1 green pepper, chopped
1 stalk celery, chopped
4 tablespoons butter or margarine
2 tablespoons flour
1 cup milk
Pepper
1/2 cup fine dry bread crumbs
2 slices bacon, fried crisp and crumbled
2 slices process American cheese, diced
1 tablespoon chopped pimiento
Paprika

Remove outer leaves from cabbage;
cut head into quarters. Place in saucepan containing about 2" boiling water.
Add 3/4 teaspoon salt, cover and simmer 10 minutes. Drain and put in
1½-quart baking dish. Cook green
pepper and celery in 2 tablespoons
butter 2 to 3 minutes. Put on cabbage.
Melt remaining 2 tablespoons butter
and blend in flour. Gradually add milk
and cook, stirring, until thickened.
Season with salt and pepper to taste.
Pour over cabbage and sprinkle with
remaining ingredients. Bake in hot
oven (400°F.) 20 minutes. Serves 6.

CURRIED CABBAGE IN BEER

3 tablespoons butter or margarine
2 teaspoons curry powder
1/2 teaspoon salt
2/3 cup beer
6 cups shredded cabbage

Melt butter in large skillet. Stir
in curry powder, salt, the beer
and cabbage. Cook, stirring occasionally, 10 minutes, or until cabbage is
tender. Good with ham and corned
beef. Makes 4 servings.

CABBAGE GOURMET

1 small head cabbage
1/2 cup Chablis or other white dinner
  wine
1/2 cup chicken broth or bouillon
1 tablespoon wine vinegar
2 tablespoons butter or margarine
1 tablespoon instant minced onion
1/4 teaspoon dried dill
1/2 teaspoon salt
Dash of pepper

Wash cabbage; shred or cut coarsely
in strips to prepare about 6 cups. Add
remaining ingredients. Cover and simmer 12 to 15 minutes. Serve with pan
liquid, which can be thickened with
flour-water paste, if desired. Makes 4
to 6 servings.

CABBAGE PIE WITH
CREAM-CHEESE PASTRY

Cream-cheese Pastry
1 large onion, chopped
1/2 cup butter or margarine
1 head cabbage, finely chopped (about
  12 cups)
2 teaspoons salt
1/4 teaspoon pepper
6 hard-cooked eggs, chopped

Prepare pastry and chill. Sauté
onion in the butter in large skillet
2 to 3 minutes. Add cabbage, salt and
pepper. Cover and cook, stirring occasionally, about 20 minutes. Add
eggs. Roll out two thirds of pastry and
line shallow 11" x 6" baking dish. Fill
with cabbage mixture. Roll remaining
pastry to fit and adjust on top of dish.
Seal edges and slit top in several places
for steam to escape. Bake in hot oven
(400°F.) 15 minutes. Turn oven temperature control to 350°F. and bake
about 20 minutes longer. Makes 6
servings. **Cream-cheese Pastry** Put 1/4
cup margarine and 1 package (3
ounces) cream cheese in bowl and let
stand until softened. Then work in
2 tablespoons sugar and 1 cup all-purpose flour. Shape in ball.

CELERY-ALMOND CASSEROLE

4 cups celery, cut in 2″ pieces
Salt
1 can (10-1/2 ounces) condensed cream
  of chicken soup
1/2 cup dairy sour cream
1 cup slivered almonds
1 can (4 ounces) water chestnuts, drained
  and sliced
Buttered soft bread crumbs

Cook celery in small amount of boiling salted water until tender but still crisp. Drain and add remaining ingredients, except crumbs. Put in greased shallow 2-quart baking dish and sprinkle with crumbs. Bake in moderate oven (350°F.) about 30 minutes. Makes 4 to 6 servings.

BRAISED CELERY WITH PEANUT-BUTTER SAUCE

3 cups sliced celery
1 medium onion, sliced
1/4 cup peanut butter
2 tablespoons soy sauce

Put celery, onion and ¼ cup water in saucepan, bring to boil and simmer, covered, 5 to 8 minutes. Drain, reserving liquid. Put vegetables in hot serving dish and return liquid to saucepan. Stir peanut butter and soy sauce into liquid. Add 3 or 4 tablespoons water to thin mixture. Heat and pour over celery. Makes 4 to 6 servings.

CREAMY CORN BAKE

1 can (17 ounces) cream-style corn
4 eggs, separated
1 teaspoon salt
1/4 teaspoon white pepper
1 cup heavy cream
Sautéed sliced fresh mushrooms
  (optional)

Put corn through sieve. Beat egg whites until stiff; set aside. Beat egg yolks until thick and add to corn with seasonings. Stir in cream. Then fold in egg whites. Pour into 1½-quart soufflé dish or casserole. Set in a pan of hot water and bake in moderate oven (350°F.) 30 minutes, or unti firm. Serve at once with mushrooms. Makes 4 to 6 servings.

SAUTEED CORN WITH GREEN ONION

Melt ¼ cup butter or margarine in skillet. Add 4 cups (about 8 ears) cut fresh corn and ½ cup sliced green onions with tops. Cook, covered, over medium heat, shaking skillet occasionally, 5 minutes. Season with salt and pepper. Makes 4 to 6 servings.

BAKED CREAMED CORN AND PEAS

5 tablespoons butter or margarine
2 tablespoons minced onion
1/3 cup minced celery
2 tablespoons flour
1 teaspoon salt
1/8 teaspoon pepper
1/2 teaspoon dried basil
1 to 2 teaspoons sugar
1-1/2 cups milk
1 box (10 ounces) frozen peas, thawed
2 cups cooked whole-kernel corn,
  drained
1/4 cup fine dry bread crumbs
1/4 cup grated Cheddar cheese

Melt 3 tablespoons butter. Add onion and celery and cook until golden. Stir in flour, seasonings and sugar. Gradually add milk and cook, stirring, until thickened. Mix vegetables lightly in greased shallow 1½-quart baking dish. Pour milk sauce over top, mixing lightly. Melt remaining 2 tablespoons butter and stir in crumbs and cheese. Sprinkle on mixture. Bake in moderate oven (375°F.) about 30 minutes. Makes 4 to 6 servings.

QUICK CORN AND MUSHROOMS

1 cup sliced fresh mushrooms or 1 can
  (4 ounces) sliced mushrooms, drained
1 tablespoon minced onion
2 tablespoons butter or margarine
3 cups (about 6 ears) cut fresh corn
1 teaspoon sugar
1 teaspoon salt
1/4 teaspoon seasoned pepper

Cook mushrooms and onion in the butter about 5 minutes. Add remaining ingredients. Sauté about 5 minutes longer. Serves 4 to 6.

MEXICAN SUCCOTASH

1 package (10 ounces) frozen baby limas,
  cooked and drained
1 can (12 ounces) whole-kernel corn,
  drained
2 eggs
2 tablespoons catsup
1/2 cup milk
1 small onion, cut up
1/2 green pepper, cut up
1 teaspoon salt
1/8 teaspoon pepper
1/4 teaspoon chili seasoning
2 tablespoons butter or margarine

Put lima beans and corn in greased 1½-quart casserole. Combine remaining ingredients in blender and whirl just until mixed. Pour over vegetables and stir. Bake in moderate oven (350°F.) 45 minutes, or until just set. Makes 4 to 6 servings.

HOW TO MAKE FRESH GRATED OR CREAM-STYLE CORN

With a sharp knife, slit down the center of each row of kernels. With dull edge of table knife, scrape out pulp and milky juice. Use in recipes as fresh cream-style corn.

FRESH-CORN CAKES

Mix 2 cups fresh cream-style corn, 1 teaspoon each baking powder and sugar, ³/₄ teaspoon salt, a dash of pepper and 1 tablespoon each melted butter and cream. Beat 2 egg yolks until thick and lemon-colored and 2 whites until stiff. Stir yolks into first mixture and fold in whites. Drop by spoonfuls onto hot, lightly greased griddle, and brown on both sides. Makes about 4 dozen 3" cakes. *Note* If cakes seem too tender to handle, stir a little flour into batter.

FRESH-CORN SOUFFLÉ

Melt 2 tablespoons butter or margarine in heavy saucepan. Blend in 2 tablespoons flour, 1¹/₂ teaspoons salt and ¹/₈ teaspoon pepper. Add 1 cup milk and cook, stirring, until thickened. Add 2 cups fresh cream-style corn and mix well. Stir in 2 egg yolks, beaten until thick and lemon-colored. Fold in 2 stiffly beaten egg whites. Pour into buttered 2-quart casserole. Bake in moderate oven (350°F.) about 30 minutes. Makes 4 to 6 servings.

CORN QUICHE

2 cups fine cheese-cracker crumbs
6 tablespoons butter or margarine
2 tablespoons flour
1/2 teaspoon salt
1/4 teaspoon celery salt
1/8 teaspoon pepper
1/2 teaspoon instant minced onion
1-1/4 cups milk
2 eggs, beaten
2 cups cooked whole-kernel corn

Mix crumbs with 4 tablespoons of the butter, melted. Reserve ¹/₂ cup for top of quiche. Line a 9" piepan with remaining crumbs, pressing down slightly to make a smooth shell. Melt remaining butter and blend in flour, seasonings and onion. Add milk and cook, stirring, until thickened. Gradually add hot mixture to eggs. Stir in corn and pour carefully into shell. Sprinkle with reserved crumbs. Bake in hot oven (400°F.) about 20 minutes. Let stand 5 minutes; then cut in wedges and serve warm. Makes 6 servings.

CREAMY SKILLET CORN

2 cups fresh cream-style corn
2 tablespoons butter
1/4 cup heavy cream
Salt and pepper
Paprika

Put corn in skillet with butter, cream, and salt and pepper to taste. Cook, stirring frequently, 5 minutes, or until mixture is fairly thick and corn is tender. Serve sprinkled with paprika. Makes 4 servings.

DOUBLE-CORN TAMALE PIE

2 medium onions, chopped
2 tablespoons vegetable oil
1 can (12 ounces) whole-kernel corn, undrained
1/2 green pepper, chopped
1 can (1 pound) tomatoes
2 teaspoons salt
1/8 teaspoon cayenne
1 cup yellow cornmeal
2 eggs, beaten
1/2 cup chopped ripe olives
1 cup coarsely chopped nuts

Cook onion in oil in kettle 2 or 3 minutes. Add next 5 ingredients and 1¹/₂ cups water and bring to boil. Gradually stir in cornmeal. Cook, uncovered, about 15 minutes, stirring frequently. Remove from heat and add remaining ingredients. Pour into shallow 1¹/₂-quart baking dish. Bake in moderate oven (350°F.) 45 minutes, or until lightly browned. Makes 6 servings.

CORN PUFF

1 cup milk
1 bay leaf
2 whole cloves
1 clove garlic
3 sprigs parsley
4 tablespoons butter or margarine
1 tablespoon chopped onion
1 tablespoon flour
1/2 teaspoon steak sauce
Seasoned salt, seasoned pepper and nutmeg to taste
2 cups cooked whole-kernel corn
3 eggs, separated
1 slice firm bread, cut in tiny dice
Paprika

Scald milk with next 4 ingredients; strain. Melt 2 tablespoons butter, add onion and cook 2 or 3 minutes. Blend in flour and steak sauce. Add milk and cook, stirring, until thickened. Season. Remove from heat and stir in corn and egg yolks. Fold in stiffly beaten egg whites and pour into shallow 1¹/₂-quart baking dish. Melt remaining butter and mix with bread cubes. Sprinkle over top of mixture. Sprinkle with paprika. Bake in moderate oven (350°F.) about 25 minutes. Serves 4 to 6.

EGGPLANT BAKED IN TOMATO SAUCE, GREEK STYLE

1 medium eggplant (1 pound)
1 can (8 ounces) tomato sauce
1 onion, chopped
1 small clove garlic, minced
2 tablespoons olive oil
1/4 teaspoon sweet basil
Salt and pepper
6 tablespoons grated kefaloteri cheese

Wash eggplant and cut off stem end. Cut in 1″ cubes and put in buttered 1½-quart casserole. Combine tomato sauce, onion, garlic, olive oil, basil, salt and pepper. Pour over eggplant. Cover and bake in moderate oven (350°F.) 30 minutes longer. Stir, sprinkle with cheese and bake 15 minutes. Makes 6 servings.

EGGPLANT PARMIGIANA

1 large eggplant
3/4 cup olive oil
2 cans (8 ounces each) tomato sauce
1/4 cup grated Parmesan cheese
1/2 pound mozzarella cheese, sliced thin

Pare the eggplant and cut it in 1/4″ slices. Sauté in the hot oil until browned on both sides. Drain on absorbent paper. Put a layer of eggplant slices in a shallow baking dish. Cover with some tomato sauce, a little Parmesan cheese and a few slices of mozzarella. Repeat until all ingredients are used, ending with mozzarella. Bake in moderate oven (375°F.) 25 to 30 minutes. Makes 4 servings.

RATATOUILLE

This Provençale casserole is as good cold as it is hot.

3 large cloves garlic
1 teaspoon salt
1/2 to 3/4 cup olive oil
2 medium eggplants
1 pound zucchini
8 large tomatoes
3 large green peppers
4 large onions
1 tablespoon salt
Pepper
2 tablespoons minced parsley
Oregano or basil

Crush garlic in salt (in a mortar) and put in a Dutch oven or casserole with the olive oil. Peel and dice eggplants, zucchini and tomatoes; dice peppers and chop onions. Put in the casserole in layers, sprinkling the salt, pepper, parsley and oregano between layers. Cook, covered, until vegetables are tender and sauce thick and rich. Correct seasoning if necessary. Makes 12 servings.

MUSHROOMS WITH SPINACH

1 can (4 ounces) mushroom stems and pieces
2 tablespoons butter or margarine
2 cups chopped drained cooked spinach
1 tablespoon Worcestershire
Dash of nutmeg
1/2 teaspoon grated lemon rind
Salt to taste
2 hard-cooked eggs, quartered

Drain mushrooms and sauté in the butter. Add to spinach with seasonings. Garnish with egg quarters. Makes 4 servings.

ANCHOVIED MUSHROOMS

Melt 3 tablespoons butter and brush on 12 mushroom caps. Broil until just tender. Cut 12 thin slices of bread into rounds and sauté them in butter until crisp and golden on both sides. Or cut rounds from buttered toast. Chop 12 anchovy fillets and mix with 1/4 cup dairy sour cream and a little chopped parsley. Top each toast round with a broiled mushroom cap, filled with a spoonful of anchovy-cream mixture. Garnish with a sprig of parsley. Makes 6 servings.

MUSHROOM PANCAKES IN BROWN SHERRY SAUCE

1/2 pound fresh mushrooms
1/4 cup butter, melted
Salt and black pepper
Dash of soy sauce
Dash of seasoning salt
Foolproof All-purpose Thin Pancakes, page 310
Brown Sherry Sauce

Grind or chop washed unpeeled firm mushrooms. Sauté in the melted butter 2 minutes, adding seasonings. Spread mixture evenly on 12 thin pancakes and roll up. Allow 2 pancakes to a serving, or 3 if the main course. Put in 4 lightly greased shallow baking dishes or in a large shallow baking dish. Top generously with sauce and put under broiler 1 or 2 minutes. **To make Brown Sherry Sauce** In a deep skillet brown 3 tablespoons each butter and flour to make a roux. Add 3 cups chicken broth, 1 tablespoon each Worcestershire and catsup, 1/4 teaspoon paprika and 1 teaspoon gravy sauce. Stir until smooth and free from lumps; bring to a boil. Reduce heat to a simmer, cover and cook slowly 20 minutes. Liquid should be reduced to about 2 cups. Add 1/2 cup heavy cream and 3 tablespoons strong dark sherry. Makes 4 to 6 servings.

PEAS AND ONION CURRY

Cook 1 box frozen peas as directed on the label. Drain off all but about 1 tablespoon liquid. Add 1 can (1 pound) onions, drained, 3 tablespoons butter or margarine and 1 teaspoon curry powder. Heat, stirring lightly once or twice. Season with salt and pepper to taste. Makes 4 to 6 servings.

FRENCH PEAS

1-1/2 tablespoons butter
1/2 cup thinly sliced mushrooms
1-1/2 cups shelled peas or 1 box
   (10 ounces) frozen peas
1 small onion, thinly sliced
1/2 teaspoon salt

Melt butter in saucepan. Add 2 tablespoons water and remaining ingredients. Cover pan tightly and cook until peas are tender. Shake pan occasionally. Makes 4 servings.

HONEY-GLAZED ONIONS

2 dozen small white onions, peeled
Salt
2 tablespoons honey
2 tablespoons catsup
3 tablespoons butter
Dash of cayenne

Cook onions in salted water 20 minutes. Drain and place in baking dish. Pour over onions a sauce made of remaining ingredients, a dash of salt and 1/4 cup water. Cover. Bake in moderate oven (350°F.) 1 hour, or until onions are mellow and glazed, basting occasionally. Makes 4 servings.

BERMUDA CASSEROLE

4 Bermuda onions, cut in 1/4" slices
6 slices day-old bread
1 cup finely crumbled blue cheese
1 cup undiluted evaporated milk or
   light cream
3 eggs, beaten
Salt
Hot pepper sauce
Butter
Paprika

Parboil onion slices in boiling water 10 minutes. Trim crusts from bread and cut bread in small squares. Butter a shallow 1½-quart baking dish. Put onion in dish and cover with bread squares. Sprinkle with the cheese. Mix milk and egg and season with salt and hot pepper sauce. Pour over ingredients in baking dish. Dot with butter and sprinkle lightly with paprika. Bake in moderate oven (375°F.) about 40 minutes. Makes 6 servings.

PEANUT-CREAMED ONIONS

18 peeled small white onions
Salt
1/2 cup salted peanuts, chopped fine
1 cup rich white sauce
Pepper
Dash of mace

Cook onions in salted water till tender. Drain and add with half of peanuts to white sauce. Season and top with remaining nuts. Bake in moderate oven (375°F.) 20 minutes. Makes 4 servings.

RUSSIAN ONIONS AND MUSHROOMS

1-1/2 cups chopped onions
2 tablespoons butter or bacon fat
1 pound mushrooms, sliced
1-1/2 teaspoons salt
1/4 teaspoon pepper
1/2 teaspoon paprika
1 tablespoon flour
1 pint dairy sour cream

Simmer onions in butter until golden. Add mushrooms and seasonings and cook slowly 10 minutes. Add flour and stir; add sour cream slowly and simmer another 10 minutes. Serve with steak or roast beef as a luncheon dish. Also good in tiny cream-puff shells as hot appetizers. Makes 6 luncheon servings.

BAKED POTATOES RECTOR

Bake large potatoes. Cut a large oval piece of skin from the top of each potato. Scrape all the potato from the shell into a warm bowl. Season potato with salt, pepper and paprika. Mash well and beat in a little heavy cream or dairy sour cream. Add some chopped green onions and fill potato shells lightly with the mixture. Put in hot oven until lightly browned.

POTATO-AND-ONION CAKE

4 medium potatoes
Butter
3 onions, chopped
Salt and pepper
Fine dry bread crumbs

Peel potatoes and slice very thin. Melt butter in heavy skillet. When hot, add alternate layers of potatoes, onions and seasonings. Sprinkle top layer with crumbs. Cook slowly until well-browned on bottom and nearly done. Turn out on flat plate. Add more butter to skillet and slide potato back into pan, brown side up. Cook until browned. Turn out to serve. Makes 4 servings.

SCALLOPED POTATOES

4 cups thinly sliced peeled potatoes
1 cup thinly sliced onion
1/4 cup all-purpose flour
1-1/2 teaspoons salt
1/4 teaspoon pepper
1 tablespoon parsley flakes
2 cups milk
1/4 cup fine dry bread crumbs
1 tablespoon butter, melted
1/2 teaspoon paprika

Toss first 6 ingredients together until potatoes are coated. Put in greased shallow 2-quart baking dish. Scald milk and pour over potatoes. Cover with foil and bake in moderate oven (350°F.) 60 minutes. Mix crumbs, butter and paprika. Remove foil and sprinkle potatoes with crumb mixture. Bake 30 minutes longer. Makes 6 servings. **Note** Vary appearance and flavor by adding 1/2 green pepper, thinly sliced, to first 6 ingredients.

ITALIAN POTATO DUMPLINGS

1 pound old baking potatoes, peeled
Salt
3/4 to 1 cup all-purpose flour
Butter or margarine
1 whole egg, beaten
1 egg yolk, beaten
Dash of nutmeg
1 cup grated Parmesan cheese

Boil potatoes in lightly salted water until tender. Drain and dry over low heat a few seconds. Sprinkle board generously with some of the flour. Force potatoes through ricer onto board (or mash potatoes and put on board). With fingers or a fork, quickly work in 2 tablespoons butter, eggs, about three fourths of the flour, 1 teaspoon salt and nutmeg. Gather up mixture and knead lightly with remaining flour and 1/2 cup cheese just until dough is smooth and pliable. Cut off egg-size knobs of dough and roll into long finger-size rolls. Cut in 1" pieces. With back of floured fork, gently roll each piece backward, then press in lightly as you roll it forward to give the characteristic shell-like indentation. Dry on towel 1 hour. In large kettle of boiling salted water, drop in some of the gnocchi (leave them plenty of floating room). Cook gently 5 to 6 minutes, or until light and slightly puffed. Remove with strainer or slotted spoon and drop into well-buttered shallow baking dish. Keep warm until all are cooked. Pour 1/3 cup melted butter over top and sprinkle with remaining 1/2 cup cheese. Put under broiler a few minutes to glaze lightly. Makes 6 servings.

POTATOES SUPREME

Cook potatoes the night before.

6 medium potatoes, peeled
Salt
1/2 cup butter or margarine, melted
2 cups shredded Cheddar cheese
1/3 cup chopped green onions
1 pint dairy sour cream
1/4 teaspoon pepper

Cook potatoes in small amount of salted boiling water until tender; drain and refrigerate, covered, overnight. Next day, grate potatoes coarsely. Mix with remaining ingredients and 1/2 teaspoon salt. Put in greased shallow 1 1/2-quart baking dish and bake in moderate oven (350°F.) about 35 minutes. Makes 6 servings.

SWISS POTATO PUDDING

1 pound potatoes, peeled
Salt
2 tablespoons butter
2 tablespoons all-purpose flour
1/2 cup grated Gruyère or aged Swiss cheese
1/2 cup grated Sbrinz or Parmesan cheese
3/4 cup milk
3 eggs, separated
Salt
Nutmeg

Cut potatoes in uniform pieces if they are large. Cook in small amount of boiling salted water until soft. Drain and mash or press through ricer. You should have a generous 2 cups potato purée. Stir in butter, flour, cheeses and milk. Beat in egg yolks, one by one. Taste and season lightly with salt and nutmeg. Beat egg whites until stiff but not dry. Fold into potato and turn quickly into buttered soufflé dish or 4-cup casserole. Bake in moderate oven (375°F.) 45 minutes, or until puffed and delicately browned. Serve at once. Makes 4 servings.

POTATO-TOMATO CASSEROLE

6 medium potatoes, peeled and diced
Salt and pepper
Butter or margarine
1 can (10-3/4 ounces) condensed tomato-rice soup
1/2 cup milk
1 tablespoon prepared mustard

Put potatoes in layers in greased 1 1/2-quart casserole, sprinkling each layer with salt and pepper and dotting with about 3 pats butter per layer. Dot top layer with butter, cover and bake in moderate oven (350°F.) about 1 hour. Heat soup and milk and add mustard. Pour over casserole and serve at once. Makes 4 to 6 servings.

GRATIN DAUPHINOIS
(Scalloped Potatoes from France)

Butter
6 medium potatoes, sliced wafer-thin
Salt
Freshly ground black pepper
Nutmeg
2 cups (about) light cream (not half-
    and-half)

Butter a shallow baking dish no
deeper than 2". Layer three-quarters
full with potato, salt, pepper and a
little nutmeg. Pour in cream just to
top of potato. Dot with 2 tablespoons butter. Bake in very slow
oven (250°F.) 1½ hours, or until
potato is tender, most of cream absorbed and top browned. Serves 6.

SAVARIN POTATOES

4 large potatoes
Butter
Port-and-Cheese Sauce

Peel potatoes and cut in thin match-
like sticks; wash and dry thoroughly.
Press into a 9" layer-cake pan. Cover
generously with melted butter. Bake
in very hot oven (500°F.) 20 minutes,
or until potatoes are tender, crisp
and browned. Turn out on a hot
serving dish. Serve with **Port-and-
Cheese Sauce.** Melt 2 tablespoons
butter. Blend in 2 tablespoons flour.
Gradually stir in 1 cup each milk and
heavy cream and cook, stirring, until
thickened. Stir in ¼ cup port wine,
1 tablespoon grated Parmesan cheese
and 2 teaspoons paprika. Season with
salt, pepper and nutmeg. Makes 4
servings.

HASH-BROWNED POTATOES

3 cups chopped cold boiled or baked
    potatoes
3 tablespoons flour
1/4 cup milk
Salt and pepper
Instant minced onion or chopped
    parsley (optional)
Bacon fat or margarine

Mix first 3 ingredients. Season to taste
with salt, pepper, and onion, if desired. Heat 2 tablespoons fat in heavy
9" skillet. Add potato mixture and
pack with spatula in a large cake.
Cook over medium heat until brown
and crusty, shaking the pan to keep
potato from sticking. Turn out on flat
plate. Wipe pan free of crumbs, and
add 1 tablespoon fat. Slide potato
back into hot pan, brown side up.
Cook until bottom is brown, packing edges with spatula and shaking
pan. Makes 4 servings.

HERBED PAN-ROASTED POTATOES

Boil peeled medium potatoes 10 minutes. Drain and arrange around roast
of meat about 1 hour before meat is
done. Turn occasionally and baste
with drippings in pan. When roast is
done, remove to hot platter. To
brown potatoes more, put under
broiler in same pan, turning to
brown. Sprinkle with paprika, minced
parsley, crumbled thyme or marjoram
and arrange around roast.

SOUR-CREAM POTATO PATTIES

2 cups grated cooked potatoes
1/2 teaspoon salt
1 cup all-purpose flour
About 1 cup dairy sour cream
Fat for frying

Mix first 3 ingredients. Add enough
sour cream to make a soft dough, as
for biscuits. Roll to ⅛" thickness on
floured board. Cut with floured 2"
cutter. Fry in small amount of hot fat
in skillet until golden brown on both
sides and done. Serves 6.

POTATOES BOULANGÈRE

2 onions, sliced thin
2 tablespoons butter or margarine
4 potatoes, sliced thin
1 can condensed consommé
1/2 teaspoon salt
1/4 teaspoon pepper
1 bay leaf
1/4 teaspoon thyme
Chopped parsley

Cook onion in butter 5 minutes. Add
remaining ingredients, except parsley. Cover and simmer 25 to 30 minutes. Garnish with parsley. Serves 4.

SCALLOPED SWEET POTATOES AND PINEAPPLE

6 medium sweet potatoes, cooked and
    peeled
1 can (13-1/2 ounces) pineapple
    tidbits, drained
2/3 cup pineapple syrup
1/8 teaspoon salt
1/2 cup maple syrup
1/4 cup butter or margarine, melted

Slice sweet potatoes and arrange alternate layers of potatoes and pineapple in a shallow 1½-quart baking
dish. Mix remaining ingredients,
bring to boil and boil rapidly 3 minutes. Pour over ingredients in dish.
Bake in moderate oven (375°F.)
about 30 minutes. Makes 6 servings.

SWEET-POTATO TOURNEDOS

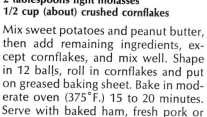Select sweet potatoes about 2" in diameter, or use canned. (Cook fresh potatoes until tender; peel and cut in pieces 2" long.) Wrap a thin slice of bacon around each potato and fasten with a toothpick. Put in shallow baking pan and bake in very hot oven (450°F.) 15 minutes; turn once so that potatoes and bacon cook evenly.

SWEETS A LA RECTOR

8 medium sweet potatoes, cooked
1/2 cup brown sugar, packed
2 tablespoons butter or margarine
1/2 teaspoon salt
1/4 teaspoon paprika
1/2 cup sherry

Peel and slice potatoes and arrange in shallow baking dish. Sprinkle with sugar and dot with butter. Add seasonings and sherry. Bake in moderate oven (350°F.) about 30 minutes. Makes 6 servings.

ALMOND SWEET-POTATO PORCUPINES

4 cups mashed cooked sweet potatoes
2 tablespoons butter or margarine, melted
1-1/2 teaspoons salt
1/2 teaspoon cinnamon
1 egg
Slivered blanched almonds
Apple butter

Beat together first 5 ingredients. Shape in 8 mounds with spoon or pastry bag on greased baking sheet. Insert a few almond slivers in each. Bake in hot oven (400°F.) about 20 minutes. Put a spoonful of apple butter in center of each. Makes 8 servings.

SWEET-POTATO SOUFFLÉ

1 cup milk
1/2 teaspoon salt
2 teaspoons sugar
2 tablespoons butter
2 cups mashed sweet potato
2 eggs, separated
1/2 cup raisins
1/2 teaspoon nutmeg
1/2 cup chopped walnuts
15 marshmallows

Scald milk with next 3 ingredients. Add to potato and beat well; add beaten egg yolks. Stir in raisins, nutmeg and nuts. Fold in stiffly beaten egg whites and pour into greased 1½-quart casserole. Top with marshmallows. Bake in slow oven (325°F.) 45 minutes, or until set. Serves 6.

PEANUT AND SWEET-POTATO BALLS

2 cups mashed cooked sweet potatoes, or 2 cans (1 pound each) dry-pack (without syrup) sweet potatoes, mashed
1/2 cup crunchy peanut butter
3 tablespoons light-brown sugar
1 egg, beaten
2 tablespoons light molasses
1/2 cup (about) crushed cornflakes

Mix sweet potatoes and peanut butter, then add remaining ingredients, except cornflakes, and mix well. Shape in 12 balls, roll in cornflakes and put on greased baking sheet. Bake in moderate oven (375°F.) 15 to 20 minutes. Serve with baked ham, fresh pork or poultry. Makes 4 servings.

PANNED MIXED GREENS

Use beet or turnip tops, cabbage, escarole, romaine, chard or spinach.

Cook 2 quarts finely chopped greens quickly in 2 tablespoons bacon fat or margarine in large, heavy saucepan 3 to 5 minutes, stirring constantly. Season to taste. Makes 4 servings.

SPINACH, FARM STYLE

4 slices bacon
1/2 cup vinegar
2 tablespoons sugar
1 teaspoon salt
1/8 teaspoon pepper
2 boxes frozen whole spinach
1 carrot, shredded

Fry bacon until crisp. Remove. Add next 4 ingredients and ¼ cup water to fat; bring to boil. Add spinach and cook, breaking up with fork. Stir in carrot and serve with crumbled bacon sprinkled on top. Serves 4.

CREAMED SPINACH

2 packages (10 ounces each) frozen chopped spinach
2 tablespoons butter or margarine
2 tablespoons all-purpose flour
1/4 cup milk
1/4 cup dairy sour cream
Nutmeg
Salt and pepper

Cook spinach according to package directions. Drain and put into blender. Melt butter over low heat, add flour and blend well. Simmer, stirring, a few minutes. Add milk and stir until blended. (It will be like a paste.) Add to spinach in blender. Whirl until smooth and fluffy. Return to saucepan and heat. Fold in sour cream and season to taste with nutmeg, salt and pepper. Makes 4 to 6 servings.

POMODORO ALLA GENOVESE

6 large tomatoes
Salt
6 anchovy fillets
8 slices Genoa salami, minced
1 cup soft bread crumbs
Mozzarella cheese
Red pepper flakes
Olive oil
Fine dry bread crumbs

Scoop pulp from tomatoes. Salt inside of shells, invert and drain. Mix tomato pulp, anchovies, salami, soft bread crumbs and 1/2 cup diced mozzarella. Season with salt and red pepper. Add 1 to 2 tablespoons olive oil, or enough to moisten. Fill tomato shells with the mixture and top each with a thin square of mozzarella. Sprinkle with fine dry crumbs and a little oil. Put in greased baking dish and add a little water to prevent tomatoes from sticking to pan. Bake in moderate oven (350° F.) 20 to 30 minutes, depending on size and ripeness of tomatoes. Makes 6 servings.

FRIED TOMATOES WITH CREAMY GRAVY

4 large tomatoes
Salt and pepper
Flour
3 tablespoons bacon or other fat
1-1/2 cups milk

Wash tomatoes, remove ends and cut in half. Dredge in 1/4 cup seasoned flour. Brown on both sides in hot fat. Remove to hot platter. Blend 1 tablespoon flour with fat in skillet, add milk and cook until thickened, stirring constantly. Add more seasoning, if necessary. Pour over tomatoes and serve at once. Makes 4 servings.

SAVORY TOMATOES, BEANS AND SQUASH

1 large onion, sliced
1 clove garlic, minced
1/4 cup minced parsley
2 teaspoons salt
1/4 teaspoon pepper
1/4 teaspoon thyme
1/4 teaspoon sage
2 tablespoons cooking oil
1 pound green or wax beans, cut
3 large tomatoes, diced
2 cups diced yellow squash

Cook onion, garlic, parsley and seasonings in oil in large skillet about 3 minutes. Add remaining ingredients. Add water to half the depth of mixture. Cover and simmer 20 minutes, or until beans are tender. Makes 4 to 6 servings.

TOMATOES WITH DILL SAUCE

1/2 cup dairy sour cream
1/4 cup mayonnaise or salad dressing
1 teaspoon snipped fresh dill or 1/4 teaspoon dried dillweed
2 tablespoons minced onion
Salt
4 large firm ripe tomatoes
Pepper
Butter or margarine

Mix first 4 ingredients and 1/4 teaspoon salt; chill. Core tomatoes and cut in half crosswise. Season cut surfaces with salt and pepper and dot with butter. Broil 3" from heat 5 minutes, or until heated through. Serve with chilled mixture. Makes 8 servings.

RED-AND-GREEN TOMATO PIE

Pastry for one deep 9" crust
Undiluted evaporated milk
4 cups sliced red and green tomatoes
1-1/2 teaspoons salt
1/8 teaspoon pepper
1/3 cup mayonnaise
1/3 cup grated Italian-style cheese
1 clove garlic, minced

Line deep 9-inch piepan with pastry, crimp edges and brush with the milk. Bake in very hot oven (450°F.) 5 minutes. Fill shell with tomatoes and sprinkle with salt and pepper. Mix remaining ingredients and spread on tomatoes. Bake in moderate oven (350°F.) 40 minutes, or until tomatoes are done and top is lightly browned. Makes 6 servings.

FRIED TOMATOES, COUNTRY STYLE

6 large beefsteak tomatoes, half-ripe if possible
Salt and pepper
Garlic salt
Fine dry crumbs
2 tablespoons each butter and bacon fat
1 tablespoon flour
1/2 teaspoon basil
1/2 teaspoon paprika
1-1/2 cups dairy sour cream
Chopped green onions

Cut tomatoes in 3/4" slices. Season with salt, pepper and garlic salt and coat with crumbs. Heat half the butter and fat in large skillet to very hot. Sauté tomatoes quickly on both sides, turning carefully. Remove and reduce heat. Add more fat to pan if needed. Add 1 teaspoon salt and next 3 ingredients, stirring. Add sour cream slowly. Heat over low heat just to thicken. Pour over tomatoes and top with green onion. Makes 6 servings.

TOMATO PUDDING

1 can (1 pound) tomato purée
1/4 cup water
1 cup light-brown sugar, packed
Seasoned salt and pepper
2 cups firm bread cubes
1/2 cup butter or margarine, melted

Mix first 3 ingredients, bring to boil and simmer 5 minutes. Add seasoned salt and pepper to taste. Put bread in greased 1½-quart casserole and pour butter over. Pour hot tomato mixture on top. Cover and bake in moderate oven (375°F.) about 30 minutes. Makes 6 servings.

ORIENTAL TOMATO SKILLET

2 tablespoons butter or margarine
1/4 teaspoon each curry powder and ginger
1/2 cup sliced onion
2 medium zucchini, cut in 1" slices
2/3 cup sliced fresh mushrooms
1 can (14-1/2 ounces) sliced baby tomatoes
Salt and freshly ground pepper

Melt butter in large skillet. Add curry powder and ginger and sauté 2 minutes. Add onion, zucchini, and fresh mushrooms. Cover and cook over medium heat 5 to 7 minutes, or until vegetables are tender but still slightly crisp. Add tomatoes and heat. Season to taste with salt and pepper. Makes 4 to 6 servings.

HODGEPODGE CASSEROLE

1 box each (9 or 10 ounces each) frozen lima beans, cauliflower, peas and cut green beans
Salt
1 can (4 ounces) sliced mushrooms, drained
3/4 cup margarine
1/2 cup all-purpose flour
1 teaspoon dry mustard
2 cups each light cream and chicken stock
2 tablespoons prepared horseradish
1/8 teaspoon hot pepper sauce
1/2 cup slivered almonds
2 cups soft stale-bread crumbs

Cook each vegetable separately in boiling salted water as directed on label. Drain and put, with mushrooms, in greased shallow 13" x 9" casserole. Melt ½ cup margarine and blend in flour and mustard. Gradually add liquids and cook, stirring, until thickened. Add next 2 ingredients and salt to taste. Pour over vegetables. Brown almonds in remaining margarine, add crumbs and toss. Sprinkle on mixture in casserole. Bake in hot oven (400°F.) 15 minutes. Makes 10 to 12 servings.

ORANGE MUSTARD SAUCE

6 tablespoons butter or margarine
1/2 cup orange juice
1 tablespoon chopped fresh parsley or 1 teaspoon parsley flakes
1 teaspoon dry mustard
Grated rind of 1 orange

Melt butter, add remaining ingredients and serve hot on cauliflower, broccoli or other vegetable. Also good on meat loaf. Makes 1 cup.

MANY-PURPOSE SAUCE

1 cup dairy sour cream
1/3 cup mayonnaise
1 can (4 ounces) sliced mushrooms, drained
2 tablespoons minced parsley
1 teaspoon celery seed
3/4 teaspoon salt
1/4 teaspoon pepper
1 teaspoon prepared mustard

Mix all ingredients. Cover and chill 1 hour or longer. Serve on hot cooked green beans, broccoli, Brussels sprouts or asparagus; baked or boiled potatoes; fried fish or chicken; cold cuts and cooked shrimps. Makes about 1½ cups.

PRETZEL CASSEROLE TOPPING

1 cup crushed pretzels
1/4 cup grated Parmesan cheese
2 tablespoons dried parsley
1 teaspoon paprika
1/4 teaspoon herb mixture or fines herbes, crumbled
Melted butter or margarine

Combine first 5 ingredients. Mix with melted butter or margarine to moisten. Sprinkle on favorite vegetable dish or casserole. Delicious on broiled tomato halves. Makes about 1 cup.

CREAMY MUSHROOM SAUCE

1 can (3 ounces) chopped mushrooms
Light cream
2 tablespoons butter or margarine
2 tablespoons flour
1/2 teaspoon steak sauce
Seasoned salt and pepper
Onion salt

Drain liquid from mushrooms into measuring cup and add enough light cream to make 1 cup. Sauté mushrooms in the butter 1 to 2 minutes. Stir in flour. Gradually add liquid and cook, stirring, until thickened. Add steak sauce, and remaining ingredients to taste. Makes 1½ cups.

PEANUT-STUFFED PEPPERS

6 green peppers, halved and seeded
Salt
Butter or margarine
1/2 cup uncooked regular rice
1/3 cup minced onion
1/2 cup chopped celery
1/8 teaspoon garlic powder
1 can (1 pound) tomatoes
1 cup chopped salted peanuts
2 tablespoons fine dry bread crumbs

Cook peppers in salted boiling water 5 minutes. Combine 1 tablespoon melted butter, 1½ teaspoons salt and next 4 ingredients in skillet. Add 1 cup water slowly as mixture begins to cook. Simmer, covered, 5 to 10 minutes. Add tomatoes and simmer 10 minutes longer, or until rice is almost done. Add more water if needed. Stir in peanuts and stuff peppers with the mixture. Sprinkle with crumbs mixed with 2 teaspoons melted butter. Set peppers in baking pan with a little hot water in bottom and bake in moderate oven (350°F.) 30 to 40 minutes. Makes 6 servings.

SQUASH MANDARIN

2 pounds yellow summer squash
Salt
2 tablespoons butter or margarine
1 can (11 ounces) mandarin-orange sections
2 tablespoons brown sugar
1/4 teaspoon nutmeg
1/4 cup canned toasted slivered almonds

Wash squash and cut in crosswise slices. Cook in small amount of boiling salted water until just tender. Drain, add butter and keep warm. Pour syrup from oranges into saucepan, add sugar and bring to boil. Boil about 5 minutes and add nutmeg. Remove from heat and add oranges. Pour over squash and sprinkle with nuts. Makes 4 to 6 servings.

KOLOKYTHIA KROKETTES
(Zucchini Pancakes, Greek Style)

3 cups grated zucchini
1 teaspoon salt
3 eggs
1 cup grated feta cheese
1-1/2 teaspoons minced fresh mint leaves
3 tablespoons flour
Pepper and butter

Mix zucchini with salt and let stand 1 hour. Squeeze out moisture. Beat eggs, add zucchini, cheese, mint, flour, and pepper to taste. Fry 1 tablespoon at a time in butter over medium heat. Brown on both sides. Makes 18 pancakes, or 6 servings.

SKILLET SQUASH AND ONIONS

2 pounds yellow summer squash
3 medium onions, sliced thin
3 tablespoons butter
1/2 teaspoon salt
1/4 teaspoon pepper

Wash squash and dice. Combine all ingredients in skillet. Cover and cook, stirring frequently, 20 to 30 minutes, or until squash and onion are tender. Makes 4 servings.

ZUCCHINI ALLA PARMIGIANA

6 medium zucchini, cut lengthwise in 1/4" slices
Salt
2 cans (8 ounces each) tomato sauce
1/8 teaspoon basil
Pepper
2 eggs, beaten
1 cup seasoned fine dry bread crumbs
Vegetable oil
1 cup grated Parmesan cheese

Sprinkle zucchini with salt and set aside. Mix tomato sauce, 1 cup water and basil; bring to boil and simmer, uncovered, about 1 hour. Season with salt and pepper. Dip zucchini slices in egg, then in crumbs. Sauté in oil until golden brown on both sides. In greased shallow 1½-quart baking dish, alternate layers of tomato sauce, zucchini and cheese, ending with cheese. Bake in moderate oven (350°F.) about 45 minutes. Serves 6.

VEGETABLE CASSEROLE, COUNTRY STYLE

1 package (10 ounces) chopped spinach, thawed
3 tablespoons vegetable oil
1 medium zucchini, diced
1/2 pound green beans, cut in 1" pieces
1 large onion, chopped
1 small clove garlic, minced
1 teaspoon dried basil leaves
3/4 teaspoon salt
1/4 teaspoon nutmeg
1/8 teaspoon pepper
4 eggs, slightly beaten
2 tablespoons grated Parmesan cheese
Paprika

Cook spinach in 2 tablespoons oil in skillet 2 to 3 minutes. Add remaining oil, 2 tablespoons water and next 3 ingredients. Cover and cook, stirring occasionally, 10 minutes, or until zucchini is tender-crisp. Add seasonings, mix well and put in greased 1½-quart casserole. Pour eggs over vegetables and sprinkle with grated cheese. Bake in moderate oven (350°F.) about 30 minutes. Sprinkle with paprika. Serves 4 to 6.

ONI FICALO

SALAD INGREDIENTS

Buy crisp young salad greens. Rinse under running cold water, drain well, wrap in foil or other moisture-proof wrapping and refrigerate. If necessary, dry with a kitchen towel before making salad. If cut fruits that darken are used, moisten them with some of the dressing or a tart juice as soon as cut.

Iceberg and Boston lettuce are the most common types of salad green used. However, a variety of greens is delicious for a green salad. Choose garden lettuce, romaine, bibb lettuce, watercress, escarole, chicory, Chinese cabbage, young dandelion greens, beet greens, spinach or other tender young greens. To vary, add radishes, green onions, chives, tomatoes, fresh herbs, cucumbers, zucchini, celery, red or yellow onion, chard, cauliflower, avocado, carrot, mushrooms or other raw vegetables. Cooked vegetables such as artichoke hearts, peas, string beans, broccoli, tiny Brussels sprouts, beets or asparagus can also be added.

No matter how good the basic ingredients, the salad will be flavorless unless bound together with a well-seasoned dressing. There are also many other ingredients that can be added to salads such as seasoned salt, seasoned pepper, lemon-pepper marinade, dried herbs, garlic and onion salts, celery salt and seed, toasted sesame seed, seasoned croutons and monosodium glutamate.

A salad may be served as an appetizer or first course, as an accompaniment to the main course or as the main course itself, depending on the ingredients. Some fruit salads may also be served as dessert.

CHINESE CHICKEN SALAD

3 cups diced cooked chicken
1 cup drained canned bean sprouts
1-1/2 cups sliced celery
1/8 teaspoon pepper
1/2 cup French dressing
2 tablespoons soy sauce
3/4 cup mayonnaise
Salad greens and ripe olives

Mix first 5 ingredients and chill. Blend soy sauce and mayonnaise. Stir into first mixture and serve on greens with a garnish of olives. Makes 4 to 6 servings.

COLD CHICKEN-HAM MOUSSE

3 egg yolks, slightly beaten
3/4 teaspoon salt
1/8 teaspoon cayenne
1 cup hot chicken broth
1 envelope unflavored gelatin
1 cup ground cooked chicken or turkey
1 cup ground cooked smoked ham
1 green onion, minced
1/4 cup mayonnaise or salad dressing
1/2 cup heavy cream, whipped
Salad greens and tomato wedges

Mix first 3 ingredients in top part of double boiler. Gradually stir in broth. Cook, stirring, over simmering water until thickened. Soften gelatin in 2 tablespoons cold water. Add to hot mixture and mix well; cool. Fold in remaining ingredients, except last 2, and pour into 1-quart mold. Chill until firm. Unmold and garnish with salad greens and tomato wedges. Makes 4 servings.

JELLIED CHICKEN

5-pound stewing chicken, cut in pieces
1 onion
2 stalks celery
1 bay leaf
Salt and pepper
Mayonnaise
Chopped fresh or crumbled dried herbs

Wash chicken and put in kettle. Add 4 cups boiling water, the next 3 ingredients and 1 teaspoon salt. Cover, bring to boil and simmer 2½ hours, or until chicken is tender. Drain, reserving liquid. Cool chicken, remove meat from bones and cut in coarse pieces. Arrange in 6 oiled individual molds or 1½-quart mold. Skim fat from liquid, strain and reduce to 2 cups by boiling, uncovered. Season to taste and pour over chicken. Cool, then chill overnight, or until firm. Unmold and serve with mayonnaise seasoned with herbs. Makes 6 servings.

HOT TURKEY SALAD

2 cups diced cooked turkey
2 cups thinly sliced celery
1 teaspoon grated onion
1/2 teaspoon salt
1/2 cup sliced canned water chestnuts
3/4 cup mayonnaise
2 tablespoons lemon juice
1 cup crushed corn chips
1/2 cup grated sharp Cheddar cheese

Mix all ingredients, except corn chips and cheese. Pile into shallow 1½-quart baking dish or 4 to 6 individual ramekins. Sprinkle with corn chips and cheese. Bake in very hot oven (450°F.) 10 to 15 minutes. Makes 4 to 6 servings.

CURRIED CHICKEN SALAD

3 cups diced cooked chicken
2 cups finely diced celery
1/3 cup slivered almonds, toasted
Juice of 1 lemon
1 tablespoon minced onion
3/4 cup mayonnaise
2 to 3 teaspoons curry powder
1 teaspoon salt
1/8 teaspoon pepper
Salad greens

Toss chicken with celery and almonds. Mix remaining ingredients, except greens, and combine with chicken mixture. Chill. Serve on greens. Makes 4 to 6 servings.

CHICKEN BREASTS VÉRONIQUE

4 chicken breasts, boned before or after
  cooking
Salt
1 onion, sliced
Dash of hot pepper sauce
1-1/2 cups heavy cream
4 egg yolks
1/2 cup chopped parsley
2 tablespoons sherry or Madeira
Watercress
Seedless grapes, halved

Cook chicken breasts in salted water with onion and hot pepper sauce. When tender, remove and cool. Discard skin and cut meat in even pieces. Chill. Place cream and egg yolks in top of a double boiler and stir over hot water until the mixture thickens. Stir in 1 teaspoon salt, the parsley and wine. Spoon the sauce over the chicken and chill. Arrange on serving dish with watercress and garnish with grapes. Good with toasted English muffins, and a peach-melon salad tossed with mustard dressing. Makes 4 servings.

JELLIED CHICKEN LOAF

2 broiler-fryers, about 3 pounds each,
  cut up
Salt
10 whole white peppercorns
1 cup celery tops
1 small onion, quartered
Curried Mayonnaise Dressing

Put 1 chicken in pressure cooker with 1³/₄ cups water, 1¹/₂ teaspoons salt and next 3 ingredients. Close cover securely. Place pressure regulator on vent pipe; set heat selector at 425°F. When pressure regulator attains a steady, gentle rocking motion, turn heat selector to left until pilot light goes out. Cook 20 minutes, then turn heat selector off and disconnect cord. Let pressure drop of its own accord. Remove chicken and cook remaining chicken in same broth according to directions above. Strain and cool broth until excess fat can be skimmed off. Correct seasonings. Discard skin and bones from chickens and put chunks of chicken in oiled 9″ x 5″ x 3″ loaf pan. Pour broth on top and mix with chicken. Chill until firm. Unmold and serve in slices, with dressing. Makes 8 servings. **Curried Mayonnaise Dressing** Mix ³/₄ cup each mayonnaise and dairy sour cream. Stir in 1 tablespoon each vinegar and curry powder. Makes about 1¹/₂ cups.

CURRIED CHICKEN SALAD II

1/4 cup chicken broth
2 to 3 teaspoons curry powder
2/3 cup mayonnaise
1 to 2 tablespoons lemon juice
2-1/2 to 3 cups julienne-cut cooked
  chicken
1 can (11 ounces) mandarin-orange
  sections, drained, or 1 can (13-1/4
  ounces) pineapple chunks, drained
1 can (8 ounces) small green peas,
  drained
1 cup thinly sliced celery
1 cup green- or red-pepper slivers
1/2 cup drained tiny pickled onions
1/2 cup chopped green onions
Toasted chopped nuts or toasted
  coconut

Simmer broth and curry powder 2 minutes; cool. Add to mayonnaise with lemon juice and blend well. Fold in chicken and arrange in center of serving platter. Chill while preparing remaining ingredients. Arrange fruit and vegetables in groups around chicken salad and sprinkle top with nuts. Good with hot rolls or toast for lunch or supper. Makes 4 to 6 servings. **Note** Turkey can be substituted for the chicken, if desired.

MEDLEY MACARONI SALAD

8 ounces macaroni
1/4 cup bottled French dressing
1 cup dairy sour cream
Salt and pepper to taste
1/2 pound bacon, cooked crisp and
  crumbled
1 cup diced cooked chicken
2 hard-cooked eggs, chopped
1/4 cup chopped pimientos
1 large tomato, diced
2 tablespoons lemon juice
1 small avocado, peeled and sliced
Crisp chicory

Cook macaroni, drain, rinse with cold water and cool. Combine dressing with sour cream, mixing well. Add macaroni and mix. Add remaining ingredients, except last 3, and toss lightly. Place in salad bowl. Sprinkle lemon juice on avocado. Garnish salad with avocado and chicory. Serves 6.

CHICKEN-AVOCADO ALL-IN-ONE

2 cups large corn chips
1 can (15 ounces) chili with beans, heated
6 cups shredded iceberg lettuce
1 can (7 ounces) green-chili sauce, chilled
1 cup grated Parmesan cheese
12 thin slices, chilled cooked chicken
2 avocados, peeled and sliced lengthwise
Radishes, tomato wedges, green onions,
  olives

Put ¹/₂ cup chips on each of 4 serving plates. Spoon hot chili onto chips. Toss lettuce with about half the green-chili sauce. Pile part of lettuce in stack over hot chili; arrange part in bed around chips. Sprinkle about 2 tablespoons cheese on each serving. Arrange chicken and avocado slices on top of lettuce stack. Sprinkle with remaining chili sauce, then with remaining cheese. Garnish each serving with remaining ingredients. Makes 4 servings.

TURKEY-POTATO SALAD

1 package (1 pound) frozen French-fried
  potatoes
1 tablespoon instant minced onion
2 cups diced cooked turkey
2 green onions, chopped
1 jar (2 ounces) sliced pimiento, drained
3/4 cup mayonnaise
1/4 cup milk
1 teaspoon prepared mustard
Salt and pepper to taste

Combine potatoes, onion and ¹/₂ cup water in skillet. Bring to boil, cover and simmer 5 minutes, or until done. Drain off any liquid; cool. Add next 3 ingredients. Mix mayonnaise, milk and mustard until smooth. Pour over potato mixture and blend gently. Season to taste. Makes 4 to 6 servings.

CHICKEN-RICE SALAD

2 cups cooked rice, chilled
2 cups coarsely diced cooked chicken
1 cup diced celery
2 chopped green onions
1 tablespoon lemon juice
2 tablespoons chopped green pepper
3/4 cup salad dressing or mayonnaise
Salt and pepper
Salad greens

Mix first 6 ingredients. Add salad dressing and mix lightly. Season to taste. Chill and serve on salad greens. Makes 4 servings.

MOLDED TURKEY SALAD

2 envelopes unflavored gelatin
2 tablespoons lemon juice
1 teaspoon sugar
1 teaspoon salt
1/2 teaspoon dry mustard
1/2 teaspoon paprika
1/4 teaspoon onion salt
1 teaspoon horseradish
4 or 5 drops hot pepper sauce
1 pint dairy sour cream
2 cups finely diced cooked turkey
1/3 cup finely diced celery
1/3 cup diced unpeeled cucumber
2 pimientos, chopped
2 tablespoons chopped green pepper
Lettuce cups
Tomato wedges
Chopped hard-cooked eggs

Soften gelatin in 1½ cups water. Heat and stir to dissolve. Add next 9 ingredients and mix well. Chill until mixture begins to set. Fold in turkey and remaining ingredients, except last 3. Pour into 8 individual molds and chill until firm. Unmold into lettuce cups and garnish with tomato wedges and chopped egg. Makes 8 servings.

MAIN-DISH RICE SALAD

1-1/3 cups packaged precooked rice
3/4 teaspoon salt
2 tablespoons dry mustard
1-1/2 teaspoons sugar
2 tablespoons wine vinegar
1/4 cup vegetable oil
1/2 green pepper, chopped
1 cup diced cooked ham
1/2 cup cooked peas
Chopped parsley
Salad greens

Prepare rice with 1⅓ cups boiling water and salt as directed on the label. Mix next 3 ingredients with 2 tablespoons cold water. Gradually beat in oil. Stir lightly into warm rice. Cool and add next 3 ingredients. Add more salt if necessary. Sprinkle with parsley and serve with greens. Makes 4 servings.

TARRAGON VEAL SALAD

Mix 2 cups of diced cooked veal with ¼ cup chopped onion, ¼ cup chopped celery and ½ cup toasted blanched almonds. Blend 1 cup mayonnaise with 1 teaspoon dried tarragon and 1 tablespoon lemon juice. Add enough mayonnaise to veal mixture to bind it. Heap on greens and garnish with remaining mayonnaise, tomatoes, ripe olives and toasted almonds. Serve with herbed French bread. Makes 4 servings.

SALMAGUNDI SALAD

2 cups diced cooked potato
3 hard-cooked eggs, diced
1 cup diced celery
1 tablespoon minced onion
1/2 cup cubed hard salami
1/2 cup cubed liverwurst
1/2 cup cubed sharp Cheddar cheese
1 cup shredded cabbage
1/4 cup olive oil
Salt and pepper
1/2 cup mayonnaise
Salad greens
Chopped parsley

Mix first 8 ingredients. Add the olive oil, and salt and pepper to taste. Mix lightly. Add mayonnaise. Serve on greens, garnished with parsley. Makes 4 servings.

OLD-FASHIONED JELLIED VEAL

2 pounds carrots, peeled
2 pounds onions, peeled
1 stalk celery
2 pounds veal shank
1 teaspoon Worcestershire
1/4 teaspoon hot pepper sauce
2 bay leaves
Salt and freshly gound pepper to taste
2 envelopes unflavored gelatin
Watercress
Radish roses

Put first 8 ingredients in kettle; Add 2½ quarts water. Bring to boil over a gentle heat. Cook very slowly until the meat falls from the bones. Strain stock through fine cheesecloth. Return to heat and cook to reduce to half its quantity. Discard all bones from the meat and cut in small even dice. When the stock is reduced to half, remove from the heat, stir in the gelatin softened in ½ cup cold water. Pour over the diced meat. Pour into 2-quart mold and chill until firm; stir occasionally while still liquid to prevent meat from sinking to the bottom. Unmold on platter and garnish with watercress and radish roses. Makes 6 to 8 servings.

PRESSED TURKEY

1 cup turkey broth
3 cups minced cooked turkey
Salt and pepper
Parsley
Mayonnaise

Mix first 2 ingredients in saucepan. Simmer until broth is almost evaporated. Season with salt and pepper and let stand until cold. Pour into oiled 3-cup mold and weight down with plate. Chill overnight. Unmold and cut in slices. Garnish with parsley and serve with mayonnaise. Serves 4 to 6.

LUAU TURKEY SALAD

4 cups cooked white turkey meat, cut in strips 2" long and 1/2" wide
2 cups thinly sliced celery
1 cup finely chopped celery tops
1/3 cup lightly toasted chopped filberts
1 teaspoon curry powder
2 teaspoons instant chicken bouillon
1 cup mayonnaise
1 to 2 tablespoons lemon juice
White pepper
Lettuce

In mixing bowl, combine first 4 ingredients, reserving 1 tablespoon filberts. Mix curry powder, bouillon and 2 tablespoons hot water until well blended. Add to mayonnaise and beat until smooth. Season with lemon juice and pepper to taste. Pour over turkey mixture; toss to blend. Put in serving dish; chill. Serve on lettuce and sprinkle with reserved filberts. Serves 6.

TURKEY LOAF WITH LIVERWURST COATING

1 (2-pound) frozen turkey roast
1/4 pound fresh mushrooms, minced
2 tablespoons butter or margarine
1/4 pound liverwurst
1 package (3 ounces) cream cheese
Garlic salt
Mayonnaise
Black olives, cherry tomatoes, watercress

Prepare turkey roast according to package directions. Chill in foil pan. Sauté mushrooms in butter until browned; cool. Combine liverwurst and cream cheese and beat in electric mixer until well blended. Add mushrooms, and garlic salt to taste and mix well. Slice chilled turkey loaf in 1/4" slices. Put slices together in shape of loaf on serving platter. Spread with mixture to cover completely. Put mayonnaise in pastry tube and flute to decorate top and sides. Garnish edge of loaf with olives, halved cherry tomatoes and sprigs of cress. Serves 8.

HAM MOUSSE

1 envelope unflavored gelatin
2 egg yolks
3/4 teaspoon salt
Dash of cayenne
1 teaspoon dry mustard
1 can (10-1/2 ounces) condensed consommé
1 cup ground cooked ham
1 slice onion, minced
1/4 cup mayonnaise
1/4 cup heavy cream, whipped
Lettuce

Soften gelatin in 3/4 cup cold water. Mix yolks, salt, cayenne and mustard in top part of double boiler. Beat until thick and lemon colored. Add consommé and cook over boiling water until mixture thickens to coat spoon, stirring constantly. Add gelatin and stir until dissolved; cool. Add next 4 ingredients. Pour into oiled 1-quart mold. Chill until firm. Unmold on bed of lettuce on serving plate. Makes 4 servings.

POTATO-HAM SALAD DELUXE

1/2 cup dairy sour cream
1/2 teaspoon salt
1/4 teaspoon seasoned pepper
2 tablespoons each vinegar and milk
2 cups diced cooked potato
1/2 cup diced celery
2 green onions, thinly sliced
About 1-1/2 cups diced ham
1/2 cup creamed cottage cheese
1 hard-cooked egg, diced
1 carrot, coarsely shredded

Mix together sour cream, salt, pepper, the vinegar and milk. Combine potato and remaining ingredients, add sour cream mixture and toss lightly. Chill. Makes 4 to 6 servings.

HAM WITH MARINATED GREEN BEANS

1 pound green beans, cut in 1" pieces
Salt
1 onion, sliced
1/2 cup sliced celery
1/2 cup sliced radishes
Pepper to taste
1/3 cup salad oil
1/4 cup vinegar
2 teaspoons dry mustard
1 to 2 tablespoons prepared horseradish
8 slices ham

Cook beans in small amount of boiling salted water until tender; drain. Add onion, celery and radishes. Mix next 5 ingredients, pour over vegetables and mix well. Cool, then chill. Serve on platter surrounded with ham slices. Makes 4 servings.

BEEF-POTATO SALAD, LORENZO

Mix 2½ cups slivered cooked beef, 3 tomatoes, quartered, 4 diced cooked potatoes, 3 diced sweet pickles, some chopped parsley, and chives and tarragon to taste. Add enough Deluxe French Dressing (page 286) to moisten to taste. Serve on bed of watercress. Makes 4 servings.

RED DOG SALAD

1 pound frankfurters, thinly sliced
1 tablespoon butter
2 cans (1 pound each) red kidney beans, drained
4 green onions, chopped
1/2 cup chopped green pepper and celery
2 tomatoes, peeled and cut in wedges
1/3 cup vinegar
1/4 cup olive or other salad oil
Salt and pepper to taste

Cook frankfurters lightly in the butter. Toss with remaining ingredients. Makes 6 servings.

TONGUE-SALAD BOATS

1 can (12 ounces) lunch tongue, chopped
1 cup chopped celery
1/2 cup chopped green pepper
1 slice onion, minced
2 hard-cooked eggs, chopped
1/4 cup chopped sweet pickle
2 tablespoons prepared mustard
8 frankfurter rolls
3/4 cup mayonnaise

Combine all ingredients, except last 2. Cut tops from rolls and remove centers. Crumble tops and centers coarsely and add to filling with mayonnaise; mix well. Heap in rolls. Makes 8 boats.

BROILED HAM SALAD

2 cups finely diced cooked ham
1-1/2 cups finely diced celery
1/4 cup lightly seasoned French dressing
1/2 cup salad dressing or mayonnaise
1/3 cup dairy sour cream
1/4 cup toasted slivered almonds
2 cups finely crushed potato chips
1 cup grated Cheddar cheese
Salad greens

Marinate ham and celery in French dressing in refrigerator 1 hour. Add next 2 ingredients and mix lightly. Put in 9" shallow baking piepan or 4 broiler-proof ramekins. Chill until almost ready to serve. Sprinkle with almonds. Mix potato chips and cheese and press on top of mixture. Put under broiler 2 or 3 minutes, or until cheese is melted. Tuck greens around edge and serve. Serves 4.

HOT CORNED-BEEF AND POTATO SALAD

1 can (12 ounces) corned beef, diced
1 large onion, chopped
1/2 medium green pepper, chopped
3 canned pimientos, chopped
1 tablespoon butter
3 cups diced cooked potato
1/4 teaspoon salt
1/8 teaspoon pepper
1/4 cup salad dressing or mayonnaise
2 cups diced process American cheese

Cook first 4 ingredients in butter until beef is lightly browned. Add remaining ingredients and cook, stirring, until cheese is melted. Serve at once. Makes 4 to 6 servings.

LAMB SALAD PLATTER

1/4 cup salad oil
1 tablespoon wine vinegar
1/2 teaspoon each salt, ground black pepper and dry mustard
1 pound thinly sliced cold roast lamb
1 large orange, peeled and thinly sliced
1 large tomato, sliced
Fresh mint sprigs
Mint Mayonnaise

Beat or shake together first 3 ingredients. Pour over lamb, orange and tomato slices in bowl. Cover and chill several hours. Arrange lamb, orange and tomato slices on a chilled platter; garnish with mint sprigs. Pass Mint Mayonnaise. Serves 4. **Mint Mayonnaise** Mix ⅔ cup mayonnaise with 4 teaspoons chopped fresh mint, or 1½ teaspoons mint flakes.

FROSTED PÂTÉ LOAF

1 envelope unflavored gelatin
2 cups tomato juice
1/2 teaspoon salt
1/2 teaspoon onion salt
1/2 teaspoon celery salt
1/4 teaspoon basil
1 can (4-1/2 ounces) liver pâté
2 packages (3 ounces each) cream cheese, softened
2 teaspoons milk
1/4 cup chopped pimiento-stuffed olives
Salad greens

Soften gelatin in tomato juice in saucepan. Add next 4 ingredients and bring to boil, stirring. Pour half into 1-quart mold and chill until firm. Meanwhile, chill remaining mixture until slightly thickened. Mash liver pâté until very soft and carefully spread on firm tomato mixture. Carefully spoon rest of gelatin over liver pâté. Chill until firm. Beat cheese and milk until blended; add olives and spread on firm mixture. Chill about 1 hour. Unmold on greens and slice. Makes 6 servings.

GREEN SALAD WITH EGGS

Mixed salad greens for 6 servings
1/4 cup olive oil
2 tablespoons lemon juice
1/4 teaspoon salt
1/8 teaspoon pepper
6 eggs, hard-cooked

Put greens in salad bowl. Mix well next 4 ingredients. Cut eggs in half lengthwise, remove yolks and mash. Slice whites. Add dressing and eggs to greens and toss well. Makes 6 servings.

SUMMER SWEETBREADS

1 pair sweetbreads
Salt
1 onion, sliced
2 cloves
1/3 bay leaf
1 sprig parsley
1 slice lemon
2 cucumbers, peeled and seeded
3 stalks celery, chopped very fine
Mustard-flavored mayonnaise
Greens, green pepper and pimiento

Poach sweetbreads in salted water with next 5 ingredients for 20 minutes. Remove sweetbreads and plunge into ice water. Peel carefully and remove fat. Cut into bite-size pieces and chill. Cut one cucumber into small dice. Add celery and sweetbreads and toss with mayonnaise. Arrange on greens and garnish with remaining cucumber, chopped, and strips of green pepper and pimiento. Makes 4 servings.

EGG-HAM-MACARONI SALAD

6 eggs, hard-cooked and diced
1-1/2 cups diced cooked ham
2 cups cooked macaroni, chilled
1/2 cup diced celery
1 sour pickle, chopped
1/4 cup chopped pimiento-stuffed olives
Mayonnaise
Salt and pepper
Salad greens

Mix first 6 ingredients. Add mayonnaise to moisten and season to taste. Serve on greens. Makes 4 servings.

PIQUANT EGG SALAD

8 eggs, hard-cooked and chilled
1/4 cup each small pickled onions and chopped sweet gherkins
1/2 cup salad dressing
1 teaspoon prepared mustard
Salad greens

Cut eggs in large chunks. Mix lightly with remaining ingredients, except greens. Serve on greens. Serves 6.

TANGY BEEF-MACARONI SALAD

8 ounces macaroni
1/4 cup butter or margarine
1 medium onion, chopped
1 jar (2-1/4 ounces) dried beef, chopped
3/4 cup dairy sour cream
1/4 cup cider vinegar
1-1/2 teaspoons prepared horseradish
Salt and pepper to taste
Crisp salad greens

Cook macaroni, drain, rinse with cold water and cool. Melt butter, add onion and beef and sauté 8 minutes, or until onion is tender. Combine all ingredients, except last, and mix well; chill. Serve on greens. Makes 4 to 6 servings.

EGGS IN ASPIC

1-1/2 tablespoons unflavored gelatin
2 cups chicken stock or canned consommé
1/2 teaspoon instant minced onion
1/2 teaspoon mixed salad herbs
1/4 teaspoon garlic powder
1 teaspoon minced parsley
Dash of cayenne
4 eggs, hard-cooked and sliced
Watercress or other salad greens

Soften gelatin in 1/4 cup cold chicken stock. Put remaining stock and other ingredients, except eggs and watercress in saucepan. Bring to boil and simmer 15 minutes. Stir in gelatin and chill until mixture begins to set. Spoon about 1/2" layer into each of four 5-ounce custard cups. Put a slice of egg in bottom of each and arrange 3 egg slices around sides of cup. Chop ends of eggs and put in center of cup. Fill with gelatin mixture and chill until firm. Unmold on cress. Serves 4.

MOLDED EGG-LOBSTER SALAD

1 envelope unflavored gelatin
2 cups milk
1-1/2 teaspoons seasoned salt
1/4 teaspoon pepper
1 teaspoon curry powder
1 tablespoon instant minced onion
3/4 cup mayonnaise or salad dressing
1 can (5-1/2 ounces) lobster, diced
1 cup diced celery
Juice of 1 lemon
6 eggs, hard-cooked
Salad greens

Sprinkle gelatin on 1 cup milk; heat, stirring to dissolve gelatin. Combine with remaining 1 cup milk, seasonings and mayonnaise; add next 3 ingredients and 4 eggs, diced. Pour into 6-cup mold and chill until firm. Unmold on greens and garnish with remaining eggs, sliced. Makes 4 servings.

BAYOU SLAW

Mix 1 cup chopped smoked tongue; 1 cup chopped cooked ham; 1 green and 1 red pepper, chopped; and 1 tablespoon minced onion. Add to 1 small head cabbage, shredded, and 1 cup mayonnaise folded into 1 stiffly beaten white. Chill. Makes 4 to 6 servings.

TROPICAL TUNA SALAD

2 cans (7 ounces) tuna, drained
1 can (1 pound 4-1/2 ounces) pineapple chunks, drained
4 ripe bananas, sliced lengthwise
Salad greens
Mustard Dressing

Arrange tuna and fruits on greens and serve with the dressing. Serves 4 to 6. **Mustard Dressing** Mix well ½ cup salad dressing or mayonnaise, ¼ cup chopped sweet pickle and 2 tablespoons prepared mustard.

SEAFOOD SALAD PLATE

Greens
Whole cooked shrimps, lobster tails, crab meat, scallops or other seafood
Lemon and tomato wedges
Cocktail sauce, curry or herb mayonnaise or Green Sauce

On greens, arrange seafood and garnish with lemon and tomato wedges. Serve with sauce. **Green Sauce** Use 1 part dairy sour cream to 2 parts mayonnaise. Add minced parsley, green onion, watercress and dill pickle to taste.

SAVORY SHRIMP MOLD

2 envelopes unflavored gelatin
2 bouillon cubes
1 pound shrimp, cooked
1/4 cup mayonnaise
1 teaspoon horseradish
1 teaspoon instant minced onion
1 tablespoon minced parsley
2 tablespoons lime or lemon juice
Dash each of Worcestershire and hot pepper sauce
1/2 cup heavy cream, whipped
Seasoned salt and pepper to taste
Salad greens

Soften gelatin in ½ cup cold water; add 1 cup boiling water and bouillon cubes. Stir until gelatin and cubes are dissolved. Chill until slightly thickened. Meanwhile, peel, clean and dice shrimp. Fold into gelatin with remaining ingredients, except greens. Chill until firm. Unmold on greens. Makes 6 servings.

CURRIED SHRIMP SALAD

Cut 2 cups chilled cooked shrimp in half lengthwise; mix with 1 cup sliced celery, 1 tablespoon each minced onion and lemon juice, ½ cup mayonnaise, 1 teaspoon curry powder, and salt and pepper to taste. Serve on greens. Makes 4 servings.

JELLIED TUNA SALAD

A jellied salad with built-in French dressing.

1 box (3 ounces) lemon-flavor gelatin
1 can (7 ounces) tuna
1 tablespoon oil from tuna
2 tablespoons vinegar
3/4 teaspoon salt
Dash of pepper
1/8 teaspoon paprika
3/4 cup finely diced celery
1 pimiento, chopped
1/4 cup chopped green pepper
2 teaspoons horseradish
Salad greens

Dissolve gelatin in 1 cup hot water. Add ¾ cup cold water and chill until slightly thickened. Drain the tuna, reserving 1 tablespoon oil. Mix oil and next 4 ingredients. Flake tuna and add with remaining ingredients, except greens. Mix well. Chill about 20 minutes. Fold into slightly thickened gelatin. Pour into 6 individual molds and chill until firm. Unmold on greens. Makes 6 servings.

MOLDED SALMON RING WITH CUCUMBERS

1 can (1 pound) pink salmon, flaked
1 envelope unflavored gelatin
2 egg yolks
3/4 cup milk
2-1/2 tablespoons lemon juice
1 teaspoon salt
1 teaspoon dry mustard
Paprika
2 tablespoons butter
1 cup dairy sour cream
Few sprigs of fresh dill, chopped
1 teaspoon seasoned salt
1 cucumber, peeled and thinly sliced
Watercress

Drain liquid from salmon into top part of small double boiler. Sprinkle with gelatin. Add next 5 ingredients and ¼ teaspoon paprika; beat with rotary beater. Add butter and put mixture over boiling water. Cook, stirring, until smooth and slightly thickened; add salmon. (Remove skin and bones, if desired.) Pour into 1-quart ring mold. Chill until firm. Unmold onto serving dish; fill center with mixture of next 4 ingredients. Sprinkle with paprika. Garnish with watercress. Makes 4 servings.

GLAMOUR CRAB SALAD

Prepare in advance, to blend flavors.

1 cup mayonnaise
1 tablespoon heavy cream
1/2 teaspoon curry powder
1 tablespoon grated onion
1 tablespoon minced parsley
1/4 cup chili sauce
2 tablespoons sherry
2 tablespoons lemon juice
1/4 teaspoon freshly ground pepper
3 pounds lump crab meat
Lettuce cups
Parsley

Mix all ingredients, except last 3. Carefully fold in lumps of crab. Chill thoroughly. Serve in lettuce cups. Garnish with parsley. Good with stuffed olives and tomato slices. Makes 8 to 10 servings.

HOT SEAFOOD SALAD

3 slices toasted white bread
1 can (6-1/2 ounces) king crab meat
1 can (5 ounces) shrimp, sliced
1/4 cup diced sweet pickles
1/2 cup mayonnaise
1 small onion, chopped
2 tablespoons chopped parsley
2 hard-cooked eggs, sliced
1/4 cup finely diced celery

Cut toast in 1/2" cubes. Remove membrane from crab meat and flake. Mix all ingredients, except last 2. Heat over hot water 20 to 30 minutes, or in hot oven 10 minutes, until piping hot. Garnish with egg and sprinkle with diced celery. Makes 4 servings. *Note* This salad can be made ahead and heated at serving time.

SEVICHE
(South American Raw-fish Salad)

1-1/2 pounds lemon sole, cut in thin
  strips
1 cup lime juice
1/2 cup olive oil
1/4 cup finely chopped onion
2 tablespoons canned green chilies,
  finely chopped
1/4 cup finely chopped parsley
1 clove garlic, finely chopped
1-1/2 teaspoons salt
1 teaspoon black pepper
Dash of hot pepper sauce
Chopped cilantro (fresh coriander)

Cover fish strips with the lime juice and refrigerate for 4 hours. Drain. Blend all remaining ingredients, except cilantro, and toss with the fish strips. Chill. Garnish with chopped cilantro. Makes 4 to 6 servings. *Note* In South America this dish is often made with tiny scallops or crab meat.

TUNA SURPRISE SALAD

2 cups cooked rice
1/2 cup dairy sour cream
1/4 cup chutney, diced
2 teaspoons curry powder
1/2 teaspoon salt
1 cup sliced celery
1 can (20 ounces) pineapple tidbits,
  drained
3 cans (about 7 ounces each) tuna,
  drained
Salad greens and toasted slivered almonds

Mix all ingredients, except the last. Chill. Arrange on greens and garnish with almonds. Makes 6 to 8 servings.

CRAB RAVIGOTE

1 pound lump crab meat
1 teaspoon salt
1/8 teaspoon cayenne
1 teaspoon prepared mustard
1 tablespoon olive oil
1 sprig parsley, minced
1 hard-cooked egg, chopped
3 tablespoons lemon juice
Ravigote Mayonnaise
Sliced lemon and pimiento strips

Gently combine all ingredients, except last 3, and heap in 4 crab shells or ramekins. Chill thoroughly. Just before serving, top with mayonnaise. Garnish with sliced lemon and pimiento strips. Makes 4 servings. **Ravigote Mayonnaise** Mix well 1 cup mayonnaise, 1 tablespoon tarragon vinegar, 1 teaspoon finely minced parsley, 1 teaspoon grated onion and a dash of cayenne.

SHRIMP SALAD, ORIENTAL

2 cups fresh bean sprouts or 1 can
  (1 pound), drained
Salt
1 can (5 ounces) water chestnuts, drained
2 cups cooked shrimps (1 pound
  uncooked shelled)
1 cup chow-mein noodles
1/4 cup minced green onions
1/4 cup minced celery
Soy Mayonnaise
Lettuce

Cook bean sprouts in boiling salted water 2 to 3 minutes. Drain and chill. (If using canned bean sprouts, rinse in cold water but do not cook.) Mince water chestnuts. Combine with next 4 ingredients and bean sprouts; toss with Soy Mayonnaise. Serve on lettuce. Makes 4 to 6 servings. **Soy Mayonnaise** Mix thoroughly 3/4 cup mayonnaise, 1 tablespoon each lemon juice and soy sauce, 3/4 teaspoon ginger juice (or 3/8 teaspoon ground ginger) and 1/2 teaspoon monosodium glutamate.

TUNA-MACARONI SALAD

1 cup elbow macaroni, cooked and
   drained
1 can (7 ounces) tuna, undrained
2 tablespoons chopped red or green
   onion
1 tablespoon capers
1/2 cup chopped green pepper
1/2 teaspoon dry mustard
1/2 cup mayonnaise
1/2 cup chicken broth
1 tablespoon lemon juice
Salt and pepper
Chopped radishes

Put drained macaroni back in sauce-pan. Add tuna with liquid, the onion, capers and green pepper. Toss to mix. Combine next 4 ingredients and mix until smooth. Pour onto macaroni mixture and mix well. Add salt and pepper to taste and put in serving dish. Garnish with radishes and chill about 1 hour. Makes 4 servings.

BLENDER TUNA MOUSSE

2 cans (7 ounces each) tuna, undrained
1 cup dairy sour cream
1/2 cup mayonnaise
Dash of hot pepper sauce
1/2 teaspoon celery salt
2 envelopes unflavored gelatin
Vegetable oil
Paprika
Marinated cooked or canned vegetables

Put first 5 ingredients in blender and whirl until smooth. Soften gelatin in ½ cup water. Dissolve over hot water or very low heat. Add to first mixture and blend well. Pour into oiled 1-quart mold lightly sprinkled with paprika and chill until firm. Unmold and serve with marinated vegetables. Makes 6 servings. **To prepare marinated vegetables,** cook and drain 1 box (10 ounces) frozen mixed vegetables. Or drain 1 can (1 pound) mixed vegetables. Season with French dressing to taste; chill.

WEST COAST TUNA SALAD

1 large or 2 medium heads romaine
2 hard-cooked eggs, chopped
3 finely minced green onions
1 can (7 ounces) tuna, broken up
6 slices crisp, cooked bacon, fat reserved
2 tablespoons or more wine vinegar
Pepper and salt

Wash romaine, dry and chill; break in pieces into a large bowl. Add next 3 ingredients with bacon, crumbled. Combine vinegar and fresh ground pepper with bacon fat in pan. Heat and pour over salad, mixing gently. Salt if necessary. Makes 6 servings.

GARLIC TUNA-RICE SALAD

1 can (7 ounces) water-packed tuna,
   drained and flaked
1 clove garlic, minced
1 jar (2-1/2 ounces) whole mushrooms,
   drained, or 1 cup sliced fresh
1/2 cup chopped parsley
1/4 cup butter or margarine
1/2 cup uncooked regular rice
Hot crusty bread

Combine tuna and garlic in salad bowl. Add mushrooms and parsley. Dot with butter and set aside while rice is cooking. Spoon hot rice on top and let stand a few minutes. Toss and serve with bread. Makes 4 servings.

TUNA COMBINATION SALAD

Salad greens
1 can (7 ounces) tuna, drained
1 hard-cooked egg, halved
2 whole canned pimientos
2 green-pepper rings
2 green onions
4 radishes
6 each carrot sticks and black olives
Tangy Dressing

Arrange salad greens on 2 individual plates. Put half the tuna in center of each plate; garnish with remaining ingredients, except dressing. Serve with dressing. Serves 2. **Tangy Dressing** Mix ¼ cup mayonnaise, ¼ teaspoon salt, ½ teaspoon lemon juice and 1 teaspoon Worcestershire.

CREAMY MOLDED TUNA SALAD

1 envelope unflavored gelatin
3/4 cup diced celery
1/4 cup each minced onion and green
   pepper
2 cans (7 ounces each) tuna, drained
1 package (3 ounces) cream cheese,
   softened
2 teaspoons prepared mustard
1 teaspoon salt
Dash of paprika
3 tablespoons lemon juice
Salad greens

Soften gelatin in ⅓ cup cold water. Add ½ cup boiling water and stir until dissolved. Combine remaining ingredients, except greens, add gelatin and mix well. Pour into oiled 1-quart mold and chill until firm. Unmold on greens. Makes 6 servings.

NIPPY RUSSIAN DRESSING

Mix 1 cup mayonnaise, 1 tablespoon horseradish, ¼ cup catsup, dash of cayenne or chili powder and 1 teaspoon grated onion. Store in refrigerator. Makes 1¼ cups.

WHOLE SALMON IN ASPIC

1 whole salmon, 6 to 8 pounds, poached
   and skinned
1 envelope unflavored gelatin
1 can condensed madrilène
Pimiento-stuffed olives
Parsley sprigs
Lemon slices

Put salmon carefully on large serving platter. Soften gelatin in ¼ cup cold water and dissolve in ¾ cup boiling water. Add madrilène and chill until slightly thickened. Arrange olive slices on salmon. Gently pour on gelatin mixture to coat fish. Chill until jelled and serve on same platter with a garnish of parsley and lemon slices. Makes 6 to 8 servings.

SALMON-CUCUMBER SALAD

2 cucumbers, peeled
1-1/4 teaspoons salt
1/4 teaspoon pepper
1 can (1 pound) salmon, well drained and
   flaked
3/4 cup dairy sour cream
1 tablespoon lemon juice
2 tablespoons minced chives or green
   onions

Quarter cucumbers, discard seed and cut in thin slices. Sprinkle with 1 teaspoon salt and the pepper; let stand ½ hour. Drain well and mix lightly with salmon. Mix sour cream, lemon juice and remaining salt. Pour over salad; sprinkle with chives. Serves 4.

CURRIED SALMON LOAF

1 box (3 ounces) lemon-flavor gelatin
1/4 cup lemon juice
1/2 teaspoon salt
2 hard-cooked eggs, sliced
1 teaspoon finely minced chives
1 teaspoon capers
1/2 medium cucumber, peeled and sliced
1 can (1 pound) salmon, drained and
   flaked
1/2 cup mayonnaise
1 teaspoon curry powder
1 teaspoon instant minced onion
Salad greens

Dissolve gelatin in 1½ cups hot water. Add lemon juice and salt and chill until slightly thickened. Pour a little of mixture into oiled 9" x 5" x 3" loaf pan. Arrange egg slices in gelatin and sprinkle with chives and capers. Chill until firm. Add a little more gelatin and cover with a layer of cucumber. Mix remaining ingredients, except greens, and spread on cucumbers. Cover with remaining gelatin and chill until firm. Unmold on greens and serve plain. Makes 6 servings.

HOT SALMON-RICE SALAD

1 can (1 pound) salmon, drained
2 cups cooked rice
1 cup thinly sliced celery
1/2 cup chopped parsley
1/4 cup sliced pitted black olives
1/2 cup mayonnaise
1/4 cup dairy sour cream
2 tablespoons lemon juice
Salt and pepper
1/3 cup thinly sliced almonds
Grated Parmesan cheese
Paprika

Break salmon into large pieces. Add next 4 ingredients. Mix well next 3 ingredients; salt and pepper to taste. Toss with salmon mixture. Divide into 6 well-greased shallow 8-ounce baking dishes and sprinkle with last 3 ingredients. Bake in hot oven (400°F.) 15 to 20 minutes, or until heated and golden brown. Serves 6.

COLD SALMON PIQUANT

1-1/2 pounds salmon fillet, skin on
1 teaspoon salt
1 tablespoon lemon juice
1 medium onion, sliced
1 teaspoon mixed pickling spice
1 small clove garlic, sliced
1/2 cup mayonnaise or salad dressing
1 cucumber, sliced
1 cup cherry tomatoes, halved

Thaw frozen salmon, if used. Sprinkle both sides with salt and lemon juice. Arrange next 3 ingredients in well-greased shallow baking dish. Put salmon, skin side up, on mixture; cover and bake in moderate oven (350°F.) 1 hour, or until fish flakes easily with fork. Remove skin and chill salmon in same dish. When ready to serve, remove serving dish and garnish with remaining ingredients. Serves 4 to 6.

COLD SALMON PLATTER

1 can (1 pound) salmon, drained
3/4 cup mayonnaise
1 tablespoon lemon juice
1 teaspoon prepared mustard
1 cucumber, peeled
1 large tomato, peeled and cut in wedges
2 hard-cooked eggs, quartered
1 tablespoon chopped fresh dill
Salt and freshly ground pepper
Paprika

Separate salmon in chunks and put in center of platter. Mix next 3 ingredients and spread on salmon. Quarter cucumber, discard seed and cut in thin slices. Arrange with tomato and eggs around salmon. Sprinkle with dill. Season vegetables and eggs lightly with remaining ingredients. Chill. Makes 4 servings.

SHRIMP MOUSSE WITH DILL-CUCUMBER SAUCE

2 egg whites
2 cups heavy cream
1 teaspoon salt
1/2 teaspoon white pepper
1/8 teaspoon nutmeg
1 package (10 ounces) cleaned shelled uncooked shrimps, thawed
Dill-Cucumber Sauce (below)

Combine egg whites, cream and seasonings in bowl. Pour one third of mixture into blender, add one third of shrimps and blend. Pour into buttered 1-quart mold or 7" x 3" x 2" loaf pan. Repeat until all is blended. Set in pan with 1" of hot water and bake in moderate oven (350°F.) about 45 minutes. Let stand 5 minutes, then turn out on serving plate. Serve with sauce. Serves 4.

DILL-CUCUMBER SAUCE

1 medium cucumber, peeled and seeded
2 tablespoons butter or margarine, softened
1 tablespoon cornstarch
1 cup light cream
3/4 teaspoon salt
Dash of white pepper
1-1/2 teaspoons lemon juice
1 teaspoon chopped fresh dill or 1/2 teaspoon dillweed

Coarsely chop cucumber in blender; set aside. Put next 5 ingredients in blender and whirl until smooth. Put in saucepan and cook, stirring, until thickened. Add cucumber and heat gently. Add remaining ingredients. A good accompaniment for shrimp, salmon and other fish dishes. Makes about 1½ cups.

SEAFOOD SALAD

2 cans (7 ounces each) chunk-style tuna, drained
1 can (8 ounces) minced clams, drained
1 can (4-1/2 ounces) medium shrimps, drained
2-1/2 cups thinly sliced celery
1/3 cup minced green onions
1 jar (2 ounces) chopped pimiento, drained
1/2 cup mayonnaise
1/2 cup dairy sour cream
1 tablespoon lemon juice
Salt and pepper
3 hard-cooked eggs, quartered
Finely chopped fresh dill or dillweed

Combine first 6 ingredients and toss lightly. Mix mayonnaise, sour cream and lemon juice. Beat until smooth. Toss with tuna mixture; season to taste with salt and pepper. Transfer to serving dish and garnish with eggs and dill. Makes 8 servings.

FLORIDA FISH MOUSSE

1 medium onion, sliced
3/4 teaspoon hot pepper sauce
2 teaspoons salt
1-1/2 pounds fish fillets (sole, flounder or other white fish)
1 envelope unflavored gelatin
6 tablespoons (1/2 can) frozen grapefruit-juice concentrate
1/2 cup mayonnaise
1 cup heavy cream, whipped
Salad greens
Pimiento, olives, capers, green pepper

In large skillet, combine 1½ cups water, the onion, ¼ teaspoon hot pepper sauce and 1 teaspoon salt. Add fillets and bring to boil. Cover and simmer 6 to 10 minutes, or until fish flakes easily with fork. Remove fish from liquid and cool; flake fish as fine as possible, removing any bits of bone, and set aside. Strain stock and cool ¾ cup; sprinkle with gelatin, then add to hot stock and stir over medium heat until gelatin is dissolved. Stir in remaining salt, the grapefruit-juice concentrate and mayonnaise; beat with rotary beater until smooth. Chill until slightly thicker than consistency of unbeaten egg white. Stir in flaked fish and gently fold in whipped cream. Turn into oiled 5-cup mold and chill until firm. Unmold on salad greens and garnish with remaining ingredients. Serves 6 to 8.

JAPANESE SHRIMP-EGG SALAD

1/2 cup uncooked rice
1 tablespoon instant minced onion
1 cup well-seasoned French dressing
1/2 pound cleaned shelled shrimps, cooked
4 eggs, hard-cooked
Salad greens
3 sweet gherkins, chopped
2 tablespoons catsup
1 tablespoon capers

Cook and drain rice. Add onion, ½ cup dressing, shrimps and 2 eggs, diced. Mix lightly with fork and chill. Put on greens in bowl; sprinkle pickle around edge. Grate separately whites and yolks of remaining 2 eggs. Sprinkle whites next to pickle and put yolks in center. Serve with remaining dressing mixed with catsup and capers. Serves 4 to 6.

AVOCADO DRESSING

Peel 1 small avocado, remove pit and mash. Add 2 teaspoons lemon juice, 2 tablespoons mayonnaise and dash of hot pepper sauce; chill. Makes about ½ cup.

CLAM ASPIC SALAD

1 envelope unflavored gelatin
1 cup tomato juice
2 tablespoons lemon juice
1/2 teaspoon salt
1 can (10-1/2 ounces) minced clams
2 hard-cooked eggs, chopped
1 tablespoon chopped sweet pickle
2 tablespoons grated cucumber
1/2 cup diced celery
Salad greens

Soften gelatin in tomato juice; heat and stir until dissolved. Cool and add lemon juice and salt; chill until slightly thickened. Fold in next 5 ingredients. Chill until firm. Serve on salad greens. Makes 4 servings.

SEAFOOD ASPIC SALAD

1-3/4 cups tomato juice
1 envelope unflavored gelatin
1 teaspoon instant minced onion
1/2 bay leaf
2 tablespoons lemon juice
1/2 teaspoon Worcestershire
1 tablespoon horseradish
1/2 cup diced celery
2 pimientos, chopped
2 cups cooked shrimp, flaked crab meat
   or lobster (alone or in combination)
Salt and pepper
Shredded lettuce
Mayonnaise

Put tomato juice in saucepan and sprinkle with gelatin; add onion and bay leaf. Heat, stirring, until gelatin dissolves. Remove bay leaf and add next 6 ingredients. Season. Pour into 6 individual molds and chill until firm. Unmold on lettuce. Serve with mayonnaise. Makes 6 servings.

SEAFOOD MOUSSE SUPREME

2 envelopes unflavored gelatin
1/4 cup lemon juice
1 teaspoon instant minced onion
1/2 teaspoon salt
Dash of hot pepper sauce
2/3 cup ripe olives, sliced thin
1 cup heavy cream
3 tablespoons mayonnaise
3/4 cup diced celery
3/4 pound crab meat
Salad greens

Soften gelatin in 1/2 cup cold water, add 1 cup boiling water and stir until dissolved. Add next 4 ingredients. Chill until syrupy. Arrange ring of olive slices in bottom of 6 individual salad molds. Whip cream stiff. Fold with remaining olives, mayonnaise, celery and crab meat into gelatin. Spoon into molds and chill until firm. Unmold on salad greens. Makes 6 servings.

TOMATOES STUFFED WITH DILLED CUCUMBERS

Cut tops from 4 ripe medium tomatoes. Scoop out pulp and sprinkle inside with salt; turn upside down and drain. Peel and dice 1 large cucumber. Season with chopped fresh dill; moisten with French dressing and fill the tomatoes. Makes 4 servings.

GARDEN POTATO SALAD

Mix lightly 3 cups sliced cooked potato, 1 cup thinly sliced celery, 1 cup thinly sliced cucumber, 1/4 cup each diced red and green pepper and 1/2 cup thinly sliced green onions. Mix 1 tablespoon malt or tarragon vinegar and 1/4 cup salad oil; add salt and pepper to taste. Add to salad. Toss lightly and chill. Serves 4.

TEXAS POTATO SALAD

4 medium potatoes
1 can condensed consommé
1 clove garlic
3 tablespoons tarragon vinegar
2 tablespoons olive or vegetable oil
1 teaspoon salt
1/4 teaspoon pepper
Few sprigs of parsley, chopped
1 small onion, chopped
1/4 cup grated Parmesan cheese
Salad greens

Cook peeled potatoes in consommé with the garlic until potatoes are tender. Drain and discard garlic. (Liquid can be saved for soups or gravies.) Dice potatoes while still warm. Mix remaining ingredients, except greens, to make dressing. Layer potatoes and dressing in bowl. Cool, then cover. Chill several hours or overnight. Serve with greens. Serves 4.

HOT POTATO SALAD

2 slices bacon
1 onion, chopped
1 tablespoon flour
1/4 cup vinegar
1/2 teaspoon salt
1 teaspoon sugar
1/8 teaspoon pepper
3 tablespoons prepared mustard
5 cups sliced cooked potato
Chopped parsley

Mince bacon and fry until crisp; remove. Cook onion in bacon fat until lightly browned. Blend in flour; add bacon, vinegar, 1/2 cup water and seasonings; bring to boil. Add potato, mixing lightly; heat. Sprinkle with parsley; serve. Or cool, refrigerate and reheat before serving. Serves 4.

SALADE PARISIÈNNE

1 cup each cooked green beans, peas
  and cauliflower
3 raw carrots, shredded
1/2 cup sliced raw mushrooms
1/2 cup diced cooked chicken livers
1/2 cup diced cooked shrimp
1 teaspoon prepared mustard
1/3 cup olive oil
Salt and pepper
Vinegar
Dash of sugar
1 tablespoon heavy cream

Mix vegetables, chicken livers and
shrimp. Put mustard in small bowl
and gradually beat in oil. Season and
add vinegar to taste. Add sugar and
cream. Pour over first mixture and
toss well. Makes 4 servings.

BEAN AND CHICKPEA SALAD

1 package (9 ounces) cut Italian green
  beans, cooked and drained
1 can (15-1/2 ounces) red kidney beans,
  drained
1 can (20 ounces) chickpeas, drained
1/2 cup shredded carrot
2 green onions, thinly sliced
1/2 cup each thinly sliced green pepper
  and celery
2 tablespoons chopped parsley
2 pimientos, chopped
Garlic Dressing (below)

Combine all ingredients in bowl and
toss well. Chill several hours. Makes 8
servings.

GARLIC DRESSING

Mix well or shake in covered jar 1/4
cup wine vinegar, 1/2 cup salad oil, 1
crushed clove garlic and 1/2 teaspoon
each seasoned salt and pepper.

MEXICAN COLESLAW

Mix 4 cups finely shredded cabbage,
1 cup diced celery, 1 large green
pepper, thinly slivered, 2 canned
pimientos cut in strips, 1 teaspoon
sugar, 1/2 teaspoon salt, 1/2 cup
chopped salted peanuts and 1/2 cup
salad dressing or mayonnaise. Serves
4 to 6.

SPICY YOGURT DRESSING

Mix well 1 cup plain yogurt, 1 hard-
cooked egg, finely chopped, 1 tablespoon lemon juice, 1/4 teaspoon curry
powder or celery seed, 1/4 teaspoon
mustard and 1/2 teaspoon salt. Chill at
least 1/2 hour. Makes about 1¼ cups.

CURRY-RHINE DRESSING

Mix well 1/4 teaspoon dry mustard,
1/4 teaspoon garlic salt, 1/2 teaspoon
curry powder, 2 tablespoons lemon
juice, 2 tablespoons domestic Rhine
wine, 1/4 cup mayonnaise and 1 cup
dairy sour cream. Cover and refrigerate. Makes about 1½ cups.

SWEET-SOUR BEAN SALAD

1 cup cooked white kidney beans,
  drained
1 can (15-1/4 ounces) red kidney beans,
  drained
1 can (20 ounces) chickpeas, drained
2 green onions, thinly sliced
1/2 cup sliced celery
1/2 green pepper, thinly sliced (or part
  red pepper or pimiento)
1/3 cup salad oil
1/2 cup vinegar
3 tablespoons sugar
1/2 teaspoon salt
1/8 teaspoon pepper
Boston lettuce

Put vegetables in large bowl. Combine remaining ingredients, pour over
vegetables and mix gently. Chill several hours or overnight. Serve on Boston lettuce. Makes 6 to 8 servings.

LENTIL SALAD

1/2 pound dried quick-cooking lentils
2 teaspoons salt
1/2 cup chopped parsley
1/2 cup minced green onion
1 clove garlic, minced
1/3 cup bottled French dressing
Salad greens
Sliced hard-cooked eggs

In large saucepan, cover washed lentils with 3 cups water and add salt.
Bring slowly to boil and simmer 30
minutes, or until tender. Drain and
chill. Add remaining ingredients, except last 2. Serve on crisp greens with
a garnish of egg slices. Serves 4 to 6.

PIQUANT MACARONI SALAD

8 ounces elbow macaroni
1/4 cup chopped green onion
1/2 cup sliced radishes
1/2 cup chopped green pepper
1/2 cup sliced celery
1/2 cup mayonnaise
1-1/2 tablespoons spicy brown mustard
1-1/2 teaspoons prepared horseradish
1 teaspoon salt
1/8 teaspoon pepper

Cook macaroni, drain and rinse in
cold water; drain again. Put in bowl
with vegetables. Mix remaining ingredients and add; toss and chill.
Makes 4 to 6 servings.

DILLY CABBAGE

3 cups shredded cabbage
1 teaspoon salt
1 turnip, shredded
1 small carrot, shredded
1 green pepper, finely diced
1/4 teaspoon dillseed
Mayonnaise-Sour-cream Dressing

Cover cabbage with salt and let stand 45 minutes. Squeeze free of water. Mix with vegetables and dillseed; add dressing to moisten. Makes 4 to 6 servings. **Mayonnaise-Sour-cream Dressing** Mix well juice of 1 lemon, 1/4 cup dairy sour cream, 1/2 cup mayonnaise, 1/4 teaspoon pepper, 1 tablespoon sugar, a pinch of thyme and a dash of paprika.

CUCUMBER-GRAPE SALAD, NEAR EAST STYLE

1 cucumber, peeled and sliced
3 cups red, purple or green grapes, halved and seeded if necessary
4 cups torn or shredded lettuce
1 tablespoon lemon juice
1 tablespoon olive oil
2 teaspoons finely chopped fresh mint or 1/2 teaspoon dried mint leaves
1 tablespoon chopped fresh dill or 1/4 teaspoon dillweed
3/4 teaspoon seasoned salt
1 cup plain yogurt or dairy sour cream

Arrange cucumber and grapes on lettuce in salad bowl. Mix next 5 ingredients. Stir into yogurt and spoon over salad. Makes 6 servings. **Note** Watercress or young spinach leaves can be substituted for the lettuce.

SWEET-SOUR CABBAGE RELISH

1 medium head cabbage, about 2 pounds
1-1/2 teaspoons (or less to taste) crushed hot red pepper
1/2 cup packed light-brown sugar
1/3 cup vinegar
2 tablespoons soy sauce
2 teaspoons salt
3 tablespoons vegetable oil

Cut cabbage in chunks, discarding core and tough outer leaves. Separate inner leaves. Mix remaining ingredients, except oil, in bowl and set aside. Heat oil in kettle over medium heat. Add cabbage and heat, stirring, until small leaves become translucent. Remove from heat and stir in seasoning mixture. Pour cabbage and liquid into large bowl. Bank around edge of bowl, leaving a well in center, so that cabbage will cool evenly. Stir occasionally while cooling and again bank around edge. When thoroughly cold, refrigerate. Makes 4 to 6 servings.

CUCUMBERS IN SOUR CREAM

2 medium cucumbers, peeled
1 medium onion, thinly sliced
1-1/4 teaspoons salt
1 cup dairy sour cream
2 tablespoons vinegar
1/4 teaspoon sugar
1/8 teaspoon paprika
1 tablespoon parsley flakes

Draw tines of fork lengthwise down cucumbers, then cut in thin slices. Add onion and sprinkle with 1 teaspoon salt. Let stand 10 minutes, then press out excess liquid. Mix sour cream, remaining 1/4 salt and other ingredients. Add to cucumbers, mixing lightly with fork. Chill thoroughly. Makes about 2 cups.

COCONUT COLESLAW

1/2 cup dairy sour cream
1/2 cup mayonnaise
1 teaspoon lemon juice
1 teaspoon salt
1/4 teaspoon paprika
1/4 teaspoon curry powder
1 cup grated fresh coconut or packaged grated (cookie) coconut
4 cups shredded cabbage
2 tablespoons minced green onion

Mix together first 6 ingredients. Stir in coconut and let stand 1/2 hour or longer. Just before serving, add cabbage and green onion and mix thoroughly. Makes 4 servings.

CUCUMBER SALAD WITH CHICKEN SHREDS

In China, sesame-seed paste is used instead of peanut butter. The sesame seeds are browned before grinding into paste. The Syrian sesame-seed paste, or tahini, available in America, is made without browning the seed. Chinese here prefer to use peanut butter, but you can use tahini if you wish. Omit oil.

2 medium narrow cucumbers
1/4 cup smooth peanut butter
1/2 cup slivered cooked chicken
1/2 teaspoon salt
1/4 teaspoon monosodium glutamate
1 tablespoon sesame oil

Peel cucumbers, leaving some green underskin. Split lengthwise and hollow out, discarding seeds. Cut diagonally in 1/4" slices (you should have about 3 cups). In small bowl, gradually add 1/4 cup cold water to peanut butter, mixing to a smooth paste. Add remaining ingredients and set aside. When ready to serve, add cucumbers and mix together lightly. Makes 2 or 3 servings.

SOUR-CREAM POTATO SALAD

1 quart diced cooked potato
1/2 cup minced mild onion
1 tablespoon chopped chives
1/2 cup diced celery
1/2 cup diced cucumber
1/2 cup thinly sliced radishes
4 hard-cooked eggs
1/2 cup mayonnaise
2 cups dairy sour cream
1 teaspoon salt
Dash of garlic salt
Dash of cayenne
1/4 teaspoon black pepper
1 teaspoon hot prepared mustard
3 tablespoons vinegar
Lettuce

Mix potato with next 5 vegetables. Dice whites of 3 eggs and add to vegetables. Mash the 3 yolks and blend with remaining ingredients, except remaining egg and the lettuce. Mix with vegetables. Chill several hours. Serve on lettuce and garnish with remaining egg, sliced. Makes 6 to 8 servings.

CALIFORNIA CHEF'S SALAD

1/2 head each lettuce and romaine
1/2 bunch watercress
1 small bunch chicory
2 tomatoes, peeled, seeded and diced
2 cooked chicken breasts, diced
6 strips crisp bacon, crumbled
1 avocado, diced
3 hard-cooked eggs, diced
2 tablespoons chopped chives
1/2 cup finely crumbled Roquefort
3/4 cup Italian-type dressing

Cut greens in small pieces into large salad bowl. Add remaining ingredients and toss well. Makes 8 servings.

RANCHO SALAD

1 can (1 pound) kidney beans
1 can (19 ounces) white beans or
    cannellini beans
1 can (1 pound) chick-peas
2 onions, coarsely chopped
2 green onions, coarsely chopped
3 pimientos, chopped
3 stalks celery, chopped
12 to 18 stuffed olives, sliced
1/3 cup chopped parsley
2 canned green chilies, chopped
Dressing
Greens and sliced tomatoes

Drain beans and chick-peas. Combine all ingredients, except greens and tomatoes; toss with the Dressing. Refrigerate salad to mellow for an hour or two. Serve on greens with a garnish of sliced tomatoes. Makes 6 to 8 servings. **Dressing** Mix 2 cloves garlic, 1 teaspoon salt, 3 to 4 tablespoons vinegar and 1 teaspoon freshly ground black pepper.

SALAD MUSETTA

A luxurious Continental salad, ideal for a buffet.

1-1/2 cups diced cooked potato
1 celery heart, diced
1 fennel heart, diced
1/4 cup diced Swiss cheese
1 heart of chicory, cut in pieces
6 artichoke hearts in oil, halved
6 mushrooms in oil, sliced
1 tablespoon capers
2 hard-cooked eggs, chopped
1/2 teaspoon salt
Freshly ground pepper
2 tablespoons wine vinegar
1 tablespoon mayonnaise
1/2 cup olive or other salad oil
Romaine

Combine first 9 ingredients and season lightly with the salt and pepper. Gradually blend vinegar into mayonnaise, then stir in olive oil. Pour over salad and toss lightly. Mound in a glass bowl rimmed with spears of romaine. Makes 4 to 6 servings.

MIAMI CHEF'S SALAD

1/2 bunch watercress
1/2 head each lettuce and romaine
1-1/2 cups orange sections
1 cup diced unpeeled apple
1-1/2 cups slivered cooked chicken
1/2 cup diced sharp Cheddar cheese
2/3 cup French Dressing, page 286

Tear salad greens into bite-size pieces. Add remaining ingredients and toss lightly. Makes 4 to 6 servings.

HERBED SLICED BABY TOMATOES

Drain 1 can (14½ ounces) sliced baby tomatoes, reserving juice for later use. Put tomatoes in small bowl. Mix 1 tablespoon olive oil and 3 tablespoons wine vinegar. Season with monosodium glutamate, seasoned salt and pepper. Pour over tomatoes and chill. Sprinkle with chopped fresh dill, marjoram, parsley, thyme, basil or other preferred fresh herb. Serve on lettuce, if desired. Makes 2 or 3 servings.

TOMATOES, FINES HERBES

Slice firm ripe plum tomatoes very thin, from the blossom end down. Layer in a large bowl, sprinkling each layer with minced parsley; finely chopped shallots or the white part of green onions; a bit of basil or oregano; salt; cracked or fresh ground black pepper; tarragon vinegar and olive oil. Chill 2 hours, then drain and heap in crisp lettuce cups.

ALSATIAN POTATO SALAD

4 to 6 potatoes
2 cups white wine
1 onion, minced
1 tablespoon white-wine vinegar
Salt and pepper
Olive or vegetable oil
Chopped parsley and fresh dill

Peel, cook and drain potatoes. While still warm, cut in thin slices into bowl. Cover with wine. Let stand a few minutes, then pour off excess wine. Add onion and vinegar to potatoes; season. Add 2 or 3 tablespoons oil and a generous amount of chopped parsley and dill. Mix lightly and serve warm or cool. (Do not chill.) Makes 4 to 6 servings.

VICHYSSOISE MOUSSE

1 envelope unflavored gelatin
1 can (12 to 14 ounces) vichyssoise
3 to 4 teaspoons horseradish
1/2 cup dairy sour cream
1 can (12 ounces) tongue, diced
1 pimiento, chopped
2 tablespoons chopped parsley
Watercress

Soften gelatin in ¼ cup water. Dissolve over hot water. Add remaining ingredients, except cress. Turn into oiled 1-quart mold. Chill until firm. Unmold on watercress. Serves 4.

CHEESE-POTATO SALAD

10 to 12 small potatoes (about 2 pounds)
Salt
6 tablespoons oil-vinegar dressing or bottled light Italian-type dressing
2 cups (1/2 pound) Swiss cheese, diced
3/4 cup diced celery
3 tablespoons minced green onion
3 tablespoons minced parsley
4 eggs, hard-cooked
1/2 cup mayonnaise
1/2 teaspoon dry mustard
Wine vinegar, if needed
Freshly ground pepper

Cook potatoes in salted boiling water until just tender but still firm. Peel while warm and cut in halves or quarters. Sprinkle with 4 tablespoons dressing. Cool and combine with next 3 ingredients, 2 tablespoons parsley and 3 eggs, chopped. Mix remaining 2 tablespoons dressing with mayonnaise and mustard and thin with a little wine vinegar if necessary. Pour over salad, mix lightly, season with pepper to taste and chill. When ready to serve, chop remaining egg fine, mix with remaining 1 tablespoon parsley and sprinkle on salad. Serves 6.

HOT MASHED-POTATO SALAD

3/4 cup mayonnaise-pickle sandwich spread
1 teaspoon salt
1/4 teaspoon pepper
1 envelope (5 servings) instant mashed potatoes
3 green onions, finely sliced
1/4 cup chopped green pepper
3/4 cup finely chopped celery
1 teaspoon prepared mustard
1 jar (2 ounces) chopped pimiento, drained
2 eggs, hard-cooked and chopped

Bring 1½ cups water to boil. Add sandwich spread, salt and pepper. Gradually add potatoes, beating with fork until well mixed. Mix in remaining ingredients, except last two. Then fold in pimiento and eggs. Serve hot. Good with frankfurters. Makes 6 servings.

MUSHROOM-RICE SALAD

1/2 pound mushrooms, sliced
2 cups cooked rice, chilled
1 cup diced tomatoes
1/2 cup chopped red onion
1/2 cup chopped green pepper
1/2 cup mayonnaise
1 tablespoon lemon juice
1/2 teaspoon salt
1/4 teaspoon hot pepper sauce
Lettuce leaves
Few sprigs of parsley, chopped

Combine first 5 ingredients in bowl. Mix mayonnaise with next 3 ingredients and add to bowl. Toss gently. Line salad bowl with lettuce and fill with salad. Sprinkle with parsley. Serve at once or chill 30 minutes. Makes 6 servings.

PINK LADY MOUSSE

1 envelope unflavored gelatin
1 can (10-3/4 ounces) condensed tomato soup
3 whole cloves
Rind of 1 lemon, in strips
1/2 teaspoon instant onion
1 teaspoon Worcestershire
1 cup cottage cheese, sieved
1 cup sour cream
1/2 cup mayonnaise
Salt, pepper and celery salt
Salad greens

Soften gelatin in ¼ cup cold water. Heat next 3 ingredients to a boil; remove cloves and lemon. Pour soup over gelatin, stirring to dissolve; cool. Beat in remaining ingredients, except greens. Pour into oiled 1½-quart mold; chill until firm. Unmold on greens. Makes 6 servings.

FATHER'S FAVORITE SALAD

1 cup elbow macaroni
2 cups (1/2 pound) Swiss or sharp
    Cheddar cheese, cubed
1 cup diced celery
1/4 cup chopped walnuts
1 cup mayonnaise
1/2 teaspoon dry mustard
1/2 teaspoon Worcestershire
Salt and pepper
Lettuce
Sliced cucumbers

Cook macaroni according to package directions. Cool and mix with remaining ingredients, except last 2. Chill 1 hour. Serve on lettuce and garnish with cucumber slices. Serves 4.

MACARONI-AND-CHEESE SALAD

2 cups small seashell macaroni
1 pound cottage cheese
1/3 cup chopped green pepper
1/2 cup chopped chives or green onion
1/2 cup sliced radishes
1/3 cup Creamy French Dressing,
    page 208
1 cup dairy sour cream
2 tablespoons lemon juice
1/4 teaspoon dry mustard
Seasoned salt and pepper

Cook and drain macaroni according to package directions. Rinse with cold water and drain well. Add next 5 ingredients and mix well; chill. Just before serving, fold in next 3 ingredients. Season to taste. Serves 6.

TOMATO ASPIC
WITH VEGETABLES

1 package (3 ounces) lemon-flavor
    gelatin dessert
2 cups hot tomato juice or hot strained
    tomatoes
2 teaspoons horseradish
2 teaspoons instant minced onion
1-1/4 teaspoons salt
Dash of cayenne
1/2 cup each cooked green beans and
    peas
1/2 cup each diced celery and radishes
    or cucumbers
1/4 cup French dressing
Crisp lettuce or other greens
Mayonnaise or other salad dressing

Dissolve gelatin in tomato juice. Add horseradish, 1 teaspoon onion, 1 teaspoon salt and the cayenne. Turn into 4 individual ring molds or 2-cup mold. Chill until firm. Mix vegetables, remaining onion, 1/4 teaspoon salt and French dressing together. Unmold aspic on lettuce. Surround with vegetables and fill centers of molds with mayonnaise. Makes 4 servings.

TWO-CHEESE RING MOLD

1 envelope unflavored gelatin
1 cup cottage cheese, mashed
1/2 cup crumbled blue cheese
1/2 teaspoon salt
2/3 cup undiluted evaporated milk
Salad greens

Soften gelatin in 1/3 cup water. Heat gently, stirring, until dissolved. Mix with remaining ingredients, except greens. Pour into 1-quart ring mold and chill until firm. Unmold on greens. Good with chicken, meat or fish salad piled in center. Makes 4 servings.

COTTAGE-CHEESE AND
VEGETABLE SALAD BOWL

1 pound cottage cheese
1 pint dairy sour cream
1 tablespoon tarragon vinegar
2 teaspoons instant minced onion
1 teaspoon sugar
1 teaspoon salt
1/4 teaspoon white pepper
1/8 teaspoon paprika
1 cup cooked mixed vegetables
Salad greens

Lightly mix all ingredients, except greens. Line bowl with greens and fill with the mixture. Serves 6.

BLUE-CHEESE AND
ORANGE SALAD

1 small head romaine
2 oranges, peeled and sliced 1/2" thick
1/2 cup sliced pitted black olives
1 wedge (3 ounces) blue cheese,
    crumbled
2 tablespoons lemon juice
6 tablespoons olive oil
Salt and pepper to taste

Wash romaine, separate leaves and dry. Break larger leaves in pieces and leave small leaves whole. Place in large bowl with next 3 ingredients. Mix remaining ingredients, pour over mixture in bowl and toss. Serve at once. Makes 6 to 8 servings.

SWISS CHEESE SALAD

1/2 pound Swiss cheese, in 1/2" cubes
6 hard-cooked eggs, chopped
3/4 cup dairy sour cream
1-1/2 teaspoons Dijon mustard
1/2 teaspoon dry mustard
1 teaspoon horseradish
Salt and pepper to taste
1 teaspoon grated lemon rind
1 teaspoon caraway seeds
Greens

Combine all ingredients, except greens. Arrange on a bed of greens. Makes 4 servings.

PINEAPPLE CHEESE MOLD

2 boxes (3 ounces each) lime-flavor
   gelatin
1 can (9 ounces) crushed pineapple,
   undrained
2 tablespoons prepared horseradish
2/3 cup undiluted evaporated milk
1 cup mayonnaise
1 cup creamed cottage cheese
Salad greens

Dissolve gelatin in 2 cups boiling water; cool. Add next 4 ingredients. Chill until slightly thickened. Fold in cottage cheese. Turn into 1½-quart mold. Chill until firm. Unmold on salad greens. Makes 8 servings.

FROZEN ROQUEFORT SALAD

1/4 pound Roquefort cheese, finely
   crumbled
1 package (3 ounces) cream cheese,
   softened
1 teaspoon vinegar
1 tablespoon chopped chives
1/4 teaspoon each paprika, salt and
   Worcestershire
Dash of cayenne
3/4 cup heavy cream, whipped
1/2 pimiento, chopped
Salad greens

Mix well all ingredients, except last 3. Fold in cream and pimiento. Pour into a refrigerator tray and freeze until firm. Cut in squares and arrange on salad greens. Serves 6.

FRUIT-COCKTAIL SALAD LOAF

Serve with crisp crackers and iced tea for a cool lunch.

1 envelope unflavored gelatin
1 can (29 ounces) fruit cocktail
1 package (3 ounces) cream cheese,
   softened
1 cup mayonnaise
1 box cherry-, black-cherry-, or
   raspberry-flavor gelatin
Salad greens

Soften unflavored gelatin in ¼ cup cold water. Drain fruit, reserving syrup. Heat ¾ cup syrup and add gelatin; stir until dissolved. Cool. Beat cheese until fluffy; blend in mayonnaise. Gradually beat in gelatin mixture. Dissolve cherry gelatin in 1 cup boiling water. Add 1 cup cold water or syrup. Chill until slightly thickened. Put half of fruit in 9" x 5" x 3" loaf pan, add 1 cup cherry gelatin and chill until firm. Pour in cheese mixture on top, chill until set. Top with remaining fruit and cherry gelatin. Chill several hours, or until firm. Unmold on greens and slice to serve. Makes 8 servings.

GARDEN LETTUCE WITH BACON DRESSING

Cook 4 slices bacon until crisp and brown; crumble. Add 2 tablespoons vinegar, 2 teaspoons sugar, 1 teaspoon salt and ¼ teaspoon pepper to fat in skillet; bring to boil. Tear 1½ quarts garden lettuce in small pieces into large bowl. Add hot dressing and toss. Serves 4.

CREAMY CABBAGE SLAW

1/4 cup sugar
1/4 cup French dressing
1/2 teaspoon salt
Dash each of pepper and cayenne
1/4 cup undiluted evaporated milk
5 cups shredded cabbage (1 medium
   head)
1/4 teaspoon poppy seed
1/4 cup chopped walnuts

Combine first 5 ingredients with 2 tablespoons water and mix well. Sprinkle cabbage with the poppy seed and toss with first mixture. Garnish with walnuts. Makes 6 servings. *Note* Peanuts can be substituted for the walnuts. If red cabbage is used, omit poppy seed.

GERMAN SPINACH SALAD

1 pound small fresh spinach leaves
1/2 cup mayonnaise
1/2 cup dairy sour cream
6 anchovies, minced
1-1/2 tablespoons chopped green-onion
   tops
1-1/2 tablespoons minced parsley
1-1/2 tablespoons vinegar
1-1/2 tablespoons lemon juice
1/2 clove garlic, minced
Cheddar-cheese cubes or garlic croutons

Wash and dry spinach. Mix with remaining ingredients, except cheese. Garnish with cheese or croutons. Makes 4 servings.

HOT STUFFED-TOMATO SALAD

6 large tomatoes
1-1/2 cups diced cooked turkey
1/2 cup sliced black olives
1/2 cup mayonnaise
1-1/2 teaspoons steak sauce
1 cup cooked whole-kernel corn
Salt to taste
2 tablespoons butter or margarine

Cut off tops of tomatoes and scoop out pulp, reserving for other use. Turn tomatoes upside down to drain. Mix remaining ingredients, except butter. Spoon into tomatoes and dot with butter. Put about 8" under broiler and broil until lightly browned on top. Makes 6 servings.

ITALIAN RAW-MUSHROOM SALAD

1/2 pound mushrooms
1/4 teaspoon each salt and pepper
1/2 teaspoon oregano
3 tablespoons lemon juice
1/2 cup olive oil

Cut stem ends from mushrooms and reserve for other use. Wipe caps with damp paper towel and slice evenly. Mix remaining ingredients, add mushrooms and toss. Let stand at room temperature about 2 hours. Makes 3 cups. *Note* Store any leftovers, covered, in refrigerator.

CRANBERRY-APPLE SALAD

1 cup cranberries
2 seedless oranges (leave 1 unpeeled)
2 apples, cored but unpeeled
About 1 cup sugar
1 box raspberry-flavor gelatin dessert
Salad greens

Force cranberries, oranges and apples through food chopper; save juice. Mix with the sugar and let stand 1 hour. Dissolve gelatin in 1 cup very hot water. Chill until slightly thickened. Add fruit mixture and juice. Pour into 8" square pan or gelatin mold and chill until firm. Cut in squares, or unmold. Serve with greens. Makes 6 to 8 servings.

PEAR SALAD WITH STRAWBERRY CREAM CHEESE

1 package (3 ounces) cream cheese, softened
1/4 teaspoon salt
1 tablespoon sugar
Dash of cayenne
1/2 cup sliced fresh strawberries
8 fresh or canned pear halves
Salad greens

Mash cheese and whip until smooth. Add next 3 ingredients. Fold in berries. Fill centers of pear halves and arrange on greens, allowing 2 halves for each plate. Makes 4 servings.

PEANUT-BUTTER WALDORF SALAD

Blend 2 tablespoons mayonnaise into 1/4 cup peanut butter; then blend mixture into 1/2 cup mayonnaise. Core and dice 5 medium unpeeled red apples. Toss with a dash of salt, 1 tablespoon lemon juice, 1 cup diced celery and 1/2 cup nuts. Add dressing and mix well. Serve on greens. Makes 6 servings.

FRUIT SALAD, AD-LIB

Try your own combinations of gelatin and frozen fruit.

Dissolve 1 box (3 ounces) blackberry- or mixed-fruit-flavor gelatin in 1 cup boiling water; add 1 box (12 ounces) frozen mixed fruits, a dash of salt and 1 tablespoon lemon juice. Stir until fruit thaws. Pour into 1 large mold or 4 individual ones and chill until firm. Makes 4 servings.

FROZEN FRUIT SALAD

1 envelope unflavored gelatin
1/4 teaspoon each salt and ginger
Juice of 1 lemon
1/4 cup honey
1/2 cup drained crushed pineapple
1 cup drained canned sliced peaches
1 cup drained canned pears, diced
1 cup sliced fresh strawberries
1 cup heavy cream, whipped
2/3 cup mayonnaise
Salad greens
Whole strawberries
Watercress or mint

Soften gelatin in 1⅓ cups syrup drained from canned fruits; heat and stir to dissolve. Add salt and ginger and next 6 ingredients. Chill until slightly thickened. Fold in cream mixed with mayonnaise. Pour into two 1-quart refrigerator trays and freeze until firm. To serve, cut each tray in 8 slices. Arrange 2 slices per serving on greens and garnish with whole strawberries and watercress or mint. Makes 8 servings.

AVOCADO RING WITH STRAWBERRIES

2 boxes (3 ounces each) lime- or lemon-flavor gelatin
1/2 teaspoon salt
2 very ripe avocados
2 tablespoons lemon juice
1/3 cup mayonnaise
3 cups fresh strawberries
Salad greens
Honey Cream Dressing

Dissolve gelatin and salt in 2 cups very hot water. Add 1½ cups cold water and chill until slightly thickened. Peel, pit and mash avocados; toss with lemon juice and mayonnaise. Add gelatin, blending well. Pour into 5-cup ring mold and chill until firm. Wash and hull berries; slice. Unmold ring on greens and fill with 2½ cups berries. Serve with dressing. Makes 6 to 8 servings.
Honey Cream Dressing Mix 1/2 cup each dairy sour cream and mayonnaise, 1 tablespoon honey and 1/2 cup sliced berries.

PEAR DE MENTHE SALAD

1 can (30 ounces) pear halves
1 can (8-3/4 ounces) seedless grapes,
    cut in halves
2 envelopes unflavored gelatin
1 tablespoon honey
Dash of salt
1/4 cup orange and lemon juice
1/4 cup green crème de menthe
1 cup dairy sour cream
1/4 cup toasted slivered almonds
Salad greens

Drain pears and grapes, reserving syrup. Set aside 6 pear halves. Dice remaining pears and mix with grapes. Soften gelatin in syrup drained from fruits; heat and stir until dissolved. Add honey and salt. Cool. Beat in juices, crème de menthe and sour cream. Chill. When partially set, fold in prepared fruit and almonds. Pour into oiled 1½-quart mold and chill until firm. Unmold on greens and encircle with pear halves, cut side up. Makes 6 servings.

GINGER-FRUIT SALAD WITH SHERRY DRESSING

1 box (3 ounces) cherry-flavor gelatin
1 cup ginger ale
1/4 cup finely chopped celery
1/4 cup finely chopped almonds
1 cup diced fresh fruit (bananas, peaches,
    plums or melon)
1 tablespoon minced crystallized ginger
Salad greens
Sherry Dressing (page 285)

Dissolve gelatin in 1 cup boiling water. Cool, add ginger ale and chill until thickened. Fold in remaining ingredients except greens and dressing. Pour into oiled 1-quart mold or 6 individual molds and chill until firm. Unmold on greens and serve with dressing. Makes 6 servings.

CRANBERRY SALAD, ORIENTAL STYLE

1 box (3 ounces) orange-flavor gelatin
1 tablespoon lemon juice
1 jar (14 ounces) cranberry-orange relish
2 tablespoons chopped crystallized ginger
1 can (5 ounces) water chestnuts, drained
    and chopped
1/2 teaspoon celery seed
1/4 cup dairy sour cream
1/4 cup mayonnaise

Dissolve gelatin in 1 cup boiling water. Add ½ cup cold water and lemon juice. Chill until slightly thickened. Fold in next 4 ingredients, pour into oiled 1-quart mold and chill until firm. Unmold and serve with a dressing of sour cream combined with mayonnaise. Makes 6 servings.

SEAFOAM SALAD

1 can (1 pound 14 ounces) pear halves
1 box (3 ounces) lime-flavor gelatin
6 ounces cream cheese
2 tablespoons milk
1/2 cup heavy cream, whipped
Salad greens

Drain pears, reserving 1 cup syrup. Heat syrup, pour over gelatin and stir until gelatin is dissolved. Beat cheese with milk until smooth and blended. Gradually beat in hot gelatin. Chill until slightly thickened. Mash pears with fork or potato masher. Fold into gelatin with cream. Turn into 1½-quart mold and chill until firm. Unmold on greens. Makes 8 servings.

FAVORITE FRUIT-SALAD DRESSING

1/2 cup honey
1/2 teaspoon ground cardamom
1 teaspoon crushed fresh or dried mint
    leaves
1 teaspoon grated lemon rind
1/4 cup lemon juice
1/8 teaspoon salt
1/4 cup salad or vegetable oil

Combine honey, ½ cup water and cardamom. Bring to boil and simmer about 3 minutes. Add mint, chill and strain. Add remaining ingredients; mix well to blend. Chill. Makes 1 cup.

FROZEN STRAWBERRY DESSERT SALAD

1 envelope unflavored gelatin
1 can (13-1/4 ounces) pineapple tidbits,
    undrained
1 tablespoon lemon juice
1/8 teaspoon each salt and ground ginger
2 tablespoons honey
1 pint strawberries, sliced
1/2 cup heavy cream, whipped
1/2 cup mayonnaise
Salad greens
Whole strawberries
Watercress (optional)

Soften gelatin in ¼ cup water and dissolve over hot water. Add pineapple and syrup, lemon juice, salt, ginger and honey and mix well. Add sliced strawberries and chill until slightly thickened. Mix cream and mayonnaise and fold into fruit mixture. Pour into oiled 9" x 5" x 3" loaf pan (pan will be about half full) and freeze until firm. Turn out on board and slice in 8 to 10 slices. For each serving, put 2 slices on greens. Garnish with whole strawberries, and watercress, if desired. If salad is frozen solid, let stand at room temperature about ½ hour after slicing. Makes 4 or 5 servings.

PINK CREAM DRESSING

Mix ¼ cup currant jelly, 1 package (3 ounces) cream cheese, softened, 1 teaspoon lemon juice and ½ teaspoon grated lemon rind. If necessary, thin with a little milk. Chill. Makes about ¾ cup.

SOUR-CREAM COOKED SALAD DRESSING

1/4 cup sugar
1 tablespoon flour
1/2 teaspoon salt
1/4 teaspoon dry mustard
Dash each of cayenne and white pepper
2 eggs, beaten
1/2 cup dairy sour cream
3 tablespoons wine vinegar

Mix sugar, flour and seasonings in top part of small double boiler. Add remaining ingredients, put over simmering water and cook, stirring, until thickened. Cool; then chill. Makes 1 cup. *Note* For a fluffy dressing for fruit or gelatin salads, fold in ½ cup heavy cream or dairy sour cream, whipped. Makes 1½ to 1¾ cups dressing.

COOKED SALAD DRESSING

For cabbage, potato or lettuce salad.

1/2 cup sugar
1 teaspoon salt
1 teaspoon celery seed
2 teaspoons dry mustard
2 tablespoons cornstarch
1/2 cup vinegar
1 egg
Undiluted evaporated milk

In top part of double boiler, mix dry ingredients. Stir in 1 cup water and the vinegar; cook over boiling water until thickened, stirring. Remove from heat and cool. Break egg into measuring cup. Add enough milk to make 1 cup. Beat with fork to break up egg yolk. Add to first mixture and beat with rotary beater until blended. Keep refrigerated.

SHERRY DRESSING

Good on fruit salads.

In top part of double boiler beat 1 egg, ¼ cup each sugar and sherry, a dash of salt, 2 teaspoons butter, juice of ½ orange and ½ lemon. Cook over boiling water until slightly thickened, stirring. Cool and chill. Just before serving, fold in ¼ cup heavy cream, whipped, or ½ cup whipped topping. Makes 1 cup.

ROQUEFORT CREAM DRESSING

Mix 1 cup dairy sour cream, 1 teaspoon lemon juice and 2 tablespoons finely crumbled Roquefort cheese; chill. Makes about 1 cup.

QUICK VINAIGRETTE DRESSING

Crush 1 clove garlic with ¾ teaspoon salt, 1 teaspoon Dijon-type mustard, 1 tablespoon minced parsley and a little fresh or dried tarragon, if desired. Put in jar with 3 tablespoons wine vinegar, plenty of freshly ground pepper and ½ cup olive oil. Cover and shake until well blended. Makes about ¾ cup.

SESAME-SEED DRESSING

Good on lettuce or fruit salad.

1/4 cup toasted sesame seed
1/2 cup sugar
1/2 teaspoon dry mustard
3/4 teaspoon each paprika and salt
Dash of hot pepper sauce
1/2 teaspoon Worcestershire
1 tablespoon instant minced onion
1 cup salad oil
2/3 cup vinegar

Combine all ingredients and whirl in blender or beat until well mixed. Keep refrigerated. Makes about 2 cups.

HONEY-LIME DRESSING

Delicious on fruit salad.

Put 1 can (6 ounces) frozen limeade concentrate, ¾ cup salad oil, ½ cup honey and ¼ teaspoon salt in electric blender and whirl a few seconds. (If blender is not available, beat or shake to mix.) Stir in 2 teaspoons celery seed. Makes 2 cups.

CHUTNEY SALAD DRESSING

Especially good on fruit salad.

1 cup salad oil
1/3 cup vinegar
1-1/2 teaspoons salt
Dash of pepper
1/4 teaspoon paprika
3/4 teaspoon sugar
1 clove garlic
2 tablespoons catsup
1 tablespoon lemon juice
1-1/2 teaspoons Worcestershire
1/4 cup chopped chutney

Measure all ingredients into a jar. Cover tightly and shake well. Chill several hours, then remove garlic. Makes 1¾ cups.

CREAMY FRENCH DRESSING

Into chilled container of electric blender (or bowl) put ³⁄₄ cup olive or salad oil, ¹⁄₃ cup vinegar, 1 egg yolk, 1¹⁄₂ teaspoons seasoned salt, ¹⁄₄ teaspoon pepper, 1 teaspoon paprika and ¹⁄₂ teaspoon sugar. Blend or beat with rotary beater until thick and smooth. Makes 1¹⁄₄ cups.

TOMATO FRENCH DRESSING

1 can (8 ounces) tomato sauce
1/2 cup salad oil
1/3 cup vinegar
2 tablespoons sugar
1 teaspoon dry mustard
1 teaspoon salt
1 teaspoon Worcestershire or steak sauce
Dash of hot pepper sauce
1 clove garlic

Put all ingredients in 1-pint jar. Cover tightly and shake until ingredients are blended. Chill several hours. Shake again before serving. Makes 1³⁄₄ cups.

FRENCH DRESSING

1/4 cup each lemon juice and vinegar
1-1/2 cups olive or other salad oil
1 teaspoon seasoned salt
1/2 teaspoon steak sauce
  or Worcestershire
1/4 teaspoon garlic powder
1/2 teaspoon sugar
1/2 teaspoon paprika

Mix all ingredients in 1-quart glass jar, cover tightly and shake until well blended. Refrigerate. Makes 2 cups.

Chiffonade Dressing Mix well ³⁄₄ cup French Dressing, 1 tablespoon minced parsley, 2 tablespoons each chopped pimiento and green pepper, 1 teaspoon instant minced onion, 1 finely crumbled hard-cooked egg and 1 tablespoon chopped cooked beet (optional). Make 1³⁄₄ cups.

Herb Dressing To ³⁄₄ cup French Dressing, add 2 teaspoons chopped fresh dill, marjoram, rosemary, summer savory or other herbs. Good on greens, seafood or meat.

Vinaigrette Dressing To ³⁄₄ cup French Dressing, add 1 chopped hard-cooked egg and 1 teaspoon chopped chives. Good on vegetables or greens.

Deluxe French Dressing To French Dressing recipe, add several split cloves garlic, ¹⁄₃ cup chili sauce, 1 tablespoon horseradish and 1 teaspoon paprika.

MAYONNAISE

2 egg yolks or 1 whole egg
1 teaspoon sugar
1 teaspoon dry mustard
1 teaspoon salt
2 tablespoons vinegar
2 cups olive oil
2 tablespoons lemon juice

Put egg yolks and seasonings in small deep bowl. Beat with rotary beater or electric mixer until blended. Add vinegar very slowly, beating constantly. Add 1 cup oil, 1 tablespoon at a time, beating constantly. Add lemon juice and remaining 1 cup oil, 1 tablespoon at a time. Refrigerate. Makes 2 cups.

Russian Dressing To ¹⁄₂ cup Mayonnaise add ¹⁄₄ cup chili sauce and 2 tablespoons pickle relish. Good on greens, meat or eggs.

Sharp-Cheddar Dressing Finely shred ¹⁄₂ pound sharp Cheddar cheese; soften at room temperature. Add 1 cup Mayonnaise, 2 tablespoons vinegar, 1 minced clove garlic, ¹⁄₂ teaspoon salt, a dash of cayenne and 2 teaspoons Worcestershire. Beat until blended. Makes about 2 cups. Good on fruit, vegetable, macaroni or potato salad.

Thousand Island Dressing Mix 1 cup Mayonnaise, ¹⁄₂ cup chili sauce, 2 tablespoons minced green pepper, 3 tablespoons chopped stuffed olives, 1 minced pimiento and 1 teaspoon grated onion or 2 teaspoons chopped chives. Makes about 2 cups. Good with seafood, greens, hard-cooked eggs or vegetables.

Green Mayonnaise Mix 2 cups Mayonnaise, ¹⁄₂ cup finely chopped spinach, ¹⁄₄ cup finely chopped parsley, 2 tablespoons chopped dill or 1 teaspoon dillweed and 2 tablespoons chopped chives.

Roquefort Mayonnaise Beat together to a thick cream 1 cup Mayonnaise, ³⁄₄ cup dairy sour cream, ¹⁄₂ pound Roquefort, crumbled, 1 teaspoon hot pepper sauce and a dash of steak sauce. Makes 2²⁄₃ cups. Good on avocado salad, lettuce wedges or atop baked potatoes.

Spanish Dressing Mix 1 cup Mayonnaise, ¹⁄₄ cup chopped roasted peanuts, ¹⁄₄ cup chopped green pepper, ¹⁄₄ cup chopped ripe olives, 2 tablespoons chopped chives, ¹⁄₂ teaspoon salt and ¹⁄₄ cup catsup. If too thick, thin with a little white wine. Makes about 1¹⁄₂ cups.

BREADS

Italian Easter Bread

Finnish Cardamom Braid

Danish Pastry

Cinnamon Snail

HOW TO BUY BREAD

Every family has its own favorite kinds of bread. But whatever the variety, for nutrition's sake, be sure to buy enriched bread, preferably made with milk. Breads made with oatmeal or whole-wheat or rye flour are very nutritious.

BREAD STORAGE

Except in hot humid weather, bread can be kept for a few days in a metal or plastic bread box. Tightly wrapped, bread stored in the refrigerator does not mold quickly but it does lose freshness. Refrigerated bread is satisfactory for toast. All breads freeze well.

TIPS FOR MAKING YEAST BREADS

Yeast Like all plants, the living cells in yeast need water, food, air and heat. They get water and food from other ingredients in any bread recipe; using sifted flour, kneading and beating provide air; the warmth of the water and the temperature of the room provide heat. When yeast becomes active, dough rises.

Kneading Use a board lightly sprinkled with flour. Rub a little flour on your hands. Shape the dough in a round ball and fold it toward you. Using heels of hands, push dough away with rolling motion. Turn one quarter-turn around. Repeat until dough is smooth and elastic.

Rising Doughs need an even temperature of 80°F. to 85°F. for rising. There are several ways to provide a warm place.
1. Set bowl on rack in an unheated oven with large pan of hot water on another rack beneath it.
2. Warm bowl with hot water and dry before greasing it for dough.
3. Fill a large pan two thirds full with hot water, put a wire rack on top and set bowl on it.
4. Set bowl in a deep pan of warm, not hot, water.
5. Put bowl in draft-free place near, not on, range or radiator.

To Speed up Rising Cover bowl with plastic wrap or set whole bowl in a large plastic bag before putting in warm place to rise.

Testing for Double in Bulk Press tips of two fingers lightly and quickly ½" into dough. If dent remains, dough is double.

Baking When baking bread in glass loaf pans, use an oven temperature 25° less than specified in recipes. This prevents formation of a thick crust (undesirable to some). Baked bread sounds hollow when bottom and sides are tapped with fingers.

Cooling Remove from baking sheet or pans and put on cake racks. Cover with towel for a soft crust; leave uncovered for crisp crust. For extra good flavor, brush hot bread and rolls with soft butter.

Freezing After bread or rolls are thoroughly cooled, wrap in foil, freezer paper, heavy-duty plastic wrap or airtight plastic bags. Press out all air by putting wrap close to bread; seal tightly. Properly frozen bread will retain its freshness for 3 months.

Thawing Thaw in original wrapper and unwrap just before serving.

TIPS FOR COOKING PANCAKES
A dry griddle or cook in fat?

If pancake batter contains enough added fat, it can be cooked on a dry or lightly greased griddle or in a skillet. Where there is little or no added fat (as in bona fide crepes or French pancakes), the batter must be cooked in fat. Do not use too much or pancakes will be greasy. Teflon-coated pans need no greasing.

How to cook pancakes

1. Heat griddle 1 or 2 minutes, or until it is so hot a drop of water will sizzle and bubble away almost immediately.
2. Drop 1 rounded tablespoonful of batter at a time onto griddle, leaving 2" to 3" between them to allow for spreading.
3. Turn only once. To check if underside is done, lift edge of cake and see if it is golden brown. Usually, when ready to turn, the top side will be full of bubbles and no longer runny.
4. Do not cook too quickly or outside will burn and inside will be moist. Do not cook too slowly or cakes may become tough.

How to freeze waffles

Cool and wrap each leftover waffle in foil and freeze. Or freeze flat and wrap. To reheat, it is not necessary to thaw. Place each unwrapped section in toaster set at light and toast until section is heated through. These waffle sections become crisp when cool. If you prefer, you can place unwrapped sections side by side on a flat cookie sheet and put under broiler until heated and sufficiently browned. Do not keep over 2 weeks in the freezer.

WHITE BREAD

1 package active dry yeast
2 cups milk, scalded
1/4 cup butter or margarine
2 tablespoons sugar
2 teaspoons salt
6 cups all-purpose flour

Sprinkle yeast on ¼ cup warm water. Let stand a few minutes, then stir until dissolved. Pour hot milk over next 3 ingredients. Cool to lukewarm and add yeast and 3 cups flour. Beat well. Add remaining flour and mix well. Turn out on floured pastry cloth or board and knead until smooth and satiny. Put in greased bowl; turn once, cover and let rise until doubled (about 1½ hours). Punch down; let rise ½ hour. Shape in loaves and put in 2 greased 9" x 5" x 3" pans. Let rise until doubled (about 45 minutes). Bake in hot oven (400°F.) about 35 minutes, or until bread is lightly browned on top and done.
Raisin Bread Follow recipe for White Bread but add 1 cup seedless raisins to dough with last addition of flour.
Individual White-bread Loaves Follow recipe for White Bread, but after first rising, cut half of dough in 6 pieces. Shape in small loaves and put in greased 4¾" x 2⅝" x 1½" pans. Let rise until doubled (about 30 minutes). Brush with melted butter and bake in hot oven (425°F.) about 20 minutes. Raise and bake remaining half of dough in greased 9" x 5" x 3" loaf pan.

CHEESE BREAD

1 package active dry yeast
2 tablespoons sugar
1-1/2 cups liquid skim milk
2-1/2 cups shredded sharp Cheddar
  cheese
1/4 cup grated raw carrot
3 tablespoons oil
1-1/4 teaspoons salt
5 to 6 cups all-purpose flour

Sprinkle dry yeast into ¼ cup very warm water. Let stand a few minutes; then stir until dissolved. Heat remaining ingredients, except flour, to lukewarm. Pour over yeast. Mix in about half of flour. Add enough more flour to make a stiff dough that will not stick to bowl. Turn out on floured pastry cloth or board and knead until smooth and satiny. Put in greased bowl; turn once, cover and let rise until doubled. Punch down and shape in 2 loaves. Put in greased 9" x 5" x 3" pans. Let rise until doubled. Bake in moderate oven (350°F.) about 40 minutes.

BATTER ANADAMA BREAD

1 package active dry yeast
1/2 cup yellow cornmeal
3 tablespoons shortening
1/4 cup light molasses
2 teaspoons salt
1 egg
2-3/4 cups sifted all-purpose flour

Sprinkle dry yeast into ¼ cup very warm water. Let stand a few minutes; then stir until dissolved. In large bowl of electric mixer stir together ¾ cup boiling water, cornmeal, shortening, molasses and salt. Cool to lukewarm. Add yeast, egg and about half the flour. Blend at low speed, then beat 2 minutes at medium speed. Stir in remaining flour. Spread in greased 9" x 5" x 3" loaf pan. Let rise until batter is 1" from pan edge. Bake in moderate oven (375°F.) 35 minutes.
Batter Oatmeal Bread Substitute ½ cup rolled oats for the cornmeal.

SEEDED BREAD SQUARES

1 package active dry yeast
Butter or margarine
1 tablespoon salt
2 tablespoons sugar
1 cup dry nonfat milk
All-purpose flour
Caraway, sesame, celery and/or poppy
  seed

Sprinkle yeast on ¼ cup warm water. Let stand a few minutes, then stir until dissolved. In large bowl, put 2 tablespoons butter, then salt, sugar and 1 cup boiling water. Mix well and add ¾ cup cold water; cool to lukewarm. Add yeast. Mix dry milk and 4½ cups flour. Add 3 cups to yeast mixture and beat with spoon until smooth. Add remaining flour mixture and, if necessary, more flour to make a dough that doesn't stick to sides of bowl and can be kneaded. Turn dough onto floured board and knead 10 minutes, or until smooth and elastic. Put in greased large bowl. Turn once, cover with waxed paper and towel and let stand 1½ hours, or until doubled in bulk. Punch down and divide in 2 equal parts. Shape in square loaves and put in 2 greased 9" square pans. Let rise ½ hour, or until doubled. Bake in hot oven (400°F.) 20 to 25 minutes. Turn out on rack. Bread can be baked the day before serving. At serving time, cut each loaf in 25 cubes. Dip all sides in melted butter and sprinkle with seed. Put in shallow pan and heat in hot oven (425°F.) 8 to 10 minutes. To serve frozen bread, thaw 1 hour at room temperature, dip in butter and proceed as directed.

BUTTERMILK RAISIN BREAD

1 package active dry yeast
1-1/2 cups buttermilk
1/2 cup butter or margarine
1-1/2 teaspoons salt
1/3 cup sugar
1 teaspoon baking soda
1 cup seedless raisins
2 eggs
5 to 5-1/2 cups all-purpose flour

Sprinkle yeast on $\frac{1}{4}$ cup warm water and let stand 5 minutes, then stir until dissolved. Scald buttermilk in top part of double boiler over simmering water. Pour hot buttermilk over next 5 ingredients in large bowl. Stir until butter is dissolved. Cool to lukewarm, then stir in eggs, yeast mixture and about 2 cups flour. Beat vigorously until blended. Gradually add more flour to make a dough that clears bowl. Turn out on floured board and knead until elastic. Put in greased bowl and turn dough over to grease top. Cover and stand in warm place $1\frac{1}{2}$ hours, or until doubled in bulk. Punch down and shape in 2 loaves. Put in 2 greased 9″ x 5″ x 3″ loaf pans. Let rise again 1 hour, or until doubled. Then bake in moderate oven (350°F.) 45 minutes, or until done. **Note** To make 1 loaf, halve ingredients and use 1 teaspoon yeast.

BUTTERMILK CHEESE BREAD

1 cup buttermilk
1/3 cup butter
1/4 cup sugar
2-1/2 teaspoons salt
1 package active dry yeast
1/2 teaspoon baking soda
1-1/2 cups shredded sharp Cheddar
   cheese
5 to 5-1/2 cups all-purpose flour

Heat buttermilk, butter and 1 cup water until butter melts. Stir in sugar and salt and cool to about 120°F. In large bowl of electric mixer, combine next 3 ingredients with half the flour. Add butter mixture and beat at low speed $\frac{1}{2}$ minute, then beat on medium-high speed 3 minutes. With wooden spoon, stir in more flour to make a soft but firm dough and turn out on floured board. Knead 7 to 10 minutes, or until smooth and elastic. Put in greased bowl and turn greased side up. Cover and let rise in warm place 1 hour, or until doubled. Punch down and shape in 2 loaves. Put in greased 9″ x 5″ x 3″ loaf pans and let rise 30 to 40 minutes, or until doubled. Bake in hot oven (400°F.) 30 to 40 minutes. Turn out on cake racks; cool before cutting.

SOUR-CREAM ONION BREAD

A Sunday brunch favorite to be served with Eggs Florentine (page 224) or Thousand Island Eggs (page 222).

1 package active dry yeast
1 teaspoon sugar
1 cup milk, scalded
Butter or margarine
1-1/2 teaspoons salt
3 cups all-purpose flour
5 large onions, sliced
2 eggs, beaten
1/4 cup dairy sour cream
3 or 4 slices bacon, cooked and crumbled
1 teaspoon caraway seed, crushed slightly

Soften yeast in 2 tablespoons warm water with the sugar. Pour milk over $\frac{1}{4}$ cup butter and 1 teaspoon salt. When lukewarm, add yeast and flour and mix well. Cover and let rise until double in bulk, about 1 hour. In the meantime, cook onion in 3 tablespoons butter until tender but not browned. Cool and stir in $\frac{1}{2}$ teaspoon salt, the eggs, sour cream, bacon and caraway seed. Punch down dough and knead until smooth. Roll out to about the size of a greased 15″ x 10″ x 1″ pan. Press into pan. Distribute onion mixture evenly on the dough. Let rise about $\frac{1}{2}$ hour, or until light. Bake in hot oven (400°F.) about 30 minutes. Cut in 3″ squares and serve hot with softened butter or margarine, if desired.

FRENCH BREAD

1 package active dry yeast
1 tablespoon shortening
2 teaspoons salt
1 tablespoon sugar
6 cups (about) all-purpose flour
1 egg white

Sprinkle yeast on $\frac{1}{4}$ cup warm water. Let stand a few minutes, then stir until dissolved. Pour 1 cup boiling water over shortening, salt and sugar in large mixing bowl. Add $\frac{3}{4}$ cup cold water and cool to lukewarm. Add yeast and gradually beat in enough flour to form a stiff dough. Turn out on floured pastry cloth or board and knead until smooth and satiny. Put in greased bowl, turn once, cover and let rise until doubled, about $1\frac{1}{2}$ hours. Shape in 2 oblong loaves about 14″ long. Put on greased baking sheets. Let rise about 1 hour, or until doubled. Brush with beaten egg white. With knife, make 3 slashes across top. Bake in hot oven (425°F.) 30 minutes. Reduce heat to 350°F. and bake 20 minutes, or until done.

SWEET DOUGH

(Basic recipe, refrigerator method)
5 to 6 cups all-purpose flour
2 packages active dry yeast
1/2 cup sugar
1-1/2 teaspoons salt
1/2 cup margarine, softened
2 eggs, at room temperature

Measure flour onto piece of waxed paper. Combine 2 cups flour and next 3 ingredients in large bowl of electric mixer. Stir well and add margarine and 1½ cups very hot tap water. Beat at low speed, scraping sides of bowl occasionally, 2 minutes. Add eggs and 1 cup flour. Beat at medium speed, scraping sides of bowl occasionally, 2 minutes, or until thick and elastic. With wooden spoon, gradually stir in enough flour to make a soft dough that leaves sides of bowl. Turn out on lightly floured board, shape in a ball and knead 5 to 10 minutes, or until smooth and elastic. Put in greased bowl. Turn once, cover with plastic wrap or put in plastic bag and let rise 1 hour, or until doubled in bulk. Punch down, knead lightly until smooth. Shape as desired, cover and let rise 30 minutes, or until doubled. Bake in moderate oven (375°F.) about 12 to 15 minutes, or until done. Remove to rack, cover with towel and cool.

GUGELHUPF

1 package active dry yeast
3/4 cup milk, scalded and cooled
4 cups all-purpose flour
1 cup butter or margarine, softened
3/4 cup granulated sugar
5 eggs
1 teaspoon salt
Grated rind of 1 lemon
1 cup seedless raisins
1/2 cup chopped blanched almonds
Confectioners' sugar

Sprinkle yeast on ¼ cup warm water. Let stand a few minutes, then stir until dissolved. Add milk and 1 cup flour and beat with spoon until smooth. Cover and let rise 1½ hours. Cream butter and granulated sugar until light. Beat in eggs one at a time. Add yeast mixture, remaining flour and salt. Beat well. Stir in lemon rind, raisins and ¼ cup nuts. Butter a 10" tube pan and sprinkle with remaining nuts. Spoon in batter, smooth top and let rise until light, about 45 minutes. Bake in moderate oven (350°F.) about 1 hour. Let stand 4 to 5 minutes. Loosen sides and turn out. Sprinkle with confectioners' sugar.

GRECIAN FEAST BREAD

Prepare 1 recipe Hot Cross Buns, page 292, omitting spices and adding 1 tablespoon grated lemon rind and ½ cup golden raisins (making 1½ cups raisins in all). After punching down risen dough, divide in thirds. Shape each in a smooth ball and put on greased large baking sheet in cloverleaf design. Flatten to 1" high and brush with vegetable oil. Let rise 45 minutes, or until doubled. Bake in moderate oven (350°F.) 25 to 30 minutes. Remove to rack, cover with towel and cool. Frost with Sweet Lemon Frosting (page 215) and decorate with almonds and candied fruit.

ITALIAN EASTER BREAD

3-1/4 cups all-purpose flour
1/4 cup sugar
1 teaspoon salt
1 package active dry yeast
2/3 cup milk
2 tablespoons butter or margarine, melted
2 eggs, at room temperature
1/4 cup each diced candied orange peel and citron
1/4 cup chopped almonds
1/2 teaspoon aniseed
5 raw eggs in shells, plain or colored
Confectioners'-sugar Frosting, page 292
Tiny multicolored candies

Measure flour onto piece of waxed paper. Combine 1 cup flour and next 3 ingredients in large mixing bowl. Add milk to butter, then gradually add to dry ingredients. Beat at low speed of electric mixer, scraping sides of bowl occasionally, 2 minutes. Add the 2 eggs and ½ cup flour. Beat at medium speed, scraping sides of bowl occasionally, 2 minutes, or until thick and elastic. With wooden spoon, gradually stir in just enough flour to make a soft dough that leaves sides of bowl. Turn out onto lightly floured board, shape in a ball and knead 5 to 10 minutes, or until smooth and elastic. Put in greased bowl. Turn once, cover and let rise 1 hour, or until doubled in bulk. Combine fruits, almonds and aniseed. Punch down dough, turn out on lightly floured board and knead in fruit mixture. Divide in half and roll each piece in a 24" rope. Twist ropes loosely together and shape in a ring on greased baking sheet. Arrange unshelled eggs in empty spaces in twist. Cover and let rise in warm place 40 minutes, or until doubled in bulk. Bake in moderate oven (350°F.) 30 to 35 minutes. Put on rack; cover with towel. Cool, frost; sprinkle with candies.

STREUSEL COFFEE CAKE

Follow recipe for Sweet Dough, page 291. After punching down dough, divide in thirds. Roll each third in a circle to fit a buttered 9″ layer-cake pan. Sprinkle each with mixture of ⅓ cup all-purpose flour, ⅓ cup sugar and ⅓ cup butter creamed together. Let rise 30 minutes, or until doubled. Bake in hot oven (400°F.) about 25 minutes. Serve warm. Makes 3.

DANISH PASTRIES

3 to 3-1/2 cups all-purpose flour
2 packages active dry yeast
1 cup cold milk
2 eggs
2 tablespoons granulated sugar
1-1/2 cups cold margarine, sliced
Filling
Confectioners' sugar

Measure flour onto piece of waxed paper. Sprinkle yeast into ¼ cup warm water and let stand a few minutes, then stir until dissolved. Blend in milk, 1 egg, sugar and about half the flour. Beat with wooden spoon until smooth. Gradually stir in more flour to make a soft dough. Turn out on well-floured board and let rest while making Filling. Then gently roll dough to a 14″ x 10″ rectangle. Cover two thirds of rectangle with slices of margarine, leaving 1″ of edges uncovered. Sprinkle with 2 tablespoons flour. Fold plain third of dough over center third; fold margarine-covered third over center to make 3 layers of dough. Press edges together. Roll again into 14″ x 10″ rectangle; repeat folding over in thirds to make 3 layers. Turn a quarter-turn to the right. Repeat rolling into 14″ x 10″ rectangle, folding and turning 3 or 4 times, to make pastry flaky. If dough becomes sticky, wrap in waxed paper and chill 10 to 15 minutes between rolling and folding. Rub flour on board and rolling pin as needed to prevent sticking. Roll to an 18″ x 15″ rectangle. Cut in 3″ squares. Put a heaping teaspoon of Filling in center of each square and fold corners to center, pinching points together. Put on baking sheets and let rise at room temperature 1½ hours, or until almost doubled in bulk. Brush tops carefully with remaining egg, slightly beaten. Bake in hot oven (425°F.) 10 to 12 minutes. Remove to rack to cool. Sift confectioners' sugar over tops. Makes about 30. **Filling** Mix 1 cup finely chopped almonds or other nuts, ½ cup sugar, 1 egg, and if desired, ½ teaspoon almond extract.

CINNAMON SNAILS

Follow recipe for Sweet Dough, page 291. After punching down, divide in 2 equal parts. Roll each to a 15″ x 12″ rectangle. Spread with softened butter and sprinkle with sugar and cinnamon to taste. Fold over lengthwise. Cut in ¾″ strips with pastry wheel. Make a slit in center of each strip 1″ from ends. Twist in snail shapes, tucking ends under. Proceed as directed. Makes about 2½ dozen. *Note* After shaping, rolls may be covered loosely with plastic wrap and refrigerated 12 to 24 hours. Remove from refrigerator; let rise uncovered until doubled. Bake as directed.

HOT CROSS BUNS

Served on Good Friday since the early days of the Christian church.
5 to 5-1/2 cups all-purpose flour
2 packages active dry yeast
1/2 cup sugar
1 teaspoon salt
1/2 teaspoon each cinnamon and nutmeg
1-1/4 cups milk
1/2 cup butter or margarine, melted
2 eggs, at room temperature
1 egg yolk
1 cup raisins, plumped in 1 cup
  hot water
Confectioners'-sugar Frosting

Measure flour onto piece of waxed paper. Combine 2 cups flour, yeast, sugar, salt and spices in large mixing bowl, stir well. Add milk to hot butter. Gradually add to dry ingredients and beat at low speed of electric mixer, scraping sides of bowl occasionally, 2 minutes. Add eggs, egg yolk and 1 cup flour. Beat at minimum speed, scraping side of bowl occasionally, 2 minutes, or until thick and elastic. With wooden spoon, gradually stir in just enough flour to make a soft dough that leaves sides of bowl. Turn out onto lightly floured board, shape in a ball and knead 5 to 10 minutes, or until smooth and elastic. Put in greased bowl. Turn once, cover with plastic wrap and let rise 1 hour, or until doubled. Drain raisins. Punch dough down, add raisins and turn out on lightly floured board; knead lightly until smooth. Divide dough in 2 equal parts. Shape in 2 rolls 12″ long and cut each in 12 equal pieces. Shape in smooth balls and arrange on greased baking sheets. Cover and let rise 30 minutes, or until doubled. Bake in moderate oven (375°F.) 12 to 15 minutes, or until done. Decorate with frosting crosses. Makes 2 dozen. **Confectioners'-sugar Frosting** Blend 1⅓ cups sifted confectioners' sugar, 1 egg white and 1 teaspoon vanilla.

CREAM COFFEE ROLLS

1 package active dry yeast
3/4 cup heavy cream
1 teaspoon salt
2 tablespoons sugar
Melted butter
1 egg, beaten
2-1/2 cups all-purpose flour
Confectioners'-sugar Frosting, page 292
Candied fruit (optional)

Sprinkle yeast on ¼ cup warm water. Let stand a few minutes, then stir until dissolved. Heat cream to lukewarm, add salt and sugar and stir until dissolved. Add ⅓ cup melted butter, yeast and egg. Add 1½ cups flour and beat well. Stir in remaining flour, cover and let rise until doubled. Punch down, cut off small pieces of dough and roll between hands to about the size of a pencil. Coil each into a 2″ muffin cup, brush with melted butter and let rise until light. Bake in hot oven (400°F.) about 15 minutes. While hot, frost. Decorate with fruit, if desired. Makes 2½ dozen.

FINNISH CARDAMOM BRAIDS

6 to 6-1/2 cups all-purpose flour
2 packages active dry yeast
1 teaspoon crushed cardamom seed
2 eggs, at room temperature
Sugar
1 teaspoon salt
1/2 cup butter or margarine, softened
1 tablespoon milk

Measure flour onto piece of waxed paper. Sprinkle yeast into 2 cups warm water in large mixing bowl. Let stand a few minutes, then stir until dissolved. Stir in cardamom seed, 1 egg, ⅓ cup sugar, salt, butter and about half the flour. Beat with wooden spoon until smooth and elastic. Gradually add enough flour to make a soft dough. Turn out onto lightly floured board and knead 5 to 10 minutes, or until smooth and elastic. Put in greased bowl, turn once, then cover and let rise 1 hour, or until doubled in bulk. Punch down, turn out onto lightly floured board and knead until smooth and free from air bubbles. Cut in 6 equal pieces and shape in even ropes 1″ wide. Using 3 at a time, make 2 braids. Put on lightly greased large baking sheet, leaving 2″ space between braids. Cover; let rise in warm place free from drafts about 30 minutes. Brush with mixture of remaining egg, beaten with milk. Sprinkle generously with sugar; bake in moderate oven (375°F.) 20 to 25 minutes, or until well browned. Put on rack; cover with soft cloth. Cool; slice.

CINNAMON LOAF

1 package active dry yeast
2/3 cup milk, scalded
1/2 cup sugar
1 teaspoon salt
Butter or margarine
2 eggs
3 cups all-purpose flour
1-1/2 teaspoons cinnamon

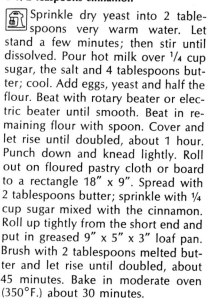 Sprinkle dry yeast into 2 tablespoons very warm water. Let stand a few minutes; then stir until dissolved. Pour hot milk over ¼ cup sugar, the salt and 4 tablespoons butter; cool. Add eggs, yeast and half the flour. Beat with rotary beater or electric beater until smooth. Beat in remaining flour with spoon. Cover and let rise until doubled, about 1 hour. Punch down and knead lightly. Roll out on floured pastry cloth or board to a rectangle 18″ x 9″. Spread with 2 tablespoons butter; sprinkle with ¼ cup sugar mixed with the cinnamon. Roll up tightly from the short end and put in greased 9″ x 5″ x 3″ loaf pan. Brush with 2 tablespoons melted butter and let rise until doubled, about 45 minutes. Bake in moderate oven (350°F.) about 30 minutes.

HONEY-OATMEAL BREAD

(Refrigerator Method)

1-1/2 cups quick-cooking (not instant) rolled oats
1/3 cup honey
1/4 cup butter or margarine
1 tablespoon salt
1 cup dairy sour cream
2 packages active dry yeast
2 eggs
4-1/2 to 5 cups all-purpose flour
Honey butter

Combine 1 cup boiling water and first 4 ingredients and stir until butter is melted. Add sour cream and cool to lukewarm. Soften yeast in ½ cup warm water. Add yeast, eggs and 2 cups flour to oat mixture and beat until smooth. Add enough more flour to make a stiff dough. Turn out onto lightly floured board and knead until elastic. Cover dough on board with towel or bowl and let rest 20 minutes. Then divide in 2 equal portions and shape in 2 loaves. Put each in a greased 9″ x 5″ x 3″ loaf pan. Cover pans loosely with plastic wrap and refrigerate 12 to 24 hours. When ready to bake, let stand at room temperature 10 minutes while oven is heating. Bake in moderate oven (375°F.) 50 minutes, or until done. Remove from pans at once and cool on rack. Slice when cold and serve with honey butter (equal parts honey and butter).

THREE-FLOUR BREAD

2 packages active dry yeast
2 cups buttermilk
1/4 cup shortening
2/3 cup light molasses
2 tablespoons caraway seed
2 teaspoons salt
2 cups all-purpose flour
2 cups each unsifted rye flour and whole-wheat flour

Sprinkle dry yeast into ¼ cup very warm water. Let stand a few minutes; then stir until dissolved. Heat buttermilk and shortening to lukewarm. Pour into large mixing bowl. Add yeast, molasses, caraway seed and salt. Beat in white flour. Gradually add rye and whole-wheat flours to form a stiff dough. Turn out on floured pastry cloth or board and knead until smooth and satiny. Put in greased bowl; turn once, cover and let rise until doubled, about 2 hours. Shape in 2 loaves and put in greased 9" x 5" x 3" loaf pans. Let rise until doubled, about 1 hour. Bake in moderate oven (325°F.) about 40 minutes, or until done.

BUTTER HORNS

1 package active dry yeast
1/2 cup milk, scalded
1/2 cup butter
1/3 cup sugar
3/4 teaspoon salt
1 egg, beaten
4 cups (about) all-purpose flour

Sprinkle yeast on ½ cup warm water. Let stand a few minutes, then stir until dissolved. Pour hot milk over butter, sugar and salt. Cool to lukewarm. Add yeast, egg and 2 cups flour. Beat well. Add more flour to make a dough that will not stick to bowl. Turn out on floured pastry cloth or board and knead lightly. Put in greased bowl, turn once, cover and let rise until doubled, about 1 hour. Divide dough in half. Roll each half out on floured board to form a circle 12" in diameter. Cut each in 12 pie-shaped pieces. Roll up from wide end and put, pointed end down, on greased baking sheets. Let rise until doubled, about 30 minutes. Bake in hot oven (400°F.) 15 minutes. Unraised dough can be refrigerated overnight. Let stand at room temperature to soften enough to roll, then proceed as directed.
Bowknots Follow recipe for Butter Horns. After first rising, cut dough in 24 pieces. Roll each piece in hands to form a pencil shape about 8" long. Tie in a loose knot. Proceed as directed.

Seeded Butter Horns Follow recipe for Butter Horns. Before second rising, brush rolls with melted butter and sprinkle with seed such as poppy, sesame or celery. Proceed as directed.

Parker House Rolls Follow recipe for Butter Horns. Roll raised dough to ¼" thickness; cut with floured 2¾" cutter. With handle of wooden spoon, make a crease in each circle to one side of center; flatten smaller half of round slightly by rolling handle of spoon toward edge. Brush with melted butter; fold thicker half over thinner half; press edges together. Proceed as directed.

Cloverleaf Rolls Follow recipe for Butter Horns. After first rising, cut dough in 24 pieces. Cut each piece in thirds and roll in a ball. Put 3 balls in each of 24 greased 2¼" muffin cups. Proceed as directed.

KOLACKY

1 package active dry yeast
4 cups all-purpose flour, spooned into cup
1/4 cup sugar
1 teaspoon salt
1 teaspoon grated lemon rind
3/4 cup butter or margarine, softened
3 egg yolks
1 cup heavy cream
Prune Filling or Apricot Filling
Sweet Lemon Frosting

Soften yeast in 2 tablespoons very warm water. Sift flour, sugar and salt. Add lemon rind and yeast and blend in butter. Blend in egg yolks beaten with cream. Store, covered, in refrigerator overnight. Put on lightly floured board and roll to ¼" thickness. Cut with 2" round cutter and put on ungreased baking sheets. Cover and let rise 1 hour, or until doubled. Make a depression in center of each and fill with about ¾ teaspoon of either filling. Bake in moderate oven (375°F.) about 12 minutes. Frost while warm. Makes 4 dozen. **Prune Filling** Cook 1½ cups pitted dried prunes in water to cover until tender. Drain and mash prunes with fork. Add ¼ cup sugar and ½ teaspoon cinnamon. Makes enough for 1 recipe. **Apricot Filling** Cook 1½ cups dried apricots in water to cover until tender. Drain and force apricots through sieve. Add ½ cup sugar. Makes enough for 1 recipe. **Sweet Lemon Frosting** Mix 1½ cups confectioners' sugar, 2 tablespoons boiling water and 1 teaspoon lemon juice.

CHEESE-FILLED ROLLS

1 package active dry yeast
Milk
Sugar
1/2 teaspoon salt
1/3 cup butter
2 eggs, 1 separated
1 teaspoon grated lemon rind
3-1/4 cups all-purpose flour
4 ounces cream cheese
1 teaspoon cinnamon

Dissolve yeast in 2 tablespoons warm water. Let stand a few minutes, then stir until dissolved. Scald ½ cup milk and pour over ⅓ cup sugar, salt and butter. Cool to lukewarm. Stir in yeast, whole egg, egg yolk and lemon rind. Beat in 1½ cups flour, then stir in remaining 1¾ cups. Cover and let rise until doubled. Punch down. Roll on floured surface to form a rectangle 14″ x 10½″. Cut in twelve 3½″ squares. Mix cheese and 1½ tablespoons milk. Spread 2 teaspoons on each square and fold in triangles. Put on greased baking sheets and let rise ½ hour, or until light. Brush with egg white beaten with 2 teaspoons water. Sprinkle with 2 tablespoons sugar mixed with the cinnamon. Bake in moderate oven (350°F.) 12 minutes.

CHRISTMAS STOLLEN

1 package active dry yeast
Butter or margarine
3/4 cup milk
Sugar
1 teaspoon salt
Grated rind of 1 lemon
2 eggs
4 cups all-purpose flour
1/2 cup chopped blanched almonds
1/2 cup chopped mixed candied fruits
1/2 cup seedless raisins
1/2 teaspoon cinnamon

In mixing bowl, dissolve yeast in ¼ cup warm water (105°F. to 115°F.). Melt ⅓ cup butter in small saucepan, add milk and heat to warm. Combine with yeast mixture, ⅓ cup sugar, the salt, lemon rind, eggs and 2 cups flour. Beat with rotary beater until smooth, cover and let rise in warm place about 40 minutes. Stir in nuts and fruit, then gradually beat in remaining flour. Turn out on lightly floured board and knead until smooth and elastic. Divide in half and shape each half in 12″ x 8″ oval. Brush with melted butter and fold lengthwise almost double. Press edges together. Put on greased large baking sheet and let rise 40 minutes, or until almost doubled. Bake in moderate oven (350°F.) 25 to 30 minutes. Brush with melted butter; sprinkle with mixture of 2 tablespoons sugar and the cinnamon.

SAVORY COTTAGE-CHEESE BREAD

2 teaspoons instant minced onion
1 package active dry yeast
Butter or margarine, softened
Salt
1 teaspoon oregano leaves
1 cup small-curd creamed cottage cheese
2 tablespoons sugar
1/4 teaspoon baking soda
1 egg
2 to 2-1/2 cups all-purpose flour

Add small amount of cold water to onion and let stand until rehydrated; drain if necessary. Soften yeast in ¼ cup warm water. In medium bowl, mix well onion, 1 tablespoon butter, 1 teaspoon salt and remaining ingredients, except flour. Add yeast mixture and mix well. Gradually add enough flour to make a firm dough. Mix well, cover with plastic wrap and let stand in warm place 1 hour, or until doubled. Punch down and put in well-buttered 1½-quart casserole. Let rise 30 minutes, or until light, then bake in moderate oven (350°F.) about 40 minutes. Turn out and brush with butter. Serve warm or cold.

FAN-TAN ROLLS

1 package active dry yeast
1/4 cup vegetable shortening
Butter
1 cup milk
1/4 cup sugar
1 teaspoon salt
2 eggs
4 cups all-purpose flour

In mixing bowl, dissolve yeast in ¼ cup warm water (105°F. to 115°F.). Melt shortening and ¼ cup butter in small saucepan, add milk and heat to warm (105°F. to 115°F.). Combine with yeast mixture, sugar, salt, eggs and 2 cups flour. Beat with rotary beater until smooth, cover and let rise in warm place about 40 minutes. Beat in remaining flour ½ cup at a time. Cover tightly and chill 2 hours. Turn dough out on lightly floured board and knead until smooth and elastic (if desired, dough can be stored covered in refrigerator 2 to 3 days). Divide dough in half. Roll each half in thin 16″ x 7″ rectangle. Brush with melted butter and, using a pastry wheel, cut lengthwise in seven 1″-wide strips. Cut strips in half crosswise and pile 7 strips one on top of the other, pressing slightly. Cut in 1″-wide pieces; place on cut end in greased muffin pans. Cover lightly and let rise in warm place 1 hour, or until doubled. Bake in hot oven (425°F.) 12 minutes. Makes about 32.

FRENCH BABAS AU RHUM

These cakes are light and tender with a delicious rum flavor.

1 package active dry yeast
1/4 cup milk
1/4 cup butter or margarine
2 egg yolks
1/4 cup sugar
1 egg
Grated rind of 1/2 lemon
1/8 teaspoon salt
1-3/4 cups all-purpose flour
Rum Syrup

Soften yeast in ¼ cup lukewarm water. Scald milk, add butter and stir until melted; cool to lukewarm. Beat egg yolks well; gradually add sugar and continue beating. Beat in egg. Add milk mixture, yeast, lemon rind and salt. Gradually add flour, beating until smooth. Cover until doubled. Stir down. Fill greased small muffin pans about two thirds full. Let rise until batter reaches top. Bake in moderate oven (350°F.) about 10 minutes. Cool. Put in shallow dish and cover with syrup. Baste several times so each one is soaked. Cover; refrigerate. Makes 24 to 36. **Rum Syrup** Mix 1½ cups water, 1½ cups sugar, ½ slice lemon, 1 slice orange, 1 stick cinnamon, 1 whole clove; simmer 5 minutes. Strain; add ¾ cup dark rum.

LITTLE BRIOCHES

2 packages active dry yeast
3/4 cup milk, scalded
1 cup butter or margarine
1/2 cup sugar
2 teaspoons salt
6-1/2 cups sifted all-purpose flour
5 eggs

Sprinkle yeast into ¼ cup very warm water. Let stand a few minutes, then stir until dissolved. Pour hot milk over butter, sugar and salt. Cool to lukewarm. Add 2 cups flour and beat well. Add yeast and beat. Cover and let rise until bubbly; stir down. Add 4 eggs and beat well. Add more flour to make a soft dough. Turn out on lightly floured board and knead until smooth and satiny. Put in greased bowl, turn once, cover and let rise 1½ hours, or until doubled. Punch down and divide in 24 pieces. From each piece, make 1 large and 1 small ball. Place large ball in well-greased 2¾" muffin cup. Indent top with thumb; press in small ball. Repeat to fill pans. Let rise 45 minutes, or until doubled. Mix remaining egg and 1 tablespoon water. Brush on rolls. Bake in moderate oven (375°F.) about 15 minutes. Makes 2 dozen.

GEORGIA RAISED BISCUITS

1 package active dry yeast
5 cups all-purpose flour
2 teaspoons salt
1 tablespoon sugar
Butter or margarine

Sprinkle yeast on 1½ cups warm water. Let stand a few minutes, then stir until dissolved. Mix dry ingredients in large bowl. Cut in ½ cup softened butter. Add yeast and mix well. Roll ¼" thick on floured board; brush with melted butter. Cut with floured 2" cutter; put on baking sheet in pairs, one on top of the other. Let rise in warm place about 1 hour. Bake in hot oven (425°F.) about 10 minutes. Makes about 5 dozen.

FARMER-CHEESE TEA RINGS

1 package hot-roll mix
2 eggs
2 tablespoons caraway seed
2 packages (7-1/2 ounces each) farmer cheese
Melted butter or margarine

Prepare roll mix, using 1 egg, as directed on the label. Let rise until double in bulk. Then knead 2 minutes. Divide dough in half. Roll each half on floured board to a 10" x 6" rectangle. Beat remaining egg; mix well with caraway seed and cheese. Brush rectangles generously with butter; spread with cheese. Roll each up from long side and shape in a ring on cookie sheet; pinch ends together. Let rise until light, about 30 minutes. Brush with butter; bake in moderate oven (375°F.) about 30 minutes. Serve warm or cold.

POTATO BREAD

2 packages active dry yeast
1 cup potato water
1 cup fresh mashed potato
2 tablespoons sugar
2 cups milk, scalded and cooled
3 tablespoons vegetable oil
2-1/2 teaspoons salt
8 cups (about) all-purpose flour

Sprinkle dry yeast into very warm potato water. Let stand a few minutes; then stir until dissolved. Add next 5 ingredients and half the flour. Beat until smooth. Add enough more flour to make a stiff dough that leaves sides of bowl. Turn out on floured pastry cloth or board; knead until smooth and satiny. Put in greased bowl; turn once, cover and let rise until doubled, about 1 hour. Shape in 3 loaves; put in greased 9" x 5" x 3" loaf pans. Let rise until doubled. Bake in moderate oven (350°F.) about 40 minutes.

WINE-GLAZED ALMOND KNOTS

1-1/2 cups milk
6 cups (about) all-purpose flour
1 package active dry yeast
4 egg yolks
2/3 cup sugar
1 cup butter or margarine, melted and
  cooled
2/3 cup chopped almonds
Grated rind of 2 large lemons
1/2 teaspoon salt
Wine Glaze
Toasted slivered almonds

Scald milk, pour into large bowl and cool to lukewarm. Stir in 4 cups flour. Soften yeast in 3 tablespoons warm water. Stir and beat into flour mixture. Cover and let rise in a warm place until nearly double in bulk, about 1 hour. Beat egg yolks with sugar until thick and light. Stir into dough. Stir in melted butter until well blended. Add almonds, lemon rind and salt. Gradually stir in more flour to make a dough that is barely firm enough to handle. Turn out on lightly floured board and knead, working in more flour until dough is just firm enough to cut without sticking. (Keep dough soft, adding no more flour than necessary.) Divide in 16 pieces. From each piece make 3 rolls about 5" long. Put side by side on board and make small braid; put in greased cup. Repeat to make 16 braided knots. Let rise in warm place until almost double in bulk, about 1 to 1¼ hours. Bake in hot oven (400°F.) about 18 minutes. Drizzle glaze over top while burns are still warm. Top with roasted slivered almonds. Makes 16 large knots. **Wine Glaze** Stir together until smooth 1½ cups sifted confectioners' sugar, 2 tablespoons white wine and 2 tablespoons melted butter or margarine.

PEANUT-ORANGE PINWHEEL ROLLS

1 package (8 ounces) crescent dinner
  rolls
1/2 cup orange marmalade
1/2 cup peanut butter (any style)
Confectioners'-sugar Frosting (page 292)

Open dinner rolls and separate in 4 rectangles. Press diagonal perforations together to seal. Combine orange marmalade and peanut butter and spread one fourth of mixture on each rectangle. Roll up jelly-roll fashion from short side. Cut each in 4 rolls. Put on ungreased baking sheet and bake in moderate oven (375°F.) 15 to 20 minutes. Drizzle confectioners'-sugar frosting over rolls while hot.

PATIO CRACKLIN' BREAD

1/2 cup crushed cracklings (French-fried
  pork rinds)
3/4 cup crushed onion snacks
1-1/4 teaspoons lemon-pepper seasoning
2 cans (8 ounces each) refrigerated
  biscuits
1/3 cup butter or margarine, melted

In small plastic bag, crush separately with rolling pin enough cracklings and onion snacks to make desired amount. Put in bowl with seasoning and mix well. Butter a 9" x 5" x 3" loaf pan. Separate biscuits, dip in the butter, then in crushed mixture on one side only. Alternating dipped and plain sides, set on edge in rows of 10 each in buttered pan (4 end biscuits can be dipped on both sides, if preferred). Sprinkle any remaining mixture and butter over loaf. Bake in moderate oven (375°F.) 20 minutes, or until a deep crusty brown. Invert on serving plate and serve hot.

ORANGE-NUT COFFEE CAKE

1 package active dry yeast
Butter or margarine
3/4 cup milk
1/2 teaspoon salt
1/4 cup sugar
1 egg
3-1/2 cups all-purpose flour
2/3 cup chopped candied orange peel
1/3 cup each chopped nuts and sugar
Pecan halves, honey

In mixing bowl, dissolve yeast in ¼ cup warm water (105°F. to 115°F.). Melt ⅓ cup butter in small saucepan, add milk and heat to warm (105°F. to 115°F.). Combine with yeast mixture, salt, sugar, egg and 1½ cups flour. Beat with rotary beater until smooth. Cover and let rise in warm place about 40 minutes. Beat in remaining 2 cups flour ½ cup at a time. Turn dough out on lightly floured board and knead until smooth and elastic. Divide in quarters. Shape each quarter to 1"-wide roll and cut in 10 pieces. In center of each piece put about ½ measuring-teaspoon orange peel, seal and shape in an even round bun. Then brush each bun with melted butter (about ¼ cup for all) and roll in mixture of nuts and sugar. Put buns close together in lightly greased 9" x 3" springform or loose-bottom pan. Let rise in warm place 1 hour, or until doubled in bulk. Bake in moderate oven (350°F.) 40 minutes, or until done (protect oven while baking with piece of foil on bottom to collect any dripping butter). Cool in pan or rack. Remove rim and decorate with pecan halves brushed with honey.

PORTUGUESE SWEET BREAD

Sugar
2 packages active dry yeast
1/2 cup lukewarm potato water
1 cup warm mashed potato
1/8 teaspoon ginger
1/2 cup milk
1/2 cup butter or margarine, melted and cooled
2 teaspoons salt
7 eggs
7 to 8 cups all-purpose flour

Add 3 tablespoons sugar and yeast to potato water and stir until dissolved. Blend in potato and ginger. Cover and let rise until doubled in bulk. Scald next 3 ingredients and cool to lukewarm. Beat 6 eggs until light. Gradually beat in 1³/₄ cups sugar. Combine yeast and egg mixtures and blend well. Stir in 2 cups flour, add milk mixture and beat until well blended. Add 2 more cups flour and beat 5 minutes. Gradually stir in more flour until dough is stiff enough to knead. Turn out on floured board and knead about 10 minutes, adding only enough flour to prevent sticking. Put dough in an oiled large bowl, turn once, cover and let rise until doubled in bulk. Punch down, put on floured board and divide in 4 pieces. Shape in round loaves and put on oiled cookie sheets or into 8¹/₂" x 4¹/₂" x 2" loaf pans. Let rise in warm place until doubled. Beat remaining egg with a few drops of water and brush on loaves; bake in moderate oven (350° F.) 40 to 50 minutes.

SAVORY BRAIDS

1 package (13-3/4 ounces) hot-roll mix
1 egg
2 tablespoons butter or margarine, melted
2 teaspoons dillweed
1 egg yolk beaten with 2 teaspoons milk or cream

Prepare mix with egg as directed on label, adding butter and dillweed to dissolved yeast mixture. After dough rises, turn out on lightly floured board and knead until smooth and elastic. Divide in 6 equal pieces. Shape each in 14"-long roll. Make 2 braids, using 3 rolls for each. Put crosswise on lightly greased baking sheet and let rise about 30 minutes. Brush with egg-yolk and milk mixture. Bake in moderate oven (375°F.) 20 to 25 minutes, or until done. Cover with kitchen towel and cool on rack. Serve in ¹/₂" slices with butter. Good toasted. Store airtight in cool place. Can be frozen. Makes two 11" x 3" loaves.

LEMON-PEPPERED CRACKLIN' BREAD

A good crunchy hot bread for a soup and salad lunch.

1 package (13-3/4 ounces) hot-roll mix
1 egg
1/2 cup butter or margarine, melted
1/2 teaspoon onion flakes
1-1/2 teaspoons lemon-pepper seasoning
2 cups finely crushed French-fried pork rinds (cracklings)

Prepare hot-roll mix with egg as directed on label. Let rise in warm place 20 to 30 minutes. Punch down and roll to about a 16" x 13" rectangle. Mix next 3 ingredients and brush on rectangle, reserving 2 tablespoons. Sprinkle cracklings on dough, reserving 2 tablespoons. Roll dough up tightly and seal. Stretch to about 22" in length and coil in well-greased 1¹/₂- or 2-quart casserole. Pour reserved butter over top and sprinkle with reserved cracklings. Let rise in warm place 30 minutes, or until light. Bake in moderate oven (350°F.) about 1 hour. Turn out; serve hot or cold.

BABKA
(Polish Easter Bread)

4 cups all-purpose flour
1 package active dry yeast
1/2 cup sugar
1 teaspoon salt
1/2 teaspoon cinnamon
1/2 cup butter or margarine
1-1/4 cups milk
5 egg yolks
1 cup golden raisins
Grated rind of 1 lemon
1/4 cup sliced blanched almonds

Combine 2 cups flour and next 4 ingredients in large bowl of electric mixer; stir well. Melt butter and add milk. (Mixture should be lukewarm.) Gradually add to dry ingredients and beat at low speed, scraping sides of bowl occasionally, 2 minutes. Add 4 egg yolks and 1 cup flour. Beat at medium speed, scraping sides of bowl occasionally, 2 minutes, or until thick and elastic. With wooden spoon, gradually stir in remaining 1 cup flour to make a soft dough. Cover and let rise until doubled in bulk. Stir in raisins and lemon rind. Put in well-greased 3-quart fluted tube pan or heavy *bundt* pan. Brush with mixture of remaining egg yolk, slightly beaten with 2 tablespoons water. Sprinkle with almonds and let rise, uncovered, 1 hour. Bake in moderate oven (350°F.) 30 to 40 minutes. Turn out of pan and turn right side up. Cool on rack.

TURBAN COFFEE CAKE

2 packages active dry yeast
1/2 cup milk, scalded and cooled
2-3/4 cups all-purpose flour
1/2 cup soft butter
1/2 cup granulated sugar
3 eggs
1 tablespoon grated lemon rind
1 teaspoon salt
1/4 teaspoon mace
2 tablespoons grated nuts
Confectioners' sugar

Sprinkle dry yeast into 1/4 cup very warm water. Let stand a few minutes; then stir until dissolved. Add milk and 1 cup flour; beat well. Cover and let rise until doubled, about 30 minutes. Cream butter and granulated sugar until light. Add eggs one at a time, beating well after each addition. Add lemon rind. Add yeast mixture and remaining 1 3/4 cups flour, sifted with salt and mace. Grease well a 9-cup turban mold and sprinkle nuts to cover the inside. Put dough in mold, cover and let rise about 1 1/2 hours, or until doubled. Bake in moderate oven (325°F.) about 45 minutes. Turn out on rack and cool. Sift confectioners' sugar lightly over top.

EASY CHRISTMAS STOLLEN

Hot-roll mix provides a short-cut method for making this traditional favorite.

1 package hot-roll mix
2 eggs
1/2 teaspoon ground cardamom seed
3/4 cup seedless raisins
1 tablespoon granulated sugar
1/2 cup confectioners' sugar
1-1/2 teaspoons milk
Candied fruit

Prepare roll mix as directed on the label, adding 1 egg and cardamom seed; let rise until double in bulk. Turn out on lightly floured board and knead in raisins. Set aside 1/3 of the dough. Divide remaining dough in 3 equal parts and roll each in a strip about 12" long; braid. Put on greased baking sheet. Divide other piece of dough into 3 equal parts and roll each into a strip about 10" long; braid. Place smaller braid on top of larger braid. Beat remaining egg with granulated sugar and 1 tablespoon water; brush surface; let rise until double. Bake in moderate oven (325°F.) 30 to 40 minutes. When cool, mix confectioners' sugar and milk; glaze top. Decorate with candied fruit. To freeze, leave stollen unfrosted. Thaw, then frost and decorate as directed.

PRONTO PUMPERNICKEL

1 package (13-3/4 ounces) hot-roll mix
2 eggs, 1 separated
1/4 cup old-fashioned molasses
Caraway or other seed
3/4 cup unsifted rye flour

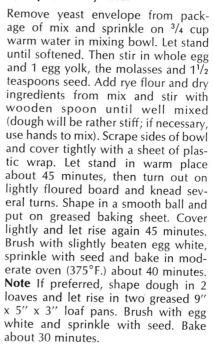

Remove yeast envelope from package of mix and sprinkle on 3/4 cup warm water in mixing bowl. Let stand until softened. Then stir in whole egg and 1 egg yolk, the molasses and 1 1/2 teaspoons seed. Add rye flour and dry ingredients from mix and stir with wooden spoon until well mixed (dough will be rather stiff; if necessary, use hands to mix). Scrape sides of bowl and cover tightly with a sheet of plastic wrap. Let stand in warm place about 45 minutes, then turn out on lightly floured board and knead several turns. Shape in a smooth ball and put on greased baking sheet. Cover lightly and let rise again 45 minutes. Brush with slightly beaten egg white, sprinkle with seed and bake in moderate oven (375°F.) about 40 minutes. **Note** If preferred, shape dough in 2 loaves and let rise in two greased 9" x 5" x 3" loaf pans. Brush with egg white and sprinkle with seed. Bake about 30 minutes.

CHEESE DIAMONDS

1 package hot-roll mix
1 egg
1 package (8 ounces) cream cheese, softened
1/4 cup sugar
3 tablespoons all-purpose flour
1 egg yolk
1/2 teaspoon grated lemon rind
1 tablespoon lemon juice
1/2 cup red jam
Chopped nuts

Prepare hot-roll mix with egg according to package directions. Turn out on lightly floured board and knead until smooth. Put in greased bowl, turn to grease top, cover and let rise until doubled in bulk. Beat cream cheese and sugar together until light and fluffy. Stir in next 4 ingredients. Roll dough in 15" square, cut in twenty-five 3" squares and put on greased baking sheets. Put 1 heaping teaspoonful cheese mixture in center of each square. Bring 2 diagonally opposite corners to center of each square, overlap slightly and pinch together. Cover and let rise 30 minutes, or until doubled. Bake in moderate oven (375°F.) 12 minutes, or until done. Heat jam until melted and brush lightly on hot rolls. Top with nuts.

YORKSHIRE PUDDING I

Old-fashioned Yorkshire pudding is cooked in the dripping pan under the roast and puffs up all around the meat. An easier way is to bake it in individual glass dishes, or a baking pan that keeps it crisp and dry. It is important, however, to use plenty of the beef drippings in preparing the pudding.

2 eggs
1 cup milk
Beef drippings
3/4 cup plus 2 tablespoons all-purpose
**   flour**
1/2 teaspoon salt

Beat eggs well, add milk and 3 tablespoons drippings. Beat in flour and salt. Blend thoroughly. Grease 11" x 7" x 1½" baking pan or custard cups with drippings and pour in batter. Bake in very hot oven (450°F.) 10 minutes, reduce heat to 350°F. and bake about 20 minutes, or until crisp and golden brown. Makes 4 to 6 servings.

HOLIDAY DOUGHNUTS

1/2 cup milk, scalded
2 tablespoons granulated sugar
Dash of salt
5 tablespoons soft butter or margarine
1 package active dry yeast
2-1/2 cups all-purpose flour
2 teaspoons cinnamon
1 egg
Raspberry or strawberry jam
Fat for deep frying
Confectioners' sugar

Pour milk over next 3 ingredients; cool. Soften yeast in ¼ cup warm water. Add to first mixture and set aside for 10 minutes. Sift flour and cinnamon into large bowl. Add yeast mixture and egg; mix well. Turn out on lightly floured board and knead until dough rounds up in a smooth ball. Put in greased bowl, turn and cover with damp cloth. Let rise in warm place until doubled in bulk, about an hour. Turn out on floured board and let rest 10 minutes. Shape dough in a roll about 12" long and cut in 12 equal pieces. Put ½ teaspoon jam in center of each and, with lightly floured hands, shape in a round bun. Let stand 20 minutes. Fry 3 or 4 at a time in hot deep fat (370°F. on frying thermometer) 3 to 4 minutes, or until golden brown, turning the doughnuts as they rise. Drain on absorbent paper and sprinkle with confectioners' sugar. Makes 12.

YORKSHIRE PUDDING II

This is an old English recipe. The batter should be made an hour or so ahead and allowed to stand.

2 eggs
1 cup plus 2 tablespoons milk
1/4 teaspoon salt
1/4 cup all-purpose flour
Drippings

Beat eggs well and add next 3 ingredients; beat thoroughly. Cover and let stand. Put drippings in 6 small custard cups or individual pottery baking dishes and put in oven to heat. Fold 1 tablespoon water into batter and fill heated containers. Bake in very hot oven (450°F.) 15 to 20 minutes, or until crisp, puffy and browned. Makes 4 servings.

BOSTON BROWN BREAD

The all-New England favorite.

Cream 2 tablespoons solid vegetable shortening, ¼ cup sugar, 1 egg and ¾ cup molasses; beat. Mix 2¼ cups whole-wheat flour, ¾ cup yellow cornmeal, 1 teaspoon salt and 1½ teaspoons each double-acting baking powder and baking soda; add alternately with 1¾ cups buttermilk to first mixture, beating until smooth. Fold in ⅔ cup seedless raisins. Spoon into 2 well-greased 1-quart molds, filling molds a little more than half full. Cover with greased lids or foil. Set molds on rack in deep kettle and add boiling water to come halfway up sides of molds. Cover and steam about 2½ hours. Makes 2.

SUGARED DOUGHNUTS

Roll them in sugar and cinnamon.

2 eggs, beaten
3/4 cup sugar
3 tablespoons shortening
3/4 cup mashed cooked sweet potatoes
1/4 cup milk
3-1/2 cups all-purpose flour
4 teaspoons double-acting baking powder
1/2 teaspoon salt
1/4 teaspoon each nutmeg and
**   cinnamon**
Fat for deep frying

Beat first 4 ingredients until well blended. Add milk and sifted dry ingredients; mix well. Chill 1 hour, or until firm enough to roll. Roll on lightly floured board to ½" thickness and cut with floured 3" doughnut cutter. Fry in hot deep fat (375°F. on a frying thermometer) until golden brown and done. Drain. Makes 30.

BUÑUELOS DE PLÁTANOS
(Mexican Banana Fritters)

4 large ripe bananas
1 egg
1/4 cup all-purpose flour
1 teaspoon each sugar and melted butter
Few grains of salt
Fat for deep frying
Confectioners' sugar

Mash 1 banana. Beat egg until very light and thick; fold in mashed banana, flour, sugar, butter and salt. Cut remaining bananas in 1" slices, dip in batter and fry in hot deep fat (360°F. on a frying thermometer) until brown on both sides. Serve with confectioners' sugar. Makes 6 servings.

APPLE FRITTERS

4 medium-size tart cooking apples, cored and peeled
Sugar
1/2 teaspoon nutmeg
2 tablespoons lemon juice
1 cup all-purpose flour
1/2 teaspoon salt
1 cup beer
Fat for deep frying

Slice apples in ½" rings. Sprinkle with sugar and nutmeg and pour lemon juice over top. Let stand 1 hour. Mix flour, salt and ½ cup beer. Then add remaining beer, beating until smooth. Dip apple slices in batter and fry a few at a time in hot deep fat (380°F. on frying thermometer) until well browned and puffy. Drain on absorbent paper and sprinkle with more sugar. Serve warm. Makes about 16.

CHEESE BLINTZES

1-1/2 cups all-purpose flour
1 teaspoon salt
5 eggs
2/3 cup milk
Shortening
1 pound cottage cheese
Dairy sour cream

Combine flour and salt. Add 1¼ cup water and mix until fairly smooth. Add 4 eggs and beat well. Add milk and mix to a thin batter. Heat a small amount of shortening in a 6" skillet. Pour in ¼ cup batter. Cook slowly until pancake is lightly browned on bottom and set on top. Turn out onto plate with browned side up. Repeat, making about 12 pancakes. Mix cheese with remaining egg. Put a spoonful of cheese in center of each pancake, fold in ends and roll. Brown in small amount of shortening. Serve with sour cream. Makes 4 servings.

CHEESE POPOVERS

2 eggs
1 cup each milk and all-purpose flour
1/4 teaspoon salt
1/4 cup grated sharp Cheddar cheese

Beat eggs with milk. Add flour and salt; beat vigorously 2 minutes. Pour batter into very hot greased custard cups or iron popover pans, filling two thirds full. Sprinkle with grated cheese. Bake in hot oven (425°F.) about 40 minutes. Serve at once. Makes 6 large popovers.

SOUTHERN GRITS BREAD

Delicious with jelly or gravy, accompanying roast pork or veal.

2 cups milk
1/2 cup hominy grits
1 teaspoon butter
1/2 teaspoon salt
1 egg, beaten

Bring milk to a boil and pour over grits, stirring to keep from lumping. Cook until thick, stirring constantly. Stir in butter until melted; add salt and egg. Pour into well-greased 9" pan and bake in hot oven (400°F.) 30 minutes, or until bread rises and top browns. Cut in wedges. Serves 6.

DOUBLE-CORN STICKS

1 cup all-purpose flour
1 cup yellow cornmeal
2 tablespoons sugar
1-1/2 teaspoons double-acting baking powder
1 teaspoon salt
1/4 teaspoon baking soda
2 tablespoons butter or margarine
1 egg
3/4 cup cream-style corn
2/3 cup buttermilk

Mix dry ingredients and cut in butter. Add remaining ingredients, mixing only enough to dampen dry ingredients. Fill well-greased corn-stick pans two thirds full. Bake in hot oven (425°F.) about 20 minutes. Makes 1 dozen corn sticks.

CORN CRISPS

1 cup cornmeal
1 tablespoon fat
1/2 teaspoon salt
7/8 cup boiling water

Mix all ingredients and make balls, using 1 rounded measuring-teaspoonful of mixture for each. Put on well-greased baking sheet about 3" apart. With moistened fingers, pat out very thin to rounds about 3" in diameter. Bake in hot oven (400°F.) about 10 minutes. Makes 2 dozen.

HUSH PUPPIES

1 cup white cornmeal
1/4 teaspoon baking soda
1/2 teaspoon double-acting baking
   powder
1/4 teaspoon salt
2 tablespoons flour
1/3 cup finely minced onion
1/3 cup buttermilk
1 egg
Lard or other fat for deep frying

Put dry ingredients and onion in small mixing bowl; stir. Add buttermilk and egg and beat until well mixed. Drop by tablespoonfuls into hot deep fat (365°F. on a frying thermometer). When golden brown on one side, turn and brown on other. Remove from fat with long-handled slotted spoon and drain on absorbent paper. Check inside for doneness. Serve at once, piping hot. Makes about 12.

SPOON BREAD

This is one of the South's greatest culinary contributions to American cookery. It makes a fine escort for most meats.

1 cup cornmeal
3 cups milk
3/4 teaspoon salt
1/4 cup butter
3 eggs, separated
1 teaspoon double-acting baking powder

Gradually add cornmeal to 2 cups boiling milk in saucepan, stirring with a wire whisk or slotted spoon. Keep stirring until mixture is very thick, switching to a wooden spoon if handy. Reduce heat. Continue cooking until most of liquid has been absorbed. Remove from heat. Add salt, butter and remaining milk beaten with egg yolks. Beat until smooth. Cover and keep at room temperature until ready to bake. Before baking, beat whites until stiff. Fold in baking powder and then fold into the prepared mush. Spoon at once into well-buttered 2-quart baking dish or soufflé dish. Bake in moderate oven (375°F.) 45 to 50 minutes, or until top is golden and mixture no longer shakes in middle when pan is moved. Do not overcook. Serve plain as a starchy vegetable, or top each portion with a teaspoon of tart jelly, such as currant, plum or grape. Makes 8 servings. **Cheesed Spoon Bread** Follow above recipe, adding 2 cups shredded sharp Cheddar cheese to the well-blended lukewarm mixture before adding egg whites.

CUSTARDY CORN BREAD

3/4 cup white cornmeal
1/4 cup flour
1 to 2 tablespoons sugar
1 teaspoon double-acting baking powder
1/2 teaspoon salt
1-1/2 cups plus 2 tablespoons milk
1 egg, well beaten
2 tablespoons butter or margarine

Mix dry ingredients. Stir in 1 cup plus 2 tablespoons milk and the egg. Melt butter in 8" square pan and pour mixture into pan. Just before baking, pour remaining milk over batter; do not stir. Bake in hot oven (400°F.) about 30 minutes. Makes 4 to 6 servings.

CHEESE-TOPPED CORNMEAL SQUARES

Cream ½ cup butter. Add 2 cups finely shredded sharp Cheddar cheese and a dash each of cayenne and Worcestershire. Beat until very fluffy; fold in 2 stiffly beaten egg whites. Bake 2 packages corn-bread mix in foil pans that come with mix and cut in 9 to 12 squares each. Put on a baking sheet and top each square with a spoonful of the cheese mixture. Bake in hot oven (400°F.) 15 to 20 minutes.

QUICK STICKY ROLLS

2 tablespoons butter or margarine
1/4 cup honey
1/2 cup broken pecans or walnuts
1 tube (8 ounces) refrigerated buttermilk
   biscuits

Melt butter in 10" piepan. Drizzle in honey, sprinkle with nuts and top with biscuits. Bake as directed on package label. Serve warm.

QUICK CRESCENT ROLLS

1 tablespoon margarine, softened
Sugar
1 egg, separated
2 tablespoons flaked coconut
1 tablespoon minced candied orange
   peel (optional)
1 tube (8 ounces) refrigerated crescent
   dinner rolls

Mix margarine, 2 tablespoons sugar, the egg yolk, coconut, and orange peel, if desired. Separate rolls into 8 triangles. Put about 1 teaspoonful of filling in center of each triangle and roll as directed. Put on lightly greased baking sheet and brush with slightly beaten egg white. Sprinkle with sugar and bake in moderate oven (375°F.) about 15 minutes. Serve warm or cool.

CRANBERRY-NUT BREAD

1/2 cup butter or margarine
1/2 cup packed light-brown sugar
1/4 cup orange marmalade
3/4 cup small-curd creamed cottage cheese (or farmer cheese, mashed)
2 eggs
Grated rind of 1 lemon
Grated rind of 1 orange
1/4 cup orange juice
2-2/3 cups all-purpose flour
3 teaspoons double-acting baking powder
1 teaspoon baking soda
1 teaspoon salt
1/4 teaspoon pumpkin-pie spice
1 cup golden raisins
1 cup cranberries, halved
1 cup coarsely chopped pecans or other nuts
Glaze

Beat first 2 ingredients until fluffy. Add marmalade and next 5 ingredients and mix well. Mix flour and next 4 ingredients and stir into creamed mixture. Fold in fruits and nuts. Spread in well-greased 9" x 5" x 3" loaf pan and bake in slow oven (325°F.) 1 hour and 15 minutes. Brush with Glaze as bread comes from oven. Let stand on cake rack 10 minutes, then remove from pan to rack to cool. Best 1 to 2 days old; can be frozen (omit Glaze; thaw before glazing). **Glaze** Mix until smooth 1 cup confectioners' sugar, 1 tablespoon melted butter and about 2 tablespoons orange juice to make a rather thin glaze.

DATE-NUT-LEMON BREAD

2 cups all-purpose flour
1-1/2 teaspoons double-acting baking powder
1/2 teaspoon baking soda
1/2 teaspoon salt
1 cup sugar
1 cup finely chopped nuts
1 package (8 ounces) pitted dates, cut in eighths
Grated rind and juice of 1 lemon
2 tablespoons margarine, melted
1 egg, well beaten

In mixing bowl, combine first 7 ingredients and mix well. Combine rind, juice, margarine and enough water to make 1½ cups mixture. Beat in egg. Pour over dry ingredients and mix just enough to blend. Spoon into well-greased and lightly floured 9" x 5" x 3" loaf pan and bake in slow oven (325°F.) 1 hour and 15 minutes, or until done. Turn out and cool. Wrap airtight and store in cool place. Serve with cream cheese. Keeps about 1 week.

RAISIN CASSEROLE BREAD

4 cups all-purpose flour
1-1/4 teaspoons salt
1-1/2 teaspoons baking soda
3/4 cup packed dark-brown sugar
1-1/4 cups raisins
2 tablespoons butter or margarine, melted
2 eggs, slightly beaten
1-1/2 cups buttermilk

Mix first 5 ingredients in bowl. Add remaining ingredients and mix only until dry ingredients are moistened. Spoon into 2 greased 1-quart casseroles and smooth tops. Bake in moderate oven (350°F.) about 45 minutes. Loosen edges and turn out on racks to cool. **Note** Bread can be frozen if desired. Is also good toasted.

PEANUT QUICK BREAD

1-3/4 cups all-purpose flour
2 teaspoons double-acting baking powder
1 teaspoon salt
1/3 cup sugar
2 tablespoons butter or margarine
1 egg
1-1/4 cups milk
1 cup chopped peanuts

Mix dry ingredients together, then cut in butter. Beat egg with milk and stir into first mixture. Stir in peanuts, pour into lightly greased 9" x 5" x 3" loaf pan and bake in moderate oven (350°F.) about 1 hour. Turn out on cake rack and cool thoroughly before cutting. Bread slices better the second day.

HAWAIIAN BANANA BREAD

1-1/4 cups all-purpose flour
1 cup sugar
1/2 teaspoon salt
1 teaspoon baking soda
1/2 cup solid vegetable shortening
2 fully ripe medium bananas
2 eggs

Sift dry ingredients into bowl. Whirl remaining ingredients in blender. Add to dry ingredients and mix just until dry ingredients are moistened. Spoon into lightly buttered and floured 9" square pan and bake in moderate oven (350°F.) 35 to 40 minutes. Remove from oven; let stand 5 minutes. Loosen edges with spatula and turn out onto cake rack covered with waxed paper. Cool to room temperature before cutting in squares. **Note** This is a very moist, spongy bread that stays fresh several days if stored airtight.

EASY COFFEE-RAISIN CAKE

1/2 cup butter or margarine, softened
1-1/2 cups packed brown sugar
1 egg
2 cups all-purpose flour
1 teaspoon baking soda
1 teaspoon each ground cloves, cinnamon and nutmeg
1 cup cold coffee
1 cup finely cut peeled apple
1 cup plumped raisins (see Note)
1 teaspoon each grated orange and lemon rinds
1/2 cup chopped nuts
Orange Glaze

Cream first 3 ingredients together until light and fluffy. Add sifted dry ingredients alternately with coffee, beating after each addition until smooth. Add remaining ingredients, except glaze, and mix well. Put in 9″ x 5″ x 3″ loaf pan lined on bottom with waxed paper. Bake in moderate oven (350°F.) 1 hour, or until done. While still warm, drizzle glaze over top. **Note** To plump raisins, put in bowl and cover with boiling water. Let stand 2 to 3 minutes; drain and dry on paper towels. **Orange Glaze** Mix 2 tablespoons frozen orange-juice concentrate and ¼ cup sifted confectioners' sugar until smooth.

CARDAMOM COFFEE CAKE

1 tablespoon cardamom pods with seed
1 tablespoon butter, softened
Fine dry bread crumbs
1 teaspoon cinnamon
Sugar
2 tablespoons chopped nuts
1 egg
3/4 cup milk, heated to lukewarm
2-1/2 cups all-purpose flour
2-1/2 teaspoons double-acting baking powder
1/2 teaspoon salt
1 cup margarine, melted

Remove cardamom seed from pods and crush; set aside. Butter (use the 1 tablespoon) 9″ square cake pan and sprinkle with bread crumbs. Shake off excess crumbs. Mix cinnamon, 1 tablespoon sugar and nuts and set aside. Beat egg until light; gradually add 1¼ cups sugar and beat until fluffy. Add cardomom seed, then add milk alternately with mixed dry ingredients. Add margarine and stir until well blended. Turn into pan and sprinkle sugar-nut mixture on top. Press down slightly; bake in moderate oven (350°F.) 35 to 40 minutes, or until cake tests done. Cool on rack. Turn out and serve in ½″ slices. Store tightly wrapped in refrigerator; keeps up to 2 weeks. Can be frozen.

QUICK OLIVE-NUT BREAD

2-1/4 cups buttermilk biscuit mix
1/2 cup sugar
1 egg, slightly beaten
3/4 cup milk
1 cup chopped walnuts or other nuts
1 cup chopped pimiento-stuffed olives

Put mix and sugar in bowl. Add egg mixed with milk; mix only enough to moisten dry ingredients. Fold in nuts and olives and put in greased 9″ x 5″ x 3″ loaf pan. Bake in moderate oven (350°F.) about 45 minutes. Turn out on rack, then turn right side up and cool thoroughly before cutting.

PEANUT-PINEAPPLE BUNS

3/4 cup packed light-brown sugar
Butter or margarine
1/2 cup salted-peanut halves
3/4 cup pineapple preserves
2 cups buttermilk biscuit mix
1/4 cup chopped salted peanuts
1/4 cup raisins

Generously grease twelve 3″ muffin cups. Mix ½ cup brown sugar, ⅓ cup melted butter and the peanut halves; divide among cups. With fork, stir preserves into biscuit mix. Knead on lightly floured board 10 turns, then roll to 16″ x 8″ rectangle. Spread with 2 tablespoons softened butter and sprinkle with chopped peanuts, remaining brown sugar and raisins. Roll tightly from long side and pinch to seal. With floured knife, cut crosswise in 12 slices. Put in prepared muffin cups and bake in hot oven (400°F.) 8 to 12 minutes. At once, invert on cake rack covered with waxed paper. Let stand 1 minute, then remove pan.

ORANGE-VELVET CRUMB CAKE

1-1/2 cups buttermilk biscuit mix
3/4 cup granulated sugar
4 tablespoons butter
1 egg
3/4 cup milk
1/3 cup packed light-brown sugar
2 tablespoons cream
1-1/2 teaspoons grated orange rind
1-1/2 teaspoons orange juice
1/2 cup flaked coconut
1/4 cup chopped nuts

Combine biscuit mix and granulated sugar. Add 1 tablespoon soft butter, the egg and ¼ cup milk; beat vigorously 1 minute. Stir in remaining milk and beat ½ minute. Pour into greased and floured 9″ round or 8″ square cake pan. Bake in moderate oven (350°F.) about 35 minutes. Mix remaining butter, melted, and remaining ingredients; spread on hot cake. Set 3 inches under broiler for 3 minutes.

BLUEBERRY MUFFINS

2-1/2 cups all-purpose flour
2-1/2 teaspoons double-acting baking powder
1/4 teaspoon salt
Sugar
1 cup buttermilk
2 eggs, beaten
1/2 cup butter or margarine, melted
1-1/2 cups washed fresh blueberries

Sift first 3 ingredients and ½ cup sugar. Add next 3 ingredients and mix only until dry ingredients are dampened. Fold in berries. Spoon into greased muffin pans; filling two thirds full. Sprinkle with sugar. Bake in hot oven (400°F.) 20 to 25 minutes. Makes 16 to 24 muffins.

APPLE MUFFINS

1-1/2 cups all-purpose flour
1/3 cup granulated sugar
2 teaspoons double-acting baking powder
1/2 teaspoon salt
1/2 cup dry nonfat milk
1 teaspoon cinnamon
1/4 cup soft shortening
1 egg
1 cup finely chopped peeled apple
1/3 cup packed brown sugar
1/2 cup finely chopped nuts

Mix first 5 ingredients and ½ teaspoon cinnamon in bowl. Add shortening, egg, ½ cup water and apple and mix quickly and lightly. Spoon batter into 12 greased 2¾" muffin cups. Mix remaining cinnamon, brown sugar and nuts and sprinkle on top. Bake in moderate oven (375°F.) about 20 minutes.

PEANUT-BUTTER MUFFINS

1-3/4 cups all-purpose flour
2-1/2 teaspoons double-acting baking powder
2 tablespoons sugar
3/4 teaspoon salt
2 tablespoons wheat germ
1/4 cup soft shortening
1/4 cup peanut butter
1 egg, well beaten
3/4 cup milk
Apricot preserves

Sift first 4 ingredients into bowl. Add wheat germ. Cut in shortening and peanut butter. Mix egg and milk and add all at once to first mixture. Stir only until dry ingredients are dampened. Spoon into greased large muffin pans, filling only two thirds full. Put about ½ teaspoon preserves in center of each. Bake in hot oven (400°F.) 25 minutes, or until done. Makes 10.

CRUMB COFFEE CAKE

Sugar
1/4 cup all-purpose flour
1/8 teaspoon cinnamon
Butter
1-1/4 cups biscuit mix
1/4 teaspoon baking soda
1 egg
3/4 cup dairy sour cream
1 teaspoon vanilla extract

Cream 3 tablespoons sugar, the flour, cinnamon and 2 tablespoons butter; set aside for topping. Combine biscuit mix, ¾ cup sugar and soda. Add 3 tablespoons melted butter, the egg and half the sour cream. Beat vigorously 1 minute. Stir in remaining sour cream and vanilla. Beat ½ minute. Pour into buttered 8" square pan. Sprinkle with topping. Bake in moderate oven (350°F.) about 35 minutes.

QUICK CARDAMOM COFFEE CAKE

2-3/4 cups all-purpose flour
1-1/2 teaspoons double-acting baking powder
1 teaspoon crushed cardamom seed
1/2 teaspoon salt
Sugar
1/2 cup margarine
1-1/3 cups light cream or milk
1/2 teaspoon cinnamon
1/4 cup finely chopped nuts

Mix first 4 ingredients and 1 cup sugar. Cut in margarine until particles are the size of peas. Add cream and stir quickly until blended. Spread in well-greased 9" square pan. Sprinkle with cinnamon mixed with 2 tablespoons sugar. Sprinkle with nuts; bake in moderate oven (375°F.) 35 to 40 minutes. Slice; serve warm or cool.

ORANGE-NUT BREAD

2-1/2 cups all-purpose flour
3 teaspoons double-acting baking powder
1 teaspoon salt
1 cup sugar
1/4 cup shortening
3/4 cup milk
1/4 cup orange juice
1 egg
3 tablespoons grated orange rind
1 cup chopped nuts

Sift dry ingredients into bowl. Cut in shortening with pastry blender or 2 knives. Add milk, orange juice and egg. Mix only enough to dampen dry ingredients. Add grated rind and nuts. Pour into greased 9" x 5" x 3" loaf pan, spread batter to corners and leave a slight depression in center. Let stand 20 minutes. Bake in moderate oven (350°F.) about 1 hour. Let stand 5 minutes, then turn out on rack. Store overnight before slicing.

APPLECAKE

1 cup all-purpose flour
1-1/2 teaspoons double-acting baking powder
1/4 teaspoon salt
4 tablespoons sugar
Butter
1 egg, well beaten
1/4 cup milk
4 cups sliced peeled tart apples
1/2 teaspoon cinnamon
1/4 teaspoon nutmeg
1/4 cup seedless raisins

Mix first 3 ingredients and 2 tablespoons sugar. Cut in ⅓ cup butter. Mix egg and milk and beat into flour. Spread in greased 10" x 6" x 2" baking pan. Arrange apple slices in overlapping rows on batter, slightly pressing down straight edges. Sprinkle with mixture of spices and remaining sugar. Brush with 2 tablespoons butter, melted; sprinkle with raisins. Bake in hot oven (400°F.) about 40 minutes.

CHEESE MUFFINS

2 cups all-purpose flour
3 teaspoons double-acting baking powder
1 tablespoon sugar
1/2 teaspoon salt
1 egg
1 cup milk
3 tablespoons butter, softened
1-1/2 cups diced sharp Cheddar cheese

Mix first 4 ingredients in medium-size bowl. Put egg, milk and margarine in blender, cover and whirl until smooth. Add cheese, cover and grind. Pour into dry ingredients and mix only until moistened. Spoon into 18 greased medium muffin-pan sections and bake in hot oven (400°F.) about 25 minutes.

SWEET CRANBERRY MUFFINS

2 cups all-purpose flour
1/2 cup sugar
3 teaspoons double-acting baking powder
1/2 teaspoon salt
1/4 cup shortening, melted
1 egg
1 cup milk
1 cup cranberries
Melted butter or margarine
2 tablespoons cinnamon-sugar

Mix flour, sugar, baking powder and salt in bowl. Add next 3 ingredients and stir to mix. Fold in cranberries and spoon into well-greased medium muffin pans. Bake in hot oven (400°F.) 20 to 25 minutes. Remove from pans, brush tops with melted butter and sprinkle with cinnamon-sugar. Serve warm. Makes 12 medium muffins.

CRANBERRY-ORANGE TEA BREAD

2 cups all-purpose flour
1-1/2 teaspoons double-acting baking powder
1/2 teaspoon baking soda
1/2 teaspoon salt
1 cup sugar
1/2 cup finely chopped walnuts
2 cups fresh cranberries, coarsely chopped
Grated rind and juice of 1 orange
1/4 cup margarine, melted
1 egg, well beaten

In mixing bowl, mix well first 7 ingredients. Combine rind, juice, margarine and enough water to make ¾ cup mixture. Beat in egg. Pour over dry ingredients and mix just enough to dampen. Spoon into greased 9" x 5" x 3" loaf pan and bake in moderate oven (350°F.) 1 hour and 10 minutes, or until done. Turn out and cool. Store airtight. Keeps about 1 week.

SOUR-CREAM MUFFINS

1 egg
1 cup dairy sour cream
1/4 cup milk
2 tablespoons butter, melted
2 cups all-purpose flour
1/4 cup sugar
2 teaspoons double-acting baking powder
1/2 teaspoon baking soda
1/2 teaspoon salt

Beat egg, sour cream and milk until light. Add butter and sifted dry ingredients. Stir only until dry ingredients are dampened. Fill 12 greased 2¾" muffin cups half full with batter. Bake in hot oven (400°F.) about 20 minutes. Makes 12.

SWEET-POTATO MUFFINS

1-3/4 cups all-purpose flour
1 teaspoon salt
3 teaspoons double-acting baking powder
1 tablespoon brown sugar
1/2 cup coarsely chopped walnuts
2 eggs, beaten
3/4 cup milk
1-1/4 cups mashed cooked sweet potatoes
1/4 cup melted butter
Cinnamon-sugar

Sift first 3 ingredients into bowl. Add brown sugar and nuts; mix well. Combine next 4 ingredients and mix well. Add to flour mixture, stirring only until dry ingredients are dampened. Fill greased 2¼" muffin cups two thirds full with batter. Bake in hot oven (425°F.) about 25 minutes. Sprinkle tops with mixture of cinnamon-sugar. Makes 1 dozen.

ORANGE PINWHEEL ROLLS

2 cups all-purpose flour, spooned into
  cup
3 teaspoons double-acting baking powder
Sugar
1/2 teaspoon salt
1/4 cup shortening
1 egg, beaten
1/2 cup milk
Grated rind of 1 large orange
2 tablespoons butter or margarine,
  melted

Sift flour, baking powder, 2 table-spoons sugar and the salt. Cut in shortening. Combine eggs and milk and add to dry ingredients, stirring with fork only until dry ingredients are dampened. Turn out on floured board and knead gently 30 seconds. Roll to a rectangle ¼″ thick. Mix ½ cup sugar with orange rind. Brush dough with melted butter and sprinkle with half the orange mixture. Roll up and cut in 24 slices ¾″ thick. Put in paper muffin cups and sprinkle with remaining orange mixture. Bake in hot oven (425°F.) 15 to 20 minutes. Makes 2 dozen.

PEANUT-HONEY SQUARES

1/3 cup peanut butter
2 cups biscuit mix
1 egg, beaten
1/4 cup honey
3/4 cup milk
1/2 cup salted peanuts, chopped

Cut peanut butter into biscuit mix with pastry blender. Mix egg, honey and milk; add to first mixture and stir just to blend. Fold in peanuts. Pour into greased 9″ square pan. Bake in hot oven (400°F.) about 25 minutes. Cut in squares.

CHEDDAR BISCUIT RING

3 cups all-purpose flour
4-1/2 teaspoons double-acting baking
  powder
1 teaspoon salt
1 cup grated sharp Cheddar cheese
6 tablespoons soft shortening
1 cup milk
Melted butter or margarine

Sift dry ingredients into bowl and add ¾ cup cheese. Cut in shortening. Add milk and stir with fork until just blended. Turn out on lightly floured board and knead a few turns. Roll to ¼″ thickness and cut in 1¾″ rounds. Butter a 1½-quart ring mold. Stand biscuits on end to fill mold. Sprinkle with ¼ cup cheese. Bake in hot oven (425°F.) 20 to 25 minutes. Serve at once.

BAKING-POWDER BISCUITS

2 cups all-purpose flour
2 teaspoons double-acting baking powder
1/2 teaspoon salt
Butter or margarine
2/3 cup (about) milk

Sift dry ingredients. Cut in ¼ cup butter. Add milk, a little at a time, to make soft dough. Turn dough out on lightly floured board and knead half a minute, or just enough to shape. Roll out ½″ thick; cut with 2″ biscuit cutter. Place on ungreased baking sheet. Brush tops with melted butter. Bake in very hot oven (450°F.) about 12 minutes. Makes 8 to 10.

MOTHER'S BISCUITS

2 cups sifted cake flour
1/2 teaspoon salt
2 teaspoons double-acting baking powder
2 tablespoons butter
3 tablespoons vegetable shortening
1/2 cup (about) milk

Sift dry ingredients together. Cut in butter and shortening with pastry blender, fork or fingertips until mixture is the consistency of coarse meal. Mixing with fork, add enough milk to form a soft dough. Work gently with fingertips, turn out on floured board and pat with floured hands to ¼″ thickness. Fold over in 3 layers; pat to ½″ thickness. Cut with floured 2″ cutter. Put on ungreased baking sheets; bake in very hot oven (450°F.) about 12 minutes. Makes 12.

TOUCH O' CORN BISCUITS

1/3 cup white or yellow cornmeal
1 cup all-purpose flour
1/2 teaspoon salt
1 teaspoon sugar
1/4 teaspoon baking soda
1 teaspoon double-acting baking powder
1/3 cup solid vegetable shortening
1/3 to 1/2 cup buttermilk
Butter

Put cornmeal in mixing bowl. Sift remaining dry ingredients over meal. Mix in vegetable shortening with fingers. Add enough buttermilk to make dough suitable for rolling. Make into a ball and roll ⅓″ thick on a floured board. Cut with 2″ round biscuit cutter. Using a pancake turner, place biscuits on ungreased baking sheet, side by side but not touching. Brush tops with melted butter. Bake in very hot oven (450°F.) 12 to 15 minutes. Serve very hot with butter. Makes about 16. *Note* If desired, sprinkle before baking with any seed of your choice, such as poppy, sesame or caraway.

BUTTERSCOTCH-ALMOND BUNS

1/4 cup butter or margarine, softened
1/2 cup packed light-brown sugar
1/3 cup slivered almonds
1 tube (8 ounces) refrigerated biscuits

Mix butter and sugar well. Spoon evenly into 10 medium muffin cups along with almonds. Press a biscuit into each cup. Bake in hot oven (425°F.) 10 to 12 minutes. Leave in pan about 5 minutes, then turn out and serve warm.

APRICOT TURNOVERS

2-1/2 cups all-purpose flour, spooned into cup
1/4 cup sugar
3 teaspoons double-acting baking powder
3/4 teaspoon salt
1/2 cup butter or margarine
2 eggs
Milk
Apricot preserves

Put first 4 ingredients in bowl and cut in butter until fine crumbs are formed. Break eggs into 8-ounce measuring cup and fill with milk. Add to first mixture and stir with fork to form soft dough. Turn out on lightly floured board and knead a few turns. Roll to a rectangle 1/4" thick and, with floured knife, cut in 2 1/2" squares. Put 1/2 teaspoon apricot preserves in center of each square and fold over to form a triangle. Put on ungreased baking sheet and bake in hot oven (425°F.) about 12 minutes. Makes about 20.

BUTTERMILK BANNOCK

Bannock was formerly baked on a griddle. The word comes from the Gaelic and means "cake."

3-1/2 cups all-purpose flour
1/2 cup wheat germ
1-3/4 teaspoons baking soda
1/2 teaspoon cream of tartar
1 teaspoon salt
Melted butter or margarine
2 tablespoons dark corn syrup
1-1/2 cups buttermilk

Mix first 5 ingredients in a bowl. Combine 1/2 cup melted butter, the syrup and buttermilk; mix into dry ingredients with a fork. Turn dough out on a lightly floured board and knead gently for a few seconds. Shape into 2 thick round cakes, about 7" in diameter. Bake on greased cookie sheet in moderate oven (375°F.) 20 to 25 minutes, or until firm. Brush tops with melted butter. Cut in wedges to serve.

CURRANT SCONES

2 cups all-purpose flour
1-1/2 teaspoons cream of tartar
3/4 teaspoon baking soda
1 teaspoon salt
1/2 cup butter or margarine
1/2 cup currants or seedless raisins
1 egg
3/4 cup (about) buttermilk
1 egg yolk
Sugar

Sift first 4 ingredients into bowl. Cut in butter. Add currants, whole egg and enough buttermilk to make a soft dough. Mix and turn out on well-floured board. Knead a few turns, then roll to 1/2" thickness. Cut in 2" diamonds. Put on cookie sheets and prick tops several times with fork. Beat egg yolk with a little cold water and brush on scones. Sprinkle with sugar. Bake in hot oven (425°F.) about 15 minutes. Makes about 2 dozen.

ORANGE-PLUM TWISTS

2 cups biscuit mix
2 tablespoons granulated sugar
1 teaspoon grated orange rind
1 egg
6 tablespoons heavy cream
1/2 cup damson plum preserves
Confectioners' sugar

Combine granulated sugar and rind. Beat egg and cream and stir into first mixture with fork. Put on floured board and knead a few times. Roll out to form a rectangle 16" x 4". Spread with preserves and fold lengthwise in thirds to form a strip about 16" x 1 1/4". Cut crosswise in 1" strips. Give each strip a half twist and put on well-greased cookie sheet and bake in very hot oven (450°F.) 8 to 10 minutes. Sift confectioners' sugar over top while twists are warm. Serve warm or cold. Makes 16.

OATMEAL MUFFINS

1 cup all-purpose flour
2 tablespoons sugar
2 teaspoons double-acting baking powder
1/2 teaspoon baking soda
3/4 teaspoon salt
3/4 cup quick-cooking rolled oats
1/4 cup vegetable shortening
1 egg
1 cup buttermilk

Sift first 5 ingredients together; add oats. Cut in shortening. Add egg and buttermilk and mix only until dry ingredients are dampened. Fill greased muffin pans two thirds full; bake in hot oven (425°F.) about 25 minutes. Makes 10 large muffins.

RAISIN PRALINE COFFEE CAKE

Butter, softened
3/4 cup granulated sugar
1 teaspoon vanilla extract
3 eggs
1-1/2 cups seedless raisins, coarsely chopped
2 cups all-purpose flour
1 teaspoon double-acting baking powder
1 teaspoon baking soda
1/2 teaspoon salt
1 cup dairy sour cream
1 cup packed brown sugar
2 teaspoons cinnamon
3/4 cup coarsely chopped pecans

Cream ½ cup butter; gradually add granulated sugar; beat until light. Add vanilla, then beat in eggs one at a time. Add raisins and dry ingredients alternately with sour cream, mixing well after each addition. Spread half the batter in 9" tube pan lined on the bottom with waxed paper. Cream together ⅓ cup butter and remaining ingredients. Sprinkle half on batter. Repeat layers. Bake in moderate oven (350°F.) 50 minutes, or until done. Cool 10 minutes, then turn out on rack.

KARTOFFELKLOSSE
(Potato Dumplings)

1 pound (4 medium) baking potatoes
Salt
2 tablespoons butter or margarine
Nutmeg or pepper
1 egg, beaten
2/3 to 1 cup all-purpose flour
1/3 cup butter, melted
3/4 cup crisp bread crumbs

Boil unpeeled potatoes in salted water until tender. Drain and dry over low heat a few seconds. White hot, peel and mash or put through ricer (there will be about 2 cups potato purée). Stir in butter, 1 teaspoon salt, and a little nutmeg or pepper. Chill thoroughly. Blend in egg and enough flour to make a mixture that can be handled. On lightly floured board, scoop up spoonfuls of potato and shape in 24 plum-size balls. Roll lightly in flour as you shape. Drop half of them into deep boiling salted water. Cook gently, uncovered, 6 to 8 minutes. Remove with slotted spoon or strainer. Shake to drain thoroughly and drop into warm bowl or pan containing a little of the melted butter. Keep warm. Cook remaining dumplings, pour rest of butter over and toss gently to coat evenly. Sprinkle with crumbs crisped a few minutes in oven or skillet. Good with Sauerbraten, page 69, or boiled beef. Makes 6 servings.

EIERPANNEKOEKEN
(Dutch Egg Pancakes)

4 eggs, beaten until light
1-1/2 to 2 cups milk
2 cups all-purpose flour
3/4 teaspoon salt
Butter
Syrup, honey or molasses
Lemon juice (optional)

Combine eggs and 1 cup milk and stir into sifted dry ingredients. Gradually add enough of remaining milk to make a thin batter. Let stand at least 1 hour. Cook in very well buttered large iron or cast-aluminum skillet or on a griddle. Ladle about ½ cup batter into the skillet, just enough to cover the bottom. Brown and turn to brown lightly on other side. Add butter to pan for each pancake so that cakes brown well and become crisp at the edges. Serve with melted butter, syrup and a touch of lemon juice, if desired. Good with sausages and eggs. Makes 8.

PEANUT-BUTTER PANCAKE SAUCE

1/4 cup molasses
1/3 cup sugar
1/2 teaspoon salt
1 cup peanut butter (any style)

Mix first 3 ingredients and 1⅓ cups water in saucepan. Bring quickly to boil and boil 3 minutes, stirring until sugar is dissolved. Put peanut butter in bowl and gradually add hot syrup, beating with rotary beater until smooth. Makes 2 cups.

HONEY-PINEAPPLE BREAD

3 cups all-purpose flour
3 teaspoons double-acting baking powder
1/2 teaspoon baking soda
1-1/2 teaspoons salt
3 eggs
1/2 cup vegetable oil
1/2 cup honey
1 can (8-1/2 ounces) crushed pineapple, undrained
3/4 cup chopped pecans or walnuts

Sift together dry ingredients. Beat eggs until thick and lemon-colored. Combine oil, honey, pineapple and ½ cup water and mix with eggs. Add to dry ingredients, mixing only until dry ingredients are dampened. Fold in nuts and spread in greased 9" x 5" x 3" loaf pan. Bake in moderate oven (350°F.) 1 hour. Then reduce heat to 325°F. and bake 15 minutes longer, or until center is done. Cool in pan about 5 minutes, then turn out on rack.

DATE-BRAN BREAD

1 cup all-purpose flour
1 cup whole-wheat flour
1-1/2 cups all-bran cereal
1 teaspoon salt
2 teaspoons double-acting baking powder
1/2 teaspoon baking soda
1/2 cup molasses
1-1/2 cups milk
1 egg, well beaten
1/4 cup shortening, melted
1 cup finely cut pitted dates

Mix dry ingredients in bowl. Add remaining ingredients and mix only until dry ingredients are dampened. Pour into greased 9" x 5" x 3" loaf pan and bake in moderate oven (350°F.) about 1 hour. Turn out on rack and cool before cutting.

PEANUT-BUTTER ORANGE BREAD

2-1/4 cups all-purpose flour
3 teaspoons double-acting baking powder
1/2 teaspoon salt
1/3 cup sugar
1/2 cup peanut butter
1 egg, well beaten
1 cup milk
1-1/2 teaspoons grated orange rind
1/4 cup chopped salted peanuts

Sift dry ingredients into bowl. Cut in peanut butter. Mix remaining ingredients and add to first mixture, stirring to blend. Pour into well-greased 9" x 5" x 3" loaf pan and bake in moderate oven (350°F.) 35 to 40 minutes. Remove from pan and cool. Store airtight.

ENGLISH SAFFRON BREAD

Wonderful sliced for tea.

1 teaspoon saffron shreds
3 cups all-purpose flour
1/2 teaspoon salt
3 teaspoons double-acting baking powder
1/2 teaspoon baking soda
1/2 cup shortening
1 cup sugar
2 eggs, beaten
1/2 cup lemon juice
1/2 cup shredded lemon peel

Add 1/2 cup boiling water to saffron and steep 30 minutes. Sift dry ingredients except sugar together. Cream shortening and sugar until light and fluffy; add eggs and beat well. Combine saffron and water with lemon juice and peel. Add with dry ingredients to creamed mixture, mixing only until dry ingredients are dampened. Turn into two 7½" x 3½" x 2¼" loaf pans. Bake in moderate oven (350°F.) 40 to 45 minutes.

BANANA NUT BREAD

Beat together ½ cup vegetable oil and 1 cup sugar. Add 2 beaten eggs, and 3 bananas mashed to a pulp; beat well. Sift 2 cups all-purpose flour, 1 teaspoon baking soda, ½ teaspoon double-acting baking powder and ½ teaspoon salt. Add to first mixture with 3 tablespoons milk and ½ teaspoon vanilla. Beat well and stir in ½ cup chopped nuts. Bake in 9" x 5" x 3" loaf pan, lined on the bottom with waxed paper, in moderate oven (350°F.) about 1 hour. Cool and store airtight.

BLUEBERRY CINNAMON CAKE

Cream ½ cup butter; add 1 cup sugar and beat until light. Beat in 2 eggs, one at a time. Sift together 2½ cups sifted cake flour, 2½ teaspoons double-acting baking powder and ½ teaspoon salt. Add to creamed mixture alternately with ½ cup milk, beating until smooth. Fold in 1½ cups washed blueberries. Pour into greased 9" x 9" x 2" pan; sprinkle with 3 tablespoons sugar and 1 teaspoon cinnamon. Bake in moderate oven (375°F.) 40 minutes; cut in squares. Serve hot.

FOOLPROOF ALL-PURPOSE THIN PANCAKES

(Basic Recipe)

1/2 cup all-purpose flour
1/2 teaspoon double-acting baking powder
1/4 teaspoon salt
1 egg
3/4 cup milk
2 tablespoons butter, melted and cooled

Sift flour, baking powder and salt. Beat egg until light and very slowly add slightly warmed milk and melted butter. Gradually add liquids to dry ingredients and beat until smooth and full of bubbles. Use electric mixer, beater or French wire whisk. Grease a 6" skillet with just enough butter or cooking oil to cover the bottom; ¼ to ½ teaspoon should be sufficient for each pancake. Pour 2 tablespoonfuls of batter all at once into skillet, turning the pan until it spreads and completely covers the bottom. This takes practice, for it must be done quickly. When pancake is brown on one side, turn and brown on the other. Serve plain or fill with creamed meat, fish or vegetables. Makes 1 dozen.

ORANGE SYRUP

Put ¼ cup orange juice, 1 cup light corn syrup and 1 teaspoon grated orange rind in jar or bottle. Cover and keep refrigerated. Shake well before serving on waffles or pancakes. Makes 1¼ cups.

APPLE-WALNUT GRIDDLE CAKES

2 cups all-purpose flour
1 teaspoon baking soda
1/2 teaspoon salt
2 tablespoons sugar
2 eggs, beaten
2 cups buttermilk
2 tablespoons vegetable oil
1-1/2 cups very finely chopped peeled apples
1/2 cup chopped walnuts
Maple syrup

Sift dry ingredients. Mix eggs, buttermilk and oil; gradually add to dry ingredients; stir until smooth. Fold in apples and nuts. Bake on hot greased griddle. Serve with syrup. Makes about 20.

NEW ENGLAND BUCKWHEAT CAKES

This makes a large amount of batter but it can be refrigerated.

2 cups buckwheat flour
3/4 teaspoon salt
1/2 teaspoon double-acting baking powder
1/2 teaspoon baking soda
1 package active dry yeast
1 tablespoon maple sugar or syrup
Milk
Lard or vegetable shortening

The evening before serving these cakes, put buckwheat flour, salt and ¼ teaspoon each baking powder and soda in bowl. Add yeast mixed with 2 cups warm water; add sugar. Put in a mixing bowl, cover and leave at room temperature overnight. Next morning, add remaining baking powder and soda mixed with 1 or 2 tablespoons milk; beat to mix. If batter is too thick, add more milk, 1 tablespoon at a time. To cook cakes use a large iron skillet, preferably a 12" one. Heat and add 1 to 1½ tablespoons lard. Heat until fat smokes. Drop batter by tablespoonfuls into the fat, leaving about 2" between cakes as they spread while cooking. They require a little more fat to be added during cooking than lighter pancakes. When one side is golden brown, turn and brown on other side. These take a little longer to cook than other pancakes. Serve piping hot. Makes about 2 dozen.

ORANGE PANCAKES

Following package directions, prepare enough pancake mix to make about 12 pancakes. Add grated rind of 1 orange and sections of 2 oranges, chopped, to batter. Bake as usual and serve with Orange Syrup, at left.

LOUISIANA PANCAKES

Serve them with butter and jelly.

1-1/2 cups all-purpose flour
3-1/2 teaspoons double-acting baking powder
1 teaspoon salt
1/2 teaspoon nutmeg
1-1/4 cups mashed cooked sweet potatoes
2 eggs, beaten
1-1/2 cups milk
1/4 cup butter, melted

Sift dry ingredients into bowl. Combine remaining ingredients and add to flour; mix only until dry ingredients are dampened. Drop by spoonfuls onto hot greased griddle and fry till browned. Makes 24.

APRICOT SYRUP

Delicious served warm on pancakes, waffles or French toast.

1 box (11 ounces) dried apricots
1 cup dark corn syrup
1 cup light corn syrup
Juice of 1 lemon
Juice of 1 orange

Cook apricots in water to cover until tender. Drain and whirl in blender, or purée in food mill or force through sieve. Add ½ cup water and remaining ingredients. Bring to boil; simmer 10 minutes. Store in refrigerator. Makes about 1 quart.

BIG APPLE PANCAKES

2 cups biscuit mix
2 eggs
1/2 cup dry nonfat milk
1 cup canned apple juice
Double-apple Sauce

Blend all ingredients, except sauce, with ½ cup water. Using ⅓ cup batter for each cake, bake on hot greased griddle or in skillet until browned on both sides. Serve with sauce. Makes twelve 8" cakes. **Double-apple Sauce** Combine 1 cup applesauce, 1 cup apple juice, ½ cup packed light-brown sugar, dash of salt, ½ teaspoon cinnamon and ⅛ teaspoon ground cloves in saucepan. Cook, stirring, over medium heat 10 minutes, or until thick and syrupy. Makes about 2 cups.

OLD-FASHIONED BROWN-SUGAR SAUCE

Mix 1 cup packed dark-brown sugar, ¼ cup water and 1 tablespoon butter in small saucepan; bring to boil. Boil, stirring occasionally to prevent sticking, 2 to 3 minutes, or until sugar melts and mixture is consistency of maple syrup. Makes ⅔ cup.

SOURDOUGH PANCAKES

The lore of sourdough in the West dates back to the early pioneers. Treasured sourdough starters were carefully guarded in covered wagons and homesteaders' farm kitchens. Sourdough leavening is still a western tradition.

1/2 cup commercial sourdough starter
1 cup undiluted evaporated milk
2 cups all-purpose flour
2 eggs
1 tablespoon each sugar and vegetable oil
2 teaspoons double-acting baking powder
1/2 teaspoon each salt and baking soda

In a large bowl, combine first 3 ingredients and 1 cup warm water. Mix to blend and leave at room temperature overnight. The next morning, add remaining ingredients. Stir just enough to mix well. Bake on greased griddle over moderate heat. Turn when surface bubbles. Serves 4.

APPLE PANCAKE

3 or 4 tart apples
Butter or margarine
Sugar
1/8 teaspoon nutmeg
1/4 teaspoon cinnamon
2 eggs
1/2 cup milk
1/2 cup all-purpose flour
1/4 teaspoon salt

Peel and core apples. Slice thin and sauté in ⅓ cup butter 5 minutes. Mix ⅓ cup sugar and the spices and add to apples. Cover and cook 10 minutes. Cool. Mix eggs, milk, flour and salt. Beat with rotary beater 2 minutes. Heat 1 tablespoon butter in 10" oven-proof dish. Pour batter into pan. Bake in very hot oven (450°F.) 15 minutes. As soon as batter puffs up in center, puncture with fork, repeating as often as necessary. Lower heat to moderate (350°F.) and bake 10 minutes. Remove from oven and spoon 2 tablespoons melted butter over surface. Sprinkle with 2 tablespoons sugar. Spread apple mixture over half the surface; fold over. Spoon 2 tablespoons melted butter over top and sprinkle with 2 tablespoons sugar. Makes 6 servings.

OATMEAL GRIDDLE CAKES

2 cups milk
2 cups quick-cooking rolled oats
1/3 cup all-purpose flour
2-1/2 teaspoons double-acting baking powder
1 teaspoon salt
2 tablespoons sugar
2 eggs, separated
1/2 cup melted fat or cooking oil

Heat milk and pour over oats; cool. Sift dry ingredients. Beat egg yolks and add to oat mixture. Add fat and stir in dry ingredients. Beat egg whites until stiff and fold in. Drop by spoonfuls onto hot greased griddle and spread with pancake turner. When surface is bubbly, turn and brown on other side. Serve with syrup or honey. Makes 4 servings.

POTATO PANCAKES

A middle-Europe specialty. For crisp light texture and delicacy of flavor:
1. *Use only russet or baking-type potatoes.*
2. *After peeling, soak in cold water 2 hours before grating.*
3. *Use a minimum of flour or crumbs.*
4. *Use plenty of fat (preferably peanut oil) for frying. Heat almost to smoking point.*
5. *Serve while crisp and hot.*

2 large baking potatoes (5" to 6" long) or 3 or 4 medium
1 tablespoon grated onion
2 tablespoons flour
3/4 teaspoon salt
2 tablespoons milk
Pepper and nutmeg
2 eggs, beaten
Peanut oil or shortening

Peel potatoes and soak 2 hours in cold water. Drain, dry and grate on medium grater into a fine strainer or cheesecloth placed over bowl (there will be about 2 cups grated potato before straining). Press firmly to squeeze out all liquid, reducing amount of potato by about one third. To potato, add next 4 ingredients and a little pepper and nutmeg. Lightly stir in eggs. In large heavy skillet, heat about ¼" oil to near smoking. Drop in potato by tablespoonfuls, spreading mixture with back of spoon to make cakes thin and lacy. Cook over high heat until golden brown and crisp on each side. Drain on paper towels and keep hot in hot oven while remaining cakes are being cooked. Add additional oil, if needed, heating it before batter is added. Good with crisp bacon and applesauce, or pot roast. Makes about 1 dozen.

HONEY-RAISIN SAUCE

1 cup orange juice
2 tablespoons lemon juice
3/4 cup honey
2 tablespoons butter or margarine
1/2 cup chopped raisins
1 tablespoon cornstarch

Combine 1/3 cup water with all ingredients, except cornstarch. Bring to boil and thicken with cornstarch mixed with a little cold water. Simmer a few minutes. Serve warm on waffles or pancakes. Makes 2 cups.

SWEET-POTATO WAFFLES

2 cups all-purpose flour
3 teaspoons double-acting baking powder
1 teaspoon salt
1/4 teaspoon cinnamon
3 eggs, separated
1-1/2 cups milk
3/4 cup mashed cooked sweet potatoes
1/4 cup butter, melted
1/3 cup chopped nuts
Maple syrup

Sift dry ingredients into bowl. Beat egg whites until stiff. Beat egg yolks; add milk and potato and beat until blended. Add to dry ingredients with butter and mix well. Fold in egg whites and nuts. Bake and serve hot with syrup. Makes 5 to 6 waffles.

BUTTERMILK WAFFLES

(Basic Recipe)

3 eggs, separated
1-1/2 cups buttermilk
1/3 cup melted shortening
2 cups sifted cake flour
2 teaspoons double-acting baking powder
1/2 teaspoon baking soda
3/4 teaspoon salt
1 tablespoon sugar

Beat egg yolks; add buttermilk and shortening. Add to sifted dry ingredients; mix until smooth. Fold in stiffly beaten egg whites. Bake in hot waffle iron. Makes 5 to 6 waffles.

Apple Waffles Add to batter 2 peeled and finely chopped apples and 1 teaspoon cinnamon. Serve with maple syrup or honey.

Caraway Waffles Soak 3 teaspoons caraway seed in hot water for 10 minutes. Drain; add to egg mixture. Serve with applesauce.

Meat Waffles Add dash of pepper to dry ingredients. Add 1/2 cup diced leftover meat to batter. Serve with relish or chili sauce.

Onion Waffles Sauté 2 minced onions in a little fat; add to batter. Serve with butter.

OLD-TIMEY CRISP CORNMEAL WAFFLES

3/4 cup white cornmeal
2 tablespoons flour
1/4 teaspoon salt
1/4 teaspoon baking soda
1/2 teaspoon double-acting baking powder
1 teaspoon sugar
1 egg
1 cup buttermilk
1/4 cup lard or vegetable shortening, melted
Old-fashioned Brown-sugar Sauce (page 312), syrup or honey

Put cornmeal in mixing bowl. Add remaining dry ingredients, then add egg and milk slowly, beating with wire whisk or slotted spoon to make a smooth batter. Add lard and beat again. Have waffle iron smoking-hot. Spoon 4 heaping tablespoonfuls of batter, or enough to spread evenly over bottom, onto iron. Close and cook 2 to 3 minutes, or until waffle is golden brown outside and done inside. Serve hot with sauce. Makes 4 large waffles.

STAY-CRISP WAFFLES

(Basic Recipe)

1-1/2 cups all-purpose flour
2 teaspoons double-acting baking powder
1/2 teaspoon baking soda
1/4 teaspoon salt
1 tablespoon sugar
3 eggs, separated
3/4 cup dairy sour cream
3/4 cup buttermilk
1/4 cup solid vegetable shortening, melted and cooled
1/4 cup butter, melted and cooled

Sift dry ingredients. Beat egg yolks, sour cream and milk. Add to dry ingredients, alternating with fats. Stir until batter is smooth. Fold in egg whites, beaten stiff. Cook waffles according to directions for your particular waffle iron. Good with syrup, honey, preserves, etc. Makes 4.

Bacon Waffles Cut thin strips of breakfast bacon in half. Place one of these pieces over the top of each waffle section before closing iron. Cook till waffle is done and bacon crisp and brown.

Blueberry, Currant, Raisin, Nut or Date Waffles Add 1/2 cup blueberries, currants, raisins, chopped nuts or pitted dates (cut in thirds) to waffle batter before cooking.

Cheese Waffles Add 1/2 cup grated Parmesan or shredded Cheddar cheese to waffle batter.

EVERYDAY WAFFLES

1-1/2 cups all-purpose flour
2 teaspoons double-acting baking powder
1/2 teaspoon salt
3 tablespoons sugar
2 eggs, beaten
1-1/3 cups milk
1/3 cup vegetable oil
1/3 cup butter or margarine, melted

Combine first 4 ingredients in mixing bowl. Beat eggs and milk. Add to dry ingredients alternately with oil and butter. Stir until batter is smooth and free from lumps. Bake according to manufacturer's directions for your waffle iron. Serve with syrup, honey, preserves, confectioners' sugar, etc. Makes 3 to 6 waffles. **Note** Batter can be stored, covered, in refrigerator. Mixture will thicken when chilled and must be spread on waffle iron with spatula or spoon.

Rice Waffles Follow above recipe, decreasing flour to 1 cup and adding 2/3 cup cold cooked rice to batter. Bake as directed. Serve with syrup, honey, preserves, confectioners' sugar, etc. Good with ham, bacon or sausages.

Nut Waffles Follow recipe for Everyday Waffles, adding 1/2 cup finely chopped nuts (peanuts, pecans, walnuts, filberts or almonds) to batter. Bake as directed. Serve with syrup or as a dessert topped with ice cream, fresh or canned fruits or favorite sundae sauce.

Chocolate Waffles Follow recipe for Everyday Waffles, adding 1/2 cup semisweet chocolate pieces and 2 teaspoons vanilla extract to batter. Bake as directed. Serve topped with ice cream or whipped cream, and chocolate syrup.

OAT WAFFLES OR PANCAKES WITH MOLASSES SAUCE

1-1/2 cups buttermilk biscuit mix
1 cup quick-cooking rolled oats (not instant)
1 egg
1-1/3 cups milk
2 tablespoons vegetable oil
Molasses Sauce

Combine biscuit mix and oats. Beat egg slightly and add milk and oil. Add to dry ingredients and stir until mixed. Bake in hot waffle iron or drop batter on hot griddle. (For thinner pancakes, add a little more milk.) Serve hot with sauce. Makes four 7" waffles or 12 medium pancakes. **Molasses Sauce** Combine 1/2 cup molasses, 3/4 cup undiluted evaporated milk and 2 tablespoons butter. Heat until butter melts.

COFFEE-TOFFEE SAUCE

1 cup packed brown sugar
2 tablespoons cornstarch
1/8 teaspoon salt
1-3/4 cups hot strong coffee
2 tablespoons butter or margarine
2 teaspoons vanilla extract

Mix first 3 ingredients well in heavy saucepan. Add coffee and cook, stirring, until thickened. Remove from heat and stir in butter and vanilla. Serve warm on waffles, ice cream or cake. Makes 2 cups.

RUM-RAISIN SAUCE

1/4 cup honey
3 tablespoons butter or margarine
Grated rind of 1 lemon
1 cup golden raisins
2 tablespoons lemon juice
1/2 cup sugar
1 tablespoon cornstarch
Dash of salt
2 tablespoons dark rum

Combine first 5 ingredients and 1 cup water in small saucepan. Add sugar mixed with cornstarch and salt. Bring to boil, stirring, and simmer 4 to 5 minutes. Add rum and blend well. Good hot or cold. Makes 2 cups.

CRISP COCONUT WAFFLES

2 cups grated fresh coconut
1-1/2 cups milk
2 eggs, separated
2 tablespoons sugar
2 cups sifted cake flour
3 teaspoons double-acting baking powder
1/2 teaspoon salt
3/4 cup butter or margarine, melted
Raspberry Sauce or maple syrup

Set aside 1/2 cup coconut. Put remainder in saucepan with milk and heat to scalding. Cool to room temperature and squeeze as much liquid as possible from mixture through several thicknesses of cheesecloth; discard coconut. Beat egg whites until foamy. Gradually add sugar and beat until stiff; set aside. Beat egg yolks until thick. Add sifted dry ingredients alternately with coconut liquid, beating after each addition until smooth. Stir in butter, then fold in egg whites and reserved coconut. Bake on hot waffle iron. Waffles will be soft when removed from iron but will crisp in a few seconds. Serve with sauce or syrup. Makes about ten 7" waffles.

Raspberry Sauce Partially thaw frozen raspberries, then whirl in blender and strain to remove seed.

Anniversary Cake

TONI FICALORA

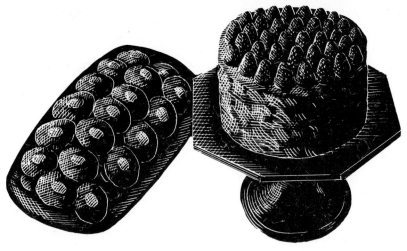

TIPS FOR MAKING AND BAKING CAKES

Equipment

For easy, accurate measurement, use a set of standard measuring spoons, a nest of measuring cups for dry ingredients and a measuring cup for liquids with a pouring lip and a rim above the 1-cup line. A rubber spatula and a sifter are essential items for preparing batter. Use shiny aluminum or glass baking pans.

For layer cakes, use pans about 1½" deep. Waxed paper, plain white or brown paper can be used to line pan bottoms. Cut paper slightly smaller than pan so that it will not touch edge but will completely cover bottom. Greasing the bottom of pan will keep the paper from slipping when batter is poured in.

Procedure

For best results, use only ingredients specified and follow directions exactly. Make all measurements level. Spoon granulated sugar and sifted confectioners' sugar into cup. Level off with flat knife. Do not shake down. Use kind of flour specified. Large eggs were used in making these cakes; substituting eggs of another size is not recommended. You can use either fresh whole milk or evaporated milk diluted with an equal amount of water. Ingredients such as shortening, milk and eggs should be at room temperature (72°F. to 80°F.) It is advisable not to double recipes.

Oven Temperature

Correct oven temperature is of great importance when baking cakes.
If your oven has no thermostatic control, try using an oven thermometer and adjusting the heat accordingly.
You may want to use a thermometer in any case to check the accuracy of your control. When baking in glass loaf pans, use an oven temperature 25° less than that specified in recipe.

STORING BAKED CAKES

Frosted cakes keep best. It's helpful to store cakes in a cake saver, deep bowl or an airtight container.

Cover the cut surface of cake with waxed paper or transparent plastic wrap; hold wrapping in place with toothpicks inserted at an angle into cake. Cakes with perishable fillings or frostings should be stored, covered, in the refrigerator. It is best to freeze cakes unfrosted.

TIPS FOR MAKING AND BAKING COOKIES

Cookie Sheets

You don't have to grease cookie sheets unless the recipe specifies it. Try the new cookie sheets that never need greasing. They come in attractive colors. If you're using aluminum sheets, shiny ones give browner cookies. Choose sheets at least 2" narrower and shorter than the oven rack so heat can circulate.

Mixing

Measure ingredients accurately. Don't make substitutions such as cocoa for chocolate, or omit ingredients. Don't use self-rising flour. Make cookies of the size specified in the recipe.

When rolling dough, be careful not to work in a lot of flour. For easier rolling, use a pastry cloth or canvas rolling-pin cover. Cut with floured cutter, using a fairly plain one if dough is soft and tender.

Baking

Space cookies to allow for spreading. Because ovens vary, watch cookies closely. Check for doneness just before minimum baking time is up. If some are thinner than others, you may have to remove them and bake the remainder a bit longer.

Cooling

Unless otherwise specified in the recipe, remove baked cookies from the sheet to a cake rack as soon as you take them from the oven. Don't stack them until they have cooled thoroughly.

Storing

Keep cookies in airtight containers. If crisp cookies become limp, heat them a few minutes in the oven to recrisp.

LEMON-ORANGE COCONUT CAKE

1 cup butter
2 cups sugar
3-1/2 cups sifted cake flour
3-1/2 teaspoons double-acting baking
powder
3/4 teaspoon salt
1 cup milk
2 teaspoons grated lemon rind
1 cup grated fresh coconut or 1 cup
canned flaked coconut
6 egg whites
Orange Filling
Lemon-Orange Butter-cream Frosting

Cream butter until soft. Gradually add 1½ cups sugar and beat until light. Add sifted dry ingredients alternately with milk, beating after each addition until smooth. Stir in lemon rind and coconut. Beat egg whites until foamy; gradually add remaining ½ cup sugar and beat until stiff but not dry. Fold into batter. Pour into four 9" layer cake pans lined on the bottom with waxed paper. Bake in moderate oven (375° F.) 15 to 20 minutes. Cool 5 minutes; then turn out on racks. Peel off paper; cool cakes. Spread filling between layers and frosting on top and sides of cake. **Orange Filling** In heavy saucepan, mix ½ cup cake flour, 1 cup sugar and ¼ teaspoon salt. Add ¼ cup water and blend until smooth. Add 1½ cups orange juice, ¼ cup lemon juice, 2 tablespoons grated orange rind and grated rind of 1 lemon. Cook, stirring, until mixture thickens and becomes almost translucent. Beat 4 egg yolks slightly and stir in small amount of hot mixture. Return mixture to saucepan and cook, stirring, a few minutes longer. Cool. Makes filling for four 9" layers.

Lemon-Orange Butter-cream Frosting

1 cup sugar
1/8 teaspoon cream of tartar
Dash of salt
2 egg whites
1 teaspoon grated lemon rind
2/3 cup softened butter
1/4 cup orange juice

In small saucepan, mix first 3 ingredients and ¼ cup water. Cook until a little of syrup dropped in cold water forms a soft ball (240°F. on a candy thermometer). Beat egg whites with rotary or electric beater until stiff but not dry. Add syrup very slowly to egg whites, beating constantly; add grated lemon rind. *Cool thoroughly.* Cream butter until light. Add egg-white mixture to butter, 2 or 3 tablespoonfuls at a time, beating well after each addition. Beat in orange juice. Makes enough for top of one and sides of four 9" layers, or tops and sides of two or three 9" layers.

ANNIVERSARY CAKE

Bake Lemon-Orange Coconut Cake as directed (at left). Then make 2 more layers, using these proportions: ½ cup butter, ¾ cup sugar, 1¾ cups flour, 1¾ teaspoons baking powder, ½ teaspoon salt, ½ cup milk, 1 teaspoon lemon rind, ½ cup coconut, 3 egg whites and ¼ cup sugar. When all layers are baked and cooled, make a 6" cardboard circle and cut around 3 of the layers, thus making 6" layers. Use scraps for puddings, etc., later. Prepare filling and frosting, making 1½ times each recipe. Reserve about 1½ cups frosting for special decorations. **To fill and frost cake** Put one 9" layer on cake plate, spread with one third of filling, add a 9" layer and spread with another third of filling. Add last 9" layer and spread with frosting. Add three 6" layers, spreading remaining filling between. Frost top and sides of cake and decorate with reserved frosting, using pastry tube. Chill. **To serve** Cut top tier in 6 wedge-shaped pieces and put on serving plates. Then cut bottom tier in 10 to 12 servings.

BURNT-SUGAR CAKE

Sugar
2/3 cup softened butter or margarine
1 teaspoon vanilla extract
2 eggs, separated
3 cups sifted cake flour
3 teaspoons double-acting baking
powder
1/2 teaspoon salt
3/4 cup milk
Burnt-sugar Frosting
Pecan halves

In small heavy skillet or saucepan, heat ¾ cup sugar, stirring, until a brown syrup forms and mixture begins to smoke. *Very gradually* stir in ¾ cup boiling water and remove from heat. Cool thoroughly. Cream butter and 1 cup sugar until light. Gradually beat in ½ cup burnt-sugar syrup. (Reserve remainder for frosting.) Add vanilla, then egg yolks, one at a time, beating well after each addition. Add sifted dry ingredients alternately with milk, beating until smooth. Fold in stiffly beaten egg whites. Pour into two 9" layer pans lined on the bottom with waxed paper. Bake in moderate oven (375°F.) about 25 minutes. Cool and frost. Top with nut halves. **Burnt-sugar Frosting** Cream ⅓ cup butter or margarine. Beat in 1 box (1 pound) confectioners' sugar, sifted, ½ teaspoon salt, 1 teaspoon vanilla, reserved burnt-sugar syrup and enough cream (about 2 tablespoons) for spreading consistency.

HONEY CHOCOLATE CAKE

A moist and very chocolate cake.

1/4 cup softened butter or margarine
3/4 cup sugar
1/2 teaspoon vanilla extract
2 eggs, separated
4 squares unsweetened chocolate, melted
1/2 cup light clover honey
2 cups sifted cake flour
1 teaspoon double-acting baking powder
1/2 teaspoon each salt and baking soda
1/2 cup buttermilk
1/2 cup milk, scalded and slightly cooled
Confectioners'-sugar Frosting (below)

Cream butter, $\frac{1}{2}$ cup sugar and vanilla. Add egg yolks and beat well. Blend in cooled chocolate. Gradually beat in honey. Add sifted dry ingredients alternately with buttermilk; beat until smooth. Beat egg whites until stiff but not dry. Gradually add $\frac{1}{4}$ cup sugar, beating until very stiff and glossy. Fold into batter; stir in scalded milk. Pour into two 9" layer pans lined on bottom with waxed paper. Bake in moderate oven (350°F.) about 30 minutes. Cool and frost.

CONFECTIONERS'-SUGAR FROSTING

Mix 2 cups sifted confectioners' sugar, $\frac{1}{2}$ teaspoon vanilla and about 2 tablespoons water until smooth. Frosts tops of two 8" layers or 1 large tube cake.

CHOCOLATE CREAM ROLL

5 eggs, separated
3 tablespoons cocoa
1 cup sifted confectioners' sugar
Dash of salt
1-1/2 teaspoons vanilla extract
1 cup heavy cream
2 tablespoons granulated sugar
Chocolate Glaze, page 440
Maraschino cherries with stems

Beat egg whites until stiff but not dry; set aside. Beat egg yolks until thick and lemon-colored. Sift next 3 ingredients and gradually beat into yolks with 1 teaspoon vanilla. Fold in whites. Pour into 13" x 9" x 2" pan lined on the bottom with waxed paper. Bake in hot oven (400°F.) about 15 minutes. Turn out on waxed paper lightly covered with confectioners' sugar. Cool and carefully peel off paper. Whip cream with granulated sugar until stiff. Add $\frac{1}{2}$ teaspoon vanilla and spread on cake. Roll up from narrow end of paper; chill. Spread top and sides with glaze and chill until firm. Decorate with cherries. Cut in slices. Makes 6 servings.

MOCHA CAKE

2 squares unsweetened chocolate
1 cup strong coffee
1-1/2 cups packed light-brown sugar
1/2 cup softened butter or margarine
1 teaspoon vanilla extract
2 eggs
1-3/4 cups sifted cake flour
1 teaspoon double-acting baking powder
1/2 teaspoon baking soda
1/2 teaspoon salt
Caramel Frosting (below)

In top of double boiler, cook chocolate and $\frac{1}{2}$ cup coffee until thick, stirring. Add $\frac{1}{2}$ cup sugar and cook 2 or 3 minutes longer, stirring; cool. Cream butter, 1 cup sugar and vanilla. Add eggs, one at a time, beating thoroughly after each addition. Beat in cooled chocolate mixture. Add sifted dry ingredients alternately with $\frac{1}{2}$ cup cold coffee; beat until smooth. Pour into two 9" layer pans lined on bottom with waxed paper. Bake in moderate oven (350°F.) about 30 minutes. Cool and frost.

CARAMEL FROSTING

In large saucepan mix 2 cups packed light-brown sugar, 1 cup granulated sugar, 2 tablespoons corn syrup, 3 tablespoons butter, a dash of salt, $\frac{2}{3}$ cup cream and 1 teaspoon vanilla. Bring to boil, cover and cook 3 minutes. Uncover and cook until a small amount of mixture forms a soft ball when dropped in cold water (236°F. on a candy thermometer). Cool 5 minutes; then beat until thick. If too stiff, add a little hot water. Frosts two 8" layers.

CHOCOLATE-FUDGE CAKE

Really moist and fudgy.

1/2 cup butter or margarine, softened
1 cup sugar
1 teaspoon vanilla extract
4 eggs
1 cup minus 1 tablespoon all-purpose flour
1 teaspoon double-acting baking powder
1 can (1 pound) chocolate syrup
1 cup chopped walnuts
Whipped cream, or vanilla or coffee ice cream

Cream butter. Gradually add sugar and vanilla; beat until light. Add eggs one at a time, beating thoroughly after each. Add sifted dry ingredients alternately with syrup, blending well; add nuts. Put in 9" tube pan lined on the bottom with waxed paper. Bake in moderate oven (350°F.) 35 to 40 minutes. Turn out on rack and peel off paper. Cool and serve with cream.

SOUR-CREAM FUDGE LAYERS

A chocolate lovers' favorite.

1-2/3 cups all-purpose flour
1-1/2 cups sugar
1/2 teaspoon salt
1 teaspoon double-acting baking powder
1/2 teaspoon baking soda
1-1/4 cups dairy sour cream
1/4 cup solid vegetable shortening
2 eggs
3 squares unsweetened chocolate, melted and cooled
1 teaspoon vanilla extract
Choco-Marshmallow Frosting (below)

Sift dry ingredients into large bowl. Add 1 cup sour cream and the shortening and stir until blended. Beat 2 minutes at medium speed of electric mixer. Add remaining sour cream and next 3 ingredients; beat 2 more minutes. Pour into two 9" layer pans lined on the bottom with waxed paper. Bake in moderate oven (350° F.) 25 to 30 minutes. Cool 5 minutes. Then turn out of pans onto wire racks and cool thoroughly. Spread frosting between layers and on top and sides.

CHOCO-MARSHMALLOW FROSTING

In top part of double boiler over boiling water, melt 3 squares unsweetened chocolate; add 16 marshmallows. Cook, stirring, until softened. Stir in $\frac{1}{8}$ teaspoon salt and $\frac{1}{2}$ cup undiluted evaporated milk. Cook until smooth. Remove from heat and gradually beat in $2\frac{3}{4}$ cups sifted confectioners' sugar; add $\frac{1}{2}$ teaspoon vanilla extract. Makes enough frosting for two 8" or 9" layers.

MIDNIGHT-LACE CAKE

A tender cake of milk-chocolate flavor.

2 squares unsweetened chocolate
1 cup milk
1/2 cup softened butter or margarine
1-1/2 cups sugar
1 teaspoon vanilla extract
2 eggs, separated
1-2/3 cups all-purpose flour
1 teaspoon double-acting baking powder
1/2 teaspoon each baking soda and salt
Soft Chocolate Frosting (above right)

Cook chocolate with $\frac{1}{2}$ cup milk until smooth and thickened, stirring. Cream next 3 ingredients; add egg yolks and beat well. Add sifted dry ingredients alternately with $\frac{1}{2}$ cup milk; beat until smooth. Blend in cooled chocolate mixture. Fold in stiffly beaten egg whites. Pour into two 8" layer pans lined on bottom with waxed paper. Bake in moderate oven (350°F.) 30 minutes. Cool; frost.

SOFT CHOCOLATE FROSTING

In double boiler over boiling water, melt 2 squares unsweetened chocolate in $^3/_4$ cup milk; beat to blend. Stir in $1\frac{1}{2}$ tablespoons cornstarch blended with $\frac{1}{4}$ cup milk, 1 cup sugar and a dash of salt. Cook, stirring often, 15 minutes, or until thick. Remove from heat; add 1 tablespoon butter and 1 teaspoon vanilla extract; cool. Frosts tops of two 9" layers.

MILK-CHOCOLATE CAKE

2-1/4 cups sugar
2 squares unsweetened chocolate, melted
3/4 cup softened butter or margarine
1 teaspoon vanilla extract
4 eggs, separated
2-1/4 cups sifted cake flour
1 teaspoon cream of tartar
1/2 teaspoon baking soda
1/2 teaspoon salt
1 cup milk
Vanilla Cream Filling (below)·
Chocolate Cream-cheese Frosting (page 321)

Add $\frac{1}{4}$ cup sugar and 3 tablespoons water to chocolate. Cream butter well. Add remaining 2 cups sugar gradually, beating until light and fluffy. Add vanilla, then egg yolks, one at a time, beating well after each addition. Blend in chocolate mixture. Add sifted dry ingredients alternately with milk, beating until smooth. Fold in stiffly beaten egg whites. Pour into three round 9" or four 8" layer pans, lined on the bottom with waxed paper. Bake 9" layers in moderate oven (350°F.) about 50 minutes, and 8" layers about 40 minutes. Let stand 5 minutes; then turn out on racks to cool. Remove paper, fill and frost.

VANILLA CREAM FILLING

1/2 cup sugar
3 tablespoons flour
1/8 teaspoon salt
1-1/2 cups milk
2 eggs, beaten
1/2 teaspoon vanilla extract

In top part of double boiler, mix $\frac{1}{4}$ cup sugar, the flour and salt. Add $\frac{1}{2}$ cup milk and stir until smooth. Pour in remaining 1 cup milk and cook over boiling water 10 minutes, or until smooth and thickened, stirring. Mix remaining $\frac{1}{4}$ cup sugar with eggs. Add hot mixture slowly, stirring. Return to double boiler and cook 5 minutes, or until very thick, stirring. Cool and add vanilla. Makes enough to fill four 8" or three 9" layers.

CHOCOLATE SHADOW CAKE

6 squares unsweetened chocolate
1-3/4 cups sugar
Soft butter or margarine
1 teaspoon vanilla extract
3 eggs
2 cups sifted cake flour
1 teaspoon baking soda
1/2 teaspoon salt
2/3 cup milk
Fluffy White Frosting (page 324)

Melt 4 squares chocolate in ¼ cup hot water in top part of double boiler over boiling water. Cook until thickened, stirring. Add ½ cup sugar and cook 2 or 3 minutes, stirring; cool. Cream ½ cup butter, remaining 1¼ cups sugar and the vanilla. Add eggs, one at a time, beating thoroughly after each addition. Add sifted dry ingredients alternately with milk, beating until smooth. Blend in chocolate mixture. Pour into two 9″ layer pans lined on bottom with waxed paper. Bake in moderate oven (350°F.) about 45 minutes. Cool and frost. When frosting is set, melt remaining 2 squares chocolate and 2 teaspoons butter. Dribble over top of cake and down the sides. Let chocolate set before cutting.

CHOCOLATE-WALNUT BUTTER CAKE

A pound-type chocolate cake that doesn't need a frosting.

Butter, softened
Walnuts
3 cups all-purpose flour
1/2 cup unsweetened cocoa
1/4 teaspoon salt
1 teaspoon double-acting baking powder
1/2 cup solid white vegetable shortening
2 cups granulated sugar
5 eggs
1 cup milk
2 teaspoons vanilla extract
Confectioners' sugar

Butter (use 1 tablespoon) a 10″ x 4″ tube pan and sprinkle bottom with ¼ cup very finely chopped walnuts; set aside. Sift dry ingredients together and set aside. Cream 1 cup butter and the shortening. Gradually add granulated sugar and beat until fluffy. Add eggs one at a time, beating well after each. Add dry ingredients alternately with milk and vanilla. Mix in ⅓ cup chopped walnuts. Turn into tube pan. Bake in moderate oven (325°F.) 1 hour and 20 minutes, or until done. Let rest on rack 5 minutes before turning out. Cool and store, well wrapped in plastic wrap, in cool place. A few days' storing improves flavor. At serving time, dust with confectioners' sugar.

DIVA CAKE

1 cup softened butter or margarine
1-1/2 cups sugar
1 teaspoon vanilla extract
2 squares unsweetened chocolate, melted
5 egg yolks, well beaten
1-1/2 cups sifted cake flour
1 teaspoon double-acting baking powder
1/4 teaspoon baking soda
1/2 teaspoon salt
1/2 cup dairy sour cream or buttermilk
2 tablespoons strong coffee
2 egg whites, beaten stiff
Scotch Chocolate Frosting (page 329)

Cream first 3 ingredients. Blend in cooled chocolate. Beat in egg yolks. Sift together dry ingredients and add alternately with sour cream; beat until smooth. Add coffee. Fold in egg whites. Pour into two 9″ layer pans lined on bottom with waxed paper. Bake in moderate oven (350°F.) about 30 minutes. Cool and frost.

DUTCH CHOCOLATE CAKE

1-1/2 cups sifted cake flour
2 teaspoons double-acting baking powder
1/4 teaspoon salt
1/2 teaspoon cinnamon
1/2 teaspoon ground cloves
3 squares unsweetened chocolate, grated
3/4 cup finely chopped walnuts
3/4 cup butter
1-1/2 cups sugar
4 eggs, separated
3/4 cup grated peeled cooked potato, chilled
1/2 cup milk
Rum Frosting (page 332)

Sift together first 5 ingredients. Mix with chocolate and walnuts. Beat butter and sugar together until creamy and light. Beat in egg yolks one at a time. Stir in potato. On low speed of mixer, blend in dry mixture alternately with milk. Beat after each addition until smooth. Beat egg whites until stiff but not dry; fold into batter. Turn into greased lightly floured 9″ tube pan or two 9″ layer pans. Bake tube cake in moderate oven (350°F.) 1 hour, layers at 375°F. 25 to 30 minutes. Cool on wire racks and spread with Rum Frosting, letting it run down sides.

GLOSSY CHOCOLATE FROSTING

Melt 6 squares unsweetened chocolate. Add 1½ cups sifted confectioners' sugar and 5 tablespoons hot water; beat well. Add 1½ cups more sugar. Gradually beat in 6 egg yolks. When smooth and blended, beat in ½ cup soft butter or margarine. Makes enough frosting for tops and sides of three 9″ layers.

CHOCOLATE CREAM-CHEESE FROSTING

1/4 cup butter or margarine, softened
8 ounces cream cheese, softened
3 squares unsweetened chocolate, melted
Dash of salt
1 teaspoon vanilla extract
3 cups sifted confectioners' sugar
1/3 cup light cream

Cream butter. Blend in next 4 ingredients. Add sugar alternately with cream, beating thoroughly after each addition. Makes enough to frost top and sides of four 8" or three 9" layers.

RED DEVIL'S FOOD CAKE

3/4 cup butter or margarine, softened
2 cups sugar
2-2/3 cups sifted cake flour
1-1/2 teaspoons double-acting baking powder
3/4 teaspoon each baking soda and salt
1-1/3 cups milk
3 eggs
3 squares unsweetened chocolate, melted and cooled
1-1/2 teaspoons red food coloring
1 teaspoon vanilla extract

Cream butter. Sift dry ingredients into butter. Add 1 cup milk and mix until flour is dampened. Beat 2 minutes. Add remaining milk and remaining ingredients. Beat 2 minutes. Pour into three 8" layer pans lined on the bottom wtih waxed paper. Bake in moderate oven (350°F.) 30 to 35 minutes. Cool and frost as desired.

GRANDMA'S CHOCOLATE CAKE

Yeast makes this one different.

1 cup softened butter or margarine
2 cups sugar
1-1/2 teaspoons vanilla extract
3 eggs, separated
3 squares unsweetened chocolate, melted
1-1/4 teaspoons dry yeast
2-2/3 cups all-purpose flour
1/2 teaspoon salt
1 teaspoon baking soda
Rich Mocha Frosting (above right)

Cream first 3 ingredients. Add egg yolks and beat until light. Blend in cooled chocolate. Dissolve yeast in 1/3 cup warm water. Add to mixture with sifted flour and salt. Fold in stiffly beaten egg whites. Cover; let stand in warm place about 4 hours. Add soda dissolved in 3 tablespoons hot water; beat well. Pour into three 9" layer pans lined on bottom with waxed paper. Bake in moderate oven (350°F.) 35 minutes. Cool; frost.

RICH MOCHA FROSTING

Cream 1/4 cup butter or margarine. Add 3 egg yolks; beat well. Add 4-1/2 cups sifted confectioners' sugar, 3/4 cup cocoa, 1/4 teaspoon salt and 1 teaspoon vanilla. Gradually beat in enough strong coffee to make frosting of spreading consistency. Frosts tops and sides of three 8" or 9" layers.

CHOCOLATE-FILLED EIGHT-LAYER CAKE

6 eggs, separated
1-1/4 cups sugar
2 tablespoons lemon juice
2/3 cup all-purpose flour
1/4 cup cornstarch
1/2 teaspoon salt
Chocolate Frosting

Beat egg yolks until thick. Gradually beat in sugar and 1 tablespoon lemon juice. Sift in next 3 ingredients; add remaining lemon juice and beat until smooth. Fold in stiffly beaten egg whites. Spread evenly in two 15" x 10" x 1" pans lined on the bottom with waxed paper. (If only one pan is available, other half of batter can wait.) Bake in moderate oven (375° F.) 10 to 15 minutes. Turn out on rack and peel off paper at once. Cool cakes and cut each in 4 even pieces. Spread frosting between layers and on top and sides of cake. **Chocolate Frosting** In top part of double boiler over boiling water, melt 4 squares unsweetened chocolate. Beat 4 egg yolks with 2/3 cup sugar. Stir in 1/2 cup heavy cream and add to chocolate. Cook, stirring, until thickened. Cream 1-1/4 cups butter or margarine. Beat in chocolate mixture, one tablespoonful at a time. Chill until of spreading consistency.

CREAM-CHEESE DEVIL'S FOOD

6 ounces soft cream cheese
1/2 teaspoon red food coloring
1 teaspoon vanilla extract
1 cup sugar
3 squares unsweetened chocolate, melted
2 eggs
2 cups sifted cake flour
1 teaspoon baking soda
1/2 teaspoon salt
Fluffy Brown-sugar Frosting, page 322

Cream first 4 ingredients; blend in cooled chocolate. Add eggs; beat well. Add sifted dry ingredients alternately with 1 cup water; beat until smooth. Pour into two 8" layer pans, lined on bottom with paper. Bake in moderate oven (350°F.) 30 minutes. Cool and frost.

FLUFFY BROWN-SUGAR FROSTING

In top part of double boiler put 1 cup granulated sugar, 1/2 cup packed light-brown sugar, 3 table-spoons dark corn syrup, 1/3 cup water, 2 egg whites and 1/4 teaspoon each salt and cream of tartar; mix well. Over boiling water, beat with rotary beater or electric mixer until mixture holds a peak, about 4 minutes. Remove from heat; beat in 1 teaspoon vanilla. Frosts three 8" or 9" layers.

SPICY FUDGE CUPCAKES

Wonderful for lunch boxes.

1/3 cup solid vegetable shortening
1 cup sugar
1 teaspoon vanilla extract
2 eggs
2 squares unsweetened chocolate, melted
1/2 teaspoon baking soda
2 cups sifted cake flour
1 teaspoon each double-acting baking powder and cinnamon
1/2 teaspoon salt
1/3 cup each hot water, buttermilk and molasses

Cream first 3 ingredients. Add eggs, one at a time, beating thoroughly after each addition. Blend in cooled chocolate. Add sifted dry ingredients alternately with liquids, beating until smooth. Half-fill greased 2½" cup-cake pans with batter. Bake in moderate oven (350°F.) 25 minutes. Serve plain or frosted. Makes 28.

SPICY FUDGE POUND CAKE

A delicate fine-grained cake.

2 squares unsweetened chocolate
1 cup softened butter or margarine
1 teaspoon vanilla extract
1/2 teaspoon black pepper
1/4 teaspoon nutmeg or mace
1-1/2 cups sugar
5 eggs
1-7/8 cups all-purpose flour
1 teaspoon baking powder
1/2 teaspoon salt
1/4 cup orange juice
1/4 cup minced nuts
Grated rind of 1 orange

Melt chocolate over warm water; cool. Cream next 4 ingredients until light and fluffy; gradually beat in sugar. Add eggs, one at a time, beating thoroughly after each. Blend in chocolate. Add sifted dry ingredients alternately with orange juice, mixing until smooth. Fold in nuts and orange rind. Pour into medium-size tube pan lined with waxed paper. Bake in slow oven (300°F.) 45 to 50 minutes, or until done. Let stand 5 minutes. Then turn out of pan on rack to cool.

BROWN-SUGAR FUDGE CAKE

A sweet, fine-grained cake.

1/2 cup softened butter or margarine
2-1/4 cups sifted cake flour
1 teaspoon baking soda
3/4 teaspoon salt
2 cups packed light-brown sugar
1 cup buttermilk
1 teaspoon vanilla extract
3 eggs
3 squares unsweetened chocolate, melted
Butterscotch Frosting (below)
Walnut or pecan halves

Cream butter. Sift next 3 ingredients onto butter. Add sugar, 2/3 cup but-termilk and vanilla. Beat 2 minutes. Add remaining 1/3 cup buttermilk, the eggs and cooled chocolate. Beat 2 minutes. Pour into two 9" layer pans lined on bottom with waxed paper. Bake in moderate oven (350°F.) about 30 minutes. Cool, frost and decorate with nuts.

BUTTERSCOTCH FROSTING

Over hot (not boiling) water, melt 1 package (6 ounces) butter-scotch pieces. Stir in 2 tablespoons water and remove from heat; cool to lukewarm. Beat until light 8 ounces cream cheese, 1/8 teaspoon salt and 1 tablespoon light cream. Blend in butter-scotch mixture and 1 teaspoon vanilla. Add 1 cup heavy cream, whipped. Frosts two 9" layers.

BLACK DEVIL'S FOOD

A moist, close-textured very choco-late cake.

3/4 cup softened butter or margarine
2 cups sifted cake flour
1-3/4 cups sugar
2/3 cup unsweetened cocoa
1 teaspoon baking soda
1/2 teaspoon double-acting baking powder
3/4 teaspoon salt
1 cup plus 2 tablespoons buttermilk
3 eggs
1 teaspoon vanilla extract
Fluffy Seven-minute Frosting, page 323
Pecan or walnut halves (optional)

Cream butter. Sift next 6 ingredi-ents into butter. Add 1 cup buttermilk and mix until all flour is dampened. Beat 2½ minutes at low speed of electric mixer. Add remaining 2 tablespoons buttermilk, the eggs and vanilla. Beat 2½ minutes. Pour into two 9" layer pans, lined on the bottom with waxed paper. Bake in moderate oven (350°F.) 35 to 40 minutes. Cool, frost and decorate with nuts.

FLUFFY SEVEN-MINUTE FROSTING

In top part of small double boiler, combine 2 egg whites, 1½ cups sugar, ⅛ teaspoon salt, ⅓ cup water and 2 teaspoons light corn syrup. Put over boiling water and beat with rotary beater or electric mixer 7 minutes, or until mixture will stand in stiff peaks. Add 1 teaspoon vanilla. Makes enough for tops and sides of two 9″ layers.

SOUTHERN CHOCOLATE CAKE

A reddish cake that's light and tender.

1 package (6 ounces) semisweet chocolate pieces
1/2 cup butter or margarine
4 egg yolks
2/3 cup sugar
1/2 cup milk
1 cup sifted cake flour
1-1/4 teaspoons double-acting baking powder
1/2 teaspoon baking soda
1/4 teaspoon salt
1 teaspoon vanilla extract
2 egg whites
Fluffy Seven-minute Frosting (above)

Melt chocolate and butter; cool. Beat egg yolks until thick. Gradually beat in ⅓ cup sugar and beat until very thick. Add milk alternately with flour sifted with next 3 ingredients; beat until smooth. Add chocolate mixture and vanilla. Beat egg whites until stiff; gradually beat in remaining ⅓ cup sugar. Fold into batter. Pour into two 8″ layer pans lined on bottom with paper. Bake in moderate oven (375°F.) about 25 minutes. Cool and frost.

PINEAPPLE-ORANGE CREAM CAKE

1 can (1 pound 4-1/2 ounces) crushed pineapple
1 package (3-1/4 ounces) vanilla pudding-and-pie-filling mix
Orange chiffon cake
1 pint heavy cream, whipped
Maraschino cherries with stems

Put first 2 ingredients in heavy saucepan and cook over medium heat, stirring, until very thick and translucent. Remove from heat, cool and chill well. Meanwhile, split cake in 3 layers. Add a little of the cream to pineapple mixture, then fold in remaining cream. Add ⅓ cup chopped cherries and spread generously between layers and on top of cake. Decorate with whole cherries. Store in refrigerator until ready to serve. Makes 10 to 12 servings. *Note* The pineapple replaces the milk in cooking the pudding.

SWEET-CHOCOLATE CAKE

A rich, light-colored cake.

1 package (4 ounces) sweet cooking chocolate
1 cup butter or other shortening
2 cups sugar
1 teaspoon vanilla extract
4 eggs, separated
2-1/2 cups sifted cake flour
1 teaspoon baking soda
1/2 teaspoon salt
1 cup buttermilk
Coconut Pecan Filling (below)
Semisweet Chocolate Frosting (below)

Melt chocolate in ½ cup boiling water; cool. Cream next 3 ingredients; add egg yolks, one at a time, beating thoroughly after each addition. Blend in chocolate. Add sifted dry ingredients alternately with buttermilk; beat until smooth. Fold in stiffly beaten egg whites. Pour into three 8″ or 9″ layer pans lined on bottom with waxed paper. Bake in moderate oven (350°F.) about 35 minutes. Cool. Fill and frost.

SEMISWEET CHOCOLATE FROSTING

Melt 3 packages (6 ounces each) semisweet chocolate pieces. Add 3 cups sifted confectioners' sugar, ⅓ cup soft butter, 1½ teaspoons vanilla extract and about ⅓ cup hot milk to make frosting of good spreading consistency. Beat smooth. Makes enough for top and sides of three 9″ layers.

COCONUT PECAN FILLING

In saucepan mix 1 cup undiluted evaporated milk, 1 cup sugar, 3 egg yolks, ½ cup butter or margarine and 1 teaspoon vanilla extract. Cook over medium heat 12 minutes, stirring, until mixture thickens. Add 1 can flaked coconut and 1 cup chopped pecans. Beat until thick. Makes 3 cups.

COFFEE-NUT MERINGUE CAKE

Prepare 1 box butterscotch, banana or spice cake mix as directed on the label. Pour into greased and floured 13″ x 9″ x 2″ pan. Beat 2 egg whites and dash of salt until foamy; gradually beat in ¾ cup packed brown sugar and 2 teaspoons instant coffee powder. Beat until meringue stands in peaks. Spread carefully on top of batter. Sprinkle with ½ cup chopped nuts. Bake as directed on label. Cool; serve from pan.

SILVER CAKE

2/3 cup softened butter
1-1/2 cups sugar
1 teaspoon vanilla extract
1/2 teaspoon almond extract
2-1/2 cups sifted cake flour
2-1/2 teaspoons double-acting baking
   powder
2/3 cup milk
1/2 teaspoon salt
1/2 teaspoon cream of tartar
4 egg whites

Cream first 4 ingredients until light. Add sifted flour and baking powder alternately with milk, beating until smooth. Add salt and cream of tartar to egg whites. Beat until stiff but not dry. Fold into first mixture. Pour into two 9" layer pans lined on the bottom with waxed paper. Bake in moderate oven (375°F.) 20 to 25 minutes. Cool and frost as desired.

LADY BALTIMORE CAKE

Make Silver Cake, as directed. Make Fluffy White Frosting (above right). To one third of frosting add 6 chopped dried figs and ½ cup each chopped raisins and nuts. Spread between layers. Use remaining frosting for top and sides of cake.

RAINBOW CAKE

Make Silver Cake, as directed, dividing batter in 3 parts. Leave 1 part plain, color 1 part pink and color 1 green. Alternate 3 parts in layer pans and bake as directed. Make Fluffy White Frosting (above right). Divide in 4 parts. Color one half pink, one quarter yellow and remaining quarter green. Reserve one half of pink for sides of cake. Alternate colors on bottom layer of cake and run a knife through colors to get a rainbow effect. Add top layer and repeat frostings. Spread pink frosting on sides and decorate top with crushed peppermint candy.

PINEAPPLE-GLAZE CAKE

Prepare 1 box yellow cake mix and bake in 13" x 9" x 2" pan as directed on the label. Bring to boil 1 can (13½ ounces) crushed pineapple and ½ cup packed brown sugar. With point of sharp knife, mark warm cake in 1" squares, cutting ½" deep. Spoon hot pineapple mixture over cake. Cool and serve with whipped cream. Makes 9 servings.

FLUFFY WHITE FROSTING

1-1/2 cups sugar
1/2 teaspoon cream of tartar
1/8 teaspoon salt
3 egg whites
1/2 teaspoon vanilla extract

Mix first 3 ingredients and ½ cup hot water in saucepan. Cook, without stirring, until a small amount of mixture forms a soft ball when dropped in cold water (240°F. on candy thermometer). Meanwhile, beat egg whites until stiff but not dry. Add syrup very slowly, beating constantly, until frosting is thick and holds its shape. Add vanilla. Frosts tops of three 8" or 9" layers.

PEANUT-BUTTER APPLE CAKE

1/4 cup softened butter
1/2 cup peanut butter
1 cup sugar
1 egg
1 cup plus 3 tablespoons all-purpose flour
1 teaspoon baking soda
1/2 teaspoon salt
1/2 teaspoon cinnamon
1/4 teaspoon nutmeg
1/4 teaspoon ground cloves
1 cup canned applesauce

Cream first 3 ingredients. Add egg and beat well. Sift dry ingredients and add alternately with applesauce to first mixture, stirring until smooth. Pour into 8" x 8" x 2" pan lined on the bottom with waxed paper. Bake in moderate oven (350°F.) 40 minutes, or until done. Cool 5 to 10 minutes. Turn out on rack; peel off paper.

CALIFORNIA WINE-GLAZED POUND CAKE

2 packages (17 ounces each) pound-cake
   mix
Sauterne
Grated rind of 2 oranges
1 cup golden raisins
1 cup toasted chopped almonds
1 cup sifted confectioners' sugar
Food coloring (optional)
Kumquats or candied fruit

Prepare pound-cake mix as directed on package, substituting sauterne for the water. Fold in next 3 ingredients. Pour into greased and floured 9" tube pan. Bake in moderate oven (350°F.) 1 hour and 20 minutes, or until done. Cool on rack 10 minutes before removing from pan. Glaze with confectioners' sugar mixed with enough sauterne to make it the consistency of thin cream. Tint glaze with food coloring, if desired. Decorate with kumquats. *Note* Cake can also be baked in two 9" x 5" x 3" loaf pans 50 to 60 minutes.

APRICOT-BRANDY POUND CAKE

1 cup butter or margarine, softened
2-1/2 cups sugar
1 teaspoon each vanilla, orange and rum
  extracts
1/2 teaspoon lemon extract
6 eggs
3 cups all-purpose flour
1/4 teaspoon baking soda
1/2 teaspoon salt
1 cup dairy sour cream
1/2 cup apricot brandy

Cream butter; gradually add sugar and flavorings and beat until light. Add eggs one at a time, beating thoroughly after each. Add sifted dry ingredients alternately with sour cream and brandy. Blend well. Put in greased 3-quart *bundt* or tube pan and bake in slow oven (325°F.) about 1 hour and 15 minutes. Cool in pan on rack. Store airtight.

PETITS FOURS

Make cake with mix or use bought pound cake or other firm-textured white or yellow cake. Cut slices about ³/₄" thick. Then cut cake in shapes with small cutters. Put together sandwich-fashion with jam, jelly or Currant Glaze, page 326. To frost and decorate, put petits fours on rack with tray underneath. Spoon Petit-four Frosting over cakes until they are smoothly coated. Scrape up frosting that drips into tray, beat smooth and reuse, adding a few drops of water, if necessary. When frosting is firm, decorate, using a pastry tube, with Decorating Frosting, or buy colored frostings in tubes with special decorating tips to fit the tubes. **Decorating Frosting** Mix until smooth 2 parts sifted confectioners' sugar to 1 part butter or margarine. Flavor and color as desired.

Petit-four Frosting

1 cup granulated sugar
1/16 teaspoon cream of tartar
1/8 teaspoon salt
Sifted confectioners' sugar
Flavoring
Food coloring

Mix first 3 ingredients with ¹/₄ cup water. Bring to boil and cook until a small amount of mixture forms a soft ball when dropped into cold water (236°F. on a candy thermometer). Cool to lukewarm. Gradually add sugar and flavoring and beat until smooth and almost thick enough to hold its shape. Divide into 4 parts. Leave one part white and tint others pink, yellow and green.

PEAR UPSIDE-DOWN CAKE

Butter or margarine
3 tablespoons brown sugar
1 teaspoon grated orange rind
6 maraschino cherries
3 fresh winter pears, peeled, halved and
  cored
1 cup granulated sugar
1 egg
1 teaspoon vanilla extract
1-2/3 cups all-purpose flour
2 teaspoons double-acting baking powder
1/2 teaspoon salt
1/2 cup milk
Orange Sauce, page 397

Put 3 tablespoons butter in 10" x 6" x 2" glass baking pan and put in moderate oven (350°F.) until butter is melted. Blend in brown sugar and grated rind. Put a maraschino cherry in center of each pear half; arrange pear halves, cut side down, in the mixture. Cream ¹/₃ cup butter with the granulated sugar until light. Beat in egg and vanilla. Mix dry ingredients and add with milk to first mixture, beating until blended. Spread evenly on pears. Bake 45 minutes, or until done. Let stand about 5 minutes, then turn out on serving plate; serve with the sauce. Makes 6 servings.

SHENANDOAH APPLE
LAYER CAKE

Butter or margarine
1/3 cup packed light-brown sugar
Granulated sugar
1 egg
2 cups sifted cake flour
Cinnamon
1 teaspoon double-acting baking powder
1/2 teaspoon baking soda
1/4 teaspoon salt
1/8 teaspoon mace
6 tablespoons milk
1-1/4 cups drained canned apple slices,
  chopped
1/2 cup coarsely chopped pecans
Confectioners'-sugar Frosting, page 318

Cream ¹/₃ cup butter. Add brown sugar and ²/₃ cup granulated sugar; beat until light. Add egg and beat well. Sift flour with ¹/₄ teaspoon cinnamon and next 4 ingredients; add alternately with milk to creamed mixture, beating until smooth. Fold in apples. Pour into two 8" layer-cake pans lined on the bottom with waxed paper. Mix pecans and 1 tablespoon melted butter; sprinkle on batter in one pan. Mix 3 tablespoons granulated sugar and ¹/₂ teaspoon cinnamon; sprinkle on nuts. Bake in moderate oven (350°F.) about 25 minutes. Cool. Spread frosting on plain layer and top with nut layer; spread sides of cake with remaining frosting.

DUTCH APPLE CAKE

1 cup all-purpose flour
1-1/2 teaspoons double-acting baking
   powder
1/4 teaspoon salt
Sugar
Butter or margarine
1/4 cup seedless raisins
1 egg, well beaten
1/4 cup milk
3 cups peeled tart-apple slices, 1/4"
   thick
1/2 teaspoon cinnamon
1/4 teaspoon nutmeg

Mix first 3 ingredients and 2 table-spoons sugar. Cut in ¹/₃ cup butter. Add raisins and combined egg and milk; blend well. Spread in greased 10" x 6" x 2" glass baking dish. Arrange apple wedges in rows on batter. Brush with 2 tablespoons melted butter and sprinkle with spices mixed with 2 tablespoons sugar. Bake in hot oven (400°F.) 30 to 40 minutes. Cut in squares and serve warm.

MARBLE CHIFFON CAKE

4 squares unsweetened chocolate
Sugar
2-1/4 cups sifted cake flour
2 teaspoons double-acting baking
   powder
1 teaspoon salt
1/2 cup vegetable oil
7 eggs, separated
1 teaspoon vanilla extract
1/2 teaspoon cream of tartar
Chocolate Butter-cream Frosting
   (above right)

Blend 2 squares chocolate, 2 table-spoons sugar and ¹/₄ cup boiling water; set aside. Sift flour, 1¹/₂ cups sugar, the baking powder and salt. Make a well in center of dry ingredients; add oil, then egg yolks, ³/₄ cup cold water and the vanilla. Beat until well blended and smooth. In large bowl, beat egg whites with cream of tartar until very stiff peaks form. Pour egg-yolk mixture in thin stream over entire surface of egg whites, gently folding to blend. Remove one third of batter to separate bowl; gently fold in reserved chocolate mixture. Spoon half of light batter into un-greased 10" tube pan. Top with half the chocolate batter; repeat. With narrow spatula, swirl gently through batters to form a marbled pattern. Bake in slow oven (325°F.) 55 minutes. Raise temperature to 350°F. and bake 10 minutes, or until done. Invert cake in pan on rack until cold. Remove from pan; spread top and sides with frosting. Melt remaining 2 squares chocolate and cool. Drizzle over top.

CHOCOLATE BUTTER-CREAM FROSTING

Melt 4 squares, unsweetened chocolate in top of double-boiler over hot water. Beat 4 egg yolks with ²/₃ cup sugar; add ¹/₂ cup heavy cream and ¹/₈ teaspoon salt. Pour slowly over chocolate, stirring constantly. Cook over hot water 5 minutes, or until thickened, stirring. Cream 1¹/₄ cups unsalted butter; add chocolate mixture, 1 tablespoonful at a time, beating until blended. Chill until thick. Frosts 9" or 10" tube cake.

COFFEE SPICE CAKE

1/2 cup butter, softened
1 cup packed light-brown sugar
1/2 teaspoon each vanilla and lemon
   extracts
2 eggs
1-1/3 cups all-purpose flour
1-1/2 teaspoons double-acting baking
   powder
1/2 teaspoon salt
1 teaspoon cinnamon
1/4 teaspoon each ginger, cloves and
   nutmeg
1/3 cup undiluted evaporated milk
1/4 cup strong coffee
Coffee Frosting (below)

Cream butter, sugar and flavorings until light. Add eggs, one at a time, beating well after each addition. Add sifted dry ingredients alternately with milk and coffee, beating until smooth. Pour into 9" x 9" x 2" pan lined on the bottom with waxed paper. Bake in moderate oven (350°F.) 25 to 35 minutes. Cool and frost.

COFFEE FROSTING

Cream ¹/₃ cup butter. Add a dash of salt and ¹/₂ teaspoon vanilla. Gradually beat in 2¹/₂ cups sifted confectioners' sugar and enough strong coffee (about 2 tablespoons) for spreading consistency. Frosts two 8" layers.

PINEAPPLE-COCONUT CAKE

Cut one 10" angel food cake horizontally in 4 layers. Drain 1 can (about 9 ounces) crushed pineapple. Put pineapple, 1 egg white, dash of salt, ¹/₂ cup granulated sugar, ¹/₄ cup confectioners' sugar and ¹/₄ teaspoon lemon extract in bowl. Beat with rotary beater or electric mixer until very stiff. Put layers together with some of the mixture, sprinkling layers with 1 can flaked coconut. Spread top and sides of cake with remaining mixture and sprinkle with more coconut. Chill. Serves 12.

BLITZ TORTE

4 egg whites
Sugar
1/2 cup softened butter or margarine
1-3/4 cups sifted cake flour
2-1/4 teaspoons double-acting baking powder
3/4 teaspoon salt
2/3 cup minus 1 tablespoon milk
1 teaspoon vanilla extract
2 eggs
1/4 cup slivered blanched almonds
Pineapple Filling (below)
Whipped cream or whipped topping

Beat egg whites until foamy. Gradually add 1 cup sugar, beating until stiff. Set meringue aside. Cream butter. Sift in 1 cup plus 2 tablespoons sugar, the flour, baking powder and salt; blend well. Add milk and vanilla; mix until flour is dampened. Then beat until well blended. Add eggs and beat well. Pour into two 9" layer pans lined on the bottom with waxed paper. Spread meringue on batter and sprinkle with nuts. Bake in moderate oven (350°F.) about 35 minutes. Cool; spread filling between layers and cream on sides.

PINEAPPLE FILLING

In top part of double boiler mix 1/4 cup sugar, 1 tablespoon flour and a dash of salt. Stir in 2 beaten egg yolks and 2/3 cup milk. Cook and stir over boiling water until thick. Add 1 tablespoon butter and 1 can (9 ounces) crushed pineapple, drained. Makes about 2 cups.

L'ORANGE ALMOND CAKE

1/2 cup each solid vegetable shortening, granulated sugar and honey
Grated rind of 1 orange
5 egg yolks
2 cups sifted cake flour
2 teaspoons double-acting baking powder
1/2 teaspoon salt
1/2 cup milk
1/4 cup each ground blanched almonds and sliced almonds
Confectioners' sugar

Cream shortening; gradually add granulated sugar, beating until light and fluffy. Add honey and orange rind and mix well. Add egg yolks one at a time, beating thoroughly after each. Add sifted dry ingredients alternately with milk, beating until smooth. Add ground nuts. Grease 9" x 9" x 2" pan, then line bottom with waxed paper and grease again. Pour mixture into pan and sprinkle top with sliced almonds. Bake in moderate oven (350°F.) 30 minutes, or until done. Sprinkle top with confectioners' sugar.

COMPANY GRAND-MARNIER CAKE

1 cup softened butter
1-1/2 cups sugar
3 eggs, separated
2 cups all-purpose flour
1 teaspoon double-acting baking powder
1 teaspoon baking soda
1 cup dairy sour cream
Grated rind of 1 orange
1/2 cup chopped nuts
1/4 cup orange juice
1/3 cup Grand Marnier
2 tablespoons slivered blanched almonds

Cream butter and 1 cup sugar until light and fluffy. Beat in egg yolks. Add sifted dry ingredients alternately with sour cream, beating until smooth. Stir in rind and chopped nuts. Fold in stiffly beaten egg whites. Pour into buttered 9" tube pan and bake in moderate oven (350°F.) about 50 minutes. Mix 1/2 cup sugar, the orange juice and Grand Marnier and spoon over hot cake in pan. Decorate top with almonds. Cool before removing from pan.

Company Orange Cake Make cake as directed above, substituting 1/4 cup orange juice for the Grand Marnier.

STRAWBERRY CAKE ROLL

1 cup sifted cake flour
1 teaspoon double-acting baking powder
1/4 teaspoon salt
3 eggs
1 teaspoon vanilla extract
1 cup granulated sugar
1/4 cup sifted confectioners' sugar
1 cup sliced fresh strawberries
1 pint strawberry ice cream, softened
1 package (1 pound) frozen sliced strawberries, thawed
2 tablespoons brandy (optional)

Sift first 3 ingredients. Beat eggs with vanilla until fluffy and light-colored. Gradually beat in granulated sugar. Stir in 1/4 cup water. Fold in reserved flour mixture carefully but thoroughly. Turn into waxed-paper-lined 15" x 10" x 1" baking pan. Bake in moderate oven (350°F.) 15 minutes, or until done. Sift confectioners' sugar evenly onto smooth dish towel. Turn hot cake onto towel and carefully peel off paper. Roll up cake from narrow end, jelly-roll fashion; cool. Add fresh strawberries to ice cream. Unroll cake and spread with ice cream mixture; reroll, wrap in foil and freeze. Thaw 10 minutes before serving. Serve sliced with sauce of frozen berries, mixed with brandy, if desired. Makes 8 servings.

BLOND FRUITCAKE

Grated rind of 1 lemon
1 cup chopped mixed candied fruit
1/2 cup each currants, golden raisins and chopped pecans or walnuts
1 package (8 ounces) cream cheese, slightly softened
1 cup butter, slightly softened
1-1/2 cups granulated sugar
4 large eggs
2-1/4 cups sifted cake flour
1-1/2 teaspoons double-acting baking powder
Confectioners' sugar

Butter a 10" Bundt or tube pan and set aside. Combine rind, fruit and nuts and set aside. Beat cream cheese and butter until fluffy. Gradually beat in granulated sugar. Add eggs one at a time, beating well after each. Gradually add flour sifted with baking powder; stir until well blended. Fold fruit-nut mixture into batter and pour into pan. Bake in slow oven (325°F.) 1 hour and 20 minutes, or until done. Let stand in pan on rack 5 minutes, then turn out on rack to cool. Store, well wrapped in plastic wrap and aluminum foil, in cool place. Before serving, dust with confectioners' sugar. Cake freezes well.

TOMATO-SOUP CAKE WITH CREAM-CHEESE FROSTING

2 cups sifted all-purpose flour
1-1/3 cups sugar
4 teaspoons double-acting baking powder
1 teaspoon baking soda
1-1/2 teaspoons ground allspice
1 teaspoon cinnamon
1/2 teaspoon ground cloves
1/2 cup solid vegetable shortening
1 can (10-3/4 ounces) condensed tomato soup
2 eggs
Cream-cheese Frosting

Sift first 7 ingredients into large bowl of electric mixer. Add shortening and soup and beat at low to medium speed 2 minutes, scraping sides and bottom of bowl constantly. Add eggs and 1/4 cup water and beat 2 minutes longer, scraping bowl frequently. Pour into two 9" layer pans lined on bottom with waxed paper. Bake in moderate oven (350°F.) 25 minutes, or until done. Let stand in pans on cake racks 10 minutes, then turn out, peel off paper and turn cakes right side up; cool. Spread frosting between layers and on top of cake. **Cream-cheese Frosting** Beat together 1/4 cup softened margarine and 1 package (3 ounces) softened cream cheese. Add 2 1/4 cups sifted confectioners' sugar; beat until spreading consistency.

CARROT CAKE WITH CREAM-CHEESE FROSTING

4 eggs, separated
1-1/2 cups vegetable oil
2 cups sugar
1-1/2 cups lightly packed grated carrot
2-1/2 cups sifted cake flour
2-1/2 teaspoons cinnamon
1-1/2 teaspoons baking soda
1 teaspoon salt
Cream-cheese Frosting (below left)

In large mixing bowl, beat egg yolks. Add 1 tablespoon hot water and next 3 ingredients and mix well. Sift in dry ingredients and mix well. Fold in stiffly beaten egg whites. Pour into greased 13" x 9" x 2" baking pan. Bake in moderate oven (350°F.) about 45 minutes. Cool in pan, then top with frosting. Cut in squares.

PRUNE CUPCAKES

1/2 cup butter or margarine
1 cup sugar
1 teaspoon vanilla extract
2 eggs
1 cup pitted cooked prunes
1-1/2 cups all-purpose flour
1/2 teaspoon salt
1-1/2 teaspoons double-acting baking powder
1 teaspoon cinnamon
1/4 teaspoon ground cloves
1/2 cup milk
1/2 cup chopped nuts

Cream butter; gradually add sugar and vanilla; cream until light. Add eggs, one at a time, beating well after each. Fold in prunes. Add sifted dry ingredients alternately with milk, beating well; add nuts. Half-fill greased 2 1/2" muffin pans; bake in moderate oven (375°F.) 20 minutes. Makes 21.

BANANA LOAF CAKE

1/2 cup butter or margarine, softened
3/4 cup packed light-brown sugar
3/4 cup granulated sugar
1 teaspoon vanilla extract
1 whole egg
1 egg yolk
1 cup mashed very-ripe banana
2 cups all-purpose flour
1 teaspoon double-acting baking powder
1/2 teaspoon each baking soda and salt
3/4 cup buttermilk

Cream butter; gradually add sugars and beat until fluffy. Add vanilla, whole egg and yolk; beat well. Blend in banana. Add mixed dry ingredients alternately with buttermilk, beating after each addition until smooth. Pour into well-greased 9" x 5" x 3" loaf pan and bake in slow oven (325°F.) 55 minutes, or until done. Cool in pan on cake rack 10 minutes.

COFFEE-MOLASSES LAYER CAKE

1/2 cup butter or margarine, softened
1 cup packed brown sugar
2 eggs
1/2 cup molasses
1/2 cup cold coffee
2 cups all-purpose flour
2 teaspoons double-acting baking powder
1/2 teaspoon salt
1/2 teaspoon pumpkin-pie spice or mixed spices
1/2 recipe Fluffy Frosting, below right

Cream butter and sugar until light and fluffy. Add eggs one at a time, beating thoroughly after each. Mix molasses and coffee and add alternately with sifted dry ingredients to first mixture, beating after each addition until smooth. Put in two 9" layer pans lined on bottom with waxed paper. Bake in moderate oven (350°F.) 25 minutes, or until done. Turn out on racks and peel off paper. Turn right side up and cool thoroughly. (Layers will not be thick.) Spread frosting between layers and on top and sides of cake.

COFFEE ALMOND-DATE LOAF

2 cups sifted all-purpose flour
3 teaspoons double-acting baking powder
1/2 teaspoon salt
2/3 cup sugar
1/3 cup chopped blanched almonds
3/4 cup finely cut pitted dates
1/4 cup minced candied ginger
1 cup cold strong coffee
1/8 teaspoon baking soda
1 egg, well beaten
2 tablespoons shortening, melted

Sift first 4 ingredients. Stir in nuts and fruit. Combine remaining ingredients and add all at once to dry ingredients. Stir only enough to dampen. Put in 9" x 5" x 3" loaf pan lined on bottom with waxed paper. Bake in moderate oven (375°F.) about 45 minutes. Let stand 5 minutes, then turn out on rack and peel off paper. Cool.

SCOTCH CHOCOLATE FROSTING

In top part of double boiler over boiling water, melt 3 squares unsweetened chocolate in 1/4 cup undiluted evaporated milk; stir until smooth. Add 1 cup packed light-brown sugar; stir until it melts. Remove from heat; beat in 1 egg, 1/4 teaspoon salt and 1/2 teaspoon vanilla extract. Gradually beat in 2 cups sifted confectioners' sugar. Frosts tops and sides of two 8" or 9" layers.

ORANGE-COCONUT CAKE WITH FLUFFY FROSTING

Have all ingredients at room temperature.

1 cup butter
2 cups sugar
3-1/2 cups sifted cake flour
3-1/2 teaspoons double-acting baking powder
3/4 teaspoon salt
1 cup milk
2 teaspoons grated lemon rind
Grated fresh coconut or canned flaked coconut
6 egg whites
Orange Filling
Fluffy Frosting

Cream butter until soft. Gradually add 1½ cups sugar and beat until light. Add sifted dry ingredients alternately with milk, beating after each addition until smooth. Stir in lemon rind and 1 cup coconut. Beat egg whites until foamy; gradually add remaining ½ cup sugar and beat until stiff but not dry. Fold into batter. Pour into four 9" layer-cake pans lined on bottom with waxed paper. Bake in moderate oven (375°F.) 15 to 20 minutes. Cool 5 minutes, then turn out on racks. Peel off paper and cool cakes. Spread filling between layers and frosting on top and sides of cake. Sprinkle generously with coconut.

Orange Filling

In heavy saucepan, mix ½ cup cake flour, 1 cup sugar and ¼ teaspoon salt. Add ¼ cup water and blend until smooth. Add 2 tablespoons grated orange rind and grated rind of 1 lemon, 1½ cups orange juice, and ¼ cup lemon juice. Cook, stirring, until mixture thickens and becomes almost translucent. Beat 4 egg yolks slightly and stir in small amount of hot mixture. Stir into mixture in saucepan and cook, stirring, a few minutes longer. Cool.

Fluffy Frosting

1-1/2 cups sugar
1/2 teaspoon cream of tartar
1/8 teaspoon salt
1/2 cup egg whites (about 4)
1/2 teaspoon vanilla or almond extract

In saucepan, combine first 3 ingredients and ½ cup hot water. Cook without stirring until small amount of mixture forms a soft ball when dropped in very cold water (240°F on candy thermometer). Meanwhile, beat egg whites until stiff but not dry. Add syrup very slowly to egg whites, beating with mixer at high speed. Add flavoring.

DAFFODIL CAKE

1 cup egg whites (8 or 9)
1/2 teaspoon salt
1 teaspoon cream of tartar
1 cup sugar
1 cup sifted cake flour
1 teaspoon vanilla extract
4 egg yolks
Grated rind of 1/2 orange
Yellow-jacket Frosting (below)

Beat egg whites with salt until frothy. Add cream of tartar and beat until stiff but not dry. Gradually add sugar and beat until very stiff and glossy. Fold in flour in thirds. Add vanilla. Beat egg yolks until thick and lemon-colored. Divide batter in half. Fold egg yolks and rind into one part. Put by tablespoonfuls into an ungreased 9" or 10" tube pan, alternating the yellow and white mixtures. Bake in slow oven (300°F.) about 1 hour; invert on rack to cool. Remove from pan and spread top and sides of cake with Yellow-jacket Frosting.

YELLOW-JACKET FROSTING

In saucepan, mix 1²/₃ cups sugar, 3 tablespoons light corn syrup and ¹/₂ cup water. Cook without stirring until a little of the mixture forms a hard ball when dropped in cold water (250°F. on a candy thermometer). Beat 3 egg yolks and ¹/₄ teaspoon salt until thick and lemon-colored. Gradually add syrup and beat until thick and of spreading consistency. Add grated rinds of ¹/₂ orange and ¹/₂ lemon and 1 teaspoon lemon juice. Makes enough frosting for large tube cake or two 9" layers.

PINEAPPLE LOAF CAKE

1/2 cup butter or margarine
1 cup sugar
2 eggs, separated
1/2 teaspoon vanilla extract
1/2 teaspoon grated lemon rind
2/3 cup undrained crushed pineapple
1-3/4 cups all-purpose flour
1-1/2 teaspoons double-acting baking
  powder
1/4 teaspoon baking soda
1/4 teaspoon salt
Pineapple Frosting (above right)

Cream butter until light and fluffy. Gradually add sugar and beat well. Beat in egg yolks and flavorings. Add pineapple and sifted dry ingredients; beat well. Fold stiffly beaten egg whites into batter. Pour into a 9" x 5" x 3" loaf pan lined with waxed paper. Bake in moderate oven (350°F.) about 50 minutes. Cool and frost.

PINEAPPLE FROSTING

Soften 3 tablespoons butter or margarine in bowl; gradually beat in 2¹/₂ cups sifted confectioners' sugar, 1 tablespoon lemon juice, ¹/₄ cup drained crushed pineapple and enough pineapple syrup to make frosting of spreading consistency. Frosts tops of two 8" layers.

PEANUT-BUTTER CAKE

1/3 cup softened butter or margarine
2-1/4 cups sifted cake flour
1-1/2 cups sugar
3 teaspoons double-acting baking powder
1 teaspoon salt
1/3 cup peanut butter
1 cup milk
2 eggs
1 teaspoon vanilla extract
Chocolate Peanut-butter Frosting (below)

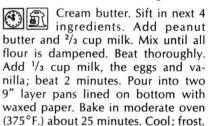

Cream butter. Sift in next 4 ingredients. Add peanut butter and ²/₃ cup milk. Mix until all flour is dampened. Beat thoroughly. Add ¹/₃ cup milk, the eggs and vanilla; beat 2 minutes. Pour into two 9" layer pans lined on bottom with waxed paper. Bake in moderate oven (375°F.) about 25 minutes. Cool; frost.

CHOCOLATE PEANUT-BUTTER FROSTING

Cream together ¹/₂ cup peanut butter and ¹/₃ cup unsweetened cocoa. Add 2²/₃ cups sifted confectioners' sugar, ¹/₄ teaspoon salt, 1 teaspoon vanilla and about ¹/₂ cup cream. Beat until smooth. Frosts two 9" layers.

KENTUCKY PANTRY CAKE

1 cup butter or margarine, softened
2 cups sugar
5 eggs
1 cup seedless blackberry jam
2-3/4 cups all-purpose flour
1 teaspoon baking soda
1/2 teaspoon salt
1/2 teaspoon each cloves and allspice
1 cup buttermilk
1 cup chopped nuts
1 cup chopped dates or raisins
Caramel Frosting, page 318
Whipped cream

Cream butter and sugar until light. Add eggs, one at a time, beating well after each addition. Beat in jam. Add sifted dry ingredients alternately with buttermilk, beating until smooth. Stir in nuts and dates. Pour into four 8" layer pans lined on the bottom with waxed paper. Bake in moderate oven (325°F.) about 25 to 30 minutes. Cool and spread frosting between layers; top with cream.

SUN-KISSED APPLE CAKE

1/2 cup solid vegetable shortening
1 cup packed light-brown sugar
1 cup canned applesauce
2-1/4 cups all-purpose flour
1/2 teaspoon each salt and baking soda
1 teaspoon double-acting baking powder
1/2 teaspoon each ground cloves and
   cinnamon
1/4 teaspoon nutmeg
1 cup chopped walnuts
Lemon Frosting (below), or
   confectioners' sugar

Cream shortening and brown sugar until light. Add applesauce. Mix dry ingredients and gradually beat into first mixture. Add nuts and pour into 9" x 5" x 3" loaf pan lined on bottom with waxed paper. Bake in slow oven (325°F.) 1 hour, or until done. Let stand on cake rack about 5 minutes, then turn out and peel off paper. Turn right side up. Cool; frost, or sprinkle with confectioners' sugar.

LEMON FROSTING

Mix 2 cups sifted confectioners' sugar, 1 teaspoon grated lemon rind, a little yellow food coloring and enough lemon juice to moisten. Frosts tops of two 8" layers or 1 large loaf.

FESTIVE WALNUT CAKE

3/4 cup Niagara-type wine or sherry
2 cups seedless raisins
4 cups all-purpose flour
2 teaspoons double-acting baking powder
1/2 teaspoon salt
1 teaspoon nutmeg
6 eggs
1 cup butter
2 cups sugar
1/2 cup molasses
1/4 cup orange juice
1 teaspoon vanilla extract
4 cups chopped walnuts
Confectioners'-sugar Frosting, page 318

Pour wine over raisins. Set aside. Sift next 4 ingredients. Beat eggs until thick. Cream butter and sugar until light and fluffy. Beat in eggs. Drain raisins, reserving liquid. Add liquid, molasses and orange juice alternately with dry ingredients to creamed mixture, beating until smooth. Add vanilla, raisins and walnuts. Line a 10" tube pan with waxed paper. Spoon in batter. Bake in very slow oven (275°F.) 3 hours. Cool 15 minutes on rack before removing from pan. Then turn out on rack and cool thoroughly. Spread with frosting, allowing some to run down sides.

SOUR-CREAM GINGERBREAD

1/3 cup softened butter or margarine
1/2 cup packed light-brown sugar
1/2 cup molasses
2 eggs
1/2 cup dairy sour cream
1-2/3 cups sifted cake flour
1 teaspoon baking soda
1/4 teaspoon salt
1 teaspoon ginger
Granulated sugar

Cream butter and brown sugar until fluffy; beat in molasses. Add eggs, one at a time, beating well after each addition. Sift next 4 ingredients; add alternately with sour cream, beating until smooth. Grease a 9" x 9" x 2" baking pan and sprinkle the inside with granulated sugar. Pour in batter and sprinkle top with more sugar. Bake in moderate oven (350°F.) about 30 minutes. Serve warm or cold. Makes 8 servings.

JUBILEE FRUITCAKE

1-1/2 cups seedless raisins
3/4 cup golden raisins
1-1/2 cups dried figs, thinly sliced
1-1/2 cups diced citron
1 cup sliced candied cherries
1 tablespoon cinnamon
1 teaspoon ground cloves
1/8 teaspoon black pepper
2 teaspoons rum flavoring
1/2 cup thick orange marmalade
1/4 cup sweet sherry
1-1/3 cups butter or margarine, softened
1-1/2 cups sugar
4 eggs
3 cups all-purpose flour
1 teaspoon double-acting baking powder
1/2 teaspoon baking soda
1-1/2 teaspoons salt
3/4 cup chopped roasted unblanched
   almonds
3/4 cup chopped walnuts
Topping

Mix well first 11 ingredients. Cream butter; gradually add sugar and beat until light. Add eggs one at a time, beating thoroughly after each. Sift next 4 ingredients; stir ½ cup into butter mixture. Add fruits, nuts and remaining flour mixture and mix well. Pour into 2 well-greased 1½-quart casseroles. Spread with Topping. Cover with lids or foil and bake in very slow oven (250°F.) 3 to 3½ hours, keeping a shallow pan of water on bottom shelf of oven while baking. Loosen around edge of casseroles and let stand on rack 15 minutes. Unmold and turn cakes right side up. Cool thoroughly; store airtight. **Topping** Mix ½ cup each golden raisins, chopped roasted unblanched almonds, chopped walnuts, finely cut citron and sliced candied cherries; add ¼ cup honey and ¼ teaspoon ground cloves.

DARK CHOCOLATE FRUITCAKE

2 packages (15 ounces each) raisins
1/2 cup chopped mixed candied fruit
1 cup hot black coffee
1 cup grape juice
2 teaspoons cinnamon
1 teaspoon each nutmeg and ground
  cloves
1/4 teaspoon ginger
1 cup solid vegetable shortening
2 squares unsweetened chocolate
1/2 cup maraschino cherries with syrup
1 cup chopped nuts
4 eggs
2 cups packed dark-brown sugar
4 cups all-purpose flour
1 teaspoon salt
2 teaspoons baking soda
Sherry or brandy

Put raisins, candied fruit, liquids and spices in saucepan and bring to boil. Simmer 5 minutes, remove from heat and stir in shortening and chocolate; cool. Slice cherries and add with syrup and nuts to first mixture. Beat eggs slightly. Gradually add sugar and beat until light and foamy. Add sifted dry ingredients alternately with fruit mixture, stirring until well blended. Pour into two 9" x 5" x 3" loaf pans lined on the bottom with waxed paper. Bake in slow oven (300°F.) 1½ to 1¾ hours. Let stand in pans on rack until cold. Turn out and peel off paper. Wrap in cloths moistened with sherry and store at least 2 weeks. Remoisten cloths when necessary.

MARVEL DATE CAKE

1/2 cup butter or margarine, softened
3/4 cup packed brown sugar
2 eggs
1-3/4 cups all-purpose flour
2 teaspoons double-acting baking
  powder
1/2 teaspoon salt
1 teaspoon cinnamon
1/2 teaspoon nutmeg
1/2 cup milk
1 tablespoon dark rum
8 ounces pitted dates, cut up
Rum Frosting (above right)

Cream butter and add sugar; cream until light and fluffy. Add eggs one at a time, beating thoroughly. Mix dry ingredients and add to first mixture alternately with combined milk and rum, beating after each addition until smooth. Stir in dates. Put in 9" tube pan lined on the bottom with waxed paper. Bake in moderate oven (350° F.) about 50 minutes. Cool 5 minutes, then turn out on rack and peel off paper. Cool thoroughly, then frost top and sides of cake.

RUM FROSTING

Cream 2 tablespoons butter. Add 2 cups sifted confectioners' sugar and 1 tablespoon dark rum. Gradually beat in enough cream or milk to make frosting of spreading consistency.

LITTLE WHITE FRUITCAKES

1 cup solid vegetable shortening
1 cup sugar
5 eggs
2 cups all-purpose flour
1 teaspoon salt
1-1/2 teaspoons double-acting baking
  powder
1/4 cup pineapple juice
1/2 cup each chopped candied cherries,
  finely cut citron, and orange and lemon
  peel
1/2 cup each chopped pitted dates,
  chopped dried figs and chopped
  dried apricots
1-1/4 cups chopped candied pineapple
1 cup golden raisins
2 cups flaked coconut
2 cups sliced blanched almonds

Cream shortening and sugar. Add eggs, one at a time, beating well after each addition. Sift 1½ cups flour, the salt and baking powder. Add alternately with pineapple juice to first mixture. Stir ½ cup flour into fruit; add with coconut and almonds to the batter. Mix only until well blended. Pour into paper baking cups in muffin pans and bake in slow oven (275°F.) 50 minutes. Cool and store airtight. Makes thirty-two 2" cakes.

OLD-FASHIONED SPICE CAKE

1/2 cup solid vegetable shortening
1 cup granulated sugar
3 eggs
1-1/3 cups all-purpose flour
1 teaspoon baking soda
1/2 teaspoon salt
2 teaspoons cinnamon
1 teaspoon each ginger and ground
  cloves
1 cup dairy sour cream
1 teaspoon crushed cardamom seed
  (optional)
Fine dry bread crumbs
Confectioners' sugar (optional)

Cream shortening. Gradually add granulated sugar and beat well. Add eggs one at a time, beating thoroughly after each. Sift next 5 ingredients; add alternately with sour cream, blending well. Add cardamom, if desired. Grease well a 2-quart fluted tube pan, sprinkle with crumbs and shake out excess. Put batter in pan and bake in slow oven (325°F.) about 50 minutes. Let cool in pan on rack 10 minutes before turning out. Cool and sprinkle with confectioners' sugar, if desired.

OLD-TIME SOUTHERN FRUITCAKE

1 pound butter, softened
3 nutmegs, grated, or 2 teaspoons ground nutmeg
Sugar
12 eggs, separated
2 tablespoons dark molasses
Juice of 1 orange
4 cups all-purpose flour
2-1/2 teaspoons double-acting baking powder
1 teaspoon salt
1 pound (4 cups) pecan halves
1/2 pound (1-1/2 cups) blanched almonds
1 pound candied cherries
1 package (15 ounces) raisins
2 slices each red and green candied pineapple, diced
1 slice white candied pineapple, diced
2 ounces each diced candied orange and lemon peel
1/2 pound pitted dates, halved
1/2 pound dried figs, diced
1/4 pound citron, diced
1/2 cup crushed peppermint-stick candy
1 cup bourbon

Cream butter with nutmeg; gradually add 1¼ cups sugar; beat until light. Add egg yolks beaten until thick. Add molasses and beat well. Add orange juice alternately with 1 cup flour sifted with baking powder and salt; blend thoroughly. Mix well remaining flour with nuts and fruits. Stir into the first mixture. Reserve 2 tablespoons crushed candy and add remainder with bourbon to batter. Beat egg whites until peaks form. Gradually beat in 1 cup sugar and beat until stiff. Fold into batter, using fingers. Grease well and flour three 9" loose-bottomed pans with tubes. Put batter in pans and sprinkle with remaining crushed candy, putting most of it around the tubes or toward the outer edge. Bake in very slow oven (250°F.) about 3½ hours. Cool in pans on racks. Store airtight.

HAWAIIAN GINGERBREAD

2 cups all-purpose flour
1-1/2 teaspoons each baking soda and ginger
1/2 teaspoon salt
1 cup molasses
1/3 cup butter or margarine
1/2 cup buttermilk
1 egg
1/2 cup snipped soft pitted prunes
Pineapple-Cream Sauce (above right)

Mix dry ingredients together. Bring molasses and butter to boil; cool. Stir in dry ingredients, buttermilk, egg and prunes. Put in greased 9" square pan and bake in moderate oven (350°F.) about 35 minutes. Cut in squares, serve warm with sauce. Makes 6 large or 9 small servings.

PINEAPPLE-CREAM SAUCE

Beat 2 egg yolks, ¾ cup sifted confectioners' sugar, 1 teaspoon vanilla and dash of salt until thick and smooth. Fold in 1 cup cream, whipped. Drain 1 can (13½ ounces) crushed pineapple and fold pineapple into cream mixture. Serve at once or chill until ready to use. Makes about 2½ cups.

CANDIED FRUITCAKE

2 cups all-purpose flour
2 teaspoons double-acting baking powder
1/2 teaspoon salt
1 pound (2-1/2 cups) candied pineapple, coarsely cut
2 cups candied cherries
3-1/2 cups pitted dates, coarsely cut
4 eggs
1 cup sugar
2 pounds (8 cups) pecan halves

Sift first 3 ingredients into large bowl. Add next 3 ingredients. Mix well with hands to coat each piece of fruit with flour. Beat eggs until frothy and gradually beat in sugar. Add with nuts to fruit and mix well. Grease and line with brown paper 2 deep 9" springform pans; grease paper. Divide dough into pans and press down firmly with fingers. If necessary, rearrange fruit and nuts to fill any empty spaces. Bake in very slow oven (275°F.) 1¼ hours. Let cakes stand in pans about 5 minutes. Turn out; pull off paper. Cool. Dough can also be baked in small paper baking cups, filling them full. Bake about 40 minutes in slow oven (300°F.).

PRALINE CAKE

1 cup butter, softened
1/2 cup solid vegetable shortening
1 pound light-brown sugar
2 teaspoons vanilla extract
5 eggs
3 cups all-purpose flour
1/4 teaspoon baking soda
1/2 teaspoon double-acting baking powder
3/4 cup milk
2 cups chopped pecans
Confectioners' sugar

Cream first 4 ingredients until light and fluffy. Add eggs, one at a time, beating well after each addition. Add sifted dry ingredients alternately with milk, beating until smooth after each addition. Stir in nuts. Pour into well-greased heavy *bundt* pan (a scalloped 3-quart tube pan). Put in cold oven; turn heat control to 300°F. Bake about 1 hour and 40 minutes. Let stand 5 minutes, then turn out on rack to cool. Sift confectioners' sugar lightly over top. Store airtight.

MELT-IN-THE-MOUTH COOKIES

1/2 cup butter
1 cup packed light-brown sugar
1 teaspoon vanilla extract
1 egg
3/4 cup all-purpose flour
1 teaspoon double-acting baking powder
1/2 teaspoon salt
1/2 cup finely chopped nuts

Cream butter and add next 3 ingredients; beat until light. Add sifted dry ingredients and nuts. Drop by scant measuring-teaspoonfuls onto cookie sheets. Bake in hot oven (400°F.) about 5 minutes. Cool 1/2 minute. Remove to racks. Store airtight. Makes about 8 dozen.

BROWN-EDGED COOKIES

1 cup softened butter
2/3 cup sugar
1 teaspoon vanilla extract
2 eggs
1-1/3 cups all-purpose flour
1/4 teaspoon salt

Cream butter; add next 3 ingredients and beat until light. Add flour and salt; mix well. Drop by half-teaspoonfuls onto greased cookie sheets. Bake in moderate oven (350° F.) about 10 minutes. Store airtight. Makes about 3 dozen.

COCONUT OATMEAL CRISPS

3/4 cup softened butter
1/2 cup granulated sugar
1-1/2 cups packed light-brown sugar
1 teaspoon vanilla extract
2 eggs
1 teaspoon double-acting baking powder
1/2 teaspoon baking soda
1 teaspoon salt
1 cup minus 1 tablespoon all-purpose flour
2-1/2 cups quick-cooking rolled oats
1 cup flaked coconut

Cream butter, sugars and vanilla until light. Beat in eggs, one at a time. Add sifted dry ingredients and oats; mix well and fold in coconut. Drop by teaspoonfuls on baking sheets; bake in moderate oven (375° F.) 10 minutes. Store airtight. Makes 6 dozen.

PEANUT BUTTEROONS

Gradually beat 2/3 cup sifted confectioners' sugar into 1/2 cup peanut butter. Fold in 2 stiffly beaten egg whites. Drop from teaspoon onto foil-covered cookie sheet and bake in moderate oven (375° F.) 10 minutes. Makes 18.

ORANGE WAFERS

1/2 cup softened butter
3/4 cup sugar
1 egg
1 teaspoon grated orange rind
1 tablespoon orange juice
1-1/3 cups all-purpose flour
1/2 teaspoon double-acting baking powder
1/4 teaspoon salt

Cream butter; add sugar and egg and beat until light. Add remaining ingredients; mix well. Drop by level measuring-teaspoonfuls onto cookie sheets. Press flat with the bottom of a glass wrapped in cheesecloth wrung out of cold water. Bake in moderate oven (375°F.) about 7 minutes. Store airtight. Makes about 8 dozen.

SESAME WAFERS

1-1/2 cups packed light-brown sugar
3/4 cup melted butter
1 egg
1 teaspoon vanilla extract
1 cup toasted sesame seed
1 cup plus 3 tablespoons all-purpose flour
1/4 teaspoon double-acting baking powder
1/4 teaspoon salt

Mix first 4 ingredients; stir in remaining ingredients. Drop by half-teaspoonfuls on buttered cookie sheets, allowing for spreading. Bake in moderate oven (375°F.) 10 minutes. Remove from pans at once. Store airtight. Makes 60.

SOFT CHOCOLATE COOKIES

2 eggs
1 cup sugar
2 teaspoons vanilla extract
2 squares unsweetened chocolate, melted and cooled
2 cups sifted cake flour
1/2 teaspoon salt
1/2 teaspoon each double-acting baking powder and baking soda
1 cup dairy sour cream
Sour-cream Chocolate Frosting
Chopped green pistachio nuts

Beat eggs until thick and lemon-colored; gradually beat in next 3 ingredients. Add sifted dry ingredients alternately with sour cream, beating until smooth. (Batter will be thin.) Drop by teaspoonfuls on ungreased cookie sheets and bake in moderate oven (350°F.) about 8 minutes. Cool and frost. Sprinkle with nuts. Makes about 5½ dozen. **Sour-cream Chocolate Frosting** Melt 1 package (6 ounces) semisweet chocolate pieces over hot, not boiling, water. Cool slightly and blend in 2/3 cup dairy sour cream and 1 teaspoon vanilla.

FLORENTINES

Combine ¹/₂ cup heavy cream, 3 table-spoons butter and ¹/₂ cup sugar in saucepan and bring to boil. Remove from heat and stir in 1¹/₄ cups finely chopped almonds, ¹/₃ cup sifted all-purpose flour and ³/₄ cup finely chopped candied orange peel. Drop by tablespoonfuls on greased and floured cookie sheet, keeping cookies 3″ apart. Bake in moderate oven (350°F.) about 10 minutes. Cool 5 minutes. Remove carefully with spatula to cake rack. Cool. Spiral melted chocolate over cookie tops and decorate with tiny colored candies. Makes about 2 dozen cookies.

SWEET-POTATO DROPS

1/2 cup butter or margarine
1/4 cup sugar
1 egg
1/2 cup light molasses
1 cup grated raw sweet potato
1 teaspoon grated orange rind
2 cups sifted all-purpose flour
1/2 teaspoon salt
1/2 teaspoon baking soda
1 teaspoon double-acting baking powder
1/2 teaspoon ground ginger
1/3 cup buttermilk
1 cup sliced pitted dates
1/2 cup chopped nuts

Cream butter and sugar. Add next 4 ingredients; beat well. Add sifted dry ingredients and buttermilk; mix well and stir in dates and nuts. Drop by teaspoonfuls onto greased cookie sheets and bake in moderate oven (375°F.) 12 to 15 minutes. Makes 4 dozen.

BUTTERSCOTCH CRISPS

1 package (6 ounces) butterscotch pieces
1/3 cup butter
1/4 cup sugar
1/4 cup corn syrup
1 egg
1 teaspoon vanilla extract
2 cups sifted all-purpose flour
1 teaspoon baking soda
1/4 teaspoon salt
Nut halves

Combine butterscotch pieces, the butter, sugar and corn syrup in saucepan. Put over medium heat, stirring until pieces melt. Cool 5 minutes. Beat in egg and vanilla. Add sifted dry ingredients and mix well. Drop by measuring-teaspoonfuls on cookie sheet. Put piece of walnut in center of each. Bake in moderate oven (350°F.) 8 minutes. Makes 6 dozen.

CRANBERRY DROP COOKIES

1/2 cup butter or margarine
1 cup granulated sugar
3/4 cup packed brown sugar
1/4 cup milk
2 tablespoons orange juice
1 egg
2-1/3 cups all-purpose flour
1 teaspoon double-acting baking powder
1/4 teaspoon baking soda
1/2 teaspoon salt
1 cup chopped nuts
2-1/2 cups coarsely chopped cranberries

Cream butter and sugars together. Beat in milk, orange juice and egg. Mix together next 4 ingredients. Add to creamed mixture and mix well. Stir in nuts and cranberries. Drop by teaspoonfuls onto greased baking sheet and bake in moderate oven (375°F.) about 12 minutes. Makes about 6¹/₂ dozen.

CHRISTMAS JEWELS

1/2 cup heavy cream
3/4 cup sugar
2 ounces candied orange peel, finely diced
2 ounces candied lemon peel, finely diced
1 tablespoon finely diced angelica
1 cup finely chopped blanched almonds
1/4 cup all-purpose flour
Dash of salt

Mix cream and sugar; add remaining ingredients and mix lightly. Drop by teaspoonfuls onto well buttered cookie sheets. Bake in moderate oven (350°F.) 10 to 12 minutes. Let stand a few minutes before removing from cookie sheets with sharp knife. Store airtight. Makes 3 dozen.

PINEAPPLE DROP COOKIES

1/2 cup butter or margarine
1 cup packed light-brown sugar
1 egg
1 teaspoon vanilla extract
2 cups sifted all-purpose flour
1 teaspoon double-acting baking powder
1/2 teaspoon baking soda
1/2 teaspoon salt
3/4 cup undrained crushed pineapple
1/2 cup each seedless raisins and chopped nuts

Cream butter until light and fluffy. Gradually add sugar beat well. Beat in egg and vanilla. Stir in shifted dry ingredients, fruit and nuts. Drop by teaspoonfuls onto greased cookie sheets and bake in moderate oven (375°F.) 12 minutes, or until lightly browned. Makes about 4 dozen cookies.

FUDGE WAFERS

1 cup softened butter
1 cup sugar
1 egg
2 squares unsweetened chocolate, melted
1 tablespoon vanilla
1-1/3 cups all-purpose flour
1/4 teaspoon salt
Brazil-nut slices

Cream butter; add sugar and egg and beat until light. Blend in chocolate and vanilla. Add dry ingredients; mix well. Drop by scant teaspoonfuls onto cookie sheets. Press a nut slice in center of each. Bake in hot oven (400°F.) about 10 minutes. Store airtight. Makes about 7 dozen.

CHOCOLATE DROPS

1/2 cup softened margarine
1 cup sugar
1 whole egg and 1 egg yolk
3 squares unsweetened chocolate, melted
1/2 cup milk
1/2 teaspoon vanilla extract
1-2/3 cups all-purpose flour
1/2 teaspoon each baking soda and
  double-acting baking powder
1/4 teaspoon salt
1 cup seedless raisins
1 cup chopped walnuts
Quick Mocha Frosting

Cream margarine; gradually beat in sugar, egg and egg yolk, chocolate, milk and vanilla. Add sifted dry ingredients. Fold in raisins and nuts. Drop from teaspoon on buttered cookie sheets. Bake in moderate oven (375°F.) 12 minutes. Top with frosting. Makes 48. **Quick Mocha Frosting** Cream 3 tablespoons butter with 1 cup sifted confectioners' sugar, 2 tablespoons cocoa, 1½ tablespoons cold coffee and ½ teaspoon vanilla.

BRAZIL-NUT MACAROONS

5 egg whites
1/4 teaspoon cream of tartar
1/2 teaspoon salt
1 teaspoon vanilla extract
1-1/4 cups sugar
1-1/2 cups flaked coconut
1 cup finely chopped Brazil nuts
1/4 cup diced candied orange peel
Halved candied cherries

Beat egg whites until foamy; add next 3 ingredients. Gradually add sugar and beat until mixture is glossy and stiff enough to hold its shape. Fold in coconut, nuts and orange peel. Drop from teaspoon onto well-buttered cookie sheet. Put a cherry half in center of each. Bake in slow oven (325°F.) 20 minutes. Store in airtight container. Makes 48.

TOASTED FILBERT KISSES

Beat 3 egg whites to soft moist peaks; gradually beat in 1 cup sugar and ⅛ teaspoon salt. Continue beating until mixture is very thick and glossy. Fold in 1 teaspoon grated lemon rind, ½ teaspoon cinnamon and 1 cup toasted ground filberts. Drop from teaspoon on buttered cookie sheets. Bake in slow oven (275°F.) 20 to 25 minutes. Makes 72. *To toast filberts* Spread nuts in shallow baking pan containing 1 teaspoon melted butter. Brown in hot oven (400°F.), stirring every 5 minutes. Turn out on brown paper to cool.

WASPS' NESTS

1 cup granulated sugar
1 pound unblanched almonds, slivered
5 egg whites
1/8 teaspoon salt
1 teaspoon vanilla extract
1 pound confectioners' sugar, sifted
4 ounces unsweetened chocolate, melted

Cook granulated sugar and ½ cup water until syrup spins a thread (284°F. on a candy thermometer). Add nuts slowly and continue stirring until all syrup is absorbed. Beat egg whites until frothy; add salt and vanilla. Continue beating until whites are very stiff; gradually beat in confectioners' sugar. Fold in nuts and chocolate. Drop from teaspoon onto well-buttered cookie sheets. Bake in slow oven (300°F.) 20 to 25 minutes. Makes 120.

FRUITED CHRISTMAS CRISPS

1 cup softened butter
1/2 cup granulated sugar
1/3 cup packed light-brown sugar
2 eggs
Grated rind of 1 lemon
1-1/2 cups all-purpose flour
1/4 cup seedless raisins
1/4 cup slivered almonds
1/4 cup diced candied cherries
1/4 cup each finely diced candied
  orange peel and citron
3 tablespoons honey
1/2 teaspoon cinnamon

Cream butter; gradually beat in both sugars. Add eggs, one at a time, beating well after each addition. Add grated lemon rind and flour. Drop from teaspoon onto buttered cookie sheets. Spread thin with knife dipped in cold water. Mix remaining ingredients; top each cookie with a little of mixture. Bake in moderate oven (375°F.) 8 minutes, or until lightly browned. Store airtight. Makes 60.

CHOCOLATE MERINGUES

3 egg whites
1/4 teaspoon salt
1 cup sugar
1/2 cup ground blanched almonds
1/2 teaspoon vanilla
1 cup semisweet chocolate pieces,
  melted and cooled

Beat egg whites and salt until stiff. Gradually beat in sugar until mixture is very stiff and glossy. Fold in remaining ingredients. Drop by teaspoonfuls onto greased cookie sheets and bake in moderate oven (350°F.) 15 minutes. Makes about 4 dozen.

CHRISTMAS MERINGUES

2 egg whites
1/8 teaspoon salt
1 cup sugar
1 tablespoon lemon juice
1-1/2 cups ground Brazil nuts
Maraschino cherries

Beat egg whites until stiff but not dry. Add salt and gradually beat in sugar and lemon juice; continue beating until very stiff. Measure $1/3$ cup and reserve. Fold nuts into remainder. Drop by tablespoonfuls onto brown-paper-covered cookie sheets. Top each with small amount of reserved meringue and a bit of cherry. Bake in very slow oven (275° F.) about 35 minutes. Remove at once from cookie sheets. Store airtight. Makes $3^1/2$ dozen.

CITRUS SANDWICH COOKIES

1/2 cup butter or margarine, softened
1/2 cup sugar
1 egg, beaten
1/3 cup honey
2 cups all-purpose flour
1 teaspoon baking powder
1 teaspoon salt
Candied lemon peel or citron
Citrus Frosting

Cream butter and sugar until light and fluffy. Beat in egg and honey. Add sifted dry ingredients and mix well. Drop by measuring teaspoonfuls onto greased cookie sheets and flatten with fork dipped in cold water. Decorate with strip of lemon peel or citron and bake in slow oven (325°F.) about 12 minutes. Cool on cake rack. Then sandwich with Citrus Frosting between. Makes about 5 dozen filled cookies. **Citrus Frosting** Cream $1/4$ cup softened butter or margarine. Add 1 teaspoon each grated orange and lemon rinds and a dash of salt. Gradually add 2 cups sifted confectioners' sugar and mix well. Add 1 tablespoon honey, and a little lemon juice if necessary to make mixture of good spreading consistency.

SAND TARTS

1 cup softened butter or margarine
1 cup sugar
2 tablespoons brandy
1 egg
1 package (6 ounces) semisweet
  chocolate pieces, ground
1-7/8 cups all-purpose flour
1/8 teaspoon salt

Cream butter and sugar with brandy until light; beat in egg. Add remaining ingredients and mix well. Drop by teaspoonfuls on ungreased cookie sheets and bake in moderate oven (350°F.) about 15 minutes. Makes about 7 dozen.

CHOCOLATE ALMOND DROPS

3 eggs
1/4 teaspoon salt
1-1/2 cups sugar
1/2 cup all-purpose flour
1-1/2 cups almonds, blanched, toasted
  and ground
1 package (6 ounces) semisweet chocolate pieces, ground fine
1-1/2 teaspoons vanilla

Beat eggs and salt well; gradually add sugar and continue beating until very thick and lemon-colored. Add remaining ingredients and mix well. Chill about 1 hour. Drop by half-teaspoonfuls onto foil-covered cookie sheets. Bake in slow oven (325°F.) about 25 minutes. Makes about 84.

GLAZED MINCEMEAT MOUNDS

1 cup all-purpose flour
1/4 teaspoon each salt, baking soda
  and nutmeg
1/2 teaspoon cinnamon
1/2 cup coarsely chopped pecans
1/3 cup softened butter or margarine
1/3 cup packed dark-brown sugar
1 egg
1/2 cup mincemeat (see page 433)
1 tablespoon dairy sour cream or
  buttermilk
Vanilla Glaze, page 353

Mix dry ingredients, add nuts and set aside. Cream butter and sugar, using an electric mixer; beat in egg. Combine mixtures, add mincemeat and sour cream and mix by hand. Drop batter by heaping teaspoonfuls to form mounds on cookie sheet, leaving 2" between mounds. Bake in hot oven (400°F.) 10 to 12 minutes, or until the cookies are done in the middle; break one open to see. Remove from oven and spread while warm with Vanilla Glaze. Loosen mounds from pan with a pancake turner. Remove to rack to cool. Store airtight. Makes about 2 dozen.

ROLLED BRANDY WAFERS

1/2 cup molasses
1/2 cup butter
1-1/2 cups sifted cake flour
1/4 teaspoon salt
2/3 cup sugar
1 tablespoon ginger
3 tablespoons brandy

Heat molasses to boiling; add butter. Add sifted dry ingredients gradually, stirring constantly. Stir in brandy. Drop by half-teaspoonfuls 3" apart onto greased cookie sheets. Bake, 6 cookies at a time, in slow oven (300°F.) 8 to 10 minutes. Cool 1 minute. Remove with spatula; roll at once around handle of wooden spoon. Store airtight. Makes about 5 dozen.

APPLE OATMEAL COOKIES

1/2 cup butter or margarine
2/3 cup sugar
2 eggs
1 cup all-purpose flour
1 teaspoon each double-acting baking
  powder and cinnamon
1/2 teaspoon each nutmeg and salt
1 cup rolled oats
1 cup chopped well-drained canned
  apples
1 cup coarsely chopped walnuts

Cream butter and sugar until light. Add eggs, one at a time, beating well after each. Add sifted dry ingredients, oats and apples to first mixture and beat well. Fold in nuts. Drop by teaspoonfuls onto greased cookie sheets. Bake in moderate oven (350°F.) about 15 minutes. Makes about 42.

SCOTCH ROCKS

2-3/4 cups all-purpose flour
1/2 teaspoon ground cinnamon
1 teaspoon each mace, nutmeg, allspice
  and baking soda
2 cups chopped raisins
1 cup softened butter or margarine
1-3/4 cups packed light-brown sugar
3 eggs, beaten
1-1/2 teaspoons vanilla extract
1 teaspoon rose water (optional)
2 tablespoons cold strong coffee
1-1/2 cups chopped nuts

Sift 2½ cups flour with spices and soda. Dredge raisins with remaining ¼ cup flour. Cream butter and sugar until light. Add next 5 ingredients. Add flour, working until raisins and nuts are well distributed through the dough. Drop by teaspoonfuls on greased cookie sheets. Bake in moderate oven (350°F.) until slightly browned, about 15 minutes. Makes about 7½ dozen.

OATMEAL LACE COOKIES

1 cup softened butter
2/3 cup sugar
1 teaspoon grated orange rind
1/2 teaspoon vanilla extract
2 eggs
1/2 cup sifted all-purpose flour
1/2 teaspoon salt
1 cup rolled oats
1/2 cup flaked coconut

Cream butter; gradually beat in next 3 ingredients. Add eggs, one at a time, beating well after each addition. Add remaining ingredients. Drop by half-teaspoonfuls onto buttered cookie sheets; flatten with knife dipped in cold water. Bake in moderate oven (350°F.) 10 to 12 minutes, or until edges are lightly browned. Do not overbake. Store airtight. Makes 96.

CHOCOLATE PEANUT-BUTTER DROPS

1/4 cup each softened shortening and
  peanut butter
Sugar
1 egg
3/4 cup all-purpose flour
1/4 teaspoon baking soda
1/2 teaspoon salt
1/8 teaspoon nutmeg
1/4 teaspoon cinnamon
1/2 cup rolled oats
1 package (6 ounces) semisweet chocolate pieces

Cream shortening, peanut butter and ½ cup sugar until light. Beat in egg. Add sifted dry ingredients and ¼ cup water; mix well. Fold in oats and chocolate. Drop from teaspoon on sheet. Bake in moderate oven (375°F.) about 12 minutes. While still warm, roll in sugar. Makes 48.

SWEDISH CURLED ALMOND WAFERS

3/4 cup finely ground unblanched almonds
1/2 cup unsalted butter
1/2 cup sugar
1 tablespoon flour
Dash of salt
2 tablespoons heavy cream

Mix all ingredients in small heavy saucepan. Heat, stirring, until butter melts. Drop by teaspoonfuls about 3" apart onto buttered and floured cookie sheets. Bake 6 cookies at a time in moderate oven (350°F.) 7 minutes, or until edges begin to brown but centers are still bubbling. Cool 1 or 2 minutes; then loosen with a thin knife and roll at once around handle of wooden spoon. Lay, joined side down, on racks to cool. Makes about 3 dozen.

NUT-FILLED COOKIES

Shelled whole filberts (about 12 dozen)
Red and green candied cherries and
    pitted dates (about 12 dozen alto-
    gether)
1/2 cup softened butter or margarine
1-1/2 cups packed light-brown sugar
2 eggs
1 teaspoon vanilla extract
2-1/3 cups all-purpose flour
1 teaspoon double-acting baking powder
1 teaspoon baking soda
1/2 teaspoon salt
1/2 teaspoon cinnamon
1/4 teaspoon nutmeg
1 cup dairy sour cream
Brown-butter Frosting (optional)

Lightly toast nuts in slow oven (325°F.) 10 minutes; cool. Stuff cherries and dates with whole nuts. Cream butter and sugar until fluffy. Beat in eggs and vanilla. Add sifted dry ingredients alternately with sour cream. Stir in stuffed fruit. Drop from spoon onto greased cookie sheets, allowing one stuffed cherry or date per cookie. Bake in hot oven (400° F.) 8 to 10 minutes; cool. Top with Brown-butter Frosting, if desired. Makes about 12 dozen. **Brown-butter Frosting** Lightly brown ³/₄ cup butter. Remove from heat and gradually beat in 4¹/₂ cups sifted confectioners' sugar and 2 teaspoons vanilla. Add ¹/₃ cup water and beat.

LECKEREI
(German Cookies)

1 cup sugar
1/2 cup honey
1/4 teaspoon salt
2 teaspoons each cloves and cinnamon
1/4 cup each finely diced candied or-
    ange and lemon peel
1/4 cup finely diced citron
1 egg, well beaten
1 teaspoon baking soda
2 tablespoons brandy
1 teaspoon grated lemon rind
1 cup chopped almonds
2-3/4 cups all-purpose flour

Bring ¹/₂ cup sugar and the honey to boil over low heat; cool. Add salt, spices, fruits and egg. Add soda dissolved in brandy and remaining ingredients. Knead until well blended. Chill 1 hour. Roll on lightly floured board to ¹/₂"-thick rectangle. Put on cookie sheet covered with greased brown paper. Bake in moderate oven (325°F.) 30 minutes. While hot, brush with syrup made by cooking ¹/₂ cup sugar and ¹/₄ cup water until mixture spins a thread (234°F. on a candy thermometer). Cut at once in 2¹/₂" x 1" strips. Pack in airtight container to ripen for about 5 weeks before serving. Makes 72.

SOUR-CREAM DROP COOKIES

1/4 cup softened butter
1 cup sugar
1 egg
1-7/8 cups all-purpose flour
1/2 teaspoon salt
1/2 teaspoon baking soda
1 cup dairy sour cream
Cinnamon-sugar mixture (make or buy)

Cream butter and sugar until light; beat in egg. Add sifted dry ingredients alternately with sour cream; beat until smooth. Drop by rounded teaspoonfuls onto greased cookie sheets. Sprinkle with cinnamon-sugar mixture. Bake in moderate oven (375°F.) about 15 minutes. Makes about 5 dozen cookies.

LIZZIES

1/4 cup margarine
1/2 cup packed light-brown sugar
2 eggs
1-1/2 cups all-purpose flour
1-1/2 teaspoons baking soda
1-1/2 teaspoons cinnamon
1/2 teaspoon nutmeg
1/2 teaspoon cloves
1 pound raisins soaked in 1/2 cup
    bourbon for 1 hour
1 pound pecan halves
1/2 pound citron, diced
1 pound candied cherries

Cream margarine; gradually beat in sugar. Add eggs, one at a time, beating well after each addition. Add sifted dry ingredients. Add raisins in bourbon and remaining ingredients. Drop from teaspoon on buttered cookie sheets. Bake in moderate oven (325°F.) about 15 minutes. Store in airtight container. Makes 120.

SWEET BITS

4 cups all-purpose flour
1 teaspoon double-acting baking powder
1/4 teaspoon salt
1-3/4 cups sifted confectioners' sugar
1 cup butter, softened
5 hard-cooked egg yolks, sieved
1 whole egg
Grated rind and juice of 1/2 lemon
1 egg white, slightly beaten
Finely chopped nuts

Sift first 4 ingredients; cut in butter. Add next 3 ingredients; knead well. Roll to ¹/₄" thickness and cut with floured Christmas cutters. Put on cookie sheet and brush with egg white; sprinkle with nuts. Bake in moderate oven (350°F.) about 15 minutes. Makes 4 to 5 dozen. *Note* To cook egg yolks, drop whole yolks in simmering water and cook about 5 minutes.

CHOCOLATE-FILLED ALMOND HEARTS

3/4 cup butter or margarine, softened
1 cup sugar
1/2 teaspoon each vanilla and almond
    extracts
3 eggs
2-2/3 cups all-purpose flour
1 teaspoon double-acting baking powder
1/2 teaspoon salt
Blanched almonds, whole or split
2/3 cup semisweet chocolate pieces,
    melted

Cream butter, sugar and flavorings until light and fluffy. Beat in 2 eggs. Add sifted dry ingredients and beat until smooth. Chill 1 hour, or until firm enough to roll. Roll a small amount of dough at a time on floured board to 1/8" thickness. Keep remaining dough chilled until ready to use. Cut in heart shapes, using a 2¼" cutter. Beat remaining egg with fork and brush on half the cookies (about 20); put a blanched almond in the center of each. Bake all cookies in moderate oven (375°F.) 8 to 10 minutes. Remove to racks to cool. Spread cooled plain cookies with chocolate and top with almond-decorated cookies. Let stand until chocolate is firm. Store airtight. Makes about 40.

RAISIN-FILLED COOKIES

1/2 cup butter or margarine, softened
3/4 cup sugar
1/2 teasoon vanilla extract
1 egg
1-1/2 cups all-purpose flour
1/4 teaspoon salt
1/4 teaspoon double-acting baking
    powder
1 tablespoon cream or milk
Raisin Filling or Fruit Filling (above right)

Cream butter. Gradually add sugar and vanilla; beat until light. Beat in egg. Add sifted dry ingredients and cream; mix well. Chill several hours, or until firm enough to roll. Roll a small amount at a time to 1/8" thickness on lightly floured cloth or board; cut in 3" rounds. Keep remaining dough chilled until ready to use. Put half the rounds on cookie sheet and top each with a teaspoonful of filling. Top with remaining rounds. With floured fork, press edges together and prick tops. Bake in hot oven (400° F.) 10 to 12 minutes. Makes about 1½ dozen. **Raisin Filling** In saucepan, mix ½ cup sugar, 1 tablespoon flour and dash of salt. Add ½ cup water and 1 cup chopped seeded raisins. Cook, stirring, until thickened and blended. Add 1 teaspoon grated lemon rind and cool. Makes about 1 cup.

FRUIT FILLING

4 dried figs
1/3 cup pitted dates
3/4 cup dried apricots
6 dried peaches
1/2 cup semisweet chocolate pieces
1/4 cup each candied cherries and
    citron
2/3 cup honey
1/8 teaspoon each allspice and
    cinnamon

Force first 6 ingredients through food chopper. Add honey and spices and mix well. Refrigerate while dough chills.

Jam Circles Prepare dough for Raisin-filled cookies. Cut half of cookies with 1¾" cutter. Cut remainder with 1¾" doughnut cutter. Bake as directed. Put pairs together with red jam or jelly. Makes about 6 dozen.

LEBKUCHEN FROM NUREMBERG

1 cup honey
1 egg, well beaten
Grated rind of 1 lemon
2 tablespoons lemon juice
2/3 cup packed dark-brown sugar
1/2 cup almonds, slivered
1/2 cup minced citron
2-1/4 cups all-purpose flour
1 teaspoon cinnamon
1/2 teaspoon each ground cloves, all-
    spice, mace, freshly grated nutmeg,
    baking soda and salt
2/3 cup sifted confectioners' sugar
1/4 teaspoon vanilla extract
1 egg white, stiffly beaten
Blanched almonds, citron or angelica
    (optional)

Heat the honey just under boiling point in a saucepan. (Use a full-flavored honey such as clover or orange-blossom.) Cool to lukewarm. Add egg and next 4 ingredients. Mix nuts and citron with ¼ cup flour. Mix remaining flour with spices, soda and salt. Combine the honey mixture with dry ingredients. Add the nuts and citron and mix with hands. Put in bowl, cover with foil or waxed paper and set in the refrigerator for 12 or more hours. Divide dough in quarters and roll each into a 6" x 4½" rectangle. With pastry wheel, cut each into six 3" x 1½" cookies. Place 2" apart on a buttered cookie sheet. Fold confectioners' sugar and vanilla into beaten egg white; spread on cookies. Decorate with halves of blanched almonds and thin slivers of citron or angelica, or leave plain. Put in hot oven (400°F.). Reduce heat at once to 375°F. and bake 15 to 20 minutes, or until cookies just test done. Do not bake until hard and dry; these should be chewy and moist. Makes 24.

MANDELKRANZE
(German Almond Circles)

Cream 1 cup butter; gradually beat in 1 cup sugar. Add 2 eggs, one at a time, beating well after each addition. Add grated rind of 1 lemon, $1^7/8$ cups all-purpose flour and 1 cup chopped blanched almonds. Chill. Roll out $1/8$" thick on lightly floured board; cut with $2^1/2$" doughnut cutter and put on ungreased cookie sheets. Brush with unbeaten egg white and sprinkle with 2 tablespoons sugar mixed with $1/3$ cup chopped blanched almonds and 1 teaspoon ground cinnamon. Bake in hot oven (400°F.) 8 minutes, or until lightly browned. Store airtight. Makes 5 dozen.

LIGHT ORNAMENTAL SUGAR COOKIES

2 cups all-purpose flour
1 cup sugar
1/4 teaspoon salt
1/2 teaspoon double-acting baking powder
1/2 cup softened butter
1 egg
2 tablespoons brandy, whiskey or rum
1/2 teaspoon vanilla extract
Ornamental Frosting (below)

Sift first 4 ingredients together. Add butter and mix with fingers as for piecrust. Mixture will form coarse crumbs. Add egg, liquor and vanilla. Knead until dough holds together. Cover ball of dough; chill until firm. Divide in thirds; roll out one third at a time, $1/4$" thick for Christmas-tree ornaments or $1/8$" thick for a dessert cookie. Cut with fancy cutters and place on lightly buttered cookie sheets. Allow space between cookies for spreading. Make hole for hanging on tree with toothpick after 3 minutes of baking. Bake in hot oven (400°F.) 5 to 10 minutes, or until cookies are done inside. Cool and serve plain, or spread with Ornamental Frosting and decorate as desired. Makes 6 dozen thin cookies.

ORNAMENTAL FROSTING

This frosting will get unusually hard and glossy. It is durable, adhesive and not apt to crack. It can be made ahead and put, tightly covered, in refrigerator for several days. Make one batch at a time, using an electric mixer if possible. Beat 1 egg white, 1 cup sifted confectioners' sugar and $1/2$ teaspoon cream of tartar until frosting is very thick but will still flow easily through icing tubes or paper decorating cones. If necessary, a little sugar may be added.

DARK ORNAMENTAL SUGAR COOKIES

2-1/2 cups all-purpose flour
1 teaspoon cinnamon
1/2 teaspoon nutmeg
1/4 teaspoon ground allspice
1 tablespoon ginger
1/2 teaspoon salt
1/2 teaspoon baking soda
1/4 cup granulated sugar
1/3 cup dark unsulfured molasses
1/2 cup butter
1/3 cup packed brown sugar
1 egg
Ornamental Frosting (below left)

Sift first 8 ingredients together. Heat molasses to boiling point and remove from heat. Add butter and brown sugar and stir until butter melts. Pour over flour mixture, stirring well. Add egg and knead until dough holds together. Chill slightly. Roll small amounts of dough with floured rolling pin on a floured board or between sheets of floured waxed paper. Roll dough $1/4$" thick to use for Christmas-tree ornaments; roll $1/8$" thick for a dessert cookie. Cut with floured cutters. Place cookies 2" apart on floured pans and bake in moderate oven (350°F.) 8 to 10 minutes, or until cookies are done inside. Remove cookies from pan as soon as baked. Cool and frost. Makes about 6 dozen thin cookies.

ITALIAN MUSCATELS

Butter
1 cup unblanched almonds
1 cup sugar
2 tablespoons dried grated orange peel
1-1/3 cups all-purpose flour
1-1/2 teaspoons double-acting baking powder
1-1/2 teaspoons cinnamon
1-1/2 teaspoons allspice
1/2 cup muscatel wine
Italian Glaze
Colored sugar

Melt $1/2$ teaspoon butter in skillet; add almonds and brown over low heat. Cool and chop almonds. Cream $1/2$ cup butter; gradually beat in sugar. Add orange peel and almonds. Sift flour with baking powder and spices; add alternately with wine to butter mixture. Chill 1 hour. Turn out on sugared board; pat or roll gently to $1/3$" thickness. Cut with $1^1/2$" scalloped cookie cutter; put on buttered cookie sheets. Bake in moderate oven (350°F.) 12 to 15 minutes. While hot, frost and sprinkle with colored sugar. Makes 96. **Italian Glaze** Add 1 teaspoon lemon juice to 2 unbeaten egg whites; stir in sifted confectioners' sugar until of spreading consistency.

FILHOS
(Portuguese Cookies)

2 eggs, slightly beaten
2 tablespoons port or Madeira wine
1/2 teaspoon vanilla extract
3 tablespoons granulated sugar
3 cups all-purpose flour
1/2 teaspoon salt
1 tablespoon melted butter
Fat for deep frying
Confectioners' sugar

Mix first 7 ingredients with 6 tablespoons water. Roll out paper-thin and cut in 2" squares. Make a cut in one corner and pull the opposite corner through. Fry in hot deep fat (375° F. on a frying thermometer) 2 minutes, or until golden brown. Drain on absorbent paper and sprinkle with confectioners' sugar. Makes about 10 dozen.

FATTIGMAN'S BAKKELS

4 egg yolks
1/4 cup heavy cream
1/3 cup granulated sugar
1-1/2 cups all-purpose flour
1/4 teaspoon salt
Dash of mace
Fat for deep frying
Confectioners' sugar

Beat egg yolks until light; add cream and sugar and beat well. Add next 3 ingredients. Roll small amount of dough at a time to a little less than 1/8" thickness. Cut in 3" x 1" strips with pastry wheel, cutting ends diagonally. Make a lengthwise slit in the center of each strip and pull one end through. Fry in hot deep fat (350°F. on a frying thermometer) 2 minutes, or until lightly browned, turning once. Drain on absorbent paper. Cool; sprinkle with confectioners' sugar. Store airtight. Makes 4 dozen.

CREAM-CHEESE FOLDOVERS

1 cup butter, softened
8 ounces cream cheese, softened
2 cups all-purpose flour
1/4 teaspoon salt
Confectioners' sugar
Red jelly or jam

Cream butter and cheese until light and fluffy; blend in flour and salt. Chill several hours. Roll 1/8" thick on board sprinkled with confectioners' sugar. Cut in 2" squares and spread with jelly. Fold one corner to within 1/2" of opposite corner. Put on ungreased cookie sheet. Bake in moderate oven (350°F.) almost 15 minutes. Do not brown. Sprinkle with more confectioners' sugar if desired. Store airtight. Makes 4 dozen.

SOFT GINGER CUTOUTS

1/2 cup molasses
1/2 cup sugar
1/2 cup soft butter or margarine
2-2/3 cups all-purpose flour
2 teaspoons ginger
1/2 teaspoon salt
1 teaspoon baking soda
1/2 cup buttermilk

Cream first 3 ingredients well. Add sifted dry ingredients alternately with buttermilk; mix until smooth. Chill several hours. Roll out on floured board to about 1/4" thickness. Cut with floured fancy cutters. Bake in moderate oven (375°F.) about 15 minutes. Cool and decorate as desired. Makes 5 to 6 dozen.

SILVER DOLLARS

Cream 1 cup butter; gradually beat in 1 cup sugar, grated rind of 1 lemon, 1 tablespoon lemon juice, 2 cups sifted cake flour and 1/2 pound blanched almonds, ground. Chill several hours. Roll out 1/8" thick on floured board. Cut with small floured fancy cutters; put on ungreased cookie sheets. Bake in moderate oven (375° F.) 10 minutes. While hot, roll in Vanilla Sugar. Sprinkle with colored sugar. Store airtight. Makes 48.
Vanilla Sugar At least 1 day before baking, add 2 teaspoons vanilla to 1 cup confectioners' sugar. Vanilla will cake the sugar, so it must be rolled and sifted before being used.

CHOCOLATE PINWHEEL COOKIES

1/2 cup softened butter or margarine
3/4 cup sugar
1 teaspoon vanilla extract
1 egg
1-1/2 cups all-purpose flour
1/4 teaspoon double-acting baking powder
1/4 teaspoon salt
1 square unsweetened chocolate, melted

Cream first 4 ingredients until light and fluffy. Blend in sifted dry ingredients. Divide dough in half and blend chocolate into one part; chill both doughs until firm enough to roll. Roll each part on floured board or wax paper to rectangle 16" x 6". Invert chocolate dough on white dough; press together gently with rolling pin. Peel off paper. Roll up like a jelly roll, being sure center is tight. Wrap and chill overnight. Slice 1/8" thick; set on ungreased cookie sheets. Bake in moderate oven (350° F.) 10 to 12 minutes, or until very lightly browned; remove to rack to cool. Store airtight. Makes about 36.

WALNUT SHORTBREAD

1 cup butter, softened
1 cup sifted confectioners' flour
1 teaspoon vanilla extract
2-1/4 cups all-purpose flour
Walnut halves

Cream butter; gradually beat in sugar and vanilla. With hands, work in flour and knead until dough forms ball. Chill thoroughly. Roll 1/2" thick on lightly floured board. Cut with 2" fancy cutter. Decorate with nuts. Bake on ungreased cookie sheets in moderate oven (350°F.) 20 to 25 minutes. Makes 24.

ITALIAN TIER COOKIES

2-1/3 cups all-purpose flour
2-1/2 teaspoons double-acting baking powder
1/2 teaspoon salt
1/4 cup sugar
2/3 cup solid vegetable shortening
2 teaspoons vanilla extract
7 tablespoons milk
1-3/4 cups sifted confectioners' sugar
Red and green food colorings
Candied fruit

Sift first 4 ingredients. Cut in shortening. Add vanilla and milk; mix well. Set aside in a covered bowl for 1 hour. Roll to 1/8" thickness and cut 2 dozen round cookies in each size: 2", 1 1/2" and 1". Bake in hot oven (400°F.) 8 to 10 minutes. Cool. Mix the confectioners' sugar with 2 tablespoons water. Divide in half and tint one part red, the other green. Put cookies together in 3 tiers with colored frosting between cookies and on top. Decorate with candied fruit. Makes 2 dozen tier cookies.

PEANUT WHIRLS

1/2 cup solid vegetable shortening
1/2 cup smooth peanut butter
1 cup sugar
1 teaspoon vanilla extract
1 egg
1-1/4 cups all-purpose flour
1/2 teaspoon baking soda
1/2 teaspoon salt
2 tablespoons milk
1 package (6 ounces) semisweet chocolate pieces, melted and cooled

Cream first 4 ingredients until light. Beat in egg. Add sifted dry ingredients and milk. Chill until firm enough to roll. Turn out on lightly floured board or cloth and roll into a rectangle 14" x 11". Spread with chocolate, roll as for jelly roll and chill 1/2 hour. Warm slightly. Cut in 1/4" slices and put on cookie sheets. Bake in moderate oven (350° F.) about 10 minutes. Makes about 42.

FROSTED HONEY JUMBLES

1/3 cup softened butter or margarine
1/4 cup packed brown sugar
1/2 cup honey
1 egg
3-1/4 cups all-purpose flour
1 teaspoon ginger
1/2 teaspoon each cinnamon, nutmeg, baking soda and salt
1 tablespoon strong coffee
1/2 cup dairy sour cream
1/2 recipe Fluffy Seven-minute Frosting, page 323
Candied cherries, angelica, multicolored candies, colored sugar

Cream first 4 ingredients until light. Add sifted dry ingredients, coffee and sour cream; mix well. Roll thin on lightly floured board or cloth and cut with 2 3/4" doughnut cutter. Bake in moderate oven (350°F.) 8 to 10 minutes. Cool, frost and decorate as desired. Makes about 7 dozen.

MELTING MOMENTS

Cream 1 cup softened butter; gradually beat in 1/3 cup sifted confectioners' sugar. Add 2/3 cup cornstarch and 1 cup all-purpose flour; mix well. Chill 1 hour. Form into 36 small irregular heaps on cookie sheet. Bake in moderate oven (350°F.) until light brown on the bottom, about 15 minutes. Cool; glaze with Wine Glaze, page 351. Makes 36.

SWISS CRISPS

1 cup softened butter
Sugar
1 egg yolk
1 tablespoon grated semisweet chocolate
1/4 teaspoon salt
1-1/4 teaspoons cinnamon
1-1/2 tablespoons Grand Marnier or Cointreau
2-1/2 cups all-purpose flour
1/2 teaspoon double-acting baking powder
Finely chopped almonds (optional)

Cream butter and 1 cup sugar; add egg yolk, chocolate, salt and 1/4 teaspoon cinnamon. Add next 3 ingredients. Mix with hands until dough holds together. Chill dough until firm enough to roll. Roll very thin on floured board, using a small amount of dough at a time. Cut into fancy shapes. Set on cookie sheet 1/2" apart. Sprinkle with 2 tablespoons sugar mixed with 1 teaspoon cinnamon, or with chopped almonds, if desired. Bake in moderate oven (350°F.) 10 to 12 minutes, or until lightly browned. Loosen at once with a pancake turner; let stand until cool. Store airtight. Makes about 12 dozen small cookies.

HAZELNUT CRESCENTS

1 cup softened unsalted butter
1 cup granulated sugar
1 cup hazelnuts or pecans, grated or
  finely ground
2 cups all-purpose flour
1/4 teaspoon salt
2 tablespoons vanilla extract
Confectioners' sugar

Cream butter and granulated sugar. Add next 4 ingredients, mixing with fingers as for piecrust. Add about 1 tablespoon ice water, if needed, to hold mixture together. Using teaspoonfuls of dough, shape in little crescents. Place 2" apart on cookie sheets and bake in slow oven (300°F.) 20 to 25 minutes, or until cookies are faintly brown outside and done inside; break one open to see. Remove from oven and dust heavily with confectioners' sugar. Cool to room temperature before storing airtight. Makes about 8 dozen.

GOLD COOKIES

1/2 cup softened butter or margarine
1 cup sugar
1 teaspoon vanilla extract
4 egg yolks
1-1/3 cups all-purpose flour
2 teaspoons double-acting baking powder
1 cup finely chopped nuts
4 teaspoons cinnamon

Cream first 3 ingredients until light. Beat in egg yolks and sifted flour and baking powder. Shape dough in ¾" balls and roll in mixture of nuts and cinnamon. Put on cookie sheets and bake in moderate oven (375°F.) 12 to 15 minutes. Makes about 60.

GINGER STICKS

3 eggs
1-1/8 cups packed light-brown sugar
3 cups all-purpose flour
1/2 teaspoon double-acting baking
  powder
1/2 teaspoon salt
1 teaspoon cinnamon
1 teaspoon ground cloves
3/4 cup diced candied ginger
Granulated sugar

Beat eggs until thick and lemon-colored; gradually beat in sugar. Add sifted dry ingredients and ginger. Chill 1 hour. Turn out on a sugared board and form into a roll 2" in diameter; cut in 2" lengths and roll each to a rope the size of a crayon. Cut in 1½" sticks and put on buttered cookie sheets. Bake in slow oven (300°F.) 8 to 10 minutes or until done. Store in airtight container. Makes 144.

MOCHA NUT FANCIES

1/2 cup margarine
1/2 cup granulated sugar
1/2 cup packed light-brown sugar
1/2 teaspoon vanilla extract
2 tablespoons instant coffee
1 egg
1 cup all-purpose flour
1/4 teaspoon salt
1/2 cup finely chopped pecans

Cream margarine; gradually beat in next 5 ingredients. Add remaining ingredients. Chill. Form into marble-size balls; put on cookie sheets. Bake in moderate oven (350°F.) 10 minutes, or until lightly browned. Store in airtight container. Makes 60.

BONBONS

Put 1 pound pitted dates and ½ pound walnut meats through food chopper twice. Shape 72 small balls. Beat 3 egg whites stiff; add ¾ cup sugar gradually and continue beating until mixture holds its shape. Add 1 teaspoon vanilla extract. Divide meringue in half; tint one half pink and other half green. With a teaspoon, roll date balls in meringue; put on buttered cookie sheets. Swirl meringue on top of each bonbon. Bake in very slow oven (250°F.) 30 minutes. Store airtight. Makes 6 dozen.

GERMAN PFEFFERNUSSE

2-3/4 cups all-purpose flour
3/4 teaspoon double-acting baking
  powder
3/4 teaspoon each salt, allspice, mace
  and cardamom
1/4 teaspoon black pepper
3/4 teaspoon baking soda
1/8 teaspoon ground aniseed
1 cup honey
3 tablespoons solid vegetable shortening
1 egg
Anise Frosting

Sift dry ingredients. Heat honey (do not boil) and add shortening; cool. Beat in egg. Stir in dry ingredients just until blended. Let dough stand 10 minutes. Shape in 1" balls. Place on lightly greased cookie sheets. Bake in moderate oven (350°F.) 13 to 15 minutes. Cool and frost. Store airtight a week to ripen. Makes 60. **Anise Frosting** Combine 1 egg white, 2 teaspoons honey and ¼ teaspoon ground aniseed. Gradually add 1½ cups sifted confectioners' sugar, beating until smooth. Put 12 to 14 cookies in a bowl, add 2 tablespoons frosting and stir to frost all sides of cookies. Lift out with a fork onto rack. Repeat until all are frosted.

GLAZED ALMOND COOKIES

1 cup softened butter or margarine
1 cup sugar
1/2 teaspoon each almond and vanilla
  extracts
2 eggs, separated
3/4 cup chopped blanched almonds
2-2/3 cups sifted cake flour
1/2 teaspoon salt
48 unblanched whole almonds

Cream butter, sugar and flavorings until light. Beat in egg yolks and next 3 ingredients; mix well. Roll in 1" balls, dip in unbeaten egg whites and put 2" apart on greased sheets. Put a whole almond in center of each ball and push down to flatten cookie. Bake in moderate oven (350° F.) about 10 minutes. Makes about 48.

CINNAMON WREATHS

1 cup softened butter or margarine
Sugar
2 egg yolks
2-7/8 cups all-purpose flour
3/4 teaspoon salt
1/4 cup sherry
1/2 teaspoon cinnamon

Cream butter and ²/₃ cup sugar; add egg yolks and beat until light. Add sifted flour and salt alternately with sherry; mix well. Force through a pastry tube onto cookie sheets in the shape of 2" wreaths. Bake in moderate oven (375° F.) about 10 minutes. Sprinkle warm cookies with mixture of 2 tablespoons sugar and the cinnamon. Makes about 40.

ADELE'S COOKIE-PRESS COOKIES

1-1/2 cups softened butter
1 cup sugar
1 tablespoon vanilla extract
2 eggs, separated
3-3/4 cups all-purpose flour
1/4 teaspoon salt
Chopped nuts and multicolored candies

Cream butter, sugar and vanilla until light and fluffy. Add egg yolks, flour and salt. Mix well. Force through cookie press onto ungreased cookie sheet. Brush the top of each cookie with egg whites beaten slightly with 2 tablespoons water. Decorate with chopped nuts or candies as desired. Bake in hot oven (400° F.) until cookies are golden brown on top and done inside; break one open to see. Baking time will depend on thickness of cookie—thin cookies take 5 to 6 minutes, thick ones, 8 to 15 minutes. Cool slightly, then remove from sheet with spatula or pancake turner. When cool, store airtight. Makes about 8 dozen.

MELT-AWAYS

1 cup softened butter
1-1/4 cups sifted confectioners' sugar
1 teaspoon vanilla extract
1 cup all-purpose flour
2 tablespoons cornstarch
1/4 teaspoon salt
1 cup chopped walnuts or pecans
1 bar (9-3/4 ounces) milk chocolate,
  melted

Cream butter; gradually beat in sugar and vanilla. Add sifted dry ingredients. Fold in nuts and chocolate. Shape in 120 balls, using 1 teaspoon dough for each cookie. Put on greased cookie sheets, allowing room for spreading. Bake in very slow oven (250°F.) 40 minutes. Store airtight. Makes 120.

BLACK-EYED SUSANS

1/2 cup softened butter or margarine
1/2 cup granulated sugar
1/2 cup packed brown sugar
1 egg
1 teaspoon vanilla
1 cup moist smooth peanut butter
1-1/2 cups all-purpose flour
1/2 teaspoon each baking soda and salt
Semisweet chocolate pieces

Cream first 6 ingredients; beat until light. Add sifted dry ingredients and mix well. Force through spritz gun or cookie press onto cookie sheets to make flower designs. Put a chocolate piece in center of each. Bake in moderate oven (350°F.) about 15 minutes. Makes about 5 dozen.

TOASTED-ALMOND FINGERS

1 cup butter or margarine, softened
1/2 cup sifted confectioners' sugar
1 teaspoon vanilla extract
1 egg
1-7/8 cups all-purpose flour
1/4 teaspoon salt
1 cup toasted almonds, finely chopped
1 package (6 ounces) semisweet chocolate pieces
1 tablespoon solid vegetable shortening
Additional toasted almonds, finely
  chopped (optional)

Cream first 3 ingredients until fluffy. Add egg and beat well. Add next 3 ingredients; mix well. Wrap in waxed paper and chill until hard, about 30 minutes in freezer or several hours in refrigerator. Using measuring-tablespoonfuls of dough, shape in 2" fingers and put on cookie sheet. Bake in slow oven (325°F.) 17 minutes, or until done. Cool on cake rack. Melt chocolate and shortening over hot water. Carefully dip in one end of each finger; put on waxed paper to dry. Sprinkle with nuts, if desired. Store in cool dry place. Makes 48.

BOURBON BALLS

1 package (6 ounces) semisweet chocolate pieces
Sugar
3 tablespoons light corn syrup
1/3 cup bourbon
1 package (7-1/4 ounces) vanilla wafers,
   finely crushed
1 cup finely chopped walnuts

Melt chocolate over hot water. Remove from heat and stir in 1/2 cup
sugar and the corn syrup; blend in
bourbon. Add crumbs and nuts and
blend well. Shape quickly in 1" balls
and roll in sugar. Ripen in airtight container several days before serving.
Makes about 4 1/2 dozen.

MOLASSES CRINKLES

The water makes them crinkle.

3/4 cup softened butter
1 cup packed light-brown sugar
1 egg
1/4 cup molasses
2 cups plus 2 tablespoons all-purpose
   flour
1 teaspoon double-acting baking powder
1 teaspoon baking soda
1 teaspoon each cinnamon and ginger
1/2 teaspoon cloves
1/4 teaspoon salt
Granulated sugar

Cream first 4 ingredients until light.
Sift remaining ingredients, except
granulated sugar. Add to creamed
mixture and mix well; chill. Roll in
1" balls and dip in granulated sugar.
Put 3" apart on lightly greased
cookie sheets. Sprinkle each cookie
with 2 or 3 drops water. Bake in
moderate oven (375°F.) 8 to 10 minutes. Makes 48.

DAIQUIRI BALLS

1 cup semisweet chocolate pieces
1/2 cup dairy sour cream
Confectioners' sugar, sifted
1/2 pound vanilla wafers, crushed
1/4 teaspoon salt
3 tablespoons cocoa
1 tablespoon each grated lemon and
   orange rind
2-1/2 tablespoons lemon juice
1-1/2 tablespoons maple syrup
1/4 cup rum
1 cup finely chopped pecans

Melt chocolate over hot water; cool.
Add sour cream and refrigerate
overnight. Form into 54 balls, about
1/2 teaspoon each. (These will be
used as centers.) Combine 1 cup confectioners' sugar with remaining ingredients; mix well. Form balls the
size of walnuts around the chocolate
centers. Roll in confectioners' sugar.
Store airtight. Makes 54.

PEANUT COOKIE BALLS

1/4 cup crunchy peanut butter
3/4 cup softened butter
1/4 cup molasses
Sugar
2 cups all-purpose flour
2 cups chopped lightly salted peanuts
1 teaspoon vanilla extract
1 teaspoon cinnamon

Cream first 3 ingredients and 2 tablespoons sugar until light; add flour,
peanuts and vanilla and mix well.
Chill dough until firm. Shape in 1"
balls and put on greased cookie sheet.
Bake in moderate oven (350°F.) 15
to 18 minutes. While warm, roll in
mixture of 1/2 cup sugar and the cinnamon. Makes 4 dozen.

ITALIAN NUT BALLS

1/2 cup softened butter
1/3 cup sugar
1 egg, separated
1/4 teaspoon each vanilla and almond
   extracts
1 cup all-purpose flour
1/2 teaspoon salt
3/4 cup chopped pistachio nuts
1/2 cup apricot jam

Cream butter; beat in sugar, egg yolk
and flavorings. Add flour sifted with
salt. Form into 36 small balls, using
about 1/2 tablespoon of dough for
each. Dip in slightly beaten egg
white; then roll lightly in nuts. Put
on buttered cookie sheets. With
fingertip, make depression in center
of each cookie. Bake in slow oven
(300°F.) 25 minutes. While warm,
fill centers with jam. Makes 36.

SCOTCH DREAMBOATS

1 package (6 ounces) butterscotch
   pieces
1/2 cup softened butter or margarine
3/4 cup sugar
1 egg
1 teaspoon grated orange rind
1 cup all-purpose flour
1/2 teaspoon baking soda
1/2 teaspoon salt
1 cup quick-cooking rolled oats
Flaked coconut
Gold dragées, or other decorations

Melt butterscotch pieces over hot,
not boiling, water; cool 10 minutes.
Cream next 4 ingredients until light.
Add sifted flour, soda and salt and
mix well. Stir in butterscotch, oats
and 1 cup flaked coconut. Shape in
1" balls, roll in coconut and put on
greased cookie sheets. Decorate with
dragées. Bake in moderate oven (350°
F.) about 15 minutes. Makes about 5
dozen.

OATMEAL-RAISIN COOKIES

1 cup butter or margarine, softened
1-1/2 cups sugar
1 cup seedless raisins
2-1/2 cups quick-cooking rolled
  oats (not instant)
1-1/2 cups all-purpose flour
1 teaspoon baking soda

Cream butter; gradually add sugar and cream until light and fluffy. Stir in raisins. Add oats sifted with flour and baking soda. Mix well, using hands. Shape in 1″ balls, trying to cover raisins. Put 1″ apart on lightly greased baking sheets. Bake in moderate oven (375°F.) 15 minutes, or until golden brown. Let cool slightly before removing to rack. Store airtight in cool place. Makes about 8 dozen.

PEANUT CRESCENTS

3/4 cup plus 2 tablespoons butter
1/4 cup granulated sugar
2 cups all-purpose flour
1 teaspoon vanilla extract
1/2 cup coarsely crushed salted peanuts
  (see Note)
Confectioners' sugar

Cream butter and granulated sugar well. Add flour and 1 tablespoon water and mix well; then add vanilla and peanuts. Wrap in waxed paper or plastic and store in refrigerator overnight. Next day, shape mixture in crescents, using about 1 teaspoonful dough for each. Put on ungreased sheets and bake in moderate oven (350°F.) about 15 minutes. Roll in confectioners' sugar while warm. Makes about 72. **Note** Crush peanuts with rolling pin. Do not use blender.

COCONUT-RUM COOKIES

1 cup all-purpose flour
1/4 teaspoon baking soda
1/3 cup sugar
2/3 cup grated (cookie) coconut
1/2 cup butter or margarine
Rum Glaze

Mix first 4 ingredients in bowl. Cut in butter with pastry blender until particles are very fine. Gather into a ball, then divide in 3 parts. Shape each part in rope ³/₄″ wide. Place lengthwise on greased cookie sheet several inches apart. Bake in moderate oven (375°F.) about 10 minutes, or until golden brown. Brush with Rum Glaze while still warm. Cut diagonally in 1″ cookies. Makes about 3 dozen. **Rum Glaze** Mix 1 cup sifted confectioners' sugar with 1 tablespoon light rum and 2 teaspoons water until smooth.

CHRISTMAS CHERRIES

1/2 cup softened butter
1/3 cup packed light-brown sugar
1 egg yolk
1/2 teaspoon vanilla extract
2 teaspoons each grated lemon and
  orange rinds
1 tablespoon lemon juice
1 cup sifted all-purpose flour
1/2 teaspoon salt
1/2 cup ground walnuts
Vanilla Glaze (page 353)
24 candied cherries
Angelica

Cream butter; gradually beat in sugar. Add egg yolk, vanilla, fruit rinds and lemon juice. Add next 3 ingredients. Chill at least 1 hour. Form into 48 small balls, put on greased cookie sheet and bake in moderate oven (350°F) 15 to 18 minutes. Put a little glaze in center of each. Top with half a cherry and a stem of angelica. Makes 4 dozen.

SPECULAAS
(Dutch Spice Cookies)

These traditional cookies taste even better after ripening for a week. They keep and ship well.

2 cups all-purpose flour
3/4 cup granulated sugar
1/4 teaspoon salt
1 tablespoon cinnamon
1 teaspoon freshly grated nutmeg
1/2 teaspoon ground cloves
1 teaspoon ground cardamom or ginger
1 teaspoon unsweetened Dutch-process
  cocoa
1/2 teaspoon double-acting baking
  powder
Grated rind of 1/2 lemon
1/2 cup softened butter
1 egg
Dairy sour cream (about 3 tablespoons)
Confectioners' sugar (optional)

Put first 10 ingredients in a large bowl; mix well. Mix in butter with fingers or pastry blender to form coarse crumbs. Add egg and mix again. Add just enough sour cream to hold mixture together and make a stiff but not crumbly dough that rolls easily. Divide the dough in half and press onto two 14¹/₂″ x 12¹/₂″ cookie sheets without sides; roll dough ¹/₈″ thick. The dough should be even and near edge of the pans. Cut the dough in strips (2″ x 3″) with a pastry wheel or a dull knife and bake in moderate oven (375°F.) 15 minutes, or until cookies test done; break one open to see. Do not overbake. Remove from oven, recut with pastry wheel and loosen cookies with a spatula. Dust with confectioners' sugar if you wish. Store airtight. Makes about 4 dozen.

NORWEGIAN ROYAL CROWNS

2 hard-cooked egg yolks
1/4 teaspoon salt
1/2 cup softened butter
1/4 cup sugar
1/4 teaspoon almond extract
1 cup all-purpose flour
Candied cherries (optional)

Force egg yolks through coarse sieve; add salt. Cream butter; add sugar and flavoring. Beat until light. Add egg yolks and flour; mix well. Force through crown design of cookie press onto greased cookie sheets. Decorate with "jewels" of candied cherries or other fruit, if desired. Bake in moderate oven (375°F.) about 10 minutes. Store airtight. Makes about 1½ dozen.

COCONUT OATMEAL COOKIES

1/2 cup softened butter or margarine
1 cup packed light-brown sugar
1/2 teaspoon vanilla extract
1 egg
1 cup rolled oats
1 cup plus 3 tablespoons all-purpose flour
1 teaspoon double-acting baking powder
1/2 teaspoon baking soda
1/2 teaspoon salt
1 can flaked coconut
Colored sugar

Cream first 3 ingredients until light; beat in egg. Add oats, sifted dry ingredients and coconut; mix well. Chill several hours. Shape in balls about the size of a small walnut and put on cookie sheets; flatten slightly with floured bottom of tumbler. Sprinkle with colored sugar. Bake in moderate oven (375°F.) 10 to 12 minutes. Makes 60.

BERLINER KRANSER
(Norwegian Butter Cookies)

1 hard-cooked egg yolk
1 raw egg yolk
1/2 cup sugar
1/2 teaspoon vanilla extract
2 cups sifted cake flour
1/2 teaspoon salt
1/2 cup softened butter or margarine
1 egg white, slightly beaten
Red and green sugar

Mash egg yolks together until smooth. Beat in sugar and vanilla. Add next 3 ingredients; mix well. Chill several hours. Break off small pieces of dough and roll each into a strip about 7" long and the diameter of a pencil. Shape into a pretzel, looping ends. Set on greased cookie sheet. Brush with egg white and sprinkle with colored sugar. Bake in moderate oven (350°F.) 8 to 10 minutes; do not brown. Makes about 24.

APRICOT CHEWS

Blend ²/₃ cup sweetened condensed milk, 2 cups flaked coconut, dash of salt and 1 cup finely chopped dried apricots. Shape in 24 balls and put on greased cookie sheets. Bake in moderate oven (350° F.) 12 to 15 minutes. Remove at once from sheet. Makes about 2 dozen.

CHOCOLATE SPRITZKUCHEN

1 cup softened butter
2/3 cup sugar
3 egg yolks
2 squares unsweetened chocolate, melted
1 teaspoon vanilla
2-1/2 cups all-purpose flour
1/4 teaspoon salt
Colored decorations

Cream butter and sugar; beat in egg yolks until light. Blend in chocolate and vanilla. Add flour and salt; mix well. Force through spritz gun or cookie press. Decorate. Bake in hot oven (400°F.) 7 to 10 minutes. Store airtight. Makes about 6 dozen.

FRENCH JEWEL-BROOCH COOKIES

1-1/8 cups all-purpose flour
1/3 cup sugar
1/2 cup softened butter
1 egg yolk
1/2 teaspoon vanilla extract
Garnishes

Mix flour and sugar; cut in butter to form coarse crumbs. Add egg yolk and vanilla; mix with the fingers or a pastry blender until dough holds together. Form into a ball and chill 20 minutes, or until stiff enough to handle. Using a measuring half-teaspoon, shape in balls with floured palms and put 1" apart on cookie sheet. Using little finger, punch a hole halfway into ball; press in one of the garnishes. Bake in moderate oven (350° F.) 15 to 20 minutes, or until cookies are golden brown. Cool to room temperature in pans. Remove with a spatula. Store airtight. **Garnishes** Crystallized cherries cut in quarters, stiff jam or jelly (seeded black- or red-raspberry jam is delicious), bits of candied ginger, tiny cubes of candied orange or lemon peel or citron, semisweet chocolate pieces, almond halves. Or bake cookies without filling centers, then put a dab of chocolate frosting into the depression of cooled cookies and top with a blanched-almond half.

TUTTI-FRUITIES

1-1/4 cups all-purpose flour
1/2 cup softened butter or margarine
3 tablespoons confectioners' sugar
2 eggs, beaten
1/2 cup granulated sugar
1/2 teaspoon double-acting baking
   powder
1/4 teaspoon salt
1 teaspoon vanilla extract
3/4 cup chopped nuts
1/2 cup flaked coconut
1/2 cup diced well-drained maraschino
   or candied cherries

With hands, mix 1 cup flour, the butter and confectioners' sugar until well blended. Spread in 8" square pan. Bake in moderate oven (350°F.) about 20 minutes. Mix ¼ cup flour and remaining ingredients. Spread over baked mixture. Bake about 25 minutes. Cool; cut in 16 squares.

DUNDEE TEA BARS

1/2 cup softened butter or margarine
1/2 cup sugar
1 teaspoon vanilla extract
2 eggs
1-1/3 cups all-purpose flour
1 teaspoon double-acting baking powder
1/4 teaspoon salt
1/2 teaspoon nutmeg
3/4 cup chopped candied mixed fruit
1/4 cup raisins
Lemon Glaze

Cream first 3 ingredients until light. Beat in eggs. Add sifted dry ingredients and fruit; mix well. Pour into a 9" square pan lined on the bottom with waxed paper. Bake in moderate oven (325°F.) 25 to 30 minutes. Turn out on rack and peel off paper. Turn right side up and brush with glaze. Cool and cut in 24 bars.
Lemon Glaze Mix ¼ cup sifted confectioners' sugar, 1 teaspoon water and ½ teaspoon lemon juice.

CRANBERRY-ORANGE SQUARES

3 cups all-purpose flour
3/4 cup sugar
1 tablespoon grated lemon rind
3/4 teaspoon vanilla extract
1 cup softened butter or margarine
3 egg yolks
Cranberry-Orange Filling (above right)

Mix first 4 ingredients. Cut in butter and add egg yolks and 1 to 2 tablespoons water to hold mixture together. Shape in a ball, wrap in waxed paper and chill ½ hour. Press two thirds of dough on bottom of 13" x 9" x 2" pan. Spread filling on mixture. Crumble remaining dough over filling. Bake in hot oven (425°F.) about 20 minutes. Cool and cut in bars. Makes about 30 bars.

CRANBERRY-ORANGE FILLING

Cut 3 unpeeled oranges in quarters. Force through food chopper with 3 cups cranberries, using medium blade. In saucepan, mix 2¼ cups sugar, 3 tablespoons cornstarch and ½ teaspoon ginger. Add fruit mixture. Bring to boil and cook, stirring constantly, 15 minutes, or until thickened. Cool and stir in ¾ cup chopped nuts; chill.

HUNGARIAN PECAN BARS

2 cups plus 2 tablespoons all-purpose
   flour
1/4 teaspoon salt
1 cup granulated sugar
1 cup softened butter
2 egg yolks
1 tablespoon brandy
4 cups finely chopped pecans
1/2 cup packed light-brown sugar
1-1/2 teaspoons cinnamon
4 egg whites
Confectioners' sugar (optional)

Sift flour, salt and ½ cup granulated sugar. Blend in butter; add the egg yolks and brandy. Pat evenly in 15" x 10" x 1" pan. Bake in moderate oven (350°F.) 15 minutes. In heavy saucepan, put remaining ½ cup granulated sugar, pecans, brown sugar, cinnamon and egg whites. Cook, stirring, over low heat until sugars dissolve. Increase heat and cook until mixture no longer clings to sides of pan. Spread on baked mixture. Bake 15 minutes longer. Cool slightly. Cut in 3" x 1" bars. Dust cookies with confectioners' sugar, if desired. Store airtight. Makes 50.

RASPBERRY DELIGHTS

1 cup plus 3 tablespoons all-purpose flour
1/2 teaspoon salt
Sugar
1 teaspoon double-acting baking
   powder
Butter
1 egg yolk
2 tablespoons brandy or milk
3/4 cup thick raspberry jam
2 eggs
2 teaspoons vanilla extract
2-1/2 cups flaked coconut

Sift flour with salt, 1 teaspoon sugar and baking powder; blend in ½ cup butter. Add egg yolk and brandy. Pat into buttered 11" x 7" x 2" pan and spread with jam. Beat eggs until thick and lemon-colored; beat in 1½ cups sugar, the vanilla and 6 tablespoons melted butter. Add coconut. Spoon over jam. Bake in moderate oven (350°F.) 35 minutes. Cool. Cut in 77 squares.

COCONUT DELIGHTS

1/2 cup butter, softened
1-1/4 cups all-purpose flour
3 tablespoons confectioners' sugar
2 eggs, beaten
1 cup granulated sugar
1/2 teaspoon double-acting baking
    powder
1/4 teaspoon salt
1/2 teaspoon vanilla extract
3/4 cup chopped nuts
1/4 cup flaked coconut
1/2 cup maraschino cherries, quartered

Mix butter, 1 cup flour and confectioners' sugar. Press in bottom of 8″ square pan. Bake in slow oven (325°F.) 20 minutes. Mix remaining ¼ cup flour and other ingredients and spread on pastry. Bake about 30 minutes longer. Cool and cut in 16 squares.

CINNAMON-NUT SQUARES

1 cup butter or margarine, softened
1 cup sugar
1 egg, separated
2 cups all-purpose flour
1 tablespoon cinnamon
1/4 teaspoon salt
1 cup finely chopped pecans, filberts or
    unblanched almonds

Cream butter; gradually add sugar and continue creaming until light and fluffy. Add egg yolk, flour, cinnamon and salt and mix well. Spread in buttered 15″ x 10″ x 1″ pan. Brush with lightly beaten egg white. Sprinkle with nuts, then press nuts into surface. Bake in slow oven (300°F.) about 50 minutes. Cut in 48 squares while still hot. Store airtight in cool place.

CHILDREN'S FAVORITE BARS

2 eggs, separated
1-1/2 cups packed light-brown sugar
1/3 cup butter or margarine, softened
1-1/2 cups all-purpose flour
1 teaspoon double-acting baking powder
1/4 teaspoon salt
1 package (6 ounces) semisweet
    chocolate pieces
1/2 cup chopped nuts
1 teaspoon vanilla extract

Beat egg yolks until thick. Add ½ cup brown sugar and the butter and beat until light and fluffy. Add dry ingredients and mix well. (Mixture will be crumbly.) Press into 13″ x 9″ x 2″ pan. Beat egg whites until very stiff. And remaining 1 cup sugar and mix well. Stir in remaining ingredients and spread on first mixture in pan. Bake in slow oven (325°F.) about 30 minutes. Cool in pan and cut in 30 bars.

GINGER-PEAR BARS

3/4 cup softened butter or margarine
1 cup packed light-brown sugar
2 cups all-purpose flour
1 teaspoon salt
1/2 teaspoon baking soda
1/2 cup finely chopped nuts
1-1/2 cups flaked coconut
Ginger-Pear Filling

Cream butter and sugar until light and fluffy. Add sifted dry ingredients, nuts and coconut; mix well. Press three fourths of mixture into lightly greased 9″ square pan. Cover with filling. Sprinkle remaining one quarter mixture over top. Bake in moderate oven (350°F.) 35 to 40 minutes. Cool and cut in bars about 2″ x 1″. Makes 3 dozen bars. **Ginger-Pear Filling** Force enough peeled fresh pears through food chopper to make 1 cup. Put in saucepan with 1½ teaspoons cornstarch, ½ cup sugar and 1 tablespoon chopped crystallized ginger. Bring to boil and simmer 20 minutes, stirring frequently. Add ½ teaspoon grated lemon rind and 1½ teaspoons lemon juice. Cool to room temperature. **Ginger-Apple Filling** Substitute an equal amount of tart apples for the pears.

GLAZED ORANGE-SHORTBREAD SQUARES

3 cups all-purpose flour, lightly spooned
    into cup
1/2 cup cornstarch
1 cup sugar
Grated rind of 1 orange
1/4 teaspoon salt
1 cup butter or margarine
1/3 cup orange juice
Orange Glaze
2 squares unsweetened chocolate

Put the flour, cornstarch, sugar, orange rind and salt in bowl and mix well. Cut in butter until particles are very fine. Add orange juice and toss to mix. Gather mixture together and work quickly with hands until crumbs form a dough. With lightly floured fingertips, press evenly on bottom of lightly buttered 15″ x 10″ x 1″ pan. Bake in moderate oven (350°F.) 25 minutes, or until golden brown. Cool and spread with Orange Glaze. Let stand until set. Melt chocolate over hot water, cool and drizzle chocolate over glaze with teaspoon. Let stand until firm, then cut in 48 squares. Store airtight in cool place. **Orange Glaze** Mix until well blended and creamy 2 cups sifted confectioners' sugar and ¼ cup orange juice.

HERMITS

3/4 cup softened butter or margarine
1-1/2 cups packed light-brown sugar
1/2 cup molasses
3 eggs
4 cups sifted cake flour
1 teaspoon salt
1 teaspoon cinnamon
1 teaspoon nutmeg
1/2 teaspoon cloves
1/2 teaspoon allspice
1/2 teaspoon mace
1/4 cup strong coffee
1 cup chopped nuts
1 cup each raisins and currants
Confectioners' sugar

Cream butter and sugar until light; beat in molasses. Add eggs, one at a time, beating thoroughly after each. Sift flour, salt and spices and add to first mixture alternately with coffee, beating until smooth. Fold in nuts and fruit. Pour into 15" x 10" x 1" pan lined with waxed paper. Bake in moderate oven (350°F.) about 20 minutes. Turn out on rack and peel off paper. Slip onto cutting board and cut in 35 bars about 3" x 1¹/₂". Sprinkle with confectioners' sugar. These will stay moist a long time.

PORTUGUESE WALNUT SQUARES

1/2 cup softened butter
3/4 cup packed light-brown sugar
1 egg
1/2 teaspoon vanilla extract
2 tablespoons milk
Port or Madeira wine
Walnuts
6 tablespoons all-purpose flour
1/2 teaspoon double-acting baking
    powder
Wine Glaze

Cream butter and sugar, using electric mixer. Beat in egg, vanilla, milk and 2 tablespoons port. Whirl in blender or grind or grate 1 cup nuts. Place nuts and dry ingredients in a mixing bowl and stir. Fold in butter-egg mixture; do not overbeat. Spoon into a lightly buttered and floured 9" square cake pan. Bake in moderate oven (350°F.) 15 to 20 minutes, or until cake is just done. Remove from oven and brush top immediately with 2 to 3 tablespoons port. Cool to room temperature and spread with glaze. Sprinkle with chopped walnuts and let stand until firm. Cut in 16 squares. **Wine Glaze** Mix well 1 cup sifted confectioners' sugar, dash of salt, 1 tablespoon softened butter and about 1 tablespoon port to make mixture of spreading consistency. Tint a light pink with a little red food coloring.

SAUCEPAN FRUIT BARS

1 cup butter
1-1/2 cups sugar
2 eggs
2-3/4 cups all-purpose flour
1/2 teaspoon baking soda
1/2 teaspoon salt
1/2 teaspoon each nutmeg, cinnamon
    and cloves
1/4 cup buttermilk
1 cup each raisins and currants
Lemon Glaze

Melt butter in saucepan. Add sugar and eggs and beat well. Add sifted dry ingredients and buttermilk; mix well. Stir in fruit. spread in greased 15" x 10" x 1" pan. Bake in moderate oven (350°F.) about 25 minutes. Brush with glaze; cool in pan. Cut in 2" x 1" bars. Makes 45. **Lemon Glaze** Mix 1 cup sifted confectioners' sugar and 4 teaspoons lemon juice.

CHOCOLATE BUTTERSCOTCH BARS

2/3 cup shortening, melted
2-1/4 cups packed light-brown sugar
1 teaspoon vanilla extract
3 eggs
2-2/3 cups all-purpose flour
1/2 teaspoon salt
2-1/2 teaspoons double-acting baking
    powder
1 cup chopped nuts
1 cup (6 ounces) semisweet chocolate
    pieces

Mix first 3 ingredients. Add eggs, one at a time, beating thoroughly after each. Add sifted dry ingredients, nuts and chocolate. Spread in greased 15" x 10" x 1" pan. Bake in moderate oven (350°F.) about 25 minutes. While warm, cut in 50 bars.

RICH ALMOND MERINGUES

1 cup softened butter
1/2 cup almond paste
1/2 cup packed light-brown sugar
1 egg
1-7/8 cups all-purpose flour
3/4 cup raspberry jam
3 egg whites
3/4 cup granulated sugar
1/2 cup flaked coconut
1/2 cup slivered almonds

Cream butter with almond paste; gradually beat in brown sugar and egg. Blend in flour. Pat in lightly buttered 13" x 9" x 2" pan. Bake in moderate oven (325°F.) 20 minutes. Spread with jam. Beat egg whites until frothy; gradually beat in granulated sugar and beat until very glossy and stiff. Fold in coconut and nuts; spread over jam. Bake about 20 minutes longer. Cool in pan. Cut in 54 squares. Store airtight.

LEOPOLD SCHNITTEN

Cream ½ cup softened butter; add ½ cup sugar and beat until fluffy. Put 1 cup unblanched almonds through finest blade of food chopper; add to creamed mixture. Sift 1 cup minus 1 tablespoon all-purpose flour and ½ teaspoon each cloves and cinnamon; add to butter mixture. Pat into buttered 13" x 9" x 2" pan. Bake in moderate oven (350°F.) 20 to 25 minutes. While hot, sprinkle with mixture of 3 tablespoons sugar and 1 teaspoon cinnamon. Cut in 54 squares. Store airtight.

BUTTER CHEWS

3/4 cup softened butter or margarine
3 tablespoons granulated sugar
1-1/3 cups all-purpose flour
3 eggs, separated
2-1/4 cups packed light-brown sugar
1 cup chopped nuts
3/4 cup flaked coconut
Confectioners' sugar

Cream butter and granulated sugar; blend in flour. Pat in bottom of 13" x 9" x 2" pan. Bake in moderate oven (350°F.) 15 minutes. Beat egg whites until stiff but not dry; set aside. Beat egg yolks until thick and lemon-colored. Beat in brown sugar. Stir in nuts and coconut. Fold in egg whites and spread over first mixture. Return to oven and bake 25 to 30 minutes longer. Cool and dust with confectioners' sugar. Cut in 20 bars.

ORANGE TEMPTATIONS

1 navel orange
1 cup seeded raisins
1/2 cup softened butter
1 cup granulated sugar
1 egg
2 cups all-purpose flour
1/2 teaspoon double-acting baking
   powder
1/4 teaspoon salt
1-1/2 cups sifted confectioners' sugar

Cut orange in half and squeeze out about 2 tablespoons juice; reserve. Force remainder, including rind, with the raisins through food chopper. Cream butter; add sugar and egg. Beat until light. Add next 3 ingredients and mix well. Stir in orange mixture. Spread in greased 13" x 9" x 2" pan. Bake in hot oven (425°F.) about 25 minutes. Mix reserved juice with confectioners' sugar until smooth. Spread on baked mixture while still warm. Cool and cut in 35 squares. Store airtight.

SERBIAN WALNUT STRIPS

Mix 1 pound walnuts, ground, and 1 cup granulated sugar. Add 1 teaspoon lemon juice and 3 unbeaten egg whites; knead until mixture sticks together. Pat out on sugared board to a rectangle 3" wide and ½" thick. Beat 1 egg white stiff; gradually beat in ¾ cup sifted confectioners' sugar. Spread over walnut mixture. Cut in 1½" x ¾" strips. Arrange on well-buttered cookie sheets. Bake in very slow oven (200°F.) 20 minutes. Store airtight. Makes 72.

PECAN CRISPS

1 cup softened butter
1 cup packed light-brown sugar
1 teaspoon vanilla extract
1 egg, separated
1-7/8 cups all-purpose flour
1/2 teaspoon salt
1 teaspoon cinnamon
1 cup finely chopped pecans

Cream butter and sugar until light. Beat in vanilla and egg yolk. Add sifted dry ingredients and ½ cup nuts; mix well. Press into greased 15" x 10" x 1" pan and brush top with slightly beaten egg white. Sprinkle with ½ cup nuts. Bake in moderate oven (350°F.) about 25 minutes. While warm, cut in 50 bars. Remove at once to rack.

CHOCOLATE TRIPLE PLAY

Butter
1/4 cup granulated sugar
1 square unsweetened chocolate
1 teaspoon vanilla extract
1 egg, beaten
2 cups fine graham-cracker crumbs
1/2 cup chopped walnuts
1 cup flaked coconut
2 tablespoons instant vanilla-pudding-mix
   powder
3 tablespoons milk
2 cups sifted confectioners' sugar
4 squares semisweet chocolate

Put ½ cup butter, the granulated sugar, unsweetened chocolate and vanilla in top part of double boiler; cook over boiling water until well blended. Add egg and cook 5 minutes longer, stirring. Add next 3 ingredients. Press into buttered 9" x 9" x 2" pan. Cool; chill 15 minutes. Cream ½ cup butter until fluffy; beat in pudding mix and milk. Add confectioners' sugar gradually and beat until smooth. Spread over first layer. Chill 15 minutes. Melt semisweet chocolate and 1 tablespoon butter over low heat. Spread over second layer. Chill until firm. Cut in 81 squares. Keep in refrigerator.

SOUR-CREAM MOLASSES SQUARES

1 cup butter
1/2 cup sugar
1 cup light molasses
1 egg
3-1/2 cups sifted cake flour
1 teaspoon baking soda
1 teaspoon each cinnamon and ginger
3/4 teaspoon salt
1/2 cup dairy sour cream
Sour-cream Frosting
Chopped nuts

Cream butter and sugar until light. Beat in molasses and egg. Add sifted dry ingredients and sour cream and beat until smooth. Spread in greased 15" x 10" x 1" baking pan. Bake in moderate oven (350°F.) about 30 minutes. Cool in pan. Spread with frosting. Sprinkle with nuts, pressing down into frosting. Cut in 35 squares. **Sour-cream Frosting** In heavy saucepan, mix 1 cup dairy sour cream, 2 cups sugar and dash of salt. Cook rapidly over high heat, stirring vigorously, about 10 minutes, or until small amount of mixture forms a soft ball when dropped in very cold water (236°F. on candy thermometer). Remove from heat, add 1/2 teaspoon vanilla and beat until smooth and creamy. Spread quickly.

FROSTED MINCEMEAT DIAMONDS

1 tablespoon softened butter
1-1/2 cups packed brown sugar
2 eggs
2 tablespoons molasses
1-7/8 cups all-purpose flour
1/2 teaspoon each salt and baking soda
1 teaspoon each cinnamon and cloves
1/4 teaspoon nutmeg
Chopped nuts
1/4 cup seeded raisins, chopped
1 box (9 ounces) mincemeat, broken up with fork
Vanilla Glaze (double recipe)

Mix first 4 ingredients well. Add sifted dry ingredients and 3 tablespoons water; mix until smooth. Add 1/3 cup chopped nuts, the raisins and mincemeat. Spread thin in 2 greased 13" x 9" x 2" pans. Bake in hot oven (400°F.) 12 to 15 minutes. Spread with glaze while warm. Sprinkle with chopped nuts. Cool and cut in 2" diamonds. Makes 4 to 5 dozen. **Vanilla Glaze** In a mixing bowl, place 1 1/2 cups sifted confectioners' sugar, a dash of salt, 1 teaspoon vanilla, 2 tablespoons melted butter or margarine and about 2 tablespoons cream or undiluted evaporated milk to make a smooth paste; stir briskly. Glaze can be refrigerated a few hours before using, if desired.

DATE DELIGHTS

3 eggs
1 cup honey
1 teaspoon vanilla extract
1-1/3 cups all-purpose flour
1 teaspoon double-acting baking powder
1/4 teaspoon salt
1 cup finely cut dried apricots
1-1/4 cups (8 ounces) cut pitted dates
1 cup chopped nuts
Confectioners' sugar

Beat eggs until light; add honey and vanilla. Beat until blended. Stir in remaining ingredients, except sugar. Bake in greased 13" x 9" x 2" pan in moderate oven (350°F.) about 45 minutes. Cool in pan. Cut in 3" x 1" bars; roll in sugar. Makes 39.

NEWTON SUGAR SQUARES

1 cup softened butter or margarine
1-1/4 cups sugar
2 eggs
1-7/8 cups all-purpose flour
1/4 teaspoon baking soda
1/4 teaspoon salt
1 teaspoon ginger
2 tablespoons buttermilk

Cream butter with 1 cup sugar; add eggs and beat until light. Add sifted dry ingredients and buttermilk; mix well. Spread in greased 15" x 10" x 1" pan. Sprinkle with 1/4 cup sugar. Bake in hot oven (400°F.) about 20 minutes. Cool; cut in 40 squares.

CHOCOLATE LEBKUCHEN

1-1/4 cups sugar
3/4 cup honey
2 cups (12 ounces) semisweet chocolate pieces
1 cup chopped unblanched almonds
1/2 cup finely chopped mixed candied fruit
2 eggs, well beaten
1/4 cup orange juice
2-2/3 cups all-purpose flour
2 teaspoons cinnamon
1 teaspoon ground cloves
2 teaspoons ground cardamom
1 teaspoon baking soda
1 teaspoon double-acting baking powder
Lemon Frosting, page 331
Red candy shot
Green sugar

Combine sugar, honey and 2 tablespoons water in large saucepan. Bring to a boil. Remove from heat; cool. Stir in chocolate and next 4 ingredients. Blend in sifted dry ingredients. Store dough in tightly closed container at room temperature for 3 days to ripen. Spread in greased and floured 15" x 10" x 1" pan. Bake in moderate oven (325°F.) 35 to 40 minutes. Cool. Frost; cut in diamonds. Decorate with shot and sugar. Makes about 4 dozen.

DOUBLE-FROSTED BROWNIES

5 squares unsweetened chocolate
1/2 cup butter or margarine
1 cup sugar
1 teaspoon vanilla extract
2 eggs
1/2 cup all-purpose flour
1/4 teaspoon salt
1/2 cup chopped nuts
White Fudge Frosting

Melt 2 squares chocolate and butter in saucepan. Add sugar and vanilla; mix well. Beat in eggs one at a time. Blend in next 3 ingredients. Spread in greased 11″ x 7″ x 1½″ baking pan. Bake in moderate oven (350°F.) 20 to 25 minutes. Cool in pan. Spread with frosting. Melt remaining chocolate and spread on frosting. Refrigerate to harden. When firm, cut in small squares. **White Fudge Frosting** Put 1½ cups sugar, ⅓ cup butter and ½ cup medium cream in heavy saucepan. Bring to boil and cook until a small amount of mixture forms a soft ball when dropped in very cold water (236°F. on a candy thermometer). Set in pan of cold water until cool. Add 1 teaspoon vanilla and beat until creamy and of spreading consistency.

CHEESECAKE BROWNIES

3 ounces unsweetened chocolate
6 tablespoons butter
1-1/4 cups sugar
1-1/2 teaspoons vanilla extract
1 tablespoon cornstarch
3/4 cup cottage cheese
3 eggs
1/2 teaspoon lemon juice
1/2 cup all-purpose flour
1/2 teaspoon double-acting baking
  powder
1/4 teaspoon salt
1/2 cup chopped nuts
1/2 teaspoon almond extract

Melt chocolate and 4 tablespoons butter over hot water; cool. Cream 2 tablespoons butter, ¼ cup sugar and ½ teaspoon vanilla. Beat in cornstarch, cheese, 1 egg and lemon juice. Set aside. Beat 2 eggs until thick. Gradually beat in 1 cup sugar. Stir in chocolate mixture, the flour, baking powder and salt. Then mix in nuts, 1 teaspoon vanilla and the almond extract. Spread half the batter in buttered 9″ square pan. Pour cheese mixture over top. Spoon remaining chocolate batter over top. (Do not attempt to cover cheese mixture completely.) With spoon, swirl 2 mixtures together. Bake in moderate oven (350°F.) 35 to 40 minutes. Cut in 16 squares while warm.

FROSTED PEANUT BROWNIES

1/2 cup crunchy-style peanut butter
1/4 cup softened butter or margarine
1 cup packed light-brown sugar
2 eggs
1 teaspoon vanilla extract
1/2 cup sifted all-purpose flour
1/4 teaspoon salt
1 cup chopped salted peanuts
Quick Chocolate Frosting
Tiny multicolored candies

Cream first 3 ingredients until light. Add eggs, one at a time, beating thoroughly after each. Stir in next 3 ingredients. Fold in peanuts. Put in greased 8″ x 8″ x 2″ pan and bake in moderate oven (350°F.) 30 to 35 minutes. Cool in pan. Then spread with frosting and sprinkle with tiny candies. When frosting is firm, cut cake in 2″ squares. Makes 16 brownies. **Quick Chocolate Frosting** Put ½ cup undiluted evaporated milk and dash of salt in saucepan and bring just to boil. Stir in 1 package (6 ounces) semisweet chocolate pieces and 1 teaspoon vanilla. Beat until smooth. Cool slightly.

THE BEST BROWNIES

1/3 cup butter or margarine
2 squares unsweetened chocolate
1 cup sugar
1/2 teaspoon vanilla extract
2 eggs
2/3 cup all-purpose flour
1/4 teaspoon salt
3/4 cup chopped nuts

Melt butter and chocolate in saucepan over low heat, stirring; cool. Beat in sugar and vanilla. Add eggs, one at a time, beating well after each addition. Add remaining ingredients. Spread in buttered 8″ x 8″ x 2″ pan. Bake in slow oven (325°F.) about 25 minutes. Cool; cut in 16 squares.

DATE TEMPTATIONS

1 package (8 ounces) pitted dates
1 cup pecans or walnuts
Sifted confectioners' sugar
2 eggs, beaten
1/2 teaspoon salt
1 tablespoon vegetable oil
1 tablespoon lemon juice
1/4 cup sifted all-purpose flour
3/4 teaspoon nutmeg

Force dates and nuts through food chopper, using medium blade. Add 1 cup confectioners' sugar, the eggs and salt; mix well. Add remaining ingredients and mix thoroughly. Spread in greased 9″ square pan. Bake in moderate oven (350°F.) about 30 minutes. Cool partially, cut in 18 bars and roll in confectioners' sugar.

CHOCOLATE RINGS

Cream 1 cup butter; gradually beat in 1 cup sifted confectioners' sugar and 2 teaspoons vanilla extract. Add 1½ cups all-purpose flour, ½ teaspoon baking soda and 1 cup quick-rolling rolled oats. Chill 1 hour. Shape in 2 rolls 1½" in diameter; roll in chocolate shot. Wrap in waxed paper; chill several hours, or overnight. Cut in ¼" slices. Bake in slow oven (325°F.) 10 minutes. Store airtight. Makes 60.

BLACK-WALNUT WAFERS

Cream ½ cup butter; gradually beat in ½ cup sugar. Add 2 egg yolks, one at a time, beating well after each addition. Blend in 1½ cups all-purpose flour. Add 1 cup minus 2 tablespoons chopped black walnuts. Pack into 4 buttered 6-ounce frozen-juice cans. Freeze or chill thoroughly. Remove from cans and slice thin. Bake in moderate oven (375°F.) 8 to 10 minutes. Cool. Frost with Black-walnut Icing. Makes 3 dozen. **Black-walnut Icing** Add ⅛ teaspoon salt and ¼ teaspoon cinnamon to 1 unbeaten egg white; stir in sifted confectioners' sugar until of spreading consistency. Add 2 tablespoons chopped black walnuts.

CHERRY-BLOSSOM COOKIE TARTS

1 cup butter or margarine, softened
1-1/2 cups sugar
1 egg, beaten
1-7/8 cups all-purpose flour
1 jar (4 ounces) red maraschino cherries
1-1/4 cups prepared almonds (grind, whirl in blender or chop very fine)
2 egg whites
2 teaspoons lemon juice

Cream butter with ½ cup sugar until fluffy; beat in egg. Gradually blend in flour. Wrap dough in waxed paper and chill until firm. Shape chilled dough in 4 rolls 10" long. Cut each roll in 15 pieces. With thumb dipped in flour, press dough into 1½" tart pans, leaving small depression in center of each tart. Drain cherries, reserving 2 tablespoons syrup. Mix syrup with 1 cup sugar and remaining ingredients, except cherries. Fill tart depression with half a teaspoon of almond mixture and top with a cherry quarter. Bake in moderate oven (350°F.) 20 to 30 minutes, or until browned around edges. Makes 5 dozen.

LITTLE TEA CAKES

2 eggs
1/2 cup dairy sour cream
1 cup honey
1/2 cup butter or margarine, melted
1-7/8 cups all-purpose flour
1 teaspoon salt
1/2 teaspoon baking soda
1/2 teaspoon cream of tartar
1/2 teaspoon each mace and cardamom
1/2 cup sifted confectioners' sugar
Chopped pecans, almonds or filberts

Beat eggs well. Then beat in next 3 ingredients, blending thoroughly. Sift next 4 ingredients and spices, add to egg mixture and mix until smooth. Spread in greased 15" x 10" x 1" pan and bake in moderate oven (350°F.) about 30 minutes. Spread while warm with confectioners' sugar mixed with 2 tablespoons water to a smooth paste. Sprinkle with nuts. Cool in pan and cut in 50 pieces.

CARDAMOM COOKIES

1 cup softened butter
1 cup sugar
1 teaspoon ground cardamom
1/2 cup dairy sour cream
3-3/4 cups all-purpose flour
1/4 teaspoon each salt and baking soda

Cream butter and sugar until light. Add remaining ingredients; mix well. Shape in 2 long rolls 2" in diameter on waxed paper. Roll up and chill overnight. Cut in ⅛" slices; bake in moderate oven (375°F.) 8 to 10 minutes. Store airtight. Makes 120.

BLACK FOREST PFEFFERNUSSE

5 eggs
2 cups packed brown sugar
Grated rind of 1 lemon
3 tablespoons strong coffee
5-1/4 cups all-purpose flour
2 teaspoons double-acting baking powder
1/2 teaspoon each salt, pepper, mace and nutmeg
1 teaspoon each cloves and allspice
1 tablespoon cinnamon
1/8 teaspoon ground cardamom
1 cup ground almonds
1/2 cup chopped citron
1/4 teaspoon anise seed
Apricot brandy

Beat eggs until thick; gradually beat in sugar. Add remaining ingredients, except brandy; mix well. Chill. Shape in rolls 1" in diameter. Cut slices ½" thick. Let stand in cool place to dry overnight. Turn cookies over and put a drop of brandy on each to make cookies pop and become rounded. Bake in slow oven (300°F.) about 20 minutes. Store airtight. Makes 8 dozen.

LEMON CARAWAY COOKIES

1/2 cup softened butter
1 cup sugar
1 egg
1-1/4 teaspoons caraway seed
Grated rind of 1/2 lemon
2 tablespoons lemon juice
2-1/3 cups all-purpose flour
1/2 teaspoon baking soda
1/2 teaspoon salt

Cream butter. Add sugar and egg; beat until light. Add next 3 ingredients and sifted dry ingredients; mix well. Shape into a roll 2" in diameter; chill. Cut in ⅛" slices. Bake on greased cookie sheets in hot oven (400°F.) about 10 minutes. Store airtight. Makes 6 dozen.

PRUNE REFRIGERATOR COOKIES

1 cup softened butter or margarine
1 cup packed brown sugar
1/2 cup granulated sugar
2 eggs
1 tablespoon vinegar
1 teaspoon vanilla extract
3-3/4 cups chopped cooked prunes or dates
4 cups all-purpose flour
1 teaspoon baking soda
1 teaspoon salt
1 cup chopped nuts

Cream butter and sugars; add eggs, one at a time, and beat until light. Add next 3 ingredients and sifted dry ingredients; mix well. Add nuts. Shape into 3 rolls about 2" in diameter. Wrap in waxed paper and chill overnight. Cut in ⅛" slices and bake in hot oven (400°F.) about 12 minutes. Makes about 12 dozen.

RUM BUTTER COOKIES

1 cup softened butter or margarine
Sugar
3 egg yolks
1/2 teaspoon vanilla extract
1/4 teaspoon almond extract
2-1/2 tablespoons rum
2-1/2 cups all-purpose flour
1-1/2 tablespoons powdered dried orange peel

Cream butter and ¾ cup sugar until light. Beat in next 4 ingredients. Gradually add flour, kneading in last cup. When smooth, shape in rolls about 2" in diameter, wrap in waxed paper and chill overnight. Cut in ¼" slices and roll each slice between hands to form a ball. Roll balls in mixture of ¼ cup sugar and the orange peel; put on cookie sheet and flatten with a tumbler dipped in the sugar-orange mixture. Bake in moderate oven (350°F.) 10 to 12 minutes. Store airtight a day or two to bring out the rum flavor. Makes about 60.

BUTTERSCOTCH MAPLE COOKIES

1/2 cup softened butter or margarine
1/2 cup packed light-brown sugar
1/2 cup granulated sugar
1 egg
2-1/3 cups all-purpose flour
1/2 teaspoon salt
1/2 teaspoon baking soda
1 teaspoon cinnamon
Maple syrup
Almond halves

Cream butter and sugars until light; beat in egg. Add sifted dry ingredients. Stir until mixture forms a ball. Divide dough into 3 parts. Shape each on waxed paper in a roll about 2" in diameter. Chill until firm. Slice ¼" thick. Put on greased sheets. Brush with maple syrup. Place almond half on each cookie. Bake in hot oven (400°F.) 10 minutes, or until golden brown. Makes about 40.

NEAPOLITANS

1/2 cup softened butter or margarine
3/4 cup granulated sugar
1 egg
1 teaspoon vanilla extract
1/2 teaspoon almond flavoring
1-7/8 cups all-purpose flour
1/2 teaspoon salt
1/4 teaspoon baking soda
3/4 cup finely chopped raisins
12 chopped candied cherries
Chocolate Dough

Cream butter; add next 4 ingredients and beat until light. Add sifted dry ingredients, 2 tablespoons water and the fruits; mix well. Prepare Chocolate Dough; pack half into waxed-paper-lined 9" x 5" x 3" loaf pan. Pack fruited dough firmly in pan for center layer; then top with remaining Chocolate Dough. Chill at least 24 hours. Turn out, cut in thirds lengthwise, then cut crosswise in ¼" slices. Bake in hot oven (400°F.) 10 minutes. Makes 8 dozen.

Chocolate Dough

1 cup softened butter or margarine
1-1/2 cups packed dark-brown sugar
2 eggs
2-3/4 cups all-purpose flour
1/4 teaspoon salt
1 teaspoon baking soda
1/2 teaspoon cinnamon
1/2 teaspoon cloves
1 cup finely chopped nuts
6-ounce package semisweet chocolate pieces, finely chopped

Cream butter. Add sugar and eggs; beat until light. Add sifted dry ingredients, nuts and chocolate; mix well.

PEANUT CHOCOLATE FUDGE

1/4 cup peanut butter
1/2 cup undiluted evaporated milk
1 cup marshmallow cream
1-1/4 cups sugar
1/2 teaspoon salt
1 package (6 ounces) semisweet
   chocolate pieces

In saucepan mix all ingredients, except chocolate. Put over low heat and cook, stirring until blended. Bring mixture to a full boil, stirring. Boil 3 minutes, stirring constantly. Remove from heat, add chocolate and stir until blended. Pour into buttered 8" square pan. Cool and cut. Makes about 1½ pounds.

QUICK CHOCOLATE FUDGE

1/4 cup butter or margarine
3 squares unsweetened chocolate
1/2 cup light corn syrup
1 teaspoon vanilla extract
1 pound confectioners' sugar, sifted
1/3 cup dry nonfat milk
1/2 cup chopped nuts

Melt butter and chocolate over boiling water. Stir in corn syrup, vanilla and 1 tablespoon water. Sift sugar and milk together; add a third at a time, blending well. Remove from heat and stir in nuts. Spread in buttered 8" square pan and let stand until firm. Cut in squares. Makes about 1¾ pounds.

KNEADED CHOCOLATE FUDGE

2 tablespoons butter or margarine
2 squares unsweetened chocolate
1 cup milk
3 cups sugar
1/4 cup honey or light corn syrup
1/8 teaspoon salt
1 teaspoon vinegar
1 teaspoon vanilla extract
1/2 cup chopped nuts

Melt butter and chocolate in milk in saucepan. Beat to blend. Add next 3 ingredients. Bring to boil, cover and boil 2 minutes. Uncover and cook, without stirring, until a small amount of mixture dropped in very cold water forms a soft ball (238°F. on a candy thermometer). Remove from heat and add vinegar. Let stand until lukewarm. Add vanilla and nuts; beat with a wooden spoon until mixture becomes thick and loses its gloss. Quickly turn out on buttered plate and knead with fingers 4 to 5 minutes. Shape in 2 rolls, each about 2" in diameter. Wrap in waxed paper and store in cool place. Cut in slices. Makes 1½ pounds.

TWO-TONE TRUFFLES

2 cups finely chopped nuts
1-1/2 cups sifted confectioners' sugar
1 egg white
1 tablespoon Cointreau or rum
1-1/2 cups semisweet chocolate pieces
3/4 cup sweetened condensed milk
1 tablespoon butter

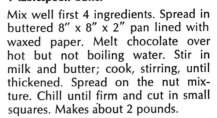

Mix well first 4 ingredients. Spread in buttered 8" x 8" x 2" pan lined with waxed paper. Melt chocolate over hot but not boiling water. Stir in milk and butter; cook, stirring, until thickened. Spread on the nut mixture. Chill until firm and cut in small squares. Makes about 2 pounds.

CHRISTMAS FUDGE

2/3 cup (1 small can) undiluted
   evaporated milk
2 tablespoons butter or margarine
1-2/3 cups sugar
1/2 teaspoon salt
2 cups (4 ounces) miniature
   marshmallows
1-1/2 cups (9 ounces) semisweet
   chocolate pieces
1/2 cup chopped pistachio nuts
1/4 cup crushed peppermint sticks

Mix first 4 ingredients in saucepan. Bring to boil and cook 4 to 5 minutes, stirring constantly. (Begin timing when mixture bubbles.) Remove from heat and add next 3 ingredients. Stir briskly until marshmallows are melted. Pour into buttered 8" square pan and sprinkle with candy. Cool thoroughly until firm and cut in squares. Makes about 2 pounds.

SOUR-CREAM CHOCOLATE FUDGE

2 cups granulated sugar
1 cup confectioners' sugar
1 cup dairy sour cream
3 squares unsweetened chocolate
1/4 teaspoon salt
1 tablespoon butter or margarine
1 teaspoon vanilla extract
1 cup chopped nuts

Mix first 5 ingredients in heavy saucepan. Bring to boil, stirring occasionally. Reduce heat and cook, without stirring, until small amount of mixture forms a soft ball when dropped in very cold water (234°F. on a candy thermometer). Add butter and vanilla and cool to lukewarm. Add nuts and beat until mixture is thick and loses its gloss. Pour into buttered 8" square pan and let stand until firm. Cut in squares. Makes about 1¾ pounds. *Note* Sour-cream candy mixtures tend to scorch. Use an asbestos mat, if available.

PENUCHE

Mix 2 pounds light-brown sugar, 1 cup undiluted evaporated milk, ½ cup butter or margarine and ¼ teaspoon salt. Cook, stirring, until sugar is dissolved. Cook without stirring until a small amount of mixture forms soft ball in cold water (238°F. on a candy thermometer). Remove from heat and cool to lukewarm. Add 1 teaspoon vanilla, 1½ cups chopped nuts and ¾ cup halved candied cherries. Beat until thick. Pour into buttered 9″ square pan. When firm, cut in squares. Makes 3 pounds.

COCONUT-POTATO CANDY

1/2 pound marshmallows
1/4 cup butter or margarine
1/2 teaspoon salt
1 cup (2 servings) prepared instant mashed potatoes (omit butter and salt in preparation)
1 tablespoon vanilla extract
Red, green and yellow food colorings
3 pounds (about) confectioners' sugar
3 cans flaked coconut
Pecan halves
Candied cherries

Mix first 3 ingredients in top part of double boiler; cook over boiling water, stirring occasionally, until marshmallows melt. Remove from heat and stir in potatoes and vanilla. Divide mixture in 3 parts; tint each part a different color. Sift 1 pound sugar; blend with 1 can coconut into each part. (Use a little more sugar, if nec--essary.) Shape in balls and put on waxed paper. Top each ball with a pecan half or candied cherry. Chill until firm. Makes about 5 pounds.

PEANUT-BUTTER FUDGE

1/2 cup light corn syrup
3/4 cup peanut butter
1/2 cup butter, softened
1/2 teaspoon salt
1 teaspoon vanilla extract
4 cups (about) sifted confectioners' sugar
3/4 cup chopped nuts plus halves for tops of squares
Halved red candied cherries

Beat first 5 ingredients in bowl until blended. Gradually beat in confectioners' sugar, making a very stiff mixture. Turn out on board and knead until well blended. Gradually work in chopped nuts. Press into buttered 8″ square pan. Mark off in squares and put a nut or cherry half in the center of each. Chill until firm before cutting. Makes about 2 pounds.

PECAN PRALINES

3 cups packed light-brown sugar
1/4 teaspoon cream of tartar
1/8 teaspoon salt
1 cup milk
2 tablespoons butter or margarine
1 teaspoon vanilla extract
2-1/4 cups pecan halves

Mix first 4 ingredients in saucepan. Stir over low heat until sugar is dissolved. Cook, without stirring, until small amount of mixture forms a soft ball when dropped in very cold water (236°F. on a candy thermometer.) Cool to lukewarm. Add remaining ingredients and beat until creamy. Drop from large spoon onto waxed paper and let stand until firm. Makes about 1¾ pounds.

CARAMEL CORN

1 cup sugar
1/2 cup dark corn syrup
1 teaspoon vinegar
1/4 teaspoon salt
1 tablespoon butter
1 teaspoon vanilla extract
1 teaspoon baking soda
1-1/2 quarts popped corn
1/2 cup salted peanuts

Mix first 5 ingredients in 2-quart saucepan. Cook over medium heat, stirring, until mixture boils. Boil gently until mixture becomes brittle when dropped in cold water (290°F. on candy thermometer). Remove from heat and stir in vanilla and soda. Pour over corn and peanuts and mix well. Store in airtight container. Makes about 6 cups.

GOLD NUGGETS

1-1/2 cups sugar
3 tablespoons orange juice
1/4 teaspoon cinnamon
1/4 cup grated orange rind
2-1/2 cups walnuts or other nuts

Mix sugar and orange juice with ¼ cup warm water; stir to dissolve sugar. Cover pan and boil 1 minute to steam down sugar crystals from sides of pan. Remove cover and cook without stirring until a small amount of mixture forms a soft ball when dropped in very cold water (240°F. on a candy thermometer). Remove from heat. Add remaining ingredients. Stir with a fork until mixture becomes creamy. Turn out onto a sheet of waxed paper or onto a lightly buttered baking sheet. Separate the nuts with a fork. Cool and store airtight. Makes 2½ cups.

ARAB DATES

1/2 cup honey
1/2 cup chopped toasted almonds
1/4 cup chopped candied citron
1/2 cup chopped walnuts
1 pound pitted dates
Sugar

Mix first 4 ingredients. Stuff dates with the mixture. Roll in sugar and store airtight.

CANDIED GRAPEFRUIT PEEL

Cover peel of 1 large grapefruit with cold water. Bring to boil and cook until tender, pouring off the water and adding fresh cold water several times. Drain. Cut peel in thin strips with scissors. Boil 1 cup sugar and ½ cup water until it threads (230°F. on candy thermometer). Add peel and cook over low heat until syrup has been absorbed. Roll each strip in sugar to coat. Cool; store airtight.

THIN MINTS DELUXE

3 cups sugar
2-1/2 tablespoons light corn syrup
Dash of salt
1/4 teaspoon cream of tartar
1/2 teaspoon glycerin (buy in drug store)
1 tablespoon white vegetable shortening
Wintergreen and peppermint extracts
Red and green food colorings

Mix sugar with 1½ cups water in saucepan. Bring to boil, stirring, until sugar is dissolved. Cover tightly 3 minutes to steam down crystals. Add next 3 ingredients. Cook without stirring until small amount of mixture forms a soft ball when dropped in very cold water (236°F. on a candy thermometer). Cool to lukewarm. Then beat with electric mixer or by hand until very thick. Knead by hand until smooth and creamy. Store in covered container about 24 hours. Divide in half. Put half in double boiler and add ¼ teaspoon glycerin and 1½ teaspoons shortening. Add a few drops wintergreen extract and red coloring to tint a delicate pink. Put over hot water and stir constantly until melted. (Mixture should be just about as hot as the finger can stand. If too hot, mints will be hard and white spots will form on them. If not hot enough, they will be too soft.) Drop from teaspoon onto waxed paper to make thin round mints. Let harden. Repeat with other half of mixture, adding peppermint and tinting fondant a delicate green. Makes about 6 dozen.

ROCKY ROAD BARS

Cut 10 marshmallows in quarters. Arrange in buttered 9″ x 5″ x 3″ loaf pan. Fill spaces between marshmallows with ½ cup broken walnut meats. Melt 1 package (8 ounces) semisweet chocolate squares and pour over contents of loaf pan. Cool until firm and cut in 15 bars.

PEANUT CHEWS

1/2 cup honey
3/4 cup maple syrup
Dash of salt
1/4 teaspoon baking soda
1/4 teaspoon cream of tartar
1 cup roasted peanuts

Mix first 3 ingredients in saucepan. Cook until small amount of mixture forms a hard ball when dropped in very cold water (255°F. on a candy thermometer). Remove from heat; stir in remaining ingredients; stir to coat evenly. Pour into buttered 8″ square pan, let stand until firm and cut in squares. Makes about ½ pound.

SPICED MIXED NUTS

1-1/2 cups unsalted mixed nuts
1/4 cup vegetable oil
2 cups sifted confectioners' sugar
1-1/2 tablespoons egg white, slightly beaten
1/2 teaspoon each ginger and nutmeg
1/2 teaspoon cinnamon
1-1/2 teaspoons brandy flavoring

Put nuts on cookie sheet and heat in moderate oven (350°F.) about 15 minutes. Meanwhile, blend remaining ingredients. Stir in nuts, coating nuts thoroughly. Spread out on cool cookie sheet to dry. Separate nuts. Makes about 2½ cups.

CARAMEL APPLES ON A STICK

In heavy saucepan mix 1 cup sugar, ½ cup light corn syrup, 1 large can sweetened condensed milk and ⅛ teaspoon salt. Stir until sugar is well blended. Cook slowly, stirring gently, until a small amount of the mixture forms a soft ball when dropped in cold water (234°F. on a candy thermometer). Remove from heat and stir in 1 teaspoon vanilla extract; cool slightly. Insert wooden skewer in stem end of each of 4 to 6 washed and dried red eating apples. Working quickly, dip apples in caramel and twirl until well coated. Put apples stem side up on a buttered plate or waxed paper to harden. Makes 4 to 6.

MARZIPAN STRAWBERRIES

1 box (3 ounces) strawberry-flavor
  gelatin
1 tablespoon confectioners' sugar
2/3 cup blanched almonds
2/3 cup sweetened condensed milk
1 package (7 ounces) grated coconut
1-1/2 teaspoons granulated sugar
Red food coloring
1/2 teaspoon almond extract

Sift 1½ tablespoons of the gelatin with the confectioners' sugar. Set aside. Force almonds through food chopper, using fine blade. Add next 3 ingredients, a few drops of food coloring, the almond flavoring and remaining gelatin. Mix thoroughly and shape in strawberries. Roll in gelatin mixture. Chill until firm. Then store, covered, at room temperature. Makes about 36. *Note* Leaves can be cut from green construction paper and fastened to strawberries with half a green toothpick or a piece of plastic-covered wire.

DIVINITY DROPS

1/2 cup light corn syrup
2-1/2 cups sugar
1/4 teaspoon salt
2 egg whites
1 teaspoon vanilla extract
1 cup coarsely chopped nuts
Red candied cherries, halved
Angelica or green candied cherries

In saucepan mix corn syrup, sugar, salt and ½ cup water. Cook, stirring, until sugar is dissolved. Continue cooking, without stirring, until a small amount of mixture forms a firm ball when dropped in cold water (248°F. on a candy thermometer). Beat egg whites until stiff but not dry. Pour about half the syrup slowly over whites, beating constantly. Cook remainder of syrup until a small amount forms hard threads in cold water (272°F.). Add slowly to first mixture and beat until mixture holds its shape. Add vanilla and nuts; drop by dessert-spoonfuls onto waxed paper. Decorate with cherry halves and angelica. Let stand until firm. Makes about 1½ pounds.
Chocolate Divinity Prepare Divinity Drops, adding 1 package (6 ounces) semisweet chocolate pieces with vanilla and nuts. Proceed as directed.
Holiday Divinity Add ¼ cup each chopped candied cherries and pineapple with the nuts.
Ginger Divinity Prepare Divinity Drops, using 2 tablespoons preserved-ginger syrup and 6 tablespoons water for the liquid. Add ½ cup finely diced ginger with the nuts.

DOUBLE-ALMOND TOFFEE

1 pound butter
2-1/2 cups sugar
1-1/2 cups whole unblanched almonds
1-1/2 cups semisweet chocolate
  pieces
1-1/2 cups lightly toasted chopped
  almonds

In large heavy skillet, melt butter and add sugar. Cook, stirring, over highest heat until mixture foams vigorously. Reduce heat to low and cook, stirring, 5 minutes longer. Add almonds, increase heat to high and cook, stirring, until nuts begin to pop. Reduce heat and cook, stirring, 7 minutes. (If mixture darkens too quickly, remove from heat but stir the full 7 minutes.) Pour into 15" x 10" x 1" jelly-roll pan and cool. Melt half the chocolate over hot water, spread over candy and sprinkle with half the chopped almonds; cool. Flip cooled candy sheet out of pan. Melt remaining chocolate and spread over other side of candy; sprinkle with remaining almonds. When cool, break in pieces. Store airtight. Makes 3 pounds.

ALMOND NOUGAT

1-1/2 cups light corn syrup
2 cups sugar
1/4 teaspoon salt
2 egg whites
1/2 teaspoon almond extract
Green food coloring
1/4 cup butter or margarine, softened
1 cup toasted unblanched almonds

Mix first 3 ingredients with ¼ cup water in heavy saucepan. Cook, stirring, until sugar is dissolved. Cook, without stirring, until a small amount of mixture forms a hard ball when dropped in very cold water (250°F. on a candy thermometer). Beat egg whites until stiff but not dry in large bowl of electric mixer. Gradually beat in about one fourth (not more) of hot syrup and continue beating until mixture holds its shape. Cook remaining syrup until a small amount separates in hard brittle threads when dropped in very cold water (300°F.). Gradually beat into first mixture and continue beating until mixture begins to hold its shape. Add flavoring and food coloring to tint a delicate green. Beat in butter and continue beating until very thick and satiny. Stir in nuts and press into buttered 8" square pan, smoothing top. Let stand until firm, then turn out and cut in 1" squares. Wrap each piece in waxed paper or plastic. For best flavor, store several days airtight in cool place. Makes about 1½ pounds.

CHOCOLATE PEANUT-BUTTER STICKS

1 package (8 ounces) semisweet chocolate squares
6 tablespoons peanut butter
1 teaspoon vanilla extract
1 cup wheat germ

Melt chocolate and blend in peanut butter and vanilla. Stir in wheat germ. Press into buttered 8" square pan and chill until firm. Cut in 4" x 1" sticks. Makes 16.

NUT BRITTLE SQUARES

Butter the outside bottom of an 8" square pan and sprinkle evenly with 1 cup rather finely chopped Brazil nuts, filberts, California walnuts, pecans, peanuts or other nuts. Set pan, nut side up, on a tray. Put 1 cup sugar in heavy skillet and heat, stirring, until golden brown and syrupy. At once pour evenly over nuts. When slightly cooled, remove in one piece and cut in 2" squares. Makes ½ pound.

TURTLETTES

3/4 pound pecan halves
1 recipe Creamy Caramel Mixture
1 package (12 ounces) semisweet chocolate pieces

Arrange groups of 4 pecan halves on buttered cookie sheet. Spoon about 1 teaspoon caramel mixture in center of each group of nuts, half covering each nut, to resemble turtles. Let stand about 10 minutes. Melt chocolate and spread some on each turtlette. Let stand until set, then wrap in plastic. Makes about 4 dozen.

Creamy Caramel Mixture

2 cups light cream
2 cups sugar
1 cup light or dark corn syrup
1/2 teaspoon salt
1/3 cup butter or margarine
1 teaspoon vanilla extract

Heat cream to lukewarm in large heavy saucepan. Pour out 1 cup and reserve. Add next 3 ingredients to cream in saucepan. Cook, stirring, until mixture boils. Add reserved cream very slowly so mixture does not stop boiling. Cook 5 minutes, stirring. Stir in butter, about 1 teaspoon at a time. Reduce heat and cook, stirring almost constantly, until a small amount of mixture forms a firm ball when dropped in very cold water (248°F. on a candy thermometer). To prevent scorching, use a thick asbestos mat under pan near end of cooking time. Remove from heat and gently stir in vanilla; cool slightly.

HOLIDAY FRUIT CANDY

3 cups sugar
1 cup light corn syrup
1-1/2 cups heavy cream
1/8 teaspoon salt
1 teaspoon vanilla extract
1/2 pound each pecan and walnut halves and whole Brazil nuts
1/2 pound whole candied cherries
1/2 cup diced candied pineapple

Mix first 4 ingredients in saucepan. Bring to boil and cook, without stirring, until small amount of mixture forms a soft ball when dropped in very cold water (236°F. on a candy thermometer). Remove from heat and let stand 5 minutes. Add vanilla and beat until slightly thickened. Add nuts and fruits and stir until thick. Pack into well-buttered 9" x 5" x 3" loaf pan and let stand overnight, or until firm. Turn out and cut in thick slices, then in smaller pieces, as desired. Makes about 4½ pounds.

CRUNCHY CEREAL PATTIES

5 cups assorted unsweetened crisp ready-to-eat cereals
4 cups miniature marshmallows
1/3 cup peanut butter
1/4 cup butter
1/2 cup semisweet chocolate pieces

Put cereals in large greased bowl. Melt together next 3 ingredients in top part of double boiler over hot water, stirring occasionally until smooth. Pour over cereal, stirring until evenly coated. With buttered hands, shape mixture in fifteen 3" patties; put on waxed paper. Melt chocolate and use to decorate tops. Chill until firm. Makes 1½ pounds.

GUMDROP SQUARES

4 envelopes unflavored gelatin
Sugar
1/8 teaspoon salt
2 tablespoons lime or lemon juice
3 drops yellow, green or red food coloring
1 teaspoon orange or lemon extract

Sprinkle gelatin in ¾ cup cold water in saucepan. Let stand 5 minutes, then add ¾ cup boiling water, 2¼ cups sugar and the salt. Bring to a full boil over low heat, stirring. Remove from heat and stir in remaining ingredients. Pour into 8" square pan rinsed with cold water. Let stand at room temperature overnight. Next day, dip pan in hot water for a moment to loosen mixture. Turn out onto waxed paper sprinkled with sugar. Cut in squares and roll in sugar. Makes about 1½ pounds.

CHOCOLATE RAISIN-NUT CLUSTERS

Melt 1 package (12 ounces) semisweet chocolate pieces over warm water and cool to lukewarm. Add ¼ teaspoon salt, 1½ cups toasted finely chopped filberts or other nuts and 1½ cups golden raisins; blend thoroughly. Drop in clusters into small foil or paper candy cups. Cover lightly with plastic wrap and put in cool dry place to harden. Makes about 6 dozen.

SKILLET CEREAL SNACKS

1/4 cup each honey and butter or
   margarine
1/4 teaspoon salt
2 cups miniature marshmallows
1 teaspoon vanilla extract
3 cups puffed dry cereal

In skillet, combine first 3 ingredients. Cook over low heat, stirring, until marshmallows are melted. Remove from heat and stir in vanilla and cereal. Press into buttered 9" square pan and let stand until firm. Cut in squares. Makes 16 squares.

HUNGARIAN CHRISTMAS BALLS

1 cup sugar
Grated rind of 2 oranges
2 tablespoons orange juice
1 teaspoon lemon juice
1 cup finely ground walnuts
1/2 cup finely chopped candied fruits
1/2 cup Dutch-process cocoa

Over low heat, melt sugar with next 3 ingredients. Cool. Add walnuts and fruits and work until well mixed. Pinch off pieces of dough and roll into ¾" balls. Roll in cocoa until covered. Makes 30.

FRENCH SWEETS

1/4 cup honey
4 squares unsweetened chocolate
1 cup each ground seedless raisins
   and dates
1 cup chopped nuts
1-1/2 teaspoons vanilla extract
Sugar

Heat honey but do not boil. Remove from heat, add chocolate and stir until blended. Add fruits, nuts and vanilla; mix well. Dip fingers in a little cold water and pat mixture to ½" thickness in a waxed-paper-lined 8" square pan. Sprinkle lightly with sugar. Let stand in refrigerator overnight. Cut in 1" squares. Makes about 1¼ pounds.

OLD-FASHIONED MOLASSES TAFFY

Mix 1 cup unsulfured molasses, 1 cup sugar, 1 tablespoon butter or margarine and dash of salt in heavy saucepan. Put over low heat and stir until sugar is dissolved. Cook over medium heat until a small amount of mixture separates in hard but not brittle threads when dropped in very cold water (270°F. on a candy thermometer). Pour onto greased platter. As edges cool, fold toward center. When cool enough to handle, press into ball with lightly buttered fingers. Pull until light in color and very firm. Stretch into a long rope ½" in diameter; cut in 1" pieces. Wrap each piece in waxed paper or plastic wrap. Makes about 1¼ pounds.

TWICE-GLAZED ORANGE SLICES

Combine 1 cup granulated sugar and ½ cup water in large heavy skillet. Heat, stirring, until sugar is dissolved. Add 12 seedless-orange slices, ¼" thick, arranging so they lie flat. Bring to boil. Remove from heat and cool. Spoon syrup over fruit. Repeat boiling and cooling process 6 or 7 times, or until all syrup has been absorbed. Remove slices and put on rack. Let stand overnight. Combine ½ cup sifted confectioners' sugar and ¼ cup water in a small saucepan. Heat till sugar dissolves. *Do not boil.* Cut orange slices in half and dip in warm syrup. Drain and return to rack to cool and dry. Store airtight in cool dry place. Makes 2 dozen pieces.

CHOCOLATE CARAMELS

3 cups packed light-brown sugar
1-1/2 cups molasses
3/4 cup butter or margarine
3 tablespoons flour
6 squares unsweetened chocolate
1-1/2 cups milk
1-1/2 teaspoons vanilla extract
Almonds (optional)

Bring first 4 ingredients to boil and boil 5 minutes. Add chocolate and milk. Cook, stirring frequently, until a small amount of mixture forms a firm ball when dropped in very cold water (248°F. on a candy thermometer). Add vanilla and pour into buttered 9" square pan. Cool and cut in squares. Put squares in bonbon cups and top with an almond. Or, wrap a number of caramels in a strip of clear plastic, twisting plastic and tying with ribbon to separate caramels. Makes about 2½ pounds.

AFTER-DINNER (PULLED) MINTS

1-1/2 cups sugar
2 tablespoons light corn syrup
1/4 teaspoon peppermint or mint extract
Few drops of food coloring

Mix sugar, corn syrup and $1/2$ cup water in saucepan. Cook, stirring, until sugar is dissolved. Cover and cook 3 minutes to steam sugar crystals from sides of pan. Uncover and cook, without stirring, until small amount of mixture forms a very hard ball when dropped in bowl of very cold water (260°F. to 262°F. on a candy thermometer). During cooking, wipe down sides of pan with a spatula wrapped in damp cheese-cloth to remove crystals. Remove from heat and pour into buttered pan. When candy is cool enough to handle, pour flavoring and coloring into center and fold corners over. Pull with fingers until mixture is satiny and quite firm. Pull into long strips $1/2''$ in diameter; cut in $1/2''$ to $1''$ pieces. Layer pieces in bowl, separating layers with waxed paper. Cover and store overnight, or until creamy. Makes about $1/2$ pound.

SUGARPLUMS

1 cup golden raisins
1 cup diced dried apricots
1 cup nuts
2 tablespoons light corn syrup
1/8 teaspoon almond extract
2 packages (12 ounces each) pitted prunes
Granulated sugar
Candied green-pineapple strips or sliced green candied cherries

Force first 3 ingredients through coarse blade of food chopper. Add corn syrup and almond extract and work with hands until well blended. Shape in 2 rolls 13" long and 1" in diameter. Cut crosswise in $1/4''$ slices. Shape slices in small balls and put one in cavity of each prune. Roll in sugar and decorate with a strip of candied pineapple or slice of cherry. Arrange in airtight box in single layers with waxed paper between; store in cool place. Makes $2^1/2$ pounds.

COFFEE SUGARED PECANS

2 cups pecan halves
1/3 cup sugar
1-1/2 teaspoons instant-coffee powder
1/4 teaspoon cinnamon
Dash of salt

Combine all ingredients in saucepan. Bring to boil and boil about 3 minutes, stirring, until liquid is absorbed and turns to sugar. Cool on waxed paper.

PEANUT BRITTLE

A light, porous brittle.

1 cup light corn syrup
1 cup sugar
1 tablespoon margarine
1/4 teaspoon salt
2 cups raw Spanish peanuts (see Note)
1 teaspoon baking soda

Put first 4 ingredients in saucepan over medium heat and stir until sugar is dissolved. Add peanuts and cook, stirring, 15 to 20 minutes, or until peanuts are a light golden brown (296°F. on candy thermometer). Remove from heat and stir in soda (mixture will foam). Spread quickly on well-greased baking sheet. When cool, break in pieces. Makes about $1^1/2$ pounds. **Note** Raw (unroasted) peanuts are available in nut shops, health-food stores and occasionally in supermarkets.

SPARKLING JELLY CANDIES

1 bottle liquid pectin
1/2 teaspoon baking soda
1 cup sugar
1 cup light corn syrup
1/4 teaspoon vanilla extract
Food coloring
Tiny multicolored candies, colored sugar, toasted coconut, silver dragees, finely chopped nuts or granulated sugar

Combine pectin and 2 tablespoons water in 2-quart saucepan. Stir in baking soda (mixture will foam slightly). Mix sugar and corn syrup in another saucepan. Place both saucepans over *high heat* and cook both mixtures, stirring alternately, until foam has thinned from pectin mixture and sugar mixture is boiling rapidly—about 3 to 5 minutes. Pour pectin mixture in a slow, steady stream into boiling sugar mixture, stirring. Boil, stirring, 1 minute longer. Remove from heat and stir in vanilla and coloring to tint desired shade. Pour at once into buttered 9" square or 9" x 5" x 3" loaf pan. Let stand at room temperature until mixture is cool and firm—about 3 hours or overnight. Invert pan onto waxed paper. Cut candy in desired shapes with cutters or knife dipped in warm water. Roll in tiny multicolored candies. Let stand overnight, uncovered, at room temperature; before packaging or storing. Makes about 1 pound. **Crème de Menthe Candies** Increase last boiling time to 2 minutes, and after removing from heat, omit vanilla and add $1/4$ cup green crème de menthe. **Nut Candies** Add $1/2$ cup chopped walnuts to cooked mixture and pour into small molds.

POPCORN BALLS

4 quarts popped corn
2 cups coarsely chopped pecans
1 cup butter or margarine
1-1/3 cups sugar
1/2 cup light corn syrup
1 teaspoon vanilla extract

Mix first 2 ingredients in 6-quart mixing bowl. Melt butter in small heavy saucepan and add sugar and corn syrup. Bring to boil, stirring, and simmer 3 minutes. Add vanilla and blend well. Pour over popcorn and nuts, mixing constantly. Let stand 2 minutes to cool. With hands dampened in cold water, shape in 2½″ balls and arrange on baking sheet to set. Wrap each in plastic wrap and store in cool dry place. Makes about 20.

BLACK-WALNUT BRITTLE

1/2 cup light or dark corn syrup
2 cups sugar
1/4 teaspoon salt
3 tablespoons butter or margarine
1 cup coarsely broken black walnuts
1 teaspoon vanilla extract

Mix first 4 ingredients with ⅓ cup water in saucepan. Bring to boil, stirring until sugar is dissolved. Add nuts and cook, stirring almost constantly, until a small amount of mixture separates in hard brittle threads when dropped in very cold water (300°F. on a candy thermometer). Add vanilla and pour onto buttered baking sheet to cool. When cold, break in irregular pieces. Makes about 1¼ pounds. **Almond Brittle** Follow recipe for Black-walnut Brittle, substituting 1 cup blanched almonds, split, for walnuts.

VIENNESE CHOCOLATE CONFECTION

1 egg
1/2 cup sugar
2 cups ground blanched almonds
1/2 cup slivered blanched almonds
1 cup grated sweet cooking chocolate
    (about 1-1/2 packages, 4 ounces each)
1/2 cup finely diced citron
Superfine granulated sugar, white or
    colored

Beat egg and sugar until fluffy. Add next 4 ingredients. Heat mixture in top of double boiler over hot water until warm, stirring constantly until well blended. Cool. Lightly spread a baking board or sheet of waxed paper with superfine sugar. Put mixture on it and, between sugared hands, shape into a sausage about 11″ long. Roll in sugar. Dry in cool place overnight. Cut in thin slices. Makes about 1½ pounds.

GREEK CHOCOLATE BALLS

1/2 pound walnut meats
1/2 pound sweet cooking chocolate
9 pieces zwieback
1/2 teaspoon cinnamon
Confectioners' sugar
2 tablespoons rose water

Put first 3 ingredients through fine blade of food chopper. Add cinnamon, 1½ tablespoons sugar and rose water. Form into 36 small balls. Roll in sugar. Store balls airtight. Makes 36.

PEANUT-BUTTER AND PRUNE SQUARES

1-1/4 cups vanilla-wafer crumbs
1/2 teaspoon double-acting baking
    powder
1/4 teaspoon salt
1/2 cup peanut butter (any style)
2 eggs, well beaten
2/3 cup maple-blended syrup
1 cup pitted cooked prunes, in fourths
Granulated or confectioners' sugar

Mix first 3 ingredients, then mix peanut butter, eggs and syrup until smooth. Add prunes, then add to crumb mixture. Grease 8″ square pan and line with waxed paper. Pour in batter and bake in moderate oven (350°F.) about 30 minutes. Turn out of pan and peel off paper. Cut in 16 squares and roll in sugar. **Note** To make crumbs, put wafers in plastic bag; crush with rolling pin.

EASY PEANUT FUDGE

3/4 cup riced hot cooked potato
1/2 cup peanut butter
1 teaspoon vanilla extract
1/8 teaspoon salt
3-1/2 to 4 cups sifted confectioners'
    sugar
1/2 cup chopped chocolate-peanut
    candy bar

Mix first 4 ingredients; add enough sugar to make a stiff mixture. Fold in candy and spread in buttered 8″ or 9″ piepan. Chill and cut in pieces. Makes about 1½ pounds.

COFFEE-PEANUT STUFFED DATES

1 teaspoon instant-coffee powder
1/4 cup peanut butter, any style
About 21 pitted dates
Confectioners' sugar

Mix coffee and 1 teaspoon water. Add to peanut butter and mix well. Use to stuff dates; roll in confectioners' sugar.

HARRY HARTMAN

Flambéed Oranges with Strawberries

THE APPROPRIATE DESSERT

A good dessert can be the happy climax to a meal and can also help to round it out nutritionally. If the day's menus have been short on milk, eggs or fruits, the omission can be rectified by dessert at dinner. The dessert should be geared to the rest of the meal and can supplement a light meal or add a delicate finish to a heavier one. The high point of a light meal might be a gorgeous cheesecake. Fruit is often the best choice, and a basket or bowl of fresh fruit can be used as a centerpiece as well. Cheese and crackers go well with a ripe pear or apple. Ice cream is convenient, wholesome and universally popular.

BROWNIE PUDDING 'N' SAUCE

Sift ½ cup all-purpose flour, 1 teaspoon baking powder, ½ teaspoon salt, ⅓ cup sugar and 1 tablespoon Dutch-process cocoa. Add ¼ cup milk, 1 tablespoon melted butter and ½ teaspoon vanilla. Stir in ¼ cup chopped nuts; pour into deep 9″ piepan. Mix ½ cup packed brown sugar and 2 tablespoons cocoa; sprinkle on batter. Pour ¾ cup boiling water over top. Bake at 350°F. about 35 minutes. Serve with cream, plain or whipped. Makes 4 to 6 servings.

CRANBERRY-APPLE CRISP

Serve warm with cream or vanilla ice cream.

2 cups fresh cranberries
3 cups coarsely chopped peeled apples
1 cup granulated sugar
1-1/2 cups rolled oats
1 cup packed brown sugar
1/2 cup butter or margarine
1/2 teaspoon salt

Combine first 3 ingredients. Turn into buttered 9″ piepan or 8″ square baking dish. With pastry blender or fingertips, work together remaining ingredients to make a crumbly mixture. Sprinkle on fruit. Bake in moderate oven (350°F.) 1 hour. Makes 6 to 8 servings.

CHOCOLATE SOUFFLÉ

A dessert classic.

2 squares unsweetened chocolate
2 cups milk
1/2 cup sugar
1/3 cup flour
1/2 teaspoon salt
2 tablespoons butter or margarine
1 teaspoon vanilla extract
4 eggs, separated
Sweetened whipped cream

Melt chocolate in milk in top part of double boiler over boiling water. Beat until blended. Mix sugar, flour and salt; stir in small amount of chocolate mixture. Return to double boiler and cook, stirring, until thickened; cook 5 minutes longer. Remove from heat and stir in butter and vanilla; cool slightly. Beat egg whites until stiff. Beat egg yolks until thick and lemon-colored. Stir yolks into chocolate mixture; fold in whites. Pour into buttered 1½-quart soufflé dish or casserole. Put in pan of hot water and bake in moderate oven (350°F.) 1 hour and 15 minutes, or until firm. Serve at once with whipped cream. Serves 6 to 8.

BAKED APPLES WITH WINE

Core 6 large baking apples and peel a 1″ strip from stem end. Put in baking dish. In each cavity, put 2 tablespoons honey, 1 tablespoon seedless raisins and 2 split blanched almonds. Put 1 cup water in dish and bake, uncovered, in moderate oven (350°F.) 30 minutes. Remove from oven and baste with syrup in bottom of dish. Pour 1 tablespoon muscatel wine over each apple. Bake 20 minutes, or until done, basting frequently with the syrup. Serves 6.

LEMON-SOUFFLÉ BREAD PUDDING

2 cups crust-trimmed bread cubes
3/4 cup sugar
Juice and grated rind of 1 lemon
1/2 cup melted butter
4 eggs, separated
2/3 cup milk
Whipped cream
Nutmeg

Mix together first 3 ingredients. Stir in butter. Beat egg yolks until thick and lemon-colored; add milk and pour over the bread. Fold in stiffly beaten egg whites. Pour into a buttered 1½-quart casserole. Bake in a moderate oven (350°F.) for 30 minutes. Serve hot with cream flavored with freshly grated nutmeg. Makes 6 servings.

ORANGE MARMALADE SOUFFLÉ WITH SUPER SAUCE

4 egg whites (yolks used in sauce)
Sugar
3 tablespoons orange juice
1 tablespoon brandy
1/4 cup orange marmalade
Butter
Super Sauce
Toasted almond slivers

Beat egg whites until stiff but not dry; gradually beat in ¼ cup sugar and continue beating until mixture stands in peaks. Fold in orange juice, brandy and marmalade. Butter a 2-quart double boiler, including the cover, and sprinkle generously with sugar. Pour in pudding and place over boiling water. Cover and cook 50 to 60 minutes. (Do not remove cover.) Turn out on serving plate. Pour Super Sauce over soufflé and sprinkle with toasted almond slivers. Makes 6 servings. **Super Sauce** Beat 4 egg yolks and ⅓ cup confectioners' sugar until thick and lemon-colored. Fold in ¼ cup orange juice, 2 tablespoons brandy and ¾ cup heavy cream, whipped. Makes about 2 cups.

ORANGE SOUFFLÉ

1 can (6 ounces) frozen orange-juice
  concentrate, thawed
Butter or margarine
3 tablespoons flour
4 eggs, separated
Pinch of salt
Sugar

Add enough water to orange juice to make 1 cup of liquid. Melt 3 tablespoons butter and blend in the flour. Slowly add liquid, stirring, and cook until thickened; cool slightly. Add egg yolks beaten until light. Beat egg whites with salt until stiff but still moist. Fold half of whites into orange mixture rather thoroughly; then fold in rest very lightly. Sprinkle bottom and sides of buttered 2-quart soufflé dish lightly with sugar. Pour in mixture and bake in moderate oven (375°F.) about 30 minutes. Makes 4 to 6 servings.

CREPES SUZETTE

Put out the lights when you flame the crepes if you wish. It is very dramatic.

Grated rind of 1 orange and juice
Grated rind of 1 lemon and juice
1 cup sugar
1/4 cup butter
1/4 cup dark rum
1/4 cup curaçao or Triple Sec
1/2 cup French brandy (Cognac)
French Dessert Pancakes at right

Cook rinds and juices in a small saucepan with sugar 5 minutes, or until syrupy, stirring occasionally. This can be done ahead; complete the sauce just before serving. Melt the butter in either 12" iron skillet placed over low heat on top of the stove, electric skillet, or a chafing dish with a shallow pan (the same size as the skillet). Add fruit syrup and let bubble. Add rum, curaçao and half the brandy and simmer again to blend. Have cooked French Dessert Pancakes ready beside the skillet or chafing dish. Put 1 pancake at a time into bubbling sauce. Using 2 forks, fold the edges together to an envelope. Push to one side and add the next crepe. Continue until all have been properly shaped. (Or transfer each shaped crepe to a flat baking dish and keep warm in a 350°F. oven.) Return crepes to skillet; add last 1/4 cup brandy. Heat until just warm but do not boil. (Brandy must be warm to flame.) Ignite; tilt the pan back and forth until all the liquor has burned out. Serve at once. Makes 4 to 6 servings, allowing 2 or 3 crepes for each person.

FRENCH-FRIED CAMEMBERT

6 wedges (1-3/4 ounces each)
  Camembert cheese, chilled
2 eggs, slightly beaten
Fine dry bread crumbs
Vegetable shortening for deep frying

Cut each wedge in half lengthwise. Dip in eggs and crumbs. Fry in hot deep shortening (400°F. on a frying thermometer) for just 1/2 minute. Serve at once. Good with chilled grapes or apple slices. Serves 6.

FRENCH DESSERT PANCAKES

Crepes can be made ahead and reheated on top of stove, in the oven or in a chafing dish.

1/2 cup all-purpose flour
2 eggs, well beaten
2 teaspoons French brandy (Cognac) or
  bourbon whiskey
2 tablespoons confectioners' sugar
3/4 cup milk
Butter

Sift flour and add eggs and brandy. Beat in sugar alternately with milk; add 1 teaspoon melted butter. Beat well with electric mixer or egg beater. This batter is very thin, about the consistency of thick cream. Heat a 6" skillet. Add 1/2 teaspoon butter, or more if needed. When melted and sizzling, pour 1 or 2 tablespoonfuls of the batter all at once into the pan, tilting the skillet until the batter completely covers the bottom of pan. When one side of crepe is brown, turn and brown on other side. If holes appear in pancake add a little more batter to "patch" the hole. Makes 10 or 11 crepes, or 4 or 5 servings.

HUNGARIAN CHEESE PANCAKES

Soak 1/3 cup currants or slivered seeded raisins overnight in 2 tablespoons rum or brandy. Prepare French Dessert Pancakes, above. Mix currants and rum with 1 cup cottage cheese, 1/4 cup confectioners' sugar or more to taste, 1 egg yolk, grated rind of 1/2 lemon and 1/2 teaspoon vanilla. Spread by the spoonful on the pancakes and roll; turn ends into roll and secure with toothpicks if necessary. Dip each roll in mixture of 1 egg beaten with 1 tablespoon milk; then roll at once in a mixture of half fine dry bread crumbs and half ground almonds. Brown in melted butter in hot skillet. Serve hot with sweetened and flavored whipped cream. Allow 2 rolls per serving; remove toothpicks. Makes 5 to 6 servings.

CREPES DREI HUSAREN

Butter
2 tablespoons all-purpose flour
1/2 cup milk
2 tablespoons granulated sugar
4 eggs, separated
2 teaspoons vanilla extract
1/8 teaspoon salt
Raspberry Purée
1 cup heavy cream, chilled
3 tablespoons sifted confectioners' sugar

Melt 2 tablespoons butter in skillet or saucepan. Stir in flour. Then slowly pour in the milk and cook, stirring constantly, until smooth and the consistency of medium white sauce. Remove from heat; with a wire whisk beat in sugar, egg yolks and 1 teaspoon vanilla. (If desired, this can be made a few hours ahead, but do not refrigerate; cover and leave at room temperature. Crepes are best if made and baked at the last moment, however.) Use 4 shallow glass or pottery baking dishes 6" in circumference and 1" deep, or foil piepans. Brush dishes with melted butter. When you are ready to cook, beat egg white with the salt until stiff; fold in half of the whites. Then quickly fold in the other half. Pour batter into dishes and place in hot oven (400°F.). Cook until tops are lightly browned and crepes no longer shake, or about 5 to 10 minutes. Loosen edges and turn upside down on a dessert plate. Pour a generous amount of Raspberry Purée over them. Surround with dabs of cream whipped fairly thick and flavored with confectioners' sugar and remaining vanilla. Makes 4 servings. Crepes can also be served with preserves. **Raspberry Purée** Wash and drain 1 pint ripe red raspberries. Place in the blender with ½ cup sugar and whirl until thoroughly blended. Strain through a fine-meshed wire strainer.

STRAWBERRY WHIP

1 cup strawberries washed, hulled and
    sliced
Dash of salt
1 egg white, at room temperature
1 cup confectioners' sugar

Put strawberries in small bowl of electric mixer with the salt, egg white and confectioners' sugar. Beat until very stiff. Serve with custard sauce or as a topping for dessert pancakes, waffles, angel cake or fruit. Makes 4 servings.

SWEDISH PANCAKES WITH LINGONBERRY CREAM (Plattar med lingongradde)

A Swedish pancake pan is cast-iron with seven ¼"-deep depressions 3" in diameter. It is necessary, since batter is runny and must be held in molds.

1 cup all-purpose flour
2 tablespoons sugar
1/4 teaspoon salt
3 eggs, beaten
3 cups milk
1/4 cup butter or margarine, melted
1/2 cup heavy cream, whipped
1/2 cup lingonberry preserves

Mix flour, sugar and salt. Mix eggs and milk and add to dry ingredients. Heat Swedish pancake pan slowly. Brush individual sections of hot pan with melted butter. Stir batter, then put about 1 measuring-tablespoonful into each section. Brown on both sides. Pile pancakes on top of each other and transfer to hot serving platter. Keep platter warm over pan of boiling water. Mix whipped cream and preserves and serve with pancakes. Makes 8 servings. **Note** Pancakes can be served with sugar and other preserves instead of whipped cream and lingonberry preserves.

BANANA CREPES WITH CHEESE SAUCE

1-1/3 cups all-purpose flour
3 eggs
1 tablespoon vegetable oil
1/2 teaspoon salt
Milk
8 all-yellow small bananas, peeled
Few drops Angostura bitters
Salt, pepper and cayenne
1/2 pound Gruyère or Swiss cheese,
    shredded
1 cup thick white sauce
Melted butter or margarine
1/2 cup cream (or milk)

Mix first 4 ingredients with about 1½ cups of milk to make a smooth batter. Chill 1 hour, then add enough more milk to make batter the consistency of slightly whipped heavy cream. Bake batter on one side only in small skillet to form 8 crepes about 6" in diameter. Put a banana on each crepe, sprinkle with bitters, seasonings and about 3 tablespoons cheese. Add 1 tablespoon white sauce and roll crepe around banana. Arrange in greased shallow baking dish; brush with butter. Bake in hot oven (400°F.) 15 minutes. Stir remaining cheese and cream into remaining white sauce, pour over crepes and return to oven 8 minutes, or until bananas are tender and sauce is just beginning to brown. Makes 8 servings.

DESSERT TOMATOES

Select firm, ripe red tomatoes. Cover with boiling water; drain and peel. Chill several hours. Cut in thick slices. Serve ice cold in chilled dishes with heavy cream and a sprinkling of fine granulated sugar.

STEAMED CHOCOLATE PUDDING

A cakelike pudding, served with sauce or whipped cream.

1-1/2 squares unsweetened chocolate
3 tablespoons butter or margarine
1/2 cup sugar
1 egg
1/2 teaspoon vanilla extract
1 cup all-purpose flour
1-1/2 teaspoons baking powder
1/4 teaspoon salt
1/2 cup milk
Foamy Sauce, page 399

Melt chocolate and butter in 2-quart saucepan. Remove from heat. Stir in sugar, egg and vanilla. Add sifted dry ingredients alternately with milk. Pour into well-greased 1-quart pudding mold. Cover and put on rack in kettle. Add boiling water to come halfway up sides of mold. Cover kettle; steam pudding about 1½ hours. Serve hot with sauce. Serves 6.

PLUM PUDDING

1/2 cup sugar
3 cups all-purpose flour
1 teaspoon baking soda
1-1/2 teaspoons salt
1/2 teaspoon each ginger, cloves and
   nutmeg
1 teaspoon cinnamon
1/2 cup each currants and raisins,
   soaked overnight in 1/3 cup brandy
2/3 cup chopped mixed candied fruit
1 apple, grated
1/2 cup chopped nuts
1 cup finely chopped suet
1-1/2 cups milk
1/2 cup molasses
1/2 cup brandy
Brandy Hard Sauce (page 398) or Super
   Sauce (page 367)

Sift dry ingredients and add fruits and nuts. Stir in next 3 ingredients. Pour into 1 buttered 2½-quart mold or two 1½-quart molds. Cover tightly with lid or double thickness of waxed paper or foil. Secure paper or foil with rubber bands or string. Put on rack in large kettle and add boiling water to come halfway up sides of mold. Cover kettle and steam 3 hours. Unmold on serving plate and decorate with holly sprig. Pour heated and flaming brandy over top. Serve with either sauce. Makes 8 servings.

BAKED APPLE TAPIOCA

Peel and slice 3 large tart apples and put in shallow baking dish. Mix juice of 1 lemon and 3 cups water. Pour over apples; cover and bake in moderate oven (375°F.) about 45 minutes. Mix 1 cup packed brown sugar, ½ cup quick-cooking tapioca, ½ teaspoon salt, ¼ teaspoon mace and 2 tablespoons melted butter. Stir into apples. Cover and bake 15 minutes, stirring once. Serve at once with cream. Makes 6 servings.

STEAMED CARROT PUDDING

1 cup coarse dry bread crumbs
1 cup packed brown sugar
1/2 cup all-purpose flour
1 teaspoon each baking powder and
   baking soda
3/4 teaspoon salt
1 teaspoon cinnamon
1/2 teaspoon each nutmeg and allspice
1 egg
1/2 cup diced candied orange peel
1 cup golden raisins
1 cup grated peeled raw carrot
1 cup grated peeled raw potato
1 cup chopped peeled tart apple
1/2 cup butter
Hard Sauce, page 398, or Foamy Sauce,
   page 399

Combine in order given all ingredients, except sauce; mix well. Pack into greased 1½-quart pudding mold. Cover and steam 4 hours, or until done. Serve warm, topped with sauce. Makes 8 to 10 servings.

RICE IMPERIAL

1 cup candied fruit
1/4 cup brandy
1 cup uncooked rice
1/4 teaspoon salt
2 cups milk
1 envelope unflavored gelatin
4 egg yolks
1 cup sugar
1 teaspoon vanilla extract
Heavy cream

Soak fruit overnight in brandy. Cook rice in boiling water to cover about 10 minutes. Drain. Add salt and 1⅓ cups milk; cook until rice is tender. Cool. Meanwhile sprinkle gelatin on ⅔ cup cold milk in top of double boiler. Add egg yolks, sugar and vanilla. Cook over simmering water, stirring constantly, until thickened. Cool; add to rice. Fold in brandied fruit and 1 cup heavy cream, whipped. Pour into 1½-quart mold and chill until firm. Unmold and decorate with whipped cream. Makes 6 to 8 servings.

BAKED ROSY RHUBARB

Cut 1 pound unpeeled rhubarb in 1" lengths. Mix in shallow baking dish with 1 cup sugar and ¼ cup water. Bake in moderate oven (350°F.) 35 minutes, or until rhubarb is just tender. Chill and serve. Makes 4 servings.

ITALIAN STRAWBERRIES

Sprinkle 2 or more tablespoons sugar over 4 cups washed and hulled strawberries; cover with ¾ cup dry wine or orange juice. Chill before serving. Makes 4 to 6 servings.

MERINGUE KISSES CHANTILLY

Prepare 1 box (6½ ounces) fluffy white frosting mix as directed on the label, using only ⅓ cup water. Fold in ½ cup chopped nuts or flaked coconut. Drop by rounded teaspoonfuls onto brown paper on cookie sheet. Bake in moderate oven (325°F.) about 20 minutes. Cool and remove from paper with sharp knife. To serve, put flat sides of 2 meringue kisses together with 2 heaping teaspoonfuls Cream Chantilly. Top with partially thawed frozen raspberries. Makes 8 to 10 servings. **Cream Chantilly** Whip 1 cup heavy cream, 1½ cups sifted confectioners' sugar and 1½ teaspoons vanilla extract.

PARTY FRUIT DESSERT

You must make this the day before.

1 box (3 ounces) lime-flavor gelatin
1 cup fine graham-cracker crumbs
1/4 cup butter or margarine, melted
1 box pineapple-flavor gelatin
1/4 cup sugar
2 cups heavy cream, whipped
1 can (8 ounces) pineapple tidbits, drained
1 can (8 ounces) sliced peaches, drained
1 cup miniature marshmallows
10 maraschino cherries, halved

Dissolve lime gelatin in 1 cup boiling water. Stir in ½ cup cold water. Pour into 8" square pan and chill until firm. Mix crumbs and butter. Press on bottom of 9" springform or loose-bottomed pan; chill. Dissolve pineapple gelatin and sugar in 1 cup boiling water; add ½ cup cold water and chill until slightly thickened. Cut firm lime gelatin in cubes. Fold cubes, whipped cream and remaining ingredients into pineapple gelatin. Pour into springform pan and chill overnight. Remove sides of pan before serving. Makes 12 servings.

HILLBILLY PUDDIN'

Fruit (see Note)
Sugar
1/4 cup cornmeal
1/4 cup flour
3/4 teaspoon baking powder
1/8 teaspoon salt
1 egg
3 tablespoons milk
1/4 teaspoon vanilla extract
6 tablespoons butter, melted
1/2 teaspoon cinnamon
Vanilla ice cream or whipped cream

Sweeten frozen or fresh fruit with sugar to taste, using ½ to ¾ cup sugar, depending on kind of fruit. Mix in bowl next 4 ingredients and ⅓ cup sugar. Combine egg, milk and vanilla. Stir into first mixture to form a smooth batter. Add fruit. Pour butter into 1-quart casserole. Sprinkle with cinnamon. Spoon in fruit batter and bake in hot oven (400°F.) about 20 minutes. Reduce heat to 350°F. and bake 15 to 25 minutes longer, or until firm. Serve warm with ice cream. Makes 4 servings. *Note* For fruit, use 1 box (1 pound) thawed frozen blueberries, sliced strawberries, rhubarb or peaches. Or use 2 cups pitted fresh red cherries, sliced peaches, rhubarb or plums.

STRAWBERRY CHARLOTTE

A classic French masterpiece.

2 envelopes unflavored gelatin
3/4 cup sugar
1/4 teaspoon salt
4 eggs, separated
2 boxes (10 ounces each) frozen sliced strawberries
2 teaspoons grated lemon rind
2 tablespoons lemon juice
10 ladyfingers
Heavy cream, whipped
Fresh strawberries

In top of double boiler beat gelatin, ¼ cup sugar, the salt, egg yolks and ½ cup water. Add 1 box strawberries. Cook over boiling water, stirring, until gelatin is dissolved and berries thawed. Remove from heat; add remaining box of strawberries, lemon rind and juice. Stir until berries are thawed. Chill, stirring occasionally, until mixture mounds when dropped from spoon. Split ladyfingers and stand around edge of 9" springform or loose-bottomed pan. Beat egg whites until stiff. Gradually beat in remaining ½ cup sugar. Fold into gelatin mixture with 1 cup cream, whipped. Pour into pan and chill until firm. Remove from pan and garnish with more whipped cream and strawberries. Makes 10 to 12 servings.

APPLE-RAISIN COBBLER

3 medium tart cooking apples
1/4 cup raisins
1/4 cup packed brown sugar
1/4 cup granulated sugar
2 tablespoons corn syrup
1/4 cup soft butter or margarine
1/2 teaspoon salt
1/2 teaspoon cinnamon
1 small box yellow-cake mix

Peel, core and cut apples in thin slices. Arrange in 9" x 9" x 2" pan. Mix remaining ingredients, except cake mix; sprinkle on apples. Prepare cake mix as directed on label and pour over first mixture. Bake as directed. Cut in squares and serve. Makes 9 servings.

BANANAS FLAMBÉ

Melt 1/4 cup butter in top pan of chafing dish over direct heat. Cut 6 peeled ripe bananas in half lengthwise; sprinkle with 2 tablespoons brown sugar and a dash of cinnamon. Cook until bananas are lightly browned. Turn and sprinkle again with sugar and cinnamon. When soft, add 1/4 cup rum and ignite. Spoon sauce on bananas. Makes 4 servings.

OLD COLONY GINGERBREAD WAFFLES

These waffles are delicious for dessert topped with cinnamon-flavored whipped cream or Mock Devonshire Cream, page 399.

1 cup plus 1 tablespoon all-purpose flour
1-1/4 teaspoons double-acting baking powder
1/4 teaspoon baking soda
1 teaspoon ginger
1/4 teaspoon each cloves and nutmeg
3/4 teaspoon cinnamon
1/8 teaspoon salt
1/3 cup butter and solid vegetable shortening (mixed)
1/3 cup packed dark-brown sugar
1/2 cup dark molasses
1 egg, well beaten

Sift dry ingredients. Add shortenings to 1/2 cup boiling water and stir until dissolved; add sugar and molasses. Cool to room temperature. Add to dry ingredients with egg and beat until batter is smooth. Pour into waffle iron. Use about 3/4 cup batter for each waffle (depending on size of iron). Serve one section to a person. Extra batter can be refrigerated for several days in a covered container. Cooked sections can be frozen and reheated in toaster. Makes 2 large waffles or 8 servings. *Note* These waffles become crisp as they cool.

GOLDEN CHEESECAKE

1-2/3 cups fine graham-cracker crumbs
1/3 cup butter or margarine, melted
2 envelopes unflavored gelatin
3/4 cup sugar
1/2 teaspoon salt
1/3 cup milk
3 eggs, separated
2 packages (8 ounces each) cream cheese
1-1/4 cups puréed cooked sweet potatoes
1 cup heavy cream, whipped
2 teaspoons vanilla extract
1 teaspoon grated orange rind

Mix crumbs and butter; reserve 1/4 cup. Press remainder on bottom of 9" springform pan. Chill. Soften gelatin in 1/2 cup cold water in top part of small double boiler. Add 1/2 cup sugar, the salt, milk and slightly beaten egg yolks. Cook over boiling water, stirring, until slightly thickened. Pour over cheese and potatoes; beat until smooth and blended. Cool. Beat egg whites until foamy; add 1/4 cup sugar and beat until stiff. Fold into cheese mixture with cream and flavorings. Pour into prepared pan, sprinkle with reserved crumbs and chill until firm. Makes 12 servings.

JELLIED CHEESECAKE

3 cups cornflakes
1/3 cup butter or margarine, softened
1/2 teaspoon cinnamon
1 cup sugar
2 envelopes unflavored gelatin
1/2 teaspoon salt
2 eggs, separated
1 cup milk
1 pound (2 cups) fine-curd creamed cottage cheese
Grated rind and juice of 1 lemon
1 cup heavy cream, whipped
1 can (22 ounces) cherry pie filling (optional)

Crush cornflakes fine with rolling pin (or whirl in blender). Mix with butter, cinnamon and 1/4 cup sugar. Press firmly on bottom of buttered 9" springform pan. In top part of double boiler, beat gelatin, 3/4 cup sugar, the salt, egg yolks and milk with rotary beater until blended. Put over simmering water and cook, stirring, until mixture is slightly thickened and coats metal spoon. Remove from heat and cool. Force cheese through ricer or coarse sieve. Add cooled gelatin mixture, lemon rind and juice. Fold in stiffly beaten egg whites and cream. Pour into pan and chill several hours, or until firm. If desired, heat pie filling, spread on top and chill. Remove sides of pan and set cake on serving plate. Makes 10 to 12 servings.

FLAMBEED ORANGES WITH STRAWBERRIES

4 large thick-skinned oranges, peeled, cut in segments and drained
Spiral of orange peel
2 tablespoons butter or margarine
1/3 cup sugar
2 tablespoons frozen orange-juice concentrate
2 tablespoons Grand Marnier
Fresh or thawed frozen strawberries
Pistachio nuts

Arrange orange segments in small skillet and put spiral of peel in center. Heat gently. Meanwhile, mix next 3 ingredients in small heavy saucepan. Bring to boil over medium heat, stirring constantly. Simmer 5 minutes, or until lightly browned, bubbly, thick and glossy. Pour at once over hot orange segments and heat 1 minute. Heat liqueur over boiling water. Remove oranges from heat, pour liqueur over and ignite. Serve on strawberries with a sprinkling of pistachio nuts. Makes 4 servings. *Note* Oranges are also good on vanilla ice cream.

LEMON CAKE PUDDING

It has a cakelike top and a delicious lemon sauce beneath.

1 cup sugar
3 tablespoons soft butter
3 tablespoons flour
2 eggs, separated
Juice and grated rind of 1 lemon
1 cup milk

Cream sugar and butter; add flour, beaten egg yolks, rind and juice and milk. Mix well and fold in stiffly beaten egg whites. Pour into 1-quart casserole. Put in pan of hot water and bake in moderate oven (325°F.) about 1 hour. Makes 4 servings.

SWEET-POTATO PUDDING

1/4 cup butter or margarine
1/2 cup packed brown sugar
2 eggs, separated
1/4 cup milk
1/2 teaspoon salt
1/4 teaspoon nutmeg
1/8 teaspoon each ginger and cinnamon
1 cup mashed cooked sweet potato
Hard Sauce (page 398), Foamy Sauce (page 399) or cream

Cream butter and sugar together. Add well-beaten egg yolks and next 5 ingredients. Fold in stiffly beaten egg whites and turn into 1½-quart casserole. Bake in moderate oven (350°F.) 40 minutes. Serve warm with sauce or cream. Makes 4 servings.

BLUEBERRY CRISP

4 cups fresh blueberries, washed
1 teaspoon grated lemon rind
3/4 cup packed brown sugar
1/2 cup all-purpose flour
1/4 teaspoon cinnamon
1/4 cup butter or margarine, softened
Cream (optional)

Put berries in shallow baking dish or deep 9" piepan. Sprinkle with lemon rind. Blend remaining ingredients, except cream; sprinkle on berries. Bake in moderate oven (375° F.) 25 minutes. Serve warm, with cream, if desired. Serves 6.

DOUBLE-BOILER CHOCOLATE PUDDING

In top part of double boiler, combine 2 or 3 squares unsweetened chocolate, 1 cup milk, ½ cup sugar, ½ teaspoon cinnamon and ⅛ teaspoon salt. Heat over simmering water until chocolate is dissolved. Beat with rotary beater until smooth. Then add 3 unbeaten eggs all at once and 1 teaspoon vanilla extract; beat 1 minute. Cover and cook 40 minutes. Serve warm with whipped cream. Makes 4 servings.

APPLES BAKED IN LEMON CUSTARD

Wash and core 4 small baking apples. Peel top third. Put in 1½-quart baking dish. Cover and bake in moderate oven (350°F.) 30 to 45 minutes, or until tender. Beat together 1 egg, ⅓ cup sugar, ¼ cup milk, grated rind of 1 lemon, 1 tablespoon lemon juice and 3 tablespoons melted butter. Add any juice from apples and mix well. Pour over apples and bake, uncovered, 10 minutes. Put in dishes and serve at once with custard sauce in pan. Serves 4.

PINEAPPLE BREAD PUDDING

1 can (9 ounces) crushed pineapple
2 cups soft stale-bread crumbs
2 cups milk, scalded
1/2 teaspoon salt
2 eggs, beaten
1/3 cup honey
1 tablespoon lemon juice
Lemon Hard Sauce, page 398

Drain pineapple and add enough water or other fruit juice to syrup to make ¼ cup. Combine syrup and pineapple with remaining ingredients, except sauce; mix well. Pour into 1½-quart baking dish. Bake in moderate oven (325°F.) about 45 minutes. Serve with sauce. Makes 4 servings.

BANANA-GINGERBREAD DESSERT

4 or 5 fully ripe medium bananas, peeled
  (2 cups mashed)
3 tablespoons lemon juice
1 package (14 ounces) gingerbread mix
1 cup golden raisins
Vanilla ice cream

Sprinkle bananas with lemon juice and mash with potato masher; measure 2 cups. Add to gingerbread mix and beat with electric mixer at medium speed until well mixed. Fold in raisins and put in greased 6-cup ring mold. Bake in moderate oven (350°F.) about 45 minutes. Let stand in mold 5 to 10 minutes, then unmold and serve slightly warm with center filled with ice cream. Makes 8 servings.

PEACH CRISP

6 or 7 large peaches, peeled and sliced
Juice of 1 lemon
1 cup all-purpose flour
1 cup packed brown sugar
1/2 cup butter or margarine
Hard Sauce (page 398)

Put peaches in greased shallow 2-quart baking dish and sprinkle with the lemon juice. Mix flour and sugar. Cut in butter with pastry blender or fingers until mixture is crumbly. Press on top of peaches and bake in moderate oven (375°F.) 25 minutes, or until peaches are tender. Serve warm with Hard Sauce. Makes 6 servings.

CHEESE-PRUNE PUDDING

1 package (8 ounces) regular or imitation
  cream cheese, softened
1/4 cup butter or margarine
1/4 cup granulated sugar
4 eggs, separated
Grated rind and juice of 1 lemon
3/4 cup finely cut ready-to-eat pitted
  prunes
1 cup dairy sour cream
1/3 cup coarsely shredded sharp Cheddar
  cheese
Light cream (optional)

Cream first 3 ingredients in mixing bowl until light and fluffy. Beat in egg yolks, lemon rind and juice, then fold in prunes and sour cream. Beat egg whites until stiff but not dry and fold into first mixture. Pour into buttered 2-quart casserole and sprinkle with Cheddar cheese. Set casserole in pan of hot water and bake in moderate oven (350°F.) 45 minutes, or until set. Serve slightly warm, with light cream, if desired. Makes 6 servings.

PEACH DUMPLINGS

1/2 cup packed brown sugar
1/8 teaspoon each ground nutmeg and
  cinnamon
Salt
2 tablespoons lemon juice
1-1/2 cups all-purpose flour
1-1/2 teaspoons double-acting baking
  powder
1/2 cup solid vegetable shortening
Milk
4 small firm-ripe peaches, halved or 2
  medium peaches, quartered
1/4 cup granulated sugar
1 tablespoon butter or margarine
Cream

Mix brown sugar, spices, 2/3 cup water, dash of salt and the lemon juice in bowl and set aside. Mix 3/4 teaspoon salt and next 2 ingredients. Cut in shortening. Add 1/3 cup milk and stir with fork until dry ingredients are moistened. Roll out on lightly floured board to form a 12″ square. Cut in 4 smaller squares. Put a peach half or quarter in center of each square. Sprinkle with granulated sugar and dot with butter. Moisten edges of pastry squares and fold corners over fruit. Brush with milk, put in shallow baking dish and pour reserved brown-sugar syrup around dumplings. Bake in very hot oven (450°F.) 10 minutes. Reduce heat to 375°F. and bake about 30 minutes longer. Serve warm with cream. Makes 4 servings.

CRANBERRY PUDDING CAKE

1-1/2 cups cranberries
Sugar
2 teaspoons cornstarch
Butter or margarine
Dash of nutmeg
1 cup plus 2 tablespoons all-purpose flour
2 teaspoons double-acting baking powder
1/2 cup milk
1/2 cup chopped dates
1/2 cup raisins
1/2 cup chopped nuts
Heavy cream or ice cream

Put cranberries in saucepan with 1 1/3 cups water and cook until berries pop. Mix 1 cup plus 2 tablespoons sugar with the cornstarch and gradually stir into berries. Cook, stirring frequently, 5 minutes. Remove from heat and add 1 tablespoon butter and the nutmeg. Put in greased 8″ square pan. Mix flour, baking powder and 1/2 cup sugar. Cut in 1/4 cup butter until mixture is the texture of cornmeal. Add milk and mix well. Stir in fruits and nuts. Drop by tablespoonfuls into hot cranberry mixture and bake in slow oven (325°F.) about 50 minutes. Serve warm with cream. Makes 8 servings.

BLENDER APPLESAUCE

Mix 1/2 cup light corn syrup, 1/8 teaspoon salt and 1/4 cup lemon juice. Peel, core and slice 6 eating apples into mixture, stirring to keep apples coated. Blend in electric blender until smooth. Chill. Serves 4.

TOPSY-TURVY CHERRY PUDDING

Serve with whipped cream or ice cream.

1-1/4 cups sugar
2 tablespoons butter
1 cup all-purpose flour
1 teaspoon baking powder
1/8 teaspoon salt
3/4 cup milk
1 can (1 pound) red sour cherries

Cream 1 cup sugar with the butter. Sift flour, baking powder and salt; add alternately with milk to butter mixture. Pour into a buttered shallow baking dish. Combine undrained cherries with remaining 1/4 cup sugar. Heat to boiling. Pour over batter. Bake in moderate oven (350°F.) 30 minutes. Makes 6 servings.

DELI PRUNE DESSERT

1/2 cup butter
1/2 cup sugar
4 eggs, separated
3/4 cup uncooked soft prunes, finely chopped
1 cup cottage cheese, sieved
1 cup dairy sour cream
1 tablespoon lemon juice

Cream butter and sugar until light and fluffy; beat in egg yolks. Add remaining ingredients, except egg whites. Beat egg whites until stiff but not dry. Fold into first mixture. Pour into buttered 2-quart casserole and set in pan of hot water. Bake in moderate oven (350°F.) 1 hour, or until set. Makes 6 servings.

HONEY-PRUNE PUDDING

1 cup chopped pitted cooked prunes
1/2 cup honey
1/2 cup chopped nuts
Grated rind of 1 lemon
1/2 cup milk
1 tablespoon butter, melted
1/2 cup coarse dry bread crumbs
1 teaspoon double-acting baking powder
Light cream

Mix all ingredients, except cream. Pour into 1-quart baking dish. Set in shallow pan of hot water and bake in moderate oven (350°F.) about 35 minutes. Serve warm or cold with light cream. Makes 4 servings.

MOLASSES CAKE PUDDING

1/2 cup solid vegetable shortening
1 cup sugar (granulated or packed brown)
2/3 cup molasses
1-1/2 cups sifted cake flour
3/4 teaspoon baking soda
1/4 teaspoon salt
1 teaspoon ginger
1-1/2 cups soft bread crumbs
1 cup buttermilk
1 egg, beaten
Lemon Sauce, page 399

Cream shortening and sugar until light; beat in molasses. Sift dry ingredients and add to first mixture with crumbs and buttermilk. Beat 1 minute; add egg. Pour into greased 8" x 8" x 2" pan and let stand 30 minutes. Bake in moderate oven (350°F.) about 45 minutes. Serve warm with Lemon Sauce. Serves 8.

BLUEBERRY BUCKLE

1/4 cup butter
3/4 cup sugar
1 egg
2 cups all-purpose flour
2 teaspoons baking powder
1/2 teaspoon salt
1/2 cup milk
2 cups washed fresh blueberries
Crumb Topping

Cream butter, add sugar and beat until light. Add egg and beat well. Add sifted dry ingredients alternately with milk, beating until smooth. Fold in berries. Sprinkle with Crumb Topping. Bake in greased 9" x 9" x 2" pan in moderate oven (375°F.) about 35 minutes. Makes 6 to 8 servings. **Crumb Topping** Blend 1/4 cup soft butter, 1/2 cup sugar, 1/3 cup all-purpose flour and 1/2 teaspoon cinnamon.

MERINGUE CAKE PUDDING

3 cups 1/2" stale-cake cubes
1/2 cup sugar
2 eggs, separated
2 whole eggs
3 cups milk, scalded
1/4 teaspoon salt
1 teaspoon vanilla or rum extract
1/2 cup semisweet chocolate pieces

Put cake in 1 1/2-quart casserole. Combine 1/4 cup sugar and the egg yolks with next 4 ingredients; mix well and pour over cake. Set in pan of hot water and bake in moderate oven (350°F.) 50 minutes, or until firm. Sprinkle with chocolate. Beat the 2 egg whites until foamy; gradually add 1/4 cup sugar and beat until stiff. Spread lightly on pudding, covering top completely. With casserole still in hot water, bake in hot oven (400°F.) 5 minutes, or until golden. Serve warm. Makes 6 servings.

APPLE TORTE

Beat 1 egg with ⅔ cup sugar. Add ½ teaspoon vanilla extract, ⅛ teaspoon salt, 1 teaspoon baking powder and 2 tablespoons flour; blend. Fold in 1 cup chopped nuts and 1 cup minced peeled tart apples. Pour into buttered 8" layer pan and bake in moderate oven (350°F.) about 35 minutes. Cut in wedges and serve warm with whipped cream. Makes 4 to 6 servings.

APPLE-CRANBERRY COMPOTE

Put 3 cups sliced peeled eating apples, 3 cups washed fresh cranberries and 2 cups orange sections in alternate layers in 2-quart casserole. Heat 1 cup sugar and ¼ cup water to boiling; pour over fruit. Cover and bake in moderate oven (350°F.) about 1 hour. Makes 6 servings.

CHERRY DUMPLINGS

1 can (1 pound) pitted red sour cherries
1 cup sugar
1 cup sifted cake flour
1 teaspoon baking powder
1/4 teaspoon salt
Grated rind of 1 orange
1/3 cup milk
2 teaspoons butter, melted

Put undrained cherries and ¾ cup sugar in large deep skillet and bring to boil. Sift ¼ cup sugar, flour, baking powder and salt. Add remaining ingredients and mix lightly. Drop from tablespoon into boiling mixture, making 4 to 6 dumplings; cover and cook gently 20 minutes. Serve warm. Makes 4 to 6 servings.

CHERRY ROLY-POLY

1 cup biscuit mix
2 teaspoons butter
1/4 cup light cream
Melted butter
1 can (1 pound) red sour cherries
2 tablespoons diced candied lemon peel
Cherry Sauce, page 398

Blend together biscuit mix and butter; add cream and stir well. Turn out on a lightly floured board; knead for 30 seconds. Roll into a rectangle ¼" thick. Brush with melted butter; top with 1 cup drained cherries (use rest of cherries and juice in sauce) and lemon peel. Roll as for jelly roll. Place on buttered baking sheet; brush with melted butter. Bake in hot oven (425°F.) for 20 minutes. Slice and serve hot with Cherry Sauce. Makes 6 servings.

APPLES BAKED IN CREAM

Peel, core and slice cooking apples. Arrange in buttered shallow baking dish, sprinkling each layer with sugar, and cinnamon or nutmeg. Bake, uncovered, in moderate oven (350°F.) about 20 minutes. Barely cover with medium cream and bake 20 minutes or until apples are tender.

CUSTARD RICE PUDDING

1/2 cup cooked rice
3 eggs, beaten
1/2 cup sugar
1/4 teaspoon salt
1 teaspoon vanilla
1-1/2 teaspoons grated lemon rind
1/2 cup raisins
3-1/2 cups milk
Nutmeg

Mix all ingredients, except nutmeg. Pour into shallow baking dish and sprinkle with nutmeg. Set in pan of hot water and bake in slow oven (300°F.) about 1½ hours. Serve warm or cool, plain or with a sauce. Makes 6 servings.

CARAMEL-PEAR DUMPLINGS

1 can (1 pound 13 ounces) pear halves
2/3 cup sugar
Dash of salt
2 tablespoons butter or margarine
1 teaspoon vanilla extract
Dessert Dumplings
Plain or whipped cream

Drain pears, reserving syrup. Cook ⅓ cup sugar slowly in large skillet with oven-proof handle, stirring, until golden-brown syrup forms. Add remaining sugar, salt, butter, vanilla and pear syrup. Bring to boil and boil 2 minutes. Arrange pear halves, rounded side down, in skillet. Drop dumpling batter by tablespoonfuls onto pear halves. Bake in hot oven (425°F.) about 15 minutes. Let stand a few minutes, then turn out on hot serving plate. Serve with cream. Makes 8 servings.

Dessert Dumplings

2 cups cake flour
1/2 cup sugar
1-1/2 teaspoons baking powder
1/2 teaspoon salt
1 tablespoon butter or margarine, melted
1/2 cup plus 2 tablespoons milk

Sift dry ingredients into bowl. Add remaining ingredients and mix quickly just until dry ingredients are moistened. Makes 8 servings.

CHEESE-APPLE-NOODLE PUDDING

1-1/2 cups wide noodles, cooked
1 can (1 pound) sliced apples, undrained
1 cup cottage cheese
1/2 cup dairy sour cream
1 cup raisins
1/4 cup granulated sugar
1/2 teaspoon cinnamon
1/2 cup packed dark-brown sugar
1/4 cup fine dry bread crumbs
2 tablespoons soft butter or margarine
Cream

Mix first 7 ingredients and pour into buttered 2-quart casserole. Mix sugar, crumbs and butter until crumbly. Sprinkle on first mixture. Bake in moderate oven (375°F.) about 20 minutes. Serve warm with cream. Makes 6 to 8 servings.

CALIFORNIA PRUNE MOLDS

1 box (3 ounces) orange- or
    lemon-flavor gelatin
1 tablespoon grated lemon rind
3 tablespoons lemon juice
1/4 cup sugar
1/4 cup rum or 2 teaspoons rum
    flavoring
1 cup diced pitted plumped dried
    prunes (see Note)
1/4 cup chopped walnuts
3/4 cup heavy cream, whipped

Dissolve gelatin in 1 cup boiling water. Add ½ cup cold water and next 4 ingredients. Chill until slightly thickened. Fold in remaining ingredients and pour into individual molds. Chill until firm; unmold in serving dishes. Makes 6 or 7 servings. *Note* To plump prunes, let them stand in water to cover for 2 hours.

PUMPKIN CUSTARD WITH SHERRY GINGER CREAM

2 cups canned pumpkin
1 cup packed light-brown sugar
1 tablespoon flour
1/4 teaspoon salt
1 teaspoon each ginger, cinnamon and
    nutmeg
2 tablespoons butter
1-1/2 cups milk
4 eggs, slightly beaten
1 cup heavy cream, whipped
1 tablespoon sherry
1/4 cup chopped preserved ginger

In saucepan mix first 7 ingredients. Cook, stirring constantly, 5 minutes. Cool slightly; pour over eggs. Pour into well-buttered 1½-quart casserole. Place in pan of hot water. Bake in moderate oven (350°F.) 1 hour, or until set. Combine remaining ingredients; serve on custard. Serves 6.

BLUEBERRY SKILLET COBBLER

1 can (15 ounces) blueberries
Sugar
2 teaspoons quick-cooking tapioca
Dash of salt
1 cup biscuit mix
2 tablespoons butter, melted
1/4 cup milk
Cinnamon
Cream (optional)

In skillet mix berries, sugar to taste, tapioca and salt. Let stand while preparing biscuit dough with biscuit mix, 1 tablespoon sugar, the butter and milk. Heat berries and drop dough from tablespoon on mixture. Sprinkle with cinnamon. Cover and cook over very low heat about 20 minutes. Serve warm, with cream, if desired. Makes 4 servings.

BUTTERSCOTCH APPLES

6 large tart apples, peeled cored and
    sliced
Brown sugar
1-1/2 teaspoons cinnamon
1/4 teaspoon nutmeg
Flour
1/4 cup orange juice
1/4 cup butter or margarine

Heap apples in greased 8" round baking dish 2" deep. Mix ½ cup packed brown sugar, the spices and 2 tablespoons flour. Sprinkle on apples and pour orange juice over top. Blend ½ cup packed brown sugar, the butter and ⅓ cup flour with fork until crumbly. Spread on apples. Cover with foil and bake in hot oven (425°F.) 20 minutes. Remove foil and bake about 15 minutes longer. Makes 6 servings.

APPLE PANDOWDY

3 cups sliced apples
1/3 cup packed brown sugar
1/4 teaspoon each cinnamon and nutmeg
1/4 cup butter or margarine
1/3 cup granulated sugar
1 egg
3/4 cup all-purpose flour
3/4 teaspoon baking powder
1/4 teaspoon salt
1/3 cup milk
Cream

Put apples in 1-quart baking dish. Sprinkle with brown sugar and spices. Bake in moderate oven (375°F.) 30 minutes, or until apples are soft. Cream butter; gradually add granulated sugar and beat until fluffy. Add egg and beat well. Add sifted dry ingredients alternately with milk, beating until smooth. Spread on cooked apples. Bake 30 minutes. Serve warm with cream. Makes 4 servings.

CREAMY RICE PUDDING

1/4 cup uncooked rice (not processed or precooked)
1/2 cup granulated sugar or packed brown sugar
1/2 teaspoon salt
3 cups milk
1 cup light cream
3/4 cup raisins (optional)
2 teaspoons vanilla extract

Mix first 3 ingredients in 1½-quart baking dish. Stir in milk, cream, and raisins, if desired. Bake in slow oven (275°F.) about 2½ hours, stirring every 15 minutes. Add vanilla 15 minutes before pudding is done. Serves 4.

SWEET SCRAMBLED RICE

1/4 cup raisins
1/4 cup rum
1 cup uncooked rice
1/4 teaspoon salt
Sugar
3 cups milk
2 tablespoons chopped nuts
Grated rind of 1 lemon
1 egg, beaten
1/2 cup butter
Cinnamon

Soak raisins in rum several hours. Cook rice, salt and 1 cup sugar in the milk in top part of double boiler over boiling water 30 minutes, or until rice is tender and milk is absorbed, stirring occasionally. Add raisins, nuts, lemon rind and egg. Melt butter in skillet, add rice mixture and cook, letting brown crust form. Turn and brown remainder. Sprinkle with sugar and cinnamon. Makes 4 to 6 servings.

LEMON-CREAM RICE PUDDING

3 cups milk
1/2 cup uncooked rice
1 cup sugar
Grated rind of 1/2 lemon
1-1/2 tablespoons lemon juice
3/4 teaspoon salt
4 eggs, separated
Bright red jelly

Heat milk in top part of double boiler. Stir in rice, cover and cook over simmering water 30 minutes, or until rice is tender. Beat ½ cup sugar, next 3 ingredients and egg yolks together. Stir in small amount of hot mixture. Put back in double boiler and cook, stirring, 2 or 3 minutes, or until mixture coats a metal spoon. Pour into shallow 1½-quart baking dish. Beat egg whites until foamy; gradually add ½ cup sugar and beat until stiff. Pile lightly on pudding. Bake in hot oven (400°F.) about 5 minutes. Top with jelly. Serves 6.

SWEET-POTATO APPLE CRISP

1 can (1 pound 4 ounces) apple slices
2 cups very thinly sliced peeled sweet potatoes
2 tablespoons lemon juice
1 teaspoon cinnamon
1/2 teaspoon salt
1/2 cup all-purpose flour
1/2 cup packed brown sugar
1/3 cup butter

Drain apples and add enough water to make 6 tablespoons liquid. Alternate layers of apples and potatoes in shallow 1½-quart baking dish. Mix liquid with lemon juice, cinnamon and salt; pour over first mixture. Combine flour and sugar; cut in butter. Sprinkle over top. Cover and bake in moderate oven (350°F.) 30 minutes. Uncover and bake 15 minutes. Makes 6 servings.

FRENCH PEAR PUDDING

Flour
2 tablespoons granulated sugar
1 cup dairy sour cream
1 egg, beaten
1 teaspoon vanilla extract
1 can (1 pound) sliced pears
1/4 cup packed brown sugar
1/2 teaspoon nutmeg
2 tablespoons butter
Cream

Mix 1 tablespoon flour with next 4 ingredients. Drain pears and arrange slices in shallow 1½-quart baking dish. Pour sour-cream mixture over pears. Bake in moderate oven (350°F.) 15 minutes. Mix ⅓ cup flour, brown sugar, nutmeg and butter until mixture resembles coarse meal. Sprinkle on pears. Bake 15 minutes. Serve warm or cool with cream. Serves 4.

GINGER PEAR CRUMBLE

1-1/2 cups gingersnap crumbs (thirty 2" cookies)
1/4 cup butter, melted
1 can (30 ounces) pear halves
1 tablespoon lemon juice
1/2 cup packed brown sugar
1/4 teaspoon salt
1/2 teaspoon cinnamon
1/4 teaspoon nutmeg
Cream or vanilla ice cream

Mix crumbs and melted butter; put half in 1½-quart baking dish. Drain pears, reserving ¼ cup syrup. Put pears on crumbs and sprinkle with mixture of lemon juice and pear syrup. Mix sugar, salt and spices; sprinkle on pears. Top with remaining crumbs. Bake in moderate oven (350°F.) about 25 minutes. Serve warm with cream or ice cream. Makes 6 servings.

ALMOND-APRICOT GLAZED FRUITS

1/4 cup dried apricots
1/4 cup granulated sugar
1 tablespoon lemon juice
1 can (1 pound) peach halves, drained
1 can (1 pound) apricot halves, drained
1/2 cup ground blanched almonds (can be chopped in blender)
1/2 cup sifted confectioners' sugar
1 egg white
Chopped pistachio or other nuts
Light cream

Combine first 3 ingredients and 1½ cups water in small saucepan, bring to boil, cover and simmer 15 minutes, or until soft. Force through sieve or purée in blender until smooth. If not of spreading consistency, add small amount of water; set aside. Arrange other fruits, rounded side up, in buttered 9" glass piepan. Mix nuts, sugar and egg white to a paste, spread over fruits and bake in moderate oven (375°F.) 15 minutes, or until golden; cool. Spread with apricot purée, sprinkle with pistachios and serve with cream. Makes 6 to 8 servings.

BANANA-CHOCOLATE FLAN

1 cup all-purpose flour
1/4 teaspoon salt
2 tablespoons sugar
1/3 cup butter or margarine
1 egg yolk
3 fully ripe bananas, sliced
1 container (17-1/2 ounces) frozen dark-chocolate-flavor pudding, thawed and lightly stirred

Put first 3 ingredients in mixing bowl and cut in butter to form coarse crumbs. Add egg yolk and work together quickly to form ball. Press into 9" loose-bottomed flan pan. Prick bottom with fork and bake in moderate oven (375°F.) 12 minutes, or until golden brown. Cool on cake rack and remove rim. Arrange bananas in shell, reserving a few for decoration. Cover with pudding and top with remaining banana slices. Serve at once. Makes 6 to 8 servings.

STRAWBERRIES WITH TROPICAL SAUCE

1 cup plain yogurt
1/2 cup drained crushed pineapple
3 tablespoons honey
1 tablespoon lemon juice
3 small firm-ripe bananas
Slightly sweetened strawberries

Put all ingredients, except berries, in blender container, cover and blend at low speed 10 seconds. Serve on berries. Makes about 2½ cups sauce.

TURKISH DREAMS

1/2 cup melted butter or margarine
4 round shredded-wheat biscuits
1/2 cup honey
1/4 cup sugar
1/8 teaspoon salt
2/3 cup chopped nuts
2 teaspoons rose water or 1 teaspoon vanilla

Pour melted butter over biscuits in shallow baking dish. Bake in hot oven (425°F.) about 20 minutes. Bring ¼ cup water and remaining ingredients, except flavoring, to boil. Add flavoring and spoon over biscuits. Serve warm or cold. Makes 4 servings.

INDIVIDUAL STRAWBERRY SHORTCAKES

4 cups all-purpose flour
5 teaspoons double-acting baking powder
1/4 cup sugar
1-1/2 teaspoons salt
Butter or margarine
2 eggs, well beaten
1 cup (about) milk
2 to 3 quarts sweetened sliced strawberries
2 cups heavy cream, whipped and sweetened
Nutmeg

Mix first 4 ingredients in bowl. Add ⅔ cup softened butter and cut in with pastry blender or 2 knives. Mixing with fork, add eggs and enough milk to make a soft dough. Turn out on lightly floured board and knead 20 turns. Pat or roll lightly to ½" thickness and cut in 12 rounds with floured 3" cutter. Put on ungreased baking sheet and bake in very hot oven (450°F.) 12 to 15 minutes. Split while hot and spread with butter. Spoon strawberries between halves and over top; add some of strawberry syrup if desired. Serve at once with whipped cream, flavored to taste with nutmeg. Makes 12 servings.

LAYERED ORANGE DELIGHT

2 cups puffed-rice cereal
1 cup heavy cream, whipped
2 cans (11 ounces each) mandarin oranges, drained

At serving time, put half the cereal in serving dish. Cover with half the whipped cream, then with mandarin oranges, reserving a few for decoration. Add remaining cereal, then remaining whipped cream. Decorate with reserved oranges. Makes 6 servings.

TOASTED PEACHES AND CREAM CAKE

Season 2 cups fresh peaches with sugar and lemon juice to taste. Chill several hours. Split 8" white-cake layer and place bottom half on heat-proof plate. Add a layer of fruit, then top half of cake and more fruit. Spread evenly with 1 cup dairy sour cream, whipped. Sprinkle with cinnamon and 1/2 cup packed brown sugar. Put under broiler about 5 minutes. Makes 4 servings.

PEACH CRISP

6 or 7 large peaches
Juice of 1 lemon
1 cup all-purpose flour
1 cup packed brown sugar
1/2 cup margarine
Hard Sauce, page 398

Peel and slice peaches into shallow 2-quart baking dish; sprinkle with lemon juice. Mix flour and brown sugar. Cut in margarine with pastry blender or fingers until crumbly. Press over peaches. Bake in moderate oven (375°F.) 25 minutes, or until peaches are tender. Serve warm with Hard Sauce or cream. Makes 6 servings.

PEARS BURGUNDY

1/3 cup sugar
1/3 cup currant jelly
1/2 cup pear liquid
1/4 teaspoon red food coloring
1 can (29 ounces) pear halves, drained
1/3 cup Burgundy
Dairy sour cream
Cinnamon

About 1/2 hour before serving time, put first 4 ingredients in saucepan. Cook over low heat until jelly is melted, stirring occasionally. Add pears and heat. Cover and simmer while serving main part of meal. When ready to serve, add Burgundy and pass sour cream sprinkled with cinnamon. Makes 4 servings.

SKILLET APPLESAUCE BROWN BETTY

Melt 1/4 cup butter or margarine in skillet; add 4 cups small stale-cinnamon-raisin-bread cubes. Cook slowly, stirring, until lightly browned. Add 1/2 cup packed brown sugar, 1 jar (15 ounces) applesauce, 1/2 teaspoon cinnamon and a dash of salt. Heat, stirring lightly. Serve warm with **Orange Hard Sauce:** Cream together 2 tablespoons soft butter, 1/2 teaspoon grated orange rind and 1/2 cup confectioners' sugar. Serves 4.

BAKED INDIAN PUDDING

A traditional, long-baking New England pudding.

4 cups milk
5 tablespoons yellow cornmeal
2 tablespoons butter
1/2 cup packed brown sugar
1/2 cup molasses
1 teaspoon salt
1/2 teaspoon each ginger, cinnamon, nutmeg and mace
2 eggs, beaten
1 cup light cream
Vanilla ice cream

In top part of double boiler over direct heat, bring to boil 3 cups milk. Mix 1 cup cold milk with cornmeal and stir slowly into hot milk. Put over boiling water and cook 20 minutes, stirring occasionally. Add butter, sugar and molasses. Remove from heat and add salt and spices. Stir in eggs and pour into 1 1/2-quart baking dish. Bake in slow oven (300°F.) 2 to 2 1/2 hours, stirring occasionally the first hour. Then pour light cream over top and finish baking without stirring. Serve warm with ice cream. Makes 6 to 8 servings.

BABA AU RHUM (Rum Cake)

1 package active dry yeast
2 cups all-purpose flour
4 eggs
1/4 cup sugar
1 teaspoon grated lemon rind
1/2 teaspoon salt
1/2 cup soft butter
Rum Syrup
Whipped cream

Soften yeast in 1/2 cup warm water. Add 1/2 cup flour and beat until smooth with a rotary or electric beater. Add eggs, one at a time, beating very thoroughly after each addition. Then beat in remaining flour, the sugar, lemon rind and salt. Cover and let rise in a warm place 45 minutes. Add butter a small amount at a time, beating after each addition until thoroughly blended. Pour into a well-buttered 5-cup fluted mold with a tube and let stand 10 minutes. Bake in moderate oven (375°F.) 35 to 40 minutes. Let stand 5 minutes, then turn out on serving plate. Prick with fork and spoon syrup over baba, making sure all surfaces are covered. Let stand until syrup is absorbed. Fill center with whipped cream. Makes 6 to 8 servings. **Rum Syrup** Put 1 cup sugar and 1/2 cup water in saucepan. Bring to boil and cook, stirring, until sugar is dissolved. Cool; stir in 1/3 cup rum.

CHEESECAKE SUPREME

Crumb Crust (page 419) (use graham-cracker crumbs)
5 packages (8 ounces each) cream cheese, softened
1-3/4 cups sugar
3 tablespoons flour
Grated rind of 1 lemon
Grated rind of 1/2 orange
1/4 cup heavy cream
5 whole eggs
2 egg yolks
Canned apricots and pineapple, fresh strawberries, grapes and blueberries
Glaze
Fresh mint leaves

Prepare graham-cracker crust. Butter a 10" springform pan 2¼" deep (or use a 9" springform pan 3" deep). Press crumb mixture onto bottom and sides of pan. Beat cheese until fluffy; blend in sugar mixed with flour. Add grated rinds and cream. Beat smooth. Add eggs and yolks, one at a time, beating well after each. Turn into crust. Bake in very hot oven (500°F.) 10 minutes. Turn temperature control to 200°F.; do not open oven door. Bake 1 hour longer. Remove from oven and set in draft-free place until cool; then chill. Remove sides of pan and put cake on serving plate; keep chilled. Cake can be made a day in advance, but fruit and Glaze should be put on the same day cake is served. Reserve fruit syrups for Glaze. Arrange 4 or 5 apricot halves around center of cake. Set quarter-slices of pineapple around them; border cake with 6 or 7 strawberries, halved, alternating with a dozen grapes. Mound about ⅓ cup blueberries in very center. Spoon Glaze over fruit; chill. Garnish with mint. Makes 12 servings. **Glaze** Combine pineapple and apricot syrups drained from fruit to make ¾ cup. Add 1 tablespoon lemon juice. Mix 1 tablespoon cornstarch with 2 tablespoons cold water in saucepan; add juices and cook, stirring, until thickened. Add a drop of yellow food coloring, if desired.

Pineapple Cheesecake Prepare Cookie Shell dough, page 419, and chill. Roll one fourth of dough onto a greased 9" springform pan; trim edges. Bake in hot oven (400°F.) 8 minutes, or until golden; cool. Divide remaining dough in thirds and roll each third into a narrow strip ⅛" thick. Grease sides of pan and fit strips around, pressing firmly to seal joints; trim. Fit sides of pan over bottom. Prepare filling as directed in Cheesecake Supreme, turn into prepared crust, bake and chill. Remove sides of pan. Cover top with Pineapple Glaze. Serves 12.

Pineapple Glaze Bring to a boil 1 can (9 ounces) crushed pineapple, ¼ cup sugar, ¼ cup water and 1½ tablespoons lemon juice. Blend 1 tablespoon cornstarch and 1 tablespoon water; stir into fruit. Cook, stirring, until thickened. Cool slightly.

BANANA MERINGUE PUDDING

1 cup sugar
1/3 cup cornstarch
3/4 teaspoon salt
3 cups milk
3 eggs, separated
1-1/2 teaspoons vanilla extract
24 small or 18 large vanilla wafers
3 large ripe bananas

In the top part of double boiler, mix ⅔ cup sugar, the cornstarch, salt and milk. Put over boiling water and cook, stirring, until thickened. Cover and cook 10 minutes, stirring occasionally. Add small amount to egg yolks, stirring. Put back in double boiler and cook 2 minutes, stirring. Cool and add vanilla. Arrange alternate layers of wafers, banana slices and pudding in 1½-quart casserole, ending with pudding. Beat egg whites until foamy; gradually add ⅓ cup sugar and beat until stiff. Pile lightly on pudding. Bake in 400°F. oven 5 minutes. Makes 6 servings.

ZABAGLIONE

5 egg yolks
3/4 cup sugar
1/8 teaspoon salt
1/2 cup Marsala, port or sherry wine

In top of a double boiler, beat egg yolks with 1 tablespoon water until they are foamy and light. Whisk in sugar, salt and wine. Beat a few minutes over hot, not boiling, water until thickened and fluffy. Pile into sherbet glasses; serve hot. Makes 6 servings.

Zabaglione with Fresh Strawberries or Peaches Prepare Zabaglione. Cool and fold in 5 stiffly beaten egg whites. Pile in a pretty serving bowl and garnish with sliced and sweetened fresh fruit.

Chocolate Sabayon Prepare Zabaglione. Stir 2 ounces grated sweet chocolate into hot dessert just before serving.

Frozen Sabayon Prepare Zabaglione. Cool and add 1 pint heavy cream, whipped, ¼ cup diced candied cherries, ½ cup diced candied pineapple and ½ cup chopped pecans. Freeze in parfait glasses and garnish with candied cherries and bits of angelica. Or pour into trays or mold and freeze. Makes 10 to 12 servings.

GRAPES SAUTERNE WITH SOUR CREAM

Sprinkle chilled seedless grapes with sauterne. Top with dairy sour cream and a little brown sugar.

WINTER FRUIT COMPOTE WITH CUSTARD SAUCE

1/2 pound mixed dried fruit
1 piece of lemon rind
Custard Sauce, page 399
1/4 cup toasted slivered almonds, or
  other nuts, chopped

Cover fruit and rind with water in small saucepan and slowly bring to boil. Cover and simmer until fruit is soft but still holds its shape. Chill in the liquid. In glass bowl, make layers of fruit and custard sauce, ending with sauce. Sprinkle almonds on top. Serve cold. Makes 4 servings.

CRÈME LOUISA

1 cup heavy cream
1/2 cup milk
1/2 cup sugar
Dash of salt
1 envelope unflavored gelatin
1 cup dairy sour cream
1/2 teaspoon almond flavoring or 2
  tablespoons brandy or strawberry
  liqueur
Crushed and sweetened strawberries

Combine first 4 ingredients in saucepan and cook over low heat until sugar is dissolved. Remove from heat. Add gelatin softened in 1/4 cup cold water and stir until dissolved. Beat in sour cream and flavoring with a rotary beater, just until thoroughly blended and smooth. Pour into individual molds. Chill until firm. Unmold and serve with berries. Makes 4 to 6 servings.

RICOTTA CONDITA

A creamy Italian dessert.

1 pound ricotta cheese
1/2 cup milk
3 tablespoons Strega or other liqueur
3 tablespoons chopped candied lemon
  or orange peel
3 tablespoons chopped pistachios
1/4 cup confectioners' sugar
Coarse granulated sugar and/or
  pulverized espresso coffee beans

Beat cheese with milk until smooth. Blend in next 4 ingredients. Beat until smooth and creamy. Spoon into sherbet glasses and chill. Just before serving, dust with sugar and/or coffee. Makes 6 servings.

MANDARIN-ORANGE MOLD

2 cups canned tangerine juice
1 box orange-flavored gelatin dessert
1 can (11 ounces) mandarin oranges,
  drained

Heat 1 cup juice, pour over gelatin and stir until dissolved. Add remaining 1 cup juice. Chill until thick but not firm. Add oranges and chill until firm. Makes 4 servings.

WINE FRUITS

Put 2 cups dried fruits in a 1-quart jar. Use dried apricots, peaches, pears with cores cut out, apples, currants, figs with stems removed, raisins, prunes, or a combination. Pour 2 cups medium (fine) or sweet (cream) sherry over fruits. Cover and let stand at room temperature 1 week or longer, then refrigerate. Serve chilled as a fruit compote topped with whipped cream. Or cut fruits coarsely and serve with the marinade as a sauce for pound cake. Replenish jar with dried fruits and wine as fruits are used.

SCOTTISH FLOATING ISLANDS

3 egg whites
3 tablespoons red-currant jelly
1-1/2 cups heavy cream
1/4 cup sugar
1/2 teaspoon grated lemon rind
1/2 cup sherry, chilled

Beat egg whites until almost stiff. Gradually beat in jelly until a stiff meringue is formed. Whip the cream with the sugar and lemon rind. Carefully fold in the sherry. Pour into a glass serving bowl. Spoon meringue islands on top. Serves 6 to 8.

RIJNWIJNVLA
(Rhine Wine Whip)

4 eggs, separated
1/2 cup sugar
1 tablespoon grated lemon rind
1/4 cup lemon juice
1/2 cup minus 1 tablespoon Rhine wine
Vanilla wafers or ladyfingers

Beat egg whites until stiff but not dry. Place yolks and sugar in a saucepan and beat until thick and fluffy. Gradually beat in lemon rind, juice and wine. Place over low heat (or use a double boiler). Stir with a wooden spoon until mixture begins to thicken. Do not boil. Continue to heat while gently folding in egg whites. Pour into a bowl to cool. Chill. Serve with vanilla wafers or ladyfingers. Makes 4 to 6 servings.

CHOCOLATE RASPBERRY CREAM

2 cups heavy cream
1/2 teaspoon vanilla extract
1 package (4 ounces) sweet cooking
  chocolate, grated fine
3 cups fresh raspberries or 2 packages
  (10 ounces each) frozen raspberries,
  thawed and thoroughly drained
1/4 cup sugar (omit if frozen berries are
  used)

Whip cream with vanilla. Blend in chocolate. Reserve a few raspberries for garnish. Sprinkle sugar on remaining berries and fold into cream. Spoon into individual serving dishes or large glass serving bowl. Chill thoroughly. Decorate with reserved berries. Makes 6 to 8 servings.

ORANGE CARAMEL PUDDING

1-1/4 cups sugar
2 tablespoons butter
6 eggs, separated
1/4 cup flour
1-1/4 cups orange juice

Stir ¹/₂ cup sugar in saucepan over low heat until sugar melts and forms a brown syrup. Pour into 1¹/₂-quart casserole. Cream butter with remaining ³/₄ cup sugar until light. Add egg yolks, one at a time, beating well after each. Add flour and mix well. Stir in orange juice. Fold in stiffly beaten egg whites. Pour over syrup in casserole. Set in pan of hot water and bake in moderate oven (350°F.) about 1 hour. Cool; chill. Makes 6 servings.

SOUR-CREAM DEVONSHIRE PEARS

1 can (1 pound 13 ounces) pear halves
Juice of 1 orange
Juice of 1/2 lemon
1/4 teaspoon ground ginger
1 stick cinnamon
3 whole cloves
1 cup currant jelly
Red food coloring
1 cup heavy cream
1/2 cup dairy sour cream
2 tablespoons sugar
1 teaspoon vanilla extract

Drain pears, reserving syrup. In saucepan, mix syrup with orange and lemon juices and spices. Let stand 1¹/₂ hours. Add pears and simmer until thoroughly heated. Cool and chill. Beat jelly until smooth. Add small amount of red coloring and 3 tablespoons liquid from chilled pears. Remove pears to serving dish and cover with the jelly mixture. Whip heavy cream until stiff. Fold in remaining ingredients and spoon in a circle on pears. Makes 8 servings.

FRESH-FRUIT COMPOTE

1 cup sugar
1 lemon, sliced
4 firm peaches, peeled and halved
4 pears, peeled, cored and halved
4 plums (see Note)
8 apricots

Put the sugar, lemon and 2 cups water in saucepan, bring to boil and simmer 5 minutes. Add peaches and pears, cover and simmer 5 minutes. Prick skins of plums and add with apricots to mixture. Cover and simmer 5 minutes, or until all fruit is tender. Cool, then chill. Makes 8 servings. *Note* If purple plums are used, cook separately in a little syrup and add just before serving.

BUTTERSCOTCH PARFAIT

1/4 cup cornstarch
1/4 teaspoon salt
2 cups milk
2 eggs, slightly beaten
1 package (6 ounces) butterscotch morsels
3 tablespoons butter
2 teaspoons grated orange rind
1 teaspoon vanilla extract
Whipped cream
Toasted coconut or chopped almonds
  (optional)

Mix first 2 ingredients in saucepan. Stir in milk and cook, stirring, until smooth and thickened. Stir a little into eggs, then return to saucepan. Cook, stirring, 1 minute longer. Remove from heat and add remaining ingredients, except last 2. Stir until morsels are melted and blended. Spoon into parfait glasses, alternating with cream; chill. Top with coconut or almonds, if desired. Serves 6.

COFFEE CUSTARD WITH CARAMEL GLAZE

Caramel Glaze
6 eggs
5 tablespoons sugar
1/4 teaspoon salt
1 cup strong coffee
1 cup cream
3 tablespoons sherry

Prepare Caramel Glaze and line 1¹/₂-quart casserole. Beat eggs slightly; add remaining ingredients and mix well. Pour into glaze-lined dish. Set in pan of hot water and bake in moderate oven (350°F.) 40 to 45 minutes, or until a silver knife inserted in the custard comes out clean. Cool completely. Makes 6 servings. **Caramel Glaze** Caramelize ³/₄ cup sugar in a heavy saucepan and pour into a 1¹/₂-quart casserole, tilting to completely coat inside.

PASCHA

An East Indian dessert of creamed, almondy cottage cheese, delicious with toasted pound cake.

2 egg yolks
1/2 cup sugar
1 pound dry cottage cheese (farmer cheese)
1/3 cup butter or margarine
1/3 cup heavy cream
Grated rind of 1 lemon
1/4 teaspoon vanilla extract
1/2 teaspoon almond extract

Beat egg yolks and sugar. Add next 4 ingredients; mix well. Put in saucepan, bring to boil and simmer, stirring, 5 minutes. Cool slightly and add flavorings. Line strainer or colander with several thicknesses of cheesecloth and stand in bowl deeper than strainer. Pour in mixture and tie cloth. Cover and refrigerate. Let drain until moisture drips out. Untie, turn out on plate and remove cloth. Makes 6 to 8 servings.

PEANUT-PUDDING SQUARES

1 package (3-3/4 ounces) butterscotch pudding-and-pie-filling mix
2 cups milk
1-1/4 cups coarse graham-cracker crumbs
1/4 cup sugar
1/4 cup creamy peanut butter
3 tablespoons soft butter or margarine

Prepare pudding mix with the milk as directed on package; set aside. Combine remaining ingredients and mix well. Spread ¾ cup crumb mixture in greased 8" square pan. Cover with 1 cup cooled pudding. Alternate layers of crumb mixture and cooled pudding, ending with crumb mixture. Chill about 4 hours before serving. Makes 6 servings.

POTS DE CREME

2 squares unsweetened chocolate
3/4 cup sugar
1 egg
1/8 teaspoon salt
3/4 cup heavy cream
1 teaspoon vanilla extract

Melt chocolate in top part of double boiler over boiling water; add sugar, egg and salt and mix until smooth. Add ¼ cup cream and cook over boiling water 8 minutes, stirring. Remove from water and stir in vanilla. Chill. Fold in remaining ½ cup cream, whipped. Pour into 6 *pot de crème* cups or serving dishes; chill until firm. Makes 6 servings.

COFFEE-RAISIN RICE PUDDING

1 cup packaged precooked rice
1 cup coffee
1/2 cup golden raisins
1/2 cup chopped walnuts
Dash of salt
1/8 teaspoon nutmeg
1/2 cup packed light-brown sugar
1 cup heavy cream, whipped
Instant-coffee powder

Prepare rice according to package directions, using coffee instead of water. Stir in remaining ingredients, except last 2, and mix well; chill. Fold in whipped cream, reserving enough for decoration. Put in large bowl or individual serving dishes and top with remaining cream and a sprinkle of instant coffee. Refrigerate. Makes 4 to 6 servings.

FRENCH FUDGE PIE

1 cup sugar
1/2 cup butter or margarine
1 cup miniature marshmallows
2 squares unsweetened chocolate
2 eggs, well beaten
1/2 teaspoon salt
1/2 cup all-purpose flour
1 teaspoon vanilla extract
1/2 teaspoon almond extract

Put first 4 ingredients in top part of small double boiler and heat over boiling water, stirring, until smooth and blended. Add eggs and beat well with electric mixer or by hand. Add remaining ingredients, mix well; pour into buttered 9" piepan. Bake in moderate oven (325°F.) 30 minutes. Cool; then chill. Makes 4 to 6 servings. **Note** Pie can be sprinkled with chopped nuts before baking, if desired.

TANGY TEMPTATION

1 box lemon pudding-and-pie-filling mix
3/4 cup sugar
2 eggs, separated
1 can (8 ounces) frozen tangerine juice
1/2 cup heavy cream, whipped

Combine pie-filling mix and ½ cup sugar in saucepan; gradually stir in 1½ cups water. Cook, stirring constantly, until mixture thickens. Beat egg yolks with ¼ cup water; add hot mixture slowly. Return to saucepan and cook a few minutes longer. Add tangerine juice and stir until melted. Beat egg whites with 2 tablespoons sugar until stiff. Fold into hot mixture; chill and fold in cream sweetened with remaining 2 tablespoons sugar. Makes 4 to 6 servings.

RASPBERRY-GLAZED PEACHES

Put partially thawed frozen raspberries in blender and blend until thick. Serve over chilled canned or fresh peach halves.

BANANA FLUFF PUDDING

1 envelope unflavored gelatin
4 medium bananas
1 tablespoon grated orange rind
1 cup orange juice
2 tablespoons lemon juice
Dash of salt
3/4 cup confectioners' sugar
1 cup heavy cream, whipped

Soften gelatin in 1/4 cup cold water; dissolve over hot water. Mash bananas and add next 5 ingredients. Add gelatin and chill until slightly thickened. Fold in whipped cream. Chill well. Makes 6 to 8 servings.

BLUEBERRY FLUMMERY

Put 2 cups fresh blueberries in saucepan with 1 cup water and simmer 5 minutes. Put through sieve or whirl in blender. Add water to make 2 1/2 cups. Mix 1/4 cup cornstarch, 3/4 cup sugar and 1/8 teaspoon salt; add to sieved berries. Cook, stirring, until thickened and clear. Add juice of 1/2 lemon. Cool, stirring occasionally; chill. Serve with sour cream. Makes 4 servings.

COEUR À LA CRÈME

A French gelatin dessert with an unusual texture.

1 envelope unflavored gelatin
1/4 cup cold milk
1 pound creamed cottage cheese
6 ounces cream cheese, softened
1-1/2 teaspoons vanilla extract
3/4 cup heavy cream
1/2 cup sugar
Cherry-Pineapple Sauce

Soften gelatin in cold milk. Stir over low heat until gelatin is dissolved. Force cottage cheese through sieve or beat at high speed of electric mixer until fairly smooth. Beat in cream cheese, dissolved gelatin and vanilla. Beat cream with sugar until stiff. Fold into first mixture. Pour into heart-shaped or other 5-cup mold and chill until firm. Unmold; serve with sauce. Makes 6 servings. **Cherry-Pineapple Sauce** Mix 1 can (8 ounces) crushed pineapple, 1/2 cup sliced maraschino cherries and 1/4 cup maraschino-cherry liquid. Chill.

JELLIED APPLESAUCE

Apple, orange and lemon gelatin blend well with applesauce, too.

Dissolve 1 box (3 ounces) black-raspberry or other flavor gelatin in 1 1/2 cups boiling water. Chill until slightly thickened. Fold in 1 cup sweetened applesauce and pour into 8" square pan. Chill until firm. Unmold and cut in cubes. Serve with soft custard or whipped cream. Makes 4 servings.

STRAWBERRY-HONEY PARFAIT

1 package (3 ounces) strawberry-flavor gelatin
1 cup undiluted evaporated milk
1/4 cup honey
Grated rind and juice of 1 lemon
15 ladyfingers, split
1 package (10 ounces) frozen sliced strawberries

Dissolve gelatin in 1 cup hot water. Chill until partially set. Pour milk into refrigerator tray and freeze until mushy. Turn into chilled bowl and whip until stiff. Add honey, lemon rind and juice. Beat until well blended. Fold in gelatin and chill until set. Just before serving, arrange 5 ladyfinger halves around edge of each sherbet glass. Spoon dessert into glasses and top with partially thawed strawberries. Serves 6.

COCONUT CREAM MOLD

2 envelopes unflavored gelatin
1 cup scalded milk
1 cup sugar
1 teaspoon vanilla extract
1/4 teaspoon salt
1 pint heavy cream, whipped
1 can flaked coconut
Fruit
Hot Butter-Cream Sauce

Soften gelatin in 1/2 cup cold water. Dissolve in scalded milk; add sugar and stir until dissolved. Chill until mixture just begins to thicken. Fold in next 4 ingredients. Pour into a 2-quart ring mold. Refrigerate for at least 4 hours. Unmold on large serving plate and decorate with maraschino cherries with stems, small bunches of grapes or with other fruit in season. Serve with sauce. Makes 8 servings. **Hot Butter-Cream Sauce** Mix 1 tablespoon flour and 1/2 cup sugar; add 1/2 cup dark corn syrup, 1/3 cup light cream, 2 tablespoons butter and 1/8 teaspoon salt. Bring mixture slowly to a boil. Simmer about 5 minutes. Serve warm. Makes about 1 cup.

PALM SPRINGS AMBROSIA

2 large grapefruit
1/4 to 1/2 cup confectioners' sugar
1 cup pitted fresh dates
1 package (4 ounces) shredded coconut
1/2 cup chopped walnuts
White port wine (optional)

Working over bowl to collect juice, peel, section and seed grapefruit. Cut sections in half, sprinkle with sugar to taste and let stand 10 minutes. Cut dates in half or snip with kitchen shears. Lightly toss sweetened grapefruit, dates, coconut and walnuts. Put in shallow dish and add reserved grapefruit juice. Chill several hours. Spoon into champagne or sherbet glasses; top each serving with 1 tablespoon port, if desired. Serves 4 to 6.

CHERRY ANGEL PIE

4 egg whites (yolks used in filling)
1/8 teaspoon salt
1/2 teaspoon cream of tartar
1 cup sugar
Cherry Filling
Fresh or maraschino cherries with stems

Beat egg whites and salt until foamy; add cream of tartar. Continue beating, adding sugar gradually until mixture is very stiff. Spread a layer 1" deep on bottom of greased 9" piepan. Spread an even layer around sides of pan and pipe remainder in rosettes around edge. Bake in very slow oven (250°F.) 1 hour; turn off heat and let stand in oven 1 hour longer; cool. Pile Cherry Filling in meringue shell; chill 12 hours. Decorate with fresh cherries. Makes 6 to 8 servings. **Cherry Filling** Drain 1 can (1 pound) pitted red sour cherries in syrup, reserving 1/2 cup syrup. Put syrup in saucepan with 1 tablespoon cornstarch and 2 tablespoons sugar. Cook, stirring, until thickened. Add small amount of mixture to 4 slightly beaten egg yolks. Return to saucepan and cook 1 to 2 minutes, stirring. Add 1/4 teaspoon almond extract and cherries; chill. Whip 1 cup heavy cream until stiff and fold in.

Chocolate Angel Pie Prepare meringue shell as directed for Cherry Angel Pie. Fill with **Chocolate Filling:** Melt 3 squares unsweetened chocolate in top of double boiler over boiling water. Beat 4 egg whites, 1/2 cup sugar, 1/8 teaspoon salt and 2 tablespoons water; stir into chocolate. Cook, stirring constantly, until very thick. Remove from heat, add 1 teaspoon vanilla and cool. Fold in 1 cup heavy cream, whipped, and pour into meringue shell. Chill overnight. Makes 6 to 8 servings.

STRAWBERRY PARTY DESSERT

Dissolve 1 box (3 ounces) strawberry-flavor gelatin in 1 1/4 cups very hot water. Add 1 pint strawberry ice cream and stir until melted. Chill until partially set. Add 8 ounces angel food cake pulled into pieces. Spoon into sherbet dishes and chill. Serves 8.

SYLLABUB

Combine 2 cups heavy cream, 1 cup sugar, 1/2 cup sherry and grated rind and juice of 1 lemon in deep bowl. Beat at medium to high speed 6 minutes, or until stiff but not curdled. (Mixture should be very stiff.) Set a very fine large sieve over another bowl. Pour mixture into sieve. Refrigerate about 1 hour. Spoon froth that remains in sieve into sherbet glasses. Good with thin crisp cookies. Makes 6 servings.

BAVARIAN CREAM

1 envelope unflavored gelatin
1 cup milk
4 eggs, separated
1/2 cup sugar
1/4 teaspoon salt
1 teaspoon vanilla extract
1 cup heavy cream, whipped
Fruit, or crème de menthe and coconut

In top of double boiler soften gelatin in milk. Add beaten egg yolks, 1/4 cup sugar and the salt. Cook over simmering water, stirring constantly, until thickened and smooth. Add vanilla. Cool. Stir occasionally to prevent a crust from forming. Beat egg whites until partially stiff, add 1/4 cup sugar gradually and continue beating until stiff and glossy. Fold into custard with whipped cream. Pour into 2-quart mold and chill until firm. Unmold and serve with fresh fruit as desired, or crème de menthe and coconut. Makes 8 servings.

Chocolate Bavarian Cream Prepare Bavarian Cream, adding 2 squares unsweetened chocolate, melted, to custard with vanilla.

Praline Bavarian Cream Prepare Bavarian Cream, adding 3/4 cup Praline along with the meringue and whipped cream. **Praline** In a heavy skillet, place 1 cup unblanched almonds, 1 cup filberts and 2 cups sugar. Cook gently over low heat until sugar melts and caramelizes and skins of nuts burst. Pour on lightly buttered cookie sheet to cool. When brittle, break into small pieces, place in towel and pound to a powder. Keeps indefinitely in tightly covered glass jar.

PINEAPPLE ANGEL PIE

3 eggs, separated
Salt
1-1/2 cups granulated sugar
1 teaspoon vanilla extract
1-1/2 teaspoons vinegar
2 teaspoons cornstarch
1 tablespoon lemon juice
1 can (8-1/2 ounces) crushed pineapple, undrained
1 cup heavy cream
2 tablespoons sifted confectioners' sugar
1/2 cup grated coconut

Beat egg whites with ⅛ teaspoon salt until stiff but not dry. Gradually beat in ½ cup granulated sugar. Add ½ teaspoon vanilla. Gradually add ½ cup more sugar alternately with vinegar, beating well after each addition until stiff and glossy. Spread in greased and floured 9" shallow baking dish. Build up edges slightly to leave a hollow in center. Bake in slow oven (275°F.) 30 minutes. Increase heat to 300°F. and bake 30 minutes longer. Cool. Meanwhile, in top of double boiler, beat egg yolks, cornstarch and a dash of salt until thick and lemon-colored. Gradually beat in remaining ½ cup sugar alternately with lemon juice; add pineapple. Cook over hot water, 10 minutes, or until thick, stirring constantly. Pour into bowl and cover with waxed paper; press wax paper on top of mixture to prevent a skin from forming. Chill. When ready to serve, whip cream stiff; fold in confectioners' sugar and ½ teaspoon vanilla. Fill meringue shell with pineapple mixture and spread cream on top. Sprinkle with coconut. Makes 8 servings.

BANANA-FIG PUDDING

Fill dessert dishes with crumbled fig bars and sliced bananas. Top generously with soft whipped cream and chopped walnuts or almonds.

BANANA-ANGEL FLUFF

1 package (2 ounces) whipped-topping mix
1 cup marshmallow cream
1/3 cup drained maraschino cherries, halved
1 can (20 ounces) pineapple chunks, drained
2 ripe bananas, diced
3 cups angel-food cake cubes

Prepare topping mix as directed on package. Add marshmallow cream and mix thoroughly. Fold in remaining ingredients gently but thoroughly. Pile in dessert dishes and chill 1 to 2 hours. Makes 5 or 6 servings.

STRAWBERRY REFRIGERATOR CAKE

7 or 8 whole ladyfingers
1 package (6 ounces) or 2 packages (3 ounces each) strawberry-flavor gelatin
1-1/2 cups crushed strawberries
1 tablespoon lemon juice
1/2 cup sugar
1/8 teaspoon salt
2 cups heavy cream
Whipped cream
Whole strawberries

Put a 3" strip of waxed paper around inside of 8" or 9" springform cake pan. Split ladyfingers and cut tips from one end so halves will stand. Arrange, rounded end up, around edge of pan. Add 2 cups boiling water to gelatin and stir until dissolved. Mix strawberries, lemon juice, sugar and salt and add to gelatin. Chill until mixture begins to set, then whip cream and fold into gelatin mixture. Carefully spoon into lined pan and chill until firm (at least 5 hours or overnight). Remove sides of pan and put cake on serving plate. Decorate with whipped cream and whole strawberries. Makes 10 or more servings.

CASSATA NAPOLITANA

1-1/2 pounds ricotta cheese
1/3 cup sugar
1/2 cup light cream
1 teaspoon vanilla extract
1/4 teaspoon almond extract
1/4 cup semisweet chocolate pieces, chopped
1/4 cup chopped toasted almonds
2/3 cup finely diced mixed candied fruit
One 9" or 10" sponge cake or 2 sponge layers, chilled
1/4 cup rum
Frosting
Candied cherries (optional)

Combine first 5 ingredients. Rub through a sieve or whirl in blender until smooth. Add chocolate, nuts and fruit; chill. If a whole cake is used, cut in 2 layers. Place 1 layer on serving plate and spread with filling. Top with remaining layer. Sprinkle with rum. Wrap and chill until shortly before serving time. Frost top, reserving some of Frosting to tint pink and swirl on cake with pastry tube. Decorate with candied cherries, if desired. Makes 8 to 10 servings. **Frosting** Mix 1 egg with 2 cups sifted confectioners' sugar, 1 teaspoon almond extract and 1 tablespoon lemon juice. Add a few drops of water for spreading consistency if necessary.

SCOTCH TRIFLE

1 sponge layer
1 cup strawberry, raspberry or other jam
6 macaroons
1/3 cup cream sherry or Marsala
1/3 cup orange juice or fruit syrup
Soft Custard
1 cup heavy cream, whipped
1/4 cup sugar
1 teaspoon vanilla extract
1/4 teaspoon almond extract
2 tablespoons chopped toasted almonds
Fresh strawberries (optional)

Split the sponge layer in half horizontally and spread thickly with jam. Cut in small fingers. Crumble the macaroons. Arrange alternate layers of sponge fingers and crumbled macaroons in a glass serving dish. Sprinkle each layer with sherry and fruit juice. Pour the cooled custard over the trifle. Cover and chill. At serving time whip cream and add sugar and extracts; spread over the chilled trifle. Sprinkle with chopped nuts and decorate with fresh strawberries, if desired. Makes 6 to 8 servings. **Soft Custard** In top part of small double boiler, beat together with rotary beater 2 eggs, dash of salt, 3 tablespoons sugar and 1½ cups milk. Cook over simmering water, stirring, until slightly thickened. Cool.

CITRUS SNOW PUDDING, OLD-FASHIONED CUSTARD SAUCE

1 envelope unflavored gelatin
1/2 cup sugar
1/4 teaspoon salt
3/4 cup grapefruit juice
1/4 cup orange juice
Juice of 1/2 lemon
Grated rind of 1 orange
4 egg whites (yolks used in sauce)
Orange sections (optional)
Old-fashioned Custard Sauce

Soften gelatin in ¼ cup cold water, then dissolve in ¼ cup hot water. Add ¼ cup sugar, the salt, fruit juices and rind. Chill until mixture begins to set. Beat egg whites until foamy. Gradually add remaining sugar and beat until stiff. Beat gelatin mixture into egg whites and pour into 1½-quart mold. Chill until firm. Unmold, and decorate with orange sections, if desired. Serve with sauce. Makes 4 to 6 servings. **Old-fashioned Custard Sauce** Scald 2 cups milk in top part of double boiler over simmering water. Beat 4 egg yolks with 6 tablespoons sugar. Stir in small amount of milk; put back in double boiler. Cook over simmering water, stirring, until mixture thickens and coats a metal spoon. Cool and add ½ teaspoon vanilla.

DELLA ROBBIA FRUIT RING

2 packages (6 ounces each) or 4 packages (3 ounces each) any red-colored gelatin
7 cups drained canned fruit, such as pineapple, pears, peaches, apricots, mandarin oranges and pitted cherries; fresh or frozen blueberries; grapes, pears and orange sections
Whole blanched almonds or other nuts
Holly or other fresh green leaves

Dissolve gelatin in 4 cups hot water and add 3½ cups cold water. (Do not use fruit juices drained from fruits.) Chill until mixture begins to set. Arrange some fruit and nuts in a pattern in bottom of 14- to 16-cup ring mold. Cover with a layer of gelatin and chill until set. Combine remaining fruit, whole and cut-up, and remaining gelatin and fill mold. Chill overnight. Unmold and garnish with leaves. Makes 16 servings.

CRÈME DE MENTHE PEARS

Drain 1 can (1 pound 13 ounces) pear halves. Put 1 to 2 teaspoons crème de menthe in bottom of each serving dish. Put a pear half, cut side up, in dish. Combine 1 cup heavy cream, whipped, with ½ cup dairy sour cream, 2 tablespoons sugar and 1 tablespoon vanilla. Swirl on pears and sprinkle with a little grated semi-sweet or sweet chocolate. Serves 8.

POACHED PEARS WITH RASPBERRY PURÉE

In large kettle, combine 1 cup sugar, 2 cups water and juice of 1 lemon. Cover and bring to boil. Peel 6 whole pears, leaving stems on but removing end cores. Put in boiling syrup, cover and simmer until tender; chill. Whirl 1 package (10 to 12 ounces) frozen raspberries, partially thawed, in blender and serve on pears. Makes 6 servings.

PINEAPPLE MOUSSE

1 box pineapple- or lemon-flavor gelatin
Dash of salt
1 can (1 pound 4-1/2 ounces) crushed pineapple
1 cup heavy cream, whipped
Maraschino cherries (optional)

Dissolve gelatin in 1 cup very hot water; add salt and pineapple. Chill until thickened but not firm. Fold in cream. Pour into 1½-quart mold; chill until firm. Unmold; garnish with cherries, if desired. Makes 6 servings.

PEACH COMPOTE

1/4 cup light corn syrup
1/2 cup orange juice
1/8 teaspoon almond extract
6 large firm-ripe peaches, peeled and
  halved
2 tablespoons honey
2 tablespoons rum or peach brandy

Bring first 3 ingredients to boil. Add peaches a few at a time, and poach, simmering gently until barely tender. Remove peaches to bowl. Boil syrup until very thick, add honey and pour over peaches; chill. Add rum just before serving. Makes 6 servings.

PEARS MOCHA

1 can (29 ounces) pear halves
1-1/2 teaspoons instant-coffee powder
1 package (6 ounces) semisweet
  chocolate pieces, melted
1/2 teaspoon vanilla extract
1/2 cup heavy cream, whipped
1/4 cup chopped walnuts

Drain pears, reserving syrup, and chill. Dissolve coffee powder in 1/4 cup hot pear syrup and add to chocolate. Beat until cool and smooth but not firm. Fold with vanilla into whipped cream. Arrange pear halves in 4 to 6 dessert dishes, top with chocolate mixture and sprinkle with nuts. Serve at once. If desserts must stand, chill pears and sauce separately. If sauce becomes too thick, thin with a little pear syrup. Makes 4 to 6 servings.

ROSY RHUBARB COMPOTE

1 cup sugar
2 tablespoons honey
1 teaspoon grated orange rind
2-1/2 cups fresh rhubarb, cut in 1-1/2"
  pieces
Fresh strawberries (optional)

Mix first 3 ingredients with 1/4 cup water in 2-quart saucepan. Bring to boil and simmer 6 to 8 minutes. Add rhubarb, slowly bring again to boil and simmer 3 minutes, or until pieces are soft and translucent but still whole. Chill. Serve with a few fresh strawberries, if desired. Makes 4 servings. **Note** Use leftover syrup for cooking fresh pears or peaches.

FROZEN FRUITS WITH KIRSCH

Partially thaw frozen mixed fruit. Add kirsch to taste. Sprinkle with chopped fresh mint and serve at once.

BANANA MOUNDS WITH STRAWBERRIES

1 cup dairy sour cream
1/2 teaspoon cinnamon
2 tablespoons maple or maple-blended
  syrup
3 firm-ripe bananas
1 cup flaked coconut
1 pint strawberries, hulled, sliced and
  sweetened

Mix first 3 ingredients. Cut bananas in 1" chunks, dip in sour-cream mixture, then roll in coconut. Put in serving dish and surround with strawberries. Chill at least 30 minutes. Makes 6 servings.

STRAWBERRIES AND SOUR CREAM

1 pint strawberries, washed and hulled
1 tablespoon sugar
1/4 pound marshmallows, diced
1 cup dairy sour cream

Set 4 attractive whole berries aside in refrigerator for decoration. Have remaining berries at room temperature, slice and mix with sugar. Let stand 10 minutes. Fold marshmallows and berries into sour cream and chill at least 1 hour. Pile lightly in sherbet glasses and top each with a whole berry. Makes 4 servings.

STRAWBERRIES CHANTILLY

1 quart strawberries
2 cups heavy cream
1/2 cup grated sweet cooking chocolate
2 tablespoons sifted confectioners' sugar
2 tablespoons light rum

Hull berries and arrange in bowl. Whip cream until foamy and barely thickened. Fold in chocolate, confectioners' sugar and rum; chill. Serve as sauce for strawberries. Makes 6 servings.

FRUIT CREAM DESSERT

1 can (1 pound) fruit cocktail, well
  drained
1 can (8 ounces) mandarin oranges,
  well drained
1 cup dairy sour cream
1 tablespoon lemon or lime juice
Flaked or shredded coconut

Mix all ingredients, except coconut, and put in serving bowl. Sprinkle with coconut and chill. Makes 4 to 6 servings.

LEMON MOUSSE IN ORANGE SHELLS

6 oranges
4 eggs, separated
1/2 cup sugar
Grated rind of 1 lemon
3 tablespoons lemon juice
1 cup heavy cream, whipped
Minted Leaves and Stems, below

Slice off tops of oranges about 1" down from stem end and reserve. Using a small sharp knife, remove pulp from oranges and cut in small pieces, discarding white membrane. (Drain off juice and reserve for other use.) Beat egg yolks until thick; beat in next 3 ingredients. Put in top part of double boiler over simmering water and cook, stirring, 5 minutes, or until very thick. Put in large bowl to cool. Fold in stiffly beaten egg whites, cream and orange pieces. Spoon about 1/2 cup mixture into each orange cup. Chill several hours. Arrange 2 minted leaves and a stem on each orange top and place on oranges. Makes 6 servings.

MINTED LEAVES AND STEMS

In mixing bowl, beat 1/4 cup small-curd creamed cottage cheese and 3 cups sifted confectioners' sugar. Add more sugar if needed to make a stiff workable mixture. Tint a delicate shade of green. Flavor with 1/4 teaspoon peppermint or wintergreen extract. Knead stiff mixture several turns. Sprinkle board generously with granulated sugar. Cover mixture with a piece of waxed paper and roll to about 1/2" thickness. Remove paper, turn mixture over and roll to 1/4" thickness. With small knife, cut leaves and make indentations to resemble veins. Roll small balls to make stems.

MOUSSE AU CHOCOLAT
(Chocolate Mousse)

1 package (6 ounces) semisweet chocolate
  pieces
6 eggs, separated
Grated rind of 1 orange
1/3 cup sugar
Whipped cream, sweetened

Melt chocolate in top part of double boiler over hot water. Beat egg yolks lightly and stir into chocolate. Heat several minutes, but do not let water in double boiler come to a boil. Add orange rind and sugar and cool slightly. Beat egg whites until stiff and fold into the chocolate mixture thoroughly. Pour into individual serving dishes and chill several hours. Serve with whipped cream. Makes 6 servings.

STRAWBERRIES ROMANOFF

1 quart strawberries
1/4 cup sugar
1/2 pint vanilla ice cream
1 cup heavy cream, whipped
1/4 cup Cointreau

Wash berries, hull and sprinkle with sugar. Chill at least 3 hours. Just before serving, soften ice cream slightly and beat until fluffy; fold into cream with Cointreau and strawberries, reserving a few to put on top. Serve at once. Makes 6 to 8 servings.

JELLIED PEACH MELBA

1 box (3 ounces) raspberry-flavor gelatin
1 box (12 ounces) frozen raspberries
6 canned or fresh peach halves
1 pint vanilla ice cream

Dissolve gelatin in 1 cup very hot water. Add berries and stir gently until thawed. Chill until slightly thickened. Put a peach half, rounded side up, in bottom of each of 6 individual molds. Pour gelatin over peach halves and chill until firm. Unmold; top each with a scoop of ice cream. Makes 6 servings.

MANGO SPECIAL

Put half a ripe mango in each sherbet glass. Top with pineapple sherbet and fill glasses with chilled champagne.

FROZEN FRUITS WITH KIRSCH

Partially thaw frozen mixed fruit. Add kirsch to taste. Sprinkle with chopped fresh mint and serve at once.

SHERRY ALMOND SNOW

1 envelope unflavored gelatin
3 egg whites
1/8 teaspoon salt
1/2 cup sugar
1/4 teaspoon almond extract
3 tablespoons sherry
1/3 cup toasted almond slivers
Sherry Custard Sauce (page 398)

Soften gelatin in 1/4 cup cold water; dissolve in 1/3 cup boiling water. Chill until it just begins to thicken. Beat until frothy. Beat egg whites with salt until stiff; gradually beat in sugar. Add almond extract, sherry and frothy gelatin. Pour into 1 1/2-quart mold, alternating layers of gelatin mixture and almonds. Chill for at least 4 hours. Unmold and serve with Sherry Custard Sauce. Makes 6 servings.

JELLIED WINE

1/2 cup sugar
1 envelope unflavored gelatin
2 tablespoons lemon juice
1 cup rosé or red wine
1/4 cup sherry
Whipped cream

Mix sugar and gelatin. Add 1/2 cup boiling water and stir until gelatin dissolves. Add next 3 ingredients and blend well. Pour into four 4-ounce molds and chill until firm. Unmold and serve with whipped cream. Makes 4 servings.

LIME GELATIN WITH LEMON CREAM MOLDS

1 package (3 ounces) lime-flavor gelatin
1/4 cup sugar
2 egg yolks
1 cup heavy cream
1 tablespoon lemon juice
1 teaspoon grated lemon rind
1 envelope unflavored gelatin
1 lime or lemon, thinly sliced

Dissolve lime gelatin in 1 cup boiling water, then stir in 1 cup cold water. Pour into shallow round serving platter 10" to 12" in diameter. Chill until set. Combine sugar, egg yolks and cream. Beat with whisk or rotary beater until mixture coats a spoon. Add lemon juice and rind. Soften unflavored gelatin in 1/4 cup cold water. Dissolve over low heat and pour into egg-cream mixture, stirring; blend well. Rinse six 4-ounce molds with cold water and divide mixture evenly among them. Chill until set. Unmold on lime gelatin. Decorate with lime slices. Makes 6 servings.

BRANDIED COFFEE JELLY

2 envelopes unflavored gelatin
2 cups hot strong coffee
1/2 cup sugar
2 tablespoons lemon juice
2 tablespoons brandy
Sour-cream Sauce

Soften gelatin in 1/2 cup cold water. Add hot coffee and sugar and stir until sugar and gelatin are dissolved. Add lemon juice and brandy, pour into 8" square pan and chill several hours, or until firm. Cut in cubes and serve with sauce. Makes 4 to 6 servings. **Sour-cream Sauce** Combine 1 cup sour cream, 1/4 cup packed light brown sugar and 1/8 teaspoon cinnamon. Beat until sugar is dissolved.

JELLIED MOCHA DESSERT

1 envelope unflavored gelatin
2 cups milk
2 packages (1 ounce each) chocolate-fudge-flavor shake mix
1 teaspoon instant coffee powder (See Note)
1/4 teaspoon vanilla extract
Whipped cream or chocolate sauce

In small saucepan, soften gelatin in 1/2 cup milk. Heat gently, stirring, until gelatin is dissolved. Beat in remaining milk and next 3 ingredients. Pour into serving dishes or bowl; chill until firm. Serve with whipped cream or chocolate sauce. Makes 4 servings. **Note** If freeze-dried coffee is used, dissolve in hot gelatin mixture before adding remaining milk.

FRESH-PLUM SAUCE

Cut fresh red plums in quarters and remove pits. Put in blender and whirl until puréed. Add a little corn syrup and lemon juice and sweeten to taste with sugar.

DANISH RUM PUDDING WITH RASPBERRY SAUCE

1 envelope unflavored gelatin
1 cup sugar
1/4 teaspoon salt
1-1/4 cups milk
4 eggs, separated
1/4 cup light rum
1 cup heavy cream, whipped
Fresh strawberries (optional)
Raspberry Sauce

In top part of double boiler, mix gelatin, 1/2 cup sugar and salt. Stir in milk and heat to scalding. Beat egg yolks slightly and gradually stir in milk mixture. Put over simmering water and cook, stirring, until mixture coats a metal spoon. Add rum, cool, then chill until mixture begins to set. Beat egg whites until foamy, then gradually add remaining 1/2 cup sugar and beat until stiff. Fold with whipped cream into first mixture. Pour into 2-quart mold rinsed with cold water and chill 4 hours or overnight. Unmold and fill center with strawberries, if desired. Serve with the sauce. Makes 8 servings. **Raspberry Sauce** Thaw 1 box (10 ounces) frozen raspberries. Put in saucepan and crush. Stir in 1 teaspoon cornstarch mixed with a little cold water. Put over low heat and cook, stirring, until slightly thickened. If not sweet enough for taste, add a little sugar. Chill.

PEACH BAVARIAN

1 envelope unflavored gelatin
1-1/2 cups puréed peeled firm-ripe
   peaches (see Note)
2 tablespoons lemon juice
1/3 cup sugar
1/4 teaspoon salt
1 teaspoon grated orange rind
1/4 teaspoon almond extract
1 cup heavy cream, whipped
Sweetened sliced peaches

Soften gelatin in ¼ cup cold water, then dissolve over hot water. Combine the peaches, lemon juice, sugar, salt, orange rind and almond extract. Add to gelatin. Chill until mixture begins to set. Beat well with rotary beater, then fold in cream. Put in 1-quart mold and chill several hours, or until set. Unmold and serve with sweetened sliced peaches. Or chill mixture, spoon into serving dishes and top with sliced peaches. Makes 6 servings. **Note** To make peach purée, whirl about 2 cups diced, pitted and peeled firm-ripe peaches in blender; or force through sieve or food mill.

SNOW PUDDING WITH STRAWBERRY SAUCE

1 envelope unflavored gelatin
3/4 cup sugar
1/8 teaspoon salt
Grated rind of 1 lemon
1/4 cup lemon juice
3 egg whites
Strawberry Sauce
Toasted sliced almonds

Soften gelatin in ¼ cup cold water. Add ½ cup sugar, the salt and 1 cup boiling water; stir to dissolve gelatin and sugar. Add rind and juice and chill until partially set. Beat egg whites until almost stiff; gradually add remaining ¼ cup sugar, beating until stiff. Add gelatin mixture and beat until well blended. Chill until firm. Using large serving spoon, mound in glass serving bowl, drizzle sauce on top and sprinkle with nuts. Makes 6 to 8 servings.

Strawberry Sauce

Wash, hull and slice 1 pint strawberries and purée in blender or by hand. In top part of double boiler, mix 3 egg yolks, 3 tablespoons sugar, ¼ cup water and strawberry purée. Cook, stirring, over hot water until thickened and foamy. Flavor with ½ teaspoon strawberry extract; chill. If too pale, tint with a few drops red food coloring, if desired.

JELLIED GINGER SOUR CREAM WITH PINEAPPLE

1 envelope unflavored gelatin
1 pint dairy sour cream
Grated rind of 1 lemon
1 tablespoon lemon juice
1/4 cup sugar
1/4 teaspoon ginger
1 can (13-1/4 ounces) crushed pineapple,
   chilled

Soften gelatin in ¼ cup cold water and dissolve over low heat. Beat into sour cream with next 4 ingredients. Pour into 2½-cup mold rinsed with cold water. Chill until set. Unmold and serve topped with pineapple. Makes 4 or 5 servings.

PEAR-ORANGE MOLD

2 packages (3 ounces each) orange-flavor
   gelatin
1 can (8 ounces) mandarin oranges,
   drained and syrup reserved
1 can (8-3/4 ounces) sliced pears, drained
   and syrup reserved
1/2 cup pecans
1 can (1 pound 13 ounces) pear halves
Red food coloring
Mint sprigs

Dissolve gelatin in 2 cups hot water. Add ¾ cup cold water. To reserved orange syrup add enough reserved pear syrup to make 1 cup; add to gelatin, stirring slightly, and chill until mixture thickens. Add oranges, sliced pears and nuts. Pour into 6-cup mold and chill overnight. Chill pear halves and drain. Dilute food coloring with a little water and rub on pears to give a blush. Unmold dessert on serving plate; surround with pear halves standing on end (cut a little off wide end if necessary). Decorate with mint. Makes 6 to 8 servings.

BANANA-STRAWBERRY DESSERT

1 box (3 ounces) strawberry-banana or
   strawberry-flavor gelatin
Grated rind of 1 lemon
1/2 cup heavy cream, whipped
4 fully ripe medium bananas, sliced
Additional banana slices and/or fresh
   strawberries

Dissolve gelatin in 1 cup boiling water. Add 1 cup cold water and lemon rind and chill until thickened but not firm. Fold in cream. Alternate layers of gelatin mixture and banana slices in parfait glasses or dessert dishes. Decorate with fruit. Makes 6 servings.

FROZEN ORANGE CREAM DELUXE

1 can (6 ounces) frozen orange juice, thawed
1 envelope unflavored gelatin
3/4 cup sugar
1/8 teaspoon salt
1/2 cup Grand Marnier liqueur, curaçao or Triple Sec
1 pint heavy cream, whipped

Beat orange juice and 1½ cups water until blended. Put ¼ cup in small saucepan. Sprinkle with gelatin and let stand 5 minutes. Dissolve over hot water or very low heat. Add to orange juice with sugar, salt and liqueur; fold in cream. Pour into refrigerator tray and freeze, stirring once or twice. Makes about 8 servings.

TROPICAL SHERBET

1 can (9 ounces) crushed pineapple
1 can (6 ounces) frozen strawberry-lemon punch
2 cups dairy sour cream, whipped
2 egg whites, stiffly beaten
1 tablespoon minced preserved ginger
Fresh strawberries

Drain juice from pineapple and add to punch and sour cream. Turn into freezing tray and freeze to a mush. Remove from freezer and beat in chilled bowl. Fold in egg whites, pineapple and ginger. Return to trays and freeze. Top each serving with a berry. Makes 6 servings.

FRENCH VANILLA ICE CREAM

Make this in the old-fashioned freezer.

6 egg yolks
2 cups milk
1 cup sugar
1/4 teaspoon salt
2 cups heavy cream
1 tablespoon vanilla

In top part of double boiler beat egg yolks and milk with rotary beater. Add sugar and salt; cook over simmering water, stirring constantly, until mixture is thickened and coats a metal spoon. Let cool, then add cream and vanilla. Freeze in a crank-type freezer. Makes about 1½ quarts.
Peach Ice Cream Prepare French Vanilla Ice Cream, substituting 1 teaspoon almond extract for vanilla. Partially freeze. Add 2 cups sweetened crushed fresh peaches (or use thawed frozen). Finish freezing.
Berry Ice Cream Prepare French Vanilla Ice Cream, omitting vanilla. Partially freeze. Add 2 cups sweetened crushed fresh raspberries (or use thawed frozen). Finish freezing.

COCONUT SNOWBALLS

Shape any flavor ice cream into balls; roll quickly in flaked coconut. Put in freezer until firm. Serve with chocolate or other sauce.

PINEAPPLE MILK SHERBET

Mix 1¾ cups milk, ½ cup sugar, 1 can (9 ounces) crushed pineapple, 2 tablespoons lemon juice and ¼ cup orange juice. Stir until sugar is dissolved. Pour into 9″ x 5″ x 3″ loaf pan; freeze, stirring twice. Serves 6.

STRAWBERRY SHERBET

1 egg, separated
1/2 cup dry instant nonfat milk
1/3 cup sugar
3 tablespoons lemon juice
1 cup sweetened sliced fresh strawberries or 1 box (12 ounces) frozen sliced berries, thawed

In small bowl of electric mixer, beat egg white, milk and ⅓ cup water until fluffy. Gradually add sugar, then lemon juice, beating until stiff. Stir in egg yolk, then fold in berries with their syrup. Pour into freezing trays or loaf pan and freeze until firm. Makes 6 servings.

PEANUT-BUTTER ICE CREAM

Good with hot fudge sauce, topped with salted peanuts.

2 egg yolks
1 tall can (13 ounces) undiluted evaporated milk
1/2 cup peanut butter
2/3 cup sugar
Dash of salt

Beat egg yolks well. Blend in remaining ingredients and turn into freezer tray. Freeze until frozen 1″ along edges of tray. Turn into chilled bowl and beat until smooth and fluffy. Return to tray and freeze until just firm. Makes 4 to 6 servings.

CRANBERRY MOUSSE

1 package (3 ounces) cream cheese, softened
1/4 cup sugar
1/8 teaspoon salt
1 cup heavy cream, whipped
1 can (1 pound) whole cranberry sauce

Beat cream cheese until fluffy; stir in sugar and salt and fold into cream. Add cranberry sauce and mix lightly. Pour into refrigerator tray and freeze until firm. Serves 6.

SPUMONI

2 cups milk
5 egg yolks, slightly beaten
1/8 teaspoon salt
1 cup sugar
1 teaspoon vanilla
1 cup heavy cream, whipped
8 maraschino cherries, finely chopped
2 tablespoons minced candied orange
  peel
8 slivered blanched almonds
2 tablespoons brandy

In top part of double boiler mix milk, egg yolks, salt and ³/₄ cup sugar. Cook over simmering water, stirring constantly, until mixture is thickened and coats a metal spoon. Cool; add vanilla. Pour into refrigerator tray and freeze until almost firm. Line a 2-quart melon mold with frozen mixture. Fold remaining ¹/₄ cup sugar into cream with remaining ingredients. Fill center of mold, cover and freeze in freezer until firm. Wrap in hot cloth a few minutes and unmold on serving plate. Cut in wedges. Makes 6 to 8 servings.

FROZEN VANILLA CUSTARD

Freeze in the refrigerator or freezer.

2 cups milk
3 eggs, beaten
3/4 cup sugar
1/8 teaspoon salt
1 cup heavy cream, whipped
1 tablespoon vanilla

Heat milk in top part of double boiler over boiling water. Mix eggs, sugar and salt. Gradually stir in hot milk. Return to double boiler and cook over simmering water, stirring constantly, until mixture thickens and coats a metal spoon. Remove from heat and cool. Fold in cream and vanilla. Pour into refrigerator tray and freeze until firm. Makes 6 servings.

Frozen Banana - Raisin - Rum Custard Prepare Frozen Vanilla Custard, omitting vanilla. Partially freeze. Meanwhile soak 1 cup finely chopped raisins in ¹/₃ cup light rum 10 minutes. Fold raisins, 1 cup mashed ripe banana and ¹/₂ cup chopped maraschino cherries into partially frozen ice cream. Freeze until firm. Makes 8 servings.

Frozen Caramel Custard Use recipe for Frozen Vanilla Custard, decreasing milk to 1³/₄ cups and vanilla to 2 teaspoons. Increase sugar to 1 cup. Cook half of sugar in small heavy skillet until golden brown and syrupy. Cool slightly; gradually add ¹/₄ cup water and cook, stirring, until syrup is melted. Add to custard mixture and proceed as directed.

BISCUIT TORTONI

2 eggs, separated
1/2 cup sifted confectioners' sugar
2 tablespoons sherry or rum
1/2 teaspoon vanilla extract
1 cup heavy cream, whipped
1/2 cup plus 3 tablespoons crushed
  almond macaroons
1/4 cup maraschino cherries, drained
  and chopped

Beat egg whites until stiff and in peaks. Beat egg yolks with sugar until fluffy. Stir in sherry and vanilla. Fold into whites. Fold in whipped cream, ¹/₂ cup almond macaroons and the cherries. Put mixture in 4-ounce paper dessert dishes. Sprinkle each with a little of the remaining macaroons. Freeze until firm. Serve in paper dishes. Makes 6 to 8 servings.

CHERRIES JUBILEE

1 can (17 ounces) dark sweet cherries
2 tablespoons sugar
Dash of salt
1 tablespoon cornstarch
1/3 cup rum or brandy
1 quart vanilla ice cream

Drain cherries, reserving syrup, and pit. Add water to syrup to make 1 cup. In saucepan mix sugar, salt and cornstarch; add syrup. Cook over low heat until slightly thickened. Add cherries and heat. Add liquor, ignite and spoon over ice cream. Serves 4.

STRAWBERRY-ALMOND ROLL

1 box frozen strawberries, thawed
8 tablespoons sugar
1 teaspoon unflavored gelatin
Red food coloring
3 tablespoons chopped blanched
  almonds
1/4 teaspoon almond extract
1/2 cup heavy cream, whipped

Force berries through sieve. Add 5 tablespoons sugar and enough water to make 2 cups. Sprinkle gelatin on 1 tablespoon cold water and let stand 5 minutes. Dissolve over hot water. Stir into berry mixture. Pour into refrigerator tray and freeze until mushy. Add small amount of red food coloring. Beat well and turn into a 28-ounce can. (It will not fill can.) Put in freezer or freezing compartment of refrigerator until almost firm. Pack mixture onto sides of can, leaving center hollow. Combine remaining sugar, the nuts, flavoring and whipped cream; pour into center. Cover with waxed paper; freeze. To serve, run a spatula around inside of can; wrap in hot cloth until dessert slides out. Cut in slices. Serves 4.

FROZEN ANGEL RING WITH PEACHES

Prepare 1 box (6½ ounces) fluffy white frosting mix as directed on the label. Whip 1 cup heavy cream until stiff. Fold into cooled frosting with ¼ teaspoon each vanilla and almond extracts. Spoon into 1½-quart ring mold and freeze until firm. Dip mold in pan of warm water, then unmold ring on serving plate. Fill center with 1 box frozen sliced peaches, partly thawed. Makes 6 servings.

WINE PEACHES WITH ICE CREAM

8 firm ripe peaches
1 cup each sherry and port wines
Sugar
1 tablespoon red-currant jelly
1 quart vanilla ice cream

Peel peaches, cut in halves and remove pits. Heat wines and 2 tablespoons sugar and add 4 peach pits. Carefully add peach halves to mixture and simmer gently 30 minutes. Remove pits. Remove peaches and chill in flat dish. Cook liquid down to form a thick syrup, adding jelly and more sugar to taste. Chill. To serve, put 2 peach halves in each serving dish and fill with ice cream. Top with sauce. Makes 8 servings.

ICE CREAM BROADWAY ROLL

4 eggs
Sugar
1/2 cup sifted cake flour
1/2 teaspoon double acting baking powder
1/4 teaspoon salt
1 teaspoon cinnamon
1/4 teaspoon baking soda
2-1/2 squares unsweetened chocolate, melted
1 quart vanilla ice cream

Beat eggs slightly. Gradually add ⅔ cup sugar and beat until thick and lemon-colored. Add sifted flour, baking powder, salt and cinnamon and blend well. Blend 3 tablespoons sugar, the soda and 3 tablespoons water with chocolate; fold into batter. Grease 15½" x 10½" x 1" pan, line with waxed paper and grease again. Pour in batter. Bake in moderate oven (375°F.) about 15 minutes. Turn out on damp towel; remove paper carefully. Roll lengthwise with towel; cool. Unroll. Spread with softened ice cream and reroll. Freeze until firm. Cut in slices to serve. Makes 8 servings.

ORANGE SNOWDRIFT

1 envelope unflavored gelatin
1 cup pineapple juice
1-1/2 cups sugar
1 cup orange juice
Juice of 1 lemon
4 packages (3 ounces each) cream cheese, softened
1/2 teaspoon almond extract
1/4 teaspoon salt
1/2 cup toasted slivered blanched almonds
1 cup heavy cream, whipped

Sprinkle gelatin on pineapple juice in saucepan. Add sugar; heat, stirring, until gelatin and sugar are dissolved. Cool. Add juices. Blend cheese with almond extract, salt and almonds; stir into gelatin and fold in cream. Pour into freezing trays and freeze until firm. Makes 8 servings.

APRICOT-BRANDY ICE CREAM

1 package (10 ounces) frozen or 1 pound fresh peaches
2 tablespoons sugar (optional)
1 pint peach ice cream
1/3 cup apricot brandy

Whirl thawed peaches in blender. If fresh peaches are used, peel, slice and add sugar; whirl in blender. Combine peach purée with softened ice cream and stir in brandy. Work quickly, especially if fruit is not cold. Refreeze in bowl or parfait glasses. Makes 4 servings.

ITALIAN COFFEE BOMBE

Sugar
1/8 teaspoon salt
1 teaspoon flour
2 egg yolks, beaten
1/2 cup milk
1/3 cup Italian or other very strong coffee
1 tablespoon Cointreau or other liqueur
1/2 teaspoon vanilla
2 cups heavy cream

Mix ¼ cup sugar, the salt and flour in small saucepan. Add egg yolks, milk and coffee; mix well. Cook until slightly thickened, stirring constantly. Chill. Add Cointreau and vanilla. Add 2 tablespoons sugar to cream and whip. Line 1-quart mold with half of whipped cream. Fold remaining cream into coffee mixture and pour gently into center of mold. Freeze until firm. Put a cloth wrung out of hot water on mold to loosen; unmold onto serving plate and slice. Makes 6 to 8 servings.

AVOCADO ICE CREAM WITH RASPBERRY SAUCE

3 egg yolks
3/4 cup milk
1/8 teaspoon salt
3/4 cup sugar
1 cup heavy cream
2 ripe avocados
Green food coloring
1 box (12 ounces) frozen raspberries, thawed

In top part of small double boiler, beat egg yolks and milk slightly. Add salt and sugar and cook, stirring, over simmering water until mixture thickens and coats a metal spoon. Remove from heat and cool. Whip cream until thickened. Peel avocados and slice. Add a slice at a time to cream, beating at medium speed. Fold into custard mixture and add a few drops of coloring. Pour into freezing tray and freeze until firm. Whirl berries in blender until foamy, or force through sieve. Serve as a sauce for ice cream. Makes 4 servings.

FROZEN STRAWBERRY MOLDS

Dissolve 1 package (3 ounces) strawberry-flavor gelatin in 1 1/2 cups hot water. At once stir in 1 pint softened strawberry ice cream. Pour into 4 individual molds and chill until firm. Unmold and serve with whipped cream. Decorate with fresh strawberries. Makes 4 servings.

FROZEN LEMON CHEESECAKE

3 eggs, separated
2/3 cup sugar
1/4 teaspoon salt
1/3 cup milk
1 envelope unflavored gelatin
4 packages (3 ounces each) cream cheese, softened
1 large lemon
2/3 cup heavy cream, whipped
1 cup gingersnap crumbs
1/4 cup melted butter

Beat egg yolks with 1/3 cup sugar, the salt and milk. Cook in top part of double boiler over hot water, stirring until mixture coats spoon. Add gelatin softened in 1/3 cup cold water; stir until dissolved. Cool. Beat cheese until light; add grated lemon rind and juice. Add to custard. Make meringue with egg whites and remaining 1/3 cup sugar. Fold with whipped cream into custard. Mix crumbs with butter; press firmly on bottom of 9" springform pan. Carefully pour custard on crust. Freeze until firm. Makes 8 to 10 servings.

STRAWBERRY BAKED ALASKA

1 quart or 2 pints brick strawberry ice cream
Sponge or pound cake
3 egg whites
Dash of salt
3/4 cup marshmallow cream
1 teaspoon vanilla extract
1 box (1 pound) frozen sliced strawberries, thawed

Have ice cream very hard. If pints are used, put together to form one oblong block. Cut 1"-thick slice of cake to fit bottom of block and put cake on a board or oven-proof dish. Put ice cream on cake. Beat next 4 ingredients until stiff. Quickly spread meringue on top and sides of ice cream and cake. Bake in very hot oven (450°F.) 2 or 3 minutes, or until lightly browned. Slice and serve at once with thawed sliced strawberries. Makes 6 servings.

GRAPE LIME ICE

Boil 2 cups water and 1 cup sugar 5 minutes; cool. Add 1 cup grape juice and juice of 2 lemons. Pour into refrigerator tray and partially freeze. Remove from tray to chilled bowl. Beat until fluffy and light. Return to refrigerator tray and freeze until firm. Serves about 6.

ORANGE BUTTERMILK SHERBET

Mix 3 tablespoons sugar, 1 teaspoon grated orange rind, 1/2 cup orange juice, 1/3 cup light corn syrup, 1 1/2 cups buttermilk and 1 tablespoon lemon juice and pour into refrigerator tray; partially freeze. Turn into chilled bowl and beat until fluffy. Return to tray and freeze until firm. Makes 4 servings.

LEMON-LIME SHERBET

1 envelope unflavored gelatin
2 cups milk
2 cups light cream
1/4 teaspoon salt
1/4 cup sugar
1 can (6 ounces) frozen lemon-and-lime ade, partially thawed

In small saucepan, sprinkle gelatin on 1/2 cup milk. Dissolve over hot water or very low heat. Mix with remaining ingredients. Freeze in refrigerator trays until frozen 1" in from edge of tray. Turn into chilled bowl and beat with mixer until smooth but not melted. Return to trays and finish freezing. Serves 6.

RED-AND-WHITE DELIGHT

2 cups creamed cottage cheese
Juice of 1 lemon
1 cup sugar
2 cups dairy sour cream
2 boxes frozen raspberries, partially
   thawed

Force cheese through fine sieve. Add lemon juice and sugar and beat smooth. Add sour cream and mix well. Pour into refrigerator tray and freeze until firm. Cut in serving pieces and serve with raspberries. Serves 8.

MAPLE PARFAIT

6 egg yolks
2/3 cup maple syrup
1/8 teaspoon salt
1 pint heavy cream, whipped

In top part of small double boiler beat egg yolks and syrup. Add salt and cook over simmering water until slightly thickened, stirring constantly. Cool. Fold in whipped cream. Pour into refrigerator tray and freeze until firm. Makes 6 servings.

STRAWBERRY ICE-CREAM-SUNDAE CAKE

1 quart strawberry ice cream,
  slightly softened
Two 8" sponge-cake dessert layers
1 package dessert-topping mix
1 quart strawberries, sliced and
  sweetened, or 1 box (12 ounces) frozen
  sliced strawberries

Pack ice cream into 8" round cake pan lined with waxed paper. Refreeze. Remove paper and put ice cream between cake layers. Press down so that all sides are even. Prepare topping mix according to package directions and spread on top and sides of cake. Freeze. Remove from freezer about 1/2 hour before serving. Garnish with strawberries. Makes 8 servings.

ORANGE SAUCE

1 cup sugar
5 tablespoons flour
1/8 teaspoon salt
Grated rind of 1 orange
Juice of 1/2 lemon
1/2 cup orange juice
3 egg yolks
1 teaspoon butter
1 cup heavy cream, whipped

In a heavy saucepan mix together first 3 ingredients. Add next 4 ingredients. Cook over low heat, stirring, until thickened and smooth; add butter and cool. Fold in whipped cream. Makes about 2 1/4 cups.

FROZEN MARBLE PIE

Crumb Crust, page 419
1 egg white
1/2 teaspoon salt
1/2 cup sifted confectioners' sugar
2 cups heavy cream, whipped
2 tablespoons sherry
1 square unsweetened chocolate, melted
1 teaspoon vanilla

Prepare Crumb Crust with chocolate-cookie crumbs and chill. Beat egg white and salt until frothy; gradually add confectioners' sugar and continue beating until stiff and glossy. Fold in cream. Divide mixture in half and add sherry to one part. Fold cooled chocolate and vanilla into remainder. Spoon mixtures alternately into crust. Freeze. Serves 6.

CHOCOLATE ICE CREAM SODA

Gradually stir 1/2 cup cold milk into 2 tablespoons Chocolate or Cocoa Syrup (page 398). Pour into tall glass; add 1 or 2 scoops chocolate or vanilla ice cream. Fill glass with chilled carbonated water; stir gently to mix.

PINEAPPLE ICE CREAM SODA

Half-fill each glass with cold pineapple juice. Add a scoop of vanilla ice cream and fill glass with cold ginger ale. Sprinkle top with toasted flaked coconut.

STRAWBERRY ICE CREAM SODA

Into a large glass, put 1/3 cup frozen or crushed sweetened fresh strawberries, 3 tablespoons milk and a large scoop of strawberry ice cream. Almost fill glass with chilled carbonated water. Stir.

COFFEE ICE CREAM SODA

Pour 1/4 cup Coffee Syrup (page 398) into tall glass. Add 2 tablespoons heavy cream and stir in a little chilled carbonated water. Put 1 or 2 scoops coffee ice cream in glass and fill with carbonated water, stirring gently to mix.

BUTTERSCOTCH SAUCE

Combine 2 cups packed light-brown sugar, 1/2 cup undiluted evaporated milk, 1/4 teaspoon salt, 1/3 cup light corn syrup and 1/3 cup butter or margarine in saucepan. Bring to boil and cook rapidly 3 minutes to 220°F. on a candy thermometer. Serve hot or cold. Makes 2 cups.

SYRUPS FOR ICE CREAM SODAS

They can also be used as sauces for sundaes, puddings and cakes.

Chocolate Syrup Put 3 squares unsweetened chocolate and ²/₃ cup water in saucepan. Bring to boil and simmer, stirring, until thick and well blended. Add ¹/₂ cup sugar and a dash of salt and boil gently, stirring, 2 minutes. Add ¹/₂ cup corn syrup and bring again to boil. Remove from heat and add ¹/₂ teaspoon vanilla. Pour into jar, cool, cover and refrigerate. Makes about 1¹/₂ cups.

Cocoa Syrup In saucepan, mix 1 cup dry unsweetened cocoa, ³/₄ cup sugar, ¹/₄ teaspoon salt and ¹/₂ cup corn syrup. Gradually stir in 1¹/₄ cups water and put over low heat, stirring until smooth. Boil gently, stirring, 3 minutes. Add ¹/₂ teaspoon vanilla and pour into jar. Store, covered, in refrigerator. Makes about 2 cups.

Coffee Syrup In saucepan, dissolve ¹/₄ cup instant-coffee powder in ¹/₂ cup hot water. Blend in 2 cups dark corn syrup and ¹/₄ teaspoon salt. Bring to boil and simmer 5 minutes. Remove from heat, skim and add 2 teaspoons vanilla. Store, covered, in refrigerator. Makes 2 cups.

SHERRY CUSTARD SAUCE

3 egg yolks, slightly beaten
2 tablespoons sugar
1/2 cup milk
Dash of salt
1/4 teaspoon vanilla extract
1/2 cup heavy cream, whipped
1-1/2 tablespoons sherry

In top part of double boiler over simmering water, cook, stirring, first 4 ingredients until mixture coats a spoon. Cool. Fold in vanilla, whipped cream and sherry. Makes 1³/₄ cups.

HARD SAUCE

Cream ¹/₂ cup soft butter with 1¹/₂ cups sifted confectioners' sugar until light and fluffy. Add 1 teaspoon vanilla or 2 tablespoons rum or brandy. Chill. Makes about 1 cup.

Lemon Hard Sauce Prepare Hard Sauce, omit vanilla and add 1 to 2 teaspoons lemon juice and a little grated lemon rind.

BRANDY HARD SAUCE

Cream 1 cup unsalted butter and 2 cups sifted confectioners' sugar; beat in 1 teaspoon vanilla and ¹/₄ cup brandy. Makes about 1³/₄ cups.

CHERRY SAUCE

1/2 cup sugar
1/8 teaspoon salt
1-1/2 teaspoons potato flour or cornstarch
3/4 cup cherry juice
1/4 cup drained canned red sour cherries
1 tablespoon butter
1 tablespoon lemon juice

Mix first 3 ingredients; stir in cherry juice. Cook over low heat 5 minutes, stirring constantly. Add remaining ingredients. Serve hot. Makes 1¹/₄ cups.

DOUBLESWEET FUDGE SAUCE

1 can (14 ounces) sweetened condensed milk
1 jar (7 ounces) marshmallow cream
1/3 cup milk
1/4 cup butter
1/4 teaspoon salt
1 teaspoon vanilla extract
1 package (6 ounces) semisweet chocolate pieces

Combine first 5 ingredients in saucepan. Cook, stirring, over low heat until mixture thickens slightly and almost boils. Stir vigorously to prevent burning. Remove from heat; stir in vanilla and chocolate pieces. Stir until chocolate has melted and sauce is smooth. Makes about 4 cups.

BITTERSWEET CHOCOLATE SAUCE

4 squares unsweetened chocolate
1 cup sugar
3/4 cup undiluted evaporated milk
1/4 teaspoon instant coffee powder
1/8 teaspoon salt
1/2 teaspoon vanilla extract

Melt chocolate over boiling water. Stir in sugar. Cover and cook ¹/₂ hour, stirring once or twice. Add remaining ingredients and beat vigorously with spoon until smooth and thick. Cover and keep warm until ready to serve. Makes about 1²/₃ cups. *Note* Sauce keeps well in refrigerator. Reheat when ready to serve.

ORANGE HARD SAUCE

Blend ¹/₄ cup butter, softened, with 1 cup sifted confectioners' sugar, 1 teaspoon grated orange rind and 2 to 4 tablespoons fresh orange juice to make a smooth sauce. Or substitute 1 or 2 tablespoons Grand Marnier, curaçao or Triple Sec for some of the orange juice. Cover and chill until firm.

MOLASSES TOFFY SAUCE

Put 1 cup packed brown sugar, $1/3$ cup molasses, $1/4$ cup butter and $1/8$ teaspoon salt in saucepan. Cook, stirring, until sugar is dissolved. Stir in $1/2$ cup light cream. Keep warm over boiling water. Makes $1 1/2$ cups.

LEBANESE RAISIN-NUT SAUCE

Serve on vanilla pudding or plain cake.

Mix in saucepan $1 3/4$ cups light corn syrup and 1 cup mixed light and dark seedless raisins. Bring to boil and simmer 2 or 3 minutes. Remove from heat and add $1/2$ teaspoon cinnamon, dash of salt and $1/2$ cup pine nuts (or $1/2$ cup chopped nuts). Makes 2 cups.

FOAMY SAUCE

In double boiler, cream 1 cup sifted confectioners' sugar and $1/2$ cup soft butter or margarine. Add 2 egg yolks, beaten. Cook over simmering water, stirring, until thickened. Remove from heat. Fold in 1 tablespoon brandy or rum and 2 stiffly beaten egg whites. Serve warm. Makes 4 to 6 servings.

CUSTARD SAUCE

Scald $1 1/2$ cups milk in top of double boiler over simmering water. Mix $1/8$ teaspoon salt, 2 eggs or 3 egg yolks and 3 tablespoons sugar. Stir in small amount of hot milk, put back in double boiler and cook, stirring, until thickened. Cool and flavor sauce with vanilla or almond extract, or grated rind of 1 lemon. Makes 2 cups.

MOCK DEVONSHIRE CREAM

Soften 3-ounce package of cream cheese to room temperature. Blend with 2 to 3 tablespoons heavy cream or dairy sour cream. When smooth, fold in 2 tablespoons confectioners' sugar and $1/2$ teaspoon vanilla. Makes $1/2$ cup.

APRICOT-BRANDY SAUCE

Mix together $1 1/2$ cups apricot jam, $1/2$ cup water and 3 tablespoons sugar. Simmer for 10 minutes, stirring often. Add 2 tablespoons apricot, peach or other brandy. Makes 2 cups.

LEMON SAUCE

Mix in saucepan $1/2$ cup sugar, $1/8$ teaspoon salt and 2 tablespoons cornstarch. Gradually stir in 1 cup boiling water. Cook, stirring, until thickened. Remove from heat; stir in 2 tablespoons butter, juice of 1 lemon and 1 teaspoon grated rind. Serve warm. Makes $1 3/4$ cups.

Orange Sauce Substitute 1 cup orange juice for boiling water, and reduce lemon juice to 1 tablespoon.

Vanilla Sauce Prepare Lemon Sauce, omitting lemon juice and rind. Add 1 teaspoon vanilla extract.

THIN CHOCOLATE GLAZE

Melt together $1/4$ cup butter and 4 squares unsweetened chocolate. Beat in $1/4$ cup boiling water, 2 cups sifted confectioners' sugar, $1/8$ teaspoon salt and $1/2$ teaspoon vanilla extract. Beat well. Makes enough to cover tops and sides of two 9" layers.

PEANUT CHOCOLATE SAUCE

Serve it warm on vanilla ice cream, plain cake or pudding.

Melt $2 1/2$ squares unsweetened chocolate in $1/2$ cup milk. Add dash of salt and $3/4$ cup packed light-brown sugar. Cook, stirring, until sugar is dissolved. Remove from heat and add $1/2$ teaspoon vanilla and $1/4$ cup crunchy peanut butter. Makes about $1 1/2$ cups sauce.

CRÈME DE MENTHE CHERRIES

Serve as a sauce for ice cream, vanilla pudding or other desserts.

Drain 2 jars (8 ounces each) green maraschino cherries, reserving $1/4$ cup of the syrup. Mix cherries with $1/2$ cup green crème de menthe and reserved syrup. Makes about $1 1/2$ cups.

PINEAPPLE-GINGER SAUCE

1 can (8-1/2 ounces) crushed pineapple
3/4 cup pineapple juice
1/2 cup sugar
1/4 cup light corn syrup
2 dashes Angostura
2 tablespoons chopped preserved ginger
1/2 cup coarsely chopped macadamia nuts

Combine all ingredients, except nuts. Bring to boil and simmer about 15 minutes. Cool and add nuts. Serve on ice cream, cake, pancakes or waffles. Makes about 2 cups.

PEANUT-BUTTER TOPPING

1/2 cup peanut butter, creamy or chunky
1 cup light corn syrup
1/2 cup salted peanuts, coarsely chopped

Mix all ingredients thoroughly and store in tightly covered jar. Serve on cake or ice cream. Makes about 1½ cups.

CREAMY BANANA TOPPING

1 fully ripe banana, diced
1 cup thawed frozen whipped topping
1 tablespoon milk
1 teaspoon vanilla extract

Gently fold all ingredients together and use as topping for plain cakes or pudding. Makes about 1¼ cups. Will keep 1 to 2 hours in refrigerator.

STRAWBERRY SATIN SAUCE

2 eggs, separated
1-1/2 cups sifted confectioners' sugar
Dash of salt
1 teaspoon each vanilla and lemon juice
1 pint fresh strawberries
1 tablespoon granulated sugar

Beat egg whites until foamy. Gradually add half the confectioners' sugar, beating until stiff and glossy. Beat egg yolks with remaining confectioners' sugar, salt, vanilla and lemon juice until thick and light-colored. Fold into whites. (Complete recipe at once or cover mixture and chill a few hours.) Shortly before serving, slice berries, toss with granulated sugar and crush lightly with fork. Fold into egg sauce. Good on tortes, cakes or puddings. Makes 10 servings.

VANILLA-COFFEE LIQUEUR

1-1/2 cups packed brown sugar
1 cup granulated sugar
1/2 cup instant-coffee powder
3 cups vodka
1/2 vanilla bean, split, or
   2 tablespoons vanilla extract

Combine sugars and 2 cups water. Bring to boil and boil 5 minutes. Gradually stir in coffee, using a wire whisk; cool. Pour into a tall bottle, jar or jug; add vodka and vanilla and mix thoroughly. Cover and let stand at least 2 weeks. Remove vanilla bean. Good as after-dinner liquer, over fruit or ice cream. Can also be used to flavor Bavarians or eggnog pies. Makes about 5 cups.

MELBA SAUCE

1 package (10 ounces) frozen raspberries
1/2 cup currant jelly
1/2 cup sugar

Combine all ingredients in saucepan and bring to boil. Simmer 20 minutes, or until of desired thickness. Pour into sterilized jar and seal. Makes about 1 cup.

COCONUT-PINEAPPLE SAUCE

1/4 cup butter or margarine
3/4 cup packed brown sugar
1 can (8-1/2 ounces) pineapple tidbits
1/2 cup flaked coconut

Put butter in saucepan with brown sugar and heat, stirring, until butter is melted and blended with sugar. Drain syrup from pineapple and add enough water to make ½ cup (or add pineapple juice, if available). Add to first mixture and bring to boil. Add pineapple and coconut, bring to boil and simmer about 4 minutes. Serve warm on ice cream or creamy puddings. Makes about 2 cups.

CHOCOLATE CRINKLE CUPS

Fill them with ice cream, whipped cream or sherbet.

Melt 6 squares semisweet chocolate in top of double boiler over hot water. Place 6 to 8 paper cups (3″ to 4″ in diameter) in muffin pan. With a spoon, line inside of cups with chocolate, coating all folds evenly. Put muffin pan in refrigerator until ready to use. Quickly peel paper off cups. Decorate filled cups with chocolate curls.

RUM-RAISIN SAUCE

1/4 cup honey
3 tablespoons butter or margarine
Grated rind of 1 lemon
1 cup golden raisins
2 tablespoons lemon juice
1/2 cup sugar
1 tablespoon cornstarch
Dash of salt
2 tablespoons dark rum or 1 teaspoon
   rum extract

Combine first 5 ingredients and 1 cup water in small saucepan. Add sugar mixed with cornstarch and salt. Bring to boil, stirring, and simmer 4 to 5 minutes. Add rum and blend well. Makes 2 cups. Store, covered, in refrigerator. Reheat to serve on ice cream, plain cake, bread or rice pudding. Recipe can be doubled, if desired.

NORMAN KARLSON

He-man Longboy

BREAD FOR SANDWICHES

Hot or cold, at home, school or office, sandwiches are a national lunchtime favorite.

Choose the bread carefully. Packaged sliced bread is fine for picnic or lunchbox sandwiches, but for tea or cocktail sandwiches, unsliced bread is best.

It should be at least 24 hours old to slice easily. Ready-cut slices can be sliced again with a thin sharp knife.

Varying the kind of bread avoids monotony for those who eat sandwiches frequently. Choose whole-wheat, raisin, oatmeal, rye, Boston brown bread, cracked-wheat, pumpernickel, nut bread, orange bread, hero loaves, seeded and sandwich rolls.

SANDWICH STORAGE

Keep prepared sandwiches well covered and refrigerated until time to serve them. Plates of sandwiches can be covered with waxed paper, foil or plastic, wrapped in a damp cloth and refrigerated. Waxed-paper or plastic envelopes are convenient for enclosing individual sandwiches.

SANDWICH FILLINGS

Many prepared fillings are available: deviled ham; luncheon-meat spread; corned-beef spread; liver pâté; cream cheese with pimientos, with olives and pimientos, with pineapple, with chives and with Roquefort; chicken spread; chipped-olive spread; blue-cheese spread; bacon-cheese spread; smoke-flavored cheese spread and many others. Hot meat and poultry sandwiches can be varied by serving them open-faced with sauce or gravy such as cheese sauce, meat-loaf sauce, tomato sauce, sour-cream sauce, spaghetti sauce, curry sauce, brown or mushroom gravy or à la king sauce. Many sauces and gravies are available in cans or packages.

FOR A CROWD

1 medium head of lettuce averages 16 leaves. 1 pint of mayonnaise spreads about 50 average slices of bread if you use 1 1/2 teaspoons (1/2 tablespoon) per slice.

1 pound of softened butter or margarine spreads about 96 slices if you use 1 teaspoonful per slice.

1 pound of cheese averages 16 slices.

CREAM-CHEESE, LIVERWURST AND MUSHROOM SANDWICHES

Mash together 8 ounces soft cream cheese and ¾ pound liverwurst. Brown 1 can (3 ounces) drained chopped mushrooms lightly in 3 tablespoons butter or margarine. Add to cheese mixture with 1 tablespoon instant minced onion, 2 tablespoons Worcestershire, ½ teaspoon salt, ⅛ teaspoon pepper and ½ cup undiluted evaporated milk. Makes filling for 4 sandwiches.

BEEF-AND-BEAN BURGERS

4 ounces dried beef
1 can (8 ounces) kidney beans, drained
1/3 cup mayonnaise
1/4 cup sweet-pickle relish
2 tablespoons minced onion
1 tablespoon prepared mustard
4 sandwich rolls
1/2 cup shredded Cheddar cheese

Cover beef with boiling water. Drain and shred. Mash beans slightly; mix with beef and next 4 ingredients. Split rolls and toast. Spread meat mixture on rolls and sprinkle with cheese. Broil 5 minutes, or until cheese melts. Makes 4 servings.

DEVILED-HAM SWISS ROLLS

6 frankfurter rolls
Mustard
Butter or margarine
12 thin slices Swiss cheese
1 can (4-1/2 ounces) deviled ham
12 dill-pickle strips

Split rolls almost through lengthwise and cut in half crosswise. Spread with mustard and butter. Spread cheese with a layer of deviled ham. Put a pickle strip at one end of each cheese slice and roll as for jelly roll. Press cheese roll into each frankfurter roll. Makes 6 servings.

HAM SALAD ROLLS

2 cups finely diced cooked ham
2 cups finely shredded cabbage
1/2 cup diced celery
1/2 green pepper, minced
1 hard-cooked egg, chopped
2 tablespoons prepared mustard
Dash of onion salt
8 frankfurter rolls
Salad dressing
Sweet-pickle slices

Mix first 7 ingredients. Open rolls; remove some crumbs from centers and add to first mixture. Moisten salad with dressing and fill rolls. Garnish with pickle. Makes 8 servings.

LAMB-TARTAR SANDWICHES

Mix ½ cup mayonnaise, ½ teaspoon instant minced onion, a dash of cayenne, 1 teaspoon minced parsley and 1 tablespoon each chopped stuffed olives, capers and pickle relish. Spread on 4 slices white bread. Top with slices of cold roast lamb, lettuce leaves and 4 slices bread. Serves 4.

CABBAGE-SALAD SUPPER SANDWICH

2 cups finely shredded raw cabbage
1 small carrot, cooked and sliced
1/2 cup cooked or canned peas
1/4 pound cooked ham or veal, cut in thin strips
Pinch each of rosemary, basil and paprika
2 tablespoons mayonnaise
2 tablespoons heavy cream, whipped with fork
Salt and pepper
8 slices dark rye bread, buttered

Mix first 5 ingredients. Combine mayonnaise with the whipped cream and fold into the mixture. Add salt and pepper to taste. Heap high on bread and serve open-faced. Serves 4.

GRILLED LUNCHEON-MEAT SANDWICHES

1 can (12 ounces) luncheon meat, finely diced
1/2 cup chopped celery
1 small onion, minced
1/2 cup chopped black olives
2 hard-cooked eggs, chopped
1/3 cup mayonnaise
8 slices white bread
8 slices Cheddar cheese

Combine first 6 ingredients. Spread on bread and top with a cheese slice. Broil slowly until cheese is bubbly. Makes 8 servings.

HOT HERO SANDWICHES

Cut 1 pound hot Italian sausage in ½" chunks and brown lightly in heavy skillet. Add 3 tablespoons olive oil, 4 large green peppers cut in strips and ½ teaspoon salt. Simmer until peppers are cooked but not brown. Cut each loaf in half horizontally. Put bottom slices on baking sheet. Divide cooked mixture evenly on bread. Add oil from skillet to each; top with layer of grated Parmesan cheese and bread tops. Cut each loaf in 3 pieces crosswise. Heat in moderate oven (400°F.) 5 minutes. Makes 6 sandwiches.

CORNED-BEEF POORBOYS

1/4 cup mayonnaise
2 tablespoons dairy sour cream
2 dill pickles, finely chopped
2 teaspoons minced capers
4 oblong hard (hero) rolls, split
Lettuce leaves
4 servings thinly sliced cooked corned beef
3 tomatoes, sliced
4 tablespoons finely chopped green onion
Salt and pepper
1 cucumber, peeled and sliced

Mix first 4 ingredients and spread on both halves of rolls. Cover bottom halves with lettuce, beef and tomato slices. Sprinkle each with 1 tablespoon green onion and with salt and pepper. Top with cucumber slices and season again. Cover with top halves of rolls. Makes 4 servings.

MONTE CRISTO SANDWICHES

For each sandwich, use 3 slices bread. Butter 1 slice and cover with a slice each baked ham and cooked chicken. Butter both sides of second bread slice. Put on meat and cover with a generous slice of Swiss cheese. Butter third slice and put on cheese; press slightly and secure with a toothpick. Trim off crusts and cut in half diagonally. Mix 3 slightly beaten eggs, 1/3 cup milk and 1/8 teaspoon salt (makes enough for 4 servings—eight 3-layer triangles). Dip sandwich triangles into egg mixture. Sauté in butter in skillet until golden brown on all sides, adding more butter when necessary. Remove toothpicks. Two triangles make a generous serving.

PORK AND CURRIED-COLESLAW SANDWICHES

8 thin pork chops, boned
Salt and pepper
Flour
1 tablespoon butter
1-1/2 teaspoons curry powder
1/4 cup mayonnaise
2 tablespoons vinegar
4 cups finely shredded or chopped cabbage
4 sandwich rolls, split and toasted

Roll chops in seasoned flour and fry in greased skillet until browned and done. Remove and keep hot. Melt butter in skillet; blend in 2 teaspoons flour and the curry powder. Add 1/3 cup water, the mayonnaise and vinegar. Cook, stirring, until slightly thickened. Add cabbage and cook a few minutes longer. Arrange chops on bottom rolls and top with slaw. Add roll tops. Makes 4.

CORNED-BEEF-SALAD SANDWICHES

Mix 1 cup chopped cooked corned beef, 1/2 cup finely chopped celery, 2 tablespoons minced onion, 1/2 cup mayonnaise and 2 tablespoons prepared mustard. Good with rye bread. Makes filling for 4 large sandwiches.

FRANKFURTER SANDWICHES WITH ONION-CHILI SAUCE

1 cup minced onion
2 cloves garlic, minced
1/4 cup butter or margarine
1/2 teaspoon salt
1/8 teaspoon pepper
1-1/2 teaspoons Worcestershire
1-1/2 tablespoons prepared mustard
1-1/2 teaspoons sugar
1/2 cup chili sauce
1 pound frankfurters
Thick slices of Italian bread, toasted

Cook onion and garlic in the butter until golden. Add remaining ingredients, except last 2; heat through. Add frankfurters split lengthwise and simmer 5 minutes. Serve with sauce between toasted bread slices. Makes 4 servings.

LIVER-AND-BACON SANDWICHES

Cook 8 slices bacon until crisp. Remove bacon and pour off some of the fat. With fork, prick 1 pound chicken livers. Cook in fat until browned on both sides. Force through food chopper, using medium blade; put bacon and 1 peeled small onion through food chopper. Add 2 tablespoons prepared mustard and enough mayonnaise or salad dressing to moisten. Season to taste with salt and pepper. Spread between 8 slices bread. Serve with tomato wedges. Makes 4 servings.

ROAST BEEF ON RYE

1/2 cup dairy sour cream
1 tablespoon dry onion-soup mix
1 teaspoon horseradish, drained
1/4 teaspoon salt
Dash of pepper
12 slices cold roast beef
8 slices rye bread, buttered
4 lettuce leaves
4 slices garlic dill pickle

Mix first 5 ingredients. Lay 3 slices beef on each of 4 buttered bread slices. Top with lettuce leaf and a spoonful of sour-cream mixture. Cover with second bread slice. Cut diagonally and serve with a garnish of dill pickle. Makes 4 servings.

HOT HAM ROLLS

Mix ground ham with minced celery, prepared mustard and mayonnaise. Remove crusts from soft bread and spread with ham mixture. Roll up and secure with toothpicks. Brush with melted butter and bake in hot oven (400°F.) until golden.

ITALIAN HAM SANDWICH

1 medium loaf Italian bread
1-1/2 cups finely chopped ham
2 tablespoons mayonnaise
1 tomato, sliced
Grated Parmesan cheese
Oregano leaves

Cut bread in half lengthwise. Spread bottom layer with ham mixed with mayonnaise. Top with tomato slices and sprinkle with cheese and oregano. Bake in hot oven (425°F.) 10 minutes, or until heated. Cut in crosswise slices. Makes 4 to 6 servings.

TENNESSEE SLOPPY JOES

1 pound ground beef
1 medium onion, chopped
1/2 cup diced celery
1/4 cup chopped green pepper
2 tablespoons Worcestershire
3 tablespoons catsup
Dash of hot pepper sauce
Salt and pepper to taste
Toasted sandwich rolls

Brown meat lightly in skillet, breaking up with fork. Pour off excess fat. Add 1 cup water and remaining ingredients, except rolls. Bring to boil, cover and simmer 20 minutes, adding more water if necessary. Serve on rolls. Makes 4 servings.

FRENCH-FRIED HAMBURGER SANDWICHES

Salt and pepper
3/4 pound ground beef
8 slices fresh bread, crusts removed
2 eggs, beaten
3/4 cup milk
Fat for deep frying

Season meat; shape it in 4 patties. Put each patty between 2 slices of bread, pressing together with hands. Seal edges with tines of fork dipped in hot water. Dip each sandwich in mixture of eggs and milk. Put in wire basket and fry in hot deep fat (375°F. on a frying thermometer) until bread is golden brown. The meat will be rare. (If you prefer the meat medium or well done, cook patties first.) Makes 4 servings.

NICK'S SPECIAL SANDWICHES

1 small onion, minced
1 tablespoon butter
1 can (1 pound) corned-beef hash
Salt and pepper
1 cup diced sharp Cheddar cheese
8 slices rye bread
1/2 cup chili sauce

Sauté onion in butter in skillet until lightly browned. Add hash and brown quickly, stirring. Season with salt and pepper. Add cheese, cover and cook slowly 2 minutes. Toast bread. Put hash mixture between slices. Top each sandwich with chili sauce. Serve at once. Makes 4 servings.

MEAT-LOAF SANDWICHES

1 loaf French bread (cut in half if long)
1 cup milk, scalded
1 pound ground beef
1 egg, beaten
1 small onion, minced
1-1/2 teaspoons salt
1/4 teaspoon pepper
2 teaspoons horseradish
3 tablespoons catsup
2 tablespoons each minced green pepper
  and celery

Cut thin slice from top of loaf of bread. Scoop out as much of inside as possible, leaving a shell. Add 2 cups of crumbs to milk. Mix in remaining ingredients. Pack firmly into hollowed-out loaf, smoothing top. Put on baking sheet and bake in moderate oven (350°F.) about 1½ hours. Last few minutes in oven, cover loaf with top. Cut in 6 to 8 servings.

SWEET-AND-SOUR HAMBURGER SANDWICHES

1 pound ground beef
1/4 pound ground pork
1 teaspoon salt
1/4 teaspoon pepper
6 slices canned pineapple
6 green-pepper rings
1 tablespoon soy sauce
1/3 cup packed brown sugar
1 tablespoon Worcestershire
1/2 teaspoon ground cloves
1/3 cup wine vinegar
6 sandwich or other rolls

Mix first 4 ingredients. Shape in 6 patties and brown on both sides in greased skillet. Pour off fat. Put a pineapple slice on each patty and top with a green-pepper ring; mix next 5 ingredients and pour over patties. Cover and simmer 15 minutes. Serve hamburgers between split rolls with some of the sauce. Makes 6 main-dish sandwiches.

HAMBURGERS HOFBRAU

2 poorboy breads
Softened butter or margarine
1-1/2 pounds ground beef
1/4 cup catsup
1-1/2 tablespoons prepared mustard
1-1/2 tablespoons steak sauce
Garlic and onion salt as desired

Cut breads in half lengthwise, then crosswise, to make 8 pieces. Spread with butter and with mixture of remaining ingredients. Broil to desired doneness. Makes 6 to 8 servings.

BARBECUED HAM FINGERS

Cut one can chopped ham in 8 strips. Brush with mixture of 1/2 cup bottled barbecue sauce and 2 tablespoons mustard-pickle relish. Broil until heated through and bubbly. At the same time toast 4 frankfurter rolls, partly split and buttered. Put 2 ham fingers in each roll. Makes 4 servings.

BARBECUED LAMB SANDWICHES

1 pound ground lamb
1/2 teaspoon garlic salt
1/4 teaspoon curry powder
1 can (6 ounces) tomato paste
2 tablespoons brown sugar
3 tablespoons lemon juice
2 tablespoons chopped parsley
1 teaspoon Worcestershire
Salt and pepper to taste
6 sesame or poppy seed rolls, split

Brown lamb with garlic salt and curry powder in skillet. Add 1/2 cup water and remaining ingredients, except rolls. Simmer, uncovered, 3 or 4 minutes. Serve on rolls. Makes 6 servings.

WESTERN LONGBOYS

1 small onion, chopped
1/3 cup chopped green pepper
1 cup chopped cooked ham
Butter or margarine
6 eggs, slightly beaten
1/2 cup milk
1/2 teaspoon salt
1/4 teaspoon pepper
French bread

Sauté first 3 ingredients in 3 tablespoons butter in large skillet. Mix remaining ingredients, except bread. Pour into skillet. Scramble gently 2 or 3 minutes, or until set. Meanwhile, cut bread in four 6″ lengths. Split, butter and toast. Serve eggs between bread lengths. Makes 4 servings.

LUNCHBOX CORNED-BEEF ROLLS

1 can (12 ounces) corned beef, chilled
6 buttered sandwich rolls
4 hard-cooked eggs, coarsely chopped
1/2 cup diced celery
1 green onion, finely sliced
1/4 cup mayonnaise
2 teaspoons prepared mustard
2 tablespoons drained sweet-pickle relish
1/4 teaspoon salt
Lettuce leaves

Slice corned beef to fit rolls. Wrap and chill. Combine eggs, celery and onion. Mix mayonnaise with mustard, pickle relish and salt, add to egg mixture and stir to mix. Pack in individual containers to top corned beef in rolls when ready to eat. Chill. Put lettuce leaves in small plastic bags to top filling just before serving.

FRANKFURTERS IN BISCUITS

1-1/2 cups all-purpose buttermilk biscuit mix
Prepared mustard
8 frankfurters (about 1 pound)
Pickles (optional)

With fork, stir biscuit mix and 1/3 cup water to form soft dough. Gently smooth in a ball on floured board and knead 5 turns. Roll in 12″ circle and cut in 8 wedges. Spread each with mustard. Make a slit in each frankfurter and insert a thin strip of pickle, if desired. Put a frankfurter on each wedge and roll up, beginning at wide end. Put on ungreased baking sheet and bake in very hot oven (450°F.) about 15 minutes. Delicious hot or cold. Makes 8.

STUFFED BREAD

2 cups ground cold meat mixture (rare beef, ham, pork or veal)
2 pickles, finely chopped
3 tablespoons minced onion
3 tablespoons minced parsley
Dash of hot pepper sauce
2 hard-cooked eggs, chopped
1 tablespoon Worcestershire
Mayonnaise
1 large loaf crusty French or Vienna bread
Butter

Mix ground meat with next 6 ingredients; mix well with mayonnaise to make a stiff paste. Cut both ends from the bread and remove crumbs with fork, leaving a shell about 1/2″ thick. Brush the interior well with soft butter and then force the meat mixture firmly into the bread so there are no air holes in filling. Wrap in foil and chill several hours before slicing. Makes 6 servings.

QUICK SLOPPY LUIGIS

1 pound ground beef
1/4 cup chopped onion
1/8 teaspoon oregano
1 can condensed minestrone soup
1/2 cup water
1/3 cup catsup
4 sandwich rolls, split and toasted

Brown beef and onion lightly. Add remaining ingredients, except rolls, and simmer about 5 minutes, stirring occasionally. Serve on rolls. Serves 4.

CORNED-BEEF SANDWICHES WITH MUSTARD DRESSING

Spread 8 large slices rye bread with prepared mustard, then cover with thinly sliced corned beef and over-lapping thin Cheddar-cheese slices. Spread with Mustard Dressing to within 1/2" of edges. Put under broiler until dressing is bubbly and cheese is melted. Garnish with pimiento strips, if desired. Makes 8 sandwiches. **Mustard Dressing** Mix thoroughly 1 cup mayonnaise, 3 tablespoons prepared mustard, 1 tablespoon prepared horseradish, 1 teaspoon Worcestershire, 1/2 cup well-drained pickle relish and a dash of hot pepper sauce.

WESTERN SANDWICHES

4 eggs
2 tablespoons minced onion
1/3 cup chopped green pepper
2 tablespoons butter
Salt and pepper
8 slices bread

Beat eggs slightly. Add onion and green pepper. Heat butter in 10" skillet. Pour in egg mixture. Cook over low heat until eggs are just firm. Sprinkle with salt and pepper. Cut into 4 wedges and place between bread or toast slices. Serves 4.

HOT PICKLED WESTERN ROLLS

2 cups ham, cut in short thin strips
1 pound sharp Cheddar cheese, shredded
2 pimientos, chopped
1/3 cup chopped green olives
1 tablespoon mustard-pickle relish
1/4 teaspoon each onion salt and pepper
Dash of garlic salt
1 teaspoon Worcestershire
1 can (8 ounces) tomato sauce
16 sandwich or frankfurter rolls

Mix all ingredients, except rolls. Split rolls and fill with mixture. Wrap each in a piece of foil. Heat in moderate oven (350°F.) about 15 minutes. Makes 16 servings.

POTATO-SALAD AND HAM SANDWICHES

Put a slice of baked or broiled ham and a layer of potato salad between slices of bread. Spread both sides of sandwiches with softened butter or margarine. Grill slowly until browned on both sides.

PILLOWS WITH ITALIAN HAM

Make sandwiches with sliced mozzarella cheese and sliced prosciutto. For each 2 sandwiches allow 1/4 cup of milk, 1/4 cup of flour and 1 egg. Dip the sandwiches in the milk, then in the flour and finally in the egg. Fry on both sides in olive oil and cut each in 4 triangles. Serve at once.

ITALIAN SAUSAGE SANDWICHES

They taste like pizza.

1 pound sweet or hot Italian sausage, thinly sliced
4 seeded hard rolls, split
1 can (8 ounces) spaghetti sauce with mushrooms, heated
4 slices mozzarella cheese

Brown sausage slices and put on bottom halves of rolls. Top with spaghetti sauce, mozzarella cheese and top halves of rolls. Serve at once. Makes 4 sandwiches.

HE-MAN LONGBOY

A meal in itself with meat, vegetables and cheese.

1 long thick loaf French or Italian bread
1 clove garlic, cut
Softened butter or margarine
1/2 pound sliced bologna
1/2 pound sliced Italian salami
1/2 pound sliced cooked smoked tongue
1/2 pound thinly sliced cooked ham
Chicory
2 large firm ripe tomatoes, cut in thick slices
1 large Spanish onion, thinly sliced
12 slices Muenster cheese
6 strips crisp bacon
Green olives

Slice off top third of loaf horizontally. Rub cut sides of both pieces with garlic and spread with softened butter. On bottom piece, arrange layers of meat, vegetables and cheese. Garnish with bacon and olives. Cut in serving pieces; cut top piece to match and arrange on longboy. Good served with pickle relish, mustard, dill pickles, pickled red peppers, French dressing and potato sticks. Makes 6 to 8 servings.

HOT CHEESE SANDWICH

Put thin-sliced mild cheese (like mozzarella or Monterey Jack) and canned peeled green chilies between slices of buttered French bread. Grill until bread is browned and cheese is soft.

CREAM-CHEESE EGG ROLLS

Blend 1 package (8 ounces) soft cream cheese, 3 chopped hard-cooked eggs, 1 grated small onion, 1/2 teaspoon salt, 1/4 teaspoon pepper and 1/2 cup sliced stuffed olives. Scoop out some crumbs from 8 split sandwich rolls. Fill with cheese mixture; put halves together. Serve with watercress or other greens. Serves 8.

COTTAGE-TOMATO TRIANGLES

Cook 1 chopped green pepper in 2 tablespoons butter in large skillet until tender; remove. Make 6 sandwiches with 1½ cups cottage cheese and 12 slices bread; cut in half diagonally and brown on both sides in more butter in skillet. Put sandwiches on a hot platter. Add 1 can condensed tomato soup to skillet with green pepper and salt and pepper to taste. Bring to boil and pour over sandwiches. Makes 4 servings.

CHEESE-OLIVE-RAISIN SANDWICHES

2 packages (8 ounces each) cream cheese, softened
2 tablespoons French dressing
1/4 cup chopped pimiento-stuffed olives
1/2 cup seedless raisins
16 slices bread, buttered

Blend cheese and dressing until smooth. Add olives and raisins. Spread on 8 bread slices. Top with remaining slices. Makes 8 sandwiches.

MUSHROOM-CHEESE SANDWICHES

1/2 pound mushrooms, chopped
2 tablespoons butter or margarine
1 cup grated Cheddar cheese
1 egg, slightly beaten
8 slices bread
2 medium tomatoes, sliced

Sauté mushrooms in butter about 5 minutes. Add cheese and egg and mix well. Toast bread on one side. Spread mushroom mixture on untoasted side. Top with tomato slice and put under broiler 5 to 8 minutes, or until heated. Makes 4 open-faced sandwiches.

CHILI-CHEESE SANDWICHES

Trim crusts from 6 slices bread; toast on one side. Spread untoasted side with mayonnaise; top with onion rings. Cook 1/4 cup chopped green pepper 5 minutes in 2 tablespoons butter; stir in 1/2 cup chili sauce. Spread on sandwiches and top each with 2 thin slices of Cheddar cheese. Broil until cheese is melted and bubbly. Makes 6 servings.

HOT TOMATO-RABBIT SANDWICHES

2 small cloves garlic
1/2 teaspoon salt
1-1/2 cups milk
2 tablespoons butter or margarine
2 tablespoons flour
1 cup grated sharp Cheddar cheese
1 tablespoon prepared mustard
4 slices toast
8 thin tomato slices
8 slices bacon, cooked until crisp

Mash garlic with salt and add to milk; strain. Melt butter; blend in flour. Stir in milk and cook over low heat, stirring, until thickened. Add cheese and mustard and stir until cheese is melted. Arrange toast on platter and top with tomato slices. Cover with cheese sauce and garnish with bacon. Makes 4 sandwiches.

ALMOND SOUFFLÉ SANDWICHES

Plan on knives and forks for these.

2 eggs, separated
1/2 teaspoon Worcestershire
1/2 cup chopped almonds
1/2 cup shredded Cheddar cheese
1 tablespoon mayonnaise
1 tablespoon chopped parsley
1/2 teaspoon salt
4 slices toast

Beat egg yolks until thick. Add next 5 ingredients. Beat egg whites with salt until stiff and fold in yolk mixture. Pile lightly on toast. Heat under broiler until puffy and lightly browned. Makes 4 sandwiches.

HOT VEGETARIAN BOYS

Split four 6" lengths of French bread. Brush with olive oil and sprinkle with garlic salt. Slice 1 pound mozzarella cheese. Cover 4 lengths of bread. Add some pimiento slices. Peel and slice 1 medium eggplant 1/2" thick. Roll in flour and brown on both sides in hot fat. Season and put in overlapping slices on remaining halves of bread. Serve open. Serves 4.

BOLOGNA-SWISS SANDWICH

Grind bologna and season to taste with chopped sour pickle. Moisten with mayonnaise and spread on split sandwich rolls. Put halves together with watercress and slices of process Swiss cheese.

DOWN-EAST SANDWICH PLATE

Mash 1 can (1 pound) Boston-style baked beans. Spread on 4 slices buttered toast. Add drained coleslaw, salt and pepper and a little catsup, if desired. Top each sandwich with 2 hot cooked sausage links and a second slice of buttered toast. Serve with pickles or olives. Serves 4.

CRISP CODFISH-CAKE SANDWICHES

Mix 6 cups finely shredded cabbage, 1 tablespoon vinegar, ½ cup mayonnaise, 2 pimientos cut in strips and salt and pepper to taste. Make 4 bread-and-butter sandwiches with 8 large slices rye bread; cut in halves and put 2 halves on each plate. Shape 2 cans (10½ ounces each) codfish-cake mixture in 12 balls. Fry in hot deep fat (375°F. on a frying thermometer) until golden brown. Top each sandwich with coleslaw and 3 codfish balls. Garnish with small sweet gherkins. Makes 4.

HOT PERCH SANDWICHES

6 sandwich rolls
2 tablespoons pickle relish
1 onion, minced
3 tablespoons mayonnaise
1 tablespoon prepared mustard
1 egg, beaten
Salt and pepper
1 pound ocean-perch fillets
1/2 cup fine dry bread crumbs
Vegetable oil
6 slices tomato

Split rolls and remove some of the centers. Mix next 4 ingredients; spread on rolls. Mix egg, ½ teaspoon salt and ⅛ teaspoon pepper. Dip fish in egg mixture and roll in crumbs. Sauté in hot oil until well browned. Arrange on rolls, top with tomato; season. Replace tops; wrap in foil. Warm in moderate oven (350°F.) 10 minutes. Makes 6 servings.

Fish-stick Sandwiches Substitute 1 box fish sticks, thawed, for the fried perch, allowing 2 sticks per sandwich. Proceed as directed.

SEAFOOD CLUB SANDWICHES

8 slices white bread, toasted
Soft butter or margarine
Lettuce leaves
1 can (7 ounces) tuna, drained and flaked
1 jar (3-1/4 ounces) smoked oysters
Whole cooked shrimp
Hard-cooked egg slices
Sliced tomatoes and cucumbers
Tartar sauce

Spread toast with butter and top 4 slices with lettuce. Add tuna, then more lettuce. Arrange oysters, reserving several for garnish, on second layer of lettuce. Cover with remaining toast, secure with picks and cut sandwiches in thirds. Garnish with oysters and remaining ingredients. Serve with tartar sauce. Makes 4 sandwiches.

BAKED TUNA-CHEESE LOAF

1 can (7 ounces) tuna, drained
1 teaspoon instant minced onion
2 tablespoons chopped sweet pickle
1 cup grated sharp Cheddar cheese
1 loaf French or Italian bread (about 12" long)
1/4 cup butter or margarine
1 teaspoon prepared mustard or 1/4 teaspoon dry mustard

Mix first 4 ingredients. Cut bread in half lengthwise. Remove a small amount of the crumbs. Spread inside with butter, mustard and tuna filling. Put loaf together, wrap in foil and bake in moderate oven (350°F.) about 20 minutes. Cut in 4 crosswise pieces.

TUNA-CHEESE-PECAN SANDWICHES

1 package (8 ounces) cream cheese
2 tablespoons lemon juice
1/4 teaspoon monosodium glutamate
1/2 cup mayonnaise
1/2 cup chopped ripe olives
1 can (7 ounces) tuna, drained and flaked
12 slices white bread, buttered
6 slices whole-wheat or cracked-wheat bread, buttered
Softened butter or margarine
1 cup salted pecan tidbits or coarsely chopped salted pecans
Sweet-pickle sticks

Blend first 4 ingredients until smooth; add olives and tuna. Spread 6 slices white bread with tuna filling; cover with whole-wheat slices. Spread with tuna filling and top with remaining white bread. Trim crusts and cut each sandwich in 4 triangles. Spread inside edges of triangles with filling. Then dip each edge in pecans. Garnish with sweet-pickle sticks. Makes 6.

MOZZARELLA SANDWICHES, ITALIAN STYLE

8 slices bread
4 slices mozzarella, about 1/4" thick
All-purpose flour
2 eggs, slightly beaten
Olive oil
Anchovy Sauce (optional)

Trim crusts from bread. Dip mozzarella in flour and put 1 slice between 2 slices bread. Dip sandwiches in beaten egg and sauté in hot olive oil in skillet, turning to brown both sides and to melt cheese. Serve with the sauce, if desired. **Anchovy Sauce** Heat together ¼ cup each olive oil and butter. Add 4 cloves garlic, minced, and sauté 2 to 3 minutes. Add 2 cans (2 ounces each) anchovies, drained. Cook, stirring, until disintegrated; add ¼ cup chopped parsley. Makes ¾ cup.

CRAB-MEAT OLIVE SANDWICHES

1 can (6-1/2 ounces) crab meat, drained, boned and flaked
1-1/2 cups grated process American or mild Cheddar cheese
1 tablespoon instant minced onion
1/3 cup sliced pimiento-stuffed olives
1 cup dairy sour cream
12 slices rye bread

Mix all ingredients, except bread. Spread between bread slices. Makes 6 sandwiches.

GRILLED HAM AND CHEESE

Spread slices of bread with deviled ham. Put thin slice of process American cheese between bread slices. Grill in butter on griddle.

SHELLFISH-BACON-EGG SANDWICHES

8 slices buttered toast
3/4 cup minced bacon
1 small onion, minced
1/2 cup chopped green pepper
1 cup lobster, crab meat or shrimp
8 eggs, slightly beaten
1/2 teaspoon salt
1/8 teaspoon pepper

Cut 4 slices toast diagonally in triangles. Arrange 1 whole slice and 2 triangles on each of 4 plates. Cook bacon until crisp. Add onion and green pepper; cook 2 or 3 minutes. Add shellfish and heat. (If more fat will be needed to cook eggs, add 1 tablespoon butter and let melt.) Mix last 3 ingredients and stir into fish mixture. Cook, stirring, until eggs are scrambled to desired doneness. Serve at once on toast. Makes 4 servings.

SHRIMP-CHEESE SANDWICHES

1 can (4-1/2 ounces) shrimp
1 package (3 ounces) cream cheese, softened
1/4 cup toasted slivered almonds
1 tablespoon lemon juice
2 tablespoons chopped ripe olives
1/4 cup drained crushed pineapple
4 slices each buttered white and whole-wheat bread

Drain shrimp; rinse and chop fine. Mix with remaining ingredients, except bread. Spread on white bread and top with whole-wheat bread. Makes 4 sandwiches.

SHRIMP BURGERS

1 box (12 ounces) frozen cleaned shelled cooked shrimp
3 tablespoons butter or margarine
3 tablespoons all-purpose flour
3/4 cup milk
1 cup cooked rice
1/2 cup grated sharp Cheddar cheese
1 tablespoon instant minced onion
1 teaspoon salt
1/8 teaspoon pepper
1/2 teaspoon curry powder
Fine dry bread crumbs
Fat
6 sandwich rolls, split, toasted and buttered
Chutney (optional)

Thaw shrimp and cut in small pieces. Make a sauce with next 3 ingredients. Add shrimp, rice, and next 5 ingredients. Chill and shape in 6 patties. Roll in crumbs and fry in small amount of hot fat in skillet until golden brown on both sides. Serve between roll halves, with chutney, if desired. Makes 6 servings.
Lobster Burgers Substitute an equal amount of finely diced lobster for the shrimp in the above recipe.

INDIVIDUAL TUNA PIZZAS

1/3 cup mayonnaise
1/2 teaspoon salt
1/4 teaspoon each dried oregano and basil
1 teaspoon instant minced onion
1/2 cup finely diced celery
2 cans (7 ounces each) tuna, drained
8 English-muffin halves or 6 slices toast
1/2 can (8-ounce size) tomato sauce
Grated Parmesan cheese

Mix all ingredients, except muffins, sauce and cheese. Pile on muffins. Spoon tomato sauce on top and sprinkle with cheese. Put under broiler until heated and lightly browned. Makes 4 servings.

TUNA CREAM-CHEESE SPECIALS

1 package (8 ounces) cream cheese,
  softened
1 can (8-1/2 ounces) crushed pineapple,
  drained
1/4 cup chopped pimiento-stuffed olives
1/4 cup chopped nuts
1 can (7 ounces) tuna, drained and flaked
16 slices bread, buttered

Mix all ingredients, except bread.
Spread between bread slices. Makes
8 sandwiches.

TUNA-AVOCADO SANDWICH

Peel and slice 1 large ripe avocado.
Arrange on 4 slices toast. Spread
with mayonnaise, cover with lettuce
leaves; top with 1 can (7 ounces)
tuna, flaked. Put 2 crisp cooked half-
slices of bacon on each, cover with
top slice of toast and cut in diagonal
halves. Makes 4 sandwiches.

SMOKED-SALMON ROLLS

Slice white bread thin and remove crusts. Cover with sliced
smoked salmon and sprinkle with
freshly ground black pepper. Roll up,
fasten with picks at each end and
grill until bread is lightly browned.

SHRIMP OMELET SANDWICHES

8 slices buttered toast
8 eggs
2 teaspoons soy sauce
1/2 teaspoon salt
1/2 teaspoon monosodium glutamate
1/3 cup butter or margarine
1 tablespoon minced chives or green
  onion
3/4 cup minced green pepper
1 can (8-3/4 ounces) pineapple tidbits,
  well drained
1 medium tomato, chopped
1-1/2 cups chopped cooked shrimp
4 slices baked ham or 8 thin slices
  prosciutto

Halve 4 slices toast diagonally.
Arrange 1 whole slice with 2
halves on opposite sides for each
sandwich. Beat next 4 ingredients.
Melt butter in large heavy skillet. Add
chives and green pepper; cook 2 or
3 minutes. Pour in egg mixture. When
set around edges, lift with spatula to
allow uncooked egg to run under.
When bottom is fairly firm, add pineapple, tomato and shrimp. Fold one
half of omelet over filling; cook 5
minutes, or until mixture is cooked
through. Arrange ham on toast and
top each slice with a serving of
omelet. Makes 4 servings.

CRAB-MEAT TOMATO STACKS

1/2 pound crab meat, flaked
1/2 cup diced celery
2 teaspoons chopped pimiento
2 tablespoons chopped green pepper
1/4 teaspoon salt
Dash of pepper
1/2 cup dairy sour cream
12 slices sandwich bread
Soft butter
4 thick tomato slices
2 tablespoons grated onion
1 cup grated sharp Cheddar cheese

Combine first 7 ingredients. Trim
crusts from bread; brush the slices
with butter. Spread 4 slices of bread
with crab filling, top with 4 more
slices of bread and cover each with
a tomato slice. Top with third slice
of bread, sprinkle with onion and
grated cheese and put on cookie
sheet. Bake in hot oven (400°F.) 10
to 12 minutes. Makes 4 servings.

EGG-SALAD SANDWICHES DELUXE

Shell 6 hard-cooked eggs and mash
yokes with 1 cup grated sharp Cheddar cheese. Add minced whites, 2
teaspoons instant minced onion, 2
tablespoons catsup, ½ teaspoon dry
mustard, ½ teaspoon Worcestershire,
a dash of hot pepper sauce, ¼ cup
mayonnaise and 2 small cans (or 1
large can) deviled ham. Mix thoroughly and spread between 8 slices
buttered white bread or toast. Makes
4 sandwiches.

TRIPLE-DECKER EGG-SALAD SANDWICHES

5 hard-cooked eggs
3 tablespoons mayonnaise
2 tablespoons minced sweet pickle
1/2 teaspoon pepper
12 slices white bread
6 slices tomato
6 slices whole-wheat bread, buttered
2 cans (4-1/2 ounces each) sardines in
  oil, drained
Lemon juice
Butter

Chop 4 eggs. Cut remaining egg in
6 slices. Mix chopped egg with mayonnaise, pickle and pepper. Spread
on 6 slices white bread. Top with
tomato slices. Cover with whole-
wheat bread, then egg slices and
sardines. Sprinkle with lemon juice
and top each sandwich with white
bread, spread with butter. Makes 6
large sandwiches.

SWISS-CHEESE, EGG AND ANCHOVY SANDWICHES

1/4 cup soft butter or margarine
3 tablespoons very finely chopped
 watercress
1 teaspoon lime juice
Dash of hot pepper sauce
8 large slices rye or whole-wheat bread
4 hard-cooked eggs, chopped
1 can (2 ounces) flat anchovies, drained
 and mashed
1 teaspoon instant minced onion
1/4 teaspoon dry mustard
1/4 cup mayonnaise or salad dressing
4 slices Swiss cheese

Blend first 4 ingredients. Spread on 4 slices bread. Mix next 5 ingredients and spread on remaining bread. Top with cheese and cover with watercress-buttered bread. Makes 4.

CHICKEN-ALMOND SANDWICHES

1 can chicken spread
1 package (3 ounces) cream cheese
1/2 cup toasted chopped almonds
1/4 cup minced candied ginger
1 tablespoon mayonnaise
Dash of salt
8 slices whole-wheat bread

Mix all ingredients, except bread, and chill several hours to blend flavors. Remove from refrigerator a half hour before serving. Remove crusts from bread; spread filling between slices and cut in quarters. Makes 4 servings.

TURKEY OR CHICKEN SANDWICH LOAF

3 cups chopped cooked turkey or chicken
1 cup chopped celery
1/2 teaspoon grated onion
1 cup mayonnaise
Salt and pepper
1 loaf (1 pound) sliced soft white bread
1/2 cup butter or margarine, softened
2/3 cup crumbled blue cheese (about
 4 ounces)
1 package (3 ounces) cream cheese,
 softened
1 tablespoon milk
Watercress

Mix first 4 ingredients, season to taste and use for filling. Trim crusts from bread and place 3 slices in a row on sheet of foil or wax paper. Butter slices and spread with filling. Add 3 more slices, butter them and spread with filling; continue until each stack has 6 slices. Press loaf together firmly. Beat cheeses and milk together until smooth. Spread on top and sides of loaf. Chill several hours, or overnight. Cut in slices to show layers of bread and filling; garnish with watercress. Makes 6 to 8 servings.

CURRIED EGG SANDWICHES

Mix 8 hard-cooked eggs, chopped; 1/2 cup mayonnaise; 1 teaspoon curry powder, or more to taste; 1/2 cup chopped stuffed or ripe olives; 1/2 teaspoon salt and 1/4 teaspoon pepper. Spread between buttered bread slices. Makes filling for 8 sandwiches.

HOT TURKEY SANDWICHES WITH MUSHROOM SAUCE

Presented this way, leftover turkey is almost better than new.

8 slices toast
Sliced cooked turkey
2 cans condensed cream of mushroom
 soup
1/2 cup shredded sharp Cheddar cheese
8 slices bacon, partially cooked
Hot mashed potato

Cut 4 slices toast in halves diagonally. For each sandwich, put 1 whole slice toast with a half on each side in baking dish or individual ovenware plate. Cover toast with turkey. Mix soup and 1/2 cup water. Heat, stirring, until smooth. Spoon sauce over turkey and sprinkle with cheese. Top with bacon. Make a border of mashed potato around each sandwich. Put under broiler until cheese is melted and potato is lightly browned. Makes 4 main-dish sandwiches.

HOT CHEESE-CHICKEN SANDWICH, LA SALLE

6 slices white bread
6 tablespoons butter
Thin slices of cooked chicken
1/2 cup blue or Roquefort cheese
 crumbled
3 tablespoons flour
3/4 teaspoon salt
1/4 teaspoon pepper
1/4 cup heavy cream
1-3/4 cups milk
1 teaspoon instant minced onion
2 egg yolks, beaten
1/4 cup grated Parmesan or Romano
 cheese

Cut crusts from bread and spread slices with 2 tablespoons butter. Arrange flat in shallow baking dish. Top with chicken and sprinkle with crumbled cheese. Melt remaining butter and blend in flour and seasonings. Add liquids and onion and cook, stirring, until thickened. Stir small amount into egg yolks. Return mixture to saucepan and cook 2 to 3 minutes, stirring. Pour over ingredients in baking dish. Sprinkle with grated cheese. Bake in hot oven (425°F) 15 minutes, or until golden brown. Serves 6.

CHILLED CHICKEN ROLLS

Trim crusts from thin slices of whole-wheat bread. Flatten on damp towel with rolling pin. Spread with softened butter and ground cooked chicken mixed with mayonnaise, salt and pepper; roll up. Tuck a sprig of watercress in each end, wrap in waxed paper, then in damp towel; chill.

CHICKEN CLUB SANDWICHES

18 slices white bread, trimmed
Softened butter or margarine
Lettuce
24 tips chilled cooked asparagus
6 large slices chilled cooked chicken breast
Salt and pepper
Mayonnaise
24 slices crisp bacon
6 chilled hard-cooked eggs, sliced

Spread bread with butter. Cover 6 slices of bread with lettuce, asparagus and chicken. Season. Cover each with bread slice, buttered side down. Spread top side with mayonnaise. Cover with bacon and egg slices. Top with remaining bread, buttered side down. Cut sandwiches in quarters. Makes 6 sandwiches.

BREADS FOR SANDWICHES

Loaves to Buy White (sliced or unsliced; round; soft or firm), French, Italian, Greek, Jewish, Vienna, potato, seeded, salt-free; whole-wheat, cracked-wheat, oatmeal, protein, gluten, health, bran; rye (dark or light, sweet or sour, soft or firm, plain or seeded, sliced, thin-sliced or unsliced, salty), Swedish, German, Jewish, American, Bavarian; pumpernickel—light or dark, sliced or unsliced; cornmeal, anadama, salt-rising, onion, honeyflavored, cheese; raisin or cinnamon-raisin swirl, Boston brown, nut, date-nut, orange-nut.

Loaves to Make See Index under *Breads, Yeast,* for White, Cheese, Seeded Bread Squares, Potato, Batter Anadama, Three-flour, Honey-Oatmeal, Cinnamon Loaf. See *Breads, Quick,* for English Saffron, Date-Bran, Banana Nut, Boston Brown, Orange-Nut and Peanut-butter Orange.

Rolls for Sandwiches White, whole-wheat, rye, Italian, French, hard and soft dinner rolls, hamburger and frankfurter buns, finger rolls, long rolls for heros and poorboys, English muffins, crumpets, biscuits, corn bread, brioches and bagels.

OPEN-FACED GOLDENROD SANDWICHES

Separate yolks and whites of 4 hard-cooked eggs. Chop whites and add to 2 cups Medium White Sauce (page 157). Heat thoroughly and pour over 6 to 8 slices toast. Sprinkle with egg yolks put through ricer and garnish with parsley. Makes 3 to 4 servings.

OPEN-FACED SHRIMP SANDWICHES

12 large cooked shrimp
1/2 cup crumbled blue cheese
1/8 teaspoon paprika
1/4 cup cream
3 tablespoons vinegar
1/2 cup mayonnaise
4 slices toast
Shredded lettuce
1 large tomato, peeled and sliced
4 ripe olives
2 hard-cooked egg yolks, sieved
1 tablespoon chopped parsley

Mince 4 shrimp and mix with next 5 ingredients. Top each toast slice with lettuce, then a tomato slice. Spoon first mixture over all. Put an olive in center. Split whole shrimp lengthwise and arrange around olive. Mix egg yolk and parsley and sprinkle around edge of sandwich. Makes 4.

OPEN-FACED SANDWICH TOPPINGS

1. Alternating slices of tongue and Swiss cheese with mustard and a thin slice of tomato.
2. Slices of thinly cut salami arranged in a pattern, garnished with a tiny gherkin or pickled onion.
3. Slices of white meat of chicken garnished with a wedge of tomato or a green-pepper ring centered with a slice of stuffed olive.
4. Thin slices of rare roast beef with a small bowknot of pimiento and a slice of gherkin.
5. Paper-thin slices of prosciutto with a green-olive garnish.
6. Thin fillets of herring with a thin slice of dill pickle.
7. Thin slices of smoked salmon with an onion ring and capers.
8. Whole boneless skinless sardines with a slice of lemon and a slice of hard-cooked egg.
9. Thinly sliced cucumber and green pepper on bread spread with dairy sour cream and prepared mustard.
10. On slices of rye bread put shredded lettuce, sliced tomatoes, Swiss cheese and cooked chicken. Serve with Thousand Island dressing; top with crisp bacon slices.

OPEN-FACED BLT's

6 large slices rye bread, buttered
3 cups finely shredded lettuce
3 tomatoes, thinly sliced
1 cup bottled thick creamy blue-cheese
   salad dressing
12 slices crisp cooked bacon
12 pitted black olives

Put a slice of bread on each plate. Top with lettuce and 3 or 4 tomato slices. Cover with dressing and top with bacon and olives. Makes 6 open-faced sandwiches.

LIME SALMON-SALAD SPREAD

Mix 1 can (1 pound) pink salmon, drained; 1 medium apple, diced; 1/3 cup salad dressing; 2 tablespoons lime juice; and salt and pepper to taste. Makes 1½ cups of spread.

TANGY TUNA SPREAD

Flake 1 can (7 ounces) tuna. Add 2 tablespoons softened butter or margarine, 2 tablespoons lemon juice, 1/8 teaspoon celery seed and 2 tablespoons sweet-pickle relish. Good on pumpernickel. Makes about 1 cup.

CREAM-CHEESE AND CAVIAR SPREAD

Soften 1 package (8 ounces) cream cheese with fork. Add 1/2 cup salad dressing, a dash of hot pepper sauce and 1/2 teaspoon grated onion. Fold in 1 can (4 ounces) caviar and mix well. Serve with freshly ground pepper. Makes 1 cup.

SAVORY CHEESE SPREAD

Blend 1/2 pound shredded process American cheese, 1/4 cup soft butter or margarine, 1 tablespoon chili sauce or catsup, dash of salt and pepper, 1/2 teaspoon dry mustard and 1 tablespoon instant minced onion. Chill. Soften at room temperature to spreading consistency. Makes 2 cups.

DEVILED BLUE-CHEESE SPREAD

1/2 cup crumbled blue cheese (about
   3 ounces)
2 cans (4-1/2 ounces each) deviled ham
1/4 cup chili sauce
1/2 teaspoon hot pepper sauce
Toast rounds, buttered

Blend first 4 ingredients together. Spread on toast rounds. Serve cold or toasted under the broiler. Makes about 1½ cups spread.

PEANUT-BUTTER-PLUS FILLINGS

Add any of the following to peanut butter:
1. Crushed pineapple, well drained.
2. Apple butter, grated Cheddar cheese and lemon juice.
3. Mashed banana and mayonnaise.
4. Chopped dates and orange juice to moisten.
5. To 1/3 cup peanut butter, add 1 orange, peeled and diced, 1 tablespoon each honey and mayonnaise and a dash of salt.
6. To 1 jar (12 ounces) peanut butter, beat in 1/2 cup milk and 1 package (6 ounces) semisweet chocolate pieces melted with 3 tablespoons water. Chill. Soften 15 minutes before spreading. Makes about 2½ cups spread.

WATERCRESS-PLUS FILLINGS

Chop fine 1/2 bunch washed cress. Add any one of the following and mix well. Each makes enough spread for 4 sandwiches.
1. Drain and mince 1 can (3½ ounces) sardines; add 2 teaspoons lemon juice and 1/8 teaspoon salt.
2. Blend one half cup chopped ripe avocado, 2 tablespoons cream cheese, 1 teaspoon lemon juice and 1/4 teaspoon salt.
3. Mix 3 chopped hard-cooked eggs, 1/4 cup minced celery, 1/2 teaspoon salt and 2 tablespoons mayonnaise.
4. Mince 1/4 pound bologna; add 3 tablespoons mayonnaise and 1/8 teaspoon salt.

PICNIC BREAD

Spread sliced bread with mixture of 1 cup grated cheese, 1/4 pound butter and 1 tablespoon prepared mustard. Put the loaf back together, wrap in foil and heat on grill for about 30 minutes, turning at least once.

PEANUT-BUTTER GARLIC BREAD

An American version of a continental favorite.

1/4 cup peanut butter
1/4 cup soft butter or margarine
1 clove garlic, crushed
1/8 teaspoon salt
1 medium loaf French or Italian bread

Mix first 4 ingredients. Slice bread in 1" slices not quite through bottom of loaf. Spread peanut-butter mixture between slices. Wrap in foil; bake in hot oven (400°F.) 10 to 15 minutes.

HERBED LOAVES

Cut long loaves of French bread in 2 or 3 lengthwise slices; spread each slice with seasoned butter. Use ½ pound butter and 2 tablespoons fresh or 1 teaspoon dried herbs, (try rosemary, tarragon, basil or oregano). Cheese, sesame seed or poppy seed can also be mixed with the butter. Put layers together, slice crosswise, wrap in foil and heat through on grill. Serve very hot.

ROMANO FRENCH BREAD

Slice French bread almost through bottom crust. Spread slices with mixture of 1 cup finely grated Romano cheese, ⅓ cup mayonnaise and some chopped parsley. Wrap in foil and heat over coals or in oven.

ANCHOVY ITALIAN BREAD

Split Italian bread lengthwise. Brush with olive oil and sprinkle with garlic salt and a few chopped anchovies. Broil until lightly browned.

ORANGE DATE-NUT FINGERS

Cook 1 cup pitted dates, ⅔ cup water and a dash of salt 10 minutes, stirring frequently. Cool and spread on slices of orange-nut bread. Cut in finger shapes. Makes enough spread for 24 small sandwiches.

CREAM-CHEESE AND HONEY SANDWICHES

Beat together 3 tablespoons honey and 1 package (3 ounces) softened cream cheese until light and fluffy; add ⅓ cup finely chopped nuts and grated rind of 1 orange. Spread between slices of lightly buttered whole-wheat bread. Makes 4.

RED-AND-WHITE TEA TRIANGLES

Mix 1 package (3 ounces) cream cheese, softened, and ⅔ cup finely chopped maraschino cherries. Cut 1 can (8 ounces) date-nut or orange-nut roll in 12 slices. Spread about 2 tablespoons cheese mixture on each of 4 bread slices. Cover with 4 more slices. Put a slice of well-drained pineapple on each sandwich and top with remaining bread. Secure sandwiches with picks and cut each in 4 triangles. Makes 16 triangles.

PINEAPPLE FINGERS

Remove crusts and cut bread in strips 3" long x 1½" wide and 1½" thick. Toast on 3 sides. Put strips on baking sheet untoasted side up; lay pineapple stick on top. Sprinkle with mixture of brown sugar and a little cinnamon; dot with butter. Brown under broiler.

RUMMY STICKS

Cut bread in ¾" slices, then in ¾" strips. Sprinkle with rum. Dip strips in butter and roll in mixture of 3 parts granulated sugar to 1 part cinnamon; or ½ cup confectioners' sugar, ½ cup packed brown sugar and 1 tablespoon cinnamon. Toast strips under broiler on 4 sides or put in hot oven (400°F.) for 8 minutes. These are good put together with applesauce.

SHAPES FOR SANDWICHES

An electric knife or one with a serrated blade is good for slicing.

Ribbon Put 1 slice white bread on 1 slice dark bread, spreading filling between slices; repeat. Press together, wrap and chill. Trim crusts if necessary and cut in ½" slices.

Checkerboard Prepare and cut ribbon sandwiches in ½" slices. Stack 3 ribbon sandwiches so white and whole-wheat sections alternate; spread more filling between sandwiches. Wrap and chill. Slice ½" thick.

Ribbon Loaf Trim crusts from 6 slices bread and stack with fillings as for Ribbon Sandwiches. Cream 1 package (3 ounces) softened cream cheese with a few drops milk until of spreading consistency. Spread on top and sides of loaf. Wrap, chill and cut in ½" slices to show ribbons.

Rolled Sandwiches Trim crusts from soft bread slices. Flatten lightly with rolling pin. Spread with watercress or parsley butter or desired filling and roll up. Wrap and chill.

Pinwheel Sandwiches Use an unsliced loaf of soft bread. Trim off crusts and slice horizontally in layers ½" thick. Flatten lightly with rolling pin. Spread each layer with butter or mayonnaise and desired smooth filling. Put a sweet or sour pickle at end of each slice and roll each one up like a jelly roll. Wrap, chill and cut in ½" slices.

BASIC FRENCH TOAST

8 slices bread
2 eggs
2/3 cup milk
1/4 teaspoon salt
Butter or margarine

Dip bread or soak a few minutes in mixture of eggs beaten lightly with milk and salt. Brown on each side in butter in hot skillet or griddle. Serve hot. Good with syrup, fruit sauce, brown or maple sugar, and dusted with confectioners' sugar.

French-toasted Ham Sandwiches Prepare 4 sandwiches, spreading butter and prepared mustard on bread and putting a thin slice of ham and Swiss cheese in each. Dip both sides in egg mixture and sauté as directed.

French-toasted Peanut-butter and Bacon Sandwiches Make 4 sandwiches, spreading bread with butter and peanut butter and putting 2 slices crisp bacon in each one. Dip and sauté as directed.

Fruited French-toasted Sandwiches Prepare 4 sandwiches of raisin bread, spreading with butter and apple butter. Dip in egg mixture and sauté as directed. Sprinkle hot toasted sandwiches with chopped nuts and sifted brown sugar.

Bragging Banana Toast Prepare 8 slices Basic French Toast. Slice 3 medium bananas and arrange a layer on 4 slices of toast. Dust with nutmeg. Cover with second slice of toast. Serve with maple syrup. Makes 4.

PEANUT-BUTTER SURPRISE TOAST

12 slices white bread
Butter or margarine
1/2 cup crunchy peanut butter
6 slices cooked ham
3 bananas, sliced
1/2 cup marshmallow cream
2 eggs, slightly beaten
3/4 cup milk
Vegetable oil
Strawberry jam or maple syrup

Spread 6 slices bread with butter, then with peanut butter; top each with slice of ham and a few banana slices. Spread remaining 6 slices of bread with marshmallow cream; put on bread, marshmallow side down. Dip bread in mixture of eggs beaten with milk. Brown on both sides in hot oil in skillet or on griddle. Serve hot with strawberry jam or maple syrup. Makes 6 servings.

APRICOT HONEY TOAST

2 eggs, beaten
2/3 cup apricot nectar
Honey
8 slices white bread
Butter, bacon fat or vegetable oil

Combine eggs, apricot nectar and 2 tablespoons honey in shallow bowl. Dip each bread slice in apricot mixture, coating both sides. Grill or pan-fry bread on both sides in hot butter. Serve with honey. Makes 4 servings.

ANGEL TOAST

Cut angel shapes from sliced white bread, using cookie cutters. Dip in sweetened condensed milk, then sprinkle with flaked coconut or chopped nuts. Bake on greased cookie sheet in moderate oven (350°F.) for 10 to 15 minutes.

CINNAMON TOAST DELUXE

1-pound loaf fresh white bread
1 cup butter or margarine
1 cup fine granulated sugar
1 tablespoon cinnamon

Slice bread diagonally; sauté slowly in butter until golden brown, adding more butter as needed. Shake in paper bag containing mixture of sugar and cinnamon. Makes 8 servings.

Caramel Toast Slice bread as directed. Mix sugar and cinnamon with water to a paste; spread on bread before sautéing. Omit shaking in bag.

CHOCOLATE CINNAMON TOAST

Blend together 1/2 cup unsweetened cocoa powder, 1/3 cup butter or margarine, melted, 1 teaspoon cinnamon and 6 tablespoons sugar. Spread on hot, crisp-toasted white bread.

RED DOG TOAST

2 eggs
1/2 teaspoon salt
1/4 teaspoon paprika
1/2 cup condensed tomato soup
6 slices bread
Butter or drippings
Parsley or chives, minced

Beat first 4 ingredients until light. Dip bread in this mixture and sauté in hot butter or drippings until browned. Serve sprinkled with minced parsley or chives. Serves 3.

Lemon Meringue Pie

PIES, PASTRIES

FOR PERFECT PIE CRUST

Some people say a pie is only as good
as its crust. The pastry should be tender,
golden brown and taste of good fat.
If you are an amateur at pie-making,
make a good but simple filling
and concentrate on the pastry.
This chapter offers a number of recipes
for pie crust; choose the one that is
most convenient for you (or use one of
the many good pie-crust mixes on
the market). Before starting to make
pastry, be sure that you have the right
equipment—a board, rolling pin, wire
pastry blender, mixing bowl, measuring
cups and spoons, canvas cover for the
board and stockinet cover for the rolling
pin. Select a regulation piepan with a
slanting rim. A pan measuring 8″ across
the top will hold enough pie for 4;
a 9″ pie will serve 6 or more.
Pastry browns best on the bottom when
baked in a glass pie plate or dull-finish
aluminum piepan. If you bake in a foil
piepan, put it on a baking sheet so
that bottom crust will brown evenly.

Freezing Pies

● Pie shells can be frozen baked or
unbaked. Frozen baked shells will keep
4 months; unbaked shells, 2 months.
To thaw baked shells, unwrap and let
stand at room temperature. Or put in
350°F. oven about 6 minutes. Unbaked
shells can be baked in the frozen state.
● Fruit pies are best if baked before
freezing.
● Do not freeze custard, cream or
meringue pies. Custard and cream fillings
separate; meringues toughen and shrink.
● Freeze pies first, then wrap and store.
Use heavyweight plastic wrap and seal
with freezer tape, heavy-duty foil, sealed
with a tight double fold, plastic bags
or other airtight containers. Label and
date. Pies will keep 4 to 6 months.
Store chiffon pies only 1 month.
● To heat baked pies, unwrap and let
stand 30 minutes; heat in 350°F. oven
just until warm.
● To thaw chiffon pies, unwrap and let
stand at room temperature 2 to 4 hours.
Chiffon pies may be eaten while
still partially frozen.

STANDARD PASTRY

Mix 2 cups of all-purpose flour and 1 teaspoon of salt. Cut in ²/₃ cup solid vegetable shortening or ¹/₂ cup of lard. Add 4 to 5 tablespoons cold water, a few drops at a time, mixing with a fork and using only enough water to make a ball of dough with no dry flour left in the bowl. Enough for one 2-crust 8″ or 9″ pie or two shells, or twelve 4″ to 5″ rounds.

Variations of Standard Pastry

Cheese Cut ¹/₃ cup grated Cheddar into the flour with shortening.
Nut Substitute ¹/₂ cup finely ground walnuts or pecans for ¹/₂ cup flour.
Coffee Add 1 tablespoon instant-coffee powder to flour and salt.
Spice Add 1 teaspoon cinnamon, ¹/₂ teaspoon nutmeg and dash of cloves.
Sesame Add ¹/₄ cup toasted sesame seed.

CRUMB CRUST

Mix 1¹/₄ cups fine crumbs (packaged crumbs can be used) and ¹/₄ cup soft butter or margarine. With graham crackers, add ¹/₄ cup sugar; with cornflakes, 2 tablespoons sugar; with chocolate or gingersnap crumbs, 1 tablespoon sugar. Press into 9″ pie-pan. Bake in moderate oven (375°F.) 8 minutes. For a graham-cracker crust that cuts without crumbling, add 1 egg to the graham-cracker mixture and flute edges of shell. Bake in moderate (350°F.) about 10 minutes. *Note* Packaged 9″ graham-cracker and chocolate crumb crusts in foil pans are available.

FLAKY PASTRY

4 cups all-purpose flour
1-3/4 cups solid vegetable shortening (not oil)
1 tablespoon sugar
2 teaspoons salt
1 tablespoon vinegar
1 egg

With fork, mix the first 4 ingredients. In small bowl, beat ¹/₂ cup of water and remaining ingredients together. Add to first mixture and blend with fork until dry ingredients are moistened. With hands, mold dough in a ball and chill at least 15 minutes. Refrigerated dough can be rolled at once. Dough can be stored in refrigerator up to 3 days, or frozen until ready to use. Makes two double-crust 9″ pies and one 9″ shell.

CREAM-CHEESE PASTRY

Mix 2 cups all-purpose flour and ³/₄ teaspoon salt. Work in ²/₃ cup solid vegetable shortening and 12 ounces cream cheese. Enough for one 2-crust 8″ or 9″ pie or two shells. Especially good for open fruit pies—cherry, peach, blueberry, boysenberry—or for citrus-flavored chiffon pies.

COOKIE SHELL

Mix 1 cup of all-purpose flour, ¹/₂ teaspoon of salt and 1 tablespoon sugar. Blend in 6 tablespoons butter or margarine. Beat together 1 egg yoke, 1 tablespoon water and 1¹/₂ tablespoons lemon juice or rum. Blend into flour mixture with fork. Shape in a ball and chill. Roll ¹/₄″ thick and fit in piepan or layer pan.

OIL PASTRY

(For those who like to use a liquid shortening.)

Mix 1³/₄ cups of all-purpose flour and 1 teaspoon of salt. With fork, stir in ¹/₂ cup vegetable oil. Sprinkle with 3 tablespoons cold water and mix to a ball. Roll between 2 sheets of waxed paper, wiping counter with damp cloth to keep paper from slipping. Makes one 2-crust 8″ or 9″ pie. For one shell, use 1 cup plus 2 tablespoons flour, ¹/₂ teaspoon salt, ¹/₃ cup oil and 2 tablespoons water.

TART PASTRY

Use for tart shells or open fruit pies.
2 cups all-purpose flour
3 tablespoons sugar
3/4 cup butter or margarine
1-1/4 teaspoons grated lemon rind
3 hard-cooked egg yolks, mashed
2 raw egg yolks
1/2 teaspoon salt

Make a well in center of flour, working on a table or in a bowl. Put all remaining ingredients in well. (Butter should not be ice cold, nor so soft it is oily.) Using fingertips, make a paste of center ingredients, gradually incorporating flour to make a firm, smooth ball of paste. Work as quickly as possible so butter won't become greasy. When bowl or table top has been left clean, chill dough until firm enough to roll between sheets of waxed paper. Makes twelve 4¹/₂″ rounds to fit over backs or inside 3¹/₂″ tart pans. Bake in hot oven (425°F.) 10 minutes. Cool before removing from pans.

BOILING-WATER PASTRY

Easy-to-handle pastry for beginners.

Put ⅔ cup of solid vegetable shortening in bowl. Gradually add ⅓ cup of boiling water, creaming with fork until well mixed. Add 2 cups all-purpose flour and 1 teaspoon salt, mixing thoroughly with fork. Enough for one 2-crust 8″ or 9″ pie or two shells or twelve 4″ to 5″ rounds. Extra pastry can be rolled out and frozen.

PUFF PASTE

1 pound unsalted butter
4 cups all-purpose flour
1 teaspoon salt
1 tablespoon lemon juice

Shape the butter into a brick about 5″ x 5″ x ¾″. Roll butter in 3 tablespoons of the flour, coating all sides. Wrap in waxed paper and chill. Put remaining flour in a large bowl. Make a well in the center. Add salt and lemon juice. Gradually add cold water, using only enough to make a rather firm, slightly sticky dough, usually about 1¼ cups. Knead dough thoroughly on floured board 20 minutes. Pound it on the table at intervals to achieve the right consistency. It should be very elastic and smooth. Form it into a ball; place on well-floured cloth. With a rolling pin, make the ball of dough into the shape of a four-leaf clover. Roll ends out, leaving the center thick. Well-rolled, the dough will have a thick cushion in the center and four thinner "petals." Put brick of butter in the center of the four-leaf clover. Fold "petals" over dough by stretching them over butter and sealing all the edges so that the butter is completely enclosed. Wrap in waxed paper and chill for 20 minutes. On well-floured cloth, gently roll out the block of dough as evenly as possible into a rectangle that is about ¼″ in thickness and about 3 times as long as it is wide. Do not roll over ends in the length but when dough is long enough, roll it lightly in the width, flattening ends to same thickness as the rest of the dough. Fold dough into thirds, making three layers, and chill for 20 minutes. Turn folded sides toward you, roll out dough and fold again into thirds. (Rolling, folding, and turning is called a "turn.") It is necessary to make a total of 6 turns, after which the dough is ready for use. The dough should be chilled between each turn and again before baking.

MERINGUE

Beat number of egg whites specified in recipe with ⅛ teaspoon salt per white until frothy. Gradually add sugar, using 2 tablespoons for each egg white, and beat until stiff but not dry. Pile lightly on pie, being sure filling is completely covered. Bake in hot oven (400°F.) 5 minutes, or until lightly browned.

NEVER-FAIL MERINGUE

This meringue cuts beautifully and never gets sticky.

1 tablespoon cornstarch
3 egg whites
6 tablespoons sugar
Dash of salt
1 teaspoon vanilla extract

Blend cornstarch and 2 tablespoons cold water in saucepan. Add ½ cup boiling water and cook, stirring, until clear and thickened. Let stand until completely cold. With electric mixer at high speed, beat egg whites until foamy; gradually add sugar and beat until stiff but not dry. Turn mixer to low speed; add salt and vanilla. Gradually beat in cold cornstarch mixture. Turn mixer again to high speed and beat well. Spread meringue on filled pie shell. Bake in moderate oven (350°F.) about 10 minutes.

BUTTERSCOTCH CREAM PIE

1/2 cup granulated sugar
2 cups milk
1/4 cup butter
1/2 cup all-purpose flour
3/4 cup packed brown sugar
1/2 teaspoon salt
2 eggs
Baked 9″ pie shell
1 cup heavy cream, whipped
Toasted slivered almonds

Put granulated sugar in small heavy saucepan or skillet and cook without stirring until sugar melts and becomes golden brown. Remove from heat and add ⅓ cup hot water slowly; cook without stirring until sugar dissolves. Add milk and heat almost to boiling. Melt butter in top part of double boiler. Remove from heat and add mixture of flour, brown sugar and salt; beat in eggs. Slowly add caramel-milk mixture. Cook over boiling water until thickened, stirring constantly; cover and cook 10 minutes, stirring occasionally. Cool to room temperature. Pour into baked shell. Chill several hours. Spread with whipped cream; sprinkle with nuts.

UPSIDE-DOWN APPLE PIE

1/2 cup walnut halves
1/4 cup butter, melted
1/3 cup packed light-brown sugar
Pastry for 2-crust 9" pie
1/2 cup granulated sugar
1 can (20 ounces) apple slices, drained
2 tablespoons flour
1/2 teaspoon cinnamon
1/8 teaspoon nutmeg
1/4 teaspoon salt

Arrange nuts, flat sides up, in butter in deep 9" piepan. Pat brown sugar over nuts and cover with a circle of pastry rolled ¹/₈" thick; trim edges. Mix remaining ingredients and pour into piepan. Adjust top crust and seal edges. Bake in moderate oven (375°F.) about 40 minutes. Cool 5 minutes; then turn out on plate. Serve warm, plain or with whipped cream or ice cream.

OLD-TIME APPLE PIE

1/2 recipe Flaky Pastry, page 311
3/4 to 1 cup sugar
1 teaspoon cinnamon or nutmeg
1 teaspoon grated lemon rind
6 to 7 cups sliced peeled tart cooking
 apples
1-1/2 tablespoons butter or margarine
Cream, ice cream, whipped cream or
 Cheddar-cheese slices (optional)

Line 9" piepan with pastry. Mix next 3 ingredients, add to apples and mix well. Heap in lined pan and dot with butter. Adjust top crust and cut slits for steam to escape. Seal edges and flute. Bake in hot oven (425°F.) 30 to 40 minutes, or until crust is well browned and apples are soft. If edge gets too brown during baking, cover with foil last 10 minutes. Serve warm or cold with cream, if desired.

PRALINE APPLE PIE

2-1/2 cups sliced peeled apples
1/3 cup granulated sugar
1/4 teaspoon each nutmeg and cinnamon
Unbaked 9" pie shell
2 tablespoons honey
1/2 cup packed brown sugar
2 tablespoons butter or margarine
1 egg, beaten
1/2 cup pecans

Combine apples, granulated sugar and spices. Put in pie shell. Bake in hot oven (400°F.) 15 minutes. Mix next 3 ingredients; bring to a boil. Add egg and nuts. Remove pie from oven and pour honey mixture over top. Return to 400°F. oven 10 minutes. Then reduce heat to 325°F. and bake 25 to 30 minutes longer, or until pie is set and apples are soft. Serve warm.

APRICOT CREAM-CHEESE PIE

1 can (1 pound 14 ounces) apricot halves
1/4 cup apricot syrup
1-1/2 teaspoons unflavored gelatin
1 package (3 ounces) soft cream cheese
1/4 cup sugar
1 can (6 ounces) undiluted evaporated
 milk, well chilled
2 tablespoons lemon juice
Baked 9" pie shell
Red food coloring
Mint sprigs

Drain apricots, reserving ¹/₄ cup syrup. Set aside 6 halves for garnish. Cut remaining apricots in small pieces. Soften gelatin in syrup and dissolve over hot water. Beat cheese until creamy; gradually beat in sugar and gelatin. Whip chilled milk until fluffy, add lemon juice and beat until stiff. Blend into cheese mixture and fold in diced apricots. Pour into baked shell. Give each reserved apricot half a red "cheek" by brushing a little food coloring dissolved in water on each. Arrange on pie. Chill until firm. Just before serving, garnish with mint sprigs.

FRESH-COCONUT CREAM PIE

1 fresh coconut, grated (see page 424)
2 cups milk
Sugar
1/4 teaspoon salt
3 tablespoons cornstarch
4 eggs, separated
1 tablespoon butter or margarine
1 teaspoon vanilla extract
Baked 9" pie shell
1/4 teaspoon cream of tartar

Reserve 2 cups grated coconut. Add milk to remaining coconut (there should be about 1 cup). Bring to boil, stirring, and let stand 20 minutes. Strain through fine sieve, pressing to extract all liquid. Add more milk if necessary to make 2 cups. Mix ¹/₃ cup sugar, the salt and cornstarch and add to beaten egg yolks. Stir in milk, add butter and cook over low heat, stirring constantly, until mixture thickens; let bubble a little. Cool. Stir in vanilla and 1 cup reserved coconut. Pour into pie shell. Beat egg whites until frothy, add cream of tartar and continue beating until stiff. Gradually add ¹/₂ cup sugar, beating constantly. Spread on pie filling. Sprinkle with remaining coconut. Bake in slow oven (325°F.) 15 minutes, or until coconut is lightly browned. Turn off heat, open oven door and let pie stand in oven 10 minutes. Remove from oven and let pie stand until it reaches room temperature before serving.

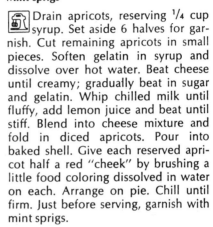

DEEP-DISH CRANBERRY-APPLESAUCE PIE

4 cups cranberries
1 cup sugar
1 teaspoon cinnamon
2 tablespoons flour
2 cups canned applesauce
1 package (10 ounces) pie-crust mix
Cream or vanilla ice cream

Force cranberries through coarse blade of food chopper. Add next 4 ingredients and mix well. Put in buttered shallow 1½ quart baking dish. Prepare pie-crust mix as directed on label. Roll out about 1″ larger than top of baking dish. Fit on dish, cut slits in top for steam to escape, fold edges under the flute. Bake in hot oven (425°F.) 30 to 40 minutes, or until browned. Serve with cream.

APPLESAUCE-MALLOW PIE

(Make the day before)

2 cups canned applesauce
1/2 pound (about 32) large
    marshmallows, diced
2 teaspoons grated orange rind
1 teaspoon grated lemon rind
1 tablespoon lemon juice
1/2 cup chopped walnuts
1 cup diced pitted dates
Baked 9″ pie shell
1 cup heavy cream, whipped

Heat applesauce. Add remaining ingredients, except last 2. Mix well and let stand at room temperature, stirring occasionally, until marshmallows are partially dissolved and softened. Pour into shell and chill overnight. Just before serving, spread whipped cream on pie.

TURNOVER APPLE PIE

5 cups thinly sliced peeled tart apples
1/2 package (10-ounce size) pie-crust
    mix, prepared
Sugar and cinnamon
2 tablespoons butter or margarine
Vanilla ice cream or whipped cream

Fill 9″ piepan with apple slices. Roll out pastry, fit over apples and trim edge. Bake in hot oven (425°F.) 25 minutes, or until apples are soft. Remove from oven and turn upside down on warm serving plate. Lift up piepan. Scrape out apples remaining in crust and mix with apples left in pan, mashing with spoon. Add ½ cup sugar, ⅛ teaspoon cinnamon and 1 tablespoon butter. Spread apple mixture on crust and dot with remaining butter. Sprinkle with sugar and cinnamon. Put in warm place until butter is melted. Serve warm with ice cream.

PEANUT-BUTTER APPLE PIE

1/4 cup peanut butter
1/3 cup sugar
1 tablespoon flour
1/4 teaspoon salt
1/4 teaspoon cinnamon
3 cups canned apples, or 4 cups
    sliced peeled apples
1 tablespoon lemon juice
Pastry for 2-crust 9″ pie

Mix all ingredients, except pastry. Line piepan with half the pastry. Add filling. Adjust top crust and bake in hot oven (425°F.) about 40 minutes.

APPLE-COCONUT PIE

1 can (1 pound 4 ounces) sliced apples,
    drained
1 cup sugar
1 teaspoon grated lemon rind
1/2 teaspoon cinnamon
1/4 teaspoon nutmeg
Unbaked 10″ pie shell
3 eggs, beaten
1/2 teaspoon salt
3/4 teaspoon vanilla extract
1-1/2 cups milk
1/2 cup flaked coconut

Chop apples. In saucepan mix with ½ cup sugar and next 3 ingredients. Cook slowly, stirring, 5 minutes, or until apples are translucent. Spread in shell. To eggs, add next 3 ingredients and remaining ½ cup sugar. Sprinkle with coconut and bake in hot oven (400°F.) about 45 minutes. Cool before serving.

APPLE PIE WITH SPECIAL PASTRY

2-1/4 cups all-purpose flour
3/4 teaspoon salt
3/4 cup chilled rendered chicken fat
6 tablespoons milk
1 egg white, slightly beaten
Sugar
6 medium apples
6 tablespoons orange juice
6 tablespoons lemon juice
1-1/2 teaspoons cornstarch
1 tablespoon butter, melted

To make pastry, mix flour and salt; cut in fat. Gradually add milk, mixing with fork to form a ball; chill. Roll a little more than half of pastry to ⅛″ thickness and line 9″ piepan. Brush with egg white and sprinkle lightly with sugar. Peel and grate apples. Mix with juices, ¾ cup sugar, the cornstarch and butter. Put in pastry-lined pan. Roll out remaining pastry, cut in ½″ strips and arrange lattice-fashion on pie. Sprinkle lightly with sugar. Bake in hot oven (400°F.) 10 minutes. Reduce heat to 350°F. and bake about 20 minutes longer.

ORANGE-PRUNE PIE

Pastry for 2-crust 9" pie
1-1/2 boxes (12 ounces each) pitted
   prunes, about 2 cups
1/2 cup golden raisins
1/3 cup sugar
1 tablespoon cornstarch
2 cups orange juice
Grated rind of 1 lemon
2 tablespoons butter or margarine
Whipped cream or softened ice cream
   (optional)

Line 9" piepan with pastry and fill with prunes and raisins. Mix sugar and cornstarch in small saucepan. Slowly stir in orange juice and cook, stirring, until mixture comes to boil. Add lemon rind and butter and cool. Pour over fruit in pan. Adjust top crust, flute edges and prick top. Bake in hot oven (400°F.) about 35 minutes. Cool thoroughly before cutting. Serve with a dollop of whipped cream or with ice cream, if desired.

EARLY AMERICAN FRESH-PEAR PIE

Especially delicious served warm.
3/4 cup sugar
2 tablespoons flour
1/2 teaspoon each nutmeg and
   cinnamon
6 cups thinly sliced peeled ripe pears
Pastry for 2-crust 9" pie
2 tablespoons butter

Mix first 3 ingredients; add pears and mix lightly. Line piepan with half of pastry. Add filling and dot with butter. Adjust top crust. Bake in hot oven (425°F.) about 50 minutes. Serve warm or cold.

FRESH-PEAR CHEDDAR PIE

Grated sharp Cheddar cheese is sprinkled on pie filling before adjusting lattice strips.
4 cups sliced peeled firm pears
3/4 cup sugar
3 tablespoons all-purpose flour
1/4 teaspoon nutmeg
1/2 teaspoon cinnamon
Dash of salt
Grated rind and juice of 1 lemon
Pastry for 2-crust 9" pie
1 tablespoon butter
1/2 cup grated sharp Cheddar cheese

Mix first 6 ingredients. Add lemon rind and juice. Put in pastry-lined 9" piepan. Dot with butter and sprinkle with cheese. Adjust pastry strips on pie, lattice fashion. Bake in hot oven (425°F.) 20 minutes. Reduce heat to 350°F.; bake about 20 minutes. Serve slightly warm or cold.

SOUR-CREAM PEAR PIE

1 can (1 pound) sliced pears
Unbaked 9" pie shell
3 tablespoons flour
Sugar
1/4 teaspoon ginger
3/4 teaspoon nutmeg
1 cup dairy sour cream
1 can (1 pound) pear halves
Red food coloring

Drain sliced pears, reserving syrup for later use. Put pears in pie shell. Mix flour, 2/3 cup sugar, the ginger, 1/4 teaspoon nutmeg and sour cream. Pour around pears. Mix 1 tablespoon sugar and remaining nutmeg and sprinkle on top. Bake in hot oven (400°F.) about 30 minutes. Cool. When ready to serve, drain pear halves. Dilute a few drops of food coloring with a little water; rub on pear halves to give blush. Arrange pears on pie.

DEEP-DISH APPLE PIE

Mix 3 tablespoons quick-cooking tapioca, 3/4 cup granulated sugar, 1/3 cup packed brown sugar, 1/4 teaspoon salt, 1 teaspoon cinnamon, 1/2 teaspoon nutmeg and 5 cups sliced tart apples. Pour into deep 8"-square baking dish. Roll pastry 1/8" thick to fit top of 8" dish. Cut several slits near the center. Arrange crust on apples. Bake in hot oven (425°F.) about 35 minutes. Break up top crust with fork and serve with whipped cream spiced with nutmeg. Makes 6 servings.

HERBLINGEN CASTLE APPLE PIE

Butter
1-1/2 cups all-purpose flour
1 tablespoon grated almonds
1 tablespoon fine dry bread crumbs
4 medium eating apples
2 cups light cream
3 egg yolks
3 whole eggs
1/8 teaspoon salt
1/2 cup sugar

To make pastry, cut 1/2 cup butter into flour with pastry blender. Add just enough water to hold mixture together. Shape in a ball, roll out and fit in 10" piepan. Fold edges under and flute. Sprinkle almonds and crumbs in shell. Peel and slice apples into shell. Bake in moderate oven (375°F.) 10 minutes. Beat next 4 ingredients lightly together and pour over apples. Bake in moderate oven (350°F.) 30 minutes, or until firm. Sprinkle with sugar and pour 2 tablespoons melted butter over top. Put in 450°F. oven about 5 minutes.

TO PREPARE FRESH COCONUT

To prepare fresh coconut, pierce holes in end of coconut and drain off liquid. Put coconut in shallow pan in moderate oven (350°F.) 20 to 30 minutes, or until shell cracks in several places. Remove from oven and pound with hammer to crack shell open. Remove coconut meat and cut off black outer shell. Grate meat on grater or whirl a few small pieces at a time in a blender until finely grated or shredded. If fresh coconut is not available, substitute 2 cans (3½ ounces each) flaked moist coconut.

CHESS PIE

Raisins, dates and walnuts in a brown-sugar-and-cream mixture.

2 eggs
1-1/2 tablespoons all-purpose flour
2/3 cup packed brown sugar
1/2 teaspoon salt
1 teaspoon vanilla extract
1 cup heavy cream
1/2 cup seedless raisins
1 cup cut-up pitted dates
1 cup broken walnut meats
Unbaked 9" pie shell

Beat the eggs until thick and lemon-colored. Mix the next 3 ingredients. Add to eggs and beat well. Stir in remaining ingredients, except pie shell. Spoon into shell. Bake in moderate oven (350°F). 50 minutes, or until a silver knife inserted in center comes out clean. Cool.

YAM CUSTARD PIE

It has a coconut meringue topping.

2 cups cold mashed cooked or canned
   yams
3 eggs, separated
Sugar
2 tablespoons melted butter
1/2 teaspoon salt
1 cup milk
Unbaked 9" pie shell
1/2 teaspoon vanilla extract
1/4 cup coconut

Beat potato and egg yolks together with spoon or electric mixer until light and fluffy. Add ½ cup sugar, butter, salt and milk. Mix well and pour into pie shell. Bake in moderate oven (350°F.) 40 minutes, or until set. Beat egg whites until foamy; gradually beat in 6 tablespoons sugar and continue beating until stiff. Add vanilla and pile lightly on pie. Sprinkle with coconut. Bake in hot oven (425°F.) 5 minutes. Cool.

ONE-BOWL PUMPKIN PIE

1-3/4 cups canned pumpkin
1 can (14 ounces) sweetened condensed
   milk
2 eggs
1 teaspoon cinnamon
1/2 teaspoon each salt and ginger
1/4 teaspoon nutmeg
1/8 teaspoon cloves
Unbaked 9" pie shell

Put all ingredients, except pie shell, in a bowl with ½ cup hot water and beat until blended. Pour into shell. Bake in moderate oven (375°F.) 45 to 50 minutes.

PUMPKIN PIE

1-1/2 cups canned pumpkin
1 can (14-1/2 ounces) undiluted
   evaporated milk
3/4 cup packed light-brown sugar
1/2 teaspoon salt
1/2 teaspoon ground ginger
1 teaspoon cinnamon
Dash of cloves
2 tablespoons butter
2 eggs (1 white stiffly beaten)
1/2 teaspoon lemon extract
Unbaked deep 9" pastry shell
Grating of nutmeg

In saucepan combine the first 8 ingredients. Mix well and heat until butter is melted. Pour over slightly beaten egg and egg yolk; add flavoring. Fold in stiffly beaten egg white. Cool. Pour into unbaked shell; top with grated nutmeg and bake in very hot oven (500°F.) 8 minutes. Reduce heat to moderate (325°F.); bake 25 to 30 minutes longer. Cool.

PUMPKIN CHIFFON PIE

1 envelope unflavored gelatin
2/3 cup sugar
1/2 teaspoon salt
1/2 teaspoon ginger
3 eggs, separated
1/2 cup Triple Sec or Cointreau
1-1/4 cups canned pumpkin
1/2 cup heavy cream, whipped
Crumb Crust, page 419 (use gingersnaps)

In top part of double boiler, mix gelatin, ⅓ cup sugar, the salt and ginger. Stir in ¼ cup water; then beat in egg yolks, one at a time. Add Triple Sec and stir over boiling water until gelatin is dissolved and mixture is slightly thickened. Remove from heat. Stir in pumpkin. Cool. Beat egg whites until stiff but not dry. Gradually add remaining ⅓ cup sugar and beat until very stiff. Fold in gelatin mixture and whipped cream. Turn into shell. Chill until firm. Garnish with additional whipped cream and candied ginger, if desired.

SOUR-CREAM BUTTERSCOTCH PIE

You don't have to cook this filling first.
1-1/2 tablespoons flour
1-1/2 cups packed light-brown sugar
1/2 teaspoon salt
1-1/2 cups dairy sour cream
3 egg yolks
1-1/2 teaspoons vanilla extract
2 tablespoons melted butter or margarine
Unbaked 9" pie shell

Mix first 4 ingredients. Add to beaten egg yolks, vanilla and butter. Pour into shell and bake in very hot oven (450°F.) 10 minutes. Reduce heat to 350°F. and bake about 30 minutes. Top with Meringue, page 312; bake.

CRANBERRY RIBBON PIE

1 envelope unflavored gelatin
1/2 cup orange juice
1 can (1 pound) whole-cranberry sauce
1 teaspoon grated lemon rind
1 cup heavy cream
1/8 teaspoon salt
1/2 cup confectioners' sugar
Baked 8" pie shell

Soften gelatin in the orange juice; dissolve over hot water. Stir one-half of gelatin mixture into cranberry sauce; add lemon rind. Chill until partially set. Whip cream until foamy; add salt and sugar and beat until stiff. Fold in remaining gelatin mixture and chill. Spread half of cranberry mixture on bottom of pie shell; cover with half of cream. Repeat layers and chill until firm.

CRANBERRY-ALMOND CRUNCH PIE

It has a bottom layer of cranberry-flavored cream cheese.
1 package (8 ounces) cream cheese, softened
1 can (1 pound) whole-cranberry sauce
Unbaked 9" pie shell
Brown sugar
3 tablespoons cornstarch
1/8 teaspoon salt
1/3 cup all-purpose flour
1/2 cup diced almonds, toasted
1/4 cup butter or margarine

Blend cheese with ½ cup cranberry sauce. Spread in pie shell. Mix ½ cup packed brown sugar, the cornstarch and salt. Blend with remaining cranberry sauce. Pour into shell. Mix flour, almonds, 3 tablespoons sugar and the butter to a crumbly consistency. Sprinkle on pie. Bake in moderate oven (375°F.) about 40 minutes. Cool; then chill.

CRANBERRY-RAISIN PIE

1-1/2 cups sugar
1/4 cup orange juice
1/4 teaspoon salt
3 cups cranberries
1 cup seeded raisins
1 tablespoon cornstarch
1 teaspoon each grated orange and lemon rind
2 tablespoons butter or margarine
Pastry for 2-crust 9" pie

Bring the first 3 ingredients and 2 tablespoons water to a full boil in saucepan, stirring until sugar is dissolved. Add cranberries and cook, stirring occasionally, until berries pop open. Add raisins. Blend cornstarch and 2 tablespoons water. Add to berry mixture and cook until thickened, stirring. Remove from heat and stir in fruit rinds and butter. Pour into bottom crust. Moisten edges with water and cover with top crust. Make slit to allow steam to escape. Press edges together with tines of fork. Bake in hot oven (425°F.) about 25 minutes. Serve warm or cold.

LEMON SPONGE PIE

3/4 cup sugar
1/4 cup melted butter or margarine
1/4 cup flour
Grated rind and juice of 2 lemons
1 cup milk
2 eggs, separated
1/8 teaspoon salt
Unbaked 9" pie shell

Mix first 5 ingredients and egg yolks. Beat egg whites with salt until stiff but not dry. Fold into first mixture. Pour into pastry-lined piepan and bake in moderate oven (350°F.) 40 minutes. Cool.

LEMON CREAM PIE

1/3 cup all-purpose flour
2 tablespoons cornstarch
3/4 cup sugar
1/4 teaspoon salt
2-1/2 cups milk, scalded
4 egg yolks, beaten
1/2 cup lemon juice
2 teaspoons grated lemon rind
3 tablespoons butter or margarine
Yellow food coloring
Baked 9" pie shell
Whipped cream

In heavy saucepan, mix first 4 ingredients. Gradually stir in milk and cook, stirring, over medium heat until thickened. Stir small amount of mixture into egg yolks; then combine the two mixtures and cook, stirring, 1 minute. Add lemon juice, rind and butter. Stir in a few drops of food coloring and pour into baked shell; chill. Top with whipped cream.

SLICED-LEMON PIE

1-3/4 cups sugar
1/2 cup all-purpose flour
1/4 teaspoon salt
3 small lemons
Pastry for 2-crust 9" pie
2 tablespoons butter

Mix well the first 3 ingredients. Add 1¼ cups of boiling water and beat with rotary beater until smooth. Grate rind of 1 lemon and add to first mixture. Cut peel and white membrane from all 3 lemons and discard with seeds. Slice lemons paper-thin. (There should be about ⅔ cup lemon slices.) Stir into first mixture. Line 9" piepan with half the pastry, pour in filling, dot with butter and adjust top crust. Bake in very hot oven (450°F.) 10 minutes. Reduce heat to 350°F. and bake about 45 minutes longer. Serve warm.

LEMON AMBROSIA PIE

1 teaspoon salt
1 cup all-purpose flour
1/3 cup shortening
1 can (3-1/2 ounces) flaked coconut, toasted and cooled
Milk
1-1/3 cups sugar
6 tablespoons cornstarch
2 eggs, separated
2 tablespoons butter
1 teaspoon grated lemon rind
1/3 cup lemon juice
1 teaspoon vanilla extract
1 envelope unflavored gelatin
1 cup light cream

To make the crust, mix ½ teaspoon of salt and the flour. Cut in shortening. Add ½ cup coconut. Blend in 3 tablespoons milk, or enough to make a dough that will form a ball. Roll out between 2 sheets of waxed paper to fit 9" piepan. Crimp edges and bake in hot oven (400°F.) 10 to 12 minutes. Cool. In top part of double boiler, mix the remaining ½ teaspoon salt, the sugar and cornstarch. Gradually stir in 1½ cups boiling water. Cook over direct heat, stirring, until smooth and thickened. Put over boiling water and cook, covered, 10 minutes. Stir small amount into beaten egg yolks, then combine the two mixtures in double boiler and cook, stirring, 2 minutes. Add butter, rind, juice and vanilla. Take out 1 cup filling and set aside. Soften gelatin in ¼ cup cold water and stir into remaining filling. When dissolved, stir in cream. Chill until thickened and fold in stiffly beaten egg whites. Pour into shell, chill until firm. Spread reserved filling on pie; top with rest of coconut. Chill.

FROZEN LEMON PIE

4 eggs, separated
Grated rind of 1 lemon
1/3 cup lemon juice
2/3 cup sugar
1 cup heavy cream, whipped
1/8 teaspoon salt
1/3 cup fine graham-cracker crumbs

In the top part of double boiler mix egg yolks, the lemon rind and juice and sugar. Cook over hot water until thickened, stirring. Cool. Fold in cream and egg whites, beaten stiff with salt. Butter a 9" piepan and sprinkle with half the crumbs. Pour in lemon mixture and sprinkle with remaining crumbs. Freeze until firm.

LEMON MERINGUE PIE

Sugar
Salt
6 tablespoons cornstarch
Grated rind of 1 lemon
1/4 cup butter
3 eggs, separated
Lemon juice
Baked 9" pie shell

Mix 1¼ cups sugar, ⅛ teaspoon salt and the cornstarch. Add 2 cups boiling water and rind. Cook until thickened, stirring; simmer 10 minutes. Add butter but do not stir. Gradually stir into egg yolks mixed with ½ cup lemon juice. Strain into pie shell and bake in hot oven (400°F.) 10 minutes. Add ⅛ teaspoon salt and 1 teaspoon lemon juice to egg whites and beat until stiff. Gradually add 6 tablespoons sugar, beating until very stiff. Pile lightly on pie; spread to edge. Reduce heat to 350°F. and bake 18 minutes. Cool.

KEY LIME PIE

1/4 cup lime juice
1 envelope unflavored gelatin
1 cup sugar
1/4 teaspoon salt
4 eggs, separated
Freshly grated lime rind
Baked 8" pastry shell or crumb crust
Sweetened whipped cream

In the top part of small double boiler, put the lime juice and ½ cup water. Soften gelatin in liquids. Add ½ cup sugar, the salt and egg yolks. Beat slightly to blend. Cook over simmering water, stirring constantly until mixture is thickened and coats a metal spoon. Remove from heat and add 2 teaspoons rind. Chill until thickened but not firm. Beat egg whites until foamy; gradually add remaining ½ cup sugar, beating until stiff. Fold into gelatin. Pile lightly in shell; chill until firm. Spread with cream; sprinkle with lime rind.

LIME CHIFFON PIE

1 envelope unflavored gelatin
1/2 cup sugar
1/2 cup lime juice
2 drops green food coloring
1/2 teaspoon grated lime or lemon rind
1/4 teaspoon salt
3 egg whites
1/2 cup light corn syrup
Baked 9″ pie shell

Sprinkle gelatin on ¹/₂ cup cold water in small saucepan. Let stand a few minutes to soften. Add sugar and stir over very low heat until gelatin and sugar are dissolved. Remove from heat and stir in lime juice, food coloring and grated rind. Chill to the consistency of unbeaten egg white. Beat salt with egg whites until stiff but not dry. Gradually add corn syrup, beating until stiff and glossy. Fold chilled gelatin mixture into beaten whites; chill, stirring occasionally, until thick enough to pile up (about ¹/₂ hour). Pile lightly into baked shell and chill until firm.
Lemon Chiffon Pie Follow above recipe, substituting lemon juice and rind for lime. Use yellow food coloring.

LIME-COCONUT MERINGUE PIE

Lime and coconut are a delicious combination.

Sugar
1/3 cup cornstarch
1/2 teaspoon salt
3 eggs, separated
1 tablespoon grated lime rind
Lime juice
3 tablespoons butter or margarine
Flaked coconut
Baked 9″ pie shell

In top part of small double boiler, combine ¹/₂ cup sugar, cornstarch, salt and ¹/₄ cup cold water. Mix until smooth and blended. Stir in 1¹/₄ cups hot water. Cook, stirring, over boiling water until thickened. Cover and cook, stirring occasionally, 5 minutes, or until very thick. Beat egg yolks with ¹/₂ cup sugar. Stir in a small amount of hot mixture; then combine the two mixtures in double boiler, stirring vigorously. Cook, stirring, 2 or 3 minutes longer. Remove from heat and stir in lime rind, ¹/₃ cup lime juice, the butter and ¹/₂ cup coconut. Pour into shell. Beat egg whites until foamy; add 1 teaspoon lime juice. Gradually add 6 tablespoons sugar and beat until stiff but not dry. Pile lightly on pie and sprinkle with coconut. Bake in moderate oven (350°F.) about 10 minutes. Let stand until cold.

BLUEBERRY PIE WITH CREAM-CHEESE TOPPING

Wash and drain 1 quart fresh blueberries. Put in saucepan with grated rind and juice of 1 lemon. Cover and cook 5 minutes. Mix ³/₄ cup sugar, 3 tablespoons cornstarch and ¹/₄ teaspoon salt. Stir into berries and cook, stirring, until thickened. Cool and pour into baked 9″ pie shell. Beat 3 ounces cream cheese with 2 tablespoons cream; decorate cold pie.

STRAWBERRY BAVARIAN PIE

Rich with a cup of heavy cream in the filling, but light, thanks to fluffy beaten egg whites.

1 cup all-purpose flour
Granulated sugar
Grated rind of 1/2 lemon
1/2 cup cold butter or margarine
1 egg yolk, slightly beaten
1 envelope unflavored gelatin
1/4 teaspoon salt
1 cup milk
2 eggs, separated
2 teaspoons vanilla extract
1 cup heavy cream, whipped
1 pint strawberries, washed, hulled and sliced
Confectioners' sugar

To make pastry, put flour, ¹/₄ cup granulated sugar and the lemon rind in bowl. Cut in butter. Mix in egg yolk with hands. Chill while preparing filling. Then roll out about two thirds of pastry on lightly floured board and use to line a greased 9″ piepan. Flute edge and bake in moderate oven (375°F.) 12 to 15 minutes, or until light brown. Shape remaining pastry into a roll and cut in 10 to 12 equal pieces. Roll each piece into a pencil-size rope 4″ long. Shape ropes into half circles on greased cookie sheet. Bake at 375°F. 10 to 12 minutes. Let shell and half circles stand until cold. To make filling, mix gelatin, ¹/₄ cup granulated sugar and the salt in top part of double boiler. Add milk and egg yolks and beat slightly to blend. Cook over simmering water, stirring, until slightly thickened. Remove from heat and add vanilla. Cool, stirring occasionally to prevent skin from forming on top. Beat egg whites until foamy; gradually add ¹/₄ cup sugar and beat until stiff but not dry. Fold into gelatin mixture with the cream; chill until thickened but not firm. Pour into cold shell and chill until firm. Arrange half circles of baked pastry around edge, putting rounded sides up for a basket effect. Put berries on top; sprinkle with confectioners' sugar.

BLUEBERRY LATTICE PIE

(Using frozen berries)

1/4 cup quick-cooking tapioca
1/4 cup granulated sugar
2 tablespoons brown sugar
1/4 teaspoon salt
1/8 teaspoon cinnamon
1/2 cup blueberry syrup
2 boxes (12 ounces each) frozen
    sweetened blueberries, thawed and
    drained
1 tablespoon lemon juice
Pastry for unbaked 8" pie and
    lattice strips
1 tablespoon butter

Mix all ingredients, except last 2. Line
8" piepan with pastry. Pour in berry
mixture. Dot with butter. Cut strips
of pastry with pastry cutter or knife.
Lay across pie, lattice fashion. Press
edges together with fork. Bake in hot
oven (400°F.) 45 minutes.

JELLIED STRAWBERRY-CREAM PIE

2 packages (3 ounces each) strawberry-
    flavor gelatin dessert
1 package (10 ounces) frozen strawberries
1 can (15-3/4 ounces) crushed pineapple,
    well drained
1/2 cup chopped walnuts
1 cup dairy sour cream
Baked deep 9" pie shell
1/2 cup heavy cream, whipped
Fresh strawberries

Dissolve gelatin in 1½ cups boiling
water. Add frozen strawberries (undrained). Chill until thickened. Add
pineapple and nuts; fold in sour
cream. Pour into pie shell and chill
until firm. Decorate with whipped
cream and fresh berries.

STRAWBERRY SNOWBANK PIE

1 quart strawberries
Baked 9" pie shell
1-1/4 cups sugar
1/2 teaspoon cream of tartar
Pinch of salt
2 egg whites
1/2 teaspoon vanilla extract

Wash and hull strawberries; arrange
in pie shell, putting prettiest berries
in center. Mix sugar, ½ cup water
and cream of tartar in saucepan. Cover and bring to boil. Uncover and
cook until syrup spins long threads
(240°F. on a candy thermometer).
Add salt to egg whites and beat until
stiff. Gradually pour syrup on whites,
beating constantly until mixture forms
stiff peaks. Add flavoring and pile on
pie, leaving center uncovered. Cool,
but do not refrigerate.

RASPBERRY CREAM PIE

12 ounces cream cheese
1/2 cup sugar
2 eggs
Unbaked 9" pie shell with high rim
1 cup dairy sour cream
2 packages (10 ounces each) frozen
    raspberries, thawed
5 teaspoons cornstarch
1 cup heavy cream

Cream together first 3 ingredients until smooth and blended.
Pour into pie shell. Bake in moderate oven (375°F.) 30 minutes, or
until filling is firm. Let stand on
cake rack until cold. Spread with
sour cream and chill 1 hour. Meanwhile, mix berries and cornstarch in
saucepan; cook, stirring frequently,
until thick and clear. Cool to room
temperature. Whip cream and fold
into raspberries. Spoon on pie; chill.

RHUBARB PIE

3 tablespoons flour
1 to 1-1/4 cups sugar
1/4 teaspoon salt
4 cups diced fresh rhubarb
Grated rind of 1 orange
1/4 cup orange juice
Pastry for 9" pie shell and lattice strips
2 tablespoons butter or margarine

Mix flour, sugar, and salt with the
rhubarb. Add orange rind and juice.
Turn into shell; dot with butter. Cover with strips of pastry, lattice fashion.
Bake in very hot oven (450°F.) 20 minutes. Reduce heat to moderate (350°
F.); bake about 20 minutes.

RHUBARB CUSTARD PIE

1 package (1 pound) frozen unsweetened
    rhubarb
2 tablespoons flour
Sugar
Unbaked 9" pie shell
3 eggs, separated
1/2 cup milk
1/8 teaspoon salt
1/4 teaspoon almond extract (optional)

Thaw rhubarb just enough to break
up solid block. Mix with flour and
¾ cup sugar. Put in pie shell. Beat egg
yolks slightly. Add milk, salt, and
flavoring, if desired. Pour over rhubarb mixture. Bake in a very hot oven
(450°F.) 10 minutes. Reduce heat to
325°F. and bake 30 minutes longer,
or until set. Cool slightly. Beat egg
whites until foamy; gradually add 6
tablespoons sugar and beat until stiff
but not dry. Pile lightly on pie. Bake
in moderate oven (350°F.) about 10
minutes. Serve warm or cold. If frozen sweetened rhubarb is used, reduce sugar in filling to ½ cup.

ORANGE AND CREAM-CHEESE PIE

4 or 5 oranges, peeled and cut in chunks, (about 2 cups)
Sugar
1 cup finely ground or crushed gingersnaps
1/3 cup butter or margarine, melted
2 tablespoons cornstarch
1 package (3 ounces) cream cheese
1 tablespoon milk
2 oranges, peeled and thinly sliced
Whipped topping, or heavy cream, whipped

Mix orange chunks and 1/2 cup sugar and chill. Mix gingersnaps, 1/4 cup sugar and butter. Press firmly with fingers or back of spoon on bottom and sides of 9″ piepan; chill. Mix cornstarch and 1/3 cup sugar in saucepan. Drain syrup from orange chunks, adding water to make 1 cup. Stir into cornstarch mixture. Cook, stirring, over medium heat until thick and clear; cool. Beat cream cheese and milk together until smooth. Spread on bottom and sides of pie crust. Cover bottom evenly with drained orange chunks. Pour about half the cooked syrup over chunks, top with orange slices and glaze with remaining syrup. Chill several hours. Then serve with whipped topping.

PEAR CREAM PIE

1 can (16 ounces) pear halves
1/2 cup packed brown sugar
1/3 cup all-purpose flour
1/4 teaspoon salt
3/4 cup milk
2 eggs, slightly beaten
2 tablespoons butter or margarine
1/2 tablespoon vanilla extract
9″ Crumb Crust (page 419)
1/2 cup heavy cream
3 tablespoons granulated sugar
1/4 teaspoon cinnamon
2 tablespoons chopped pecans

Drain pears, reserving 3/4 cup syrup. Blend brown sugar, flour and salt with a small amount of pear syrup. Add remaining pear syrup and milk. Cook over low heat, stirring, until thickened. Cover and cook, stirring occasionally, 15 minutes longer. Add a little of the hot mixture to beaten eggs; blend slowly with remaining hot mixture. Cook a few minutes longer. Remove from heat. Add butter and vanilla; cool. Pour into Crumb Crust. Chill thoroughly. Whip cream with 1 tablespoon granulated sugar and cover top of pie. Mix together remaining 2 tablespoons sugar, cinnamon and pecans. Dip drained pear halves in mixture and arrange on pie.

ROSY-TOPPED PEACH CREAM PIE

1 package (3-1/4 ounces) vanilla pudding-and-pie-filling mix
2 cups milk
Baked 9″ pie shell
1 can (30 ounces) sliced cling peaches, well drained
1-1/2 teaspoons cornstarch
3 tablespoons grenadine
Toasted whole almonds
Whipped cream

Prepare pie filling with milk according to package directions. Cool slightly, then pour into baked pie shell and cool completely. Arrange peach slices pinwheel fashion on top of pie filling. Blend cornstarch with 1/4 cup cold water in saucepan. Add grenadine and cook over low heat, stirring, until clear and slightly thickened. Cool, then spoon carefully over peach slices. Place almonds in center and pipe whipped cream around edges.

PEACH CREAM PIE

Unbaked 9″ pie shell
3 tablespoons all-purpose flour
1/3 cup sugar
1/8 teaspoon salt
1/4 teaspoon ground nutmeg
3/4 cup medium cream
3-1/2 cups sliced peeled firm-ripe peaches

Chill pie shell and prick a little with fork. Bake in hot oven (400°F.) about 6 minutes. Mix next 4 ingredients, add cream and mix well. Put peaches in shell and pour cream mixture over fruit. Bake in hot oven (400°F.) 40 minutes, or until set; cool.

DEEP-DISH PEACH PIE

1/4 cup sugar
1/2 cup packed light-brown sugar
1/8 teaspoon mace
1-1/2 tablespoons quick-cooking tapioca
4 cups sliced peeled firm-ripe peaches
2 tablespoons lemon juice
Pastry for 1-crust pie, unbaked
Cream

Combine first 4 ingredients. Add peaches and lemon juice and toss gently to mix. Turn into 9″ square baking dish. Roll pastry to about an 11″ square. Put over peaches, pressing to side of dish. Cut a few slits in top with knife to permit steam to escape. Bake in hot oven (425°F.) 40 minutes, or until crust is browned and filling is bubbly. Serve with cream while still warm.

RHUBARB-PINEAPPLE PIE

All-purpose flour
Sugar
Grated rind of 1/2 lemon
Butter
1 egg yolk, slightly beaten
1 can (15-3/4 ounces) crushed pineapple
3 cups fresh rhubarb, cut in 1/2" pieces

To make pastry, put 1½ cups flour, 2 tablespoons sugar and the lemon rind in bowl. Cut in ¾ cup butter. Mix in egg yolk and work pastry quickly together with hands. Chill. Meanwhile make filling. Drain pineapple, reserving syrup. In large saucepan, mix ⅓ cup flour and 1 cup sugar. Add ¼ cup pineapple syrup. Cook over low heat, stirring constantly, 3 or 4 minutes. Add rhubarb and cook gently until rhubarb is soft but pieces are still whole, 2 or 3 minutes. Add pineapple and mix lightly. Cool. Roll out about two thirds of pastry on lightly floured board. Fit into 9" pie-pan, trim edges and press to edge of pan with thumb. Prick with fork dipped in flour. Bake in moderate oven (375°F.) 12 to 15 minutes; cool. Pour filling in and dot with 2 tablespoons butter. Roll out remaining pastry and cut in ¾" strips. Adjust on pie to form a lattice. Press a strip of pastry around edge. Bake 15 to 20 minutes longer, or until lattice is golden brown. Serve slightly warm.

CHERRY ALMOND PIE

The Almond Cream Topping is a delicious new idea for cherry pie.

2 cans (1 pound each) unsweetened pitted sour cherries
1 cup sugar
1/4 cup cornstarch
1/8 teaspoon salt
1 tablespoon butter
1/8 teaspoon cinnamon
1/8 teaspoon almond extract
Few drops of red food coloring
Baked 9" pie shell
Almond Cream Topping

Drain cherries well, reserving ⅔ cup juice. In saucepan, mix next 3 ingredients. Gradually stir in juice. Bring to boil and cook, stirring, until thick and clear. Add cherries and next 4 ingredients. Cook, stirring gently, until very thick. Cool and pour into shell. Chill. Spread with topping just before serving. For **Almond Cream Topping,** whip ⅔ cup heavy cream until almost stiff. Add 2 teaspoons sugar, ¼ teaspoon vanilla extract and 1 or 2 drops almond extract. Beat stiff.

CHERRY BAVARIAN PIE

Try a sprinkle of nutmeg over this.
1 cup undiluted evaporated milk
1 can (1 pound) pitted red sour cherries
3/4 cup sugar
1 envelope unflavored gelatin
3 tablespoons lemon juice
Red food coloring
Baked 9" pie shell

Chill evaporated milk in freezer tray until ice crystals form around edge. Drain cherries, reserving liquid. In saucepan, mix sugar and gelatin; gradually add liquid and heat, stirring until sugar and gelatin are dissolved. Remove from heat and add lemon juice and cherries. Chill until thickened, but not firm. Add a few drops of red coloring. Whip milk until stiff and fold into first mixture. Pile in baked shell and chill until firm.

SOUR-CREAM RAISIN PIE

1 cup sugar
1/2 teaspoon cinnamon
1/4 teaspoon powdered cloves
1/8 teaspoon nutmeg
1/8 teaspoon salt
1 cup dairy sour cream
1 egg, beaten
1 teaspoon vinegar
1 cup chopped raisins
Pastry for 8" pie shell and lattice strips

Mix first 5 ingredients. Add remaining ingredients, except pastry, and mix well. Pour into pastry-lined piepan. Cover with pastry strips, lattice fashion. Bake in very hot oven (450°F.) 15 minutes. Reduce heat to 350°F. and bake 15 minutes longer. Cool.

GOLDEN RAISIN PIE

Sugar
1 tablespoon cornstarch
1/2 teaspoon each salt, ginger and cinnamon
1/4 teaspoon each ground cloves and nutmeg
3 eggs, separated
1/2 cup light corn syrup
1 cup dairy sour cream
1 cup golden raisins
2 to 3 teaspoons grated orange rind
Baked 8" pie shell

In top part of small double boiler, mix ¼ cup sugar, the cornstarch, salt and spices. Stir in egg yolks and next 4 ingredients. Cook over simmering water, stirring, 10 minutes, or until very thick. Pour into shell. Beat egg whites until foamy. Gradually add 6 tablespoons sugar and beat until stiff. Spread on hot filling, covering edges well. Bake in hot oven (400°F.) 5 minutes, or until golden brown. Cool before cutting.

PEACH-ALMOND CREAM PIE

3-1/2 cups sliced peeled fresh peaches
2/3 cup sugar, or to sweeten
1/4 cup all-purpose flour
1/4 teaspoon nutmeg
Unbaked 9" pie shell
1 cup heavy cream
1/4 cup sliced almonds

Toss peaches gently with sugar, flour and nutmeg. Turn into pie shell. Pour cream over peaches. Bake in hot oven (400°F.) 35 minutes. Remove pie from oven and sprinkle with almonds. Return pie to oven and bake 5 minutes longer. Cool. *Note* Nectarines or apricots can be substituted for the peaches.

PINEAPPLE AMBROSIA PIE

1-1/4 cups fine graham-cracker crumbs
1/2 cup flaked coconut
1/3 cup butter or margarine, melted
1 package (3 ounces) orange-flavor gelatin dessert
1 cup orange sherbet
1 can (15-3/4 ounces) crushed pineapple, drained
Whipped heavy cream

Mix first 3 ingredients and press into 9" piepan. Bake in moderate oven (350°F.) 10 minutes. Cool thoroughly. Dissolve gelatin in 1 cup boiling water. Add ½ cup cold water, then stir in sherbet until melted. Add pineapple. Chill until thick and pour into pie shell. Chill 3 hours, or until firm. Decorate with whipped cream.

PINEAPPLE-RAISIN PIE

Sugar
3 tablespoons cornstarch
1/4 tablespoon salt
1 can (15-3/4 ounces) pineapple spears
1-1/2 cups dairy sour cream
3 eggs, separated
1 cup seedless raisins
Baked 9" pie shell

In top part of double boiler, mix ½ cup sugar, the cornstarch and salt. Add syrup drained from pineapple, sour cream and egg yolks. Stir, then beat with rotary beater until smooth. Cook over simmering water, stirring, until very thick and smooth. Remove from heat and cool slightly. Dice pineapple, add with raisins to filling and pour into shell. Beat egg whites until foamy. Gradually add 6 tablespoons sugar and beat until stiff but not dry. Pile lightly on filling, covering completely. Bake in hot oven (400°F.) 5 minutes, or until golden brown. Cool before cutting.

PINEAPPLE CREAM-CHEESE PIE

1/2 cup well-drained crushed pineapple
Baked 10" pie shell
12 ounces cream cheese
3/4 cup sugar
1 tablespoon flour
1/8 teaspoon salt
4 eggs
1/4 cup each heavy cream and milk
1 teaspoon vanilla extract

Spread pineapple in bottom of shell. Mash cheese and beat in next 3 ingredients. Beat eggs slightly; add cream, milk and vanilla. Stir into cheese mixture. Pour into shell and bake in moderate oven (350°F.) 30 minutes, or until firm. Cool; chill.

SOUR-CREAM PRUNE MERINGUE PIE

1 cup finely diced cooked prunes
1-1/2 cups dairy sour cream
1/2 cup sugar
1 teaspoon cinnamon
1/2 teaspoon ground cloves
1/4 teaspoon nutmeg
3 eggs, separated
Unbaked 9" pie shell
Never-fail Meringue (page 420)

Mix first 6 ingredients. Stir in beaten egg yolks. Pour into shell and bake in hot oven (425°F.) 10 minutes. Reduce heat to 325°F. and bake about 20 minutes longer. Use egg whites to prepare meringue. Bake as directed.

BANANA MERINGUE PIE

Sugar
6 tablespoons all-purpose flour
1/4 teaspoon salt
2-1/2 cups milk
3 eggs, separated
1 tablespoon butter or margarine
1/2 teaspoon vanilla extract
2 or 3 ripe bananas
Baked 9" pie shell
Dash of salt
1/4 teaspoon cream of tartar

Mix ½ cup sugar, the flour and salt in top part of double boiler. Add milk and cook over boiling water until thickened, stirring constantly. Cover and cook 10 minutes longer, stirring occasionally. Beat egg yolks. Add a small amount of milk mixture slowly to yolks; return to double boiler and cook 2 minutes, stirring. Remove from heat; add butter and vanilla. Cool. Slice bananas into shell; pour cooked mixture over them at once. Add salt and cream of tartar to egg whites; beat until stiff. Gradually add 6 tablespoons sugar, continuing to beat until very stiff. Pile lightly on pie; spread to edge. Bake in slow oven (325°F.) about 18 minutes.

PRUNE-WHIP PIE

1 pound prunes, cooked, pitted and
    cut up
1/2 cup sugar
3/4 cup chopped nuts
1/8 teaspoon salt
1 teaspoon grated lemon rind
1 tablespoon lemon juice
2 egg whites
Baked 9" pie shell
1/2 cup heavy cream, whipped
Few drops of almond or rum extract

Mix first 6 ingredients. Fold in stiffly
beaten egg whites. Pour into pie shell
and bake in moderate oven (325°F.)
30 minutes, or until set. Cool. Flavor
cream and spread on pie.

CONCORD GRAPE PIE

7 cups stemmed Concord grapes
3 tablespoons cornstarch
1-1/2 cups sugar
1/4 teaspoon salt
Grated rind of 1 orange
Pastry for unbaked 9" pie shell and
    lattice strips

Wash the grapes; slip skins from pulp
and reserve the skins. Heat pulp
to boiling and rub through coarse
sieve to remove seeds. Combine
cornstarch, sugar, salt and rind; add
grape pulp. Cook until thickened,
stirring constantly. Add skins; cool.
Pour filling into shell; cover with
strips of pastry, lattice fashion. Bake
in very hot oven (450°F.) 10 minutes;
reduce heat to moderate (350°F.) and
bake about 25 minutes.

PEACH MELBA PIE

1 cup all-purpose flour
Cornstarch
1/4 cup confectioners' sugar
1/4 teaspoon salt
1/2 cup butter or margarine
1 can (29 ounces) sliced cling peaches,
    drained
1/4 cup bottled raspberry syrup
1 teaspoon lemon juice
Red food coloring
1/2 cup heavy cream, whipped

To make crust, mix flour, 1/4 cup cornstarch, the sugar and salt. Cut in butter. Work together with hands and
roll pastry to a 7" circle. Then press
on bottom and sides of 9" piepan.
Flute edges with fork. Chill 15 minutes. Then bake in slow oven
(325°F.) about 20 minutes. Let stand
until cold. Put peaches in shell. Mix
raspberry syrup and 1/4 cup water;
blend in 1 teaspoon cornstarch.
Cook, stirring, until slightly thickened. Add lemon juice and a little
food coloring. Pour over peaches.
Chill and decorate with cream.

CREAMY BANANA-NUT PIE

*It should be eaten within a few hours
after preparation.*
1/4 cup lemon juice
3-1/2 cups sliced ripe bananas
    (4 medium)
1 envelope unflavored gelatin
1/2 cup sifted confectioners' sugar
1/2 teaspoon ginger
1/4 teaspoon salt
1 cup heavy cream, whipped
1 cup chopped pecans
Baked deep 9" pie shell

Combine 2 cups water and lemon
juice. Add bananas, cover and refrigerate 1 hour. Soften gelatin in 1/4
cold water; dissolve over hot water.
Drain bananas and beat until almost
smooth. Stir in gelatin and sugar
mixed with ginger and salt. Fold in
cream and 3/4 cup nuts. Pour into shell
and sprinkle with remaining 1/4 cup
nuts. Chill until set.

PEACH PARFAIT PIE

1 box (3 ounces) peach- or lemon-
    flavor gelatin
1 pint peach or vanilla ice cream
2 fresh peaches, peeled and diced
    (1 cup)
1/4 cup sugar
Baked 9" pie shell, chilled
1/2 cup heavy cream

Dissolve gelatin in 1¼ cups hot water.
At once add ½ cup ice cream and stir
until blended. Repeat using all of
ice cream. Chill until almost firm.
Mix peaches with sugar and fold into
mixture. Pour into baked shell and
chill until firm. Whip cream and
spread on pie.

ORANGE-PINEAPPLE
CHIFFON PIE

1 envelope unflavored gelatin
2/3 cup sugar
3/4 cup orange juice
3 eggs, separated
1 teaspoon grated orange rind
1 can (9 ounces) crushed pineapple,
    drained
1/2 teaspoon salt
Baked 9" pie shell

Mix gelatin and 1/3 cup sugar in
top part of small double boiler.
Beat in orange juice and egg yolks.
Cook over simmering water, stirring,
until thickened. Remove from heat
and add orange rind and pineapple.
Chill until almost set. Beat egg whites
with salt until foamy; gradually add
remaining 1/3 cup sugar and beat until stiff, but not dry. Fold into first
mixture. Pile lightly in shell and chill
until set.

HOME TOUCHES FOR BOUGHT MINCEMEAT

Any kind of bought mincemeat can be used. Prepare packaged mincemeat as directed before measuring. To each 2 cups of bought mincemeat add: 1/2 cup shredded peeled apple, 1 teaspoon (or more to taste) mixed spices (especially cinnamon, nutmeg and coriander), 2 tablespoons diced citron, 2 tablespoons diced candied orange peel, 2 tablespoons diced candied lemon peel, 2 teaspoons orange juice, 1 teaspoon lemon juice, 2 tablespoons whiskey or brandy, 1 to 2 tablespoons (to taste) rum or sherry. Mix well, cover and let stand at least 24 hours before using.

SWEET-POTATO PECAN PIE

1/4 cup soft butter
1/4 cup packed brown sugar
1/8 teaspoon salt
3 eggs
3/4 cup dark corn syrup
1-1/4 cups mashed cooked sweet potato
1 teaspoon vanilla extract
1-1/2 cups pecans
Unbaked 9" pie shell

 Cream butter and sugar. Beat in next 5 ingredients. Add 1 cup nuts and pour into shell. Sprinkle 1/2 cup nuts over top. Bake in moderate oven (375°F.) 50 to 55 minutes.

NEVER-FAIL CUSTARD PIE

2-1/4 cups milk
1/2 cup sugar
1/2 teaspoon each salt and vanilla
Grating of nutmeg
3 eggs
Unbaked 9" pastry shell

Scald milk; add sugar, salt, vanilla and nutmeg. Mix well. Gradually pour over slightly beaten eggs, stirring constantly. Grease a deep 9" piepan with cooking oil; pour in custard mixture. Put pan in larger shallow pan and pour in hot water to depth of about 1". Bake in slow oven (300°F.) 55 minutes, or until set. Remove pan of custard from water; let stand until cold, then chill. Bake pastry shell in a piepan exactly like the one containing custard; cool. Just before serving, carefully loosen custard from sides of pan, using a small spatula. Shake gently to loosen custard from bottom; carefully and quickly slide firm custard from pan into the baked shell. Allow custard filling to settle down into the crust a few minutes before serving.

Coconut Custard Pie Use the above recipe, sprinkling custard just before baking with 1/2 cup flaked coconut.

MINCEMEAT PIE WITH CHEESE CRUST

1-1/2 cups all-purpose sifted flour
1/2 teaspoon salt
1/3 cup shortening
1/2 cup shredded process American cheese
4 cups prepared mincemeat
1/4 cup brandy (optional)

Sift flour and salt; then cut in shortening. Add the cheese and toss with fork to blend. Sprinkle with cold water (about 2 tablespoons). Mix with fork until dry ingredients are moistened. Press into a ball. On floured board, roll 2/3 of dough to 1/8" thickness; press into 9" piepan. Fill with mincemeat, mixed with the brandy, if used. Roll remaining dough and cut in strips 1/2" wide. Arrange on pie, lattice fashion. Trim lattice edges and crimp edges of crust with fingers. Bake in hot oven (400°F.) 20 minutes, or until lightly browned.

CHOCOLATE CHIFFON PIE

Crust
1-1/2 cups graham-cracker or zwieback crumbs
1/3 cup unblanched almonds
6 tablespoons sugar
1/4 cup light cream
1/2 cup melted butter or margarine
1/2 teaspoon cinnamon

Filling
1 envelope unflavored gelatin
4 eggs, separated
1 cup bought chocolate sauce
1/8 teaspoon salt
1 teaspoon vanilla extract
1/2 cup sugar
Whipped cream
Shaved semisweet chocolate

Blend crumbs at low speed until very fine. Add almonds and blend fine at low speed. Remove from blender and mix thoroughly with remaining crust ingredients. Pat firmly into lightly buttered 10" piepan. Prick bottom several times with fork tines. Bake in moderate oven (375°F.) 12 to 15 minutes. Cool. Soften gelatin in 1/4 cup cold water. Add 2 tablespoons hot water and stir until dissolved. Put egg yolks in blender, add gelatin, cover and blend at low speed until thoroughly mixed. Add chocolate sauce, salt and vanilla; blend at high speed 4 or 5 seconds, or until thoroughly blended. Chill until partially thickened. With rotary beater, beat egg whites until foamy. Gradually add sugar and beat until very stiff. Fold into chocolate mixture. Pour into shell and chill. Decorate with cream and chocolate.

BLACK BOTTOM PIE

4 teaspoons cornstarch
1/8 teaspoon salt
1 cup sugar
4 eggs, separated
2 cups milk, scalded
1 package (6 ounces) semisweet
    chocolate pieces
2 teaspoons vanilla extract
Baked 9" pie shell
1 envelope unflavored gelatin
1/4 teaspoon cream of tartar

In top part of double boiler, mix cornstarch, salt and ½ cup sugar. Beat egg yolks and stir in milk. Add to first mixture and cook, stirring, over simmering water until mixture thickens and coats a spoon. Remove from heat, measure 1 cup and pour over ½ cup chocolate pieces. Beat with fork until smooth. Add 1 teaspoon vanilla, cool and pour into shell. Chill. Soften gelatin in ¼ cup cold water, add remaining hot mixture and stir until gelatin is dissolved. Add 1 teaspoon vanilla and chill until thickened. Beat egg whites until foamy; add cream of tartar and beat until almost stiff. Gradually add remaining ½ cup sugar and continue beating until stiff. Fold into gelatin mixture and pour over chocolate layer. Sprinkle with remaining ½ cup chocolate, chopped. Chill until firm.

CHOCOLATE-TOPPED CUSTARD PIE

Unbaked 9" pie shell
4 eggs
1/2 cup sugar
1/2 teaspoon salt
Grating of nutmeg
1/2 teaspoon vanilla extract
Milk
1/2 cup semisweet chocolate pieces

Brush pie shell with small amount of slightly beaten white from 1 egg. Add white to remaining eggs and beat slightly with next 4 ingredients. Scald 2¼ cups milk; pour over eggs. Mix well and pour into shell. Bake in hot oven (425°F.) 25 to 30 minutes. Cool. Melt chocolate and stir in 2 tablespoons milk. Spread evenly on pie.

Caramel Custard Pie Follow above recipe but caramelize the sugar. (To do this, heat sugar in heavy skillet over low heat, stirring until brown and syrupy.) Gradually stir into hot milk until blended. Proceed as directed. Omit topping, if desired.

Coconut Custard Pie Follow above recipe. Top unbaked pie with ½ cup flaked coconut in place of chocolate.

MARBLED CHOCOLATE-RUM PIE

1 envelope unflavored gelatin
1 cup sugar
1/8 teaspoon salt
2 eggs, separated
1 cup milk
1/4 cup rum
12 ounces semisweet chocolate pieces
1 cup heavy cream
1 teaspoon vanilla extract
Baked deep 9" pie shell

In top part of double boiler mix gelatin, ¼ cup sugar and the salt. Beat in egg yolks, milk and rum. Cook over boiling water, stirring, until slightly thickened. Remove from heat and stir in chocolate until thoroughly blended. Chill until thickened but not set. Beat egg whites until they are foamy; gradually add ½ cup sugar and beat until very stiff. Fold into chocolate mixture. Whip cream with remaining ¼ cup sugar and the vanilla until stiff. Alternate the two mixtures in pie shell; swirl with spoon. Chill until firm.

CHOCOLATE PECAN PIE

Good with whipped or ice cream
1/2 cup sugar
1 cup dark corn syrup
1/4 teaspoon salt
1 tablespoon all-purpose flour
2 eggs
1 tablespoon butter or margarine, melted
2 squares unsweetened chocolate, melted
1 teaspoon vanilla extract
1-1/4 cups pecan halves
Unbaked 9" pie shell

Beat together first 5 ingredients. Add next 4 ingredients and mix well. Pour into pastry shell. Turn some of nuts rounded side up. Bake in slow oven (300°F.) 50 to 60 minutes, or until just set. Cool.

CHOCOLATE SPONGE-CAKE PIE

3/4 to 1 cup sugar
2 tablespoons flour
1/4 teaspoon salt
3 eggs, separated
2 squares unsweetened chocolate, melted
1 cup milk
1 teaspoon vanilla extract
Unbaked 9" pie shell
Ice cream or whipped cream (optional)

Mix first 3 ingredients. Beat egg yolks until thick and lemon-colored. Stir into first mixture with chocolate. Add milk and vanilla; blend with rotary beater. Beat egg whites until stiff; fold in. Pour into pie shell. Bake in very hot oven (450°F.) 10 minutes. Reduce heat to 350°F.; bake 30 minutes, or until set. Cool.

HUNTSVILLE CHEESE PIE

Unbaked 8" pie shell
1/2 cup butter, at room temperature
1 cup sugar
2 eggs, separated
1-1/2 teaspoons white cornmeal
2 tablespoons heavy cream
1/2 teaspoon vanilla extract
Dash of salt

Bake shell in very hot oven (450°F.) 10 minutes, or until baked but not browned. Cream butter, sugar and egg yolks together. Add cornmeal mixed with cream and vanilla. Fold in egg whites beaten with the salt until stiff. Pour into baked shell and bake in hot oven (400°F.) 5 minutes. Reduce heat to 350°F. and bake 10 to 12 minutes longer, or until filling is just set. Serve slightly warm.

UNBAKED BANANA-CHEESE PIE

1 package (8 ounces) soft cream cheese
1 cup dairy sour cream
1 cup mashed banana
1 box (3-3/4 ounces) vanilla instant
    pudding
1 teaspoon vanilla extract
9" Crumb Crust (page 419)

Beat cheese until fluffy. Gradually beat in sour cream. Add remaining ingredients, except crust, and beat at low speed until blended. Pour into crust; chill until firm.

PEANUT-BUTTER CHIFFON PIE

1 envelope unflavored gelatin
1/2 cup sugar
1/4 teaspoon salt
1 cup milk
2 eggs, separated
2/3 cup smooth peanut butter
1 cup dairy sour cream
Baked 9" pie shell
Peanut-butter Topping (page 400)
    or sweetened whipped cream
1/2 square semisweet chocolate

In top part of small double boiler, mix gelatin, 1/4 cup sugar and the salt. Add milk and egg yolks and beat with rotary beater until blended. Put over simmering water and cook, stirring, until mixture thickens slightly and coats a spoon. Remove from heat, pour into bowl and beat in peanut butter. Cool thoroughly. Beat egg whites until foamy. Gradually add remaining 1/4 cup sugar and beat until stiff. Stir sour cream into gelatin mixture; then fold in egg whites. Pile lightly into shell and chill until firm. Decorate with preferred topping and semisweet-chocolate curls.

BUTTERMILK COCONUT PIE

3 eggs
1-1/2 cups sugar
1/2 cup margarine, melted
1-1/3 cups flaked coconut
1/3 cup buttermilk
1 teaspoon vanilla extract
Unbaked 9" pie shell

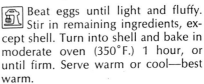 Beat eggs until light and fluffy. Stir in remaining ingredients, except shell. Turn into shell and bake in moderate oven (350°F.) 1 hour, or until firm. Serve warm or cool—best warm.

OLD-FASHIONED IRISH POTATO PIE

Unbaked 9" pie shell
3 eggs, separated
Sugar
1 cup riced cooked potatoes
1 cup hot milk
1 tablespoon pure vanilla extract
Nutmeg (optional)

Bake shell in hot oven (450°F.) 10 minutes. Beat egg yolks well and add 1 cup sugar, the potatoes, milk and vanilla. Pour into shell and sprinkle with nutmeg, if desired. Bake in moderate oven (350°F.) 30 minutes, or until golden. Beat eggs whites until foamy throughout. Gradually add 6 tablespoons sugar and beat until stiff. Spread on pie and bake in hot oven (400°F.) 5 minutes, or until golden brown. Cool before cutting. **Note** Meringue is not traditional and can be omitted, if preferred.

FROZEN EGGNOG PIE

2 cups pretzel crumbs
1/2 cup melted butter
3 egg yolks, slightly beaten
1 cup sugar
1/4 teaspoon salt
1/2 cup milk
3 tablespoons rum
1/2 teaspoon nutmeg
3 egg whites
1 cup heavy cream, whipped

Prepare crumbs by crushing pretzels fine in blender or grinder. Mix with butter and press into buttered 9-inch piepan; chill. In top part of small double boiler, mix egg yolks, 1/2 cup sugar, the salt and milk. Cook over simmering water, stirring constantly, until slightly thickened. Remove from heat and add rum and nutmeg; cool. Beat egg whites until almost stiff. Gradually beat in remaining 1/2 cup sugar. Fold with cream into egg mixture. Pile lightly in pie shell and freeze.

SHOOFLY PIE

3/4 cup dark molasses
1/2 teaspoon baking soda
1/4 teaspoon salt
1-1/2 cups all-purpose flour
1/4 cup butter or margarine
1/2 cup brown sugar, packed
Unbaked 9" pie shell

Mix the first 3 ingredients with ¾ cup boiling water. In another bowl, mix next 3 ingredients. Pour one third of molasses mixture into shell. Sprinkle with one third of flour mixture. Continue, ending with flour. Bake in moderate oven (375°F.) 35 minutes. Serve warm or cold.

SOUTHERN PECAN PIE

1/2 cup sugar
1 cup dark corn syrup
1/4 teaspoon salt
1 tablespoon flour
2 eggs
1 teaspoon vanilla extract
1 tablespoon butter, melted
1-1/4 cups pecan halves
Unbaked 9" pie shell

Beat together first 5 ingredients. Add next 3 ingredients. Pour into shell. Turn up rounded side of some pecans. Bake in slow oven (300°F.) 1 hour, or until set. Cool.

CHOCOLATE CREAM PIE

1 cup all-purpose flour
1/8 teaspoon salt
2 tablespoons cocoa
8 tablespoons sugar
Grated rind of 1 orange
1/3 cup plus 1 tablespoon butter or margarine
3 eggs, separated
1 tablespoon cornstarch
1 cup milk
1 cup semisweet chocolate pieces
1 tablespoon vanilla extract
2 tablespoons pistachio nuts (optional)

To make pastry, mix flour, salt, cocoa, 2 tablespoons sugar and the orange rind. Cut in butter. Mix in 1 egg yolk with hands. Roll out dough to a 7" circle. Then press into 9" piepan, covering edges. Chill 15 minutes. Bake in slow oven (325°F.) 25 to 30 minutes. Put 2 egg yolks, the cornstarch and milk in top part of small double boiler; beat until blended. Add chocolate; cook over boiling water until thickened, stirring. Remove from heat; add vanilla. Pour into shell. Beat egg whites until foamy; gradually add remaining sugar; beat until stiff but not dry. Pile lightly on pie and sprinkle with nuts, if desired. Bake in moderate oven (350°F.) 10 minutes. Cool; chill.

GOLDEN CARROT PIE

2 cups puréed cooked carrots, about 1-1/2 pounds before cooking
1 cup clover honey
3/4 cup undiluted evaporated milk
1/2 teaspoon each salt, nutmeg and ginger
1 teaspoon cinnamon
1/8 teaspoon ground cloves
3 eggs, slightly beaten
Unbaked 9" pie shell, chilled
Whipped cream
Toasted sliced almonds

Combine first 3 ingredients, salt and spices. Stir in eggs and pour into shell. Bake in hot oven (400°F.) 40 to 45 minutes, or until set. Cool on rack 30 minutes, then chill. Top with cream and almonds.

HONEY PECAN PIE

1/4 cup butter or margarine
1/2 cup sugar
2 tablespoons flour
1/4 teaspoon salt
3 eggs
1 cup honey
1 teaspoon vanilla extract
1-1/4 cups coarsely chopped pecans
Unbaked 9" pie shell

Cream first 4 ingredients until light. Add eggs, one at a time, beating thoroughly after each. Add honey, vanilla and nuts; mix well. Pour into shell. Bake in slow oven (300°F.) 70 minutes, or until firm. Cool, cut and serve with whipped cream, if desired.

THREE CREAM FILLINGS

Vanilla Cream Filling

3 cups milk
3/4 cup sugar
6 tablespoons cornstarch
1/2 teaspoon salt
3 eggs, beaten
1 tablespoon butter
2 teaspoons vanilla

Scald milk in top of double boiler over boiling water. Mix next 3 ingredients. Stir into milk. Cook, stirring until thick. Cover; cook 10 minutes longer. Add small amount of mixture to eggs; return to double boiler; cook 5 minutes. Add butter and vanilla. Put in bowl and sprinkle small amount of sugar over top to prevent skin from forming. Chill.
Chocolate Cream Filling Use above recipe. Melt 3 squares unsweetened chocolate in the milk and beat until smooth. Proceed as directed above.
Fluffy Cream Filling Use either recipe above, reducing milk to 2½ cups. Just before using, fold ½ cup heavy cream, whipped, into chilled mixture.

GLAZED CHERRY TARTS

Prepare Tart Pastry, page 419, and Vanilla Cream Filling, page 436, adding 1/2 teaspoon almond flavoring to filling. Drain 1 can (1 pound) pitted red sour cherries, reserving 3/4 cup juice. In saucepan mix 1/4 cup sugar, 2 tablespoons cornstarch, 1/8 teaspoon salt. Add cherry juice. Cook, stirring, until thickened. Add cherries and 1 tablespoon lemon juice. Add red food coloring to tint desired shade. Cool. Before serving, fill tart shells; top with cherry mixture. Makes 12.

LATTICE STRAWBERRY TARTS

Browned pastry strips contrast attractively with the berry filling.

1 recipe Standard Pastry, page 419, or Tart Pastry, page 419
1 quart strawberries
1 cup sugar
2 tablespoons cornstarch
2 tablespoons butter or margarine

Cut pastry to fit 6 shallow 4" tart pans. Wash and hull berries. Cut larger ones in halves; leave small ones whole. Add mixture of sugar and cornstarch. Pour into lined tart pans. Dot with butter. Arrange strips of pastry, lattice fashion, over tarts. Bake in very hot oven (450°F.) 10 minutes; then bake 20 minutes, or until berries are done and pastry is nicely browned. Makes 6 servings.

PINEAPPLE-APRICOT CREAM TARTS

Bake 4 shallow 4 1/2" tart shells, using pastry mix or your favorite pastry; cool. Prepare 1 box vanilla pudding-and-pie-filling mix as directed on label, cool slightly and divide into shells; chill. About 1 hour before serving, drain 4 slices pineapple. Put 1 on each tart. Top with **Apricot Glaze** Heat 1/2 cup apricot preserves until runny and strain onto pineapple. Chill.
Fruit Tarts, Second Method Prepare tart shells as above. Sprinkle cooked shells with ground almonds and fill with sweetened ripe fruit. You can use strawberries, raspberries, sliced or halved peaches, pitted cherries, grapes, etc. Brush with Apricot Glaze (above) or Currant Glaze (below) and top with sweetened whipped cream, if you like. **Currant Glaze** Heat 1/2 cup currant jelly until runny; add 1 tablespoon Cognac or kirsch. Cook 2 minutes. Cool slightly and brush on top of the fruit.

DEVONSHIRE STRAWBERRY TARTS

Cream cheese is covered with whole berries and a strained-berry filling.

1 quart strawberries
1/4 cup cornstarch
Dash of salt
3/4 cup sugar
1 package (3 ounces) cream cheese
2 tablespoons milk
6 baked shallow 4" tart shells

Wash and hull berries; put half through sieve. Add enough water to sieved berries to make 1 1/2 cups. Mix cornstarch, the salt and sugar; stir in sieved berries. Cook 5 minutes, or until thick, stirring constantly. Cool. Mix cheese with milk; spread in bottom of tart shells; cover with whole berries, tips up; top with cornstarch mixture. Chill. Makes 6 servings.

GLAZED GRAPE TARTS

3 tablespoons cornstarch
1/2 cup sugar
Pinch of salt
1-1/2 cups orange juice
Red food coloring (optional)
2 cups seeded or seedless grapes
6 baked shallow 4" tart shells
Whipped cream

Mix first 3 ingredients in saucepan; stir in orange juice. Cook until thick, stirring constantly, about 5 minutes. Add a little red coloring, if desired; cool. Shortly before serving, put grapes in tart shells; cover with orange-juice mixture. Top with whipped cream. Makes 6 servings.

LEMON-BUTTER TARTS

This lemon-butter filling is also sometimes called lemon curd or lemon cheese. It can be used as a cake filling or in place of jam. And for those who dislike lemon pies rigid with cornstarch, this is the filling!

1/2 cup butter
2 tablespoons grated lemon rind
1/2 cup lemon juice
1-1/2 cups sugar
3 whole eggs
3 egg yolks
8 baked 3" tart shells
Heavy cream (optional)

In the top of a double boiler, melt the butter. Stir in the lemon rind, juice and sugar. Beat the eggs and yolks together until thick; blend into lemon mixture. Cook, stirring constantly, over hot water until mixture is very thick. Chill before using. Spoon into baked tart shells and top with whipped cream. Makes 8.

SURREY ALMOND TARTS

2/3 cup fine white-bread crumbs
2/3 cup sugar
1/4 teaspoon salt
1 tablespoon flour
1/2 teaspoon double-acting baking
 powder
1/3 cup butter or margarine
2 eggs, separated
1 teaspoon almond extract
2 tablespoons milk
6 to 8 unbaked medium tart shells
Strawberry jam
Slivered almonds

Mix together first 5 ingredients. Cut in butter until fine and uniform in texture. Add egg yolks, almond extract and milk and beat well. In separate bowl, beat egg whites until stiff; gently fold in almond mixture. Spread bottom of each tart shell with strawberry jam to depth of 1/8". Pour mixture over jam and sprinkle generously with almonds. Bake in hot oven (425°F.) 10 minutes. Reduce heat to 350°F. and bake about 15 minutes longer. Cool before serving.

GRASSHOPPER TARTS

Decorate these tarts to suit the holiday. Use red candied cherries in winter and green cherries or tinted coconut for spring and summer.

1 envelope unflavored gelatin
1/2 cup sugar
1/8 teaspoon salt
3 eggs, separated
1/4 cup green crème de menthe
1/4 cup white crème de cacao
1 cup heavy cream, whipped
6 to 8 baked medium tart shells,
 or baked 9" shell
Additional whipped cream and shaved
 chocolate (optional)

In top of double boiler, mix together gelatin, 1/4 cup sugar and salt. Stir in 1/2 cup cold water. Put over boiling water, stirring, until gelatin is dissolved. Beat egg yolks slightly. Pour a small amount at a time of hot gelatin mixture into egg yolks and mix well. Put back over boiling water and cook, stirring, until slightly thickened. Remove from heat and stir in liqueurs. Chill, stirring occasionally, until mixture is consistency of unbeaten egg whites. Beat egg whites until foamy. Gradually add remaining 1/4 cup sugar and beat until stiff. Fold gently into gelatin mixture, then fold in whipped cream and mix lightly until blended. Put about 3/4 cup filling in each tart shell, or pour all of filling into 9" pie shell. Chill until firm. If desired, top with whipped cream and shaved chocolate.

KENTUCKY DERBY TARTS

2 eggs
1 cup granulated sugar
1/4 cup butter or margarine, melted
2 tablespoons bourbon
1/2 teaspoon vanilla extract
1/2 cup all-purpose flour
1/2 cup semisweet chocolate pieces,
 melted
1/2 cup chopped pecans
6 unbaked medium tart shells
Confectioners' sugar
Whipped cream
12 pecan halves

Beat eggs slightly. Add granulated sugar and beat in well. Add butter, bourbon and vanilla. Gradually add flour, mixing well. Stir in chocolate and nuts and divide among tart shells. Bake in moderate oven (350°F.) about 25 minutes. Cool, then dust lightly with confectioners' sugar. Top each tart with whipped cream and 2 pecan halves.

FROZEN RASPBERRY TART

Almond Pastry (below)
1 package (10 ounces) frozen
 raspberries, thawed
1 cup sugar
2 egg whites
1 tablespoon lemon juice
1/8 teaspoon salt
1-1/2 cups heavy cream
1/2 teaspoon almond extract
Chopped pistachios, sliced almonds or
 other nuts

Prepare and bake pastry; cool. Set a few raspberries aside for decoration and put remainder with the syrup, sugar and next 3 ingredients in large bowl of electric mixer. Beat until stiff. Whip 1 cup cream and fold with almond flavoring into first mixture. Pour onto crust in pan and freeze until firm. When ready to serve, put on serving platter. Remove rim of pan and decorate tart with remaining 1/2 cup cream, whipped, the nuts and reserved raspberries. Serve in wedges. Makes 8 to 10 servings.

ALMOND PASTRY

1/4 cup butter or margarine, softened
2 tablespoons sugar
1 egg yolk
3/4 cup all-purpose flour, lightly spooned
 into cup
1/4 cup minced blanched almonds

Cream first 3 ingredients until light. Stir in flour and almonds until well mixed. Press onto bottom of 9" springform pan 3" deep. Bake in hot oven (400°F.) 12 minutes, or until golden brown.

BANANA-AMBROSIA TARTS

Prepare 1 box (3¼ ounces) vanilla pudding-and-pie filling mix with 2 cups milk as directed on label; cool. Pour into eight 4″ baked tart shells. Peel and section 4 oranges. Just before serving, slice 2 or 3 ripe bananas. Arrange fruit on pudding in shells. Top with flaked coconut and maraschino cherries. Makes 8.

STRAWBERRY CREAM TARTS

Also good with blueberries.
Tart Pastry (page 419)
Pastry Cream (page 440)
Whole ripe strawberries, hulled
1 cup apricot preserves

Fit Tart Pastry in two 9″ piepans; or twelve 3½″ or 6 large shallow tart pans. Patch broken pieces with fingertips and chill shells. Bake in very hot oven (450°F.) 10 minutes. Turn control to 400°F. and bake 5 to 8 minutes longer; cool. Spoon a layer of cooled Pastry Cream into shells and top with strawberries. Heat apricot preserves until runny. Strain and spoon over fruit to glaze top. Chill. Makes 12 servings. *Note* Leftover pastry cream can be refrigerated and used for other tarts or cakes.

SWISS APPLE TART

Tart Pastry, page 419, or Standard Pastry, page 419
1/3 cup butter
8 large cooking apples, peeled and cut in eighths
Sugar
1 teaspoon vanilla extract
2 apples, peeled and sliced thin
Juice of 1 lemon
1 egg
3 to 4 tablespoons heavy cream
1 cup jelly or preserves

Line a 10″ flan ring or piepan with pastry and chill. Melt butter in skillet and add 8 apples. Cover and cook, stirring occasionally, until apples are just soft. Add ⅓ cup sugar and the vanilla and break the apples in small pieces. Cool slightly and spoon into pastry. Cook thinly sliced apples in 1 cup water with lemon juice about 5 minutes. Drain apples and dry. Arrange slices in a pattern on top of pie. Sprinkle with sugar. Bake in hot oven (425°F.) 10 minutes. Reduce to 350°F. and bake 20 minutes. Beat egg and cream and pour over tart. Bake about 10 minutes longer. Heat jelly or preserves until runny; strain preserves. Spoon carefully over top to glaze. Serve tart warm.

CHESTNUT-CHOCOLATE VANILLA TARTS

You can buy chestnut cream at gourmet food or specialty stores.
1 square unsweetened chocolate
3 tablespoons butter
1 teaspoon vanilla extract
3/4 cup canned sweetened chestnut cream
1/2 package (about 1/3 cup) instant vanilla-pudding mix
1 cup heavy cream
6 baked shallow 4-1/2″ tart shells
Sweetened whipped cream

Melt chocolate in top of double boiler over hot water. Combine thoroughly with butter. Cool. Stir in vanilla. Blend with sweetened chestnut cream until very smooth. Chill. Beat vanilla-pudding mix and the heavy cream until thoroughly blended and fluffy, scraping the bottom of the bowl frequently. Chill. Divide chestnut-chocolate filling evenly among the 6 tart shells; repeat with the vanilla filling. Top each tart with whipped cream, or decorate with piped swirls of whipped cream, using pastry bag. Makes 6 servings.

RAISIN-NUT STRUDEL

Simpler to make than a true strudel.
4 cups all-purpose flour
3 teaspoons baking powder
1/2 teaspoon salt
Sugar
1/2 cup vegetable oil
1/4 cup butter or margarine, melted
1/4 cup orange juice
1 teaspoon vanilla extract
3 eggs
1/3 cup tart jelly
1 cup soft white raisins
1 cup chopped nuts
12 maraschino cherries, diced
1 teaspoon cinnamon
1 egg white, slightly beaten

Sift first 3 ingredients and ¾ cup sugar into bowl. Make a well in center and add next 5 ingredients. Mix to form a soft dough. Knead a few times on floured board to form a smooth dough. Cut in 4 equal parts. Roll each to form a circle about ¼″ thick. Spread each with a thin coat of jelly. Sprinkle with raisins, nuts and cherries. Mix ¼ cup sugar and the cinnamon and sprinkle some lightly over fruits and nuts. Roll tightly and put on greased cookie sheet. Prick with fork and brush with egg white. Sprinkle with remaining cinnamon-sugar mixture. Bake in a moderate oven (350°F.) 45 minutes, or until golden brown. Cool and cut in slices. Makes four 8″ rolls.

PETITS PUFFS

Use recipe for Eclairs, below. Measure 1¼ teaspoons of dough onto greased baking sheet. Continue, placing same-size puffs 2" apart. Bake in hot oven (400°F.) about 20 minutes. Fill and frost. Makes 8 dozen.

ÉCLAIRS

1/2 cup butter or margarine
1/4 teaspoon salt
1 cup all-purpose flour
4 large eggs, beaten
Chocolate Cream Filling, page 436,
    Vanilla Cream Filling, page 436, or
    whipped cream
Chocolate Glaze

In saucepan, heat 1 cup water, butter and salt to full rolling boil. Reduce heat and quickly stir in flour, mixing vigorously with wooden spoon until mixture leaves the sides of pan in a ball. Remove from heat and add eggs in 6 additions, beating after each addition until mixture is very smooth. (An electric mixer at a low speed makes this procedure easier.) Force mixture through pastry tube onto greased baking sheets; or shape with spatula in 16 fingers, 4" x 1", 2" apart. Bake in hot oven (400°F.) 40 to 45 minutes. Remove at once to racks and cool away from drafts. Split and fill. Spread tops with glaze. Makes 16. **Chocolate Glaze** Melt together 2 tablespoons butter and 2 squares unsweetened chocolate. Stir in 1 cup sifted confectioners' sugar and 2 tablespoons boiling water. Beat until smooth but not stiff.

APPLE TWISTS

Standard Pastry (page 419)
2 tablespoons butter or margarine
3 tart apples, cut in sixths
Fat for deep frying
1/4 cup sugar
1/2 teaspoon cinnamon

Roll pastry into ½" thick rectangle; dot with butter and roll as for jelly roll. Roll again into rectangle, fold from sides toward center, making 3 layers; fold from ends toward center, making 9 layers in all. Wrap in waxed paper and chill. Roll into rectangle 18" x 11" and cut in eighteen 1" strips. Wind strip of dough around a wedge of apple, overlapping dough and pinching ends together. Repeat until all strips are used. Fry in hot deep fat (375°F. on frying thermometer) about 10 minutes. Drain on brown paper. Mix sugar and cinnamon. Roll twists in the mixture.

PASTRY CREAM

5 egg yolks
2/3 cup sugar
1/3 cup all-purpose flour
2 cups hot milk
1 teaspoon vanilla extract (or other
    flavoring)

Beat yolks until thick and gradually beat in sugar. Continue beating until mixture forms a ribbon when you lift the beater. Beat in flour until well blended. Add hot milk in a thin stream, beating constantly. Put mixture in top part of double boiler over simmering water and stir with a wire whisk until smooth and flour is cooked. Remove from heat and beat in vanilla; cool slightly. Makes 2½ cups.

COTTAGE-CHEESE DANISH PASTRIES

1 cup milk, scalded
Sugar
1 teaspoon salt
1-1/4 cups butter or margarine
1 package active dry yeast
3 eggs
1 teaspoon vanilla extract
Dash of nutmeg
3-1/2 to 4 cups all-purpose flour
1 egg yolk, slightly beaten
1 teaspoon grated lemon rind
1 package (7-1/2 ounces) farmer cheese,
    or 1 cup cottage cheese, sieved
Sliced or chopped almonds

Pour scalded milk over ⅓ cup sugar, the salt and ¼ cup butter in large bowl; cook to lukewarm. Soften yeast in ¼ cup warm water and stir into first mixture. Add 2 eggs, ½ teaspoon vanilla and the nutmeg. Beat well; then beat in 3 cups flour. Add more flour to make a soft dough. Cover and let rise until double in bulk about 1 hour. Meanwhile, soften 1 cup butter slightly at room temperature. Roll dough to form a square about ¼" thick. Dot with half the butter, leaving a 2" border. Fold over and dot with remaining butter; seal edges. Roll and fold 3 times, or until butter is thoroughly rolled into dough. Then roll dough to a little less than ½" thickness. Cut in 3" squares. Mix ½ teaspoon vanilla, egg yolk, lemon rind and cheese. Put a teaspoonful in center of each square; fold 2 opposite corners over and press to seal. Put on greased baking sheets. Brush with 1 egg beaten with 2 tablespoons sugar and sprinkle with almonds. Let rise until light. Bake in very hot oven (450°F.) about 10 minutes. (Watch closely.) Makes 2 dozen Danish pastries.

NUT PASTRIES

1 cup soft butter or margarine
3 cups all-purpose flour
1 package active dry yeast
3 egg yolks
1 cup dairy sour cream
1 teaspoon vanilla extract
Nut Filling
Confectioners' sugar

Cut butter into flour. Soften yeast in 2 tablespoons warm water. Add to flour mixture with remaining ingredients, except filling and sugar. Mix thoroughly and chill a few hours. Roll dough to 1/8″ thickness on floured board. Cut in 3″ squares. Put 1 teaspoon filling in center of each square. Moisten edges of pastry with water and pinch corners up and together. Bake on ungreased cookie sheets in moderate oven (375°F.) about 15 minutes. Cool and sprinkle with sugar. Makes about 4 dozen. **Nut Filling** Force 4 cups walnuts through food chopper, using medium blade. Add 1 cup sugar, 3 tablespoons vanilla and 1/2 cup milk; mix well.

FILLED BUTTERHORNS

2 cups all-purpose flour
1-1/2 teaspoons granulated sugar
1/2 teaspoon salt
1/2 cup butter or margarine
1 package active dry yeast
1/4 cup dairy sour cream, heated and
  cooled
2 egg yolks
Confectioners' sugar
Filling

Mix first 3 ingredients. Cut in butter. Sprinkle yeast on 2 tablespoons lukewarm water. Let stand a few minutes; then stir until dissolved. Blend sour cream and egg yolks. Add yeast and mix well. Stir into flour mixture and blend well. Cover and refrigerate at least 3 hours, but not more than 24. Remove from refrigerator and let stand at room temperature until soft enough to handle. Divide dough in 4 balls. Roll one section at a time on board sprinkled with confectioners' sugar; roll from center to edge to form an 8″ circle. Cover each circle not quite to edges with one fourth of the Filling. Cut each in 8 wedges. Roll up from rounded edge to point. Put on baking sheet. Bake in moderate oven (375°F.) 15 to 20 minutes. Cool and store airtight. Makes 32. **Filling** Beat 2 egg whites until stiff peaks are formed. Gradually add 1/2 cup sugar and 1/2 teaspoon vanilla, beating until glossy. Fold in 1/2 cup finely chopped nuts.

SOUTH AMERICAN COCONUT PASTRIES

2 cups all-purpose flour
1/2 teaspoon baking powder
1/2 teaspoon salt
1/2 cup butter
5 tablespoons orange juice
1 egg white
Coconut Filling

Sift dry ingredients into bowl; cut in butter. Mix in orange juice, a little at a time, until ball of dough is formed. (Dough will be rather dry.) Press together lightly. Wrap in waxed paper and chill 1 hour. Roll the dough 1/8″ thick on a lightly floured board. Cut with a 3 1/2″ cookie cutter. Put 1 teaspoon Coconut Filling on half of each round. Moisten edges and fold over. Seal edges with a fork. Arrange on greased baking sheet and brush with slightly beaten egg white. Bake in hot oven (425°F.) 10 minutes, or until delicately browned. Makes 1 1/2 to 2 dozen. **Coconut Filling** Mix 1 1/2 cups flaked coconut, 1 tablespoon cornstarch, 1/3 cup sugar and 3/4 cup undiluted evaporated milk. Cook over low heat, stirring 5 minutes. Add 2 beaten egg yolks and 3 tablespoons melted butter, stirring. Stir over low heat 2 minutes. Cool.

HUNGARIAN CHEESE PASTRIES

1/2 cup plus 1 tablespoon soft butter or
  margarine
1-2/3 cups all-purpose flour
1/8 teaspoon salt
1 egg yolk, beaten
Heavy cream (about 1-1/2 tablespoons)
Filling
Confectioners' sugar
Black-currant or other jelly

To make pastry: Cut butter into flour and salt. Add egg yolk, mixing with fork. Add just enough cream to hold mixture together. Chill overnight. Roll about one third of dough to form an 8″ square a little more than 1/8″ thick. Put in 8″ x 8″ x 2″ pan. Roll more dough to form strips about 1″ wide. Fit around sides of pan. Pour in Filling and level top. Roll out remaining dough and cut in 3/4″ strips. Put on Filling, lattice-fashion. Bake in moderate oven (350°F.) about 40 minutes. Cool on rack. Just before serving, sift confectioners' sugar over top. Cut in 2″ squares and garnish each with jelly. Makes 16. **Filling** Press 1 pound dry cottage cheese through fine sieve. Add 1/4 cup sugar, grated rind of 1/2 lemon, 2 egg yolks and 2 tablespoons melted butter. Beat 4 egg whites stiff with 1/4 teaspoon salt. Fold into mixture.

NAPOLEONS

Prepare Puff Paste, page 420, and roll 1/8" thick. Cut in 6 strips 3" wide and 14" long. Put on cookie sheets, covered with 2 layers of brown paper, and prick with fork. Cover with another cookie sheet to keep flat. Bake in very hot oven (450°F.) 5 minutes. Reduce heat to moderate (350°F.) and bake 15 minutes longer. Remove top cookie sheet; bake 15 minutes longer, or until pastry is dry and brown. When cold, trim off edges. Make 2 piles of 3 strips each, putting well-chilled Vanilla Cream Filling, page 436, between the layers. Chill and cut each crosswise in 3 pieces about 4" x 2". Spread a thin confectioners'-sugar frosting on top; draw lines of chocolate frosting across top, using writing tip with pastry bag or toothpick. Chill.

PINEAPPLE FRITTERS

1 cup all-purpose sifted flour
2 tablespoons sugar
1 teaspoon baking powder
1/4 teaspoon salt
1 egg, beaten
1/3 cup milk
1 cup drained crushed pineapple
Fat for deep frying

Sift dry ingredients into bowl. Add next three ingredients and mix well. Drop by tablespoonfuls into hot deep fat (370°F. on a frying thermometer) and fry until golden brown and done. Serve as dessert with cinnamon and sugar, or with thin custard or orange sauce. Or serve with syrup for breakfast with ham or bacon. Makes 12.

BANBURY TARTS DE LUXE

1/4 cup each currants, seedless raisins
  and chopped candied pineapple
1/2 cup chopped dates
1/3 cup chopped nuts
1 cup packed light-brown sugar
2 eggs, slightly beaten
2 tablespoons flour
1/4 teaspoon salt
Grated rind and juice of 1 lemon
Flaky French Pastry (page 34)
1 egg yolk
1 tablespoon milk

Mix well all ingredients, except last 3. Roll pastry to 1/8" thickness and cut in twenty-four 4" squares. Put about 1 tablespoon of the mixture in the center of each square and fold the corners to meet in center. Brush with egg yolk beaten with milk; bake in very hot oven (450°F.) 12 to 15 minutes. Makes 2 dozen.

BLUEBERRY TURNOVERS

In saucepan mix 1/4 cup sugar, 1/8 teaspoon salt and 1/3 cup flour. Add 2 tablespoons orange juice and 1 can (14 ounces) blueberries with syrup. Cook, stirring, until very thick; cool. Prepare Tart Pastry, page 419. Roll and cut in twelve 4½" rounds. Put 2 tablespoons blueberry mixture on half of each round, moisten edges and fold over. Seal edges with a fork. Fry in small amount of fat until golden brown on both sides.

CHRISTMAS CRULLERS

4 egg yolks
Confectioners' sugar
3 tablespoons soft butter or margarine
1 tablespoon brandy
2 teaspoons grated lemon rind
1/4 teaspoon salt
1-1/4 cups all-purpose flour
Fat for deep frying

Beat egg yolks until thick and lemon-colored. Beat in 1/2 cup sifted confectioners' sugar and the butter. Blend well and add remaining ingredients, except fat. Work dough quickly on floured board until smooth. Chill thoroughly. Roll out on floured board to 1/8" thickness. Cut in strips 3" x 1". Cut a 1" slit in center of each strip and slip one end through slit. Fry in hot deep fat (375°F. on a frying thermometer) until light brown on both sides. Drain on absorbent paper. Sprinkle with confectioners' sugar; store airtight. Makes about 50.

DUTCH DOUGHNUTS

Sprinkle them with confectioners' sugar.

1-1/2 packages active dry yeast
3 cups all-purpose flour
2 eggs
1-1/4 cups lukewarm milk
2 tablespoons sugar
1 teaspoon salt
2 tablespoons raisins
1 tablespoon chopped candied orange
  peel
1-1/2 teaspoons grated lemon rind
Fat for deep frying

Soften the yeast in 3 tablespoons lukewarm water in a deep bowl. Put flour in another bowl. With a wooden spoon, stir in eggs, one by one. Slowly add milk. Stir until smooth. Add next 5 ingredients and yeast. Mix well. Cover and let rise in warm place until doubled in bulk, about 1½ hours. Drop from tablespoon in hot, deep fat (370°F. on frying thermometer); fry until brown. Makes 18.

Turnip Relish

range-Cucumber Relish

Pepper Relish

Beet Relish

Sweet Cucumber Relish

Zucchini Pickles

HARRY HARTMAN

Lady Ross Relish

Lemon Relish

Chili Relish

Yellow-tomato Preserves

SHOPPING FOR PICKLES & PRESERVES INGREDIENTS

Every market offers a selection of
excellent commercial pickles, preserves,
jams, jellies and relishes.
But when you're in the mood for
something different, something more
distinctive, consider one of the recipes
in this chapter.

For preserving, select firm fruit and
vegetables, free from blemishes and
spots. If ripe fruit is called for, be sure
it is thoroughly ripe but not overripe
or jellies won't set. Wash all foods just
before you use them.

For pickling, use a good clear standard
vinegar, free from sediment, one with
4 to 6 percent acidity; strength of vinegar
is usually shown on the bottle label.
If vinegar or brine is too weak, the pickles
will spoil or become soft. Distilled
white vinegar is best for preserving
the color and crispness of foods.

Use a pure granulated salt for pickling.
Granulated salt containing less than
1 percent chemicals is satisfactory.

Use soft water if possible.
Large amounts of calcium and other salts
found in many hard waters may
interfere with the fermentation and
pickling processes. High iron content in
water may cause food to darken.
If hard water must be used, boil,
skim off scum and let water stand

24 hours. Ladle water off the top, leaving
the sediment in the bottom.

White corn syrup or honey can replace
half the sugar called for. Use 1 cup
for each cup of sugar replaced.
Stir frequently during cooking.

Pickling Equipment

Select jars or glasses without nicks or
cracks. Wash jars and lids thoroughly.
Sterilize jars for pickles by boiling in
water to cover 15 minutes; treat lids and
rubbers, if used, according to manufacturer's directions. Let stand in water
until needed. Jars and glasses used
for jellies, jams and spreads need not be
sterilized, just brought to a boil.
Use a wooden spoon and a large shallow
kettle for cooking. Fill jars with hot
pickles and preserves to within ¼" of
top. Always follow the manufacturer's
directions for sealing the jars. Use
crockery, glass, earthenware or stainless
steel for brining, but not aluminum or
any chipped enamelware. If cucumbers,
peppers and onions are to stand
overnight in salt solution, put in
refrigerator to prevent fermenting.

STORAGE

When cold, label jars with name and
date and store in cool, dark, dry place.
Jellies and jams may need a little time
to set, and most develop best flavor
after standing a few weeks.

FRESH KOSHER-STYLE DILL PICKLES

3 cups white vinegar
6 tablespoons pure granulated salt
Fresh or dried dill
Garlic
Mustard seed
30 to 36 pickling cucumbers, 3″ to 4″ long

Combine vinegar, 3 cups water and salt in saucepan and bring to boil. Put a generous layer of dill, 1/2 to 1 clove garlic, sliced, and 1 1/2 teaspoons mustard seed in bottom of each quart jar. Wash cucumbers and pack into jars. When half filled, add another layer of dill and complete filling of jars. Fill to within 1/2″ of top with boiling brine. Put caps on jars, firmly screwing bands tight. Process 15 minutes (pickles will shrivel some in processing but will plump later on standing).

SWEET PICKLE STICKS

Firm medium pickling cucumbers
3-3/4 cups white vinegar
3 cups sugar
3 tablespoons pure granulated salt
4-1/2 teaspoons celery seed
4-1/2 teaspoons turmeric
3/4 teaspoon mustard seed

Wash cucumbers and cut in sticks. Cover with boiling water and let stand 4 to 5 hours. Then drain and pack solidly into 6 pint jars. Mix remaining ingredients in saucepan; bring to boil and boil 5 minutes. Pour over cucumbers, filling to within 1/2″ of top. Put on caps and firmly screw bands tight. Process 5 minutes.

SEVEN-DAY ONION PICKLES

1 gallon tiny white onions
4-1/2 cups pure granulated salt
1 teaspoon powdered alum
  (buy in drugstore)
1 quart white vinegar
2 teaspoons mixed pickling spice
2-1/4 cups sugar

Scald onions and peel. Put in crock with 3/4 cup salt and water to cover and let stand overnight. Next day, drain thoroughly; add 3/4 cup salt and boiling water to cover; let stand overnight. Repeat on third, fourth, fifth and sixth days. On seventh day, drain onions and wash thoroughly in cold water. Return to crock and add alum. Cover with boiling water and let stand until cold. Drain and pack in 7 hot sterilized pint jars. Bring vinegar, spice and sugar to boil, stirring to dissolve sugar. Pour over onions to within 1/2″ of top. Seal and process 5 minutes.

MUSTARD PICKLES

1 large cauliflower, broken in florets
1 quart cubed cucumbers
1 quart small white onions, peeled
2 sweet red peppers, sliced
1 cup pure granulated salt
1/4 cup dry mustard
1/2 cup packed brown sugar
1 quart cider vinegar
1/2 teaspoon celery seed
2 teaspoons mustard seed
1 teaspoon each whole cloves, allspice
1/4 cup all-purpose flour
1 teaspoon ground turmeric

Arrange vegetables in layers in large bowl, sprinkling each layer with salt. Let stand overnight; drain. Mix mustard and brown sugar in large kettle. Add 1 cup water, the vinegar and seed. Add spices tied in cheesecloth bag. Bring to boil, add vegetables and simmer until tender. Mix flour and turmeric to a paste with a little cold water. Stir into pickles and cook 5 minutes longer. Remove spice bag and pack pickles in 4 or 5 hot sterilized pint jars. Seal and process 5 minutes.

BEST-EVER PICKLED ONION RINGS

Large sweet onions
2 cups white vinegar
1 cup sugar
1 teaspoon each mustard seed, celery
  seed and ground turmeric
1/4 teaspoon powdered alum (buy in
  drugstore)

Peel and slice 1/8″ thick enough onions to fill a wide-mouthed quart jar. Bring remaining ingredients to boil and pour over onions. Cool, then cover and refrigerate. Let stand several days before serving. Will keep several months.

CANDIED DILL PICKLES

1 quart processed dill pickles
1/2 cup tarragon vinegar
2-3/4 cups sugar
2 tablespoons mixed pickling spice
1 can (4 ounces) pimientos, diced

Drain pickles and cut in 1/4″ slices. (Use a crinkle cutter if available.) Mix pickle slices, vinegar and sugar. Add spice tied in cheesecloth bag. Let stand at room temperature, stirring occasionally, until sugar is dissolved, about 4 hours. Return half the pickles to the quart jar; add spice bag. Add pimiento and remaining pickles. Fill jar with the syrup. Cover and refrigerate at least 4 days before serving. Remove spice bag after 1 week, if desired. Makes 1 quart.

CRYSTAL PICKLES

Let them stand a few days before serving.

Mix 3 cups thinly sliced, drained sour pickles (24 ounces) and 2 cups sugar, stirring until sugar is partially dissolved. Let stand a few days, stirring a few times. Makes 3 cups. *Note* Process dill pickles can be used, if sour pickles are unavailable.

GREEN-TOMATO PICKLE

4 quarts thinly sliced green tomatoes
1 quart thinly sliced onions
1/3 cup cooking salt
3 cups vinegar
1 teaspoon whole allspice
1 tablespoon whole black peppercorns
1 teaspoon celery seed
1 tablespoon mustard seed
1 tablespoon dry mustard
1/8 teaspoon cayenne
1 lemon, thinly sliced
3 cups packed brown sugar

Put tomatoes and onions in large bowl. Sprinkle with salt, cover and let stand overnight. Drain. Heat remaining ingredients to boiling. Add tomatoes and onions. Bring to boil and simmer about 10 minutes, stirring gently several times. Pour into hot sterilized jars and seal. Makes about 5 pints.

PICKLED PEACHES

With roast beef or turkey these are reputation-makers for club or family dinners.

6-3/4 cups sugar
1 pint white vinegar
5 sticks cinnamon
2 tablespoons whole cloves
6 pounds peaches (24 to 26 medium)

Combine sugar, vinegar and 1 cup water in kettle, stirring down crystals from sides of pan. Add cinnamon and cloves tied in cheesecloth. Bring to boil; boil 5 minutes. Meanwhile, cover peaches with boiling water; let stand 1 minute; cool quickly under running water. Peel and put in pan of slightly salted water to prevent browning, or dissolve ascorbic acid tablets in water according to package directions. Do not let stand more than 20 minutes. Add peaches 8 to 10 at a time to syrup; simmer 10 minutes, or until tender. Lift out into 5 hot sterilized pint jars, filling 1/2" from top. Put lids on to keep peaches hot. When all jars are filled, open spice bag and put 1 cinnamon stick in each jar. Bring syrup to boil and pour over peaches, filling jars to top. Seal jars at once.

DILLED CARROTS AND GREEN BEANS

Serve as an hors d'oeuvre or relish.

1 pound carrots
2 cans (1 pound each) green beans, vertical pack, drained
2 cloves garlic, split
1-1/2 cups wine vinegar
4 tablespoons salt
2 tablespoons crushed hot red pepper
1/2 cup snipped fresh dill or 2 tablespoons dillweed

Peel carrots, cut in strips and cook until limp; drain. Pack beans and carrots into 4 hot sterilized 1-pint jars, dividing garlic cloves among them. Bring last 4 ingredients to boil with 1½ cups water, pour over vegetables and seal.

GALA SPICED FRUIT

Fruit is studded with whole cloves in syrup of cinnamon and brandy.

1 can each (1 pound each) peach halves, pear halves and apricot halves
2 teaspoons whole cloves
1 stick cinnamon
2/3 cup packed brown sugar
1/3 cup vinegar
2 tablespoons brandy
1/2 cup maraschino cherries with stems, drained

Drain syrup from peaches, pears and apricots into saucepan. Add 1 teaspoon cloves and the cinnamon. Stud fruit with remaining cloves. Bring syrup to boil and boil rapidly until reduced to 1½ cups. Add sugar and vinegar and simmer 5 minutes. Stir in brandy. Add studded fruit and cherries, bring to boil and spoon into hot sterilized jars. Seal. Makes 4 half-pints.

ZUCCHINI PICKLES

Build an antipasto plate around these with tuna, olives, chick-peas, artichokes and hard-cooked eggs.

2 pounds small zucchini
2 medium onions
1/4 cup salt
1 pint white vinegar
1 cup sugar
1 teaspoon celery seed
1 teaspoon turmeric
1/2 teaspoon dry mustard
1 teaspoon mustard seed

Wash and cut unpeeled zucchini and peeled onions in very thin slices into crock or bowl. Cover with water and add salt. Let stand 1 hour; drain. Mix remaining ingredients and bring up to boil. Pour over zucchini and onion. Let stand 1 hour. Bring to boil and cook 3 minutes. Pack in 3 hot sterilized pint jars and seal.

FESTIVAL RELISH

2 unpeeled oranges, quartered and
　seeded
2 unpeeled apples, quartered and cored
1 pound cranberries
2 cups sugar

Force oranges and apples through coarse blade of food chopper, reserving extra juice for other uses. Grind cranberries and add with sugar to other fruits. Mix well and let stand several hours to ripen. Store covered in refrigerator. Good with roast turkey, chicken, duck, pork or fried liver. Makes about 4 cups.

CORN RELISH

2 green peppers
2 sweet red peppers
1 cucumber
1/2 pound white onions
3 large tomatoes
1 teaspoon turmeric
1 quart white vinegar
2 cups fresh whole-kernel corn
4 stalks celery, diced
2 tablespoons salt
2 cups sugar
1/4 cup whole light mustard seed

Cut open peppers and remove seeds and fiber. Cut peppers in small dice. Peel cucumber, onions and tomatoes; cut in small dice. In kettle, blend turmeric with a little vinegar. Add remaining vinegar and all other ingredients. Bring to a boil and simmer, uncovered, 50 or 60 minutes, or until fairly thick. Pour into hot sterilized jars and seal. Makes about 2 quarts.

PICNIC RELISH

Also good with pork roll, bologna or baked beans.

3 pounds medium green tomatoes (about
　10)
4 medium red apples
3 sweet red peppers
4 onions, peeled
4-1/2 teaspoons salt
1-1/2 teaspoons pepper
1-1/2 teaspoons cinnamon
3/4 teaspoon ground cloves
2-1/2 cups sugar
1 pint white vinegar

Wash tomatoes and remove stem ends. Core apples; do not peel. Remove cores and seeds from peppers. Force apples and all vegetables through the coarse blade of food chopper. Combine remaining ingredients and bring to boil in kettle. Add vegetables and simmer, uncovered, 30 minutes, or until thick, stirring occasionally. Pack into 4 or 5 hot sterilized pint jars and seal.

CABBAGE-BEET RELISH

Mix 2 cups chopped pickled beets, 3 cups chopped green cabbage, 1 chopped onion, 2 teaspoons salt and 1 tablespoon celery seed. Store, covered, in refrigerator several days before serving. Makes about 5 cups.

APRICOT-HORSERADISH RELISH

To serve with sliced cold meats.
1/3 cup cider vinegar
1/2 cup sugar
2/3 cup bottled horseradish, undrained
6 whole cloves
1 cup seedless raisins
1 cup chopped dried apricots
1/3 cup sliced, blanched almonds

Combine vinegar, 1 cup water, sugar, horseradish and cloves. Boil 5 minutes. Add fruits and nuts; simmer 15 minutes more. Cover and refrigerate. Makes about 2 cups.

TOMATO-FRUIT RELISH

30 large ripe tomatoes (about 12 pounds)
6 medium peaches
6 medium pears
2 large onions
3 cups sugar
1-1/2 cups chopped celery
3 tablespoons salt
1 quart white vinegar
2 tablespoons mixed pickling spice

Peel first 4 ingredients and chop fine. Add next 4 ingredients, and pickling spice tied in a piece of cheesecloth. Boil, uncovered, 1 to 1½ hours. Remove spice bag. Pour into hot sterilized jars and seal. Makes about 5 pints.

CRANBERRY-FILBERT RELISH

1 can (20 ounces) crushed pineapple
2 cups sugar
1 pound (4 cups) cranberries
2 oranges
1/2 cup seedless raisins
1/2 cup chopped candied ginger
1/2 cup toasted chopped filberts

Drain pineapple. Measure syrup and add enough water to make 2 cups. Add sugar to liquid and bring to boil, stirring until sugar is dissolved. Add cranberries and cook 5 minutes. Grate rind of 1 orange. Remove segments from both oranges. Add rind, segments, raisins, pineapple and ginger to cranberry mixture. Simmer, stirring frequently, 25 minutes, or until thick. Add nuts, pour into hot sterilized jars and seal. Makes about 6 half-pints.

PEPPER RELISH

6 red peppers
6 green peppers
6 onions, peeled
2 cups white vinegar
1-1/2 cups sugar
2 tablespoons salt
1 tablespoon mustard seed
1 tablespoon celery seed

Split peppers and remove seeds. Chop peppers and onions coarsely, cover with boiling water and let stand 5 minutes; drain. Cover again with boiling water and let stand 10 minutes; drain. Combine remaining ingredients and boil 5 minutes. Add vegetables and boil 10 minutes. Pack into hot sterilized jars; seal. Makes 4 pints.

SWEET CUCUMBER RELISH

Especially good with frankfurters.

8 large, ripe cucumbers
1/4 cup salt
4 sweet red peppers, seeded and cored
4 large onions, quartered
4-1/2 teaspoons each celery seed and mustard seed
2-1/2 cups sugar
1-1/2 cups white vinegar

Peel and slice cucumbers into crock or glass bowl. Add salt and mix well. Let stand overnight in refrigerator. Drain and force through coarse blade of food chopper with peppers and onions. Put in kettle; add remaining ingredients. Bring to boil and cook, uncovered, stirring occasionally, about 30 minutes. Pack into 3 hot sterilized pint jars and seal.

LADY ROSS RELISH

4 cups chopped peeled cucumber (2 large)
4 cups chopped onion
1 large cauliflower, chopped
1-1/2 green peppers, chopped
1-1/2 sweet red peppers, chopped
1/4 cup salt
4 cups packed brown sugar
3 cups white vinegar
2 tablespoons mustard seed
1/4 cup dry mustard
1-1/2 teaspoons turmeric
1/4 cup flour

Mix first 6 ingredients and let stand overnight. Drain thoroughly. Bring next 5 ingredients to boil in kettle. Blend flour with about 1/4 cup water to make a smooth paste. Stir into boiling mixture. Add vegetables, bring again to boil and simmer 10 minutes. Pour into hot sterilized jars and seal. Makes about 5 pints.

INCREASING RECIPES

Follow recipes as given. Batches of chili sauce, relish and pickles can be doubled if the cooking time is increased, but jams or jellies using bottled or powdered pectin should not be changed in any way or they may not set. If more is desired, make another batch.

CHILI RELISH

2 quarts chopped peeled tomatoes
1 cup chopped green onion
1/2 cup each coarsely ground sweet red and green pepper
1 teaspoon crushed dried red pepper
1 cup sugar
1-1/2 teaspoons salt
1-1/2 teaspoons white mustard seed
1/2 teaspoon cinnamon
1-1/4 cups white vinegar

Combine all ingredients in large kettle, bring to boil and simmer, stirring frequently, 3 to 4 hours, or until thick. Pour into hot sterilized jars and seal. Makes about 4 half-pints.

BEET RELISH

1 quart finely chopped cabbage
1 quart cooked beets, in strips
1 cup chopped onion
2 cups sugar
1 tablespoon black pepper
1 teaspoon salt
1/4 teaspoon cayenne
1 cup grated fresh horseradish
White vinegar

Mix all ingredients, except vinegar. Add enough cold vinegar to cover mixture. Store, covered, in refrigerator (the flavor improves on standing). Makes 4 pints.

ORANGE-CUCUMBER RELISH

1-2/3 cups chopped sweet red pepper
1-2/3 cups chopped green pepper
4 cups chopped peeled cucumber
1/4 cup salt
3 oranges
2 cups white vinegar
2 cups packed brown sugar
1/2 teaspoon mustard seed
1/2 teaspoon celery seed

Mix peppers, cucumber, salt and 1/2 cup water and let stand overnight. In morning, drain and discard liquid. Squeeze most of juice from oranges and reserve for other use. Force pulp and rind through coarse blade of food chopper. Combine all ingredients and bring to boil. Simmer about 10 minutes. Pour into hot sterilized jars and seal. Makes 3 to 4 pints.

APPLE CHUTNEY

To serve with curried meat or poultry.

2 cans (1 pound 4 ounces each) apple slices
2 cups seedless raisins, chopped
1 cup minced onion
1-1/2 pounds packed brown sugar
2 cups cider vinegar
2 tablespoons salt
1 box (2-3/4 ounces) mustard seed
1/4 cup chopped preserved ginger
1/8 teaspoon cayenne
2 cloves garlic, minced

Combine all ingredients and cook slowly for 1 hour. Pack quickly in hot sterilized jars to within 1/8" of top. Seal at once. Makes 3 pints.

PEACH CHUTNEY

A spicy condiment of fruit seasoned with garlic, ginger and vinegar.

3-1/2 cups sugar
2 cups white vinegar
1 quart chopped peeled firm peaches
1-1/2 cups raisins or dried currants
1 clove garlic, minced
4 pieces whole dried ginger or 3 pieces preserved ginger, chopped

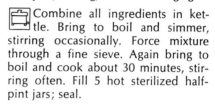Heat sugar and vinegar to boiling in large kettle. Add peaches, raisins and garlic. Add whole ginger, tied in cheesecloth bag, or add chopped ginger. Bring to boil and cook slowly, uncovered, 2 hours, or until thick, stirring occasionally. Remove whole ginger. Ladle into 4 hot sterilized half-pint jars and seal.

CHILI SAUCE

Delicious on eggs or meat.

4 quarts chopped peeled ripe tomatoes (about 6-1/2 pounds)
2 cups chopped onion
2 cups chopped sweet red pepper
1 hot pepper, chopped
1 teaspoon ground ginger
1 teaspoon ground nutmeg
2 tablespoons celery seed
1 tablespoon mustard seed
1 bay leaf
1 teaspoon whole cloves
2 tablespoons crushed cinnamon stick
1 cup packed brown sugar
3 cups white vinegar
2 tablespoons salt

Put vegetables and ground spices in large kettle. Add seeds and whole spices tied in cheesecloth bag; bring to boil and cook, uncovered, until reduced one-half, stirring frequently. Add sugar, vinegar and salt and simmer 5 minutes, stirring. Remove spice bag and fill 6 hot sterilized pint jars; seal.

HOT CONDIMENT SAUCE

A thick, spicy steak sauce.

2 quarts chopped ripe tomatoes (4 to 5 pounds)
2 carrots, chopped
3 onions, chopped
4 sweet red peppers
1 quart white vinegar
1 teaspoon pepper
3/4 cup packed brown sugar
2 tablespoons salt
1/2 teaspoon cayenne
2 teaspoons each ground cloves, allspice, nutmeg, cinnamon and ginger

Combine all ingredients in kettle. Bring to boil and simmer, stirring occasionally. Force mixture through a fine sieve. Again bring to boil and cook about 30 minutes, stirring often. Fill 5 hot sterilized half-pint jars; seal.

LEMON RELISH

6 thin-skinned lemons
1 teaspoon ground sage
1-1/2 cups sugar

Trim yellow peel from 2 lemons. Cut in fine strips and cover with boiling water; drain and reserve. Cut peel and white membrane from all lemons and cut lemons in thin slices. Remove seeds and put slices in bowl. Mix sage and sugar in small saucepan. Add 1 cup water, bring to boil and boil 4 minutes, or until thick. Add lemon strips and pour over lemon slices, cover and chill. Serve with roast pork or other meats. Makes about 2²/₃ cups.

TURNIP RELISH

15 medium white turnips (about 3 pounds)
3 sweet red peppers
6 green peppers
3 large onions
1/2 cup salt
1 pint white vinegar
3 cups sugar
1 tablespoon white mustard seed
1 tablespoon celery seed
1/2 teaspoon crushed dried red pepper

Peel turnips and cut in pieces. Remove seed and white membrane from red and green peppers and cut peppers in pieces. Peel and cut up onions. Force all through coarse blade of food chopper. Sprinkle with salt and let stand 2 hours. Drain and squeeze dry. Mix remaining ingredients in kettle and bring to boil. Add vegetables, bring to boil and simmer, uncovered, about 1 hour. Pour into hot sterilized jars and seal. Makes 4 half-pints.

GOLDEN NUT CONSERVE

1 package (11 ounces) dried apricots
1 can (20 ounces) crushed pineapple
2/3 cup seedless raisins
1/2 cup finely chopped nuts
2 tablespoons lemon juice
4 cups sugar
1/2 bottle liquid fruit pectin

Soak apricots in water to cover at least 4 hours; drain. Chop apricots and mix with remaining ingredients, except pectin, in large kettle. Bring to boil, stirring, over high heat. When bubbling rapidly over entire surface, boil hard, stirring constantly, 1 minute. Remove from heat and stir in pectin. Ladle quickly into hot sterilized jars; seal. Makes 7 half-pints.

HONEYDEW CONSERVE

One of the prettiest conserves, a clear light green.

2 limes, sliced
3 cups sugar
3 cups diced peeled honeydew melon

Remove seeds from limes. Put limes and 1 cup water in electric blender and run until lime is finely cut. (Or force lime through fine blade of food chopper and add 1 cup water.) Pour mixture into kettle and cook, covered, 10 minutes. Add sugar and honeydew. Bring to boil and simmer, uncovered, 30 minutes, or until thick, stirring frequently. Ladle into 5 hot sterilized 6-ounce glasses. Cover with melted paraffin.

PLUM CONSERVE

Tossing orange rind with sugar to draw out flavor makes this unusually good.

3 pounds (about 1-3/4 quarts) blue plums or fresh prunes
3 medium oranges
1-1/2 cups seeded raisins, chopped
1-1/4 cups seedless raisins
6 cups sugar
1/2 cup chopped nuts

Remove pits from plums. Peel oranges, reserving rinds, and dice pulp. Combine raisins, plums and orange pulp. Add 5½ cups sugar and mix well. Let stand overnight in refrigerator. Cook orange rind in boiling water until tender. Cut off and discard white inner lining. Dice remaining rind and sprinkle with ½ cup sugar. Let stand overnight in refrigerator. Combine both mixtures in kettle, bring to boil and cook, stirring frequently, 30 minutes, or until thickened. Add nuts 5 minutes before removing from heat. Turn into 7 hot sterilized 6-ounce glasses. Cover with melted paraffin.

PIQUANT PINEAPPLE AND BEETS

1/2 cup crushed pineapple
2 tablespoons vinegar
2 tablespoons sugar
2 tablespoons cornstarch
1 can (1 pound) sliced or diced beets, drained
2 tablespoons butter or margarine
Salt and pepper

Bring pineapple and vinegar to boil. Mix sugar and cornstarch and stir into mixture. Cook, stirring, until thickened. Add beets and butter; heat well and season to taste. Serve hot as a relish. Makes 4 servings.

TOMATO BUTTER

So good with crackers for an afternoon snack!

5 pounds tomatoes
1 teaspoon salt
3-1/2 cups packed light-brown sugar
1/2 teaspoon ground allspice
1-1/2 teaspoons each ground cloves and cinnamon

Wash, core and peel tomatoes and cut in small pieces. Put in kettle with salt and cook 15 minutes. Remove from heat and measure. Return 2 quarts to kettle with remaining ingredients and simmer slowly, stirring occasionally, 1 hour, or until very thick. Pour into hot sterilized jars and seal. Makes about 6 half-pint jars.

GREEN-TOMATO MINCEMEAT

7 pounds green tomatoes
4-1/2 cups sugar
1 tablespoon each cinnamon and ground cloves
1/2 teaspoon nutmeg
1/2 cup vinegar
1/2 teaspoon salt
1/2 cup ground beef suet
1 package seedless raisins
Grated rind and juice of 1/2 orange
1-1/2 tablespoons lemon juice

Wash and trim tomatoes. Chop fine or force through coarse blade of food chopper. Drain off liquid and cover tomatoes with cold water. Drain again and cover with boiling water. Drain well and put in kettle with remaining ingredients. Bring to boil and simmer, uncovered, stirring occasionally, 20 to 25 minutes, or until thick. Pour into hot sterilized jars and seal. Makes about 5 pints, or enough for 3 or 4 pies.
For Pie Put 3 cups mincemeat in pastry-lined 9" piepan. Dot with 1 to 2 tablespoons butter. Adjust top crust and bake in hot oven (425°F.) about 30 minutes.

GREEN-TOMATO PRESERVES

A Pennsylvania Dutch "sour."

Cover 11 cups chopped green tomatoes (about 5 pounds) with hot water and boil 5 minutes. Drain and add 8 cups sugar. Let stand 3 hours or longer. Drain syrup into a kettle; bring to boil and cook rapidly until it spins a thread. Add tomatoes and 2 thinly sliced lemons; cook 10 minutes until thick and clear. Pack in 4 hot sterilized pint jars and seal.

YELLOW-TOMATO PRESERVES

5 pounds yellow pear tomatoes
1 lemon, sliced very thin
1 teaspoon ginger
5 pounds (11-1/4 cups) sugar
1/4 teaspoon salt

Pour boiling water over tomatoes. Let stand 3 minutes, drain, rinse in cold water and drain again. Discard lemon seeds and cut slices in halves. Add ginger, sugar and salt and let stand overnight. Drain and cook syrup until very thick. Add tomatoes and simmer until thick. Pour into hot sterilized jars and seal. Makes about 4 half-pint jars.

OVEN PEAR PRESERVES

2 pounds winter pears
1 lemon
4 cups sugar
2 tablespoons chopped candied ginger

Peel, core and quarter pears. Force through food chopper, using medium blade. Using fine blade, force lemon through food chopper. Add to pears with sugar and ginger. Cover and let stand overnight, then bring to boil. Put in moderate oven (375°F.) 10 minutes. Reduce heat to 300°F. and cook 1 hour, or until thick and amber-colored. Pour into hot sterilized jars and seal. Makes about 5 half-pint jars.

SPICED FRUIT SALAD

A delicious relish spiced with zesty cinnamon.

1 can (29 ounces) fruit cocktail
1 cup packed light-brown sugar
1/3 cup white vinegar
2 cinnamon sticks (2″ each)

Drain fruit cocktail. Combine cocktail syrup with brown sugar, vinegar and cinnamon and simmer 10 minutes. Pour over fruit cocktail. Pour into hot sterilized jars and seal. Chill. Makes 2 pints.

SPICED ORANGE WEDGES

Oranges simmer in clove- and cinnamon-flavored syrup.

6 medium oranges
2-1/2 cups sugar
3/4 cup vinegar
1 teaspoon whole cloves
3 sticks cinnamon

Cover oranges with water. Bring to boil and boil 20 minutes, or until quite tender. Drain and cut into eighths. Combine remaining ingredients with 2 cups water, stirring until mixture boils. Add orange pieces and simmer about 20 minutes. Pack into 3 hot sterilized pint jars and seal.

GINGERED PEARS

You use both ground and crystallized ginger.

2 cans (1 pound 13 ounces each) pear halves
1 cup packed light-brown sugar
1-1/2 cups granulated sugar
Grated rind and juice of 2 lemons
3 teaspoons ground ginger
1/2 cup diced candied ginger
1/2 teaspoon ground cinnamon
1 bottle (4 ounces) maraschino cherries, drained

Combine 1 cup pear syrup with sugars, lemon rind and juice. Add spices. Boil gently 5 minutes. Add drained pears and cherries and cook until pears are heated through, about 10 minutes. Pack in sterilized jars; seal. Makes 3 pints.

CRYSTAL TOMATOES

Delicious with pot roast on a cold November night.

2-1/2 pounds green or underripe tomatoes
4-1/2 teaspoons slaked lime powder (buy in drugstore)
1-3/4 cups sugar
2 sticks cinnamon
1/2 teaspoon nutmeg
2 pieces whole dried ginger
1/2 teaspoon salt
2 cups white vinegar

Cut tomatoes in 1/4″ slices and put in bowl. Add lime dissolved in 1 quart water. Stir. Let stand overnight in refrigerator. Next day, drain and rinse tomatoes in several changes of cold water; drain. In kettle, mix sugar, spices tied in cheesecloth bag, salt, vinegar and 1/2 cup water. Bring to boil and boil 5 minutes. Add tomatoes and cook, uncovered, 20 minutes, or until syrup is thick and tomatoes clear. Pack in 5 hot sterilized half-pint jars and seal.

LIME MARMALADE

Paper-thin lime slices plus lime pulp in this pretty marmalade.

5 limes
1/4 teaspoon baking soda
1 box powdered fruit pectin
4 cups sugar

To prepare fruit, slice 1 lime paper-thin. Add 3 cups water and soda. Bring to boil and simmer, covered, 20 minutes. Peel and discard rind from 4 limes. Chop pulp very fine and add to undrained cooked sliced lime. Simmer, covered, 10 minutes longer. Measure 3 cups into large saucepan. Add pectin and mix well. Cook over high heat until mixture comes to a hard boil. Cook gently 1 minute. At once stir in sugar. Bring to a full rolling boil and boil 1 minute, stirring. Remove from heat and skim off foam with metal spoon. Then stir and skim 7 minutes to cool slightly to prevent fruit from floating. Ladle quickly into hot sterilized glasses. Cover at once with hot paraffin. Makes about 6 medium glasses.

GRAPEFRUIT-SAVORY JELLY

Dried herbs are used in this recipe, which has three variations.

Canned grapefruit juice
2 tablespoons dried savory
3 cups sugar
1/3 cup lemon juice
Red and yellow food colorings
1/2 bottle liquid fruit pectin

Bring 1 cup grapefruit juice to boil and pour over savory. Cover and let stand 20 minutes. Strain through several thicknesses of cheesecloth. Add enough more grapefruit juice to make 1 cup liquid. Put liquid, sugar and lemon juice in saucepan and mix well. Bring to boil, stirring. Add a few drops of each coloring. Add pectin and mix well. Bring to a full rolling boil, stirring. Boil hard 1/2 minute, stirring. Remove from heat and skim off foam with metal spoon. Pour jelly quickly into glasses and cover at once with hot paraffin. Makes 4 small glasses.

Orange-Marjoram Jelly Use above recipe, substituting orange juice for the grapefruit juice and marjoram for the savory.
Grape-Thyme Jelly Use recipe for Grapefruit-Savory Jelly, substituting grape juice for the grapefruit juice and thyme for the savory.
Cider-Sage Jelly Use recipe for Grapefruit-Savory Jelly, substituting cider for the grapefruit juice and sage for savory.

NEW ENGLAND CRANBERRY-ORANGE JELLY

It has honey in it.

Pick over, wash and drain 1 quart cranberries. Put in saucepan with 2 cups boiling water and grated rind of 1 orange. Bring to boil and simmer, covered, 20 minutes. Force through fine sieve. Bring to rapid boil; stir in 1 cup sugar and 3/4 cup honey. Boil 3 minutes. Pour into 3 or 4 hot sterilized glasses. Cover with paraffin.

LOUISIANA HOT-PEPPER JELLY

This goes well with meat.

In large saucepan mix 1 cup water, 2 teaspoons hot pepper sauce (or more if a very hot jelly is desired), 1/3 cup lemon juice and 3 cups sugar. Bring to boil, stirring. Add 1/2 bottle fruit pectin and a small amount of red coloring, stirring well, until mixture comes to a full rolling boil. Boil hard 1/2 minute. Remove from heat; skim. Pour into 4 hot sterilized 5-ounce glasses and cover with paraffin.

HOLIDAY JELLY

Made with cranberry juice and cider.

2 cups sweet cider
2 cups bottled cranberry juice
4 cups sugar
1/2 bottle fruit pectin

Combine cider, juice and sugar in a large saucepan and mix well. Put over high heat and bring to a boil, stirring constantly. At once stir in pectin. Then bring to a full rolling boil and boil hard 1 minute, stirring constantly. Remove from heat, skim off foam and pour quickly into glasses. Cover at once with hot paraffin. Makes six 8-ounce glasses.

APPLE-JUICE JELLY

The color of your jelly will depend on the soft-drink mix you choose.

7 cups sugar
2 cups bottled apple juice
1 envelope instant soft-drink mix
  (any fruit flavor)
1 bottle fruit pectin

Mix first 3 ingredients with 2 cups water in very large saucepan. Put over high heat and bring to a boil, stirring. At once stir in pectin. Then bring to a full rolling boil and boil hard 1 minute, stirring. Remove from heat, skim off foam with metal spoon and pour jelly quickly into hot sterilized glasses. Cover with hot paraffin. Makes 11 glasses.

AMBROSIA MARMALADE

4 oranges
2 lemons
1 lime
Sugar
2 cups toasted flaked coconut

Cut ends off fruit. Quarter fruit and cut in thin crosswise slices. Put in large heavy saucepan with 2 quarts water. Bring to boil and simmer, uncovered, 40 minutes, or until peel is tender. Measure and add an equal amount of sugar. Put half the mixture in second large heavy saucepan (this shortens cooking time). Bring to boil and boil gently over medium heat about 30 minutes. Combine in one saucepan and add coconut. Pour at once into hot sterilized jars and seal with paraffin. (Mixture will be thin but thickens when cold.) Makes about 8 cups.

PEACH-ORANGE MARMALADE

18 medium peaches
6 oranges
10 cups sugar

Scald, peel and dice peaches. Squeeze the juice from oranges and grind skins, using medium blade. Combine ingredients, cover and let stand overnight. Cook over low heat, stirring until sugar is dissolved. Bring to boil and cook over moderate heat 1 hour, stirring frequently to prevent scorching, until clear and thickened. Pour into hot sterilized jars and seal at once. Makes about 3½ quarts.

SPICED TOMATO MARMALADE

2 lemons
1 orange
1 can (35 ounces) Italian-style tomatoes
6-3/4 cups sugar
1/4 teaspoon salt
Three 1" pieces dried gingerroot
  or 1/2 teaspoon ground ginger
1/2 teaspoon ground allspice

Peel lemons and orange, discarding all white part that clings to peels. Cut peels in thin strips; cover with water, bring to boil and simmer 10 minutes; drain. Section citrus fruit, discarding seeds and membrane. Put fruit in 3-quart saucepan. Add peel, tomatoes, sugar, salt and ginger. Mix well, bring to boil and cook rapidly, uncovered, stirring occasionally, 40 minutes, or until thick. Add allspice and cook 5 minutes longer. Pour into hot sterilized half-pint jars and seal. Makes 6 jars.

CRANBERRY-CLARET JELLY

3-1/2 cups sugar
1 cup bottled cranberry juice
1 cup claret wine
1/2 bottle fruit pectin

Put sugar in top part of double boiler. Add cranberry juice and wine; mix well. Put over rapidly boiling water and stir until sugar is dissolved, about 2 minutes. Remove from heat and stir in fruit pectin. Skim off foam and pour quickly into glasses. Cover at once with ⅛" paraffin. Makes 6 medium glasses.

BEET-RASPBERRY JELLY

3 cups beet liquid (see Note)
2 envelopes (0.15 ounces each)
  unsweetened raspberry soft-drink
  mix (4 teaspoons)
4 teaspoons lemon juice
1 package (1-3/4 ounces) powdered
  pectin
4 cups sugar

Combine first 3 ingredients in heavy kettle. Stir in pectin. Turn heat on high and quickly bring to hard boil, stirring occasionally. Add sugar all at once, bring to full rolling boil and boil hard, stirring, 1 minute. Remove from heat and skim off foam, using a metal spoon. Pour at once into hot sterilized jars to within ½" from top. Cover with ⅛" melted paraffin. When cool, cover with loose-fitting lids. Makes 5 medium glasses. **Note** To obtain beet liquid, wash, scrub, slice and quarter fresh beets. Cover with water and cook until tender. Drain off liquid. Remove skins and use beets as desired. Or use liquid drained from canned unseasoned beets.

PARADISE JAM

4 cups coarsely chopped very ripe pears
1 can (8-1/2 ounces) crushed pineapple
  (undrained)
10 maraschino cherries, chopped
1 orange, peeled and chopped
1 tablespoon aniseed
6 cups sugar
1/2 bottle liquid pectin

Put pears in large saucepan and cook 3 minutes. Add the pineapple with liquid, the cherries, orange and aniseed and bring to boil. Stir in sugar, bring to boil and boil hard 1 minute. Remove from heat and stir in pectin. Stir and skim 5 minutes to cool slightly; this prevents fruit from floating. Ladle into hot sterilized jars and seal. Makes about 8 half-pint jars.

JUNE JAM

Fresh rhubarb and pineapple are combined with strawberries.

3 cups shredded fresh pineapple
2 cups cut fresh rhubarb
4 cups hulled washed strawberries
Dash of salt
4-1/2 cups sugar

Put pineapple in large preserving kettle and cook without added liquid 10 minutes. Add rhubarb, berries and salt; cook 20 minutes. Add sugar, bring to boil and boil rapidly, stirring frequently, 25 to 30 minutes, or until thick. Skim off foam and pour into hot sterilized jars. Seal with hot paraffin, cover with lids and store in a cool place. Makes about 6 half-pint jars.

SPICED PEACH-AND-BLUEBERRY JAM

This makes a blue-ribbon addition to your jam cupboard.

4 pounds peaches
1 quart blueberries, washed
5-1/2 cups sugar
1/2 teaspoon salt
2 sticks cinnamon
1 teaspoon whole cloves
1/2 teaspoon whole allspice

Peel and pit peaches. Force through coarse blade of food chopper. Combine berries, peaches and 1/2 cup water in kettle; bring to boil. Cover and simmer 10 minutes, stirring occasionally. Add sugar and salt, and spices tied in a cheesecloth bag. Bring to boil slowly, stirring until sugar dissolves. Boil rapidly 10 minutes, or until fruit is clear. Remove spice bag. Ladle into 8 hot sterilized 6-ounce glasses. Cover with melted paraffin.

BLENDER CITRUS MARMALADE

A fine marmalade because the rinds are puréed.

4 large oranges
2 lemons
1/8 teaspoon soda
5 cups sugar
1/2 bottle fruit pectin

Peel oranges and lemons. Whirl 1/3 of peel at a time with 1/2 cup of water each time in blender 10 seconds. Add soda to peel, bring to boil and simmer 20 minutes. Squeeze juice from oranges and lemons. Add to rind and cook 10 minutes longer. Add sugar. Bring to boil and boil 1 minute. Remove from heat; stir in pectin. Cool 10 minutes. Put in hot sterilized glasses and cover with hot paraffin. Makes 6 or 7 glasses.

JAM AND JELLY TIPS

When making jelly with added pectin, a stiffer product can be obtained by using 1/4 cup less juice. For softer jelly, use 1/4 cup more juice.

Paraffining jams and jellies is not necessary if they are to be stored no longer than 2 months. Just cover glasses with tight lids and store in refrigerator.

CHRISTMAS JAM

Ingredients are available all year.

1 package (11 ounces) dried apricots
1 can (30 ounces) pineapple chunks
1 jar (8 ounces) maraschino cherries
6 cups sugar

In large saucepan, combine apricots, pineapple and syrup, cherry syrup and 3 1/2 cups water. Let stand 1 hour. Cook slowly until apricots are tender. Add sugar and cook slowly, stirring often, until thick and clear (216°F. on candy-jelly thermometer). Add cherries, cut in quarters, and cook a few minutes longer (220°F.). Pour into hot sterilized jars and cover with melted paraffin. Makes 6 half-pint jars.

PIMIENTO JAM

3 cans (7 ounces each) pimientos drained
2-1/4 cups sugar
1-1/2 cups white vinegar
3 tablespoons grated lemon rind
1/8 teaspoon hot pepper sauce

Mince pimientos fine. Cook with remaining ingredients, stirring until sugar is dissolved. Simmer, stirring occasionally, until of jam consistency, about 20 minutes. Pour into hot sterilized jelly glasses. Cover with paraffin. Makes 3 glasses.

PEAR HONEY

A sunny-colored dress-up for toast and rolls.

3 pounds firm ripe pears (6 to 8 large)
1 cup undrained canned crushed pineapple
5 cups sugar
Red and yellow food coloring

Peel, core and slice pears; force through fine blade of food chopper. Combine with pineapple and sugar in kettle. Bring to boil and simmer, uncovered, 20 minutes, or until thick, stirring frequently. Stir in a few drops each red and yellow coloring. Ladle into 6 hot sterilized 6-ounce glasses. Cover with melted paraffin.

Pineapple-Strawberry Delight

Luscious Mocha Cake

Graham-cracker Brownie Bars
Vanilla-Currant Cookies

Crab-Vegetable Mélange

Curried-peach Chicken

MIDORI

CALORIE CHART
EDIBLE PORTION, 3½ OUNCES

Food	Calories
Almonds, roasted salted	627
Apples, raw unpared	58
Apple butter	186
Apple juice, bottled	47
Applesauce, canned sweetened	91
Apricots, canned, solids and light syrup	66
Apricots, dried sulfured, uncooked	260
Asparagus, cooked spears	20
Avocados	167
Bacon, Canadian, cooked	277
Bacon, cooked, drained	611
Bananas, raw	85
Beans, baby lima, cooked	111
Beans, dry red, cooked	118
Beans, dry white, cooked	118
Beans, green, cooked	25
Beans, wax, cooked	22
Beef:	
chuck, pot-roasted	327
club steak, broiled	454
flank steak, braised	196
lean beef, ground, cooked	219
porterhouse steak, broiled	465
rib, roasted	440
round, broiled	261
round-bone sirloin steak, broiled	387
rump, roasted	347
T-bone steak, broiled	473
Beets, cooked	32
Beet greens, cooked	18
Blueberries, raw	62
Bluefish, baked	159
Bran flakes with raisins	287
Brazil nuts	654
Breads:	
French or Vienna	290
Italian	276
raisin	262
rye, American	243
white	269
whole-wheat	243
Broccoli, cooked spears	26
Brussels sprouts, cooked	36
Butter	716
Buttermilk	36
Cabbage, raw	24
Cabbage, cooked	20
Carrots, raw	42
Carrots, cooked	31
Cashew nuts	561
Cauliflower, raw	27
Cauliflower, cooked	22
Celery, raw	17
Cheeses:	
American, pasteurized process	370
natural blue, or Roquefort type	368
Cheddar, domestic	398
cottage, creamed	106
cottage, uncreamed	86
cream	374
Parmesan	393
Swiss, domestic	370
Swiss, pasteurized process	355
Cherries, raw red sour	58
Cherries, raw sweet	70
Cherries, canned:	
sweet, solids and light syrup	65
Chicken:	
dark meat, roasted, without skin	176
fryer, fried	250
light meat, roasted, without skin	166
stewing chicken, stewed	369
Chili con carne, canned, with beans	133
Chocolate syrup, thin	245
Clams, raw soft, solids and liquid	54
Clams, canned, solids and liquid	52
Corn, sweet:	
kernels cooked on cob	91
cream-style, canned	82
whole-kernel, canned, drained	84
Cornflakes	386
Crab, canned	101
Crackers:	
graham, plain	384
saltines	433
Cranberry-juice cocktail	65
Cranberry sauce:	
canned, strained	146
homemade, unstrained	178
Cream:	
half-and-half (cream and milk)	134
heavy	352
light	211
Cucumbers, raw, pared	14
Doughnuts, cake type	391
Eggplant, boiled	19
Eggs:	
fried	216
hard-cooked	163
omelet	173
poached	163
scrambled	173
Filberts	634
Flounder, baked	202
Fruit cocktail, canned, solids and light syrup	60
Grapefruit, pulp	41
Grape juice, bottled	66
Haddock, fried	165
Halibut, broiled	171
Honey, strained	304
Lamb:	
leg, roasted	319
loin chops, broiled	420
rib chops, broiled	492
shoulder, roasted	374
Lard	902
Liver:	
beef, fried	229
calf's, fried	261
chicken, simmered	165
Lobster, cooked	95
Macaroni, cooked tender	111
Mackerel, Atlantic, broiled with butter	236
Margarine	720
Marmalade, citrus	257
Melons:	
cantaloupe	30
honeydew	33
Milk, cow's:	
whole	65
skim	36
Noodles, cooked	125
Oatmeal, cooked	55
Ocean perch, fried	227
Okra, boiled	29
Olives, black	129
Olives, green	116
Onions, boiled	29
Oranges, raw peeled	49
Oysters, raw Eastern	66
Oysters, fried	239
Oyster stew:	
frozen diluted with milk	84
Parsnips, boiled	66
Peaches, raw	38
Peaches, canned, solids and light syrup	58
Peanut butter	581
Peanuts, roasted salted	585
Pears, raw	61
Pears, canned, solids and light syrup	61
Peas, boiled	71
Peppers, green sweet	22
Pineapple, raw	52
Pineapple, canned, solids and light syrup	59
Plums, raw hybrid	48
Plums, canned purple, solids and light syrup	63
Pork, fresh:	
loin, roasted	362
loin chops, fried	357
spareribs, braised	440
Pork, smoked:	
ham, light cure, baked	289
Potato chips	568
Potatoes:	
baked	93
boiled	76
French-fried	274
mashed with milk and fat added	94
Pretzels	390
Prune juice, bottled	77
Prunes, tenderized, cooked fruit and liquid, unsweetened	119
Raisins	289
Raspberries, red	57
Rhubarb, cooked, sweetened	141
Rice, cooked brown	119
Rice, cooked white	109
Rutabagas, cooked	35
Salad dressing, mayonnaise type	435
Salmon, broiled fresh	182
Salmon, canned red sockeye, solids, liquids	171
Sardines in oil, drained solids	203
Sauerkraut, canned solids and liquids	18
Sausage:	
bologna	277
deviled ham, canned	351
frankfurters, cooked	304
luncheon meat	294
pork sausage, bulk or links, cooked	476
salami, dry	450
salami, cooked	311
Scallops, steamed	112
Shrimps, French-fried	225
Spaghetti, cooked tender	111
Spinach, cooked	23
Squash:	
acorn, baked	55
butternut, mashed	41
summer, cooked	14
winter, mashed	38
zucchini, cooked	12
Strawberries	37
Sugar, brown	373
Sugar, granulated	385
Sweet potatoes:	
baked	141
boiled	114
candied	168
Swordfish, broiled	174
Tomatoes, raw	22
Tongue, beef, braised	244
Tuna in oil, drained	197
Turkey, roasted	263
Turnips, cooked	23
Veal:	
shoulder, braised	235
loin, broiled	234
rib, roasted	269
Walnuts, English	651
Whitefish, baked stuffed	215

LOW-CALORIE COOKING

With weight-watching almost a national pastime, the chances are that you and/or some member of your family has become (or should become) conscious of calories. It may be that someone needs to lose weight, or merely doesn't want to gain any. In either case, it's up to you as the meal planner to see that a certain restraint is exercised. Actually, in a society where food is so plentiful and physical exercise so relatively minimal, it makes sense in general to concentrate your daily eating on lower-calorie foods.

To do this, obviously you must know which foods they are—and they may not always be the ones you think. Everyone knows that a hot fudge sundae with whipped cream and pecans is likely to put on pounds, but not everyone is aware that a serving of one vegetable may contain several hundred calories while another may contain practically none. So the first thing to do is to know your onions (40 calories) from your mushrooms (15 calories) and your pizza (150 calories) from your pike (80).

With relative caloric counts in mind, you can set about planning meals that are appetizing, attractive and satisfying and still allow the dieter to lose or maintain weight. Don't imagine your family is alone—the odds are that half your friends are engaged in the same mathematics, so even at cocktail parties it's thoughtful to offer at least one appetizer that doesn't add to the waistline.

BROILED COD PIQUANT

4 cod fillets fresh or thawed (1-1/2 pounds)
1/3 cup low-calorie Italian-style dressing
Paprika
4 lemon slices
4 anchovy fillets
1 tablespoon capers
Parsley sprigs

Marinate fish fillets in the dressing 1 hour, turning once. Sprinkle both sides with paprika. Broil 3 minutes on each side. Garnish with lemon slices topped with anchovy fillets rolled around capers and with parsley. Makes 4 servings.

About 134 calories, 2 grams carbohydrate, 27 grams protein and 2 grams fat, per serving.

DOS FOR WATCHING WEIGHT

DO eat a good breakfast to prevent late-morning fatigue and overeating later in the day.

DO eat slowly to gain a satisfied feeling before leaving the table. Eat salad first to take an edge off appetite.

DO keep slivers of low-calorie fresh vegetables on hand for nibbling between meals.

DO use salt lightly in cooking and none at the table.

DO select thin-sliced bread; try low-calorie gluten and protein breads. Low-calorie mayonnaise makes a good spread.

DO choose fresh fruit for dessert. If sweetening is needed, add a little vanilla extract; you will need less or no sugar. Try a sprinkle of salt on grapefruit.

DO cut excess fat off meat. Roast, broil or grill lean meats.

DO use nonstick pans or skillets for browning, if possible.

DO eat four or five small meals a day rather than three large ones. You won't feel so hungry.

DO choose skim milk, low-calorie margarine, low-calorie dressings for salad, cottage cheese without added cream, low-calorie dairy sour cream and low-calorie yogurt.

SCALLOP-PINEAPPLE KABOBS

1 pound fresh or thawed frozen scallops
2 tablespoons lemon juice
1 tablespoon vegetable oil
2 cups fresh pineapple chunks
1 green pepper, cut in chunks
1 cup cherry tomatoes
Salt, pepper and paprika

Marinate scallops 30 minutes in mixture of lemon juice and oil, then drain. Thread scallops alternately on 6 skewers with pineapple, green pepper and tomatoes. Broil about 8 minutes; do not turn. Sprinkle with seasonings. Makes 6 servings.

About 135 calories, 15 grams carbohydrate, 12 grams protein and 3 grams fat, per serving.

INDIVIDUAL SHRIMP-EGG CASSEROLES

1 tablespoon margarine
1-1/2 tablespoons all-purpose flour
1-1/2 cups skim milk
1 teaspoon Dijon-type prepared mustard
1 tablespoon minced green onion
1 tablespoon minced parsley
2 tablespoons minced green pepper
Dash of cayenne
1 teaspoon lemon juice
Salt and pepper to taste
1-1/4 cups peeled cooked shrimps
2 hard-cooked eggs, diced
2 tablespoons grated Parmesan cheese

Melt margarine in saucepan over low heat. Blend in flour and cook about 1 minute. Gradually add milk and cook, stirring, until smooth and slightly thickened. Add remaining ingredients, except last 3, and simmer 3 minutes. Carefully fold in shrimps and eggs. Pour about 1/2 cup in each of 5 small broiler-proof ramekins. Sprinkle with cheese and broil about 3" from heat 3 to 4 minutes. Makes 5 servings.

About 161 calories, 7 1/2 grams carbohydrate, 16 1/2 grams protein, and 7 1/2 grams fat, per serving.

Food Values for Crab Meat and Shrimp

Crab Meat 3 ounces canned, 85 calories, 1 gram carbohydrate, 15 grams protein, and 2 grams fat.

Shrimp 3 ounces canned, 100 calories, 1 gram carbohydrate, 21 grams protein, 1 gram fat.

WATER-BROILED FISH FILLETS WITH EGG SAUCE

1-1/2 pounds fresh fillet of haddock, cod or scrod
Lemon juice, salt, pepper and paprika
1 teaspoon margarine
2 hard-cooked eggs, chopped
2 tablespoons minced green onion
2 tablespoons minced green pepper
1 tablespoon minced parsley

Rinse fish quickly under running cold water and drain on paper towels. Cut in 4 or 5 portions and arrange, skin side down, in 11" x 7" broiler-proof baking pan. Fold tail parts double so all portions are of same thickness. Pour boiling water over fish to half its thickness. Sprinkle with lemon juice, salt, pepper and paprika. Broil about 3" from heat 12 minutes, or until fish is opaque and flakes easily with fork. Remove fish from broth. Heat 1/3 cup broth and remaining ingredients and serve on fish. Makes 6 servings.

About 127 calories, 1 gram carbohydrate, 23 grams protein and 3 grams fat, per serving.

SEAFOOD COCKTAIL SAUCE

Mix 1/2 cup tomato juice, 1 teaspoon horseradish, 1/2 teaspoon each Worcestershire, vinegar, salt and lemon juice, and a little chopped parsley; chill. About 21 calories, 4 grams carbohydrate, 1 gram protein, no fat, for 1/2 cup.

MUSTARD-GLAZED MEAT LOAF WITH MUSHROOMS AND SHREDDED CARROTS

2 pounds ground round
Salt and freshly ground pepper
Catsup
1 medium onion, minced
2 egg whites, slightly beaten
1 tablespoon prepared mustard
3 cups coarsely shredded carrot
8 medium fresh mushrooms

Mix beef with 1 1/2 teaspoons salt, 1/2 teaspoon pepper, 1/4 cup ice water, 1/3 cup catsup, the onion and egg whites. Beat well. In a shallow 2-quart baking dish, shape mixture in a loaf about 10" x 4". Bake in moderate oven (375°F.) 30 minutes. Spread top with a mixture of the mustard and 1 tablespoon catsup. Put carrot around the loaf and arrange mushrooms on top. Sprinkle lightly with salt and pepper. Bake 30 minutes longer. Serves 8.

About 245 calories, 8 grams carbohydrate, 24 grams protein and 13 grams fat, per serving.

MUSHROOM, GROUND-BEEF AND GREEN-BEAN CASSEROLE

1 cup chopped onion
1 tablespoon vegetable oil
1/2 pound fresh mushrooms, sliced
1 pound ground round
1 teaspoon salt
1/4 teaspoon ground black pepper
1 teaspoon basil leaves, crumbled
1 cup beef broth
2 tablespoons tomato paste
1 can (1 pound) cut green beans, drained
4 servings (2 cups) seasoned instant mashed potatoes
1 tablespoon grated Parmesan cheese

In large nonstick coated skillet, sauté onion in hot oil until transparent. Add mushrooms, beef and seasonings. Cook, stirring frequently, until meat is browned. Add broth and tomato paste. Simmer a few minutes, then add beans. Pour into shallow 2-quart broiler-proof baking dish. Spread mashed potatoes on top and sprinkle with cheese. Broil until lightly browned. Makes 6 servings.

About 275 calories, 18 grams carbohydrate, 26 grams protein and 12 grams fat, per serving.

OVEN-CRUSTED CHICKEN

1 chicken (about 2-1/2 pounds), quartered
1/4 cup evaporated skim milk
Salt and pepper
1/2 cup cornflake crumbs
3/4 teaspoon crushed rosemary leaves

Dip chicken pieces in milk and sprinkle both sides with salt and pepper. Dip in cornflake crumbs mixed with rosemary, coating both sides. Arrange chicken pieces on rack in shallow baking pan. Add water to pan to depth of $1/4''$. Bake in moderate oven (350°F.) 1 hour, or until tender. Makes 4 servings.

About 290 calories, $7\frac{1}{2}$ grams carbohydrate, $21\frac{1}{2}$ grams protein and 4 grams fat, per serving.

CURRIED PINEAPLE CHICKEN

1 tablespoon margarine
2 teaspoons curry powder
2 tablespoons all-purpose flour
1-1/2 cups chicken broth
2 cups cooked diced chicken meat
  (skin removed)
1 cup canned unsweetened pineapple
  chunks
Chopped parsley

Melt margarine over low heat in saucepan. Sprinkle with curry powder and flour. Simmer, stirring, a few minutes. Gradually add chicken broth, stirring until thickened. Simmer a few minutes. Add chicken and pineapple and heat. Sprinkle with parsley. Serves 4.

About 147 calories, 10 grams carbohydrate, $14\frac{1}{2}$ grams protein and 5 grams fat, per serving.

VEAL BIRDS

4 slices (3/4 pound) veal scallops, 1/4"
  thick
Salt and white pepper
Grated rind of 1 lemon
4 cooked medium carrots
1 can (10-1/2 ounces) condensed chicken
  broth
1-1/2 tablespoons tomato paste
Minced parsley

Season veal slices lightly with salt and pepper. Sprinkle with lemon rind. Place a cooked carrot on top of each. Roll up and fasten with toothpick. Combine chicken broth with tomato paste in small skillet. Bring to boil and simmer a few minutes. Add veal rolls, cover and simmer 15 to 20 minutes, or until meat is tender. Remove toothpicks. Sprinkle with parsley. Serves 4.

About 214 calories, $6\frac{1}{2}$ grams carbohydrate, 25 grams protein and $10\frac{1}{2}$ grams fat, per serving.

ROAST STUFFED CORNISH HENS

2 Cornish hens
Choice of stuffings

Wipe birds inside and out with wet paper towel. Fill cavity of hens with preferred stuffing and tie ends of legs together. Put on rack and roast in hot oven (425°F.) $1\frac{1}{4}$ hours, or until tender. If first stuffing is used, baste occasionally with mixture indicated in recipe. If second stuffing is used, sprinkle with salt or butter-flavor salt before roasting. Makes 2 servings.

Been-sprout Stuffing

1 can (1 pound) bean sprouts, drained
1/4 cup chopped water chestnuts
1 cup chopped celery
2 tablespoons soy sauce
2 tablespoons lemon juice
1 tablespoon margarine, melted

Mix first 3 ingredients with 1 tablespoon each soy sauce and lemon juice. Use as stuffing. Mix remaining soy sauce, lemon juice and the margarine and use as baste.

About 221 calories, 16 grams carbohydrate, 25 grams protein and 9 grams fat, per serving.

Carrot-Celery Stuffing

1/3 cup chopped onion
1 tablespoon margarine
1 cup chopped celery
1-1/2 cups shredded carrot
3 tablespoons chopped parsley
1 tablespoon instant chicken bouillon

Sauté onion in margarine. Add other ingredients and cook gently 5 minutes.

About 232 calories, $12\frac{1}{2}$ grams carbohydrate, $22\frac{1}{2}$ grams protein and 9 grams fat, per serving.

CHICKEN WITH ZUCCHINI

1 broiler-fryer (about 2-1/2 pounds),
  cut up
Salt and pepper
1/2 teaspoon paprika
1 medium onion, sliced
3 medium tomatoes, peeled and diced
1 pound zucchini, sliced
1/2 teaspoon dried oregano

Sprinkle chicken with a mixture of 1 teaspoon salt, $1/8$ teaspoon pepper and the paprika. Broil 15 minutes, turning once. Remove chicken to 3-quart casserole. Add remaining ingredients. Cover and bake in moderate oven (350°F.) 50 to 60 minutes, or until chicken is tender. Makes 4 servings.

About 275 calories, 13 grams carbohydrate, 31 grams protein and 10 grams fat, per serving.

CURRIED PEACH CHICKEN

1 broiler-fryer (about 2-1/2 pounds),
  cut up
1 medium onion, quartered
1 teaspoon salt
5 whole black peppercorns
2 bay leaves
Parsley
2 tablespoons flour
2 teaspoons curry powder
1/4 cup lemon juice
Salt and pepper
1 can (1 pound) low-calorie sliced
  peaches, drained

Cover chicken with water; add next
4 ingredients and 2 sprigs parsley.
Bring to boil and simmer 30 minutes.
Remove chicken from broth and keep
warm. Boil broth to reduce it to
1½ cups. Cool; remove excess fat.
Remove skin from chicken and arrange chicken on a hot platter. In
saucepan, mix flour, curry powder
and broth. Bring to boil, stirring.
Simmer 5 minutes and add lemon
juice; season with salt and pepper
and pour over chicken. Garnish with
peaches and parsley. Serves 4.

About 295 calories, 16 grams carbohydrate, 31 grams protein and 10
grams fat, per serving.

SKILLET VEAL CHOPS WITH GREEN BEANS

6 loin veal chops
1 teaspoon sugar
Salt and pepper
1/2 teaspoon oregano
2 medium onions, sliced
1 can (4 ounces) sliced mushrooms,
  undrained
1 cup chicken broth
1 jar (4 ounces) pimientos, chopped
1 package (10 ounces) frozen green beans

Sprinkle chops with sugar and brown
on both sides in hot skillet. Season
with salt, pepper and oregano. Add
next 3 ingredients. Cover; simmer 20
minutes. Add pimientos and beans.
Simmer 10 minutes. Serves 6.

About 219 calories, 9 grams carbohydrate, 21 grams protein and 11 grams
fat, per serving.

POTATOES FOR CALORIE-COUNTERS

Sprinkle boiled potatoes with one of
the following: chopped parsley,
chives, paprika, sage, thyme, marjoram, rosemary or basil.
  In baked potatoes, use 1 tablespoon of low-calorie dairy sour cream
or ¼ cup low-calorie yogurt (only
30 calories each).

CRAB-VEGETABLE MELANGE

1 cauliflower (about 1-1/2 pounds)
Salt
1 package (10 ounces) frozen Brussels
  sprouts
1 tablespoon butter or margarine
2 tablespoons flour
1 cup skim milk
1 package (7 ounces) frozen Alaska
  king crab meat
Pepper and paprika

Break cauliflower in large flowerets.
Cook in lightly salted boiling water
10 minutes, or until tender but still
crisp. Cook sprouts as directed on
the package; drain and keep warm.
Melt butter and blend in flour. Gradually add milk and cook, stirring, until thickened. Simmer 4 to 5 minutes.
Add crab meat and season with salt,
pepper and paprika. Bring to boil.
Arrange vegetables on hot platter.
Pour sauce over top and sprinkle
lightly with paprika. Makes 6 servings.

About 94 calories, 9 grams carbohydrate, 10 grams protein and 2
grams fat, per serving.

GREEN BEANS AND STEWED TOMATOES

1 can (1 pound) cut green beans
1 can (10 ounces) stewed tomatoes
1 small onion, minced
2 tablespoons minced parsley
1/2 teaspoon salt
Dash of pepper
1 teaspoon steak sauce

Drain beans, add remaining ingredients and simmer 10 to 15 minutes.
Makes 6 servings.

About 28 calories, 6 grams carbohydrate, 1 gram protein and no fat,
per serving.

DEVILED BEETS

1 tablespoon margarine
1/4 teaspoon dry mustard
1/4 teaspoon ground cloves
2 tablespoons vinegar
1 tablespoon brown sugar
1/2 teaspoon salt
1/2 teaspoon paprika
1 teaspoon Worcestershire
3 cups diced cooked beets

Melt margarine, mix in seasonings
and beets and heat. Makes 6 servings.

About 65 calories, 11 grams carbohydrate, 1 gram protein and 2 grams
fat, per serving.

MEAT-VEGETABLE SOUP

1 pound ground round
2 cans (10-1/2 ounces each) condensed
  beef broth
1 package (10 ounces) frozen
  Brussels sprouts
1/4 cup finely chopped green pepper
1 leek, thinly sliced
8 medium fresh mushrooms, thinly sliced
1 tablespoon catsup
1/2 teaspoon each dried thyme and
  marjoram
Salt and pepper to taste
1/4 cup minced parsley

In heavy saucepan, cook meat, stirring, until well browned. Add 2⅓ cups water and remaining ingredients, except parsley. Bring to boil and simmer 10 to 15 minutes. Sprinkle with parsley. Serves 4.

About 196 calories, 10 grams carbohydrate, 21 grams protein and 8 grams fat, per serving.

CELERY WITH TOMATOES

1 small onion, chopped
1 small green pepper, chopped
1 teaspoon oil
1 cup canned tomatoes
Pinch of basil
3/4 teaspoon salt
1/2 teaspoon cracked pepper
12 small stalks celery, halved

Sauté onion and green pepper lightly in oil. Add remaining ingredients, bring to boil and cook, covered, 10 to 15 minutes, or until celery is tender. Makes 4 servings.

About 40 calories, 8 grams carbohydrate, 2 grams protein and no fat, per serving.

EGG-VEGETABLE PUFF

4 eggs, separated
1/2 teaspoon salt
1/4 cup skim milk
Pepper
1 teaspoon butter or margarine, softened
1-1/2 cups drained cooked well-seasoned
  spinach or zucchini

Beat egg whites with salt until very stiff. Beat yolks with milk and pepper to taste until foamy. Fold in whites until well blended. Preheat a 9″ to 10″ skillet with cover over low heat. Grease with butter. Spread vegetables over bottom of pan. Pour egg mixture over. Cover tightly and cook over low heat 8 minutes, or until puffy. Unmold on hot platter. Serves 4.

About 113 calories, 3 grams carbohydrate, 8½ grams protein and 7½ grams fat, per serving.

CHINESE STEAMED EGGPLANT

1 large or 2 small eggplants (about 1
  pound)
3 tablespoons cider vinegar
3 tablespoons light-brown sugar
2 teaspoons sesame or vegetable oil
1 tablespoon soy sauce
1/2 to 1 tablespoon minced gingerroot
1 teaspoon minced garlic (optional)

Remove stem and peel eggplant. Cut in 6 to 8 wedges. Spread in steaming tray with holes and set in wok. Add 3 cups water to wok and set on circle stand. Steam over medium-high heat 8 to 10 minutes, or until tender. Add remaining ingredients, mix well and serve. Also good cold. Serves 4. **Note** If wok is not available, put eggplant in colander and steam, covered, over a saucepan of boiling water.

About 87 calories, 16 grams carbohydrate, 1½ grams protein and 2 grams fat, per serving.

RATATOUILLE

1 can (1 pound) tomatoes, drained and
  juice reserved
1 clove garlic (optional)
2 cups diced yellow or green summer
  squash, or zucchini
1 green pepper, diced
Salt and pepper

Put tomato juice in skillet with garlic. Bring to boil, add squash and green pepper and simmer 5 minutes. Add tomatoes and heat. Season to taste with salt and pepper. Makes 4 servings. Serve hot or cold.

About 44 calories, 9½ grams carbohydrate, 2 grams protein and ½ gram fat, per serving.

SAUERKRAUT WITH VERMOUTH

1 can (27 ounces) sauerkraut, drained
  and rinsed
1 medium onion, chopped
1 tart apple, chopped
1 can (10-1/2 ounces) condensed chicken
  broth
1-1/3 cups dry vermouth or dry white
  wine
1 teaspoon caraway seed

Put first 3 ingredients in heavy kettle or Dutch oven. Add broth, 1 can water, wine and caraway seed. Bring to boil, cover and simmer 2 hours. Frankfurters or lean cooked spareribs can be added during last ½ hour of cooking. Makes 6 servings.

About 43 calories, 9 grams carbohydrate, 9 grams protein and 1 gram fat, per serving, without meat.

CHINESE ASPARAGUS SALAD

2 pounds fresh asparagus
3 tablespoons soy sauce
1/4 teaspoon monosodium glutamate
1 teaspoon sesame oil

Cut off tough white part of asparagus and trim off small lower leaves. Wash well and drain. Cut, rolling (cut diagonally, turning asparagus with left hand while cutting with right), in 1 1/2" lengths. Plunge asparagus into 6 cups boiling water in saucepan over high heat. When water comes again to boil, drain asparagus and plunge into cold water until thoroughly cold; drain well. When ready to serve, mix with next 2 ingredients and sprinkle with oil. Makes 4 servings.

About 50 1/2 calories, 7 1/2 grams carbohydrate, no protein and 1 gram fat, per serving.

GREEN-BEAN AND CARROT SALAD

Cook 1 pound whole fresh green beans in small amount boiling salted water until tender. Drain and chill. Peel 3 medium carrots and cut diagonally with waffle cutter. (Slice or cut julienne, if preferred.) Cook in small amount of boiling salted water until tender-crisp. Chill. Serve vegetables with Piquant Salad Dressing, page 466. If desired, garnish dressing with 1 radish, chopped. Makes 8 servings.

About 32 calories, 6 grams carbohydrate, 2 grams protein and no fat, per serving, without dressing.

EVAPORATED-SKIM-MILK DRESSING

1/2 cup undiluted evaporated skim milk
1/2 teaspoon dry mustard
1/2 teaspoon paprika
2 tablespoons lemon juice
1 teaspoon salt
1-1/2 teaspoons sugar
Dash of coarsely ground pepper
1/4 cup minced onion
1/4 cup minced parsley
1/4 cup skim-milk cottage cheese

Chill milk, bowl and beater, then whip milk until stiff. Mix next 3 ingredients; add to milk after it starts to thicken. Fold in remaining ingredients. Ideal for coleslaw, cold cooked broccoli and green beans. Makes about 1 1/2 cups.

About 30 calories, 4 grams carbohydrate, 3 grams protein and no fat, per 1/4 cup.

CELERY SALAD

1/2 bunch large celery ribs, slivered
1 carrot, slivered
1 tablespoon gingerroot, peeled and finely shredded (optional)
2 teaspoons salt
3 tablespoons soy sauce
1/4 teaspoon monosodium glutamate
1 teaspoon sesame oil

Soak first 3 ingredients with the salt in ice water to cover 1/2 hour, then drain. Cover and refrigerate until ready to serve. Just before serving, mix next 2 ingredients, then toss with vegetables. Spoon oil over top. Makes 4 servings.

About 30 calories, 7 1/2 grams carbohydrate, 1 gram protein and 1 gram fat, per serving.

TOMATO DRESSING

Combine 1 cup tomato juice, 1/4 cup each salad oil and vinegar, 1 teaspoon each salt and dry mustard, 1/4 teaspoon onion salt and 1 tablespoon steak sauce. Beat with rotary beater until well blended. Good on green salads. Makes 1 1/2 cups.

About 24 calories, 1/2 gram carbohydrate, trace of protein and 1/2 gram fat per tablespoon.

CHERRY-TOMATO AND ONION SALAD

Romaine
2 cups cherry tomatoes, sliced
1/4 cup minced red onion
2 tablespoons lemon juice
1 tablespoon dry vermouth
Freshly ground black pepper
1/4 teaspoon crumbled oregano leaves
1/4 teaspoon salt

On platter, make a layer of romaine torn in bite-size pieces. Arrange tomatoes in center and sprinkle with onion. Beat together remaining ingredients and pour on top. Chill and toss before serving. Makes 4 servings.

About 39 calories, 7 1/2 grams carbohydrate, 1 gram protein and no fat, per serving.

CUCUMBER SAUCE

Mix 1 container plain yogurt with 1 grated small cucumber. Stir in 1 tablespoon chopped fresh dill and salt to taste. Chill. Stir before serving. Makes 1 1/2 cups.

About 8 calories, 1 gram carbohydrate, 1 gram protein, no fat per tablespoon.

JELLIED CHIFFON FRUIT SALAD

1 can (20 ounces) unsweetened crushed
  pineapple, well drained, with juice
  reserved
1 package (3 ounces) low-calorie lemon-
  flavor gelatin
1/2 cup finely diced celery
1/3 cup low-calorie creamy dressing
1/2 cup instant nonfat dry milk powder
2 tablespoons lemon juice
Watercress or lettuce

Add enough water to pineapple juice
to make 1 cup. Bring to boil, simmer
2 minutes and pour over gelatin. Stir
until dissolved, then chill until consistency of unbeaten egg white. Combine pineapple, celery and dressing
and mix well. Add to gelatin. Chill
bowl and beater. Put milk in bowl
with 1/2 cup ice water and whip 3
minutes, or until soft peaks form.
Add lemon juice and beat 3 minutes,
or until stiff. Fold into gelatin mixture.
Spoon into 6-cup ring or other mold
and chill 3 hours or overnight. Unmold and fill center with watercress.
Or unmold on bed of lettuce. Makes
6 servings.

About 96 calories, 14 grams carbohydrate, no protein and no fat, per
serving.

FRENCH TOMATO DRESSING

1 package old-fashioned French-dressing
  mix
1-1/2 cups tomato juice
1/4 cup malt vinegar
1/4 cup salad oil

Empty all ingredients into a screw-top
quart jar. Cover, shake and chill.
Makes 2 cups.

About 22 calories, 1 gram carbohydrate, no protein and 2 grams fat, per
tablespoon.

BLUE-CHEESE SALAD DRESSING

2 ounces blue cheese, crumbled
1/4 cup dry white wine
1/4 cup buttermilk
1/2 cup skim-milk cottage cheese
1/4 teaspoon salt
Dash of cayenne
1/4 teaspoon powdered caraway seed
  (optional)

 Combine all ingredients until
smooth and creamy (blender can
be used). Makes 1 cup.

About 24 calories, 1/2 gram carbohydrate, 2 grams protein and 1 gram fat,
per tablespoon.

MIMOSA CHICKEN SALAD

2 cups diced cooked chicken (skin
  removed)
1 cucumber, peeled, cut in half lengthwise and seeds removed
1/2 green pepper, cut in fine strips
1/2 cup creamed cottage cheese
1/2 cup buttermilk
1 teaspoon prepared mustard
2 tablespoons minced green onion
3/4 teaspoon salt
Freshly ground pepper
Lettuce
1 hard-cooked egg, sieved

Combine first 3 ingredients. Whirl
cheese and buttermilk in blender
or beat until smooth. Add mustard
and next 3 ingredients and blend well.
Pour on top of chicken mixture and
mix carefully. Spoon into lettuce in
serving dish. Garnish with egg. Makes
4 servings.

About 140 calories, 7 1/2 grams carbohydrate, 13 1/2 grams protein and 4
grams fat, per serving.

PINEAPPLE-CABBAGE
SALAD RELISH

1 cup canned unsweetened crushed
  pineapple, undrained
Juice of 1 lemon
4 cups finely chopped cabbage
2 tablespoons minced parsley
Salt and pepper

Combine ingredients and chill. Makes
6 servings.

About 42 calories, 10 grams carbohydrate, 1 gram protein and no fat, per
serving.

FRUIT-SALAD DRESSING

1 teaspoon butter
1 egg yolk, beaten
1/2 cup orange juice
Juice of 1/2 lemon
1/2 teaspoon salt
1 tablespoon sugar
1 tablespoon prepared mustard
1/4 cup dry nonfat milk

Melt butter in top of small double
boiler; add next 6 ingredients. Cook,
stirring, until thickened; cool. Beat 1/4
tary beater or electric mixer until mix-
cup ice cold water and the milk with
rotary beater or electric mixer until
mixture stands in peaks. Fold into
first mixture. Makes about 1 1/2 cups
dressing.

About 12 calories, 2 grams carbohydrate, 1 gram protein and no fat, per
tablespoon.

YOGURT DRESSING

1 teaspoon dry mustard
1/2 teaspoon sweet paprika
Dash of dried horseradish
1 cup plain yogurt
2 teaspoons honey
1/4 cup lemon juice
Grated lemon rind to taste

Mix all ingredients thoroughly; chill. Makes 1¼ cups.

About 20 calories, 3 grams carbohydrate, 1 gram protein and .5 gram fat, per 2 tablespoons.

GREEN SALAD WITH MARINATED MUSHROOMS

1/4 pound mushrooms, thinly sliced
1 tablespoon salad oil
2 tablespoons lemon juice
1 tablespoon wine vinegar
4 cups mixed salad greens, torn in small pieces
Salt and pepper
1 small red onion, sliced in rings
Chopped parsley

Marinate mushrooms in mixture of next 3 ingredients in refrigerator ½ hour. Toss with greens and salt and pepper to taste. Garnish with onion rings and parsley. Makes 4 servings.

About 70 calories, 6 grams carbohydrate, 2 grams protein and 4 grams fat, per serving.

JELLIED TUNA SALAD

1 envelope unflavored gelatin
1/2 teaspoon dry mustard
1/2 teaspoon salt
1/2 teaspoon instant minced onion
2 tablespoons sugar
1 tablespoon lemon juice
1-1/4 cups buttermilk
Yellow food coloring (optional)
1/2 cup diced celery
1 can (3-1/4 ounces) tuna, drained and broken in small pieces
Salad greens
Cooked Salad Dressing, page 361

Soften gelatin in ¼ cup water. Dissolve over hot water. Blend in mustard, next 5 ingredients and a few drops coloring. Chill until thickened but not firm. Fold in celery and tuna. Pour into 4 individual molds and chill until firm. Unmold on salad greens. Serve with dressing. Makes 4 servings.

About 86 calories, 5 grams carbohydrate, 12 grams protein and 2 grams fat, per serving.

CALORIE-COUNTER'S COLESLAW

Mix 3 cups finely shredded cabbage (white or red), ½ cup chopped green pepper, ½ cup thinly sliced carrots, ½ cup grated or thinly sliced cucumbers, ½ cup minced parsley and a little vinegar. Season. Serves 6.

About 21 calories, 4 grams carbohydrate, 1 gram protein and no fat, per serving.

ORANGE-CUCUMBER SALAD

2 medium cucumbers, peeled and thinly sliced
1 teaspoon salt
1/8 teaspoon white pepper
2 medium oranges, peeled and sectioned
1/2 cup finely chopped green pepper
2 tablespoons chopped parsley
1 cup skim-milk cottage cheese
1/4 cup skim milk
1/2 teaspoon thyme
Salad greens

Sprinkle cucumbers with salt and pepper. Toss with next 3 ingredients. Beat cottage cheese, skim milk and thyme until smooth. Spoon over salad, or serve separately on crisp greens. Makes 6 servings.

About 70 calories, 9 grams carbohydrate, 8 grams protein and no fat, per serving.

DEVILED EGGS IN ASPIC

4 hard-cooked eggs
1 tablespoon low-calorie mayonnaise
Salt and pepper to taste
Dash of paprika
1/2 teaspoon curry powder
2 envelopes unflavored gelatin
2 bouillon cubes
1 tablespoon each lemon juice and tarragon vinegar
Lettuce

Cut eggs lengthwise; remove yolks and mash. Beat in next 4 ingredients with a fork. Fill whites with mixture and chill. Soften gelatin in ¼ cup cold water; add 2 cups boiling water and bouillon cubes, stirring to dissolve. Season to taste. Add lemon juice and vinegar. Pour a small amount into 1-quart mold and chill until thickened. Cool remaining mixture. Press eggs, rounded side up, into chilled aspic. Cover with remaining aspic and chill until firm. Unmold on lettuce. Makes 4 servings.

About 135 calories, 1 gram carbohydrate, 10 grams protein and 9 grams fat, per serving.

SALMON SALAD MOLDS

1 can (1 pound) salmon
1 envelope unflavored gelatin
1 vegetable bouillon cube
1/4 cup minced celery
1 tablespoon capers
1 tablespoon lemon juice
Salad greens
Mask and chopped green onion (both
  optional)

Drain salmon, reserving liquid in measuring cup. Add enough water to liquid to equal 1/2 cup. Sprinkle gelatin on liquid. Dissolve bouillon cube in 1/2 cup boiling water and add to salmon liquid, stirring until gelatin is dissolved. Flake salmon gently and toss with celery, capers and lemon juice. Add salmon-liquid mixture. Spoon into 4- to 5-ounce custard cups or individual molds and chill until firm. Serve on greens. If desired, mask molds before serving. Makes 4 servings.
Mask Unmold salads on cake rack on waxed paper. In small saucepan, combine 2/3 cup low-calorie creamy-type salad dressing (such as French, green goddess or Russian), 1/3 cup water and 1 envelope unflavored gelatin. Heat gently, stirring, until gelatin is dissolved. Put over ice water and chill, stirring. When mixture begins to thicken, spoon quickly over molds. If mixture becomes stiff, reheat to soften and chill again. Sprinkle molds with chopped green onion. Makes 4 servings.

About 178 calories, 2 grams carbohydrate, 24 grams protein and 7 grams fat, per serving without mask.

SILHOUETTE SALAD

1 envelope unflavored gelatin
1 can (10-1/2 ounces) condensed cream
  of chicken soup
1 tablespoon lemon juice
Dash of pepper
1 can (5 ounces) chicken, diced
1/2 cup diced celery
1/4 cup chopped green pepper
2 tablespoons chopped pimiento
1 teaspoon instant minced onion
Salad greens

Soften gelatin in 1 cup cold water. Dissolve over hot water. Beat gelatin with soup, lemon juice and pepper. Chill until thickened but not set. Fold in remaining ingredients, except greens. Pour into 1-quart mold and chill until firm. Unmold on greens. Makes 4 servings.

About 139 calories, 8 grams carbohydrate, 11 grams protein and 7 grams fat, per serving.

ORIENTAL SHRIMP-CHEESE SALAD

18 cooked cleaned shelled medium
  shrimps
5 tablespoons orange juice
1 teaspoon soy sauce
1-1/2 teaspoons sugar
1/2 teaspoon onion salt
Ground ginger
Dash of dry mustard
1/4 cup Cooked Salad Dressing (page 285)
6 lettuce cups
1-1/2 cups creamed cottage cheese

Marinate shrimps in mixture of 4 tablespoons orange juice, 1/2 teaspoon soy sauce, 1 teaspoon sugar, 1/4 teaspoon onion salt, 1/8 teaspoon ginger and the dry mustard. Cover and refrigerate 2 hours. Mix dressing with remaining 1 tablespoon orange juice, 1/2 teaspoon each soy sauce and sugar, 1/4 teaspoon onion salt and a dash of ginger. Cover and chill. Put a lettuce cup on each of 6 individual plates. Mound 1/4 cup cheese in center of each leaf. Press 3 shrimps in base of each mound. Pour 1 tablespoon chilled mixture over each salad. Makes 6 servings.

About 113 calories, 8 grams carbohydrate, 18 grams protein and no fat, per serving.

TUNA-VEGETABLE SALAD

2 cans (7 ounces each) water-packed
  tuna, drained
1 can (15 ounces) water-packed artichoke
  hearts, drained
1 can (1 pound) cut green beans, drained
1 cup diagonally sliced celery
1/3 cup low-calorie Italian-style salad
  dressing
Tomato wedges and salad greens

In bowl, gently toss all ingredients, except last 2. Spoon onto platter or individual plates and chill well before serving. Garnish with tomato wedges and greens. Makes 6 servings.

About 198 calories, 13 grams carbohydrate, 11 grams protein and 1 1/2 grams fat per serving.

MARINATED TUNA

1 can (7 ounces) water-packed tuna
1/4 cup each minced parsley and red
  onion
1/4 cup lemon juice
Black pepper to taste

Separate tuna in chunks. Combine remaining ingredients and pour on top; chill. Makes 4 servings.

About 75 calories, 2 grams carbohydrate, 9 1/2 grams protein and 1 gram fat, per serving.

PIQUANT SALAD DRESSING

1/2 teaspoon dry mustard
Dash of monosodium glutamate
1/4 teaspoon seasoned salt
1/2 teaspoon celery salt
1 tablespoon flour
1/2 cup nonfat milk
1 egg yolk, beaten
3 tablespoons vinegar
Few drops of noncaloric liquid sweetener

In top part of small double boiler, mix seasonings and flour. Add milk and cook over boiling water, stirring, until thickened. Stir in egg yolk and cook 1 minute longer, stirring. Remove from heat and stir in vinegar and sweetener. Cool; chill. Makes 2/3 cup.

About 17 calories, 1 gram carbohydrate, 1 gram protein and 1 gram fat, per tablespoon.

FROZEN PEACH DELIGHT

2 egg whites
1/4 cup confectioners' sugar
1 can (8 ounces) low-calorie sliced peaches, drained
2 teaspoons lemon juice
1/2 teaspoon vanilla extract
1/4 teaspoon almond extract

Beat egg whites until stiff but not dry. Gradually add sugar, beating constantly until well blended. Whirl peaches in blender or force through sieve. Add remaining ingredients and gently fold in egg whites. Turn into freezing tray of refrigerator and freeze until firm. Makes 4 servings.

About 72 calories, 16 grams carbohydrate, 2 grams protein and no fat, per serving.

APPLE SNOW

2 cups grated peeled apple
3 tablespoons lemon juice
2 tablespoons granulated sugar
Dash of salt
Dash of nutmeg
3 egg whites
1/4 cup confectioners' sugar
1/4 teaspoon cinnamon

Combine first 5 ingredients. Beat egg whites until they form soft peaks. Gradually beat in confectioners' sugar. Then gently fold in apple mixture. Sprinkle with cinnamon and serve at once. Makes 6 servings.

About 81 calories, 18 grams carbohydrate, 2 grams protein and no fat, per serving.

COOKED SALAD DRESSING

In top part of small double boiler, mix 1/2 teaspoon salt, 1/4 teaspoon each dry mustard and paprika, a dash of cayenne, 2 tablespoons vinegar, 1/4 cup skim milk, 1 egg, beaten, and 1/4 teaspoon liquid noncaloric sweetener. Put over hot water and cook, stirring, until thickened. Cool and chill. Makes 1/2 cup.

About 13 calories, no carbohydrate, 1 gram protein and 1 gram fat, per tablespoon.

STRAWBERRY FLUFF

2 envelopes strawberry-flavor dietary gelatin dessert
1 tablespoon lemon juice
1 package (2 ounces) whipped topping mix
1/2 cup nonfat or skim milk
6 fresh strawberries

Dissolve gelatin dessert in 1 1/2 cups hot water. Add lemon juice and chill until thickened but not firm. Prepare topping mix as directed on the label, using the 1/2 cup milk. Reserve 1/2 cup; fold remainder into thickened gelatin and pile in 8" piepan. Chill until firm. Decorate with reserved topping and unhulled strawberries. Makes 6 servings.

About 81 calories, 5 grams carbohydrate, 4 grams protein and 5 grams fat, per serving.

ROSY RHUBARB SHERBET

1 teaspoon unflavored gelatin
1 package (1 pound) frozen rhubarb in sugar syrup
1/4 cup light corn syrup
1/8 teaspoon salt
1 tablespoon grated lemon rind
1 tablespoon lemon juice
Red food coloring
2 egg whites, stiffly beaten

Soften gelatin in 1/2 cup water and dissolve over low heat. Cook rhubarb 3 to 4 minutes. Press through a sieve to make 1 cup purée. Combine rhubarb, gelatin mixture, and next 4 ingredients and a few drops food coloring. Pour into a loaf pan and freeze until mushy. Beat with a rotary or electric beater until fluffy. Fold in egg whites. Return to loaf pan and freeze until firm. Makes 1 quart, or 6 servings.

About 104 calories, 24 grams carbohydrate, 2 grams protein and no fat, per serving.

BROILED GRAPEFRUIT HALVES

Cut grapefruit in half crosswise. Remove center membrane and cut around the sections. Sprinkle tops with 1 teaspoon honey and dot with 1 teaspoon butter. Heat slowly under broiler.

About 94 calories, 16 grams carbohydrate, 1 gram protein and 4 grams fat for each half.

ROSY MELON DESSERT

1 envelope (4-serving size) low-calorie strawberry- or lemon-flavor gelatin
1/4 cup Cointreau or orange juice
1 cup melon balls or cubes

Dissolve gelatin in 1 cup boiling water. Add liqueur and $^3/_4$ cup cold water. Chill $1^1/_3$ cups of mixture until thickened, then fold in melon balls. Pour into serving dish and chill until set but not firm. Chill remaining $^2/_3$ cup mixture until slightly thickened. Then set bowl of gelatin in larger bowl of ice and water and whip until thick. Pour over set gelatin and chill until firm. Makes $3^1/_2$ cups, or 6 servings.

About 33 calories using Cointreau, 2 grams carbohydrate, 1 gram protein and no fat, per serving.

ORANGE-BUTTERMILK SPONGE

2 envelopes unflavored gelatin
2 cups buttermilk
1 cup orange juice
2 tablespoons lemon juice
1/4 cup honey
2 egg whites, stiffly beaten
Orange slices or sections

Soften gelatin in $^1/_4$ cup cold water and dissolve over hot water. Stir into buttermilk and combined fruit juices and chill until partially set. Beat in honey until foamy, then fold in egg whites. Turn into 5-cup mold and chill until firm. Unmold and decorate with orange slices. Makes 6 servings.

About 117 calories, $22^1/_2$ grams carbohydrate, 7 grams protein and no fat, per serving.

STRAWBERRY-YOGURT FREEZE

Combine 1 cup plain yogurt, 2 cups fresh strawberries, halved, $^1/_4$ cup honey and 1 tablespoon lemon juice. Whirl in blender until smooth. Pour into ice-cube tray and freeze until firm around edges. Makes $2^3/_4$ cups.

About 45 calories, 11 grams carbohydrate, 1 gram protein and $^1/_2$ gram fat per $^1/_4$ cup.

LIME-GRAPE DESSERT

2 envelopes low-calorie lime-flavor gelatin
1/2 cup plus 2 tablespoons bottled unsweetened grape juice
30 seedless green grapes

Dissolve gelatin in 1 cup boiling water. Remove $^1/_2$ cup of mixture to small bowl and add $^1/_2$ cup cold water. Chill until slightly thickened. Add grape juice to remaining gelatin and fill 4 sherbet glasses. Chill until firm. Beat thickened gelatin until frothy and double in bulk. Let stand in bowl of ice water until mixture holds its shape, stirring occasionally. Fold in grapes and pile lightly on firm gelatin. Chill until firm. Makes 4 servings.

About 56 calories, 10 grams carbohydrate, 4 grams protein and no fat, per serving.

LEMON MOUSSE

2 tablespoons cornstarch
1/4 teaspoon salt
1 cup sugar
1 cup skim milk
3 egg yolks, slightly beaten
Grated rind of 1 lemon
1/3 cup lemon juice
2-1/2-ounce box (2 envelopes) low-calorie whipped-topping mix

In top of double boiler, mix cornstarch, salt and sugar. Add milk, put over boiling water and cook, stirring frequently, about 15 minutes. Pour slowly over egg yolks, stirring. Mix well and put back in double boiler. Cook, stirring, 1 minute. Add lemon rind and juice and chill. Prepare topping mix with water as directed on label, omitting vanilla. Fold into chilled mixture, pour into refrigerator trays and freeze until firm. Serves 10.

About 127 calories, $24^1/_2$ grams carbohydrate, 2 grams protein and 2 grams fat, per serving.

QUICK PINEAPPLE SHERBET

Freeze 1 can (20 ounces) pineapple chunks in unsweetened juice until solidly frozen. Put under running hot water 1 minute before opening. Then put frozen chunks in blender and whirl. Stop blender occasionally and, with rubber spatula, work fruit down slowly until of sherbet consistency. Serve with fresh berries in season, if desired. Serves 4.

About 73 calories, $17^1/_2$ grams carbohydrate, no protein and no fat, per serving.

LUSCIOUS MOCHA CAKE

1 package (14-1/2 ounces) angel-food
  cake mix
1 package (3-3/4 ounces) chocolate
  fudge whipped dessert mix
1 cup cold coffee
2 tablespoons chopped pistachio nuts
Unsweetened baking chocolate

Bake cake according to package directions; cool. To make frosting, follow directions on dessert-mix package, substituting coffee for milk and
water. Chill 10 to 15 minutes, or until
of spreading consistency. Spread cake
with frosting; decorate top with nuts.
Using a vegetable peeler, shave a
little chocolate in "curls" on top of
cake. Makes 12 servings.

About 186 calories, 37 grams carbohydrate, 5 grams protein and 2 grams
fat, per serving.

PINEAPPLE-STRAWBERRY DELIGHT

2 cans (8-1/2 ounces each) low-calorie
  pineapple tidbits
1 can (16 ounces) low-calorie apricot
  nectar
2 packages (1/2 ounce each)
  strawberry-flavor dietary gelatin
  dessert
1 tablespoon grated lemon rind
Low-calorie Whipped Topping
12 fresh strawberries
Mint sprigs

Drain pineapple, reserving liquid.
Mix liquid, apricot nectar and
enough water to make 4½ cups. Put
in saucepan with gelatin dessert.
Bring to boil and stir until dissolved.
Add lemon rind and chill until
slightly thickened. Whip until fluffy,
fold in pineapple and pour into a
1½-quart mold. Chill until firm. Unmold and decorate with topping,
strawberries and mint sprigs.

About 64 calories, 14 grams carbohydrate, 2 grams protein and no fat,
per serving including topping.

Low-Calorie Whipped Topping

Combine ¼ cup cold water, 1 tablespoon lemon juice, 3 tablespoons
nonfat dry-milk granules, and noncaloric sweetener to taste; put bowl
and mixer beaters in refrigerator.
When chilled, beat mixture until stiff
enough to stand in peaks. Use at
once. Makes about 1 cup.

About 80 calories, 12 grams carbohydrate, 8 grams protein and no fat,
for whole recipe.

TANGY ORANGE MOLD

2 envelopes unflavored gelatin
2 tablespoons grated orange rind
1 cup orange juice
2 cups buttermilk
2 tablespoons sugar
1 teaspoon vanilla extract
Green grapes and low-calorie
  mandarin-orange sections (optional)

Soften gelatin in 1 cup water and
dissolve over low heat. Mix next 5
ingredients with gelatin. Pour into 1-
quart mold and chill until set. Unmold and decorate with grapes and
mandarin orange sections, if desired.
Makes 6 servings.

About 75 calories, 12 grams carbohydrate, 6 grams protein and no fat,
per serving.

GRAHAM-CRACKER BROWNIE BARS

2 cups fine graham-cracker crumbs
1/2 cup chopped pecans
1/2 cup semisweet chocolate pieces
1/4 cup granulated sugar
1/4 teaspoon salt
1 cup skim milk
1 tablespoon confectioners' sugar

Mix all ingredients, except last. Turn
into lightly greased 9" x 9" pan. Bake
in moderate oven (350°F.) 30 minutes. Cut in 40 bars while warm.
Sprinkle with sugar.

About 46 calories, 6 grams carbohydrate, 1 gram protein and 2 grams
fat, per bar.

VANILLA-CURRANT COOKIES

1 cup all-purpose flour
1/4 teaspoon baking powder
1/8 teaspoon salt
1/4 cup sugar
1/4 cup butter or margarine
2 tablespoons currants
1/2 teaspoon vanilla extract
1 egg

On board, mix first 4 ingredients.
Cut in butter and sprinkle with currants. Add vanilla and egg and work
quickly together to form a ball.
Shape in a roll 12" long, wrap in
waxed paper and chill until firm. With
a sharp knife, cut roll in ¼" slices.
Put on lightly greased cookie sheet
1" apart and with a fork dipped in
flour make a lattice pattern on each
cookie. Bake in moderate oven
(375°F.) 12 to 15 minutes. Remove
at once from sheet. Makes 3 dozen.

About 38 calories, 4 grams carbohydrate, 1 gram protein and 1 gram fat,
per cookie.

HOW TO COMPOSE MENUS

Meal planning can be a chore or a challenge depending on how knowledgeably you approach it. If mapping out the week's menus is boring or frustrating to you, it may be that you're just not going about it right. Here, some simple ground rules for approaching the task for both family fare and meals for company.

DOS

• Do keep within your budget—within reason. But operate on a weekly rather than a daily allowance.

• Do plan ahead. There's really no reason why anyone should have to shop for groceries every day. Furthermore, a well-thought-out order allows you to do some double cooking, then freeze or refrigerate half for another day.

• Do make use of seasonal foods, not only because they're bargains but because they are almost always at their most delicious when the supply is greatest.

• Do make a shopping list, so nothing is forgotten and the temptation to buy on impulse is minimized. But keep the list flexible enough so you can substitute a special bargain if you run across one.

• Do plan the way you are going to use leftovers and be imaginative. Browse through cook books and magazines looking for recipes that will make the second appearance just as spectacular as the first.

• Do make one dish your point of departure. This needn't be the entrée. If you're serving a filling dessert like strawberry shortcake make the rest of the meal relatively light. If the soup is rich and hearty, the main course should be something simple. And if one dish is highly spiced, try to keep the others fairly bland. Everything on the menu should harmonize even when it's merely a soup-and-sandwich lunch for the children.

• Do keep family meals to two, or at most three, courses. In most cases an entrée and dessert should be adequate, though on occasion you may want to add a first course of soup, fruit or seafood, or a special salad course. And some nights it's fun (and easy) to make a one-course meal of a family favorite—minestrone or fish chowder served with hot bread, or boiled lobster with side dishes of celery and ripe olives will please everyone. Then, if you like, serve mints or candied fruit with coffee instead of dessert.

• Do try new dishes. One new recipe a week is a good rule of thumb—but never more than one in any meal. Introduce your family to foods they've never tasted —lamb kidneys, sweetbreads, scallops; shallots, eggplant, fennel. You may find some doubting Thomases on the first go-around, but this is a good way to teach young people the many and varied pleasures of eating.

• Do consider nutrition, but don't make a big issue of it. Doctors agree that if meals are well balanced nutritionally, there is no need for extra vitamins or other food supplements. All you have to do is serve foods from the four basic groups every day. These include 2 cups or more milk for adults and 3 to 4 cups for children (part of this can be cheese or foods cooked with milk); 4 or more servings of cereal, bread, or foods such as macaroni (all whole-grain, enriched or restored); 4 or more servings from the fruit-vegetable group, including 1 citrus each day, 1 dark green or deep yellow at least every other day, and 2 or more servings of others, including potato; 2 or more servings lean meat, or 2 eggs, 1 cup cooked dry beans or $1/4$ cup peanut butter. To fully meet energy needs, select additional foods, which could be fats or sweets. Using these groupings, serve the foods your family likes best without mentioning their nutritional value. Somehow the less said about how good something is for you, the more pleasure in eating it.

• Do mix methods of cooking. Apart from obvious exceptions such as a New England boiled dinner or a mixed grill, try not to have all the foods at one meal cooked the same way—all fried, all baked or all boiled. Combine a baked potato and stewed tomatoes with a broiled hamburger, or poached fish with shoestring potatoes and a raw vegetable salad.

• Do serve hot things hot and cold things cold—but don't go to extremes. Of course you'll want to warm the plates for hot food, but don't get them so hot they burn the fingers or further cook food already done to your liking. Have cold plates for cold food but don't ice everything. Many fruits and desserts are best served at room temperature.

• Do suit the plate to the serving. A small serving on a large plate looks meager; conversely a large helping on a small plate is crowded and hard to handle. Never make servings enormous regardless of the size of the plate. It is likely to overwhelm modest appetites; besides, you can always serve seconds.

• Do vary textures, making sure there's something crisp and crunchy in every meal. Some easy suggestions: celery, radishes, water chestnuts, nuts, Chinese noodles, or apples.

DON'TS

• Don't use an ingredient more than once in a menu. That is, don't serve tomato soup and tomato sauce at the same meal, or cream soup, creamed sweetbreads, and ice cream.

• Don't repeat colors. Not only is a one-color meal uninspiring to look at, foods of the same color are likely to be of similar tastes and textures. Even if you were served a dinner of white fish, mashed potatoes and cauliflower, blindfolded, it would taste insipid. But if you substitute some brown shoestring potatoes and green beans, the whole meal brightens. If you find that, inadvertently, you've planned a dinner without color variation, add a garnish to pick it up; a sprig of watercress, a slice of tomato or pickled beet, even a dash of paprika or minced parsley, adds instant eye appeal to a monochromatic plate. And speaking of plates, remember that your china is part of your color scheme too. So unless you have several sets to complement different menus, it's wise to choose a white or natural background to harmonize with whatever food you're serving.

Although most of the foregoing rules apply equally to family and company meals, there are a few special dos and don'ts when you are having guests.

DOS FOR COMPANY

• Do consider the occasion, the season, the size of your dining table and the amount of help available when planning a dinner for company. These will help you decide whether the meal should be formal or informal, sit-down or buffet, indoors or out. They will also give you some guidance in what the menu should be.

• Do keep a file of guests—when you entertained them, what and how much you served, and how it all worked out. This may seem unnecessary because you don't do that much entertaining, but it can be helpful on a number of scores. It can remind you that it's been much longer than you thought since you invited old acquaintances to dinner. It can save you from presenting an identical meal to the same people twice in a row. And it can star your success and flag your failures so you can repeat the first and avoid the second. It also gives you a place for a permanent record of special preferences you've observed or been told about, as well as any pet hates, food allergies, etc.

• Do write out the menu before you start to cook or even shop, and when meal preparation begins be sure to refer to it. Many a hostess has found some carefully prepared delicacy untouched in the refrigerator after the guests have departed. Which may prove, since it wasn't missed, that we are all inclined to plan too much food, or too many different kinds of food for a party.

• Do prepare as much of the meal as you can ahead of time. If something can be frozen, make it a day or a week in advance of the party. If it can be refrigerated overnight or for several hours, prepare it the day before, or early on party day. Try to plan meals that require a minimum of attention after the guests have arrived so that it takes you only a few minutes to handle the final steps.

• Do try the practice of having two parties two days in a row—it has so many advantages. The flowers are still fresh, the silver still shining, the coat closet still cleared, on the second day. And if you serve the same menu, most of the cooking is already behind you and the food needs only reheating for the second wave of guests.

DON'TS FOR COMPANY

• Don't be ostentatious. If your budget is modest, don't serve guests luxury items that will dent it for weeks to come. Naturally you'll take special pains to have something extra-good, but that doesn't necessarily mean extra-costly. A delicious casserole will please everyone just as much as a Beef Wellington, and such obvious extravagances as fresh caviar can very well make guests uncomfortable.

• Don't make every dish an elaborate one. A fancy dish really calls for simple accompaniments, while a succession of foods ringed with garnishes, sauced in wine and herbs, or squiggled with a pastry tube can be downright overpowering.

• Don't serve too much. Many women seem to think that the longer the guest list the more different dishes they must serve. But it stands to reason that if three courses are enough for four people they are also enough for forty. Even if you're serving buffet, plentiful amounts of a few foods are all you really need. If the table threatens to look bare, fill it with flowers, candles or fruit arrangements, and napkins and tablewear attractively set out.

• Don't, under any circumstances, try out new recipes on guests. The hazards are simply too great. Either stick to tried and true favorites or, if you run across a dish that sounds exciting, prepare it for the family—your most honest critics—before you present it to company.

• Don't serve exotic controversial foods unless you're very sure of your guests' tastes. *Tripes à la mode de Caen* may be an exciting gastronomical experience to some, a guest's nightmare to others. Since many people are, or think they are, allergic to seafood, to play it completely safe, choose beef, ham, veal or poultry.

OUTDOOR EATING

- A small sharp paring knife is a handy item to take to a picnic. For safety's sake, carry knife in a plastic toothbrush holder.
- Stack paper plates for a picnic with a sheet of waxed paper between plates. Serve the first course on the paper, which keeps food from soaking into the plate, and after the first course, remove the paper and use the plate for dessert (saves work and paper).
- Carry unpeeled hard-cooked eggs and soft fruits such as plums in egg cartons.
- Empty plastic pill bottles make good containers for dressings, catsup, mustard, etc. Wash thoroughly before using.
- Put salt in an empty seasoning or tenderizer jar. This will give you a handy shaker and the screw top will keep salt from spilling.
- Freeze individual cans of flavored bouillon (or fruit or vegetable juice) and pack them frozen. By lunchtime, they'll be the right temperature for drinking. Pack miniature can openers.
- Fill wide-mouthed vacuum containers with ice cream, refreeze, wrap in foil or pack with canned ice and they'll keep until lunchtime. Put gelatin desserts and frozen puddings in these containers too.

BARBECUE COOKERY

A barbecue or cookout is undoubtedly the most popular of American parties, and the easiest on the hostess. Space is no problem (you can even cook in an open garage!) The service can be as informal as you like, and in nine cases out of ten the man of the house takes over a substantial part of the cooking.

Fancy equipment isn't necessary—a surprising variety of foods can even be cooked on a small hibachi, or Japanese grill, and vegetables, salads and breads can be prepared inside and brought out when the meat has been cooked. On the other hand, you may prefer a really large grill, big enough to accommodate most of the meal for a crowd. Just be sure that all the equipment—tongs, long fork, charcoal, lighter fluid, and serving implements—as well as seasonings and sauces are set out before the guests arrive.

In addition to the "dining" table or tables, which can be anything from garden umbrella tables to long boards on sawhorses, you'll probably need some serving space for those dishes that don't come direct from the grill and, if you're planning an after-dark meal, some illumination—hurricane lamps on the table, or torches on poles stuck in the ground.

For the most carefree and casual get-togethers, paper plates are in order (though you should avoid using them for runny dishes such as chili), and paper napkins, disposable plastic glasses and cups keep breakage and cleanup to a bare minimum. And when the informal feast is finished, *do* let your company help clear the table and get rid of the throwaways in suitable containers you've provided.

TIPS FOR BARBECUEING

1. Brush grill with oil before using. Be sure that it has been well cleaned.

2. Meat should be at room temperature. Take out of the refrigerator at least 1 hour before cooking.

3. Cheaper cuts of meat are enhanced greatly by a liberal sprinkling of tenderizer, or marinating before cooking.

4. For steaks allow 1/2 to 3/4 pound per person. One or two large steaks may be cut after grilling into serving pieces or strips. Individual steaks are fine for a small group.

5. Roasts are excellent for a large group. Any type can be cooked on a revolving spit. Balance is important. Be sure the meat is centered securely on the spit. Slow fires are best for cooking. The roast may be marinated before being spitted, or basted with any of your favorite barbecue sauces while cooking.

6. Handle meat or chicken with tongs instead of a fork. Don't jab with forks or knife to turn or test.

BARBECUE MENUS

COLD TOMATO-CLAM SOUP

Mix 2 chilled cans (10³/₄ ounces each) condensed tomato soup, 1 bottle clam juice and 2 soup-cans (2³/₄ cups) cold water. Add lemon juice to taste and garnish with sliced lemon and chopped parsley. Serves 6.

EASY CLAM CHOWDER

1 package (3-1/5, 5-1/2 or 5-5/8 ounces)
  scalloped potatoes
1/2 cup dry nonfat milk
2 tablespoons butter, margarine or
  bacon fat
1 can (8 ounces) minced clams,
  undrained
Salt and pepper
Parsley flakes (optional)

Put potatoes in kettle with 4 cups water and next 2 ingredients. Bring to boil, cover and simmer over fire or low heat 15 minutes, or until potatoes are tender (leave cover slightly ajar so mixture doesn't boil over). Add clams and salt and pepper to taste. Sprinkle with parsley, if desired. Makes 4 servings.

LUNCHEON SAUSAGE-POTATO SOUP

1 medium onion, chopped
1 carrot, finely chopped
1 stalk celery, minced
3 tablespoons butter or margarine
1-1/2 cups diced potato
1 teaspoon salt
Dash of pepper
2 knackwurst or 4 frankfurters, cooked
Chopped parsley

Cook first 3 ingredients slowly in butter, about 10 minutes, stirring often. Add next 3 ingredients and 3 cups water. Bring to boil, cover and simmer 45 minutes. Add sliced knackwurst and heat. Sprinkle with parsley. Makes 2 generous servings.

TUNA-CORN CHOWDER

2 cans (7 ounces each) tuna
2 tablespoons instant minced onion
2 cups diced peeled potatoes
1 can (1 pound) cream-style corn
3 cups milk
2 teaspoons salt
2 tablespoons parsley flakes
1/2 teaspoon hot pepper sauce

Drain 2 tablespoons oil from tuna. Sauté onion in the oil, stirring, a few minutes. Add 1 cup water and potatoes, cover and cook 10 minutes over fire or low heat. Add tuna and remaining ingredients and heat thoroughly, about 10 minutes. Makes 6 generous servings.

HEARTY CORN SOUP

1 enveope chicken-gravy mix
1 tall can evaporated milk
1 can (1 pound) cream-style corn
1 teaspoon prepared mustard
1/3 cup bacon-flavor bits

Put 1 cup water and first 4 ingredients in saucepan and bring to boil over fire or heat, stirring. Sprinkle with bits. Makes 4 servings.

GAZPACHO

1 medium cucumber
2 ripe tomatoes
3 tablespoons minced onion
1/2 cup diced green pepper
2 tablespoons olive oil
2 tablespoons cider vinegar
2 cups tomato juice
Salt and pepper to taste
Chopped parsley to taste
1 clove garlic, cut

Peel cucumber, remove seed and chop. Peel tomatoes and chop. Combine all ingredients, except garlic. Put garlic on toothpick and add to mixture. Chill several hours, then remove garlic. Spoon into chilled wide-mouthed vacuum container, adding an ice cube or two. Makes 4 to 6 servings. **Note** Mixture keeps a day or two. Or halve recipe for 2 to 3.

BACKPACKER'S ALL-IN-ONE

5 cups instant cereal such as grits or
  oatmeal (any combination)
4 cups dry nonfat milk
1 cup plain wheat germ
2 cups sesame-seed meal
1/2 cup ground or minced filberts,
  almonds, pecans or Brazil nuts
1/2 cup dehydrated date nuggets,
  packaged chopped dates, currants or
  finely chopped figs or raisins
1 cup hard dehydrated apple nuggets
  or 1 package Gravenstein applesauce
2 cups packed dark-brown sugar
1/2 cup brewer's yeast
2 teaspoons cinnamon

Spread cereals on baking sheet and toast in warm oven (250°F.) about 20 minutes. Mix with remaining ingredients. Makes about 12 firmly-packed cups. To prepare, put ³/₄ cup mix in serving bowl or cup; stir in enough boiling water to make cereal consistency; let stand in warm place about 5 minutes. Serve plain or with reconstituted whole milk. Crumbled bacon bar may be sprinkled on top. **Note** Sesame-seed meal and brewer's yeast can be bought in health-food stores; apple and date nuggets in mountaineering supply or sporting-goods stores.

ROAST PORK AND SQUASH

1 envelope (about 1-1/2 ounces)
  onion-soup mix
4 to 5 pounds pork-loin roast, trimmed
  of excess fat
3 tablespoons all-purpose flour
Salt and pepper
Steamed acorn-squash rings
Canned whole apricots

Put 30″ x 18″ piece heavy-duty aluminum foil in 13″ x 9″ x 2″ baking pan. Sprinkle soup mix lengthwise in center of foil. Lay roast, fat side down, on soup mix. Fold foil and seal securely in center and at ends, raising ends slightly. Bake in slow oven (300°F.) 3½ hours, or until meat is very tender. Remove to heated platter and keep warm. Add enough water to drippings to measure 2 cups and pour into saucepan. Blend flour with small amount of cold water until smooth. Add to mixture in saucepan and bring to boil, stirring until thickened and smooth. Season to taste with salt and pepper. Serve with the gravy, squash and apricots. Makes 6 to 8 servings.

WINE 'N' HONEY RIBS

1 can (8 ounces) tomato sauce
1/2 cup red wine
1/4 cup honey
1/2 cup red-wine vinegar
1 teaspoon onion salt
1 teaspoon garlic salt
1/8 teaspoon ground cloves
4 pounds beef short ribs

Combine all ingredients, except ribs, and mix well. Lay ribs in shallow glass dish and pour sauce over top. Refrigerate overnight. Remove from refrigerator and cook on grill, brushing frequently with sauce, 1½ to 2 hours, or until very tender. Remaining sauce can be reused. Makes 4 to 6 servings.

GRILLED MINTED LAMB CHOPS

6 double loin lamb chops
Salt, pepper and dried rosemary
1/4 cup butter or margarine, melted
1/2 cup dry white wine
1 teaspoon Worcestershire
1/4 cup mint jelly
2 tablespoons finely chopped fresh mint

Sprinkle chops with salt, pepper and rosemary. Put on grill 6″ above gray coals and cook, turning occasionally, 15 minutes. Mix remaining ingredients and heat in saucepan on grill until jelly is melted. Brush chops with the mixture and cook, brushing with glaze every few minutes, 15 minutes, or until chops are done. Serves 6.

BARBECUED PORK-LOIN ROAST

3-1/2-pound (or larger) pork-loin roast
Soy sauce
1 teaspoon each powdered ginger, dry
  mustard and dried orange peel
1/2 teaspoon seasoned salt
1/2 teaspoon (or less) powdered garlic
1/4 teaspoon curry powder
2 tablespoons each honey and catsup
1 tablespoon wine vinegar

Have butcher bone, roll and tie roast. Push spit rod through center of roast, balancing weight as evenly as you can. Tighten the holding forks. Brush surface of roast with soy sauce. Combine spices and rub on roast. Insert meat thermometer at angle into heaviest part of roast; be careful it does not rest on rod. Cook meat about 4″ above heat 1 hour. Combine remaining ingredients. Begin brushing over meat every 15 to 20 minutes during remainder of cooking. Cook meat about 2 hours (or 185°F. on meat thermometer). Makes 8 servings.

GLAZED PORK CHOPS WITH FRUIT

1/2 cup each honey and lemon juice
2 tablespoons brown sugar
2 tablespoons soy sauce
1/2 teaspoon ground cloves
1/2 teaspoon grated lemon rind
1/2 teaspoon salt
6 loin pork chops, 1″ to 1-1/4″ thick
2 large oranges, peeled and sliced
1/2 each medium cantaloupe and honeydew, peeled and cut in chunks

Combine first 7 ingredients in saucepan and heat. Put chops on greased grill about 5″ above low heat and grill 15 minutes, or until well browned on one side. Turn and grill, brushing occasionally with glaze, 12 to 15 minutes, or until well done. Thread fruit on skewers, brush with glaze and warm on grill 3 to 5 minutes. Makes 6 servings.

SMOKY LINKS WITH BEANS AND APRICOTS

3/4 cup finely chopped dried apricots
1 package (12 ounces) smoky links
1 can (28 ounces) pork and beans in
  tomato sauce
2 tablespoons brown sugar

Cover apricots with boiling water and let stand 5 minutes; drain. Cut links in bite-size pieces. Combine all ingredients, bring to boil and simmer over fire or low heat 20 minutes, or until apricots are tender. Makes 6 servings.

BARBECUED BROILED CHICKEN I

Basic directions for broiling indoors.

Wash broiler-fryer halves or quarters and dry on absorbent paper. Arrange, skin side down, on rack in broiler pan. Brush chicken with preferred barbecue sauce and put in preheated broiler 7" or 8" from heat. Broil, brushing occasionally with sauce, 30 minutes. Turn, brush again with sauce and broil 15 to 30 minutes longer, depending on size of chicken. **Caution** High-sugar sauces, such as those made with molasses, honey, catsup or chili sauce, have a tendency to burn easily, so partially broil chicken before brushing with sauce.

BARBECUED BROILED CHICKEN II

Basic directions for broiling on grill outdoors.

Wash broiler-fryer halves or quarters and dry on absorbent paper. Arrange skin side up, on grate set 3" to 6" from heat (set 6" from heat if high-sugar sauce is used for brushing). Brush chicken with preferred barbecue sauce and cook, turning and brushing occasionally, 45 minutes to 1¼ hours, or until tender (time depends on weight and distance from heat).

BARBECUE SAUCES FOR CHICKEN

Spicy Barbecue Sauce Heat ½ cup butter or margarine, 1 teaspoon salt, 2 tablespoons cider vinegar, 1 teaspoon sugar, 1 tablespoon Worcestershire, 1 teaspoon onion salt, ¼ teaspoon pepper and ½ cup water until butter is melted. Makes 1 cup.

Curry Barbecue Sauce Mix ½ cup melted butter or margarine, 2 tablespoons curry powder, 1½ teaspoons garlic salt, 1 tablespoon dry mustard, 2 tablespoons steak sauce and ⅔ cup wine vinegar. Makes about 1¼ cups.

Herb Barbecue Sauce Mix 1 cup catsup, ½ cup water, 3 tablespoons tarragon vinegar, 1 tablespoon steak sauce, dash of garlic salt, and ¼ teaspoon each ground marjoram, oregano and thyme. Makes about 1⅔ cups.

Sherry Barbecue Sauce Mix 1 cup sherry, ½ cup vegetable oil, 2 tablespoons Worcestershire, 1 tablespoon each onion powder, dry mustard and brown sugar, 1 teaspoon garlic salt and ½ teaspoon each salt and pepper. Makes 1½ cups.

COUNTRY CAPTAIN

2 tablespoons butter or margarine
1 broiler-fryer, cut in serving pieces
1 onion, thinly sliced
1 green pepper, slivered
1 clove garlic, minced
1 cup chicken bouillon
1-1/2 teaspoons curry powder
Salt and pepper
3/4 cup toasted slivered almonds
1/4 cup currants or raisins

Heat butter in oven-proof skillet and brown chicken pieces. Remove chicken. In remaining butter, cook next 3 ingredients until lightly browned. Add bouillon, curry powder and salt and pepper to taste. Add browned chicken, cover and bake in moderate oven (350°F.) 45 minutes. Remove from oven, add almonds and currants and simmer on top of range 5 minutes. Makes about 4 servings.

MEDITERRANEAN CHICKEN

1/2 cup olive oil
1/2 cup white wine
1/4 cup honey
1/4 cup white-wine vinegar
2 teaspoons garlic salt
1/2 teaspoon oregano
1 lemon, thinly sliced
1 orange, thinly sliced
2 broiler-fryers, split

Mix thoroughly all ingredients, except chicken. Pour over chicken in glass bowl and refrigerate overnight. Warm to room temperature before grilling. Grill over coals, basting frequently with marinade, 45 minutes, or until done. Add fruit slices the last few minutes of cooking to heat through. Makes 4 servings.

HERB-BUTTERED TURKEY

1/2 cup butter or margarine, softened
1/2 teaspoon dillweed
1/2 teaspoon dried oregano
Hickory-smoked salt
10- to 12-pound turkey
Seasoned pepper

Blend butter with herbs and ¼ teaspoon hickory-smoked salt; set aside. Remove giblets and neck from turkey for use another time. Sprinkle inside of bird with smoked salt and seasoned pepper. Lift skin from breast and spread about half the herb butter over meat. Pat skin down, gently stretching it back into place. Cover and refrigerate several hours. When ready to barbecue, truss turkey and prepare for spit cooking. Cook over coals, brushing now and then with remaining herb butter, 2 to 2½ hours. Makes 8 to 10 servings.

ALBACORE EN BROCHETTE

2 pounds fresh albacore
1 slender loaf French bread
1/4 pound butter, melted
1/4 cup olive oil
3 tablespoons lemon juice
1 teaspoon salt
Bay leaves

Slice albacore 3/4" thick, remove skin and cut meat into pieces slightly smaller than the diameter of the bread. Slice bread thin. Mix remaining ingredients, except bay leaves, and marinate fish for 1 hour. Put a slice of bread on a skewer, a slice of fish and a bay leaf; repeat until each skewer holds 3 slices of fish and 4 of bread. Do not push too close together. Grill about 15 minutes, basting with remaining marinade and turning until browned on all sides. Serves 6.

GRILL-BAKED STUFFED SALMON

5- to 7-pound whole salmon
Lemon juice and salt
1/2 teaspoon pepper
3/4 cup each chopped green pepper, celery and onion
1/4 cup minced parsley
Pinch each thyme and marjoram
1/4 cup vegetable oil
Parsley sprigs
Melted butter

Wipe fish inside and out with lemon juice and sprinkle with salt. Stuff cavity with mixture of 1 teaspoon salt, the pepper and remaining ingredients, except last 3. Sew together securely to hold in stuffing. Put fish on piece of chicken wire, making a basket. Grill over medium fire, turning and basting with oil mixed with 1 cup water, 1 1/2 hours, or until done. Most of skin will remain on wire. Garnish with parsley sprigs and sprinkle with lemon juice and butter. Makes 4 to 6 servings.

GRILLED ASPARAGUS

Put 1 package (10 ounces) frozen asparagus in center of square of heavy foil. Sprinkle with 1/2 teaspoon salt and 1/8 teaspoon pepper and dot with 1 tablespoon butter. Seal well and put on grill over hot coals. Cook, turning several times, 25 to 30 minutes, or until done. Makes 3 servings.

GRILLED SUMMER SQUASH

Slice small crookneck squash, zucchini, pattypan or other summer squash onto squares of double foil. Season with butter, salt, pepper and garlic powder. Seal and grill over medium fire 10 to 15 minutes, or until tender.

HOT CORN SALAD

1 package (10 ounces) frozen cut corn
1 cup sliced celery
1 tomato, diced
1/3 cup chopped green pepper
1/3 cup sliced green onions
1/2 cup sliced pitted black olives
1/4 cup bottled creamy dressing

Cook corn according to package directions. Drain and mix with remaining ingredients. Return to fire to heat through. Makes 4 to 6 servings.

ONIONS IN THE COALS

Count 1 sweet Spanish onion per serving. Put, unpeeled, at edge of coals. Roast, turning occasionally, 45 minutes to 1 hour. To serve, remove charred outer layer, dot with butter and sprinkle with salt and pepper.

SLICED POTATOES IN FOIL

Peel baking potatoes and cut in fairly thin slices (about 1/8" thick). Wrap each half potato, sliced, in double foil with 1 tablespoon butter and salt and pepper to taste. Put packages on coals and roast 20 to 30 minutes, or until done. Serve in foil, cutting open with scissors. Tiny new potatoes can be done the same way, each foil package containing 3 or 4, unpeeled. After cutting open, sprinkle with minced parsley and pass more butter.

HERBED POTATOES

4 medium potatoes, thinly sliced
1/4 cup butter or margarine, melted
1 tablespoon each chopped parsley and chives
1 teaspoon dillseed
1/2 teaspoon salt
1/4 teaspoon monosodium glutamate

Mix all ingredients together and wrap tightly in 15" length of heavy foil. Cook on grill, turning occasionally, 15 to 20 minutes. Makes 4 servings.

BARBECUED BEANS

2 cans (21 ounces each) pork and beans in tomato sauce
2 tablespoons instant minced onion
1/4 cup bottled barbecue sauce
1/4 cup chili sauce
1/4 cup molasses
8 slices cooked bacon

Combine all ingredients, except last, in pot. Bury bacon slices in beans. Heat over coals or low heat until bubbly. Serve in bowls with spoons. Serves 6 to 8.

TOASTED ANGEL FOOD

Cut wedges of unfrosted angel-food cake and toast over medium fire until golden brown. Serve hot with spoonful of sour cream and some brown sugar.

BAKED APPLES

Core cooking apples and fill with mixture of cut-up dates, finely chopped nuts, cut-up marshmallows and cinnamon-sugar mixture. Place each apple on square of foil, gather up sides and twist together. Bake on coals, turning occasionally, 45 minutes to 1 hour.

BANANA YUM-YUMS

Cut stem from bananas. Slit lengthwise through all except bottom skin. Spread gently and sprinkle with brown sugar. Close banana and wrap in foil. Put on grill and cook about 15 minutes.

WINE-FRUIT KABOBS

2 ripe peaches or nectarines, cut in large chunks
1 pear, cut in large chunks
1 banana, cut in 6 chunks
1/2 small cantaloupe, peeled and cut in 2″ chunks
1/4 cup butter or margarine, melted
1/4 cup red dessert wine
1/4 teaspoon ginger
Juice and grated rind of 1 small orange

Push fruit chunks onto skewers. Mix remaining ingredients and brush on fruit. Put skewers 8″ above gray coals on greased grill. Cook, brushing with wine mixture, about 5 minutes. Makes 6 servings.

CHOCOWICHES

For each serving, spread a slice of bread with peach or apricot jam, then sprinkle with flaked coconut and semisweet chocolate pieces. Top with second slice of bread and wrap in foil, leaving ends open. Put on grill and heat, turning, until bread is toasted and chocolate melted.

GRILLED PINEAPPLE

Cut a ripe fresh pineapple in 6 or 8 (depending on size) lengthwise wedges, cutting through leaves. Brush with melted butter and broil over medium fire until hot and slightly browned. Serve at once. Canned pineapple can be substituted.

POUCH PUDDING WITH CREAMY ORANGE SAUCE

1 can chocolate-nut or date-nut roll
1 package (3 ounces) cream cheese
2 tablespoons orange juice
3 tablespoons confectioners' sugar (sift if necessary)
1 teaspoon grated orange rind

Remove both ends of bread can and push bread out. Wrap in foil and seal tightly. Heat, turning often, 15 minutes, or until heated through. Meanwhile, soften cream cheese and blend in orange juice. Then add sugar and rind and stir until smooth. Serve on hot sliced bread. Makes 4 servings.

STRAWBERRY-MANDARIN-CHEESE DESSERT

1 pound (2 cups) creamed cottage cheese
1 pint strawberries, washed, hulled and sliced
2 tablespoons confectioners' sugar
Grated rind of 1 orange
1 can (11 ounces) mandarin oranges, drained

Make a layer of cottage cheese in serving dish. Carefully mix remaining ingredients and spoon on top. Chill at least 1 hour before serving. Makes 4 to 6 servings.

STRAWBERRIES IN FOIL

Wash 1 quart fresh strawberries, remove hulls and slice in bowl. Sprinkle with 3/4 cup superfine sugar and let stand 1/2 hour. Divide berries among 6 squares of double foil, add 2 teaspoons Cognac to each and seal well. Put packages on grill and cook over slow fire 7 to 8 minutes. Serve warm over ice cream, or top with cold whipped cream.

INDIVIDUAL STRAWBERRY-LADYFINGER DESSERTS

1/4 cup vanilla instant-pudding mix
3/4 cup milk
1/2 teaspoon vanilla extract
6 ladyfingers, split
1 pint strawberries, washed, hulled and sliced
2 to 3 tablespoons confectioners' sugar

Combine first 2 ingredients until smooth, then chill until set. Add vanilla and beat until smooth. Put 3 ladyfinger halves on each of 4 individual dessert plates or in small bowls. Spread with vanilla custard and spoon strawberries sweetened with the sugar on top; chill. Makes 4 servings.

NATURAL FOODS

The most nourishing family diet includes as many natural foods as possible, since these contain all their healthful original vitamins and minerals. Obviously, in today's world most of us cannot eat solely unprocessed foods, so these recipes use both strictly natural foods and foods that, though not "natural," are nutritious.

TIPS FOR BETTER NUTRITION

• Plan menus to include some of the "basic four" every day. They are:
1. Meats, poultry, fish and eggs—at least two servings every day. Beans, peas and nuts have good food values and can sometimes be substituted.
2. Milk and dairy products (directly or in cooking)—at least two cups milk every day or the equivalent in ice cream, cheese or other dairy foods.
3. Breads and cereals—at least four servings every day. Use whole-grain. Remember pasta, rice and grits are cereals, not vegetables.
4. Fruits and vegetables—at least four servings every day, including a dark-green or deep-yellow vegetable for vitamin A at least every other day, and a citrus fruit or other fruit or vegetable for vitamin C every day.
• When you select a natural food, bear in mind that it's best when it is fresh. Natural grains contain the fresh germ and, like any fresh food, should be stored in the refrigerator.
• Make your own breads frequently and include flours such as unbleached all-purpose, stone-ground whole-wheat, rye, buckwheat and soy; rolled oats; cornmeal; wheat germ; seed meals; etc.
• Include a variety of hot whole-grain cereals and sprinkle them with toasted seed; wheat germ; nuts; raisins or other dried fruit; and meals such as sesame, sunflower or coconut.
• Serve brown rice and whole-grain pasta when available.
• Sweeten cereals, breads, fruits, custards and puddings, etc., with honey, sorghum, pure maple syrup, brown sugar or blackstrap molasses.
• Buy unsulfured dried fruits.
• Serve variety meats frequently.
• When snacks are called for, serve fresh or dried fruits; nuts; toasted grain breads or crackers spread with honey or pure peanut butter; carob "cocoa"; cookies or candy made with natural sweets and nuts, fruits or seed.

TOASTED-OAT CEREAL

2 cups old-fashioned rolled oats
1 cup plain wheat germ
1/2 cup slivered almonds
1/4 cup cold-pressed oil
1/2 cup honey

Combine first 3 ingredients in 15" x 10" x 1" baking pan. Drizzle with oil and honey and mix so that all pieces are coated. Spread evenly in pan. Bake in very slow oven (250°F.), stirring occasionally, 1½ hours. Cool and break apart any chunks. Store in airtight container. Serve with milk, and fruit, if desired. Makes about 1 quart.

ZIPPY TOASTED PUMPKIN SEED

1 can (14 ounces) pumpkin seed
2 tablespoons Worcestershire
2 tablespoons butter, melted
2 tablespoons grated Parmesan or
　Romano cheese
Salt to taste

Mix all ingredients and put in jelly-roll pan. Toast, stirring every 5 minutes, in moderate oven (375°F.) 15 minutes, or until toasted. **Note** Fresh pumpkin seeds can be used, if available. Toast unwashed seed until golden.

TOASTED SUNFLOWER SEED

Spread shelled seed in piepan or on cookie sheet with sides and put in moderate oven (350°F.). Toast, stirring occasionally, 10 to 15 minutes, or until golden brown.

WHOLE-WHEAT CHEESE APPETIZERS

1 cup fine shredded sharp Cheddar
　cheese
1/3 cup butter
1 cup whole-wheat pastry flour
1/8 teaspoon cayenne
1/4 teaspoon salt

Combine all ingredients in mixing bowl and gather together with hands in a ball. Shape in roll 1¼" wide; chill. With serrated knife, cut in ⅛" slices. Bake on ungreased baking sheets in moderate oven (375°F.) 8 to 10 minutes. Makes about 4 dozen.

SALT STICKS

Cut sliced rye bread in ½-inch strips. Brush with melted butter or margarine. Toast in hot oven (400°F.) 8 to 10 minutes, or until lightly browned. Sprinkle with coarse salt.

RYE WAFERS

1/2 cup butter, melted and cooled
1 cup rye flour
3/4 cup all-purpose flour
1 teaspoon double-acting baking powder
1 teaspoon sugar
1/2 teaspoon salt
2 teaspoons cumin seed
1/2 cup milk

In mixing bowl, combine all ingredients and mix until smooth. Chill 1 hour. Divide in 2 parts and roll each out on lightly floured board until very thin. Cut in 3" x 2" rectangles with sharp knife or pastry wheel. Put on baking sheets and bake in moderate oven (375°F.) 8 to 10 minutes, or until well browned. Cool on rack. Store airtight in cool place. Makes about 4 dozen.

WHEATEN CHEESE CRACKERS

1 cup minus 2 tablespoons all-purpose flour
1/4 teaspoon baking soda
1/2 teaspoon salt
1/2 cup stone-ground yellow cornmeal
Wheat germ
1/2 cup butter
1/2 cup grated sharp Cheddar cheese
1/4 cup milk
1 tablespoon white vinegar

Mix first 4 ingredients and ¼ cup wheat germ in bowl. Cut in butter until mixture resembles coarse meal, then stir in cheese. Mix milk and vinegar and add, mixing lightly until dry ingredients are just moistened. Knead slightly on lightly floured board and roll to ⅛" thickness. Cut in 2¼" x 1¼" rectangles and prick with tines of fork. Sprinkle with wheat germ and put on lightly greased baking sheets. Bake in moderate oven (375°F.) 12 to 15 minutes. Remove to racks to cool. Makes 5 to 6 dozen.

BLUE-CHEESE AND NUT SPREAD

1 cup coarsely shredded blue cheese
1/3 cup margarine
1 tablespoon (or more) Worcestershire
1/2 cup finely chopped nuts
Finely chopped parsley (optional)

Combine first 3 ingredients and cream until well blended. Add nuts and mix well. Serve on crackers. Or spread on white-bread rounds or triangles and bake in hot oven (400°F.) 15 minutes; sprinkle with parsley and serve hot as appetizers. Or serve larger rounds or triangles with salads or soups. Store airtight in refrigerator and bring to room temperature before serving. Makes about 1 cup.

DILL DIP

1 teaspoon dry mustard
1 tablespoon lemon juice
1 cup mayonnaise
1 cup dairy sour cream
1 tablespoon fresh chopped dill or 1 teaspoon dillweed
1/4 teaspoon salt

Combine first 2 ingredients and stir until smooth. Add remaining ingredients and mix well. Serve with raw vegetables as an appetizer. Makes 2 cups.

HERB YOGURT DIP

1 teaspoon caraway seed
1 cup plain yogurt
1 tablespoon chopped green onion
1/4 teaspoon basil leaves, crushed

Pour boiling water over caraway seed, let stand about 5 minutes, then drain. Add seed to yogurt with green onion and basil. Chill several hours. Use as a dip for various raw vegetables. Makes 1 cup.

SALMON-STUFFED EGGS

2 eggs, hard-cooked
1/3 cup canned red or pink salmon
1 teaspoon milk
Salt and pepper to taste
Sweet-pickle relish
1 teaspoon red caviar
Paprika (optional)

Cut eggs in half lengthwise and remove yolks. In small bowl, mix yolks, salmon, milk, salt, pepper and 2 tablespoons relish until well blended. Stuff whites with the mixture. Garnish each half with ¼ measuring teaspoonful caviar and a sprinkling of relish, or dust with paprika.

TERIYAKI ALMONDS

4 cups blanched almonds (1-1/4 pounds)
1/4 cup butter or margarine
2 tablespoons soy sauce
2 tablespoons sherry
1/4 to 1/2 teaspoon ground ginger
Garlic salt

Put almonds in 13" x 9" x 2" pan and toast in slow oven (300°F.) 20 minutes. Meanwhile, melt butter in small saucepan. Add soy sauce, sherry and ginger and stir to blend. Pour mixture over almonds and toast, stirring occasionally to get an even coating, 15 to 20 minutes longer. Sprinkle with garlic salt to taste and spread out on paper towel to dry and cool. Store in cool place or freeze. Makes 4 cups.

BEAN SOUP WITH ITALIAN SAUSAGE

3 cups dried red kidney or other red
  beans
3/4 pound sweet Italian sausage
2 large onions, chopped
1 bay leaf
1/2 teaspoon dried thyme leaves
Few sprigs parsley
1 can (29 ounces) tomatoes
1-1/2 teaspoons seasoned salt
1/4 teaspoon pepper
1 green pepper, chopped
2 cups diced potato
Salt

Cover washed beans with 2½ quarts
water, bring to boil and boil 2 minutes.
Cover and let stand 1 hour. Cut sausage in ¼″ slices and brown in skillet.
Add sausage and sausage fat to beans
with next 7 ingredients. Bring to boil
and simmer, covered, until beans are
tender. Add green pepper and potato;
cook 15 minutes. Salt to taste. Makes
about 3 quarts.

CREAM OF CHICKEN SOUP AUX FINES HERBES

1 fryer, cut up
4 cups water
2 chicken bouillon cubes
1 bay leaf
1 each onion, celery stalk and
  peeled carrot
1/2 cup butter
1/2 cup all-purpose flour
2 cups each milk and light cream
1/2 teaspoon each dried thyme, marjoram
  and chives (or fresh herbs to taste)
1/8 teaspoon ground nutmeg
1/2 teaspoon turmeric
3/4 cup cooked brown rice
Salt and pepper
Chopped parsley and toasted sesame seeds

Put first seven ingredients in kettle,
bring to boil and simmer, covered,
1½ hours, or until chicken is tender.
Remove skin and bones from chicken
and cut meat in bite-size pieces. Strain
broth and reserve. In same kettle, melt
butter and blend in flour. Add milk
and cream and cook until thickened,
stirring constantly. Add chicken broth,
chicken, herbs, nutmeg, turmeric and
rice. Heat well. Season to taste. Serve
with a sprinkling of parsley and sesame seeds. Makes about 2½ quarts.

CURRIED SHRIMP BISQUE

Combine 1 can (10½ ounces) condensed cream of shrimp soup, 1 cup
milk and ½ cup light cream. Add
1 can (4½-ounces) shrimp, drained,
rinsed and chopped. Add 1½ teaspoons curry powder, 3 drops hot pepper sauce and 2 tablespoons sherry.
Heat through, stirring. Serves 4.

CREAM OF LENTIL SOUP

1 pound dried lentils
2 tablespoons instant bouillon
1 onion, chopped
1 clove garlic, minced
1 carrot, chopped
1 stalk celery, chopped
1/4 teaspoon dry mustard
1/4 pound Genoa bologna, hard salami
  or boiled ham, cut in thin strips
Salt and pepper
1 cup cream

Wash lentils and soak overnight in 3
quarts water; do not drain. Add bouillon, vegetables and mustard. Bring to
boil and simmer, covered, 2 hours, or
until lentils are very tender. If desired,
force through sieve. Add meat; season
to taste; simmer 10 minutes. Add
cream just before serving. Makes 2
quarts.

YELLOW-PEA SOUP WITH PORK

1 smoked pork butt, 2 to 3 pounds
1 cup coarsely chopped onion
1 pound dry yellow split peas
1 teaspoon dried thyme
1 bay leaf
1/2 teaspoon coarse black pepper
1 teaspoon salt

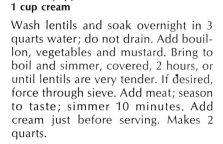 Put pork butt and onion in
large kettle or Dutch oven
and add 3 quarts water. Bring to boil,
cover and simmer 1½ hours, or until
meat is tender. Remove meat and skim
off all but about 2 tablespoons fat
from broth. Slice meat very thin and
set aside. Wash peas, drain and add
to broth with remaining ingredients.
Bring to boil, cover and simmer, stirring occasionally, 1½ hours, or until
mixture becomes almost a purée. Add
meat and heat. Makes 6 servings.

TON-JIRU (Japanese Pork Soup)

1/4 pound lean pork
1 can (7 ounces) bamboo shoots
6 large mushrooms
1 cup bean sprouts or raw peas
4 cups chicken stock
Shoyu (soy sauce) or salt
2 green onions, minced

Slice pork as thin as possible. (At Japanese markets it can be bought already
sliced. The meat is usually frozen, then
sliced on a machine.) Combine all ingredients, except shoyu and onions,
and simmer, covered, 15 minutes, or
until pork is cooked. Add shoyu to
taste and serve with a little onion
sprinkled on each serving. Makes 6
servings.

PEPPERS STUFFED WITH CORNMEAL AND BEEF

4 large firm green peppers
2 tablespoons bacon fat or butter
1/2 pound ground lean beef (raw or cooked)
Salt and pepper
Worcestershire sauce
2 tablespoons olive oil
3 cups tomato juice
1 clove garlic, crushed
2 teaspoons chili powder
6 tablespoons white cornmeal
Dash of honey

Cut off tops of peppers and reserve. Trim white membrane from peppers, remove seeds and wash. Heat fat in skillet; add beef, season with salt, pepper and 1 teaspoon Worcestershire and brown lightly. Add 1 cup water, cover and simmer 1 hour, or until most of water has evaporated. In another skillet, heat oil and add 2 cups tomato juice, garlic and chili powder. Bring to hard boil and gradually add cornmeal, beating constantly to avoid lumping. Simmer 15 minutes, or until thick, stirring occasionally. Add meat mixture and cook slowly until stiff enough to use as filling for peppers. Check seasoning. Fill peppers with the mixture, adjust tops and secure with toothpicks. Set in small casserole or baking dish. Season remaining tomato juice with Worcestershire, salt and honey. Pour into dish with peppers. Bake in moderate oven (375°F.) 40 to 50 minutes, basting every 10 minutes with tomato juice in dish. Serves 4.

THE POOR PARSON'S NOODLE DISH

3 tablespoons bacon fat
2 onions, minced
1/2 cup minced green pepper
2 cans (4 ounces each) sliced mushrooms, drained
4 cups ground cooked meat
3 cups beef bouillon
3 tablespoons flour
Dash of hot pepper sauce
1 teaspoon salt
1/2 teaspoon pepper
1/2 teaspoon thyme, basil or other favorite herb
8 ounces medium noodles, cooked

Melt bacon fat and sauté onions and green pepper until soft. Push to one side and add mushrooms. Sauté 5 minutes, covered. Add meat and cook 5 more minutes. Add bouillon. When boiling, thicken with flour mixed with 1/4 cup water to a smooth paste. Stir in seasonings. Simmer 15 minutes, stirring occasionally. Add noodles and heat. Serves 6 to 8.

HOT BEEF-AND-LIMA BAKE

1 cup uncooked brown rice
1 pound ground beef
2 tablespoons bacon fat or margarine
1 can (1 pound) lima beans, undrained
1 can (1 pound) tomatoes
1 envelope onion-soup mix
1 tablespoon celery flakes
2 tablespoons catsup
1 teaspoon each chili powder and salt
1 beef bouillon cube

Cook and drain rice. Cook beef in bacon fat until it loses its red color, breaking up meat with fork. Add rice and remaining ingredients. Pour into 2-quart casserole and bake, uncovered, in moderate oven (350°F.) about 30 minutes. Add more bouillon if too dry. Makes 6 servings.

FAR EAST HAMBURGER DINNER

4 medium onions, minced
1 clove garlic, minced
2 tablespoons butter or margarine
1 pound ground lean chuck
1 tablespoon flour
2 tablespoons chopped raisins
1/4 cup chopped almonds
1 teaspoon ginger
3 teaspoons curry powder
1 beef bouillon cube
1 cup cooked peas
Seasoned salt and pepper
Hot cooked rice

Cook onion and garlic in butter until golden. Add meat and brown lightly, breaking up with fork. Blend in flour. Add next 5 ingredients and 1 1/4 cups water. Bring to boil and simmer, covered, 15 minutes. Add peas and salt and pepper to taste and heat. Serve on rice. Makes 4 to 6 servings.

SAVORY STUFFED BEEF HEART

1-1/4 cups uncooked brown rice
Few celery leaves, chopped
3 onions, chopped
1 teaspoon poultry seasoning
Salt and pepper
1 beef heart
2 tablespoons cold-pressed oil
2 cups beef bouillon or water

Mix rice and next 3 ingredients and season to taste with salt and pepper. Trim heart and remove large tubes, excess fat and blood vessels. Season well inside and out with salt and pepper. Fill with some of rice mixture and sew edges together. Brown well in the oil in heavy kettle or Dutch oven. Cover and cook slowly without added liquid 2 hours. Remove meat and pour off all fat. Put remaining rice mixture in kettle, add bouillon and season to taste. Put heart on top, cover and simmer 1 hour longer. Serves 8.

BROWN BEANS, SWEDISH STYLE

1 pound dried Idaho or Swedish brown
   beans
1/3 cup each white vinegar and molasses
1 teaspoon salt
1/3 cup heavy cream (optional)

Bring 6 cups water to boil in kettle or Dutch oven. Add washed beans and boil 2 minutes. Cover, remove from heat and let stand 1 hour. Then bring again to boil and simmer, covered, 2½ hours, or until very tender. Add vinegar, molasses and salt. Stir in cream, if desired, or add water if too thick. (Beans will have a mild sweet-sour taste.) Serve with meatballs, pork or other meat. Serves 6.

LASAGNA WITH MEATBALLS

3/4 pound lean ground beef
1/2 teaspoon salt
1/4 teaspoon pepper
1 teaspoon grated lemon rind
2 tablespoons olive oil
3 cups favorite tomato sauce
1 pound lasagna, cooked and drained
1 pound ricotta or cottage cheese
1 pound mozzarella cheese, cubed
1-1/2 cups grated Parmesan

Mix first 4 ingredients and shape in small balls. Brown in hot oil. Cover bottom of a large 2″ to 3″ deep baking dish sparingly with tomato sauce. Line with lasagna. Dot with half the cheeses. Spread with half remaining sauce; top with meat. Cover with remaining lasagna, sauce and cheeses. Bake in moderate oven (350°F.) about 45 minutes. Cool slightly. Makes 10 to 12 servings.

HOME-FRIED SPAGHETTI WITH EGGS

8 ounces whole-wheat spaghetti
Salt
4 large eggs
1/8 teaspoon pepper
2 teaspoons instant minced onion
1/4 cup grated Parmesan cheese
1/4 cup butter
2 tablespoons Toasted Sunflower Seed
   (page 479)

Cook spaghetti in boiling salted water 12 minutes, or until tender; drain. Beat together ½ teaspoon salt and next 4 ingredients. Add spaghetti and mix well. Heat butter in 10″ to 12″ skillet and pour in spaghetti mixture. Sprinkle with sunflower seed. Cook over medium heat until firm and well browned on bottom. Invert on cookie sheet without sides and slip back into skillet. Brown underside. Cut in wedges. Makes 4 to 6 servings.

SAUTÉED BROWN RICE AND MUSHROOMS

1 medium onion, minced
1/4 cup minced green pepper
1/2 pound mushrooms, coarsely chopped
1/4 cup butter
3 cups cooked brown rice
3/4 teaspoon salt
1/4 teaspoon pepper
1/2 teaspoon chili powder

Sauté onion, green pepper and mushrooms in butter in skillet 5 minutes, or until mushrooms are cooked and liquid is evaporated. Add remaining ingredients and cook, stirring gently, until lightly browned. Makes 4 servings.

WALNUT-RICE FRITTERS

1 cup all-purpose flour
1 teaspoon double-acting baking powder
1 teaspoon salt
3 eggs, slightly beaten
1/2 cup milk
2 tablespoons cold-pressed oil
2 cups cooked brown rice
1/2 cup chopped walnuts
Fat for deep frying
Maple syrup

Sift dry ingredients into bowl. Add eggs, milk and oil; beat until smooth. Stir in rice and nuts. Drop by spoonfuls into hot deep fat (365°F. on a frying thermometer) and fry until golden brown and done. Serve very hot with syrup. Makes about 22.

BAKED SOYS

1 pound dried soybeans
1-1/2 teaspoons salt
1 medium onion, chopped
1 small green pepper, chopped
2 stalks celery, finely diced
1/4 cup catsup
1 teaspoon dry mustard
3 tablespoons blackstrap or other
   unsulfured molasses
1/4 cup bacon fat or other fat or oil
   (soy, safflower, etc.)
1/4 cup packed brown sugar

Put beans with 6 cups water in kettle or Dutch oven. Bring to boil, uncovered, 2 minutes. Cover and let stand 1 hour. Then add 1 teaspoon salt, bring again to boil and simmer, covered, about 2 hours, adding more water if necessary. Then add vegetables and cook until beans are tender. Drain, reserving 1½ cups liquid; add water to make up amount if necessary. Put bean mixture in greased shallow 2-quart baking dish. Mix liquid, remaining salt and other ingredients, except brown sugar, and pour over beans. Sprinkle with sugar; bake, uncovered, in hot oven (400°F.) about 1 hour. Serves 6 to 8.

BAKED APPLESAUCE BROWN BREAD

2 cups whole-wheat flour
1 cup stone-ground cornmeal
3/4 teaspoon salt
1 teaspoon baking soda
1 cup buttermilk
1 cup blackstrap or other unsulfured molasses
3/4 cup canned applesauce
3/4 cup seedless raisins

Mix first 4 ingredients in bowl. Add buttermilk and molasses and beat with spoon until smooth. Fold in applesauce and raisins and spread in greased 9″ square baking pan. Bake in moderate oven (350°F.) about 35 minutes.

FRUITED WHEAT BISCUITS

2 cups whole-wheat flour
1/4 cup soy flour
3 teaspoons double-acting baking powder
1/2 teaspoon baking soda
1 teaspoon each sugar and salt
1/2 cup butter, softened
1/2 cup dairy sour cream
1/2 cup mashed ripe banana
1/4 cup (about) milk

Put dry ingredients in bowl. Cut in butter until mixture resembles cornmeal. Add next 2 ingredients and enough milk to hold mixture together. Stir with fork only until dry ingredients are moistened. Turn out on lightly floured board and knead 10 turns. Roll gently to 1/2″ thickness and cut in rounds with 2″ cutter. Put on ungreased baking sheet, prick with fork and bake in hot oven (450°F.) 10 minutes, or until well browned. Serve at once. Makes about 20.

SAVORY CASSEROLE BREAD

2/3 cup chopped green onions with tops
3 tablespoons cold-pressed oil
2 cups buttermilk biscuit mix
1 cup chopped cooked ham
2 eggs, slightly beaten
2/3 cup milk
1/2 teaspoon prepared mustard
1-1/2 cups grated sharp Cheddar cheese
2 tablespoons sesame seed
3 tablespoons butter or margarine, melted

Sauté onion in 1 tablespoon oil about 2 minutes. Combine biscuit mix and ham. Mix remaining 2 tablespoons oil, eggs, milk, mustard, onion and half the cheese. Add to ham mixture and stir until mixed. Spread in greased round 10″ casserole 1″ to 1 1/2″ deep. Sprinkle with remaining cheese and seed, then pour butter over top. Bake in moderate oven (375°F.) 35 to 40 minutes. Makes 6 to 8 servings.

OATMEAL-DATE-NUT BREAD

1-1/2 cups all-purpose flour
1/2 teaspoon salt
1/2 teaspoon double-acting baking powder
1 teaspoon baking soda
3/4 cup quick-cooking rolled oats (not instant)
1 egg
1/2 cup sugar
1 cup dairy sour cream
1/3 cup molasses
1 cup each pitted dates and walnut meats

Mix first 5 ingredients in bowl. Put egg and next 3 ingredients in blender, cover and whirl until smooth. Add dates and nuts, cover and chop. Add to dry ingredients and mix only until moistened. Put in greased 9″ x 5″ x 3″ loaf pan and bake in moderate oven (350°F.) about 45 minutes. Cool.

CINNAMON-RAISIN MUFFINS

1-1/2 cups whole-wheat flour
1/3 cup packed brown sugar
3 teaspoons double-acting baking powder
1/2 teaspoon salt
1 teaspoon cinnamon
1/2 cup plain wheat germ
3/4 cup seedless raisins
2/3 cup milk
1/3 cup soy or other cold-pressed oil
2 eggs, slightly beaten

Mix dry ingredients in bowl. Add remaining ingredients and mix only until dry ingredients are moistened. Fill greased 2 1/2″ muffin-pan sections two-thirds full; bake in hot oven (400°F.) about 20 minutes. Makes 12.

WHOLE-WHEAT RAISIN BREAD

2 envelopes active dry yeast
2 teaspoons salt
1/4 cup blackstrap molasses
1/2 cup seedless raisins
3 cups whole-wheat flour
1 cup plain wheat germ
1 cup soy flour
3 cups (about) all-purpose flour

In large mixing bowl, dissolve yeast in 3 cups warm water (105° to 115°F.). Stir in salt and next 5 ingredients. Add all-purpose flour 1 cup at a time and beat with wooden spoon until smooth and elastic. Cover with sheet of plastic and let rise in warm place free from drafts 1 hour, or until doubled in bulk. Knead on lightly floured board until smooth and elastic (at least 10 minutes). Divide in 2 parts and shape in loaves. Put in 2 greased 9″ x 5″ x 3″ loaf pans. Cover and let rise in warm place about 1/2 hour. Bake in moderate oven (375°F.) 35 to 40 minutes. Turn out on rack; brush tops with warm water. Cover with towels; cool.

OPEN-FACED CHEDDAR SANDWICHES

1 cup finely shredded Cheddar cheese
1/4 cup slivered black olives
1/4 teaspoon dry mustard
1/4 teaspoon caraway seed
3 slices whole-grain bread
Mayonnaise

Mix first 4 ingredients. Spread bread with mayonnaise, then with cheese mixture. Broil until cheese is melted and lightly browned.

COTTAGE-CHEESE SANDWICH FILLING

1 cup cottage cheese
2 tablespoons each finely chopped radish and cucumber
1 tablespoon finely sliced green onion

Mix all ingredients together and spread on whole-wheat or other bread. Makes about 1¼ cups filling.

CHEESY EGGS ON ROLLS

6 eggs, hard-cooked and chopped
2 cups shredded sharp Cheddar cheese
1 tablespoon steak sauce
4 large rolls
Bacon Curls

Combine eggs, cheese and sauce. Spoon onto roll halves. Just before serving, broil until browned and bubbly. Serve topped with Bacon Curls. Makes 4 servings. **Bacon Curls** Place 8 slices bacon on rack of broiler pan. Bake in hot oven (400°F.) 10 minutes, or until limp. Remove from oven, curl bacon strip around fork and secure with toothpick. Slide off fork and return to broiler pan; continue baking about 5 minutes. Gently remove picks.

EGG-SALAD SANDWICHES

1 package (8 ounces) cream cheese, softened
1/4 cup minced onion
1/4 cup finely chopped green pepper
3 tablespoons chili sauce
2/3 cup chopped walnuts
5 hard-cooked eggs, finely chopped
1/2 teaspoon salt
Dash of pepper
12 slices bread
Butter or margarine, softened

Mix thoroughly all ingredients, except last 2. Spread 6 slices bread with mixture. Spread remaining bread with butter and close sandwiches. Makes about 2½ cups filling, or enough for 6 sandwiches.

PEANUT-BUTTER SANDWICH FILLINGS

1. Mix ½ cup peanut butter and 1 can (8 ounces) crushed pineapple, drained. Add a little pineapple syrup if necessary to moisten.
2. Mix ½ cup peanut butter, ¾ cup finely shredded carrot, ¼ cup chopped raisins and 3 tablespoons mayonnaise.
3. Mix ½ cup peanut butter, ¼ cup drained pickle relish, 1 tablespoon pickle liquid, a dash of hot pepper sauce and 2 tablespoons bacon-flavor protein bits.

PEANUT-HONEY TRIANGLES

1/2 cup peanut butter
3 tablespoons honey
3 tablespoons chopped peanuts
2 teaspoons grated orange rind
4 slices toast

Blend peanut butter and honey, then stir in next 2 ingredients. Spread on toast and cut slices diagonally in triangles.

THIN BOYS

6 long French rolls
Mayonnaise or salad dressing
1 pound creamed cottage cheese
2 cucumbers, peeled and sliced
French dressing
Salt and pepper
4 large ripe tomatoes, sliced
1 bunch radishes, sliced
2 bunches green onions, chopped, or 3 large sweet onions, sliced
6 slices sharp Cheddar cheese
1/2 bunch watercress
Lettuce or other salad greens

Split French rolls lengthwise. Spread each half liberally with mayonnaise. Pile half of cottage cheese on roll bottoms. Arrange cucumber slices on cheese. Drizzle with French dressing and dust with salt and pepper. Put remaining cottage cheese and remaining ingredients, except last 2, in layers, sprinkling each layer with dressing and seasonings. Add cress, lettuce and roll tops. Makes 6 sandwiches.

TUNA-ALMOND SPREAD

1 can (7 ounces) tuna
1/4 cup unblanched almonds, chopped
1/2 cup salad dressing
1 tablespoon lemon juice
Salt and pepper to taste

Mix all ingredients and store, covered, in refrigerator until ready to use. Makes about 1½ cups.

ALOHA SALAD

3 avocados, halved and peeled
2 tablespoons lemon juice
1 can (1 pound) unsweetened pineapple
 chunks, drained
Shredded salad greens
Aloha Dressing
1/3 cup flaked coconut, toasted

Brush cut surfaces of avocados with lemon juice. Fill center of each half with pineapple chunks and put on greens on individual salad plates. Top each with 2 tablespoons dressing and sprinkle with coconut. Makes 6 servings. **Note** Other fruits such as canned pear and peach halves or bananas can be substituted for the avocados and lemon juice omitted. **Aloha Dressing** Mix 1 cup flaked coconut, 1½ cups mayonnaise, 3 tablespoons milk, 1½ tablespoons lemon juice and 1 teaspoon curry powder. Makes about 2 cups.

HONEY FRENCH DRESSING

1 cup cold-pressed oil
1/2 cup catsup
1/3 cup each vinegar and honey
1 teaspoon each salt, paprika and grated
 onion
1 clove garlic, halved

Put all ingredients in 3-cup salad-dressing bottle and shake well. Let stand 10 minutes, then remove garlic. Makes 2 cups.

BANANA WALDORF SALAD

1 large red apple, unpeeled
1/2 cup diced celery
1/4 cup mayonnaise
2 fully ripe medium bananas
Salad greens
1/2 cup walnut halves

Dice apple in bite-size pieces and toss with next 2 ingredients. Peel bananas and cut in ¼″ slices. Add to first mixture and mix lightly. Arrange salad greens on each of 4 to 6 plates, add salad and garnish with nuts. Makes 4 to 6 servings.

HERB YOGURT DRESSING

1 cup plain yogurt
1/4 cup finely chopped celery leaves
1/4 cup minced parsley
1/4 cup mayonnaise
3 green onions, thinly sliced
1 tablespoon lemon juice or vinegar
Salt and pepper
1 tablespoon prepared horseradish
1 teaspoon honey

Mix all ingredients. Serve with green salad or as a sauce for cold meat or fish. Makes about 1½ cups.

HOMEMADE YOGURT

1/4 cup plain yogurt
1 quart nonfat milk (fresh or made from
 package)

Let yogurt stand at room temperature 3 to 4 hours. Heat milk to 120°F. on candy thermometer (do not overheat). Cool to 90°F. Add yogurt and mix thoroughly. Put in bowl or 4 individual containers. Do not stir or move containers. Cover and keep barely lukewarm until a curd has formed. Store in refrigerator. Makes 1 quart.

BANANA-ORANGE SALAD WITH LEMON DRESSING

3 large California oranges, peeled
2 large fully ripe bananas
Lemon Dressing
Salad greens
1/3 cup chopped walnuts
3 tablespoons chopped watercress or
 parsley

Slice oranges in cartwheels. Peel bananas and slice in half lengthwise, then cut in 2″ pieces. Marinate fruit in dressing at least 30 minutes. Then arrange on greens and sprinkle with nuts and watercress. Serve with remaining marinade. Makes 6 servings.

Lemon Dressing

1/3 cup lemon juice
1/2 cup safflower or other cold-pressed
 oil
1 tablespoon honey
1 teaspoon each salt, paprika and
 prepared mustard
1/2 teaspoon celery seed
1/4 teaspoon pepper

Put all ingredients in tightly covered jar and shake well. Makes about 1 cup.

TOMATOES FILLED WITH VEGETABLE SALAD

1 package (10 ounces) frozen peas and
 carrots, cooked
1 cup finely chopped celery
1/4 cup chopped fresh parsley
1/4 cup bottled green-goddess or other
 salad dressing
1 teaspoon lemon juice
1/2 teaspoon seasoned onion salt
Salt
6 medium tomatoes, peeled
Lettuce cups

Combine first 6 ingredients and ½ teaspoon salt; chill. Cut thin slice off top of each tomato, then cut each tomato from top almost to bottom, making 6 wedges. Press wedges open to form petals. Sprinkle with salt. Place on lettuce cups and spoon chilled salad into center of each. Makes 6 servings.

RAISIN AND APPLE-BUTTER PIE

1-1/2 cups seedless raisins
2 eggs, well beaten
1 cup apple butter
1/3 cup sugar
1/4 teaspoon salt
1 teaspoon vanilla extract
1/4 teaspoon baking soda
1 cup buttermilk
Whole-Wheat Pie Shell (below)

Cover raisins with hot water and let stand about 10 minutes to plump; drain well. Mix well next 5 ingredients. Stir soda into buttermilk, then fold with raisins into apple-butter mixture. Pour into pie shell and bake in moderate oven (375°F.) 10 minutes. Reduce heat to 350°F. and bake about 40 minutes longer. Cool well before cutting.

WHOLE-WHEAT PIE SHELL

1-1/4 cups whole-wheat flour
1/2 teaspoon salt
1/2 cup solid white vegetable shortening

Put flour and salt in bowl, then cut in shortening with pastry blender or 2 knives. Mixing with fork, add enough cold water to hold mixture together. Pull into ball and roll on floured board to 1/8" thickness. Fit in 9" piepan, trim edges and flute. Prick with fork and bake in very hot oven (450°F.) about 12 minutes.

APPLE CRISP

4 cups sliced peeled tart apples
1/2 cup seedless raisins
1/2 cup sweet apple cider, or 1/2 cup water and juice of 1 lemon
1 cup packed brown sugar
1/2 cup margarine, softened
1/4 cup dry nonfat milk
1/4 cup quick-cooling rolled oats (not instant)
6 tablespoons all-purpose flour
1 tablespoon plain wheat germ
1 teaspoon cinnamon
Whipped dessert topping or vanilla ice cream

Put apples and raisins in buttered 1½-quart baking dish. Pour cider over top. Mix remaining ingredients, except topping, with hands until crumbly. Sprinkle on apples and raisins, covering completely. Bake in moderate oven (350°F.) 30 minutes, or until apples are tender. Serve with topping. Makes 6 servings.

Pear Crisp Use 4 cups sliced peeled firm pears, water and lemon juice, and ½ cup packed brown sugar.

WALNUT-APPLE MATRIMONIAL CAKES

1-1/2 cups all-purpose flour
1-1/2 cups packed brown sugar
1 cup finely chopped walnuts
1 cup sugar-honey wheat germ
1 teaspoon double-acting baking powder
1/2 teaspoon baking soda
1/4 teaspoon salt
3/4 cup butter or margarine, softened
2-1/2 cups finely chopped peeled apple
6 tablespoons apple juice
1 cup golden raisins
1 tablespoon cornstarch

Combine flour, 1 cup brown sugar and next 5 ingredients. With wooden spoon or hands, blend in butter until mixture is well combined and crumbly. Pack two thirds of mixture on bottom of 9" baking·pan. Set aside remainder for topping. Combine apple, half the apple juice and remaining ½ cup brown sugar in saucepan; cook over low heat until apple is translucent. Stir in raisins. Combine cornstarch with remaining 3 tablespoons apple juice and stir into mixture; cook until thickened. Chill. Spoon over crumb crust in pan. Sprinkle reserved crumb mixture over top. Press down. Bake in moderate oven (350°F.) about 45 minutes. Cool and cut in 16 squares.

CRUSTLESS APPLE PIE

8 large apples, peeled, cored and cut in thin wedges (8 cups)
1/2 cup granulated sugar
1 teaspoon cinnamon or nutmeg
1/2 cup packed brown sugar
1/2 cup whole-wheat pastry flour
1/4 cup butter
Pinch of salt
Cream or ice cream

Toss together first 3 ingredients and put in buttered shallow 2-quart baking dish. Mix remaining ingredients, except cream, until crumbly. Sprinkle over apples and bake in hot oven (400°F.) about 30 minutes. Serve with cream. Makes 6 servings.

PRUNES DELUXE

1 pound prunes
2-1/4 cups apple cider
3 tablespoons honey

Soak prunes overnight in cider. Put over low heat, bring to boil and simmer 20 minutes. Add honey and simmer, covered, 10 minutes longer. Cool and store in refrigerator. Makes about 4 cups.

ARAB DATES

1/2 cup honey
1/2 cup chopped toasted almonds
1/4 cup chopped candied citron
1/2 cup chopped walnuts
1 pound pitted dates
Sugar

Mix first 4 ingredients. Stuff dates with mixture and roll in sugar. Serve as a confection. Dates keep well if stored in airtight container.

OLD-FASHIONED APPLE COOKIES

1/2 cup butter, softened
1-1/3 cups packed brown sugar
1 egg
1/4 cup apple juice
1 cup finely chopped peeled cored apples
2 cups whole-wheat pastry flour
1/2 teaspoon salt
1 teaspoon baking soda
1/2 teaspoon ground cloves
1 teaspoon cinnamon
1 cup seedless raisins
1 cup chopped walnuts or other nuts

Cream butter and sugar until blended. Add egg and beat well. Beat in juice. Add next 6 ingredients and mix well. Then fold in raisins and nuts. Drop by rounded teaspoonfuls about 2″ apart on greased baking sheets and bake in moderate oven (375°F.) about 13 minutes. Remove to racks. Makes 48.

CRISP HONEY COOKIES

1/2 cup butter or margarine
1/2 cup clover honey
1-3/4 cups all-purpose flour
1 teaspoon baking soda
1/2 teaspoon cinnamon
1/4 teaspoon each ground cloves and allspice
1/3 cup wheat germ
Honey-Lemon Frosting

Cream butter and honey. Sift together flour, soda and spices; mix in wheat germ. Combine dry ingredients with creamed mixture. Chill about 1 hour. Roll on lightly floured board to about 1/8″ thickness. Cut with floured cookie cutter and put on greased cookie sheets. Bake in moderate oven (350°F.) 8 to 10 minutes. Cool on rack; spread thinly with frosting. Makes about 3 dozen. **Honey-Lemon Frosting** Mix 3/4 cup sifted confectioners' sugar, 1 tablespoon honey and about 1 tablespoon lemon juice to make frosting of thin spreading consistency.

CAROB-NUT COOKIES

1 cup all-purpose flour
2 tablespoons plain wheat germ
1/2 teaspoon baking soda
1/2 teaspoon salt
1/2 cup butter, softened
6 tablespoons granulated sugar
6 tablespoons brown sugar
1/2 teaspoon vanilla extract
1 egg
1 package (6 ounces) carob nuggets
1/2 cup coarsely chopped nuts

Mix first 4 ingredients. Cream butter and sugars together. Add vanilla and egg and beat well. Add dry ingredients and mix well. Stir in carob and nuts. Drop by teaspoonfuls 2″ apart on ungreased cookie sheets. Bake in moderate oven (375°F.) 10 to 12 minutes. Remove at once from sheets to racks. Makes about 4 dozen.

HONEY DATE-NUT BARS

3 eggs
1 cup honey
2 teaspoons grated lemon rind
1/4 teaspoon salt
1 cup all-purpose flour
1 teaspoon double-acting baking powder
1 package (8 ounces) chopped dates
1 cup chopped pecans or walnuts
Confectioners' sugar

In mixing bowl, beat eggs until light and foamy. Add next 3 ingredients and mix well. Mix flour and baking powder and add with dates and nuts to egg mixture; mix well. Grease 13″ x 9″ x 2″ baking pan and line bottom with waxed paper. Spread batter in pan and bake in moderate oven (325°F.) about 40 minutes. Let stand a few minutes, then loosen around edges with knife. Turn out on board to cool. Wrap in foil, seal and let ripen in cool place several days. Cut in 1/2″ strips, then cut crosswise 3 times to form bars about 2″ x 1/2″. Makes about 9 dozen. Store in airtight container. Just before serving, sprinkle with confectioners' sugar.

FRUIT-NUT LOAF

Using coarse blade, force through food chopper 1/2 pound each seedless raisins, pitted dates, currants, dried apricots, walnuts and blanched almonds. Mix well with 1/4 cup orange juice and press firmly into lightly oiled 9″ x 5″ x 3″ loaf pan. Cover tightly with plastic wrap and let stand 3 days at room temperature. Unmold and cut loaf lengthwise in 2 parts. Store leftovers well wrapped in plastic wrap in cool place. Makes about 3 pounds.

Cheesecake Supreme

B

D

Dessert Sauces

Desserts. *See also* Cake; Cookies; Pie

E

F

G

H-I

J

K

L

O

P

S

Salad Dressings

Salad(s)

NOTES

NOTES

NOTES

NOTES

NOTES

RECIPE SYMBOLS

Here's your key to the symbols printed at the beginning of recipe directions. The blender, fryer, Dutch oven, grinder, knife, mixer and skillet drawings tell you when these electrical appliances can be put to good use in making the recipes. The clock-face symbol denotes time-saving recipes and the penny bank indicates money-saving dishes.

 BLENDER

 DEEP-FAT FRYER

 DUTCH OVEN

 GRINDER

 KNIFE

 QUICK AND EASY

 LOW COST

 MIXER

 SKILLET

Tables of Measures and Weights
LIQUID MEASURE

1 dash	= 6 drops
1 teaspoon	= 1/3 tablespoon
1 tablespoon	= 3 teaspoons
1 tablespoon	= 1/2 fluid ounce
1 fluid ounce	= 2 tablespoons
1 jigger	= 3 tablespoons
1 jigger	= 1-1/2 fluid ounces
1 gill	= 1/2 cup
1 cup	= 1/2 pint
1 cup	= 16 tablespoons
1 cup	= 8 fluid ounces
1 pint	= 2 cups
1 pint	= 16 fluid ounces
1 fifth	= 25 fluid ounces
1 quart	= 2 pints
1 quart	= 4 cups
1 quart	= 32 fluid ounces
1 gallon	= 4 quarts
1 gallon	= 16 cups
1 gallon	= 128 fluid ounces

DRY MEASURE

1 dash	= less than 1/8 teaspoon
1 teaspoon	= 1/3 tablespoon
1 tablespoon	= 3 teaspoons
1/4 cup	= 4 tablespoons
1/3 cup	= 5 tablespoons plus 1 teaspoon
1/2 cup	= 8 tablespoons
2/3 cup	= 10 tablespoons plus 2 teaspoons
3/4 cup	= 12 tablespoons
7/8 cup	= 14 tablespoons
1 cup	= 16 tablespoons
1 pint	= 2 cups
1 quart	= 4 cups
1 peck	= 8 quarts
1 bushel	= 4 pecks

AVOIRDUPOIS WEIGHT

1 ounce	= 28 grams
1/4 pound	= 4 ounces
1/2 pound	= 8 ounces
1 pound	= 16 ounces